The Papers of
HENRY CLAY

The Papers of
HENRY CLAY

Robert Seager II
Editor

Richard E. Winslow III
Associate Editor

Melba Porter Hay
Assistant Editor

Volume 7
SECRETARY OF STATE
January 1, 1828–
March 4, 1829

THE UNIVERSITY PRESS OF KENTUCKY

*"My ambition is that we may enter a new
and larger era of service to humanity."*

Dedicated to the memory of
JOSIAH KIRBY LILLY
1861–1948
President of Eli Lilly and Company
Founder of Lilly Endowment, Inc.

Whose wisdom and foresight were
devoted to the service of
education, religion, and
public welfare

ISBN: 0-8131-0057-7
Library of Congress Catalog Card Number: 59-13605

Copyright © 1982 by The University Press of Kentucky

Scholarly publisher for the Commonwealth,
serving Berea College, Centre College of Kentucky,
Eastern Kentucky University, The Filson Club,
Georgetown College, Kentucky Historical Society,
Kentucky State University, Morehead State University,
Murray State University, Northern Kentucky University,
Transylvania University, University of Kentucky,
University of Louisville, and Western Kentucky University.

Editorial and Sales Offices: Lexington, Kentucky 40506-0024

CONTENTS

PREFACE

With this volume an entirely new staff of editors and researchers has taken responsibility for *The Papers of Henry Clay*. In addition to those people mentioned on the dust jacket and title page, the names and labor of others who contributed constructively to the Clay Papers project during the transition period must gratefully be noted.

Chief among these contributors was Mary Wilma M. Hargreaves, retiring senior editor, who did much to break in the incoming senior editor. Her patience in this regard was Jobian. Ably assisting her in the orientation of new staff members in 1979 was Richard A. Bland, then assistant editor. The newcomers were Mary Barbara Allen who served in the summer and fall of 1979 as assistant editor, and Mackelene G. Smith who joined the staff as research and editorial assistant in the fall of 1979, replacing Renée A. Piper. Margaret A. Spratt has served the Clay Papers as research associate since July, 1981. Contributing to the project in many useful ways, mainly with typing and proof-reading, have been Sheila Breeding and Ingrid Hansen.

Readers of the six previous volumes in the series will notice that in this volume the editorial philosophy of the project has undergone fundamental rethinking. In addition, the format of the book has been redesigned and significant mechanical changes have been made in the text. All of the latter have to do with an eye to cost efficiency and with the intention of bringing the project, commenced thirty years ago, to a reasonably early conclusion.

In addition to documents excluded by the editors of previous volumes (see 6: iii–iv), the new editors have chosen not to print other materials deemed marginal or peripheral to an understanding of Clay's ideas and activities. These include the records of his daily financial transactions, his routine legal papers, and numerous letters of application and recommendation written to him. Routine letters of introduction, gratitude, regret, transmittal, inquiry, and acknowledgment have also been excluded. All of the excluded items, however, have been listed in a calendar at the end of the volume; and the general subject matter of each calendared item has been noted.

Further, letter headings have been modernized and standardized, and salutations and subscriptions have been eliminated. No costly efforts have been made to identify obscure figures who are referred to in passing and then disappear forever from Clay's correspondence. Redundant volume and page numbers have not been used in the citations of encyclopedias and dictionaries arranged alphabetically. Abbreviations have been employed in the footnotes, as explained below.

More substantial changes in Volume 7 include the following: Most incoming mail has been summarized with a view toward saving space and controlling publication costs. Incoming letters dealing with identical subjects have been summarized and grouped as a single entry (for example, see p. 10). To reduce staff labor costs, footnotes have generally been utilized as sparingly as possible and executed in as brief compass as is consistent with providing the reader with an adequate historical context in which to understand the thrust and meaning of a given letter. To reduce the number of footnotes in Volume 7, cross-references to documents found in Volumes 1–6 have been bracketed into the text. Cross-references within Volume 7 have been footnoted in the primary documents and bracketed into the texts of the summarized documents. Except in the instance of proper names, the editors have not called attention, with the usual [sic], to the hundreds of misspelled words encountered in these letters. The reader may be certain, however, that misspelled words have been transcribed and printed just as they appear in manuscript. Otherwise, in matters of form and style the new editors have continued the sound practices employed by their predecessors (6: v–vi).

A final significant change in this volume will be noted in its index. Volume 7 includes a combined name and subject index. The subject part of this index, incidentally, has permitted the use of fewer cross-references within the volume. At the end of Volume 7 the reader will also find a subject index for Volumes 1 through 6. It should be used in conjunction with the name index appearing in those six volumes. The compilation of the subject index for Volumes 1–6 has been the dreary task of the present senior editor (Samuel Johnson would call him a "harmless drudge"), who hopes that its belated appearance will result in rendering all seven of the volumes now in the series somewhat more useful and efficient to use as scholarly research tools. He hopes too that researchers finding significant errors or omissions in the subject index of Volumes 1–6, as surely they must, will be kind enough to bring such failures to his attention.

Finally, the editors sincerely thank the Lilly Endowment, Inc., for its generous support of the early volumes in the series. We wish also to thank the National Historical Publications and Records Commission, the University of Kentucky Research Foundation, and the University Press of Kentucky for the funds that have made possible the editing and publishing of this particular volume at this particular time.

Robert Seager II
June, 1982

SYMBOLS & ABBREVIATIONS

The following symbols are used to describe the nature of the originals of documents copied from manuscript sources.

AD	Autograph Document
AD draft	Autograph Document, draft
ADI	Autograph Document Initialed
ADS	Autograph Document Signed
AE	Autograph Endorsement
AEI	Autograph Endorsement Initialed
AES	Autograph Endorsement Signed
AL	Autograph Letter
AL draft	Autograph Letter, draft
ALI	Autograph Letter Initialed
ALI copy	Autograph Letter Initialed, copy
ALI draft	Autograph Letter Initialed, draft
ALS	Autograph Letter Signed
ALS draft	Autograph Letter Signed, draft
AN	Autograph Note
AN draft	Autograph Note, draft
ANI draft	Autograph Note Initialed, draft
ANS	Autograph Note Signed
Copy	Copy not by writer (indicated "true" if so certified)
D	Document
DS	Document Signed
L	Letter
L draft	Letter, draft
LI draft	Letter Initialed, draft
LS	Letter Signed
N	Note
N draft	Note, draft
NS	Note Signed

The following, from the *Symbols Used in the National Union Catalog of the Library of Congress* (9th ed., rev.; Washington, 1965), indicate the location of the original documents in institutional libraries of the United States.

CSmH	Henry E. Huntington Library and Museum, San Marino, California
CtY	Yale University, New Haven, Connecticut
DLC	Library of Congress, Washington, D.C.
DLC-HC	Library of Congress, Henry Clay Collection

DLC-TJC	Library of Congress, Thomas J. Clay Collection
DNA	United States National Archives Library, Washington, D.C. Following the symbol for this depository the letters A. and R. mean Applications and Recommendations; M, Microscopy; P. and D. of L., Publication and Distribution of the Laws; R, Reel; and RG, Record Group.
ICHi	Chicago Historical Society, Chicago, Illinois
IHi	Illinois State Historical Library, Springfield, Illinois
InHi	Indiana Historical Society, Indianapolis, Indiana
InU	Indiana University, Bloomington, Indiana
KyLoF	Filson Club, Louisville, Kentucky
KyLxT	Transylvania University, Lexington, Kentucky
KyU	University of Kentucky, Lexington, Kentucky
MB	Boston Public Library, Boston, Massachusetts
MdHi	Maryland Historical Society, Baltimore, Maryland
MH	Harvard University, Cambridge, Massachusetts
MHi	Massachusetts Historical Society, Boston, Massachusetts
MiD-B	Detroit Public Library, Detroit, Michigan, Burton Historical Collection
MoU	University of Missouri, Columbia, Missouri
MWA	American Antiquarian Society, Worcester, Massachusetts
NBu	Buffalo and Erie County Public Library, Buffalo, New York
NBuHi	Buffalo Historical Society, Buffalo, New York
NcD	Duke University, Durham, North Carolina
NHi	New York Historical Society, New York City
NjP	Princeton University, Princeton, New Jersey
NN	New York Public Library, New York City
NNPM	Pierpont Morgan Library, New York City
NRU	University of Rochester, Rochester, New York
OClWHi	Western Reserve Historical Society, Cleveland, Ohio
OHi	Ohio State Historical Society, Columbus, Ohio
PHi	Historical Society of Pennsylvania, Philadelphia, Pennsylvania
PPiU	University of Pittsburgh, Pittsburgh, Pennsylvania
PU	University of Pennsylvania, Philadelphia, Pennsylvania
RHi	Rhode Island Historical Society, Providence, Rhode Island
ScHi	South Carolina Historical Society, Charleston, South Carolina
THi	Tennessee Historical Society, Nashville, Tennessee
ViHi	Virginia Historical Society, Richmond, Virginia
ViU	University of Virginia, Charlottsville, Virginia

The following abbreviations are used in the footnotes of this volume:

AQR	*American Quarterly Review.*
ASPFR	*American State Papers, Foreign Relations.*
ASPN	*American State Papers, Navy.*

BDAC	*Biographical Dictionary of the American Congress.* Washington, D.C., 1928.
BDEAJ	*A Biographical Dictionary of Early American Jews.* Joseph R. Rosenbloom, Lexington, Ky., 1960.
CAB	*Cyclopedia of American Biography.* J. G. Wilson and J. Fiske, Appleton, N.Y., 1888.
CDC	*Century Dictionary Cyclopedia.* B. E. Smith and W. D. Whitney, Century, N.Y., 1911.
DAB	*Dictionary of American Biography.* A. Johnson, N.Y., 1927.
DBF	*Dictionnaire de Biographie Francaise.* J. Balteau, M. Barroux, and M. Prevost, Paris, 1933.
DEP	*Diccionario Enciclopedica Del Peru.*
DH	*Delaware History.*
DNB	*Dictionary of National Biography.* L. Stephen and S. Lee, Oxford, 1885.
GEPB	*Grande Enciclopedea Portuguesa e Brasileira.* Lisbon and Rio de Janerio, 1935–1960.
HRDUSA	*Historical Register and Dictionary of the United States Army.* . . . F. B. Heitman, Washington, D.C., 1965.
JSAH	*Journal of the Society of Architectural Historians.*
JSH	*Journal of Southern History.*
LHQ	James A. Padgett, "Letters of James Brown to Henry Clay," *Louisiana Historical Quarterly* (January, 1937), 20:58–136, (October, 1941), 24:921–1177.
MHM	*Maryland Historical Magazine.*
MVHR	*Mississippi Valley Historical Review.*
NAR	*North American Review.*
NBG	*Nouvelle Biographie Générale.* J. Hoefer, Paris, 1852.
NCAB	*National Cyclopedia of American Biography.* N.Y., James T. White & Company, 1898.
NCE	*New Catholic Encyclopedia.*
OHQ	*Ohio Historical Quarterly.*
PMHB	*Pennsylvania Magazine of History and Biography.*
Richardson, MPP	*Messages and Papers of the Presidents.* J. D. Richardson, Washington, D.C., 1896.
RKHS	*Register of the Kentucky Historical Society.*
SCHM	*South Carolina Historical Magazine.*
USMA, Register	*Register of Graduates, United States Military Academy.* West Point Alumni Association, 1960.
VMHB	*Virginia Magazine of History and Biography.*
WMQ	*William and Mary Quarterly.*
WPHM	*Western Pennsylvania Historical Magazine.*

Note: Volume and page numbers of dictionaries, encyclopedias, and registers arranged alphabetically are not included in citations.

The Papers of
HENRY CLAY

From JAMES COOLEY, Lima, no. 11, January 1, 1828. Reports that several American seamen, along with some British mariners, have been impressed onto the Peruvian Frigate " 'Presidente' (or Protector)"; that a complaint on this matter was made to him on November 17, 1827, and since that time correspondence, which he encloses, has passed between him and the Peruvian Government. Adds that on November 27 the Peruvian Government replied that "two of the individuals had been given up upon producing their protections, & that the others named had formerly been in the Peruvian service & consequently had lost the right of being reclaimed by their Government." Notes that by the time he received this information, the *Presidente* had sailed. Since he could do nothing more at the time, he waited for the return of Commodore Jacob Jones, then absent at Valparaiso. States that upon Jones's return, Cooley learned that he was uninstructed and unwilling to assume responsibility in the matter. Comments that the Peruvians "seem to entertain the idea that foreigners who are found in the country without protections they have a right to treat as natives." Advises: "It is certainly desirable that some rules should be laid down for the government of the officers & agents of the U.S. in cases of this sort, especially on such distant services." Expresses opinion that impressment will continue as long as Peru has need for a naval force, because the "natives in general" will not "make good sailors," and that some naval force will be necessary to prevent foreign control of the carrying trade along the Pacific coast and to prevent seizures by Spanish privateers. Reports that the British Government has instructed its officials "not to permit the impressment of any British subject," and that its navy has been authorized "to take out forcibly, if necessary, all British subjects who might be impressed." Adds, in a postscript, that he has just learned that 15 impressed Americans are on board the *Presidente*. ALS. DNA, RG59, Dip. Disp., Peru, vol. 1 (M–T52, R–T1). Received June 4, 1828.

To LAFAYETTE   Washington, January 1, 1828
I recd your friendly letter of the 10h. of October last, and you will observe from the publication (of which I send you herewith a Copy [6:1394–6]) that I have taken the liberty of submitting it to the public. Although I presumed, from my appeal to your recollection of the conversation which you relate [6:872–5, 1132–5], that you expected I might publish that part of your letter which concerned myself, I doubted whether I ought to publish the residue of it. But after reading it again and again, it did not appear to me that it would in any manner compromise you; and being very unwilling to publish an extract, I finally

1

decided to submit the whole of it to the public. I shall be happy if I receive your approbation of this step. I was further induced to take it by the consideration that even the private opinions and thoughts of Genl. Lafayette, are, in some sort, public property. The paragraph relating to [Simon] Bolivar created most doubts with me; but when I remarked how delicately and cautiously you had expressed yourself concerning him, I thought that no injury could happen by the publication. Indeed I indulged the hope that, if your letter should ever meet his eye, it might possibly contribute to recall him from his ambitious projects to the duties of patriotism, and liberty.

I thank you, most cordially, my dear General for the testimony which you have borne in my behalf. A witness so beloved by the American people, and so disinterested, can not fail to make a deep impression. And I think I may fairly conclude that your evidence will give the finishing stroke to a calumny which owes its origin and its propagation to the excitement of the period.

In respect to the U. States, you are so well informed through the public prints and your other correspondents that I can add but little to your stock of information. The weak part of our Constitution, I fear, is that which relates to the election of a Chief Magistrate. It is that, you know, on which the enemies of our system chiefly build their hopes; as it has been the source of the most apprehensions with the American patriot. We are now putting this provision of our Constitution fairly to the test, and I sincerely hope that it may pass safely through the experiment. Some months ago, when I last wrote you, I felt very confident of the re-election of Mr. Adams; and I still think that he will succeed. But some late events, I must confess, induce me to regard the event as being far from certain [6:360-3].

In both houses of Congress there are majorities (quite small) against the Administration. In the history of our Government, heretofore, the fact has often occurred that, in one, or the other house of Congress, there was a majority against the Executive; but this, I believe is the first time when such a majority existed in both. And yet, I do not anticipate any thing unfavorable to the Administration from this anamoly. This is partly owing to the elective character of both the Executive and Legislative departments of our Government, but principally to the personal nature of the present majorities. That is, they are not opposed to the measures but to the head of the Administration, & desire a change of the one without that of the other.

In all other respects, our Country remains prosperous, and continues to make rapid advances. The progress of many branches of manufacturing has been very great, notwithstanding the demand for further protection against foreign competition which is made in behalf of some particular articles.

My opinion of the ambitious views of Bolivar remains unchanged [6:872-5], although I think it not improbable that he may have changed his designs, upon the discovery of their impracticability. The degree and the success of the resistance to his projects in Peru was not expected by him. They have called to their head a most virtuous and patriotic Citizen (General [Jose] La Mar [sic, Lamar]) who has commenced his administra-

2

tion of the Peruvian Govt. under very flattering auspices. In Colombia too Bolivar encountered an opposition which he did not expect [6: 956-7, 1054, 1242-3]. From these and other causes, I should not be surprized if he renounced his splendid projects of power and empire, and aims at the truer glory of establishing the Liberty as well as the Independence of his Country. Such at least is my anxious hope.

I congratulate you, most cordially, on the brighter prospects of Greece. For, altho' the allies may not be disposed to do all for her that her friends could wish, the destruction of the Fleet of the Turks must relieve her for the present, and she may hope a good deal from the improbability of the three great powers agreeing in any scheme which would render her condition less happy than under the Turks [6:780-2, 1241, 1334-5].

We have not yet heard from your elections in France [6:438-9, 1132-5; 1256-9]. In yours, I need not say, that I take a lively interest, mixed with no inconsiderable portion of apprehension that, whatever may be the result, your happiness may not be promoted by it. You know what you allowed me to take the liberty of saying to you, prior to your departure from this Country. We all here are so anxious that you should have a calm and serene close of that life which has been so dear to us, that you must excuse us for any solicitude which we may feel about any occurrence which may possibly disturb its tranquillity.

I pray you to make my warm regards to your son [George Washington Lafayette], and to all your family....

ALS. NNPM.

From AMBROSE H. SEVIER, Washington, January 1, 1828. Recommends that someone other than a resident of Arkansas be appointed as Governor of the Territory. Argues that party political disputes are often so violent in Arkansas that they end in "bloodshed—street fights and unlimited and almost unqualified denunciations," and that the post should therefore go to a non-partisan appointee. Specifically rules out Robert Crittenden, for whom "I have an unconquerable hatred," and suggests instead William Carroll of Tennessee as a "suitable nominee." ALS. DNA, RG59, A. and R. (M531, R2). Published in Carter, *Territorial Papers,* 20:822-4. George Izard was reappointed Governor of the Territory. For Sevier, see *BDAC.*

From DANIEL WEBSTER
Washington,
January 1, 1827 [i.e., 1828]

After company went out last night, and I had packed up my trunk,[1] I sat down and read your letter[2] through. Probably, I should have voted against any further publication; but I am now fully satisfied this will do good. The statement is clear, and the evidence irresistible. I am satisfied, upon my conscience, that the whole business originated with General J. himself; whether through mistake, or from intention, I do not say.

Printed in Calvin Colton, *Clay Correspondence,* 4:156. Misdated January 1, 1827, by Colton. 1. Webster was preparing to leave for New York to visit his wife who was seriously ill. She died on January 21, 1828. 2. *A Supplement to the Address ... to the Public,* December 29, 1827.

From THOMAS HAMMOND   Sharpsburg, Md., January 2, 1828

Permit me though not a personal acquaintance, yet in some degree a connexion,[1] to address you. The deep interest felt in your prosperity will I am sure be an ample apology for this intrusion. You are aware that this Electoral district has been and still may be deemed Jac[k]sonian. Powerful exertions are making to stem the tide of opposition and the friends of the Administration are not without hope that at the next Election it will be with you. Your character has been basely assailed and by him too who is held up by his friends as the very paragon of all that is honourable and just. Your friends know how to appreciate your worth; but your enemies have yet to learn. Your late address [6:1394-6] has not reached us a; notice of it in the public journals came to hand by this days mail. If you can without inconvenience or subjecting yourself to censure forwd a few copies to be distributed through this end of our county much good may result. But few persons are in the habit of receiving public journals in this neighbourhood by their own agency. Yet the [Washington *United States*] Telegraph I find distributed every where by the partizans of the General which exerts much influence on the minds of the ignorant and unenlightened rabble   The truth requires only to be known to be believed and when known the effects will be evident.

ALS. DLC–HC (DNA, M212, R3).   1. Hammond was a nephew of Dr. Richard Pindell, a connection he mentions in the closing of this letter.

From WILLIAM SAMPLE   Washington, Pa., January 2, 1828

This day Mr [Thomas] M[c]Giffin, mentioned to me that he had received a line from you in which you signified that you had not heard from me on the subject of Gen. Jackson's expressions about "*corruption*" and "*bribery*". I must confess sir, that I have been remiss in the performance of my promise. Since I received your last letter, in which you informed me, that the statement I had made would not do to go forth to the public, I intended, day after day, to visit Mr [Edward] MGlaughlin [*sic,* McLaughlin], but circumstances beyond my controul have prevented my going.

I still feel determined to see Mr MGlaughlin and if possible, get from him a certificate of the statement, as to the fact as it transpired at the time. I am aware now, that MGlaughlin, is a Jacksonite, & a man not of the most correct and retentive memory; but if he has any recollection and more especially, if he has the *disposition,* to remember, he must recollect the facts, of his being introduced to Jackson, his expression to him and the general's laconic, but emphatic reply.

I think the last time I was in your company you told me that you designed, at a proper time, making a public expose, embracing such facts as were susceptible of proof and demonstration; that you would embrace the one that took place between Jackson and MGlaughlin, with the mass of others you had and were in expectation of receiving. With a view to aid you in this, I was desirous of procuring a certificate from Mr MGlaughlin's own hands and then forwarding you a copy of the same, retaining the original here for the purpose of stumping the advocates of the general in our own neighborhood—

We have nothing new, here, in the political field—the Jacksonites

4

are making a noise in consequence of the president's not noticing the "American System" in his message [6:1302–04]—but, their noise, is mere sound, and I hope that the contest will end in that which may be best for the real interest of our common country. Our delegates have went on to Harrisburgh [*sic*], according to previous concert, to form an electoral ticket friendly to Mr Adams [6:1049–51].

On the next page, I have made out the statement you wanted at more length, and detail than it formerly appeared....

[Enclosed statement] On Tuesday the 22d day of March 1825, when Gen. Andrew Jackson was on his way from Washington City to his residence in Tennessee, he with a number of the citizens of Washington, Pa. and of the county, were in the public house of Mr. [John] Chambers, innkeeper, West Alexandria, Pa. Mr Edward MGlaughlin, a citizen of Donegall township Washington County, Pa called at the public house of Mr Chambers, in the town of West Alexandria, for the special purpose of seeing Gen. Jackson. Mr E MCLaughlin was introduced to the general, and after the common salutation of shaking hands, Mr MGlaughlin said "Well general we done all we could for you here, but the rascals at Washington cheated you out of it." To this expression, General [Ja]ckson, made the following reply—"Indeed, my old friend, there was *cheating* and *corruption* and *bribery* too—the editors of the National Intelligencer[1] were *bribed* to suppress the publication of honest George Kremer's letter [4:113–4]." Mr MGlaughlin's introduction was at his own solicitation, in a public house, in the presence of a room full of gentlemen and the interchange of expressions in the same public house and also, in the presence of a large and promiscusous company—Samuel Workman[2] esq. Thomas Morgan[3] Joseph Henderson esquirs Josiah Truesdell William Sample and others, present.... [P.S.] Should you chose to change the arrangement of the foregoing statement, in any way to please yourself, you have my permission, retaining the declaration of E. MG and A. Jackson as put down.[4]

DLC-HC (DNA, M212, R3). Endorsed by Clay: "With a Certificate of a conversation of Genl Jackson."   1. Joseph Gales and William W. Seaton, Jr.   2. Samuel Workman, briefly editor of the *Reporter* in Washington, Pa., served variously as Washington County treasurer and county sheriff (1824–1827), and was a member of the State legislature in 1828–1830. In 1840, the year before his death, he was appointed postmaster in Washington by Van Buren. Crumrine, *History of Washington County, Pennsylvania*, 484; U.S. Sen., *Executive Journal*, 5:253,256.   3. Thomas Jefferson Morgan, a lawyer and newspaper editor in Washington, Pa., later led a volunteer company, "Morgan's Rifles," to fight in Texas (1836). Nominated by Jackson, Morgan also served as postmaster of Washington during the Martin Van Buren administration. He was the son of Col. George Morgan, hero of the American Revolution. Crumrine, *History of Washington County, Pennsylvania*, 310,508; U.S. Sen., *Executive Journal*, 4:568,571.   4. The postscript appears on the envelope.

From JOHN SERGEANT   Baltimore, January 2, 1828
I am still detained here, but determined at all events to go to Washington to morrow. Mr. [Daniel] Webster, who arrived here last evening, gave me one of your publications [6:1394–6]. I have read it with great satisfaction. It is triumphant as a refutation; but it is a great deal more than that. The time is come for a general elevation of tone. Circumstances require it, and are just now favorable. Your pamphlet, and the letters of your

friends are sufficiently of this character, and in that point of view, invaluable. The measure I proposed for the Harrisburg convention (in my letter a day or two ago) will be, if adopted, in the same spirit, and *every measure* ought, henceforward, to be in accordance with this system [6:1049-51, 1401-03]. All this, we can talk over more at large, this hint being enough for the present.

Your publication, besides, will oblige Genl. Jackson and his *friends* to come out with some answer, or subject themselves to the most dangerous of all imputations, that of fear.[1] If they adopt the former course, I think I see plainly where it will lead. My notions of this whole fiction of corrupt bargaining are perhaps peculiar, but time (not very distant) will determine whether they are correct or not. This publication will accelerate the disclosure of the truth, and the truth will do no credit to any of our adversaries, and will bring signal discredit upon some of them. That the whole is a fiction, *no one*, I believe, now doubts. Your reputation is secure. Malice and uncharitableness may prevail a little longer, but they must inevitably yield to the force of truth.

It is for us (I repeat) now to shew, that we feel that we have the truth on our side, not by vindictiveness and violence, but by a firm and open course of conduct,

ALS. InU. Letter marked "(Private)." 1. For the Jacksonian counter-attack, see the Washington *United States Telegraph* of January 1, 2, and 11, 1828. The latter carried a report of the Jackson Central Committee of Washington, dated January 8, sharply attacking Clay's *Address* of December 29, 1827 and promising an early reply. See also Bassett, *Jackson Correspondence*, 3:389-90.

From JONATHAN WARNSLEY, Weston, [West] Virginia, January 2, 1828. Protests against the possible re-appointment of Benjamin Reeder as United States marshal for the Western District of Virginia. States: "He is addicted to inebriety. He has heretofore acceded to applications of Young men who reside in this [Lewis] County, to be summoned as Jurors to attend in different distant counties, whither they had private business." ALS. DNA, RG59, A. and R. (M531, R7). See 5:167.

To JOHN QUINCY ADAMS, January 3, 1828. Transmits "copies and extracts of letters" in response to the resolution of the Senate of December 19, 1827, requesting of the President "any information obtained from the British Government, with regard to the establishment of light houses, light vessels; Buoys and other improvements to the navigation within their jurisdiction, opposite the coast of Florida, or so much thereof as he may communicate without injury to the public interest." Copy. DNA, RG59, Report Books, vol. 4, p. 215. Published, with enclosures, in *ASPFR*, 6:753-7.

To JOHN M. FORBES Washington, January 3, 1828
I should have, long since, noticed the subject which formed the principal topic of your conference with the President [Rivadavia] of the Argentine Republic, in August of the year before last (a minute of which, together with your correspondence on the same subject with the Minister of Foreign Affairs of that Republic, is transmitted with your despatch No 40

[5:670]) if the arrival of a Minister from Buenos Ayres had not been expected. In both the minute and the correspondence above referred to, it is stated that such a minister was about to be sent to the United States; but as he has not arrived, and as we have heard nothing, of late, about him, I will not longer delay communicating to you the views which are entertained by the President of the United States, on the two enquiries with which Mr [Francisco] de la Cruz concludes his note to you. Those enquiries relate to the declaration of the late President of the United States [James Monroe], contained in his message to Congress, of the 2d. December 1823 [3:542], against the interference of Europe with the affairs of America. At the period of that declaration, apprehensions were entertained of designs, on the part of the Allied Powers of Europe to interfere, in behalf of Spain, to reduce again to subjection, those parts of the Continent of America which had thrown off the Spanish yoke. The declaration of the late President was that of the head of the Executive Government of the United States. Although there is every reason to believe that the policy which it announced was in conformity with the opinion both of the nation and of Congress, the declaration must be regarded as having been voluntarily made, and not as conveying any pledge or obligation, the performance of which foreign nations have a right to demand. When the case shall arrive, if it should ever occur, of such an European interference as the message supposes, and it becomes consequently necessary to decide whether this country will or will not engage in war, Congress alone, you well know, is competent, by our Constitution, to decide that question. In the event of such an interference, there can be but little doubt that the sentiment contained in President Monroe's message, would be still that of the People and Government of the United States.

We have much reason to believe that the declaration of Mr Monroe had great, if not decisive, influence, in preventing all interference, on the part of the Allied Powers of Europe to the prejudice of the new Republics of America. From that period down to the present time, the efforts of the Government of the United States have been unremitted to accomplish the same object. It was one of the first acts of the present administration to engage the head of the European Alliance, the late Emperor Alexander [I], to employ his good offices to put a stop to the further effusion of human blood, by the establishment of a peace between Spain and those new Republics. Entering fully into the views of the United States, he did give his advice, to that effect, to the Spanish Government. His successor, the Emperor Nicholas [I], is known to march in the same line of policy which was marked out by his illustrious brother.

Not long after President Monroe's declaration, Great Britain took the decided step of acknowledging the independence of several of the new Republics [4:94]. More recently France, and other European Powers, have given indications of their intention to follow the example of the United States [5:24].

It may then be confidently affirmed that there is no longer any danger whatever of the contingency happening, which is supposed by Mr Monroe's message, of such an interference on the part of Europe,

7

with the concerns of America, as would make it expedient for the Government of the United States to interpose.

In respect to the war which has unhappily been raging between the Argentine Republic, and the Emperor of Brazil [Pedro I], the President has seen it with great regret, and would be very glad to hear of its honorable conclusion. But that war cannot be conceived as presenting a state of things bearing the remotest analogy to the case which President Monroe's message deprecates. It is a war strictly American in its origin and its object. It is a war in which the Allies of Europe have taken no part. Even if Portugal and the Brazils had remained united, and the war had been carried on by their joint arms, against the Argentine Republic, that would have been far from presenting the case which the message contemplated. But, by the death of the late King of Portugal [John VI], and during the greater part, if not the whole, of the period of the war, the condition of Portugal has been such as to need succor, rather than be capable of affording it to the Brazils.

The general policy of the United States is that of strict and impartial neutrality in reference to all wars of other Powers. It would be only in an extreme case that they would deviate from that policy. Such a case is not presented by the present war.

You will communicate in the most friendly manner, the substance of this despatch to the Government near which you reside.

Copy. DNA, RG59, Dip. Instr., vol. 12, pp. 49-52 (M77, R7).

From JAMES H. McCULLOCH, Custom House, Baltimore, January 3, 1828. Acknowledges receipt of Clay's letter of December 29, 1827. Reports that the Argentine brig *Flor de Mayo* has arrived at Baltimore, "but with neither Prize or prize goods." States: "The vessel is in balast & put in for repairs & refreshments; to the supply of which she will be strictly confined." ALS. DNA, RG59, Misc. Letters (M179, R66).

From JOHN G. ROBERTS, Richmond, Ky. January 3, 1828. Mentions a correspondence with Clay [not found] "18 Mos. or 2 yrs. since" respecting the whereabouts of his father-in-law, Alexander MacKae. Notes that his wife is "quite uneasy" and inquires if MacKae is "engaged in the public service in Europe."

Disclaims any involvement in politics except "in fearlessly expressing my opinions," and proclaims "you sir . . . have been my choice since the commencement of the Elections . . . for President after the expiration of Mr. Monroes term . . . and you are still my favorite." States: "I am delighted you have again addresse'd the public [6:1394-6], surely it will carry conviction to the minds of all unprejudiced persons of your purity of conduct & intention." ALS. DLC-HC (DNA, M212, R3).

From WILLIAM TUDOR, Lima, no. 82, January 3, 1828. Submits his consular report for the period ending December 31, 1827. Notes that the number of American vessels in the trade has declined, "but the general result . . . has been much more advantageous than in some previous periods." Mentions, specifically, profits from sales of flour and "plain cottons," as well as "Two or three cargoes from China . . . belonging to American merchants," and "one or two considerable parcels of quicksilver . . . from Europe." Reports a proposal, to be considered by the Peruvian Congress in connection with a projected treaty with Chile, for a new tariff which would be injurious to U.S. commerce. Expresses doubt that the treaty will be made but warns that importation of wheat from Chile will reduce the demand for American flour. Recommends that Stanhope Prevost, whom James Cooley has placed in charge of the office [6:1352-3], be appointed consul. ALS. DNA, RG59, Cons. Disp., Lima, vol. 2 (M154, R2). Received September 3, 1828. The projected Peruvian treaty with Chile did not materialize.

From ALEXANDER BURTON, Cadiz, January 4, 1828. Submits his consular report for the last six months. Notes that, despite his "Repeated remonstrances," vessels from American ports "continue to be excluded" from Cadiz from May 15 to November 15 by regulations imposed by French occupying forces and points out that "the subject is now in the hands of the Minister of the United States at Madrid [Alexander H. Everett]." Interprets renewal of contracts for the subsistence of the French troops for the current year to mean that these forces are unlikely to leave "as long as the English Forces remain in Portugal." Comments on the recent abundant harvest and the continued ban on "importation of Bread Stuffs." Reports the departure for Havana of "The Ship of the Line 'Soberano'" with a convoy of "four transports loaded with masts, spars, and munitions of war." ALS. DNA, RG59, Cons. Disp., Cadiz, vol. 4 (M-T186, R4).

From SAMUEL A. FOOT, "Senate Chamber," January 4, 1828. Inquires "whether under the Resolution of Congress the Public documents ordered to be distributed to the Several Colleges—have been distributed to the Washington College in Hartford Ct." ALS. DNA, RG 59, Misc. Letters (M179, R66).
The Resolution, dated December 23, 1817 [3 *U.S. Stat.,* 473], ordered the distribution of sets of certain "state papers and public documents" to various state and federal officials, to the Library of Congress, and to "each University and College in the United States." A second resolution on the subject, May 24, 1828 [4 *U.S. Stat.,* 321], limited the number of the educational institutions so favored.

From BENJAMIN GRUT, New York, January 4, 1828. Transmits, on his "arrival from Maracaybo," a copy of the November 11, 1827 "number of the Gazette of Colombia" containing news "that order had been restored among the troops at Guyaquil." Also encloses "an address to the People of Colombia, from . . . Genl. [Francisco de Paula] Santander." ALS. DNA, RG59, Misc. Letters (M179, R66). Santander's address is dated October 28, 1827.

From **WASHINGTON M. HAXTON,** New York, January 4, 1828. Requests a copy of Clay's Address of December 29, 1827; anticipates "great pleasure from the perusal of a Document which refutes in So masterly a manner the Vilifications of desperate antagonists." AN. DNA, RG59, Misc. Letters (M179, R66). Haxton was an attorney doing business at 7 Frankfort St., New York City.

From **THOMAS M. RODNEY,** Havana, January 4, 1828. Acknowledges receipt of Clay's letter of November 20, 1827 with enclosures. Reports having been informed by "the Capt. General [Francisco Dionisio Vives]" that "Thomas Hampstead [*sic,* Hempstead]" is not "in or about the Havana." Notes the probability that Hempstead "may have been sent out in the expedition [6:1336] from Cadiz, which . . . is expected at Porto Rico," and states that he has "therefore made Copies of the papers received" and will send "them to the Consular Agent [William Simmons, Jr.] of the United States for that Port." LS. DNA, RG59, Cons. Disp., Havana, vol. 5 (M–T20, R5). Received January 29, 1828.

On February 19, 1828, Charles S. Hempstead wrote Clay, acknowledging receipt of a copy of Rodney's letter of January 4 concerning his brother Thomas and asking to be notified if the State Department should receive further information. ALS. DNA, RG59, Misc. Letters (M179, R66).

Writing on July 3, 1828, Charles Hempstead asked Clay if the American Minister to Spain, Alexander H. Everett, had been able to provide any information about his brother. *Ibid.*

The following day, Alexander Everett wrote from Madrid reporting that Spanish authorities had assured him that "no such person" was being held at Cadiz. ALS. DNA, RG59, Dip. Disp., Spain, vol. 29 (M31, R29). Received September 4, 1828.

Cornelia Hempstead wrote on September 3, 1828, asking if additional information had been received. ALS. DNA, RG59, Misc. Letters (M179, R66).

On October 21, 1828, Charles Hempstead wrote Clay once more, acknowledging receipt of two letters from the State Department containing extracts of Everett's dispatch and expressing his distress in learning that Spanish authorities had denied having any knowledge that Thomas Hempstead had ever been held their prisoner. Enclosed letters to the U.S. Consuls at Cadiz, Alexander Burton, and Havana, Thomas M. Rodney, asking them to pursue the matter. *Ibid.*

From **ROBERT TILLOTSON,** New York, January 4, 1828. States that on receipt "this morning" of Clay's letter of December 31, 1827 he "ascertained that the armed vessels referred to . . . had already sailed from the waters of the United States." Declares "There is too much reason to believe that the officers commanding those vessels have in the augmentation of their force, by the shipment of men, violated the laws of this Country." Promises "a particular report" as soon as he "can obtain the facts." ALS. DNA, RG59, Misc. Letters (M179, R65). Letter is misdated January 4, 1827. Clay acknowledged receipt of this letter on January 8 and asked Tillotson to send his report as soon as possible. Copy. DNA, RG59, Dom. Letters, vol. 22, p. 119 (M40, R20). See also, Clay to Rebello, Jan. 29, 1828.

To JOHN QUINCY ADAMS, January 5, 1828. Transmits, in response to a House of Representatives resolution of December 17, 1827, correspondence with Great Britain "relative to the free navigation of the River St. Lawrence [5:451–64]"; also various documents "connected with that subject, and explanatory of the same." Copy. DNA, RG59, Report Books, vol. 4, p. 215. Published with enclosures in *ASPFR*, 6:757–77.

From VINCENT GRAY, Havana, January 5, 1828. Again warns against the appointment of George Byron Shields as U.S. commercial agent at Sisal, Mexico. States that Shields is wanting in principle, is engaged in illegal trade, and that his appointment would "do little more than legalize the Shamefull Scenes of frauds in Conbrand Trade, carried on there in Drawbackgoods." ALS. DNA, RG59, Cons. Disp., Havana, vol. 5 (M-T20, R5). Received January 20, 1828. Letter marked "Private & Confidential."

From JOHN T. KIRKLAND   Cambridge, Mass., January 5, 1828
I have been desired to express my opinion respecting Mr. Professor [Alva] Woods as a candidate for the Presidency of Transylvania University [6:460–2, 485].

I am considerably acquainted with that gentleman. He was four years a member of our College [Harvard], where he took his degree in 1817. About four years after he was appointed a Professor of Mathematicks in the Columbian College in Washington. He was afterwards removed to the same chair in Brown University in Providence, previous to which he travelled in Europe.

He is a ripe scholar, well grounded in the several parts of elementary knowledge. He is a good diciplinarian, without any tincture of severity. In manners he is quite gentlemanly. He has as little bigotry as any Baptist I know. In this view I think him the best qualified for the office of President of any one I am acquainted with in New England, or have heard of in the other states. I think you cannot do better than to choose him.

ALS. KyLxT. On January 12, Clay forwarded this letter to John Bradford in Lexington with his compliments. AN. KyLxT.

To GEORGE FREDERICK LIST   Washington, January 5, 1828
I received, in due course of the Mail, your letter with a packet for Genl. Lafayette, and a Copy of your speech delivered before the Pennsa. Society.[1] The packet was forwarded with our public despatches. I derived much gratification from the perusal of your Speech, as I had previously from your letters to Mr. Ingersoll.[2] I am very glad that a good cause has found a good advocate.

ALS. KyU.   1. *Professor List's Speech, Delivered at the Philadelphia Manufacturers' Dinner, November 3.* Philadelphia, 1827.   2. Charles Jared Ingersoll, vice president of the

Pennsylvania Society, to whom List wrote twelve solicited letters attacking the free-trade theories of Adam Smith and J. B. Say. These were published serially in the Philadelphia *National Journal,* July 10 to July 30, 1827, and later in the same year were reprinted by the Society under the title, *Outlines of a New System of Political Economy.* Clay congratulated List on this volume. See Margaret Esther Hirst, *Life of Friederick List....* (New York, 1909), 41–55.

From JOHN MARSHALL   Richmond, Va., January 5, 1828

I thank you for the copy of your address [6:1394–6] on the charges made against you respecting the election of President, which I have read with the more pleasure because it combines a body of testimony much stronger than I had supposed possible, which must I think silence even those who wish the charges to be believed. . . .

ALS. DLC–HC (DNA, M212, R3).

From JOHN MORRISON, *ET AL.*, Key West, January 5, 1828. State, in the form of a memorial, that on December 20, 1827 they "saved His Britannic Majesty's Schooner Nimble, together with the persons on board the Spanish Brig Gu[e]rrero from the Coast of Africa, laden with Negroes, both of which were ashore on the Florida Reef"; that the *Nimble,* after being repaired, was brought to Key West. Note that Lieutenant Edward Holland, of the *Nimble,* refused to agree to submit the matters of salvage to arbitration or to "any other adjudication than that of a Court of Admiralty." Report that the memorialists acceded to his demands, took depositions, and submitted them to Holland for corroboration. Add that he not only refused to look at the depositions but "in defiance of all law . . . made Sail," leaving the "Memorialists without any compensation for their arduous toil, and expense, in saving him and his Vessel & Crew from inevitable destruction." Mention that not knowing the proper course to follow, they brought to Key West "the Negroes taken from the Wreck of the Brig" and turned them "over to the high Civil Authority." Have learned, however, that the collector of the port, William Pinkney, intends submitting a claim for himself, to the exclusion of the memorialists, "for the bounty allowed to Citizens for Capture [of] Vessels laden with Negroes from the Coast of Africa."

Inform Clay that each of them commands "a vessel, and pursues the Wrecking business." Appeal to him for help and call attention to supporting documents transmitted with their memorial. Copy. DNA, RG59, Misc. Letters (M179,R66). In addition to Morrison, the memorialists, all salvage captains working out of Key West, were Charles Grover, Samuel Sanderson, and John Walker.

Commissioned July 26, 1826, Edward Holland subsequently commanded other small Royal Navy vessels engaged in anti-slave trade activities on the U.S. coast.

For the disposition of slaves brought into the U.S. in this manner, see 4:220, 255; the law of March 3, 1819 authorizing bounty payments is in 3 *U.S. Stat.,* 533.

Captain Sanderson's subsequent claim in February, 1836, for a bounty payment of twenty-five dollars each for the 121 slaves he had rescued from the *Guerrero* made no headway in Congress. *House Docs.*, 24 Cong., 1 Sess., no. 76, *passim.*

From SAMUEL L. SOUTHARD, Navy Department, January 5, 1828. Acknowledges receipt of letters referred by Clay to the Navy Department from "John Scott, Theodore Hunt, and Wilson P. Hunt [6:1212, 1301, 1318], recommending Messrs. John Perry & Co. who are desirous of "Contracting for a Supply of Cannon Shot, and Shells for the Navy." States that Perry and Company may compete when the Department invites bids through the "public News-Papers" and, if their offers are "as favorable as others, [they] will receive a portion of the Contract." Copy. DNA, RG45, Navy Dept., Letterbooks, vol. 1821–31, p. 284.

From JONATHAN THOMPSON, Custom House, New York, January 5, 1828. Acknowledges receipt of Clay's letter of December 25, 1827. Reports that the Argentine brig *General Brandizen,* George C. Dekay, commanding, and her prize the Brazilian brig of war *Casique,* arrived at New York on December 12, 1827, and that customs officials visited both vessels and were told that they had come to New York "in distress." Explains that he informed Dekay that "the rights of hospitality would be extended to his vessels, in the same manner that was extended to the vessels of all other nations, but that our laws would not permit his force to be augmented, nor the number of his men increased." Dekay, who said he was a native of New York City, denied any intention to augment his force or to recruit men and on December 24 called and "stated that his vessels were ready for sea." Adds that the Customs House barge and officer, George Howard, were sent to inspect them; that the officer's report, dated December 28, indicated that the Argentine vessels had departed for sea. However, on December 29 Thompson, investigating reports that they were anchored "outside the Hook" and there taking on men, found the reports to be true. States that he therefore "directed additional bargemen to be employed night and day, to examine the vessels apparently bound to Sandy Hook, for seamen, that might have been shipped; and to detain them." Notes that he "also ordered the Revenue Cutter below [to Sandy Hook], for a similar purpose" and that he learned on December 31 from Thomas Goin that Dekay had employed Goin and "his partner William P. Hallett, to ship men for his vessels." Learned also that the vessels were last sighted by the revenue cutter in the early morning of January 1, when it encountered them near Long Branch and pursued them "as far as the Floating Light."

Maintains that he, Thompson, has done all in his power "to prevent violation of the laws, not having the power to call out the Army & Navy for assistance." Expresses the opinion that American commerce and the Navy "are losing every year many valuable seamen who are enticed and secretly sent out of the country, many of whom perish in foreign climes." Concludes: "There appears to be no way to check this evil, unless by punishing those who aid and assist in procuring and sending them on board foreign armed vessels." Encloses copies of the documents obtained during his investigation, retaining the originals so that they may be used if the President deems it proper "to order legal proceedings against any of the parties." ALS. DNA, RG59, Misc. Letters (M179, R66).

At this time, Dekay, an American, was serving as a captain in the Buenos Airean navy. See, *DAB*. Goin was a notary in New York; he was partner to Hallett who was a merchant and lawyer there.

On April 29, 1828, Jose S. Rebello assured Clay that Hallett, although a partner of Goins, had not been involved in the *General Brandizen* matter and was thus innocent of charges being brought against him by the U.S. government. Rebello to Clay, April 29, 1828. ALS, in Portuguese, with trans. in State Dept. file. DNA, RG59, Notes from Brazilian Legation, vol. 1 (M49, R1).

From WILLIAM H. D. C. WRIGHT, Rio de Janeiro, January 5, 1828. Encloses another letter from the Minister of Foreign Affairs, the Marquis of Aracaty, concerning the payment of duties on stores landed there for the American naval squadron [6:1400-01]. Reports that the government intends to require such duties, regardless of nationality, on all supplies shipped commercially. Suggests "that all that is necessary to give an American Merchantman the Transport Character, is that she be provided with two or four guns, wear a pennant, that on entering the port she refuse the Custom House visit calling herself a Transport, and that an Officer comes in charge of the stores." States that the transit duty amounts to six percent upon an established evaluation. ALS. DNA, RG59, Cons. Disp., Rio de Janeiro, vol. 3 (M-T172, R4). Received March 10, 1828. An endorsement by Clay on wrapper (AE), "Translations to be made—And Copies to be sent to Mr [Samuel L.] Southard," seems to apply to notes by Aracaty dated December 18, 1827 and January 3, 1828.

From JAMES MADISON   Montpellier, January 6, 1828
I have duly recd. the copy of your Address [6:1394-6] politely forwarded to me. Although I have taken no part in the depending contests and have been led to place myself publicly on that ground, I could not peruse the appeal you have made without being sensible of the weight of testimony it exhibits, and of the eloquence by which it is distinguished.

Having occasion to write to Mr. [Henry Peter] Brougham on a subject[1] which interests our University [Virginia], I take the liberty of asking your friendly attention to the letter which I enclose. I hope it may find an early conveyance from the Department of State with dispatches about to be destined for London. Should that not be the case, Mr. [Daniel] Brent will cause you the trouble of giving the intimation, that a duplicate may seek some other channel. It is desirable that the letter should reach Mr. B with as little delay as may be.

ALS. DLC-HC (DNA, M212, R3).   1. Regarding an attempt which was finally successful in June, 1828 by the University of London to engage the services of George Long, professor of ancient languages at the University of Virginia. Henry Peter Brougham, later Lord Brougham, chairman of the Council of the British institution, acted as intermediary in the matter. See Philip Alexander Bruce, *History of the University of Virginia, 1819-1919.* 5 vols. (New York, 1920-1922), 2:146-8.

From WILLIAM PHILLIPS   Philadelphia, January 6, 1828
I must beg your indulgence for occupying your attention, necessarily taken up by affairs of the greatest national importance, particularly at this crisis—But Sir You I am sure will allow me upon the eve of my departure from the US [6:1061, 1099-100, 1128-31], to express to you my unfeigned gratitude, for the prompt & liberal manner you acted to me when I had the honor of a personal interview in August of last year[1]—I hope it is not too late to wish you a happy new year, and that it may close with as complete a triumph, over your relentless political persecutors, as your most ardent friends can desire—The celebrated Canal Contractor [Aaron H.] Palmer is about taking the benefit of the insolvent act in N York;[2] so that I may chaunt a *Requiem*, over my $3000. advanced—I have no claims of any kind or description upon the Government any farther than that I was induced to make these advances by the Representative of the Government of the US. Col [John] Williams [6:159-60, 865], which he will Substantiate upon reference if necessary—I shall leave town tomorrow, and expect to meet The Honl. Mr. [William B.] Rochester in Omoa, when he may reckon upon any assistance I can render; my ulterior destination is Guatamala [*sic*, Guatemala]—the City.

ALS. DNA, RG59, Dip. Disp., Central America, vol. 1 (M219, R2).   1. The thrust of this interview is not known.   2. The New York State bankruptcy law of 1801, the subject of the U.S. Supreme Court decision (1827) in *Ogden* v. *Saunders* (12 Wheaton 213).

From SAMUEL L. SOUTHARD, "Navy Department," January 7, 1828. Acknowledges receipt of Clay's note of January 2 and returns Nathaniel Hart's letter. States that "The views of this Department upon the cultivation & preparation of Hemp were fully presented in reports made to the Senate on the 5th. January 1825, and to the House of Representatives of the 20th. Decemr. 1827," which reports "may be found among the printed documents." Adds that "if a Contract were entered into with Mr. Hart or any one else, no advances could be made under existing laws." Copy. DNA, RG45, Navy Dept., Letterbooks, vol. 1821-1831, p. 285.

    The hemp report of January 5, 1825, is in *Sen. Docs.,* 18 Cong., 2 Sess., no. 12; that of December 20, 1827, is in *House Docs.,* 20 Cong., 1 Sess., no. 22. The 1823 law governing advances to contractors is in 3 *U.S. Stat.,* 723-4.

To CHARLES R. VAUGHAN, January 7, 1828. Acknowledges receipt of Vaughan's note of December 26, 1827, and quotes Section 4 of the Act of Congress of January 7, 1824 [4:116, 644]. States, by direction of the President, that "it would be deemed a compliance with the intention of Congress, if the Government of Hanover would declare through Mr. Vaughan, or in some other authentic form, that no discriminating duties of tonnage or impost are imposed or levied within the ports of the Kingdom of Hanover, upon vessels wholly belonging to Citizens of the United States, or upon merchandize the produce or manufacture thereof imported in the said Vessels." Copy. DNA, RG59, Notes to Foreign Ministers and Consuls, vol. 3, pp. 412-4 (M38, R3). AN, draft. CSmH.

From JOHN YOUNG, St. Louis, January 7, 1828. States that he is now a resident of Galena, Illinois, and that as a consequence of the Winnebago War, the people of this mining area have formed a Committee of Safety and appointed James Craig as their agent "to carry their claims ag[ains]t. the Government & their petitions for the relief of certain Grievances to Washington." Declares: "The growing wealth & the immense increase of Population in that section of the country, imperiously demands a change of Rule by which these mining districts have been governed—" Adds: "The fostering care which you have always taken of our interest, in the western country, even from Kentucky to the western boundary of Missouri when it was in Danger, has encouraged me on this occasion to solicit your aid." In a postscript, recommends James Craig to negotiate a treaty between the U.S. and the Winnebago Indians and to survey the land boundaries. ALS. DNA, RG59, Misc. Letters (M179, R66). For Federal administration of lead mine leases in the Galena area, see White, *The Jeffersonians*, 515–6; William J. Peterson, "The Lead Traffic on the Upper Mississippi, 1823–1848," *MVHR* (June, 1930), 17:73.

From ALEXANDER H. EVERETT, Madrid, no. 94, January 8, 1828. Reports that King Ferdinand VII remains at Barcelona but is expected to return to the capital "about the last of this month." Mentions that a "project of a general amnesty" is now under consideration by the Council of Castille, the members of which are in disagreement as to "whether it shall take effect from the year 1808 and include the Afrancesados or partizans of the Napoleon Government, or only apply to the adherents to the Constitution of 1820."

States that the Russian Minister to Spain, Pierre d'Oubril, has gone to Barcelona to deliver a letter from Emperor Nicholas I to Ferdinand VII complimenting the latter "upon his success in quelling the late insurrection." Adds that the letter also contains "some friendly but urgent advice to the King to improve the period of tranquillity which is now likely to ensue for introducing the necessary reforms in the administration." Notes that he has learned from d'Oubril that the Emperor is assuring the "other powers of Europe" that he will [not?] use the results of the Battle of Navarino [6:1241] to effect "any object of aggrandisement or exclusive in national interest."

Reveals that the "last accounts" from Turkey indicate that war appears inevitable and that should war commence the British Ministry "will assume anew a purely Tory complexion"; also that Lord Goderich "has already offered his resignation, and only holds his place until a new arrangement can be made." Concludes that the Russians "have terminated a brilliant campaign in Persia by a most advantageous peace, which has at this moment the additional convenience of leaving their armies entirely at liberty to act against Turkey [5:691–2; 6:1334, 1343–4]." ALS. DNA, RG59, Dip. Disp., Spain, vol. 28 (M31, R29). Received March 16, 1828.

The Afrancesados, also called "Josefinos," were Spaniards who had supported King Joseph Bonaparte during the French occupation of

Spain in 1808–1813. Ivan F. Paskevich commanded Russian forces in Persia.

From JEPTHA GARRIGUS   Gallatin, Ind., January 8, 1828

all the difference I know in men is in there conduct and I never respect a man because he Has got a little money in his pocket or a little more learning than another, and I ne[e]d not tell you that nearly all the schooling I got was under the forge Hammer in New Jersey, but sir I have a rite to judge of men and of measures, and I once thought that there was scarce such a man on earth as Henry Clay. But how different now. I think Perhaps your Political damnation is not yet sealed but what If you were to go back to God and the people you might Be forgiven, Sir you have been the cause of having a Presedent Elected that was not the peoples choice Particular in the west. if you had of hung to the West nothing but death could of prevented you From being presedent someday, and perhaps yet if you would leave that Eastern faction and return To your old democratic Station the west might awaken the third great Era of your life as public man. I should, think there was not anything so degrading to your feelings as to be upheld by such a combination of aristocracy as one now vendicating your conduct. to wit Charles Hammon[d], of Cincinnati for one and maney more equil as Notorius. I know of but one of all the old eastern Faction but what are well pleased with you and how changed are they with you. Sir a friend of mine in Ohio one of the Electors at the last Presedential Election assured me as him Clay did not get into the House that him Clay would not interfere on either side But would stand nuteral between Genl. Jackson and Adams, that you would not risk your standing in the west to join the East in particular and how mutch better would you have felt today had that of been the case. you would not of had to of went Through the State of Kentucky to of tried to of propect up a fallen reputation nether would you of had such a powerfull opposition there. Sir stop and think Before you farther go is it not better for a man to confess This rong than to persist in that rong. this from him that was on[c]e your friend. [P.S.] If you wish to know who it is that has so much Impudence I refer you to Col T. H. Blake of Terrehaute [*sic*] and John Woods Esq of Hamilton Ohio

ALS. DLC-HC (DNA, M212, R3). Garrigus at this time was justice of the peace in Parke County. He served three terms in the Indiana lower house in the late 1830s and early 1840s. Dorothy Riker, ed., *Executive Proceedings of the State of Indiana, 1816–1836* (Indianapolis, 1947), 551, 553; Dorothy Riker and Gayle Thornbrough, *Indiana Election Returns, 1816–1851* (Indianapolis, 1960), 238, 248, 260.

To ARCHELAUS M. HUGHES   Washington, January 8, 1828

I received your letter of the 3d ultimo, and I assure you that although I have not the pleasure of a personal acquaintance with you, the perusal of it excited a lively interest and sympathy. I had before heard that there was much persecution and proscription in Tennessee, on account of political opinion, but I had no idea it was carried to the lengths which you describe.

With respect to the particular object of your letter, that of obtaining a clerkship in the Department of State, or some other public employment that would support your family, I regret to have to inform you that, at present, there is no vacancy at my disposal. It is not my practice to make promises in advance; all, therefore, that I can say *is,* that in the event of a vacancy arising, I will give to your application full consideration. Colonel [Andrew] Erwin, from Tennessee who is now in my house [6:1379–80] has spoken of you in terms which have augmented the interest excited by the perusal of your letter.

The pressure of business does not allow me to notice, particularly, various other topics of your letter. With respect to the Presidential election, there is enough of hope and probability of an issue favorable to our civil institutions, to animate patriotism, and stimulate the highest exertions of all who are friendly to the durability of the Republic. We have already, since the commencement of the new year, received from several quarters encouraging information. A friend from Pittsburg[h] writes me, that on the first day of the new year, the election for their local officers, terminated in favor of the Administration.[1] He adds, that at the last Presidential election, Mr. Adams did not get twenty votes in that city.

LS. THi. Hughes, of Dresden, Tenn., an anti-Jackson man, was later (1830s) clerk of the Tennessee state senate and an unsuccessful candidate for the U.S. House. One Jacksonian described him as the "most violent and foul-mouthed oposition man you ever heard." Weaver, ed., *Polk Correspondence,* 4:95–6, 332.   1. The front-running local candidate on the Adams ticket polled 537 votes. His counterpart on the Jackson slate received 401. The election, "which turned decidedly on the presidential question," brought out about a third more Pittsburgh voters than usual. *Niles' Register* (January 12, 1828), 33:315.

From DAVID B. OGDEN   New York, January 8, 1828

On my return home yesterday from Poughkeepsie where I have been for a few days attending the Court of Chancery, your address to the People of the United States [6:1394–6] was put into my hand. Believing as I have always done that the charge of corruption brought against you and Mr. Adams at the last election was false and malicious in the extreme, and thinking that no man in the country not blinded by prejudice or misled by party feelings gave it any credence—I felt sorry that you had deemed it necessary to make any further address to the public on the subject—But having read your address, I cannot withold from you the expression of the pleasure I have derived from its perusal. You have collected a mass of evidence as to the purity of your intentions and the patriotism of your conduct upon the late Election, which I did not suppose you could have collected and which must be considered as conclusive upon every fair and candid mind, if any such mind ever had a doubt upon the subject—And you have traced up the origin of the slander to its source—In this you have performed a great public duty—If the People of this country ever for a moment believe that a man capable of originating such a slander, for the purpose of promoting his own ambitious views is a proper man for the head of this government, then my dear Sir, it seems to me, that we must despair of the Republic—

But the People are seldom governed by sober reflection—Their passions and prejudices are first roused and excited by artful men, and what on earth is so resistless as an infuriated populace?

Excuse me for troubling you with this. I could not forbear writing to

thank you for having made this last appeal to the public—It ought to produce a feeling of heartfelt indignation every where against the au-thors & propagators of the slanderous tale.

ALS. DLC-HC (DNA, M212, R1).

From WILLIAM PLUMER, JR.   Epping, N.H., January 8, 1828

The deep interest which I take in the success of the Administration, of which you form so essential a part, has prompted me repeatedly to write you on the subject; I have hitherto forborn to do so principally from an unwillingness to intrude upon your time with the mere expression of my opinions. I cannot however refrain from expressing to you the very high gratification which I have just received, from the perusal of your trium-phant vindication of yourself against the base charges of corruption & intrigue, brought against you in the late Presidential election. To all generous minds your Address [6:1394-6] must be as pleasing as it is conclusive & unanswerable. To me it was unnecessary, as a mere vindica-tion of your conduct, because I never had any doubt as to the propriety of your conduct on that occasion. From my situation at the time, I pos-sessed more than common opportunities of knowing what took place in relation to this important transaction: & my anxiety for Mr Adams's success did not suffer me to omit any opportunity of informing myself minutely on the subject. My intercourse with the friends of the several candidates, particularly with those of Mr Adams, Mr Crawford & your-self, was constant, intimate, & extensive. With many of them, I conversed freely & frequently on this subject, & the result of all that I heard, that I saw, & that I knew, was a conviction, founded on innumerable facts & observations, that, in this difficult & delicate juncture, your conduct was marked by great purity of motive, by a deep sense of duty, & by much prudence & discernment in the course proper to be pursued.

It was my practice, while a Member of Congress, to note down, on my return home, in a journal which I kept for that purpose, every thing of an interesting nature which had occurred during the session. From this journal I take the liberty to send you some extracts,[1] which go to sustain various statements contained in your late Address [6:1394-6]. The first is under date of "June 1824", & was written immediately on my return from Washington which I left on the 27th of May. It is as follows.

"I spoke but twice to Mr Clay on the subject of the Presidential Election. The first was with respect to the Caucus, against which he declared himself; but professed to be governed, in this whole matter, entirely by the advice of his friends. The other conversation related to General Jackson. It was soon after Pennsylvania declared for the Gen-eral. He spoke with equal & good sense of this subject. It was, he said, truly discouraging to see the people so intoxicated & deluded by a little military glory—that a man totally unknown to the civil history of the country—who knew nothing of the laws, or the Constitution—who, in short, had, no other recommendations than what grew out of his fortu-nate campaign at New Orleans, should be thought of for President of the United States—& was preferred by so many to all others & at a time too, when some of the ablest men the country had ever produced (he did not

mean, he said, to include himself in the number), men who had grown gray in the civil departments of the Government, in Congress, in Diplomatic missions, & in the Cabinet, were before the public as candidates for that office—was, he said, such a symptom of the diseased state of public sentiment, as must appear equally alarming & discouraging, whether viewed by those who saw the highest objects of laudable ambitions snatched from them by a military chief, or by those calmer observers who look with philosophic or prophetic eyes into the causes of the permanence or decay of our free institutions."

I not only considered those remarks of your as eminently just; but I spoke of them, at the time, to some of my friends, as indicating very clearly your intention to support either Mr Adams or Mr Crawford, in preference to General Jackson, should you ever be called upon to decide between them.

What was my own view, in relation to yourself, appears from the following extract, under the same date with the last, ''If Mr Adams succeeds, he cannot do a better or a wiser thing than to bring Mr Clay into the Cabinet, as Secretary of State.'' This opinion was, I know common, even at that early period, with the friends of Mr Adams—so that your appointment, the next year, to that office, was neither strange, or unexpected by them. Their sense of your fitness for that office is no afterthought, growing out of your vote for Mr Adams, but an act of justice, rendered to your talents & your standing while you were still a rival candidate.

The following extract relates to your determination not to suffer your name to be used as an obstacle to prevent an election by the House. It confirms very strongly the statement of Mr [Josiah S.] Johnston, referred to in your Address. This extract is from the Journal, already quoted, under date of ''March 1825'', & was written immediately on my return from the session of 1824-5. ''General [Duncan] M'Arthur of Ohio told me that, meeting Mr Clay one day, when it was supposed he would receive the votes of Louisiana, he told him that if he came into the House, as one of the three candidates, it would be by so small a vote from the people, that he found that his friends could do him very little service there—that Mr Clay answered he hoped he should not be returned to the House as one of the candidates, since his election, (if it could take place,) would be contrary to the expressed opinion of a vast majority of the people; & that, if he should be returned to the House, by receiving the votes of Louisiana, he should think it his duty, under such circumstances to decline the support of his friends; & use his own influence in favor of one of the other candidates.'' This must have been prior to the 16th of December, when information reached the City of the votes of Lousiana not being for you.

I could give you many other extracts from my Journal on this subject, if it were necessary; but I will trouble you with only one more, which relates to Mr [Daniel Pope] Cooke [sic, Cook] of Illinois; whose death [6:1223] put it out of your power to obtain any statement from him on the subject of his vote. It is from the Journal, already quoted, under date of ''March 1825''; & is as follows—''For some time, Mr Cooke kept his sentiments very much to himself; but it was no sooner known that Ken-

tucky & Ohio would vote for Mr Adams, than Mr Cooke gave way to his long cherished partiality for Mr Adams, & determined to vote for him. He told me that, at one time, he thought it almost certain that every Western State, except Illinois, would vote for General Jackson; which, with the aid of other states upon which his friends relied, would have secured his election; that, under this impression, he could not see that his vote would be of any advantage, in that event, to Mr Adams; but that the moment he learned the intended course of Mr Clay & his friends, he "determined to vote for Mr Adams, let the consequences to himself be what they might." That Mr Cooke was, from the beginning, in favour of Mr Adams, is very generally known. Of this fact, he himself informed me, as early as the winter of 1822–3, &, I think, the year before.

If the preceeding extracts should be of any use to you, it will be a source of much satisfaction to me. They are certainly entitled to more entire credence than any statement which I could now make, from mere recollection; as they were written, at the time, for my own use only, & with no expectation that they would ever be seen by any other person. A desire to contribute something however small, towards repelling charges against your character cruel as they are unfounded, is my only motive for making this communication; which must be as unexpected to you, as it is spontaneous on my part. . . .

DLC-HC (DNA, M212, R3). 1. Portions included in *A Supplement to the Address of Henry Clay . . .*, June 10, 1828; also see Clay to Plumer, January 24, 1828.

From JOEL R. POINSETT, Mexico, no. 113, January 8, 1828. Reports that negotiations "were renewed this day" and that he expects to conclude the "Treaty of Friendship, Navigation, and Commerce favorably and promptly." States that the Chamber of Deputies insists upon the insertion of an article confirming that part of the Spanish–American Treaty of 1819 setting the limits [boundaries] of the territories of the two contracting parties [2:678, 803–16]. Points out that since the Mexican negotiators, Jose Ignacio Esteva and Juan Jose Espinosa de los Monteros, have informed him that he could not consent to the inclusion of that article "it would be useless to discuss the other articles of the Treaty," he has consented. However, since the article on boundaries was to be perpetual, while the rest of the treaty was to have a definite time limit, he had proposed, and it was agreed upon, that the two concerns be divided into "distinct conventions."

Reveals further that he had hinted, in a private conversation with one of the plenipotentiaries, "at a remuneration in money to the Mexican Government as an inducement to extend our boundary to the Rio del Norte." Reports, however, that his Mexican counterpart had replied that such an arrangement, which would be interpreted as a dismemberment of Mexican territory, would be unconstitutional. Consequently, he has agreed to the Mexican position on the subject of territorial limits.

ALS. DNA, RG59, Dip. Disp., Mexico, Vol. 3, (M97, R4). Received February 23, 1828.

Distinct conventions were decided upon. The January 12, 1828, Treaty of Limits with Mexico accepted the Sabine-Red River boundary line as defined in the 1819 U.S. treaty with Spain. But not until April 5,

tion concluded.

1831, was the U.S.-Mexican Treaty of Amity, Commerce, and Naviga-

From PETER B. PORTER   Albany, N.Y., January 8, 1828

I received your "Address [6:194-6]" by yesterday's mail, for which I thank you. It is a triumphant vindication, and I am glad that it has come out, because I think it has traced the calumny, pretty satisfactorily, to the source from whence it no doubt originated: It was not necessary how-ever to your justification in the mind of one honourable man. Your favour of the 29th Ult. was received several days since, and it affords some consolation to see, through the mists in which we are enveloped, that light is beginning to beam in some other parts of the Union.

This is a day of great parade & circumstance and all the authorities, civil & military are preparing to do honor to the battle of Orleans, & its *hero*. The Jackson spirit is, if possible, more violent & outrageous here, than it ever was in Pennsylvania. The symptom is favourable, for the greater the effervescence, the sooner it will subside. You may have ob-served that our Governor [De Witt Clinton], in his late message, recom-mends that the President should be eligible for one term only, and, in support of his recommendation, evidently, but darkly, alludes not only to the management & intrigues which may happen in future elections, but to those which have heretofore been employed. This part of the message was referred, by our Senate, no doubt by previous concert, to a committee of three—two of whom, [Robert] Bogardus & [John] C. Spencer are outrageous Jackson Clintonians.[1] They, yesterday, made a report, which I have not yet seen, but which, it is said, repeats in strong & positive terms, the charge of intrigue & corruption against you & Mr. Adams. It was accompanied with resolutions which I have seen, and which assert, in substance, that the election of Genl. Jackson, who was the undoubted choice of the people, was defeated by intrigue & man-agement. The Report produced a strong sensation in the Senate, and will produce a still stronger one should the resolutions be adopted & sent to our house, of which however I doubt.[2]

The course adopted by the House of Reps. on the 31st Ult. in rela-tion to the Tariff,[3] is producing good effects, and has opened the eyes of many honest men who had been persuaded by [Martin] Van Buren &c that the Jacksonians were friendly to an increased rate of duties. The people of the interior of this State are alive to the subject; and it is by the influence of the tariff question, if by any thing, that the administration can be sustained here.

Letters were received, last week, from V. Buren & [Silas] Wright[4] by their friends here, advising that a Legislative Caucus be immediately held for the purpose of nominating Jackson.[5] Some steps have been taken to sound the members accordingly—but I am of opinion that we shall be able to keep it off until some more decisive information is ob-tained in regard to the fate of the tariff. [Peter]. R. Livingston, who is very popular with the members will take a decided stand with us on this point. In your next letter to me, say something accidentally, that will be personally flattering to him, & which I may shew him, in confidence [Clay to Porter, January 14, 1828]. (Burn this)

I have in my possession, copies of the whole series of Maps made by our surveyors under the 6th & 7th articles of the Treaty [of Ghent], & which rightfully belong to the Government. Maj. [Donald] Fraser, our late Secretary—a very worthy man, in moderate circumstances, & in very delicate health owing to the hardships he suffered during the late war, is desirous of obtaining the privilege of making reduced copies from them with a view to publication. Will there be any objection to granting him this privilege?[6] P. S. 5. OClock P.M. The Jackson celebration turns out to be quite a lean affair, although a great noise has been made about it, & still more will be made tomorrow—*in the Newspapers.*[7]

ALS. InU. Letter marked *"Confidential."*   1. For Robert Bogardus, a New York City lawyer, see *CAB.* Charles Stebbins, of Madison County, was the third member of the committee.   2. The resolutions in the state Senate urged amendments to the U.S. Constitution limiting presidential tenure and preventing the choice of presidents by the U.S. House of Representatives in any "event or contingency." The resolutions did not reach the N.Y. House. Albany *Argus,* January 8 and 11, 1828.   3. On December 31, 1827, the U.S. House of Representatives resolved to empower its Committee on Manufactures to investigate "the present condition of our manufactures" and to report its findings back to the House. *Register of Debates,* 20 Cong., 1 Sess., 873–89. An analysis of the 102 to 88 vote showed, as *Niles' Register* explained its meaning, the "hostile character" of the resolution from the standpoint of those who favored protective tariffs, particularly "for protection in the growth and manufacture of wool, etc." *Niles' Register* (January 5, 1828), 33:289.   4. For the long and varied political career of Silas Wright, at this time a Canton, New York congressman, see *DAB.*   5. On January 31, such a caucus, attended by 23 state senators and 87 assemblymen, was held. Albany *Argus,* February 1 and 2, 1828.   6. Fraser seems not to have followed through on this venture.   7. The Albany *Argus* of January 9 reported that the anniversary of the Battle of New Orleans was joyfully celebrated at a dinner, attended by 350 persons, and was followed by a ball.

From THOMAS L. L. BRENT, Lisbon, no. 49, January 9, 1828. Encloses "a translation of the speech made . . . by the Infanta Regent," Isabel Maria, to "The Royal Session for opening the ordinary General Cortes . . . as prescribed by the Constitution on the 2d. January." Notes: "She encourages them to persevere in the zeal heretofore displayed in the service of their country and in the consolidation of the constitutional System, as it is expected of them by the Emperor [Peter IV]." Summarizes briefly the proceedings in the Cortes thus far. Reports that on "The day after Christmas," when "the diplomatick Corps waited upon the Infanta Regent, to offer the compliments of the season," he "never saw the court thinner: the nobility having preferred waiting on the Queen [Carlota Joaquina]; and upon a lady who had been the nurse of the Infante Dom Miquel to whom he has occasionally written from Vienna." Continues: "It is worthy of observation that previous to it's being decided that he was to be Regent she was only visited by two of the nobility." States that "The Bank [of Lisbon] has resumed payment in metal . . . of it's small notes [6:1361-2]" and that "It's failure has not been" as injurious "as had been anticipated." Adds that "Miguel left Vienna the 6th. of last month and reached Paris the 20th." LS. DNA, RG59, Dip. Disp., Portugal, vol. 7 (M43, R6). Received March 11, 1828.

From FRANCIS T. BROOKE   Richmond, January 9, 1828
Our convention [6:923-6] is going on Slowly though as yet harmoniously two committees were formed to day one to make out an electoral ticket and the other to report an address &c—our numbers increase daily it is

23

to day more than 200, I have placed on the latter committee the best talents we have, and I hope for the best but am not Sure that I shall be intirely gratified, it is proposed that after the committee reports we shall have Some good Speeches illustrating the address or resolutions, though taking different grounds on which no question will be taken in which Some defence of the admn will be introduced to be decided on by the people—I wish I had your talents or some of Bonapartes guard, though I have no cause to complain except of the people in Galleries—[1]

ALS. InU.   1. Obscure reference.

From HENRY & DAVID COTHEAL, New York, January 9, 1828. Appeal for government assistance in the case of their schooner, the *Ben Alam,* which, having obtained a license agreeably to Colombian law "to trade on the Mosquito Shore," was seized at the Chagres River in October, 1827, and charged with smuggling. State that they have been informed that "vessel and cargo were both condemned and the Captain & Supercargo condemned to six years labour on the public works," and that the charge of illicit trading is without foundation. ALS. DNA, RG76, Misc. Claims, Colombia. Last page of the document is torn and a part of it is missing.

Endorsed (AEI) by Clay on cover to the effect that Beaufort T. Watts, Chargé in Bogota, would be instructed to take the case up with the Colombian government, but that "some evidence had better be furnished, if it can be obtained."

On February 18, the Cotheals submitted documents for their claim. Three days later, February 21, they transmitted an affadavit of Silas Kellogg, Supercargo of the *Ben Alam,* noting that "The papers most wanted from Panama are the copy of condemnation and the proceedings of the Court, to know on what grounds the Schooner was condemned." Both letters in *ibid.*

The Cotheals inquired on June 20 if William Henry Harrison, the new American Minister to Colombia, would be instructed to take up the case of the *Ben Alam.* Note that the State Department has already certified copies of all documents pertaining to the case and that the originals presumably can be obtained from the New York underwriter who insured the ship. Ask also if Alexander H. Everett, U.S. Minister in Madrid, has pressed the claim against Spain for the *Mosquito* and its cargo. *Ibid.*

On October 13, the Cotheals asked Clay if and when William Henry Harrison will sail from New York on his mission as U.S. Minister to Colombia. Wish verbally to explain to him "the nature of the piratical act we complain of" in the "condemnation of our Schooner Ben Alam at Chagres." ALS. DNA, RG59, Misc. Letters (M179, R66). Complain futher, on October 23, that in spite of previous correspondence with the Department on the *Ben Alam* claim, they had discovered in a conversation with Harrison in New York that "he has never heard of our case nor has he any papers relating to it." Ask that Harrison's departure from New York be delayed until Clay can instruct him on the matter. LS. DNA, RG76, Misc. Claims, Colombia.

On October 27, Clay transmitted documents in the case to Harrison and instructed him to take it up with the Colombian government on the "earliest proper occasion." LS. DNA, RG84, Foreign Service Posts, Mexico (MR17, frames 313-5). For eventual settlement of the case, see *Sen. Docs.,* 35 Cong., 2 Sess., no. 18, p. 125.

From EDWARD KING   Columbus, Ohio, January 9, 1828
The Jackson forces made their appearance here yesterday to the number of 160—they have made out their ticket E. A Brown at the head.[1] But they are quarrelling among themselves—Some of the new converts require *pap.* They wont give it—Others have received it, which meets with the disapprobation of those who have borne the heat and burden of the day—Your Capital address [6:1394-6] arrived at the very nick of time. I assembled about 50 of our friends & read it to them—And took order & subscription for 5000 copies to be distributed through the State in newspaper form—it will be ready on the 14th for distribution— Ohio is safe

ALS. DLC-HC (DNA, M212, R3).   1. Ethan A. Brown of Hamilton County who headed a slate of sixteen Jackson electors. Columbus *Ohio State Journal,* January 9 and 12, 1828.

From JOEL R. POINSETT, Mexico, no. 114, January 9, 1828. Reports that "The party in opposition to the government of Mexico and to the existing federal institutions, known here by the name of the *Scotch* party [5:649; 6:880], having been defeated in all the elections and failed in all their political combinations and attempts to regain the power they had lost, have at length appealed to arms." Admits that, although "not ignorant" of the designs and determination of this party, he "could not believe, that, aware as they must have been of their weakness, they would hazard so much upon ... so remote a prospect of success." Notes the beginning of the insurrection on December 23, 1827 under "one Manuel Montano," and comments on the demands, including one for the expulsion of "the Envoy of the United States," announced by the rebels. Traces succeeding events: the appointment of General Vicente Guerrero to lead the government forces; "the clandestine departure of the Vice President, General Nicolas Bravo, who placed himself at the head of the malcontents"; the raising of "the standard of revolt" by General Miguel Barragan, Governor of Veracruz; and the capture by Guerrero of the leaders of the insurrection. Professes to be "at a loss to account for the conduct of the Members of the diplomatic corps," who "openly advocated the cause of the insurgents and publicly expressed their wishes for the success of General Bravo." Predicts that the British Chargé, Richard Pakenham, and the French Consul General, Alexandre Martin may "some day" feel the public indignation their course has aroused. Encloses documents that "give ... a view of ... this revolutionary movement and of the alarm that prevailed in the government." Expresses his belief that "The triumph of the liberal party is now secure." LS. DNA, RG59, Dip. Disp., Mexico, vol. 3 (M97, R4). Received February 23, 1828.

For the history of this uprising, see Bancroft, *Mexico,* 5:37-40; for Nicolas Bravo, see *CAB.*

From **ROBERT TILLOTSON,** New York, January 9, 1828. Refers to the report communicated by "The Collector of this Port . . . this day [*sic*, January 5] . . . to the Department of State . . . as containing all the information that could be collected regarding the illegal augmentation of the crew of the Buenos Ayrean Brig of War General Brandison [*sic*, Brandizen] and her prize while lying in this Port [6:1406]." Promises, should sufficient evidence "be obtained of the direct agency of persons residing in this District . . . to submit the same to the next Grand Jury of this District." ALS. DNA, RG59, Misc. Letters (M179, R66). Cf. above, Thompson to Clay, Janaury 5, 1828.

From **PHILIP YOST, JR.**   New Orleans, January 9, 1828.
[Discusses his application for the position as U.S. Consul at Port au Prince, Haiti. Continues:]

Yesterday was a great day among the Jacksonites—[1] and they done their utmost to make the best of it—but a poorer display I have never seen—They tryed to get up a dinner, and fixed the tickets of Admission at 6$. but Could not get a sufficient quantity made up. and had to reduce the price to 3$. when about 6 Hours before dinner the Subscription was filled or rather amtd to about 475 persons, and the Managers had to obligate themselves to [John] Davis [2:691][2] to pay the Balance—You need not fear Louisiana She will hang fast to the present administration if proper Steps are taken—I was an officer in the Army at the time when Jackson was here, was in both engagements—[3] but unfortunately have never been named among them although I think my Services justifyed it Col. [William] Piatt [3:6] of Cina [Cincinnati]. is here who was a Qrmaster Genl. at the time he comes as the Jackson Delegate from Cina. You surely must be aware that this said Piatt made his fortune through Jackson who Signed returns for Sundries furnished the Army which never was done, and he made about 25 or $30.000 by it if you will examine the documents of the campaign. here which was allowed to Piatt by Special Act of Congress as well as yourself when this Claim Passed[4]—Please let me hear from you on the subject of my appointment. I shall give you the news of this. City occaisianally

ALS. DNA, RG59, A. and R. (M531, R8).   1. Thirteenth anniversary of the Battle of New Orleans.   2. John [or Jean] Davis ran a combined theater-ballroom-hotel at 38 Orleans. See Nelle Smither, "A History of the English Theater at New Orleans, 1806–1842," *LHQ* (January, 1945), 28:90; Joseph G. Tregle, Jr., "Early New Orleans Society: A Reappraisal," *JSH* (February, 1952), 18:28.   3. Army records indicate that 1st Lt. Yost, 1st Regiment, was "dropped" from the service on January 1, 1815, a week before the final battle. *HRDUSA.*   4. The "Special Act of Congress" was passed on February 19, 1814. It allowed Piatt the pay of Deputy Quartermaster General from July 17, 1811, to January 27, 1812. 6 *U.S. Stat.,* 128. The vote on the bill was apparently by voice.

From **THOMAS L. L. BRENT,** Lisbon, no. 50, January 10, 1828. Reports that the departure of Frederico Torlade de Azumbuja for the U.S. has been further delayed [4:524; 6:313-4], but that Candido Jose Xavier, the Minister of Foreign Affairs, has informed him that Torlade will soon be departing. Notes that Torlade has recently informed him that no commercial treaty "would be made with any power, until some

26

arrangements in contemplation, arising out of the revision of the last commercial Treaty between Portugal and Great Britain [5:85] should be brought to a conclusion." ALS. DNA, RG59, Dip. Disp., Portugal, vol. 7 (M43, R6). Received March 11, 1828. The U.S. Treaty of Commerce and Navigation with Portugal was not concluded until August 26, 1840.

To FRANCISCO TACON, Philadelphia, January 10, 1828. Acknowledges receipt of Tacon's letter of December 21, 1827. States that "assuming all the facts stated by Mr. [Hilario de Rivas y] Salmon to be true, they do not present a case which could authorize the President to interpose. The case made out is that of a private injury, committed on the property of a foreign subject, by a citizen of the United States with the aid of a private Merchant vessel [*Mary*] engaged in ordinary navigation [5:160]. In such a case the President has no power to interfere; but I am happy to be able to add that the Tribunals of the United States are competent to afford full redress, and would no doubt administer it, upon a proper appeal to them." Adds that he has "abstained from all investigation into the correctness of the facts communicated by Mr. Salmon" but that the President "would feel himself bound to make" the same decision as Clay now communicates even if all the facts stated by Rivas y Salmon "were fully established." Copy. DNA, RG59, Notes to Foreign Ministers and Consuls, vol. 3, pp. 415–6 (M38, R3). ALI, draft, in CSmH.

On January 15, Tacon acknowledged receipt of the letter and stated that he had transmitted it to his government. LS. DNA, RG59, Notes from Spanish Legation, vol. 9 (M59, R–T12).

From A MEMBER
OF THE CONVENTION   Richmond, January 11, 1828
I am an humble individual but an American Citizen. You Sir occupy a conspicuous station before the people of this nation, rendered more interestingly so by the malignaty of your enemies. All regard to decorum & the principals of honour have been violated in the attacks upon your reputation. I deem it then an act of justice, mere justice to place you in possession of a fact which if given to the publis; will develope in its true colours the character of your most violent & vindictive enemy. There is in this city a letter from Judge [Nathaniel W.] Williams of Tennessee declaring that at the time that A[a]ron Burr was inlisting his army in the west to consummate the treason his disappointed ambition had caused him to conceive: that Genl. Andrew Jackson did offer to him, Williams a Captains Commission in that Army.[1]

For information I refer you to the Revd. John Kerr [5:300–01] who says[2] he has the letter to Saml Branch[3] of Buckingham, Thos S. McClelland of Nelson, Saml Pannill[4] of Campbell, and Frances B Deane jr[5] of Cumberland, to all of whom Mr Kerr mentioned the fact, sayaing that the letter was addressed to Nathaniel Kerr of Pittsylvania [Va.]. all of those gentlemen are now in the city of Richmond and members of the convention.

Judge Nathaniel Williams is the brother in Law of Mr. Kerr.

ALS. DLC-TJC (DNA, M212, R10). On the Convention, see 6:923–6, and Brooke to Clay, January 9, 1828.   1. See 6:409–10. For Jackson's connection with Williams, see also

Bassett, *Correspondence of Andrew Jackson*, 3:391–2, 402. 2. For John Kerr, see Macomb to Clay, misdated May 4, 1826 in 5:300–01; it should be dated May 4, 1827. 3. Branch was a student at Hampden–Sydney College about 1806 and was later Commonwealth's attorney of Buckingham, Va. He was a trustee of the college from 1820 until his death in 1847. J. B. Henneman, "Trustees of Hampden–Sydney College," *VMHB* (October, 1898), 6:182–4; A. J. Morrison, ed., *College of Hampden–Sydney Dictionary of Biography, 1776–1825* (Hampden–Sydney College, 1921), 142–3. 4. Samuel Pannill (1770–1861) was for many years president of the Roanoke Navigation Company. See *WMQ* First Series (October, 1897), 6:113. 5. Francis Browne Deane, Jr., of Cartersville, Va., had been a student at Hampden–Sydney College in 1812, was later a trustee of the school for ten years, and was one of the organizers of the Tredegar Iron Works in Richmond in the mid-1830s. He died about 1860. See Henneman citation in note 3, above, and Morrison, *Dictionary*, 171.

From ROBERT SCOTT   Lexington, January 11, 1828

Herewith please receive your Accounts with Colo. [James] Morrison's Estate, and with me for the quarter ending with the 31 Ulto—[1]

In the specie Acct. with the estate, you will perceive I have charged you with 6 months interest on 17900$—of the T[ransylvania]. University legacy in your hands—I am not satisfied with this charge, because the money might as well remain in your hands as in Bank where it would have produced nothing—I was induced however to make it as it is, to prevent your enemies from having a shadow of complaint on this subject, for they have made themselves very busy with it, and would I believe injure you in that or any other way if possible—[2] If you direct it, I will change the charge as you may think right—In addition to the balance of Cash on hand according to the specie Acct is 2108$. recd. of the Boswells [Joseph and George; 3:668] since the close of the quarter and which will appear in the next Acct

In your A/C with me, you will perceive I have charged two advances of 50$ ea made T. W. Clay—I had no authority for this except his stating you had authorized him to draw upon you—and this I deemed quite sufficient, because he is very studious and reads almost constantly unless when necessarily out on business—From the Acct last referred to you will perceive also, that the charges for repairs &c. on your houses &c., are pretty heavy—particularly on that [5:601–02, 618] lately occupied by Mr. Smith—When incurring these charges I did not go hastily into them, but consulted your friends Kennedy & Smith[3] and we have done in this respect what we beleived most for your interest and hope you will approve it—The house and lot on Poplar Row is now rented to Jos. Ficklin for one year @ 175$ [6:1366]—

I have not been at Ashland for some time, Theo. W. Clay is there every two or three days and both him and Mr [John H.] Kerr says the Jack ["Ulysses"] and Jenny ["Calypso"] are thriving finely [6:1296]—

ALS. KyLxT. No. 1 of this date. 1. Omitted by editors. 2. Allegations that Clay mismanaged the legacy of James Morrison to Transylvania University, to his own profit and benefit, surfaced repeatedly during his political career. See, Van Deusen, *Clay*, 226; Lexington *Kentucky Gazette*, September 21, 1827. The bank reference is obscure. 3. Probably Matthew Kennedy.

From ROBERT SCOTT   Lexington, January 11, 1828

Your two favors of the 26 Novr. and one of the 24th Ulto. came to hand in due course. There not being any thing in them requiring an immediate reply and being somewhat hurried when the two first arrived, deferred acknowleding their receipt until now—

When your letter relative to the baging concern came to hand, Tho. W. Clay informed me he was about writing to you, and as it was intended he should have an interest in it, I requested him to mention to you, that Mr. Henley and myself were of opinion, that to render to each of the partners a just and suitable equivelant in proportion to his Services &c. in the concern, your proposition or specification of terms of partnership required some modification[1]—These were, that Mr. Henley should be allowed in addition to 1/3d. part of the profits the sum of 160$ so as to render his personal services and attention to the business equal to the sum of 400$. including 6 pr. ct. interest on 4000$. being 1/3rd. of the capital to be advanced by you and by myself—And to my self for keeping the Accounts &c. the sum of 150$—These allowances I conceive are but nearly reasonable—as Mr Henley will of course have to attend to the whole drudgery of the business—And as to him, are not near so favorable as those made to Mr. [John] Bruce in the concern of Morrison, Bruce & Gratz—In that concern, [James] Morrison & [Benjamin] Gratz advanced 12,000$ ea and Bruce but 6,000$ [3:443]—the house he resided in belonged to the concern and he occupied it free of rent—they allowed him also, his fuel, meal and meat at the expense of the concern, and he had the cooking and washing done with his own women—All these together, were considerably more advantageous than what I propose for Mr. Henley—And as to what I propose for myself as compensation for keeping the Accounts &c. is I think so very moderate, that on reflection, you will at once accede to it—I am sure you wish for nothing but what is just and equitable between us, but your time and attention is so much occupied by more important affairs that I presume this subject has not had much of your attention—

We have not as yet fixed upon the stile of our firm, because from the inveteracy of your enemies, we were not satisfied of what would be most agreeable to you on that subject—

We have in operation, seven Looms, but are going on rather heavily in consequence of the Scarcity and high wages of experienced hands— and excessive wetness of the weather, which last circumstance has kept up the price of Hemp, it being now @ 6 to 6 $50 per 112 lb—

Please let me hear from you on the subject of this letter as soon as you can with convenience—

Mr. [William G.] Duncan of Louisville, has been engaged to attend to the interest of Colo. Morrison's estate there in the suit of [George] Nicolas's heirs [3:844] and Messrs. [Richard] Chinn and [Robert] Wickliffe here—

Your letter to Jas. Erwin Esqr. was forwarded a day or two after its reception, together with one from me explaining to him the transactions to which your refers.

As yet, nothing further has been done with Mr. [Robert S.] Todd in relation to renting to him the Tamy. Mill[2]—I will attend to what you direct relative to Messrs. [Louis] Marshall and [James E.] Davis—

ALS. KyLxT. No. 2 of this date.   1. This short-lived partnership of Robert Scott, Ozborne Henley, and Clay in the cotton bagging business, was initiated by Scott and

Henley in October of 1827. Lacking sufficient capital, they included Clay in the partnership by an Agreement, dated April 25, 1828. Under terms of the Agreement Clay and Scott were to advance the firm $600 each. Henley was to manage the factory for the annual salary of $160; Scott was to keep the accounts for the annual salary of $150, while Clay was exempted from "any of the labors or business of the concern." ADS, in Scott's hand. DLC–TJC (DNA, M212, R16). This partnership was dissolved by an Agreement of November 18, 1829. See also Clay to Scott, January 22, 1829. 2. Above, 4:758–9; Agreement, March 1, 1828. An endorsement to the agreement, dated February 23, 1828, authorized Scott to recover the property on March 1, 1828.

To FRANCIS PRESTON BLAIR   Washington, January 12, 1828

I have had no reason to be dissatisfied with your conduct, which has been, in respect to our intercourse, manly and honorable.

Extract. Washington *Daily Globe,* October 12, 1844. The full Clay to Blair letter of January 12, 1828, has not been found, but see Blair's reference to its subject matter in Blair to Clay, February 4, 1828. This extract from it was used by Blair prior to the presidential election of 1844 when the charge of a corrupt bargain between Clay and Adams in 1824 was again raised as a campaign issue, and Blair, although a Democrat partisan in 1844, sought once again to disassociate himself from the accusation. For the political circumstances and correspondence surrounding the reappearance of the Clay-Blair exchange sixteen years earlier, see Washington *Daily Globe,* October 12, 1844, and *Niles' Register* (October 12, 1844), 67:84–5. See also, 6:1106–07, 1163–4.

From JAMES BROWN, Paris, no. 78, January 12, 1828.

Encloses copies of his letter "to the Minister of Foreign Affairs, Baron de Damas, and the reply dealing with the subject of discriminating duties imposed at Havre on vessels and cargoes belonging to citizens of the United States, merely because those vessels had on their voyage touched at the ports of a third power [5:624, 639–40, 678; 6:977–82]. Confesses to have been "not a little mortified, after a delay of five months, to find that the answer evaded the main point . . . namely the repayment of the duties." States: "It would seem that this Government is willing to allow our vessels hereafter to touch for orders on their voyage to France, but not to refund the duties already exacted under an unfair interpretation of The [June 24, 1822] Convention [3:53]." Promises to "renew" his "claim for restitution, and obtain if possible a definitive answer." ALS. DNA, RG59, Dip. Disp., France, vol. 23 (M34, R26). Received March 6, 1828. The copies enclosed are of Brown's note to Damas, August 1, 1827, and Damas' reply, December 31, 1827.

From CHRISTIAN GOEHRING, Leipzig, Saxony, January 12, 1828.

Transmits consular report, calling attention to the increase in exportations to the U.S. Urges that the U.S. not "put the value of the Saxon Thaler to 71 Cents at the Custom house," a step which he has been informed in under consideration. Suggests that the old rate of 69 cents is preferable and that the higher figure would encourage "The manufacturers and Merchants of this Country" to "find means of avoiding" it. ALS. DNA, RG59, Cons. Disp., Leipzig, vol. 1 (M–T214, R1). Received February 16, 1828. Endorsed by Clay: "Send a Copy of this to Mr. [Richard] Rush."

To ANDREW MARSCHALK   Washington, January 12, 1828

Your letter, both of the 13th. ulto.[1] and the 20th. of Augt. last, have been received. The President is obliged by your attention to the Moorish

Slave, now in the possession of Mr. Thomas Foster [6:158]. The object of the President being to restore Prince [Abduhl Rahahman], the slave mentioned, to his family and Country [Morocco], for the purpose of making favorable impressions in behalf of the United States, there is one difficulty in acceding to the conditions prescribed by Mr. Foster, which I understand to be, that Prince shall not be permitted to enjoy his liberty in this country, but be sent to his own, free from expense to Mr. Foster, who is pleased to ask nothing for the Manumission of Prince on those conditions.—

I have, therefore, to request that you will complete, the humane agency, which you have so kindly undertaken, by calling upon Mr. Foster, assuring him that the above conditions shall be complied with, and receiving the custody of Prince from him. You will then be pleased to send Prince to this City, either by the river or by the sea, as you may determine to be most convenient, for the purpose of his being transported to his Native Country. In order to defray the expenses of decently, but plainly clothing him, if it should be necessary, and those incident to his voyage and journey to this place, you are authorised to draw upon me, at sight, for a sum not exceeding two hundred dollars. And I have to request that you will have the goodness to render me an Account of the disbursements, you may make under this authority.—[2]

Copy. DNA, RG59, Dom. Letters, vol. 22, pp. 120-1 (M40, R20). 1. I.e., December 18, 1827, not published, but noted in connection with Marschalk to Clay, August 20, 1827. 2. On January 3, 1829, Clay wrote Ralph Randolph Gurley, head of the American Colonization Society, that he was pleased to learn "that Prince is on his way to New York" to embark on the ship *Harriet* which has been chartered by the Colonization Society to convey emigrants to Africa. LS. DLC-Records of the American Colonization Society (DNA, M212, R20). Clay informed John Mullowny, U.S. Consul at Tangier, on January 7 that Mullowny's suggestion of returning Prince to his own country had "received the Presidents approbation." Mentions, however, that Prince "expressed a strong desire of going to Liberia," and the President "thought proper to yield to his inclinations." Order Mullowny to inform the government of Morocco of these events. Copy. DNA, RG59, Cons. Instr., vol. 3, p. 32 (M78, R3). The same day in a letter to Dr. Richard Randall, agent of the Colonization Society, Clay repeated that Rahahman's preference was to go to Liberia, but added that once Prince and his wife were in Liberia, the President would prefer that they "should be sent to that part of Africa in which his relations reside, which is understood to be Timboo," if they can be persuaded to go voluntarily. Authorizes the expenditure of $500 for their transport to "Timboo," or $250 for their subsistence if they stay in Liberia, because "he may, from his great age . . . become a charge upon the colony." Requests that the actions of the President in attempting to restore Rahahman to his native country "be diffused as extensively as practicable." *Ibid.*, p. 31A. Document, with official State Department seal, is in *ibid.*

To JOEL R. POINSETT   Washington, D.C., January 12, 1828

Information has reached this Department that there exists some impediment in the United Mexican States, particularly the Province of Texas, to the recovery of debts and property due, and belonging to citizens of the United States, from Mexican inhabitants [6:593-4]. Upon inquiry of Mr [Pablo] Obregon, he informed me that he was not aware of any such impediment; but that, on the contrary, he believed the tribunals were alike open to foreigners and natives, for the prosecution of all their rights. A Resolution, on this subject, calling for information from the President, was adopted by the House of Representatives, on the 2nd instant, which assumes the existence of such an impediment.[1] I am, therefore, directed by the President to instruct you to inquire into the actual state of the fact. If you should find, upon such inquiry, that the alledged impediment does exist, you will by a representation to the Mexican Government, require its immediate removal. The considerations of justice and policy, as well as of comity, in favour of leaving open the Courts of Justice in all civilized countries, to foreigners, as well as natives, are so obvious that the President cannot doubt that the Government of the United Mexican States will acknowledge, and yield to, their force. It will occur to you to state that the Constitution and laws of the United States have been so attentive to the rights of foreigners, as to make express provision that the courts of the United States shall have jurisdiction in all cases to which they are parties.

The negotiation with which you are charged, and to the early renewal of which the President now confidently looks has the security to reciprocal access to the Courts of Justice of the two countries among its objects.[2] You will recollect that this subject is provided for in the tenth Article of our treaty with Colombia and the twelfth of that with Central America [4:127, 878-9]. Even if you should find no existing obstacle in the administration of justice to foreigners, it will be expedient to insert a similar provision in the treaty which you are expected to conclude. But the motives for its insertion will be much stronger if your investigations should lead to the ascertainment of any existing impediment.

LS. DNA. RG84, Foreign Service Posts, Mexico (R17). L draft, with interlineations by Clay, in DLC–HC (DNA, M212, R8). No. 26.   1. The resolution, introduced December 27, 1827, passed January 2, 1828, asked what arrangements, if any, had been made with the Mexican government to "enable citizens of the United States to recover debts and property belonging to them, from persons absconding from the United States, and taking refuge within the limits of that Government"; also, what steps had been taken to establish the U.S. boundary between Louisiana and the province of Texas. *Register of Debates*, 20 Cong., 1 Sess., 96, 108.   2. See, 4:167; 5:543-4; 6:285-90, 542, 880, 1120, 1250-1, 1347-8; Poinsett to Clay, January 8, 1828.

From PETER B. PORTER, Albany, January 13, 1828. Warns against the appointment of Thomas J. Oakley [6:467-8] who, it is rumored, is to be given the office of United States Attorney for the Southern District of New York, for the purpose "of purchasing him up for the Administration." States that Oakley is "cold, unprincipled & treacherous" and "He was elected as a Tariff man, & has thus far given the measure the true Jackson support."

Recommends that either James Lynch or Ogden Edwards be appointed to the office. Describes Lynch as a successful lawyer, "until within the last two or three years, during which he has been engaged in money transactions in Wall Street." States also that Lynch is a nephew of Peter R. Livingston and that the latter "would be much gratified with the appointment."

Concludes: "There is nothing new here. The Resolutions mentioned in my last [January 8], as having been introduced into the Senate by [Robert] Bogardus & [John C.] Spencer, were followed, two days after, by a substitute offered by Mr [Charles] Stebbins, the third man of the committee. It recommends the same amendments to the Constitution, but divests the original report as well as resolutions of all personality. The Senate have refused to take up the subject, & it will probably rest where it is for several weeks. The attempt too to get up a Legislative Caucus, is I believe, for the present, abandoned." ALS. InU. Letter marked "Confidential."

To JOHN QUINCY ADAMS, January 14, 1828. Reports in response to a House resolution of January 2, 1828, which requested information on negotiations with Mexico. These concern recovery of American property carried into Mexico by "persons absconding from the United States, and taking refuge within the limits of that [Mexican] Government"; and the need "to establish the boundary of the United States between the State of Louisiana, and the province of Texas." States that inquiry was made of the Mexican Minister, Pablo Obregon, about impediments to the recovery of such property. Declares that Obregon said "he was not aware of the existence of any such impediment, but that . . . he believed the tribunals of his country were open alike to foreigners and inhabitants, for the recovery of their debts and the prosecution of all their rights"; also that "an instruction has been addressed to the Minister of the United States at Mexico to inquire into the true state of the fact, and, if necessary, to make such representations or remonstrances as its actual conditions may call for [Clay to Poinsett, January 12, 1828]." Reports that Poinsett, at the beginning of his mission to Mexico "was charged with a negotiation relating to the territorial boundary between that Republic and the United States, in its whole extent . . . [4:171–3]." Adds that "no definitive arrangement on that subject has yet been concluded," and that "it would be premature to publish the correspondence that has passed between the two Governments." LS. DNA, RG59, Report Books, vol. 4, p. 216; also in *ASPFR*, 6:822–3.

   The House Resolution of January 2, 1828, was not published in either the *Annals of Congress* or the *House Journal* for that date; however, Adams took note of it on January 15. See, *House Exec. Doc.* 61, 20 Cong., 1 Sess., p. 3.

From FRANCIS T. BROOKE   Richmond, January 14, 1828
I have not written you for Some days Such has been the State of my health that I could hardly do more than write to my wife [Mary Champe Carter Brooke]—I have been afflicted with a painful indolent and anomalous Swelling on the pan of one of my knees, and am now Suffering under it, though I Shall to day with my friend Colo[ne]l [Hugh] Mercer leave Richmond for my home, you will have Seen and See our proceedings here [6:923–6] in better form by the pens of others than I can now give to them—to remain at my post and to exert what power I had to produce harmony and the happy result to which we have brought our affairs left me no time for anything else, I hope you will be pleased with our address to the people of Virga and resolutions, the address is defective in omitting to notice the objections to the course of the government as to the west India trade, also the mission to Panama,—not owing to any difference of opinion on these Subjects but to the want of time there being Some impatience manifested by the convention, you will perceive that the convention has Substituted me for the central

committee to express its wishes to the Electors on its ticket—this as regards Mr Madison & Mr Monroe is a very delicate Subject [6:1356], I have written to the latter an inofficial note,[1] in which after using all the arguments I was capable of to induce him to accept—I have informed him that I shall not depart from the usage heretofore respected by the central committees here which has been to postpone the communication to the Electors to a period after which in case of refusal vacancies may be filled up—Judge [Archibald] Stuart has promised me to return by Montpellier [sic, Montpelier] and to See Mr Madison—my object is to keep the names of these gentlemen on our ticket as long as possible and to give them full time to reflect on the consequences of a refusal to Serve, and to give them the advantage also of any events that may occur, before they decide, an earlier communication than usage warrants would imply doubt of their acceptance which would be injurious to us and will be avoided un[less—ms. defaced] Some urgency should require it, it is possible the Caucus to night may put them on its ticket,[2] if so I shall be in Some degree perplexed but I shall exercise my best judgment to avoid its effects—will you do me the favour to Shew this to my friends [Samuel L.] Southard [James] Barbour [William] Wirt & [John] Taliaferro and give me the council which you all think best, from Barbour I have expected a letter but received none.

ALS. InU.   1. Brooke to Clay, February 28, 1828.   2. The caucus of the Legislature on the evening of January 14 nominated Jackson for President and John C. Calhoun for Vice President. Neither Madison nor Monroe was placed on the Jackson slate of presidential electors. Richmond *Enquirer*, January 15, 1828.

From NINIAN EDWARDS, Belleville, Illinois, January 14, 1828. Transmits two receipts for taxes on Clay's lands which he has paid. States that Clay probably has been charged too much. Explains: "The tax upon land not patented, is in proportion to the amount paid on it. Yours have, until the last year, been taxed as patented lands. If the whole instalments have not been paid, you will be entitled to a warrant of the Treasury for what you have overpaid." Advises that, since Edwards may change his residence in the future, Clay entrust the payment of his taxes to "Wm. H. Brown esq of Vandalia an Atto at law, the clerk of the Federal court, the real Editor of the Vandalia Intelligencer, an honorable high-min[d]ed gentleman, & as warm a political friend, as you have in the Union." ALS. DLC-TJC (DNA, M212, R13).

Part of this tax bill was paid the following day by Edwards [Edwards to Clay, two memoranda, January 15, 1828; neither published herein]. ADS, in DLC-TJC (DNA, M212, R16).

On August 18 James Hall wrote Clay from the Treasurer's Office in Vandalia to report that a tax refund of $112.74 was due him and that $108.72 had been applied to his taxes for 1828, 1829, 1830, & 1831, leaving a balance of $4.02 which is "at your disposal." ALS. DLC-TJC (DNA, M212, R13). A receipt from Hall of the same date for $108.72 indicates that Clay's lands amounted to about 1360 acres. The acreage of his five lots and their locations, all but one in 14N.10W., were: 160 acres, SE6; 598 acres, Sec. 7; 160 acres, SW8; 281 acres, W.½18; and 160 acres, SE12, 14N. 11W. *Ibid.* (R16).

From ARIEL KENDRICK, Cornish Flat, N.H., January 14, 1828. Solicits a contribution to the Baptist church in Claremont. Notes that the "Presidential question excites an astonishing interest" in New England, but wonders why so much morality and piety is involved in the debate. Says that the newspapers are not always speaking the truth and asserts that "No privilege in this nation is more shamefully abused than is freedom of the press." Rejoices that the Vermont Legislature has endorsed "the general administration especially as the people of that State are known to be high toned 'Republicans'"; thinks also that Governor Ezra Butler of Vermont is "a most excellent man." Condemns the "measures of Mr. [Martin] Van Buren" [6:453-4] and the sharp attacks of Cornelius P. Van Ness on "our illustrious President" [6:408-09, 432]. Wishes however, that the President would "give the *Billiard Table* [6:24-6] to him in whose service it is employed (I mean Satan)" and replace it with some "elegant Bibles" scattered throughout his house. Has heard that the post office in Cornish Flat "was about to fall into other hands" and recommends merchant Newton Whittlesey, "a moral and religious man of good education," for the job. Assures Clay that Whittlesey "is a federalist—we both agree now as to the Administration." ALS. DNA, RG59, Accounting Records, Misc. Letters. Letter erroneously dated December 14 by Kendrick. On October 31, 1827 the Vermont lower house had endorsed the re-election of John Quincy Adams by a vote of 164 to 33. See, *Niles' Register* (November 17, 1827), 33:180. For Ezra Butler, see *DAB*.

From ROBERT KERCHEVAL   Chillicothe, January 14, 1828
It gives me great pleasure to furnish you with the enclosed Copy of a correspondence[1] between Alexander Robinson [*sic*, Robertson] Esq—a highly respectable Citizen of this (Ross) County[2] and myself; detailing his recollections of a Conversation which occured between you & him, whilst travelling together from Srewsberry's[3] tavern to Staunton in Virga. in Nov 1824:—by which he substantiated the fact of your expressed determination to Vote for Mr. Adams in Nov 1824.[4] Our friend Mr. [William] Creighton is personally acquanted with the character of Mr. Robinson and will cheerfully corroborate what I have said of it.

I sir, rejoice and your friends here all rejoice at the signal triumph which you have obtained over your enemies in your recent publication [6:1394-6]. If there are any who still affect to doubt the purity of your motives in Voting for Mr. Adams, I envy neither their feeling nor their sense of moral justice.

With my best wishes for your health, and my ardent prayers for your final and complete triumph over all your enemies, both political and personal. . . .

ALS. DLC-HC (DNA, M212, R3). 1. Robertson to Kercheval, January 12, 1828, published in *Supplement to the Address of Henry Clay*, June 10, 1828, pp. 18-19. 2. Alexander Robertson, a private in the War of 1812, had migrated to Ross County [Chillicothe], Ohio, from Augusta County, Virginia, in 1798 and had taken up farming. He remained in this location and occupation until his death in 1840. *History of Ross and Highland Counties, Ohio* (Cleveland, 1880), 98, 259. 3. Samuel Shrewsberry's tavern was on the Great Kanawha River in western [West] Virginia. 4. The House vote for President was held on February 9, 1825.

From WILLIAM B. LAWRENCE, London, no. 18, January 14, 1828. Discusses pending changes in the Cabinet and speculates at length on who is to replace whom and why. Reports that Prince Don Miguel arrived in London on December 30 but has yet made no "declaration favorable to the Constitutional system" in Portugal or given assurances that a "liberal Ministry" will be appointed there. Notes that some of the probable members of the new British ministry are hostile to the Treaty of London of July 6, 1827, and that there may be changes in Britain's Eastern policy because these members will not "continue their sanction, to the occupation of Moldavia and Wallachia by Russia." Transmits the third volume of "Hertslett's [*sic*, Hertslet's] Commercial Treaties." Observes that the 1826 British–Mexican commercial treaty [5:1005] includes a most-favored-nation clause applicable in "the British dominions out of Europe," and suggests that since this treaty and earlier ones with Buenos Aires [4:104] and Colombia [4:364–5] came "at the time when Great Britain refused even to negotiate with us on the subject of Colonial Trade [they] may not be unworthy of notice as throwing additional light on the policy of this country toward the United States." Adds that Buenos Aires has defaulted on its English debt. ALS. DNA, RG59, Dip. Disp., Great Britain, vol. 35 (M30, R31). Received March 17, 1828. Wellington, who replaced Lord Goderich as Prime Minister at this time, remained in power until November 16, 1830. For Lewis Hertslet and his commercial treaties series, see *DNB*.

To PETER B. PORTER Washington, January 14, 1828
I duly received both your favors of the 3d. and 8h. instant. Your report under the 7h. article of the treaty of Ghent [6:1208–10] has not yet been received, nor that of Mr. [Anthony] Barclay [6:1383].[1] If the latter gentleman has annexed to his report exparte affidavits not submitted to the Board, their effect ought to be counteracted by others, if to be obtained, of an opposite tendency. Or we must object to their reference to the Sovereign Arbitrator. I shall be glad to receive your observations on Mr. Barclay's report.

I see no objection to the privilege desired by Majr. [Donald] Fraser of making copies, on a reduced scale, from the maps in your possession, made by the surveyors under the 6h. & 7h. articles of the treaty of Ghent, for the purpose of publication.

I am glad to learn that the friends of the American System are beginning to open their eyes in your quarter to the dangers with which it is threatened. All that surprizes me is that they have not before perceived it. Of its reality no one here can or I believe, sincerely, does doubt. If they will only reflect that the most considerable portion of the party (that from the South) which supports Genl. Jackson is opposed to the system, and will also take along the fact that the residue of that party (from the middle states and the East) already manifests a disposition to modify their opinions so as to accommodate them to the South, all doubt as to the consequences which would follow their success must vanish.

Our cause begins to arouse its friends to the West, in Pennsa., and in Virginia & North Carolina, to the highest exertions. If the results of the late elections in N. York [6:1185–6] had not inspired the other party with the most extravagant joy, the Country would now be perfectly tranquil. Those results were so unexpected, that we are still anxiously looking towards your State for their probable consequences.

What course, in the present state of things, does P[eter]. R. Livingston Esq. pursue? And [Erastus] Root? And the C. Justice, [John] Savage? I have no personal acquaintance with Mr. Livingston, but I entertain a high respect for him, and a warm gratitude for his firm & efficient support of me heretofore. All unite in ascribing to him talents of the first order. With Root and Savage, you know, I served in the H. of R. I think I have heard that the latter was opposed to Genl. Jackson.

The Admon Convention has just closed its Session at Richmond [6:923–6]. They have taken up Mr. [Richard] Rush as the Candidate for V.P. and have published an eloquent address breathing (I am told) a true Roman spirit.

[William B.] Rochester is here, but leaves us in a few days.

I shall be glad to hear often from you.

ALS. NBuHi. Letter marked "(Private & Confidential)." 1. This report was hand-carried from New York to Clay on February 26, 1828. Joseph Delafield to Clay, February 26, 1828. ALS. DNA, RG76, Northern Boundary: Treaty of Ghent, 1814, Arts. VI & VII.

To JOHN QUINCY ADAMS, January 15, 1828. Responds to a resolution of the Senate of January 9, referred to him by the President, which requested information relating to the importation of American goods into the colonies of France and the duties thereof when the goods are carried in American vessels. Reports from a translation of an ordinance of February 6, 1826, governing the trade of Martinique and Guadeloupe, "That by the tables annexed to the ordinance, it will be seen that a number of articles, the produce of the United States, are admitted into those colonies, and the Terms of their admission: that by the third and seventh articles of the ordinance, the importation of the produce thus receivable is allowed in foreign, as well as national, vessels; and it is expressly declared, by the seventh article, that foreign vessels 'shall not be subject to higher tonnage duties, port charges, payment of light money, or other charges of the same nature, than those to which national vessels shall be subject.'" LS. DNA, RG59, Report Books, vol. 4, pp. 216–7; also in *ASPFR*, 6:825. The French ordinance of February 5, 1826, is found in *Sen. Docs.*, 20 Cong., 1 Sess., no. 89, pp. 1–11.

To FRANCIS T. BROOKE   Washington, January 15, 1828
I am sorry to learn that you are indisposed and suffering much pain from a swelled knee; but I hope you will soon get over it.[1]

I congratulate you on the proceedings of your Convention [6:923–6]. I was particularly gratified that you were made its President. I hear the most flattering accounts of the Address to the People which the Convention has adopted. Altho' I am eager to see it, I have not yet had an opportunity of perusing it. But I am prepared in advance, to make my grateful acknowledgments for the friendly notice which is taken of me.[2] I am rendered quite happy by the kind feelings which have been contemporaneously expressed towards me by my native & my adopted State. The Address of the Convention in the latter [6:1120-3] I send[3] you herewith, and after you are done with it, I will thank you to hand it over to [John H.] Pleasants who may possibly think proper to publish it or parts of it in the [Richmond *Constitutional*] Whig. All, I hope and believe, will yet go well. The New Year has been characterized by many cheering incidents.

ALS. KyU. 1. See above, January 14, 1828. 2. "The Address to the People" issued by the Adams convention in Richmond denied that there was any evidence linking Clay to a bargain with Adams in 1825 to secure the post of Secretary of State. Richmond *Enquirer*, January 17, 1828. 3. "An Address to the Freeman of Kentucky. From a Convention... Friendly to the Re-Election of John Quincy Adams...," published in the Lexington *Kentucky Reporter*, January 9, 1828, insisted that Clay had not been guilty of a corrupt bargain with Adams in December, 1824.

From SAMUEL LARNED, Santiago de Chile, no. 65, January 15, 1828. Reports having had two conferences on the subject of the claims of United States citizens against Chile, one with Vice President Francisco Antonio Pinto Diaz, who is acting as "Chief Magistrate," and another with "the new Minister of Foreign Relations, Mr. [Carlos] Rodriguez"; and that both officials expressed a willingness to pursue the matter further. States that "Some disturbances" occurred recently in the Provinces of Aconcagua and Colchagua because of municipal elections but that peace has been restored in the former province and probably soon will be in the latter. Reports that the election for deputies to the Constituent Congress was held on January 12 and 13 and that it is believed that "in this city the candidates of the liberal party have been chosen by a large majority." Adds that Bolivia is "in a state of great ferment" and that it is "highly probable" that a revolution may soon occur there. Notes further that Mariano Egana, "the Chilean Minister in London, has been recalled, and a Consul General appointed as a substitute." ALS. DNA, RG59, Dip. Disp., Chile, vol. 2 (M-T2, R2). Received May 1, 1828.

From SOLOMON SIBLEY, Detroit, January 15, 1828. Reports that the Grand Jury of the Circuit Court, in session at Detroit, has drawn up and forwarded to the Department of State charges against him, as well as "a remonstrance against ... [his] reappointment as a Judge of the Territory [5:768-9]." Denies these charges, specifically and in detail, and requests that he be given a copy of the remonstrance and the names of his "accusers." ALS. DNA, RG59, Misc. Letters (M179, R66); also in Carter, *Territorial Papers*, 11:1151-2. Other details of the case are in *ibid.*, 1144-5.

From THEODORE WYTHE CLAY Lexington, January 16, 1828
Your time I hope is not trespassed upon by my letters; I got yr. pamphlet [6:1394-6] & perused it with infinite pleasure; my opinion is that no man who regards honor or himself can [be found] so reckless as to re-iterate the foul & exploded charges of [Andrew] Jackson [George] Kremer [George] McDuffie &ca. The public of this nation or any other free one ever regard with pleasure a man in whom they have reposed confidence come out of such a business overwhelming his enemies with ridicule & contempt; and no tenacity that is dignified in its port & bearing but what is hailed with pleasure. Whilst I consider myself fairly involved in all the

technicalities & subtleties, as well as fine specimens of ratiocination of the hon[ora]ble profession to which I am but yet in the vestibule, I am by no means an inattentive, or unconcerned observer of passing events.

It has had a wonderful effect here and will go on to do so. I have heard no one urge that there was any ground left for the Genl, to stand upon but odium & disrepute.

They shall have hot & unremitted fire in this quarter: & I deem it well to be so; because the shameful effects of elections may [th]ereby be somewhat obviated, by getting public sentiment well drawn up. Strong as they may be here they are but a poor dodging set. [William T.] Barry flies from some subjects that he will find it hard to carry in company to The Guber[nator]ial chair: He has committed himself agst Internal Imps & the Tariff: I do not for my soul see how [they] are to get along with their war here. [John M.] McCalla I have now no doubt if not the author of the numbers concerning the Morrison end[o]w[ment], is the in-stigator,[1] or cats paw of Barry. He [McCalla] is an unfortunate young man. Honest I believe but vilely under the influence of bad men. He went so far as to appear before the Leg[islat]ive Committee of the Col-lege,[2] on the subject, and by [Richard H.] Chinn, (a worthy fellow) was sent out with great discomfiture; and is, I hear being caught or next to it in a lie direct. He is done over. The rest of the Phalanx there, I know well; they are a headstrong set, and with whom not much can be done in any way. They dare not argue: they cannot write: and they will not fight as men. We have nothing to fear there. Preacher Hall[3] is a miserable fellow. Under the sacred garb of the ministry of the Gospel; he hides a hideous form. But he is now torn from his ambuscade. & not to be feared. I shall deliver a little address Feb. 22nd if well.[4]

I have agitated with a few confidential friends a scheme, which to my mind is frought with utility: It is to appoint, by legislature [a] body o[r] Board of Overseers—or Superintendants to the College: with the duty of meeting once a year at Commencement, to take in consideration the general Interests of the College; to recieve a full Report from The Trus-tees of its concerns and to pass it to the Legislature when required; with no powers of an executive Character whatever. This I Think will be of this great advantage. They are to be taken, one from each county of the state; or any moderate number from each Congressional District. It will secure a formidable body of friends who will be proud of their avoca-tion; and no one ill result can accrue: Something must be done. The State neither can nor will grant much pecuniary assistance. I think this to[o] ought to be passed this winter.[5]

Those who have this thing at heart, and are at liberty to act should stand forward now or never.

The Report of The trustees was able & Satisfactory.[6]

Give Love to Mother & the boys. . . . PS. I shall take infinite pleasure in having The books I wanted & any thing interesting that you have to spare me. A re[port has] circulated the rounds that you were to go to the court of St. James. It could not be so for various reasons I thought unanswerable.

ALS. DLC-TJC (DNA, M212, R10). MS faded; transcription of words in brackets is some-times uncertain.   1. Scott to Clay, Janaury 11, 1828.   2. Ky. Sen. *Journal* ... 1827–

39

1828, pp. 364–6.   3. The Reverend Nathan H. Hall (1783–1858), born in Franklin County, Va., famed revivalist, was pastor of the First Presbyterian Church in Lexington from 1823 to 1847. At the time of his death he was pastor of the Presbyterian Church in Columbia, Mo. Joseph Wilson, *Presbyterian Historical Almanac and Annual Remembrance of the Church* (n. p., 1860). 2:72. See also, *RKHS*, (October, 1942), 40:373.   4. No record of young Clay's "Oration in the Methodist Church," at the invitation of the Lexington Light Infantry Company, has survived, if indeed the address was actually given as planned. Lexington *Kentucky Reporter*, February 20, 1828.   5. Aside from routine legislative reviews of tuition and faculty salaries, and the reelection of the existing trustees, the state legislature took no major action on Transylvania University during the 1827–1828 session. Ky. Sen. *Journal . . . 1827–1828*, pp. 364–79.   6. Not found; but see Sonne, *Liberal Kentucky, 1780–1828*, 208–9, 257–9; and 6:257.

From JOHN M. FORBES, Montevideo, no. 56, January 16, 1828. States that the Government of Buenos Aires remains "in the same state" as when he left the city—"Mr [Manuel] Moreno having withdrawn from the ministry and no successor having been appointed, General Don [Juan] Ramon [Gonzales] Balcarce, Minister of War, being charged with all the other departments."

Reports that the cargo of the brig *Ruth* has been condemned and quotes from the decision of the Prize Court. Points out that an appeal has been entered and is pending; and that Mr. Lees, the supercargo of the *Ruth*, was approached by an agent of the original court and made to understand "that, in case a certain sum intimated should be paid, a sentence of restitution should be pronounced." Notes that he has written the government to complain of the outcome of the case and that a copy of his complaint is enclosed; expresses optimism that since "the Court of appeals is composed of very respectable men," and will be presided over by the Minister of War, General Balcarce, the "Sentence of the Prize Court will be reversed." Comments that his health has improved and that he will return to Buenos Aires as soon as he can obtain passage. Adds: "Our countrymen here are all looking with great anxiety for the arrival of the President's message, always a most interesting document, but, at the present moment, peculiarly so in relation to our affairs in this quarter." LS. DNA, RG59, Dip. Disp., Argentina, vol. 3 (M69, R4). Received April 30, 1828; also in Espil, *Once Anos en Buenos Aires*, 486–88. For Adams's message, as it related to Latin America and the war between Brazil and Buenos Aires, see Richardson, *MPP*, 2:384–6.

From CHRISTOPHER HUGHES   Brussels, January 16, 1828
An American Gentleman, Mr. Shillaber,[1] has just called on me, to have his passport *vise*, (vouched:) without which, he could not travel through france; and to inform me, that he leaves Town immediately, for United States, via, Calais, & Liverpool. I have only a half-hour to write you a hurried Letter; you will receive it with your usual indulgence.

I enclose you, the closing Letters concerng Mr. [Richard] Ward, and his projects; about which, I wrote to you, some time ago [6:1323–5, 1389–92], through the Legation, at London. I now send Nos. 1. 2. & 3. and that affair is finished. Mr. Ward may be a very clever man; he is a very hypocondriacal one; at all events, I have written to you *all* I know about him. He sailed, on the 8th. from Antwerp for U. States, as he says, in his last Letter; (No. 2.) His Son is a very intelligent & promising young man; & I recommend him to your kindness & protection.[2]

I have been frequently in Holland, since the Court went to the Hague; There was a Grand Audience, on the New Year's day; at one [O']Clock; when the King [William I] received *all* the Corps Diplomatique. His Majesty, [a]s he invariably is, was very courteous to me; He asked many questions about the United States; among others, "Which is your most prosperous and flourishing Town, Mr. Hughes?" "That, which had the happiness to be founded by Your Majesty's Countrymen, New York." My answer was pronounced to be happy; and it certainly is *true;* it circulated, among my Colleagues & throughout the Court; and I had to produce statistical *proof,* that I was no *Courtier;* no difficult task, on a recurrence to the rapid and almost unsurpassed growth of the trade & population of N.Y. My neighbour, on the *Right* (the new French Envoy;) wasted his breath, in an extravagant and unmerited eloge of the Posting facilities of this Kingdom; the King listened to [Louis–Toussaint] the Marquis de la Moussaye; but the King, & all of us, (not excepting the Marquis himself;) knew it was all *Flummery!* For it is some 40 per Ct. inferiour to, & quite as dear as, the Post-Establishment in France; All my Colleagues post, however, but me; I am the *only one* who travels in the Diligence; (not being able to afford a Gentlemanlike conveyance;) & go to Court, in a Hackney Coach! The expenses of living have become enormous here; and at the Hague, they are greater than in England. The fraud, the uncontrollable larceny, practised upon all the members of the corps Diplomatique, by the corrupt servants, & trades-people with whom they are in league, surpass all discussion! I assure you, that do our best, and we are robbed and almost mined; I mean, *my family.* I am almost *in despair!* We have no extravagance; as to a carriage, I should as soon think of swimming over the atlantic; Mrs. [Laura Sophia Smith] Hughes never goes into Society, not being able to bear the expense of dress! I am obliged to withdraw from it, from down-right Shame, at not being able to make any *return;* we have dismissed our Cook (& one man servant). & live on the daily supplies of a Restauranteur; not being able to keep-house, & bear the expenses & frauds of the kitchen; we keep *one* man & *two* women Servan[ts] and yet, with all this, I have been obliged, in settling up the year (1827.) anticipate my Salary, for ½ a year; there are Balls & parties, to which I am *absolutely obliged* to go; My wife stays at Home; I walk, rain or Snow, with a pair of dry Shoes, in my Servants pocket; & change in the *Entry!*—[n]ot affording 10 or 12 francs, for a Hackney Coach! We have as I have, said, reduced our house, down to the commonest *necessities* of Life, [a]nd, by the strictest economy & every possible denial, we *may* be able to *live,* & that is all! House Rent, schooling, Doctors—servants—the fact of being *game,* (so soon as you are a diplomat) for every rogue & scoundrel of a tradesman, who sells you the necessaries of Life—and the inconceivable augmentation of [e]xpenses, prices, charges, & *corruption of the servant Class,* in [co]nsequence of the Myriads of expensive *English,* Established here, together with the expensive *extra's* of the Royal Residence at the Hague, [w]ill explain to you all this; & before God, I am sometimes, almost *in despair;* & lament, in my heart, that the idea of *public Life* ever entered into my brain! And yet, with all this weight on my mind, I observe (as far as human being *Can* observe;) every act & conduct, and discretion, that belongs to him, who represents his Country at a foreign Court; I may boldly say, no man stands higher, in the universal estimation of all classes of Society; The Royal Family treat me, with marked kindness; my Colleagues cherish me, & honour me with their respect & Confidence; & the Grandees of the Realm, actually *seek* me out & shower upon me their courtesies & their favours! *Upon my honour,* all this is true & not exaggerated! If I were Minister, I might be able to *live* Genteely & as becomes one, in such a place, as I occupy; without doing *more,* than merely meeting the inevitable expenses of a Gentlemanlike House.—

I have given you a sad Jeremiad; and, I dare say, you will be vexed with me, for plaguing you with my distresses, & mortifications; you will be angry with me, for a moment only; for after *that,* you will remember me; and you will recollect, how sincerely I am attached to you; and you know that I am made of good stuff; and I *know* how kind your feelings for me have ever been! And yet, many efforts have been made, to estrange me from you; and to make me believe that you take no interest in me; I have *never* yielded to them; and, I shall live & die, truly attached to you; and convinced, in my heart, that, (putting your eminent public qualities aside; a Subject upon which, our own country, and the world, have pronounced but *one* opinion) ther[e] does not live, a purer hearted, more generous and excellent man, & *friend,* or any one, whose soul & whose sentiments are more concentered in his Countries welfare and honour, than you; I shall always feel for you, the affection of a younge[r] Brother, or a protege; & nothing can, or *shall,* estrange me from you!—

I have told you, how it would go, with the [Lord] Goodrich [*sic,* Goderich] Ministry; His Lordship is not a man to Rule a Storm, or guide public affairs in *troublous* times; He is a man, himself, to be ruled by *women,* & by *Cousins!* The Commercial & Shipping interests of England, are all opposed to [William] *Huskisson's system;* his libera[lity,] his reciprocity, & his free competition; I have heard, that the powerful [Nathan Meyer] Rotschild [*sic,* Rothschild], should have said, (not many days ago, at a dinner in London, where Huskisson's resignation was the topic;) "that, if Mr. Huskisson would leave England and promise never to return, or to *meddle* in its politics, He, (Rotschild) would find procure for him, 100,000£ Stg. on the Royal Eschange, before 12 o'Clock the next day; and present them to Him!"—Lord Wellington will Rule England; He has the greatest power over the King [George IV]; who is dazzled, (as are our people;) by *Military Glory!* He will rule, through *Mr.* [Robert] *Peel;* for, to Mr. *Peel,* they *must* come; He has more talents & weight, than all the others put together! It will be evil for us, if *Lord Grey* get power! He hates *America & Americans* & I know it.

ALS, DNA, RG59, Dip. Disp., Netherlands (M42, R-T12). Received March 19, 1828. Letter marked "Private." 1. Possibly John Shillaber. 2. Ward wrote Clay and, reminding him that Hughes had assured Ward's son of his specific recommendation, solicited for the younger Ward a position in the State Department "as a Writing Clerk." Letter not dated. LS. DNA, RG59, A. and R. (M531, R8).

From JOSEPH POLLARD, Greenville, Ky., January 16, 1828. States that he is a veteran of the Revolution and a "poor" man who needs a job; seeks appointment as secretary of Arkansas Territory [3:234-5]. Adds:

"The electioneering campaign for electors in this section of country has commenced with much activity & zeal on both sides The event I think doubtfull I hope tho the Adams Tickett will succeed unwearied Exertions will be used by us to insure success [6:360-3]." ALS. DNA, RG59, A. and R. (M531, R6).

Aside from his service in the Virginia 2nd Continental Line during the Revolution, Pollard has not been further identified. He notes, however, that "I received no other compensation for my services in the campaign of 1781 than some deprecated paper money which was consumed in my house about 2 years ago."

To BARON STACKELBERG, Washington, January 16, 1828. Reports that the President, with the advice and consent of the Senate, has ratified the Treaty of Commerce and Navigation with Sweden, concluded on July 4, 1827 [6:761-2]. Requests an interview at one o'clock on January 18, to exchange ratifications. Copy. DNA, RG59, Notes to Foreign Ministers and Consuls, vol. 3, p. 416 (M38, R3). ALI, draft, in CSmH.

Stackelberg acknowledged Clay's note the same day and inquired whether or not American ratification applies to the separate article [6:762]. LS, in French. DNA, RG59, Notes from Swedish Legation, vol. 3 (M60, R2).

The next day, January 17, Clay acknowledged receipt of Stackelberg's note of the previous day and assured him that the American ratification applies to the separate article as well as to the body of the treaty. Copy. DNA, RG59, Notes to Foreign Ministers and Consuls, vol. 3, p. 417 (M38, R3).

From CHARLES S. TODD   Stockdale,[1] Ky., January 16, 1828
I had the satisfaction of writing to you shortly after our meeting in the County[2] to appoint Delegates to the Convention at Frankfort [6:1120-3], and of expressing a wish to receive your views as to the Vice Presidency.—I did expect to receive them before the adjournment of the Convention—but a conversation with Mr. [Robert] Wickliffe to whom, I understood you had written on that subject induced myself and others not to make any nomination[3]—although we had some difficulty in consequence of the proposition of Mr. [Isham] Talbot to nominate Mr. [William H.] Crawford. He was, however, prevailed upon to withdraw it. I see that the Convention in Ohio [6:1199-201], also, has concluded to await the Course of events upon that subject.

I was favored on yesterday by the receipt of your late address [6:1394-6] and hasten to return you my grateful acknowledgements for the Masterly manner in which you have vindicated yourself and fastened the iniquity of the slander on General Jackson. It is proposed to republish it extensively in this State.—While on this subject and referring to that part of your address where "you have no doubt that in your promiscuous & unreserved intercourse among your acquaintances in this State, others not recollected by you could bear testimony to the undeviating and settled determination of your mind." I beg leave to mention to you the substance of a conversation between you, my father [Thomas Todd] & myself at his house on the day, or a few days before you started from Frankfort on your journey to Washington early in November 1824.—I did not know that you contemplated a publication on the subject, or I would have long since communicated it to you and shall rejoice exceedingly if you shall think it worthy of your attention[4]—

We were speaking of the prospects as to the Presidential election and the rumor of the proposed resolution by the Legislature to instruct the Kentucky Delegation to vote for General Jackson [3:902] was noticed—you deprecated the idea as being in the highest degree embarassing and hoped it would not be adopted. The whole conversation impressed on my mind the firm conviction with which you seemed to be animated that you could not vote for General Jackson under any circumstances whatever.—I recollect well that you foreboded the direst consequences to the Country in the event of his Election; that it would be an administration of fury and of violence.

The Cause is prospering here—great zeal and talent was collected in the Convention and a solemn determination manifested among its members to carry that energy into the approaching Canvass. The friends of the administration are already aroused to a sense of their condition and of the necessity for a vigorous effort, while the considerate men of the Jackson party are pausing to reflect. I do believe, most firmly, that Mr. Adams will receive the entire vote of the State [6:360-3].

I will procure the speech of David White at the dinner given to you at Shelbyville, which was written out by himself and published [4:515] in the [Shelbyville] Compiler, in which he bears testimony to the purity of your conduct.

I should have been pleased to have learned something as to your health—on this subject I feel much the greatest solicitude. . . . P.S. Metcalfe will do well in this County, even among some of the Jacksonites.[5]

ALS. DLC-HC (DNA, M212, R3).   1. The name of Todd's estate in Shelby County, Ky.   2. Not found. However, the Shelby County meeting was probably held in late October or November, 1827.   3. Not found. On the Vice-Presidential nomination see 6:923-6.   4. See below, Todd to Clay, February 18, 1828.   5. Thomas Metcalfe, the pro-administration candidate for Governor, beat William T. Barry in Shelby County in the August election by a count of 1087 to 821. Louisville *Public Advertiser*, August 23, 1828.

From CHARLES R. VAUGHAN, Washington, January 16, 1828. Reports that he has received an answer, a copy of which is enclosed, from the Governor General of Canada, the Earl of Dalhousie, to the inquiry made at Clay's request concerning Nathaniel Snelson [6:1348-9]. States: "It appears . . . that Snelson is not at present to be found in any of the gaols in the Province of Lower Canada . . . nor is there any reason for believing, that he has ever been in confinement there." LS. DNA, RG59, Notes from British Legation, vol. 15 (M50, R15).

On January 17 Clay sent Vaughan's letter and enclosure to John Brockenborough, "President of the Bank of Va. Richmond," noting that there was reason to believe that the supposition about Snelson "was erroneous." Copy. DNA, RG59, Dom. Letters, vol. 22, p. 124 (M40, R20).

From JAMES G. BIRNEY, Huntsville, Alabama, January 18, 1828. Recommends Francis W. Armstrong, although he differs with him "in political opinions and wishes," for reappointment as United States marshal for Alabama [6:1367].

Adds: "I do not suppose, that a Ticket for Administration—Electors, will be run at the ensuing election, in this State. Jacksonism is, I believe *fastened* on us; and how indispensable it is considered by those, who are not *fixed* in honesty and want office, you, yourself may have some opportunity of knowing." ALS. DNA. RG59, A. and R. (M531, R1).

The Jackson ticket, against virtually token Adams opposition, swept Alabama in the November, 1828, election by a 13,384 to 1,629 margin. The state legislature in 1827 had nominated the General for President by a 54 to 8 vote. Abernethy, *Formative Period in Alabama*, 121.

To THOMAS L. L. BRENT, Lisbon, no. 6, January 18, 1828. Reports having received a letter from Charles W. Dabney [6:1347] on the subject of the American vessel *London Trader*. States: "Should there be a failure to obtain redress through the local government, to which an appeal has been made, you will bring the case before the Portuguese Government, and urge, in strong, but respectful language, indemnity to be made to the injured American Citizens." Copy. DNA, RG59, Dip. Instr., vol. 12, p. 55 (M77, R7). ALI, draft, in DLC-HC (DNA, M212, R8).

On April 12, in dispatch no. 62, Brent acknowledged his receipt of this letter on April 9. He reported that he had mentioned the matter to the Minister of Foreign Affairs, the Count of Vila Real, who advised him to await further information from Dabney before he formally asked the Portuguese Government for redress. LS. DNA. RG59, Dip. Disp., Portugal, vol. 7 (M43, R6). Received June 4, 1828.

To FRANCIS T. BROOKE   Washington, January 18, 1828
I have duly recd. your favor of the 14th. inst. prior to which I addressed a short letter to you at Richmond.[1]

The proceedings of your Convention [6:923-6] have been seen here with the greatest satisfaction. They are all marked by wisdom and discretion. The address is admired by everybody, and fully realizes the high expectation which was formed when it was understood who was to compose it.

The duty assigned you as to the communication to Messrs Madison & Monroe is very delicate; but it appears to me that, by giving them before-hand sufficient notice of your intention here after to make an official communication to them, you have adopted the most prudent course. I am apprehensive that they will decline, which I should very much regret. If they do, it will be very desirable that it should not be done in such manner as to injure our cause.

Our news from the west is very cheering. Ohio is beyond all doubt safe. So is Indianna, and I think Illinois. Our friends in K. are very confident of success, as is exhibited by a proposition in the Legislature, proceeding from them, for a General ticket.[2] It was not decided when I last heard from Frankfort.

[Samuel L.] Southard [h]as just returned from Annapolis I have not yet seen him.

Copy. DLC-TJC (DNA, M212, R13).   1. Clay to Brooke, January 15, 1828.   2. On February 12, 1828, the Kentucky General Assembly set the election date for Monday,

November 3, providing also that voters would select "fourteen Electors for President and Vice President" on a statewide basis rather than by district as formerly done [3:784]. See Ky. Gen. Assy., *Acts . . .* 1827–1828, p. 165.

To WILLIAM B. LAWRENCE   Washington, January 18, 1828
My [Jared] Sparks, who will present you this letter, is a gentleman of high literary attainments, and great worth and respectability. He goes to Europe for the purpose of collecting papers and information which he supposes may be acquired in the public offices there, connected with the settlement and history of this country [6:899–900, 962]. The confidence reposed in him is evinced by his having been selected to arrange and publish the Washington papers, and by his having been, also, designated, with the approbation of the President, to examine into the mass of our diplomatic confidential correspondence, during our Revolutionary period, and to point out such parts of it as may be now beneficially published—The intimate connection between the two above objects and that which takes him to Europe, is very obvious—I recommend him to your friendly attentions. And as he will be desirous of obtaining access to such of the public archives of the Government near which you reside, as may serve to illustrate the history of our country, I have to request that you will endeavor, informaly and unofficially, to procure [it?] for him. His purpose being one which must command the approbation of both Governments, no objection to the grant of such access is anticipated.

Copy. MH. Addressed to Lawrence in London, England. Letter marked "Private and inofficial."

From LEVI LINCOLN, Boston, January 19, 1828. Refers to the President's annual message [December 4, 1827] with reference to the Northeast Boundary issue and to "the Character of alleged Acts of aggression" by Britain "upon the territory within the line of jurisdiction claimed by the United States [6:994–5, 1055, 1251]." Notes that the issue remains one of "deep Concern" to the people of Maine and Massachusetts and that the boundary line, as defined in the treaty of 1783, had a "clear and precise designation." Admits that while "Treaties are not to be Controlled by metaphysical subtleties," the British claim to territory rightfully belonging to Massachusetts is fallacious and unjust. For this reason, Massachusetts "will seek the means to retain this valuable territory" and expects the national government to protect her, "as a member of the Confederacy," from being "spoiled of her possessions." Asks for further information to pass on to the state legislature, now in session, for their advice. LS. DNA, RG76, Northeastern Boundary: Misc. Papers, Env. 4, item 20. For Adams's remarks on the boundary question, see Richardson, *MPP*, 2:381.

From GEORGE ROBERTSON   Lancaster, Ky., January 19, 1828
The unreserved freedom of this communication is allowed by our acquaintance, and demanded by very recent intelligence. My principles, and my opinion of yours will neither require, nor tolerate any further or other apology.

46

By a letter received from Mr. [Robert P.] Letcher last night (written in a confidence which I shall not violate by this to you, otherwise I would not write it) I am informed that hints from some (to Mr. L.) unknown and unascertainable quarter had been made to you, questioning the sincerity and constancy of my humble support of the Administration, and my satisfaction with the late recommendation of Genl. [Thomas] Metcalfe for Governor [6:1380–1].

In relation to the first charge, my feelings will suffer me only to say, that no man in the United States has felt more solicitude for the prosperity and success of this administration that I have,—And no one according to the measure of his abilities, and the extent of his theatre, has attempted more for its advancement. Of the efficiency of what I have done or tried to do, it is not for me to give an opinion—and no one else can be acquainted with the facts which would enable him to judge.

You and Mr. Adams were my first and second choices—And Genl. J never was and never could be under any circumstances the object of my preference. These opinions were never withheld or dissembled either before or since the presi[dentia]l. election. My political opinions have ever been and shall ever continue to be unalloyed by selfishness. I had never any selfish aim in any opinion which I have ever publicly avowed. This is more than most politicians will accredit. But I would repeat it with the most solemn asseverations. I mean never to become variant from my established principles of action. The administration is as good as I expected or had any just reason to hope that it would be. Its general tenor I approve. Some things I have not approved. But they are comparativily unimportant and such as the best men must necessarily differ about. I contributed, honestly and disinterestedly, all I could to the election of Mr. Adams; and I know that my efforts had at least some effect. I have not repented—I would pursue the same Course if the drama were to be reacted.

I would not notice the second charge, if it did not contain an implication unworthy of me, and unwarranted by any act of my whole life—(viz) that I was dissatisfied with Genl. M's nomination because I desired that honor myself.

I not only did not desire it for my self, but I had done every thing in my power for the last year to avoid a dilemma in which I might have to choose between a surrender of my principles or duty and the acceptance of a nomination for a place which I never could *personally* desire, and an election to which could almost ruin me. During the last winter our party in the Legislature were unfortunate in their solications, often repeated and sometimes in very large bodies, that I should consent to be run—I peremptorily and perserveringly refused—. Ever since, I had almost daily, solicitations by letter and personal application. I went to Frankfort, principally for the purpose of avoiding a nomination by the Convention [6:1380–1]. I was anxious for Mr [John J.] Crittenden to offer and no doubt was entertained untill the 3rd. day of the convention, that he would consent to be the Candidate—I was doing what I could for him and Davy Trimble and a few others were urging the pretensions of Metcalfe, as superior to those of Crittenden. They objected to the latter; 1st. that he had opposed the Occupant System [3:91]—and made a

Speech agt. the occupant Act of 1812—2nd. that he had been charged with a design to compromise the reorganisations controversy [3:902][1] on grounds incompatible with the principles and interests of the party to which he was attached:—3rd. That he was in favor of Genl. J—in preference to Mr. A. and would still admit the Genls. fitness for the office. And insist that he is a fine old fellow &c. These objections I felt the force of, and admitted, but endeavored to obviate Many on the North Side, Some in the Green river and the Middle district[2] with not more than three or four exceptions seemed still very anxious for me to suffer my name to be used in opposition to that of Mr. C—I refused possitively and pressed them to unite on him—and when it was believed that all objections and preferences would be waived and that he would be nominated, he addressed a note to the Committee unconditionally refusing! In *all* this time, there seemed no one for Metcalfe except Trimble and some of the Green river delegates who had been relief men [3:146]. The Northern District I was frequently told by members from it were unanimously opposed to him. But at last there was a determination evinced to yield an apparent acquiescence in the wishes of the relief administration members—. And the Genl. was nominated—so far as he or my self can be personally concerned, no one could have more Cause of gratification than I have. The office will suit him—It would not suit me—He is one of my favorites—And if the office will advance or gratify him, no one will rejoice more than I shall. His nomination relieves me from an alternative which would have been extremely disagreeable to me. *I could have been nominated without any difficulty*—The middle district and my own [Fourth] Cong[ression]al District voted for Genl. M. more unanimously than any other part of the State. I will not fatigue you with a narration of all the facts which I could give you on this subject—They would be more curious than useful. I have only given you this outline to shew how uncharitable and unjust those must be who suspect me for any *personal* dissatisfaction with the nomination. I believed and yet believe that we had stronger—much stronger men—I considered it our duty as well as obvious interest to run an anti-relief man—We would thus have been consistent and faithful to our Creed, and been, I have no doubt, invincible—

The old court Jackson men would have supported an old Court[3] popular Adm. candidate, unanimously agt. [William T.] Barry—But they will not vote for Metcalf[e]—I have hopes that some of them may; but generally they will not—

I was apprehensive that when we had nominated Metcalfe the other party would have taken up an old court man; they said they would, and seemed exceedingly rejoiced and relieved by our nomination. And if they had selected an old court Candidate instead of Barry, I have no sort of doubt they would have beaten us. I hope however and believe that Metcalf[e] can beat Barry.[4] No man, not even [John] Rowan or [Joseph] Desha, is so odious with the old court part as Barry is—And relief Adn. men, will vote for any adn. candidate, they are tired of the relief system. In these lines I am not in any degree, mistaken; I would have no excuse for being mistaken on such a subject. Hence you may infer the importance of running an old court adn. candidate and the only objection I had to the nomination that was made and even that I have no recollection of ever expressing. The only occasion of mortification or regret, to me personally, which the incidents of the last year have furnished has been the opportunity of which some insidious men by reason of the use made of my name have meanly availed themselves, to snarl at me and misinterpret my motives and best intended acts. And the attempt to make the impression that I was disappointed in not being nominated for Govr. is perfectly in character. There are three of four Choice Spirits who smile in my face and are meditating by day and by night how to blast what little of character and the modicum of popularity I may possess. I know them and have marked them long ago—I see, although I have not felt their Lilliputian Missiles. Two of these Iagos (who always cover their operations agt. me with the mark of simulated friendship) were very busy with the members of the Convention, in sly attempts to make the impression that I am odious in this quarter! Hearing delegates say from other sections of the State, that they had come resolved to nominate me (if I would consent) These kind friends would tell them that they were my friends,—but they must yeild all local and personal preference—for I was unpopular at Home and could get very few votes in my own end of the State. (Mr. L. will tell you how true this is—Even the most of the Jacksons would vote for me in all this region—) They were afraid I would be nominated notwithstanding my known opposition to it—any they feared that such a testemonial would give me some factitious strength. They were not counteracted. My Confidential friends knew my wishes and interest and were desirous that the convention should unite on some other person. But the world does not know these things and hence many may be made to believe that I was desirous to be nominated and failed for want of strength—and those loveing friends of mine, flatter themselves with an imaginary triumph over me. This I can't help and would not if I could. My conscience is in repose. I want nothing and I would not care if the world knew it—There has been no moment in the last 10 years when I would voluntarily have accepted any office under the State Constitution. I have been perfectly satisfied and mean to be with my humble lot. I envy no man his political honors or preferment. Happiness is found only in Contentment—and that is found any where else than in high Station. The puerile apprehension that I might be in some aspirant's way, has converted into enemies men who would otherwise be my warm friends; and has induced them to employ means to harrass me. Whilst I would be glad to get out of their way, I intend that my peace shall not for one moment be distrubed by their envy, malignity or machinations. I believe I know one thing that few men ever did or will understand—I know my friends—I know my enemies. Suffer me here to give you a hint—I fear you do not even yet know your friends and your enemies. I call those enemies who support and flatter us while in prosperity, but are prepared to desert us as soon as adversity renders their support of value to us. Such self interested–adulatory–hollow hearted–miscalled–friends do us much more harm than open undisguised enemies, whose batteries are unmasked. May God deliver you from them. Of course mine are few and they can do *me* no essential injury.

Therefore I will not misemploy the omnipotence of Jehovah by invoking it in my case. I must "work out my own salvation"—or if I perish very few will fall with me. My political life has been irksome and inglorious and unprofitable. I have no inclination to protract its vexations and its cares. I expect therefore, to withdraw from political strife, and devote the remainder of a misspent life to a large family, already too long neglected. I ought to settle in some more eligible place if I could, but I am unadvised on this subject, and of course undetermined.

I do not know whether your informant is one of those very Pragmatical gentleman to whom I have alluded—I do not desire to know who he is or what were his motives. He has been greatly mistaken. If Mr. L. had not told me that you seemed inclined to doubt his information, I should not have felt myself authorised to say a word to you on the subject.

My only object in this dissutory and very free communication is to relieve myself from the burthen of uneasing feeling, produced by Mr. L['s] letter. I have written as I should have spoken only not so fully and directly—The last office I could desire would be that of Govr. of Ky.—I prevented my own nomination—and am now suspected for being uncandid in my uniform declarations, and for coveting the honor of being selected! This is provoking but ought not to be regarded by one whose whole life has been a struggle agt. ungenerous opposition and unjust reproach. I wish to be in no man's way. I mean to pull down no one. This I never have done, although I have helped to put a few up. It is time that I should look to my own concerns. I never had the advantage of any adentitious support. I have lived so far on my own resources, and expect to do so as long as I shall live—

Already the busy inventiveness of some, has attributed to me a design to offer for the US senate, and is conjureing up means of counteraction and annoyance. I do not desire that station. I do not know that I shall ever desire it. I know one thing—and that is—I would not turn on my heal for it. A Seat in the Senate of the Union is an exhalted place of honor and distinction for any man. But if I ever attain it, it will be without my solicitation. Besides I never could contemplate with any satisfaction or direct hope of enjoying it, a place which will not be vacated in less than two years.[5] My uneasy friends may therefore have peace on that subject, if they will.

In the same Spirit I have been charged with being a candidate for the District attorneyship   And a mission to Colombia—You know these suspicions are unjust. I was not an applicant either directly or indirectly for either of those offices—I refused to be recommended for the attyship—and requested Mr. Letcher by letter not to suffer my name to be used, but to recommend another gentleman—What he did I know not—I never felt concern enough to inquire.[6] In relation to the other— all I know is that without any agency or wish of mine, it was asserted as I have learnt since, at Washington that the mission to Colombia would be offered to me, and seemed to be calculated on in this country. How this delusion originated I know not. It is all a mystery to me. I'm sure I never asked for that mission or any other station in the foreign service. If either of those offices had been offered to me I cannot say what I should have done. Mr. [Richard C., Jr.] Anderson in his lifetime wrote to me that he intended to come home, and desired me to succeed him—to which I replied that if it were then offered to me I would not undertake the mission. What I would under other circumstances have done or thought, I am unable now to say. So much for speculations about my desire of office—That I am ambitious I own. But my ambition is of a peculiar Cast. It is not the ambition of office—but of usefulness and reputation free from reproach and above suspicion. And I would desire no office in the world, any further than it might give me a fair chance to attain these ends. The suspicions expressed of my application for office have been inexpressibly disagreeable to me, and no doubt will be terribly detrimental. But I only allude to them now, in connexion with the other subject to aid your own sagacity to ascertain how things are going on here—to know "what is what and who is who"—and to shew you that a system is in operation here, entended if possible to render me ridiculous. It is managed by a very few and with the body of the people although I am not popular in the vulgar sense, I am in as favorable standing as I deserve or desire. I never grasped at popularity. I have long known its capriciousness and evanescence. It can only be required by great Deeds or mean and unremitted subserviences—and is only worth having and will last only, when atchieved by the former.

I am unwilling to believe that you felt any doubt about the incorrectness of the communication made to you by the unknown informant. I know I should do you great injustice by doubting whether or not you gave credence to it—and I repeat, that if I had supposed you believed it, I should certainly have spared you the trouble of reading this long letter. Whatever may be thought or stated to the contrary by any, I have given to you the naked, plain truth which I cant most abundantly prove. But it is a delicate subject, and I can speak on it to only a very few—And I have never before been as open in relation to it as I am now with you. It is useless to be otherwise—To play the diplomatist on such a subject would betray a fastidiousness and fear of being egotistical which I do not feel.

"Prosperity makes friends—adversity tries them."—If you are destined to go down, you will see the aphorism most signally exemplified—I am unwilling to be more explicit—and I might do injustice—. I thank you for your address [6:1394–6]. It *must* do good.

As long as you continue what I believe you are—I shall be what I have been—if you rise higher or if you sink lower, not a flattering but sincere friend. . . .

ALS. DLC-HC (DNA, M212, R3). At this time Robertson was Secretary of State of Kentucky [2:676].   1. For Crittenden's role in the reorganization controversy, see Albert D. Kirwan, *John J. Crittenden: The Struggle for the Union* (Lexington, Ky., 1962), 56–64. 2. The names given the three presidential electoral districts. The Green River district was also referred to as the "Southern" district, and the "North Side" was also called the "Northern" district. See 3:784.   3. For a summary of the Relief vs. anti-Relief party struggle and the related Old Court vs. New Court party controversy, see Kirwan, *Crittenden*, 53–5. 4. Metcalfe defeated Barry by the close margin of 38,940 to 38,231. Frankfort *Argus of Western America*, August 27, 1828.   5. Richard M. Johnson's Senate seat was filled by George M. Bibb in 1829. Johnson was elected to the U.S. House.   6. On the recommended appointment as Federal attorney, see 6:16–7, 40, 65. No letter from Letcher in reference to Robertson's nomination has been found.

From CHARLES R. VAUGHAN   Washington, January 19, 1828
I thank you for your loan of the message of the Governor of Maine,[1] and as I am still disappointed of being able to procure a Copy of it through the Newspapers I take the liberty of asking your permission to keep your Copy—If you cannot conveniently allow me to do so, I will return it immediately.

ALS. DLC–HC (DNA, M212, R3). Letter marked "Private."   1. For Enoch Lincoln's annual message to the legislature, delivered on Janaury 3, 1828, see Henry S. Burrage, *Maine in the Northeastern Boundary Controversy,* (Portland, Me., 1919), 138–40.

From JOEL R. POINSETT, Mexico, January 20, 1828. Reports protest of American merchants in Veracruz against an order from the Mexican Customs house there, ordering the merchants to provide an inventory of their stocks within eight days for the purpose of collecting an internation duty on them. Argues the order "is contrary to the interests of trade, and to the usages of all commercial Nations ... nor does the spirit of the law justify this measure," because the law never intended recovery of such a duty on goods which might be sold or consumed in the port rather than sent into the interior. Predicts that Mexico will revise the measure when it understands the paralyzing effect it will have on its commerce. Suggests that the most equitable solution for the merchants and the Mexican government would be "to equalize the duties both on goods now existing in the port and such as may be imported before the 20th February next [when a new, lower tariff would go into effect], so that they may all be brought into the market on a fair and equal competition." Copy. DNA, RG59, Dip. Disp., Mexico, vol. 4 (M97, R5). Enclosed in Poinsett to Clay, July 12, 1828, no. 131, in which he states that the matter was "satisfactorily arranged by the passage of a law equalizing the duties as suggested in my note [of January 20]." LS. *Ibid.* Received August 25, 1828.

From GEORGE B. ADAMS, Alicante, Spain, January 21, 1828. Encloses "a list of American vessels which have paid the Tarifa Light duty since the impost of one dollar P[er] ton was laid on Vessels belonging to Citizens of the U.S." States: "The Royal Decree of 12 March [18]18 did not fully explain" that the light duty was included in the tonnage, and that he, "through the ... diligent exertions" of Mr. Alexander H. Everett, has obtained "a clear elucidation of the ... Decree" and a refund of money collected for the light duty since imposition of the tonnage charge. Adds that the sum recovered, "$110. less $25.," has been sent to Robert G. Shaw, Boston, for disposition under Clay's direction. Attributes the decline in American trade to Cadiz province to the nearly prohibitive tonnage duty paid by American vessels. ALS. DNA, RG59, Cons. Disp., Alicante, vol. 1 (M–T357, R1). Received July 11, 1828.

From JOSEPH BALESTIER & COMPANY, New York, January 21, 1828. States that Mexico's determination "to authorise the licensing of Privateers by Commodore [David] Porter, for the purpose of sending in for trial, vessels having on board Spanish property, renders it necessary that Citizens of the United States . . . should have the means of protecting their property by legal documents, proving ownership and neutrality." Points out that documentation by "a Spanish magistrate, would be very questionable in the court of a nation, at war with Spain." Recommends the establishment of consulates or commercial agencies at Guayama, Ponce, and Mayaguez, all on the island of Puerto Rico, and suggests that William H. Tracy, Thomas Davidson, and Sampson C. Russell be appointed at those ports, respectively. Adds that "our importations of the produce of that Island, in 1827, added upwards of Two hundred Thousand Dollars to the revenues, and, if not molested and vexed by Privateers of nations at war with Spain, we have every reason . . . to expect an increase the present year." LS. DNA, RG59, A. and R. (M531, R2).

Tracy was appointed consular commercial agent in Guayama on January 26, 1828. Clay to Tracy, January 26, 1828. Copy. DNA, RG59, Cons. Instr., vol. 2, pp. 457-59 (M78, R2). Russell was simultaneously appointed agent at Mayaguez. Clay to Russell, January 26, 1828. *Ibid.* Davidson was similarly appointed at Ponce. Clay to Davidson, January 26, 1828. *Ibid.* "J. Balestier" acknowledged, on February 11, receipt of the appointments, "which documents" he promised "to forward . . . by the earliest conveyance." ALS. DNA, RG59, Misc. Letters (M179, R66). No letter of transmittal from Clay to Balestier has been found.

From JOSEPH KENT   Annapolis, January 21, 1828
I thank you for your very kind & friendly favour of the 15th. Inst.— Every effort was made here by the opposition to prevent my reelection, but in vain—in the end abandoned all opposition & gave me every vote in the Senate!![1]—

Our prospects certainly have improved & I am much gratified to find you in such good spirits—Mr. [Richard] Rush's nomination will probably render us stronger in Pena. than that of any other person except Govr. Shoultz [*sic,* John A. Shulze]—The Richmond address [6:923-6] is an excellent one & must have a powerful effect in the Ancient Dominion—

Will Mr. Maddison [*sic,* James Madison] & Mr. Munroe [*sic,* James Monroe] consent to serve on the Electoral Ticket?[2]—

Your address [6:1394-6] must be conclusive with all honest men— You have provend a negative farther perhaps than was ever done before, and Col. [Thomas H.] Bentons late letter [6:1342] has corroborated every thing you have adduced—Should Genl. Jackson succeed it will destroy altogether my confidence in the good sense of the People, on the durability of our institutions—If the People can be so imposed on as to be induced to subvert an upright administration without complaint, they can be led a step farther & be induced by the same means to subvert a Govt. under which they have experienced and they feel happiness & prosperity—

Judge [Samuel L.] Southard accompanied by a few friends from Washington spent a day with me last week—I was gratified to find among them our young friend Mr. [William C. C.] Claiborne—He informed me you were all well—

ALS. DLC-HC (DNA, M212, R3). 1. Governor Kent was re-elected on January 7, 1828. He received 80 votes, there also being 13 blank ballots, and was sworn in three days later. Baltimore *American and Commercial Advertiser,* January 9, 1828. 2. Brooke to Clay, February 28, 1828.

From SAMUEL B. BARRELL, Boston, January 22, 1828. Feels that he has accomplished the objects of his Madawaskah mission [6:1282-4] and trusts that his final report [February 11, 1828] will be satisfactory, "both to the Administration and the Country," but requests a personal interview with Clay before actually preparing the report. Notes that there has been "much excitement" over the arrest and imprisonment of John Baker [6:1272-3]. Says that he saw and spoke with Baker in Fredericton and that he sees no reason for the U.S. government to "interfere with the proceedings against him" by New Brunswick authorities. Believes, however, that there will be "no further obnoxious measures" by New Brunswick against "American settlers at the Madawaskah" until the boundary is definitely settled, and expects there will be "no new acts of an offensive nature" by the settlers. ALS. DNA, RG76, Northeast Boundary (KyU., Special Roll, frames 665-8).

From FRANCIS P. BLAIR   Frankfort, Ky, January 22, 1828
You will have heard from some other hand that resolutions have been introduced into the [Ky.] Senate upon the subject of the late presidential election[1]—Genl. [James] Allen of Green [County] has introduced a resolution (in addition to these brought forward by Beatty[2] [*sic*]) for the purpose of broaching an enquiry before an opinion is expressed on the fairness of the election. some of the members of the Senate have told me that they designed to call on me to say upon what grounds I made the declaration to [Amos] Kendall &c. that you would be made Secretary of State before the happening of the event. The Commit[tee] of enquiry it is proposed shall have the power to send for persons & papers.

    If the resolution should pass, & any enquiries should be made of me, I will frankly state to the Committee, that I consider the proceeding wholly unauthorized, & will refuse to say whether I have or have not information of any kind on the subject. I will not be put to the question—

ALS. DLC-HC (DNA, M212, R3). 1. See 6:1106-07; and Blair to Clay, February 4, 1828. The resolution of James Allen, introduced on January 18, was prompted by a resolution offered by Martin Beaty in the committee of the whole. The Beaty resolution expressed "deep concern and feeling of just indignation" with the various efforts underway in the nation "to blast the reputation of the distinguished members of Congress from this State who voted for John Q. Adams to be president of the United States." It noted, too, that the "charges of bargain, sale and corruption, in the election of John Q. Adams are utterly false and malicious," and were being voiced for "party purposes" designed to elevate Jackson to the presidency. Allen's resolution asked that the committee of the whole "be authorized to examine into, and investigate the transactions embraced in the foregoing resolution." Taken up again January 25 on a motion by Francis Lockett, an amended version of the resolution was passed and an inquiry was held from January 31 through February 2. Subsequently, Beaty's resolution, tacked on to an omnibus internal improvements measure, passed on February 7. For the legislative history of the resolutions and the investigation, see Ky. Sen., *Journal* ... 1827-1828, pp. 207-08, 254, 256-7, 298-9, 302-10, 335-9, 347-9; and Ky. House of Reps. *Journal* ... 1827-1828, p. 382. 2. Martin Beaty, of Wayne County, served in the State Senate from 1824 to 1828 and again in 1832. Subsequently, he served in Congress. See *BDAC.*

To CHURCHILL C. CAMBRELENG

Washington,
January 22, 1828

I have the honor to inform you, in answer to the enquiry which is made in the Letter to you,[1] which is herewith returned, that a Despatch has just been received at this office from Mr. [Joel R.] Poinsett, which confirms the authenticity of the published notice of Commodore [David] Porter [6:1344], as contained in the printed slip furnished by your Correspondent, and contains a translation of the Notice, itself.

This Department has no information of any Law of the Imperial Government of Brazil, which places the duties on imports from all Nations at fifteen per Cent, without regard to Treaties, or of the passage of any other recent Law of that government upon that subject.

LS. DLC-HC (unbound).   1. The previous day, Cambreleng had written: "If you can give me any information on the subject referred to in the enclosed letter and extract [neither found] you would much oblige me as well as our Commercial interest—generally for whose use it is required—" Cambreleng to Clay, January 21, 1828. ALS. DNA, RG59, Misc. Letters (M179, R66).

From WILLIAM B. LAWRENCE, London, no. 19, January 22, 1828. Discusses pending changes in the Cabinet, the internal politics involved, and the role of King George IV in the matter. Notes that the "most extraordinary part of the new arrangements" is the continuation of William Huskisson as Colonial Secretary and Lord Dudley as Foreign Secretary. Suggests that because of this the ministerial changes are "wholly unimportant to us," since the same people still direct the Government's policy toward the U.S. Points out that it is not yet known "how the discordant opinions" of Prime Minister Wellington and Foreign Secretary Dudley on the Treaty of July 6, 1827, will be resolved. ALS. DNA, RG59, Dip. Disp., Great Britain, vol. 35 (M30, R31). Received March 4, 1828. For the Anglo–French–Russian Treaty of London of July 6, 1827, called the "Greek Treaty," see [6:780-2].

From CHARLES R. VAUGHAN, Washington, January 22, 1828. Complains on the basis of information enclosed, received from Lt. Edward Holland, Commander of H. M. Schooner *Nimble,* that the Collector of Customs at Key West, William Pinkney, has "taken possession of some Negroes which the Commander had been obliged to send into that Port on board a hired American sloop, after having engaged and run ashore [on December 19, 1827] on the Coast of Florida a Spanish Armed Brig [*Guerrero*] engaged in the Slave Trade." Complains further that the Collector has also demanded duty payments on "some goods" taken out of the captured and wrecked Spanish vessel. Also encloses copies of Holland's correspondence with the Collector. Reports that the Collector has justified taking the slaves "upon the grounds that the Spanish Brig was wrecked and that the Slaves were brought within the limits of the United States, before the captured vessel had been taken formal possession of" by the *Nimble.* Notes that the Collector has suggested to Holland that the case be "referred to a Judicial Tribunal at St. Augustine." Thinks the Collector's explanations and proposed legal disposition of the case are entirely "erroneous" and asks that Clay give directions "to relieve

Lieutenant Holland from any further proceedings against him." ALS. DNA, RG59, Notes from British Legation, vol. 15 (M50, R15). Pinkney's letter to Holland, December 25, 1827, is in *ibid*. See above Morrison, *et al*. to Clay, January 5, 1828.

From WILLIAM WOODBRIDGE, Detroit, January 22, 1828. Reports, as Secretary of State of Michigan Territory, that since "our whole system of statutory law has been repealed—& with some or no variation reenacted," he has had difficulty preparing and forwarding the executive and legislation proceedings of the territorial government. Hopes that rumors that he is to be replaced as Secretary are not true because it would be to him "a source of deep humiliation." Asks for funds to pay a clerk to assist him in catching up on the paperwork of his office. ALS. DNA, RG59, Misc. Letters (M179, R66). Published in Carter, *Territorial Papers*, 11:1156-7. The reasons for the rewriting of the territorial statutes are found in James V. Campbell, *Outlines of the Political History of Michigan* (Detroit, 1876), 416-7. The principal reason was to eliminate unpublished laws not contained in the statutes.

From WILLIAM B. LAWRENCE, London, no. 20, January 23, 1828. Forwards an article on the "West India question" made available to him by the editors of "Parliamentary Review, a work published annually as a Companion to the Parliamentary abstracts." Thinks it represents "the first defense, which has appeared in England, of the course pursued by the United States on that subject," and notes that "It charges, as you will observe, Mr. [William] Huskisson and his late associates with having violated in respect to us those principles, by which they have so frequently asserted that their Commercial policy was governed."

Complains that British postal regulations slow down the forwarding of legation mail, personal and official, from Liverpool. Encloses a letter to Jonathan Thompson, Collector of Customs in New York, suggesting that Thompson instruct the masters of the Liverpool packets sailing from New York to put all U.S. legation and consular mail in separate bags and insist that British postal officials in Liverpool promptly forward such parcels to their destinations. Asks Clay to consider placing such mail under the "law of nations" by designating the master of "regular Liverpool Packets" as diplomatic *"Couriers"* and issuing passports to them.

Concludes with the assurance that while the new Cabinet appointees were not listed in last evening's newspapers, the names given in his dispatch number 19 [above, January 22] are "known to be correct." ALS. DNA, RG59, Dip. Disp., Great Britain, vol. 35 (M30, R31). The enclosure, Lawrence to Thompson, January 23, 1828, is in *ibid*.

To JONATHAN THOMPSON   Washington, January 23, 1828
Your letter of the 5th. instt. with the accompanying papers, relating to the Buenos Ayrean privateer, the General Brand[i]zen and her prize, has been received. It is to be regretted that they increased the number of their crew whilst in our Waters. As soon as an attorney is appointed for

the District, you will be pleased to lay the whole case before him, for the purpose of his determining upon the propriety of his instituting prosecutions against the persons, who may have afforded any assistance to the Commander of the privateer in augmenting his force.—

I transmit you herewith, a copy of a translation of Mr. [Jose S.] Rebello's note of the 31st. ulto., [6:1405] from a perusal of which, you will perceive that he attributes to you the opinion, or declaration that, if the privateer departed with no more men than she brought into port, there would be nothing illegal, although she had changed a part of her original crew for others. As I cannot but be persuaded, there is some mistake in relation to your opinion, or declaration, I have to request such explanation as you may have to offer.—

Copy. DNA, RG59, Dom. Letters, vol. 22, pp. 128–9 (M40, R20).

From NICOLAS NAVONI, Constantinople, January 24, 1828. Recalls his "communications" with Luther Bradish and the Porte "For the purpose of concluding a Treaty of Commerce between the United States and the Sultan," and expresses a belief that the "favourable disposition" which he has "perceived in the Ottoman Government" authorizes him to renew the "communications... which have been for some time suspended." States that Bradish, when he left, authorized Navoni "to continue to solicit a categorical answer from the Porte to his last note." Encloses that authorization and a "historical narrative of ... [his] conversations with the Reis Effendi, the Minister of Foreign Affairs."

States that the Porte is suspicious of innovations in negotiations, especially with "Christian Powers of whom they are generally distrustful," but that now "they consider themselves as released from their obligations to the Preponderant Powers that have influenced them—obligations which they would willingly destroy forever. Reports that the Turks are especially happy to be relieved of "the surveillance" which England "has exercised over them with regard to [a] proposed treaty with the United States of America."

Suggests that if "the United States is not willing to appoint and dispatch a Plenipotentiary, openly, Mr. [David] Offley might... be charged with full power to prosecute this business" and that "the Porte would be pleased with this arrangement." Continues: "It is the earnest wish of the Porte to conclude a treaty but ... their overtures and propositions are not merely commercial." Explains that his own "agency ... in this business, took its rise in an invitation addressed to ... [him] by the Porte during the residence here of Mr. Bradish," and that his "occupations and ... study of the oriental languages have rendered ... [him] for many years familiar with" Ottoman laws, policy and "the Grandees of the Empire." Adds that he offered his "services to Mr. Bradish ... [in] the hope of being one day" named "Interpreter to the Embassy of the United States."

Transmits also four documents: "the Danish Treaty recently concluded," "a letter from the Danish Consul [J. de Jongh] at Smyrna," "an appeal from the Sultan to the Mussalman people," and "a copy of a letter from Mr. Bradish, in which he flatters ... [Navoni] with the hope of obtaining the good will of the Government of the United States." Copy.

DNA, RG59, Dip. Instr., Turkey, vol. 1, pp. 48–50 (M77, R162). Navoni was referred to as "Dragoman American Legation in Constantinople."

Negotiated by Charles Rhind, David Offley, and Commodore James Biddle, USN, a Treaty of Commerce and Navigation was finally concluded with the Ottoman Empire on May 7, 1830. Parry, *Treaty Series*, 81:7–24. The Danish–Turkish Treaty of Commerce and Navigation, was concluded October 16, 1827. *Ibid.*, 77:449–52. The Sultan's appeal, dated December 20, 1827, pointed to wrongs suffered at the hands of Russia and called on his people to resist a foe determined to crush the true religion that was Islam. Creasy, *History of the Ottoman Turks*, 512.

To WILLIAM PLUMER, JR.   Washington, January 24, 1828

I have received and perused with particular satisfaction your obliging letter of the 8th inst. I thank you most cordially for the interest you take in my affair. My late Address [6:1394–6] is doing much good, unless my correspondents are deceived as to its effects.

Since its publication I have rec'd important additional evidence on several of the points which it states, and I shall be determined by future events as to the use to be made of it.

That which your Journal and your memory enable you to supply is very striking.

I have a general recollection of having conversed with you on the subject of the Presidential election, altho' I cannot, from my own memory, recall the particulars of the conversation, but the fact of your having recorded them in the summer of 1824, shortly after your return from Congress, places out of all doubt, and beyond the possibility of cavil, the genuineness of the conversation, and that fact communicates a high additional interest to the testimony, which the conversation bears.

If you could feel at liberty to address a note to some reputable Editor of a Newspaper, communicating the two extracts from your Journal, respecting our conversation, which you have transmitted to me, that voluntary & spontaneous exhibition of the proof would render it, I think, more impressive than if it were brought out in the first instance by me. I should be obliged if you could think it proper so to present it to the public; but if you have the smallest doubt of the propriety of that course, I beg of you not to adopt it.

It is not I think material to state what your Journal records respecting Mr. [Daniel P.] Cook, although I believe it to be perfectly true.

The Jackson party had almost gained Mr. Cook to their cause by erroneously representing the delegations of certain Western States to be favorable to the General, when they were decidedly hostile to his election. I thank you for the privilege which you kindly give to use the extracts which you have sent me. I will avail myself of it hereafter, if necessary.

I congratulate you on the late decided improvement in the prospects of Mr. Adams' re-election. Everywhere there is a better tone, & greater confidence. I shall be much disappointed if the West do not give him a larger vote than both he & I together had in that quarter, at the last election.[1]

I seize with pleasure the opportunity to assure you of the friendly recollections which I retain of our intercourse during our mutual service in the public Councils. And I pray you to convey my friendly regards to your father [William Plumer], with whom also I had the honor to serve in Congress.

Printed in *PMHB*, (1882), 6:355. 1. This is a difficult comparison to evaluate; but see, Schlesinger, Israel, and Hansen, *History of American Presidential Elections*, 1:409, 492.

From FRANCISCO TACON, Philadelphia, January 24, 1828. Surveys, and supports with enclosed documentation, the history of ownership of "20,000 arpents of land, situated in the new settlement of St. Helena on the western bank of the river St. Vincent Otiekfan, the most northern part of the land being sixteen miles, little more or less, to the South of the Boundary Line between the dominions of" Spain and the United States. Concludes that the land is now owned by the "present Marquis of Casa Irujo, an officer in the first department of State," and requests "the special acknowledgement and confirmation of this right of property . . . which is assured by the 8th. Article of the Treaty of the 22d. of February [1819]." ALS, in Spanish with trans. in State Dept. file. DNA, RG59, Notes from Spanish Legation, vol. 9 (M59, R-T12).

Carlos Fernando Martinez de Irujo had been born in Washington, D.C., when his father was Spanish minister there. A professional diplomat, he became Secretary of State for Spain in 1832. His land was situated near what is now Port Vincent in Livingston Parish, La.

Article VIII of the Adams–Onis Treaty of February 22, 1819, confirmed Spanish land grants dated before January 24, 1818. See Parry, *Treaty Series*, 70:8.

To JOHN Q. ADAMS   Washington, January 25, 1828
Mr. Clay's respects to the President and informs him that Mr. Storrs[1] has called to express his strong convictions of the utter inexpediency of the appointmt.[2] of Mr. Talmadge [*sic*],[3] which he thinks would be very mischievous. Mr. Storrs is of the opinion that either Mr. [John] Duer[4] or Mr. [Ogden] Edwards would be decidedly the best selection.

ALS. MHi–Adams Papers, Letters Received (MR484). 1. At this time, Henry Randolph Storrs (1787–1837) was a U.S. Representative from New York. *BDAC.* 2. As U.S. Attorney for the Southern District of New York. 3. Possibly Frederick A. Tallmadge (1792–1869), at this time a New York City lawyer. *BDAC.* 4. Duer was formally appointed on February 1, 1828, not in 1827, as *DAB* has it, or as indicated in 5:108. He was sent his commission on February 4. Clay to Duer, February 4, 1828. Copy. DNA, RG59, Dom. Letters, vol. 22, p. 136 (M40, R20); see also U.S. Sen. *Executive Journal*, 3:594-5. On February 11, Duer acknowledged receipt and acceptance of his commission. LS. DNA, RG59, Accept. and Orders for Comms. (M-T645, R2).

To JOHN Q. ADAMS   Washington, January 25, 1828
The Secretary of State, to whom has been referred a resolution of the House of Representatives of the 2d instant,[1] requesting the President of the United States to communicate to that House, "if the public interest permit, the recent correspondence between the Governments of the United States and Brazil, and any other documents in the Department of

State connected with the subjects of discussion between the two Governments," has the honor to submit to the President the copy of a recent correspondence between the Charge d'Affaires of Brazil and this Department upon the subjects of discussion between the two Governments.

Printed in *ASPFR*, 6:823; also in DNA, RG59, Report Books, vol. 4, p. 217.   1. Introduced on December 27, 1827; adopted January 2, 1828. U.S. H. of Reps., *Journal*, 20 Cong., 1 Sess., 95, 108.

From CHARLES EDMONDSTON & JOHN GEDDES, Charleston, S.C., January 25, 1828. Submit copy of a memorial from John Morrison and others [January 5, 1828]. Express opinion that the memorialists have rendered "highly meritorious services" to both "His Brittanic [*sic*] Majesty's schooner Nimble and to the Spanish Brig Guerrero and the people that were saved from the Wreck of the latter and that the Memorialists are richly entitled to a liberal compensation for these services." Request that the United States Government and the British Minister, Charles R. Vaughan, order an investigation so that the facts of the case may be brought before an appropriate tribunal.

State the opinion, in regard to the portion of the case dealing with "the negroes carried into Key West and there put into the custody of the highest Civil Authority in the place," that American law and "sound discretion properly vested in the head of Department" will produce everything "which justice may require." Request that this aspect of the case be turned over to the Secretary of the Treasury, Richard Rush, if it comes under his jurisdiction. ALS, by Edmondston, signed also by Geddes. DNA, RG59, Misc. Letters (M179, R66). See Vaughan to Clay, January 22, 1828. Edmondston was a naturalized citizen who was prominent in the Charleston mercantile and insurance businesses. See "The Schirmer Diary," *SCHM* (April, 1965), 66:121; (April, 1968), 69:142; (July, 1969), 70:199; (January, 1977), 78:72.

To LEVI LINCOLN, January 26, 1828. Acknowledges receipt of Lincoln's letter of January 19. Reports having received a letter [January 22, 1828] from the special agent, Samuel B. Barrell, commissioned to investigate the Northeastern boundary controversy, and promises to transmit a copy of Barrell's report upon its receipt.

Encloses a copy of the convention concluded with Great Britain on September 29, 1827 [6:1100–01]. Reports that the Senate has advised its ratification, but requests, as ratifications have not yet been exchanged, that Lincoln "consider the Copy of it as confidentially communicated." Copy. DNA, RG59, Dom. Letters. vol. 22, p. 131 (M40, R20).

From ALEXANDER H. EVERETT, Madrid, no. 96, January 27, 1828. Transmits translation of a note from Manuel Gonzales Salmon "on the indemnity question." ALS. DNA, RG59, Dip. Disp., Spain, vol. 28 (M31, R29). Received March 26, 1828.

Salmon, in his letter of January 16 to Everett, based his argument for refusing to consider an indemnity convention on the contention that the Latin American republics were in fact still Spanish colonies and that trade with them by foreigners was restricted. On this ground, Salmon defended the Spanish blockades of these colonies. He also stated that the American citizens "were not ignorant of these prohibitions; they well knew the risk to which they exposed themselves, and consequently have no ground on which to rest a claim for indemnification for any losses or damages which they may have suffered." Further, he asserted that Americans were engaged in the contraband trade. Copy. *Ibid.* See also Everett to Clay, February 21, 1828.

From JOSEPH STORY   Washington, January 27, 1828
I feel great difficulty in interfering with the choice of a District Attorney for New York—But a good appointment is so important to the Administration, that I almost feel that entire Silence would be criminal—I have heard, that Mr [Frederick A.] Talmadge [*sic,* Tallmadge] has been thought of, as on the whole the most suitable candidate—I have long considered him as a most doubtful friend of the Administration from information, which reached me before I left home—And my inquiries here have led me to the knowledge that he is deemed a man of a wavering mind, & by his temperament little adapted to give any aid to the Administration, even when he is an open supporter. I find that Judge [Smith] Thompson thinks that Mr Ogden Edwards would be the best appointment, & next to him Mr [John] Duer would be the best—This latter gentleman I know well from his high character & talents, & his present very high standing in the State—In a professional view he is perhaps second to no man in the State; & he is an open, decided, & stedfast friend of the Admin—I believe his appointment would give very general satisfaction, I do not say universal, because that is impossible, but quite as much as any which could be made, & far more than the appointment of Mr Tallmadge—

I write you with out the Solicitation of any one; but from a sense of duty, & an anxious desire at this critical juncture to add my mite to the assistence of the administration—

If you think my views of any importance you are at liberty to suggest them to the President; but at the same time it is not my wish to enrol[l] myself among the Solicitors for any of the Candidates upon the present occasion—

ALS. DNA, RG59, A. and R. (M531, R2). Letter marked "Private and Confidential."

From JOHN B. BERNADOU, Philadelphia, January 28, 1828. Complains of "erroneous and unlawful" fees levied on his brigs *Emily* and *Sophia* at Havre and Bordeaux, and at St. Ubes, Portugal. Notes that freight rates "are now so reduced that Ship owners are Compelled, to save themselves, to Look Carefully on any Item of expenditure." Asks: "How am I to be refunded?" ALS. DNA, RG59, Misc. Letters (M179, R66). For Bernadou see *NCAB,* 9:495.

From THEODORE HUNT   Saint Louis, January 28, 1828
The course of conduct pursued toward you by some of your political Enemies, I feel most sensibly—I have heard this morning, that in the Telegraph received last night,[1] a piece appeared (supposed in this

Town, to be written by Col [Thomas H.] Benton) calling upon you to permit him to make public, *all* the conversations held with you, on the Presidential question; and stating his willingness to do so, provided you release him from secrecy—As He may be the Author, I have thought it proper to inform you of the following facts—

When a statement appeared in the public prints, in this place, with regard to a decliration, made by Coln Benton in Virginia as to your having stated to him, prior to the 15 Decr 1824 that you would *not* vote for General Jackson [6:1342]—Two of his devoted friends, Mr John Smith, Mr Arther L. McGinnes, both of this Town, asserted that Mr Benton had prior to his departure for Washington last fall, made the same statement to them—This can be proven without dificulty—and further it can be proven, that Mr Benton held out a different opinion to others.

Having married the Daughter of Judge [Jean Baptiste Charles] Lucas, it might be supposed (*were it known that I am your informant*) that it is alone from feelings of hostility to Mr Benton, that I give the information; I therefore give you the names of those, to whom a reference can be made.—Colo. John O Fallen [*sic*, O'Fallon] said to me, in Public, that Mr John Smith, had made the statement to him; and I believe the fact, of Mr McGinnes's having made a similar statement, can be proven by the same gentleman; it can also be proven by others—

Mr Isaac McGirk told me of Mr Bentons having made the different statment refered to, Mr McGirk named to whom He Mr B had made it, but I do not now remember their names, with certainty—In confirmation of his Mr McGirks statement—I am told by good authority that Major Thomas Biddle, fell in company with two or three gentlemen who were present when He Mr Benton had his conversation in L[ake]. Charles; and that they related it, to Major Biddle—Mr McGirk is a friend, and correspondent of Mr [David] Barton's—

With respect to the 2d edition of "Kreemers [*sic*, Kremer's] letter", to viz, that [6:816-7] of H Mondays [*sic*, Munday's], which was got up in this Town, and Mondays doing no more than sign his name to what was written for him; from the knowledge of one or two persons who were present (to viz, Major [William] Christy) when this letter was written it is pretty well known, who wrote it—When I look around me and see the ingratitude, and duplicity with which some persons act, it makes me sick—You I hope my Dear Sir, will not consider me officious, but will attribute this letter to motives of friendship towards you—

ALS. DLC-HC (DNA, M212, R3).   1. Washington *United States Telegraph*, December 11, 1827.

From RICHARD HAWES, JR.   Winchester, Ky., January 29, 1828 [Discusses some minor business relations with Clay involving legal fees and rent payments. Continues:] We entertain a confident belief that we shall suc[ceed] in our elections for this year. I was a member of the adm[on] Convention on the 17th. Decr. [6:1120-3], and it appeared to me that the assem[bla]ge of talents and influence there arrayed, with ordinary industry & Concert, must prevail. In the Northern & most of the Middle Electoral districts we have the Anti relief party, almost "en masse" and in the Southern we are informed that we make great inroads on the relief party [3:146, 902]. The methodists & presbiterians in this quarter are unanimously for us; the Babtists under the influence of [Jacob] Creath & Vardanum [*sic*]¹ who now as of old are the obedient servants of J. P.² are generally against us. The Legislature will rise in about 2 weeks. Nothing as yet done with the Admon resolutions, or the apportionment Bill. You have no doubt heard of the cause of the mortifying defeat in the election of Speaker. A vain giddy youth when we had certain victory before us, permitted masonic friendships, to turn him traitor to his party & constitutents [6:1362-4]. The general ticket plan will pass without opposition, as both parties appear to be for it[.]³

We have recd. your address [6:1394-6] with great pleasure. I think it would have had a better effect at an earlier day. It however sweeps all before it, and we have the isolated subjects of discussion before the people of "the American System" & the qualifications of the Candidates. If we Can effect a fair trial on the former of these questions at our polls we must be triumphant here as well as in the other states or a majority of them [6:360-3].

ALS. DLC-TJC (DNA, M212, R13).   1. For Jeremiah Vardeman, see John H. Spencer, *A History of Kentucky Baptists From 1769 to 1885, Including More than 800 Biographical Sketches.* 2 vols. (Cincinnati, 1885), 1:233-9.   2. John Pope.   3. Blair to Clay, January 22, 1828; Clay to Brooke, January 18, 1828.

From THOMAS McGIFFIN   Washington, Pa., January 29, 1828
Yours of the 21st Inst was recd on the 27th and in reply I have the pleasure of informing you, that so far as regards the Revd Doct. Andrew Wylie there is no *peace to* be made—he is entirely satisfied with the reference to his name and has this day promised to give me his written narrative "over his own signature" within, say 8 or 10 days¹—His only difficulty is in the recollection of the *terms* and the names of those present—The *import* is distinctly recollected as from that conversation his impressions were strongly formed against you—I have furnished him with all your statements and the last containing the evidence and I am much gratified in being able to state to you that his unfavourable impressions are thereby removed Both these—his *first & latter impression,* I intend, if practicable, to have embraced in his narrative He is a man of some talents and standing among his clerical brethren as well as in Society at large and of consequence his impressions maybe of some use to lead others to a similar result—The general impression I believe is on all hands, that you have been injured and were there half as much honesty as there is rancor among politicians, this opinion would be generally expressed in public as fully as it now is in private conversation—I have seen [William] Sample who says he will endeavour to obtain the written statement promised by him² Will you permit me in that spirit of candor and friendship which you know I feel, to ask why it was that you omitted to take any notice of the alledged meeting of the Kentucky (at least) Delegation at which you were reported to have made the "Anthony" speech?³ and also the Amos Kendal[l] disclosures or rather statements [6:1071-2, 1131-2]—especially those which alledge your correspondence on the subject of your appt.—before the election? I know you cannot so

far misunderstand me as to suppose that these omissions make any impression on my mind—The suggestion is only made in the possible conclusion that they had escaped your attention

I do consider Mr. [Richard] Rush's defense of the Tariff [6:1302-05] a very good one, and the only dissatisfaction is that the President did not *endorse the* paper—Had he in any way identified himself with it, I should have been content—Had *you* been President I admit this wou[l]d not at all have been necessary to establish the *fact* of your being a Tariff-man—your whole public life is plenary evidence upon that subject—But even in your case, may I be permitted to ask you, with the *Constitutional injunction* to recommend such subjects as you might deem of national importance—*could* you or would you have omitted the Tariff and Internal Improvements? especially at this time when a greater effort than was ever before made, is making to prostrate both interests? And that too upon a principle—that of constitutional construction, which if *true* must put the question at rest? But Mr. Adams never has in any public official act placed his opinions on these questions before the nation in an *unquestionable shape*—The *principal* evidence which he ever has given is that of your selection—however as regards Mr. Rush's report—*he* may have never seen it—Rush reports directly to Congress and *may* be *setting up for himself*—But I regret the omission *especially* on the ground that—admitting that he is favorable, which I still hope is the case,—it had the *appearance* of *catching* Virginia and North Carolina—an inference much more strong and plausible than would have been the charge of his intending to *catch* Penna, had he spoken out plainly in favour of the American System—This was expected by *every* body—friend & foe and was triumphantly defensible under the *Consitutional injunction.* And altho I admit, in answer to one of your inquiries, that he would not have thereby changed one Jackson *partizan,* yet I *know* he would have *retained* and *obtained many* who were *not partizans,* but were *pausing*   This I know is, and much more, *has* been the case with *many* very many of our Citizens—who as the case now stands are lost to our side—and if they ever should be reclaimed Mr Adams will not be entitled to the credit of it—I admit that we must look pretty much to the course of our adversaries for the evidence to convince our Citizens in regard to this question but I should really have been glad that we could have pointed to the Official act of our (*locum tenens*) *chief* for the *conclusive* evidence of his devotion to the great *cause* of the country and contrasted *that* with the *doubtful* and equivocal attitude of his rival. *Many,* no doubt many thousan[ds] believe that it matters little what cou[r]se th[e] friends and advocates of a man take—provid[ed] *he* becomes President, he can & will *contradict* everything—But I will not trouble you wi[th] any further crude remarks upon this matter—it [is] passed and however destructive to our prospects perhaps cannot—it seems will not, be *mended*—However much I may regret it, I shall never desert the ship while you are on board, altho I conf[ess] I would much rather cause a mutiny and throw the present Captain overboard & take the *Mate* for Commander.—

I have this day written to Mr. [Joseph] Lawrence and enclosed a recommendation signed by upwards of 70 of our most respectable Citizens in behalf of my son [6:1305-06][4]—I have stated to him that I had, according to his own suggestion, written to you upon the subject & that you were kind enough to say that you would co-operate so far as you could with propriety and asked of him to see you—If he should fail, will you have the goodness to speak to him upon the subject? *Inter nos,* I cannot now have full confidence in this man altho, I am compelled to make him the chann[el] of communication—His course upon a late occasion has put it out of the question for me implicitly to rely on him and especially in this case as Sample is a rival applicant. They affirm here that they have his first pledge and seem to have no doubt of success—Be it so—w[e] only had his *pledge,* whether first or last I know not, nor do I care—a pledge is a pledge and I shall hold him to a strict account—I have asked of him to say whether I may rely upon [word missing] to present an application in my son's behalf to the Penna Delegation and also to many from Ohio, who I believe are friendly & who would act *thro'* him, but most probably not against him? Will you please keep an *Eye* on him—It is a small matter—altho, of considerable importance to me and *everything* to my *young-hopeful,* as he has set his heart upon success, and I am really sorry and ashamed to trouble you with it—As matters stand however I must either abandon the object or rely upon you & you alone—If it were a matter exclusively my own I would not hesitate a moment in relieving you from all importunity, but being a father you can easily imagine my present predicament—Do what you think is right I will thank you if I succeed and if I fail my regard will remain not only unchanged but undiminished—

ALS. DLC–HC (DNA, M212, R3).   1. For inclusion in *A Supplement to the Address . . . to the Public,* pp. 6–7. See June 10, 1828.   2. See January 2, 1828, and enclosure. 3. Reference obscure; but see Clay's statement to having "most earnestly entreated them" in Clay to Blair, Jan. 8, 1825 [4:10].   4. Nathaniel W. McGiffin was admitted to the U.S. Military Academy as a cadet in 1830 but was not graduated. William Sample's son, David, was not admitted. *Register of Graduates and Former Cadets of the United States Military Academy* (West Point, N.Y., 1960), 186. Hereafter cited as USMA, *Register.*

From JOSE S. REBELLO   Washington, January 29, 1828
I had on the 25th. ultimo, the honor to inform you that immediately upon the receipt of your Note of the 17th. of the same month, the necessary orders were directed to the Custom house officers at New York, to prevent any violation of the laws of Neutrality of the United States, on the part of the Buenos Ayrean Privateer, the General Brand[i]-zen, or her prize, whilst within our jurisdiction. Without such orders, it would have been the duty of the Officers of the Customs to have prevented any such violation as far as was practicable, and their known vigilance authorizes the belief that they would have faithfully performed their duty. But those orders were nevertheless, given, to furnish an additional proof to the Government of the Brazils of the desire of that of the United States to conform to the wishes of its Representative here, and to enforce a strict and impartial neutrality.

Immediately on the receipt of your Note of the 31st. ultimo, communicating the statement that the above mentioned Vessels had augmented their force in the port of New York, I addressed Instructions [6:1406] to the Attorney of the United States [Robert Tillotson] to investigate the transaction, and if he should find that there had been any violation of our Laws to institute the necessary proceedings for bringing the guilty to punishment. I am now enabled by the report of that officer to communicate to you such information and explanations, in respect to the Privateer and her Prize, above mentioned, as will, I trust, prove entirely satisfactory to yourself and your Government.

Those vessles arrived in the port of New York, on the 12th. ultimo, and after being immediately visited by the Custom house officer, reported that they came in, in distress. Their Commander [George C. DeKay] was informed by the Collector [Jonathan Thompson] that the rights of hospitality would be extended to them, but that our laws would not permit his force to be augmented, or the number of his men increased. The Commander professed to be well acquainted with his duty in that respect, I transmit herewith a copy of a Letter from him to the Collector of the Port exhibiting the vigilance with which the operations of the vessels were executed on the part of our officers and containing a recognition of his obligations to observe, with strictness, our Laws and regulations. On the 24th. ultimo, the Commander of those Vessels having stated that they were ready to proceed to Sea, the Collector of the Port directed the proper officer to board and visit them, and I now, also, transmit herewith, a copy of the report made by that officer on the occasion. Those vessels afterwards dropped down and came to anchor on the bar, or just within Sandy Hook, below the City of New York. Whilst in that situation, the Collector was informed that they were receiving reinforcement of men. In consequence additional barge-men were directed to be employed, night and day, to examine the vessels apparently bound to Sandy Hook, for seamen that might have been shipped; and to detain them. The Revenue Cutter was also, ordered below, for a similar purpose. I, likewise transmit you herewith, a Copy of a Letter from the Surveyor of the Port of New York to the Collector, manifesting the diligence with which those vessels were watched during their visit, and shewing that some men who were intended to be put on board the Privateer, clandestinely, were arrested in their progress and discharged. When it was discovered by the Collector that an attempt was making to evade our Laws, the Revenue Cutter was sent near Long Branch, in pursuit of the Privateer and her prize; but upon discovering her approach, they hove up their anchors and made sail. The Cutter continued the pursuit until she lost sight of them in the night.

From the preceding narrative, and the perusal of the documents referred to, you must be convinced that every precaution was employed, to prevent any breach of our Laws, and, especially to guard against any augmentation of the force or Crews of the Privateer or her prize. If the number of their crews has been increased, it was done without the consent or knowledge of the Officers of the Port of New York; was an inexcusable abuse of the rights of hospitality, and took place under such clandestine circumstances as that it could not have been detected or prevented.

Upon full consideration of all the circumstances attending the transaction, I am persuaded that there is no just ground of complaint against the officers of the Government of the United States, at the port of New

York; that their conduct, on the contrary has been marked by a vigilant attention to the discharge of their duties, and the enforcement of our Laws, and that they have not been actuated by any unfriendly spirit towards His Majesty the Emperor of Brazil [Pedro I].

The Government of the United States, and its officers, in the discharge of their neutral duties towards His Majesty the Emperor of Brazil, and the Republic of Buenos Ayres, have not, in any instance, allowed themselves to be influenced, in the smallest degree, by any considerations derived from the nature of the political institutions existing in those Countries. I must take the occasion to say, that it appears to me to be unadvisable in the course of that diplomatic correspondence which it may be necessary to carry on between the two Countries, in consequence of complaints which the one may have against the other to refer to the forms of their respective Governments. Allusions to those forms on the one side, may beget similar allusions on the other, and this discussion, instead of being limited to facts, and cases of real grievance, may be extended to abstract questions relating to forms of Government.

I have to request that you will communicate this note to Your Government. . . .

Copy. DNA, RG59, Notes to Foreign Ministers and Consuls, vol. 3, pp. 418–21 (M38, R3). L draft, in CSmH, under date of January 23, 1828.   1. Tillotson to Clay, Jan. 4, 1828.

From JOSEPH RICHARDSON, Washington, January 29, 1828. At the request of Benjamin Delano, Kingston, Massachusetts, the Congressman inquires "concerning the disposition that has been adopted in the case of the Schooner, Only Son, and Cargo, of which Jacob Fuller was master, upon which an outrage was committed [in July, 1822] at Halifax in Nova Scotia." Adds that "The papers belonging to this case were sent to the Department of State in 1822 or 1823." ALS. DNA, RG76, Misc. Claims, Great Britain. Endorsed by Clay on cover: "Mr. [Daniel] B[rent] will be pleased to examine into this case and inform HC."

For subsequent developments of this rather unusual case, see Richardson to Clay, February 7, April 10, January 11, 1829. *Ibid.* The vessel, while standing off Halifax, "calling for advice and bound for a market," had been forced by British authorities to enter the port, pay duties, and sell her cargo. The case was not settled until 1853 when "full" damages of $1000 were paid. *Sen. Docs.,* 35 Cong., 2 Sess., no. 18, p. 7. For Richardson, See *BDAC.*

From JAMES RIDDLE, Pittsburgh, January 29, 1828. Asks for Clay's intervention with Secretary of War James Barbour with regard to a disciplinary case at West Point involving Cadet James H. Stewart, son of Mathew Stewart, "our Register and Recorder of this City & County." Concludes that "As to thing[s] Political I do assure you we are doing well in west Penna." ALS. DNA, RG94, Application Papers of Cadets. Clay endorsement on attached sheet: "Reappd Feby 18 1828." ALS. DNA, RG94, Application Papers of Cadets. Cadet Stewart was not graduated with his class of 1831. USMA, *Register,* 184.

To **BENJAMIN W. ROGERS,** New York, January 29, 1828. Sends, in response to Rogers's letter of January 21, brought him by Fulgence Chegaray, "an extract from a letter of instructions [October 23, 1827] transmitted by this Department to Mr. [William] Tudor." Promises that "in case the further good offices of the Department could promote the success of this reclamation, they will be promptly and cheerfully afforded." Copy. DNA, RG59, Dom. Letters, vol. 22, p. 132 (M40, R20). Rogers was President of the New York and South American Steamboat Association in New York. His January 21 letter included a memorial [not found] of the Association which apparently asked for protection and assistance to American shipping in Brazil, and the settlement of outstanding U.S. claims there. Chegaray was an agent of the Association. LS. DNA, RG76, Misc. Claims, Brazil.

From **JONATHAN THOMPSON,** "Custom House New York, Collectors' Office," January 29, 1828. Acknowledges receipt of Clay's letter of January 23 and its enclosures. Defends himself against Jose Silvestre Rebello's charges. Refers to Thompson's letter to Clay of January 5, which stated that only two members of the *General Brandizen's* crew "were shipped in this [New York] port; and they were put on shore." Denies having said that a belligerent could "replace in Neutral ports its invalids and deserters." Asserts that the "charge of connivance" is without foundation.

Suggests that Rebello should reflect upon the fact that his Emperor, Peter I, has received "Two Frigates of the largest class, One small Frigate, and several other vessels of War, and their crews, American Citizens, within a few years past from the United States." Adds: "This probably may not be considered by him a violation of the Laws of Neutrality." LS. DNA, RG59, Misc. Letters (M179, R66).

From **MARTIN VAN BUREN,** "Committee Room [U.S. Senate]," January 29, 1828. Requests, on behalf of the Senate Judiciary Committee, "copies of the instructions given by the President, to Andrew Ellicott Esquire," the U.S. commissioner appointed to run the boundary line between the U.S. and the Spanish territory of Florida, "in conformity" with the Treaty of San Lorenzo "and also of the report made by him either separately, or in conjunction with the Commissioner of the Government of Spain [6:987–8]." ALS. DNA, RG59, Misc. Letters (M179, R66).

From **WILLIAM B. LAWRENCE,** London, no. 21, January 30, 1828. Transmits a copy of "the speech of the King [George IV], yesterday delivered ... to ... Parliament," the "larger portion" of which was devoted to foreign relations. Points out that "The intention to withdraw the British troops from Portugal ... is formally stated and the Treaties with Brazil and Mexico are officially announced." Notes that "the most important part of this State paper relates to the affairs of the East," and that "the policy of the country with respect to the Turkish mediation has been most materially changed." Characterizes an Order in Council, published in The London *Gazette* of "last evening" [enclosed], allowing

"American vessels, arriving in ballast, to take Salt and fruit from the Island of Anguilla to any part of the world," as a "petty concession," and "of little consequence, except as affording an additional indication of the British system." States, with regard to colonial trade, that he has "no reason to believe that the present [Wellington] Administration has the least intention to recede." Expresses his belief that "this Government has never assigned the true reason, which induced them to suspend our intercourse with the West Indies" and asserts: "It grew out of the state of things in England and resulted from nothing which was done or omitted on our part." Adds, by way of explanation: "The Reciprocity Treaties with several of the powers of Europe were extremely unpopular with the Ship owners, at the same time that the Order in Council of July 27, 1826 [5:632–4] was issued and Mr [William] Huskisson looked out for some measure, which, while it tended to conciliate them, might be defended with the friends of free trade on grounds, other than those of a change of principles. Of the misunderstanding in the United States of the meaning and intention of the Act of 1825 [5:629–32], he therefore gladly availed himself." ALS. DNA, RG59, Dip. Disp., Great Britain, vol. 35 (M30, R31). Received March 17, 1828.

To JOSEPH R. REVENGA   Washington, January 30, 1828
I have received the Letter which Your Excellency did me the honor to address to me, on the 25th. of September of the last year [6:1069], by the directions of the Liberator President [Simon Bolivar] on his assumption of the exercise of the national executive power of the Republic of Colombia: The object of Your Excellency's letter is to explain to the satisfaction of the Government of the United States the reasons which induced the publication at Caracas of a communication from Mr. [Beaufort T.] Watts, Chargé d'Affaires of the United States near the Republic of Colombia [6:684–5].

There is no one point in the foreign relation of the United States about which their Government has ever been more solicitous, than that of scrupulously avoiding all interference in the internal affairs of another nation. This rule of conduct, which has been invariably observed by the Government of the United States, is founded upon the double motive of self respect, and respect for foreign powers. As we could ourselves tolerate no interference in our affairs by any foreign power; we suppose no foreign power would admit of any interference, on our part, in its affairs.

The communication of Mr. Watts, to which your Excellency refers, was made without instruction; and the first information of it which reached the Government of the United States, was received through the channel of the public prints. In *making that communication* Mr. *Watts was no doubt actuated* by *a zealous interest which* he *took* in *the affairs* of *Colombia, and he was probably* also *influenced* by the *laudable object* of *healing, rather than exciting, intestine divisions.* Your Excellency does the Government of the United States no more than justice in supposing that it takes a deep concern in whatever relates to the prosperity of the Republic of Colombia. It has, consequently, seen, with regret, late events occurring within the bosom of that Republic, whose tendency appeared to be to impair its happiness; and it hails with joy the restoration of a more auspicious state of things. Although the Government of the United States cherishes these sentiments, it could not have allowed itself to take any part in the internal transactions of Colombia the proper estimate of which belonged exclusively to her own Government and people.

Whilst I feel that the occasion calls for these explanations, I take great pleasure in being the organ of expressing the satisfaction of the President of the United States with the reasons assigned in Your Excellency's letter for the publication of Mr. Watts communication. One half of the objection to that communication is removed by the ascertainment of the fact that it gave no dissatisfaction to the Government of the Republic of Colombia; and with respect to the other half relating entirely to the United States, the President is disposed to overlook it, under all the circumstances of the case.

With assurances of the most sincere and undiminished friendship, on the part of the United States, for the Republic of Colombia, I beg leave. . . .

LS. ScHi.

From GEORGE W. SLACUM, Alexandria, Va., January 30, 1828.

Transmits a letter received from his "agent in Buenos Ayres" and requests that it be filed "as a communication from . . . [his] Consulate." ALS. DNA, RG59, Cons. Disp., Buenos Aires, vol. 3 (M70, R4). No date of receipt.

The enclosure, addressed to Slacum by Robert Kortright, "Acting Consul of U.S.," Buenos Aires, October 10, 1827, reports violations of American neutral rights during the war between Buenos Aires and Brazil in the cases of "The Brig Annah of New York," "The Schooner Hazard," "The Brig Ruth of Philadelphia," and "The Brutus . . . of New York." Lists also a number of vessels which he suspects have been sold but which still sail under United States colors.

From FRANCIS T. BROOKE
Near Fredericksburg, Va.,
January 31, 1828

Believe not that my tardiness in writing you is any proof of any abatement of my faithful recollection of you, I have been Sorely afflicted with an abcess on my knee I am now better and Shall be in Richmd I hope in a few days—I have no answer to my last letter to Mr Monroe from which I infer he means to let me have my own way or is as I requested consulting with Mr Madison[1] I shall know Shortly and will inform you—Some of our Friends in Penna ought to contrive to Send Some of [the] important documents in German into the valley of Virginia depend on it it is of great importance—our address will be published in German at Winchester [Va.] and will have a good effect—the debate on Chiltons resolutions[2] ought not to be Slightly passed over, it Speaks volumes and a good use ought to be made of it—but I am Sending coals to Newcastle—it is barely possible that during our vacation in April I will Spend a few days with you I have much too much to Say to you on paper—

ALS. InU. Endorsed by Clay: "Politics." 1. Above, 6:1356; below, Brooke to Clay, February 28, 1828. 2. The resolution of Rep. Thomas Chilton of Ky. looked toward investigating the possibility of reductions in the cost of operating the executive agencies of the U.S. government for the ostensible purpose of more rapidly paying off the public debt, but also as a political device that might embarrass the Adams administration. Offered on January 22, modified on January 26, passed in amended form on February 6, the final version provided for the appointment of a "Select Committee" of seven to study the problem of where and how reductions in government expenses might best be made. The debate on this measure is found in *Register of Debates*, 20 Cong., 1 Sess., 1064–8, 1084–90, 1122–51, 1253–74, 2275–458. The final report of the House, May 15, 1828, stated that Cabinet officers, all of whom had testified that reductions were impossible, had been uncooperative and that the number of U.S. government clerks could be reduced by one-third. *House Reports*, 20 Cong., 1 Sess., no. 259.

To HEZEKIAH HUNTINGTON, "Attorney U.S. District of Connecticut, Hartford," January 31, 1828. Reminds him of his letter of April 30, 1827, in which he expressed an intention to submit a statement explaining his "official conduct." States: "No such statement, however, having yet been received from you, I am directed by the President to state that, if you do not immediately furnish one, he shall think it his duty to enter upon the examination of the Matters charged against you, and decide upon them without it [6:331–2]." Copy. DNA, RG59, Dom. Letters, vol. 22, p. 134 (M40, R20). Huntington responded to this on February 6, pointing out that he was gathering together his evidence and would lay his defense "before the President, as soon as tis possible." ALS. DNA, RG59, Misc. Letters (M179, R66).

Huntington submitted an 11 page letter written on May 3 and 19, 1828, defending himself against the charges and "the *wretches* who pursued me." *Ibid.*

To PETER B. PORTER Washington, D.C., January 31, 1828
I defered answering your letter of the 13h. inst. which I duly recd. until I could communicate something to you conclusive about the office of district Attorney. The person you apprehended would be pressed (Mr. [Thomas Jackson] Oakley) was not urged on the President. He has concluded, under all circumstances, to nominate Mr. [John] Duer of the City of N. York, who was recommended by more than two thirds of the representation from your State, including gentlemen of both parties, and most of the friends of the Administration. The President would probably have nominated Judge [Ogden] Edwards but for that fact and the personal infirmity of the Judge. There were very opposite opinions expressed by gentlemen from New York; and no selection could have been probably made which would have given universal satisfaction. I shall be glad if this should prove acceptable to our friends.

I beg you to communicate to me freely, and without reserve, your opinions as to appointments and measures within your State. I need not say that the opinion of no friend would have more weight with me, and I will add, according to my belief, with the President also. The Administration has been much in want of such a judgment as your's and such information as you possess respecting N. York affairs.

I hear that you are effecting wonders in advancing the cause of the Administration at Albany. I am glad to be able to say to you that its prospects have brightened every where of late. They began to change with the New Year, and their improvement has been ever since great and progressive.

What do you think of the Correspondence respecting the Navigation of the St. Lawrence? It has been much mutilated in the publication, but it will be intelligible to you.[1]

I shall be glad to hear from you as often as convenient.

ALS. NBuHi. Letter marked ("Private & Confidential.")   1. On the St. Lawrence issue, see 5:443, 451–64; and Clay to Adams, January 5, 1828. The Washington *Daily National Journal* of February 11, 1828, was one of the newspapers which printed a truncated version of the Anglo–American correspondence on the issue. See also *Niles' Register* (February 16, 1828), 33:411–28.

From CHARLES SAVAGE, Omoa, Federation of the Centre of America, January 31, 1828. Reports the flight of the commandant of the town on a British vessel, the continued proximity of San Salvador troops, the removal of American property to ships in the harbor for safety, and the rupture of communications with Guatemala. States his intention to leave for Guatemala City in two days. ALS. DNA, RG59, Cons. Disp., Guatemala, vol. 1 (M–T337, R1). Received March 8, 1828.

From THOMAS L. L. BRENT, Lisbon, no. 51, February 1, 1828. Refers to the arrival of Dom Miguel in London and the expectation that he would not leave that city before January 22. Reports that "The Ultraroyalist party are mortified beyond measure that he should have taken that rout[e] and that he should come on with the additional title of Lieutenant of the Emperor Dom Pedro and not under that of Regent merely, with the express recognition of his right to it as alone derived from the Constitution." Notes other circumstances contributing to the disappointment of this group, which, however will gain "a momentary advantage" from the violence of political parties, the opposition "to all reforms," the economic stagnation of the country, and the widening gap between national revenues and expenses. Observes that the advantage enjoyed by the ultraroyalist party "can not but be Transient," for, despite the difficulties faced by "the constitutional party, a spirit is displayed in the House of Deputies beyond what" he had expected.

Comments on the neglect of Prince Miguel by his father, John VI, and the change for the better of the former "since his residence in Vienna," where, however, the "opinions and impressions" received by him "will have been all unfavorable to free principles of government." Questions Miguel's capacity to govern. Remarks that since the adoption of recent measures by Spain [6:1280; 1334; 1335] "the portuguese refugees in the depots have remained perfectly quiet." LS. DNA, RG59, Dip. Disp., Portugal, vol. 7 (M43, R–T6). Received April 4, 1828.

To ALEXANDER H. EVERETT, no. 12, February 1, 1828. States that the commissioners, Andrew Ellicott and Stephen B. Minor, appointed under the Treaty of 1795 with Spain [Pinckney's Treaty] to fix the boundary between the United States and the Floridas, "terminated their labors in 1800, and are believed to have made a report of Their proceedings to their respective Governments," but that no copy of the report can be found in the archives of the United States. Explains the need, in the settlement of the Georgia–Florida boundary, "to ascertain the fact with certainty, whether a report was made, or not, by the Commissioners, and, if it were, to obtain a copy of it [6:987–8]." Instructs Everett to "make an official application to the Spanish Government, to ascertain if a report was made . . . and, if it was, to procure a copy of it." Copy. DNA, RG59, Dip. Instr., vol. 12, p. 56 (M77, R7). No date of receipt.

From JOSE SILVESTRE REBELLO, Washington, February 1, 1828. Acknowledges receipt of Clay's note of January 29 and adds that "from . . . [the enclosures] it is to be deduced that the Officers of the Government of the United States" in the Port of New York had done all "in their power" to prevent the privateer from abusing the hospitality permitted by "the Laws of Nations." Promises to transmit a copy of the note to his Government and to make no allusion in future correspondence with the United States "to the form of the two Governments, this being under the Conviction that an equal resolution will allways be in the Minds of the greatest part of the individuals of this Country." ALS, in Spanish, with trans. in State Dept. file. DNA, RG59, Notes from Brazilian Legation, vol. 1 (M49, R1).

To FRANCIS T. BROOKE   Washington, February 2, 1828
I am sorry to learn by your letter of the 31st. Ulto. that you have continued to be afficted with the complaint in your knee; but as you proposed going to Richmond (where I address you) I hope you have by this time recovered from it.

Our late information from Albany is highly encouraging. The partizans of [DeWitt] Clinton and [Martin] V.B. are beginning already to display their suspicions and jealousies of each other; and my correspondents assure me that there is very little prospect of an union between them to nominate a P. and V.P. In the mean time it is stated that a powerful reaction has taken place throughout the State.[1]

I shall be glad to have the earliest information of the decision of Mess [James] Madison and [James] Monroe, as to their names continuing on the Electoral ticket.

Should you be able to execute your intention of visiting this City, I pray you to come at once to my house, where we have plenty of room for such accommodations as we shall take pleasure in affording you. It would add to Mrs. Clay's gratification and my own, if you would bring Mrs Brooke with you.

ALS. KyU.   1. Porter to Clay, January 13, 1828.

From THOMAS E. WAGGAMAN, Baltimore, February 2, 1828. Reminds Clay that in early 1827, when he was a resident in Virginia, he had applied for the "humble employment of Lockgate keeper on the Banks of the James River" but had failed in his quest. Remarks: "I have no friend in Congress to urge my suit with the present Administration—On that subject I differ with my Virginia friends—and if the delusion under which the Public is laboring, results in the explusion of the most enlightened and virtuous Citizens of the Country from the Administration of its Government, I for one am willing to be numbered with the minority, and shall take comfort in 'the fact that the race is not always to the Swift nor the Battle to the Strong.'" Says he will take any post available and notes that even the "relentless severity" of Tiberius Caesar did not prevent him from assisting the descendants of Roman patriots. "My children too, are the offspring of some of those who stood foremost in the hour of trial in our own Country." ALS. DNA, RG59, A. and R. (M531, R8). On March 29, Waggaman, writing from the "General Post Office" in Washington, where he had temporary employment, applied unsuccessfully for the permanent job of Superintendent of the Patent Office. ALS. DNA, RG59, A. and R. (MR8).

From WILLIAM H. D. C. WRIGHT, Rio de Janeiro, February 2, 1828. Forwards copy of a Brazilian decree requiring that a bond be posted by neutral vessels landing at Montevideo. States that the bond is aimed at preventing neutral trading with Buenos Aires. Objects that the decree attempts to extend Brazilian authority to the high seas and is "too palpable a violation of the Sovereignty of Other Powers to admit of any justification." Learns from Commodore James Biddle that the cargo of the brig *Ruth* has been condemned at Buenos Aires. Observes that the war has been confined to Buenos Aires's privateering raids on Brazilian and neutral shipping, but reports that a campaign "is expected shortly to open in the South" since the army of Buenos Aires is advancing in large numbers upon Rio Grande. Has heard nothing of William Tudor's whereabouts. ALS. DNA, RG59, Cons. Disp., Rio de Janeiro, vol. 3 (M-T172, R4). Published in *ASPFR*, 6:1068. Received April 1, 1828. In another dispatch on February 2, Wright transmitted a printed copy of the Anglo–Brazilian Treaty of Amity and Commerce [4:768; 5:235] that had been signed at Rio de Janeiro on August 17, 1827, and ratified in London on November 10, 1827. *Ibid.* Received March 30, 1828. See Parry, *Treaty Series,* 77:375–93.

From FRANCIS PRESTON BLAIR   Frankfort, February 4, 1828
I was called on Saturday before the Senate to give evidence in the enquiry produced by [Martin] Beattys Resolution,[1] or rather Ben:Hardins for I believe he is the real author—I refused to be sworn for reasons which I submitted in writing of which I send you a copy[2]—I objected on principle to the right assumed by the body to pry into my private confidential correspondence for political offences—My friends in politics appear offended at the course I felt myself bound in honor to take & some seem to think that I have been influenced to save myself from the exposure of my own conduct by the letters I wrote myself to Washington on the subject of Mr Adams election.[3] I was however actuated solely by what appeared to me to be right in the matter without any consideration of your or my individual interest—The Senate by a vote almost unanimous supported me in the position I had taken—[4]
    I exerted all the influence I had with my party to prevent this inves-

tigation, because I thought the whole proceeding wrong, & I was gratified to perceive that they were willing, as I think all sides should have been to put down this species of legislative electioneering. Genl [James] Allen's resolution giving power to send for persons & papers would have slept on the table & the other resolution would have been acted on but for the interposition of [Francis] Lockett an administration Senator who called up Allens resolution when it had been agreed by the Jackson party that they should rest on the table.[5] And at the threshold of the enquiry when the witnesses were called a motion was made by Mr [John] Pope to lay the resolutions on the table until the last of July & he pledged himself that he would follow by it up by moving to expunge the resolution[6] which had called for the enquiry from the Journal Whatever be the consequences of the present unprecedented proceeding in the Senate[7] they ought of right to fall on the administration party which has urged them with great pertinacity; especially [Ben] Hardin & [Robert] Wickliffe—

I recd. your letter of the 12th. of last month. I would not hesitate on my own account for a moment to make the spontaneous publication you desire. But you will consider whether the seriousness of the late enquiry here will not make it improper for me now to volunteer a statement & whether it would be advantageous for me to become a witness at all. Would it not give some claim to your opponents to call me out or increase the force of the call already made on you to do it? From some proof which [William] Tanner has given the old fishery & Navigation business [3:204, 236-8] will be brought up[8]—[Amos] Kendall & others know that I wrote pieces on that Subject, & I want to avoid altogether all reference to me about it, & as you made me your confidant in regard to that as well as to other matters, I do not think that any party should be furnished with any pretext to penetrate our private intercourse[9] & claim a right to know through me the various views entertained by you in conducting the complicated [1824] canvass. I do not know however what course the late proceeding here will it necessary for you to adopt. I have always thought myself that there was no criminality in the members of Ky. ascertaining who were to be Adams' counsellors before they voted for him as it has been proved before the Senate that it was that vindication offered by some before their constituents.[10] The public would never have considered Such a care of the western interests by the western members a corrupt bargain but for the mystery that was [hung?] round it—I know I advised it my self, & predicated all my efforts in favor of Mr Adams' here upon that result which I supposed I had good grounds to anticipate—Nothing has ever cost me more anxiety than the statement which I made to Mr Kendall on that subject to obtain his support & concurrence in effecting the object which Mr. [Robert P.] Letchers letter to Mr. [John J.] Crittenden first induced me to suppose was essential to your interests [4:41; 6:1071-2]—Kendall's letter to you & Mr Crittenden's response [6:1071-2; 1131-2; 1206-07] having fixed the eye of curiosity on me has subjected me to much questioning by those who are now my intimates—I have given to all private the same answer that I have given to the *public* enquiry—From *me* it shall never be understood otherwise than that the objection to the publicity of a private correspondence has proceeded from me & has been prompted by *principle* & a wish to put down an attempt which would commit a sacrilege on social intercourse.—a piracy upon all friendly commerce—P.S. In looking over your letters recently I find one dated immediately before the election before the House & subsequent to that I sent you—It contains an indication of the course you had resolved on & some strictures upon the conduct of [DeWitt] Clinton, [John C.] Calhoun & [William H.] Crawfords friends [4:9-10, 46-7]—If you have no copy of it & wish it, I will send it to you—

ALS. DLC-HC (DNA, M212, R13).   1. Blair to Clay, January 22, 1828.   2. Not found; but in his statement, Blair asserted that he refused to be sworn because the investigation was not "a subject constitutionally cognizable" by the Senate and because his information "was obtained in the course of friendly communication and a private correspondence" which he "deemed confidential." Ky. Sen. *Journal* . . . 1827-8, p. 308.   3. See 4:41; and Ky. Sen. *Journal* . . . 1827-8, p. 308.   4. No vote has been found on the motion which discharged Blair from providing testimony. However, a motion to reconsider it failed by a vote of 18 to 8. Ky. Sen. *Journal* . . . 1827-8, pp. 308-10.   5. For Lockett's role, see Blair to Clay, January 22, 1828. Francis Lockett, a Virginia-born officer in the War of 1812 who had taken up residence in Kentucky in 1807, was at this time a member of the State Senate. E. Polk Johnson, *A History of Kentucky and Kentuckians.* 3 vols. (Chicago, 1912), 2:717.   6. The adjective "offensive," modifying "resolution" is struck through in the original. No resolution to expunge is found in the Ky. Sen. *Journal.*   7. Blair to Clay, January 22, 1828. For further details on the "unprecedented proceeding," see Frankfort. *Argus of Western America,* January 30, 1828; Lexington *Kentucky Reporter,* February 8, 1828; Ky. Sen. *Journal* . . . 1827-8, pp. 337-9.   8. William Tanner [4:258], sometime editor of several Kentucky newspapers, was at this time editor of the Harrodsburg *Central Watchtower.* In 1823, Clay had contributed $100 ($75 of which was funneled through Thomas Smith) to help pay for Tanner's printing of Amos Kendall's pamphlet attacking Adams's stance on the fisheries and Mississippi navigation issues during the Treaty of Ghent negotiations. Frankfort *Argus of Western America,* February 13, 1828. For Tanner's journalistic career, see *KHSR,* 36:60, 155, 250; 38:61; Lexington *Kentucky Reporter,* February 6, 1828; Willard R. Jillson, *Early Frankfort and Franklin County, Kentucky* (Louisville, 1936), 124.   9. Blair's "pieces" and any correspondence between Clay and Blair on the subject have not been found.   10. Several members of the Kentucky delegation had supported the U.S. House election of Adams, over Jackson, in February, 1825, in their belief that Adams would appoint Clay as Secretary of State, that Clay, as a cabinet member, would thus better be able to protect western interests for the next four years, and that he might even succeed to the presidency. They had little confidence, however, that Jackson would so favor Clay. See, Frankfort *Argus of Western America,* February 6 and 13, 1828.

From JOHN BLAIR, Chairman of House Committee on Expenditures in the Department of State, February 4, 1828. Requests that Clay supply the Committee with a detailed accounting of all State Department expenditures and disbursements, specifically including "contingent expenses of all Missions abroad" as well as those for "Foreign intercourse." Asks for a breakdown of monies spent from the regular appropriation [4 *U.S. Stat.,* 214] and from the contingency fund. ALS. DNA, RG59, Misc. Letters (M179, R66). On February 5, Blair again wrote, pointing out that the Committee had already examined the Department's accounts through 1824, but not for 1825. *Ibid.*

From WILLIAM H. CRAWFORD   Wood Lawn,[1] February 4, 1828 Inclosed is a letter for Mr [Joel R.] Poinsett our minister in Mexico, which I will thank you to forward to Mr Poinsett with as little delay as is consistent with your convenience The object of the letter is obtain from him some of the productions of Mexico which will probably succeed in the Southern & Western States. Perhaps an intimation from the Secretary of State on this subject may be productive of good effects.

I hope you know me too well to suppose that I have countenanced the charge of corruption which has been reiterated against you. The truth is I approved of your vote for Mr Adams when it was given [4:11]; & should have voted as you did between Jackson & Adams. But candour compels me to say, that I disapproved of your accepting an office from him [4:74, 90]. You ought I think to have forseen that his administration could hardly fail to be unpopular. Those who know his temper, disposition & political opinions, entertained no doubt upon the subject. By accepting the office of Secretary of State from him, you have indubitubly connected your fortunes with his. And it appears to me that he is destined to fall as his father [John Adams] did, & you must fall with him. This State [Ga.] could not have been driven under the banners of Jackson by any other course of measures than that pursued by the administration towards it [4:501–02]. Mr Adams general measures, altho very exceptionable would not have ranged the State under Jackson's Standard. Mr. Adams has professed to consider the federal government limited by the enumerated powers.[2] Yet he has recommended to Congress to erect light houses to the skies [4:872]. A recommendation utterly inconsistent with the idea of the government's being limited by the enumerated powers. This recommendation appears to me can be supported by no other construction than that Congress can do any thing which is not expressly forbidden by the constitution. The whole of his first message to Congress is replete with doctrines which I hold [to] be unconstitutional.

ALS. DLC–HC (DNA, M212, R3). Endorsed by Clay on cover: "W. H Crawford Esq Approving H C. vote for Mr. Adams." 1. Crawford's plantation, near Lexington, Georgia. 2. In his first Annual Message. Richardson, *MPP*, 2: 315.

To PHILIP R. FENDALL Washington, February 4, 1828
Mr. Clay requests Mr. Fendall to examine the authorities in the Library (Wheaton on Captures[1] and Lee[2]) to ascertain whether a capture at Sea is considered as Complete before the Captor takes actual possession of the prize. Will the striking of the flag, or making a light at night and ceasing to fire, be deemed such a surrender as to vest a right in the Capture without his taking possession of the antagonist vessel?

AN. KyU. Endorsed on verso: "Clay, H. Washington 4th. Feby. '28." Letter marked "Private." 1. Henry Wheaton, *A Digest of the Laws of Maritime Captures and Prizes* (New York, 1815). 2. Possibly Thomas Lee, *A Dictionary of the Practice in Civil Actions, in the Courts of King's Bench and Common Pleas. . . .* 2d ed. (London, 1825); or his *Cases Argued and Adjudged in the Court of King's Bench, at Westminster, in . . . the Reign of His Late Majesty, King George the Second. . . .* 2d ed. (London, 1825).

To WILLIAM B. LAWRENCE, London, no. 4, February 4, 1828. Referring to dispatch no. 6 [6:1249–51] states that it is U.S. policy to reimburse the expenses of owners of foreign vessels "in furnishing subsistence to American mariners taken from wrecks at sea and brought into port," coming under the law for the relief of distressed seamen. Recommends, therefore, that Colonel Thomas Aspinwall, U.S. consul at London, be authorized to reimburse the owners of the *Black River* packet in such a situation involving American seamen, and notes that this case "will form a good rule in analogous circumstances." Copy. DNA, RG59, Dip. Instr., vol. 12, p. 66 (M77, R7).

To MARTIN VAN BUREN   Washington, February 4, 1828
After I had made the necessary inquiries and obtained the requisite copies to enable me to answer your letter of the 29th ultimo, requesting, at the instance of the [Senate] Judiciary Committee, copies of the instructions given by the President to Andrew Ellicott, Esq. respecting the running of our Southern boundary, and of his report, it occurred to me that there was an irregularity in the form of application for those documents,[1] which was, perhaps, not adverted to by the Committee. It is in the call being made directly on the Department of State by a Committee of the Senate, for instructions given by the President, instead of being addressed to the President himself. Although, in the particular case, there might be no public inconvenience or objection to this more compendious mode of arriving at the information, or obtaining the papers desired, it is not the customary course, and if adopted in this instance, would establish a precedent that might operate injuriously in other cases. If you concur in these views, will you have the goodness to obtain the passage in the Senate, of the usual resolution, calling upon the *President* for the papers?[2] There shall not be one moment's delay, on my part, in complying with it.

LS. DNA, RG59, Report Books, vol. 4, p. 218. ALI draft, in DLC–HC (DNA, M212, R3). Letter marked "Private and inofficial."   1. Clay read to Adams a draft of this letter and the President fully concurred with him on the point of the irregularity in the Committee's procedure. Adams, *Memoirs,* 7:421.   2. Van Buren replied on February 6, 1828: "I think you are right & will pursue the course you propose." ANS. DNA, RG59, Misc. Letters (M179, R66).

From ELISHA WHITTLESEY, Washington, February 4, 1828. Cites losses of property and lives, in the navigation on Lake Erie, "from the want of a light house on Long Point in Upper Canada." Suggests that "measures . . . be taken, either to induce the British Government to" act, "or to permit under suitable regulations, this Government to do it." Offers to provide evidence of the need for a light, and promises to solicit a resolution from the House of Representatives relative to the matter if Clay considers such a step useful. ALS. DNA, RG59, Misc. Letters (M179, R66). Clay forwarded a copy of this letter to Charles R. Vaughan on February 6, noting that the U.S. had erected several lighthouses on the American side of Lake Erie, to the benefit, of both British and American navigation and commerce, and suggesting that Vaughan might want to direct the attention of the British Government to the utility of building a lighthouse on Long Point. Copy. DNA, RG59, Notes to Foreign Ministers and Consuls, vol. 3, p. 428 (M38, R3).

On January 24, 1829, Whittlesey, writing to Clay again from Washington, reiterated this suggestion and inquired about the disposition of his earlier attempts on this matter. Having conversed during the recess of Congress "with many Gentlemen on this subject, owners of vessels, and commission merchants all of whom concur in the absolute necessity of having the Point lighted," Whittlesey felt that Peter B. Porter would also be interested. ALS. DNA, RG59, Misc. Letters (M179, R67).

Clay replied to Whittlesey on January 27, 1829 that "this Department is still unacquainted with the result of the Application which it made to the British Government . . . in relation to the Establishment of a Light upon Long Point." LS. Courtesy of Charles E. and Betty D. Eastin, Lexington, Ky.

Whittlesey notified Clay on February 1 that he had received information that a bill was before the Upper Canada [Ontario] Parliament "to authorize the erection of a light house on Long Point" and that it was expected to pass the assembly. ALS. DNA, RG59, Misc. Letters (M179, R67).

From EDWARD EVERETT, Washington, February 5, 1828. By direction of the House Committee on Foreign Affairs, requests documents relating to U.S. support of James Devereux's claim against the Portuguese government having to do with the loss of his brig *Osprey* and her cargo at Bahia [4:526]. ALS. DNA, RG59, Misc. Letters (M179, R66).

On the same day, in a letter marked "Private," Everett requested this information "as soon as conveniently practicable." *Ibid.* Devereux was a Salem, Mass. shipper.

From ABRAHAM B. NONES, Maracaibo, February 5, 1828. Reports alarm among the people, occasioned by "an account, of a Spanish Expedition under Commodore [Angel] Laborde having Sailed for this Coast, and . . . rumors of the rising of the Blacks, and disaffected, in the neighbouring province of Coro." Adds that "this Department [Maracaibo]" has been placed under martial law, under which numerous arrests, without explanations of charges, have been made. States that "the enemy merely has run along the coast," and that nothing more has been heard of the "pretended revolution or rising in Coro." Notes that "these events are considered as a mere prelude to some great change or plan, about to be carried into effect at the point of the bayonet, and most probably by orders from Bogota. . . ." Charges that "the people are completely overawed," and that "the Grand Convention [6:860-1] to which deputies from the Liberal party" were elected, will probably not be allowed to meet. Alludes to the prevailing distress, the inability of the government "to furnish rations," the call upon "Merchants Native & Foreigners" for loans, and the threat to levy a forced loan, which "has alarmed all the foreigners. . . ." Observes that "our Treaty [4:127-8] is . . . Silent on this Subject, Yet the same is so completely provided for in the British Treaty [4:365] that . . . in case of need, [he] will insist on its leaning towards our Citizen's" under the most favored nation provision of the U.S. treaty with Colombia. Has heard hints that "Citizens of the U.S. could be called on for Militia Duty," prohibited under the British Treaty, and asks "to be instructed . . . on this Subject as early as possible." Attributes the "unfriendly disposition on the part of the . . . Intendant & Commandant General (both of whom are Newly appointed here) towards us" to "our known republican principles & character. . . ." Describes the deplorable state of business, commerce, and agriculture and asserts that "all Confidence [is] destroyed." LS. DNA, RG59, Cons. Disp., Maracaibo, vol. 1 (M-T62, R1). Received March 1, 1828.

To TIMOTHY PICKERING, Salem, Massachusetts, February 5, 1828. Notes that Andrew Ellicott, both in his *Journal* published (at Philadelphia) in 1803 and in a letter to Pickering dated March 22, 1800, alludes to the drafting of reports by himself and his colleague, Stephen B. Minor, as commissioners "for running the Boundary Line between the Territories of the United States and those of Spain, agreeably to the provisions of the Treaty of San Lorenzo, of October 1795, between the United States and Spain." States that the report "prepared for this Government, if one was ever so prepared is not now to be found amongst the Archives of this Office [6:987-8; Clay to Everett, February 1, 1828]." Inquires "whether such a Report was made to the Government of the United States" while Pickering headed the State Department and, if so, whether he recalls "what disposition was made of that Document." LS. MHi. See also Van Buren to Clay, January 28, 1828.

To FRANCISCO TACON, Philadelphia, February 5, 1828. States that, having communicated to Hilario de Rivas y Salmon on April 24, 1827 the President's decision on the [West Florida property loss] claim of Juan Miguel de Losada [5:827], "it was thought to be unprofitable to prolong the discussion." Hence Clay has not responded to the Spanish note of May 10, 1827. Acknowledges receipt, however, of Tacon's note of December 20, 1827, which caused the President "from respect to the opinion of His Majesty [Ferdinand VII]" to re-examine the matter. Regrets to report that as the result of the reconsideration the President has concluded that Losada "has no just demand upon the American Government." Reviews the facts in the Losada vs. Joseph E. Caro dispute and suggests that the issue be "left to the ordinary administration of justice" in U.S. courts. Copy. DNA, RG59, Notes to Foreign Ministers and Consuls, vol. 3, pp. 423-8(M38, R3). L, draft, in CSmH. See also Tacon to Clay, February 9, 1828.

To HENRY CLAY, JR.   Washington, February 6, 1828
I saw Majr. Worth[1] who gave us the most flattering and encouraging accounts about you, concurring with those which we receive from all other quarters. Indeed my dear child you are a great blessing to me, and I am sure if you knew what a Source of happiness you are to me, by your present praise worthy conduct, you would persevere in it, if you had not the super-added motive of its conducing to your own lasting good. I find that you still occasionally perplex yourself with the question of what pursuit you shall finally engage in it. On that subject I can only repeat, what I have so often told you, that when you quit West point, if you improve the opportunities afforded you there, you may enter on any career you prefer. You may study the profession of law, if you should desire it. It is a mistake to suppose that it will be too late. If I had my choice, it would be to begin the study of that profession at 20 or 21, in

prefe[ren]ce to any other age, and continue at it four or five years.[2] But if you should like the profession of arms, you will have it in your power to continue in it. Calculating upon the ordinary course of human events, our Country will be in War, when you are in the prime of life, say some where between 25 and thirty five.[3] In that contingency how many opportunities of advancement will present themselves? I say, therefore, continue with assiduity your present studies. They will form a capital on which you may operate advantageously in civil or military life, according to your choice.

Let me know what sum is necessary to pay your debts at the Point, and I will remit it to you.[4]

I have not heard from Thomas [Hart Clay] for a long time; and I am almost afraid to hear from him [6:385-6]. I have understood indirectly that he has left Arkansas; but whither he has gone I know not. Theodore [Wythe Clay] is at Lexington. . . .

ALS. Henry Clay Memorial Foundation, Lexington, Kentucky. 1. William Jenkins Worth, commandant of cadets and instructor in infantry tactics at the United States Military Academy, 1820-1828. See *DAB*. 2. Clay's own study of law had begun when he was eighteen or nineteen years of age and had lasted only about one year. Van Deusen, *Life of Henry Clay*, 12, 14. 3. Henry Clay, Jr. was killed in action at the Battle of Buena Vista in the Mexican War, less than two months before his thirty-sixth birthday. 4. On March 2, Clay sent his son $150.

From AMOS KENDALL, Frankfort, February 6, 1828. States that John J. Crittenden, in his address [6:1206-07] admits to having seen letters from Clay to common friends during January 1825, but denies remembering having seen anything in any of them which suggested a bargain between Adams and Clay. Asserts that among the letters that Crittenden saw were those which Francis P. Blair did not reveal [Blair to Clay, February 4, 1828]. Continues: "Hence, I feel authorized to charge and I *do* charge, that you [Clay] ascertained from Mr. Adams himself, that if elected by your influence and the votes of the west, he would 'associate you with him in the executive department;' that you communicated this fact to F. P. Blair, Esq. in a private letter or letters, written and received in January 1825, suggesting to him the propriety of procuring as many of Mr. [David] White's constituents as practicable to write to him instructing him to vote for Mr. Adams." Asks Clay to demand that Blair reveal the truth. Copy. Frankfort *Argus of Western America*, February 6, 1828.

From WILLIAM B. LAWRENCE, London, no. 22, February 6, 1828. Discusses developments in British policy in the Russian–Turkish crisis over Greece. Reports that from his private "sources of information" he has learned that in December, 1827, "propositions were made by Russia to England and France to cooperate with her land forces in carrying into effect the common object of the alliance" of July 7, 1827 [Treaty of London]. Notes that a favorable British overture to this approach was interrupted by the resignation of Lord Goderich's ministry on January 8. States, however, that the arrival of the new Wellington government has improved the prospects for peace.

Pledges his assistance in carrying out the intent of a proposed bill in Congress [6:962] designed to "obtain from the public offices here [London] transcripts of documents relating to our Colonial history." ALS. DNA, RG59, Dip. Disp., Great Britain, vol. 35 (M30, R31). Received March [27?], 1828. A House bill to appoint an agent to procure from the British Plantation Office and other repositories copies of such "documents as will serve to illustrate the early history of the States of this Union" was reported to the House from the Committee of Ways and Means on February 8, 1828; there it subsequently died. U.S. H. of Reps., *Journal,* 20 Cong., 1 Sess., 271.

From ISAAC THOMAS, New Orleans, February 6, 1828. Explains his interest in the claim of Henry de la Francia for arms and ammunition sold to Col. Reuben Kemper, agent of the West Florida convention. Notes that the U.S. Government has assumed responsibility for these payments [6 *U.S. Stat.,* 139], and that Spanish opposition to the claim has held up settlement. Requests a brief statement on the status of the case.

Concludes with the political observation that "The presidential vote of this State is every day growing more doubtfull—altho the heated friends of each say there is no doubt.—I am sorry that our opinions divide on the subject—I was with you before, and when it is necessary wil[l] be again—but I cannot bring myself to support Mr. Adams altho I have no very warm side for Jackson—My friends are divided and I will not attempt to exercise my influence over them." ALS. DNA, RG59, Misc. Letters (M179, R66).

On March 10, 1828, Clay's office forwarded Col. Thomas's request to the Treasury Department, asking for a report on the Francia case. It was the opinion of Stephen Pleasonton, Fifth Auditor, expressed to Clay on March 12, that the claim had earlier been rejected as "inadmissible," and that without new authority from Congress, the Department "could not again act upon the case." Pleasonton to Clay, March 12, 1828 [two letters of this date]. Copy. DNA, RG59, Dom. Letters, vol. 22, pp. 157–8 (M40, R20); copy. DNA, RG217, Records of the Fifth Auditor, Letters Sent to the Sec. of State, vol. 2, pp. 249–50. For Thomas, see *BDAC,* for Kemper, see *DAB.* See also Clay to House of Representatives, April 19, 1828. For the background of the claim and its subsequent settlement, see Cox, *West Florida Controversy,* 658; and *Sen. Reports,* 20 Cong., 1 Sess., no. 51.

From WILLIAM TUDOR, "At Sea" no. 84, February 6, 1828. Reports that he took passage, at Lima, for Valparaiso, where he hopes to find further transportation. Cites the five months in which Clay's communications were on their way to Lima "as a case to shew the advantage of establishing the communication with Peru, & the adjoining countries thro' Panama [5:226, 402–03]." Closes his "long correspondence from Peru," with a summary of various events that occurred in the final two months of his residence, during which an illness prevented his communicating at the time. Discusses the work of the Peruvian Congress, which, in "its prolonged session," has settled "the most difficult chapters" of the Constitution and, in addition, has considered "the project of a treaty with Chile" and a new tariff, both of which threaten the commercial interests of the United States. Describes his own efforts, through conversations with Peruvian officials and through publications, to influence these last mentioned proceedings. Gives details of an unsuccessful revolt in the Department of Ayacucho and of a conspiracy, discovered in Lima, "to seize the heads of the government, disperse the Congress, & place the whole controul of affairs in the hands of [Manuel Lorenzo de] Vidaurre." Adds that when he left Lima, the trial of the "conspirators was proceeding according to the usual, tardy process. . . ." Characterizes as an "event of the most favorable kind for Peru," a reported insurrection of "two chosen battalions of [Antonio Jose de] Sucre's army. . . ." Expresses optimism, despite fears of factionalism in the country, concerning the future of Peru and praises Jose de Lamar, who "is in every respect the opposite of Bolivar."

Adds in a postscript, dated February 11, that he has reached Valparaiso. ALS. DNA, RG59, Cons. Disp., Lima, vol. 2 (M154, R2). Received September 18, 1828. Letter marked "Confidential."

The Lima conspiracy, planned for January 25, 1828, was designed to crown a native Indian colonel, one Linavibca, as King of Peru. For his part in this plot, Vidaurre was temporarily exiled to the U.S. See *Niles' Register* (June 28, August 9, 1828), 34:287,384; also, Prevost to Clay, April 26, 1828.

From FRANCIS T. BROOKE   Richmond, February 7, 1828
I have received your kind letter of the 2d instant, I shall be very happy if it Shall be in my power to visit you in April and I shall present to Mrs Brooke Mrs Clays polite invitation to accompany me, though I fear in vain—Since I came here I have been advised forth with to write to Messrs Monroe & Madison it is thought that I owe it to the convention to leave nothing for imputation upon them, and I have concluded to do so in a few days, I can readily perceive there will be some recoil of public opinion but it Seems to be unavoidable and we must make the most of it, the news from N York is very cheering—I have written to Gen P[eter] B Porter and expect to hear from him in a day or two, as Soon as I hear from Messrs Monroe & Madison I will apprise you of it,[1] the total failure at New Orleans[2] is a great damper to the opposition here—and has increased the confidence of our friends—I begin to think Virginia will be with us—unless Something Should occur more disastrous than the refusal of Mr Monroe & Mr Madison to accept we shall do well [6:862–4]—Present my cordial respects to Mrs Clay—

ALS. InU.   1. February 28, 1828.   2. Yost to Clay, January 9, 1828.

To JAMES FAIRLIE   Washington, February 7, 1828
Judge [William B.] Rochester delivered to me your letter of the 29h. Decr.[1] and being anxious to converse with Mr. [Samuel L.] Southard (who was absent some days) fully on the subject of it, I postponed answering it until I had that opportunity. He informs me that your son[2] stands well in the Navy, but I regret to be obliged to add that he thinks the public service will hardly require a new appointment of Purser for twelve months to come. He has promised me that whenever one is made he will give to your wishes, and to mine, which I have emphatically expressed to him, the most friendly consideration. I will endeavor to bear

the thing in mind, and hope you also will take care to keep me reminded of it. I do not often interfere, at all, in the administration of the duties of other departments, particularly in respect to appointments, but I am some times induced to make an exception to the rule, and there is no friend for whom I would sooner do it than yourself.

I request you will communicate my best regards to Mrs. [Thomas A.] Cooper. . . .[3]

ALS. PPiU. Letter marked "Private and Inofficial." 1. Not found. 2. Probably Robert Y. Fairlie, who served as Midshipman in the Navy from 1816 until his resignation in 1823. 3. Wife of the famous tragedian; for the Fairlie–Cooper connection, see Seager, *And Tyler Too*, 123–4.

From WILLIAM PHILLIPS, Omoa, Federation of the Centre of America, February 7, 1828. Reports his arrival on January 15, 1828. States: "We are anxiously expecting the arrival of" William B. Rochester, an event "that will contribute much to the safety of the lives & property of these citizens of the US, who are unfortunately engaged in commercial pursuits with this illfated country. It is scarcely in the power of words, to convey an adequate idea of its present situation—" Summarizes recent events: "The Commandant in chief [Arrasola] of this important port ran away about ten days ago, and robbed the national chest, not leaving one disposable dollar behind." Reports that his successor, "in order to keep the troops quiet," has seized cargo from a French vessel and sold it. Adds that troops from Honduras and San Salvador [6:26, 822–3] have approached the city "and yesterday . . . demanded the fortress to surrender," and that all communication with the interior "is cut off." Further, it is reported that "the S Salvador troops have [Manuel Jose] D'Arce penned up in Guatemala." Notes that "the Salvr. force have possession of every hold in Central America but *Omoa & Guatemala*." Suggests that "a National vessel of some description" be sent to Truxillo occasionally to protect United States citizens. ALS. DNA, RG59, Cons. Disp., Central America, vol. 1 (M219, R2). Received March 8, 1828.

From JOEL R. POINSETT, Mexico, no. 115, February 7, 1828. Transmits "copies of the Treaty of Limits, and of the Protocols of the conferences held with the Mexican Plenipotentiaries [Sebastian Camacho; Jose Ignacio Esteva] upon that subject." Explains that he "did not insist upon introducing the article respecting the obligation of the parties to restrain the Indian tribes [4:173] . . . because it is inserted in the Treaty of Amity, Commerce and Navigation, which . . . [he is] about concluding." Notes, further, that he did not oppose Mexican wishes "to adopt the limits as settled by the Treaty of Washington [2:678]." In view of efforts of "Agents of certain European Powers" to portray the United States as "the natural" enemy of Mexico, desirous of depriving "them of a portion of their territory," he thought it necessary to proceed cautiously and on "the question of limits, to endeavor, if any change were made, that it should be at the suggestion" of Mexico. Believes that in this manner would "the honorable dealing of the United States, in this respect . . . be manifest." States that he will "send the original Treaty by . . . [his] Secretary, Mr. Edward T. Tayloe, together with that of Amity, Commerce, and Navigation." Reports, with regard to the latter treaty, that he has established "all the important points, according to the resolutions of the Senate [6:285-90]," except for "the principle of free ships making free goods," which is still being negotiated. Adds that in order to meet the President's wish, in treaties with these new States, "to establish the principle of perfect reciprocity in commerce, in preference to that of the most favored nation [4:168-70, 804-05]" he has proposed that the U.S.-Mexican accord include Articles V and VI of the 1827 treaty between Mexico and Great Britain [5:1005]. Observes that "This will render it necessary to prolong the duration of the Treaty" and expresses a hope that "the Senate will not object." LS. DNA, RG59, Dip. Disp., Mexico, vol. 3 (M97, R4). Received March 10, 1828. See, Poinsett to Clay, February 22, 1828; and Parry, *Treaty Series,* 78:35-42.

From **JAMES RAY,** "near Newark, Del.," February 7, 1828. Encloses documents relating to Spanish seizure of his brig, *James Lawrence* [4:376, 842], at Havana, and asks that the claim be pursued in Madrid. Cites another case in which Spanish authorities "falsified their own records" and asserts that "they now do the same at the Havanna to protect pirates and free booters, & rob us of our property." ALS. DNA, RG76, Misc. Claims, Spain. Endorsed by Clay (AEI) on cover: "Mr. [Daniel] Brent will examine and inform me what instructions were given to Mr. [Alexander H.] Everett in this case."

To **CHARLES R. VAUGHAN,** February 7, 1828. Informs him that the Senate has "given its advice and consent" to the three Conventions, concluded and signed at London, on August 6 and September 29, 1827 [6:826-7; 854-5; 1072-3; 1100-01]. Asks, since these documents contain no provision concerning exchange of ratifications, whether Vaughan is empowered to make the exchange or has "any knowledge of the views and expectations of the British Government on that subject." Copy. DNA, RG59, Notes to Foreign Ministers and Consuls, vol. 3 (M38, R3).
    Vaughan replied to this letter on February 8, stating that he had no instructions on ratification procedures, but suggesting that the exchanges could be accomplished as soon as the U.S. ratifications were presented in London. LS. DNA, RG59, Notes from British Legation, vol. 15 (M50, R15); also in Manning, *Diplomatic Correspondence . . . Canadian Relations,* 2:683.

From **THOMAS L. L. BRENT,** Lisbon, February 8, 1828. Reports that "the dispositions of the Infante don Miguel have more and more developed themselves as unfriendly to the Constitution." Cites appointments of certain of its enemies, and notes that "The Count of Villa real [*sic,* Vila Real] who had been charged ad interim is now appointed Minister of foreign Affairs." ALS. DNA, RG59, Dip. Disp., Portugal, vol. 7 (M43, R6). Received May 9, 1828.

From ALEXANDER CALDWELL Wheeling, Va.,
February 8, 1828

I regret that I had it not in my power to have forwarded the enclosed at an earlier day. It would not have been unworthy of appearing in the appendix to your pamplet.[1] It exhibits the "hero [Andrew Jackson]" in a most un hero like point of view—as the inventor of a fals hood and the falsifier of dates in order to vilify his rivals.

with the highest satisfaction, I congratulate you on the effect produced by your pamphlet. In removing doubts as to your political integrity, in confirming the wavering in their good opinions, and in confounding your enemies, it has had a powerful influence. nevertheless, in my judgment, its results will be more propitious to your fame than decisive of the next Presidential election. Thousands will continue to adhere to Jackson who will not hesitate to acquit you of all censure in regard to the late election. Many, very many, are too firmly harness to the Car of Jackson to admit of a recovery of their liberties until the delusion under which they labor shall have passed away. At the same moment that the voters deposit their tickets in the balot boxes for Jackson, they will proclaim their entire confidence in you, and disbelief of all the Charges brought against you. Under Such circumstances will be given nine–tenths of the votes which Jackson will receive in this County.[2]

In case you shall obtain other testimonials, and make a further publication, will it not be sufficent in copying the enclosed to commence with "I do certify that I heard Mr. [Thomas] Sloane state that he was one of a Committee &C"

ALS. DLC-HC (DNA, M212, R3). Endorsed by Clay on cover: "{With Mr. Bennetts statement}." 1. 6:1394-6. The enclosure, Isaac Bennett to McKee and Caldwell, does not accompany this letter. 2. Ohio County, Va., now West Va.

To CHARLES EDMONSTON & JOHN GEDDES, February 9, 1828. Acknowledges receipt of their letter of January 25. Reports that he has "prepared a note to Mr. Charles R. Vaughan [February 18, 1828], presenting the claim and asking his concurrence in such measures, as it might be expedient . . . to fix the amount of salvage." Notes, however, that "Vaughan verbally informed me that he had no communication on the subject from Lieut. [Edward] Holland, and as he can have no instructions relative to the case, he will, probably, decline the requested cooperation, and refer the matter to the British Government." Promises, in that event, that "instructions will be given to the Representative of the U. States in England [William B. Lawrence] to pursue the claim." Informs them that the claim for salvage involving "the Guerraro [*sic, Guerrero*] . . . does not belong to this Department, but appertains to other branches of the Government." Copy. DNA, RG59, Dom. Letters, vol. 22, pp. 139-40 (M40, R20).

On March 31, 1828, Edmonston acknowledged receipt of this letter. He stated that the claimants "desire to have their rights under their claim, if possible, put in a train of determination and adjustment in this Country," and expressed hope that Charles R. Vaughan would "sanction such a course of settlement." ALS. DNA, RG59, Misc. Letters (M179, R66).

To ALBERT GALLATIN, February 9, 1828. Informs him " that the Senate has given its advice and consent to the ratification of the three Conventions concluded by . . . [him] with the British Government last year [6:826–7; 854–5; 1072–3; 1100–01]." Solicits his services, "on the contingency of the arbitration taking effect according to the stipulations of the Convention respecting our Northeastern boundary." States that the President proposes, "if it be agreeable to" Gallatin, to associate with him a citizen of Massachusetts or Maine. Requests that he furnish "a list of such acts of British authority" as should be obtained and, in addition, "a statement of all the evidence which" should be laid before the arbiter. Assures him that he "will be paid out of the contingency fund for foreign intercourse, or by an appropriation, which it is presumable Congress would make, for the purpose, on application." LS. NHi–Gallatin Papers (MR15). Copy, in DNA, RG59, Dip. Instr., vol. 12, pp. 58–9. L draft, partly in Clay's hand, in CSmH; also in Manning, *Diplomatic Correspondence . . . Canadian Relations*, 2:144–5. Letter marked "Confidential."

From JOEL R. POINSETT, Mexico, no. 116, February 9, 1828. Reports that, as he had predicted [Poinsett to Clay, January 9, 1828] the civil war has ended with the defeat of the rebels. States that Generals Nicolas Bravo and Miguel Barragan are prisoners and the "general government has received congratulations from all the States in the Union." Indeed, "even the Legislature of . . . [Veracruz] has retracted its opinions in the most disgraceful manner. . . ." Encloses translation of a letter from that legislature to Sebastian Camacho, the Secretary of State of the Republic, and a translation of their "manifesto to their constituents." States: "This country is now perfectly tranquil, and the Federal government much stronger than ever," but its finances "continue in a distressful state." Promises to send by Edward T. Tayloe "the Memorials of the several ministers, and a sketch of the present state of the country."

Forwards letters from William Tudor, who, in a communication to Poinsett, indicated that Peru was about to ask Great Britain to intervene "to save that country from the violence threatened by [Simon] Bolivar." Relays the opinion, at Tudor's request, that the British "cabinet is much more likely to favor the designs of Bolivar than to counteract them. . . ."

Acknowledges receipt of Clay's dispatch No. 25 [6:1284–6] and promises to convey to the Mexican Government the President's "views with regard to the conduct of the Legislature of Vera Cruz."

Expresses gratification for the President's approval of his conduct and states that he will not terminate his mission "until the Treaties [Poinsett to Clay, February 22, 1828] are ratified," after which he will turn his "attention to the Congress of Tacubaya [6:248] and endeavor to induce the Members now here to take some definitive measures in relation to it." Promises a more detailed report on the Congress soon. LS. DNA, RG59, Dip. Disp., Mexico, vol. 3 (M97, R4). Received March 10, 1828.

From **FRANCISCO TACON,** Philadelphia, February 9, 1828. Acknowledges receipt of Clay's note of February 5. Asserts that the important feature of the Losada vs. Caro case "is not so much the value of Losada's claim, as the important principle that the American tribunals have no right to arraign or judge the *official conduct* of a *public* agent of His Catholic Majesty [Ferdinand VII](particularly in cases purely Spanish, in whatever light considered)." Cites the case of Spanish Vice Consul Joseph Nicholas de Villavazo "still pending at New Orleans [5:209]" as another instance in which "American tribunals appear to have arrogated to themselves an authority over the functionaries of H. M. in this country." Asks: "Would not the mere fact of Losada making a defence have been an acknowledgement of the *jurisdiction* of the Court of Escambia [County, Fla.] over the *official* acts of a Spanish public functionary, which jurisdiction is precisely the point in dispute?" Develops his argument further, and concludes by asking Clay to request the President to reconsider the matter. LS, in Spanish, with trans. in State Dept. file. DNA, RG59, Notes from Spanish Legation, vol. 9 (M59, R–T12).

From **BEAUFORT T. WATTS,** Cartagena, no. 41, February 10, 1828. Acknowledges receipt of Clay's "communication upon the subject of the American Brig Morris [6:1135-6]" and his "note thro' Mr. Holden [*sic*, John W. Holding] relating to a disputed claim between himself and Mr. [Joseph] Karrick [6:1036-7]." Refers to his dispatch number 28 [6:560], in which Clay will find that he has acted, in the latter case, in accord with instructions. Encloses copies of his correspondence with Jose M. Restrepo, Minister of the Interior, on the subject of a railway across the Isthmus of Panama, which he had been "urged to solicit by an association of Citizens in New York [William Radcliff and others]." Encloses also a translation of a speech in the Colombian Senate dealing with Simon Bolivar's "resignation"; the letter from Bolivar to Clay [6:1298-9], a translation of which he had sent in his last dispatch [November 21, 1827]; and letters to be forwarded to various persons relative to their private claims.

States that the national convention, scheduled to meet on March 2 at Ocana [6:1378] will probably be delayed because of the great distances some members have to travel. Deplores "the angry feelings of party" and cites the election, to the convention, of both the Vice President, Fransisco de Paula Santander and his "hateful enemy," Dr. Miguel Pena, as well as the separatist feeling in some provinces. Reports having learned, by a letter "from a private source," that Santander called on Bolivar before leaving for the Convention in order to learn his "opinions in relation to reform." Says that Bolivar recommended "a strong–strong, strong government," expressed his opposition to Federation, declare that he "had no idea of recommending" the Bolivian Constitution "to Colombia," and stated his intention of retiring to private life and going to Europe. Reports that "Great dangers now threaten the Republic—The enemy is cruising along the coast [cf. above, Nones to Clay, February 5, 1828] issuing his proclamations inviting the people to return to the allegiance of Ferdinand [VII], whilst there is nothing but disunion within." ALS.

DNA, RG59, Dip. Disp., Colombia, vol. 4 (M–T33, R4). Received March 14, 1828.

For the Convention of Ocana, which was scheduled for March 2, 1828, postponed to April 9, and broke up in confusion on June 10, see 6:723–4; Santander to Clay, June 17, 1828; and *Annual Register,* 1828, 70:255–8.

From JAMES BARBOUR, "Department of War," February 11, 1828. States that, upon receipt of information sent him by Clay in December [6:1369], he "immediately directed the Agent of the Six Nations [Jasper Parrish] to take Such Steps as would tend to ensure the future good conduct of that portion of the tribe." Encloses "A copy of the instructions . . . and of the report of the Agent who visited St. Regis. . . ." Copy. DNA, RG107, Military Books, vol. 12, p. 336. The enclosures have not been found; nor is it clear which one of several agents visited St. Regis, N. Y.

From SAMUEL B. BARRELL, Washington, February 11, 1828. Reports at length on his mission, undertaken "in pursuance of the instructions . . . received from the Department of State [6:1282–4]," and encloses numerous documents. Observes that John Baker is charged with "exciting sedition among the French settlers at Madawaskah, and endeavoring to obstruct the passage of the British mail upon the River St. John" and "is also imprisoned on civil process" growing out of a judgment confessed by him in 1821 [6:1272–3]. Notes that settlers on the Aroostook "are about forty in number, nine of whom are citizens of the United States, and the residue are British subjects." Adds that none of the settlers has "any other title to the land occupied, than that which arises from possession." Contends that the statements of William Dalton and Jonathan Wilson [6:1273–4] are false; that "The population of Madawaskah amounts to about two thousand, and is almost exclusively French." Concludes: "The undersigned recommended to the American settlers at Madawaskah, forbearance and moderation in their future proceedings during the pendency of the existing negotiations between their Government and that of Great Britain in relation to the disputed territory:—assuring them that if their conduct should be inoffensive & peaceable, they might rely upon the protection of their Government: and he has the satisfaction to believe that reliance may be placed upon the assurances he received from the settlers generally, that they would hereafter abstain from all acts of individual violence and from all unnecessary collision with the authorities of the neighboring Province [New Brunswick]." ADS. DNA, RG76, Northeast Boundary (KyU., Special Roll, frames 669–91); also in *ASPFR,* 6:839–42.

To THE CONGRESS OF THE UNITED STATES, February 11, 1828. Submits annual report on the pay of clerks in the Department of State and disbursements from the contingency fund. Notes, with reference to the latter, that $2,519.93 was spent for transcribing and copying "voluminous records, books, and maps, relative to the Northeastern boundary line of the United States [6:609–10]." LS. DNA, RG59, Report Books, vol. 4, pp. 220-4.

From JOSEPH PULIS, JR., Malta. No. 1 of this date, February 11, 1828. Reports giving aid in the amount of $66.92 to distressed American seamen who had been involved in bringing the Greek frigate *Hellas* out from New York [5:389; 6:14]. Explains that while they had "no right to claim Consular assistance," he decided "to take care of them" because "of their distressing situation." LS. DNA, RG59, Cons. Disp., Malta, vol. 1 (M–T218, R–T1). Received May 22, 1828.

From JOSEPH PULIS, JR., Malta. No. 2 of this date, February 11, 1828. Reports the arrival, on January 9, of the Count Capo d'Istria, who "on the 14th. continued his voyage for Egina in order to take the command as President of Greece." Reports also the expulsion of "all the Franks" from Constantinople and the removal of the Armenians to "the interior of Asia." Adds that "the Jews only were allowed to remain at Constantinople, where the Sultan [Mahmud II] is exclusively occupied in preparations of war." Notes: "They say that the Count Capo d'Istria and the Admirals of the Allied Powers have adopted such measures as to destroy all the pirates [6:1306]." LS. DNA, RG59, A. and R. (MR3). Received May 22, 1828.

The expulsion, "on a very brief notice," of the Europeans from Turkey was interpreted as a preparation for war. Some 12,000 Armenians were also banished "to their own country, never again to revisit the capital." *Annual Register,* 1828, 70:223.

From JAMES J. DEBESSE, La Rochelle, France, February 12, 1828. Reports that the vessel *Imperial,* of New York, upon entering La Rochelle, "accidentally took the ground on a bank" and, condemned as "unworthy of repairs" by the "Tribunal of Commerce" of La Rochelle, was sold at auction on December 22, 1827. States that he was absent when the crew was discharged, and that his agent, erroneously in Debesse's opinion, insisted on the payment of three months' extra wages. Asks whether or not the Act of Congress of February 28, 1803, requires payment of extra wages when a vessel is involuntarily sold [4:372]. States that he has already posed the question to James Brown, who, believing it settled by the State Department circular of July 1, 1805, instructed him to retain the money until receipt of instructions from the Secretary of State. ALS. DNA, RG59, Cons. Disp., La Rochelle, vol. 1 (M–T394, R1). No date of receipt.

Debesse, a resident of La Rochelle, served as United States consul at that port from 1825 to 1835.

From WILLIAM PHILLIPS, Omoa, Federation of the Centre of America, February 12, 1828. Reports that "The panic existing here" when he arrived "has subsided in some measure," and "some of those people that had fled . . . are . . . returning." States that the party of President Manuel Jose Arce has reportedly "obtained some partial success," but that he [Phillips] anticipates a protracted contest and "an *exhaustion* of all the physical resources of this fairest portion of the Southern Continent." Encloses papers from Guatemala confirming "the above gloomy forebodings." ALS. DNA, RG59, Dip. Disp., Central America, vol. 1 (M219, R2). Received March 27, 1828.

From TIMOTHY PICKERING, Salem, Massachusetts, February 12, 1828. Acknowledges receipt of Clay's letter of February 5. States that he has no recollection of Andrew Ellicott's report and that the circumstances mentioned by Clay lead him "to think that no such Report . . . came to the department of state" during his incumbency. Notes that Ellicott's "printed journal" indicates that "Ellicott and his company" arrived in Philadelphia on May 18, 1800, prior to which date President John Adams had removed Pickering from office. Suggests that Clay consult John Marshall, Pickering's successor, if he has not already done so. Mentions that "All" of Ellicott's "papers are probably in the hands of som[e] member of his family," and that the information desired from Ellicott's report can be found in the printed journal. ALS. DNA, RG59, Misc. Letters (M179, R66).

To JOHN QUINCY ADAMS, February 13, 1828. Reports, in response to a Senate Resolution of February 11 [U.S. Sen. *Journal*, 20 Cong., 1 Sess., 147], referred by the President to the Secretary of State, "the instructions requested, contained in a letter from Timothy Pickering, Secretary of State, under date the 14th day of September, 1796, addressed to Andrew Ellicott, Commissioner, and Thomas Freeman, Surveyor, to run and mark the line between the United States and Spain, in conformity with the treaty of San Lorenzo el Real [the Pinckney Treaty]." States that Ellicott's report, also called for, has not been found. Cites Ellicott's printed journal and a letter (a copy of which is also enclosed) from Ellicott to the Secretary of State, March 22, 1800, relative to the preparation of the report and observes: "Whether, in point of fact, it [the report] was finished, and transmitted to the Department of State, cannot, now, be here ascertained." Adds that the United States Minister in Spain, Alexander H. Everett, has been directed "to procure a copy of the report, if it be among the archives of the Spanish Government." Copy, signed. DNA, RG59, Report Books, vol. 4, pp. 219–20. Draft, partially in Clay's hand, in DLC–HC (DNA, M212, R3). Also in *Senate Docs.*, 20 Cong., 1 Sess., no. 104, p. 5. For Freeman, see *DAB*. See, also, Clay to Adams, February 29, 1828.

From JAMES BROWN, Paris, February 13, 1828. Discusses in detail changes in the structure of the French government and relays rumors about expected appointments thereto. Notes that the speech of King Charles X on February 5 was received with "repeated acclamations," especially that portion touching on the Battle of Navarino. Believes that the new government is, however, stable enough to justify renewing negotiations on U.S. claims under the Louisiana treaty [5:29–31] and asserts that he will raise with Count Pierre La Ferronnays, the new Foreign Minister, his earlier proposal to Baron Damas to submit the issue to arbitration. Reports that Turkey and Russia continue to prepare for war, while England and France are "exerting themselves to preserve peace." Notes that it seems certain that French troops will be withdrawn from Spain "before the end of March" and that U.S. trade "may at last escape from the oppressive quarantine imposed on it in the ports of Cadiz and Barcelona by the French commanders." LS. DNA, RG59, Dip. Disp., France, vol. 23 (M34, R26). Received March 26, 1828. Marked "Private."

From THOMAS W. FOX, Plymouth, England, February 13, 1828. Transmits consular report, expressing regret concerning the lack of American trade, and reports that trade generally is dull. Notes deficiency in the wheat crop in many parts of England, the expectation that the importation of foreign grain will be needed before the next harvest, and local anxiety for a new corn law to protect British growers. ALS. DNA, RG59, Cons. Disp., Plymouth, vol. 1 (M-T228, R-T1). No date of receipt. Fox, a native of England, was United States consul at Plymouth from 1823 to 1854 and again in 1859.

From JAMES HAMILTON, JR., "Chairman," Washington, February 13, 1828. Quotes "a resolution adopted yesterday by the Committee on Retrenchment" and calls attention "to that part of it, relating to . . . [Clay's] Department, from which the Committee will be happy to receive, the information required": "Resolved that the Chairman of the Committee address a letter to the Head of each of the Executive Departments, and of the Post Office Department, requesting information whether, in their opinion, there be any officers in either of those Departments, whose services may be dispensed with, without detriment to the public interest, or if the salaries of any of them, can be reduced, consistently with justice & propriety; and in general whether any of the expences, incident to those Departments, can be reduced, without impairing the efficacy of their operations." LS. DNA, RG59, Misc. Letters (M179, R66).

Hamilton wrote again on March 3, transmitting a supplementary resolution of that date by the House Committee on Retrenchment which directed Clay to respond to the initial February 12 request. ALS. DNA, RG59, Misc. Letters (M179, R66). See also Clay to Hamilton, February 29, 1828.

From PETER B. PORTER   Albany, February 13, 1828
I should have replied sooner to your favour of the 31st Ult. but that, having recently returned from Saratoga springs, where I had been to see some friends & improve my health which has not been good, I was met by an hundred calls of business all pressing on me at the same time.

When I wrote you last,[1] I was of opinion that the Jackson men in our Legislature had abandoned, at least for the present, all idea of a caucus. Such indeed, I am persuaded, *was* their determination, which however was changed by positive instructions from Washington not to lose the favourable moment. They secretly got up a paper pledging the signers to it to hold a caucus for the purpose of nominating Jackson, and procured the signatures of some two or three more than half the members—They then published an invitation for a meeting of the "Republican Members" without intimating its object. The consequence was that a large number assembled, the Jackson Resolutions were immediately introduced & passed, but no count called, and every member present was put down as a Jackson man.[2] I was out of town at the time of this proceeding, but I know that a large number of those who attended, are, and will continue to be, opposed to the election of Gen. Jackson. Among others I would name P[eter]. R. Livingston who is a man of considerable political influence—who attended & was counted, but who took no part in the proceedings & will support the administration.

The friends of the Admn. have had meetings during the last week, and have concluded to call a State Convention, to assemble at this place in May, for the purpose of passing on the presidential question.[3] The notice will not appear immediately, as it was deemed advisable, preparatory to the call, to write to some of the most prominent men in different parts of the State for the use of their names.

What will be the political effect of Mr Clinton's death[4] cannot be exactly foreseen. It will probably attach to the Admn many of his friends who would otherwise have adhered to him. On the other hand it may secure to Genl. J. some of our democrats who were resolved not to travel the same political path with Mr. C.

Much, in this state, will, I am satisfied, depend on the progress & fate of the Tariff Bill. If it fails in consequence of the hostility of the Jackson party generally, the effects will be great: But if it succeeds they will contrive to monopolise the credit of its passage. The State convention is put off untill May, in order that it may act under a full knowledge of the fate of that measure.

I received a copy of Mr [Anthony] Barclays report [6:1383] only two days ago. As soon as I have had time to examine it, I will write you on the subject. From the partial reading[5] I have given it, I find that it is weak, jesuitical & imprudent, and that its reasonings are all founded on evidence which he has gratuitously introduced, & which never was exhibited to the Board. what is worse the most material part of it is false.

No complaint can be made against the President for his appointment of a District Attorney [John Duer], although I am inclined to think that a different selection would have produced more political effect.

ALS. InU. Letter marked "(Confidential)."   1. January 13, 1828.   2. Porter to Clay, January 8, 1828.   3. A gathering of the friends of Adams met in Albany on March 26 and issued a "Circular" calling for an Adams nominating convention to meet in Albany on June 10–11, 1828. Washington *Daily National Journal*, June 16, 1828. See also Porter to Clay, March 26, 1828.   4. DeWitt Clinton died on February 11, 1828.   5. The phrase "partial reading" is substituted for "slight examination," which is struck through.

From THOMAS M. RODNEY, Havana, February 13, 1828. Encloses "a copy of a letter . . . received from the collector at Key West." Comments that there are no United States vessels of war at Havana and does not expect any to visit there in the near future. Details Spanish capture of the Mexican brig of war *Guerrero*. States that the *Guerrero* was "officered and mand almost entirely by American Seamen." Reports that upwards of 400 houses were destroyed by a fire that raged thirty-six hours and that, according to his understanding, lumber will now be admitted to Havana free of duty. LS. DNA, RG59, Cons. Disp., Havana, vol. 5 (M–T20, R5). In the enclosure William Pinkney complains that, in the face of Mexican violations, he is "without the means to enforce respect to the sovereignty & neutral character of the United States" and requests that Rodney "communicate this letter to the Commander of any United States Vessel of war which may be in Havana in order that a recurrence of such mortifying circumstances may be prevented in future."

From JAMES BARBOUR, War Department, February 14, 1828. Replies "to Mr Clay's note, endorsed on Mr David Schaeffers letter of the 9th. Inst. addressed to Mr Clay [not found], stating 'he had seen in the [Washington *Daily*] National Intelligencer, that an appropriation has been made by Congress, for the completion of a Survey of the road from Zanesville [Ohio] to Missouri' and requesting information whether a Superintendent is to be appointed." States that the bill has not been enacted, but, if Schaeffer wishes to recommend anyone for appointment, that person's name will be placed on file for consideration. Returns Schaeffer's letter. Copy. DNA, RG77, Misc. Letters Sent, vol. 4, p. 482.

David Frederick Schaeffer, a Lutheran clergyman, was at this time secretary of the General Synod and editor of the *Lutheran Intelligencer*. *DAB*. The Washington *Daily National Intelligencer* on February 8, 1828, had reported a resolution of the House of Representatives calling upon the Secretary of War to release the report of the commissioner earlier appointed to locate the route of the National Road [4:33]. Jonathan Knight, a Pennsylvanian [see *DAB*], had filed the report as commissioner on February 1, and it was submitted to Congress on February 16, 1828. *House Docs.*, 20 Cong., 1 Sess., no. 149.

To JOHN J. CRITTENDEN   Washington, February 14, 1828
I have delayed answering your last favor,[1] under the hope that I might have it in my power to communicate to you some more certain information than I am able to transmit, respecting public affairs. In regard to N. York, the late Caucus nomination of Genl. Jackson was the first consequence of the packed elections to their Legislature last fall [6:1185–6]. So far from discouraging our friends there, it is believed that good will come out of it. They speak, with great confidence, of a result next fall that will give Mr Adams a large majority of the Electoral vote of that State [6:360–3]. Our prospects are good in Pennsa. Virginia, and especially in North Carolina. If our friends, without reference to false rumors and idle speculations, every where do their duty, the issue of the present contest will, in my opinion, be certainly favorable to Mr Adams. All that we want is a tone of confidence corresponding with the goodness of our cause.

Is it not strange that no member of the Court, nor any bye stander, should have given me any account of my trial before the Senate of K.?[2] With the exception of one short letter, before it began, and another after its commencement from a friend, residing some distance from

Frankfort, I have received no satisfactory information about the extraordinary proceeding. Of the result I am yet unaware. I hope, if I am to be hung, I shall be duly notified of time and place that I may present myself, in due form, to my executioner. But to be serious. Was it not a most remarkable proceeding? I never doubt the good intentions of my friends, but in this instance I am afraid their zeal and just confidence in my integrety have hurried them into some indiscretion. By admitting the investigation, have they not allowed, what no man of candor and of sense believes, that there may be ground for the charge? At this distance it is difficult to judge correctly, but it seems to me that it would have been better to have repelled the resolution of Genl. [James] Allen with indignation. I make however no reproaches; I utter no complaints. Resignation and submission constitute my duty, and I conform to it cheerfully[.]

I perceive that Mr [Francis P.] Blair refused to be sworn. I persuad-[ed] myself that his resolution was dictated by honor, and his personal regard for me.[3] Still I fear that malice will draw, from his silence, stronger conclusions to my prejudice than could have been done, if he had exhibited my letter.[4] Should that appear to him and you to be the case, I should be glad that you would have the letter itself published. There is nothing in it but its levity that would occasion me any regret on account of its publication. The public will however make a proper allowance for a private and friendly correspondence never intended for its eye.

We shall have the Tariff up in Congress next week. I anticipate a tremendous discussion. The Jackson party is playing a game of brag on that subject. They do not really desire the passage of their own measure; and it may happen, in the sequel, that what is desired by neither party commands the support of both.[5]

ALS. DLC–HC (DNA, M212, R3). 1. The most recent Crittenden to Clay letter recovered is dated November 28, 1827; Clay responded to it on December 16. 2. Blair to Clay, January 22, 1828. 3. Blair to Clay, February 4, 1828. 4. Clay to Blair, January 8, 1825; see Blair to Clay, March 4, 1828. 5.6: 876-7. A bill had been recommended by the Committee on Manufacturers on January 31, 1828. U.S. H. of Reps., *Journal,* 20 Cong., 1 Sess., 236. The debate on the measure, running from March 4 to April 22, is reported in *Register of Debates,* 20 Cong., 1 Sess., 1727–2472. See also, Taussig, *The Tariff History of the United States,* 8th ed. (New York, c. 1931), 86–103.

From ELIJAH LARKIN, "Post Office, Neville, Ohio," February 14, 1828. Protests, on behalf of a group of citizens of Feestown, Clermont County, the appointment of Robert Chalfant as local postmaster. Maintains that Chalfant is not well qualified for the office and is, moreover, a supporter "of the Military Chieftain [Jackson]!!" Notes that the citizens of Feestown feel "unbounded confidence in the integrity an[d] judgment" of Postmaster General John McLean but believe "that some designing person or persons have by 'Intrigue and Management,' or in some way underhand[edly] procured the appointment" of Chalfant. ALS. DNA, RG59, Misc. Letters (M179, R66).

Larkin, for 40 years postmaster of Neville, served also in two minor judgeships in Clermont County. J. L. Rockey and R. J. Bancroft, *History of Clermont County, Ohio* (Philadelphia, 1880), 357–8. Little is known of Chalfant save that he was a supporter of Jackson in Ohio as early as 1824. Stevens, *Early Jackson Party in Ohio,* 179.

From WILLIAM B. LAWRENCE, London, no. 23, February 14, 1828. Discusses the recent changes in the British Cabinet, tracing the fall of the Goderich government to "irreconcilable" differences in the old Cabinet between William Huskisson and John Charles Herries. Notes that the Colombian minister to Great Britain, Jose Fernandez Madrid, has been in London since last April and has still not been presented at Court. Says that while this delay has officially been "represented as accidental," he feels that the "present Government is not, at all events, so strongly impressed, as Mr. [George] Canning was, with the importance of encouraging in every manner the strongest interest in the New American States." Notes that only Brazil, Colombia, Mexico, and Buenos Aires are represented here and that the latter two are represented only by Chargés—Vincent Rocafuerta and Juan Francisco Gil. ALS. DNA, RG59, Dip. Disp., Great Britain, vol. 35 (M30, R31). Received March 16, 1828.

From JOAQUIN CAMPINO, Baltimore, February 15, 1828. Reports that the Government of Chile has appointed him Minister Extraordinary and Plenipotentiary to the United States, and that he has "this day" arrived in Baltimore. States that since his health is "somewhat impaired," he will remain in Baltimore "a short time in order to recover it," but that he will soon arrive in Washington to present his credentials to the President. ALS, in Spanish, with trans. in State Dept. file. DNA, RG59, Notes from Chilean Legation, vol. 1 (M179, R66).

On February 16, Clay acknowledged receipt of the letter and offered "congratulations" to Campino upon his arrival. Copy. DNA, RG59, Notes to Foreign Ministers and Consuls, vol. 3, pp. 429–30 (M38, R3).

From THOMAS McGIFFIN   Washington, February 15, 1828
I am at length enabled to enclose you the statement of the Revd. Doct. [Andrew] Wylie—[1]It is not *precisely* such as I had good reaons to expect, altho I believe substantially sustaining that which I gave you "white man is very uncertain" truly and hence there is still a leaning and an effort to sustain former opinions, notwithstanding a distinct verbal admission that Jackson has totally failed in the proof and that as an honorable man he ought at once to withdraw the charge   The hopes of the party are evidently kept up for the present in the expectation that the developements of the central Committee of your City will put them on their feet again—Even this Revd. Gentleman is looking to that and therefore could not be prevailed on now to *put on paper* his former & present impressions of the transaction—I am induced to believe you have already obtained from [William] Sample all that is obtainable in relation to Jacksons conversations at Alexandria [Pa.].[2] He has made two efforts to obtain the signatures of those present to a statement of that conversation, but has failed altho it was admitted to be correct—Having his own however I am well satisfied there is no *hazard* in relying on it—You judged entirely correct when you supposed it was not necessary to say to me that you ought not to be held responsible by your friends for appointments made in the other departments—I had endeavoured as *strongly* and forcibly as

96

I could to relieve you from all complaints in the quarter you mention and believe I was at least partially successful—Relying implicitly upon your friendly liberality of disposition I ever have & trust I ever shall take for granted that you have done all that it was proper for you to do and that when you have not accomplished what was asked for, it was because having a *view* of the *whole* ground you thought it ought not to be granted and *most* probably directed correctly—And in reference to my sons appointment[3] I shall barely repeat that if he is successful I shall *thank* you for it and if not I shall charge his defeat to what I know will be the fact viz the influence of Mr [Joseph] Lawrence in behalf of the son of his *Type setter*—Since I commenced this letter Doct. Wylie has called on me and has substituted another statement for the one I then had—It is substantially the same, but adds a partial & prospective *change of opinion*—This I am glad of because it was due to himself and will not certainly be injurious to you—I *know* the public mind is prepared for a *reaction* and is only now *pausing* in expectation of the promised *Bulletin* from the Central Committee when it does come I trust you will be prepared at once to give it its *quietus*—I shall be looking for both with much anxiety—After much delay I have Sample under *way* in the republication of 1000 of your last address—and shall distribute them as *judiciously* as possible—They must & will do good—If you have occasion to publish anything more I should be glad to see it as early as convenient to you, in order that it may be republished & distributed here   Let the Antidote follow the poison as soon as possible—Will the Yankees *swallow* the projected Tariff? They must or fall in the trap which is evidently laid for them and will *thereby* inevitably loose their President—This *necessity* is in my judgment much increased by the unfortunate omiss[ion] of the Presidt to speak out plainly on this ques[tion in] his message—This you see still *sticks* with me—In order to relieve Mr Wylie from the *appearance* of volunteering in this matter I was obliged to address him a note requesting it as from you—Hence it appears in the garb in which you have it—My name can be dropped in the the [*sic*] publication of it, if by any possibility it should be considered as injurious—You know I am a *Federalist*.

ALS. DLC–HC (DNA, M212, R3).   1. McGiffin to Clay, January 29, 1828.   2. Sample to Clay, January 2, 1828.   3. McGiffin to Clay, January 29, 1828.

From DAVID OFFLEY, Smyrna, February 17, 1828. Encloses letter [above, January 24] from Nicholas Navoni. States that he informed the Porte that he is "not authorized to enter into any negociations" regarding a commercial treaty. Adds that he does, however, "contrive to receive frequent indirect communications from the Reis effendi [Saida Efendi] on that subject." Reports that the Turks are disposed to negotiate now because of "a communication made to the Sultan [Mahmud II] by the former Capudan now Seraskier Pacha [Chosrew–Mehmed–Pacha]—the Sultan's orders thereon" and the opinion entertained by the Porte that "if a treaty of friendship existed between the two nations they would be allowed to have vessels of war built in the United States so to replace those destroyed at Navarino." States that "representatives of the Seraskier Pacha gave orders to the Reis Effendi to conclude a treaty with the United States and particularly to grant all privileges enjoyed by the

French and English." Says he told the Turks, that if they would inform him "in an official manner of the present friendly disposition of the sublime Porte to terminate a treaty of friendship and commerce," he would transmit the information to the American Government.

Requests that instructions be "given to the Commanders of American vessels of war on this station that they should give Convoy to American merchant vessels bound to Ports not blockaded loaded with merchandize not contraband" to obtain a "most valuable trade." ALS. DNA, RG59, Dip. Disp., Turkey, vol. 1 (M46, R2). No date of receipt.

From WILLIAM E. ALLEN, New York, February 18, 1828. Reports that an Englishman desires to invest from $80,000 to $150,000 in a factory in New York state, but to succeed must acquire a patent or patents for certain "extremely advantageous Processes." Inquires whether or not Congress would by "Express Law" exempt him from the ordinary residence requirement and if it would be necessary for him to become an American citizen. ALS. DNA, RG59, Misc. Letters (M179, R66).

From THOMAS H. BAIRD   Washington, Pa., February 18, 1828 [Complains of the way his brother, William Baird, had been passed over for an appointment as a postmaster in favor of Joseph Henderson, apparently because of the influence of Joseph Lawrence with Postmaster General John McLean. Admits that while Henderson is "very capable," the appointment was "unfortunate . . . as it regards the cause of the administration in this county [Washington]." In addition, "when I was informed that you declined interfering, my feelings were hurt & my friendship wounded.—As to the president I have experienced sentiments of disapprobation only." Will continue to support Adams, however, "because I wish to avoid a dreadful evil to the country"; and even though "I shall experience my share of the bitter denunciation & persecution which already distinguishes Pennsylvania Jacksonism." Continues:]

I think we can yet gain the victory. In my late journey to Harrisburgh [sic, Harrisburg], I went down by the southern route & returned by the Northern road.—I [am] well satisfied that a great change is progressing in this state—and if vigorous & well directed efforts are made, our cause will be successful. But one event has occurred to lessen this confidence. This was the late election in Cumberland & Perry counties in which the Jackson candidate for senator had a large majority. I am assured however that this result was greatly owing to the personal unpopularity of the Adams' candidate.[1]—I received a letter a few days ago from Somerset county stating that the German preachers were coming out for the administration. If we get the dutch we are safe.—In this part of the country the people are waiting with anxiety the fate of the tariff bill. I think it has been contrived as a "ruse de guerre" upon our New England friends.—If they take it however *cum more:* if they vote for it with all its objectionable features to *their* interests—the battery will be unmasked & we will see who are really the friends of the "American

System".—And should it turn out as I anticipate, we will put down Jacksonism in Pennsylvania.—Governor [William B.] Giles' late communication to the Virginia legislature I am inclined to believe will operate favorably here.[2]—

But I beg your pardon.—I find I have written a long letter about a small matter. . . .

ALS. DLC–HC (DNA, M212, R3).   1. Jesse Miller defeated Peter Ritner in a special election for state senator held on January 29. For Miller, see *BDAC*. Ritner was an ironmaker whose brother Joseph was later (1835) governor of Pennsylvania. *PMHB*, 98:208.   2. The message and report of Governor Giles of February 8, 1828, condemned, among other things, the tariff on agricultural commodities. *Niles' Register* (February 16, 1828), 33:405. The Legislature, however, voted on February 18, by 112 to 77, not to take up the issue. *Ibid.* (March 1, 1828), 34:6; see also Richmond *Enquirer*, February 23, 1828.

From ISAAC D. BARNARD, Washington, D.C., February 18, 1828. States his understanding that the British will cease to exact disciminating duties on the tonnage of American vessels in Canadian ports if the United States "will abolish the like duty on the tonnage of British vessels in the American ports of the Northern and Northwestern Frontiers of the United States." Adds that, because of its importance to "the Lake Navigation," he wishes to accomplish "that object" during the "present Session of Congress." Concludes: "The object of my note is, to ask of you, if not improper, whether the government has any wish to continue the discriminating duties . . . and whether it would object to their being abolished?" ALS. DNA, RG59, Misc. Letters (M179, R66). Clay responded on this same day that the duties could be discontinued "provided the British Government will adopt the principle of reciprocity and admit our vessels in the British ports on the Lakes on the same terms with Canadian vessels." DS, by Clay. DNA, RG59, Report Books, vol. 4, p. 221. This arrangement was finally worked out in June, 1854, in the Reciprocity Treaty with Great Britain. Parry, *Treaty Series,* 112:31–7.

To WILLIAM H. CRAWFORD   Washington, February 18, 1828
I received your letter of the 4th instant, and will take pleasure in having forwarded the letter which it enclosed to Mr [Joel R.] Poinsett with the first publick despatches. I should not hesitate to intimate to him my wish that he would comply with your request for the Mexican seeds &c, if I were not persuaded that it would be altogether unnecessary for me to second any expression of your desire to him. Our Country needs much the multiplication of the products of the earth, as well as of industry otherwise applied. And he deserves well of it who will introduce a new, or more successfully cultivate, an old article of agriculture.

I do, my dear Sir, know *you* too well to suppose that you ever countenanced the charge of corruption against me. No man of sense and candor—at least none that knew me—ever could or did countenance it. Your frank admission that you would have voted as I did between Mr Adams and Genl Jackson, accords with the estimate I have always made of your intelligence, your independence, and your patriotism. Nor am I at all surprised or dissatisfied with the expression of your opinion that I erred in accepting the place which I now hold. When two courses present themselves in human affairs, and one only is pursued, experience develops the errors of the selection which has been made. Those which would have attended the adoption of the opposite course can only be matter of speculation. Thus it is in the case referred to. We see, or think we see, distinctly, the errors of the alternative which I embraced. But are we sure that if I had chosen the other, I should not have been liable to greater hazard or more animadversion? The truth is, as I have often said, my condition was one full of embarrassments, whatever way I might act. My own judgment was rather opposed to my acceptance of the Department of State, but my friends, and let me add two of your best friends (Mess [Louis] McLane of Delaware and Mr [John] Forsyth) urged me strongly not to decline it. It was represented by my friends that I would get no credit for the forbearance, but that, on the contrary, it would be said that that very forbearance was evidence of my having made a bargain, though unwilling to execute it. The office, they thought, was an office of the nation, not of the actual presidential encumbent; and I was bound to look to the good of the Country, and not to regard any personal objections which I had to him. Can you who have contributed, said they, to the election of Mr Adams decline the Department of State? Will you not be charged if you do, with having co-operated in the election of a man, of whom you think so ill, that you will not serve in one of the highest places in the publick councils with him? Even if he should be wanting in any of the requisite qualifications for the station to which he has been elevated, you are the more bound, for that very reason, to accept in order to endeavor to guard the country against any danger from his mal-administration. Your enemies have sought, by previous denunciation, to frighten you. They do not believe that you have acted otherwise than from motives of the purest patriotism; but they wish to alarm you, and prevent your entering the Department of State. These and other similar arguments were pressed on me, and after a week's deliberation I yielded to their force. It is quite possible that I may have erred. And you may be right in predicting, as a consequence of my decision, that being identified with Mr Adams' Administration, if he falls, I also shall fall. Should such be my fate, I shall submit to it, I hope, with the fortitude of a philosopher, if not with the resignation of a Christian I shall at least have no cause of self-reproach. For I will undertake to affirm (and I appeal with confidence to Him who knows best the human heart for the truth of the affirmation) that throughout my publick life, in the many trying situations in which I have been placed, I have been guided exclusively by the consideration of the good of my country. You say that I ought to have foreseen that Mr Adams' Administration could hardly fail to be unpopular. I certainly did not foresee that the tree would be judged of otherwise than by its fruits. But the popularity of a particular course or proceeding (although I will not pretend that I have been altogether regardless of it) has not been the deciding motive with me of my publick conduct. Is the measure right? will it conduce to the general happiness, and the elevation of the national character? These have been always my first, and most anxious inquiries.

I had fears of Mr Adams' temper and disposition; but I must say that they have not been realized; and I have found in him, since I have been associated with him in the Executive Government as little to censure or condemn, as I could have expected in any man. Truth compels me to say that I have heartily approved of the leading measures of his Administration, not excepting those which relate to Georgia. I have not time, if I had ability and it were necessary, to vindicate them. But, my dear sir, I must invoke your frankness and justice to re–consider the only exceptionable measure which you have specified, that of his recommendation of lighthouses to the skies. It is not the metaphor, I presume, but the thing (an Observatory) which has provoked your censure. And can you justly censure Mr Adams for a recommendation which almost every previous President has made? If there be no power in the General Government to authorize the erection of an Observatory within the limits of a State, is there none to sanction its location in *this* District? The message,[1] I believe, was silent as to the place where it should be built. But I will dwell no longer on publick affairs. I should not have touched the topic but for your friendly allusion to it. I turn from it with pleasure to the recollection of our amicable relations. Whatever you may have though[t] or may have been sought to be infused into your mind, my friendly feelings toward you have never ceased. And although our correspondence has been interrupted four or five years, I have always entertained a lively solicitude for your welfare, and availed myself of every opportunity to inquire particularly about your health and situation. I have heard with unaffected pleasure of the improvement of your health. That it may be perfectly reestablished, and that you may be long spared for the benefit of your family and the good of your Country, is the sincere wish of. . . .

Copy. DLC–HC (DNA, M212, R3). Another copy, dated February 10, is in *ibid*. Still another copy, dated February 18, is in KyU. Printed in Colton, *Clay Correspondence*, 4:192–5, under date February 18; extract printed in *ibid*., 1:395, under date February 10.
1. Annual Message, December 6, 1825, in Richardson, *MPP*, 2:313–4.

To GEORGE W.   Washington, February 18, 1828
FEATHERSTONHAUGH
I was extremely gratified to learn, from your letter of the 12th inst. that you had returned in safety from Europe [5:426]. The reception with which you met on the two sides of the British Channel, from the American Ministers[1] corresponded with that which our countrymen generally experienced. I am happy to learn that that which Mr. and Mrs. [James] Brown gave you, was warm and cordial.

You find our country, on your return, exhibiting one of its most unpleasant aspects; that of an universal agitation and excitement relative to the election of a Chief Magistrate. In this struggle, which has already continued so long, and which, with increased ardor must be protracted yet another year, all the worst passions are displayed. I hope the same Providence who has so often smiled upon us will carry us securely through it.

The late event at Albany is one of great importance. Governor [DeWitt] Clinton had some great qualities, and his name will be perpetually identified with the history of his country.

I am happy to learn, from you and other friends, that there is an abatement of the extraordinary political fever which raged with so much violence in some parts of New York last Fall. My confidence in the correctness of the ultimate decision of the People has been very great; and I cannot doubt that if the exertions of the friends of the Administration are equal to the goodness of their cause, they will yet prevail.

The subject of the protection of our own industry will probably be taken up this week in the House of Representatives.[2] It is difficult to resist the conclusion that the bill which has been reported was framed, purposely, to create divisions among the friends of the American System, and thus to defeat the measure. I hope the discussions in the House of Representatives will be so conducted as clearly to manifest to the country, who are friendly and who are opposed to the protection of its industry. You must not be surprised if you see those who are, and always have been, opposed to any protection whatever, voting, on this occasion, for the highest amount of it. The danger is, that by a combination between that class and some professed friends, but secret foes, of the System, the bill may be finally lost.

It gives me great pleasure to be assured by you that you have returned without any change in your former opinions, personal or political. . . .

LS. KyU.   1. Albert Gallatin and James Brown.   2. Clay to Crittenden, February 14, 1828.

From ALBERT GALLATIN, New York, February 18, 1828. Responds to Clay's letter of February 9, 1828, outlining the "necessary preparations for the arbitration" of the Northeast Boundary, now that the U.S. Senate has approved the Convention [6:1100-01]. Reports that he has drafted a preliminary account of those negotiations on the boundary in which he personally had participated, including "all the arguments and all the evidence laid before the late Commission [1:1006; 4:182]" and "embracing every topic." Suggests ways of reorganizing the evidence presented to the previous Commissioners, and recommends that the governors of Maine, Massachusetts, Vermont, New Hampshire, and New York be sent a copy of the August 6, 1827, Convention together with "my statement of evidence" and a request that they submit to the State Department "any further evidence in their possession as is not embraced in the Statement and they may deem material." Refers to his letter to Clay of December 12, 1827 with reference to his continuing conviction that "the ultimate decision as to what evidence should be laid before the Arbiter, must be reserved to the Government of the U.S.," and to his concern over "the measures necessary to collect information in the British provinces." Recommends a timetable for the submission of additional relevant documents to the Department of State. Discusses what geographical surveys, presented to the earlier Commission, should be "laid before the Arbiter." Thinks it best to make two copies of "all the said Surveys and of the map *A*."

Has the "strict conviction" that the Maine boundary line claimed by the U.S. is in "strict conformity with the letter of the treaty of 1783 and with the intentions of the parties," and that Great Britain has not the "shadow of a claim" to territory thus properly belonging to the U.S.

Offers his personal services to Clay "in making the necessary preparations for the arbitration and in preparing the statements according to the stipulations of the Convention . . . without an official appointment, and without any compensation."

Considers it quite important that the "selection of evidence and delineation of highlands on the transcript of the Map *A*" be done with particular care. Copy. NHi–Gallatin Papers (MR21).

To WILLIAM PLUMER, JR.   Washington, February 18, 1828

I have received your favor of the 18th [*sic*, 8th] inst. with its enclosure, which I have deliberately examined & considered. No improvement of it suggests itself to me, and I therefore return it without any proposed alteration, under the hope that you may have it published.[1]

Mr. [Alexander] Robertson, near Chillicothe in Ohio, has recently presented voluntarily to the public his testimony of my avowed preference of Mr. Adams over Gen'l Jackson;[2] and I think its effect will be better than if it had been offered even by myself in the first instance. Of the several conversations between us, to which you testify, I have no recollection but that which occurred on the occasion of LaFayette's reception [3:893–4]. Still I have not a doubt of the substantial correctness of your report of them.

On the side of Mr. Adams, yours will be the first testimony offered in my exculpation; and on that, as well as on other accounts, it will command particular attention.

The late event at Albany is highly important in every aspect of it. Of Mr. [DeWitt] Clinton it may be justly said that he has associated his name forever with the history of his Country; and so much can be said of but few.

I hope & believe that even his death (since that was inevitable) may conduce to the benefit of his country.

My best respects to your father [William Plumer]. . . .

Copy. *PMHB*, 6:355–6.   1. See, *A Supplement to the Address of Hency Clay. . .* , 15–8. 2. *Ibid.*, pp. 18–9.

From CHARLES S. TODD   Stockdale [Shelby Co.], Ky.
                                        February 18, 1828

Your esteemed favor of the 31st. Ulto. has been received and I hasten to send you the enclosed statement.[1] So much of it as relates to the Conversation with Gov. [Isaac] Shelby occurred at different times in the Course of your visit, in the presence of Mrs. [Letitia Shelby] Todd and Mrs. [Susanna Hart] Shelby and the same views of the conduct and character of General Jackson were repeatedly stated by him to me in different conversations. That part in relation to the Chickasaw Treaty[2] has also been communicated to me by Gov. Shelby and has been often mentioned by Thos. H Shelby[3] who was present. George Graham Esq of your City arrived just at the moment and Gov. Shelby took him aside, informed him of the project of General Jackson and his friends and requested him to examine the land and report it to the President who by the terms of the Treaty had the preemption. Graham did so and the Government took the land at the price stipulated. By which means, the object of the intrigue was defeated.—It would be well to converse with Mr. Graham on the subject and to examine the Treaty itself as to the details.

The opinion of my father [Thomas] and of Gov. Shelby may have some effect upon the next contest in Kentucky.—You can use the statement entire or confine it singly to the conversation with my father. Though I should prefer its being used entire as I feel a perfect conviction, and so Mrs. Shelby has expressed herself, that if Gov. Shelby were now living, he would not hesitate to make a public statement if necessary to prevent the election of General Jackson who, he said to me one day, would make a *very good* President for the State of Tennessee: as he had not mind or temper to look beyond his immediate personal friends to the promotion of the great interests of the Country—

How will your indignation rise on seeing the disgraceful conduct of the Jackson party of the Senate in the late investigation?[4] There seems to be but one opinion as to the impropriety of that course—it is a complete abortion, involving the Managers in deeper infamy—What think you of the moral obliquity and perfidy Of [Amos] Kendall & [Francis P.] Blair. The latter of whom particularly holds out the idea that he was in your confidence, retails the slander to Kendall who publishes it and then refuses to speak before the Senate because, forsooth, what he pretends to know has been derived confidentially? We should suppose he had been studying the part of Iago in Othello—he has certainly acted the character to the life though your conduct has been as pure as was that of the murdered Desdemona:—I cannot sufficiently express my detestation of the conduct of your avowed & of your *secret* foes in this State.

I was particularly pleased with the spirit and point shewn in the statements of [Thomas] Metcalfe [William L.] Brent and [Duncan] McArthur, the latter of whom alone has ventured to say, what the witnesses of General Jackson have proved, that the attempt at bargaining was on their side. This fearless course was to be expected from the blunt dependent character of my old friend whom I knew well in the War. The contest has assumed a character which, in my opinion, calls on the Members of Congress from the States originally supporting Mr. Adams to come out with their statements on the subject—Is such a course in contemplation?

I hope our friends in Kentucky will do their duty—there is yet time to disabuse the public mind of the gross delusions which have been practised on it. The course of General Jackson's friends as to the Tariff is working well and is winnowing the chaff from the wheat.—In this County we hope to maintain our ground, while, in Henry we are gaining advantages daily—[5] The [Shelbyville] "Advocate" conducted by Miller is making a valuable impression on the public mind. He deserves credit for his zeal and ability though I fear he is declining rapidly with a consumption. We shall be at a loss to supply his place. "Old rifle [probably Joseph LeCompte]" seconded by the character of Stone Mason [Thomas Metcalfe] cannot be resisted. I will thank you to assure him that his friends will be true to him in his absence.

We have nothing yet as to your health. Be pleased to present us affectionately to Mrs. Clay. . . . P.S. I have purposely avoided stating the authority for the Conversation with Gov. Shelby. I have given the private history in this letter with which the public has nothing to do. I will vouch for the statement being substantially correct. although the conversation both with Gov. Shelby & with my father *in all their details* may have escaped your recollection.

ALS. DLC–HC (DNA, M212, R3). Letter marked "Confidential." No. 1 of this date.
1. Next letter, below. Printed in Clay, *A Supplement to the Address . . . to the Public . . .* , 9–11. Cf. below, June 10, 1828; and *Niles' Register* (July 5, 1828), 34:308.　　2. Parry, *Treaty Series,* 69:287–91. The treaty was signed on October 19, 1818.　　3. Shelby (1789–1869), son of Governor Isaac Shelby, was for a time the latter's private secretary. Most of his life was spent on his estate, "Grasslands," south of Lexington, where he gained prominence as a cattle breeder. Howard Galloway, *The Shelby Family . . .* (Mobile, 1964), 58; and Richard L. Troutman, "Stock Raising in the Antebellum Bluegrass," *RKHS,* (January, 1957), 55:19.　　4. Blair to Clay, January 22; February 4, 1828.　　5. Adams carried Shelby County 1,099 to 946 in the 1828 presidential canvass; Jackson swept Henry County by a 672 to 338 count. Jasper B. Shannon and Ruth McQuown, *Presidential Politics in Kentucky, 1824–1948* (Lexington, 1950). 6.

From CHARLES S. TODD　　　　Shelby [Co.], Ky., February 18, 1828
Adverting to that part of your late address [6:1394-6] in which you remark "you have no doubt that in your promiscious and unreserved intercourse among your acquaintances in this State, others not recollected by you, could bear testimony to the undeviating and settled determination of your mind." I deem it an act of duty and of justice to inform you that a conversation of the tendency alluded to, occurred between you, my late father [Thomas] and myself at his house in Frankfort a few days before you started from that place on your journey to Washington early in November 1824. I was not aware that you had it in contemplation to make a publication on this subject[1] or I would have long since communicated the circumstance to you.—

We commenced the conversation by an enquiry of you as to the prospects of the Presidential Election and particularly as to the import of the latest information on an event which we regarded with great solicitude, that of your being returned by the electoral college to the House of Representatives—You were of opinion that this result would depend chiefly on the vote of Louisiana and the relative extent of the vote for yourself and Mr. [William H.] Crawford in the State of New York.— Predicated on the idea of your exclusion from the House my father enquired as to the actual and most received opinion of the state of Mr. Crawford's health and intimated a preference of that distinguished individual on the Contingency supposed, should his health be considered as sufficiently firm to enable him to discharge the arduous and complicated duties of President. You spoke of the last intelligence as to his health being very unfavorable and concurred in the kind opinion expressed of him by my father—A comparison was then entered into as to the respective qualifications of Mr. Adams and General Jackson. My father mentioned having some prejudices against Mr. Adams which, however, he admitted were not of a character to impeach his patriotism or his fitness for the office both of which were acknowledged. He expressed a desire to have a Western President but did not think that in this aspect of the case, we should effect this object by the election of General Jackson as neither he nor his immediate friends could be relied on as favorable to what was called the Western policy. He regarded General Jackson, moreover, as disqualified by his temper, his Education and habits to discharge, satisfactorily, the duties of the office of President. In these views you appeared to concur and requested us to exert any personal influence we might have with the Legislature in preventing the introduction or adoption of a resolution [3:902] to instruct the Kentucky delegation to vote for General Jackson. You deprecated the idea as being in highest degree embarassing and hoped it would not be adopted. The whole conversation impressed on my mind the firm conviction with which you seemed to be animated that you could not nor ought not to vote for General Jackson under any circumstances whatever. I recollect distinctly that you foreboded the direst consequences to the country in the event of his election; that it would be an administration of fury and of violence; as had been forcibly stated by the author of an interesting pamphlet [3:845-6, 871] just published in New York and to which you adverted. As contrasted with the pretensions of General Jackson you referred to the ability and long experience of Mr. Adams in the civil affairs of the Nation and mentioned the incident of a friendly argument with him in his office on your leaving Washington in 1821.22.[2] but in which you differed in opinion as to the most suitable time to recognize the Independence of the new Governments south of the United States. I took occassion here, to speak of the high opinion of Mr. Adams's patriotism and abilities produced on my mind by the opportunity afforded of judging of them when engaged in the service of the U. States abroad; which tended in a great degree to remove the prejudices imbibed from the misrepresentations of his political conduct at an early period of the Government.

In appropriate connexion with the preceding narrative, I can state the substance of a Conversation of like tendency had between yourself and our venerated friend the late Gov. [Isaac] Shelby at his residence as early as the month of July 1824. He commenced the conversation by asking what you thought of the prospects of General Jackson in the approaching election. You replied by stating that you did not beleive he would be elected: and spoke freely and fully of his conduct and qualifications, very much in the manner you had treated of them in your public speeches; that you did not expect from him or his Counsellors any friendly feeling towards Kentucky or the great Western interests which she had so prominently Supported and that you had strong apprehensions that his Administration would be a reign of fury and of turbulence—Gov. Shelby then remarked that he concurred entirely in these views and proceeded to communicate to you, what he had never mentioned out of the circle of his immediate family, the great change effected in his mind towards General Jackson by his conduct at the Chikkasaw Treaty[3] in 1818. that the high estimation in which he had theretofore regarded the temper, the discretion, judgment and disinterested patriotism of General Jackson, had been greatly lessened by his conduct on that occassion. He said, his rash hot headed temper, if it had not been restrained, would have cost the Nation Double the sum for which the land was ultimately purchased and he had so permitted the integrity of his principles to be the dupe of an intrigue as to propose on behalf of his personal friends, then present, to secure for them a reservation of the Big Spring and a valuable tract of land around it—To this proposition, he, Gov. Shelby, opposed an indignant refusal, but at length consented to its partial adoption with the understanding that the Government should have the preemption right at the price stipulated. He, accordingly, caused the necessary information to be transmitted to the President who promptly accepted the reservation on behalf of the Government. In conclusion, Gov. Shelby remarked, in a tone and style peculiar to himself, that he beleived there were 500 men in the Union with stronger claims & qualifications to the Presidency than those possessed by General Jackson. From repeated and full conversations which I had the satisfaction of subsequently holding with my revered father and my venerated father in Law [Isaac Shelby] I am persuaded, that had you voted for General Jackson it would have greatly impaired the confidence in you which had been implicit and exalted, and in the friendship which had been unclouded, during a period of 30 years of intimate intercourse.—You will concur with me in the belief that no two individuals in the western States, out of Tennessee, were so thoroughly apprized of the *real character and qualifications* of General Jackson as were these two departed patriots—

ALS. DLC-HC (DNA, M212, R3). No. 2 of this date. Also in *Niles' Register* (July 5, 1828), 34:308.   1. See Clay, *A Supplement to the Address . . . to the Public*, 9-11. See below, June 10, 1828.   2. The conversation took place on March 9, 1821. Adams, *Memoirs*, 5:324-6, 495-6.   3. Todd to Clay, Oct. 10, 1828; Parry, *Treaty Series*, 69:287-91.

To CHARLES R. VAUGHAN, Washington. No. 1 of this date, February 18, 1828. Reviews the circumstances in the case of the wrecked Spanish slave vessel *Guerrero* in response to Vaughan's note of January 22, 1828. Points out that with "respect to Mr. Vaughan's demand of the surrender of the African Negroes" cast up on U.S. territory, the "negroes, without any fault of theirs, or any act of the Government of the United States, have come within its jurisdiction, and must now be disposed of according to its laws." Asserts that the future of the shipwrecked slaves now rests with the U.S. courts, to which Great Britain might appeal and that to permit this appeal, the slaves will be "detained a reasonable time." If there is no appeal, the Negroes will be returned to Africa "as freemen." Asserts that Lt. Edward Holland, RN, in transporting some of the rescued slaves from U.S. territorial waters to "foreign ports," had violated an Act of Congress of March 3, 1825 [4 U.S. *Stat.*, 132-3] prohibiting such transport. In so doing, Holland has "subjected himself to censure." Concludes with the hope that "the British Government will bestow such animadversion upon that officer as his conduct merits." Copy. DNA, RG59, Notes to Foreign Ministers and Consuls, vol. 3, pp. 430-3 (M38, R3).

To CHARLES R. VAUGHAN, Washington. No. 2 of this date, February 18, 1828. Transmits a copy of the memorial of John Morrison and others of January 5 and its enclosures. States that Lieutenant Edward Holland has conceded to "the right of salvage," and that "the only question appears to have been as to the amount of it." Notes: "The parties agreed to leave that question to some competent American Tribunal," but "Holland afterwards refused to execute that arrangement, and sailed from the United States."

Expresses expectation that Vaughan has "some communication from Holland on the subject" and that Vaughan will be willing to "co–operate in such measures as may be necessary to ascertain the just amount of indemnity to which the Memorialists are entitled." Copy. DNA, RG59, Notes to Foreign Ministers and Consuls, vol. 3, pp. 434–5 (M38, R3).

To FRANCISCO TACON, February 19, 1828. Replies to Tacon's note of January 24 concerning the West Florida land grant of the Marquis of Casa Irujo, Carlos Fernando Martinez de Irujo. States that Congress passed a series of acts, the first dated May 8, 1822, to provide for the ascertainment of Florida claims and that the validity of each claim was to have been determined by a Board of Commissioners, or by Congress. Adds that the Marquis was required to exhibit his claim in accordance with the laws and if he has fulfilled the requirements of the law, "there is no doubt" that the claim will be respected by Congress and the courts, but if he has not, Congress must determine the validity of the claim, upon application by the Marquis. Copy. DNA, RG59, Notes to Foreign Ministers and Consuls, vol. 3, pp. 435–6 (M38, R3).

From SAMUEL LARNED, Santiago de Chile, no. 66, February 20, 1828. Reports that Congress will convene on February 25 in Santiago and that "a great majority of its members" belong to the Liberal party. States that disturbances in Quillota, growing out of the recent elections, "as well as those of Colchagua, have been at length happily adjusted." States that "commotions in Bolivia," which broke out in late December, have been suppressed, but that "President [Antonio Jose de] Sucre can, however, no longer confide in his Colombian troops; and will, in all probability, soon find it necessary to abandon that country to its own direction." Relates that the Spanish privateer brig *Greek,* of 18 guns and 175 men, and commanded by "the noted Marteli," has captured several vessels of "these new States." Notes that William Tudor arrived at Valparaiso on February 10, en route to Rio de Janeiro. ALS. DNA, RG59, Dip. Disp., Chile, vol. 2 (M–T2, R2). Received June 21, 1828.

To WILLIAM B. LAWRENCE, London, no. 3, February 20, 1828. Conveys by the hand of Nathaniel B. Blunt the three conventions with Great Britain [6:826–7, 859–60, 1100–01] negotiated by Albert Gallatin in 1827 and recently ratified by the U.S. With reference to selecting an arbiter of the Maine boundary, as provided by Article I of the Northeastern Boundary Convention [6:1100–01], the U.S. insists on, in order of preference, the Emperor of Russia [Nicholas I], the King of Denmark [Frederick VI] or the King of the Netherlands [William I]. Notes, however, that if, "as it appears to us, at this distance, to be highly probable, from recent information, hostilities have been commenced with Turkey, the fact of Great Britain and Russia being allies in the prosecution of that war, might render somewhat doubtful the expediency of our agreeing to the choice of the Emperor Nicholas as arbiter." Still, he does not believe that Great Britain would necessarily object to the selection of Nicholas I. In any event, "The President is not now prepared to authorize the selection of any sovereign or state, other than one of the three mentioned above." L, with interlineations and signature. DLC–HC (DNA, M212, R8); also in Manning, *Diplomatic Correspondence . . . Canadian Relations,* 2:145–7.

From WILLIAM SHALER, Algiers, February 20, 1828. Acknowledges receipt of Clay's dispatch of August 13, 1827, which granted Shaler a leave of absence, and states that he will leave Algiers as soon as he conveniently can. Adds that he understands that Richard B. Jones wishes to succeed him, but that he will not know whether or not he will resign until he has returned to the United States. ALS. DNA, RG59, Cons. Disp., Algiers, vol. 11 (M23, R–T13). Received May 1, 1828. Letter marked "Private."

From JAMES TAYLOR, Lexington, February 20, 1828. Reminds Clay that he owes the U.S. government some $2600 as security for the late James T. Eubank, that he has regularly paid the interest on the sum, but that now the U.S. Treasury wants a $500 payment on the principal. Reports that he is in serious financial difficulty, and argues that since Eubank died a heroic death in action in the War of 1812 the debt should be forgiven by a grateful government. Requests that Clay ask General William Henry Harrison about Deputy Quartermaster Eubank's service record in the certainty that "he will unite with you in asking the indulgence now requested." ALS. DNA, RG206, Solicitor of the Treasury, Letters Received, Misc. "T."

From CHARLES R. VAUGHAN, Washington, February 20, 1828. Transmits a copy of a petition of Henry Beamish of St. Andrews, New Brunswick. States that Beamish apparently bought flour in the United States for delivery at Eastport, Maine, and then sent part of it on to St. Andrews in "open boats"; that one boat, carrying 44 barrels of flour, valued at 220 dollars, "went adrift" in the Bay of Passamaquoddy and later was seized by a customs officer at Lubec. Requests that Clay investigate the case. LS. DNA, RG59, Notes from British Legation, vol. 15 (M50, R15).

On February 29, Clay sent a copy of this note to Richard Rush, asking for information from the Treasury Department that would enable him to answer Vaughan's complaint as well as furnish Beamish with whatever relief "may be within the competency" of the State Department. Copy. DNA, RG59, Dom. Letters, vol. 22, p. 150 (M40, R20).

Rush responded on March 1, citing the Act of Congress of May 15, 1820 and that of March 3, 1797 governing the legal and administrative procedures by which the Secretary of the Treasury might make financial restitution in claims cases like that in which Beamish was involved. D. DNA, RG59, Misc. Letters (M179, R66).

To **CHARLES R. VAUGHAN,** Washington, February 20, 1828. Submits the report of Samuel B. Barrell, the U.S. agent sent to investigate "disturbances among the settlers" in the disputed area along the Maine–New Brunswick border, especially the case of the "arrest, deportation, and detention in confinement, at Frederickton, of John Baker [6:1272-3], a Citizen of the United States." Expresses concern over the "long delay" in reaching a final settlement on the boundary question, but states his disagreement with Vaughan's contention that Great Britain has the right to maintain sovereignty over "the territory in dispute" until the entire issue is settled. Reviews the status of the disputed area, "an uninhabited waste" in 1783, the settlements that slowly grew in the region, the initial disinterest of both governments in those peaceful settlements, and his belief that "the actual occupancy" of British settlers at Madawaska did not extend to "the uninhabited portions of the adjoining waste." Claims that John Baker's settlement "appears to have been made outside of the Madawasca settlement," was therefore not within New Brunswick's claimed jurisdiction at Madawaska proper, and that Baker's arrest "on the disputed ground" and his confinement "in a loathsome jail" in Frederickton "cannot be justified." Reports that he has been instructed by the President "to demand the immediate liberation of John Baker, and a full indemnity for the injuries which he has suffered in the arrest and detention of his person."

Informs Vaughan, further, that the President cannot "view with satisfaction" New Brunswick's "exercise of jurisdiction . . . over the settlement on the Aroostook." Reviews the brief history of the settlement there by citizens of both nations. Concludes that "The Undersigned must protest, in behalf of his Government, against any exercise of acts of exclusive jurisdiction by the British authority, on the Madawasca, the Aroostook, or within any other part of the disputed territory before the final settlement of that question." Conveys also "the Presidents expectation that Mr. Vaughan will make such representations as will prevent, in future, any such jurisdiction from being exerted." Copy. DNA, RG59, Notes to Foreign Ministers and Consuls, vol. 3, pp. 436-40 (M38, R3); also in Manning, *Diplomatic Correspondence . . . Canadian Relations* (together with Barrell's Report), 2:148-63.

From FRANCIS T. BROOKE   Richmond, February 21, 1828
At your instance I Some time Since wrote a letter to Gen P[eter] B Porter but have received no answer, how is that my letter may have miscarried but I fear to write again—lest in these times of change he too may have gone about we are very anxious to know Something of N York especially Since the death of Mr [DeWitt] Clinton on that, there is Some Speculation here, You will See in the [Richmond *Constitutional*] Whigg of today a pretty accurate acct of the condition of things in Virginia—The report of the committee on the late message of the Governor [William B. Giles] will be attempted to be taken up to day—I have this moment Seen a Substitute by one of the Jackson members who I perceive is fast coming over, which I would rather Should not be adopted at this time, though it contains much more correct principles than the report—as I think that will work a greater change in the public mind, what does Mr [John]

Randolph mean by so often referring to your letter to me[1][,] the public has Seen it, does he mean it to be understood that it has not been Seen—I conclude the latter, which ought to be put right

ALS. InU.   1. Brooke and Clay apparently thought Randolph's reference was to Clay to Brooke, January 28, 1825 [4:45-6], a letter which had been published in 1825 and was reprinted on March 28, 1828; but cf. below, Brooke to Clay, March 8, 1828. For Randolph's remarks on the matter in the House on February 1, 1828, see *Register of Debates*, 20 Cong., 1 Sess., 1324-5, 1332.

From ALEXANDER H. EVERETT, Madrid, no. 97, February 21, 1828. Transmits copy of a note to Manuel Gonzales Salmon in reply to the latter's communication on a proposed Convention of Indemnities [4:299-300]. States: "The refusal of this Government to allow the claims of the United States, given as an answer to a proposal to negotiate upon those of the two Governments on each other which had already been accepted, was grossly irregular in form as well as unjust in substance." Asserts that he perceives the "real object" of the Spanish Government to be delay and that he feels that he can prevent delay most effectively by treating the subject as fully as possible at every opportunity. Notes that he has argued "that there is no doubtful question of law or politics involved in the claims, and that they are founded in various irregular and illegal proceedings of the Spanish authorities for which the Government is incontestibly responsible." Continues: "But as it may appear hereafter that controverted points of public law are nevertheless involved in some few of the cases, I have taken care to avoid any implied admission of the pretensions of Spain in regard to them, by shewing incidentally that the trade with the Independent Provinces on the Gulf of Mexico had been opened to neutrals by various public acts as well of the authorities in America as of the Metropolitan Government; and that the pretended blockade of all the ports on the Gulf declared by Genl. [Francisco Tomas] Morales was in every respect illegal." Expresses the opinion that the Spanish Government will use some "frivolous pretence" to create a new delay. LS. DNA, RG59, Dip. Disp., Spain, vol. 28 (M31, R29). Received May 8, 1828.

To COUNT CHARLES JULES DE MENOU, February 21, 1828. Requests "to be informed whether there has been any recent imposition of duties on American produce or American Vessels, admitted in the island of Martinique or whether there has been any alteration in the Ordonance of the King of France [Charles X] of the fifth day of February 1826." Copy. DNA, RG59, Notes to Foreign Ministers and Consuls, vol. 3, p. 441. (M38, R3).

From ROBERT PORTER & SON [JOHN], Wilmington, February 21, 1828. Report that the "Delaware Watchman [*American Watchman and Delaware Advertiser*]" no longer exists and that the editor of the "Patriot [*Delaware Patriot and American Watchman*]," its successor, "is a declared enemy" of the administration, who has stated that he does not want the contract to publish the laws, but if it is offered he will accept it "and continue to abuse the government." Adds that "a complete system of exclusion [has] been adopted here by the *opposition*, relative to the 'Delaware [State] Journal,'" which the Porters publish, and that this boycott is aided by the Collector and the Attorney General. Notes that "even our Sheriff refuses to insert his Sales," although the Delaware *State Journal* has "nearly as many subscribers (distinct persons) as both the papers (Oppositionists,) in which he publishes." ALS. DNA, RG59, P. and D. of L.

From CHARLES R. VAUGHAN, Washington. No. 1 of this date, February 21, 1828. Acknowledges receipt of Clay's note of February 18 "communicating the decision of the Government relative to the Negroes seized by the Collector of Customs [William Pinkney] at Key West." States his refusal to acquiesce in the contention that the capture was illegal because it was made within the territorial jurisdiction of the United States. Argues that the United States and Great Britain are both engaged in the suppression of the slave trade and that "their operations, in future, cannot but be embarrassed by the declaration, that the pursuit of their common Enemy, the Dealer in Slaves, must cease, whenever he shall place himself within the territorial jurisdiction of one of the Powers not actually engaged in the pursuit." Reminds Clay that Lieutenant Edward Holland was authorized only to detain the Spanish brig and to take it in for adjudication before a mixed commission; also, that because the vessel was "well armed and manned," it could legally be detained prior to the "Action which left both Vessels upon the Rocks." Adds that the Negroes taken off the wreck by the British officer "may be fairly considered as on their way to adjudication before a Mixed Commission, when they were seized by the Collector at Key West." Expresses satisfaction with Clay's assurance that the slaves will be ultimately returned to their native country whether they be held by the United States or delivered up to Great Britain. Declines the Secretary's offer to "detain the Negroes for a reasonable time, should it be thought adviseable to obtain the decision of a Court of Justice," since "he has not any instructions in what manner to proceed." Is satisfied, however, that "duties are not believed to be legally chargeable upon Goods taken from the Spanish," but expresses regret "that a censure is called for, upon the conduct of Lieutenant Holland" because he does not believe that the Act of Congress of March 3, 1825, applies "to prize goods on board one of His Majesty's Ships of War." LS. DNA, RG59, Notes from British Legation, vol. 15 (M50, R15).

From CHARLES R. VAUGHAN, Washington. No. 2 of this date, February 21, 1828. Acknowledges receipt of Clay's note of February 18 regarding the salvage of the British schooner *Nimble*. Promises to transmit the note and its enclosures "to the Admiral [Charles E. Fleeming] commanding His Majesty's Naval Force in the West Indies . . . in order that the question of Salvage may be adjusted as soon as possible, if it has not been already submitted to the Tribunal established at Pensacola." LS. DNA, RG59, Notes from British Legation, vol. 15 (M50, R15).

   In a letter to Clay, May 9, 1828, Vaughan encloses documents relating to the salvage of the *Nimble*, pointing out that the reason for the delay in settling the claim of the American seamen has been their unwillingness to accept "a fair or reasonable sum," or submit their case to a competent tribunal. Announces that the British navy will send a vessel to Key West to investigate the matter further and to attempt to work out a settlement. *Ibid.*

To FRANCIS T. BROOKE   Washington, February 22, 1828
Your favor of yesterday is received. Genl. [Peter B.] Porter had been ill and absent from Albany. He had returned however and I have a late letter from him.[1] All accounts concur that the political effect of Mr. [DeWitt] Clinton's death will be favorable to the Administration; and intelligence generally from that State [N.Y.], especially from the Western portion of it is very cheering.

I really do not know (and who does?) what Mr. R. [John Randolph] means by his allusion to my letter addressed to you [4:45-6].[2] I do not think there is any necessity for you or myself saying any thing on that subject. As to his statement of a conversation which he represents himself to have held with me, he has been so contradictory in the H. about it, that, although my first impression, when I heard of it, was to have authorized a counter statement, my friends think it is not worthy of such a notice. If I take any of it, I shall do it in some other way, and at a future day.

I have a curious but very friendly letter from Mr. [William H.] Crawford,[3] in which he says he never countenanced the calumny against me; that he would have voted as I did between Jackson & Adams &c. I have answered it[4] in the most friendly terms, combating however some of his opinions.

The enquiry in the Senate of K. has terminated with the adoption of resolutions friendly to the Admon & myself.[5] My friends there claim a decided & triumphant victory.

ALS. KyU.   1. February 22, 1828.   2. Brooke to Clay, February 21, 1828.   3. February 4, 1828.   4. February 18, 1828.   5. Blair to Clay, January 22, 1828.

To NICHOLAS BIDDLE   Washington, February 22, 1828
There is $7681.50 standing to the credit of Bishop [Philander] Chase, Mr. [Bezaleel] Wills and myself, for the use of the Theological Seminary of the Protestant Episcopal Church in the Diocese of Ohio [5:717-8; 6:358-9, 707-08]. Whilst it remains there it is unproductive. We are not prepared at this time to decide what stock it would be expedient to invest it permanently in, and are therefore, anxious to make a temporary arrangement, in the mean time to secure some interest or dividend upon the money. We have concluded to take the liberty of requesting the favor of you to convert it into some stock of the Government of the U. States which you may deem best, and for that purpose transmit the enclosed check.[1] We have entire confidence in your judgment as to the stock which it will be most advisable to purchase. We should be glad from the benevolence and piety of the object of the capital, if the operation could be performed without expense; but on that subject we submit to whatever you may think right and proper. Please to have the stock taken in the corporate name of "the Theological Seminary of the Protestant Epis-

copal Church, in the Diocese of Ohio." Bishop Chase will remain in this city until we can have the pleasure of hearing from you, and we will thank you to transmit the evidence of stock, under cover, to H. Clay.

LS. DLC-HC (DNA, M212, R9). Signed also by Philander Chase.   1. Not found.

From JOHN CUTHBERT, Hamburg, February 22, 1828. Reports that the convention [6:1370-1] between the United States and the Hanseatic Republics "was yesterday ratified by the Senate and Freemen of Hamburg without one dissenting voice, and so soon as the ratified copy's are received from Lubeck and Bremen, the whole will be forwarded to Mr. [Vincent] Rumpf [*sic*, Rumpff] to be exchanged at Washington." ALS. DNA, RG59, Cons. Disp., Hamburg, vol. 3 (M-T211, R3). Received May 1, 1828.

From WILLIAM B. LAWRENCE, London, no. 24, February 22, 1828. Summarizes the recent budgetary debates in Parliament and repeats his earlier opinions on the causes of the collapse of the Goderich Cabinet. Reports the news that the Turkish government has taken a stronger line with Russia on Greek affairs, but that the new Wellington government has still made "no determination . . . as to Turkish affairs." Transmits a copy of "Bouchette's [*sic*, Bouchett] Topography of Canada," published in 1815, a work which Clay may find useful "on account of the North Eastern Boundary question." Adds that the book, as well as an accompanying map by the same author, who was the Surgeon General of Lower Canada, was "almost immediately suppressed" following publication because they could be "construed favorable to our claims." Reports that when Albert Gallatin was in London "all our efforts to purchase the book were unavailing and only one copy of the map could, after great difficulty, be procured." ALS. DNA, RG59, Dip. Disp., Great Britain, vol. 35 (M30, R31). Received April 2, 1828. The book by Joseph Bouchett (1774–1841) was *A Topographical Description of the Province of Lower Canada, with Remarks Upon Upper Canada, and on the Relative Connexion of Both Provinces With the United States of America.* London, 1815.

From JOEL R. POINSETT, Mexico, no. 117, February 22, 1828. Transmits, by Edward T. Tayloe, a Treaty of Limits, signed January 12, and a Treaty of Amity, Commerce, and Navigation, signed February 14. Notes that, in the latter, "all the alterations suggested by the Senate of the United States, have been introduced, except that in relation to the duration of the Treaty." Explains that he did not insist upon that alteration because the fourth article of the Treaty provides that, at the end of six years, "such important points as may require revision and a special convention, shall be taken into consideration." Reports that he preferred a term of five to nine years for carrying into effect the fifth and sixth articles but that the Mexican plenipotentiaries, Sebastian Camacho and Jose Ignacio Esteva, objected on the ground "that the term of ten years had been adopted in all their Treaties, where the principle of perfect reciprocity had been introduced," that such an alteration might jeopardize ratification by the Mexican Congress, and that a statement of term was unnecessary, "as the instant the principle went into operation with one nation, it would of course be extended to us." ALS. DNA, RG59, Dip. Disp., Mexico, vol. 3 (M97, R4). Received April 16, 1828; also in *ASPFR*, 6:948.

The Treaty of Limits was ratified by Mexico on April 28 and by the United States on April 30; but because these delays made it impossible to exchange ratifications on May 12, as stipulated in the treaty, an additional article had to be written and the treaty re-submitted to the United States Senate. In the meantime, Mexican objections to the proposed Treaty of Amity, Commerce, and Navigation led to its rejection and re-negotiation. Both it and the additional article revising the date for exchange of ratifications on the Treaty of Limits were finally signed on April 5, 1831, and became effective one year later. Miller, *Treaties*, 3:405, 411–5, 599–628. See also Poinsett to Clay, Jan. 8, 1828.

From THOMAS L. L. BRENT, Lisbon, February 23, 1828. Reports that the arrival of Miguel, on February 22, "passed off very quietly" despite apprehensions that a "disturbance" might ensue and that tomorrow Miguel will "take the oath to the Constitution before the Cortes." Notes that the British vessels which brought Miguel, plus others, "are destined to take away the british troops," with three regiments going to the Mediterranean and another to England. ALS. DNA, RG59, Dip. Disp., Portugal, vol. 7 (M43, R6). Received April 28, 1828.

From ROBERT CAMPBELL, Genoa, February 23, 1828. Notes an increase in tonnage, though not in the value of imports at this port. Calls attention to the exportation of Italian hemp, which "is found" superior to the Russian and which is valued at about $130 per ton. ALS. DNA, RG59, Cons. Dip., Genoa, vol. 1 (M–T64, R1). Received April 29, 1828.

From ALBERT GALLATIN, New York, February 23, 1828. Transmits "a general Statement of all the evidence," which, with the exception of extracts from the Arguments of the Agents [William C. Bradley; Ward Chipman] and from the reports of the Commissioners appointed in pursuance of the fifth Article of the Treaty of Ghent [Cornelius P. Van Ness; Thomas Barclay], might be useful "to lay before the Arbiter." Notes that "the extracts aforesaid" may be added to "the Statements" at any time. Remarks that he has "inserted in the accompanying Statement, not only all the new evidence which the investigation of the subject had suggested, but also all that, which, on perusing the arguments, reports and documents of the late Commission," he had considered "applicable to the question." Notes it is in reference to making extracts from "the Arguments and reports" that he has "suggested the propriety of directing a clerk to run through the whole and to make a list of all that is quoted as evidence." Suggests those "volumes to which the clerk employed may confine his attention. . . ." Observes that "the accompanying Statement . . . is a first rough copy," but says his observations "are sufficient to point out all that is to be done, the general object of the evidence, and the several questions which may arise respecting the evidence which may be omitted, that which ought to be communicated, and that of which authentic copies should be demanded." Adds: "I think that this Statement will satisfy you that, with the assistance I may give and in the manner in which I have proposed to give it, there will be no difficulty in performing all that is necessary to be done during the course of this year." Notes, further, that "it will not be necessary to transmit . . . a copy of the accompanying Statement to the States of Vermont, New Hampshire, and New York. An application to Vermont would be a matter only of Courtesy. What should be communicated to, and asked from the other two States is very limited and pointed out in the observations on the evidence." Requests, in a postscript, that certain published documents be sent to him. ALS. DNA, RG76, Northeast Boundary (KyU., Special Roll, frames 45-6). Copy in NHi–Gallatin Papers (MR15). The enclosure, entitled "Evidence respecting the North Eastern Boundary of the United States with Observations," covers 12 manuscript pages (frames 47-53).

From FRANCIS JOHNSON   Bowling Green, Ky., February 23, 1828
Your favor of the 6 Inst was Recd on my return home, on the night before last. You are before this apprized that I left here very unexpectedly on the second of Feby for Frankfort. The address [6:1394-6] was not then published, & I trusted to a friend here to have Doctr Jones' & Mr Keel's certificates added.[1] The one had been obtained before I left home, the other I obtained today. The pamphlet having been published without these I send them enclosed to you with a letter addressed to _____[2] To be filled up. I had first contemplated addressing it to the Editor of the [Washington *Daily National*] journal—for publication together with the statements of Doctr Jones and Mr Keel. I submit to your discretion what direction to give them—and to fill up the address. Perhaps you would prefer its being addressed to yourself—if so, it will be only necessary to strike out after the words "refered to" on the second line "in Mr. Clay's address" and insert "in your address"—or perhaps you had rather publish the statements without my letter: You will take such course as your prefer—the only reason which could induce me to suppose any note from me would be at all proper, is that in my letter to Doctr [Tobias] Watkins of 22d May [6:1394-6], I stated that I did not "think we ought to believe Genl Jackson had made such charges without good proof"—when the Genls letter appeared declaring the Origin was at his own fire side [6:718-9, 763-79, 839-40, 1394-6] &c—then for the first time, did I hear of his having made these charges here; Mr Keel I believe was the first person, who mentioned it to me—and expressed his astonishment, that the Genl. should deny he had made the charge at his fire side only.
   The statements are not precisely the same and the reason is, they were different conversations, for it seems he took occasion to repeat the charge of Bargain &c, frequently—shortly after the publication of the Genls letter of the 18th. July [6:839-40, 1394-6], to Mr Trotter, who wrote a letter to Mr [Charles] Hammond for publication, a copy of which I have seen detailing particuarly by the Genls conversation, giving, his

116

manner &c but it has not been published—Mr Trotter is not now here—when he returns I shall get a statement from him—those sent however will answer the purpose of establishing the fact.

As I said to you in my letter from Frankfort, our friends have great confidence of success in the state, and they appear to be impressed with the necessity of the utmost exertion—If proper exertions are made throughout the state by our friends we must succeed—We have undoubtedly gained friends in this quarter, But the change is yet slow and few—Yet I think it must be steady—The prospects in Virginia, will have some affect here—and those of Pennsa is cheering—all that is necessary here, is exertion—If the Report of the retrenchment Committee,[3] shall be as it, cannot otherwise be, favorable to this Admn—it will help us—The Tariff Bill as expected, is by no Means satisfactory—Cotton Bagging is omitted—The duties on course wollens seems insufficient—It will answer but little purpose to exclude the raw Hemp, when the Manufactured article is permitted at low duties—The duty on Iron, which is becoming a great article in this quarter of the state, is put on proportion to that on Raw Hemp—Such as it is, I do presume the Southern gentlemen intend not to pass it—

A few nights ago on my way home, I lodged in the neighborhood of Mr [Thomas] Chilton's father [The Rev. Thomas J. Chilton] & relations—I was there informed his relations said he had gone over to the administration, and was sending your pamphlets into his district—but I immagine it is a mistake—The *man* [Joel Yancey] from this district has dealt largely in [Samuel D.] Ingham's pamphlets—The [Washington *United States*] Telegraph and the New York enquirer—

As to whether I shall be a candidate for the Legislature depends pretty much on circumstances—In the first place I do not wish to come in collision with any of my friends for the office—if they will all offer the truck I shall take it—if not, I had perhaps better remain out of the Canvass—But on the other hand, believing as I do that I can unite more votes than any other, it is a great enducement, to the Service of the Cause for me to come out—Upon this I shall determine in the course of next week. The Circuit Court commences on Monday—

Pardon me, for repeating my solicitude that you should pay especial attention to your health—I pray God that we may live to triumph over Your enemies—

ALS. DLC-HC (DNA, M212, R3). Endorsed by Clay: "with statements of Genl Jackson's conversations at Bowling Green K." Letter marked "Private." 1. The statements of John Keel and Cuthbert T. Jones were subsequently published in Clay, *A Supplement to the Address . . . to the Public*, 7–8. Cf., below, June 10, 1828. 2. Name of addressee not supplied. 3. Brooke to Clay, January 31, 1828.

From WILLIAM B. LAWRENCE, London, no. 25, February 23, 1828. Encloses an "Order in Council, dated 13th instant, and first published in the Gazette of last evening," which "extends to Pictou and Sydney, in the province of Nova Scotia, the provision respecting free ports contained in the act of 1825 [5:629–32] entitled 'An act to regulate the trade of the British possessions abroad.'" ALS. DNA, RG59, Dip. Disp., Great Britain, vol. 35 (M30, R31). Received April 2, 1828.

From FRANCIS T. BROOKE   Richmond, February 25, 1828

The intelligence from K[entucky] is truly pleasing[1] I hope there is no doubt that the lower house will concur in the resolution, it will have a good effect in Virginia, I am Surprised after what has been Said of the opinions of Mr [William H.] Crawford that he Should have written you at all, and much gratified that he too gives the lie to the calumny—[2] would he have any objection to this being known, or are you at liberty to permit me to Speak of it, I wish when you write Genl [Peter B.] Porter you would mention my letter to him and its object—it may have miscarried—there is nothing new here [William B.] Giles message as you See by the papers has produced much consternation among the opposition[3] and its effect will be very favorable to us—the legislature would have risen to day probably but they have laid hold of a Silly communication from Chancellor Taylor and will waste Some time on it, he has behaved very badly but I do not believe they will fix any conduct on him of so Serious a character as to be noticed by impeachment, but there is no knowing what they may do—[4]

ALS. InU.   1. Blair to Clay, January 22, 1828.   2. Crawford to Clay, February 4, 1828.   3. Baird to Clay, February 18, 1828.   4. Creed Taylor, chancellor of the Virginia Superior Court, had addressed a letter to the House of Delegates to explain why he had not obtained from his clerk the security bond required by a recent Virginia law. The letter prompted an investigation of Taylor's conduct from the date of his appointment to the bench. After this investigation, which revealed no intentional misconduct, the issue was recommitted to the Committee for Courts of Justice. There it lay when the session of the legislature ended. Lynchburg *Virginian*, March 3, 1828. For Taylor, who continued as chancellor until 1831, see *DAB*.

From THEODORE W. CLAY   Lexington, February 25, 1828

I should have acknowledged earlier the super added favor you have conferred on me, by the money you let me have. The truth is I have been and am but an indifferent financier; this is on the fair way I trust to be remedied. I shall use it to the best advantage, & thank God my wants are just at this moment to be gratified by it.

We have no news cince the close of the legislature, & its extraordinary & absurd proceedings;[1] unavoidable however to the better part. We think the J[ack]son party is loosing ground constantly. Genl. [Thomas] Metcalfe whose character & course of life I admire, will beat [William T.] Barry; but with a considerable contest. I am now of opinion myself, that he will find a strong weapon to use by remaining if not to the last hour, towards the end of the Session of Congress. There is not much danger of apathy on the part of his friends: Tho' B. & his adherents are busy huckstering about their retail political squibs and small ware. I observe with pleasure, they are bitter & waspish to an extreme. Our friends here are warm & animated. Whilst my studies, perhaps erroneously, have been such, & my turn & habit of mind is such, that I, exercising without reserve the freedom of opinion & of speech, cannot sit down under the idea that such men as are offered, shall preside over the destinies of my country, I have yet the prudence neither to say nor to do any thing which shall not be wholly upon my own responsibility, and entirely my own. Much as I am devotd to you, I trust you will ratify the feeling, that were any final decision to be made, I could entertain and manifest that fervent attachment without doing any thing which in my opinion would hazard or compromit my coutry. I am a free citizen, of a free country, bound by its laws, owing it my services if they can be of any use, and interested as much as another. I feel it my right & my duty to raise my still small voice, to avoid what I think would be a destructive course for her; I shall therefore push the war into the enemy's camp, and proclaim my bold & solemn protest with my reasons, on all decent & proper occasions. I perceive the govt. have been grossly misrepresented & abused by my little trip to the south. The contemptible organ of the bankrupt party here has recd. from W[ashing]ton no doubt his acct which is designedly false;[2] but I shall adopt more potent means for giving the lie to its shameful falsehoods, than by degrading myself to a controversy with such poltroons. But I weary you I fear A little about myself, & I will commend me to my dear parents with an overflowing heart. I have been treated generously by your friends here. I love the place, & shall not leave it. Many of our citizens are more worthy than I had any idea; & I fear they are in danger of misplacing kindness on your account. Mrs [Mary Austin] Holley is here & is I think an excellent woman. I have recd pleasure from her society. She lives with her son-in law young [William M.] Brand, a good young man. I think that family a most worthy one.

I addressed some of our citizens the 22nd Inst, & they have been kind enough to think better of me than I deserve—I wish I was safely moored into the happy haven of matrimony. I think my expenses are above my capital stock but I do think I could be of more use to my country & certainly more happy myself, if I were established. Ashland is not, I am certain doing as much as it could if one who entered more fully into your interest & its, were in its occupation. My health is very good, but I do fear that it will never enable me to undergo the steady, constant task of reading law, & travelling from point to point under all circumstances without fail. I have just thought in common with one or two particular friends that a guerrilla paper here such as we have had before, tho' not to interefere with Smith can do good.[3] Patrick Henry protested agst the influence of Washington, from laudable motives tho' without application in that particular place. The bagging business is going on with alacrity. Mr. Scott[,] Henley & myself have just thought upon some articles of agreement to be entered into,[4] Such will be submitted to you on your arrival if not before. Scott advanced the capital of his private funds so far. Not liking to check on that of the estate, without hearing from you. The articles are entirely equalising to us all. On your part a vote by yr. ag[en]t in all matters. Scott. $150 for Clerksship &c Henley for overseeing &c $160. I think these moderate myself.

To last for 5yrs, neither to have the liberty to retire or To draw any stock without the consent of the rest or to do any act; & in case of death, the survivors to make reasonable provision for decedents, interests, or to continue if meet.

In case one of the partners advance more than his part by consent however, he is entitled to interest 6 per cent. $6000 to be advd by you & Scott. S. has gone on & advanced—should a less sum be advanced by one or the other, as yet no provision on our pact; & from what you said you would not immediately advance $6000, an interest of 6 per cent allowed to half the difference advanced by the others I should thank you to attend to this as your opinion will decide us. They are equal and entirely safe to all.

Give my love to my Mother, & tell her that we are all very anxious she should come out this summer. . . . PS. I can with confidence assure that we will be equal to the management of the concern; & could yield with great advantage a greater capital. To own the labor & to save the rents &c—Outgoings without any incomings.

ALS. DLC–TJC (DNA, M212, R10). 1. Blair to Clay, January 22, 1828. 2. The Lexington *Kentucky Gazette* had charged Theodore W. Clay with receiving more than $1,200 as a messenger to Mexico, and with going there on the same vessel as John Sergeant, one of the ministers to the Panama Congress. On February 21, the Washington *United States Telegraph* repeated the *Gazette* story and stated that the allegation had circulated in Washington "some weeks past." The *Telegraph,* although expressing indignation at "$1205.50 for 107 days!!!," conceded that Clay and Sergeant had taken passage on different vessels. See above, 6:307. 3. Thomas Smith was editor of the Lexington *Kentucky Reporter.* The earlier "guerrilla paper" was probably the Lexington *Kentucky Whig,* a weekly which ran from September 22, 1825 to September 14, 1826. The proposed one was the Lexington *Anti–Jackson Bulletin and Message of Truth,* a weekly which began publication on August 30, 1828, and shut down after the presidential election with issue 8. 4. Scott to Clay, January 11, 1828.

From JOSEPH KENT, Annapolis, Md., February 25, 1828. Informs Clay that he has no further interest in being appointed Treasurer of the United States. Thinks "better political effect" would probably stem from the appointment of someone from New York or Pennsylvania, rather than a man from Maryland; but cautions that "Maryland has received nothing from Mr. Adams that I recollect during his administration, whilst N. York & Pennsylvania has been repeatedly favoured as well as Va." Says he has heard it rumored that the Treasury post has already been offered "to an individual [William Clark] but little known, and who has not been able to sustain himself at home or who has not subserved in the remotest degree the interests of the President." ALS. DLC–HC (DNA, M212, R3). Letter marked "(Private & confidential)." William Clark, recently ousted Treasurer of the state of Pennsylvania, was appointed Treasurer of the United States and served in that capacity from June, 1828 to November, 1829. See *BDAC.*

From LEVI WOODBURY, February 25, 1828. Transmits, by direction of the Commerce Committee, a U.S. Senate resolution, adopted February 25, 1828, which instructed the Committee on Commerce "to enquire whether any and if any, what legislative measures ought to be adopted in consequence of the French Ordinance of 5h. February, A. D. 1826 [6:301], regulating trade with the Islands of Guadaloupe and Martinique." Asks Clay to provide the historical background the Committee will need to guide it in its legislative task. AN. DNA, RG59, Misc. Letters (M179, R6).

From BARON PAUL DE KRUDENER, *ca.* February 26, 1828. Reports that he has heard of the publication, by Isaac Hill, of a pamphlet "which has made some noise in the debates of Congress, and which seems to be destined to attract more notice than is desirable." Notes that in addition to attacks against the Administration, it contains "calumnies ... insulting to the memory of the late Emperor Alexander [I]." Enquires whether the American Government "has no means within its reach to suppress such a scandal, and to lead to the punishment of those who render themselves guilty of it." States that the pamphlet "is of a nature calculated to spread through every city" of the United States "odious falsehoods concerning the character of" Alexander and that these "calumnies" are compatible "neither with the justice due to the dead, nor with the benevolent feelings which unite the Russian and American nations, nor with the respect which, on every principle of civilization, the two nations reciprocally owe to each other's Governments." Points out that "Switzerland is as republican and as free as America, still no such atrocious imputations could be published there." Adds that he must report the "libel" to the Russian Government, which may give him "some directions on the subject" and consequently asks Clay for "explanations ... as to the nature of the satisfaction which it might be practicable to obtain." N, in French, with trans. in State Dept. file. DNA, RG59, Notes from Russian Legation, vol. 2 (M39, R2). Headed: "Verbal Note."

The "calumny" was that while serving as Minister to Russia, Adams had supplied one of his household servants, Martha Godfrey, for the Tsar's carnal appetites. The charge appeared in the pamphlet, *Brief Sketch of the Life, Character and Services of Major General Andrew Jackson, by a Citizen of New England*. Concord, N. H., 1828. See further, Samuel F. Bemis, *John Quincy Adams and the Union* (New York, 1965), 147. The pamphlet was likely written for Isaac Hill by Jonathan Russell.

To FRANCIS T. BROOKE   Washington, February 27, 1828
Your favor of the 25h. inst is recd. The H. of R. of K. having been limited to an adjournment on a fixed day [February 13], when the resolutions came to it from the Senate, there was not time to act on them, and it adjourned without taking them up.[1] My friends there think we have gained a great victory. It will possibly lead to some further publications that may render it more decisive. The general ticket has passed;[2] so that the entire vote of Kentucky may, I think, be now anticipated.[3]

Mr. [William H.] Crawford's letter to me [February 4] has been seen by several of my friends and has been spoken of, I understand, generally in this City. I should regret that the subject should get into the Newspapers, but with that exception I do not know that I ought to object to its being mentioned. It is not *confidential;* and in my opinion does Mr. C. as much credit as it does me.

I will, when I write to Genl. [Peter B.] Porter, express to him the information that you have recd. no answer to your letter.

ALS. KyU.   1. Blair to Clay, January 22, 1828.   2. Clay to Brooke, January 18, 1828.   3. 6:747–9.

From JAMES BROWN, Paris, No. 80, February 27, 1828. Reports that he has taken up with the new Foreign Minister, the Count de La Ferronnays, successor to the Baron de Damas, the subject [6:1392] of his letter to Damas of December 19, 1827, in which he had expressed his hope that the "negotiation for indemnity," which had been "unexpectedly arrested by the interposition on the part of France of her claim under the 8th. article of the Louisiana treaty [3:382-3; 6:1013-4]" might be resumed. Asked, further, that "the proposal which I had made, to submit the question under that article to arbitration," also be discussed. Explained to the Foreign Minister the view of President Adams that France's delaying tactics have worked "a grievous hardship" on American citizens "unjustly deprived of their property by acts of the French authorities." Count Ferronnays responded that having been long out of the country, while serving as Ambassador to Russia, he would need time to study these issues. Having done this, he would "give me his definitive answer." Brown notes that he "cannot suppress a hope that we shall meet in the diposition of the present ministry, a more favorable course of proceeding . . . than we experienced from the last." Hopes, too, that the new Foreign Minister will be more reasonable, and "will not unnecessarily retard the settlement of this by insisting that we shall surrender our rights under the Louisiana treaty" in order to obtain satisfaction. ALS. DNA, RG59, Dip. Disp., France, vol. 23 (M34, R26). Received April 26, 1828. For Pierre–Louis–Auguste Ferron, Comte de La Ferronnays, see Hoefer, *NBG*.

Article VIII of the Louisiana Cession Treaty of 1803 read: "In future and forever after the expiration of the twelve years, the ships of France shall be treated upon the footing of the most favoured nations in the ports above mentioned." Article VII provided that "for a space of twelve years" French and Spanish ships would be admitted to the "port of New Orleans, and in all other legal ports of entry within the ceded territory, in the same manner as the ships of the United States coming directly from France or Spain, or any of their colonies, without being subject to any other or greater duty on merchandise, or other or greater tonnage than that paid by the citizens of the United States."

From THOMAS McGIFFIN   Washington, Pa., February 27, 1828
Having behaved consistently well during this winter in not troubling you with more than one letter—I am inclined to risk another—I have two objects in view in writing you at this time—*one* which my judgment and feelings approve and the other not having the sanction of either—

In the first place I again request of you to say whether it will comport with your feelings & convenience to give your old friends in this place an opportunity of paying the usual tribute of respect to you as you return to Kentucky? And if so when we may expect you? There is but one opinion or desire by your friends here upon this subject—Notwithstanding the late successful Tornado of Jacksonism we still are anxious to give our Testimony to the worth of and [illeg. word] respect for you & our personal devotion to you—If you shall agree to stay a day or two with us & cannot now fix the precise time you will be good enough to give us that precise day as early as you can—Our friends at Union Town as also at Wheeling are anxious to have a similar opportunity—The main object is in relation to my son Nathaniel's being placed at West Point—[1] This subject I had determined never to renew but his continued and anxious importunities induce me to name the matter to you—that if contrary to

122

any expectation or belief on my part the attainment of his desires be now practicable, it may be done—He is still under 18 years—has graduated at our College,[2] but is too young to commence the study of any profession—The fact is his head is so full of this project that he cannot be induced to *quiet* himself, or give it up untill it be certainly established that he cannot succeed—which of course will be after the 4th of March

ALS. DLC–HC (DNA, M212, R3). Addressed to Clay at Washington, D.C.   1. Nathaniel W. McGiffin was admitted to the U.S. Military Academy in 1830 but was not graduated. USMA, *Register*, 186.   2. Washington College, now Washington and Jefferson College.

From CHARLES R. VAUGHAN, Washington, *ca.* February 27, 1828. Acknowledges receipt of Clay's note of February 20 and its enclosures. Challenges Clay's contention that the disputed territory came into the possession of the United States by the Treaty of 1783. Argues that the limits of the United States "are still undefined . . . and . . . remain to be settled by a Reference to a friendly Sovereign [6:1100–01]," and that "the Sovereignty and Jurisdiction of the disputed Territory, rests with Great Britain, until that Portion of it designated in the Treaty of 1783, shall have been finally set apart from the British Possessions, as belonging to the United States."

Recalls that in 1783 New Brunswick was not a separate province, but part of Nova Scotia. Concedes that "on the West of Nova Scotia some Difficulty might have arisen" regarding the boundary between it and Massachusetts because of the uncertainty of the limits of Acadia, which France had ceded to Great Britain in 1713. Disputes, however, the "Pretensions of Massachusetts, to the Territory upon the Madawaska, which lies to the North of St. John's, and falls into that River at a Distance from its Source," because it is still uncertain whether, once the "North West Angle of Nova Scotia shall have been determined," the boundary between the United States and Great Britain "will intersect any Portion of the Madawaska Territory." Argues that British occupation in the meantime will have no effect on the final settlement of the dispute, by strengthening the British claim or by invalidating American rights under the Treaty of 1783. Reminds Clay that Maine's census of the Madawaska region in 1820 became the subject of a remonstrance by the British Government.

Denies that John Baker has been treated severely, but promises to transmit Clay's note to the British Government and to the Lieutenant Governor of New Brunswick, Sir Howard Douglas. States that the settlers in the Aroostook settlement will remain under British jurisdiction until the dispute is settled. Complains that in all the newspapers he has seen from the State of Maine, the "disputed territory is invariably represented as "Part of that State." LS. DNA, Notes from British Legation, vol. 15 (M50, R15). Dated "February 1828"; received February 28. Also in *ASPFR*, 6:1016–7.

To THURLOW WEED   Washington, *ca.* February 27, 1828
I hasten to acknowledge the receipt of your obliging letter of the 29th ult. and to return you my thanks for the highly interesting information

which it contains. All our late accounts from N. York are most cheering. Those from Kentucky are also very encouraging. There will be fought (in the month of August next) the first great Presidential battle of the current year.[1] Any favorable demonstrations in N. York will have much influence in K.

The statements in the papers respecting a late letter which I have rec'd from Mr. [William H.] Crawford[2] are true, but I do not want at this time any thing published about it as coming from me.

Copy, NRU. The manuscript of this letter was at one time in possession of the late Mrs. Thomas G. Spencer, a descendant of Thurlow Weed. The present locus of the manuscript is unknown. The typed copy of the letter carries the date, February 7, 1828. On the basis of internal and other evidence, however, the editors think a date late in February is more likely.   1. The Thomas Metcalfe vs. William T. Barry gubernatorial contest. See Robertson to Clay, January 19, 1828.   2. Crawford to Clay, February 4, 1828.

From FRANCIS T. BROOKE   Richmond, February 28, 1828
I have received answers to my Circular from Mr Madison & Mr Monroe which you will See in the Whig next week,[1] they decline to accept the appointmt as was apprehended, though with the expression of Sentiments if not perverted rather flattering to the friends of the administration—The fact is, that they have used an expression Susceptable of construction more favorable to genl Jackson than was intended, they Speak of the high estimation in which they held both of the candidates which may be interpreted now and not then as was intended—It is painful to me ever to missemploy your time, but I must request the favour of you if you have any message for England or France to take into consideration the claims of a friend and relative, it is Lieut L N Carter[2] of the Marine Corps he is anxious to fill Such an appointmt and you know his qualifications for it, in making th[e] request I beg you will not understand me as imputing that it is to embarrass you in the Smallest degree in the discharge of that portion of your duty which must be so arduous all I mean to say is that it will be very gratifying to me, if it accords with that duty—

ALS. DLC-HC (DNA, M212, R3). Endorsed by Clay: "Messrs. Madison & Monroe decline to be Electors."   1. For Brooke's circular of February 8 and the responses to it by Madison and Monroe, both dated February 22, see *Niles' Register* (March 8, 1828), 34:25-6. The *Register* reprinted the correspondence from the Richmond *Constitutional Whig* of March 1.   2. Landon N. Carter entered the Marine Corps in 1824 and rose to the rank of captain shortly before his death in 1847. Callahan, *Navy List,* 683.

From JAMES BROWN, Paris, no. 81, February 28, 1828. Notes that he has been out of the U.S. for four years and away from "private concerns" that need his "attention," and that his health "although much improved is not yet completely re-established." Asks permission to resign his post as U.S. Minister and leave Paris on September 15. ALS. DNA, RG59, Dip. Disp., France, vol. 23 (M34, R26). Received April 26, 1828.

From JAMES BROWN   Paris, France February 28, 1828
You may recollect that some months ago I expressed to you in a private letter [6:1027-9] my willingness to leave my present situation provided it could be filled by some person whose appointment would better suit

the views of the President. The kind answer I received to that letter [6:1193–5] might have induced me to remain another year in Europe had not the long indisposition of Mrs. Brown and her anxious desire to see her relations and friends induced me to take a different resolution. My private affairs also which have necessarily been neglected during my long absence from home require immediate attention. I have therefore in a letter which will go by the Packet of the 1st. March requested you to ask that the President will be pleased to give me permission to leave France on the 15 of September next. The day I have named is a period as late as would permit me to hope for a safe and comfortable passage and to reach the American Coast before the winter commences. I shall at that time be able to embark on board of one of the largest and most commodious Packets in the line commanded by a polite and practised Seaman. As it is not my intention again to return to Europe the President can decide whether it will be most eligible to appoint a Successor who shall arrive in France either before or soon after I may sail for the United States, or to name some person to be left in charge of the duties of the Legation. It is probable that with all the delay we experience in obtaining answers on propositions having in view the adjustment of our Claims I may obtain an answer to my proposal of an Arbitration [6:1013–4] and have time should it be accepted to sign a Convention for that purpose. Should it be rejected any efforts to take up our claims on a different basis may as well be made by a new Minister as by me. I earnestly entreat you to obtain for me the Presidents determination in order that I may make the necessary preparations for my voyage. I have already suffered so much by one winter voyage in coming to France that I am unwilling to undertake another at that season.

I hope the President will not experience any embarrassment in consequence of the necessity imposed on me of returning to the United States. I know that much has been said respecting the two missions to England [6:413–4] and said I believe without any other motive than that of injuring Mr Adams election.[1] My stay however has been longer than that of many other Ministers who have preceded me and certainly long enough to spend with all the economy I could use the full amount of Salary and outfit. Perhaps in the present state of European affairs it will be well always to have a Minister at this Court. It is here that every important event passing in Europe is known at the earliest period, and if I mistake not the signs of the times great events are in preparation on this Continent. The theater of them will be far removed from us at first but may be brought nearer by subsequent events.

Having mentioned the State of Mrs. Brown's health as one of my reasons for wishing to resign my charge, it may be necessary with you to be more particular on that subject. As long ago as last July she discovered a tumor on her right breast which gave her no alarm but which in a few weeks assumed such an appearance that I thought it necessary to take the advice of the ablest Physicians. They immediately prescribed a strict regimen with other remedies and recommended that she should not go to parties which would require any alteration in her dress. She has now for six months been confined at home and although some diminution in the size of the tumor is perceptible yet much time must elapse, and great care must be taken before it can be removed. In the mean time she has constant fears that it may so far increase as to prevent her from returning to her friends and country and therefore she is unwilling to prolong her stay in France. Her situation here added to her social and hospitible disposition rend[e]rs it impossible that she can enjoy quiet and repose both of which are so necessary to the re establishment of her health. My own health is not so good as it has been during the last eighteen months. I have given you this statement in *confidence* because I know that if particulars were known to her mother and sisters[2] they would immediately imagine the worst and suffer the greatest anxiety. At her mothers advanced age and after all the afflictions she has survived we must not give so severe a shock to her happiness.

The turn which the affairs in the East have taken has been as unforeseen as it is embarrassing to England and France [6:1040-4]. These powers under the impression that Turkey would yield without a struggle and that Russia might in that case be baffled in her ambitious projects have by the Treaty of the 6 July [6:780-2] tied themselves to the Emperors [Nicholas I] car and must either follow him in the Conquest of the Turks or violate their Treaty stipulations and begin a general war on the Continent. The Russians are delighted with the present state of things and their troops are rapidly accumulating on the frontier. The Turks are animated by the same hostile spirit and as [sic, are] hastening to meet them. I can hardly think it possible that war can be avoided. This war would be exceedingly unpopular in England and not much less unpopular in France. In both Countries peace is desirable, and in both the precarious standing of Ministers and the want of confidence in their talents renders war a cause[3] of the greatest alarm—Russia alone finds every thing favorable to her projects and may now consider herself as having obtained the consent of the great powers to carry them into effect.

Mr [Daniel] Sheldons health is a little improved but is still very delicate. He is exceedingly emaciated, has frequent fevers, and really only lives because he has more self command than any person I have ever known. I need not tell you how much I regret all this because he is really a man of information and talents united to much prudence and sterling integrity.

If the Count de la Fernonays [sic, Ferronnays] should agree to the basis of an arbitration, I think he will wish to have the question under the Lousiana Treaty stated as broadly as was done by Mr Hyde de Neuville in his correspondence with Mr. Adams—that is to say that France ought always to have the same privileges gratuitously for her vessels in Louisa. as are are [sic] enjoyed by other Nations in consequence of such nations having given the United States an equivalent [3:382-3]. In case of his insisting on such a submission I wish to know what answer I ought to give to the proposal. Mr de Neuville is now in favor with a majority of the Chamber and will probably be consulted on this question by this Minister of Foreign Affairs.

Should the leave to return be granted and the situation of Mrs. Brown's health be so bad as to forbid her to embark this fall, I shall probably travel to Nice or some part of Italy where she may be tranquil and enjoy a fine Climate[.] I have not had a line from you since the opening of the Session. I have however heard from some of my friends that your health had considerably improved. I have seen your statement in relation to the slanders circulated against you [6:1394-6]. To those who judged impartially it was not necessary. It appears conclusive. But will party spirit ever reason.

Will you be so good as to send a small package to Madam [Charlotte] Mentelle by some private and safe conveyance[?] It is a work in Pottery which may be of use to her husband [Augustus W. Mentelle].

Mrs. Brown joins in affectionate remembrances to Mrs. Clay who is I hope passing a pleasant winter

ALS. DLC-HC (DNA, M212, R3). Printed in *LHQ*, 24:1083-6.   1. Alleged misuse of the State Department contingency fund was a Jacksonian campaign charge leveled against Adams and Clay. *Register of Debates*, 20 Cong., 1 Sess., 1173-4.   2. Susannah Gray Hart; Susanna Hart Price and Lucretia Hart Clay.   3. The word "matter" is struck through and the word "cause" substituted.

From WILLIAM B. LAWRENCE, London, no. 26, February 28, 1828. Comments on the most-favored-nation dimensions of the British treaty with Brazil, signed August 17, 1827, the public and personal economic extravagancies of George IV, the continuing debate in Parliament on the "Catholic question," and the related repeal of the Test and Corporation Act of 1673. Announces that the supposed "manifesto of the Porte" is now regarded as "genuine," although it "can hardly be received as a declaration of war" by the Turks, and although it goes far toward "unmasking the profound duplicity which has long governed the Ottoman scoundrels." Notes, however, that the Turkish manifesto has damaged the Porte's cause in London and has undercut some earlier pro-Turkish sympathy in Britain that stemmed from the Turco-Egyptian disaster at the naval Battle of Navarino. Reports that since the receipt of the Ottoman manifesto the "Greek Treaty [Treaty of London, July 6, 1827] has become more popular" in Britain. ALS. DNA, RG59, Dip. Disp., Great Britain, vol. 35 (M30, R31). Received April 17, 1828. The Anglo-Brazilian commercial treaty of 1827 in is Parry, *Treaty Series*, 77:375-93. The Sultan's "manifesto" of December 1827, intended only for circulation within the Ottoman Empire, spoke of a possible holy war to maintain Islam in southeast Europe and denounced the Turco-Russian Convention of Ackerman (October 7, 1826) in which Turkey had agreed to withdraw her troops from the Danubian principalities and provide freedom of passage to Russian vessels at the Straits [5:937]. C. M. Woodhouse, *The Greek War of Independence* (London, 1952), 117. The manifesto was used by Russia as the formal reason for its declaration of war against Turkey in April, 1828. See, also, 6:1343-4; and *Niles' Register* (April 12, 1828), 34:107.

From JOSEPH MARTI Y NIN, Santa Cruz de Tenerife, February 28, 1828. States that Consul Payton Gay has returned. Reports that a scheme exists among some American captains and traders in Tenerife and some persons in America whereby illegal drawbacks have been procured through the use of fraudulent certificates and that Gay has frustrated their plans. Adds that they have consequently complained to Clay

[5:698] and have employed influential men in America to have Gay removed. ALS. DNA, RG59, Cons. Disp., Tenerife (M–T690, R1). No date of receipt.

From JOHN YOUNG Greenup County, Ky., February 28, 1828
.... I have lately returned from a Six weeks trip through Fleming Bath Montgomery Madison Garret [*sic*, Garrard] Rockcastle Pul[aski] Lincoln Mercer Jessamine Woodford Fayette and Clarke [*sic*, Clark] in those Counties there is much stir about Religion amongst, t[he] Baptist, Presbiterians [*sic*, Presbyterians], and Methodist, which I think is opperating powerfully in favour of the present administ[ration] the People are saying they will keep as much wickedness of the Cabbinet as possible and are saying if G[enl]. Jackson [is] Elected President it must be designed of Heaven as an [illeg. word] Judgment on the United States which may God [illeg. word]. NB. it is reported but not yet believed that G. Jackson has Joined society & is very Zealous may the devil over [illeg. word] himself

ALS. DNA, RG59, Misc. Letters (M179, R66). Virginia-born Young, who migrated to Palmyra, Greenup County, in 1784, subsequently served for a time as county surveyor. Nina M. Biggs and Mabel L. Mackoy, *History of Greenup County, Kentucky* (Louisville, 1951), 18, 26–8, 94.

To JOHN QUINCY ADAMS, February 29, 1828. Responds to "a resolution of the House of Representatives of the 18th instant requesting the President to communicate to the House copies of the instructions ... to Thomas Pinckney ... in pursuance of which the treaty of San Lorenzo el Real was entered into ... so far as said instructions relate to the designation of the dividing line between the territories of Spain and the United States." Submits extracts from Edmund Randolph's letter of instructions to Thomas Pinckney, November 28, 1794, and material "from a report referred to therein." NS. DNA, RG59, Report Books, vol. 4, pp. 222–3; also in *ASPFR*, 6:836–8. Cf. above, Clay to Adams, February 13, 1828. The House action is in U.S. H. of Reps., *Journal*, 20 Cong., 1 Sess., 305–6, 313.

From JAMES BROWN Paris, February 29, 1828
I wrote you yesterday under considerable depression of spirits arising from the state of Mrs. Browns health, and fear that my letter may have expressed my fears and awakened your apprehensions too strongly. Her case although a deep cause of uneasiness is more so from what we *fear* than from what she feels. Her complaint has never given her any pain and the tumor on her breast is less extensive and softer than it was some weeks ago. Her physicians who have just seen her give her strong hopes that by care, respose, confinement to the house, and the use of proper remedies, it can be dispersed never to return. She has great firmness and generally good spirits. Never had any person more reason to know how much she is loved and esteemed by, as well our Countrymen now in Paris, as by the European friends she has made since her arrival. Every evening she receives fifteen or twenty persons, who call to converse with her, and express their hopes that she will soon be able to join in the gay

parties of the season. She has lost much of her flesh from confining herself to a low diet, but preserves her general health and appetite and rides out every day for exercise. Had I not read too much on the subject of diseases of the breast it is probable my mind would have been less affected by her situation. Fortunately she perseveres in hoping that she will ultimately recover but is too anxious, from the apprehensions that she neglects her country men, not being able to assemble parties at home for their amusement My letter asking for leave of absence[1] has been written on account of her fears of an increase of her complaint and of her apprehension that she may innocently give offense to our fellow citizens here by not extending to them the attentions they have been accustomed to receive from her. We have both every reason to be pleased with our standing here as well at Court & with the diplomatic corps as with the society of Paris generally. I have given you this particular statement to allay any alarm which my letter of yesterday might have occasioned either to you or to any other of our numerous friends. You shall hear from me by every opportunity and be fully informed of the progress of this unfortunate case. We have the advantage here of the best medical advice and of a tolerably good Climate. I shall consult fully and candidly [with] the celebrated Doctor Dupuytren[2] and write you his opinion by the ship which will sail on the 15th. His reputation is of the highest order and his advice will either dispel or confirm my fears. You who know how great is my attachment to her and how richly she merits it by the possession of every grace and every virtue which can fix the human heart will judge of my sollicitude respecting her and my willingness to sacrifice ambition and every other passion where her health or happiness are at stake—Mr. [Daniel] Sheldon appears to waste away gradually without any suffering—He eats well, digests and sleeps well, and yet is wasting away with a slow and constant fever. I really feel for him for he is intelligent safe and honorable. His prudence and self command are such that I have great hopes the warm weather will restore him to his usual health which has never been robust—

For the last two month our travellers have nearly all been Jacksonians and consequently have led all Paris to believe that the election of their favorite was secure. Our papers from Washington which ought to have arrived by the New York Packet of the 15 were not placed on board at New York and have only been received this day with those down to the 25 Inst. which came by the Packet of the 1st. Inst. I had a letter from my friend J[osiah]. S. Johnston which represents Mr Adams as gaining very rapidly in Virginia Pennsylvania and North Carolina—Kentucky I think is safe—Time will do much for Mr Adams. His conduct in office has been irreproachable—The passions of the people have been excited by intolerable clamor and misrepresentation. They will e'er long cool down and with the return of good temper we shall have a return to reason and justice. Preserve my dear friend your temper and with it your health and all will soon be well with you—I am afraid my excellent sensitive sister[3] has had her feelings severely tried but I am sure she has not been found wanting. Give our love to her. . . .

ALS. DLC-HC (DNA, M212, R3). Printed in *LHQ*, 24:1086-8.   1. Brown to Clay, no. 81, February 28, 1828.   2. Guillaume Pierre-Buffiere Limousin Dupuytren (1777-

1835), former chief surgeon of the Hotel Dieux, was made a Baron by Charles X and appointed a member of the Academy of Medicine. See *Grand Larousse Encyclopedia*.
3. Lucretia Hart Clay, his wife's sister.

From ALBERT GALLATIN, New York, February 29, 1828. Reports that he has discovered, annexed to the third report of the Parliamentary Committee on Emigration, a "Map of the British Possessions in North America, compiled from documents in the Colonial Department." Expresses the opinion that the map deserves special attention, because it was prepared by a Committee of which Wilmot Horton, Undersecretary of State for the Colonial Department, was chairman and "with an eye to the question at issue between" the United States and Great Britain. States that, although the map shows the same boundary between the United States and the British possessions as are shown on "Map A," boundaries between the British provinces are altered so as to demonstrate that the northwest angle of Nova Scotia is "far north" of where the British claim the north western boundary of Nova Scotia to have been. Notes that the map indicates that no Act of the Crown extended the limits of New Brunswick over the Madawaska settlements and points out that the map and report will be useful when information is gathered for the arbiter regarding New Brunswick. ALS. DNA, RG59, Northeast Boundary (KyU., Special Roll, frames 53–4). The map in question was appended to the June 29, 1827 "Third Report from the Select Committee of the House of Commons, in 1827, on Emigration from the United Kingdom," in Great Britain, House of Commons, *Sessional Papers, 1826–1827*, no. 550, pp. 225–879. For Sir Robert John Wilmot Horton, see *DNB*.

To JAMES HAMILTON   Washington, February 29, 1828
I have received the letter which, as Chairman of the Committee of the House of Representatives on Retrenchment, you did me the honor to address to me on the 13th instant, transmitting a copy of a resolution which had been adopted by the Committee; and having given the subject embraced in the resolution attentive examination, and the most respectful consideration, I beg leave now to communicate my answer, to be laid before the Committee. The resolution, in substance, calls for the expression of my opinion, first, whether there be any officers in the Department of State whose services may be dispensed with, without detriment to the public interest; secondly, whether the salaries of any of them can be reduced, consistently with justice and propriety; and, thirdly, in general, whether any of the expenses incident to this Department can be reduced, without impairing the efficacy of its operations.
    As to the two first objects of inquiry above mentioned, my opinion is, that there can be no reduction in the number of officers employed in the Department of State without detriment to the public interest; nor in the salaries of any of them without injustice or impropriety. Within a few years past there has been a great increase in the general business of this Department, arising from the progressive increase of the wealth and population of the country, and from the establishment of Independent Governments upon this continent. The number of permanent American

missions which we now send from this country is equal to the number that we send to continental Europe. And the public interest has required the creation of various consular and other commercial agencies in this hemisphere, but not in the same proportion. Although those missions were authorized, and several of them had proceeded to their residences, during the preceding Administration, most of them have left the United States, and much the greater part of the other appointments referred to, have been made, during the present Administration. These foreign agencies have greatly extended the correspondence of the department, created a necessity for numerous translations from foreign languages, required much additional copying, and otherwise added to the labors of the Department   The committee will readily comprehend that the new duties arising from the above causes have rendered indispensable additional assistants to perform them, but the number of persons employed in the Department has not been increased in any thing like an equal proportion with the increase of its business. So far from its being expedient to discharge any of those persons, the public service would be promoted by some addition to the number of clerks in the Patent Office; and an increase in the salary of its Superintendent [William Thornton], which has heretofore been repeatedly proposed, is again respectfully recommended. The receipts in that Office are quite adequate to cover every expenditure already authorized; and any that its additional wants may require. In respect to those wants I beg leave to refer to a letter which the Superintendent, though confined by a long and dangerous illness, has recently felt it his duty to address to me, and which, under the designation of the letter A.[1] accompanies this communication.

Before I proceed to answer the third and last inquiry of the Committee, whether any of the Expenses incident to this Department can be reduced without impairing the efficacy of its operation, I ask permission to present some general and explanatory observations in respect to the disbursements of the public money which are made through the Department of State. Those disbursements are made out of appropriations of two kinds: First, those in which both the amount of the appropriation and its particular object are specified; and, secondly, those in which, although the amount of the appropriation is limited, and the general purpose of it is mentioned, its particular object is not, definitively, stated. The salaries of our diplomatic agents form an example of the first description of appropriation, as the contingent expenses of Foreign Intercourse do of the latter. The first depends, exclusively, upon the pleasure of Congress; and it is only over the last that a discretionary power is, or can be, exerted by the Executive, through the Department of State, in a course of administration. During my service in the Department, I have endeavored to enforce the most rigid economy which appeared to me compatible with the public interest. Particular items of expenditure will vary from year to year, according to exigencies; and the amount of disbursement will, consequently, be greater or less. There has been, for example, a vast deal of extra copying in the Department, during the two or three last years. The papers relating to our northeastern boundary, consisting of upwards of twenty manuscript volumes, and numerous maps and other detached papers, have been twice transcribed in that time [5:495, 781; 6:1205-06]. But the total amount of appropriations for the service of this Department, has been progressively diminishing during the three last years. On that subject, as well as the Expenditures of the Department, I beg leave to present to the Committee, from the document marked B. accompanying this letter, the three following views.

The first is a comparison of the amount of appropriations made during each of the three last years of the preceding administration, with that made during the three first years of the present, applicable to public service through the agency of this department.

Last Administration.	Present Administration.
1823, ... $154,800	1826, ... $350,932
1824, ... 309,350	1827, ... 290,550
1825, ... 336,050	1828, ... 89,550
$800,200	$731,032.

The cause of the smaller amount of appropriation for the year 1823, compared with several succeeding years was that the sum of $100,000, which, by the act of 4th May, 1822, was appropriated for such missions to the Independent Nations on the American Continent, as the President of the United States might deem proper [3:186], had remained in the Treasury unexpended. The appropriation for 1825 is placed under the last Administration, because it was in fact made, and the estimates for the public service were prepared under that Administration, although the disbursement of it took place, in conformity with those estimates, under the present.

The aggregate amount of appropriations during the latter term of three years is less, by $69,168, than in the former; and, excluding the appropriation in 1826 of $40,000 for the Panama Mission [5:171], (of which $26,953.52 only was expended,) which will not be an occasion of permanent expenditure, during each successive year of the latter term, the amount appropriated, in comparison with the year immediately preceding, has progressively decreased, until that for the service of the present year has declined as low as $89,550, a little more than one-fourth of the amount appropriated in the last year of the preceding Administration. I do not wish to be understood as stating that the smallness of the sum appropriated for the current year is attributable to permanent retrenchments, and is therefore to be regarded as the standard for future years; but it is the effect of economical savings from former appropriations, all of which might have been disbursed if there had been a disposition to indulge in extravagance [4:814-16; 5:932-3; 6:1306-07].

The next view which is now offered to the Committee is that of a comparison[2] of the actual expenditures during the three last years of the past, and the same period of the present, administration. The expenditures of

Last Administration.	Present Administration.
1822, ... $173,879.51	1825, ... $306,731.74
1823, ... 314,668.56	1826, ... 255,296.20
1824, ... 270,731.27	1827, ... 287,463.42
$759,279.34	$849,491.36

132

The amount during the latter term exceeds that of the former by $90,212.02; but this difference may be satisfactorily accounted for. In the first place, there was a remittance, in the month of December last, of $70,000 to our European bankers [Baring Brothers], which is charged to the service of the year 1827, although, in point of fact, it will be disbursed in the year 1828. In the next place the expenditure of the year 1822 amounted only to the sum of $173,879.51, because the sum appropriated to the missions to the New American Nations was not applied in that year. It was in succeeding years that those missions were despatched, and it has been only since the commencement of the present Administration that all of them have been put in operation, and that the entire expense, therefore, of maintaining the whole of them has been incurred. A comparison of the expenditure of the two last years of the past Administration with two years of the present Administration, though, for the reason just mentioned, still operating unfavorably to the latter, will be more just. The aggregate amount of the expenditures of the years 1823 and 1824 was $585,399.83; and the average of each year was $292,699.91½. The aggregate amount of the expenditures of the years 1825 and 1826 was $562,027.94; and the average of each year was $281,013.97. The average expenditure of each of the three years of the present Administration being $283,163.78⅔, although including the before mentioned recent remittance, and the expense of the mission to Tacubaya, is less than the average of the two last years of the past Administration.

The preceding views of appropriation and expenditure are exclusive of the salaries of the Secretary and clerks employed in the Department.

I have stated that the small amount of appropriation required for the service of the present year, was the result of economical savings out of previous appropriations. This will be manifest from the last view, which I now take the liberty of presenting to the Committee, of the appropriations and expenditures during the years 1825, 1826, and 1827, under those heads of appropriation in the application of which a discretionary control is exercised through the Department of State. Those heads are, first, Contingent Expenses of Foreign Intercourse; secondly, Intercourse with Barbary Powers; thirdly, Relief and Protection of American Seamen; and, fourthly, the Contingent Expenses of the Department. The total amount of appropriations under the first head, for the three years of 1825, 1826, and 1827, was $111,000; and the total amount at the service of the Department, including a balance of appropriation for the year 1824, and, also, some small items of repayment was $127,420.05; the actual disbursement during the three years 1825, 1826, and 1827, was $80,567.97, leaving an unexpended surplus of $46,852.08. The total amount appropriated during the same three years for Intercourse with the Barbary Powers, was $80,000. And the entire sum at the disposal of the Department, including a balance of the sum appropriated for 1824, was $100,450. The actual expenditure during those three years was $55,700.29; leaving an unexpended balance of $44,749.71. The total amount for the Relief and Protection of American

Seamen, at the disposal of the Department, during the same three years was $99,678.84. The total expenditure was $87,698.17; leaving an unexpended balance of $11,980.67.—The total amount at the command of the Department for its Contingent Expenses, during the same period of three years, was $97,863. The actual expenditure for the same term being $90,305, left a surplus of $7,558.

The third and last view is taken from a summary statement of moneys appropriated and expended under certain heads of appropriation, for the years 1822, 1823, 1824, 1825, 1826, and 1827 which is hereto annexed, designated by letter C., to the whole of which the attention of the Committee is respectfully invited.

During the present Administration there has been a permanent reduction in the grade of two, and a temporary reduction in another of our missions on this continent, from that of an Envoy Extraordinary and Minister Plenipotentiary to a Chargé d'Affaires.[3] And I am induced to believe that one or two of our American Missions may be abolished,[4] at a day not very distant, without injury to the public interest. In respect to those branches of expenditure which have been placed, by long established usage, under the control of the Executive, any retrenchment of which they are susceptible, must, from the nature of the case, depend upon the exercise of a sound and responsible discretion. Without being able now to state to the Committee any particular reduction which can be made in those branches of expenditure, I can only assure them that, so far as the application of that discretion depends upon me, I shall continue to be animated by the desire I have ever felt to observe all practicable economy.

Without being perfectly sure that the inquiries of the Committee extended beyond the officers immediately concerned in the Department of State, and the expenses incident to it within the city of Washington, I thought it safer to act on the supposition of their having contemplated a more comprehensive inquiry into the disbursements of the public money, wherever made, and the utility of existing officers wherever their sphere of action may be, under the direction of the Department of State. . . . P.S.—5th March, 1828.—This letter was prepared at the time it bears date; but its transmission has been delayed from that time to procure the certified statements from the Treasury which accompany it, and which from the press of business, could not be procured until this day.

Copy, signed. DNA, RG59, Report Books, vol. 4, pp. 223–7. Dispatch of letter delayed to March 5.   1. Document A not found. Remainder of enclosure was published in *House Reports*, 20 Cong., 1 Sess., no. 259, pp. 47–56.   2. This comparison was included at the suggestion of Adams. Adams, *Memoirs*, 7:454.   3. These reductions involved Buenos Aires, Chile, and Colombia. See 3:335, 377; 4:179; 5:572, 856, 863; 6:1306–07.   4. The U.S. mission to the Federation of the Centre of America was discontinued in 1829.

To CHARLES R. VAUGHAN, Washington, February 29, 1828. Transmits the report of Charles S. Daveis, agent of the State of Maine, to investigate disturbances in the disputed territory. Copy. DNA, RG59, Notes to Foreign Ministers and Consuls, vol. 3, p. 441 (M38, R3). Daveis's report, which details oppressions dealt to American citizens by the British Government in the disputed territory, is published in *ASPFR*, 6:936–44.

In late February, 1828, Clay wrote Vaughan that he could not supply two additional copies of Daveis's report, because he did not have them. Promises, however, that he will apply to the Maine delegation for them, "and if it should be successful you shall be supplied with them." ALS. All Souls College, Oxford Univ.

To FRANCIS T. BROOKE   Washington, March 1, 1828

I was prepared to anticipate the declension, communicated in your letter of the 28h. Ulto. of Mess. Madison and Monroe, to serve on your electoral ticket. I regret that there should be any thing ambiguous in the terms which they have employed to express their refusal, 'though, in that also, I am not much disappointed. It will, for the moment, produce a bad effect, but I am persuaded that it will soon pass off. Our prospects are better at this time than they have been for many months.

You will have seen the allusion made in K. to a correspondence between Mr. [Francis P.] Blair and myself, and the defiance which has been thrown out as to my allowing the publishing of it. I have a copy of the letter [4:9–10], on which reliance is placed. It is written in a style of playfulness and friendly familiarity which constitutes the only objection I could possibly have to its publication. I shall let them go on making confident assertions in regard to its contents, and *perhaps* I may hereafter cause it to be published. With honorable men, it will do me good rather than harm. By the bye, this is not a bad time to have the letter published, which you did me the favor to submit to my inspection last fall [6:1058–9].

At present we have no messenger to send abroad. We rarely employ one to go to France or England, on account of the great regularity of the packets. I will bear in mind your wish concerning your nephew [Landon N. Carter], should an occasion arise to despatch a messenger.... P.S. You see [John] Randolph, like the Porcupine, is ejecting his malignant arrows in every direction, not allowing you to escape. You should not mind him.

ALS. KyU.

From O. V. KING   Portland, March 1, 1828

I have just learn'd that the question of the "North Eastern boundary" is referred to the umperage of the Emperor of Russia [Nicholas I], and that an Agent is to be appointed from this State to manage our cause & that Judge Preble[1] is a candidate—Now all that know me, are ready to attest, that I was a strenuous advocate for and have been and still am a firm supported of the General administration—But if Judge Preble shall be appointed as agent to Russia on that business, he being the most violent opposer of the administration in this State & the advocate of Jackson, the silent writer of Hickory published in the [Portland *Eastern*] Argus and alway[s] ready to dance to the "cry tune corruption" I shall feel myself bound by every thing which I hold dear to oppose Mr Adams's reelection and I hesitate nothing in saying that his appointment would be met by general dissatisfaction and, that it would prove detrimental to the cause of Mr Adams at least in part of the State—Mr [Charles S.]

Daveis I would recommend as a Gentleman every way qualified to discharge the duties of such an officer

LS. DNA, RG59, A. and R. (M531, R2).   1. For Judge William Pitt Preble, see Ronald F. Banks, *Maine Becomes a State: The Movement to Separate Maine from Massachusetts, 1785–1820* (Middletown, Conn., 1970), *passim;* and *DAB.* Judge Preble and Albert Gallatin, were appointed "Agents in the negotiations and upon the umpirage relating to the northeastern boundary of the United States" on May 9, 1828. U.S. Sen., *Executive Journal*, 3:608–9. For their instructions in this assignment, see Clay to Gallatin and Preble, May 19, 1828; and Clay to Preble, May [26?], 1828.

To PETER B. PORTER   Washington, March 1, 1828

I received, in due course of the Mail your favor of the 13h Ulto. as I did that also which communicated the death of Mr. [DeWitt] Clinton. Our intelligence from N. York, since that event, is very favorable. I should be glad to receive your opinion as to its probable influence.

The Tariff[1] will be taken up next week. Public opinion is manifesting itself very strongly against the measure, as reported by the Manufacturing Committee. In that shape it is the vilest of cheats. With the professed purpose of protecting our Woolen manufactories, it demolishes them. With the purpose avowed of encouraging the growth of wool it destroys the Home market. What, think you, in N. York of the bill? I am apprehensive that the *first* impression there was too favorable to it. Does that continue?

I have a letter [February 28] from Judge [Francis T.] Brooke this morning, in which he states that Mess. Madison and Monroe decline serving on the Electoral ticket, but in a manner which he thinks is flattering to the Administration. We shall see their letters next week.

By the way, Judge Brooke tells me that he has not received any answer from you to a letter which he wrote. I think it would be well to address him a letter, at your leisure.

AL. NBuHi.   1. 6:876–7; Clay to Featherstonhaugh, February 18, 1828

From STANHOPE PREVOST, Lima, March 1, 1828. Details the funeral of James Cooley who died February 26 "after a violent bilious attack." Reports that before his demise, Cooley arranged for all his official papers to be turned over to Prevost; promises to preserve them intact and transfer them to William Radcliff whose arrival is anticipated "hourly." ALS. DNA, RG59, Misc. Letters (M179, R66). Received August 13, 1828. Duplicate in DNA, RG59, Cons. Dip., Lima, vol. 2 (M154, R2).

To ROBERT S. TODD, Lexington, March 1, 1828. Agreement in which Clay leases to Todd, for five years, at the rate of $240 per year, "his large Stone building in the lower part of the Town of Lexington, called the Tammany Mill" and the rest of the buildings on its lot "including the dwelling houses fronting the street or Alley leading from Water to Hill Street—" ADS, by Robert Scott for Clay. KyLxT. The final payment was made March 1, 1833.

From FREDERICK J. WICKELHAUSEN, Bremen, March 1, 1828. Acknowledges receipt of State Department certificate which affirms that "no deduction whatsoever is exacted from persons or property that are or is removing from the U. States." States that the Oldenburg government has reciprocated with a similar document. Advocates a change in legislation to require that ships' captains provide consuls with a complete crew list when in port. Reports that a treaty of amity and commerce between the Hanseatic Republics and Brazil has been concluded [6:82], and that the "Citizen Convention" of Bremen "yesterday" ratified the treaty with the United States [6:273-7]. LS. DNA, RG59, Cons. Disp., Bremen, vol. 2 (M–T184, R2).

From **THOMAS L. L. BRENT,** Lisbon, no. 52, March 2, 1828. Reports that Miguel arrived on February 22, took the oath on the 26th, and that party activity has increased, with both the ultra–royalists and the constitutionalists watching Miguel to detect the course he intends to pursue towards the constitution. Notes that Miguel has dismissed the entire ministry and appointed new members, most, if not all, of whom "are opposed to the present system." States that the new ministry consists of: the Duke of Cadaval as prime minister; Jose Antonio de Oliveira Leite de Barros, as minister of the interior, and ad interim of marine; Luis de Paula Furtado do Rio de Mendonca, as minister of ecclesiastical affairs and justice; the Count of Vila Real, as minister of war and ad interim of foreign affairs; and the Count of Lousa (Diogo de Meneses d'Eca) as minister of finance. Reports that Great Britain has announced that it will withdraw its troops from Portugal and that the withdrawal is underway. LS. DNA, RG59, Dip. Disp., Portugal, vol. 7 (M43, R6). Received May 9, 1828. For Oliveira Leite, see Espasa, *Enciclopedia;* for Lousa and Mendonca see *GEPB.*

From **ALEXANDER H. EVERETT,** Madrid, no. 98, March 2, 1828. Encloses translation of a recent "decree making some alterations in the regulations affecting the trade between this kingdom and the different parts of America; and in the duties levied here on articles imported from that quarter." Reports that King Ferdinand VII is recovering from "another attack of the gout" and rumor has it that he may stay in Barcelona "until summer." Manual Gonzales Salmon, however, has indicated that he believes the King will go to Aranjuez "soon after Easter." Notes that Catalonia hardly needs the royal presence as the province continues to be tranquil. Adds that recent accounts indicate that "Col. Bossoms [*sic*, Busson]. . . . the most notorious of all the ostensible chiefs of the conspiracy had just been taken and shot."

Relates that the evacuation of Spain "by the French army has been agreed upon between the two Governments" and that the troops will probably leave Cadiz "before the end of April." Discusses a memoir written by Count Ofalia, Spanish minister to London, to the King, on the Latin American question. Reports that "the object of the Memoir was to recommend an immediate pacification on the best terms that can be obtained." Notes that "the Count may have acted under the instigation of the British Government" and that the Council of State probably will not report favorably on the memoir because "persons of influence" are generally "adverse to an acknowledgment of the independence of the new States" and events during the past year, especially the expulsion of the Spaniards from Mexico, have fostered that feeling. Reports that the amnesty, mentioned in his preceding dispatches, [6:1245-6; and January 8, 1828] has not yet been carried into effect, and expresses doubt that "a bona fide Amnesty, sufficiently extensive to be of any great value can be finally carried through." LS. DNA, RG59, Dip. Disp., Spain, vol. 28 (M31, R29). Received May 8, 1828.

The commercial decree, dated February 21, 1828, was published in the Washington *Daily National Intelligencer*, May 13, 1828.

From ROBERT MONROE HARRISON, Grenada, March 2, 1828. Reports his arrival at this place on February 24, after visits at Tobago, Trinidad, and St. Vincent. Comments on these islands individually, including Grenada, relative to their population, productions, necessary imports, sources of supply, trade with the United States, and local desire for reopening intercourse with the U.S. Briefer notes on these topics are also provided with regard to St. Christopher, Nevis, and Montserrat, "three of the poorest of the colonies."

Encloses statistics on the imports from the U.S. and British North America to Tobago, Trinidad, and St. Vincent during the period immediately preceding the trade interdict [4:180]. Notes that "taking the average state of the markets since the Interdict, the price of American productions in general have not risen much, nor will they so long as the circuitous trade [U.S. to St. Barts] is allowed, and the introduction of our articles into the British North American Colonies as they are at present." Remarks that British West Indian planters generally feel that "the loss of the Barter trade . . . is of the most serious consequence."

Concludes that the vessels reported in his letter of December 24 as seized at Barbados, coming from Martinique with American goods, have been restored intact, and no similar seizure has been reported. The Dutch, however, have barred American vessels from the Port of Nicaria, where they supplied vessels from Demera, "which depended a good deal in getting various articles it stood in need of in that circuitous way." LS, postscript, AE. DNA, RG59, Cons. Disp., Barbados, vol. 1 (M-T333, R1). No date of receipt.

From JOHN BARNEY, "House of Representatives," March 3, 1828. Fearing that "Privateers now in the Waters of the United States, . . . not knowing the repeal of the instructions given by the Buenos Ayres Govt. to send in for adjudication vessels bound to [the] Brazils [6:1213-15], may capture and detain our Merchantmen immediately after getting to Sea," renews his "request that the information transmitted by Mr. [John M.] Forbes may be published." ALS. DNA, RG59, Misc. Letters (M179, R66). No earlier request from Barney relative to this matter has been found.

To NICHOLAS BIDDLE   Washington, March 3, 1828
We have received your obliging letter of the 25h. Ulto. inclosing a Certificate for $7624:31[1] in the 4½ per Cent Stocks of the U. States, which you

have had the goodness to purchase, by our request, for the [Kenyon] Theological Seminary of the Protestant Episcopal Church of the Diocese of Ohio, with the amount standing to our credit in the B[ank]. of the U.S. We are greatly indebted for your prompt and kind attention to our request in making this investment, and entertain entire confidence in your judgment in the selection of the Stock. We beg your acceptance of our acknowledgments also for your having caused the purchase to be made, without expence to the Seminary; and for the kind offer which you have made to have the accruing dividends drawn without charge to the Institution, of which it will not fail to avail itself. For your friendly services Bishop Chase promises you the prayers of the Church, and both of us tender our sincere thanks. . . .

ALS, by Clay, signed by Bishop Philander Chase. NNPM.   1. The figure $7681.50 is used in Clay and Chase to Biddle, February 22, 1828.

From GEORGE G. BARRELL, Malaga, March 4, 1828. Believes that the amount of U.S. imports at Malaga "is of so trifling a nature as almost to amt. to a prohibition of American productions—the same will hold good throughout Spain, until we have some well founded commercial Treaty, based on reciprocal advantages." Adds that Spanish duties "fluctuate from day to day" and that this has been the situation throughout the entire kingdom for many years. ALS. DNA, RG59, Cons. Disp., Malaga, vol. 2 (M217, R2). No date of receipt.

From FRANCIS P. BLAIR   Frankfort, March 4, 1828
I recd. your letter of the 15 ult. & send you a copy of that which you desire to see.

Mr [John J.] Crittenden showed me a letter from you to him[1] upon the subject of publishing your letter of the 8 of Jan:1825, & consulted me on the propriety of making it public. I told him frankly that I did not concur that it would be advantageous to you to make the publication. There are certain passages in it that would expose you to every species of attack. "Ridicule would find Bye=words." in it to render the president contemptible, & to make the world beleive that you yourself despised him. Serious arguments would be founded on the different appeals made to you by the friends of the returned candidates, to prove that while one invoked you by *the interests of the West,"* and another by *"the hopes of the Republican party"*; you would listen only to the voice of him who held out the invitation *of your own future interests"* which are brought into view in connexion with *"your fitness for any Station"* while the favor, & favorable opinions of Mr Adams are at the same time presented as the means of attaining both—Besides this there is towards the conclusion of the letter a declaration that your friends were actuated by the beleif that their wishes for you would be more likely to be accomplished by bestowing their votes on Mr Adams than on General Jackson—This they have denied as their motive & having denied it, the public have been induced to impute an impurity to the influence under which they acted which if they had boldly avowed at first & persisted in to the last, would have been their best ground of vindication. The proofs embodied in your pamphlet [6:1394-6] would have made it apparent, that you made up your mind [illeg. word] without reference to the appointment of secretary & before any concert to ally parties would have been made at Washington—But your letter to me might be now used to prove that you exerted an influence over hesitating members at a time when the advances of Mr Adams or his friends might be assigned as having an operation on your mind—& this fact would seem to conflict with a statement made in a short letter of yours in which you expressly deny that you would exert such an influence & say that you would not hold that man as your friend who could be so operated on—This although I think I understand could not be readily explained to the public or satisfactorily to [David] White who would not like to be exposed to his constituents—.

I do not think that the inferences which suspicion makes with regard to my refusal to give evidence will have any important bearing on the contest in *Kentucky*—From it the administration men come to conclusions unfavorable to me—the Jackson men look to my conduct as ruinous to you—but so long as the uncommitted portion of the people see nothing of the correspondence between us they will found no decision on its data. A hesitating person will not settle his opinion on invisible ground, and the rest are fixed to condemn you or me already   The common law is full of common sense & among the fruits of that code of custom & experience the following maxim is found—"De non apparentibus, et non existentibus eadimus est ratio."[2]

You will not understand me as expressing my own wishes[3] in the suggestions I have offered—The publication of the letter would releive me from the crimination of political opponents, & the suspicions & curiosity of political friends. From the last however I hope I have not much to fear, for I am too decisive a partizan to be long suspected by those I serve—And I trust that the leading administration prints will drop the discussion of the letter & cease to abuse, if it, should be your intention to let the matter sink into oblivion—as it regards permanent effect I have nothing to apprehend. The grounds I urged to the [Kentucky] Senate are sufficient to vindicate my course to all men of all parties when the time of temperate reflection shall return. In making up your decision upon the subject will you be solely guided by considerations of your own interest, & do what your feeling, may prompt without reference to mind—My opinions I have frankly given because they were asked in a spirit of confidence which I would not respond to in any otherwise than in the honesty of my heart—I have presented the harshest aspect of your letter, not because I interpret it thus unkindly, but because you ought to consider it in that light in which it will be held up to the public view by the worst of your enemies—

I never in my life have experienced such a discord in my feelings as late events have occasioned—I beleive no man more ardently wishes the triumph of his party than I do—Yet it is a subject of the deepest regret to me that its success should be made to depend in any degree on circumstances which may be used to cast a blemish on a name associated with all the attributes, of the spirit & honor of a Christian. I must confess that I felt the utmost chagrin at the conduct of those in the Senate who called themselves your friends. They were apprized before [James] Allen's resolution[4] was called up by them that I should be compelled to take the attitude I assumed before the Senate—Before the enquiry was begun I told Mr Crittenden what I should do; & John Green who came to me & told me that a certain person (not named by him) had said that I had read your letters to him, was solemnly assured by me that there was not the least foundation for the Statement & that although your letters to me said nothing about your being appointed Secretary yet they were of a confidential nature, & that I could not think of exposing them even at the bidding of the Senate. And yet Green urged on the enquiry & contributed to produce the present delemma—He also by an allusion in the Senate to your letters & an insinuation that I had exposed them, drew me into an explanation in Self-defense & thus unnecessarily associated your name with the correspondence which was not mentioned as yours in the objections I made to the Senate. The array of prosecutors & defenders was enough to fill my mind with surmises as to the motives which got up the proceedings—Your ancient enemy [John] Pope managed on one side—while the meanest & most vindictive & most vulgar of these who were set up as your adversaries pretended to defend you—[Benjamin] Hardin & [Robert] Wickliffe press on the accusation & in their resolution presuppose " a full examination of all the evidence adduced" by way of inviting an investigation, & putting your opponents upon the plan of bringing to a focus at Frankfort all the flying reports about imputed Management in the Country—I could scarcely suspect any person upon earth of such detestible chicane & contrivance but such a pair of as Hardin & Wickliffe, but I do confess that I have sometimes considered as within the range of probability that they wished to settle the gloom of suspicion around you to revenge themselves for the insults & injuries which their malignant envy has induced them to beleive you have wantonly put upon them—while by assuming the attitude of your defenders could at once lay claim to your gratitude & the support of your friends—They did not mean to urge the matter so far as to ruin the cause of Mr Adams—but reckoning upon the worst that might happen they have [illeg. word] to secure a position which would enable themselves to profit by your fall, & rise upon your ruins—If you should die under their management, they have taken care that they shall be called on to administer upon the property [?] you may leave—Pope introduced a Janus faced Resolution[5] into the [Kentucky] Senate intended to vindicate Adams from the affair of the Mississippi & the fisheries, & to charge you as a calumniator; & in case of failure to fix the censure on Adams by the vote of the majority & present you to the world as the prosecutor—In vindicating Adams[,] Pope was perfectly at home, but Ben Hardin showed his enmity to you by joining with Pope in denouncing the charge brought against Adams as a Slander. & vindicating his conduct at Ghent—In this he ov[er] reached himself as he will find one day—when the [Jonathan] Russel[l] letter was called for in congress [3:219-26] Hardin himself asserted that Adams had *betrayed* the interest of the West in the negotiation & he re[ite]rated the declaration in the Legislature in 1824 when all the documents had been laid before the public[6]—But enough—it is not my pl[ace] to write politics to you—we cannot see things in the same light or you would not, have turned a deaf ear &

refused to mediate a peace & save your old friends from their oppressors merely becau[se] you thought they had indulged in relief whims & judge breaking freaks some what unconstitutionally—The only persons who looked upon the Scene in the Senate with hearts of Sorrow were those who once idolized you & who had been cast off to make room in your affections for the Wickliffe[s] Hardins [Thomas] Marshalls, [John] Greens the Richmond & Garrard[7] printers &c &c

In conferring with Mr Crittenden yesterday we differed about a matter of fact concerning which I think I cannot be mistaken—He says that it was in consequence of the letter of the 8 [January, 1825] from you, & the inferences that he & I drew from it that your interest would be promoted by the vote of Kentucky going for Mr Adams & at my instancy th[at] he was induced to give up his preference reluctantly for Jackson & th[at] these considerations induced him to write to White—My recollections of [the] matter is that he came to my house & told me that Mr. [Robert P.] Letcher had wr[itten] a letter to him in which the election of Mr Adams was spoken of as probable &c &c. & desiring him to speak to me for the purpose of getting letters to White to induce him to go with the Kentucky delegation in support of Mr Adams—I am persuaded that I had written to White & sent the letters of others to him before I received your letter of the 8th. Jan: & that I told you in my reply [4:41] that I had anticipated the wish expressed in that letter by sending communications as requested by Mr Crittenden. If I seem certain of any thing depending on memory it is the truth of the Statement I have made. I should be glad to know from Letcher & from you whether you remember the circumstances because I should be sorry Crittenden should think me capable of such a fabrication, Although there is really no inducement which could lead to the invention[8] of such a story—I never mentioned it to any body since the time of the communication with me but I think I referred to it in a letter to you—If you have the letter I wrote in reply to yours of the 8 it will shed some light on the subject—Do me the favor to write to me on this subject—

ALS. DLC–HC (DNA, M212, R3). 1. February 14, 1828. 2. "The reasoning must be the same with respect to the things which do not appear, as to things which do not exist." 3. Following the word "wishes" is the phrase, struck through, "or feelings." 4. Blair to Clay, January 22, 1828. 5. On February 6, 1828. Ky. *Senate Journal* ... 1827–8, pp. 336–7. 6. Hardin statement not found. 7. Richmond, Ky. (Madison Co.) and Garrard Co. in Kentucky. 8. Following the word "invention" is the phrase, struck through, "on my part."

To JOHN BLAIR, House of Representatives, March 4, 1828. Acknowledges receipt of Blair's letters of February 4 and 5. Transmits a statement of the Department's continguent expenses for 1825–7. States that the vouchers supporting every expenditure are on file in the office of the Register of the Treasury. Encloses a letter from the Fifth Auditor, Stephen Pleasonton, with an explanatory letter from the Register, Joseph Nourse, which indicates "all the disbursements made out of the appropriation for the Contiguent Expenses of Foreign Intercourse" from the beginning of the administration until the end of 1827. Notes that those items which were allowed on Clay's special approval are distinguished from those which were not. Adds that, since no item among the accounts of the continguent expenses for the missions abroad had been allowed by his special approval, he is not furnishing a statement regarding that appropriation. Describes the procedure whereby domestic disbursements of the Department are made through an agent, Richard Forrest, who is also a departmental clerk. Transmits a statement showing the disbursements, made by his particular authority, from the "appropriation for the Continguent Expenses of Foreign Intercourse," and states that the "principal item" there has been the compensation of bearers of dispatches. Explains the reasons for hiring these messengers.

Cites several examples including "Theodore W. Clay [who] was engaged, in March last, to carry back to Mexico . . . [a treaty] after it had been submitted to the Senate; and, also, to carry other confidential despatches to Mr [Joel R.] Poinsett, and despatches to Mr. [John] Sergeant, who had left the United States the preceding November."

Describes the procedure whereby bearers of dispatches are remunerated. LS. DNA, RG59, Report Books, vol. 4, pp. 230–3; also in *House Reports*, 20 Cong., 1 Sess., no 226, pp. 14–7.

From ALEXANDER BURTON, Cadiz, March 4, 1828. Encloses a copy of a Spanish decree which regulates "Commerce between America, and Spain in either Foreign or Spanish vessels, on a more liberal footing than heretofore," along with a new tariff and an explanation of the decree. ALS. DNA, Cons. Disp., Cadiz, vol. 4 (M–T186, R4). For the enclosures, dated February 21, 1828, published in *Diario Mercantil de Cadiz* of March 4, see *ibid*.

From JOHN J. CRITTENDEN   Frankfort, March 4, 1828
I have received your letter of the 14th of Feby:—

The late inquisition held upon you in the Senate was to my mind the most remarkable & extraordinary proceeding. I am entirely satisfied that neither [James] Allen nor his party, desired the adoption of his resolution—[1] They naturally calculated that their political opponents would reject it, & all that they wished or expected to gain, was the wretched advantage of those vauntings & misrepresentations which their partisans would have founded upon its rejection—Your friends allowed themselves to be goaded & precipitated into the measure without much reflection—I thought it was a great indiscretion—I thought too upon principle, that the whole procedure was a most alarming & flagrant violation of justice & the Constitution—It is in vain that the Constitution has prohibited the passing of bills of attainder if such proceedings are to be warranted—I thought that your friends ought to have rejected it scornfully, & I expressed that opinion—But the inconsiderate zeal of your friends, & their confidence in your integrity determined them to indulge even the lawless inquisition of your enemies—I had all the confidence that they had, & perhaps more, for I thought that your vindication was already so complete & triumphant, that Allen's resolution deserved only to be treated as an effort of malice & cast off with contempt.

But all that is now past—And I think that this persecution or prosecution, can not in its results be prejudicial to you—It shews the malignity

& malice with which you are pursued, & ought to provoke the indignant sympathy of Kentuckians at least—The proceeding before the [Kentucky] Senate had not even the dignity of a solemn mockery—It was the subject of jest & merriment for the Lobby—The active prosecutors seemed ashamed of their dirty work—And the discouraging answers they were continually receiving from their chosen witnesses excited a laughter in the bye standers that the officers of the House could but illy repress—

This was the impression which the scene & the proceeding made on my mind—I think it did not make upon the audience, & I did not suppose it could make upon the world any unfavourable impression as to you or your cause—And at the conclusion of the affair, I did beleive it would operate favourably for you—I do not beleive it is operating against you in Kenty:—So far as my intelligence through the State extends it is of the most cheering & encouraging character—The friends of the Administration are more confident of success in Kenty:, than they have been for a long time past—

The Central Committee appointed by the [Adams] Administration Convention have determined to address the people.[2] This Mock trial before the Senate & the evidence adduced before it will form one of its principal topics—It has been rendered more necessary by the false & garbled statement which has been given to the public in an address of the Jackson Committee, which you will see in the [Frankfort] Argus—[3]

On Monday last I had a conversation with Mr [Francis P.] Blair respecting your letter to him of the 8th of January 1825 [4:9-10], the publication of which you refer to our discretion—He seemed to think that there was no necessity for its publication, & that it would be unadviseable, as it might be tortured into constructions unfavourable to you—And that we ought to leave it to your better judgment to decide upon the matter, & to publish it in your own manner, if it should be deemed proper—My anxiety to avoid the responsibility of deciding on the subject, & the distrust of my own judgment, more perhaps than any thing else, induced me then to concur in the opinion that that would be the better course—And that no injury could result from the idle surmises that might be indulged from Blair's refusal to be sworn, or to disclose that letter—And we concluded that I should write you to that effect—I have since almost changed my opinion, & been confirmed in the determination to procure a copy of that letter & publish it at once—Mr Blair had it with him at our conversation, & I examined it carefully—If "reason & justice" had not in a great degree "lost their sway," there could be found in it no ground for serious censure—And evil as are the times, I can not think that its publication would be seriously injurious to you—In the confidence that it was not to be published, the Argus appeals to it as containing positive evidence of the bargain &c and so does the address of the [Kentucky] Jackson Committee—I have too made some of my confidential friends, (who are also your friends), acquainted with the contents of that letter in order to obtain their advice—They all declared at once for its publication—they thought it would benefit you—They did not seem to be so very decided, whether I should cause it to be published here at once & without delay,

144

or should wait to hear from you again, so as to afford you the opportunity of publishing it yourself, & in a manner perhaps that might be [more] effectual & imposing than we could do it. So the matter now rests in our consideration—A few days will determine my course—I have not got a copy of the letter from Mr. Blair—The instant that the determination is made, you shall again hear from me—

I have been witnessing with some satisfaction, that the Argus, the Jackson Committee & their associates, have been of late concentrating all their charges, & their hopes of proof upon that letter of yours—I say I witnessed it with satisfaction, because I hoped that the publication of it, if you should be compelled to make it, would cut off at once the hundred heads of the Hydra—There has been a rumour here for some days, said to be founded upon letters from Jackson men at Washington, that you intended to publish your letter to Mr. Blair—This rumour preceded your last letter to me—I think it occasions some concern among your enemies here. They begin to be a little apprehensive that its publication may falsify all the slanders they have predicated upon it—I can not but notice a short paragraph in the last Argus [February 27], (since my last conversation with Mr Blair) in which they are pleased so far to soften their tone, as to say they do not expect to find in that letter *positive proof* of *the bargain in so many words* &c In the address of the Jackson Committee here written only a few days before, and no doubt by [Amos] Kendall himself, they say "they do not doubt that *full proof* of a direct bargain is in the hands of Mr Blair"—Blair['s] situation must be an unpleasant one—And rendered more delicate by what the Jacksonites are continually saying in order to confirm their insinuations against you, that he ought himself to be condemned if the evidence in his hands does not support all that they have predicated upon it—. In this state of the case, I was utterly astonised when in the conversation between Blair & myself first referred to above, he for the first time through out a suggestion that pending the presidential election I had told him that I had recd From Robt: P Letcher a letter in which I was desired to request him (Blair) to write to our representative [David] White to induce him to vote for Adams &c &c I at once disavowed any recollection of having told him any such thing or of having recd such a letter—And denied his statement—He still seemed to insist on—And says that in his answer to your letter of the 8th Jany: 1825 [4:41], (the one so often above alluded to) he makes some reference to the letter of Letcher of which he says I had told him Is this so? If it be, it is very strange & unaccountable—I am under the strangest delusion if I ever recd such a letter from Letcher or ever told Blair that I had—I have written to Letcher by this mail enquiring if he has any recollection of ever having written me such a letter— Can it be that [Francis] Preston [Blair] is beginning, when he sees the time approaching when your letter to him may be published, to provide a retreat for himself upon some other letter or imagined ground of suspicion? And that when your letter may be published we shall hear of another, & another, if not from you, from some friend supposed to be acting or writing in confidence & privity with you? This difference between Blair & myself is known as yet only to ourselves, unless he has communicated it—Beleiving that he is mistaken, honestly mistaken, I wish to correct his error, & prevent a new ramification of the vilest of slanders—If Letcher will say that he wrote me such a letter, & Blair's letter to you makes reference to it, I must conclude that I am forgetful & wrong, but both these circumstances must concur to convince me—I wish to know of you whether Mr Blair's letter to you contains such a reference?

I am really ashamed of the manner, matter, & length of this letter—more especially as it is addressed to a secretary of State—

I wish you all the success, I think you deserve. . . . P.S. If you should see the Jackson address to which I have alluded, you will see that it states that your friends here had a copy of your letter to Blair—this might induce you to beleive that I had kept a copy from the one I sent you—Be assured that I did not—The statement is doubtless entirely false.

ALS. NcD.   1. Blair to Clay, January 22, 1828.   2. Address not found; see Wickliffe to Clay, March 25, 1828.   3. Frankfort *Argus of Western America,* February 20, 1828.

From ROBERT MONROE HARRISON, Grenada, March 4, 1828. Reports that he has been able to complete his "observations on all the Windward Islands and Colonies" without his movements being particularly noticed, except in St. Vincent and Grenada. Explains that in the latter instances he was known to Government officials, who feted him, which occasions caused newspaper speculation regarding the purpose of his tour. Denounces American journalists who defame their Country and cites specifically the New York *Evening Post,* from which newspaper "all (or nearly so) of the *vile things* said of our Government and public authorities in the West Indies, and much in England," are read. Notes, also, that the New York *Albion,* "a paper in the pay of the British Government," is advertised in the West Indies as "a paper exclusively in the British *interest.*"

Inquires regarding the delay in receipt of his exequatur. Explains that, because of illness he has been compelled to use a copyist. Asks, on grounds of depleted health from extended duty in the tropics that he be given a post in Greece, if consular relations should be opened there. LS. DNA, RG59, Cons. Disp., Barbadoes, vol. 1 (M-T333, R1). Received April 22, 1828.

From ABRAHAM B. NONES, Maracaibo, March 4, 1828. Reports that an anonymous address to the officers of the army has enjoyed wide circulation and that the army has sent a petition to Simon Bolivar urging him to take charge of the government, with or without the approval of the Grand Convention at Ocana. States that the army has sent a delegation to represent the military at Ocana. Notes that the army is having difficulty supporting itself, as the revenue has decreased as a result of the depression in trade to that Country. Says that while all apprehension of an invasion by Angel Laborde has subsided [6:1336], the Department remains under marital law. Observes that the Ministers of War and Foreign Relations have resigned and that their resignations have been accepted. LS. DNA, RG59, Cons. Disp., Maracaibo, vol. 1 (M-T62, R1). Received April 2, 1828.

From JOSE SILVESTRE REBELLO, Washington, March 4, 1828. Informs Clay that the Argentine privateer *Flor de Maio* has apparently added to its strength, while in the port of Baltimore, by "substituting real bulwarks" to the existing false ones and by increasing the number of its "sails, boats &c—." Requests that Clay "direct the officers of that port to reduce the said privateer to her former condition, equal in every respect to that in which she was at the time of her arrival." Reminds Clay that if the privateer sails from Baltimore in a condition to continue its cruise without touching at an Argentine port for supplies, Brazil will interpret its stay in Baltimore as a "mark of indulgence" of Brazil's enemy. LS, in Portuguese, with a trans. in State Dept. file. DNA, RG59, Notes from Brazilian Legation, vol. 1 (M49, R1).

From HENRY WHEATON, Copenhagen, no. 3, March 4, 1828. States that a "satisfactory arrangement" has been made in relation to the three vessels—*Ariel, Fair Trader,* and *Minerva Smyth*—detained at Kiel in 1810 [5:386], and that John Connell has received the indemnity and is on his way to the United States [6:590-1, 616-27]. Reports that Count Ernst Heinrich Schimmelmann has been ill and that none of the diplomatic corps has seen him for "several weeks," but that he, Wheaton, will resume his conferences with the Count on the subject of the general claims as soon as possible. Expresses opinion that he will succeed in achieving only a compromise and that he will accomplish that only if he is authorized to conclude an agreement whereby the Danish Government "should agree to pay to the Government of the United States a gross sum for the entire claims." ALS. DNA, RG59, Dip. Disp., Denmark, vol. 1B (M41, R3). Received May 9, 1828.

To LEVI WOODBURY, U.S. Senate, March 4, 1828. Acknowledges receipt of Woodbury's note of "the 26th ultimo [*sic*, February 25]." States that the French Minister, Baron de Mareuil, personally delivered the ordinance of February 5, 1826, to the State Department on June 21 of that year. Says that the minister made no "proposal or demand" then that the United States reciprocate to French vessels the privileges which the ordinance extends to American vessels. Notes that the ordinance, revocable at the whim of the French government, was regarded as having been promulgated with a view to French interests, not as an accommodation to any foreign power, and that the ordinance does not apply to other French colonies, but exclusively to Guadaloupe and Martinique.

Reports that the Convention of June 24, 1822 [3:53], applies only to France, not to its colonies. States that the "equality" it provides between the vessels of the two nations had not become reality when the ordinance of 1826 took effect and, in fact, did not do so until October 1827. Adds that the French government has complained of disadvantages to French shipping under the Convention and has indicated a desire to open negotiations to improve "commercial intercourse" and that the United States government has indicated a willingness to consider French proposals in a "friendly spirit."

Indicates that the French government has ruled that an American vessel, carrying American produce, forfeits the privileges of the Convention "by merely touching at the port of a third power, although only for information, and without breaking bulk." Reports that the American Minister in Paris, James Brown, has remonstrated against the decision, but has not secured a reversal of it, as yet; that, on the contrary, when the question arose as to whether vessels from France, carrying a French cargo, lost their privileges by touching at French islands, President Adams ruled that they did not.

States that vessels carrying island products directly from the French island to the United States are liable to alien duties and that, if the Commerce Committee believes that French vessels in the direct trade from Guadaloupe and Martinique should be allowed equality with American vessels, it should propose a bill "to that effect," since the President does not have power under existing law to accomplish the change by proclamation.

Concludes that recent reports of a change in the "ordinances disadvantageous to the commerce and navigation of the United States" have not been confirmed. LS. DNA, RG59, Report Books, vol. 4, pp. 228–30; also in *ASPFR,* 6:827–8.

From WILLIAM H. D. C. WRIGHT, Rio de Janeiro, March 4, 1828. Encloses a copy of a decree requiring that neutral vessels leaving Montevideo be bonded to prevent their entering any Argentine port. Transmits correspondence relating to the impressment of seaman Joseph Anderson Lyons, the bonding of prize vessels, and the burning of the brig *Brutus.* States that the impressment of Lyons was based on unjust principles, one of which required proof of citizenship as a prerequisite for avoiding the press gang. Observes that peace negotiations between Brazil and Buenos Aires are currently being conducted under British mediation. Reports that he has learned, confidentially, that Buenos Aires requested that negotiations be arranged through the mediation of the Colombian Minister, Leandro Palacios, but that the Brazilian Emperor, Pedro I, informed Palacios that he preferred the mediation of the United States. Adds that Palacios's dispatches were held up and did not arrive before the negotiations were begun under British mediation. Details the terms proposed to Brazil through Palacios: suspension of hostilities, mutual withdrawal from the Banda Oriental, mediation of Great Britain, twelve–month grace period should a settlement fail to materialize, and the right of the inhabitants of the Banda Oriental to choose the power with which they will unite. Says the Emperor is willing to withdraw his army from the Banda Oriental, retaining Montevideo. ALS. DNA, RG59, Cons. Disp., Rio de Janeiro, vol. 3 (M–T172, R4). Received April 20, 1828. See Tudor to Clay, August 28, 1828 and Parry, *Treaty Series,* 79:1-11, for the end of the Buenos Aires (Argentine)–Brazilian conflict.

To WILLIAM B. LAWRENCE, no. 5, March 5, 1828. Comments on "the importance of using . . . before the Arbiter who may be appointed under the late North Eastern boundary Convention [6:1100–01] . . . 'the third report from the Select Committee on Emigration' laid before Parliament during the last year, together with the accompanying 'map of the British possessions in North America, complied from documents in the Colonial Department.'" Requests him to "purchase two copies of that Report, *with the accompanying map*"—one for the State Department, and the other for "the archives of the Legation." Copy. DNA, RG59, Dip. Instr., vol. 12, p. 66 (M77, R7). L, draft, in DLC-HC (DNA, M212, R8); also in Manning, *Diplomatic Correspondence . . . Canadian Relations*, 2:164–5.

From JOHN McLEAN, "Post Office Department," March 5, 1828. States that the removal of the Patent Office from the building housing "the General Post Office" is necessary "unless some other building shall be provided for" the latter. Notes that he has applied to the House Ways and Means Committee for an appropriation of $12,000 to be used in constructing "a building for . . . the City Post Office and the Patent Office." Reports that "a Company whi[ch] owns the building lately occupied by Cong[ress] near the Capitol" has proposed to the Committee that it be purchased for use by the Patent Office, and that he had informed the Committee that he would consult Clay "as to [the] location of the Patent Office." Requests a reply, which "shall be transmitted to the Committee. . . ." ALS. DNA, RG59, Misc. Letters (M179, R66). During the reconstruction of the United States Capitol, following the War of 1812, Congress met in a brick building erected for the use of that body by a group of private citizens on the site now occupied by the Supreme Court. Constance McLaughlin Green, *Washington Village and Capital, 1800–1878* (Princeton, 1962), 67. For the construction in 1836–40 of the Patent Office building, see Louise Hall, "The Design of the Old Patent Office Building," *JSAH*, (March, 1956), 15:27–30.

McLean repeated on May 31 his complaint of the lack of space in the building housing the Post Office and Patent Office, the uncomfortable working conditions for his clerks, and the restriction of "public business." To alleviate this unhealthy condition, he suggested to Clay that Congress make an appropriation to rent "the building near the Capitol" to accomodate the Patent Office. See, further, McLean to Clay, May 31, 1828. ALS. DNA, RG59, Misc. Letters, (M179, R66).

From JOSEPH HILL CLARK   London, March 6, 1828
[Letter commences with a seven and a half page discussion of current British and European political and economic affairs; and with growing Russo-Turkish diplomatic tensions. Continues:]
I hope to see published in the U.S. the speach of Mr [Henry Peter] Brougha[m] on the motion for an address in answer to the Kings speach,[1] it ought to open the eyes of some of our people to the wanton folly of sporting with our own institutions in the means they used to promote the election of Genl. Jackson—I do assure you if such should be the unfortunate issue of the next election, our character will sink dreadfully in the estimation of all those in Europe who have been looking to our Country as the last hope & refuge of all that is enlightened & wise in Government, they hope & expect that we are too sensible a people to

shut our eyes to the monstrous absurdity, of electing a man, who sets all laws at defiance, who is unable to controul his own violent passions and who has shown himself utterly incapable of civil employment, to place such a man as this in a place in which he can do so much mischief merely because he has done one clever thing at N[ew]. O[rleans]. as commander, argues they say, such a total want of foresig[ht] & for which our Countrymen have so much credit, it is difficult for them to believe, that, on the occasion the people of the U.S. will be found wanting in this particular.

I enclose you a drawing of the model of a Steam carriage which I have seen in operation in this City; and it is my opinion Corroborated by all who have seen it, that it will answer the purpose intended; a coach built after this model will be ready for the road in about a month—The patentees informed me that they had procured a patent in France, and they were desirous to obtain one in the U.S. but it seems our laws do not permit a foreigner taking out a patent, or a Citizen without he is the original inventor—[2] in this Country the patent laws are opened to all of every Nation & clime—

In case of War between Russia & Turkey [6:1343-4], would not an appointt. of some kind other be usefull to our trade at Constantinople—the produce of the Black Sea must be brought to Europe—and we can do it cheaper than any other people—

I have to beg your pardon for prosing thus long, with a promise however that I will not again commit the like fault—

ALS. DNA, RG59, Misc. Letters (M179, R66).   1. Brougham's speech in Parliament of February 7, 1828, was in answer to that of George IV on January 29, 1828. Hansard, *Parliamentary Debates*, 18:2-4, 4-83, 127-258.   2. Laws relating to aliens taking out U.S. patents are found in 1 *U.S. Stat.*, 318-23 (February 21, 1793), and 2 *U.S. Stat.*, 37-8 (April 17, 1800).

From WILLIAM B. LAWRENCE, London, no. 27, March 6, 1828. Reports that the Convention [6:1370-1] between the U.S. and the Hanse Town Republics, Lubeck, Bremen, and Hamburg, was approved in Hamburg on February 21. Notes that the denunciation of the Russo-Turkish Convention of Ackerman [5:937] by the Sultan in the recent "Turkish Manifesto [Lawrence to Clay, February 28]" has sounded a very serious note in the Eastern issue. Reviews British and Russian diplomatic agreements and maneuvers in bringing on the Treaty of Ackerman in October, 1826. Points out that Britain "entertains great apprehensions" that Russia will now "proceed on her own private quarrel" with the Porte, notwithstanding the "restraints on territorial aggrandizement" at Turkey's expense to which she had agreed in the subsequent "Greek Treaty [Treaty of London, July 6, 1827]." Reports that the British government has received from Charles R. Vaughan, its Minister in Washington, dispatches announcing U.S. Senate ratification of "the Commercial Convention [6:826-7] and of the Convention to regulate the reference to arbitration of the North East Boundary question [6:1100-01]." ALS. DNA, RG59, Dip. Disp., Great Britain, vol. 35 (M30, R31). Received April 23, 1828. For the Anglo-Russian involvement in the preliminary arrangements leading to the Convention of Ackerman, see Woodhouse, *The Greek War of Independence*, 115-27.

To JOHN McLEAN, March 7, 1828. States, in reply to McLean's letter of March 5, that he will be glad "to co-operate in any measures that may induce to the convenience of . . . [McLean's] Department" and that, if "the Patent office . . . is to remain attached to this [State] Department," the existing inconvenience resulting from the location of the former some distance from the latter "will be a little increased by the removal of the patent office to the proposed building on Capitol Hill." Refers to the possibility of the establishment of a Home Department [5:72–3, 109–12], to which the Patent office would probably be connected, and concludes: "I shall conform, cheerfully, to any disposition which Congress may make of the matter." Copy. DNA, RG59, Dom. Letters, vol. 22, p. 153 (M40, R20).

From THOMAS L. L. BRENT, Lisbon, no. 53, March 8, 1828. Reports that he "waited on" the Count of Vila Real, in consequence of the latter's recent appointment [as acting Foreign Minister]. States that Vila Real informed him "that a piratical vessel had been fitted out and armed in the United States," that it had already "captured a Brazilian vessel," and that it was expected "to proceed to the coast of Portugal to cruize against her commerce." Adds that Vila Real asked him to inform the United States government of the situation. Promises to explain more fully after he learns the name of the vessel. LS. DNA, RG59, Dip. Disp., Portugal, vol. 7 (M43, R6). Received May 9, 1828. On March 13, in his dispatch no. 55, Brent informed Clay that he had not yet been able to see Vila Real in order to learn more about the pirate vessel. *Ibid.* See also Brent to Clay, March 28, 1828.

From THOMAS L. L. BRENT, Lisbon, no. 54, March 8, 1828. States that he believes the visit of Frederico Torlade de Azambuja will be important in the eventual conclusion of a "commercial arrangement advantageous to both" nations. Reports that he has consequently, with a view to preventing postponement of Torlade's departure, addressed him a note, which, with Torlade's reply, is enclosed. ALS. DNA, RG59, Dip. Disp., Portugal, vol. 7 (M43, R6). Received May 9, 1828.

From FRANCIS T. BROOKE   Richmond, March 8, 1828
I was much gratified by Seeing Mr [David] Whites publication in the [Richmond *Constitutional*] Whig to day [6:1206-07]—it will have very good effect as he was relied on as knowing all about the Corrupt Bargain—I wish you would publish your letter to [Francis P.] Blair [4:9–10], of that you are the best judge—I have not the least objection to publishing your letter to me of the 4 of Feb 1825 [4:55-6; Brooke to Clay, February 21, 1828] and am ready when called on, I have Spoken of it often, and hoped that Mr [Thomas] Ritchie would call for it, if he could be tempted to do that, it would have an excellent effect—I do not feel Mr Rs [John Randolph] Slanders but am vexed with Ritchie for publishing them and have with drawn my name from his paper [Richmond *Enquirer*], I gave him a hint, in the piece in to days [Richmond *Constitutional*] Whig Signed Veritas—and I Suppose he will declare war against me,[1] I have no ill will against him but I owed to

myself not to be made to contribute to the circulation of abuse of myself—I wish I could See the documents on the Subject of the execution of the Six militia men [5:739], I am not Satisfied with the report of the committee[2]—my friend [Chapman] Johnson now takes a deep interest in your affair—[Benjamin Watkins] Leigh is terribly hampered he loves Johnson but fears Randolph his condition is truly pitiable—

ALS. InU.   1. Editorial, Richmond *Enquirer,* March 14, 1828.   2. The February 11, 1828, Report of the House Committee on Military Affairs exonerated Jackson for his court martial trial and excecution of six U.S. [Tennessee] militiamen for desertion in Mobile on December 5, 1814. *House Reports,* 20 Cong., 1 Sess., no. 140, pp. 6–8. The Report was read and tabled.

To ALBERT GALLATIN, March 8, 1828. Acknowledges receipt of Gallatin's letters of February 18, 23, and 29, and their enclosures. States that, since the treaties which Gallatin negotiated [6:826–7, 859–60, 1100–01] have been ratified by the Senate, the President felt obligated to transmit them promptly to England for exchange of ratifications, despite the fact that delay would have allowed more time to prepare for arbitration. Says that the messenger carrying them probably embarked from New York on March 1 so that the exchange will probably occur between April 1 and 15; consequently, the "demand upon the British Government must be made" during the first half of October. Meanwhile, an agent will be selected, who, after an association with Gallatin, may be sent to Europe to "superintend the arbitration" for the United States. Reports that the agent, William Pitt Preble, who will be appointed soon, may be sent to Canada to make an investigation before he goes to Europe.

Transmits the recently published report of the Joint Select Committee of the Maine legislature regarding the Northeastern Boundary and suggests that it may supply Gallatin "with some useful suggestions." States that he will cause to be transmitted a copy of "Map A." as well as the books which Gallatin requested.

Reports that the President agrees with Gallatin that "it will be more expedient" to secure a special appropriation for the funds to implement the convention rather than "to draw from the Contingent Fund of Foreign Intercourse," and that such an act will be requested during the present or early in the next session of Congress. Accepts Gallatin's offer to provide a "sketch" of the instructions for the agent who will go to Canada. Promises to send a copy of the February 11, 1828 report of the agent, Samuel B. Barrell, who has recently returned from New Brunswick, as soon as it is published. LS. NHi–Gallatin Papers (MR15). LS, draft, in CSmH; copy in DNA, RG59, Dip. Instr., vol. 12, pp. 67–9 (M77, R7); extract in Manning, *Diplomatic Correspondence . . . Canadian Relations,* 2:165–6. The Senate confirmed Gallatin and William Pitt Preble as agents on May 5. U.S. Sen., *Excecutive Journal,* 3:608–09. For the Maine Legislature's report, *Resolves of Maine,* see *Niles' Register* (February 23, 1828), 33:428–30 and Henry S. Burrage, *Maine in the Northeastern Boundary Controversy* (Portland, Me., 1919), 138–42.

From JOEL R. POINSETT, Mexico, no. 118, March 8, 1828. Transmits protocol of a conference held with Sebastian Camacho "at his request" to explain some doubtful points on the proposed treaty of amity, commerce, and navigation [Poinsett to Clay, February 22, 1828]. States that he "used very strong language" in discussing the article on fugitive slaves, because he "thought it politic." LS. DNA, RG59, Dip. Disp., Mexico, vol. 3 (M97, R4). Received April 22, 1828. No specific article on fugitive slaves appeared in the treaty when it was finally concluded on April 5, 1831.

From WILLIAM TAYLOR, Veracruz, March 8, 1828. Reports that he has returned to Veracruz following a tour through the country, and that few improvements have been undertaken. Expresses belief that the dominance of the Yorkinos over the Escoseses depends largely on the former's ability to procure money for the government. Contends that the rise of the Yorkinos has been favorable to American interests. Notes that the Yorkinos "scarely felt themselves warm in their seats, before they resumed their negotiations and concluded a Treaty with Mr. [Joel R.] Poinsett. . . ." Relates news of the capture of the Mexican brig *Guerrero* off Havana. Reports that the brig *Bravo* of 18 guns sails tomorrow with two privateers for the coast of Cuba and that the *El Congresso* of 64 guns and the *Libertad,* "now cut down to a Corvette," are in Veracruz port. ALS. DNA, RG59, Cons. Disp., Veracruz, vol. 1 (M183, R1). Received March 28, 1828.

To ALVA WOODS   Washington, March 8, 1828
I have received your letter of the third instant. My advice to you is that, if you are not decided at once to accept the Presidency of Transylvania, you proceed to Lexington before coming to a final determination. The best route will be to proceed by Balto. or this place to Wheeling and thence down the Ohio river in a Steam boat. You can get from here to Lexington in eight or nine days. In the hope of seeing you here in your way thither, I shall forbear at this time from entering into those details which your letter requests. I will say in the general that I think Transylvania offers a fine field for useful exertion; and that it presents no formidable obstacles to its becoming one of the most respectable literary institutions in the U. States. And I do believe that the means which it possesses, and the arrangements which the Trustees have the power of making, are such as to afford reasonable security for a liberal compensation to the President.

ALS. RHi.

From JOEL R. POINSETT, Mexico, no. 119, March 9, 1828. Reports that the former Secretary of State, Sebastian Camacho, will not resume that office because President Guadalupe Victoria has yielded to Liberal party opposition to him. Adds that Juan de Dios Canedo will become Secretary of State while Camacho has been appointed minister to the Tacubaya Congress. States that, in addition, the cabinet includes: Jose Ignacio Esteva for Treasury; Miguel [*sic,* Manuel] Gomez Pedraza for War and Marine; and "probably" Juan Jose Espinosa de los Monteros for Grace and Justice. Notes that Jose Miguel Ramos Arizpe will likely leave the administration. Describes Canedo as "a man of specious rather than of solid talents," but predicts, after having a "perfectly satisfactory" first interview with him, that some of the many claims now pending will be brought "to a speedy issue." Reports that he received "some days ago" a memorial from the American merchants in Veracruz and Tampico regarding the new tariff. Expresses the opinion that Mexican officials "misinterpreted the law and attempted to compel the foreign merchants to pay at once the internation duty upon all goods at this time in the several ports of the Republic." Notes that through his intervention, "the matter was arranged to the satisfaction of the merchants by the Congress."

Reports that Manuel Rincon has gone to assume the governorship of Veracruz with the hope of compelling the people of that state to obey the "laws of the actual government," which they now refuse to do. Adds that the insurgents on the Pacific are "still in arms" but do not engage in hostilities and that the war in Guatemala continues without prospect of "speedy termination." LS. DNA, RG59, Dip. Disp., Mexico, vol. 3 (M97, R4). Received April 22, 1828.

From JOHN QUINCY ADAMS, Washington, March 10, 1828. Patent affirming the fact that Clay has purchased 160 acres of land in "South West quarter Section Eight, in Township fourteen, North of Range ten West," near Vincennes, Indiana. DS. DLC–TJC (DNA, M212, R10).

To FRANCIS T. BROOKE   Washington, March 10, 1828
I have received your favor of the 8h. inst. If you do not, I do, feel the attacks on you, because I fear that they are the effect of our long standing friendship. Their effect is less, it is true, considering the quarter from which they proceed. [John H.] Pleasants of the [Richmond *Constitutional*] Whig has not the merit of first evincing a thorough knowledge of that being [John Randolph]—Mr. Jefferson long ago understood him, when he made an allusion to the same physical defect. We ought to be ashamed of ourselves in refle[c]ting that such a *thing* should be capable of inflicting any pain.

I wish my letter to you of 4 Feb 1825 [4:55–6] could be drawn out. But how is that to be done? I have a copy of mine to Blair [4:9–10], mentioned by you, and although there is a playfulness, not to say levity, about it, which renders it perhaps unfit for the public eye, I do believe that good rather than evil would attend its publication. The difficulty, and the only difficulty with me, is whether I ought to lend any sanction to such a violation of private intercourse; and whether, after yielding to it there would not be other and further appeals and insinuations, to deceive public credulity. If I authorize its publication, I do not think the time has yet arrived when that ought to be done. I will, if I do not forget it, send you hereafter a Copy of the letter. Since the publication of my address [6:1394–6], I have received a large mass of additional evidence, to the same tenor. Some of it is as strong, if not stronger than any which is now before the public. Ought I to publish it?[1] I am afraid, on the one hand, of teazing the public; and on the other, of omitting any thing that is due to the occasion.

You are assailed for the first time seriously. May I take the liberty of suggesting that you should not allow the wanton attack to affect you, in the smallest degree? Above all, you should not permit yourself to use one expression, or to perform any act hastily. An unsullied character of more than three score years' duration can surely successfully withstand the imbecile assaults of a miserable _____.

I will send you a Copy of the Report of the Comee. respecting the six militia.[2]

I am sorry for [Benjamin W.] Leigh—quite as much on his as on public account. The gratification of private antipathy will never be allowed, before God or Man, as a sufficient motive for the neglect of patriotic duty. And if he fears R [John Randolph]. more even than he hates Mr. Adams, the world and his own conscience will both condemn him [6:636–7].

Our accounts are truly encouraging. From N. York the current of favorable intelligence is steady, unchecked and such as to justify a confident anticipation of our success. The Kentucky prospects too are good; and, if, as I believe, we shall succeed there, we shall owe our good fortune, in no small degree, to our Virginia friends.

ALS. KyU.   1. *A Supplement to the Address ... to the Public, passim.* Cf. below, June 10, 1828.   2. Brooke to Clay, March 8, 1828.

To ALBERT GALLATIN, March 10, 1828. Urges him to read an article on the Northeastern Boundary controversy "in the next North American Review." LS. NHi–Gallatin Papers (MR15). Also in Manning, *Diplomatic Correspondence ... Canadian Relations,* 2:166. The article, "Northeastern Boundary," published in the *NAR* (April, 1828), 24:421–44, is a book–review essay on *Considerations of the Claims and Conduct of the United States, respecting their Northeastern Boundary, and the Value of the British Colonies in North America* (London, 1826), and on *Letters on the Boundary Line,* "By Verax," published in the St. John [New Brunswick] *Gazette,* 1827. After discussing the disputed region's history since 1604, with an extended treatment of various French and British surveys and boundary studies, the reviewer concluded: "We find nothing to invalidate in any degree the claim made by our [U.S.] government." *Ibid.,* 444.

From SAMUEL MIFFLIN   Lebanon, Pa., March 10, 1828
I think in some of my communications I have said, that the Election in Penn: November next, would be decided by the German population.—I am not singular in this opinion, or in the belief, that a spirit of enquiry is commencing among them, which is likely to lead to the happiest results.—

Independently, of the difficulty of circulating information among a class of people, who do not understand the common language of the Country, those, who are in the habit of reading the news of the day, were induced, by the silence or the flat denial of the Opposition papers, of the charges brought against the General to believe, them entirely groundless. But fortunately, for the cause of our Country, his supporters, have been driven into a defence & justification, of their Idol, & thus, the parties having fairly Joined issue I cannot doubt, but the verdict, will be in favor of the correct course pursued by the present Ad[ministration]. Indeed, we have in this County [Lebanon] several instances when the

Militia & Bentons affair [5:739; 6:1342] have already made converts & to me the declaration, of a Jackson man, "Many are falling off from us, but I can not find, that any are joining us."—

Strange as it may appear, the simple fact that Mr. Adams speaks the German language, is calculated to make a favorable impression. Altho., the knowledge that such is the case being very limited its operation must necessarily be equally limited—

However unwilling to use any unfair means (& indeed our cases do not require there aid) it has struck me, if some opportunity should better rise which would give a plausible ground, for addressing a letter of Mr. A. in German & he would answer it, in the same language, that it will be the means of conveying to the Germans a knowledge which would produce a much stronger impression, in his favor than you can be aware of.

I am fully sensible of the correct & prudent course, which he has observed, in relation to the pending question & possible he may be averse even to make use of this innocent engine [?], to secure his reelection; but I trust should occasion offer, for addressing him such a letter, he will so far relax from the rigid rule, he had adopted, as to reply to it, in the same language.—

For my own part taking a view of the means used by the opposition to pull down virtue & talent & put in their place ignorance & vice, I cannot but consider, every measure, consistent with truth, & calculated to defeat a conspiracy, against the cause of one['s] Country is justifiable.—

Should you think proper to reply, to the main object of this letter, you can do so, by simply saying "Your wish can or cannot be complied with"—Letters, which are never written do not tell tales—& were I disposed to follow the example of the follower of the [illeg. word] Don Quixote. I could give you many other reasons, why, my wish should be complied with, but as I believe it is a rule, in law, when the ground is sufficient to sustain a cause, it is unnecessary to adduce others. . . . [P.S.] I am not without a hope that I may have occasion to visit Washington before the S. C. breaks up—Can I procure a copy of the Militia documents[1]

ALS. DLC–HC (DNA, M212, R3). Addressed "(Private)" on attached sheet.   1. Brooke to Clay, March 8, 1828.

From NICHOLAS NAVONI, Constantinople, March 10, 1828. Transmits "a Bulletin of all that has occurred [in Turkey], from the 1st. Feby, to the 10th. March, . . . for the purpose of being sent . . . to the different cabinets of Europe." Encloses translation of the declaration of the Porte "to the Greek Patriarch and Synod, in which it supposes the fact of having received a petition, soliciting the pardon of the Greeks in the Morea and other places in rebellion." ALS, in French, with trans. in State Dept. file. DNA, RG59, Dip. Disp., Turkey, vol. 1 (M46, R2). Received August 6, 1828.

From CHARLES SAVAGE, Guatemala City, March 10, 1828. Reports his arrival as of February 23, finding the President, Manuel Jose Arce, in retirement, the Secretary of State, Juan Francisco de Sosa, absent in the army, and the Federal compact apparently a dead letter. Describes the composition of the Federation of the Centre of America, the economy and political attachment of the various states, the recent victories of the Guatemalan forces, the background of the differences between the executive authority and the congress, with the latter body supported by San Salvador. Notes that no exactions have been made of Americans here but that exorbitant demands have been coerced on the British, French, and other merchants. Requests instructions on his course should such a move be made against Americans, pending the arrival of a Chargé d'Affaires from the United States. ALS. DNA, RG59, Cons. Disp., Guatemala, vol. 1 (M–T337, R1). Received May 7, 1828. At "midnight" on this same date, Savage again wrote, enclosing Government newspapers dated March 4 and 9, 1828, which announced victory by Government forces over the insurgents. *Ibid.* Received May 7, 1828.

From BEAUFORT T. WATTS, Cartagena, no. 42, March 10, 1828. Reports that a rebellion led by Jose Padilla of the navy has recently been suppressed. States that it was adjunct to the "revolution effected by [Jose] Bustamante in Lima [6:684–5], and lately attempted at La Paz in Bolivia," and that Padilla has fled towards Ocana in order to confer with Francisco de Paula Santander who is believed to be part of a conspiracy in Peru and Colombia whose object it is "to prostrate President [Simon] Bolivar." Points to the recently detected plot of Manuel Lorenzo de Vidaurre in Lima, "the object of which was the subversion of the governments of Peru and Bolivia, disunite the South of Colombia (Guayaquil) and to consolidate an Empire under the sovereignty of a descendant of the Incas [Linavibca].—"
Laments the unsettled political situation in Colombia and attributes it to the circumstances which prompted the Spanish American revolutions—not a desire to be free of Spain but rather Spain's prostration by Napoleon. Reviews Bolivar's early involvement in the revolution, the earlier activities of Francisco de Miranda, and the relationship between the Colombians and the Spanish cortes. Details the financial distress of the country. ALS. DNA, RG59, Dip. Disp., Colombia, vol. 4 (M–T33, R4). Received April 28, 1828. See, above, Tudor to Clay, February 6, 1828.

From NATHANIEL WILLIAMS, Baltimore, March 10, 1828. Acknowledges receipt of Daniel Brent's letter regarding the Argentine privateer *Flor de Maio*. Reports that he has investigated and found "no addition of any kind . . . to the military equipments of this vessel." Details repairs made to the vessel, noting that while the vessel had bulwarks when it entered port, they were in poor condition and new ones were built. ALS. DNA, RG59, Misc. Letters (M179, R66). For Brent's letter of March 6 to Williams, see DNA, RG59, Dom. Letters, vol. 22, pp. 152–3 (M40, R20); see, also, Rebello to Clay, March 4, 1828.

From JAMES BROWN   Paris, March 12, 1828
You will perceive by the despatch which you will receive with this letter that changes are still going on in the Ministry, and that the Administra-

tion which has been very unsettled ever since the dissolution of the late Chambers is yet fixed upon no solid or permanent foundation. It is said the King [Charles X] only changed the [Cound de] Villele administration from a belief that it could not obtain a majority in the Chambers, and that the address censuring their conduct met with his disapprobation. Indeed it has been reputed I know not with what truth, that he at first talked of declining receiving it, upon which the new Ministers intimated that should he take that step they would immediatley tender their resignations. It has been the intention of some of the members of the two chambers to prepare and present Articles of impeachment against M de Villele but I rather think this design will be abandoned. The new elections which are ordered in consequence of the elections of several members to more than one Department will it is believed strengthen the liberal party who have offered Candidates for each of them. The constitution which was in some danger seems now to be secure and reflecting men consider themselves more confirmed in their rights than they have hitherto been. M [Hyde] de Neuville had entered the Hotel of the Marine and had appointed the last Tuesday for his first reception. A melancholy accident however compelled him to postpone it. Immediately before her proposed change of residence Madame de Neuville entered the house of one of her neighbours to take leave but in returning down stairs fell through a trap door which unfortunately was opened into the cellar and fractured her thigh and received contusions in several parts of her body. You will easily believe how much we all sympathize in the sufferings of this excellent lady. It is said that circumstances inspire a hope of her recovery.

Mrs. Brown's health has greatly improved since the date of my last letter, and we now hope that although some months may elapse before the cause of her complaint entirely disappears yet that it may be attended with no serious consequences. We have had an unusually mild winter and an early spring. I had felt much uneasiness at not hearing from New Orleans for some time but was, a day or two ago, relieved by a letter from my nephew [John B. Humphreys] who gives me the most satisfactory accounts of the place and informs me that we have this year made five hundred thousand weight of the very finest sugar, and a large quantity of molasses. A considerable quantity of the first had been sold at six and a half cents. My crop of the preceding year was the same in quantity and sold at that price. My good fortune so far as a planter is perhaps without a parralel and my planting for the next year promises an increase of revenue. I am very sorry that you had not purchased when you visited New Orleans [2:689–95] and commenced a similar establishment. I hope the leave I asked to return to America will not occasion any embarrassment to the government but that it may be made useful to the Presidential election. It is unfortunate that Virginia had not sooner endeavored to stir up the friends of Mr. Adams. The address of Chapman Johnston [sic, Johnson] displays much talent and cannot fail to produce considerable effect.[1] Mr [Langdon] Cheves does not seem to have done much for General Jackson in the vicinity of Lancaster if I may judge from the result of the late elections in that quarter.[2] Your vindication [6:1394–6] is conclusive if men would reason but those who have assailed you without proof will endeavor to destroy you because they have wantonly and wickedly wounded you. Examples of this kind are to be found in every country. Time will do justice to your motives and character.

Although Mr de Neuville has formerly been unfriendly to our claims yet knowing his ambition to become a Minister and the probability that he might succeed, and having always found him friendly to me, I have when he was in disgrace at Court always received and treated him as an old acquaintance. I have some hope that he will relax in his opposition to us more especially as he has always professed a great affection for our Country and its institutions and has often alluded to them in the Chamber of deputies in terms of high approbation. From Mr de Villele I easily perceived that we had nothing to hope. It is possible this Government may object to submitting the question under the treaty without submitting our claims also. I am by no means very sanguine in my hopes that they will do any thing. Perhaps the affairs in the East may end in a war in which event they may consider it their interests to make us their friends. It would seem now that if the Porte persists the combined powers will overrun and then divide Greece and Turkey. The distribution of the spoil will be a point of some difficulty, but by means of one or two Congresses of sovereigns, that may be satisfactorily arranged. A report was circulated at the Exchange yesterday that the Russians had crossed the Pruth [6:1343-4] and a small decline in the stocks followed it.

Great as Mrs. Brown['s] wish is to see her friends and to live quiet she yet feels that she will not have in America, Physicians to consult in whom she will have equal confidence with the distinguished Surgeons and Physicians who now attend her. Although she has not joined in evening parties abroad yet such is the attachment of her friends to her that even at this season of gayeity and dissipation she never passes an evening without social visits from the most affectionate and agreeable society. Her courage never forsakes her and her general health is good.

I have not received a line from you since October. Where will you spend the Summer and at what time will you leave Washington? I have been delighted to learn from some of my correspondents that your health is better than formerly. Mr. [Josiah Stoddard] Johnston writes now that you have had a pleasant society during the Winter. I hope Mrs. Clay is pleased with her fine house.[3] It gave me great pain to hear that Mrs. Adams health had declined.[4] Her brother [Thomas B. Johnson] is at Rouen and I believe passes his time very agreeably. Mr. Adams has the satisfaction of finding that his most bitter enemies can find nothing to blame in his administration since their unjust censures on the Panama Mission [5:117-8] and the conduct of the Colonial question [5:630-2].

Give my love with that of Mrs. B. to Mrs. Clay. . . .   P S Will you be so obliging as to request Mr [Stephen] Pleasonton to examine my last years accounts as soon as convenient and write me if he finds them correct. Mr [Daniel] Sheldons health declined so rapidly that it became absolutely necessary that he should change the air—He has gone for a few weeks to Marseilles and as he has been on two former occasions restored by a short excursion I hope he will now regain his usual strength. He has engaged a son [Isaac Cox Barnet] of Mr [Charles]

Barnet our Consul, to act in his place during his absence. I could find no other American now in Paris sufficently well acquainted with the french language to answer the purpose—He [Charles Barnet] is consul at Antwerp but the duties are performed by a Vice Consul.

March 13

The Budget was presented yesterday and excited much surprize and disatisfaction. You will find it in the number of the [Paris] Constitutionel [*sic, Constitutionnel*] which I now enclose. The news which that paper contains respecting the East is generally credited. The French troops will in five days embark for Greece. I was told last evening that the King [Charles X] on being informed that his late Ministers were censured in the address of the Chamber of Deputies intimated an intention of dissolving the Chamber and placing other Ministers at the head of Affairs, but was dissuaded from it. He did not agree to receive the Committee appointed to present the address until five oClock in the afternoon. Our Ship which sailed on the 14th ulto. has not yet arrived. I wish the Newspapers for Mr [Christopher] Hughes and Mr [Henry] Middleton could be sent to them without coming by way of Paris. Those to the former after a short delay can be sent by American travellers going to Brussels but I have no means of forwarding Mr Middletons except occasionally by a Russian Courier, and the Documents and Newspapers are so voluminous that I can hardly ask the Ambassador [Pozzo Di Borgo] to Charge himself with them.

ALS. DLC-HC (DNA, M212, R3). Printed in *LHQ*, 24:1088–91.   1. See above, 6:1385–6. The address of the Richmond Anti–Jackson Convention, apparently written by Johnson, is in the Richmond *Enquirer*, January 17, 1828.   2. Langdon Cheves resided in Lancaster, Pa., from 1826 to 1829. See Sergeant to Clay, December 30, 1827, for the political situation in Lancaster County.   3. The so–called "Decatur House." See 6:385–6. 4. Adams, *Memoirs*, 7:453, 455.

From HENRY PRATT, Philadelphia, March 12, 1828. Solicits Clay's attention to the "most unjustified outrage committed under the Authority of the Buenos Ayres Government upon" his brig *Ruth* and her "valuable cargo." Expresses disappointment that "such reclamations" have not been made "by the United States representatives Civil or Naval at Buenos Ayres; as would have induced that Government to Know that there was a safeguard for the rights and property of American Merchants trading to that quarter which Could not be disregarded with impunity—" Criticizes John M. Forbes and "the Commander of the Sloop of War Boston [Beekman V. Hoffman]" for abandoning "the vessel and cargo . . . to their fate." Encloses copies of documents pertaining to the case and requests Clay's early, and efficient intervention in his behalf. LS. DNA, RG76, Misc. Claims, Buenos Aires.

The following day, March 13, Clay instructed Forbes "to make an immediate and urgent demand of full satisfaction and indemnity" for the *Ruth*, stating that its capture "is an outrage which requires immediate and full indemnity," because the "pretended" Buenos Airean blockade of the coast of Brazil does not justify such a seizure. Copy. DNA, RG59, Dip. Instr., vol. 12, pp. 69–70 (M77, R7).

On March 14 Clay informed Pratt of his instructions to Forbes. Copy. DNA, RG59, Dom. Letters, vol. 22, p. 159 (M40, R20).

On April 22 Clay sent Forbes a duplicate of the instructions of March 13 and admonished him to "urge the demand . . . with additional earnestness and solemnity." Copy. DNA, RG59, Dip. Instr., vol. 12, p. 100 (M77, R7).

Pratt again wrote Clay on June 27, pressing for a full indemnity for the *Ruth* and insisting that Forbes be alerted to his duty. Expresses the hope that "the flagrant and outrageous . . . decision" of the lower court in Buenos Aires in condemning the ship will be "corrected in a higher tribunal." ALS. DNA, RG76, Misc. Claims, Brazil.

To JOSE SILVESTRE REBELLO, March 12, 1828. States that the district attorney at Baltimore, Nathaniel Williams, was instructed "to enquire into the circumstances complained of" in Rebello's note of March 4. Encloses a copy of the March 10 reply received from Williams, noting that "it would seem" that the public law had not been violated in the repairs made to the *Flor de Maio* and that the Collector of the Customs, James H. McCulloch, had ordered "a strict inspection . . . to prevent her receiving any augmentation of Stores or Men. . . ." Copy. DNA, RG59, Notes to Foreign Ministers and Consuls, vol. 3, p. 442 (M38, R3).

From THOMAS L. L. BRENT, Lisbon, no. 56, March 13, 1828. States that the Regent, Miguel, has shown himself to be "hostile to the new institutions" and "completely" under the control of the Queen Carlota Joaquina. Reports that the Count of Vila Real has been "removed from the war department and appointed Minister of Foreign Affairs instead of being ad interim" and that the Count of Rio Pardo, an anticonstitutionalist, has replaced him at the War Department. Adds that changes in military personnel have strengthened the position of those opposed to the Constitution and that no newspapers in favor of the Constitution "have been allowed to appear" while "others have been established that are violent in their opposition to it."

Notes that, in the Cortes, the House of Peers has been "nearly . . . passive" while the House of Deputies has passed resolutions supportive of the constitution. Reports that the British army has suspended its evacuation. Continues, under date of March 14, stating that Miguel has dissolved the Cortes without giving cause and adding that it is believed that Miguel intends "to be declared absolute King." LS. DNA, RG59, Dip. Disp., Portugal, vol. 7 (M43, R6). Received May 4, 1828.

To JAMES COLLIER   Washington, March 14, 1828
I received your favor of the 13t instant. I think your friend at Russellville [Ky.] must be somewhat mistaken as to the want of papers conveying political information in his district, although I perceive it is not well supplied with those, on one side, as it would be, if it had a different representative. The same mail that brought your letter, brought also the Russellville paper containing my Address [6:1394–6];[1] so that I presume it has been extensively circulated.

Our friends from K in Congress are, I believe, diffusing intelligence as much as they can. The number at work on the other side is certainly much against our cause. But I am happy to tell you that the accounts from K are encouraging.

ALS. CtY.   1. The Russellville *Weekly Messenger* ran Clay's *Address* of December 29, 1827, in its issues of January 2, February 2, and February 9, 1828.

From WILLIAM B. LAWRENCE, London, no. 28, March 14, 1828. Refers to his dispatch of March 6 with reference to probable Russian foreign policy moves. Recently received information does not indicate, however, the "precise manner, on which that power proposes to avenge herself on Turkey for the violation of the Treaty of Akkerman [*sic*, Ackerman] [5:937]," only that the receipt of the Turkish Manifesto at St. Petersburg seems to suggest the early commencement of hostilities, and that Russia's felt obligation to Britain and France in this regard is not yet clear. Thinks British policy is peaceful, "that war of any kind is greatly deprecated and that, in the present state of the finances, it would require the most powerful considerations to induce either the nation or the Administration to enter voluntarily into measures, which would occasion expenditures that would take away all hope of even a future diminuation of existing burthens." Adds that Britain does not "consider the Turkish manifesto, by itself, a sufficient cause for her [Russia] acting offensively against the Porte." Encloses a copy of an article from the Paris *Le Constitutionnel* stating that the Mr. George H. Richards mentioned therein had once been a government clerk in Washington and in 1827 was employed in the London legation. Notes that when Richards received a passport for Greece and Italy, Lawrence understood that he was travelling under the auspices of the Philhellenic Committee. Adds, however, that he [Lawrence] has denied that Richards is an agent of the United States. LS. DNA RG59, Dip. Disp., Great Britain, vol. 35 (M30, R31). Received April 28, 1828.

The article from *Le Constitutionnel* of March 7 charges that Richards was negotiating a pact with Turkey whereby the United States would receive commercial advantages in return for a promise that it would aid Turkey should the latter become involved in war with the European powers. For the Philhellenic Committee(s), see Dakin, *British and American Philhellenes During the War of Greek Independence, 1821–1833, passim.*

From ENOCH LINCOLN, Worcester, Mass., March 14, 1828. Transmits copy of a petition, dated Houlton Plantation, March 3, and signed by Joseph Houlton and 11 others, complaining of the indictment by the supreme court at Fredericton, New Brunswick of 13 Americans "for opposing a British Officer in taking Arnold's Cow." LS. DNA, RG76, Northeast Boundary (KyU., Special Roll, frame 222). Copy of petition enclosed in *ibid*. The cow seems not to have been consulted in this crisis of nationality. For details, see *ASPFR*, 6:936–7.

From JOSEPH HILL CLARK   London, March 15, 1828
[Discusses at length the sugar tariff question now before Parliament. Continues:]

There is little doubt that warlike operations have already commenced between Russia & Turkey.

It is now a favorite belief in this Country that the Turks have lost that enthusiasm, that military ardour, & that self devotion to the cause of their Religion, which at one time carried them conquerers to the gates of Vienna; altho their present situation may not indicate that they are animated by the same chivalrous spirit, yet who can say what a war for the preservation of national existance & national Religion may not bring forth? it would be as difficult to fix a period for its termination, or to name that Power which may not find it necessary to take part in the Contest....

ALS. DNA, RG59, Misc. Letters (M179, R66).

To HOUSE OF REPRESENTATIVES, March 15, 1828. Transmits, in response to a House resolution of February 19, copies of maps "exhibiting surveys and delineations" of as much of the Northern and Northwestern boundaries as he thinks is required by the resolution. Also refers the House to the decision, [6:1208-10] dated June 18, 1822, of the Joint Commissions under the Treaty of Ghent, "for a further and full explanation of the... boundary line, as agreed upon and established." Copy. DNA, RG59, Report Books, vol. 4, p. 234.

From DANIEL HUGUNIN, Oswego, New York, March 15, 1828. Interprets act of Congress of March 1, 1823, as authorizing the President to issue a proclamation diminishing the duties on trade with Upper Canada. Requests Clay's influence in securing such a proclamation. ALS. DNA, RG59, Misc. Letters (M179, R66). For Hugunin, see *BDAC*. For the law he mentions, see *3 U.S. Stat.*, 740-2.

To ENOCH LINCOLN, March 15, 1828. Transmits a copy of Samuel Barrell's report of February 11, 1828. Notes that the United States has returned the arbitration convention to Great Britain "with the ratification on the part of the United States" and that ratifications will be exchanged between April 1 and 15. Adds that within nine months following ratification, documentation to be used before the arbiter must be assembled. Requests that Lincoln bring to his attention any public documents or records he believes will support the American title. Copy. DNA, RG59, Dom. Letters, vol. 22, pp. 159-60 (M40, R20). Also on March 15, Clay made the same request of Levi Lincoln, Governor of Massachusetts, and in addition asked him for copies of several specified documents, on file in the public offices of Massachusetts. *Ibid.*, pp. 160-2.

From JOEL R. POINSETT, Mexico, no. 120, March 15, 1828. Reports that, because the New York packet was late, he did not receive Clay's letter of January 12 until March 14. States that he thinks the belief embodied in the resolution of the House of Representatives that an impediment existed in Mexican courts to the recovery of property by citizens of the United States from Mexican citizens "originated in some mistake or in some partial act of injustice." Adds that he had an interview with the Minister of Foreign Relations, Juan de Dios Canedo, who assured him that Mexican courts "were open to foreigners for the recovery of their debts and property, whether from each other, or from Mexican citizens, and that . . . no distinction had ever been made in the courts . . . between a native or foreign suitor and that if in particular cases, injustice has been committed this government . . . would take the requisite measures to afford redress to the aggrieved party and to punish the offenders." States that since he is aware of no impediment as described, he expressed satisfaction with the explanation. Notes that, in the 14th. article of the commercial treaty which he recently concluded with Mexico, a provision is made that "the tribunals of Justice shall be free and open to the citizens of both countries respectively for their judicial recourse, on the same terms which are usual and customary with the citizens of the country in which they may be." LS. DNA, RG59, Dip. Disp., Mexico, vol. 3 (M97, R4). Received April 22, 1828; also in *Niles' Register* (June 7, 1828), 34:245.

From PETER B. PORTER   Albany, March 15, 1828

I recieved several days since, your favour of the 1st Inst, and my apology for not having written you oftener is, that I have been suffering for several weeks with a severe cold which has affected my head and created some aspect apprehension of an inflammation of the brain—of course I have deemed it prudent to abstain as much as possible from mental exertion. I am now, however, nearly recovered.

The death of Mr. [DeWitt] Clinton will, without doubt, operate favourably to the Administration; and many of his adherants, who had no other inducement than their personal attachment to him to support Genl. Jackson, will now abandon the cause of the latter—altho' great exertions are making by the Jackson party, who are now the regents of the State, to retain them by a liberal distribution of offices, and the political favours. The controul which Mr Clinton & [Martin] Van Buren & their partisans had over the political presses & other party machinery of the State, had enabled them to create a general belief that the great body of the Republicans were in favour of the election of Genl. Jackson; and to *this belief* alone is to be ascribed most of the numerous but reluctant conversions to a cause against which the better judgment & whole moral sense of the community revolted. The people, however, are beginning to be undeceived; and a strong reaction has commenced. I think I run no hasard in assuring you that a decided majority of the electoral votes of the state will be for Mr. Adams [6:360–3].

The Tariff is the favourite measure of the people of this State, and its merits & bearings are well understood by the most intelligent part of them—But I am afraid that our adversaries will be able to gull many of the ignorant, by their hollow & hyporcritical cant about the interests of the wool grower the farmer &c &c

To morrow, or the next day, I will write to you on the subject of Mr [Anthony] Barclay's report. Indisposition alone has prevented me from doing it sooner. P.S. Will you have the goodness to give such a direction to the enclosed letter to Judge [Francis T.] Brooke as will enable it to find him, & send it to the P. office? I understand that a District Attorney is about to be appointed at Detroit. without claiming any right to give advice in relation to such an appointment you will excuse me for saying that in my opinion Mr Henry S. Cole, whose name will be laid before the President, is probably as qualified for, and as deserving of the office as any candidate that may be presented.[1]

ALS. DLC–HC (DNA, M212, R3). Addressed "private."   1. Cole did not receive the appointment. See further, 5:754, 793.

From WILLIAM H. D. C. WRIGHT, Rio de Janeiro, March 15, 1828. Corrects statement in earlier dispatch that Joseph Anderson Lyons was detained by Brazilian authorities. Transmits copy of decree of April 29. 1826 by which Emperor Pedro I abdicated the crown of Portugal [5:310]. Includes correspondence on that subject with the Marquis de Aracaty, Brazilian Minister of Foreign Affairs. Encloses copy of a letter he has received from William Tudor, announcing his appointment as Chargé d'Affaires to Brazil and explaining that illness has delayed his departure from Lima for Rio de Janeiro. ALS. DNA, RG59, Cons. Disp., Rio de Janeiro (M–T172, R4). Received May 5, 1828.

From PEDRO GONZALES, New York, March 16, 1828. States that the political disturbances in Central America "seem daily to become more serious." Notes that communications from his government are intercepted and that he feels it his duty to return home to receive instructions. Adds that he will either return soon or an explanation of his absence will be made by his government. ALS, in Spanish, with trans. in State Dept. file. DNA, RG59, Notes from Central American Legation, vol. 1 (M–T34, R1).

From STANHOPE PREVOST, Lima, March 16, 1828. States that the late James Cooley appointed him temporary U.S. consul at Lima on January 7, and that he considers it his duty to fill the post until the arrival of William Radcliff. Observes, in connection with the replacement of Cooley, that "as 'Chargé des Affaires' no one can live on the Salary" in Chile. Reports that the new constitution has been completed and that "the prospect is favorable for uninterrupted tranquillity and consequent improvement of the Country...." ALS. DNA, RG59, Cons. Disp., Lima, vol. 2 (M154, R2). Received June 8, 1828.

From GEORGE MOORE, Trieste, March 17, 1828. Transmits correspondence between himself and William B. Lovett, "master of the Brig Homer of Beverley [*sic,* Beverly, Mass.]," from whom he "demanded three months extra pay for four Seamen discharged here on account of an alleged Deviation in the Voyage." States that since he and Lovett disagreed on the "construction of the shipping articles," he "left it optional" with Lovett whether to pay Moore or not "upon his own responsibility on his return to the United States," and that Lovett insisted upon paying "*under Protest.*" Asks for instructions as to whether he is obliged to accept payment with protest "thereby incurring the responsibility of being condemned to refund an amount" two-thirds of which is paid to the seamen and the remainder credited to the government.

Asks if masters who discharge seamen for alleged acts of mutiny are requires to give them wages due and three months' extra pay and if a consul is required to maintain seamen discharged under such circumstances "when they are really in distress."

Adds that the British government's contract for Italian hemp, "cleaned, packed and shipped" at Trieste, continues, but that the British have ordered 100 tons of the shorter Hungarian variety. Notes that large quantities of Italian hemp have recently been shipped to the United States. ALS. DNA, RG59, Cons. Disp., Trieste, vol. 1 (M-T242, R-T1). Received June 1, 1828.

From JOHN B. NICHOLSON   Washington, March 17, 1828
Having visited the Colony of Liberia, on my return to the United States, from a cruise in the Mediterranean, I cheerfully comply with your request, by presenting to you such views of its present condition and probable growth, as occurred to me in the course of that visit.

The soil in the possession of the Colonists is rich, and will produce a superabundance for the support of the Colony, as well as for external commerce. Sugar, coffee, cotton, rice, and various trees and plants, yielding valuable dyes and medicinal gums, can be cultivated with success.

The population is now 1200, and is healthy and thriving. The children born in the country are fine looking, and I presume can be raised as easily as those of the natives. All the Colonists with whom I had any communication, (and with nearly the whole I did communicate in person or by my officers,) expressed their decided wish to remain in their present situation rather than to return again to the United States. I cannot give you better evidence of the prosperity of the Colony, than by mentioning that eight of my crew, (colored mechanics) after going on shore two several days, applied for, and received their discharge, in order to remain as permanent settlers. These men had been absent from their country upwards of three years, and had, among them, nearly two thousand dollars in clothes and money. Had they not been thoroughly convinced that their happiness and prosperity would be better promoted by remaining among their free brethren in Liberia, they would not have determined on so momentous a step as quitting the United States, perhaps forever, where they all had left friends and relatives.

The appearance of all the Colonists, those of Monrovia as well as those of Caldwell, indicated more than contentment. Their manners were those of freemen, who experienced the blessings of liberty, and appreciated the boon. Many of them had, by trade, accumulated a competency, if the possession of from three to five thousand dollars may be called so. As a proof of the growing importance of the commerce of the country, more than 100 hogsheads of tobacco had been used during the last year and the demand was increasing. Ivory and camwood are now the prominent articles received in exchange for foreign imports; other dyewoods, and many medicinal gums and roots will be hereafter brought in, as they are already known to exist in the interior.

I take this occasion to suggest the propriety of permitting any of the Colonists to purchase an additional number of acres of land from the Agent. By permitting this, the more enterprising will be enabled to turn their attention to the culture of the coffee-tree, which grows spontaneously in the vicinity of Monrovia. In fact, the soil will produce every thing which a tropical climate will allow to arrive at maturity.

From the good order and military discipline which appear to prevail among the Colonists, I am induced to believe they could easily repel any attack which could be made upon them by any native force. They have arms, and having associated themselves in volunteer companies, have acquired the knowledge of using them with effect against any probably force which might be brought to bear upon them, by undisciplined and scattered tribes in their vicinity. It is true, they have no harbors for large vessels, as all their rivers are obstructed by bars. This is not of much consequence to their coasting trade, as they have many harbors and inlets, which are accessible to small vessels. Large vessels have also one advantage, that most of the heavy winds are off the coast, which gives them a lee and a smooth sea. Off Cape Mesurado, there is a good anchorage, and on the pitch of the Cape they have planted a battery, which will protect any vessel that may need it, from piratical depredations.

I would respectfully suggest, for your consideration, the propriety of making the principal Agent of the Colony a "Commercial Agent," as cases have occurred on the coast, where such an appointment might have proved the means of rescuing American property from the hands of foreigners, who have maintained possession of it in consequence of their being no legalized American Agent on the coast.

The importance of this Colony, as regards the native tribes of the coast, is in my estimation, great. They already begin to perceive that it is civilization and the blessings of religion, which give superiority to man over his fellow man. They had supposed it was the white skin; but now they see in their neighborhood, men of their own color, enjoying all those advantages hitherto deemed peculiar to the former. This has elicited a spirit of inquiry which must tend to their benefit. The philanthropist may anticipate the day when our language and religion will spread over this now benighted land. The slave trade will cease, as the colony progresses and extends its settlements. The very spot where now exists a free people, was a depot for the reception of manacled slaves. This fact alone is entitled to consideration, and ought to arouse the zeal of the friends of humanity every where.

Our large cities complain of the number of free blacks, who have by their petty crimes, filled their penitentiaries. Would not the colony be benefitted, by the labor of these men, and the community relieved by their transportation? I certainly think the colony is sufficiently strong both morally and physically, to prevent any injury from their admission. I do not pretend to point out the mode or character in which they ought to be received. This I leave to those who are more able to judge on the subject. I see that the colony is now, in want of numbers to clear and cultivate a country which will amply repay them for their labor.

I take leave to mention, that the climate is much like that of all similar latitudes; and as the land is rich, and most of it still in woods, we must expect that billious fevers will sometimes prevail; but I do not think it more unhealthy, to the colored people, than our extreme Southern coast; and as the soil of Liberia becomes cleared and cultivated, I have no doubt it will be found as healthy as any other Southern latitude. It was, I believe, never intended that the white man should inhabit this region of the globe; at least we know that the diseases of the climate are more fatal to him than the man of color. They luxuriate in the intense heat, while a white man sinks under its exhausting influence.

I confess, sir, that since I have visited this Colony [6:83–97], I felt a strong interest in its prosperity, and hope that it will thrive under the auspices of a society, among whom are some of our most distinguished citizens.

If what I have communicated shall prove instrumental, in the slightest degree, to sustain you in the cause of humanity, and of this degraded race, I shall rejoice that my duty called me to witness the growing prosperity of the Colony of Liberia. . . .

Copy. *Religious Intelligencer* (April 12, 1828), 12:724–5.

From WILLIAM B. ROCHESTER   Norfolk, Va., March 17, 1828

Being disappointed of going down on Saturday from the Navy Yard to Hampton roads by reason of the spindle of the Falmouth's capstan's breaking in attempting to weigh anchor and a very strong & steady Contrary wind now prevailing I think it probable the return boat from Washington may find us on Thursday in the roads if not at some point nearer to Norfolk—if therefore you have any late authentic information touching the condition of Central America which you may find time to put me in possession of I shall be gratified to receive it—I understand Mr. [Pedro] Gonsalez has written to an Englishman here that the Insurgents have taken the Castle at Omoa—

The news from N. Y. is cheering—Judge [Adam] Beatty to his son speaks well of Ken:—I say nothing of Va, for she seems bent for the Hero—I am still inclined to think Penn is to be the battle ground—as to N. Y. my opinion that Mr. A. must get about ⅔ds. of it is not changed—My respects to Mrs. Clay—I beleive I mentioned in a former letter having seen Henry Hart the day before the Delaware sailed—he was Then well

ALS. DLC–HC (DNA, M212, R3). Letter marked "(Confidential)."

To CHARLES R. VAUGHAN, Washington, March 17, 1828.

Acknowledges receipt on February 28 of Vaughan's note [ca. February 27, 1828]. States that, in reply, he would restrict himself to an "expression of his satisfaction" with Vaughan's agreement to present the case of John Baker [6:1272–3] to the governments of Great Britain and New Brunswick, "but for certain opinions and principles advanced" by Vaughan. Says he cannot concur in the assertion that, because the limits of the treaty of 1783 are "undefined and unadjusted," Great Britain retains possession of the disputed territory, because "This argument would prove that the United States are not now lawfully in possession of any portion of the territory which they acquired by the war of their Independence." Notes that neither party had actual possession of the territory at the time of the treaty of 1783 and, consequently, commends the understanding which has prevailed "to abstain from all acts of exclusive jurisdiction which might have a tendency to produce inquietude."

States that the President does not sanction the acts of John Baker, but "The acts of Baker complained of, were, however, performed by him under a belief that he was within the rightful limits of the State of Maine; and with no views of violating the territory, or offending against the laws of Great Britain." Adds that "The Provincial Government of New Brunswick, in the arrest and trial of Baker, for acts of his, some on the disputed territory, commits the very error which is ascribed to Baker, that of undertaking, in effect, to determine a National question, the decision of which should be left to the Governments of Great Britain and the United States, which are, in fact, endeavouring peaceably to settle it." Expresses the opinion that the Baker case could have been better handled through diplomatic channels, citing as an example, a case in 1818 involving squatters on the disputed territory.

States that the 1820 Madawaska census "was made in virtue of the laws of the United States, and by officers duly commissioned by them." Denies Vaughan's assertion that "there was a remonstrance against it at the time." Contends: "No trace of any such remonstrance is discernible in the records of this Department."

Protests acts of exclusive jurisdiction by New Brunswick which if allowed to continue will result in the whole area's being "brought, with its inhabitants under British subjection." Concludes by warning that the British "Government will be responsible for all the consequences, whatever they may be, to which any of those acts of jurisdiction may lead." Copy. DNA, RG59, Notes to Foreign Ministers and Consuls, vol. 3, pp. 443–51 (M38, R3); also in Manning, *Diplomatic Correspondence . . . Canadian Relations*, 2:167–72.

To CHARLES A. WICKLIFFE   Washington, March 17, 1828
Your letter of the 14th instant,[1] as Chairman of a Sub–Committee, appointed by the Committee of the House of Representatives on Retrenchment, making certain inquiries in respect to a remittance of $70,000, alluded to in my letter to the Chairman [James Hamilton, Jr.] of that Committee of the 29th ultimo, was received the day after its date; and I have now the honor to communicate the following answer.

The practice of the Department of State is to employ two banking houses, in Europe, of established credit and character, one at London, and the other at Amsterdam, to pay the expenses of the Foreign service of the Government, connected with our diplomatic corps, consular, and other public agencies. For the purpose of defraying those expenses remittances are made, from time to time, to the bankers, who regularly account to the Department. This practice is coëval with the Government.

On the 5th day of December last, requisitions were made by this Department on the Treasury, for $70,000, to be remitted to our European bankers. The communication which I made to the Chairman of the Committee of Retrenchment, in respect to the remittance, was founded on the day when the requisitions were made at this office, and not on that when the bills were actually purchased, at another office, or when they were transmitted to Europe. The prompt attention usually paid at the Treasury did not allow me to doubt that, in this instance, the requisitions had been complied with, without unnecessary delay. It appears, in point of fact, from a statement[2] from the Treasury, herewith transmitted, designated No. 1, that 39.000$ was remitted, on the 17th day of December, 1827, and $31,000 on the 17th day of January, 1828. The total amount of $70,000 was chargeable to appropriations made prior to that, for the service of the year 1828. The same Treasury Statement shews the heads of appropriation on account of which the remittance has been made, and the objects of public expenditure to which it is applicable. The bankers will give credit for the amount in their general account current.

From the time the Treasury received the above mentioned requisitions of the Department of State, or from that on which the bills were purchased, (as the one or the other mode of keeping the account happen to prevail at the Treasury,) the Department of State became chargeable, and is presumed to have been charged with the above sum of $70,000; and it must have been so charged on account of appropriations made prior to the year 1828. Its credit, therefore, with the Treasury, in consequence of those appropriations, was reduced by the amount of that sum of $70,000, from the one period or the other, above mentioned. But the disbursement of the remittance must be made in the year 1828, or at least subsequent to the year 1827. And in any account exhibiting the actual expenditures of the Department, they ought to be strictly charged to the year when incurred.

Hoping that the explanations and Treasury Statement now communicated, will afford to yourself and the Sub Committee all the information requested in your letter. . . .

Copy. DNA, RG59, Report Books, vol. 41, pp. 234–5.   1. See Wickliffe to Clay, March 14, 1828.   2. See *House Reports,* 20 Cong., 1 Sess., no. 259, p. 58.

From CHARLES J. INGERSOLL, Philadelphia, March 18, 1828. Writes on behalf of Captain John Hammond, a native of St. Johns who became a naturalized American in 1806 and who, since 1823, has been a resident of Boston. States that Hammond, commanding the brig *Mohawk,* sailed from Rio Grande, Brazil, in April, 1827, with a cargo of beef and some other articles belonging to a Brazilian subject; but that enroute to Cuba, the *Mohawk* was captured by an Argentine cruiser. Hammond, however, recovered the property. In August, Hammond put in at Santiago, Cuba, in distress. There the *Mohawk* and her cargo were again seized. Hammond was imprisoned on the charge of barratry, but was released after sixty days. Still, his brig and cargo continued to be detained pending his furnishing proof of his innocence and ownership of the property. Concludes with a request for the intervention of the government in "whatever way may be thought proper." ALS. DNA, RG59, Misc. Letters (M179, R66).

Endorsed on verso in Clay's hand: "Mr. [Philip R.] Fendall will prepare a letter to our Comml. agent at St. Iago de Cuba, [Thomas Backus] transmitting a Copy of the enclosed letter, and instructing him that , if Captain Hammond shall substantiate the case which he states, to afford him such official aid as may appear proper and conducive to his obtaining redress."

On July 31, 1828, Backus wrote, acknowledging receipt of a letter of March 25 from the State Department, enclosing Ingersoll's letter and instructing him "to afford Capt. Hammond such official aid as may appear proper and conducive to his obtaining redress." Stating that he has not attempted "to decide whether the papers prosecuted by Capt. Hammond entitle him to the aid of our govt. or not," explains that "In a case pending before the Tribunals here a commercial agent not regularly acknowledged would not be permitted to interfere." Adds that he has given Hammond his "advice and assistance in causing his papers to be laid before the Governors Tribunal . . . asking payment for his vessel and Cargo." ALS. DNA, RG59, Cons. Disp., Santiago de Cuba, vol. 1, (M-T55, R1). Received August 15, 1828.

To JOSE MARIE SALAZAR   Washington, March 18, 1828
A complaint has been received at this Department,[1] that the Consul of Colombia [Xavier de Medina] at New York requires of the Merchants at that port engaged in the trade between the two Countries to furnish him with copies of the invoices, or with the invoices themselves, from which he takes copies, before he will affix the usual Consular Certificate. This appears to be an unnecessary exposure of the Mercantile operations of each particular merchant prosecuting the trade, and enables the Consul himself to profit by the information thus acquired. It is not known at this Department whether the other Consuls of the Republic of Colombia, officiating within the United States, require the same course of proceeding. Being persuaded that your Government, on all proper occasions is ready to afford its aid in improving the commercial intercourse between the two Countries by removing unnecessary obstacles, or granting greater facilities, I have to invite your attention to the above complaint with the hope that if you view it as I do, you will apply the necessary corrective, or make suitable representation to your Government. . . .[2]

Copy. DNA, RG59, Notes to Foreign Ministers and Consuls, vol. 4, p. 1 (M38, R4).   1. The complaint, dated March 13, was from Eugene Jarrossay, a New York merchant.   2. On April 30 Salazar acknowledged receipt of Clay's letter and explained that his delay in responding resulted from the absence of the Colombian consul, Xavier de Medina, from New York, and his own desire to determine the practices of other consuls. Salazar noted that he had directed the Colombian consul to write the Colombian Consul General, Alexander Velez, whose obligation it is to correspond with the Bogota Government on commercial matters. Adds that Medina will be in Washington in a few days and will at that time confer personally with Clay about the invoices. LS, in Spanish, with trans. in State Dept. file. DNA, RG59, Notes from Colombian Legation, vol. 1 (M51, R2).

From RUFUS EASTON, St. Louis, March 19, 1828. Asks for a copy of a petition addressed to the President, signed by 23 persons, recommending his appointment as circuit judge of the proposed new Federal court for the district of Indiana, Illinois, and Missouri [6:109]. Concludes: "Enclosed [not found] you will receive the address of the administration convention held at the seat of Government in this state on the first monday of the present month [March 2]; I have no doubt of the success of the administration ticket here by a majority of about two thousand votes [6:360-3]." ALS. DNA, RG59, A. and R. (MR3).

Editorial   [March 19, 1828]

During the War which has for some time past existed between Buenos Ayres and the Brazils neutral commerce has, as is usual, suffered; but, all the rest of the world being at peace, the injuries inflicted upon it have not, as formerly, been confined to the United States, but have been extended to the maritime Powers of Europe. None of the suffering commercial Powers have yet thought proper to make war upon either of the belligerants on account of their aggressions, although all of them have probably made remonstrances. We are informed by the King of France [Charles X] in his late Speech to the Legislature, that a demand of satisfaction has been made for the injuries done to the French Commerce. Last Summer, in consequence of the Brazilian Government failing to make the prompt redress which Mr [Condy] Raguet conceived was justly due to Citizens of the United States, he demanded his passports, and returned them [6:295] without the instructions of the Executive. This was a delicate step, very seldom taken without instructions, and generally, when taken the prelude to immediate war. In this state of things, the U States being left without a diplomatic representative at Rio Janeiro, Mr [Jose S.] Rebello, on the 30h. of May last, addressed a note to the Secretary of State, requesting that a successor might be appointed to Mr Raguet, and that his conduct might be disapproved. What ought the President to have done? He had no power to make war if a case for war existed, which has not been shewn. The Secretary of State, in his note to Mr Rebello of the next day, admits that the demand of his passports, on the part of Mr. Raguet, was his personal act, for which he stood responsible to his own Government *only*, and very properly abstains from throwing any censure upon that Minister, at the instance of a foreign GOVERNMENT. And Mr Rebello is informed that the President will replace Mr Raguet by the appointment of a successor, upon the assurance which had been given, that he should be received with the consideration due to his official character, and on the further assurance being given that, in ALL cases in which injuries have been inflected on the *property* or *persons* of American citizens, contrary to the public law, a prompt arrangement will be made by the Government of Brazil, satisfactory to that of the United States. This further assurance was accordingly given in Mr Rebello's note of the 1st of June last, and he was informed by Mr Secretary Clay in reply, that a successor would be appointed to Mr. Raguet. Mr [William] Tudor, a Citizen of the United States, eminently entitled to the confidence of Government, then at Lima, was appointed to that station, his nomination has been approved by the Senate;[1] and he has probably, we understand, reached Rio Janeiro before this time.

Such is the amicable arrangement which has provoked the censure of some of the leading prints of the opposition, and especially of the New York Enquirer and its present ally the [New York] Evening Post. We think that the public will form a very different judgement of this affair If the Brazilian Government had refused to make the pledge which the Secretary of State obtained, and had taken the ground that, whenever the American Government thought proper to send a successor to Mr. Raguet, it would discuss our claims, the President could not well have

172

declined appointing a Minister, on that sole condition. By obtaining the solemn pledge that all injuries committed upon the persons or property of American Citizens shall be promptly and fully indemnified the Secretary of State annexed a condition to the sending of a successor to Mr. Raguet, on which we had not strictly a right to insist. To the redemption of that pledge, the good faith of the Government of Brazil—the security for the performance of all treaties—is committed. This arrangement is pronounced by the New York Enquirer to be a patched up affair, and our Government is charged with submitting to insult from a petty potentate, &c. The wiles of the opposition leaders, ready to take sides against their own government whenever a party object is to be accomplished, must excite, through such organs as the Enquirer, the alarm and apprehensions of the sober and reflecting. In the Colonial controversy with Great Britain [4:180; 5:630-2], the American Executive according to the opposition prints, was too firm and unyielding in support of the interests of the United States. And now that Executive which could not be awed into compliance with the terms dictated by an ambiguous act of the British Parliament [5:631-2], is alleged to have tamely submitted to the Brazilian power! With such doctrines as those, which are put forth by the Editor of the Enquirer, the peace of the country would not be perserved six months after his party should be in power.

Whilst upon this subject, we take occasion to add to our belief, that the statement that a different rule is to be applied to the public ships of the United States in the ports of Brazil, in respect to the payment of duties, from that to which the public vessels of other countries are made to conform is wholly erroneous.

Copy. Washington *Daily National Intelligencer,* March 9, 1828. Article entitled "The United States and the Brazils." AD draft, in DLC–HC (DNA, M212, R3) differs slightly in punctuation and abbreviations from the printed version; however, the substance is essentially the same.   1. President Adams nominated Tudor for the post on December 19, 1827, and a week later the Senate voted its assent. U.S. Sen., *Executive Journal,* 3:579, 583.

From PABLO OBREGON, Washington, March 19, 1828. Reports that General Manuel de Mier Teran has been appointed to do the scientific work and the surveys necessary for the execution of the treaty of limits [Poinsett to Clay, January 8, 1828] between the United States and Mexico and that Joel R. Poinsett has issued passports to him. Asks if passports from Clay are necessary for other members of the Mexican party. LS, in Spanish, with trans. in State Dept. file. DNA, RG59, Notes from Mexican Legation, vol. 1 (M54, R1).

From WILLIAM PHILLIPS, Omoa, March 19, 1828. Reports that political conditions remain unsettled as the civil war continues both in Omoa and in the interior. States that "American property here at present is much exposed, and some kind of protection would inspire confidence." Adds that "nothing but the arrival of our Minister [William B. Rochester] will prevent Americans from feeling the lash of despotism." LS. DNA, RG59, Dip. Disp., Central America, vol. 1 (M219, R2). Received April 29, 1828.

To WILLIAM B. ROCHESTER, March 19, 1828. States that the civil war has worsened and that "there is reason to believe that the residence of an Agent of this Government near that of Central America, if such a government still exists, could be attended with no possible advantage whatever at the present moment." Instructs Rochester to return home if he incurs "imminent personal risk" in trying to reach Omoa, or if, upon his arrival there, he determines his presence futile. Instructs him also to take whatever measures may be within his power to insure "the safety of the persons and property of American citizens" in Omoa. Copy. DNA, RG59, Dip. Instr., vol. 12, p. 73 (M77, R7).

On March 25, Rochester acknowledged receipt of this letter and its enclosure, Phillips to Clay, February 7, 1828, above. Rochester, writing from on board the "U.S. Sloop of War Falmouth, Middle ground, Capes of the Chesapeake," stated that he would "probably look in at Truxillo before going to Omoa." ALS. DNA, RG59, Dip. Disp., Central America, vol. 1 (M219, R2). Received March 30, 1828.

To WILLIAM TUDOR, Rio de Janeiro, no. 5, March 19, 1828. States that he assumes that Tudor has arrived at his post in Brazil and has already begun negotiations on the subject of indemnities. Instructs him to include any additional cases, if well-founded, which he has learned of from claimants, their agents, or the United States consul, William H. D. C. Wright. Transmits documents regarding the schooner *Hero* of Plymouth, Massachusetts, and details the case, which "appears to be marked by peculiar enormity." Copy. DNA, RG59, Dip. Instr., vol. 12, pp. 71–2 (M77, R7).

From FRANCIS T. BROOKE   Richmond, March 20, 1828
You will have seen in the [Richmond *Constitutional*] Whig the publication of your letter to me of the 4h Feb 1825—it has escaped the perversion of [Thomas] Ritchie so far, in his last paper [March 19] he makes only an allusion to it, in a Sarcasm as bitter as he could make it on your use of the expression, in the letter of the 28 of Januy [4:45-6]. I consulted my conscience, every generous feeling that ever inhabited his bosom Seems to be Stifled by his party feelings—he has been attempting here to explain away to Some of our mutual friends his conduct to me, but how does he do it (in the [Richmond] Enquirer before the last)[1] he makes bad worse, the abuse of Mr [John] Randolph gives me no concern as regards my own State, nor can it effect me where the Whig is read, [John H.] Pleasants gave a Short history of me which can not be contradicted, it was enough for me, but as regards the influence of office where character is not known it might have been enlarged upon to Serve the cause, this I must leave to *its* friends, as I can not meddle with it—in Virginia I cheerfully Submit as where Judge [William H.] Cabell & myself are known Mr R[andolph]s Slanders have benifited the cause, I am just about to return home and as our Court will adjourn on the 31t I shall probably not return, untill the next Term which will commence on the first day of May—These attacks upon me have increased my desire to come to Washington in April—but am not Sure that it will be in my power—

174

ALS. DLC–HC (DNA, M212, R3). 1. The Richmond *Enquirer* of March 18 accused Clay of so often using the word "conscience" as to obscure its meaning. Brooke was criticized for using the "pomp and circumstance" of his office as Judge of the Court of Appeals to "affect the votes of the people," even though the opinions of judges are entitled to no more political weight "than those of other citizens." Ritchie's *Enquirer* of April 1 also printed the Clay to Brooke letter of February 4, 1825.

From ALBERT GALLATIN, New York, March 20, 1828. Acknowledges receipt of Clay's letter of March 8. Encloses sketch of instructions for the agent who will be sent to New Brunswick. Expresses concern about the use of the word "highlands" in the "descriptive part of the boundary fixed by the treaty of 1783" because of "doubts thrown on its meaning by our own officers" and because of "the general ignorance of Natural Geography" by persons outside the United States. Urges, therefore, strengthening "the main argument, (that drawn from the terms of the treaty of 1783)" by considering the intentions of the parties when the treaty was drafted and the "construction put since upon it by the British Government and local authorities."

Expresses dissatisfaction with the report of the committee of the Maine legislature [Clay to Gallatin, March 8, 1828] for blending its argument that the United States cannot cede territory belonging to a state, together with its contention of ownership of the territory in dispute with Great Britain. Notes that although the authors of the report are substantially in accord with his own views of the dispute, the report's publication is "premature and incautious" and will "put the British Govt more on their guard." Adds list of documents annexed to, or quoted, in the report which he believes will be useful in the arbitration. ALS. DNA, RG59, Northeast Boundary (KyU., Special Roll, frames 55–7).

To PETER B. PORTER Washington, March 20, 1828
I have just received information entitled to credit that Mrs. [Harman] Blannerhaset [*sic*, Blennerhassett] (relect of the famous gentleman of that name who was concerned with [Aaron] Burr) has in her possession letters from Andw. Jackson to her husband incontestably proving the participation of Genl. Jackson in Burr's conspiracy [1:253, 256–7; 6:409–10; cf. above, Member of Convention to Clay, January 11, 1828]. How can possession of them be obtained? Should they contain the alleged proof they would be decisive of the question which now so much agitates the public. Can you contribe any means to prevail on Mrs. B. to surrender them? I have supposed, from your acquaintance at Montreal you may be able to obtain possession of them. You will at once perceive the delicate nature of the affair, and the expediency of the profoundest silence about the letters. If she has such letters, and it should be known to some of the partizans of the Hero, I have no doubt that they would get hold of them, even at the sacrifice of the life of the lady. Could you not engage some confidential person to proceed to Montreal and obtain the letters? Let me know promptly whether you can do any thing, and what it may be.

ALS. InU. Letter marked "Confidential."

From THOMAS L. L. BRENT, Lisbon, no. 57, March 21, 1828. Encloses translations of Miguel's decree which dissolved the House of Deputies and the article of the constitution which empowers the regent to do so "'in cases in which the salvation of the state may require it.'" Reports, however, that Miguel has not fulfilled the constitutional requirement to convoke a new chamber but rather has appointed a junta to prepare instructions for new elections. Cites additional evidence that Miguel intends "to restore without delay the absolute government," and to have himself declared king.

Reports that the Count of Vila Real has been replaced as foreign minister by the Viscount of Santarem, "a person of no weight of character." LS. DNA, RG59, Dip. Disp., Portugal, vol. 7 (M43, R6). Received May 14, 1828. For Santarem, see Espasa, *Enciclopedia.*

From JOHN CUTHBERT, Hamburg, March 21, 1828. Acknowledges receipt of a letter, dated November 23, 1827, from Daniel Brent, written at Clay's direction, which enclosed a memorial, critical of his official conduct and signed by 27 seamen [6:898-9]. Asserts that he knows the writer and his motives. States: "The first epithet I am accused of using, I declare to be utterly false, the second I acknowledge to have used more than once; and to more than one of them." Admits that such behavior "was not proper," although he had "ample proof of the fact." Denies that he has failed to provide protection to any seaman entitled to it. Adds that his vouchers prove that "several of the signers were boarded, lodged, cloathed and their passages paid" by Cuthbert. Agrees that before and on the date of the memorial, American vessels carried foreigners, but explains that "they were vessels not returning." States that, since he has no authority to insist that American masters ship American seamen in such circumstances, his requests that they do so have seldom been heeded. Concludes that he has begun to prepare evidence to vindicate himself. ALS. DNA, Cons. Disp., Hamburg, vol. 3 (M-T211, R3). Received May 12, 1828. Cuthbert defended himself further in a letter to Clay on April 8. *Ibid.*

From PETER B. PORTER   Albany, N.Y., March 21, 1828
Having received and read Mr. [Anthony] Barclay's seperate Report[1] under the 7th Article of the Treaty of Ghent, my first intention was, to reply to it at some length, for the purpose of exposing the falacies, or—to use a harsher, but more appropriate term—the falsehoods which it contains. My health, however, for some time past, has been such as to render me unfit to undertake the task; and I find, moreover, that I am not in possession of the necessary surveys, maps & other documents to enable me to do it satisfactorily. I have therefore concluded not to attempt a reply until you shall have had an opportunity to examine the two reports, and to advise me whether you deem a supplemental report by me, necessary, or expedient; and, if you do, what should be its form & character.

For the purpose of sustaining the British claim to St George's Island, and the western channel as the boundary Mr Barclay attempts to establish the following propositions

1st That one of the rules or principles of decision adopted by the two Commissioners [Porter and Barclay] was—That the boundary line should never intersect islands, but should uniformly pursue a water route.
2d That, by a second rule, the party to which the largest portion of any island should fall, by a line drawn across it—in such a direction as to be, at all times, equidistant from the opposite & extreme shores of the water communication, should be entitled to claim the whole island—giving however an equivalent for the smaller part in some other island.

The first proposition—That we agreed to make the boundary a water line & not to divide an island—is correct, and acknowledged to be so in my seperate report [6:1208–10, 1383].

The Second—that I recognised the principle that an equi–distant line should controul the course of the boundary, or determine, by its operation, the ownership of islands, is *not* true.

I admit that the *general* effect if [*sic, of*] the principles by which I was governed, and which are explained, at large, in my seperate report, would be, to give to each party respectively, those islands, the greater part of which lay on *its* side of an equidistant line; and this frequently corresponding result of my rule is assumed as evidence that I assented to his.

But that I did not agree to his rule as a general and abstract principle, Mr Barclay himself acknowledges in the 30th section of his report wherein he says that "It is admitted that the American Commissioner did, in terms, decline establishing the rules above specified as principles for governing the decision required. Yet he afterwards fully adopted them in practice."

Mr [David] Thompson, the British Surveyor, in his affidavit (see Mr Barclay's report Section 35) says, "that for a boundary line under the 6th article of the treaty of Ghent, the United States Commissioner [Peter B. Porter] resorted to a line as near as possible equidistant from the opposite main shores; and whenever the line intersected an island, the island was considered as belonging to the side on which the greatest part of it lay." These assertions of the Surveyor, in the extent in which they are intended to be understood, are totally unfounded. I am satisfied of being able to prove by the American Surveyor [James Ferguson] & Secretary [Donald Frazer] (and I should have exhibited such proof to the Board had I been apprised of the existance of Mr Thompson's affidavit) that I uniformly objected both theoretically and practically to the principles imputed to me by Mr Thompson: and I think, more over, that I can point out, as soon as I can have access to the maps, a dozen, or more, probably twenty, deviations from these principles.

I wish you to understand that Mr. Thompson's affidavit, on which the whole of Mr. Barclay's argument in regard to St George's island is based, was never presented to the Board, nor ever seen by me, untill I saw it in the appendix to Mr Barclay's report—although it appears from it's date, to have been taken at New York nearly a year before the last meeting of the Board.

Mr Barclay, evidently aware of the impropriety of introducing this affidavit, makes an indirect, but very weak effort, in the 33d Section of his report, to legalise it, by referring to a resolution of the Board passed Novr. 1825, by which it was declared "that such written documents as the Agents of the respective Goverments intend to submit as evidence in support of their claims (excepting the maps of the surveyors in the employ of this Commission) be first duly authenticated agreably to the forms & usage of the country in which the same are procured"—thus flattering himself, perhaps, that the Umpire who is to decide the question, would not possess sufficient segacity to discover that this resolution related to such evidence only as was to be *submitted* to the Board; and that he might, moreover, forget, that the Commissioners were directed[2] to decide "upon such evidence as should be laid before them" and that such is the tenor of the oath which we were required to take.

3d The third position of Mr Barclay, founded on the affidavit of Mr Thompson (see Section 35. of Mr B's report)—"That Saint George's Island, intersected by a middle line as near as possible equi–distant from the opposite main shores, has its greatest part on the British side of the said line." is equally incorrect if my views and those of the American Surveyors on this subject are not extravagantly erroneous. But as the questions—What is meant by an equi–distant line? and—In what manner would such a line divide St. Georges Island? are subjects of scientific principle & mathematical calculation, this proposition is, fortunately, not to be decided by the gratuitous assertions either of Mr. Thompson the Surveyor or of Mr B. himself.

I do not object to this *last* part of Mr Thompson's evidence on the ground of its *incompetency.* On the contrary, as it discloses no fact not already before the board, but is a mere mathematical calculation or deduction from surveys & maps which had been regularly presented & filed, it was undoubtedly proper for Mr. Barclay to resort to such calculations (as I have done to simular ones in my report) for the purpose of elucidating his argument.

I have no doubt but that the claim of the United States to St George's Island, and to the British Channel as the boundary, may be successfully sustained on the ground that it is the only navigable channel: But if it can be geometrically & mathematically demonstrated, (as I have reason to think it may) that the equi–distant line relied on by Mr Barclay will give more than half of the island, St George [*sic,* Georges], to the United States, then, *upon his own principles,* the controversy will be at an end, and the *whole* island will be ours; and there will be no necessity of again resorting to the other arguments & considerations by which I have endeavoured to support our claims.

The large maps returned to your department by the Board, are made[3] from trigonometrical surveys, and protracted with great accuracy & precision; and I would therefore suggest to you the expediency of making an informal reference of such sheets as embrace St. George's island to some scientific men—say the officers & professors of the Corps of Engineers—for the purpose of ascertaining their views of an equidistant line, and of its practical application to this part of the boundary.

My own impressions are that the only practicable process, in this particular case, for determining what is an equidistant line, is to assume the general course of the river or water communication (from the point where it divides, above, to where it unites again, below, the island) as the base of operation; and to call those *opposite points of the shores* which are intersected by a line at right angles with the general course.

To explain my views, I enclose you a sketch[4] of the island & river, with an equidistant line which I have hastily drawn, upon this principle, in pencil. I cannot vouch for the accuracy of the sketch, but if it be correct, an equi-distant line will give us, at least, three fifths of the island.

I must beg the favour of you, after having read the two reports, to advise me as to the course which you & the President deem it proper for me to pursue.—whether to procure new evidence to repel that which has been improperly introduced by Mr Barclay. whether merely to protest against the *ex parte* evidence introduced by him—or whether not to reply at all.

ALS. DNA, RG76, Northern Boundary: Treaty of Ghent, 1814. Arts. VI and VII.
1. *House Docs.*, 25 Cong., 2 Sess., no. 451, pp. 38–117.   2. The word "required" is struck through and the word "directed" is substituted.   3. Following this word is the phrase "with geometrical precision," which is struck through.   4. Not found.

From SAMUEL L. SOUTHARD   Navy Department, March 21, 1828
I have the honor to request a certified Copy of the bill making appropriations for the support of the Navy for the year 1828,[1] as remittances for a large amount to all our stations, are depending and the money is very much needed.

LS. DNA, RG59, Misc. Letters (M179, R66).   1. 4 *U.S. Stat.*, 254–6; see also *House Docs.*, 20 Cong., 1 Sess., no. 2, pp. 228–52.

From JOHN U. WARING   Frankfort, March 21, 1828
Your replication [6:1394–6] to the charges so often repeated against you, of corruption, &c. in the late presidential election, has been received in Kentucky with much satisfaction, by the friends of the present administration, and more particularly by your well-wishers, while it has silenced a portion of your most open-mouthed defamers.

It is a fact probably known to you, that an extraordinary effort has been made, and is making, in this country to rally the shattered ranks of a desperate party, upon the name of Jackson, although he has said that an honest jury would convict any man of perjury who would vote for the very measures that have in Kentucky been so warmly supported by them.

In your vindication [6:1394–6], you refer to a conversation had by general Jackson in Bowling Green [Ky.], upon his return from congress, after the election of Mr. Adams to the presidency. I was present at one of those conversations, when the general observed, in speaking of the late election, that *"the people had been cheated." "That the corruptions and intrigues at Washington had defeated the will of the people, in the election of their president."* I waited until this branch of the conversation was closed, and finding no palative, left the company, which was large, and composed of gentlemen and ladies of the first respectability, and at a public tavern; several followed, and his remarks became the subject of street conversation, in which I remarked that, as highly as I was disposed to think of the

179

general, particularly for his military success, I could not approve such a course—that if corruption existed, and that known to him, he surely should not have been the first to greet Mr. Adams upon his elevation; and that, if you had participated, it was his duty to have exposed it when your nomination[1] was before the senate.

It may be well to remark, that the general may have thought that he was wholly surrounded by his political friends, as he had been well received there by the citizens. . . . P.S. By a sense of duty to an injured and much persesecuted man, I have been induced to address this letter to you, and you are at liberty to use it as you may think proper: I would have communicated these facts to you at an earlier period, but believing them unnecessary after the general's letter giving up Mr. [James] Buchanan [6:839–41].

ALS. DLC-HC (DNA, M212, R3). Published in Niles' Register (July 5, 1828), 34:307; and also in Clay, *A Supplement to the Address . . . to the Public*, 8–9. Cf. below, June 10, 1828.
1. As Secretary of State, which Senator Jackson had opposed. See 4:90.

From WILLIAM H. D. C. WRIGHT, Rio de Janeiro, March 21, 1828. Details his part in prompting the Brazilian government to inform its authorities in Montevideo of the decision to discontinue exacting bonds of neutral vessels sailing from that port as previously required, the condition of which was that they not enter Buenos Airean ports. Encloses correspondence with the Minister of Foreign Affairs, the Marquis de Aracaty, on the subject of the bonds. Observes that the Marquis has expressed his "disposition to cultivate the best feelings between our governments." ALS. DNA, RG59, Cons. Dip., Rio de Janeiro, vol. 3 (M–T172, R4). Received May 24, 1828.

To JOHN Q. ADAMS   Washington, March 22, 1828
The Secretary of State, to whom has been referred a resolution of the House of Representatives of the 25th of last month, requesting the President "to send to that House copies of the instructions given by the Government of the Confederated States to its Ministers [Adams, Franklin, Jay, Laurens] by whom the definitive treaty of peace [1783] was concluded with the Government of Great Britain, so far as such instructions relate to the settlement of the boundary line of the United States, or any one of them, and also, the correspondence between said ministers with the ministers of Great Britain upon the same subject, or so much therefrom as will not be injurious to the public service," has the honor to report to the President, that it does not appear from the research which has been made in this office, which has been full and particular, that any instructions, other than those which are published in the second and third volumes of the secret Journals of Congress,[1] were given to the Ministers of the Confederated or United States, by whom the preliminary articles, or the definitive treaty of peace, were concluded with Government of Great Britain, in relation to the settlement of the boundary line of the United States, or any one of them, or that there was any correspondence, in writing, between said ministers and the Ministers of Great Britain upon the same subject. The Secretary begs leave, therefore, respectfully to refer to the said two volumes of the Secret Journal,

which were printed and published by the authority of Congress, for the information required by the Resolution of the House, so far as, they contain such information.

Copy. DNA, RG59, Report Books, vol. 4, p. 236.   1. U.S. Continental Congress, *Secret Journals of the Acts and Proceedings of Congress....* 4 vols. Boston, 1820-21.

To SAMUEL LARNED, no. 1, March 22, 1828. Transmits his commission as U.S. Chargé to Chile, together with a letter from President Adams to acting President Francesco Antonio Pinto of Chile on the subject of Heman Allen's departure from that country. Instructs Larned to persevere with efforts to adjust the claims of U.S. citizens against Chile. Copy. DNA, RG59, Dip. Instr., vol. 12, pp. 74-5 (M77, R7).

From WILLIAM B. LAWRENCE, London, no. 29, March 22, 1828. Notes that the efforts of Turkey, along with her "Asiatic neighbour," in preventing the ratification of the recently concluded treaty between Russia and Persia [5:691-2] have so far been successful, but states "Very little importance is however attached to a concert between these Mahomedan States, should it be attempted."

Reports that Russia has chosen April 12 as the date to commence "hostile operations" against Turkey and that France has not objected to the Russian decision. Says it is not certain what courses Britain and Austria will pursue. Notes that although British attitudes are probably "in accordance with those of Austria, it is not easy for England to extricate herself from the obligations" of the Treaty of London of July 6, 1827. Still, he believes that "active interference will, as far as practicable, be avoided by this Country," even though "no means will be left untried to prevent the territorial aggrandizement of Russia." The English have therefore "reinforced their garrisons in the Ionian Isles," and had they not been required by "recent occurances" to leave a portion of their army of occupation in Portugal, the reinforcements would have been larger.

States that the return of Miguel to Portugal from his stay in England proves that he "has again placed himself under the authority of the Queen, Carlota Joaquina, his mother, and of his old associates." Discusses Miguel's advisors, and the suspicions of him held by the British ambassador to Portugal, William A' Court.

Remarks briefly on British policy regarding the war between Brazil and Buenos Aires, a new law regarding dissenters, and changes in regulations respecting vessels carrying passengers. LS. DNA, RG59, Dip. Disp., Great Britain, vol. 35 (M30, R31). Received May 9, 1828.

From JESSE TURNER   Waynesboro, N.C., March 22, 1828
A rapid change in public sentiment is going on in North Carolina—Mr. [William] Gaston's able and interesting address[1] is producing the most happy effects and will no doubt aid materially in advancing the administration cause in this state Your appeal [6:1394-6] to the Citizens of the United States has also produced quite a salutory effect   None except those who are steeled against conviction and pre-determined in their belief can read it without acknowledging the baseness of the charge

proclaimed against you by the opposition candidate—perhaps no man is now living who has been more wantonly traduced than yourself but your triumph has been glorious and the reputation which you have acquired by dint of industry must shine brighter and brighter as these base calumnies recoil upon those who had the meanness to propagate them—Nothing is wanting to secure the vote of North Carolina to Mr. Adams [6:360-3] but the continued and indefatigable exertion of his friends—The Jacksonions are extremely active and though certain of succeeding will I confidently believe sustain a defeat—the leading men in the eastern part of the state are for Mr. Adams, in the western part perhaps a majority of them are for Gen. Jackson but by far the greater part of the intelligent and reading citizens are with us it is rumourd here that Mr. Gaston will get the appointment of Minister to England this would no doubt highly gratify the pride of North Carolina she is justly entitled to such an appointment for her devotion to the Federal Compact cannot be questioned. it is also due to the great talents of Mr. Gaston who would no doubt fill such an appointment ably and satisfactorily— The following counties in North Carolina would I think at this time give Administration majorities (Viz)[2] Surry, Wilkes, Iredell, Guilford, Randolph, Chatham, Johnston, Sampson, Dublin, Lenoir, Jones, Craven, Carteret, Pitt, Washington, Beaufort, Hyde, Tyrrell, Chowan, New Hanover, & Cumberland the County of Wayne will be pretty equally divided and our cause continues to gain ground daily How will the vote of Virginia go? of New York, of Maryland and of Kentucky? and upon the whole what are the prospects of the Administration

ALS. DLC-HC (DNA, M212, R3). Little is known about Jesse Turner of Waynesboro, N.C. save that he was a judge.   1. Gaston's address to the N.C. convention to nominate an electoral slate for Adams, held in Raleigh on December 20, 1827, included a refutation of various charges made against Adams and a broad-ranging attack on Jackson's lack of candor and political experience. It was serialized in the Salisbury *Western Carolinian*, March 4-25, 1828. See, also, Washington *Daily National Intelligencer*, December 29, 1827.   2. For the North Carolina vote, by county, see Salisbury *Western Carolinian*, November 25 and December 2, 1828.

To FRANCIS T. BROOKE   Washington, March 24, 1828
I received your favor of the 20h. instant. I had previously seen in the [Richmond *Constitutional*] Whig my letter to you of the 4 Feb. 1825.[1] It is believed here that its publication will do good.

I am glad that you do not allow yourself to be affected by the calumnies of Mr. [John] Randolph. Here, I assure you, they do you no prejudice, and excite no other than a feeling of detestation towards their author. The Whig has found out his sensitive part, and, if a man ever forfeited all claim to commiseration, on account of a physical misfortune and justified the allusion to it, by the wanton and unprovoked attacks which he makes upon others, Mr. R. is that man.

I hope you will not fail to visit us in April. I think you would pass a week or two here very agreeably; and you are so near home that half a day will at any time take you there. [Samuel L.] Southard and [John] Taliaferro are my next door neighbours, so that, at my house, you would be in the midst of your friends.

The general aspect of our political news continues good, especially from Kentucky and New York.

ALS. KyU.   1. Richmond *Constitutional Whig*, March 15, 1828.

From ROBERT B. CAMPBELL, Washington, March 24, 1828. States that he has been requested to inquire of the British minister in Washington, Charles R. Vaughan, whether or not the officers and men of 71st. Regiment, Scottish Highlanders, who served in the American Revolution were granted land in Canada by the British government at the end of the war, and, if so, how the heirs of the veterans may claim the land. Asks that Clay take up the matter with Vaughan. ALS. DNA, RG59, Misc. Letters (M179, R66).

On March 29, Vaughan returned Campbell's questions to Clay stating that he could not "answer one of them" and did not know "to what Department of the British Government" to send them. Suggests that Campbell hire an agent in Canada to investigate the matter. Copy. DNA, RG59, Notes from British Legation, vol. 15 (M50, R15).

To JAMES COLLIER   Washington, March 24, 1828
I received your favor of the 13h. instant. I think your friend at Russellville [Ky.] must be somewhat mistaken as to the want of papers conveying political information in his district, although I presume it is not as well supplied with those, on one side, as it would be, if it had a different representative.[1] The same mail that brought your letter, brought also the Russellville paper containing my Address [6:1394-6]; so that I presume it has been extensively circulated.

Our friends from K in Congress are, I believe, diffusing intelligence as much as they can. The number at work on the other side is certainly much against our cause. But I am happy to tell you that the accounts from K are encouraging.

ALS. CtY. Addressed to Collier in Steubenville, O.   1. Joel Yancey represented Kentucky's Tenth Congressional District, which included Russellville.

From JAMES HAMILTON, JR., House of Representatives, March 24, 1828. Transmits resolution of the House Retrenchment Committee, of this date, which instructs him to ask Clay whether or not John H. Pleasants went to Buenos Aires and Rio de Janeiro as a bearer of dispatches in 1825 [4:515-6, 754], whether or not he delivered the dispatches entrusted to his care, and, if not, what happened to them. Also inquires where Pleasants went when he left the United States, and whether or not the State Department knew that he had not been in Buenos Aires and Rio de Janeiro when it settled his accounts. LS. DNA, RG59, Misc. Letters (M179, R66).

From BARON PAUL DE KRUDENER, Washington, March 24, 1828. Transmits a report to the Imperial Ministry by the colonial administration of the Russian settlements on the northwestern coast of America. States that the report claims that William Cotting, master of the brig

183

Active of Boston, while at New Archangel, Sitka, was guilty of acts "contrary, not only to good order, generally, and to the commercial laws of the Empire; but, likewise, in direct contradiction to the stipulations" of the treaty of April 17, 1824 [4:213]. Requests that Cotting be punished and such transgressions not be allowed to occur in the future. LS, in French, with trans. in State Dept. file. DNA, RG59, Notes from Russian Legation, vol. 2 (M39, R2).

The enclosed memorial charged that, in October, 1827, Cotting had violated the treaty by trading with the natives in an area already settled by the Russians and by providing them with liquor. Copy. *Ibid.*

Two months later Clay responded to this protest, declaring that the vessel's "owners are respectable merchants" and that "they never had received the slightest intimation . . . of any irregularity committed by the master of the *Active* . . . and if he be guilty of any such irregularity it was without their instructions or authority." Reports that Congress was asked to provide "for the punishment of offenses" in such cases, and has passed a suitable act, a copy of which is being transmitted. Clay to de Krudener, May 28, 1828, in DNA, RG59, Notes to Foreign Ministers and Consuls, vol. 4 (M38, R4). The act was passed on May 19, 1828. *Register of Debates*, 20 Cong., 1 Sess., 18.

On June 1, 1828, de Krudener responded to Clay's May 28 letter with the observation that the recent act of Congress and the Treaty of 1824 should be vigorously enforced in matters such as these. De Krudener to Clay, June 1, 1828. LS, in French. DNA, RG59, Notes from Russian Legation (M39, R2).

From LEVI LINCOLN   Worcester, Mass., March 24, 1828
I have the honor to acknowledge the receipt of your communication of the date of the 15th inst, with a pamphlet accompanying it, containing a Message from the President to the Senate of the United States, with the Reports of Mr [Samuel B.] Barrell, and other Documents relating to alleged aggressions on the rights of Citizens of the United States, by the Authorities of New Brunswick &c. &c—

While on all occasions I have felt it to be my duty, in behalf of this Commonwealth, to express in earnest terms a strong interest and most anxious desire in maintaining the inviolability of the territory and for the preservation of the property so justly claimed as the right of Massachusetts and her Sister State [Maine], I have equal satisfaction in recognising in the measures adopted by the General Government, those manifestations of regard for the protection of the States and for the vindication of the National Sovereignty, alike assailed by these incroachments of a foreign jurisdiction, which are calculated to give effect to our well grounded complaints of injury, to obtain redress, and to secure from future aggression both the persons and possessions of American Citizens. In whatever it may be in my power to cooperate to these ends, I shall faithfully seek opportunity so to do.—I beg therefore, in these sentiments, to assure you, that the original Documents referred to in your communication, shall be immediately inquired for, and authentic Copies of such as are to be found in the public offices of this Government, furnished to your Department. The Executive of Massachusetts will, at all times, take a deep concern in the necessary arrangements for a just and final establishment of that *true Boundary*, which was *practically* well understood under the definitive [1783] Treaty, and comes now to be controverted only from an artificial and forced application of terms, sufficiently explicit in themselves, but which the temptations of opportunity and an adversary interest would wrest to a violent and most injurious prejudice to this section of Country.

A Copy of the Convention [6:1100-01] which you did me the favor to forward in confidence, was duly received—And I have to beg your excuse of me, that in the pressure of engagements I have delayed to this time its acknowledgement

LS. DNA, RG76, Northeast Boundary: Misc. Papers, Env. 4, item 22.

From BOYD McNAIRY   Nashville, March 24, 1828

Your letter of the 7th. has been receivd. Your views of the Presidential election have given me fresh vigor, it can not be possible that the people of Kentucky, if they understand their own interests can be for the promotion of Jackson, admitting him equally qualified; A man who done his best, & did in an official report speak derogatory of this *character* as soldier—[1]

Your favourite the American system, the people of Tennessee is opposed to, also the Hero if he had no concilement; I am certain in this state, not more than one in ten is in favour of it, and all the particular friends of the Hero violent opposed to it with few exceptions—All that is wanted, is some efficient man to tell them so, & I know no one but yourself that can make the impression strong enough—I dont know, nor would I advise if capable your resignation—but you will excuse me, when I do advise a visit to Kentucky at some time during the sumer, & it would give me great pleasure [if] you would extend your visit to Tennessee—You must not be defeated in Kentucky [6:360-3] above all other states—

My friend Mr. [Wilkins] Tannehill just returned from the Green River country, he says your friends are very sanguine, & that dayly changes are making in your favour   You will shortly see Thos. Washington w[as] brought ought [*sic*, out] as elector for Mr. Adams & he will not refuse to run & I will get a good vote in Jacksons own district—[2]I do believe all the districts in the state will have an elector. dont be astonished if Mr. Adams gets a vote in Tennessee—

ALS. DLC-HC (DNA, M212, R3). Addressed: "Private Letter."   1. Jackson had criticized the performance of Kentucky militia troops during the New Orleans campaign in January, 1815, a charge Kentuckians deeply resented and contested. See Jackson to Col. Robert Butler, May 7, 1817 in the Lexington *Kentucky Reporter*, May 28, 1817; and William G. Leger, *The Public Life of John Adair* (Univ. of Ky., Ph.D. Dissertation, 1953), 150-65.   2. The vote in Davidson County, District 7 (Nashville), Jackson's home district, was: Jackson, 5008; Adams, 715. Nashville *Republican & State Gazette*, December 12, 1828.

From JOHN M. MACPHERSON, Cartagena, Colombia, March 24, 1828. States that Colonel Beaufort T. Watts's return to the United States by the same conveyance as that of the present dispatch renders a detailed written report concerning recent disturbances in Cartagena unnecessary. Encloses two letters received from General Jose Padilla making

requests which MacPherson refused to honor, "knowing how much our Government is opposed to its agents interfering in the affairs of other states." Hopes his conduct was correct in that matter. Also encloses a printed communication from Simon Bolivar announcing the Liberator's intention to leave Bogota and setting forth "the mode in which the affairs of state will be conducted during his absence." Sends along newspaper accounts of recent disturbances in Cartagena and of General Mariano Montilla's proclamations. ALS. DNA, RG59, Cons. Disp., Cartagena, vol. 1 (M–T192, R1). Received April 27, 1828.

To PETER B. PORTER   Washington, March 24, 1828

Are you sure that no attempt will be made to repeal your [N.Y.] Electoral law, and to assume to the Legislature the power to appoint the Electors [6:1185]? Against such a movement, I think you should be constantly on your guard. Depend upon it, there is nothing too desparate for the Jackson party. Recollect how you were deceived by the Caucus nomination.[1] These suggestions are made in consequence of my having heard that a leading Southern politician has stated that such a law would be proposed, and what is more would be carried in your Legislature. The same secret arrangements that led to the Caucus nomination may be made to change your Electoral law. How would it do to propose a resolution, declaring that inquietude existing upon that subject, it was deemed proper to calm the public mind in respect to it by an explicit avowal that no such purpose was contemplated? It appears to me that the friends of the Administration in your Legislature would do well, on all fit occasions, and even to seek opportunities, to denounce such a project as the repeal of the existing Law, unless you substitute a general popular ticket.

I received your favor of the 15h. instant, and transmitted the letter which it inclosed to Judge [Francis T.] Brooke.

The Tariff is still under discussion. No one believes at present that there is any prospect of passing a proper bill on that subject. A viler cheat was never attempted on an intelligent people than the bill reported by the Committee.[2] I am glad to perceive that the public are every where beginning to understand its bearing. That was particularly desirable in your State where, I thought, when it was first reported, much misconception prevailed. In the shape in which it was reported it would destroy our Woolen manufactories, and consequently deprive us of all market for the raw material.

I trust that I need not contradict to you the story of my having got up, or contributed, to the Anti masonic spirit prevailing in your State [6:1233–5].[3] I have looked upon it as one of those delusions to which men are unfortunately sometimes exposed. If [William] Morgan has been murdered or carried into captivity, I certainly could not approve of it; but if the one or the other has been done, I presume it has been the work of some misguided individuals, which however reprehensible it may be, ought not to affect the whole order. I am myself a Mason, and although not a bright one nor a regular attendant of the Lodge, I respect the craft, and its members generally.

I have not yet received your observations on Mr. [Anthony] Barclay's report.[4]

186

ALS. NBuHi. Letter marked "Confidential." 1. Porter to Clay, January 8, 1828. 2. Clay to Crittenden, February 14, 1828. 3. For Clay's views of and participation in the Antimasonic movement, see Glyndon G. Van Deusen, *The Life of Henry Clay*, (Boston, 1937), 240–5. For a more complete consideration of the movement nationally, and its influence in the 1832 Presidential election, see Lorman Ratner, *Antimasonry: The Crusade and the Party*. Englewood Cliffs, N.J., 1969; and Charles McCarthy, *The Anti-Masonic Party*. Washington, 1903. 4. Porter to Clay, March 21, 1828.

From ALEXANDER H. EVERETT, Madrid, no. 99, March 25, 1828. Calls attention to an enclosed "memoir" he has prepared for early publication in the *North American Review* which, "from the nature of the subject may be of some little interest to the President." LS. DNA, RG59, Dip. Disp., Spain, vol. 28 (M31, R29). Received July 2, 1828.

The article, a survey of "the present aspect of the general politics of Europe," appeared in the *NAR* (July, 1828), 27:215–68.

From ROBERT SCOTT, Lexington, March 25, 1828. Discusses his handling of recent payments into and out of the George Nicholas and James Morrison estates and the suit of the heirs of Nicholas against the Morrison estate. Concludes in a postscript: "I contemplate purchasing about 100 Hogs to put in my clover and fat in the fall—I believe you have not enough on your farm. If on consulting Theodore [W. Clay] & Mr. [John H.] Kerr one should think so shall I purchase you some? I intend sending to Eagle Creek or perhaps to Indiana." ALS. DLC-TJC (DNA, M212, R13).

From CHARLES R. VAUGHAN, Washington, March 25, 1828. Acknowledges receipt of Clay's note of March 17. States that he does not understand the distinction made by Clay "between the actual and constructive possession of the disputed territory" prior to the treaty of 1783. Contends that, though part of the territory was inhabited, the plenipotentiaries at Paris intended "to leave untouched the rights of his Majesty over the province of Nova Scotia" and that until ownership is resolved, "jurisdiction must continue to be exercised within the disputed limits by the original possessors" because "joint jurisdiction" would be "impracticable." Denies that activities of American settlers in the disputed territory have infringed upon the British claim. Argues that John Baker [6:1272–3] knew he resided "within the jurisdiction of New Brunswick, as he had received the provincial bounty for corn raised upon land newly brought into cultivation." LS. DNA, RG59, Notes from British Legation, vol. 15 (M50, R15). Also in *ASPFR*, 6:1020.

On May 21, 1828, writing from Washington, Clay submitted to the President copies of the correspondence between himself and Vaughan on the subject of the John Baker case, as requested by a resolution of the House of Representatives. Copy. DNA, RG59, Report Books, vol. 4, p. 250; also in *ASPFR*, 6:1015.

To JAMES BROWN Washington, March 26, 1828

I receive your letters regularly, and peruse them with great satisfaction. I have so often had to apologize for my want of punctuality in writing to you, that I will not take up time now to make excuses, but throw myself at once upon your indulgence.

We have been greatly concerned on account of Mrs. Brown's health, and although your letter of the 13h. Feb. this day recd. represents her situation as improved, the intimation of your proabable intention to return home, should she not get better by the first of this month, admonishes us that she must be far from well. I hope perseverance in the system of medicine and regimen may complete the work of restoration of her health.

I read to the President the part of your letter relating to Mrs. Brown's situation, and your contingent intention of returning. He appeared to be sensibly affected by it, and [as] before manifested a strong interest in your case. Although there is no sort of desire that you should return, if you should do so, from the cause indicated, there can be no just complaint. If you do return, I think you had better postpone as long as you can consistently with Mrs. Brown's condition.

I never had a thought of going to England. Nor is it yet decided who is to go. I do not think Mr. Webster will, although there is no man in whom I shald have more confidence

I yet believe, strange as it may appear to you, that Mr. Adams will be re-elected. My address [6:1394-6] and other causes have produced a powerful reaction, which has been greatly aided in N. York by Mr. [DeWitt] Clinton's death. If they do not assume to the Legislature the appointment of Electors [5:988](which it is said they will not and dare not do) Mr. Adams will get a large majority of the votes of that State. And our hopes are still strong of carrying the vote of Kentucky. There is a subdued tone in the Jackson corps. They have made nothing of their majorities in Congress, neither for our annoyance, nor their advancement.

My health is as usual. That of Mrs. Clay is not good. 'though she has participated freely in the parties of the winter.

Our pecuniary condition is in a state of progressive improvement. I live within my salary.

We have been concerned about the health of our friend Genl. Lafayette. I pray you to say so to him, and deliver him my affectionate regards.

Give also our best respects to Mrs. Brown, and tell her how much we have been afflicted on her account.

ALS. KyLxT–Haupt Collection.

To JAMES HAMILTON, JR. Washington, March 26, 1828
I have received your letter of the 24th instant, containing a copy of a resolution adopted by the Committee on Retrenchment, in which they are pleased to inquire, "Did John H. Pleasants go as bearer of despatches from the United States to Rio de Janeiro and Buenos Ayres in 1825? Did he deliver the despatches to the proper authority at Rio Janeiro and Buenos Ayres? If he did not go, what became of the despatches, who bore them to the Government of Rio Janeiro and Buenos Ayres? Where did John H. Pleasants go after he left the United States? Was it known to the Department, when his account was settled and paid him, that he had not been to Rio Janeiro and Buenos Ayres, as bearer of despatches from this Government?"

In reply I have the honor to state, for the information of the Committee, that Mr. Pleasants was engaged, in the Spring of 1825, to carry to our respective Chargés des Affaires at the Brazils [Condy Raguet] and Buenos Ayres [John M. Forbes], their credentials, commissions, general instructions, and other despatches from this Department; that with that view he left the city of Richmond, the place of his residence, on the 19th day of April, and embarked at the port of New York on the 28th day of May, 1825, on board the brig William Tell, having employed the intermediate time in seeking, from Baltimore to Boston, a vessel in which he could obtain a passage; that whilst at sea, he was taken so ill as to be apprehensive of his life, which he supposed would be in imminent danger, if he continued the voyage, and meeting a vessel at sea, bound to Antwerp, he transferred himself to her, and committed the despatches with which he was charged to the care of Captain Hinman, the master of the vessel William Tell; that the despatches, both for Mr. Forbes, our Chargé d'Affaires at Buenos Ayres, and for Mr. Raguet, our Chargé d'Affaires at Rio de Janeiro, were delivered by the Captain of the William Tell; to the former gentleman on the 12th day of August, 1825, as will appear by an extract of a despatch from him, under date the 15th day of September, 1825, marked A.; and that those intended for Mr. Raguet were received by him on the 26th October, 1825, as will appear by an extract from a despatch from him, under date the 12th of November, 1825, which is marked B.

I beg leave, also, to refer to a copy of a letter from Mr. Pleasants, under date the 7th day of July, 1825, marked C. and to an extract from a letter from him, under date the 22d October, 1825, marked D., as explaining more fully the motives which induced him to change his destination, and commit the public despatches in his care to Captain Hinman. During his voyage in the Antwerp vessel, Mr. Pleasants met at sea a vessel bound to Liverpool, to which he transferred himself, and he arrived in that port on the 1st day of July, 1825. He reached the port of New York, on his return to the United States, the 22d october, 1825, bringing with him despatches for this Department from Mr. R[ufus]. King, our Minister at the court of London.

It was known at this Department, when the account of Mr. Pleasants was settled and closed, that he had not reached Rio de Janeiro or Buenos Ayres; but it was also known that the despatches which had been entrusted to him, had been received by the persons to whom they were regularly addressed; and it was believed that he had been prevented from personally delivering them by the causes already stated. Supposing .. —the affliction of disease did not occasion a forfeiture of all claim for expenses, and all compensation for services, the allowances made to him were according to established usage, which has prevailed as far back as any traces of the accounts of bearers of despatches can be discerned in the Treasury. Agreeably to that usage they are generally allowed their expenses, personal and travelling, to the port of embarcation, their passage money at sea, their expenses personal and travelling, from the port of debarcation to the places of their destination, and the like expenses and passage money on their return home; and they receive, moreover, a compensation for their services of six dollars per day, out of which they defray their expenses whilst they remain at the places to which they are sent, or stop at Washington for despatches. Upon an examination of Mr. Pleasants' account it will be seen that it has been adjusted according to those principles; and of the sum received by him, $756 was for per diem allowance, and the residue on account of expenses and passage money.

It was not believed that the visitation of Providence with which he was afflicted ought to deprive him of all allowance for expenses, and all compensation for services, but it was not thought right that the per diem should be continued during the whole period of his absence from home, and until his return to New York, on the 22d October, 1825. It was, therefore, limited to the 22d August, 1825, that being the time when it was estimated he might have returned to the United States, if, after abandoning the voyage to South America, he had sought an opportunity of coming home, instead of proceeding to Europe. It was within the discretion of the Department to have compensated him as the bearer of despatches from Mr. King; but it was not deemed proper to make him any allowance for that service.

Copy. DNA, RG59, Report Books, vol. 4, pp. 237–9.

From PETER B. PORTER   Albany, March 26, 1828

I received, last evening, your favour of the 20th in relation to Mrs [Harman] Blannerhasset [*sic,* Blennerhassett] &c. It happens that a gentleman now lodges in the same Hotel with me (Matthew L. Davis, of whom you have heard) who, in case of a mission to Montreal, would, probably, be the best man that could be selected, and would be willing to undertake it. He is extremely adroit—a gentleman in manners—and perfectly conversant with the subject & strongly in fav. of the Admon. I met also, this morning, *Col.* [Aaron] *Burr,* who arrived, from N. York, last night, & returns again this evening. Thinking that I might get some information from him, through Mr Davis, who has his entire confidence, I had a full & free conversation with the latter, and requested him to procure, in the course of the day, an interview with Col. B. which he has accordingly done. Burr does not hesitate to acknowledge that Jackson was a participater in his schemes, and he would be gratified (in consequence of the treatment lately received from him) to have him exposed; but he has still too much pride of character to become, himself, an *Informer.* He (B) is satisfied that confidential & unreserved communications passed, at that time, between the General & Blannerhasset (or rather *Mrs.* B. whom he considers as having been the better *man*) but he does not know whether she, now, possesses any evidence of such communications; or, if she does, whether she will be willing to surrender them.

Until the receipt of your letter, I was not apprised of the fact that Mrs B. is now a resident of Montreal; and, as yet, I have not ventured to hold any communication except with Mr Davis. I will, tomorrow, make some enquiries as to the certainty of her residence at Montreal, her situation &c. and if, after the information I shall obtain, it shall be deemed expedient to send on, Davis will cheerfully undertake the mission, and we shall take care that he be furnished with letters to the best & most fit people of that city. The subject, however, is one of so much delicacy & difficulty, that I can hardly, as yet, venture to anticipate any favourable result.

Our prospects in this state are cheering in the extreme; and I cannot doubt but that the Admn will have a sweeping majority. A "Circular" which you will see in our papers, signed by some 200. of the most respectable Republicans in different parts of the State, calling a convention at this place on the 10th of June, has, this day been issued.[1]

I was glad to hear by Mr McMichail [*sic*, McMichael][2] (who by the bye, was much gratified with his visit) that our friends at Washington, in case of their failing—as they doubtless will—to carry Mr [Rollin C.] Mallary's amendments,[3] have resolved to take the Tariff as reported by the Committee; in as much as, all things considered, it will probably be better than the one now in operation. My wishes on the subject are predicated on the belief (of the soundness of which, however, you can much better judge than myself) that, altho' the Jackson men may probably pass the Bill in the *House*, it will be rejected or shuffled off in the *Senate*, and the hollowness of their professions exposed to the public.

ALS. DLC-HC (DNA, M212, R3). Marked "Confidential." Envelope marked "Private." 1. See Porter to Clay, February 13, 1828; also Albany *Argus*, March 27, 1828. The Circular, signed by 212 men, called for a convention "to devise projects of further electioneering for the administration." 2. Richard McMichael represented Schenectady in the N. Y. State Senate. 3. U.S. H. of Reps., *Journal*, 20 Cong., 1 Sess., 298, 319, 508–12, 517–21.

From FRANCISCO TACON, Philadelphia, March 26, 1828. Demands restitution for the "Spanish Hermaphrodite Brig, 'Reyna Amelia'" which was captured by "one of those [Mexican] vessels which . . . find a shelter in the ports of this Union," particularly Key West. Cites the capture as "additional proof" that the neutrality practised by the United States "is not such a one as is defined by the Law of Nations, nor that which is required by treaties, and by good accord, and harmony. . . ." LS, in Spanish, with trans. in State Dept. file. RG59, Notes from Spanish legation, vol. 9 (M59, R–T12).

From ROBERT WICKLIFFE   Lexington, March 26, 1828
Mr. [Thomas] Smith has just shewn me your letter to him relative to the bargain & sale affair. I think I wrote you that I had disadvised the publication of your letter to [Francis P.] Blair or your taking any notice of the editor [Amos Kendall] or the pieces in the [Frankfort] argus[1] enough has, rely on it, been said by yourself the general effect of partial speaking upon the same point in answer to quibling, after a great effort on a jury is something like any further conniving on your part, upon the publick palate   Indeed your again appearing is an evidence or will be taken as evidence that you fear to submit you[r] cause to the people, there is a period when you should cease to play the prisoner in the trial. These are my sentiments. I delivered them with great solicitude to [John J.] Crittenden & your other friends from Frankfort I did not see [John] Harvey [*sic*, Harvie] but requested Crittenden to urge upon him my views they, except [Isham] Talbott [*sic*, Talbot], differed with me yet I hope they have not come to the conclusion to publish it   The moment it is made publick it will excite publick attention & draws it from the

contest between J[ackson] & A[dams] to yourself If we elect A. you are acquitted. If J is elected then in private life the publick will be your impartial arbiter. Your Book [6:1394–6] has had a good effect & your now publishing Blairs letter [4:41] would not only expose you to such perversions of it as your enemies might make but (as Blair from good or bad motives has refused to expose it) to the just reproach of violating your confidence towards him &c   Our Committee has a book in the press² which will I think place you upon good if not high ground in the affair & in many respects be usefull. It is writen in my loose rough way but I could prevail on no other to write it that I thought could do it better   Smith has been dilatory in its publication.   *remarkably so.* I have scolded him about it   He promises diligence &c   [Benjamin] Hardin Promised his Speech or I should have published mine³ but he is so much of a prude that he never publishes any thing untill effect is lost. My Speech would say to all except the examination[,] as it was made before the enquiry was entered upon; his embraced all & if were published would have a good effect   Our Book will embrace all & serve as a text for the *Stump* you will as well as others be furnished with copies   Pray let [Thomas] Metcalf[e] off as soon as practicable⁴

ALS. DLC–HC (DNA, M212, R3).   1. See Kendall to Clay, February 6, 1828. An *Argus* editorial of March 26 urged Clay to publish his letters to Blair impinging on the "corrupt bargain" charge [4:9–11, 46–8]. "Let the people see them Mr. Clay, and judge for themselves," said Kendall.   2. The Fayette County Corresponding Committee pamphlet, published by Thomas Smith of the Lexington *Kentucky Reporter*, was titled *Address on the Proceedings in the Senate of Kentucky against the President, Secretary of State and members of Congress and on other Subjects connected with the Approaching Presidential Election* (Lexington, [April 23] 1828). 49 pp. See Blair to Clay, January 22, February 25, 1828; and Clay to Harvie, June 5, 1828, published in Lexington *Kentucky Reporter* of July 2, 1828; see also, Lexington *Kentucky Reporter,* April 23, 1828.   3. Wickliffe delivered an address to the Fayette County Corresponding Committee on April 14, 1828. Lexington *Kentucky Reporter,* April 16 and April 30, 1828.   4. Thomas Metcalfe, the Administration candidate for governor, remained in Washington as a member of Congress. He resigned June 1, a few days after the First Session of the Twentieth Congress adjourned.

From ISAAC BARD   Greenville, Ky., March 27, 1828
I know you will not think it strange, if an unknown Friend should address a Letter to you. Have you not given yourself to your beloved Country, devoted yourself to her Cause; & may not the Citizen claim you as his Property & Inheritance? If so, why should an humble Citizen be shy & stand aloof from him whoom, he has long loved & admired?

    Will you be so kind [as] to indulge me in some dissultory remarks? When I was pursuing my Education in Lexington, I first herd you deliver an Oration at the Laying of the Cornerstone of the Hospital. As a student & a Boy, I was much pleased. Once on Poplar Row [North Mill St.], on the Pavement I met you & there were none else on the whole street, & you spoke to me so Politely & Friendly, it though a little thing, made no small Impression. The next time I saw you was when I was on at College & the Divinity School, you passed through Princeton [N. J.] siting by the Driver on an outside seat of the stage, spoke to Mr Wm Warfield,¹ who was with me coming up street. To say the least, the way you spoke to him (an acquaintance) impressed me that you, in no ordinary degree was a man; of Friendly Feeling, of Openess & urbanity of Manners.

But it is not merely the pleasing qualifications & attractions of Private Character, your Eloquence & Ratiocenation, the Boon of God; but your Political Course & those important national Principles, of Internal Improvement smiling on rising Republics, that enhance you in the approbation & give you such a scope in the affections of your Fellow Citizens. you have already established an imperishable Reputation. A wreath of Evergreens encircles your Brow, & will entwine around your name, while Time shall last. Your Reputation, the storms of Persecution have tried to carry away; but it is built on a Basis that mouldering ages cannot waste. Ethiopia, will remember your Colozenation efforts. South America & *Greece,* will couple your name with Liberty & Independence. You[r] Tariffe speech of 1824 [3:683–730], has opened the eyes of the American People & they will not forget you. Roads & Canals & Manufacturers, in fine, the American System, will hail you as their Founder & Father. Sir, if I understand Flattery it is stating, what is False. But I believe I am telling the Truth. Truth that is already written in American History. written in the Hearts & Affections of the American People, more indellible than Letters engraven on Adamant.

For many years I have re[a]d with pleasure your speeches & observed your Public Course. I have witnessed with heart–Burning & disgust, the vituperation & slander of ambitious, wicked men. In private conversation I have often plead your Cause, & of the President & of your Policy. I approve heartily, of your course. When my Friend told me, that Mr. Adams was President & you had voted for him, a sudden exultation of joy flashed through my Bosom.

We (of Greenville) had a large number of your Defences [6:1394-6] Printed at Russelville & I have spread them from my store far & wide. (for I am a Merchant & a Presbyterian Preacher) Be assured they are operating powerfully. It is the best antedote against Lying & slander, that has ever been used. Many of the Jackson men of this County (Muhlenberg) have turned completely around. We are decidedly Administration here, by a very lar[ge] majority.[2] I hope you & Mr Adams will not be discourag[ed] but keep up good spirits.

Two things are now operating against Jackson[sm]. When the J Party had the majority & the Power in Congress, they could make no Retrenchment of alleged Extravagence, & the Party in Congress & [James] Buchanan addmitting there was no Corruption. These have constituted the Pith of their Cause. Here has been their strong–Holds, to fly to be shielded, when pressed with argument. Honest Intelligent men must see the Dilemma & Ignorant men, will be overcome; as these hiding places are destroyed. "Truth will out." It is shining brighter every day & the Administration, is on the gain most every where.

In writing you this Letter, I mean no more than an expession of my Friendship for you, & my Country the Prosperity of the Nation & the welfare of Civil & religious Liberty.

I am in the Habit of Praying for you in secret & in Public. If I have any Interest at the Court of Heaven, I have tried to make it for you. Think; they did'nt say, at Hopkinsville they knew I was an Administration man from my Pray[e]r! Prayed for the Priest &c. But it is not a cause I am ashamed or afraid of; for it even "old Hickory" should be elected;

we will not give up you. You must come next. You are consecrated to your Country & you are ours.

Permit me to say, I have named my first–born so[n] Henry Clay Bard. I done it for Two Reasons. 1. As a mark of affe[ction] & Friendship for you. 2. That your Character might stimulate hi[m] to worthy Deeds.

Will you be so good as to give my Respects to Mrs Clay? Will you be so good as to give my Respects to the President, Mr Adams. To [*sic*, tell] him I pray for him & his Cabinet. May God bless Mr Clay. May God bless the President. May God guide & direct him & his Counsell[ers]. May you all fear God. Pray to him. Keep his "Commandments, that [all] may be well with you." P:S. Nearly all the leading men of this County, are your warm & devoted Friends. Judge Alney McLean, Jas. Wier, Willis Morgan, Charles Wing.[3] E. Brank & Dr. McLean &c do their best for you & the American System. My Relations at Bardstown Ky & Judge Bard near Mercersberg Penna are all warm in your Cause. I know you must be very Bisy; but, if you could for once send me a few Lines it would greatly gratify me. Any Documents or Papers to shed Light on the Election I would gladly receive to distribute or use to promote the Cause. Bear with me, for I love you.

ALS. DLC–HC (DNA, M212, R3). Isaac Bard (1797–1878), born near Bardstown in Nelson County, Ky., was a Presbyterian clergyman, storekeeper, and farmer who attended Transylvania University and was graduated from the Princeton (N. J.) Theological Seminary (1820) and Union College (1821), Schenectady, N. Y. He spent most of his adult life in Greenville, Ky. managing his farm there, and serving several Presbyterian churches in Muhlenberg County on a part–time basis. He owned large tracts of land in the Pond River country.   1. William C. Warfield (1796–1835) was born in Lexington, was involved in a stabbing incident as a young man, and ran off to Bardstown as a fugitive. There he heard Jeremiah Vardeman preach, was filled with the Holy Spirit, and gave his life to God. Returning to Lexington, he entered the ministry, was eventually ordained, and then proceeded to Princeton Theological Seminary for two years. Upon his return to Kentucky, he was active in a church in Todd County until his death.   2. The Adams–Rush ticket beat the Jackson–Calhoun ticket by a 359 to 266 margin in Muhlenberg County in the November presidential canvass. Frankfort *Argus of Western America*, November 19, 1828.   3. Judge Alney McLean served in the Ky. 14th District Court, 1821–1841, and was a presidential elector on the Clay ticket in 1824 and 1832; Willis Morgan, one of Muhlenberg County's earliest settlers, was a miller; Charles Fox Wing was Circuit Court and Muhlenberg County clerk for 50 years.

From FRANCIS P. BLAIR   Frankfort, Ky., March 28, 1828

I recd. your letter of the 15. Ins. yesterday evening—I had not copied the letter I designed enclosing to you, when I began to write the last letter I wrote you—& before I could make the copy the mail here arrived—I sent it the next day in the mail

You say that you would wish to publish my answer to your letter of the 8.,[1] if you should determine to make the letter public—I cannot object, however unpleasant it may be to have one's heart exposed naked to the world as disclosed in familiar intercourse to a friend—No personal consideration could induce me to oppose any obstacle to a full & fair developement of all the facts in relation to the [1824] presidential Election, so far as I am concerned, if you shall deem it proper that the Subject should undergo that species of Ordeal before the public,

I will not impose on you the trouble of transcribing & forwarding copies of my letters to me as you obligingly propose unless you should feel yourself constrained to introduce what passed in our private intercourse as proof to be presented to the tribunal of the public—In that event, I suppose it will be demanded of me to state what I know in relation to the matter. I would consider it therefore as a favor if you determine on that course, that you would send me copies of all the letters I wrote you having relation to the subject

ALS. DLC-HC (DNA, M212, R3).   1. Blair answered Clay's letter of January 8, 1825, on January 24. See 4:9-11, 41.

From THOMAS L. L. BRENT, Lisbon, no. 58, March 28, 1828. Transmits copy of a letter from the Portuguese Minister of Foreign Affairs, Viscount Santarem, regarding the "capture of the portuguese ship Almirante Pacheco off Cape Espichel by the corsair Independencia of Buenos Ayres," and reports that Santarem requested it be laid before the American government. LS. DNA, RG59, Dip. Disp., Portugal, vol. 7 (M43, R-T6). Received May 14, 1828.

In the enclosure, dated March 27, Santarem complained that the *Independencia,* "was manned the greater part by subjects of the United States where she was fitted out." He asked that the United States government "take measures to the end that . . . this aggression may not be any longer permitted against portuguese vessels of such corsaires which cannot be considered otherwise than as pirates." Copy, with trans. in State Dept. file. *Ibid.*

From JAMES BROWN   Paris, March 28, 1828

Matters in the East remain in the same state as at the date of my last letter.[1] At the last accounts the Porte still remained inflexible and continued his persecutions of the Armenian Catholics, and the prohibition to pass the Dardanelles. Russian preparations for war [6:1343-4] were going on with great activity, and little doubt appears to exist that the Pruth [*sic,* Prut] will be crossed before the 12 of April. The papers state that the French troops which had marched to Marseilles to embark for Greece at Toulon have received orders by Telegraph to delay their embarkation and that the transporter which had been chartered for the purpose of carrying them had been discharged after receiving indemnity. It is thought that England has been unwilling to go any further in this affair and wishes to leave Russia solely to contend with the Porte relying on the Emperors [Nicholas I] promise to abstain from all plans of agrandiz[e]ment. We learn from the papers that the difficulties which have existed between France and Algiers will be speedily adjusted. You will through the British papers receive such full accounts of the extraordinary state of things in Portugal that I need say nothing to you on that subject. It seems now pretty certain that what I have long predicted will happen   the Infante will be declared absolute King and the Charter [5:310] and British influence will be expelled from the Peninsula.

It gives me great pleasure to inform you that Mrs. Brown's complaint which has given me so much uneasiness has, thanks to her excellent Physicians, begun to assume a milder aspect and we now confidently hope will in a short time disappear. When I say a short time I mean to say a few months because it cannot be expected that an enlargement of a gland so considerable and of such long standing can be speedily removed. I have gotten over the winter without any return of Rheumatism and begin to hope that I shall be exempted from it during my life. If therefore my request for leave to return shall be calculated in any way to embarrass the Government, I will if the President wishes it remain until Spring When the season will be more propitious for the voyage. I find in the motion for retrenchment so much declamation about the expences of Ministers and particularly about those who do not remain long enough to expend their *outfits* that I shall be willing to remain more than five years from home, in which time I think it probable that the whole of the sum may be expended and that the good people of Mr [Thomas] Chiltons District may be convinced that I have not pocketted a single shilling of the publick money. I am happy in the belief that the enquiry if directed to my account would have found it moderate and I only trembled for the fifteen hundred francs laid out in preparing my carriage for the coronation. If so much has been said about twenty or thirty dollars worth of Embroidery on our coats what might not be said about a coronation carriage. The affair would have assumed a still *darker* aspect had I rendered my account of expences for the late Kings [Louis XVIII] funeral when I expended about fifteen hundred francs in covering my carriage and servants with mourning. I suppressed this and wishing only to exhibit the bright side of matters charged the publick with decorating my carriage.

I wish you would send the Newspapers and despatches to Denmark Stockholm and St Petersburg by sea rather than through this Legation. We have no Couriers and very rarely find any Americans travelling so far to the North. They are so very voluminous that Ministers sending Couriers in that direction do not wish to take charge of them. The Russian Ambassador [Pozzo Di Borgo] has hitherto been so obliging as to take charge of the Newspapers for Mr [Henry] Middleton.

It is now six months since I had the pleasure of a line from you. I am happy to find that your vindication [6:1394–6] has produced a great change in the publick opinion. You have certainly experienced a degree of persecution without a precedent. What business can the Kentucky Legislature have with the matter? Do you pass the next Summer in that State.

Mrs. B. sends her love to her sister [Lucretia Clay] to whom please make my affectionate respects. . . . [P.S.] Mr [Daniel] Sheldon writes me from Marseilles that his health is very bad. I hope the sea air will restore him.

ALS. DLC–HC (DNA, M212, R3).   Printed in *LHQ,* 24:1092–4.   1. March 12, 1828.

From CHARLES S. WAUGH   Culpeper, Va., March 28, 1828

A Virginian begs to be permitted to congratulate you on a complete victory over yr enemies; and to rejoice with thousands, that in yr. person the Ancient Dominion, has produced a Son, worthy of her proudest days.—Your talent, integrity, and firmness, will one day, Deo volente, place you in the highest office, within the gift of your Country. Persue the "even tenor of yr way," and your enemies in future will be "curs baying the Moon." Had I not thought it obtrusive, and improper, while under the excitement produced by the malevolence of your enemies, I should have troubled you with the matter of this Letter before.—Laennec[1] one of the most enlightened Physicians of France, has made a discovery by means of acoustic Instruments, of diseases of the Chest, which promises to fix an Epoch in practical Medicine.—Could I ask the favour of you when more at leisure, to inform yourself on the subject, preparitory to your laying the matter before the President.—It promises more advantages to this Country, than any on the Globe.—The great outlets to human life in this Country, are diseases of the Chest, particularly with the laboring class, and more particularly with our Slaves. The Stethoscope the Instrument used, indicates the disease, when no other method can, and with a certainty not to be credited by those uninformed.—Laennec on the diseases of the Chest is translated from the French by John Forbes;[2] will you be so good as to read his preface, when you will see my object, and be enabled with the Professional Gentlemen of yr. City to appreciate its value, and judge whether his Excellency Mr Adams shall order its use in our Hospitals.—Language cannot describe the advantages it promises to the Medical art; and I beg you to be assured it is worthy the attention of the enlighten'd head, and Cabinet, that presides over the destinies of our beloved Country.—Permit me to say one word of my self; I never did for one moment prostitute my tongue, or pen, possessing at all times more of the Fortiter in re, than the suaviter in modo.—I had made some progress in the Latin, and Greek classicks, when we adopted the Federal Constitution; connected by birth, and marriage, with the best families in Virginia; I have always had the means of correct information; pardon me for not suppressing, a conviction that a more virtuous, and enlightened Administration never existed than that which now presides over our destinies. . . . From the great desire I have to see the Stethoscope in general use, I regret that I am not professionally known to you.—Several Universities have honored me with Diplomas, among them there is one from your State, now in the hands of Colo: Robert Mallory[3] a Clark in the War Department, to which I beg yr reference.—A successfull case in Surgery, against the united judgement of the Faculty of Maryland and Virginia, has drawn from the oldest Universites of Europe, their confidence, and thanks, for the honor done to the Profession[.]

ALS. DLC-HC (DNA, M212, R3).   1. For Rene T. H. Laennec, see further, *Encyclopaedia Britannica; Micropaedia.*   2. A *Treatise of the Diseases of the Chest* . . . , trans. from the French of R. T. H. Laennec, with a preface and notes by John Forbes. 1st American ed. Philadelphia, 1823.   3. Virginia-born Robert Mallory had been a War Department clerk since 1826.

From THOMAS L. L. BRENT, Lisbon, no. 59, March 29, 1828. Reports that, after the arrival of dispatches from London of Frederick James Lamb, the British minister, the British army resumed its embarcation. States that it is "asserted that possession will be retained by the english of the forts of St. Julien [Sao Juliao de Barra] and Bugio . . : & that a ship of the line and a frigate will remain in the Tagus." Describes an attack on the garrison at St. Ubes by ultraroyalists. Notes that General Juan Carlos Saldanha arrived a few days ago from England. Details circumstances surrounding the murder of two royalist College of Coimbra professors by constitutionalist students, and discusses friction between the armed forces and Miguel. Notes that the refugee Spaniards in the country are being "marched" toward Salvaterra. LS. DNA, RG59, Dip. Disp., Portugal, vol. 7 (M43, R6). Received May 14, 1828.

From LANGDON CHEVES, Washington, March 29, 1828. States that among the documents sent to the Senate in response to its resolution of December 14, 1827 is a letter from Albert Gallatin to Clay, dated November 13, 1826 [5:923], "which refers to the *data* furnished by . . . [Cheves] for the basis of a Compromise with Great Britain under the 1st. article of the Treaty Ghent." Reports that William Wirt has referred to the data in such a manner, before the Board of Commissioners, as to cause Cheves to wish "to shew what . . . [he] did say." Requests a copy of his memorandum and permission to use it. Asks also for a copy of and permission to use the letter of the American Commissioners of September 13, 1824, "which Communicated to [the State] Department, the decision of the Mixed Commission on the question of the average values [of slaves]." ALS. DNA, RG76, Misc. Claims, Great Britain. See also 6:347.

On the same date, Daniel Brent, at Clay's direction, transmitted to Cheves the joint letter from Cheves and George Jackson to the State Department, dated September 13, 1824, which stated that the average value of slaves had been fixed under the Treaty of St. Petersburg. He also sent him the "Memoranda" which accompanied Cheves's letter of April 26, 1825 (above), and other documents. Copy. DNA, RG59, Dom. Letters, vol. 22, p. 170 (M40, R20).

From WILLIAM B. LAWRENCE, London, no. 30, March 29, 1828. Acknowledges receipt of Clay's dispatches numbers 3 and 4 of February 20 and 21, 1828. Has informed Lord Dudley by letter that he has received official notification of Senate ratification of the conventions concluded in London on August 6, 1827 [6:826-7, 859-60], and also the convention concluded on September 29, 1827 [6:1100-01]. Raised the question with Dudley as to where the ratifications are to be exchanged, and told him that he had received instructions relating to further arrangements "contemplated by the Convention [6:1100-01] respecting the North East Boundary."

A personal conversation with Dudley revealed his pleasure in learning of the Treaty of Limits [Poinsett to Clay, January 8, 1828] between Mexico and the United States.

Discusses the selection of a suitable arbiter for the Northeast Boundary, as contemplated in the recent September convention, and asks which nation Clay might now think preferable, since "the reasons for preferring Denmark to the Netherlands are still stronger than when you assigned the order in which they should respectively be proposed." Thinks the British will likely propose the Netherlands; but "I can hardly with propriety decline that power, intending hereafter to take it as a *pis-aller;* whereas, if we fail in obtaining Russia or Denmark, we can, in all human probability, have our third choice." Believes that the British will suggest that the "nomination should proceed from us."

Reports that the "affairs of the East" were discussed in the House of Commons on March 24 and in the House of Lords on March 26 and that yesterday the news of "the definitive decision of the Cabinet of St. Petersburg respecting Turkey" reached London. "I also learn that large reinforcements are preparing to be sent to support the army now on the frontier of Turkey," and that Emperor Nicholas I is apparently determined to crush the Turks in a manner "entirely distinct from the Stipulations of the Greek Treaty [Treaty of London, July 6, 1827]" which Russia "professes her wish to execute in conjunction with her allies."

Adds that Russia has renewed her earlier treaty negotiations with Persia which Turkey was instrumental in disrupting, even though the Persian monarch, Fath' Ali Shah, clearly wanted "to terminate the affair." The "movements of the Russian General [Ivan F. Paskevich] were so rapid and his success so decided, that the Schah was soon compelled to sue for peace."

Concludes that at "the King's late Levee" he had finally been presented at Court along with Vincente Rocafuerte, the Mexican Chargé, and Jose Fernandez Madrid, the Colombian Minister. Believes that rumors to the contrary, King George IV "appeared in good health" throughout the ceremony. ALS. DNA, RG59, Dip. Disp., Great Britain, vol. 35 (M30, R31). Received May 12, 1828; extract in Manning, *Diplomatic Correspondence . . . Canadian Relations,* 2:691-3. The Russo–Persian Treaty of Peace and Friendship was signed at Turkmanchai on February 10, 1828.

From WILLIAM B. LAWRENCE, London, no. 31, March 29, 1828. Acknowledges receipt of instructions of February 20, 1828, by the hand of Nathaniel B. Blunt. Reports that Prince Christoph von Lieven, the Russian ambassador to Great Britain, in a "confidential interview" yesterday, had indicated Russian willingness to assist in choosing an arbiter in the Northeastern Boundary dispute between the U.S. and Great Britain. Notes, however, that Clay's instructions on the order of preference of acceptable arbitrators had been written "before any intelligence could have reached you of the Turkish Manifesto [Lawrence to Clay, February 28, 1828], which has been supposed to change the political relations of England and Russia." That being the situation, "I took the liberty . . . of reading to the Russian Ambassador so much of my instructions as relate to the selection of the Emperor [Nicholas I]." Thinks the likelihood that "England should consent to the choice of Russia is very improbable," but that by taking the Russian ambassador into his confidence on the boundary arbitration question he had extended "a most delicate compliment which . . . may hereafter be remembered at St. Petersburg." Reports that Prince Lieven also thought it *"improbable* that Lord Dudley should accede to the choice" of the Russian Emperor. Therefore, Lawrence had "named hypothetically the different sovereigns, who might possibly be proposed by England or the United States in case Russia should be objected to." The Ambassador, in turn, spoke highly of "the personal character and upright views," both of the King of Denmark, Frederick VI, and the King of the Netherlands, William I, but "laid great stress" on the fact that the latter, given British policy in Portugal, was subservient to Great Britain. "He thought that there was no doubt that the King of the Netherlands would be seized with alacrity should I name him, and spoke of the Prussian, Frederick William III, as a Sovereign much less under British influence." ALS. DNA, RG59, Dip. Disp., Great Britain, vol. 35 (M30, R31). Received May 12, 1828; also in Manning, *Diplomatic Correspondence . . . Canadian Relations,* 2:693–5. Letter marked "Confidential."

To WILLIAM TUDOR   Washington, March 29, 1828
The President is desirous that you should negotiate, in behalf of the Government of the United States, with the Government of Brazil, a Treaty[1] of friendship, commerce, and navigation. A similar desire is understood to be entertained by the Emperor [Pedro I] on the part of his government. Circumstances, hitherto, have not favored the execution of that object; but the time has now arrived when it is supposed it may be entered upon with advantage. The manufacturers and productions of the United States, have, for some time, sustained, in the ports of the Brazils, an unequal competition with similar productions and manufactures of other foreign countries—Whilst the former have been subjected, on entry into those ports, to a duty of 24 per cent, ad valorem, the latter have been admitted at the lower rate of only 15 per cent. Against this inequality, your predecessor [Condy Raguet] was instructed to remonstrate, as you also were, by your general instructions of the 3d day of October 1827. Mr Raquet's interposition was not attended with the desired effect, and we fear that yours may be equally unsuccessful. We hope an efficacious remedy may be found in the negotiation of a Treaty. I had supposed that it might be most expedient to postpone opening such a negotiation, until after you had made a satisfactory arrangement on the subject of indemnities due to Citizens of the United States. Circumstances, however, on the spot, may recommend an earlier attempt to conclude a commercial treaty. It is submitted to your discretion to open a negotiation, at such time as may appear to you most expedient, keeping constantly in view the wish of the President to avoid unnecessary delay.

With respect to the commerce and navigation between the two countries, three different bases for an arrangement present themselves. The first is to be found in the fourth and fifth articles of the Treaty between the United States and the Federation of the Centre of America [4:878], signed at the City of Washington on the 5th. of December 1825. The second is contained in the second article of the Convention to regulate commerce between the territories of the United States and His Britannic Majesty [2:54–7], concluded at London on the 3d day of July 1815; and the third you will meet with in the second and third articles of our treaty with Colombia [4:127–8], signed at Bogota on the 3d day of October 1824.

According to the first mentioned basis, no higher or other duties would be imposed, on the importation into the ports of one country, of any article, the produce or manufacture of the other, than should be

200

paid on the like articles, being the produce or manufacture of any other foreign country. Nor would any higher or other duties or charges be imposed in either of the two countries, on the exportation from one to the other, of any article of their respective produce or manufacture, than such as should be paid on the exportation of similar articles to any other foreign country. Nor would any prohibition be imposed on the exportation or importation of any articles, the produce or manufacture of either country, to or from their respective ports, which should not equally extend to all other nations.—Such would be the principle of the basis under consideration in respect to the commerce between the two countries. It would leave each at perfect liberty, as each ought to be, to impose such duties as it wants, or its policy might seem to require, whilst it would restrain either from laying upon the produce or manufactures of the other, higher duties than are exacted from other nations on similar articles of their produce or manufactures. It would consequently remove, the existing inequality prevailing in the ports of the Brazils, to the disadvantage of the United States, of which we have more just cause to complain since there is no similar inequality operating in our ports to the prejudice of the commerce of the Brazils. What would the Government of the Brazils think if we were to make a difference of nine or ten per cent against the coffee of the Brazils in the ports of the United States?

As to the navigation between the two countries, the first basis is founded upon the most perfect equality and reciprocity. According to its principle, whatever can be imported into, or exported from the ports of one country, in its own vessels, without any regard to the place of its origin, may in like manner, and upon the same terms, and conditions, be imported or exported in the vessels of the other country. This is the most perfect freedom of navigation. We can conceive of no privileges beyond it. All the shackles which the selfishness or contracted policy of nations had contrived, are broken and destroyed by this broad principle of universal liberality. The President is most anxious to see it adopted by all nations. Since the commencement of the present administration, besides the Guatemala [Federation of the Centre of America] treaty, the principle has been embraced in treaties concluded with Denmark, Sweden, and the Free Hanseatic Cities of Europe; in the two former instances with a slight modification, not at all, however impairing its value.

2. The second basis which I have stated, found in the Convention with Great Britain, in respect to commerce and duties, both on exportation and importation, is the same as that contained in the treaty with the Federation of the Centre of America; and it would, therefore, secure to our produce and manufactures an admission into the ports of the Brazils upon as favorable terms as similar produce and manufactures of any other foreign country. But there is a wide difference between the two treaties, in relation to navigation: according to our Convention with Great Britain, its privileges are limited to the importation of the produce and manufactures of the two countries respectively, neither being permitted to import into the ports of the other, goods from any other ports of the world. Within those restricted limits, that convention secures a perfect equality and reciprocity between the vessels of the two countries.

It was a great improvement on the previous condition of the navigation of the two countries, but it falls far short of the comprehensive scope of the treaty with Central America.

3. The last basis which I have mentioned is that of the Colombian Treaty, according to which the rule of the most favored nation has been adopted. The objections to this principle are, in the first place, the difficulty of always clearly discriminating between that which is a gratuitous concession, and what is granted upon equivalent. Secondly, the difficulty of ascertaining the precise extent of commercial favors which may have been granted to all, or anyone, the most favored, of the commercial powers. And, thirdly, a grant, by the United States of all the Concessions which it has made to the most favored nation, in consideration of a similar grant from a foreign power, might far transcend the limits of a just equivalent. The most favored nation, according to the commercial policy of some States, has its commerce and navigation loaded with burthens and restrictions. But the most favored nation, according to the liberal and enlightened policy of the United States, has its commerce and navigation freed from almost all burthens and restrictions.

Of the three bases which I have described, the first is entitled to a decided preference. You will therefore use your best endeavors to get it adopted. The treaty with Central America may be taken as a model, in all its articles, for one which you are authorized to conclude with the Government of the Brazils. If the assent of that Government can be obtained to the fourth and fifth articles of that treaty, you may agree to include or omit all or any of the other articles, accordingly as you find the disposition of the other party.

Should the Government of the Brazils decline acceding to the principles of the Treaty of Central America, as a basis, your next endeavor will be to get that of the Convention with Great Britain of 1815, adopted. And if that should be agreed to, you may propose to be connected with it the various articles of the treaty with Central America.

If you cannot prevail upon the Brazilian Government to negotiate on the basis of neither the treaty with Central America, nor the Convention with Great Britain, you will lastly propose the rule of the most favored nation as contained in the treaty with Colombia; and you will offer to connect the other articles contained in the same treaty, most of which are identically the same as those contained in the treaty with Central America. That rule will, at least secure to us equal competition, with other foreign Powers, in the trade with the Brazils.

Considering the present state, and the probable future extent of the naval power of the United States, the opinion entertained by some is not without plausibility, that their interest is adverse to those liberal maritime principles for which they have ever contended since their origin as a nation. That opinion, perhaps, would be well founded, if they were likely to be frequently involved in maritime wars. But their prosperity is so evidently connected with the preservation of peace, that it is to be hoped that they will but rarely be involved in war. Whatever may really be the pecuniary interest of belligerent maritime powers, there can be no doubt that the general cause of humanity and civilization will be promoted by the adoption of those maritime principles which the United States have so perseveringly endeavoured to establish.

It is in that view of the matter that the President wishes you to propose these articles which relate to that subject, which you will find in the treaty with Central America, and to press them as long as there is any reasonable prospect of their being agreed to.

The principle of equality and reciprocity between the navigation of the two countries may be objected to, both in its more general and limited extent, upon the ground of the infancy of the mercantile marine of the Brazils, and its incompetency, therefore, to sustain an unequal competition with that of the United States; but if a competition cannot be maintained under a system of exemptions, how can it be under one of reciprocal restrictions? If one maritime Power, in its intercourse with another, endeavours to secure to its own navigation peculiar advantages, by laying burthens upon the navigation of that other, from which its own is free, countervailing legislation is the necessary consequence. Restriction begets restriction, until the parties, after a long course of irritating legislation and counterlegislation, find themselves arrived, in the end, at a point of equality, it is true, but it is an equality wither of mutual interdiction of all intercourse or of burdensome restrictions essentially impairing the value of that intercourse. When that point is at last reached, the discovery is made, by the contending parties that they had better here set out with equal and reciprocal freedom from burdens; and that each has injured himself as much, if not more than the other, by the shackles which were attempted to be put upon his navigation. It is to be hoped that the Government of the United States and the Brazils will avoid this unfriendly process of imposing burdens and restrictions upon the navigation of each other, and in their first treaty of commerce, exhibit to the world an example of equal Justice and liberality, worthy of imitation.

With respect to the duration of any Treaty on which you may be able to agree, it may be fixed for a term of about ten or twelve years. It will be well to add a clause providing against the unintentional expiration of the treaty, whatever may be the term you fix upon, similar to the stipulation contained in the eleventh Article of our late Treaty with Denmark.

A full Power is herewith transmitted to enable you to enter upon the negotiation, and to conclude the treaty to which you are authorized to agree. . . . P. S. I transmit herewith a copy of Elliott's [sic, Elliot's] Diplomatic Code [6:1102-03], embracing a collection of the Treaties and Conventions between the United States, and foreign Powers. &c.

Copy. DNA, RG59, Dip. Instr., vol. 12, pp. 77-81 (M77, R7), no. 6.   1. For the treaty, which was signed December 12, 1828, ratified March 18, 1829, and proclaimed on the same date, see Parry, *Treaty Series*, 79:249-75.

From FRANCIS P. BLAIR   Frankfort, March 30, 1828
Amidst the variety of Calls on my attention which appertain to the Sitting of the court, the remark at the close of your last letter[1] with respect to the mistake imputable to Mr [Jephthah] Dudley or myself, which was not unobserved when I read your letter, escaped my mind at the mo-

ment I was replying to it—I did not remember that there was any thing said with regard to Mr. Dudley in my letter to which you allude; but I am not surprized to be informed that the Statement which it may contain, differs from that recently given to the public by Mr. Dudley[2]—I was sitting in the Secretary's [i.e. clerk, James Stonestreet] Office pending the investigation in the [Ky.] Senate when Mr [Amos] Kendall brought in, & read to me the manuscript (then just written) containing Mr Dudleys account of my application to him—I then told those present & I think especially to Mr Kendall & the Secretary more than once declared that Mr. Dudleys recollections did not at all correspond with mine—I am persuaded that Mr Dudley has confounded in his memory,[3] impressions which have originated in his mind *since* the transactions in question with the facts which transpired at the time, or rather that he has unconsciously substituted the one for the other—

I designed also to mention to you, that the declarations recently made with regard to the course I would pursue by the Editor [Duff Green] of the Telegraph[4] are wholly unauthorized by me & that I have given no intimation which can be construed to authorize his assertions The editors of the [Washington *Daily National*] Journal & [Washington *Daily National*] Intelligencer may call till doomsday & I'll not answer them—[5]

ALS. DLC-HC (DNA, M212, R3). 1. Not found. 2. Dudley stated on the floor of the Kentucky Senate in February, 1828, that Blair had approached him in January, 1825, with reference to resolutions passed by the state Senate urging Congress to vote for Jackson for President; that Blair had urged him to write Kentucky legislators in Washington to follow Clay's lead in the matter, pointing out that were Adams elected, Clay would become Secretary of State. Dudley refused, saying he opposed the pro-Jackson resolutions and hoped further, that Clay would not accept any position in an Adams administration. In refusing a post in Adams's Cabinet, Clay would, Dudley believed, become the leading candidate in the 1828 canvass for President. Frankfort *Argus of Western America*, February 13, 1828. 3. The word "recollections" is struck through and "memory" is substituted in its place. 4. The Washington *United States Telegraph* of March 13, 1828, picking up on a piece from the Frankfort *Argus*, argued that if Clay denies that Blair was authorized to approach Dudley and Kendall [see note 2 above] Blair would be compelled in self-defense to publish the relevant correspondence. 5. Peter Force and Gales and Seaton respectively.

From WILLIAM TUDOR, Valparaiso, no. 85, March 30, 1828. Apologizes for still being on the west side of the continent. Explains that he has recovered from his illness and will soon proceed to Brazil. Reports the arrival of General Andres Santa Cruz in Chile on his way to Buenos Aires as minister from Peru. States: "This is a kind of honorary exile solicited by him; and which will serve to relieve the government of Peru, by depriving political intriguers of the presence of an individual whom they constantly pretended was acting with them." ALS. DNA, RG59, Dip. Disp., Brazil, vol. 6 (M121, R8). Received July 10, 1828.

To WILLIAM B. LAWRENCE, London, no. 6, March 31, 1828. Transmits correspondence between State Department and Charles R. Vaughan which pertains to the Northeastern boundary. Notes that the United States has demanded "the liberation of John Baker [6:1272–3] . . . and full indemnity for the wrong which he has suffered by the seizure of his person . . . and his subsequent abduction and confinement"; and that it has also "demanded that the Government of New Brunswick shall cease from the exercise . . . of exclusive jurisdiction within the disputed territory, until the question of right is settled by the two Governments." Instructs Lawrence to request officially that the British Government "interpose its authority" to enforce compliance by the provincial government of both demands. States that the United States "cannot consent to the exercise of any separate British jurisdiction within any part of the State of Maine." Adds that "if there be a persever-ance in the exercise of such jurisdiction, this Government will not hold itself responsible for the consequences." Observes that the British will probably argue that if they relinquish jurisdiction over the disputed area "disorder and anarchy . . . will ensue." Instructs Lawrence to counter that contention with the assertion that the inhabitants of the area can "institute some form of governing themselves, adapted to their condi-tion," but "whether they do or not, however, it will be competent to the Governments of Maine and New Brunswick, within their respective ac-knowledged limits, to guard against any disorders." Concludes that only an end to British jurisdiction over the territory "will supersede those precautionary measures which this government will, otherwise, feel itself constrained to adopt." Copy. DNA, RG59, Dip. Instr., vol. 12, pp. 83–4 (M77, R7); also in Manning, *Diplomatic Correspondence . . . Canadian Rela-tions,* 2:172–3.

To WILLIAM TUDOR   Washington, March 31, 1828
Since the date, on the 29th. Inst., of my letter to you, in regard to a Commercial Treaty with the Brazilian Government, I have received a copy signed at Rio de Janeiro, on the 17th day of August last, between that Power and Great Britain.[1] By the 20th Article, an exception of greater favor, to the produce of Portugal, when brought direct from Portugal, in Portuguese or Brazilian ships, is allowed than to similar British produce. Although the reason assigned for that exception is in-applicable to the United States, yet it may be insisted upon, in conse-quence of the ancient political connexion between Portugal and the Brazils, and the present connexion between the reigning families of the two countries. You will oppose it as long as there is any probability of its being successfully resisted; but if you find it necessary to yield the point, to secure the conclusion of a treaty, you are authorized to do so.

By the 19th. Article of the same Treaty, the rate of duty established for all British or British Colonial produce, is not to exceed 15 per cent. ad valorem. We should be entitled to the admission of our produce at the same rate of duty, if either of the three bases is adopted on which you are authorized to conclude a treaty. The adoption of either of them would however, leave open to possible controversy the question whether our productions were similar or not to those of Great Britain, or the most favored nation. To guard against all danger of dispute on that ground, it would be expedient to insert an additional article corresponding with the above mentioned 19th Article. Perhaps it may be required, on the other side, that we should agree, as an equivalent, to receive brasilian produce at the same rate of duty, in our ports. To such a stipulation you will not consent. It has formed no part of our foreign policy to subject this

Government to any limitation as to the amount of duty which it may think proper to impose on foreign productions, and the President cannot authorize any deviation from our established policy, in that respect. Foreign Powers have been content to treat with us upon the principle that their respective productions shall be received at the same rate of duty which is paid by the most favored nation; and what that should be, has been left to the direction of Congress. We should not ask that the Brazilian Government would subject itself to any restriction, in this particular, if it had not thought proper to adopt it, in reference to other Powers. This subject will require to be touched with much delicacy, and if you should have reason to apprehend, in the course of the negotiation, that the proposition may not be well received, you will refrain from making it, and let us depend upon the just interpretation, without it, of that one of the three principles on which you are authorized to conclude a Treaty, according to all of which we would have a right to insist upon the admission of our produce on as favorable terms as that of Great Britain.

Although I have treated, in the former instruction, of the rule of the most favored nation, as a distinct basis from the other two which are there mentioned, it will, of course, occur to you that it is not incompatible with them; but may be well incorporated in the same treaty with either of those two.

Copy. DNA, RG59, Dip. Instr., vol. 12, pp. 86-8 (M77, R7), no. 7.   1. Parry, *Treaty Series,* 77:375-93.

To PHILIP P. BARBOUR, Washington, April 1, 1828. Draws the attention of the Chairman of the House Judiciary Committee to the wording of the fifth article of the U.S.-Russian treaty of April 17, 1824 [4:213] having to do with not selling liquor and firearms to the Alaskan natives. Notes that a protest of March 24 has been received from the Russian Minister, Paul de Krudener, to the effect that American nationals have violated this provision. Suggests that the House enact legislation "as may enable the Government of the U.S. to execute the stipulations of the treaty" in good faith. ALI, draft. DLC-HC (DNA, M212, R3).

From THOMAS L. L. BRENT, Lisbon, no. 60, April 1, 1828. Reports that the evacuation of British troops continues. States that the British and the Portuguese are in disagreement over whether or not the former shall continue to occupy the "forts St. Julien and Bugio," and that animosity is felt by many Portuguese towards the British. Expresses the opinion that the British may wish to continue their presence in Portugal to thwart ultra royalist intentions to make Miguel king. LS. DNA, RG59, Dip. Disp., vol. 7 (M43, R-T6). Received May 14, 1828.

From ROBERT SCOTT   Lexington, April 1, 1828
Your favor of the 19th Ulto came to hand yesterday.[1] Something of what you have heard, occurred early in the year—it has ceased some time since and nothing has suffered in consequence except my feelings—and reputation of course[2]—the latter was to be expected, and perhaps ought

to follow—No pecuniary loss however has arisen—either in the affairs of the estate—yours, or my own—

[Discusses Clay's accounts with the estate of Col. James Morrison for the past quarter and those with himself, and submits listing of receipts and payments.][3] I have setled with [James E.] Davis &c. for the first years rent of the Tam[man]y Mill—150$ for repairs and RS. Todds note for the other 100$ payable on the 4th Septr. next, with interest from the time it fell due. I have caused a Warrant of Distress to issue for the balance of the rent—about 295$. and a sale has been made of the Machinery &c. at three months to cover the debt—

The [Kentucky] Hotel is wholly unoccupied, and no applications to lease it have been made, except that by Mr. [Zedekiah] Moore,[4] the Inkeeper, of which I have heretofore advised you—[John] McCracken positively refuses to give more than 100$ pr. year for the Stable—and as he is a good tenant and pays punctually, I agreed that he may keep it at the 100$—but subject to be relinquished by him when we can do better with it,—upon giving *reasonable* notice—

Unfortunately for our poor town, rents are decreasing—and I fear great depression in town property unless our university [Transylvania] can be resuscitated—Part of the Citizens have subscribed to the amt of 2500$ to 27-or 2800$. and the Town 500$ to pay the President—The subscription of the Citizens is for three years—and perhaps that of the town—I have understood that a Mr. [Alva] Wood[s] of Maryland has been invited by the Trustees to accept the Presidency—If he should I hope it will aid us some—But more depends upon the preceedings of Congress in the Tariff Bill, than on the University; because, if they protect our hemp manufactures and that of coarse woollens, the former would be prosperous, and have but little doubt, the latter would soon become so in our town—

We are all well.

ALS. KyLxT.   1. Not found.   2. Reference obscure.   3. Enclosure and comments thereon omitted by editors.   4. Moore had moved from Virginia to Nicholas County, Ky., about 1805. He subsequently operated a hotel at Blue Lick Springs on the Lexington-Maysville Pike. At this time, however, he was apparently living in Fayette County, although the 1840 census places him back in Nicholas County.

From SMITH THOMPSON   New York, April 1, 1828

I see by the papers some intimation that a new treasurer is about to be appointed, and the name of Mr. [John] Savage of this State has been mentioned. I have not seen him, and am unable to say how far that situation would comport with his views. I have understood for some time past that he would willingly relinquish his present office[1] if he could withdraw from it in some honorable manner. His appointment would I think be an excellent one both for the public and the political effect it would have here. I have had some conversation with his friends here, who are more particularly acquainted with his views, who are inclined to think he would accept the office but are of opinion that he would be better pleased with that of Comptroller—He held the office of Comptroller in this State for some time and gave great satisfaction, and I understand was pleased with it—Would not Judge [Joseph] Anderson like to take the office of Treasurer, the labours are less arduous and he is growing old and an little infirm. If this could be brought about I am inclined to think it would have a very salutary effect here—Judge Savage has been written to on the subject. And I would thank you to drop me a line confidentially what you think could be done on the subject. I have taken the liberty to suggest these things in consequence of what you mentioned to me when I had the pleasure of seeing you, was the wish of the administration, as it respected some appointment from this State.

ALS. DLC-HC (DNA, M212, R3).   1. New York Supreme Court Chief Justice (1823–1836) John Savage received the appointment as Treasurer of the United States on May 15. Savage to Clay, May 15, 1828. ALS. DNA, RG59, Misc. Letters (M179, R66). Two weeks later, however, he declined the appointment, stating that his acceptance would be "totally incompatible with my relations in society," and that he could not bear to leave his friends "in this part of the country." Savage to Clay, May 29, 1828. *Ibid.* He had earlier served in the U.S. House and as Comptroller of the State of New York (1821–1823). See *BDAC*.

To WILLIAM TUDOR   Washington, April 1, 1828

From late communications received at this Dept., from our Consul, Mr [William H. D. C.] Wright, at Rio de Janeiro, it is seen with surprize that the Brazilian Government persists in the measure of exacting from neutrals clearing from the port of Monte Video, bonds obliging them not to enter any Buenos Ayrean port. That measure can find no jusitifcation whatever in the usage or laws of nations. Its pretext is the violation of blockade instituted by the Government of the Brazils.—A blockage must execute itself. The presence of the force which constitutes it is the means of enforcement. The belligerant has no right to resort to any subsidiary means. Such a resort is a tacit admission of the incompetency of the blockading force to sustain the blockade, and, consequently confesses its illegality. The belligerant can have no right, especially, to exert any municipal authority, as the measure in question is, over neutral vessels to execute his belligerant designs.—The Belligerant has no more right to lay the neutral under bond to respect the rights of war, than the neutral has to lay the belligerant under the bond to respect the rights of neutrality.

What would his Imperial Majesty [Pedro I] think of a demand of the Government of the United States, if it could bring itself to make a demand, from all his cruizers that might resort to their ports, to enter into bonds with sureties, obliging them to abstain from all captures of American vessels.

The measure in question is attended with the greatest practical inconvenience. It must be often difficult, if not altogether impracticable for our traders to obtain in distant and foreign ports, the securities satisfactory to the local authority. We cannot submit to the measure. If it shall be in operation on the receipt of this despatch, you will remonstrate against it with an urgency proportionate to its manifest want both of principle and precedent. And, if necessary, you will notify the Brazilian Government that the commanders of our public vessels will be instructed to disregard and resist it.

Copy. DNA, RG59, Dip. Instr., vol. 12, pp. 88–9 (M77, R7); also in *ASPFR*, 6:1071. No. 8. On April 9, Clay sent a copy of these observations and instructions to Secretary of the Navy Samuel L. Southard. Copy. DNA, RG59, Dom. Letters, vol. 22, p. 179 (M40, R20).

From JOSHUA BOND, New York, April 2, 1828. Transmits a copy of a circular addressed by the President of Montevideo, Tomas Garcia Luniga, to the foreign consuls in that city. The circular advises the consuls that the Brazilian order requiring that vessels leaving Montevideo be bonded against touching at Argentine ports, even "for information or supplies," has been renewed. Reports that the consuls remonstrated to the President, who promised to forward the protests to the Imperial government, and that a modification of the order to limit its scope to vessels taking in cargoes at Montevideo is hoped for. ALS. DNA, RG59, Cons. Disp., Montevideo, vol. 1 (M71, R1).

To BARON PAUL DE KRUDENER, Washington, April 2, 1828. Acknowledges receipt of Krudener's note of March 24 and states that it has been submitted to the President, "who has seen with regret that the conduct of Captain William Cotting has been such as to occasion dissatisfaction to the Government of Russia." States that Cotting's alleged infractions of the 1824 treaty were "upon his own responsibility, and without any sort of warrant or authority from the Government of the United States."

Promises to instruct the U.S. attorney for Massachusetts to investigate the matter. Expresses, on behalf of the President, satisfaction with the Russian observance of the treaty provision "by which the contracting powers reciprocally reserved to themselves the right to inflict the punishments incurred, by their respective Citizens or Subjects, in instances of a contravention of the stipulations of the fifth article." Copy. DNA, RG59, Notes to Foreign Ministers and Consuls, vol. 4, pp. 4–5 (M38, R4).

On April 3 Clay transmitted to George Blake, the U.S. attorney for Massachusetts, in Boston, the report of the Russian American Company. He instructed Blake to "investigate the grounds of the complaint and institute such legal proceedings" as are appropriate, if necessary, "to vindicate the national faith." Copy. DNA, RG59, Dom. Letters, vol. 22, pp. 175–6 (M40, R20).

On May 5, Blake replied, stating that he had talked with Cotting's employers, Baker and Sons, who told him that "they had never heard from any quarter, the slightest intimation respecting any real or supposed irregularity on the part of their Captain in the course of his voyage." The Bakers showed to Blake their instructions to Cotting, which appeared to Blake "to have been drawn up with the greatest fairness and caution" and to "denote a particular solicitude, on their part, that the conduct of the Captain, should in all things, be regulated by a strict regard to the laws and usages of the country to which he was destined." ALS. DNA, RG59, Misc. Letters (M179, R66).

From HENRY MIDDLETON, St. Petersburg, no. 75, April 2, 1828. Reports that two long-standing claims, that of Israel Thorndike for the brig *Hector* and that of the Weymouth Importing Company for the ship *Commerce*, have been admitted by the Russian government. Details the negotiations concerning the cases of the two vessels, both captured in the

Mediterranean Sea in 1807, which led to a final settlement. Copy. DNA, RG59, Dip. Disp., Russian, vol. 11 (M35, R11). Received July 20, 1828. Letter also carries Old Style date of March 21, 1828.

From HEZEKIAH NILES   Baltimore, April 2, 1828

I have the honor to acknowledge the receipt of your kind letter of the 29th. This evidence of your confidence and good will, must long be remembered by me. It would be honorable to be the successor of the late Dr. [William] Thornton, and I should feel as if within my own elements, when located in the patent–office; but the situation of my present business is such that I cannot give it up, and, having reflected upon the subject, I should be often embarrassed in carrying it on, while holding a public office. Besides, I stand as pledged [two illeg. words] cannot support of the "American system," and every feeling of my heart is interested in the success of the contest which I foresee will take place in the ensuing summer. I therefore beg leave respectfully to decline the proffered appointment, which I assure you of my gratitude for the tender of it.

ALS. DNA, RG59, Misc. Letters (M179, R66). No. 1 of this date.

From HEZEKIAH NILES   Baltimore, April 2, 1828

To the preceeding, which I regard as the reply to your official offer; I would assign this first reason why I cannot accept any place at present: When the battle is over, and all things quietly settled over *as I trust that they will be,* it would be very desirable for me to retire from my present arduous business, and I shall, possibly, solicit your good offices in my behalf. It is to me very plain that nothing will be done with the tariff, in the present session. On a right understanding of the subject will depend momentous results in New York, Pennsylvania and several other states. The force of circumstances have made me a [illeg. word] man in this matter, and I shall have to take a larger share in the battle that is to be fought. It is expected of me—and I cannot disapoint my friends. The influence of the Register, is at this time, perhaps, quite equal to that of any other paper in the U.S. and rapidly extending. I have received 400 new subscribers during the *present* year, that is in 3 months, and some are sent in every day. The question concerning domestic industry has been forced by its opponents by *contrast,* as I solemnly believe, into the electioneerings of the day. The old enemies present themselves in new shapes, and never was the spear of Ithuriel more needed than now. I must do my part in exposing the truth to the people—and my means for doing this are not small. I am preparing for a fierce campaign and am perfectly satisfied that I shall render much service to the general cause being flattered with the belief that I possess most of the confidence of an an [*sic*] old friend, even of those who have "turned aside & ceased to do well." I do not fear the result if we all exert ourselves as in Combat[?]— and I trust that heaven will give you health & spare your life, to enjoy the most splendid triumph in the complete success of our policy—and be preferred through the best *sense of gratitude of your fellow citizens,* to the most honorable place in this world for which, in my opinion, nothing but the loss of life or want of will to possess it (health being assured, can deprive you of the result of the ensuing contest what it may, for either the action or re-action *must* favor you & us.

There is now sitting at my side, Mr. Aaron R. Levering.[1] He was the captain of our strongest company of volunteers during the war, and fought at Bladensburg & North Point. No one was a braver man—no one more beloved—no one who has more of the *sympathies* of the respectable people of Baltimore. His knowledge of business & acquirements are above the ordinary cast—he is steady & industrious, and has had much to do with machinery; he is also an excellant clerk and writes a good hand. But he has been unfortunate—unfortunate and yet without censure. He is connected with some of the most respectable families in this city,—and on the whole, is a gentleman fitted for the place as as [*sic*] an appointment which would have *effect* upon the feelings of the people of this city, in general, I do not think it possible to make a better selection; and he is a warm friend. I would therefore, very respectfully, ask this favor—that if no one has been agreed upon in case of my declining the appointment, that Mr. Levering may have an opportunity of presenting some recommendations to you. I am *very* very interested in this matter—as a *man* and a *politician*. Mr. L. has ten children, and is somewhat lame from a hurt. It prevents *some* labor, but does not at all incapacitate him from performing the usual affairs of life.

ALS. DLC-HC (DNA, M212, R3). The preceding Niles to Clay of the same date was probably enclosed in this letter.   1. Levering, a Baltimore stationer and warhawk, had served as Captain and commanding officer of the 5th Company, Maryland Militia, in 1814 and had subsequently been a grocer and commission merchant on the Pratt Street wharf. He died in 1852.

To PETER B. PORTER   Washington, April 2, 1828
I have received both your favors of the   [*sic*][1]   and the 26h. Ulto. and I rejoice to hear the good tidings which you send us. Prospects are brighter than they have been for a long time, in every quarter; our friends have a tone of confidence, and our opponents a corresponding depression which have not been before manifested during the Session. In proportion to the despondency of our adversaries will be the disposition of some of their leaders to resort to desparate means. I have accordingly never been without fears that they would ultimately make a great endeavor to assume to the Legislature of N. York the power of appointing the P. electors [3:476–77; 5:988]. You do not know the outrageous character of the spirit of Jacksonism. It will stop at nothing to carry the day; and our friends in N. York should be constantly on the alert. In this view of the matter I learnt from you, with high satisfaction, that it was in contemplation for some friend of the Administration to propose a Law for a general popular ticket.[2] These advantages would result from such a proposition, if rejected.

1st. It would give confidence and animation to our friends in other parts of the Union, especially if the law should be voted for by our friends & opposed by the other side. You do not I fear sufficiently appreciate in N. York the importance elsewhere of favorable demonstrations among you.

2dly. Having rejected the bill (should such be the result) by their own vote at this Session, it would deprive the Jacksonians of all pretext, at your Extra Session, to change the [electoral] Law. If you do not deprive[3] them of this ground, it will be then urged, that the State will lose its weight, if the existing law be not repealed; that N. York has the power to make the President; that the great majority of the Republican party in that State is in favor of Jackson, and that the real question is whether the Republican majority or the Federal minority shall prevail &c &c. These appeals to State pride & to party prejudices, with the aids of coaxing, cajoling, promising, and if necessary bribing, I should much fear, would produce the desired effect. But if *you* now propose an appeal to the people, by a general ticket, *they* will have the ground so taken from them, or weakened, that I should think a proposition at the Extra Session to vest the Legislature with the power could hardly be entertained.

I dare say all these things have suggested themselves to you. As you must have also thought it expedient, on all occasions, in the press, in conversation, and in debate, to denounce the project of Legislative usurpation of the choice of Electors.

The affair of Mrs. B's [Harman Blennerhassett] letters appears by your last letter to be in a good train. If she has *such* letters as have been stated their effect would be decisive.

The fate of the Tariff is uncertain, or rather I should say, I think it will not pass. If there can be no amendments made to it, I must say that I think it ought not to pass. It is a trick, and every where it is now so understood, except I fear in your State. It gives protection where it is not wanted; and it sacrifices where protection is needed. Should it not be modified, there will be near two thirds of the House against it; and the small squad of Jackson tariff men will stand in such bold relief that I think the public will not fail ultimately to pass a right judgment upon them. What I should prefer is (next to the passage of a good bill) that the present one should be modified and sent to the Senate. There is a feint hope that this may be done. We shall see in a few days.

ALS. NBuHi.   1. Number omitted. Probably Porter's letter of March 15, 1828.
2. No such bill was considered in Albany in 1828.   3. The word "strip" is struck through and the word "deprive" substituted.

From JOHN U. WARING, Lexington, April 2, 1828. Reports that Robert Scott has advised him to communicate directly on the subject of title to 600 acres of land on the Ohio River in Union County, Ky., as this property might pertain to assets involved in settling the estate of James Morrison. Summarizes some of the legal problems involved in evicting the current occupants, the increasing value of the property, and the improvements made thereon by the occupants. ALS. DLC–HC (DNA, M212, R3).

To ALBERT GALLATIN, April 3, 1828. Acknowledges receipt of Gallatin's March 20 letter, "with the accompanying sketch." States that he expects to be able to send an agent into Canada soon, and that currently an appropriation is anticipated. Notes that the government of Maine has been supplied "with copies of the reports and all the documents returned by Mr. Commissioner [Cornelius P.] Van Ness" and consequently probably has a "copy of the British Agent's argument, on the fifth article of the Treaty of 1794 [Jay's Treaty]." Reports that he has initiated a research "relative to the 'plans of the former survey of the latitude of 45° north, in 1774.'" Transmits a copy of "map A." LS. NHi–Gallatin Papers (M415). For Map A, see *ASPFR*, 6:821 and foldout preceding. Article V of Jay's Treaty asked "what river was truly intended under the name of the river St. Croix" mentioned in Article II of the Treaty of Peace of 1783. Article II had described the Northeast boundary, partly in river St. Croix terms.

From BARON STACKELBERG, April 3, 1828. Alludes to a conversation with Clay regarding "a difference of opinion respecting the true meaning of the eighth Article" of the recently concluded Treaty of Commerce between the United States and Sweden [6:1235-6]. Quotes the article, which provides reciprocal most–favored–nation privileges. Complains that the American Chargé in Sweden, John James Appleton, claims for American commerce "the privilege of the lowest rate of tonnage duty, in case of its not being uniform, on all kinds of navigation, but regulated according to localities, and the length of voyages, excepting only the trade between Sweden and Norway." States that such variations exist among the duties on tonnage in Norway, but not in Sweden. Discusses the Norwegian tariff scale, and observes that, if Appleton's claim is agreed to, "American vessels would pay less than national vessels." Expresses the opinion that "the true meaning and intent of the 8th. Article, is to secure the commerce of the respective countries against an increase of tonnage duties which might be prejudicial to it—" Explains that "the Article . . . embraces only these two cases—1st, that a Swedish or Norwegian vessel, going to, or returning from, America, would be subjected to the same tonnage duties as an American vessel going to Sweden or Norway, or returning to the United States:—and 2dly, that no other foreign vessels, carrying on the same commerce and making the same voyage, should obtain, either in Sweden or Norway, or in the United States, more favorable terms, with respect to tonnage duties—" LS. DNA, RG59, Notes from Swedish Legation, vol. 3 (M60, R2).

From ALEXANDER H. EVERETT, Madrid, April 4, 1828. Expresses the opinion, based on recently acquired information, that Count Ofalia's memoir, a subject of his last dispatch on March 2, 1828, will not produce "any important result." Reports that he has not yet seen a copy of the memoir, but that he does not now believe that it is an effort by Ofalia to foster recognition by Spain of Latin American independence. Believes that Ofalia, when he went to London, "was instructed to communicate either directly or indirectly with the agents of the American powers, and to hear their proposals, particularly with the view of ascertaining whether any of them would be satisfied with any thing short of complete independence." Adds that the memoir contains "the result of these communications accompanied by observations from the Count. . . ." Suggests that Spain, taking into consideration "the continued troubles in various parts of Spanish America," may wish to attempt "an arrangement upon a different basis from that of separation." States that the Russian Minister, Pierre d'Oubril, thinks that the "better course would be for the principal European powers in concert with the U.S. to endeavour to mediate between the two parties to [put] the war on a different principle from that of independence." Notes that the Russian's opinion is "entirely a private one"; and, to Everett, the implementation of it seems "on all accounts impracticable."

Reports that, since Spain again has the American question under consideration, he believed it expedient to show to the Russian Minister the dispatch by the Count de la Alcudia on the British plan to effect revolutions in the Canary Islands and Cuba [6:920–1]. Says d'Oubril seemed surprised but agreed that the Wellington Government will probably not pursue the project. Believes that the British threat, though not immediate, has prompted Manuel Gonzales Salmon to enquire about American policy and mentions that Everett has assured him, informally, that the United States "could not in any event permit the island of Cuba to pass into the hands of any European power other than Spain." Adds: "His precise object seemed to be to ascertain whether in the case supposed the United States would go the length should other methods fail—of employing their naval and military force in aid of the King [Ferdinand VII]. I made no scruple of assuring him that I had no doubt they would—considering this as a necessary result of their declared and well known policy."

Reports that he has received from Jose Fernandez Madrid, the Colombian minister at London, a request that Colombian armed vessels, cruising the Mediterranean, be allowed to use American consular facilities in Barbary ports to authenticate their national character and to protect themselves "against any arbitrary proceedings on the part of the Regencies of Barbary." Reports that he has provisionally granted the request, pending a decision by the President.

In a postscript dated April 11, Everett relates that the Russian Minister, d'Oubril, has just been informed that the Imperial Guard has been ordered to join the Southern Army, in reaction to "the hostile character of the late Turkish Manifesto [Lawrence to Clay, February 28, 1828]." Adds, however, that d'Oubril has been instructed to assure the Spanish that the Emperor will continue to make every effort to preserve peace." LS, with postscript in Everett's hand. DNA, RG59, Dip. Disp., Spain, vol. 28 (M31, R29). Received June 3, 1828; also, without postscript, in Manning, *Diplomatic Correspondence . . . Latin American Nations*, 3:2152–7. Letter marked "Confidential."

From WILLIAM B. LAWRENCE, London, no. 32, April 5, 1828. Encloses a copy of his official note of March 24 to Lord Dudley, and the answer thereto, respecting British ratifications of "the three conventions [6:826–7, 859–60, 1100–01]." Reports that he also spoke with King George IV on April 2 "respecting the further arrangements contemplated by the North East Boundary Convention [6:1100–01]."

Nathaniel B. Blunt, who will leave London tomorrow in order to embark on the packet leaving Liverpool on April 8, will bear the documents to Washington.

Reports, further, a conversation with Lord Dudley respecting the choice of an arbitrator for the Northeast Boundary dispute, but found Dudley unwilling to suggest a name, a hesitancy, Lawrence suggests, having to do with the current state of British policies in Europe. "Taking this view of the case, I declined mentioning the names of the Powers to which we were disposed to agree." Instead, Lawrence suggested that the "fairest mode of proceeding" would be that "each of us should put on paper the name or names of one or two sovereigns . . . and that our lists should then be compared and if it fortunately happened that the same power was selected by both, it should be the arbiter, but if otherwise, we would consider the Sovereigns or States selected by each in nomination and adopt such ulterior measures, as might then be expedient and consistent with the views of our respective Governments." Lord Dudley accepted this procedure and said that he would consult with his colleagues. "The course resolved on, I believe to be the best calculated to afford us a chance of obtaining the Arbiter that we may prefer, while if we fail in our first and second choices we may avoid in any way giving umbrage to the Sovereign ultimately selected."

Notes that he also informally discussed with Dudley the subject of impressment and expressed his hope that a European war would not break out before some arrangement between the two governments could be made on the issue. Believes that Dudley might accept as a basis for an understanding the informal proposals put forward last year by Albert Gallatin [6:1086-7].

As to European developments, informs Clay that the British intend to withdraw their forces entirely from Portugal and are reluctantly prepared to accept whatever kind of government in Portugal the Portuguese themselves select. Says that Britain considers the Russians the best judges of how most effectively to settle their "grievances" against the Turks and will therefore remain neutral in the event of war, in spite of French pressure that they "cooperate effectively against the Turks in the Morea." Notes that Britain is urging France, in return, "to confine the acts under their mediation to preventing the passing of troops from Egypt into Greece." ALS. DNA, RG59, Dip. Disp., Great Britain, vol. 35 (M30, R31). Extract in Manning, *Diplomatic Correspondence . . . Canadian Relations*, 2:696-7. Received May 14, 1828.

From HENRY MIDDLETON, St. Petersburg, no. 76, April 5, 1828. Reports that the war between Russia and Persia has ended in acquisition by Russia of Armenia and the payment by Persia of an indemnity for the cost of the war [5:691-2]. Details the capitulation of Prince Abbas Mirza, and the lack of support given him by his father the Shah, Faith 'Ali. Describes the boundaries of the new Russian province and discusses the relative strengths of the two nations during the struggle. LS. DNA, RG59, Dip. Disp., Russia, vol. 11 (M35, R11). Received July 20, 1828.

From PETER B. PORTER   Albany, April 6, 1828

I have, this moment, received your favour of the 2d Instant. Your apprehensions that our Legislature will take the choice of Electors from the people, are rest assured, without foundation. *They dare not do it.*

When I say this, I have no doubt but that the *Jackson Leaders* are ready to advise & urge such a course. But not one member in five, in either house, would consent to make a political sacrafice of himself (as he would do by consenting to such a measure) to gratify the personal ambition of [Martin] Van Buren and his friends.

The present mode of chosing Electors by districts was, as you are probably aware, adopted about three years ago by a vote of the people [3:476–7; 5:988]. Whether we shall make a proposition to the Legislature to choose by *general ticket,* as I suggested in a former letter, is not yet resolved on. The only objection to such a course is, that if *we* should recommend a departure from the mode established by the people, the *Jackson men* may siese on it as a pretext[1] for going a step further, & taking the power into their own hands.

I regret that the prospect of obtaining, from the quarter anticipated, evidence of Genl. J's participation in [Aaron] Burr's conspiracy, is likely to fail. Immediately after the receipt of your first letter,[2] I requested my confidential friend, Mr [Chandler] Starr,[3] to write to Montreal, where he was well acquainted, for information. He, this morning, handed me the enclosed letter,[4] with its enclosure,[5] from which it would seem that Mr. & Mrs [Harman] Blannerhassett [*sic,* Blennerhassett] are, at this time, both in Europe.

ALS. InU.   1. The adjective "justiafiable," modifying "pretext," has been struck through.   2. Not clear to which letter this refers; but see Morgan to Clay, April 27, 1827; A Member of the Convention to Clay, January 11, 1828; and Clay to Porter, March 20, 1828.   3. An Albany, N. Y., dry goods merchant, Starr at this time was a member of the N. Y. State Assembly.   4. Horatio Gates to Chandler Starr, Montreal, April 20, 1828. Informs Starr that Mrs. Blennerhassett has not been in Montreal for a year or more and seems to have gone abroad. Says he will continue his search for her because he "will do any thing fair and honorable to promote what I consider the good and righteous cause." Gates was a Montreal merchant who founded the Bank of Montreal and was later a member of the Legislative Council of Lower Canada.   5. P. W. Rossiter to Horatio Gates, [Montreal], Wednesday [*sic,* Sunday], March 9, n. d [1828]. Reports that he had not had a letter from Mr. or Mrs. Blennerhassett for over two years, the last when they were in Bath, England.

To WILLIAM PLUMER, JR.   Washington, April 7, 1828

I received your obliging letter of the 26th ulto. with the newspaper containing the statement which you had previously apprised me of your intention to publish.[1] I am greatly indebted to you for spontaneously presenting this valuable testimony to the public. It cannot fail to have good effect. You will have seen a contemporary evidence in the note of the Chief Justice of the U. States [John Marshall], which will associate very well with yours, in point of time.[2]

I have a mass of unpublished testimony which I consider highly important. If I should publish it, I will send you a copy of it, in conformity with your request.

The H. of R. is now on the Tariff. A gleam of hope has recently broken out that something useful may be yet done. Perhaps this day's proceedings in the House may be decisive of the fate of the measure there.[3]

I congratulate you on the result of the elections, including your own, in New Hampshire.[4] It will have an encouraging influence out of the State.

I have thought that our New England friends have not been sufficiently alive to the beneficial effect in other parts of the Union of favorable demonstrations among them. The system, on the other side, is one of manoeuvres & demonstrations, & I regret to believe in the necessity of counteracting it, by a like system on our part.

I thank you for your kind offer of service, of which I shall not hesitate to avail myself if necessary.

Be pleased to remember me kindly to your father. . . .

Printed in *PMHB* (1882), 6:356.   1. Plumer's statement was published again in Clay's, *A Supplement to the Address . . . to the Public.* . . . Cf. below, June 10, 1828.   2. Marshall was quoted in the Baltimore *Marylander* for March 22, 1828 as having said that while he had not voted for twenty years it was his "solemn duty" to vote in the coming presidential election, "for should Jackson be elected, I shall look upon the government as virtually dissolved." Beveridge, *The Life of John Marshall*, 4:462-5. Marshall denied the accuracy of this statement in a letter to the Richmond *Enquirer*, dated March 29, 1828 saying instead that he would probably vote in the presidential canvass "from the strong sense I felt of the injustice of the charge of corruption against the President & Secretary of State: I never did use the other expressions ascribed to me. . . . you are authorized to declare that the Marylander has been misinformed." Richmond *Enquirer*, April 4, 1828.   3. U.S. H. of Reps., *Journal*, 20 Cong., 1 Sess., 483-98.   4. Plumer had been elected to the State Senate.

To JOHN JAMISON   Washington, April 8, 1828

I should have been mortified at the enquiry contained in your letter of the 3d. instant, if it had been made with the view of obtaining information to satisfy yourself; because I hope you could not believe me capable of procuring advances to be made for my Son and then refusing to reimburse them.

I had a son [Theodore W.] with me in the Session of Congress 1824. With many good qualities, he was prone to indolence and dissipation. I brought him in the hope of reforming him. I was disappointed, and sent him back to Kentucky. No one but myself advanced, within my knowledge, one cent to defray his expences here, or on his return. Whilst here he engaged, as I understood, in gambling in company with Mr. [David] White of Kentucky, member of Congress and others, and lost $500. That sum I did refuse to pay. He had been a source of great expence to me, and of much unhappiness. Being indebted some what myself, and with the claims of a family which is not very small, I did not think it right to pay the gambling debts of another, at least until my own were satisfied. But no one ever advanced a dollar to him, at my instance, which remains unpaid.

This is a delicate and painful subject, which parents will know how to appreciate. I cannot consent to any publication concerning it.

Defying my enemies on all points, if they will adhere to truth, I feel perfectly invulnerable in all that relates to pecuniary transactions.

I beg you to accept my warm acknowledgments for the expression of your feelings of friendship and regard. . . . P. S. I cannot object to your shewing this letter to any gentlemen, under the restriction which has been mentioned.

ALS. KyU.   Little is known of Jamison save his residence in Charleston, Va. [W.Va.]

From J. LENOX KENNEDY, Mazatlan, April 8, 1828. Reports receipt of an official note from the Commissary General of this State, protesting against trade by several American vessels over the past two years with the Californians, "in direct opposition to a law of this Republic, reserving the right of that trade to the vessels of the country." Notes the request that captains and supercargos trading on this coast be informed that they are authorized to trade only at designated ports, that permission obtained from local authorities "will not be considered an excuse for traveling at (except in case of distress) or trading with" other ports, and that the penalty for violation of the ruling of the Supreme Government will be confiscation of vessel and cargo. ALS. DNA, RG59, Cons. Disp., Mazatlan, vol. 1 (M159, R1). Received June 5, 1828.

From JOHN KIRKLAND, Cambridge, Mass., April 8, 1828. Commenting on Alva Woods, candidate for the presidency of Transylvania University: "He is a ripe scholar, well grounded in the several parts of elementary knowledge. He is a good disciplinarian without any tincture of severity. In manners he is very gentlemanly. . . . I think you cannot do better than to choose Him." [Alva Woods], *Literary and Theological Addresses of Alva Woods, D. D.* Providence, R.I., 1868.

To JOSE S. REBELLO   Washington, April 8, 1828
I have the honour to acknowledge the receipt of your Note of the 3d. instant, communicating information of the arrival at the port of Baltimore, of the Buenos Ayrean privateer, the Schooner Juncal,[1] and expressing your expectation that the reparation of any damages which she may have experienced during her voyage, will be limited to those which proceeded from the sea, and not be allowed to extend to such as you suppose may have been inflicted in an engagement which she is represented to have had with a Brazilian transport brig [*Santista*].[2] You also state that the privateer [*Juncal*] has entered the port of Baltimore with the avowed object of buying or building vessels of war for the service of the Argentine Republic, and you are pleased to enter a formal protest against any transaction to be made by her Commander, by which an augmentation of the Naval force of that Republic, might be effected.

I have the honor to state, in reply, that whilst the same hospitality will be extended to the privateer in question, which, under analogous circumstances, would be allowed to any Vessel of War of His Majesty the Emperor of the Brazils [Pedro I], the necessary precautions will be taken to prevent any reparations, or augmentation of the force, of the Schooner, not warranted by law, and the neutral posture of the United States. In respect to the purpose which you attribute to her Commander, of purchasing or building Vessels of war, I have also to state, that nothing will be permitted contrary to our neutral duties. The building and sale of Ships appertain to the industrious pursuits of the people of the

United States, with which the Government does not interfere further than to prevent the departure of any such Vessels from our ports in a warlike condition. With such an application of the industry of the people of the United States your Government is well acquainted, and of that industry has frequently availed itself. I have now before me what I presume to be a correct copy of a Letter from you, under date the 25th. March, 1827, addressed to an eminent ship builder of the United States, in which you state, "that having done with you business to the amount of about $900,000, in the last two years, I am absolutely satisfied with your conduct. . . . The two Vessels built by you for the use of my Government, have been found, not only by me, but also by competent persons at Rio de Janeiro, the *ne plus ultra* in their building."

It is not doubted that in the valuable addition which was thus made to the naval service of the Brazilian Government, proper respect was paid to the public law and to the municipal laws of the United States. Complaints have, nevertheless, been made by the Buenos Ayrean Republic, of the building of those vessels in the ports of the United States. In declining to interpose to prevent it, this Government gave a strong proof of its friendship and impartiality to that of His Imperial Majesty, whose strong sense of justice cannot fail to enable him to perceive that the same impartiality requires that what was allowed, without molestation, to his agents, should not be forbidden to others under like circumstances.

Copy. DNA, RG59, Notes to Foreign Ministers and Consuls, vol. 4, pp. 5–7 (M38, R4). No. 1 of this date.   1. For a translation of Rebello's note of April 3, see DNA, RG59, Notes from Brazilian Legation, vol. 1 (M49, R1). On April 7, James H. McCulloch, the Collector at Baltimore, reported to Clay that the *Juncal* arrived on April 1 and listed the articles on board. He stated that the vessel had been "put under the inspection of an officer to prevent any addition to her military strength." ALS. DNA, RG59, Misc. Letters (M179, R66).   Also on June 7, Clay, not having yet received McCulloch's letter, wrote the Collector and instructed him to allow the *Juncal* "the usual hospitality" but to prevent the schooner from making "any augmentation of her force, and . . . [from] making any repairs, not warranted by law." He added that the damages which the vessel "experienced from the sea" could be repaired, but those inflicted in battle could not. In a postscript, written on the 8th., Clay acknowledged receipt of McCulloch's April 7 letter. In regard to the articles listed as constituting the *Juncal's* cargo, he advised that "if they are prize goods taken at sea, and have not been adjudged lawful prize by a competent tribunal, I should think they ought not to be admitted to entry at the Custom House; but that they might be so admitted, if they were regularly shipped in a foreign Port, according to ordinary commercial usage." Copy. DNA, RG59, Dom. Letters, vol. 22, p. 177 (M40, R20).   2. On April 7, Rebello informed Clay that the "formerly Brazilian Brig Santista," prize of the *Juncal*, had arrived in New York. He demanded that the U.S. government prevent the unloading of its cargo and any repairs except of "sea damages." LS, in Portuguese, with trans. in State Dept. file. DNA, RG59, Notes from Brazilian Legation, vol. 1 (M49, R1).   Clay acknowledged this note in his second letter of April 8 to Rebello and assured him that the necessary orders had been given "to prevent any disposition of the prize, or the goods on board, which would be contrary to the neutrality of the United States." Copy. DNA, RG59, Notes to Foreign Ministers and Consuls, vol. 4, pp. 7–8 (M38, R4).   On April 9, Clay reminded Jonathan Thompson, Collector of the Port of New York, that neither the *Santista* "nor the prize goods on board can be lawfully sold in the United States, prior to their condemnation by a competent tribunal." He added: "You will, therefore, limit our hospitality to an allowance of such supplies, and such repairs of sea damage as may be needed, without permitting any augmentation of the force of the vessel.—" Copy. DNA, RG59, Dom. Letters, vol. 22, pp. 178–79 (M40, R20).   Rebello acknowledged receipt of Clay's letter of April 8 on April 11. Still not satisfied, he asserted that neutrality involved the aiding of neither side, not the helping of both. He argued that American actions had been unjust and "unpolitical" and that they jeopardized the lucrative trade between the United States and Brazil. ALS, in Portuguese, with trans. in State Dept. file. DNA, RG59, Notes from Brazilian Legation, vol. 1 (M49, R1).   See, below, Clay to Rebello, May 1, 1828.

To EDWARD EVERETT   Washington, April 9, 1828

In answer to your letter of yesterday, I have the honor to state, confidentially, for the information of the Committee, that a Convention has been concluded between the United States and Great Britain, providing for a reference to arbitration of the dispute respecting our northeastern boundary [6:1100–01]. The exchange of the ratifications of that Convention is not known to have been yet effected; and hence, and, also, for other obvious reasons, it is proper that the subject, for the present, should be treated confidentially.

By the terms of the Convention, the parties are to reciprocally exchange schedules of the evidence, and their respective statements of the case, to be used before the arbitrator, within prescribed periods of time, which begin to run from the date of the exchange of the ratification of the Convention. I transmit, herewith, in confidence, a copy of the Convention from a perusal of which the Committee will perceive the importance of avoiding any unnecessary loss of time in making the preparation which it contemplates for the arbitration. The question which is involved is very complicated, and is rendered more difficult by the ingenuity and the exertions of the other party. To elucidate and establish our right, numerous charters, statutes, commissions, maps, and other public acts and documents are necessary; some of them extending back to the original settlement of this country. They are to be collected from the archives of Great Britain, several of the States, and from the adjoining British provinces. I also transmit, herewith, to the Committee, in like confidence copies of two letters from Mr. [Albert] Gallatin[1] which will convey some idea of the nature, variety, and importance, of the documents to be collected. The object of the bill from the Senate before the [House Foreign Relations] Committee, is to invest in the President the authority to employ the necessary agents to collect and collate our proofs, and make other needful arrangements to give effect to the arbitration.[2] It will be necessary to send one of these agents to the adjoining British Provinces, and after our case shall have been fully prepared, it is intended to send one of the agents who may be employed, and who shall have made himself complete master of the whole subject, to Europe, to superintend the arbitration should no circumstance occur to defeat it.

The Committee will perceive the necessity of the adoption of initiatory proceedings during the present session of Congress. Prior to the commencement of the next annual session, the first term prescribed in the Convention neither which the parties are to make reciprocal demands of the documents and papers with in their respective archives, will have expired. Should this communication not prove satisfactory, I shall be happy to furnish any other information in my power which the Committee may require.

I have to request a return of the papers now sent, when they shall be no longer wanted by the Committee, and I beg permission to add that if the House of Representatives concur in the expediency of the bill, its passage is desirable with as little delay as may be practicable.

LS, draft. DLC–HC (DNA, M212, R3). Marked "(Confidential)."   1. Gallatin to Clay, December 12, 1827; February 23, 1828.   2. U.S. Sen., *Journal*, 20 Cong., 1 Sess., 264, 270, 278, 292, 295, 299, 310, 318. On April 11, Everett acknowledged receipt of this letter, and reported that the House had passed legislation authorizing the employment of boundary agents. Everett to Clay, April 11, 1828. ALS. DNA, RG59, Misc. Letters (M179, R66).

From JOHN J. AUDUBON   London, April 10, 1828

The letters of recommendation[1] that you were So good as to Send me to Louisiana when on the eve of leaving America for England have procured me in this Country so much hospitable treatment and so many honors, that I feel most anxious to offer you again my Sincerest thanks.

My Publication [3:104] is now I think inSured; but I am deSirous to have it honoured with the names of Such Men and public Institutions in the United States as will crown it with everlasting Fame.—

I have taken the liberty to address the PreSident and to beg his Patronage; I am equally deSirous to obtain your name and to forward you a Copy. I Send you a Prospectus and should your many avocations permit you to recommend the work to the public Institutions & Men of Science I should Still feel more obliged to you. . . .

ALS. DNA, RG59, Accounting Records, Misc. Letters. Written from 95 Great Russel St., Bedford Square. No date of receipt.   1. Not found.

From WILLIAM B. HODGSON, Algiers, no. 5, April 10, 1828. Reports that he has taken over the direction of the consulate following the departure of William Shaler, and that he has studied the history and character of "these asiatic Turks, and of their piratical republic," as well as the Arabic, Turkish, Persian, Modern Greek, and Berber languages. Notes that the ten–month French blockade of Algiers, and the unwillingness of the French to cede "the objects of the war," even though "it is supposed that her operations here, will be subordinate to those in the Levant." Believes that U.S. status has grown "in these remote regions," to the "first rank of Nations," partly as a result of the rumor that "The U. States being recognized by Treaty [2:80] would no doubt, as friends [of Algiers], lend their powerful marine, to aid the Sultan [Mahmud II] in the present juncture of affairs." ALS. DNA, RG59, Cons. Disp., Algiers, vol. 11 (M23, R13). Received June 11, 1828.

From ROBERT MONROE HARRISON, Kingston, April 11, 1828. Reports arrival on June 30 and discusses commerce of the island. Notes that the colony will accept the British interdict [5:629–32] against its commerce with the United States as long as a circuitous trade is permitted. Lists military forces. ALS. DNA, RG59, Cons. Disp., Kingston, Jamaica, vol. 1 (M–T31, R–T1). No date of receipt.

From SAMUEL LARNED, Santiago, no. 67, April 11, 1828. Reports that the constituent congress has been in session in Santiago since February 25, that a committee has been appointed to draft a constitution, and that the ideas suggested by Larned [5:894] to the committee of the last constituent assembly will be adopted "without essential variation." Elaborates: "That is, a system, embracing the main features and essential advantages of our federal form, but avoiding, at the same time, the dangerous principle of conflicting sovereignty, and other points calcu-

lated to disturb the general harmony, and throw obstacles in the way of the legitimate and beneficial operations of the national government:—a system having a tendency also towards a more enlarged and perfect application of the municipal principle, and calculated to prepare the nation for its safe and advantageous adoption." Notes that he has declined an invitation to attend the sessions of the constitutional committee but has provided "information upon some particular points, in relation to which the light of practical experience was wanted."

Reports that a bill has been introduced in Congress "to prohibit the importation of all such articles as may be either produced or manufactured in the country, in sufficient quantity to meet the demands of consumption." Notes that "the trade of the United States to Chile, which consists principally in Flour, coarse cotton goods and cabinet wares" would be materially lessened if the measure becomes law. States: "I am . . . taking all proper and honourable measures to prevent it, and have hopes of succeeding in, at least, putting it to rest for the present." Reports that he has presented a memorial to the Chilean Government requesting a reduction of the transit fee on flour imported by American merchants and urging that the merchants be allowed to store the produce in their own warehouses rather than in expensive public magazines.

States that the new Peruvian constitution has been completed and was to have been proclaimed on March 19. Reports that Colombian troops will soon evacuate Bolivia. Adds, in a postscript, that he has just received a note from the Minister of Foreign Relations, Carlos Rodriguez, inviting him to open negotiations for a commercial convention. ALS. DNA, RG59, Dip. Disp., Chile, vol. 3 (M–T2, R3). Received August 13, 1828.

To FRANCISCO TACON, Philadelphia, April 11, 1828. Acknowledges receipt of Tacon's note and enclosure of March 26 on the status of the Spanish brig *Reyna Amelia* which had been seized by a Mexican warship and taken into Key West, Florida [Clay to Wirt, April 22, 1828]. Cites U.S. neutrality law pertaining to such captures, admits that "it is very possible that some irregularities may have been committed on the coast of Florida by both belligerents," and rules that in the instances of the *Reyna Amelia,* "no sale or disposition of the Vessel or cargo will be allowed, no violation of the public law, nor of the obligation of existing treaties, can be admitted." Wants to know why the Colombian armed schooner *Zulme,* taken by spanish warships in Florida territorial waters, has not been surrendered to U.S. authorities as demanded. Copy. DNA, RG59, Notes to Foreign Ministers and Consuls, vol. 4, pp. 8–10 (M38, R4); also in Manning, *Diplomatic Correspondence . . . Latin American Nations,* 1:295–6.

From THOMAS L. L. BRENT, Lisbon, no. 61, April 12, 1828. Reports that no doubt is longer entertained by anyone of the existence of an ultraroyalist plan to place Miguel on the throne. Details efforts of the pro–Miguel forces to accomplish their goal, including efforts " to destroy the party of the Emperor of Brazil [Pedro I]." States that enough transports have arrived to take away the remaining British troops waiting aboard the British fleet in the Tagus, and that it is not yet known how long the British will occupy the forts at St. Julien and Bugio. Adds that the Portuguese refugees in Spain have been prevented from returning to Portugal as a result of a British request to the Spanish Government. LS. DNA, RG59, Dip. Disp., Portugal, vol. 7 (M43, R6). Received June 4, 1828.

From JAMES BROWN   Paris, April 12, 1828

Mr John Connell with whom you are acquainted, on his return from Copenhagen, has remained a few days in this place and will take charge of this letter with the Newspapers for the Department of State. From these you will discover that Russian preparations for war are going on with great activity, and that the Porte is preparing his defences by strengthening his line on the Danube, and by adding to the fortifications of the Dardannelles. The troops of Russia will cross the Pruth on the 15th., and before the end of this month, the Emperor [Nicholas I] will take the command in person of the invading army. The war will be very popular in Russia, and even in Poland, the troops manifest the greatest enthusiasm in the cause. Events have been such as to place the Emperor on the ground of right, and to ensure the neutrality of England, and France. Indeed the cooperation of these powers may be claimed and expected to the extent necessary to secure the objects of the treaty of the 6th. of July [6:780–2], or in other words to effect the liberation of Greece. It is believed that the British Government has already given to the Russian Ambassador at London [Count von Lieven], assurances that it would not take part in favor of the Porte, in a war provoked by his obstinacy and rashness. Preparations are still going on for the embarkation of about 6000 men at Toulon, but their destination is not known. By some it is believed to be entended for Algiers, by others to take post in some of the Grecian Islands. The insignificance of the force would seem to contradict the first of these conjectures. It is not believed that the war will become general, and consequently the British as well as French funded stock has experienced little or no depression.

[Comments on internal French political developments. Continues:] I hope when I next write to you I shall have something to communicate on the subject of our Claims [5:29–31]. Indeed I should before this have pressed for an answer had not Mr [Hyde] de Neuville entered the Ministry. I have been anxious, as I know he will be consulted, and indeed have an overwhelming influence on the question, to find some means of disposing him to view our claims with more favor than he has hitherto done. Since his appointment I am more discouraged than ever as to the result of our proposal to arbitrate the question, as I know he has hitherto resisted every argument in favor of our claims. He takes a deep interest in the Beaumarchais claim [3:311–13], and is I believe intimate with the family of Mme. de la Rue [Amelie Eugenie Beaumarchais]. She can now entertain no hope of recovering it unless connected with the admission of our claims. Perhaps this circumstance may have some weight in our favor. The present Minister of Foreign Affairs [Pierre La Ferronnays], with who I have taken particular pains to become acquainted, appears to be a frank, honorable and intelligent man, and if left to act alone, would in my opinion be more disposed to do us justice than his predecessor [Baron Damas]. But he knows nothing of our claims, and to save himself the trouble of examining them carefully, will perhaps be disposed to submit the question to his Colleague who has already borne a part in the discussion of them. As we have every reason to consider the proposition last made as the only one short of coercive measures, I wish to give it every chance of success.

Mr [Daniel] Sheldon is still at Marseilles from whence he writes that his health is not improved. I hope he exaggerates the danger, but certainly his situation is rather alarming. I am encouraged however by the recollection, that he left us twice in nearly the same situation, and by remaining a few weeks on the sea side, returned in good health. I should deeply regret his loss. He is an honorable, safe, and well informed man. His talents are highly estimated here by all his acquaintances. A son [Charles] of our Consul Mr [Isaac C.] Barnet who is himself Consul at Antwerp has consented to remain a few weeks and attend to Mr Sheldons duties—So few of of [sic] our young Americans have a competent knowledge of the French to be of any use in that situation, that I was glad that Mr Sheldon was able to borrow Mr Barnet for a short time

Mrs. Brown health has rather improved since the date of my last letter. She continues to receive her friends every evening and sometimes has small dinner parties. Her spirits are wonderfully good considering her long confinement at home. She rides out in the morning for exercise but never goes into parties abroad. Her Medical attendants are distinguished by their talents, and are sanguine in their hopes, that with time and perseverance, her complaint may be removed. It is an encouraging circumstance, that the tumor has never encreased since she perceived it, but has on the contrary, diminished although in a very inconsiderable degree. It has given me inexpressible anxiety.

I find from the latest accounts that Mr Adams prospects of a re election are improving. It is to be regretted that the effort in his favor by your Virginia friends had been so long delayed. I fear the Jackson influence has become so rooted that you cannot eradicate it. The same may be said of Pennsylvania. If you can secure 24 votes in new York the election will be safe without those two States. If General Jackson be elected the next four years, if we may judge by the temper of his friends at the present Session, will be unusually stormy & violent. How does the *extravagant* Committee of Mr [Thomas] Chilton go on in the detection of abuses? Who is the said Mr Chilton? I think the party must have lost ground by this discussion. They have spent more money in the time consumed in the debate than would have reimbursed Mr John King's outfit, the only abuse specified in the course of the argument.

I hope soon to hear from you a pleasure I have not had since Oct.

ALS. DLC–HC (DNA, M212, R3). No date of receipt. Also printed in *LHQ,* 24:1094-7.

From DANIEL CALL   Richmond, April 12, 1828

I received your letter (enclosing certain copies) this morning after breakfast. They contain nothing but what was fair and honorable; and breathe, throughout, the stoutest integrity, and the most patriotic views; but there is occasional looseness in the expression, which your enemies would carp at; and therefore I, at first, determined to show them to nobody, until I heard from you again: Distrusting my own judgment however, and having the most perfect confidence in that of Mr [Chapman] Johnson, I shewed them to him; and he suggested the same ideas, but kept your letter and the Copies to consult Mr [Benjamin W.] Leigh (whom he expected to see at Court to day) respecting the affair.[1] I presume that I shall know the result of their deliberations tomorrow, when I shall write to you again. In the mean time, I think you had as well suspend any further circulation of them, until you do hear from me. At present the facts before the public, and the argument, are unquestionably in your favour; and it would be wrong to furnish any thing which Malice might distort.

I have just returned from North Carolina, and think that State will vote for General Jackson. A great many people of distinction will dislike it, but their fears will either keep them silent, or prevent their voting; which will be a loss to the Administration party, who are ardent, but they will probably be out numbered. . . . P.S. The Chief Justice [John Marshall] is not in town—

ALS. KyU.　1. This reference is obscure; but it probably has to do with a proposed personal answer by Clay to charges of the Jackson Central Committee relating to his letters in early 1825 to Francis P. Blair on the "corrupt bargain" issue [4:9-11, 46-8]. See Wickliffe to Clay, March 26, 1828.

To PETER B. PORTER   Washington, April 12, 1828

Your favor of the 6h. instant is received. I am glad to observe the confidence with which you speak of the impracticability of the Jackson leaders prevailing upon the Legislature to pass a law assuming to themselves the appointment of Electors. I confess that I had entertained fears on that subject.

I suppose we must abandon the pursuit of the letters supposed to be in the possession of Mrs. [Harman] B[lennerhassett].

The Tariff remains in doubt. I rather think however that it will pass the house, with the amendments which have been made. That is now my wish, and my advice.

Our news from K. continues cheering. The election of Genl. [Thomas] Metcalfe as Governor is spoken of with great confidence.

ALS. NBuHi.

From WILLIAM B. LAWRENCE, London, April 13, 1828. Regrets "not having enjoyed in America the privilege of your personal acquaintance." Nonetheless, states that he must ask Clay to forward him a letter of credit "to pay me the outfit of a Chargé d'Affaires, together with the salary attached to that grade." Complains that he has not received the pay to which he was entitled when he was promoted to the grade of Chargé on October 4, 1827, and that he has since been forced to draw on "private resources" in the amount of "a sum equal to the outfit" to meet the high cost of living in London. ALS. DNA, RG59, Dip. Disp., Great Britain, vol. 35 (M30, R31). No date of receipt. Letter marked "Private."

From JOHN M. MACPHERSON, Cartagena, Colombia, April 13, 1828. Reports that General Jose Padilla has proceeded to Ocana, where the Grand Convention is assembling [Watts to Clay, February 10, 1828]. Details the abortive attempt of Padilla's friends, a minority of the convention, to put the convention on record as approving Padilla's conduct. Notes that when Padilla returned to Cartagena, he was arrested and sent under guard to Bogota and that since then, other conspirators in the plot have been arrested and are on trial. Discusses Simon Bolivar's sending 4000 men to Cartagena to suppress the disturbances there. Thinks Bolivar may not come to Cartagena when he learns of Padilla's arrest. Reflects on Padilla's background noting that he rose from common sailor to admiral in a brief 14 years, although he cannot write a word other than his name. Concludes that he is probably but a tool of Vice President Francisco de Paula Santander. ALS. DNA, RG59, Cons. Disp., Cartagena, Colombia, vol. 1 (M-T192, R1). Received May 15, 1828.

From WILLIAM TUDOR, Valparaiso, no. 88, April 13, 1828. States that he has written General Jose de Lamar "suggesting the necessity of his sending some envoy to the U.S. especially after this unfortunate event of Mr. [James] Cooley's decease." Quotes from a letter from Lamar which indicates that, owing to the lessened threats posed by Simon Bolivar and Antonio Jose de Sucre, Peru may, in "'two or three months . . . be able to make some reforms, and count on some disposeable funds to satisfy the interest of the loans.'" Reports that he has booked passage on the ship *Star* for Rio de Janeiro, and expects to arrive there in two months. ALS. DNA, RG59, Dip. Disp., Brazil, vol. 6 (M121, R8). Received July 10, 1828. Letter marked *"Confidential."*

From JOAQUIN CAMPINO, Washington, April 14, 1828. Reports that he was called upon yesterday by Jose S. Rebello, who had been "expressly charged by Baron de Stackelberg" to give Campino "satisfaction respecting the occurrence which took place at the theatre on the night of the 10th.," and that Stackelberg requested him to withdraw his letter of complaint to the U.S. Government. States that consequently he "does not feel it his duty further to prosecute this affair" and asks Clay to return his note of April 11 [not found]. LS, in Spanish, with trans. in State Dept. file. DNA, RG59, Notes from Chilean Legation, vol. 1 (M73, R1).

On April 15 Clay acknowledged receipt of Campino's note, expressed his satisfaction that "an accomodation" had been made, and returned the requested note. Copy. DNA, RG59, Notes to Foreign Ministers and Consuls, vol. 4, p. 10 (M38, R4).

From JOHN HARVIE, Frankfort, April 14, 1828. In his capacity as Chairman of the "Central Committee appointed by the Convention of the Friends of the Administration of Kentucky assembled in this town in December last [6:1120-3]," respectfully asks for a copy of the January, 1825 Clay letter to Francis P. Blair [4:9-11] which allegedly has to do with Clay's bargain with Adams. Wants to publish this letter "as the best and most effectual means of putting down all the calumnies which have been predicated by your enemies upon its supposed contents." Is quite certain that the letter will support none of the vicious political charges currently being made by the enemies of the Administration. ALS. DLC-HC (DNA, M212, R3).

From **WILLIAM B. LAWRENCE,** London, no. 33, April 14, 1828. In response to Clay's dispatch No. 5 of March 5, 1828, forwards a copy of the "Third Report of the Emigration Committee, with a Map annexed." Reports that there has been no recent progress in selecting an arbiter for the Northeastern boundary conflict. "I shall not regret the delay, if it enables me to learn before taking any definitive step, whether the recent changes in the relative position of the different European Powers has produced any alteration in the President's views." LS. DNA, RG59, Dip. Disp., Great Britain, vol. 35 (M30, R31). Received May 14, 1828. Extract in Manning, *Diplomatic Correspondence . . . Canadian Relations,* 2:697–8.

To JAMES COOLEY   Washington, April 15, 1828
The President is desirous that you should negotiate, in behalf of the Government of the United States, with the Govt of Peru, a Treaty of Friendship; Commerce and Navigation.[1] Circumstances, hitherto, have not favored the execution of that object; but the time has now arrived when it is hoped it may be entered upon with advantages.

I had supposed that it might be most expedient to postpone opening such a negotiation until after you had made a satisfactory arrangement on the subject of indemnities due to citizens of the United States. Circumstances, however, on the spot, may recommend an earlier attempt to conclude a commercial treaty. It is submitted to your discretion to open the negotiation at such time as may appear to you most expedient, keeping constantly in view the wish of the President to avoid unnecessary delay.

With respect to the commerce and navigation between the two countries, three different bases for an arrangement present themselves. The first is to be found in the fourth and fifth Articles of the Treaty between the United States, and the Federation of the Centre of America [4:878–9],[2] signed at the City of Washington on the 5th December 1825.—The second is contained in the second Article of the Convention to regulate Commerce between the territories of the United States and His Britannic Majesty, concluded at London on the 3d day of July, in the year 1815 [2:26, 30–7]. And the third you will meet with in the 2d and 3d Article of our treaty with Colombia, signed at Bogota on the 3d day of October, 1824 [4:127–8].[3]

According to the first mentioned basis, no higher or other duties would be imposed on the importation into the ports of one country, of any articles the produce or manufacture of the other, than should be paid on the like articles, being the produce or manufacture of any other foreign country. Nor would any higher or other duties or charges be imposed in either of the two countries, on the exportation from the one to the other, of any article of their respective produce or manufacture, than such as should be paid on the exportation of similar articles to any other foreign country. Nor would any prohibition be imposed on the exportation or importation of any articles the produce or manufacture of either country to or from their respective ports, which should not equally extend to all other nations. Such would be the principle of the basis under consideration, in respect to the commerce between the two countries. It would leave each at perfect liberty, as each ought to be, to impose such duties as it wants, or its policy might seem to require, whilst it would restrain either from laying upon the produce or manufactures of the other higher duties than are exacted from other nations or similar articles of their produce or manufacture.

As to the navigation between the two countries, the first basis is founded upon the most perfect equality and reciprocity. According to its principle, whatever can be imported into, or exported from, the ports of one country, in its own vessels, without any regard to the place of origin, may, in like manner, and upon the same terms and conditions, be imported or exported in the vessels of the other country. This is the most perfect freedom of navigation—We can conceive of no privileges beyond it. All the shackles which the selfishness or contracted policy of nations had contrived, are broken and destroyed by this broad principle of universal liberality. The President is most anxious to see it adopted by all nations—Since the commencement of the present administration, besides the Guatemala [Federation of the Centre of America] Treaty, the principle has been embraced in Treaties concluded with Denmark [5:274-5], Sweden [6:48-52], and the Free Hanseatic Cities of Europe [6:1370-1]; in the two former instances with a slight modification, not at all, however, imparing its value.

2. The second basis which I have stated, found in the Convention with Great Britain, in respect to commerce and duties, both on exportation and importation, is the same as that contained in the Treaty with the Federation of the Centre of America, and it would therefore secure to our produce and manufactures an admission into the ports of Peru, upon as favorable terms as similar produce and manufactures of any other foreign country. But there is a wide difference between the two treaties in relation to navigation. According to our [1815] Convention with Great Britain, its privileges are limited to the importation of the produce and manufactures of the two countries respectively, neither being permitted to import into the ports of the other goods from any other part of the world. Within those restricted limits that Convention secures a perfect equality and reciprocity between the vessels of the two countries. It was a great improvement on the previous condition of the navigation of the two countries, but it falls far short of the comprehensive scope of the Treaty with Central America.

3. The last basis which I have mentioned is that of the Colombian Treaty, according to which the rule of the most favored nation has been adopted. The objections to this principle, are, in the first place, the difficulty of always clearly discriminating between that which is a gratuitous concession, and what is granted upon equivalent. Secondly

the difficulty of ascertaining the precise extent of commercial favors which may have been granted to all, or any one, the most favored, of the commercial Powers. And thirdly, a grant by the United States of the concessions which it has made to the most favored nation, in consideration of a similar grant from a foreign Power, might far transcend the limits of a just equivalent. The most favored nation, according to the commercial policy of some States, has its commerce and navigation loaded with burdens and restrictions; but the most favored nation, according to the liberal and enlightened commercial policy of the United States, has its commerce and navigation freed from almost all burthens and restrictions

Of the three bases which I have described, the first is entitled to a decided preference; You will, therefore, use your best endeavors to get it adopted. The Treaty with Central America may be taken as a model in all its articles, for one which you are authorized to conclude, with the Government of Peru. If the assent of that Government can be obtained to the fourth & fifth articles of that Treaty, you may agree to include or omit all or any of the other articles, accordingly, as you find the disposition of the other Party.

Should the Government of Peru decline acceeding to the principle of the Treaty of Central America, as a basis, your next endeavor will be to get that of the Convention with Great Britain of 1815 adopted. And if that should be agreed to, you may propose to be connected with it the various articles of the Treaty with Central America.

If you cannot prevail upon the Peruvian Government to negotiate on the basis of neither the Treaty with Central America nor the Convention with Great Britain, you will, lastly, propose the rule of the most favored nation, as contained in the treaty with Colombia, and you will offer to connect the other articles contained in the treaty with Central America. That rule will, at least secure to us equal competition with other foreign Powers, in the trade with Peru.

Considering the present state and probable future extent of the naval power of the United States, the opinion entertained by some is not without plausibility, that their interest is adverse to those liberal maritime principles for which they have ever contended, since their origin as a nation. That opinion, perhaps, could be well founded if they were likely to be frequently involved in maritime wars. But their prosperity is so evidently connected with the preservation of peace, that it is to be hoped that they will but rarely be involved in war. Whatever may really be the pecuniary interest of belligerant maritime powers, there can be no doubt that the general cause of humanity and civilization will be promoted by the adoption of those maritime principles which the United States have so perseveringly endeavored to establish—It is in that view of the matter that the President wishes you to propose those articles which relate to that subject, which you will find in the Treaty with Central America, and to press them, as long as there is any reasonable prospect of their being agreed to.

The principle of equality and reciprocity between the navigation of the two countries may be objected to, both in its more general and limited extent, upon the ground of the infancy of the mercantile marine of Peru, and its incompetency, therefore, to sustain an equal competition with that of the United States. But if a competition cannot be maintained under a system of exemptions, how can it be under one of reciprocal restrictions? If one maritime power, in its intercourse with another, endeavors to secure to its own navigation peculiar advantages by laying burthens upon the navigation of that other, from which its own is free, countervailing legislation is the necessary consequence. Restriction begets restriction, until the Parties, after a long course of irritating legislation and counter-legislation, find themselves arrived, in the end, at a point of equality, it is true, but it is an equality either of mutual interdiction of all intercourse, or of burdensome restrictions essentially impairing the value of that intercourse. When that point is at last reached, the discovery is made by the contending Parties that they had better have set out with equal and reciprocal freedom from burdens, and that each has injured himself as much, if not more, than the other, by the shackles which were attempted to be put upon his navigation. It is to be hoped that the Government of the United States and Peru will avoid this unfriendly process of imposing burdens and restrictions upon the navigation of each other, and in their first treaty of commerce, exhibit to the world an example of equal justice and liberality worthy of imitation.

With respect to the duration of any treaty on which you may be able to agree, it may be fixed for a term of about ten or twelve years. It will be well to add a clause providing against the unintentional expiration of the treaty, whatever may be the term you fix upon, similar to the stipulation contained in the 11th Art: of our late Treaty with Denmark.

A full Power is herewith transmitted, to enable you to enter upon the negotiation and to conclude the Treaty to which you are authorized to agree.... P. S. I transmit, herewith, a copy of Elliott's [sic, Elliot's] Diplomatic code [6:1102–03], embracing a collection of the Treaties and Conventions between the United States and foreign Powers. Although I have treated, in the preceeding instruction, of the rule of the most favored nation, as a distinct basis from the other two which are there mentioned, it will, of course occur to you that it is not incompatible with them, but may be well incorporated in the same treaty with the other two.

DLC–HC (DNA, M212, R8); also, copy. DNA, RG59, Dip. Instr., vol. 12, pp. 89–95 (M77, R7). No. 4 to Cooley.   1. Parry, *Treaty Series,* 106:143–77. The treaty was not accomplished until July 26, 1851.   2. *Ibid.,* 75:433–58.   3. *Ibid.,* 74:455–78.

To JAMES K. POLK   Washington, April 15, 1828

I have received and submitted to the President your letter of the first instant, stating that certain persons of the name of Hardin, having perpetrated a Murder within the State of Tennessee, had fled from justice, and taken refuge in the province of Texas, one of the United Mexican States, and requesting the interposition of this Government with that of Mexico, to procure the surrender of the fugitives.[1] Your letter is accompanied by a transcript of judicial proceedings which have been instituted against the accused, and by a correspondence which has taken place between an Agent sent for the purpose of obtaining the custody of the fugitives, and a Magistrate in the province of Texas, who appears to have declined causing them to be delivered up.—

We have no right, by the law of Nations, to demand the surrender of these persons, and such a demand would, probably, not be complied with. Nations sometimes reciprocally bind themselves, by treaty to deliver up fugitives from justice; but we have no treaty by which the Government of the Republic of Mexico is now bound to surrender persons of that description. The mutual surrender of fugitives from justice, in cases of murder and forgery has formed a subject of negotiation between the United States and Mexico, and has been provided for in a treaty which has been recently concluded at Mexico;[2] but the treaty has not yet been ratified by the Governments.—

Under these circumstances; the desired application would be, probably, fruitless.—The Executive has no power upon an application from Mexico, to surrender any persons escaping from that Country and taking refuge in ours. But, if it be desired, I will direct Mr. [Joel R.] Poinsett to request the surrender of the accused, and take the chances of the application.—

Copy. DNA, RG59, Dom. Letters, vol. 22, pp. 182–3 (M40, R20).   1. On April 1, Polk had written to Clay on behalf of Joseph B. Porter, whose son, Isaac H., had been among the victims of the Hardin boys—Benjamin F., Benjamin W., William, Augustine B., and Swan Hardin. Polk pointed out that all but Swan had fled to Texas and requested that the U.S. Government demand of Mexico their extradition. ALS. DNA, RG59, Misc. Letters (M179, R66). On April 21, after receiving from Clay this letter of April 15, Polk wrote again, asking that the U.S. "request" Mexico to return the fugitives. ALS. *Ibid.* On this same day, April 21, Clay instructed U.S. Minister Joel R. Poinsett in Mexico to pursue the extradition matter; and on April 28 he informed Polk of his instructions to Poinsett. Copy. DNA, RG59, Dip. Instr., vol. 12 (M77, R7); Copy. DNA, RG59, Dom. Letters, vol. 22, p. 190 (M40, R20). On June 9 Poinsett transmitted to Clay his correspondence with the Mexican government on the Hardin question and urged him to send someone to Mexico to transport the prisoners back to Tennessee. LS. DNA, RG84, Foreign Service Posts, Mexico (R17, frame 507). Poinsett also transmitted to Clay, on July 12, translations of a note from the Mexican Secretary of State, Juan de Dios Canedo, and a latter from the Governor of the State of Coahuila and Texas, Jose Maria Viesca, concerning "the arrest of the persons who are accused of having committed murder in the State of Tennessee...." LS. DNA, RG59, Dip. Disp., Mexico vol. 4 (M97, R5). Received August 28, 1828. On the Hardin murder incident, see also Weaver, *Polk Correspondence*, 1:173–5, 178–80.   2. Poinsett to Clay, February 22, 1828. As finally renegotiated and ratitifed in April 1831, the Treaty of Amity, Commerce, and Navigation contained no extradition clause.

From ROBERT SCOTT, Lexington, April 15, 1828. Reports on the recent financial transactions having to do with the management of the James Morrison estate and with regard to Clay's personal business, commercial, and legal accounts. Notes that Robert S. Todd is using the leased Tammany Mill property as a cotton mill; also that stoves have been removed from the Lecture rooms in the Kentucky Hotel "for the use of our Factory." ALS. KyLxT.

From THOMAS P. JONES, Philadelphia, April 16, 1828. Reports receiving Clay's letter of April 12, "appointing me Superintendent of the Patent Office." States he will report to Washington by April 27 to assume the post. ALS. DNA, RG59, Accept. and Orders for Comms. (M–T645, R2).

Writing to Clay from Lansingburgh, New York, on October 10, 1828, Horatio Gates Spafford expressed his satisfaction with the appointment of "my friend Dr. Jones," indicating as well his own "hope" for a place in Washington. ALS. DNA, RG59, A. and R. (MR3).

From THOMAS L. L. BRENT, Lisbon, no. 63, April 18, 1828. Reports that the remaining British troops left the Tagus on April 10 and only the forts at St. Julien and Bugio continue in British possession. Adds that the government of Portugal continues to remove officers whose loyalties are suspect and that while "an immense number of the subaltern officers of the army have been changed and some of the inferior magistrates," the provinces have offered "very little opposition to the orders of the government." Notes that popular enthusiasm for the assumption of the throne by Miguel has not materialized to the degree hoped for by the ultra–royalists and that financial and economic distress "which had been very great has been considerably increased since the arrival of the Prince." Says that the Minister of Foreign Affairs, the Count of Vila Real, has informed him that Frederico Torlade will come to the United States as Chargé d'Affaires. LS. DNA, RG59, Dip. Disp., Portugal, vol. 7 (M43, R6). Received June 17, 1828.

From ENOCH LINCOLN   Portland, April 18, 1828
I have received your several communications and should, at an earlier period have acknowledged my obligations if absence had not prevented. Domestic and private griefs, to which I have been subjected, would not, except in connexion with the former cause, have formed a part of my apology.

I pospone offering any views I entertain as to the particular arrangements of the federal administration relative to that large and valuable portion of the United States, within the limits of Maine, which is claimed by a foreign Power and omit to repeat the sentiments now, universally, as it seems, entertained in this Country, as to the injustice of the claim laid upon our territory.

It is, at present, simply, my wish to be permitted to declare to you my belief that the demand of the release of John Baker [6:1272–3] and the direction of a military force to defend the north eastern frontier of the Union are measures which ought to be and will be regarded as politic, magnanimous, and honorable, for which we shall always return a grateful recognition and affectionate remembrance to the Statesmen who, in a measure, controul the destinies of the country.—

The report of facts which was made by Mr. [Charles] Daveis, and which I had the honor to transmit was, I am satisfied, made with the intelligence and integrity, relied upon at the time of his appointment.

If any additional statements or opinions, or if any action on my part as to future measures, shall be required, I shall feel assured of his patriotic and able assistance to present all the local knowledge and discreet judgment which can be derived from this portion of the country.

LS. DNA, RG76, Northeast Boundary: Misc. Papers, Env. 4, item 23.

To **HOUSE OF REPRESENTATIVES,** Washington, April 19, 1828. Reviews and summarizes the history of the claim of Joseph de la Francia, agent for Henry de la Francia, for $11,850, plus 10% interest. The claim, dating from December, 1810, was "for arms and munitions of war, which were sold by the said Henry de la Francia to Reuben Kemper, acting as the agent of the Convention which revolted against the Spanish Government in that part of West Florida [Thomas to Clay, February 6, 1828] claimed by the United States under the cession of Louisiana." Notes that the claim had been denied in 1817, that he sees no reason to reverse that decision, and that there are no appropriated funds with which to pay the claim anyway. Copy. DNA, RG59, Report Books, vol. 4, pp. 242–4.

From HENRY MIDDLETON, St. Petersburg, no. 77, April 19, 1828. Reports that Russia continues to prepare for war on its southern frontier and that its policy includes "a line of distinction between the objects of the Treaty of London of July 6, 1827 [6:780–2] and that of obtaining for Russia a full and complete reparation of the wrongs and provocations she alledges to have received at the hands of the Porte." Adds that Sultan Mahmud II is already unpopular and that a war with Russia may cause a revolution of government in Turkey. ALS. DNA, RG59, Dip. Disp., Russian, vol. 11 (M35, R11). Also dated April 7, O.S. Received July 13, 1828.

From PAYTON GAY, Santa Cruz, Tenerife, April 20, 1828. Complains that the fulfillment of his duties has brought him "injuries [and] threats" and "character assassination" by persons here who are determined to "make my conduct suspectful to my Government." Urges Clay not to be influenced by whatever hostile representations these people might make. Complains, further, that his official letters are not being answered. LS. DNA, RG59, Cons. Disp., Tenerife, vol. 1 (M-T690, R1). Received June 14, 1828.

To HENRY MIDDLETON, no. 77, April 21, 1828. Transmits convention [6:1100–01] between the United States and Great Britain "providing for a reference to arbitration of the dispute between the two countries on our northeastern boundary." States that Emperor Nicholas I of Russia is the choice of the United States and that if he is not chosen, "it will be because of objections to his selection made by G. Britain." Adds that if Nicholas is selected he will receive official notification from the two Governments jointly or separately. Orders Middleton to take no action on the information until he receives further instructions.

Discusses unrest in the disputed territory and notes that "the President has directed a small portion of our military force to take position on our acknowledged territory, near to, but outside of, the disputed territory." Adds that, in conversations on the matter, Baron de Krudener "has evinced, on behalf of his Govt., great solicitude that peace may be preserved between Great Britain and the U. States." Instructs Middleton to "make the Russian Government suitable acknowledgements for this new evidence of the friendly interest which it takes in our peace and prosperity." Copy. DNA, RG59, Dip. Instr., vol. 12, pp. 96–8 (M77, R7). Also dated April 9, O.S.

From FRANCISCO TACON, Philadelphia, April 21, 1828. Acknowledges Clay's note of April 11, 1828 on the subject of the brig *Reyna Amelia*. Charges that the U.S. violates strict neutrality in Spain's wars with her rebellious American colonies. Specifically calls attention to the purchase by Argentine interests of the corvette *Bolivar* in New York for privateering purposes and the fact that two additional vessels are being outfitted in Baltimore for similar operations. Requests strongly that the President prevent these warships from departing American ports. ALS, in Spanish, with trans. in State Dept. file. DNA, RG59, Notes from Spanish Legation, vol. 9 (M59, R12).

For similar allegations of U.S. unneutrality from a Brazilian perspective, see Rebello to Clay, May 7, 1828. ALS, in Portuguese, with trans. in State Dept. file. DNA, RG59, Notes from Brazilian Legation, vol. 1 (M49, R1).

From WILLIAM H. D. C. WRIGHT, Rio de Janeiro, April 21, 1828. Concerning the rumors about a peace treaty between Brazil and Buenos Aires, reports that "It is now the general opinion that the terms are actually concluded. The funds of both governments have experienced a considerable rise from this belief." Refers to a letter he has received from William Tudor, dated Buenos Aires, April 5. Quotes Tudor: "There exists in the mercantile community the most distressing crisis that ever was known in this country," one occasioned by the uncertainty about peace.

Reports that Tudor will leave Valparaiso for Rio de Janeiro at "the first good opportunity." ALS. DNA, RG59, Cons. Disp., Rio de Janeiro, vol. 3 (M-T172, R4). Received June 25, 1828.

From WILLIAM B. LAWRENCE, London, no. 34, April 22, 1828. Transmits Parliamentary Papers relating to the British merchant marine. Reports that the decline in tonnage may be attributed to the "excessive speculations of 1825." States that this decrease has been brought about as well by countries having treaties of reciprocity among themselves rather than with Great Britain.

Reports no private discussions on the West India trade question [5:630–2] although it has been mentioned in the House of Commons. Quotes Joseph Hume's remarks in session that England does "the greatest injury to the Islands" by obligating them "to pay 30% more for every article" than its cost in the United States, "whilst the mother country gains nothing." Notes that no one answered him. Discusses the efforts of the ship builders to achieve "mutual prosperity and advancement" by pressuring Parliament and King George IV to promote their interests and to co–operate with the American government on the West Indian trade issue.

Reports that Lord Dudley has remained silent on the choice of an arbiter over the Northeastern boundary dispute, but that William Huskisson stated "last evening" that the matter would be laid before Parliament.

Reviews the British evacuation of Portugal and their continuing support of the Portuguese constitutionalists.

Discusses Russian preparations and plans for war with Turkey and notes, "while the bonds of friendship between Russia and England relax, those between this country and Austria become more and more intimate." Realizes that Austria, in a critical geographical position with respect to Greece and Turkey, would welcome the trade should Greece become independent.

Reveals that the British feel the "termination of hostilities" between Buenos Aires and Brazil may soon occur, resulting in the independence of Banda Oriental. LS. DNA, RG59, Dip. Disp., Great Britain, vol. 35 (M30, R31). Received May 28, 1828.

From HEZEKIAH NILES   Baltimore, April 22, 1828
I apprehended the difficulty that would restrain you, and your friends, as to the fact derived from something which had fallen from the lips of Mr. [Louis] Mc. L[ane].[1] We are bound in cases wherein the other party feels itself at liberty. But it will wear the best, and we should look ahead. I hope to live to see a complete triumph of those opinions and principles, which guide you. The subject shall, of course be not meddled with by me; or through my instrumentality. But it was pretty freely spoken of, (among friends), in Delaware.

Circumstanced as I am, and with a sole *exclusive* view to benefit the cause, I fear that I shall sometimes be placed in a rather difficult situation.[2] The [Baltimore] "Marylander"[3] has a great circulation. The merit of its *matter* belongs to the "proprietor," Mr. [Edward P.] Roberts—its general *manner*, with its distribution, is managed on behalf of the subscribers to its fund, and the general committee. In ordinary concerns, the superintendence is easy, but cases may arise wherein we know not what rightfully to do. One of these has occurred, as to a letter which will appear in tomorrow's paper, as to the general-in-chief of the army [Alexander Macomb]. The "*necessity*" of publishing this letter is strongly enforced by a gentleman whose *near* views of the affair and devotion, demand greatest respect. I could not fail to recommend the publication, but more upon *faith* than *judgment*, and hope that the first will sustain us. I have a notion, that some plan should be adopted whereby it may be certainly known what we should do in such collateral matters. The hint of this will be sufficient for you—for I tell plainly, that *you* are the rallying point, here.

The communication alluded to passed through my hands.[4] I do not seek your opinion about it, but, whether it is right or wrong, let something be done by which we may understand *your* views of like things hereafter.

The nature of the matters herein referred to are delicate—which no one can appreciate quite so well, perhaps, as yourself. [P.S.] I am the more anxious because of the greatly increasing popularity of the Marylander, and the great good which it may do, if the *prudence* of its publications shall equal the *honesty* and *zeal* of its exertion.

ALS. DLC-HC (DNA, M212, R3).   1. Reference obscure.   2. Clay to Plummer, April 7, 1828.   3. Established in December, 1827 to support the candidacy of President Adams, the paper disappeared into a merger with the Baltimore *Morning Chronicle* in January, 1829.   4. Reference obscure.

From DAVID OFFLEY, Smyrna, April 22, 1828. Relates "that the Brig Delos of and from Boston with a cargo," en route from Smyrna to Constantinople, was freely given permission, by the Porte, to proceed from the Dardanelles to Constantinople, and is expected to be allowed to enter the Black Sea. Comments that "certainly this advantage for our commerce might now be obtained without difficulty."

Reports that he has appointed Gaspar William Glavany as Agent for American commercial affairs at Constantinople. Explains he gave Mr. Glavany this title, rather than that of "vice Comr. Agent [which] would have been more regular," in order to increase his "influence with the authorities at Constantinople. . . ."

States that "perfect tranquility" reigns in Constantinople and that reports from there as late as April 17 indicate "that a war with Russia would not take place." Copy. DNA, Dip. Instr., Turkey (M77, R162) vol. 1, pp. 74-5; LS, in DNA, RG59, Cons. Disp., Smyrna, vol. 1 (M-T238, R-T1). Received July 19, 1828.

From JAMES TAYLOR   Urbana, Ohio, April 22, 1828
I have been much about since I came into this state & find the cause of the Administration good & prospering. Among those I have seen it appears to me there are two to one in its favor. I was at Batavia, Clermont, Maysville, Xenia, Springfield & this place at two of which places Courts are sitting & I had considerable opportunity of hearing the sentiments of a number of people.

I sincerely wish our state was as secure as this but I think the cause of correct principles are gaining ground & I think there will be a majority yet before the election in our favor. In our section of the country, Pendleton grant &C there can be no doubt but there is considerable change in favor of the Admn.[1] But I have been less in the interior of our state for the last week than usual. but I was at Lex: Frankfort &c. for a few days in Feby last.

I hope this will find your self Mrs Clay & the rest of your good family in good health to whom I beg to be named. . . . PS. I took the liberty of saying to Isaac Walker P[ost]. Master & Indian agent at upper Sandusky, that I understood our Govt. was endeavoring to make some arrangement with the B[ritish]. Govt. in relation to our slaves & that I was confident it would meet the approbation of our Govt. if he would aid me in recovering my slaves & to get the Indians to stop them as they pass thro their lands, & stated to him I should name the matter to both yourself & the P. M. Genl. [John McLean] that I should write on the subject.

ALS. DLC-HC (DNA, M212, R3).   1. In the election of 1828, Jackson defeated Adams by a margin of 267 to 152 in Pendleton County, Kentucky, and by 186 to 136 in Grant. Frankfort *Argues of Western America,* November 19, 1828.

To WILLIAM WIRT   Washington, April 22, 1828

The Secretary of State presents his respects to the Attorney General and will be obliged by his opinion on the following case:[1]

A Mexican vessel of War captures and brings into an American port a Spanish merchantman; the prize vessel is in a disabled condition, so that she cannot proceed, in safety, to Sea, the disability being the result of the action which terminated in her capture. Can she repair in the U. States, without violating the Laws of Neutrality and of the U. States? If the prize vessel is allowed to repair, ought the reparation to be restricted to those damages which resulted from the Sea, or may it include also those which proceeded from the action? If she cannot repair *belligerent* damage, and if, as is understood to be the Law, the Cargo cannot be sold within the U. States, what is to be done with Vessel and Cargo?[2]

AL. DNA, RG60, Letters Received from State Dept. (R14).   1. Clay to Tacon, April 11, 1828.   2. Wirt responded to Clay on April 27 from Philadelphia, where he was engaged "in some important cases for the Govt.," saying that he would answer Clay's "legal inquiries" as soon as possible. Wirt to Clay, April 27, 1828. *Ibid.*   On May 3, the Attorney General informed Clay that in his opinion "the vessel may be repaired and put in a condition to be carried to a home port of the captor for adjudication without violating the laws of neutrality or of the United States." Outlines the reasoning which persuades him to believe that "we . . . shall be much more apt to expose ourselves, justly, to the imputation of a breach of neutrality by refusing than by permitting the repairs." ALS. DNA, RG59, Misc. Letters (M179, R66).

From JAMES BROWN, Paris, no. 82, April 23, 1828. Communicates the sad news that Daniel Sheldon, Secretary of Legation, died in Marseilles on April 16 of a "pulmonary complaint" of several years duration. Characterizes him as an "excellent man" in "capacity, industry, and talents." Notes that before Sheldon left Paris for the south of France he had engaged the services of Charles Barnet, son of the U.S. Consul in Paris, Isaac C. Barnet, as Secretary of the Legation. But since the younger Barnet is already U.S. Consul in Antwerp, Brown has ordered his return there pending "the pleasure of the President" as to his possible later transfer to Sheldon's job at the Legation, a post for which he "possesses the qualifications." Awaits the President's decision. ALS. DNA, RG59, Dip. Disp., France, vol. 23 (M34, R26). Received June 3, 1828.

Writes Clay again on April 29 reporting that he has temporarily hired Mr. William A. G. Barnet, elder brother of Charles Barnet, to assume Sheldon's duties at the Legation. Asks what salary the acting Secretary of Legation should be paid. *Ibid.* Received June 3, 1828.

From JOEL R. POINSETT, Mexico, no. 121, April 23, 1828. No. 1 of this date. Reports that he has just closed a correspondence with the Mexican Government on the subject of American vessels trading at Matagorda and other ports on the Texas coast "which are not legally opened to foreign commerce." States that, by a law of September 27, 1823, all imports "into the *province* of Texas for its inhabitants were declared free of duty for six years," and American merchants have, under authority of this law, been trading in Texas ports. Says that the Mexican Government has resolved to stop the practice and that his own effort to persuade the Government to grant enough time for him to inform American merchants of the change has failed. Notes that the

Mexican Government maintains that the practice was illegal from the start. Promises to address letters to the Chambers of Commerce of New Orleans and New York informing them of the Mexican policy.

States that he has received a note from the Mexican Secretary of State, Juan de Dios Canedo, complaining of the incursions into Mexico of American "adventurers" calling themselves the "advanced guard of the Republican army." Adds that he assured the Secretary that "every proper step would be taken to repress these unauthorized incursions into Mexican territory and to punish the offenders."

Reports that the Mexican Government has also complained about American hunting parties illegally operating in Mexico and in the Mexican province of California. States that he explained that the hunters probably entered California without passports through ignorance. LS. DNA, RG59, Dip. Disp., Mexico, vol. 3 (M97, R4). Received "April [*sic,* May] 29," 1828.

On July 14, 1828, Poinsett transmitted copies of correspondence with the Mexican government concerning the American citizens who "made an irruption into the State of Coahuila and Texas." LS. DNA, RG59, Dip. Disp., Mexico, vol. 4 (M97, R5). No. 136. Received September 19, 1828.

From JOEL R. POINSETT, Mexico, April 23, 1828. No. 2 of this date. Transmits a copy of the Mexican law which permits "the export of gold and silver in bars." Expresses the opinion that it "will have a beneficial effect upon the Commerce between the United States and this Country." LS. DNA, RG59, Dip. Disp., Mexico, vol. 3 (M97, R4). Received May 29, 1828.

From JOEL R. POINSETT, Mexico, no. 124, April 24, 1828. Reports that the treaty of limits [Poinsett to Clay, January 8, 1828] has been ratified by the Mexican House of Representatives and is under consideration by the Senate. States that it is impossible for the treaty to reach Washington in time for ratifications to be exchanged during the time specified in the treaty. Blames the delay on the "extreme indolence" of the former Foreign Minister, Sebastian Camacho, who kept the treaty in his office for almost two months before sending it to Congress. Adds that the treaty of commerce with the U.S. [Poinsett to Clay, February 22, 1828] "is now under discussion in the house of Representatives."

States that the captured conspirators [Poinsett to Clay, January 9; February 9, 1828] have been banished for six years and that Vice President Nicolas Bravo, General Miguel Barragan and others "will be sent to some distant point on the western coast of South America, probably to Chile." Notes that Jose Dominguez, formerly the Mexican Minister to Panama, was nominated as minister to Great Britain, but that the Senate has rejected the nomination on the ground that an envoy might not be well received at that court because dividends due on the Mexican stock in London have not been paid. Reports that he believes the Mexican Government intends to send money to Europe to buy some of its own stock "at the present reduced prices."

Reports that the commercial arrangement with France will not be carried into effect and expresses the opinion that Mexico will not enter into any trade agreement, with any nation, "which does not virtually imply an acknowledgement of their independence." Adds that an envoy will be sent to Paris to explain the rejection of the commercial agreement and "to propose to treat with that Court on the terms of one independent nation with another." Reports also that Jose Maria de Bocanegra, "a distinguished member of the house of Deputies," will be sent as the Mexican envoy to Rome. Expresses the opinion that the decision to expel certain Spanish nationals from the country will eventually allow the nation to enjoy "a much more healthy state." LS. DNA, RG59, Dip. Disp., Mexico, vol. 4 (M97, R5). Received May 29, 1828. Extract in Manning, *Diplomatic Correspondence ... Latin American Nations*, 3:1668–9. For the 1827 Mexican "commercial arrangement" with France, see Parry, *Treaty Series*, 77:181–8.

From JOHN J. APPLETON, Stockholm, no. 27, April 25, 1828. Details the delay of the Swedish Government in issuing the orders necessary to implement its Treaty of Navigation and Commerce [6:761–2] with the United States and his efforts to speed the issuance of the order. Concludes, in a postscript dated April 29, that he has just received copies of a Royal ordinance which carries the treaty into effect. ALS. DNA, RG59, Dip. Disp., Sweden, vol. 5 (M45, R6). Received June 27, 1828.

From THOMAS L. L. BRENT, Lisbon, no. 64, April 25, 1828. Reports that orders have come from London for the evacuation of the British–held forts. Notes that the Marquis of Palmela, unpopular with Miguel and Queen Carlota Joaquina, has been recalled from his post as minister to Great Britain.

Continues dispatch under date of April 26. Reports that at a gala on the occasion of the Queen Mother's birthday, April 25, vivas were given for "Dom Miguel the first absolute king." Also, that the municipality of Lisbon, meeting the same day, "framed and laid before the Regent a representation requesting him ... to declare himself absolute king." Quotes Miguel's answer in which he stated that "such grave objects ... should be treated of by legal means." Adds that the Portuguese have assured the British that Miguel will not assume the title of king "without the consent of his brother," Pedro I of Brazil. Concludes: "Books are opened at the halls of the municipality for such of the people to sign as wish to give their vote for Dom Miguel as king. This has been done in all the cities and towns throughout the kingdom." LS. DNA, RG59, Dip. Disp., Portugal, vol. 7 (M43, R6). Received June 17, 1828. For Pedro de Sousa Holstein, Marquis [later Count and Duke] of Palmela, see *GEPB*.

From WILLIAM B. ROCHESTER   U.S.S. *Falmouth,* La Guaira,
                                    Colombia, April 25, 1828
We anchored in this bay on the 20th. inst. after a passage of nearly 4 weeks, thus protracted by almost constant head winds—I have visited

Caracas where I became acquainted with Genl. [Jose] Paez also met there with several intelligent Countrymen, no one more so than Doctr. [Samuel D.] Forsyth, who appears quite conversant with Columbian [*sic,* Colombian] politicks—I was astonished at the freedom with which many Gentlemen at publick tables and in mixed companies, comprising several officers of the Col. army, discussed the Merits and animadverted upon the pretensions of Genl. [Simon] Bolivar—Before this letter reaches Wash[i]ngton you will no doubt have seen his late proclamation addressed to the Bogotanians announcing his intention to leave the Capital for a season, & alleging that the state of the Country may more imperiously require his presence in some other quarter of the Republic— he always moves with an army at his heels—before leaving Bogota he had, by private letters, signified his intention to come immediately to Caracas, but after advancing some two or three days the late real or pretended troubles at Carthagena were seized upon as the ground for changing his destination—Doctr. F. thinks that by the time he reaches the neighbourhood of Ocana [Colombia], he will Satisfy himself there no longer exists any pressing necessity for his appearance at Carthagena and consequently that, as it will be expensive to keep his troops in motion, he will deem it expedient to bivouac them not a vast number of leagues from the point where the convention for forming a new Constitution,[1] are now holding their Session so much [for] a Military President. As it regards the rumoured troubles at C. Tis here said that [Jose] Pedillo [*sic,* Padilla](I think this is the name) the wanton spirit of the Alleged Conspiracy, denies *totis vinbus* all participation whatever in any treasonable designs, ridicules the suggestion of a private correspondence having taken place with the Government of Hayti & openly defies Genl. B. and his party to fix upon him the remotest possible evidence of guilt—

Bolivar's proclamation speaks of the convention as "the hope of the Country." It is here thought that this is for effect abroad, whilst in reality he dreads the result of their deliberations—he is aware that his opponents succeeded in electing a majr. of members & he recollects that there were 24 out of about 60 members of Congress who voted to receive his resignation of the Presidency—so far as their proceedings have been made known here they are not favourable to his supposed aim at despotick power—the Committee of Elections have reported against admitting to a Seat, one of his friends & favourites returned from his Native City (Caracas) on account of that friend & favourite having recently embezzled a large amount of publick funds, which offence the partisans of B. contend was purged by the Liberator's general amnesty when Paez was excused, caressed & promoted by him for having, in his absence, resisted the constituted authorities of the Country—

Nevertheless the prevailing opinion appears to be that B. will awe the Convention into a compliance with his views and that a Constitution Something like that of Bolivia will be adopted—if not—that the convention will be broken up without accomplishing any thing—the friends of a Republican Constitution are evidently uneasy, & if B. have sinister designs, will doubtless be constrained to yield—indeed, it seems to me, when such men as Doctr. [Pedro] Gual, Mr [Jose Maria] Salazar &c

240

continue to absent themselves without adequate ostensible motive, it is rather ominous—

There has been nothing new here from Guatemala for the last three months, except an idle story (in my able opinion, unworthy of credit,) that there is a secret understanding between Columbia & Mexico to partition and to take under their respective protection the whole of Central America! this, by the bye, is an old story newly got up—

Our Consul here (Mr. [John G. A.] Williamson) has some little trouble on his hands, through which, on account of his Station, his amiableness and the distress it gives him, I hope he will safely and honourably ride—On the night before last, he was arrested by an alcalde & two soldiers, & denied the privelege of giving bail, but hurried off to Caracas to answer before some tribunal there for an alleged breach of the peace in a personal rencontre some months ago with one of his country men, (Mr. Robertson) residing in Caracas—Mr. R is the Prosecutor—

I have been on shore this Evening for the last time nothing from Mr. Williamson since his deportation to Caracas—

As there is now some indication that the Sea breeze will be felt before long there is a prospect of our being able to weigh anchor by tomorrow morning, though uninterrupted calm for the last 48 hours, has made it impossible for any vessel with sails to stir out of the Bay

I send this by the Mary Ann which sails hence for Phila: in the course of 3 or 4 days—

During my excursion to Caracas, Capt: [Charles W.] Morgan recd. information from our Consul here, that a Schooner named Fingal, now in this harbour, had arrived here from Curacoa some 10 or 12 days previously, with a motley & numerous crew on board, under American colours but under circumstances exciting his Strongest suspicions, being unfurnished with the necessary credentials, & not having been in the U.S. for the last two years, during which her Captain & crew had under gone an entire change, besides that unfavourable reports respecting her had reached here from Curacoa—There was but one American on board who says he was recently decoyed in fact forcibly dragged into her service—

As the authorities here had taken no measures to examine into his character, Capt. M. thought proper to set on foot an inquiry and accordingly took possession of her, first having communicated with the Governor of La Guayra thro' the medium of our Consul & a Mr Pascal, the latter as interpreter, and receiving from him a verbal answer thro' the same medium, that he (the Govr.) neither wished nor intended to take any measures respecting the said vessels and that he (Capt. M.) was at liberty to resort to any steps in reference to her that the latter might deem expedient—Soon after Capt. Morgan took possession of her, I understand, (for I was not here at the time) that her Capt. & crew, with the exception of the American above spoke of, left her, tho requested to remain on board, & although three days have since elapsed, & they at the time of quitting her avowed a determination to return in a few hours, not one of them has returned—On the next morning (yesterday) Capt. M. recd. a polite note from the Govr. expressing a hope that he would not send the Fingal to the U.S. until the ordinary Port fees were paid—in reply to this Capt. M. despatched his Purser to the Govr. with a line to him and with orders to pay the port fees—

In the interim it seems that some new lights beamed upon the Govr's. imagination, for upon the Purser's presenting himself, he directed that the port fees should not be received & wrote a long prevasicating epistle to Capt. M. & requested him to restore to the *Captain & crew of the Fingal,* the possession of the Vessel, denying at the same time in toto all that passed between himself & Messrs. Williamson & Pascal, only the day before or that any thing of the kind transpired between them—The Consul [Williamson] being absent from La Guayra could not be confronted with the Govr. but Mr. Pascal says "he did not think the Govr. was such a man as to tell such a great l[i]e."

Such being the state of the case, Capt. Morgan (very discreetly in my opinion) actuated by a desire not to violate the Sovereignty of Colombia, the voluntary relinquishment of the assertions of which on the part of the Governor, had this been suddenly & capriciously recalled, & unwilling doubtless to disturb the harmony subsisting between the two Countries, notified the Govr. that he would not restore the Fingal to her Captain but that if the Constituted authorities here formally demanded her he would forth with withdraw his prize crew & yield up the vessel to their custody & jurisdiction, subject to the claim of the United States for a violation of their laws—to this propostion, I have learned since commencing this scroll, that the Governor has readily assented—

I have given you this statement as the affair might otherwise reach you in a shape more garbled and unsatisfactory and now conclude this already too long letter by tendering to you assurances of my unabated respect.... [Enclosure on verso of envelope] Capt. Morgan complts. to Mr. Clay & begs that he will say to Mr. [Samuel L.] Southard, that he has been too busy to finish communication began here for him—that he means to touch at Cartagena

ALS. DLC–HC (DNA, M212, R3). Letter marked "(un official)"; and sent "per the Mary Ann."   1. Watts to Clay, February 10, 1828.

From DAVID TRIMBLE   Greenupsburg, Ky., April 25, 1828

It is quite obvious that the "American System" has in its turn obtained the assendency over all other Subjects of conversation & Legislation. The "System" and the "opposition" to it forms the two elementary principles of the two parties. The line was drawn between the parties at the Session of 1824; if not Some years Sooner; say as Early at least as [Henry St. George] Tuckers resolutions [2:446–7] on internal Improvements. It was then a question of Medium Size; Now it is *"Sixty Cubits high."* It was the Basis of the Harrisburg Convention [6:319–21]: It is the leading Subject of debate in Congress: It is alluded to in *every debate* upon *every other* Subject. It is the leading Subject of State resolutions—some for & some against the System. It is a Standing question in the Newspapers and the principle topic of Conversation in all circles of Society public & private throughout the union. The measures in favor of the System *Stand first* among Measures of Public and National utility. The Country is divided— I hope not equally—upon it. The parties for and against it are embodied, and will not be disbanded for many years. This System had great influence in the late presidential Election. The Success of it, and of Measures connected with it inclined many Members to give up Minor objections to Mr Adams & vote for him. I have a right to say this because it is personally known to me. In fact "the System" made the President. Mr Adams had a given strength without it; but if he had been opposed to the *System* he could not have obtained the votes of the western States. I speak of the states, and the people of the State on the western waters, & not of the numbers then in Congress.

The System will make the next president and two or three Sucessors, unless the Military Name shall mislead the nation. I am sure nothing less could mislead it. If Jackson is Elected, the party which elects him may become strong enough to force three or four Presidents of the anti–American School upon the nation in Sucession. My opinion however is, that opposition to the System will diminish when we are done with Jackson. He I think will be the last of our Presidents who will be opposed to the American System of Policy. After him—or after he fails—the System will take a run of four or five Presidents. It has been the *"fashion"* of all nations for *Six thousand years* to waste their revenues upon conquests & *Military expeditions*. It will be the *"fashion"* of nations for centuries to come to expend revenue upon Internal Improvements, and Such other objects as will encourage national industry. *This is the Spirit of the age*. It will prevail over the Spirit of foreign Wars & foreign Conquests and over the military Spirit of the moment. The *action* & *reaction* of Sound principles upon the public mind will [two illegible words] Strength enough to Sustain the System and the Measures connected with it: or in other words—The Spirit of the age will Surely be strong enough to Sustain itself.

Take all this for granted, and then the question will occur—who, after Mr Adams, will be taken up & Supported by the party in favor of the System—or rather—by the *Majority of the Nation*. Events placed Mr Adams at the head of the party—and the force of events will place you there. [John] Sergeant, [Samuel L.] Southard, & [Daniel] Webster, are in the line of Sucession. I name you in alphabetical order, without pretending to predict the order in which you will come to the presidency: You certainly stand first after Mr Adams—The Death of DeWit[t] Clinton has left you an open field, clean & free from dangerous competition. If you live & have health to take the office, you will Suceed Mr Adams if he is re–elected—and I hope you will Succeed Jackson, if he should be elected over Mr Adams—which God forbid.

I repeat it—I think Jackson (if elected) will be the last of the Presidents—*Secretly* or *openly*—opposed to the American System. This view of the Subject must have occurred to you often—It ought to give you *new strength* and fresh vigor to combat with your adversaries. It ought to induce you to husband your health; for in *that* I think the greatest obstacle to your advancement will be found. I have some confidence in your *Judgment* as a Statesman; but very little in your discretion at a dinner table. A confirmed *Dyspepsy* will destroy any mans chance of coming to the Presidency. How is your health at present?

ALS. DLC-HC (DNA, M212, R3).

From **BEAUFORT T. WATTS,** New York, no. 43, April 25, 1828. Reports that before he left Cartagena he learned of "some excitement" in Bogota "in consequence of the abuses of the press." States that "the inhabitants" had asked Simon Bolivar to postpone his departure for Venezuela "until the commotion should subside" and "also solicited him to issue a decree restricting the liberty of the press for the time being." Details changes in Government personnel including the appointment of Pedro Gual to replace Jose Revenga who has resigned as Foreign Minister. States that many delegates have arrived at the Ocana Convention "but fifteen are wanting to form a quorum." ALS. DNA, RG59, Dip. Disp., Colombia, vol. 4 (M–T33, R4).

From **LUDWIG NIEDERSTETTER,** Washington, April 26, 1828. Expresses his consent to article 12 [Clay to Brown, May 17, 1828]. Proposes "adding after art. 12 also the contents of art. 18 of ... [the] last [American] treaty with Sweden [6:761–2], concerning blockades." States that he does feel authorized to make a decision regarding revival of article 23 of the 1785 treaty between the United States and Prussia, but wishes that the subject be left for future discussion. LS. DNA, RG59, Notes from Prussian Legation, vol. 1 (M58, R1). For the 1785 treaty with Prussia, see Parry, *Treaty Series,* 49:331–54.

From **JOEL R. POINSETT,** Mexico, no. 125, April 26, 1828. Reports that the Treaty of Limits [Poinsett to Clay, January 8, 1828] has been approved by the Mexican Senate, but that he will not transmit the ratification because it cannot reach Washington before the deadline for exchange of ratifications. Notes that, consequently, the U.S. Senate will have to act again on the treaty. LS. DNA, RG59, Dip. Disp., Mexico, vol. 4 (M97, R5). Received May 29, 1828.

From **STANHOPE PREVOST,** Lima, April 26, 1828. Transmits Peruvian newspapers which contain articles "in support of American flour and Domestic cottons, staple articles of our trade with Peru,—and which ignorance and English influence had combined to destroy." States that at least some of the articles were paid for by the late James Cooley and notes that the consular accounts include $102.50 for printing. Asserts that the articles achieved their principal objective, "which was to convince the Peruvians, that our coarse cottons if sold at 20 cts. no more interfered with their manufactures than English sold at the same price" and that the "principal member of the Committee of Finance" has promised to move to excise the discrimination between British and American cottons when the tariff bill is "brought forward." Encloses documents including a printed copy of the new Peruvian Constitution. Warns that the banished Manuel Vidaurre will sail for Salem in the *China,* which leaves Lima in two days, and may "attempt to palm himself off in the U.S. as other than he is." Adds: "As regards Mr. V's public character, he is a compound of the French revolutionary triumvirate of Robespierre and associates: of religious principle he is totally destitute, and his private Character is beyond exaggeration, Scandalous and unprincipled." ALS. DNA, RG59, Cons. Dip., Lima, vol. 1 (M154, R2). No date of receipt.

From HENRY MIDDLETON, St. Petersburg, no. 78, April 27, 1828. Transmits "the Russian declaration of war against the Ottoman Porte [6:1343–4], which was published late last night." Expresses the opinion that the war will be short, if not precluded entirely by a Turkish capitulation. Reports that the "reserve of the Imperial Guard" has started towards the frontier and that the Emperor, Nicholas I, will leave soon for Ismail, "where a general rendezvous is appointed for the 10th. May O. S." ALS. DNA, RG59, Dip. Disp., Russia, vol. 11 (M35, R11). Received July 2, 1828. The letter also carries the date of April 15, Old Style. A copy of the published declaration of war, in French, is in *ibid.* See further, 6:1343–4.

To JOHN QUINCY ADAMS, April 28, 1828. Transmits the papers required by a resolution of the House of Representatives of April 9, "requesting the President of the United States 'to communicate to the House, if the public interest will permit, the correspondence between this Government and Great Britain on the subject of the trade between the United States and the British colonial possessions in the West Indies and North America, as far as the same has not been heretofore communicated to Congress.'" LS. DNA, RG59, Report Books, vol. 4, p. 245; also with enclosures in *House Docs.,* 20 Cong., 1 Sess., no. 259, pp. 5–57; and in *ASPFR,* 6:963–85.

From FRANCIS T. BROOKE   Near Fredericksburg, Va.,
April 28, 1828

Its impossible for me to describe my mortification at being compelled to decline my visit to Washington—when I shall have the pleasure to See you which I certainly mean to do, in June or the first of July on my return from Richmond I will inform you of the cause of it, you have never yet Sent me the documents on the Subject of Shooting the Six militia men [5:736-9]—the letters of Genl Jackson to Genl [James] Winchester and to a gentleman in Kentuckey (whos[e] name I forget, on that Subject would be (as well as I remember, a good comentary on Mr [James] Hamiltons report[1]—they were published about July last, but what avails the abominations of the pride with Some of our fellow Citizens a Cataline would be preferred to Mr Adams, I trust however that there is a redeeming power Some where that will Save us from Such a calamity I shall return to Richmond on Tuesday where I shall be happy to hear from you

ALS. InU.   1. As indicated in Rep. James Hamilton's report on the militiamen incident (*House Reports,* 20 Cong., 1 Sess., no. 140), Jackson's letters in 1813–14 on the matter were to Secretary of War John Armstrong and to Tennessee Governor Willie Blount—not to Winchester and "a gentleman in Kentuckey." For Blount, see *NCAB,* 7:207.

From JAMES BROWN   Paris, April 28, 1828

I feel much obliged to you for having snatched a few minutes of your labors and absorbing interests during the Session to notice my letter of the 13 of Feby which I intimated to you my apprehension that the state of Mrs. Brown's health might be such as to require that I should ask the Presidents permission to return to the United States. Her prospects for some time after the date of that letter became more and more gloomy and my spirits consequently became so depressed that I actually made a request at the same time stating in a private letter to you[1] that the President could either give the permission in the form of leave of absence or immediately send out my successor. The letters which I wrote to you subsequently to the first of March have mentioned that Mrs. Brown was in a state of gradual and slow improvement and that if my stay until Spring would save the Government from any embarrassment I would cheerfully consent to prolong it to that time. It gave me pain to find that my return might in some measure interfere with the presidents wishes, and I therefore hope that those letters may arrive in time to leave him at perfect liberty to prolong my stay. I assure you that I am deeply sensible of the Presidents kindness to me and that my gratitude for his goodness is only equalled by my esteem for his virtues and talents. The death of poor Mr [Daniel] Sheldon which has made a deep inroad on our domestic happiness will, even should I obtain permission to return, induce me to remain until some one can be sent out more capable than any person I can find here to take charge of the interests of the Government.

Mr. Charles Barnet American Consul at Antwerp was in Paris at the date of Mr Sheldons departure and for a compensation offered by Mr Sheldon consented to discharge the duties of secretary of the Legation. Although I consented to the arrangement for a few weeks yet I could not feel justified in detaining him from his Consulate for a longer period. I think I shall engage the eldest son of the American Consul [Isaac C. Barnet] here Mr [William] Armand [G.] Barnet [to] remain with the Legation until Mr Sheldons successor can arrive. This young Gentleman has on two former occasions, when Mr. Sheldon left me for a few [days] discharged the duties of Secretary of Legation to my entire satisfaction. We have a considerable number of American citizens now in Paris among whom are several of great wealth and promise, and yet few or none of them have a sufficient acquaintance with the French language to discharge the duties of the office. In making a selection of a successor to Mr. Sheldon, I hope the President considers it of great importance that not a superficial but a thorough Knowledge of French should be one of the qualifications for the place. The correspondence with persons residing here who have information to ask of the Legation, and is carried on in the French language is very considerable and requires [in] a Secretary a familiarity with that tongue which is possessed by few American citizens. I met with a son of Mr. William Hunter [4:864] of Rhode Island formerly a senator who would have met with my approbation as fitted for [a] time to fill the place, but as he was only in his nineteenth year I was apprehensive he might not have all the discretion and steadiness necessary for a Post of such importance. Should the President expect me to return in September this will be to me a matter of no personal importance. [If] I should remain longer, my comfort as well as usefulness depend in some measure upon the character [and] qualifications of the person selected as Secretary of Legation. In Mr Sheldon I had an excellent friend diligent and discreet. In our family we found him a great resource. His memory was unusually rententive and he had collected a great deal of information.

It gives me great pleasure to relieve your mind and to reassure all Mrs. Brown's relatives and friends who have taken an interest in her, by informing them that her disorder seems within the fortnight to have taken a turn decidedly favorable. Her physician now seems to entertain no doubt but that the tumor may be des[iccant ?] without resorting to a surgical assistance. The fine weather has just commenced[,] it will have a happy influence, I hope, as well upon her health as her spirits. The firmness with which she has sustained herself under prospects alarming to her friends is the subject of their admiration. Whilst I, in common with many of her friends, was almost in a state of despondency she has in a great measure perserved her accustomed cheerfulness and [receives] her friends as if in perfect health. She begs me to say to Mr Adams that she is exceedingly grateful for the sympathy he was so good as to express for her sufferings which after all were not acute, but arose from apprehensions respecting the probable termination of her complaint.

I am delighted to learn that the prospects of Mr Adams election brighten, and am only sorry that Virginia wasnt sooner awakened to the due consideration of the merit of the Candidates. The largest portion of the travellers we meet here are from New York (the city) where it would seem General Jackson is very strong.

I will thank you if you fix the compensation which I ought to give to the person [W. A. G. Barnet] whom I have engaged to perform the writing of the Legation until a Secretary appointed by the President can arrive. As I can make no appointment legally I have informed the person who will do the business of the Legation that I shall leave the compensation to be allowed to the decision of the President.

Everything seemed a few weeks ago to indicate a war which before it could terminate might involve in it some of the great continental powers who might feel it their interest to support or promote the views of Russia—soon after the appearance of the porte Manifesto[2] the Emperor [Nicholas I] called on France and England to execute fully the Treaty of the 6th. of July [6:780-2], and at the same time declared his intention of commencing hostilities against Turkey which he would follow up with no views of aggrandizement, but for the purpose of exacting from that power the faithful execution of the Treaty of Ackerman [5:937] scarcely for navigation of Black Sea, and indemnity for past injuries and ins[ults]. This declaration of the Emperor excited some jealousy in England but s[eems] to have been well received in France where immediate preparations have commenced to be ready to act as circumstances might require. Thirty sail of Vessels of War with complements of men were in readiness at Toulon to receive troops on board and a large land force was collected in the south of France ready for embarkation. It is now believed that the Russians will after passing to the Danube, [halt] their march, and make their demands of the Porte supported by the continued influence of England, France and Russia who will unite in threatening[3] that if they are rejected the Emperor [will] march to Constantinople. You will perceive that this is re[newing] the attempt to frighten Turkey, but one much more powerful than that terminated in the Battle of Navarino. The general opinion here is it will be successful and that peace will follow—

You will see Mr [John] Connell who has been here for some days. He is well informed on the subject of our Claims [5:29-31] and [if] the claimants wish to have an agent he merits all their confidence—I shall in the course of a few days have a conference with Mr. [Pierre] de la Ferronnays on the subject. Mr. Connell will tell you my reasons for delaying it.

ALS. DNA, RG59, Dip. Disp., France (M34, R26). No date of receipt. 1. A second letter of February 13, 1828, above, marked "private," does not discuss Brown's possible early return to the U.S. 2. Lawrence to Clay, February 28, 1828. 3. The word "threatening" is followed by the words "the Porte," which are struck through.

To BARON STACKELBERG, Washington, April 28, 1828. Acknowledges receipt of his note of April 3. Complains of Swedish violations of Article VIII of the 1828 Treaty of Commerce and Navigation with the Kingdoms of Sweden and Norway [6:760-1]. This article provides that neither signatory will impose higher duties on the other "than those which shall be imposed on every other navigation," save in the coastwise trade of each nation and in the trade between Sweden and Norway. Points out that under Norwegian law U.S. vessels calling directly at Norwegian ports are being charged higher duties than are Swedish and Norwegian vessels calling directly at U.S. ports. Suggests that Norwegian law in this regard be brought into conformity with the Kingdom's treaty obligations, and that Swedish law be "altered so as to place the navigation of the United States on the footing which the treaty contemplates," namely, "an equality of the competition." Copy. DNA, RG59, Notes to Foreign Ministers and Consuls, vol. 4, pp. 11-5 (M38, R4).

To FRANCIS T. BROOKE Washington, April 29, 1828
I was much disappointed in not having the pleasure of seeing you. Having understood from Mr. [Richard Brooke] Maury that you would certainly be here on a particular day, I even made arrangements to get some friend to meet you at dinner.

I transmitted to Mr. [Daniel] Call copies of my letter [4:9-11] to Mr [Francis P.] Blair, which have formed the subject of news–paper animadversion,[1] and requested him to send them to some friends in Richmond. I will thank you also to look at them.

I send herewith copies of Mr [William H.] Crawfords last letter to me [February 4, 1828] and my answer [February 19], which after having perused them yourself, you will be pleased to exhibit confidentially to such of the gentleman who saw Mr Blairs letters[2] as you may think proper.

Our news from Kentucky is very good.

Copy. DLC-TJC (DNA, M212, R13). 1. Such references are found in Blair to Clay, January 24, February 11, and March 7, 1825. 2. See 4:41; 6:1403-05; and Blair to Clay, February 4 and March 4, 1828.

From JAMES BROWN, Paris, April 29, 1828. Reviews the diplomatic and military aims of England, France, Russia, and Austria, earlier allied by the Treaty of London of July 6, 1825 [6:780-2] against Turkey. Observes: "The cause of the Greeks has always been popular in France and

248

the Ministers ... seem anxious to adopt such measures as may meet the approbation of the nation." Speculates on the possible courses of action of the "great powers" against Turkey and predicts "Russia will immediately take possession of the Turkish provinces of Wallachia and Moldavia." Notes, however, that "the general opinion now is that matters will be arranged without war." Cites the belief that "the Porte, overawed by the approach of the Russian troops ... will accede to the demands" of the Austrian government.

Reports that the new elections in France "have sent liberal deputies," and have put that party in power. Believes they can "adopt measures highly beneficial to the country." LS. DNA, RG59, Dip. Disp., France, vol. 23 (M34, R26). Received June 3, 1828. Letter marked *"Private."*

To JAMES BROWN   Washington, April 29, 1828
Your despatch, under date the 28th day of Feby. last, in which you express a desire, on account of Mrs. Brown's state of health, and for other reasons of a private nature, to be permitted to return to the United States, has been received, and submitted to the President. Sincerely sympathizing with you in the cause which has induced you to form that resolution, the President does not feel himself at liberty to withhold his assent to your request; and you will, therefore, consider yourself as having his consent to your return, on the 15th of September, the day you proposed, or at any time thereafter that you may find more convenient and agreeable. Should you not receive any other direction prior to that time, you will present Mr. [Daniel] Sheldon as Chargé d'Affaires, until your successor is appointed, and commit the papers and records of the legation to his care.

The President having stood in the most intimate official relations with you, during the whole period of your mission, has had full opportunity to form an opinion as to the manner in which you have executed its duties. He charges me to say that he is entirely satisfied with the zeal and ability which you have manifested, and that he regrets the existence of any causes which should deprive the United States of your services, as their representative at the French Court.

Copy. DLC-HC (DNA, M212, R8). No. 15.

From ALEXANDER H. EVERETT, Madrid, no. 101, April 29, 1828. Transmits a "paper" which contains the substance of a proposition made to the Regent Miguel of Portugal by the British Ambassador, William A'Court, in Lisbon "as a basis for a negotiation respecting the settlement of the succession to the two Crowns of Portugal and Brazil." Expresses opinion that the paper was probably presented to Pedro and Miguel as a compromise between their two positions. Predicts, however, that "Nothing short of the most positive and determined opposition from the great powers will prevent" Miguel's being absolute king, "whether the Emperor of Brazil consents to it or not." LS. DNA, RG59, Dip. Disp., Spain, vol. 1 (M31, R29); also in Manning, *Diplomatic Correspondence ... Latin American Nations,* 3:2157–8. No date of receipt.

Terms of the British proposal included the proposition that Pedro I of Brazil agree to cede his right to the crown of Portugal to Maria da Gloria and to acknowledge Miguel as Regent according to the constitution; also that the succession in Brazil be secured to Pedro's lineal descendants, with the exclusion of Maria. See 5:310.

From WILLIAM B. LAWRENCE, London, no. 35, April 29, 1828. Reports a brief conversation with Lord Dudley at his home on April 23, pertaining to the naming of a Northeast Boundary arbiter. Mentions that Dudley offered only apologies for the delay in this matter, a delay, however, that hardly comports "with the importance of the business in question or with a proper respect for the United States." Reviews his past frustrations in getting on with this issue.

Acknowledges Clay's dispatch, no. 6, relating to the arrest of an American citizen, John Baker [6:1272-3], within the boundaries of Maine by New Brunswick authorities. Reports that he responded by writing immediately to Dudley, "requesting an early interview." Adds that since he has never spoken with Dudley on "the actual collision in the disputed territory," he does not know if Dudley shares the same "sentiments" expressed by Charles R. Vaughan, the British Minister to the United States.

Mentions that in a previous meeting Dudley raised the question of whether the U.S. had any objection to the publication of the correspondence "on the West India question" which "had not been heretofore printed. I of course replied in the negative."

Lists comparative figures showing Britain's increasingly favorable balance of trade in 1826 and 1827, but notes that these figures relate to "the official value, which, in the case of cotton manufactures especially, differs materially from current values."

Comments on the close ties of the present ministry with the aristocracy, concluding "that there is every prospect that the Duke of Wellington's administration will continue at least as long as the present reign. LS. DNA, RG59, Dip. Disp., Great Britain, vol. 35 (M30, R31). Extract in Manning, *Diplomatic Correspondence... Canadian Relations,* 2:699-700. Received June 4, 1828.

From JOHN H. PLEASANTS   Richmond, April 29, 1828
During my absence in Washington, some nos. of the Ky. Reporter came to hand & were lost—and among them particularly, the no. of the "Tennesseean [*sic,* Tennessean]," investigating that precious land speculation of the Hero.[1] I wish to publish these nos.—that one at least, and if possible, I shall hold myself much obliged to you if you can furnish it me either in the Reporter, or any other paper. To my surprise, I have not seen it republished except in one paper, & the name of that I have forgotten—

Have you read A Freeman, in the [Richmond *Constitutional*] Whig.[2] It is not dazzling, but exceedingly cogent & clear. Professor [Nathaniel Beverley] Tucker[3] is the Author. I really do not despair of Va. If we could distribute from this city, such intelligence & in such proportion as the Central Committee[4] desire, we might I believe in my conscience, carry the State. But our means are limited, and the times difficult in Va. beyond all former Experience. As it is, we shall show a very different result from that the vaunting of our foe has led the world to expect.

ALS. Courtesy of Orbra E. King, Utica, Kentucky.   1. The Lexington *Kentucky Reporter,* April 9, 1828, carried a long article on alleged improprieties in Jackson's various land dealings in the 1790s, including documents and depositions of related legal actions in 1800–20. It was signed, "A Tennesseean."   2. Brooke to Clay, May 20, 1828.   3. For the long and distinguished literary and legal career of N. B. Tucker, see *DAB.*   4. For the Adams Virginia Central Committee, the Adams "National General Committee" in Washington, and their interrelationship, see Remini, *The Election of Andrew Jackson,* 132–3. The reference here seems to be to the latter.

From JONATHAN THOMPSON, Custom House, New York, April 29, 1828. Transmits a letter from John Williams, an American Seaman, who "is detained in the Colombian Service, contrary to his inclination." Requests Clay's "consideration and direction." ALS. DNA, RG59, Misc. Letters (M179, R66). Williams's letter to Thompson, dated Puerto Cabello, March 28, is in *ibid.*

To PABLO OBREGON, Washington, April 30, 1828. Reports that the United States has approved the Treaty of Limits with Mexico [Poinsett to Clay, January 8, 1828] and that he is "ready to proceed in the exchange of the ratifications." Copy. DNA, RG59, Notes to Foreign Ministers and Consuls, vol. 4, pp. 15–6 (M38, R4).

On May 1, Obregon acknowledged Clay's note and stated that he would proceed with the exchange of ratifications upon his receipt of the treaty. LS, in Spanish, with trans. in State Dept. file. DNA, RG59, Notes from Mexican Legation, vol. 1 (M54, R1).

From WILLIAM B. ROCHESTER   Carthagena, Colombia,
                                                            April 30, 1828
This evening the Falmouth anchord. in the harbour of this place, having left La Guyra [*sic,* Guaira] on the 26h. inst.—Capt [Charles W.] Morgan says he will take in some fresh water Tomorrow & will make sail direct for Omoa the next day—if so—I hope we shall reach Omoa by the 10. May—I wrote you [April 25] whilst at Caraccas [*sic,* Caracas] a letter which you will probably receive before this one—Every thing is quiet here tho' the existing session of the [Ocana] Convention makes it quite a time of expectation with the Colombians—the better opinion here is (and it is ostensibly the desire of the Carthagenians) that [Simon] Bolivar will be made Dictator for life—as was supposed at Caracas he is stationed in the neighbourhood of Ocana—I am strengthened, by what I observe & learn here, in the hasty view taken in my Caracas letter of the designs of the great Military chief of South America—will you be good eno' to forward pr. mail to my Father [Nathaniel] the letter for him? I enclose you a file of papers containing the laws of Columbia [*sic,* Colombia] respecting the publick credit—would have undertaken a translation of them for your perusal, but it is so hot (88 Faren:) that I must e'en postpone the conclusion of this scrawl until tomorrow morning—

There is not now a single American Merchant man in this harbour— I shall leave this to be put into the hands of our consul Mr. [John M.]

McPherson [*sic*, MacPherson] who is not now at Carthagena but on a visit to the country—this place is at this time healthy—

The dispatch[1] from your Dept. forwarded to me at Norfolk, for our Consul at Porte Cabello I delivered to Mr. [Franklin] Litchfield in person at Caracas where I met with him.

Carthagena, May 1, 1828

I resume my pen at the House of Mr. McPherson who returned to town this morning, merely for the purpose of saying that I have scarcely any thing to add—To day I saw the famous Carabobo regiment paraded—a miserable looking set of Fellows they are—this is said to be the favourite Regiment of [Jose] Paez—arrived here lately from Venezuela in consequence of the recently disturbances here—but never did I see a town as large as Carthagena so perfectly calm, so little disturbed by commotions or motions of any kind—There is little or no business doing—they have no money here and scarcely any provisions—I am credibly informed that the Carabobo Regiment has not drawn any rations for two or three days!—The Military Govr. here Genl. [Mariano] Montilia an accomplished gentleman to whom I paid my respects this morning—says that all is quiet in Columbia. and going on prosperously & happily for the People—he is an admirer of [Simon] Bolivar and very hostile to [Francisco de Paula] Santander—I fear the latter is marked for a victim on account of his independent spirit moral courage & political integrety—Gel. M. says that the latest news from Guatemala—i.e. about a fortnight since from Nicaragua, is more unpropitious than any which preceded it, I could not get him to specify—to my interrogations—he would only repeat—"it is very bad"

ALS. DLC-HC (DNA, M121, R3). Marked "(private)."   1. See above, March 19, 1828; the dispatch from Clay to Litchfield, transmitted by Rochester, has not been found.

From GEORGE C. WASHINGTON, Washington, April 30, 1828. Notes that Congress has before it a bill to authorize the appointment of a Superintendent of the Penitentiary being built in the District. Strongly recommends "my friend Mr. [George] Price" for the post. Notes that Price "lives in a most important dis't of M.d. [Maryland] now considered doubtful as to the result of the pending contest—The appointment of Price would be highly popular, for he is generally known and esteemed in Fred.k. c.y. [Frederick County] and has an extensive acquaintance in Washington—he has all ways been a decided friend to the administration, and is particularly devoted to yourself. . . . The acct. he gives of the state of public opinion in his county is flattering." ALS. DNA, RG59, A. and R. (MR3). For the bill, see *Register of Debates*, 20 Cong., 2 Sess., 72-4 (Appendix). Price, a perennial office seeker, was not appointed to this position before the November election. Adams carried Frederick County, Md. with 3,574 votes to 3,044 for Jackson. *Niles' Register,* (November 22, 1828), 35:2.

From WILLIAM H. D. C. WRIGHT, Rio de Janeiro, April 30, 1828. Reports that he has secured an extension of the twelve-month period of deposit at the port of Montevideo, thus allowing American merchants to land and warehouse goods there intended for another market without having to pay duties. States that he no longer doubts that a peace treaty between Brazil and Buenos Aires has been or will be concluded very shortly. Adds that he cannot understand why the government has remained so silent on the subject, for surely it must know what good effect such a settlement would have on its public credit. Notes that recent letters from Rio Grande, "the seat of the war," relate that there is an armistice in force and that the Buenos Airean troops have retired from the front lines. Encloses correspondence on the deposit–extension arrangement. ALS. DNA, RG59, Cons. Disp., Rio de Janeiro, vol. 3 (M–T172, R4). Received June 26, 1828.

From CHARLES SHALER, Pittsburgh, May, 1828. Encloses a political broadside and assures Clay that "the good cause continues to prosper in Pennas." The broadside, dated May 1, 1828, calls for an "American System Ticket" of John Quincy Adams for President, Richard Rush for Vice President, and J. Andrew Shulze for Governor. Issued by Committee of Correspondence for Allegheny County, Pittsburgh. DLC–United States Broadsides, *Heavily Annotated.*

From THOMAS ADAMS, Philadelphia, May 1, 1828. Believes that "our good & honest cause" is gaining among the Germans in Pennsylvania. Has heard also that Edward Coleman of Lancaster County "has fallen into our Ranks with about 200 Votes—of his workman, we hope it is true." ALS. DNA, RG59, Misc. Letters (M179, R66). For Coleman, see Philip S. Klein, *President James Buchanan: A Biography* (University Park, Pa., 1962), 28-9, 36; and *PMHB*, 11:71-2.

From ALEXANDER H. EVERETT, Madrid, no. 102, May 1, 1828. Acknowledges receipt of Clay's instruction no. 12, dated February 1. States that he has consequently "made an official application to the Secretary of State [Manuel Gonzales Salmon], for a copy of the report supposed to have been made to the two Governments by the commissioners [Andrew Ellicott and Stephen B. Minor] appointed in virtue of the Treaty of 1795 [Pinckney Treaty] to run the boundary line between the United States and Florida." Reports also that the U.S. consul at Cadiz, Alexander Burton, has applied to the military authorities in that neighborhood for information regarding Major Thomas Hempstead, "and has received an official assurance in writing that no such prisoner is detained under their authority." Adds: "There is little doubt therefore that he must have made his escape soon after writing to his friends at home." States, however, that, as a precaution against "accidental error" he has requested Salmon to inform him whether or not Hempstead is being in custody anywhere in the kingdom. Encloses translations of various documents, including a circular which instructs Spanish treasury officials to take measures to insure "more effectual prevention of contraband trade." LS. DNA, RG59, Dip. Disp., Spain, vol. 28 (M31, R29). Extract in Manning, *Diplomatic Correspondence . . . Latin American Nations,* 3:2160-1. Received July 2, 1828.

To JAMES HAMILTON, JR.   Washington, May 1, 1828

I have received your letter under date this day,[1] stating that "it having been ascertained that the late Daniel P. Cook, late representative in Congress from the State of Illinois received a sum of money from the Government, during the Spring or Summer of the last year, for certain services supposed to have been either foreign or diplomatic," you are instructed by the Committee of Retrenchment, to request me to inform you where they are to look for the auditing of the sum said to have been received by Mr Cook, and, if not audited in the usual course, what was its amount.

Without admitting or denying the correctness of the information which the Committee are stated to have received, I have the honor to observe, that I am not aware of the disbursement of any[2] money, through the agency of this department, the account of which has not been, or in a regular course of settlement is not to be, audited in the usual way at the Treasury, or passed upon a certificate of the President, in conformity with the provisions of the third section of the act of the 1st May, 1810, entitled "an act fixing the compensation of public ministers and of consuls residing on the coast of Barbary, and for other purposes." I cannot presume that it was the intention of the committee to inquire into any disbursement which may have been made agreeably to that section; and all others are accessible to them, in like manner with other expenditures. I have, however, the authority of the President for saying that I will make to the Committee a *confidential* communication in relation to the expenditure, to which they are supposed to allude, if they will signify their desire for such a communication.[3] In that case, I should be glad to learn their pleasure as soon as convenient as I purpose leaving the city on the fourth instant,[4] a few days, on account of the state of my health. . . .[5]

AL, draft. DLC-TJC (DNA, M212, R13).   1. LS. DNA, RG59, Misc. Letters (M179, R66).   2. Word "any" is followed by word "public," which is struck through.
3. Acting for the Committee, Hamilton declined making application for a confidential communication. Hamilton to Clay, May 2, 1828. ALS. DNA, RG59, Misc. Letters (M179, R66).   4. Phrase "the fourth instant" is preceded by the phrase "the 6h sunday next," which is struck through.   5. Clay to Adams, May 8, 1828.

From JOHN MARSHALL   Richmond, May 1, 1828

A visit to my friends in the upper country, from which I returned yesterday, prevented my receiving your letter of the 8th of April, at an earlier day. The note you mention,[1] was drawn from me very unwillingly, and the opinion it expressed, was the necessary result of evidence on a mind not predisposed to condemn. If it draws upon me a portion of that scurrility, which has been lavished on others, I must console myself with the reflection, that I have not voluntarily intruded myself upon a controversy, which has been carried on with such unexampled virulence.

Mr. [Daniel] Call looked in upon me yesterday afternoon, and showed me your two letters [5:9–11, 46–8] to Mr. [Francis P.] Blair. We have indeed "fallen upon evil times," if the seal of confidence is to be broken, and such letters to be shown, for the purpose of injuring the writer. No fair mind can misunderstand them, or pervert their light and

254

sportive language into a confession of dishonorable views. I know not how Mr. Blair can abstain from a public vindication of your conduct, so far as it is developed in those letters.

Printed in Colton, *Clay Correspondence*, 1:389.   1. Clay to Plumer, April 7, 1828.

To PABLO OBREGON, May 1, 1828. Summarizes Obregon's complaint of April 18 relating to the capture of the Spanish privateer brig *Reyna Amelia* by the Mexican brig warship *Hermon,* the towing of the prize into Key West harbor, and the seizure there of the vessel by the Collector of the Port, William Pinkney. Supports Pinkney's refusal to permit the *Reyna Amelia* to make repairs, sell off part of her cargo to defray the expenses of repairs, and clear for a Mexican port with a prize crew on board. Points out that this "is not the first instance of an abuse of the privileges, of the hospitality of the United States by Mexican armed vessels in the same port." Informs Obregon that the neutrality stance of the U.S. is increasingly tending toward a decision to close Key West to the armed vessels of both belligerents. Reports that President Adams has directed that the *Reyna Amelia* not be turned over to Mexico and his view that the Mexican government can seek whatever relief it may feel its due in the matter in "the proper judicial tribunals" of the U.S. Concludes with the further observation that the "laws of the United States do not admit of the sale, within their jurisdiction, for any purpose, of prize goods taken by one belligerent from another and brought into their ports." Copy. DNA, RG59, Notes to Foreign Ministers and Consuls, vol. 4, pp. 22-5 (M38, R4). For Obregon's protest, see his letter to Clay, April 18, 1828, in DNA, RG59, Notes from Mexican Legation, vol. 1 (M54, R1).

To JOSE S. REBELLO, May 1, 1828. Requests to be informed whether or not Rebello knows of "the adoption of any regulations by the Government of the Brazils reducing the duty on imports from twenty four to fifteen per Cent," and asks which "commercial powers are made to pay the higher rate of duty." Copy. DNA, RG59, Notes to Foreign Ministers and Consuls, vol. 4, p. 16 (M38, R4). No. 1 of this date.

On this same day Rebello replied, stating he had "not received any official Communication respecting to the reduction of duties on importations" into Brazil and noting that "all Nations, that have not entered on peculiar treaties with the Government, are those which pay higher duties—" N, in Portuguese, with trans. in State Dept. file. DNA, RG59, Notes from Brazilian Legation, vol. 1 (M49, R1).

To JOSE S. REBELLO   Washington, May 1, 1828
The Undersigned, Secretary of State of the United States, whilst acknowledging the receipt of the Note of Mr. Rebello, Charge d'Affaires of His Imperial Majesty [Pedro I] the Emperor of Brazils, under date the 11th. [April] in answer to that of the Undersigned of the 8th. instant [*sic,* April], feels it incumbent upon him to make a few remarks, to guard against misconception, although they are not called for by any immediate practical purpose.

The Government of the United States has taken no new resolution to prevent vessels under their flag, sailing from their ports in a warlike condition. The law on this subject has remained the same during the last ten years. According to the provisions of the act of Congress, every person is prohibited from fitting out and arming, or augmenting the force, of any Vessel within the limits of the United States, to cruize against the subjects, Citizens, or property of any Prince or State, Colony, district or people with whom the United States are at peace. In instances in which the sailing of armed Vessels, belonging wholly or in part of Citizens of the United States, which is allowed in certain cases for self protection against pirates or other unlawful aggressions, the Owners are required to give bond with sufficient sureties, in double the amount of the value of the vessel and Cargo, prior to clearing, that it shall not be employed by such Owners to cruize against powers with which the United States are at peace. And in other instances, the proper officers are authorized to detain any Vessel manifestly built for warlike purposes, and about to depart from the United States, the Cargo of which Vessel shall principally consist of Arms and Amunition of war, when the number of men shipped on board or other circumstances shall indicate that such vessel is intended to be employed by the Owners to Cruize or commit hostilities against friendly powers, until the decision of the President thereon, or until the owners shall give bond and security as previously required.

This act does not forbid Citizens of the United States from trading in ships as an article of Commerce. It could not have imposed such a prohibition without an unjust restriction upon the industry of the people of the United States. Mr. Rebello admits that they have certainly the right of building and selling Ships at their perfect liberty. It is true he qualifies the right, by alleging that it must be exercised under the restriction that the ships shall not be sent directly to enable one of the belligerents to make war with advantage against the other. But this qualification cannot be supported unless Mr. Rebello is prepared to maintain that after a vendor has sold his entire interest in an article, he is nevertheless responsible for the subsequent use of that article in the hands of the purchaser, who has acquired the absolute right to it. The concession of a right to sell a ship necessarily implies a cessation of the responsibility of the original owner for its use after he has parted with it, and the creation of a new responsibility in the second proprietor. The argument founded on the increased ability of a belligerent to prosecute an existing war, by the purchase of a Ship from a neutral, if valid, would lead to a total interdict of all commerce between the neutral and that belligerent.

The Government of the Brazils, by its own practice in causing to be built in the ports of the United States the fine frigates alluded to in Mr. Rebello's letter, cited by the Undersigned in his former Note, has manifested its clear comprehension of the reciprocal right of Sale and purchase of Ships. Mr. Rebello justifies the purchase of those frigates upon the ground that they were to be used in a War which Brazil was waging for Independence.[1] The United States felt the warmest sympathy for Brazil in that struggle. But standing in a Neutral relation to both the belligerents, it was their duty to be impartial to both. The character of the War did not authorize them to violate that principle of equality. It cannot be admitted that there is any countenance in any writer on public Law, or in any established principle of international duty, to the discrimination which Mr. Rebello sets up.

But it is believed that there have been recent instances, during the war now unhappily raging between Brazil and the Argentine Republic, of the purchase by the Government of the former of Vessels built within the United States. The Undersigned cannot undertake to enumerate them; but if he has not been misinformed the Flag Ship of the Brazilian Admiral [Rodrigo Lobo][2] commanding the Squadron blockading the River Plate, was built within the United States; and as late as October last the Robert Fulton, a Vessel also built and owned in the United States was purchased for the Imperial service.

Mr. Rebello has in his last note as he had in his previous correspondence referred to the injustice of the war, as it respects Buenos Ayres. He has even gone so far as to ask the United States to consider and treat as pirates, the armed Vessels of the Republic which the Imperial Government itself has not deemed it expedient to consider piratical. But surely it ought not to be necessary to remind Mr. Rebello that, whilst the United States remain neutral, whatever sincere regrets they may feel in consequence of the War between their friends, it is not their office to decide which of them is in the wrong.

Mr. Rebello states that the Brazilian Cruizers have never visited the ports of the United States for refreshment nor to sell their prizes; that the geographical position of the United States is such as not to render it necessary to resort to their ports; and hence he argues that the hospitality of the United States ought not to be extended to the other belligerent.

Neither belligerent is allowed by the laws of the United States to sell his prizes within their ports. The rights of hospitality are equally offered to both. They could not be denied, in many cases, without a violation of the duties of humanity. If hitherto one party has resorted more than the other to the ports of the United States (and what the state of the fact really is the Undersigned is not informed) it has been probably because of the casualties of war, a turn in its fortunes may, in that respect, reverse their conditions. With respect to the geographical relations of the belligerent Countries to the United States that of the Brazils, being nearest to them, is most favorably situated to enjoy their hospitality. But the right or rather duty of a Neutral to receive and treat with friendship and hospitality the subjects and Vessels of the belligerents, does not rest on considerations drawn from territorial proximity or remoteness, nor from the degree of use which either belligerent may make of the Assylum. It depends upon the laws of nature and humanity, which only enjoin that the same right of reparation and refreshment which is allowed to one party shall be in like manner permitted to the other, when he thinks proper to avail himself of it.

It is undoubtedly true that the desire of gain sometimes prompts individuals, in the pursuit of it, to the performance of acts incompatible with the rights of belligerents. The Government of the United States, during the periods of their happy exemption from wars which have afflicted other States, has never countenanced any violation of those rights by their citizens, who have however much oftener suffered than inflicted wrongs.

On the other hand, belligerents eager to subdue each other, and animated sometimes by a spirit of vengeance, too frequently transgress the rights of Neutral powers. Some of the injuries which the Citizens of the United States have experienced in their persons and lawful commerce, during the existing war have formed the subject of a correspondence and arrangement between Mr. Rebello and the Undersigned. He regrets now to have occasion to notice a recent measure of the Government of Brazil, the requirement of bonds from the owners of American vessels clearing from the port of MonteVideo, not to violate the blockade of the ports of La Plata, for which no sanction whatever is to be found in the Public Law. In confidently anticipating a fulfillment of the arrangement just mentioned, with the good faith which should ever characterize the execution of National engagements, the Government of the United States indulges also the expectation that the measure in question will be revoked and abandoned.

Mr. Rebello concludes his Note with an intimation which the Undersigned does not clearly understand. He states that "if the people of the United States continue to exhibit so much partiality for the Enemies of His Majesty the Emperor, it is not to be comprehended how it will not terminate in bringing the lucrative commerce of the United States between Brazils to a state of jeopardy." It is altogether undeniable that the people of the United States, alike friendly to both belligerents, have manifested in their intercourse with both, a partiality for neither. They desire with each those commercial exchanges which minister to the comfort or wants of both parties. If the value of their commerce with each is to be taken as a test of partiality, and as contributing to the belligerent power of either, the test would be unfavorable to the Brazils. Mr. Rebello could hardly have intended to intimate that the commerce of the United States with the Brazils was likely to be endangered by any hostile operations upon it emanating from the authority of the Government of Brazil, because he must be aware that the United States are quite competent to afford adequate protection to their commerce against any hostile attack from whatever quarter proceeding. Commerce is mutually beneficial to the Nations between which it is carried on. And it is not, therefore, easy to understand how any injury could happen to that of the United States with the Brazils, which would not affect the commerce of the Brazils with the United States. Did Mr. Rebello mean to suggest the possibility of the adoption of municipal regulations in the Brazils unfavorable to American Commerce? They already exist. The Commerce of the United States is now exposed to restrictions and high duties, from which that of most of the great maritime powers is exempt. The United States have not resorted to countervailing restrictions and regulations, because, being sincerely desirous to cultivate the most friendly intercourse with the Emperor of the Brazils, they have foreborne under the hope that, animated by a like disposition, his Government would place their Commerce, at no distant day, upon a just and equal footing. . . .

Copy. DNA, RG59, Notes to Foreign Ministers and Consuls, vol. 4, pp. 16–22 (M38, R4). No. 2 of this date.   1. Joao Pendia Calogeras, *A History of Brazil*. Percy Alvin Martin, trans. and ed. (Chapel Hill, N. C., 1939), 72–93.   2. For Lobo, see Jean Willis, *Historical Dictionary of Uruguay* (Metuchen, N. J., 1974), 155.

To JOHN Q. ADAMS   Washington, May 2, 1828

The Secretary of State, to whom the President has refered a resolution of the Senate[1] requesting "any information he may possess concerning any regulations that may have been adopted by the Government of Brazil, relative to the reduction of the duty of twenty four per Cent, heretofore imposed in Brazil on the produce and manufactures of the United States, to 15 per Cent; or any information on the subject that he may deem proper to communicate," has the honor to report, that no information has been received at the department of State, of the reduction of the duty as mentioned. Nor has the Chargé d'affaires [Jose Silvestre Rebello] of the Emperor of the Brazils [Pedro I] received from his Government any information of the supposed reduction of the duty, as he has stated to the Department.

The resolution of the Senate admits of a construction that the higher rate of duty is applicable only to the produce and manufactures of the U. States; but that is not the case. It is collected upon all foreign produce and manufactures received in the ports of Brazil, except those of some powers with which the Government of that country has otherwise provided by treaty. The inequality between those powers and the U. States, in that respect, has formed the subject of instructions to the late Chargé d'affaires of the United States [Condy Raguet] at the Court of the Brazils, and of instructions which have been sent to Mr [William] Tudor. . . .

ALS. DLC-HC (DNA, M212, R3).   1. Passed April 30, 1828. U.S. Sen., *Journal*, 20 Cong., 1 Sess., 342.

From THOMAS L. L. BRENT, Lisbon, no. 66, May 2, 1828. Reports that the forts of St. Julien and Bugio were restored to the Portuguese on May 1, when the British naval force departed. Notes that all the newspapers except *Gazela de Lisboa* support Miguel's aspirations for the throne.

Mentions that the public was "all alive" with the approach of April 30, the anniversary of the conspiracy of Prince Miguel and Queen Carlota Joaquina against King John VI, who fled in 1824. Supporters of Miguel were rewarded with government positions.

States that Miguel has informed the foreign ministers that he intends to prevent "insults and attacks" disruptive to public order and safety by police enforcement. Reports that the plan to place Miguel on the thorne is succeeding. The number of signatures in support of Miguel, including those of public officers, clergy, and nobility, is great in Lisbon. States that the governmental Commission is said to be recommending "the establishment of the ancient Cortes" as most suitable to the monarchy. One extreme political faction wants to "have the Prince proclaimed King on May 8, the anniversary of the apparition of the Archangel Miguel." Asserts that if Miguel assumes power, he will suspend all diplomatic intercourse with the new government and await instructions. LS. DNA, RG59, Dip. Disp., Portugal, vol. 7 (M43, R6). Received July 7, 1828.

For the 1824 conspiracy against John VI, see White, *A Century of Spain and Portugal,* 100–01.

From JOHN M. FORBES, Buenos Aires, no. 57, May 2, 1828. Announces that he returned from Montevideo on March 21.

Notes that the affair of the brig, *Ruth* and cargo, is still pending in litigation, and promises "to spare no effort to hasten a final decision."

Forwards a dispatch from William Tudor, Chargé d'Affairs in Chile, who is expected to arrive in Buenos Aires by land.

Reports that the prospects of an immediate peace with Brazil, based on the report of the British ship, *Heron,* are said to be favorable. Believes, however, that such a peace would include only the independence of Banda Oriental [Uruguay]. Notes, additionally, that in a "frank" interview, the Governor of Buenos Aires, Manuel Dorrego, had declared "his distrust in the eventual success of this pending negociation," and had charged that "the proposed independence of Banda Oriental was only to serve as a veil to cover the new intrigues of the Brazilian Government." The persons designated to negotiate a compact of peace with Brazil are Pedro Feliciana Cavia and Generals Ramon Balcarce and Tomas Guido.

Continues, on May 8, that the regime has suspended an election concerning constitutional matters because of irregularities and some violence.

States in conclusion that the British frigate, *Forte,* has arrived "bringing no news of a pacific character," and reports that hopes for "an immediate peace are now disappointed." LS. DNA, RG59, Dip. Disp., Argentina, vol. 3 (M69, R4). Received August 27, 1828. Also in Espil, *Once Anos en Buenos Aires,* pp. 488–91. Extract in Manning, *Diplomatic Correspondence . . . Latin American Nations,* 1:662–3.

To GEORGE McDUFFIE, Washington, May 2, 1828. Refers to the 1825 House of Representatives resolution asking for statistics on capital crimes in the U.S. since 1789—convictions, executions, pardons. Notes that he sent a circular letter to the various U.S. District Attorneys requesting this information. Recommends that the House appropriate $7000 to cover the cost to the State Department of preparing the final report. Copy. DNA, RG59, Report Books, vol. 4, p. 247. The resolution is in U.S. H. of Reps., *Journal,* 18 Cong., 2 Sess., 129. The report was transmitted to the House on January 29, 1829; *House Exec. Doc.* 146, 20 Cong., 2 Sess.

From BOYD McNAIRY   Nashville, May 3, 1828
In the address of the [Jackson] Central Committee at Washington,[1] I see that the Hon. Ths. P. Moore [3:764] has assailed you in a Certificate with all the virulence of a violent partizan. Mr Moore seems to have forgotton his declarations when last in this place the fall or summer of the year before the last election for President. He then publickly declared in my

260

presence that he considered the State of Tennessee disgraced, by bringing out Andrew Jackson, whom he looked upon as *totally unfit for the Station,* enquired of me, if I thought his ears would be safe in Nashville for making those declarations—He was then your strong friend and regarded Genl Jackson's nomination as entended to injure your prospects in the west—This declaration was made by Mr. Moore, in the presence of many gentlemen of this place who have a perfect recollection of it. You can make what use you please of this information—

ALS. DLC-HC (DNA, M212, R3). Postmarked, Nashville, June 4. Printed versions in Lexington *Kentucky Reporter,* July 9, 1828; Frankfort *Argus of Western America,* July 30, 1828. 1. Sergeant to Clay, January 2, 1828.

To FRANCISCO TACON, Philadelphia, May 3, 1828. Acknowledges receipt of his letter of April 21, 1828 regarding the brig *Reyna Amelia.* Refers to the charge that Argentine interests have purchased the corvette *Bolivar* in New York for privateering purposes, and that in Baltimore they are fitting out a schooner for similar duties. Assures him that the U.S. District Attorney in New York [James A. Hamilton] and in Baltimore [Nathaniel Williams] are carefully investigating these matters. Maintains that in the case of the *Kensington,* the complaints of the Spanish legation "do not bear the test of solemn examination." Copy. DNA, RG59, Notes to Spanish Legation, vol. 4, pp. 26-7 (M38, R4).

From JOHN H. GROSVENOR, New York, May 5, 1828. States that in September, 1827, he had received the documents Clay had sent him on April 15, 1826. Blames the delay on his "friends in New York" who had not forwarded the material to him in China. Notes that until he received Clay's transmission he had remained as acting consular agent in Canton, having been appointed to that post by his predecessor, John R. Thomson. Reports, however, that his private business interests forced him to leave Canton in December 1827, and that he had arrived back in New York on April 1, 1828. Informs Clay that he had appointed Charles N. Talbot of New York to handle U.S. consular activities in Canton during his absence and that he intends to return to China "next Season." Encloses consular reports and "four numbers of a Newspaper [not found] entitled the 'Canton Register' (edited by an American). . . . the only newspaper which has ever been printed in China in the English language." Asks that this letter "be considered as an application for leave of absence." ALS. DNA, RG59, Cons. Disp., Canton, vol. 1 (M101, R1). For Talbot, a New York City merchant shipper, see Charles Oscar Paullin, *American Voyages to the Orient, 1690-1865. . . .* (Annapolis, Md., 1971), 37; Sydney and Marjorie B. Greenbie, *Gold of Ophir: The China Trade in the Making of America* (New York, 1937), 152.

From SAMUEL ISRAEL, Cap Haitien, May 5, 1828. Acknowledges receipt of his commission. Shares his impressions of the island, noting that commercial relations with Haiti are "friendly." Remarks that French influence on members of the government is high, that the people are not in sympathy with the high tax policies of the regime of Jean Pierre Boyer and that considerable agitation in several quarters may eventually lead to a general revolt. Suggests that U.S. armed vessels be sent to the vicinity, pointing out that the British and French "pursue this measure, considering it a small means of protection to their subjects." Reports also that U.S. trade with Haiti has "diminished considerably" during the first half of 1828. ALS. DNA, RG59, Cons. Disp., Cap Haitien, vol. 6 (M9, R66). Received May 25, 1828.

From WILLIAM B. LAWRENCE, London, no. 36, May 6, 1828. Reports sending a note to Lord Dudley, incorporating Clay's instructions, for "the release of Mr. [John] Baker [6:1272–3] with an indemnity for his sufferings," and "requesting that the British Government should abstain from the exercise of exclusive jurisdiction in the territory in dispute on our Eastern frontier." Mentions he has prepared this note with information derived from maps, Albert Gallatin's correspondence, Clay's notes to Charles R. Vaughan, various reports, and the example of the joint occupancy of the Northwestern [Oregon] Territory by the two countries. Is convinced that "Lord Dudley who is a gentlemanly scholar has not been accustomed to business, and, being of eccentric character, he has the reputation of giving less attention to ordinary forms" of governmental procedure.

Relates a recent conversation with Prince Lieven, the Russian minister to Britain, in which Lieven suggested that "Russia would not be reluctant to undertake the umpirage" of the Northeast Boundary dispute and, indeed, "desires on her part to be chosen."

Reviews the preliminary troop movements, sizes of armies, and logistical problems of the early days of the Russo–Turkish War. Mentions the role of the English fleet under Sir Edward Codrington for coordinating any combined allied sea operation. LS. DNA, Dip. Disp., Great Britain, vol. 35 (M30, R31). Extract in Manning, *Diplomatic Correspondence . . . Canadian Relations,* 2:707–09. Received June 14, 1828.

To JOHN Q. ADAMS   Philadelphia, May 8, 1828
I have the satisfaction to inform you that the judgment of the Physicians [Nathaniel Chapman and Philip Syng Physick] on my case is much more favorable than I anticipated. They believe nothing indicating immediate danger ails me; and that by abstraction from business, a journey, some attention to exercise and a little medicine my health may be re-established. Dr. Physic [*sic*] does not even think it necessary to starve me.

Much dissatisfaction has prevailed here among our active friends in regard to the recent appointment in this City.[1] I hope that it will pass away and that ultimately they will not slacken their zeal.

I cannot omit respectfully to suggest the propriety of considering the expediency of removing, after the termination of Congress, the P. M General [John McLean]. This is a suggestion not the result solely of the recent appointment, 'though if some allegations respecting the defalcations of the late post master [Richard Bache] be well founded, they afford sufficient ground for the measure. I believe that the sum of injury would fall far short of the sum of benefit from the removal. On this subject, when I return, I will have the honor of laying before you my views at large.[2]

ALS. Adams Papers, Letters Received (MR485). 1. Thomas Sargeant was appointed postmaster of Philadelphia in April. He held the job throughout Jackson's first administration. *DAB.* 2. While in Philadelphia for medical consultations, Clay visited Charles C. Watson & Sons, 92 Chestnut St., where he purchased "A Green imp[orted] Cassimere Coat" for $33.00; a velvet collar ($2.00); "A pair fine Beaver Angolo Trousers" ($10.00); and "A Buff Cassimere Vest" ($7.00). Printed bill. DLC-TJC (DNA, M212, R16).

From WILLIAM SHALER, Marseilles, May 8, 1828. Reports his arrival from Algiers en route home for reasons of health. Notes that he had left William B. Hodgson in charge of U.S. interests at Algiers. Reports that U.S.-Algerian relations are on the "most friendly footing," also that the "war between France and Algiers continues and I have reason to believe that no proposition has yet been made by either party for the conclusion of peace." ALS. DNA, RG59, Cons. Disp., Algiers, vol. 11 (M23, R-T13). Received June 28, 1828.

From JOSIAH STODDARD   Washington, May 9, 1828
JOHNSTON

Your Letter this Morning[1] has given real pleasure to all our friends & they all say God bless the Physician—The advice you have recivd is all the Physick[2] You require—You may tell the Doctor that he perfectly understands these State Cases—The prescription he has given you, would have saved [Robert Stewart] Castlereah [*sic,* Castlereagh] & [George] Canning—The cases of Kings is very different, they suffer from plethora & inaction, the Ministers from over action & reactions—

I think you should be forbid the Use of pen ink & paper—Newspapers—documents & Reports—except perhaps the [Washington *Daily National*] Intelligence[r], a few signs of the times & some Admn addresses in the Morning—They are certainly right in supposing that you do not require starving—& that exercise, regimen, ease & respite from the Cares of State, are all you require—We shall rigidly enforce the prescription—

If Genl. J. should be elected he will unintentionally do for you What your friends Can not advise—He will save your life by relieving you from the Cares of the State—

You May tell [Nathaniel] Chapman, that you Come like Napoleon, to throw yourself upon the most *powerful of your enemies*—That you have lost your health, may lost the battle, but have saved your honor—If he will preserve your health—We will win the battle—

I think the Dr. should banish you at least 30 leagues from the Capital for three months during the Summer—

I am very sorry indeed that I can not give you any News of the Tariff that will give you any ease—Maine complains of the Iron & the hemp—New England of the molasses the South of every thing—Penna. insists on the Iron Ky on the hemp—N. York on the Woolens—Penna. agrees to ease Maine on the Molasses—if she will take the Iron.

But the South insists on a *Whole* Tariff—

Maine implores—& is obstinate—N. England sickens with the Molasses & hesitates—The South tell them, it is a Naucious Medium, but will do them good, & will work–off the Tariff fever—

We shall bring the debate to a close tomorrow but I can not tell you, how Massachusetts will be she is making her Calculations to night—& the result is very doubtful—Lou[isian]a. takes no interest in the subject She Submits to their better judgement—

ALS. DLC-TJC (DNA, M212, R13).   1. The reference is probably to Clay to Adams, May 8, 1828.   2. Pun on the name of Dr. Philip Syng Physick of Philadelphia who, with Dr. Nathaniel Chapman, had diagnosed and treated Clay.

From LUDWIG NIEDERSTETTER, Georgetown, D.C., May 9, 1828. Raises the question of the possibility of abolishing all discriminating tariff duties between the two nations, a subject brought up by Prussia during the recent negotiations on the pending U.S.-Prussian commercial treaty. Notes that since April 15, 1826, no Prussian duties have been levied on U.S. vessels, not even on vessels "not coming directly from the ports of the United States, but from any other country." Notes that this concession was adopted on the expectation that a law, then before Congress, granting similar benefits to Prussia, "would be put into operation." Says that the Prussian government had agreed not to include in the pending commercial treaty an article providing for U.S. restitution of duties collected from Prussian vessels since April 15, 1826; but reminds Clay that the Prussian position had been based on the "condition that an arrangement to this effect would be made by a particular legislative act," and that Clay had agreed that he recommend such legislation to the President. LS, in French, with trans. in State Dept. file. DNA, RG59, Notes from Prussian Legation, vol. 1 (M58, R1); also in *ASPFR,* 6:945-6. On May 16, 1828, President Adams recommended to Congress that the duties on Prussian vessels arriving in U.S. ports be abolished, but the Congress took no action on the request prior to adjournment. U.S.H. of Reps., *Journal,* 20 Cong., 1 Sess., 769; *Sen. Docs.,* 20 Cong., 1 Sess., no. 196, p. 3. *ASPFR,* 6:992-4, contains the provisions of the 1828 U.S.-Prussian commercial treaty.

From THOMAS L. L. BRENT, Lisbon, no. 67, May 10, 1828. Observes that Miguel is now issuing decrees in his name alone, with the royal rubrica of his first initial, M, rather than in the name of the late King John VI.

Transmits a copy of the circular of the Viscount of Santarem announcing Miguel's intention to convoke "the three Estates of the Kingdom" to restore order. States that all the members of the diplomatic corps, except himself, have suspended diplomatic functions with Miguel's government.

Explains his course of action, declaring "the United States . . . derived no right of interference" in the Portuguese political situation, and has "nothing to do" with the conflicting claims of Pedro and Miguel to the throne, or to related controversies involving the internal affairs of Portugal. Opposes "meddling" in the entire situation. Points out that his position is different from several other envoys who "were already informed of the views of their respective governments." LS. DNA, RG59, Dip. Disp., Portugal, vol. 7 (M43, R–T6). Received July 30, 1828.

From JAMES BROWN   Paris, May 10, 1828

In my last letter [April 28] I informed you of Mr [Daniel] Sheldons death and mentioned that I had engaged the eldest son [William A. G.] of Mr [Isaac C.] Barnet to write for the Legation until the President shall have appointed a Secretary. I have no doubt but that the field for selection will be extensive and as the affair is one of some importance at this Court [,] I hope the President will take full time to examine into the qualifications of the several Candidates in order to make the best selection. Mr Barnet is capable of doing all I wish until a Successor to Mr Sheldon shall arrive even should the choice be postponed until the ensuing spring provided the President should express this wish that I should remain at this Court until that time. I would greatly prefer were it necessary to devote some of my time to supertending the duties of the Secretary to having an Individual in that place who might not possess the qualifications to fill it or whose temper and manners might render his intercourse unpleasant or unsafe. You will perceive that I have declined giving any recommendations because I was persuaded that the President would have many applications for the office and consequently from his long experience in diplomatick affairs and his Knowledge of men could make a better choice than any which it was in my power to recommend. Mr Adams [*sic*, John Adams Smith] who goes by the Packet Ship which carries this letter told me it was his intention to offer himself as a candidate. My acquaintance with him is exceedingly slight and I can only say that he appears rather *raw* in his knowledge of the world. It is possible, though I know nothing about it, that Mr Ray the brother in Law of Mr John King may also be a Candidate. He has but a very superficial acquaintance with the French language and does not appear to me to possess any habits of business. If I may judge from the Journals the favor shown to that family has not been of much service to the administration. The son of Mr Barnet has never been in the United States and although a very good young man is not likely to enter successfully into competition with persons of superior claims from their Knowledge of the interests and policy of their own Country. These are the only persons who have been spoken of here and who may perhaps be mentioned to the President. These suggestions are made in *sheer confidence*—As it is possible that in consequence of my request to return in September the President may have made arrangements to fill my place before he received my communication announcing the visible and unexpected improvement of Mrs. Brown's health and my willingness if he wished it, to remain longer at this Court, I have determined to abstain from the expression of an opinion in favor of any individual who may apply for the office.

I have received from home letters which have made me very easy on the score of my private affairs. My crop of the last year has equalled that of the preceding, amounting to 500,000 pounds of sugar and 24,000 gallons of Molasses, a part of the former was sold for Six and one half dollars per hundred weight and the whole of the latter at 22 Cents per gallon. I owe no debts that I know of unless some should grow out of that fruitful mine of litigation and loss to me my old land claims in Kentucky. [Thomas] Bodly [sic, Bodley] and his friend [William] Pogue have found me so profitable to them that I am always apprehensive they may succeed in some new attempt to make something out of me.

It gives me sincere pleasure to learn that your health continues good in spite of your laborious life and of the unparralelled attacks which have been made on your character. Keep up your spirits and your temper and you will unquestionably find a generous and redeeming reaction. It is impossible that the American people can long be the dupes of the scandalous artifices which have been employed to undermine the political standing of Mr Adams and yourself. Good God! can the American people know so little of character as to permit themselves to be persuaded that Mr Adams, whose whole life has been one of unostentatious republican simplicity, is a proud arrogant aristocrat, whilst his competitor [Andrew Jackson], who travels with the retinue of the Chieftain of a Scotish Clan, is made to pass for a plain modest and exemplary Democrat? I have felt every disposition to look at all this with indifference because I have unfeigned confidence in the wisdom of the people, but I find myself moved from my tranquil mood when I see such exaggerating in the Columns of the opposition papers. The publick mind is gradually becoming enlightened, but the opposition had made such strides in Virginia, Pennsylvania, and New York before it was met, that the result yet appears very doubtful. It must have been very gratifying to the administration to find that with all the desire to discover faults in it the opposition so totally failed of success.

Mrs. Brown's health is gradually improving, and with every appearance of a favorable termination, a load of care and anxiety is removed from my heart. Her courage and patience are the theme of general praise, as her entire recovery will be a source of delight to her numerous friends at home and abroad. I can say to you without reserve that no lady in Paris has made more friends or filled with more grace and dignity the difficult station in which she has been placed. I say difficult, because it is no easy matter to satisfy hundreds of her Countrymen, who often come to Europe with exaggerated expectations of what they have to expect from the family of their Minister. Although she is delighted at the thought of embracing her friends yet she will cheerfully consent to remain if the President wishes to prolong my residence here—

You may mention to Mrs. Adams that I have heard that Mr [Thomas B.] Johnstons [sic, Johnson] health is much improved and that he is pleased with the Eternal city. I am told that his spirits were better now than when we saw him in Paris. It appears to me that the climate and scenery of Italy will please him better than that of France.

Should we be expected home this Autumn we shall be happy to execute any commissions for you here—You surprize me when you state that you have lived on your Salary.[1] We had heard so much of your agreeable parties and know so well your hospitable disposition, that we feared you might be forced to spend a considerable sum out of your own resources. I cannot speak so favorably of our Economy although I am convinced that we live at a much lower rate than any other Minister without knowledge of French character and manners could do.

I hope you will not be compelled by business to go to the West this summer. You require some quiet, and from the state of parties there you have a poor prospect of finding it. I should think that an excursion of a few weeks to the Bedford or Berkely Springs, would be the best manner of spending the interval until the meeting of the next Congress.

Although I have had no return of the Rheumatism for the last two years yet I felt a considerable degree of torpor in my left leg, and feared at one time that it might end in a paralytic affection. I am relieved from it and hope I may enjoy a good state of health or at least as good as can be expected on the wrong side of sixty—I have not yet determined where I shall reside when I return to the United States. My business will not require my residence in New Orleans, and political life will soon cease to have any attractions for me. It is my intention to pass some time in each of our principal Cities and at Washington and to decide on my permanent place of abode. I think the President was right in delaying for some time sending a Minister to England inasmuch as the two outfits coming in such rapid succession had given a shock to the sensitive nerves of our Economists. Mr [William B.] Lawrence appears to be an attentive young man and has given me a proof of his vigilance in expressing some apprehensions that the Squadron fitting out at Toulon was destined for the conquest of Mexico in the interest of the Spanish Government, and with the view of obtaining payment of the money due from Spain to France. I have every reason to think that no such design is entertained, because the expense of the expedition would amount to more than the sum due—the success of it would be doubtful—England and the United States would frown on it, and lastly the temper of the nation at this moment is not such as would view with complacency conquests of Representative Governments for the benefit of absolute Monarchies. The doubtful state of affairs in the East, requires that France should hold herself in a state of preparation for war, and complete her Military armaments. The doctrines of the Portuguese and Spanish Governments which have always been unpopular with this nation, are now equally so with the majority of the Chamber of Deputies—Besides, the commercial relations with the New [American] Republicks are daily expanding and affording additional motives for holding only peaceful relations with them—In England they have become so conscious of the weight of this debt and the embarrassments into which a war would plunge them, that they see it in every movement of their great rival—Here I have never heard it hinted that the Toulon fleet was destined for the New World except so much of it as may be necessary to protect their commerce in that quarter.

I have this moment received a note from Mr [Thomas Pennant] Barton son of the late Doct [Benjamin Smith] Barton of Phila. in which he states his intention to apply for Mr Sheldons place in case of my not having made any recommendation. I answered him that I had not. He of course will be on the list of Candidates.   My acquaintance with him is very slight. He left Paris soon after I arrived. You will not want for Candidates. Every body thinks himself qualified, and as the Secretary hopes to reside in the family of the Minister and consequently to be at but little expence the office is considered as one of the best in the gift of the Governm't.   I have requested sir to say what allowance I shall make to Mr Barnet as he has consented to be satisfied with the decision of the President on that head.   Young Barton is well educated, polite, and speaks French like a native of Paris. I only doubt his steadiness attention and habits of business. These are essential in a Secretary of Legation.

If the place which has just become vacant shall be as much coveted in the United States as seems to be here you will be overwhelmed with Candidates. I have just received a long letter from Mr Shobel[2] in which he urges me to recommend him   Although he is a wealthy man and very capable of business generally yet I shall answer him as I have done to others that I do not intend to recommend any candidate to the President who ought when he examines the pretensions of each to chuse the best who presents himself.

Mr Fleming sent me out a Bill in Chancery in which I have even made a Drft. and requested my answer. As none of the French authorities will administer an oath I sent it back to Mr Fleming and requested that he would obtain an order of writ authorizing the consul to receive my oath. I have not since that time heard from him.

Mrs. Brown joins me in affec. greetings to all the family.... P.S. I sent my account to the Dept. down to 1st. of January last—Will you request Mr [Stephen] Pleasenton [sic, Pleasanton] to close it to that day. I enclose you the Emperors proclamation which has arrived.[3]

ALS. DLC-HC (DNA, M212, R3). Letter marked "(Confidential)." Published in *LHQ*, 24:1097–102.   1. Clay paid $200 rent per quarter for the house owned by Mrs. Susan Decatur.   2. Probably Daniel Strobel who was U.S. Consul at Bordeaux.   3. Russian declaration of war on Turkey, dated April 14, 1828, Old Style [6:1343–4] also called the Russian "Manifesto." A copy was enclosed in Middleton to Clay, April 27, 1828.

From WILLIAM H. CRAWFORD   Woodlawn, Ga., May 10, 1828
When I saw that it was proposed to Congress to make appropriations for holding a treaty with the Cherokee nation, I wrote to the agent of the cherokee nation who is a particular acquaintance & friend of mine, to ascertain the prospect of obtaining lands by treaty from that Tribe. I have just received his Answer & enclose it for your information. If his opinion prevails with the President, I would recommend John Taylor[1] Governor of So Carolina or General David R Williams of the same state. You will discover he alludes to a plan of mine in the inclosed letter. In a letter written some time last winter to the President, I explained my Ideas upon the subject to which the agent alludes   By referring to that letter you will see my views. From the accounts I have received of the Intelligence & Sagacity of the Indians I should not despair of making a treaty with them at this time, if men of high talents & established character were appointed to treat with them. In this state (if it has not sinned by and forgiveness) I would mention Augustin S Clayton[2] & Colo Wm Cumming[3] as proper men to be employed if a treaty should be attempted. [Duncan G.] Campbell & [James] Meriweather [sic][4] altho

smart men, are not the characters from whom any good could be expected from treating with the Cherokee Indians.

When I received your Answer to mine[5] in which you say every administration had recommended the erection of observatories, alias "light houses to the Skies," I was much surprized. My connexion with the two last administrations was so intimate that I thought I remembered every recommendation, at least of an extraordinary nature that had been made by them; yet I had no recollection of any such recommendation. Still I thought as your Situation gave you access to the most authentic evidence you would not have ventured an opinion of that kind without referring to the records themselves. I therefore doubted the accuracy of my own memory. Chan[ce] has however thrown in my way a volume[6] contain[in]g the annual messages of all our Presidents & have read those of the three first, & find not the most distant hint at such a recommendation. It is very improbable that a recommendation should be found in the messages which are sent to Congress during its session, as those messages are always produced by the circumstances which arise during the session.

ALS. KyLoF.   1. For Taylor, see *BDAC*.   2. For Augustin Smith Clayton, Georgia politician and judge, see *BDAC*.   3. For Cumming, a career Army officer, see *CAB*.   4. For Duncan G. Campbell, educator, sometime state legislator, and negotiator of the 1825 treaty with the Creeks, see George M. White, *Historical Collections of Georgia* (New York, 1855), 685; for James Meriwether, who had also been involved in earlier treaty negotiations with the Creeks, see *ibid.*, 503; and Charles Royce, *The Cherokee Nation of Indians* (Chicago, 1975), 94.   5. Crawford to Clay, February 4, 1828; Clay to Crawford, February 19, 1828.   6. *The Speeches, Addresses and Messages of the Several Presidents....* (Philadelphia, 1825).

From SAMUEL LARNED, Santiago de Chile, no. 68, May 10, 1828. Transmits documents "inviting me to the negotiation of a commercial treaty." Suggests that he undertake such negotiations without a delay which could only lead "to the serious injury of our trade and the jeopardy of our interests." Reports pending negotiations between Chile and Peru regarding reciprocity of foodstuffs and sugar, and notes a stipulation in the proposed treaty "that the United States are to be placed on the footing of the most favoured nation." Advocates, contrary to the attitude of Heman Allen, former U.S. minister to Chile, a "treaty... with this government." Identifies Chile, as "the most tranquil and orderly of these new republics." Points out that "the independence of Chile has not been recognized by Great Britain," but contends that a forthcoming American treaty "would have great influence in accellerating such a step on the part of the British government." States that he will avow, in the negotiation of any treaty, "the great principles of equality of favours and strict reciprocity." Reports that the Chilean Constituent Congress "is about to transfer its sittings to Valparaiso in order to avoid... all external influence." ALS. DNA, RG59, Dip. Disp., Chile (M–T2, R3). Received August 20, 1828; also in Manning, *Diplomatic Correspondence... Latin American Nations*, 2:1128–30. The U.S. did not conclude a "General Convention of Peace, Amity, Commerce and Navigation" with Chile until May 16, 1832.

To EDWARD EVERETT   Baltimore, May 11, 1828

I hope that you will not omit to propose to the Commee of Retrenchment the enquiry, about which we conversed, as to the time of the authority being given to create the expenditure in respect to secret service,
that is whether it was under the past or the present administration.[1] I
take it for granted that the enquiry will be resisted, but such a decision
may hereafter be important, in evincing the quo animo of the Commee.
On the other hand, if it be acceded to, the result will be favorable.

I am much fatigued, but still I cannot divest myself of an interest in
public affairs.

ALS. MHi. The letter was written from "Barnums" Hotel on a "Sunday evening." Clay,
enroute back to Washington from medical treatment in Philadelphia, had stopped in
Baltimore to give an important political speech on Tuesday, May 13.   1. The Retrenchment Bill was debated in the House from January 31 to February 6, 1828. The
Report of the House Select Committee on Retrenchment (economy in government) indicated that "secret service money" in the amount of $8,958.01 for 1827, up from 1,666.66 in
1826, was excessive. Sums of $3,000 (in 1823) and $2,130 (in 1824) had been spent during
the previous Monroe Administration. *Reports of Committees*, 20 Cong., 1 Sess., no. 259,
p. 11.

From PHILIP SYNG PHYSICK   Philadelphia, May 11, 1828
& NATHANIEL CHAPMAN

It is our conviction from the most deliberate examination of your case,
that your present ill health, wholly independent of any organic derangement, is the gradual effect of sedentary habits, and intense and too
long continued application to the arduous duties of your official station.

Entertaining such an impression, it appears to us, that little more is
required for your speedy & entire recovery than a temporary escape
from the influence of these causes, aided by a strict adherence to a
properly regulated regimen.

As essential to the success of every other suggestion on our part, we
must therefore insist on a suspension, as soon as it can be done with any
sort of convenience of your present engagements, and that a lengthened
journey be pursued leisurely through some healthy region of country,
and deexposed as possible to all undue excitements.

It is natural for us to suspect from the political character of the
times, and the generous devotion of your friends, that occasions may
arise to call you in social entertainments, and the delivery of formal
addresses. Every temptation of the kind we trust will be resolutely resisted, however ungracious may seem the refusal, since such indulgences
would not fail to lead to the worst consequences, utterly frustrative of
our plan of cure.

As you cannot immediately enter on the proposed journey, we do
strenuously recommend to you as the best substitute for it, to appropriate daily several hours of the interval that may elapse, to exercise and
recreative amusements. Equally have your mind and body been overworked, and while the one is to be recuited by agreeable relaxation, the
other should be fortified by active exertion.

Concerning diet, the avoidance of exposure to cold, and the use of
medicine, we have nothing to add to the verbal instructions given to you.

Continue this course unremittingly for six or eight weeks, and we can pretty confidently assure you of the restoration of health, in which result, no one will more sincerely rejoice than ourselves.

Copy. Lexington *Kentucky Reporter,* June 18, 1828.

From JAMES BROWN, Paris, no. 84, May 12, 1828. Has resumed discussion with Count Pierre de La Ferronnays on American claims [5:29-31; Brown to Clay, February 27, 1828]. The Foreign Minister has agreed to submit to the Council of Ministers Brown's letter of December 19, 1827, to Baron de Damas [6:1392-3]; but he also "observed that the American claims were large in amount, that even omitting for the present any objections he might find it necessary to make to them, he feared he could not encourage a hope that they would be satisfied, because of the present State of the Finances of France." Brown responded that "the amount of the Claims proved the extent of the injury sustained by the Claimants, but could not be urged as a reason why France might not so liquidate them," and suggested that the two nations "remove by an arbitration, an objection which had for some years been made to the discussion of our claims [5:29-31]." The Count then suggested that the U.S. claims would have a better chance of success had they been presented as part of the "general settlement which took place anterior to the evacuation of France by the Allied armies" in 1818. To this argument, "I observed that we had been neutral in the war which led to that settlement." Notes that since Count Ferronnays "did not further insist on this point, I presume he considered it as having no important bearing on the question." ALS. DNA, RG59, Dip. Disp., France, vol. 23 (M34, R26). Received June 27, 1828.

From FRANCISCO TACON, May 12, 1828. Notes with satisfaction the American inquiry "into the circumstances of the Corvette *Kensington,*" to prevent "armament, equipment and departure" against Spain as a privateer. Cites the example of the sale of the brig, *Alfred,* to French interests in violation of the spirit of neutrality. States it is "publicly known" that the *Kensington,* built at Philadelphia, would be armed and equipped "for the Mexicans, who had here a Spanish-American agent to inspect the work, make payments etc." LS, in Spanish, with trans. in State Dept. file. DNA, RG59, Notes from Spanish Legation, vol. 9 (M59, R-T12).

Earlier, on April 25, 1828, Charles J. Ingersoll, U.S. District Attorney at Philadelphia, reported to Clay that he had responded to Tacon's repeated complaints and had brought the case of the *Kensington* to court. In addition, Ingersoll had given assurances that there would be "a constant eye upon this vessel" concerning any violations. ALS. DNA, RG59, Misc. Letters (M179, R66).

From THOMAS L. L. BRENT, Libson, no. 68, May 13, 1828. Reviews political situation in Portugal. Reports that as Miguel issued a decree to convene the Cortes in his own name, this action helped prompt a decision by the diplomatic corps to suspend relations. Declares also that as

Miguel issues his decrees with different degrees of authority, he (Brent) could not continue "to recognize the government of the Prince." Has decided, therefore, to a "suspension of my diplomatic intercourse."

Continues, on May 16, that he now judges his suspension decision to have been the wisest one, since Miguel's government is one of "so undefinable a nature." LS. DNA, RG 59, Dip. Disp., Portugal, vol. 7 (M43, R–T6). Received July 30, 1828.

To CITIZENS OF BALTIMORE   Baltimore, May 13, 1828

Although I have been required, by the advice of my physicians, to abstain from all social entertainments, with their consequent excitements, I cannot leave Baltimore without saying a few words by way of public acknowledgement for the cordial congratulations with which I have been received during my present visit.[1] I am not so vain, indeed, as to imagine that any personal considerations have prompted the enthusiastic demonstrations by which my approach to this city, and my short sojourn, have been so highly distinguished. Their honoured object, has, it is true, some claims upon the justice, if not the sympathy, of a generous, intelligent, and high minded people. Singled out for proscription and destruction, he has sustained all the fury of the most ferocious attacks. Calumnious charges directed against the honor of his public character, dearer than life itself, sanctioned and republished by one, who should have scorned to lend himself to such a vile purpose, have been echoed by a thousand profligate or deluded tongues and presses. Supported by the consciousness of having faithfully discharged his duty, and defended by the virtue and intelligence of an enlightened people, he has stood firm and erect, amidst all the bellowings of the political storm. What is a public man, what is any man worth, who is not prepared to sacrifice himself, if necessary, for the good of his country?

But the demonstrations which I have here witnessed, have a higher and a nobler source than homage to an individual; they originate from that cause with which I am an humble associate—the cause of the country—the cause of the Constitution—the cause of free Institutions. They would otherwise be unworthy of freemen, and less gratifying to me. I am not, I hope, so uncharitable as to accuse the opponents of that cause with designs unfriendly to human liberty. I know that they make, many of them, sincerely other professions. They talk indeed of republicanism, and some of them impudently claim to be the exclusive Republican party. Yes! we find men who, but yesterday, were the foremost in other ranks, upon whose revolting ears the grating sound of republicanism ever fell, and upon whose lips the exotic word still awkwardly hangs, now exclaiming, or acquiescing in the cry that they are the Republican party! I had thought if any one more than all other principles characterised the term Republican party, it was their ardent devotion to liberty, to its safety, to all its guarantees. I had supposed that the doctrines of that school taught us to guard against the danger of standing armies, to profit by the lessons which all history inculcates and never to forget that liberty and the predominence of the military principles were utterly incompatible. The Republican party! In this modern new fangled and hetrogeneous party, Cromwell and Caesar have recently found

272

apologists. The judgement of centuries is reversed—long established maxims are overturn—the Ethiopian is washed white—and the only genuine lovers of liberty were the Philips—the Caesars—the Cromwells—the Mariuses and the Scyllas of former ages. It is time for slumbering patriotism to awake, when such doctrines as these are put forth from the Capitol, and from popular assemblies. It is time that the *real* Republican party, (I speak not of former divisions springing from causes no longer existing, and which are sought to be kept up by some men in particular places, only for sinister purposes)—that party, under whatever flag its members may have heretofore acted, that party which loves freedom, for freedom's sake, justly to estimate the impending perils and to proceed with an energy, and an union, called for by the existing crisis in the Republic. Regardless of all imputations and proud of the opportunity of free and unrestrained intercourse with all my fellow citizens, if it were physically possible and compatible with my official duties, I would visit every state, go to every town and hamlet, address every man in the Union, and entreat them by their love of country, by their love of liberty, for the sake of themselves and their posterity—in the name of their venerated ancestors, in the name of the human family, deeply interested in the fulfilment of the trust committed to their hands—by all the past glory which we have won—by all that awaits us as a nation—if we are true and faithful, in gratitude to HIM who has hitherto so signally blessed us—to pause—solemnly and contemplate the precipice which yawns before us! If indeed, we have incurred the divine displeasure, and it be necessary to chastise this people with the rod of his vengeance, I would humbly prostrate myself before HIM, and implore his mercy, to visit our favoured land with war, with pestilence, with famine, with any scourge other than military rule or a blind and heedless enthusiasm for mere military renown.

Gentlemen, I wish I had strength to expatiate upon this interesting subject; but I am admonished by the state of my health to desist. I pray you to accept my thanks for the sentiment with which you have honoured me, and your permission to offer one [toast] which I hope will be approved by you.

Genuine Republicans, of every faith, who true to the cause of liberty, would guard it against all pernicious examples.

Printed in Baltimore *American*, May 14, 1828.   1. Clay's invitation to speak in Baltimore, on his return to Washington from Philadelphia, where he had received medical treatment, was extended on May 6 by Luke Tiernan and 21 other prominent Marylanders, among them Hezekiah Niles, John S. Tyson, George F. Warfield, and Stevenson Archer. Tiernan to Clay, Baltimore, May 6, 1828, in Baltimore *American*, May 13, 1828. Clay's acceptance of this invitation noted an improvement in his health and asserted that his doctors in Philadelphia, Philip S. Physick and Nathaniel Chapman, had assured him that "a temporary abstraction from business, and exercise" would further benefit him. Clay to Tiernan, Philadelphia, May 8, 1828, in *ibid.* His remarks in Baltimore were delivered on Tuesday, May 13.

From WILLIAM B. LAWRENCE, London, no. 38, May 14, 1828. Reports on a May 12 meeting with Lord Dudley, regarding the selection of an arbiter of the Northeast boundary dispute. Notes that the previously agreed upon procedure to select an arbiter—"each of us presenting to the other simultaneously one or two Sovereigns or States to form a list from which an arbiter was to be chosen"—has been rejected; and that Dudley has suggested, instead, that "the names of all the powers of Christendom, from among whom there was the least probability that a selection would be made, should be placed in a glass and that as they were respectively drawn, each of us should write on a seperate piece of paper 'yes' or 'no', until we came to one in whom both concurred." Reports that he protested this change in procedure because it "tended to blend all shades of preference" which either party might have. Says that he told Dudley that had the original arrangement for selection been followed he was prepared to name the U.S. nominees immediately. Further conversation with Dudley indicated, however, that since it is unlikely that Russia, the first choice of the U.S., would be acceptable to his government, "it might perhaps be politic to name Denmark first, but I fear I should not acquit myself of my duty if the Emperor Nicholas was not pressed."

Concluded the interview with reference to recent tension on the Northeast frontier, particularly the John Baker controversy [6:1272-3] and, in light of peaceful "joint occupancy of the North West Territory" pointed out "the expediency as well as practicability of abstaining, on both sides, from exclusive jurisdiction over the disputed district." Notes that Dudley "seemed to be wholly uninformed as to the merits" of the Baker controversy.

Resumed the conversation with Dudley on May 14 with the result that "I am more and more satisfied that the indecision results from a belief that Russia will be our first selection." Explains that Lord Dudley, in mentioning British delay on the arbitration matter, made it "sufficiently obvious" that there should be a prior understanding that "no Power would be proposed with which England was likely soon to come into collision." Upon hearing this, "I made no reply from whence it could be inferred that I understood" his allusion. LS. DNA, RG59, Dip. Disp., Great Britain, vol. 35 (M30, R31). Extract in Manning, *Diplomatic Correspondence . . . Canadian Relations,* 2:710-2. Received June 14, 1828.

From WILLIAM B. ROCHESTER, Truxillo [Trujillo], Honduras, May 14, 1828. Reports his arrival on board the *Falmouth,* on May 12, and the "precarious . . . existence" of the Federal government of Central America. Notes lack of food and other provisions among the swarm of refugees who have fled from the civil war in the interior to Truxillo and also the total disruption of the local economy. Observes that the Commandant, "A Negro, living like most of his neighbors in a state of polygamy" who has "about fifty black troops, badly equipped and worse disciplined," is "indifferent and ignorant" of the nation's "present political conditions and prospects," and cares little about the outcome of the civil war. Says that there is even local sentiment for "the re–establishment of Spanish authority." Feels that to talk about a commercial treaty at this time would be pointless, and that the Commandant, "if he knows how to read," would probably not understand the principle of the most favored nation. Discusses some of the recent problems of U.S. merchant vessels in Central American waters, especially the loss of the American schooner *Harriet* while enroute from Truxillo to Havana. Reports rumors that the

"Bay of Honduras is at this time infested with pirates," but believes that the appearance of the *Falmouth* has prevented these pirates from showing themselves "in great numbers." Asks that a shallowdraft, U.S. war vessel be sent for close-in patrol of the Honduran coast for the purpose of stamping out piracy. Admits, however, that he knows of but "one Amer. citizen resident here"; and notes that the only foreign consul, a Dutch official, is making preparations to leave with his family at the earliest opportunity. Concludes: "From all the information I have been able to collect here touching on the present state of things, having reference to the internal divisions of this country, I am apprehensive that the residence at Guatemala of a diplomatic agent from our Government, if not improper at this juncture, would at least be inexpedient and useless—the civil war is certainly not at an end, neither is there any reasonable prospect of a speedy termination to it—so opposite and obstinate in their respective views" are the Guatemalan "Centralists" and the El Salvadorian "Liberalists." ALS. DNA, RG59 Dip. Disp., Central America, vol. 1 (M219, R2). Received June 22, 1828.

To NICHOLAS BIDDLE   Washington, May 15, 1828

I have the pleasure to introduce to you the bearers hereof Messs. Lavergne, and Villere,[1] two gentlemen from Louisiana who have been recommended to me in very high and favourable terms. Mr. Lavergne's object in our Northern Capitals is that of a pecuniary agency in connection with a new Bank[2] in that State in which the planters take a deep interest. Any aid which you can afford him in the accomplishment of that object, and any attentions you may render these gentlemen will oblige. . . .

LS. DLC–Nicholas Biddle Papers (DNA, M212, R20).   1. H. Lavergne, prominent banker, and Jacques Phillippe Villere, former governor of Louisiana. For Villere, see *DAB;* for Lavergne, see *Louisiana History*, 8:124–5; 16:93.   2. Probably the Consolidated Association of Planters, H. Lavergne, President, which was incorporated in March, 1827, and capitalized at $2,500,000 in February, 1828. William Graham Sumner, *A History of Banking in All the Leading Nations*, 4 vols. (New York, 1896), 1:244.

From CHARLES R. VAUGHAN, Washington, May 15, 1828. Requests "copies of certain public documents" dealing with the Northeastern boundary question, as provided by the Convention of September 29, 1827 [6:1100–01]. Also requests all the "maps surveys and delineations comprised in the atlas annexed to the Reports of the Commissioners" appointed under Article V of the Treaty of Ghent [6:656]. Notes that since there are apparently two "authentic copies" of the *Atlas* in the possession of each party, time and money might be saved were the U.S. to agree to a "simple collation and comparison" of these copies, rather than making "fresh copies" for exchange. LS. DNA, RG59, Notes from British Legation, vol. 15 (M50, R15).

On the British proposal for a time and expense–saving collation and comparison of existing copies of the *Atlas*, rather than making additional copies for exchange, a proposal accepted by the U.S. in October, 1828, see: Clay to Vaughan, June 12, 1828, Copy, extract. DNA, RG76, Northeast Boundary: Misc. Papers, Entry 72, frame 3; Vaughan to Clay, June 15, 1828, LS. DNA, RG59, Notes from British Legation, vol. 15 (M50,

R15); Gallatin to Clay, October 1, 1828, ALS. DNA, RG76, Northeast Boundary (KyU., Special Roll, frames 90-2); Gallatin to Clay, October 3, 1828, *ibid.*, frames 92-4 ["Whatever the British may do, they will not falsify the surveys in question." Instead, they will probably attempt to render inadmissable "far more important fresh evidence."]; Clay to Vaughan, October 16, 1828, LS. DNA, RG76, Northeast Boundary: Convention of 1827. See also Clay to Gallatin, October 20, 1828, LS. NHi-Gallatin Papers (MR15); Vaughan to Clay, October 20, 1828, Copy. DNA, RG76, Northeast Boundary: Misc. Papers, Env. 4, item 29; Clay to Peter B. Porter, October 20, 1828, Copy. DNA, RG59, Dom. Letters, vol. 22, p. 311 (M40, R20); Peter B. Porter to Clay, October 21, 1828, Copy. DNA, RG107, Military Books, vol. 12, pp. 380-1.

On February 2, 1829, Vaughan notified Clay that when the proposal for a simple collation of the *Atlas* had been made, the British government believed it had duplicate copies of the *Atlas*. After now finding that it has only one copy, the Foreign Office has concluded "it would be too great a risk . . . to send that one copy to the United States . . . until a Transcript . . . shall have been made of it." Gives assurance "that no time will be lost in making a Transcript . . . with a view to its collation at Washington." Copy. DNA, RG76, Northeast Boundary: Convention of 1827. See Gallatin to Clay, May 26, 1828.

From LANGDON CHEVES, JAMES PLEASANTS, & HENRY SEA-WELL, Washington, May 16, 1828. Ask Clay "to give the necessary direction to cause to be placed to the credit of Our Clerk Col. [Aaron] Ogden, the sum of two thousand Dollars from the fund appropriated for the payment of the expenses of the [Slave Indemnity Awards Commission] Committee." LS. DNA, RG59, Misc. Claims, Great Britain. See also [6:347]; and Pleasants and Sewell to Clay, August 30, 1828.

To EDWARD EVERETT   Washington, May 16, 1828
I cannot perceive the smallest objection to the proposed Call for your brother's [Alexander H.] note to the Duke del Infantado [4:767-8] and you have my entire assent to such a call, if you deem that assent at all necessary.

ALS. MHi.

From HENRY MIDDLETON, St. Petersburg, no. 79, May 16, 1828. Reports on preliminary Russian army and navy movements in the war against the Turks, and the Emperor's [Nicholas I] initial strategic and political goals in the contest. Is convinced that "the Emperor will not consent to take halfway measures," since the "improvement of the Southern provinces of his Empire depends essentially on the free navigation of the Dardanelles. He will not be contented as hitherto to enjoy this at the wish of another, if he can obtain a better security." Notes that the "road to Constantinople is open to the invader," and that there are already 400,000 troops "within a few days march of the frontier." ALS. DNA, RG59, Dip. Disp., Russia, vol. 11 (M35, R11). Received July 26, 1828. Dated May 4, 1828 O.S.

From WILLIAM B. ROCHESTER, Omoa, Honduras, May 16, 1828. Reports his arrival "this morning." Has interviewed the local Commandant "who is courteous and vastly more shrewd than the Comdt of Truxillo," but has received from him no reliable information or conjecture on the possible outcome of the civil war. Comments: "One thing is pretty evident they are here alike too deficient in physical strength and too doubtful on which side the scales of victory will finally preponderate to pledge themselves zealously and irrevocably in behalf of either party." Has found no reason to change his opinion about "the inexpediency and inutility" of sending an American diplomatic agent to Guatemala at this time. Will not tarry in this city because of pestilence, but will return home on a private schooner rather than on the *Falmouth*, stopping briefly at Belize. Regards the Federation of Central America as "virtually dissolved . . . all attempts to get together a Congress have been abandoned long since." Discusses at length the war between the Centralists and Liberalists, concluding there is "no valuable or adequate publick object, to which I might direct my attention should I proceed on my mission, unless indeed I were to attempt the part of a mediator of peace." This, however, "would, ill become a foreign agent in the absence of any instructions from his own government, and . . . in cases of domestick or civil war, is generally a vain and always a thankless undertaking." ALS. DNA, RG59, Dip. Disp., Central America, vol. 1 (M219, R2). Received June 23, 1828.

To JAMES BROWN   Washington, May 17, 1828
Upon consulting with the President he authorizes me to say that it is left entirely at your option, to return, at the time you have asked permission to return, or to postpone it until the next Spring. Whether at the one period or the other, you will commit the charge of our Affairs to Mr. [Daniel] Shelden [*sic,* Sheldon], the Secretary of the Legation, if he be still with you.

Referring to the instruction under date the 28th of May last [6:596–603], relative to a reference to arbitration of the disputed question arising under the 8th article of the Louisiana treaty [5:29–31], you are authorized, (if you cannot prevail upon the French Government to consent to the reference, in the qualified manner proposed in that instruction,) to agree to the reference of the general question involved in that dispute; that is, one so stated as to embrace all the rights claimed by France, according to her interpretation of that article. In other respects, you will consider the above-mentioned instructions unmodified.

LS. KyLoF. No. 16. A rough draft version of this letter, somewhat garbled, is found in DLC–HC (DNA, M212, R8).

To JAMES BROWN   Washington, May 17, 1828
We have been greatly concerned by the accounts received from you as to the state of Mrs. Brown's health. Your last letter of the 28h March just received relieves us a good deal from our anxiety. I hope that, by perseverance in the system of her excellent physicians, she will be finally entirely restored to health.

My health has not been so good of late, but [Philip S.] Physic [*sic*, Physick] and [Nathaniel] Chapman, whom I have just returned from consulting, at Philadelphia, assure me that there is no organic defect about me, that I have been only overworked and that by a few weeks of relaxation from business and moderate exercise I shall find my health re–established. I shall accordingly commence a long journey shortly and dedicate the whole summer, if necessary, to the care of my health. I believe I shall go by the Southern route to Kentucky.

Your brother, Dr. [Samuel] Brown,[1] who has taken suddenly a resolution to visit Europe, will put you in possession of all the current political and other news. On the subject of the Presidential election, I adhere to the opinion formerly expressed that Mr. Adams will be re–elected. Our information from Kentucky, on the vote of which State much depends, is highly encouraging. The State elections, coming on in August, precede the electoral election. They will turn, as almost all elections now do, on the agitating question of the day. [William T.] Barry and Genl. [Thomas] Metcalfe are the opposing Candidates, and we have the strongest assurances of the General's election, in which event I shall consider the ultimate decision of the State pretty certain. The opinion I have formed, excludes from our calculation Pennsa. Virginia and the other Southern States, which I think cannot be relied on for Mr. Adams, although there are hopes of the two States mentioned and North Carolina.

I have, according to your request,[2] transmitted to you the President's permission to you to return in September. I am not aware that your return will add to our embarrassments. In your last letter [March 28] you state that it is probable you may not return until the Spring, and that you would be willing to remain, if it be the desire of the President. I have not yet consulted him, but I entertain no doubt that he will acquiesce entirely in your wishes on that subject. Whether you return in the fall or the Spring your Successor will probably not be appointed until towards the close of the next Session of Congress, which you know is the short Session. After I shall have conversed with the President I will again write to you.

I am owing you a balance on the purchases in Paris which you last made for me. Had I been earlier aware of Dr. Brown's intention to visit Paris I would have remitted it by him. But there is not now time (as he proposes to sail on the 20h. instant) and I hope it may suit you to receive it when you come back.

Should the French Government offer to accept our proposal to refer the question under the Louisiana treaty [6:596–603], on condition that the reference be made without limitation or qualification, I think you had better take the question ad referendum, unless under all circumstances you should deem the delay hazardous, in which case I would accede to the proposal.

Our affairs stand well with all Foreign powers. I have lately concluded here treaties with Prussia[3] and the Hanse towns [6:1370–1], making four treaties that I have signed since I have been in office. There is no present danger of any rupture with G. Britain about our N. Eastern boundary. The dispute is to be arbitrated.

278

Mrs. Clay wishes her sister [Ann Hart Brown] to purchase for her and bring or send if an opportunity offers four dozen pair of short white Kid gloves and two or three of black. They perhaps could be put up and sent by mail.

She joins me in affectionate remembrance to Mrs. Brown.

ALS. ViU. 1. Also on this date, Clay sent Dr. Samuel Brown a passport as "Bearer of Public Dispatches" to the U.S. ministers in London and Paris. This courtesy involved transportation to Europe at public expense. Samuel Brown replied with thanks for Clay's kindness, noting, further, that Mrs. James Brown "is thought to be much better by her medical attendants." Samuel Brown to Clay, Philadelphia, May 19, 1828. ALS. DNA, RG59, Misc. Letters (M179, R66). 2. Brown to Clay, February 28, 1828. 3. Signed, May 1, 1828; ratified, March 14, 1829. Parry, *Treaty Series*, 78:279-92. See also Niederstetter to Clay, April 26, 1828.

To EDWARD EVERETT, Washington, May 17, 1828. Reports that instructions have been sent to James Brown, U.S. Minister in Paris, relative to the Beaumarchais claim [3:311-3]. Explains that in 1822 the U.S. had agreed to negotiations on this claim and that this agreement was based on an earlier instruction of May 7, 1816. At that time the then American minister, Albert Gallatin, had been authorized, in general terms, to negotiate with France a convention which would include, among other provisions, "claims of French subjects against the United States." Copy. DNA, RG59, Report Books, vol. 4, pp. 248-9. The 1816 Monroe to Gallatin instruction is in *ASPFR,* 5:284.

To WILLIAM B. LAWRENCE   Washington, May 17, 1828
Your despatches from 27 to 33, inclusively, have been received, and Mr. [Nathaniel B.] Blunt has arrived with the British ratification of the Conventions [6:826-7, 859-60, 1100-01] of last year. We are very anxious to learn whether you have come to an agreement for the designation of a Sovereign Arbitrator [for the Northeastern boundary]. I have nothing to add to former instructions on that subject. It is most desirable that the Emperor of Russia [Nicholas I] shall be agreed upon, and the King of Denmark [Frederick VI] would be our second choice. The President weighed all the considerations you have suggested respecting the King of the Netherlands [William I]. They did not seem to him to overrule the confidence which he has in the intelligence and personal character of that Monarch. As to the King of Prussia [Frederick William III], the circumstance of our having no representative near him, was not without its influence in the omission of his name.

The President has decided to allow you the usual salary and outfit of a chargé d'affairs, the Salary to commence from the 4th day of October last. An authority to the Messrs. Baring Brothers & Co., to pay you accordingly, is herewith transmitted.[1]

Copy. DNA, RG59, Dip. Instr., vol. 12, pp. 102-03 (M77, R7). Dispatch No. 7. Extract in Manning, *Diplomatic Correspondence . . . Canadian Relations,* 2:174. 1. Encloses a letter to Baring Brothers, & Co., London, May 17, 1828, requesting extension of credit to William B. Lawrence in amount of $4500 outfit and $4500 salary. Copy. *House Docs.,* 21 Cong., 1 Sess., no. 66, p. 3.

From STANHOPE PREVOST, Lima, May 17, 1828. Reports that William Radcliff took charge of the consulate on May 14. Notes the difficulty of dealing with Peruvian officials on U.S. complaints about maritime freight rates, and believes that "recent political occurrences of a war like nature, will probably suspend the adoption of any definite tariff, for a year or more." Analyzes the international situation of Peru as this relates to a fear of "approaching hostilities with Bolivar." States that Peru is about to announce a constitutional congress and an election for the Presidency, "thereby relieving Bolivar of that charge." Suspects, however, that Bolivar, is still bent on gaining "a footing again in Peru, and establishing his grand Empire, of which Lima is to be the Capital." Is confident, however, that Peru can resist invasion. Blames Bolivar for the unrest in South America, "owing altogether, solely and entirely, to his ambitious intriguing manuevers." ALS. DNA, RG59, Dip. Disp., Peru, vol. 2 (M154, R2). Received September 5, 1828.

To FRANCIS T. BROOKE   Washington, May 18, 1828

Your two favors of the 4h. and 6h. inst. reached this place during my absence on a trip to Philada. for the purpose of obtaining medical advice, which I am happy to inform you was favorable.

I cannot object to Mr. [Robert] Tripletts speaking of the contents of the letters[1] which you shewed him, 'though I do not desire, at present, that they should be published.

I will endeavor to procure and forward the documents you request.[2]

I regretted much that the considerations, to which the President felt himself bound to yield, did not seem to him to admit of the appointment [6:467–8] of our friend [John] Taliaferro.[3] N York has not, in the person of any Citizen of that State, a single representative at this place, in any one of the high executive offices. Judge [John] Savage is a man of undoubted qualifications, and standing high in the esteem of the people of that State. Under these views the President thought he ought to be appointed, and his appointment[4] has given very great satisfaction.

ALS.KyU.   1. Probably the Clay–Blair exchange of January 8 and January 24, 1825. 2. Reference obscure.   3. At this time John Taliaferro represented Virginia in the U.S. House.   4. Thompson to Clay, April 1, 1828.

From T. H. BENNETT   Boston, May 19, 1828

If I had been unacquainted with your generous nature, you would not have been troubled with this letter; but I know that a line from the humblest of your fellow citizens would be received as cheerfully, as from the richest, or most talented; and however unwilling to encroach upon your time, I could not longer refrain from addressing you.

I have this moment finished the perusal of a few observations which you made on the 13th. inst. at a private party in Baltimore.[1] In the warmth of my heart I will tell you *They are worthy of you, sir,* and that is the greatest compliment I can pay them.

Many years ago, in the House of Representatives, I heard you urge in terms as bold as eloquent the necessity of the U.S. acknowledging the independence of the South American Republics; and it fell to my lot, *after such acknowledgement,* to hear you spoken of with enthusiasm from Valdivia [Chile] to Tumbes [Peru]; and in more than one instance, to listen to a Castilian strain in which the North American advocate of the rights of the Southern Hemisphere was classed with the Balcarces, the Rondeaus, and the O'Higginses.[2]—It is strange that whilst in remote countries your name should be endeared to all—*here,* in your native land—a land so much indebted to you—a knot of envious wretches should have attempted—*more they could not do*—to sully your well-earned fame.

I know how the bare *attempt* must operate upon feeling so sensitively alive to honour as your own—I have often thought of the anxiety of mind you must have felt, and had fears that your health would give way under the relentless attacks of a party; who, I verily believe would, if they had the power, subvert our liberties. Yes, sir, the stabs at you and Mr. Adams, were made *at the nation;* and in six months more this nation will testify in a unequivocal manner, what it thinks of these Character and State Assassins.

I feel a glow of pride that the people of Philadelphia and Baltimore have come forward to solace and uphold a man so villainously beset as you have been; and you may rest assured, sir, from what I know of Boston population, that had you extended your visit to this city, you would have met with such a welcome *as you never yet experienced.*

No excuse is offered for the liberty taken in addressing you, for I believe it *was* mine, and *is* the solemn duty of every man who wishes well to his country, to lend his aid to support an honest son of that country whom a band of miscreant conspirators have unholily attempted to destroy because he stood in the way of their traitorous projects.—My blood has boiled within me, Mr. Clay, to see how you have been treated; and my heart has beat quicker to behold you gloriously triumphing over the infernal machinations of your enemies.

Go on, sir, in the manly and undaunted course you have hitherto pursued—New England is with you, almost to a man. Do not, I entreat you, let the malignant outpourings of a dastard faction weigh upon your mind a feather; for if such a thing was once imagined, you would be pursued with tenfold relentlessness. Posterity will assuredly do you justice, and I am greatly mistaken if the present generation do not do it fully.

In conclusion, sir, I sincerely trust that you may be quickly restored to health, and that you may live long, very long,—after the Jacksons and [John] Randolphs and [Thomas H.] Bentons, et id genus omne, are politically forgotten.

ALS. DLC-HC (DNA, M212, R3). Addressed: "Private." Written from "Mass. Journal Office," Boston.   1. Clay to Citizens of Baltimore, May 13, 1828.   2. For Antonio Gonzales Balcarce, Jose Rondeau, and Bernardo O'Higgins, see Irene Nicholson, *The Liberators: A Study of Independence Movements in Spanish America.* New York and Washington, 1969.

To JOHN DUER   Washington, May 19, 1828

I have just received your letter of the 17th.,[1] informing me that you had been induced, by having obtained further evidence in relation to the equipment of the Bolivar, since the date of your preceding letter, the 6th. instant, to direct that vessel and her cargo to be seized and libelled.—This proceeding is entirely approved, and is considered as a pledge, that it will be followed up effectually by you; that the neutrality of the United States may be preserved, and the culpable brought to punishment, in reference to that vessel and its equipments.—

A letter has just been received at this Office from the District Attorney of Maryland [Nathaniel Williams],[2] stating that he had filed an information against the Schooner Juncal, at Baltimore. This circumstance is mentioned to you because the two cases of the Bolivar and Juncal, are, in some degree, connected, at least, in reference to a common interest in ownership.

Copy. DNA, RG59 Dom. Letters, vol. 22, p. 202 (M40, R20).   1. Which discussed evidence of Buenos Airean violations of U.S. neutrality in the *Bolivar* case in New York and recommended that the vessel's armament be seized and libelled. DNA, RG59, Misc. Letters (M179, R66). On May 16, Clay had written Duer that he had received no "evidence" from Francisco Tacon, Spanish minister to the U.S., that would support seizure of the *Bolivar*, and that unless evidence from other sources could be obtained the vessel should be permitted to sail. DNA, RG59, Dom. Letters, vol. 22, p. 191 (M40, R20). On May 31, Duer informed Clay that there was insufficient evidence to warrant a costly trial, that the *Bolivar* should be released, but that she should be stripped of her armaments prior to sailing. DNA, RG59, Misc. Letters (M179, R66).   2. Dated May 16, 1828. See, Odgen to Clay, May 24, 1828.

To EDWARD EVERETT   Washington, May 19, 1828
I have received the letter which you addressed to me on the 17th inst. by the direction of the Committee of Foreign Affairs of the House of Representatives, requesting information, if the public interest will permit, whether any, and, if any, what, answer has been returned by the Government of France to the proposal, stated in the message of the President, at the opening of the present session of Congress, to have been made to that Government, on the part of the United States, touching the matters in controversy between the two Governments [6:596–603].

I must, in the first place, remark that I am persuaded the Committee will, on consideration, concur with me in thinking that their application ought to have been made to the President through a resolution of the House of Representatives, according to established usage, instead of being addressed directly to this Department. The constitution having confided to him the care of our foreign relations, a just execution of, and responsibility under, the trust, would seem to require that he should possess a controlling power over all correspondence connected with them. This control could not be so effectually exerted if the calls for diplomatic correspondence should be made immediately upon this Department. Such, I believe, has been the uniform sense of both branches of Congress, as well as of the Executive Department. But as I presume it was not the intention of the Committee to deviate from any established practice, nor to introduce any new principle of official intercourse with the Executive; but that, to avoid delay during the small remaining portion of the session, they have thought proper to apply at once to this Department, for the information that they wish; I have the honor, in compliance with their request, to make the following communication.

That during the ministry of the late [Damas] and present [Ferronnays] French Ministers of Foreign Affairs, Mr [James] Brown has had several conferences with them on the subject of the claims of American citizens upon France; and the proposal mentioned by the Committee as having been stated in the President's message, that no definitive answer to that proposal had been received at the date of Mr. Brown's last dispatches; and that he had addressed an official note to the French Government, on those subjects, no answer to which has been yet received at this Department.

LS. MHi.

To JOSEPH GALES   Washington, May 19(?), 1828

I send you a hasty article on the subject of the Brazilian affair, which I have not time to improve or abridge, but of which perhaps you may make something.[1]

On the other subject—the expences of our Foreign Intercourse—I have lately addressed a letter[2] to the Comee. of Retrenchment which I think will be found to contain an ample refutation of the charge of extravagance. In the mean time, until that is published, Mr. Bartletts speech[3] will probably be sufficient.

ALS. InU. Dated only "Monday night"; possibly May 12, but probably May 19. 1. Neither found nor apparently published in the Washington *Daily National Intelligencer.* 2. Probably a reference to Clay to James Hamilton, Jr., February 29, 1828. 3. Rep. Ichabod Bartlett, of New Hampshire, delivered a lengthy speech on retrenchment, and the need for economy in government in general, in the House on February 6, 1828. *Register of Debates,* 20 Cong., 1 Sess., 1401–18. For Bartlett, see *BDAC.*

To ALBERT GALLATIN &   Washington, May 19, 1828
WILLIAM PITT PREBLE

The President having, by and with the advice and consent of the Senate, appointed you agents, to assist in carrying into effect the convention [6:1100–01] concluded at London, during the last year, relative to our northeastern boundary, I have the satisfaction to transmit to you, herewith, a joint and several commission, in duplicate, evidencing your appointment and authorizing you to act in that character. I also transmit, herewith, a copy of the convention itself, which, having been duly ratified by both Governments, has been promulgated in the accustomed form.[1]

The general object of your agency will be to perform such duties, under the direction of the Department of State, in respect to the disputed boundary, as both or either of you may, from time to time, be called upon to execute. At present I will more particularly state some points to which your attention is expected to be immediately turned.

1. You will collect and collate such information and documents as enabling you to understand clearly our rights, may assist in their illustration and enforcement, and in opposing the pretensions of the other party.

2. After all the documents and information are collected, either from American sources, or from British archives, according to the provisions of the convention, you will prepare a statement of our case, according to its terms, to be submitted to the sovereign Arbitrator, after it shall have been inspected and approved at this Department.

3. You are expected likewise to prepare an answer to the statement which the British Government may propose, in conformity with the

Convention, to present to the arbitrator, when that statement shall be received by the American Government: And

4. It is expected that you will separately[2] perform such acts, connected with the business of your agency, as either of you may be directed, from this Department, to execute.

Mr. Gallatin has in his possession a transcript of the transactions of the mixed Board of Commissioners formerly appointed by the two Governments[3] to settle the dispute in the boundary, together with the arguments of the respective agents; a free access to all which will be allowed to Mr. Preble. Other documents, maps, &c. are in this Department, or may be acquired in the progress of our inquiries and investigations, which will be subject to your use.

The exchange of the ratifications, in London, took place on the 2d day of the last month. From that day, according to the provisions of the convention, the respective periods of time which are prescribed for the performance of the several acts therein mentioned, begin to run; and it is, therefore, important to keep their termination constantly in view. That which is limited for the demands which the two Governments have a right to make upon each other for public papers, will expire on the 2d of October next. We must, therefore, be prepared to make our demand in due time. I have already received from Mr. [Charles R.] Vaughan an official note [May 15, 1828], (a copy of which has been transmitted to Mr. Gallatin,) demanding, in conformity with the convention, certain papers in behalf of the British Government.

I regret that I am not now able to state the compensation to which you will be entitled for this public service. It cannot, however, be doubted that Congress will, during the present or next session, make an adequate provision on that subject.

L.S. DLC–Exec. Papers: Northeast Boundary (DNA, M212, R9); also in NHi–Albert Gallatin Papers. 1. On May 17, Clay had also transmitted a copy of Charles Vaughan's note of May 15 (above). Clay to Gallatin, May 17, 1828. NHi–Gallatin Papers (MR15). On May 19, writing from New York, Gallatin reported having obtained a copy of a map of Charles II pertinent to the controversy and his intention to search in Boston for additional relevant materials. Gallatin to Clay, May 19, 1828. ALS. DNA, RG76, Northeastern Boundary (KyU., Special Roll). 2. Clay to Preble, May 22, 1828. 3. A Board comprised of Thomas Barclay, Great Britain, and John Holmes, U.S., had rendered a decision on November 24, 1817, regarding possession of islands in the Bay of Passamaquoddy. A second Board, comprised of Barclay and Cornelius Van Ness, of the U.S., had studied the geography of the "Highlands," in the vicinity of Mars Hill, but had adjourned in deadlock on October 4, 1821. Burrage, *Maine in the Northeastern Boundary Controversy*, 89–90, 93–115.

From THOMAS W. WHITE, Richmond, May 19, 1828. Remarks that he has also consulted the "same talented physicians [Philip S. Physick and Nathaniel Chapman]" in Philadelphia whom Clay has recently seen, and urges Clay to follow their advice. Remarks that Clay's health has surely been impaired by the "peltings of the pitiless storm" brought down on him by his political enemies. Considers his Baltimore speech of May 13 "one of the happiest efforts of your life," and adds: "I am unwilling to give up the ship, while we have such a steersman as Henry Clay. . . . without you, all would be lost. . . . I conscientiously believe that it is yet in your power to save the nation." Notes, however, that in Virginia, "our degraded State, all is lost," and that it would be a waste of Clay's time to travel there; but thinks that a trip through New York "will win many hearts." Encloses an anti-Jackson poem, in French, written by his 17-year old daughter, and boasts that it is the product of but four months study of that language "and that only half an hour per day." Asks whether Clay thinks she has any talent; "if you think so, please tell me." Signs his letter, "Your ardent Friend." ALS. DLC-HC (DNA, M212, R3).

To DANIEL BRENT, Washington, May 20, 1828. Promises to pay Brent, 60 days from date, the sum of $1350. When the note was presented on July 22, 1828, at the Washington Branch of the Bank of the United States, the bookkeeper there informed Brent "that there were no funds" to cover it. Brent protested the note on July 23, the protest being notarized by Michael Nourse. ALS. DLC-TJC (DNA, M212, R16).

From FRANCIS T. BROOKE   Richmond, May 20, 1828
I am very happy to receive a letter from you, and rejoice that your health is improving—If you mean to follow what is Said to be the prescription of the faculty at Philad I Should like to know when you will begin your travels, I Shall return home about the middle of June and Should be much gratified by the pleasure of yours and Mrs Clays company at St Julien—and would return with you to Washington, I shall observe your caution as [Robert] Tripletts communication of the contents of the letters[1]—I regret that our friend [John] Taliaferro was not appointed the Treasurer [of the U.S.], I have had no letter from him for Sometime, but understand from [Samuel L.] Southard that he is very well Satisfied—I am not now so desirous to see the documents on which [James, Jr.] Hamiltons report of the execution of the Six militia men was made[2]—[John] Sloanes pamphlet[3] has placed that matter in a very clear light—and its circulation ought to be promoted—I Should like to See Burgeses pamphlet[4] in answer to [George] McDuffies report on the finances[5]—a portion of the Jackson address by the committee at Washington is published in the [Richmond] Enquirer[6]—I have not had time to read it, perhaps Something ought to be done to repel its effects—the address of the Jackson committee here[7] has been little read as I am assured from the country—The answer to it by Freeman in the [Richmond *Con-stitutional*] Whig which is written by professor [Nathaniel Beverley] Tucker though not very Strong is more than a match for it,[8] if it could be circulated in pamphlet form—your [May 13] Speech at Baltimore has had a good effect   I heard Watkins from Goochland[9] Say here the other evening that he would vote for you in preference to Jackson but he could not vote for Mr Adams—that is no uncommon Sentiment in Virginia

ALS. InU.   1. Clay to Brooke, May 18, 1828.   2. *House Reports*, 20 Cong., 1 Sess., no. 140, pp. 1-100; Pleasants to Clay, April 29, 1828.   3. [John Sloane], *Mr. Sloane's View [To the Editor of the (Washington Daily) National Journal] . . . of the Report of the Committee of Military Affairs, in Relation to the Proceedings of a Court Martial, Ordered for the Trial of Certain Tennessee Militiamen.* Washington, 1828. 16 pp.   4. Tristam Burges, *Speech of Mr. Burges, of Rhode Island, Delivered in the House of Representatives of the United States, April 21st, A.D. 1828, on the Tariff.* Washington, 1828. 90 pp.   5. *House Reports*, 20 Cong., 1 Sess., no. 185, pp. 1-36.   6. *Reply by the Jackson Corresponding Committee of the District of Columbia, to Mr. Clay's Last Address,* in Richmond *Enquirer,* May 20, 23, 27, 30; June 3, 6, 10, 13, 1828.   7. At a meeting of the Jackson Committee of Correspondence of Richmond County, Va., held on April 19, 1828, an address of the Jackson Central Committee of

285

Correspondence in Washington, directed to the people of Virginia, was read. Resolutions were passed supporting the election of Jackson through the dissemination of appropriate papers and campaign documents. Richmond *Enquirer,* April 25, 1828.   8. See Pleasants to Clay, April 29, 1828; and Richmond *Constitutional Whig,* May 10, 1828. Tucker signed himself, "A Freeman."   9. Either George W., John R., or P. L. Watkins, all members of the Anti-Jackson Corresponding Committee, which met at Goochland County Courthouse on March 17, 1828. Richmond *Constitutional Whig,* April 2, 1828.

From CHRISTOPHER HUGHES, Brussels, May 20, 1828. Commiserates with Clay over the unfairness of the recent political attacks upon him and compliments him on the "purity, the spirit, the patriotism of your character and conduct" that was revealed in his Address of December 29, 1827. Notes that "I had the boldness, perhaps the impertinence to tell you frankly when I was at home, how much I had regretted your having accepted the office of Sec. of State; I remember the manly and noble explanation you made to me of your feelings & motives; & the indignation you thundered out at the very idea of your shrinking from the great duties to which you were called, or blanching before the host of slanderers, and their diabolical charges and imputations." Reminds Clay that "what I wanted you to do, (or to have done;) was to withdraw yourself from public life:—decline *high* employment. . . ," so that his health would not break down, as had William H. Crawford's. Recalls that he had then advised him to let "Mr. Adams 2. terms pass quietly over," after which, he felt, the "eyes of our nation" would be "directed towards Lexington," and that there would then be "a *national* demand for you."

Reports that British troops in Gibraltar, earlier withdrawn from Portugal, are in readiness to depart for Greece, but feels that there will be no joint European opposition to Russian pressure on the Turks. "So long as the war between Russia & Turkey may go on and last, it is believed that the other powers may & will remain quiet." Sees greater diplomatic difficulties at war's end on the question of Russia's demand for indemnities. Notes, too, that there is a general expectation of "bloody & general struggles to take place in Portugal"—either a civil war or a Portuguese war with Spain that could well produce foreign intervention in its train.

Concludes with a lengthy exposition of recent Court gossip and social activities, and adds the news that the Netherlands has recognized the independence of Mexico. ALS. DLC–HC (DNA, M212, R3).

To JAMES MADISON   Washington, May 20, 1828
The inclosed letter has been transmitted to me by Mr. [John] Binns with a request to address a letter to you in behalf of Mr. [M.L.] Tracie,[1] the writer of it, who is desirous of filling the Greek professorship in the Virginia University. Whilst I comply with that request, I think it proper to add that I cannot offer any opinion of my own as to the competency of Mr. Tracie for the station which he solicits. Should there be a disposition to appoint him, I presume that he will be subjected to the necessary previous examinations.

ALS. CtY.   1. For Tracie, see Bruce, *History of the University of Virginia,* 2:154–5; Madison to Clay, May 24, 1828.

From GILLIES THOMPSON, Iberville, La., May 20, 1828. Offers his services to make "an Hydrographical survey of the Western Coast of Louisiana," and solicits the protection of the United States during the undertaking.

Plans to map the coast with "all its shoals, Islands, bars, Bays and Inlets, with correct soundings" around the "curve of the Bay of Mexico" to Veracruz. Notes the existence of "many valuable fertile Islands" suitable "to the culture of coffee, sugar & cotton." Mentions also the presence of "fierce and hostile . . . savages" in the area and states that the proposed survey will require "the whole of the Autumn of 1828–9" to complete and will cost $6000. Feels it is important "to give the Expedition more of a National undertaking," since it may be subject to "insult" and "imposition" in the Mexican states; suggests, therefore, that "Companies" of Marines accompany the surveyors to insure their safety. Refers to his own qualifications and acquaintances with governmental officials. ALS. DNA, RG59, Misc. Letters (M179, R66).

From WILLIAM B. LAWRENCE, London, no. 39, May 21, 1828. Reports that there has been no meeting of the representatives of the Allies—England, France, Russia—since the organization of the Wellington government [January, 1828], to discuss the "pacification of Greece." Notes, however, that King George IV's recent speech from the throne characterized the Battle of Navarino as an "untoward" action and revealed generally less hostile British views of the Porte. Calls attention to Allied pressure on the Pasha of Egypt, Mohammed Ali, "to induce recall of [Egyptian] forces which interfered with the settlement of Greece." States that England will, if possible, "refrain from any new engagements with Russia" if the "Sultan [Mahmud II] can be induced to offer moderate terms of pacification to that Power." Sees evidence of "little cordiality" between Britain and France on the Greek question as the French move closer to St. Petersburg in support of Russia's war against the Turks. Explains that the movement of a "powerful" Russian army toward the Black Sea gives the Tsar's government added strength in dealing with the future role of Turkey–in–Europe.

Comments on the debate on a new corn bill in Parliament and believes that its "scale of duties will probably effectually prevent the United States from sending any grain or flour direct to England." Observes that a temporary law, passed in the last session, requires a "certificate of origin to accompany all corn imported from the British possessions," and concludes that England's overall trade policy in this regard is "obviously to prevent the introduction of American produce through Canada."

Submits, in an enclosure, information requested by the Agricultural Society of South Carolina relative to the quantity of rice currently being imported from the United States by Great Britain, to the differences in duties on "rice in all shapes whether of the denomination of Paddy, rough rice or the common rice of commerce," and to "the specifications of the patents of the proprietor of the rice mill established here and of the Act of Parliament, if any, granting him exclusive privileges." LS.

DNA, RG59, Dip. Disp., Great Britain, vol. 35 (M30, R31); also in Manning, *Diplomatic Correspondence... Canadian Relations*, 2:713. Received July 2, 1828.

From JOEL R. POINSETT   Mexico City, May 21, 1828

The Mexican Congress adjourned today and I regret to say without having ratified the Treaty of Amity, Commerce, and Navigation.[1]

The House of Representatives rejected two articles, The one for the restoration of fugitive slaves, and the other providing for the maintenance of peace between the Indians of our respective Territories.

The first was rejected on philanthropic principles altogether, such [as] are most likely to influence the young legislators of a young nation. With the other question many considerations were urged—Among them the fear of our armed populations.

The fact however is, that at this moment the public mind is violently excited by the publication of a pamphlet being a translation of the article on Mexico published in the 4th number of the North American Review [*sic*].[2]

These people are like spoilt children and cannot bear to be chided.

I think during the extraordinary session to take place in August I shall be able to [illeg. word] both articles.

Some alarm has been excited by a report of an intended invasion from Cuba. [Angel] Laborde's squadron is expected daily, but I do not think any attempt will be made to land Troops on the Mexican shores. In other respects all is tranquil here. The Treasury still empty.

I am ashamed to say that the law permitting the export of Silver in bars or ingots, has not yet passed. It was sent to me by high authority as having passed the Senate. It will remain over to the next session when its passage will certainly take place.

LS. DNA, RG59, Dip. Disp., Mexico, vol. 4 (M97, R5). No. 127. Received July 21, 1828.   1. Poinsett to Clay, February 22, 1828.   2. The offending piece was, "Art. II–Mexico," *AQR* (December, 1827), 4:338–62. Patronizing in tone, the article attacked the character of the Mexican people, the rigidity of the social caste system, corruption within the Roman Catholic clergy, and the problems faced by British and American investors in Mexican mining ventures. Poinsett to Clay, June 4, 1828.

From WILLIAM RADCLIFF, Lima, May 21, 1828. Announces his safe arrival at Lima in 128 days from New York, following a detainment at Panama for 49 days, "owing to an interruption of the usual intercourse by a Spanish privateer" operating on the coast.

Mentions assuming the duties of Consul on May 14. Laments the death of James Cooley, the late Consul, and reports receiving all of Cooley's "public papers and property" from Stanhope Prevost, Vice Consul.

Suggests that "the commerical regulations of this Government" are not "consistant with impartiality toward our country," and resolves to attempt to change them. Notes that American "cotton fabricks," notwithstanding a duty, "have hitherto been sold at a fair profit, and in large quantities."

Observes: "The political affairs of this country remain in a very unsettled state," despite the adoption of a new constitution. States that "deep concern prevails here," concerning the possibility of war with Colombia and that "preparations are being made for defense." Believes this unrest is "imputed to the ambition and injustice of [Simon] Bolivar." Reports that a revolution has toppled the regime in Bolivia.

Declares that the government of Peru "is extremely embarrassed for want of funds," and "difficulties seem to be experienced in all its affairs." Lists resignations and removals from the cabinet.

Reports "The U.S. Squadron in this Ocean are at present employed," with the *Brandywine, Vincennes,* and *Dolphin* cruising off or calling at various Pacific ports. ALS. DNA, RG59, Cons. Disp., Peru, vol. 2 (M154, R2). Received August 19, 1828.

Writing from Washington on June 9, 1828, to William White, Clay officially verified the death of James Cooley at Lima "on the 24th day of February last." Copy. DNA, RG59, Dom. Letters, vol. 22, p. 222 (M40, R20).

To CHARLES R. VAUGHAN, Washington, May 21, 1828. Announces that William Pitt Preble, appointed as one of the American agents in the Northeastern boundary dispute, is proceeding shortly to New Brunswick "to make certain inquiries." States that Preble's visit is for the procurement of additional information. Notes that "our own offices of public record are open and accessible," and presumes "the same facilities exist in the British provinces." Requests a letter of introduction for Preble to the Lt. Governor of New Brunswick, Sir Howard Douglas. Copy. DNA, RG59, Notes to Foreign Ministers and Consuls, vol. 4, pp. 29–30 (M38, R4); also in Manning, *Diplomatic Correspondence... Canadian Relations,* 2:174–5. For Douglas, see *DNB.* For Vaughan's acknowledgment and enclosure of a letter of introduction, see Vaughan to Clay, May 22, 1828. DNA, RG59, Notes from British Legation, vol. 15 (M50, R15); also in Manning, *Diplomatic Correspondence... Canadian Relations,* 2:713–4.

From THOMAS L. L. BRENT, Lisbon, no. 69, May 22, 1828. Conveys second-hand information on conferences at Vienna pertaining to the aspirations of Miguel to the throne of Portugal. Learns that Prince Metternich apparently respects Miguel's claim. Believes that the courts in Europe desire the abdication of Pedro IV and "the total and definite separation of Brazil and Portugal." Reports the news of an uprising on May 16 at Oporto led by Constitutional Party interests and its quelling by the local governor. States that Oporto is a bastion of the Constitutional Party and of local army units still loyal to Pedro as a result of the influence of English merchants there. Feels Miguel's prospects are "gloomy," given the news from Oporto and the "entire stagnation" of the economy. Ponders that England, as an ally of Portugal, may "find herself frustrated" and "will endeavor to acquire the Island of Madeira." Asserts: "The United States will be the best judges how far their interests would be affected as a maritime nation by the possession of Madeira and the Azores Islands." Notes the various intrigues and rumors prevailing in this confused and unstable country. LS. DNA, RG59, Dip. Disp., Portugal, vol. 8 (M43, R7). Received August 9, 1828.

To JAMES ERWIN   Washington, May 22, 1828

I received your letter, dated at New Orleans on the 22d ulto, enclosing a bill drawn by Dr [Walter] Brashear for the payment due to me this year. I have forwarded the bill to Boston, and presume it will be duly honored.

My health having been bad of late, in consequence of intense application to business, I went to Philadelphia to consult Drs [Philip S.] Physick and [Nathaniel] Chapman. Their opinion of my case was much more favorable than I anticipated. They believe that, with a temporary relaxation from business, moderate exercise, and a little attention to diet, my health and strength may be reëstablished. I shall commence, according to their advice, a journey, in a few weeks, to Kentucky, which I hope to reach early in July. Mrs. Clay will remain here to receive Ann [Anne Brown Clay Erwin]. We shall be greatly disappointed if she does not come.

With respect to politics, I have little to add to what I formerly wrote, and what you will find in the newspapers. If the issue of the Kentucky elections in August should be favorable, I think Mr. Adams' reëlection is certain. On the contrary, if we fail there, there is much reason to fear the loss of his reëlection. From New York our information is most satisfactory.

Mrs. Clay and the children are well, and she joins me in presenting you, our affectionate regards. . . . P. S.—I shall write to Thomas [Hart Clay], as you advise. Mrs. [Horace] Holly had left here before your letter reached the city, but your communication to her brother [Charles Austin], met her, I have no doubt at New York.

LS. THi.

From RICHARD B. JONES   Near Philadelphia, May 22, 1828

[Regrets that he did not see Clay in Philadelphia when he was there for medical consultations. Recommends, at considerable length, that the son of Joseph Pulis, U.S. consul at Malta, be appointed to succeed his father, who is resigning the post. Continues with an analysis of Middle East politics and diplomacy, viz:]

I have news from the Levant to 11nth of March. The vessels of the Allies had been allowed to quit Constantinople on landing their cargoes, for which a receipt was given to the Masters. The Sultan [Mahmud II] ordered all the *Franks* to quit Constantinople   They were sent on board the Allied vessels. The Armenians were sent into the interior, the Jews were allowed to remain. The Sultan is extremely occupied in preparations for war and is daily occupied in inspecting his Troops; The writer adds, there is not the least appearance That the Grand Seignior will condescend to any concession in favour of the Greeks. Three Turkish line of battle ships & 11 F[r]igates have sailed from Constantinople, the remainder preparing to follow, immense efforts are made to fortify both shores of the Hellespont. Every act of English Diplomacy has been employed to effect a separation of the Pashaw [or Pasha] of Egypt [Mohammed (or Mehemet) Ali] from the Sultan, but in vain! Ibrahim Bey [Ibrahim Pasha] has lost the greater part of his troops by famin[e], the remainder still occupied Modon, Coron, Tripolizza [*sic*, Tripolitza]

290

& Patress [*sic,* Patras], waiting the arrival of Transports to conduct them to Egypt. The Greek Pirates are dispersed. The English Frigate [illeg. word] was entirely lost, crew saved, on the rocks of [illeg. word] near Candia.

If ever there was a period propitious for the introduction of american manufactured goods, cottons &c into the Turkish dominions, the time has now arrived, and I hope Government will urge their agents to effect it. Barbary alone would consume to the amount a million a year in our cotton goods alone, and the articles of commerce in return on such raw materials as we much want. wool, skins, hides, madder, Guano, Senna dye, Soda, Salt &c   They are all now much incensed against the Great Powers of Europe; and since they have been taught to respect us, they are pleased with the moderation with which our *Power* has been used.

Since my last letter the Legislature have taken from our [Pennsylvania Agricultural] Society the funds which had been assigned to us, at our next quarterly meeting, should the Society continue their existence, I will make use of the permission you gave me.[1] I have discovered that my Hor[s]e is spavined, I hope to cure him after the season is over.

ALS. DNA, RG59, A. and R. (MR3). Written from "Broodfield," Pa.   1. Obscure reference.

From LEVI LINCOLN, Worcester, Massachusetts, May 22, 1828. Forwards "copies duly authenticated, from the records and files, *as they are found to exist,*" relative to the Northeastern boundary controversy. Supplies other copies "which may be useful for reference." Offers "further assistance ... for maintaining the integrity of the territory of the nation, and for vindicating the rights of the States and their citizens, particularly interested in this country with a foreign power." LS. NHi–Gallatin Papers (MR15).

Clay acknowledged this letter and added: "It is possible that Mr. [Albert] Gallatin and Mr. [William Pitt] Preble ... may personally apply to make some researches in the Archives of Massachusetts for evidence to support and illustrate our title." Clay to Lincoln, May 30, 1828. Copy. DNA, RG59, Dom. Letters, vol. 22, pp. 207–8 (M40, R20).

To WILLIAM PITT PREBLE   Washington, May 22, 1828
I addressed a letter to yourself and Mr. [Albert] Gallatin, jointly, on the 19th instant, acquainting you and him with your appointment as agents to assist in carrying into execution the convention concluded at London, on the 29th day of December [*sic,* September] last [6:1100–01], respecting the dispute with Great Britain in our Northeastern boundary. In that letter I informed you that one of the objects of the appointment was that each of the agents should perform such separate acts as might be assigned him by this Department. I have now to request your particular attention to such a separate service. The President wishes you to proceed, as soon as convenient, to the Province of New Brunswick, for the purpose of making certain inquiries, and obtaining copies of certain documents, to guide our judgment in deciding what authentic copies of

acts of a public nature, relating to the territory in question, should be applied for, to the British Government, in conformity with the third article of the convention. It is not intended that you should, your-self, make any formal application, agreeably to the provisions of that article. Such an application must be made to the British, and not Provincial, Government. But it is supposed, without any such formal application, on your part, the information and copies wanted may be obtained.

The inquiries which we desire you to make, and the copies to be procured, are the following:

I. Have the boundaries of New Brunswick, in any respect, been altered since the province was first erected into a separate Government?

If such an alteration has taken place, has it been by virtue of an order in Council, or by a designation of limits inserted in the commission or commissions of any of the Governors, or in consequence of an agreement or understanding between the Government of that Province and that of Lower Canada?

In either case, what is the substance, and what is the date of such order in council, commission, or agreement?

Had there been, previous to such alteration, any dispute between the Governments of the two provinces, or any difficulty in ascertaining any part of the boundary between them? And was it in consequence of an application by the Provincial authorities, that the alteration or explanation, (if it has taken place,) was made by the crown?

Is there a general understanding in New Brunswick, that the Province is bounded, on the north, by the Ristigouche river? And, if so, by what authority, for what reason, and at what time, is it understood that that river was established as a boundary?

II. Has the crown made any grant of land west of the line drawn due north from the source of the river St. Croix?

If such grant, or grants, have thus been made, has any originated directly from the crown? Or have they all been made, in the usual way, by the Governor of the Province? Or have any been made by the Governor, but in consequence of any special authority or instructions emanating from the Colonial Department, or from any other organ of the crown?

This inquiry has been suggested by the following paragraph quoted, as part of a statement of the Lieutenant Governor of New Brunswick [Sir Howard Douglas],[1] in the report [March 8, 1828] of the joint Committee of the Legislature of the State of Maine, (page 50.) vizt.

"In fact, by a reference to documents in the possession of the British Colonial Department, it appears that the settlement at Madawaska, in the province of New Brunswick, was made under a grant from the crown upwards of thirty years ago, (and that) so late as the year 1810 no claim had been advanced by the United States, although the settlement had been established at the time for upwards of twenty years, under a grant from the Government of New Brunswick, and had been constantly designated the Madawaska settlement."

Although the settlement was of a much earlier date, it is not probable that the [Lieutenant] Governor could be mistaken as to the fact of a

292

grant having been made about the year 1796: but he calls it, in the same sentence, a grant from the crown, and a grant from the Government of New Brunswick. And it is important that this should be elucidated, in reference both to the documents to be applied for, and to the manner of managing the argument.

It seems that there can be no difficulty in ascertaining that point, as the settlers must have the evidence of their title, and copies of some of the grants, under which they hold, may be obtained.

III. Has the Government of New Brunswick extended its jurisdiction beyond those boundaries, which must necessarily have been those of the Province, if Mars hill had been the northwest angle of Nova Scotia?

The facts which may be ascertained under this head, are intended to be applied to two distinct branches of the argument.

(a) The exercise of jurisdiction by the Government of New Brunswick over territory lying on the waters of the river St. John's, west of the line drawn due north from the source of the river St. Croix, will prove that they did not consider that territory as being part of Canada; that they did not, therefore, consider the line, now claimed by Great Britain, which extends from Mars hill, westwardly, and divides the waters of the river St. John's from those of the Penobscot, as the southern boundary of Canada (Province of Quebec,) established by the proclamation of 1763, and the Quebec act; and, as a necessary consequence, that they considered that southern boundary to be along the ridge which divides the waters of the river St. John's from those of the river St. Lawrence: all which is precisely what the United States contend for.

Independent of grants of land and other acts of jurisdiction, both there and east of the line drawn due north from the source of the river St. Croix, the late acts of the Government of New Brunswick, towards citizens of the United States residing above the Madawaska settlement, will afford proofs of jurisdiction exercised west of the north line from the source of the river St. Croix. The application for a writ against John Baker, (page 36 of Appendix to Report of Joint Committee of Legislature of Maine,) expressly states the land on the river St. John's, between the Madawaska river and the river St. Francis, to be in the parish of Kent, county of York, province of New Brunswick. It is presumed that abundant proofs of this description may be easily obtained.

(b.) The exercise of jurisdiction by the Government of New Brunswick, over territory lying east of the aforesaid line drawn due north from the source of the river St. Croix, and northwest of any part of a line drawn due northeast from Mars hill to the Bay des Chaleurs, will prove that they have not considered Mars hill as the northwest angle of the Province, and that that northwest angle is, at all events, north of that hill. The farther north and west the jurisdiction may have been extended, the farther north it will prove that northwest angle to have been, according to the understanding of the local authorities of New Brunswick. Grants of land, and other acts of jurisdiction, should be inquired for principally in the Dalhousie settlement, and at Ristigouche, both at the bottom of Bay des Chaleurs, on the waters of the river Ristigouche, and on the St. John's river, and its tributary streams, from the parallel of Mars hill northwards, to the place where the line drawn due north from the source of the river St. Croix, crosses the river Ristigouche.

It may not be possible to enumerate all the various acts of jurisdiction of which proof may be attainable, such as enrolment of militia, appointment of magistrates, establishing of courts, and processes issuing from courts, &c. But there are two which require particular attention, vizt.

1. The erection of new counties, vizt. those of Gloucester, Northumberland, and York, and also of parishes, or other territorial subdivisions, in the upper part of those counties, northwest of the northeast line above mentioned. These, it is presumed, may be found amongst the legislative acts of the Province; and if a copy of the Provincial laws, generally, could be obtained or consulted, it is probable that they would afford other proofs of the extension of jurisdiction, as above stated.

2. Grants of land within the same boundaries. These are mentioned, not only as affording decisive proofs of jurisdiction, but as being more likely to be easily obtained than any other kind of evidence. There is a register kept of all the locations, and a map of the grants in the office of the Surveyor General of the Province. Although copies may not be obtained, access may probably be had to the map, and the names of some grantees, having grants in the quarters above designated, would be sufficient to enable the Government of the United States to apply for copies of the grants. Copies of grants may, also, be obtained from some of the grantees who may have had to sell, or for other purposes. There are, also, probably, there as elsewhere, grants of land known to every body, and respecting which sufficient information may be obtained to ground upon it an official application to the British Government.

IV. Although the information respecting old grants by the Government of Nova Scotia, may not so easily be obtained in New Brunswick, it would be desirable to ascertain there, if possible, the names of grantees, and dates of the following grants, which are wanted for a quite distinct purpose, vizt. Island of Campobello—Island of Grand Manan— (probably subsequent to 1783,) and Governor [Sir Francis] Bernard's[2] grant, so called, being, it is believed, for 100,000 acres, of a date prior to the year 1776, and extending from the river Schoodic westwardly, to the Cobnook bay. This last is the most important of the three.

The names and times of respective appointments of the Governors, of New Brunswick, from 1784 to this time, may be useful.

It is neither practicable, nor, perhaps, necessary, that you should affect any reserve or secrecy in the performance of this service. Under this impression, I have applied for and obtained a letter of introduction for you from Mr. [Charles R.] Vaughan,[3] the British Minister, to the [Lieutenant] Governor of New Brunswick, which is, herewith, transmitted, and which, I hope, may facilitate your inquiries. It is of course well known to you, and it may be urged, if necessary, that our public offices of record are open and accessible alike to foreigners and natives, and that our laws offer no impediment, not equally applicable to both, to any investigations into matters of fact which any foreigners might wish to

294

make within the United States. We have, therefore, reason to expect reciprocal facilities in any foreign, and especially British country.

Your reasonable expenses, from the time you may leave home until your return to it, will be allowed you. You will keep and render an account of them to this Department, supported by such vouchers as, from their nature, it may be practicable to procure. In order to meet them, you are authorized to draw, at sight, upon this Department, for any sum not exceeding $1000. Whatever sum you may draw will be charged to you, and must be accounted for on the settlement of your account.

It is not intended, in the specification of the preceding objects of inquiry, and the copies of documents to be obtained, to exclude others which may suggest themselves to you, as being useful in elucidating the question at issue. Your own reflections, or the researches you may make in New Brunswick, may indicate the importance of others. You will, therefore, exercise your own discretion in procuring such additional information and transcripts as may strike you to be useful.

You have been already informed, by the joint letter [May 19] to yourself and Mr. Gallatin that the exchange of the ratifications of the Convention, in London, having been made on the 2d day of the last month, the term of six months, within which we must make the formal application to the British Government for copies of such public acts as we wish to obtain from it, will expire on the 2d day of October next. Hence, it is desirable to avoid, as much as possible, all unnecessary delay.

Your acceptance of the agency has been anticipated from the communications received from your friends. I hope that we may not be disappointed in that respect. But if you should think proper to decline it, you will see the necessity of communicating the earliest information of your resolution.

LS. DLC–Exec. Papers, Northeast Boundary (DNA, M212, R9).   1. George Ramsey [see *EC*] was at this time "Captain General and Governor in Chief" of all of Canada, including New Brunswick. Douglas, as Lieutenant Governor of New Brunswick, was the chief administrative officer of that particular province.   2. *DNB*.   3. Clay to Vaughan, May 21, 1828.

To JOHN QUINCY ADAMS, Washington, May 23, 1828. Transmits to the President, in obedience to the resolution of the House of Representatives of April 30, correspondence between Condy Raguet, late U.S. Chargé in Brazil, and the Brazilian government. Notes that these documents relate to the alleged blockade of Buenos Aires by Brazilian naval forces, the "imprisonment of American citizens" by Brazil, and the circumstances which caused Raguet to demand his passports and depart Rio de Janeiro in protest over the "illegal system of blockade attempted to be enforced." Also transmits correspondence of William H. D. C. Wright, U.S. consul at Rio de Janeiro. Calls attention, further, to the fact that the documents transmitted also embrace the "embarrassment to American commerce" resulting from the "paper blockade of the whole coast of the Buenos Ayrian Republic." Reports that William Tudor, formerly U.S. consul in Lima, has been appointed to replace Raguet, but that he has been delayed by "unforeseen casualties" in reaching his new post. Encloses the most recent instruction sent by the Department to Tudor on "the subject of the blockade." Copy. DNA, RG 59, Report Books, vol. 4, pp. 250–3; also in *ASPFR*, 6:1021 and in *House Docs.*, 20 Cong., 1 Sess., no. 281, pp. 5–6.

From ALBERT GALLATIN, New York, May 23, 1828. Reports the existence of thirty–three documents for which "it might possibly be necessary to apply to the British Government." Discusses also the value and significance of various maps and charters.

Asks: "Should you apprehend that you may be absent from Washington in that month [August], I would submit that Mr. [William] Preble should be instructed to send direct to me here the result of his enquiries, and that Mr. [James] Barbour should be instructed to apply to the British Government for copies of such documents as I would write to him were necessary." Copy. NHi–Gallatin Papers (MR21).

To ALL WHO SHALL SEE THESE PRESENTS, GREETING, Washington, May 24, 1828. Appointment of Lewis Cass, Michigan Territory, and Pierre Menard, Illinois, as Commissioners to negotiate and sign treaties with the Chippewa, Ottawa, Potowatomi, Winnebago, Fox, and Sac "nations of Indians." DS. ICHi. Jointly signed by Adams and Clay. For the treaties signed, 1828–30, with various of these tribes, see Parry, *Treaty Series*, 79:74–7; 80:20–3, 34–7; 81:68–73.

From JOHN JACKSON, Washington, May 24, 1828. Seeks appointment as chief clerk in the Office of the Department of the Treasury, noting that he is a merchant and accountant, down on his luck, who needs the job badly. States that Mr. Samuel Brooks, the incumbent in the position, does not need the income; indeed, that he remits it "yearly to England to an illegitimate child he has there." Points out that Judge John Savage has written Clay in Jackson's behalf and that this gesture "removes the difficulty suggested by you, at the time I mentioned this subject to you—to wit; that you could not interfere in any appt. in any Depart. other than your own, the application coming from the appoint[in]g. power." ALS. DNA, RG59, A. and R. (MR2).

John Jackson had earlier, and unsuccessfully, sought appointment as Superintendent of the Patent Office. Jackson to Clay, April 2, 1828. *Ibid.* Samuel Brooks was British–born. *Biennial Register*, 1828, p. 22; Peter G. Washington of Virginia succeeded Brooks as chief clerk in the Office of the Treasurer. *Ibid.*, 1829, p. 23.

From JAMES MADISON   May 24, 1828
I have recd. yours of the 20th inclosing the letter from Mr [M. L.] Tracie. He had before made a direct applica– for the Classical professorship in our University, and will of course be taken into due consideration with the other Candidates. Notwithstanding the number of them, we shall not I fear find one who will *replace* as well as succe[e]d Mr [George] Long now in that chair, whose emeninent qualifications have tempted an offer from the London University which he has accepted.

We learn with great pleasure that your health, of which very unfavorable reports had prevailed, is improved, & that a compleat re-establisht. of it is pledged by the skilful physicians [Nathaniel Chapman and Philip S. Physick] you have lately consulted. With our best wishes that such may be the result, be pleased to accept the assurance of of [*sic*] our esteem and our friendly respects. Mrs. M. offers her affecte. remembrances to Mrs Clay. . . .

AL, draft. DLC-James Madison Papers (DNA, M212, R22).

From DAVID B. OGDEN, New York, May 24, 1828. Reports that Cesar Fournier, a captain in the navy of Buenos Aires, has raised the subject of the legal status of his vessel, the *Juncal,* which is now under seizure at Baltimore for "acts of piracy" in the capture of the Brazilian brig, *Lantista.* Relates the details of the last cruise of the *Juncal* before her seizure, as told him by Fournier. Asks Clay: "Is the captain of a public armed ship of a foreign nation amenable to our laws for the manner in which he conducts himself towards the property or prisoners captured by him? Is he responsible to [this] Government for his conduct or to his own government?" Reports that it is Fournier's complaint that the U.S. seizure of his vessel was the result of Brazilian diplomatic "representations," and that the seizure was particularly unneutral in light of the fact that the U.S. has allowed the Brazilians to build, arm, and equip "two first rate frigates" in American shipyards. Fournier denies, further, that adding four cannon to his battery while in the waters of the U.S. constitutes a legal reason for the forfeiture of his ship. In such cases, he claims, U.S. law "punishes the person who shall aid . . . in adding to her armament"; it does not require outright seizure of the vessel. Ogden assures Clay that Fournier "stands high in the estimation of his Government," and concludes: "I believe that if every charge in the U.S. libel be fully proved no condemnation of the vessel can be founded on them." Reports that Fournier now seems inclined to abandon his vessel and return home with the bitter conviction that the U.S. has clearly violated its neutrality in its treatment of the *Juncal.* "I shall endeavor to dissuade him from this course," Ogden promises. "But as is naturally the case of all new governments, he feels most sensibly everything which can by any possibility be construed into an insult upon his flag which represents her sovereignty." LS. DNA, RG59, Misc. Letters (M179, R66). For further details in the case of the *Juncal,* see Nathaniel Williams to Clay, May 3, May 16, May 23, 1828, in DNA, RG59, Misc. Letters (M179, R66); also Clay to Williams, May 19, May 22, 1828, in DNA, RG59, Dom. Letters (M40, R20). Captain Cesar Fournier's protests and complaints are in Fournier to Clay, May 21, May 26, 1828, in DNA, RG59, Misc. Letters (M179, R66).

On June 5, U.S. District Attorney Nathaniel Williams, writing from Baltimore, reported to Clay that at a preliminary hearing on June 4, the judge had dismissed the U.S. government's case against the *Juncal* and restored the vessel to its claimants, noting that the vessel's activities had been "directed against their lawful enemies, the Brazilians," and that there was "not sufficient ground for the charge of piracy." ALS. DNA, RG59, Misc. Letters (M179, R66).

To ROBERT WICKLIFFE   Washington, May 24, 1828

The variety in their modes of attack, and the industry of my enemies, are remarkable, if not always commendable. I observe that some of them, about Lexington, have carefully searched the records of Fayette, and extracted from them a formidable list of mortgages, which are paraded as evidence of my bankruptcy. The fairness of this proceeding, in my absence, on arduous public service, and without inquiry into the fact whether the mortgages be extinguished or not, is submitted to my fellow-citizens of Fayette. I do not consider that a man who honestly fulfils his pecuniary engagements, as entitled to any special praise, or I would not observe, that I can confidently appeal to all with whom I ever had pecuniary transactions, to bear testimony of the fidelity with which I have discharged mine. I invite the severest scrutiny into my conduct, in that respect, and request a comparison of it with that of any one of those who now assail me. I never was sued in my life for an uncontested debt—indeed I have no recollection, at this time, of having ever been sued for any ascertained debt, contested or uncontested, and whether I was principal or endorser.

[Mr. Clay then speaks of a heavy responsibility, incurred about ten years ago, as endorser for his friends—and proceeds—]

To that cause is to be attributed my temporary retirement from public life [2:795; 3:54, 548–9], and the renewal of my professional labors. I then resolved not to endorse for others, except in extraordinary cases, and not to ask others to endorse for me: and that, when it became necessary for me to give security, to pledge, in the form of mortgages, that estate which was the ultimate resource of my creditors. Hence the greater number of mortgages which have been recently so malignantly exposed to the public observation. Most of them have been long since satisfied. Among this number is one for a debt of $20,000 [2:795, 877], for the payment of which you had kindly become my surety, every cent of which has long since been discharged. There are not [sic, now] subsisting mortgages upon my estate to the amount of ten thousand dollars; and before the year expires I hope there will not remain more than one-fifth of that sum.[1] I have hitherto met all my engagements [4:38] by the simplest of processes, that of living within my income, punctually paying interest when I could not pay principal, and carefully preserving my credit.

I am not free, absolutely, from debt. I am not rich. I never coveted riches. But my estate would, even now be estimated at not much less than 100,000 dollars. Whatever it may be worth, it is a gratification to me to know that it is the produce of my own honest labor, no part of it being hereditary, except one slave, who would oblige me very much if he would accept his freedom. It is sufficient, after paying all my debts, to leave my family above want, if I should be separated from them. It is a matter also of consolation to me to know, that this wanton exposure of my private affairs can do me no pecuniary prejudice. My few creditors will not allow their confidence in me to be shaken by it. It has indeed led to one incident, which was at the same time a source of pleasure and of pain. A friend lately called on me, at the instance of other friends, and informed me, that they were apprehensive that my private affairs were embarrassed, and that I allowed their embarrassment to prey upon my mind. He came, therefore, with their authority, to tell me, that they would contribute any sum that I might want to relieve me. The emotions which such a proposition excited can be conceived by honorable men. I felt most happy to be able to undeceive them, and to decline their benevolent proposition. . . .

Copy. Lexington *Kentucky Reporter,* June 11, 1828; reprinted in *Niles' Register* (June 28, 1828), 34:295–6.   1. For Clay's financial difficulties, also occasioned partly by the panic of 1819 and the depression that followed, see Van Deusen, *Clay,* 152–3.

From SIDNEY BREESE   Washington, May 25, 1828

I called on [you] yesterday to take my leave of you but you were engaged. Deprived of the pleasure of a personal interview with you, I have thought proper to say a few words to you by letter previous to my departure, of which, I am now on the eve. In my last letter to you from Illinois I took the liberty of making some suggestions for your consideration, one of which I am satisfied could not be complied with. The other, in relation to a survey of the national road in *our* state the bidding I am in, I hope may meet with some attention. It will be said by our opponents that the government never intended to extend that road to the Bank of the Mississippi, and that the *only* way to effect that most desirable object is to elect Genl. Jackson. If possible, let the people have some evidence that we are in reality friends of that measure and determined to cary it on to the proposed extent, and that speedily. I have great hopes of our State—we will to a man do our duty and struggle zealously in support of a Cause in which is involved, in my opinion the durability of our institutions. Your friends are and will be active, and though we have much to contend against, we *count* on victory.

One thing, in the event of success, must, your friends think, be done, that is, the removal of Gov. [Shadrach] Bond & Edward Humphreys from their offices at Kaskaskia. They are both positions of [Elias Kent] Kane and hostile to the administration. Judge [Jesse Burgess] Thomas does not think that Mr. Humphreys is, I live in the same town with him and have every reason to know he is—I have no interest in their removal other than the desire to see your friends strengthened and promoted, and your enemies placed, where they should be—out of place and out of power.

I received a letter from Col. [Thomas] Mather[1] dated Philadelphia, in which he informed me he desired an appointment at the Lead Mines. I hope he may obtain it, he is a staunch and efficient friend, and will do much for us in that quarter. He will take our press there and inform the public mind on those topics they are now ignorant of. That is the most important point in our state and *must* not be neglected. The vote of that region of Country, will decide the vote of our state, and there needs only the *means* in the power of some few intelligent and lively friends to bring it in the right direction.

I am well satisfied of your friendship and disposition to do all in your power consistently with your sense of propriety to promote your friends, and I feel assured that those in our state will not be passed over.

I hope to have the pleasure of receiving a letter from you, so soon as your public business and health (which I trust will be soon restored) will permit. In closing permit me to wish you all success and to subscribe myself your friend "through evils and through good report."[2]

ALS. DLC–HC (DNA, M212, R3). Written from Brown's Hotel. Letter marked "(confidential)." 1. Sometime Illinois state legislator, Thomas Mather (1795–1853) at this time was serving as an Adams–appointed commissioner to locate a military road from Independence, Mo. to Sante Fe, and to conclude permissive easement treaties with Indian tribes along the way. Bateman and Selby, *Historical Encyclopedia of Illinois and History of Morgan County*, 356. 2. A misquotation of 2 Corinthians, 6:8.

From PETER B. PORTER   Black Rock, N.Y., May 25, 1828

It has been my calculation, as I have before apprised you, to make a journey to Washington with Maj. [Joseph] Delafield, soon after the adjournment of of [*sic*] Congress, for the purpose of closing our [Boundary] commission accounts [2:162], and also to take the advice of the Government, whither I ought to make a supplemental report, or have any further agency in the business of the Commission.

Having learnt that Congress will adjourn tomorrow, & having been recently appointed a delegate to the Administration Convention to be held at Albany on the 10th of June, my present arrangement is to attend that convention, & thence proceed immediately to Washington. But I perceive, with much regret, by the last papers, that your health is bad, in consequence of which it will be necessary for you to devote two or three months to relaxation—Of course, I may not find you at Washington as late as the 15th of June, by about which time my arrangement would bring me there.

Will you have the goodness, on the receipt of this, to drop me a line at Albany, advising me when you will probably leave Washington, and what will be your destination? I hope you may find it convenient to visit our State, the climate of which, during the warm months, would, I am persuaded, be favourable to your health.

Mrs Porter will leave home, next week, for Kentucky where she has some pecuniary affairs to settle for herself and son; and I propose to return by way of Lexington, to accompany her home. As you probably intend to visit Kentucky I wish it might so happen that you leave there about the time we do, & return with us by way of Black Rock. It would give me great pleasure to accompany you as far as Albany, where our Legislature meet again on the 9th of September, and where your friends would be much gratified to see you.

Our political prospects continue to be fair, especially in the western & northern parts of the State which constitute its principal strength. Judging of the Character of our proposed Convention, from the partial information I now possess of the names of the delegates returned, I anticipate that it will be most respectable & imposing. . . . [P.S.] I cannot forbear to repeat the hope that you will make a tour through our State, and be at Albany while the Legislature are in Session.

ALS. InU.

To PETER B. PORTER   Washington, May 25, 1828

You were yesterday nominated to the Senate as Secy. of War. You will be confirmed tomorrow.[1] I need not tell you how agreeable this arrangement is to me. I hope you will not hesitate to accept and come to us as soon as you can. I shall leave this place for Kentucky in about three weeks, and should be happy to see you here before I go, if convenient. You might come hither, get installed and return afterwards in the summer to Black Rock. [Samuel L.] Southard will be charged with the duties of the office, ad interem, as [James] Barbour immediately retires to prepare for his voyage.[2] The whole arrangement, in respect to him and you, has given great satisfaction.

Barbour wishes to sell his house and furniture to you. The house cost him, I think $9000. My opinion is that it is a fair price; and if you should think proper to buy, you would have nothing to do but to take his place in Bank. The furniture is in good taste.

[Alexander] McCoomb [sic, Macomb] was yesterday confirmed by the Senate (26 to 12) as Major General.

Mrs. Clay joins me in respects to Mrs. Porter. Tell her that we all desire her presence and society. P.S. Southard was appointed by Barbour president of the Board of Visiters at West point. He now hesitates but will probably go.

ALS. NBuHi. Letter marked "(Private and Inofficial)." 1. Clay to Porter, May 27, 1828. 2. To England, to take up his duties as U.S. Minister. Clay to Barbour, June 3, 1828.

To CHARLES PINKNEY, May 26, 1828. States that, because of Pinkney's failing health, the President has named Beaufort T. Watts his successor as Secretary to the American Minister in St. Petersburg, Henry Middleton. Expresses, on behalf of Adams, the hope that Pinkney will recover and be able to resume public employment "whenever a suitable occasion may present itself." ALI. DLC–HC (DNA, M212, R8).

Informs Watts that the Senate has approved his appointment as Secretary to the U.S. Legation in St. Petersburg and that his salary will be $2000 per annum. Clay to Watts, May 29, 1828. ALS. *Ibid.* On June 13, Clay wrote to William Willinck, Jr., "Bankers of the United States for this Department in Amsterdam," authorizing him to honor requests of Watts to draw his salary. LS. ScHi.

In a letter to Clay of June 4, written from Baltimore, Pinkney pointed out: "Having, after a severe and painful indisposition, retrieved my health, I beg you to consider me as a Candidate for public employment." ALS. DNA, RG59, A. and R. (MR3). Writing again on June 17, Pinkney notes that "There are, I believe, some vacancies in the Legations in South America. Should the President think fit to send me there I should be ever grateful to him and to yourself." Assures Clay that his health has improved and that "I can discharge my duties with the zeal they require." ALS. *Ibid.* Clay endorsed this letter, instructing Daniel Brent to inform Pinkney that there were no vacancies at present, but that when one occurs his application "will receive freindly consideration."

To ALVA WOODS   Washington, May 26, 1828
I have received information from Lexington that the impression you have left there is highly favorable to you, and that much solicitude is felt

that you should accept your appointment.[1] I have no doubt of the practicability of reviving the Institution with suitable exertions.

Copy. In [Alva Woods], *Literary and Theological Addresses of Alva Woods, D.D.*, 389.   1. As President of Transylvania University.

From C.D.E.J. BANGEMAN HUYGENS, Washington, May 27, 1828. Informs Clay that Edouard Bouiller, a native of Paris who had worked in his employ as a domestic, but had recently been discharged for misconduct, had attacked Auguste Petitjean, maitre d'Hotel to Huygens, in the street. Notes that Petitjean, a French native, had been struck in the head with a leaded cane and that the blow might have been lethal had Petitjean's hat not cushioned it. Brings this altercation to Clay's attention and hopes that justice will be done. ALS, in French. DNA, RG59, Notes from Netherlands Legation, vol. 1 (M56, R1). Trans. by Jean Charron.

On June 27, Huygens assured Clay that Bouiller was no longer in his employ and that he would not intervene in the man's behalf. *Ibid.*

From ALEXANDER H. EVERETT, Madrid, no. 104, May 27, 1828. Transmits translated copy of treaty between Spain and the Ottoman Empire, the object of which "is to open to Spanish vessels the trade to the Black Sea." Says this was stipulated in the Treaty of Ackerman [5:937]. LS. DNA, RG59, Dip. Disp., Spain, vol. 29 (M31, R29). Received August 4, 1828. The treaty is found in George F. DeMartens, *Nouveau Reçueil De Traites De L'Europe.* 19 vols. (A. Gottinque, 1829), 7:496–505.

From ROBERT MONROE HARRISON, British Brig, *Margaret,* off St. Thomas, May 27, 1828. Forwards "many additional notes and remarks" relative to his investigation of the West Indies trade. Is unable to furnish a correct list from the Custom House in Jamaica [where he was detained for almost a month] of imports from Europe, "since the colonial ports were closed to our flag." Confesses that he was misinformed concerning the European trade with the West Indies, as supposedly "vessels were arriving daily in that colony [Jamaica] . . . laden with everything which formerly came from U States and that no injury whatsoever had occurred from the no[n]-intercourse." Observes that "not a vessel came in . . . from Continental Europe" in a month, but goods came from Cuba and St. Thomas. Declares the passage to St. Thomas from Europe is "as long as sixty days and seldom less than thirty, the freights enormous, with double port charges." Criticizes "the theorists and the enemies of America in England & Elsewhere." Asserts: "The colonies are american Islands and it has been so ordained by nature that they should be dependent for their wants at least, (if not otherwise) on the US and from which they will (in spite of Parliamentary acts or orders in council) continue to receive them directly or indirectly." Copy. DNA, RG59, Dip. Disp., Special Agents, (M37, R9).   No date of receipt.

To PETER B. PORTER   Washington, May 27, 1828
I have the pleasure to inform you that your nomination as Secretary of War was yesterday confirmed by the Senate. An opposition was made to

302

it, I understand, by Mr. [John H.] Eaton, on the ground of the Address lately signed by you, as Chairman, at Albany.[1] Ten others concurred with him, on that or some other ground, in voting against you, but the nomination was supported by twenty two affirmative votes.[2] The President wrote you on the subject yesterday, and intended to have sent your commission with his letter. It was not then forwarded, for the want of some official form, and I now have the pleasure of transmitting it with this letter.[3]

Mr. [James] Barbour, who was just now with me, tells me that he would be glad to dispose of both his house and furniture to you, and that as he owes for them in bank, you can, by taking his place there, obtain them, if you wish to do so. . . .

LS. NBuHi. 1. At the March 26 meeting of the friends of Adams. Porter to Clay, February 13, March 26, 1828. 2. U.S. Sen. *Journal*, 20 Cong., 1 Sess., 500–01. Eaton's remarks on this point, if any, are not reported in the *Register of Debates*. 3. Not found. On June 21, Porter announced that having decided to accept the post, he had on this date taken the oath of office. Porter to Clay, June 21, 1828. Copy. DNA, RG107, Military Books, vol. 12, p. 357.

From LUKE TIERNAN, Baltimore, May 27, 1828. Recounts a "long conversation" with Bishop Benedict Joseph Flaget of Bardstown, Ky., to whom Clay had offered the hospitality of his home when the Bishop arrived in Washington from Baltimore on May 31. Reports that the Bishop will be unable to accept Clay's invitation, but that he "expressed a warm friendship for you and expressed his gratitude for an offer you made him of a loan of four thousand dollars which he declined, owing to the state of the currency and the unsettled and disturbed state of politics then existing." Tiernan informed the Bishop that in Kentucky there existed a political party hostile to "equity and Justice and destructive to the morals of the people, that such was the case with the relief party." To this, Flaget "made no reply but seemed to think seriously on the remark." LS. DLC-HC (DNA, M212, R3). The "political party" mentioned was the Relief or New Court party [3:902].

To NICHOLAS BIDDLE Washington, May 28, 1828
You may have observed in the [Washington *United States*] Telegraph of the 20h. inst. an article taken from a K. paper,[1] in which a formidable array of my mortgages and debts is made with the view of making me out a bankrupt. Among the mortgages are two, one to the Bank of the U.S. to secure payment of $22.000 [2:795, 877], and the other to J[ames]. Harper Cashr. &c.—to secure payment of $1666:66 [3:342]. The latter is wholly discharged. Of the former debt all is paid but about $4000 to meet which there is deposited with the Lexington [Bank of U.S.] office paper payable to me, and which becomes due this fall. I have every reason to anticipate its punctual payment, and thus the entire extinction of the mortgage. The truth is that my private affairs, materially affected by a responsibility which I incurred about 10 years ago, as indorser, have been in a state of progressive improvement since, and now stand better than they have done during any portion of that time. They are such that, if I were to die tomorrow, my resources are abundant to meet all my engagements, and to leave my family comfortable.

I have thought that it might be beneficial to me if you would cause a paragraph to be inserted, in some paper in your City,[2] making concisely the above statement in regard to the two mortgages, or simply saying that a small balance only is due on the large mortgage which paper is in deposit to meet this fall, and that the small one is discharged. It would be no more than an act of justice to add that, in all my relations with the bank, I have practised the greatest fidelity to my engagements; and that whilst most of your Western debtors have been allowed to pay off their debts in property, no such easement was ever extended to or asked by me. I presume the returns from the [Bank] office at Lexington are such as to admit of the insertion of such a paragraph, which might be signed by yourself or Mr. [William] McIlvaine, or be published as upon the authority of the Bank, without any signature.

I do not owe any bank in existence a cent, except the small balance due to the Lexn. office. Instead of being indebted to the Bank of K[entucky]. (which is one of my enumerated creditors) subsequent to the date and after the payment of my mortage to that institution, it became indebted to me to the amount of $10000 for which I actually sued it [3:344–5, 519].

I hope you will excuse the trouble I give you. . . .

ALS. DLC–Nicholas Biddle Papers (DNA, M212, R20). Letter marked "(Private)".
1. Lexington *Kentucky Gazette,* May 9, 1828.   2. Philadelphia *National Gazette,* May 31, 1828. See also Biddle to Clay, May 31, 1828.

From THOMAS L. L. BRENT, Lisbon, no. 70, May 28, 1828. Transmits a translation of the proclamation of the Regent Miguel, issued on May 23, in consequence of the revolution at Oporto, stating "the legal measure . . . will forever crush the revolutionary monster." Adds that this proclamation, offering reasons for the calling of the Cortes, appeals also to "legitimacy," and "to the honor and courage of portug[u]ese soldiers," and concludes with an offer of amnesty.

Mentions the organization of "royal volunteers," a force of 2992 men, to put down the revolt. Understands, however, that the provisional government at Oporto is "full of enthusiasm and confidence." Learns that two regiments are marching toward Oporto, but hears reports of "considerable desertion" from their ranks.

Interprets the decision of the English ambassador and his government in suspending "diplomatick intercourse" with Miguel's government as "a mark of disapprobation of England." States that, if Miguel declares himself King, the English ambassador is ordered "to depart from the country." Asserts that this policy is designed to set an example for other ambassadors. Speculates that such diplomatic pressure may force Miguel to abandon his pursuit of the throne, an act that would result in the restoration of diplomatic functions.

Submits a translation of a decree of Pedro I, King of Brazil, renouncing any claim to the Portuguese Crown [as Pedro IV] and ordering the country to be governed in the name of his daughter, Maria II, with Miguel "as Regent." LS. DNA, RG59, Dip. Disp., Portugal, vol. 8, (M43, R–T7). Received July 26, 1828.

To FRANCIS T. BROOKE   Washington, May 28, 1828

I sent the documents to you by mail requested in your favor of 20th. inst. My intention is to leave this place in about a fortnight on my contemplated journey which I propose taking through the valley of Virginia, by the White Sulphur Springs and thence by the Crab Orchard to Kentucky. I shall not return to the city until late in July or early in August. If I do not then find myself entirely re-established, I will go to some of the Sea Baths.

The last appointments of the President have given general satisfaction, as far as I have heard. I do not think that that a better arrangement could have been made. We shall loose [*sic,* lose] no strength in the Cabinet by the introduction of [Peter B.] Porter.

Our information from K. continues to be very encouraging. We must be greatly deceived if [Thomas] Metcalfe should not be elected by a respectable majority.

I hope you were pleased with the address of our friends in Congress to the people on the prospects of the election.[1]

Copy. DLC-TJC (DNA, M212, R13).   1. Printed in the Washington *Daily National Journal,* May 27, 1828.

From ALBERT GALLATIN, New York, May 28, 1828. With reference to the legal status of instructions to Richard Rush on various diplomatic questions at issue with Great Britain, when Rush served as U.S. Minister in London, argues that instructions from a government to its ministers abroad are "not Acts of a public nature," and that only the publication of such instructions by the government can "convert" such documents into public property; nor can a "confidential communication" by the Executive to the U.S. Senate be considered a "publication by Government." Maintains, therefore, that "the pamphlet printed for the use of the Senate [5:475-6] which contains the instructions to Mr. [Richard] Rush" is not a public document; hence, the British request that the pamphlet be introduced formally into the Northeast boundary arbitration proceedings should be resisted, even though a copy of the pamphlet is already in their possession.

Discusses at length the details of the grant of land to Dartmouth College as this bears on British claims; also the background of earlier U.S. legislation and regulations pertaining to the boundaries of Vermont, Maine, New Hampshire, and Massachusetts. Asks that copies of such legislative acts be sent to him. Notes that while it is "extremely desirable not to render the question still more complex," the receipt of the "various Acts" will "enable me to judge whether it is necessary to produce any counter-evidence," especially with reference to the New Hampshire boundary "which intervenes between Vermont and Maine," and which was laid out in the years 1737 and 1740. Believes he should also correspond with the governors of Massachusetts, Maine, New Hampshire, and Vermont on these questions "whenever the occasion will require it."

Claims that there is "some want of precision in the manner in which Mr. [Charles] Vaughan has stated the tenor" of Article IV of the 1827

Convention [6:1100–01] to arbitrate the boundary, particularly "in reference to the maps, surveys, or topographical delineations which have been filed with the commissioners under the 5th Article of the Treaty of Ghent." Explains his concern at length. Wonders why Vaughan seems to want the "whole atlas" of previously collected maps "annexed to the first statement and be laid before the Arbiter," since this can only complicate the problem. Remarks that of such maps there were but "few of any real importance to either party, many of them being superseded by the Map *A* as agreed to." Why, then, does Vaughan insist on comparing "the two copies of that Atlas" reposing respectively in London and Washington [Vaughan to Clay, May 15, 1828]? If the "object is to secure the identity of the copy to be delivered to the Arbiter by each party with that now in his possession, the collation and comparison should be made *both* at Washington and in London." Copy. NHi–Gallatin Papers (MR21); also, ALS. DNA, RG76, Northeast Boundary (KyU., Special Roll, frames 63–5).

From AMOS KENDALL, Frankfort, May 28, 1828. Reviews circumstances of Clay's first offer to him of a post in the State Department [4:305–06], one, as he understood it, "in which it would be expected of me to write in support of the administration." Says he could not accept the position under those conditions. Recalls that Clay had told him later that his motives in the matter had been misunderstood, but that "You then offered me a clerkship with $1000 salary, upon the express condition that I should not leave the state until after the Next August [1825] elections [4:718–9, 746–7, 943]." Admits that he had countered with a request for a salary of $1500.

In his accounts of their correspondence on this matter, notes that he has been charged with "contradiction" and "perjury" by Clay's friends in Kentucky and by the Adams administration press in Washington. Asserts that initially it was his "intention to remain neutral in relation to the administration of Mr. Adams, because I was not disposed to give you up," even though the appointment of Rufus King [as Minister to Great Britain] was "obnoxious to me." Reminds Clay, however, that in 1825 in Kentucky "A local controversy [Old Court vs. New Court] of great warmth was raging . . . and I knew you to belong to the party [Old Court] which was seeking my ruin [3:902]. Yet I did not abandon You." Charges that with the victory of the Old Court forces, Clay went on the political and patronage offensive against the New Court people, "the party to which I belonged." This caused some of "your most sincere, perservering, and warm-hearted friends . . . stung to the quick . . . to fall from you, and change their opinion both of your political and private character. No man felt your cold and ungrateful policy more than I did; but I was one of the last to say aught against you." Says he had no choice politically but to "fight or die. In neutrality I should be trampled on by your friends, distrusted by *my own*, and abandoned by every body." States that because of "my former relations with your family," he has had no desire to attack Clay's integrity. Nevertheless, in spite of his continuing personal loyalty, the *Argus* was deprived of its contract to punish the federal laws and the business was instead given to the Frankfort *Commentator*. Charges that "Your motive was cruel; but your act was kind," since it released the *Argus* from having to support the policies of the Adams administration. Affirms, further, that he has "never doubted" that "you and your friends supported Mr. Adams with a view to your own elevation, first to the office of Secretary of State and then to the Presidency." Discusses Clay's manuevers in working out his arrangement with Adams, and demands that he publish his "confidential correspondence" with Francis P. Blair [4:9-11, 46-8] "if your acts and motives" pertaining to your elevation of the post of Secretary of State are other than they appear. Reviews also the circumstances of Clay's loan of $1500 to him in 1825 [4:135-6; 5:334-5], the security he put up for the loan, and his repayment schedule. Complains that Clay's friends "reproach me with not having paid one cent of the debt, when I have already paid more than its original value, and am using every exertion to discharge the balance."

Regrets that a break between them has come. Concludes: "In you I had entire confidence. To no man did I communicate my feelings more freely or fully. For no man, at one time, would I have done so much. I regret, that by your own change of conduct and the avowal of new principles, an alienation was rendered inevitable. . . . In future I shall not suffer myself to be drawn off from exposing the abuses and corruptions of the men in power, by these relentless and perservering attacks on myself. The war shall be carried into the enemy's country, and we shall see who will escape with the least injury from the terrible ordeal which your friends have instituted." Printed in the Frankfort *Argus of Western America*, May 28, 1828.

From WILLIAM B. LAWRENCE, London, no. 40, May 28, 1828. Transmits a circular from the Marquis de Palmela, Portuguese ambassador to Great Britain, addressed to all ministers accredited to the British Court, pointing out that the "legitimate rights" of his sovereign, Pedro IV, have been undermined by the new [Miguel] government in Portugal; this communication was accompanied by a Portuguese note to the British government "which has been regarded as an official notification of the suspension of the functions of the Portuguese Ambassador." In his circular, Palmela "seemingly invites" his colleagues to attest to the fact that "he had strictly followed the line of conduct [to Pedro] which his duty imposed." Lawrence assures Clay that he had done nothing more than acknowledge receipt of Palmela's circular, this in conformity with the "the general policy of the United States with respect to Governments de facto," and because he knows nothing of the views of the President in the matter. Reports, further, that he has learned of Pedro's formal and "unqualified" abdication [5:310] in favor of his daughter, Maria da Gloria, from recent newspaper accounts and from the dispatches of Thomas L. L. Brent from Lisbon. Concludes, by saying that "it is believed by the best informed statesmen that the events of the last eighteen months have had the effect of putting an end to that influence which, for more than a century, has rendered Portugal virtually a Province of the British Empire." LS. DNA, RG 59, Dip. Disp., Great Britain, vol. 35 (M30, R31). Received July 19, 1828.

To WILLIAM HENRY HARRISON Washington, May 29, 1828
I have the honor to inform you that the President, by and with the advice and consent of the Senate, has appointed you Envoy Extraordinary and Minister Plenipotentiary to the Republic of Colombia. The President wishes you to proceed on your mission without unnecessary delay. Your instructions will be immediately prepared, and delivered to you, with your commission, when you are ready to take your departure.

The President allows you an outfit of $9000, according to law, which you have already received, and you will be entitled to a salary at the rate of $9000 per annum, which, according to usage applicable to members of Congress[1] appointed on foreign missions, will commence from the time of your appointment, unless you should unnecessarily prolong the period of your departure, in which case it will commence from the time you leave home to proceed on your mission. Your acceptance of the appointment having been already communicated to me, it will only be necessary for you to keep this Department advised as to the time when you will be ready to depart.

ALS. DLC–William Henry Harrison Papers (DNA, M212, R21).   1. Harrison was U.S. Senator from Ohio at this time.

From WILLIAM PITT PREBLE, Portland, Maine, May 29, 1828. Accepts appointment as a commissioner to prepare the Northeastern boundary dispute for arbitration [6:1100–01], notes that he cannot depart for New Brunswick for at least two weeks, and recommends that John G. Deane, a member of the Maine legislature, a man "inoffensive and unassuming in manner, but shrewd and adroit at collecting facts," be appointed to assist the commissioners. Adds: "The people of this state are all alive, as it were, on the subject of our boundary; and in the interest they feel, lose sight almost of party feelings and preferences. It is peculiarly acceptable to them therefore to see the administration take decisive measures in relation to it."

Requests copies of relevant transactions, reports, and proceedings "for the purpose of reference, but also to enable me fully to possess myself of the present state of the question." LS. DNA, RG76, Northeast Boundary: Misc. Papers, Entry 82, frames 67–9.

Answering Preble on June 12, Clay thanked him for his acceptance of the post and authorized him to employ John G. Deane as an assistant for 90 days at six dollars per day. LS. CSmH.

To GEORGE ROBERTSON, May 29, 1828. Offers him the post of Chargé d'Affairs at Lima, Peru. Declares: "Our commercial relations with Peru are always interesting, but what gives to this mission, at the present time, particular consequence, is the desire which is felt to conclude a commercial treaty with that Republic." LS. DLC–HC (DNA, M212, R8); also in DNA, RG59, Dip. Instr., vol. 12, pp. 108–09 (M77, R7).

Robertson, writing from Lancaster, Ky., declined the offer, citing his "obligations to a large family." ALS. DNA, RG59, Dip. Disp., Peru, vol. 1 (M152, R1). Received June 23, 1828.

From NICHOLAS BIDDLE   Philadelphia, May 30, 1828

I had this morning the pleasure of receiving your favor of yesterday [sic, May 28] during the Session of the Board from which I was not released in time to answer it by the return of the mail. I need not say that it will afford me great satisfaction to assist in refuting the injurious representations of your affairs, which I remember to have seen without reading, as I should have read without believing them. I began by ascertaining from the records of the Bank [of the U.S.], the accuracy of your statement, but as the returns from the offices represent only the debts of the parties, & not the paper which they deposit for collection, I cannot speak on that subject with as much distinctness as I am able to do in regard to the reduction of your debt & your fidelity in complying with your engagements to the Bank. On reflection I think it better not to publish a formal certificate, but to introduce the testimony of the Bank in a manner less direct tho' equally authoritative. With the reasons of this I need not trouble you, tho' I do not doubt that you would concur with me. You will also I hope agree in the opinion that the fittest channel here for such a communication is Mr [Robert] Walsh.[1] The relation in which he stands to the present contest will render his agency more independent & he will give a pungency & force to the contradiction which will probably secure to it a wider circulation than it could obtain through any other of our papers. I have accordingly given to him a statement which he will embody in a paragraph for tomorrow's [Philadelphia *National*] Gazette. You & he I believe do not always agree in the upper regions of politics.—but I regret to see estrangements among those whom I esteem and on this occasion, he will do you justice frankly & cordially. I trust you will be satisfied with the manner in which the subject will be presented[2]. . . .

ALS. DLC–HC (DNA, M212, R3).   1. Robert Walsh was the founder and editor, to 1836, of the Philadelphia *National Gazette*. Frederick Hudson, *Journalism in the United States, 1690–1872* (New York, 1873), 322.   2. See Philadelphia *National Gazette*, May 31, 1828.

From JAMES BROWN   Paris, May 30, 1828

The invasion of Turkey by the Russian forces which has been so long expected has actually taken place. The Russian troops passed the Pruth [sic, Prut] on the evening of the 5 Inst. and accounts dated on the 10 inform us that they had taken possession of Gallatz [sic, Galatz], Jassy, and Bucharest without meeting any resistance. Their march will be pursued to Constantinople unless a degree of resistance on the part of the Porte much stronger than any which existing preparations would lead us to expect, should be encountered, or unless by submitting to any conditions which Russia may dictate he shall avert the blow. On the 30 Ulto. the utmost apathy prevailed at the Turkish Capital, and indeed it is said, that instead of rigorous preparations for defense, complaints were publickly uttered against the policy which had brought the Empire into its present critical condition. The Emperor [Nicholas I], accompanied by the Empress, and Grand Duke Michael, left St Petersburg on the 7th to place himself at the head of the invading army which, it is said, will consist of two hundred thousand men and sixteen hundred pieces of artillery. By an unforseen and truly extraordinary combination of fortunate events, the Emperor has been placed in a situation highly favorable to the accomplishment of his plan of aggrandizement. He has now a right to require, not merely that France and England shall abstain from assisting the Porte, but also that that they shall effectually cooperate with Russia in obtaining the objects of the Treaty of the 6th. of July [6:780-2]. Austria finding herself too feeble to interpose, makes a merit of necessity, and affects to place the most unbounded confidence in the just and moderate policy of the Russian Emperor. Prussia has declared that she will maintain a neutral position, so that Russia and Turkey will be the only belligerents except in so far as the influence of England and France in favor of the Greeks may lead to hostilities. It being pretty generally admitted that Russia will extend her territory by this war, and that no European power will interpose for the present to prevent it, France and England are preparing to profit from the state of things which may grow out of this great event. In both countries means are adopted to give to their Marine a more formidable attitude, and measures are in train here to increase their standing army. Additional ships of war with a few thousand men have been sent by both nations to the Morea, the blockade has been rendered more strict; and it is now reputed that it has been extended to Alexandria, all attempts to detach the [Egyptian] Viceroy [Mohammed Ali] from the Porte having been unsuccessful. The prospects of Greece appear to brighten under the able direction of the Count Capo d'Istria and there is now some reason to hope that order and regular government will prevail in that unhappy country so long subjected to the double scourge of war and intestine factions.

[Discusses recent developments in internal French politics and remarks on the "foolish and proflegrate game" Don Miguel is playing in Portugal, giving it as his opinion that were Miguel to assume the crown "he will be deserted by" all the sovereigns of Europe and will certainly "ruin Portugal," even to the extent of provoking "a civil war." Mentions the replacement of the recently deceased Daniel Sheldon as Secretary of Legation, and fears that the event might cause him to prolong his stay in Paris until his successor arrives. Comments that his wife's health has improved and that he would be willing to remain at his post until Spring. Continues:]

I was really shocked at reading in an English newspaper this morning an account of a brutal attack made in the Capitol by [Russell] Jarvis one of the Editors of the [Washington *United States*] Telegraph on young Mr [John] Adams.[1] If General Jackson's friends commence in this strain of violence and outrage, we shall have a stormy time of it during his administration should he be elected. Will not acts like these open the eyes of the people and rally them around an administration which has been at once wise, firm, and prudent? I hope you will not go to Kentucky where I apprehend some tragic scenes will be acted in the month of August. You have many friends there but also some very bitter enemies.

Your life is of great importance to your family and you ought not rashly to expose it to danger. I presume Mr Adams is sure of a majority in that state. Our latest reports from New York are encouraging and yet the result is generally considered very doubtful. I have heard from Louisiana and am convinced that Mr Adams will obtain all the votes of that state.

I have been advised by our Physicians that the sea air and sea bathing would be beneficial to Mrs. Brown, and as I shall not obtain for some weeks an answer from the Count de la Ferronnays on the subject of our claims, I have sometimes a thought of passing two weeks about the last of June or beginning of July at Dieppe which is not more than a days ride from Paris. Should my experience of the effects of the waters be encouraging I may come up to Paris and write to you, so that not more than one Packet will leave Havre without a letter from me. We have now been nearly two years in this city without having left it for a day except on a visit of two nights to General Lafayette on the occasion of his grandaughters marriage.[2] The greater part of the Diplomatique corps leaves Paris every summer—[Christopher] Hughes it is said wishes to come on here to make a speech on the 4 July, and as I am as little inclined to parade as he is fond of it, he may be the great man of the day if he thinks fit. He is very anxious to be made a Minister and perhaps expects that if General Jackson is made President he may through the influence of his father in law[3] be sent to some more important court. [Samuel] Smith writes me making strong professions of neutrality but I can as I think perceive that he is not very friendly to the President. I do not know whether his influence is of much importance in the question. He told me in one of his late letters that the Osages [Indians] and their French guide had played upon the credulity of Hughes and myself— that [Thomas H.] Benton had told him that they were not Chiefs but had come to France to be exhibited for money. I assured him that I had known what they were and for what purpose they came out the moment they had reached Paris—that I had even read their contract—that I had taken no notice of them except that when they called at my house, uninvited, one morning, I had given them some refreshments but had expressed my disapprobation of their speculation and given them my advice to return immediately—I assured him that I had invited no company to meet them made them no *speeches* nor given them any letters of recommendations—I added that Mr Hughes was better able to say how far he had been deceived than I could say for him, but that as they had been exhibited at all the low theatres and inferior gardens at Paris, before they went to Brussels, I thought he must have known that they were a miserable set of strollers unworthy of his notice.

[Concludes with observations on his vouchers and accounts and his difficulty in communicating directly with St. Petersburg from Paris. Reports that William Huskisson and Lord Palmerston have "gone out of the Ministry."]

ALS. DLC-HC (DNA, M212, R3). Printed in *LHQ*, 24:1103–08.   1. For Jarvis, see *CAB*. John Adams was the son of and private secretary to John Quincy Adams. An account of the assault is in Adams, *Memoirs*, 7:508.   2. Louise de la Tour-Maubourg married the Comte Hector Perrone di San Martino in July, 1827.   3. Samuel Smith of Baltimore, Md.

From **WILLIAM B. LAWRENCE,** London, no. 41, May 30, 1828. Reports a shakeup in the Duke of Wellington's cabinet and the departure therefrom of William Huskisson, the Colonial Secretary, Lord Dudley, the Foreign Minister, and Lord Palmerston, the Secretary of War. Speculates at length on possible motives in the resignations, on the names of those who might fill the vacancies, and on the outcome of the continuing debate on the Corn Bill. Notes that the U.S. need have "no particular reason to regret the recent changes," save that the adjustments have slowed progress in pursuing the diplomatic objectives of the nation. Characterizes Dudley as "deficient both in industry and decision." Proposes calling on the new Foreign Minister, possibly Lord Aberdeen, as soon as he enters upon his duties, to take up again the selection of an arbiter in the Northeast Boundary dispute [6:1100–01] and the problem of the "personal liberty of an American citizen [John Baker, 6:1272–3]." On these matters, "I shall ask an early answer." Adds, in a postscript, additional information for the Agricultural Society of South Carolina on British duties on rice. LS, with postscript in Lawrence's hand. DNA, RG59, Dip. Disp., Great Britain, vol. 35 (M30, R31). Received July 26, 1828. Original without postscript received July 19, 1828.

From **W. THARP,** Washington, May 30, 1828. Announces his vigorous support of Adams's presidential candidacy. Laments that the very nature of "Politics . . . a reckless green eyed monster," has placed Clay "at the striking point" of abuse by the Jacksonians, and warns that the time has come to counterattack "your foulest accusers." Urges, specifically, that Clay "hurl the Postmaster Genl [John McLean] & his nest of conspirators from the *temple* & fill it with them who will serve the good cause," since "this is the strong hold, the Citadel & head quarters of your enemies, its baneful influence extends from one end of this vast territory to the other." Lose this opportunity and "*you give up the Ship,*" he adds. Claims also that he can "produce you a signature" that will clearly prove that the Postmaster General has been "carrying on, the most foul and extensive depredations on the public treasure with their mail contracts," and that his informant had been pressured to withdraw a particular bid, in return for which "they would give him appointment & other advantages." Notes, however, that his informant refused to "contend with this influence." Concludes with a report of his own activities against the candidacy of Jackson and his efforts to "put it to him under the fifth rib." ALS. DLC–HC (DNA, M212, R3).

From **BEAUFORT T. WATTS,** Washington, May 30, 1828. Reports on his continuing effort to secure restitution for three American vessels and their cargoes taken by a Colombian privateer [4:122–3, 654]. Recalls that in conducting this inquiry in 1824, he had traveled to Caracas to express "the views of my government," but had discovered that "the [ships'] property . . . was Spanish and was condemned" by Colombian ordinances.
    Is dismayed by the fact that the correspondence between "the late Mr. [Richard C., Jr.] Anderson and the then Minister of Foreign Affairs

312

at Bogota [Joseph R. Revenga]" ultimately resulted in Colombia's refusal to "make indemnity." ALS. DNA, RG59, Dip. Disp., Colombia, vol. 4 (M–T33, R4). Received June 9, 1828.

From NICHOLAS BIDDLE   Philadelphia, May 31, 1828
You will see in the [Philadelphia] National Gazette of today the paragraph on the subject of the mortgages.[1] In my note to you yesterday I remarked that not receiving from the offices the list of paper deposited for collection, I could not speak so distinctly on that point as on the others. And accordingly in my memorandum to Mr [Robert] Walsh I stated that for the present amount of your debt—funds, *it was understood* were already deposited &c &c   I perceive that Mr. Walsh in remoulding the article has omitted the qualification. This is not of much consequence for I have of course no doubt of the fact because it comes from you,[2] but I could not speak of it as of my own personal knowledge from documents in the Bank [of the U.S.]—, & recur to it now, that you may understand precisely my note of yesterday

The article will I think be satisfactory to [missing name] & your friend.[3]

ALI, draft. DLC–Nicholas Biddle Papers (DNA, M212, R20).   1. Clay to Biddle, May 28, 1828.   2. The phrase, "since you mentioned it," is struck through and is replaced by "because it comes from you."   3. Words "& your friend," are struck through.

From THOMAS L. L. BRENT, Lisbon, no. 71, May 31, 1828. Observes that the court and the ultraroyalist party are determined to resist the constitutionalist uprising in Oporto. Learns that the nobility is urging Prince Miguel to "go out at the head of his troops and insist upon accompanying him into the field." Remarks on the generally warm reception Miguel is receiving in his trips around the city.

Reports that the provisional government at Oporto has appointed "heads of departments, governors of Provinces and other civil and military officers." States that the Oporto regime has "eight or nine thousand troops of the line," and estimates Miguel's forces at about "four to five thousand men."

Notes the instructions to the English ambassador, Sir William A'Court, the originals of which A'Court sent to the Foreign Minister, the Viscount of Santarem. These "spoke of the conduct of the Prince in the strongest terms." Laments that this protestation "produced little effect." Indeed, when coupled with other objections of the diplomatic corps at Lisbon, it will not prevent a tentative meeting of the Cortes on June 6 which may well, according to strong rumor, support Miguel as King. LS. DNA, RG59, Dip. Disp., Portugal, vol. 8 (M43, R–T7). Received August 4, 1828.

From JOHN CUTHBERT, Hamburg, May 31, 1828. Continues defense of his conduct in office, and declares "that there has not been a single seaman in distress . . . that has not been immediately taken charge of" during the nearly nine years he has held the post. Has also paid for sick seamen's expenses in hospitals with his own funds. Mentions his strict attention to duty, having not been "out of the walls of the city" in nearly four years. LS. DNA, RG59, Cons. Disp., Hamburg, vol. 3 (M–T211, R3). Received September 1, 1828.

From CHARLES EDMONSTON, Charleston, S. C., May 31, 1828. Thanks Clay for putting him in possession of the note, with enclosures [Vaughan to Clay, February 21, 1828], of the British Minister with reference to the claim for salvage of the schooner *Nimble* [Morrison to Clay, January 5, 1828; Edmondston to Clay, January 25, 1828]. Reports that the vessel was worth $12,000 and that she carried on board $9,000 worth of gold dust and other valuable stores when she grounded. Feels that her $5,000 salvage claim was "quite moderate." Solicits Clay's "continued attention" to the claim and hopes that the whole *Guerrero–Nimble* matter will soon be adjusted. ALS. DNA, RG59, Misc. Letters (M179, R66).

To CHARLES HAMMOND   Washington, May 31, 1828
I am not sure that you have not given me the best, as I know it is the most friendly advice in your letter of the 5h. inst. And yet I cannot at present pursue it. Such is my destiny! [Philip S.] Physic[k] and [Nathaniel] Chapman believe that my frame is free from any organic defect; that I have been only overtasked; and that a long tranquil journey will re-establish my health. I shall make the experiment and be guided here after by the result. Of one thing you and my other friends may rest assured that I never will remain in any office to the discharge of the duties of which I may be incompetent, from physical causes.

The system of our opponents is to attack every prominent man in our party. None of you escape. The President, [Daniel] Webster and myself have borne the brunt. Webster has more than ever attached me to him by his disinterested and manly conduct, in respect to the mission to England.[1] I wish you would occasionally, in some suitable manner, defend him against the vile assaults aimed at him. He would take it kindly and it would otherwise have good effect.

All are now gazing upon Kentucky. If we succeed there [6:360–3], I do not entertain a particle of doubt as to the general issue.

ALS. InU. 1. Webster, the President's original choice for this post, was shunted aside because of controversy over the so–called "Adams pledge." This involved charges in the Jackson press that Webster has supported Adams in the 1824 election in return for political office. Thus Adams decided that "the moment was unfavorable" for Webster's appointment. Wiltse, *Papers of Daniel Webster,* 2:302. James Barbour was sent instead.

From BASIL HALL, Washington, [Early June, 1828]. Asks, on the eve of commencing his travels in North America, that Clay help him secure the 1827 annual reports on revenues and expenditures issued by the legislatures of the several states. Says he wants "to get at the real truth in all matters connected with this country." Thanks Clay for his "hearty frankness, & confidence on occasions of real importance," and hopes he will also let him see a copy of "your Speech on the Colonization question [6:83–97] to which you alluded the other Even[in]g." LS. DLC–HC (DNA, M212, R6). Hall's tour resulted in his *Travels in North America in the Years 1827 and 1828,* 3 vols. Edinburgh, 1829. For Captain Basil Hall, R.N., whose "frank criticism of American customs excited the utmost

314

indignation" in the U.S., see *DNB*. For the approximate dating of this letter, see Hall, *Travels*, 3:392.

To NICHOLAS BIDDLE
Washington, June 1, 1828

I am greatly obliged by your prompt attention to my request relative to my engagements with the B. U. S. as evinced in your letter of the 30h. Ulto. The mode which you suggest of bearing testimony to the fidelity with which I have observed them, and the medium through which you intend to have the fact promulgated are perfectly satisfactory. Although there has not been yet time for Mr. [Robert] Walsh's paper [Philadelphia *National Gazette*] to reach me, I have no doubt that the contemplated paragraph will contain all that is material.[1] I am not disposed to believe that gentleman ever designed me positive injustice, or that he can be actuated by any unfriendly feeling towards me, although he and I may differ as to the rules which should regulate my public conduct.

ALS. DLC–Nicholas Biddle Papers (DNA, M212, R20).   1. Biddle to Clay, May 30 and May 31, 1828.

To NICHOLAS BIDDLE
Washington, June 2, 1828.

I have before me your favor of the 31st. Ulto. and I have seen the paragraph in Mr. [Robert] Walsh's paper [Philadelphia *National Gazette*], which is perfectly satisfactory and for which I feel much indebted to both of you.

Mr. Walsh's statement of the fact, respecting the deposit of paper to discharge the balance of my debt, at the Lexington office [of the Bank of the U.S.], is stronger than I expected and stronger than it should have been, according to any information which you officially possess. But it is nevertheless conformable to the truth. The statement, however, shall in no event operate to the prejudice of the Bank.

ALS. DLC–Nicholas Biddle Papers (DNA, M212, R20).

From THOMAS L. L. BRENT, Lisbon, June 2, 1828. Announces that the party of Prince Miguel has gained advantage in the Algarve, but that "the organization of the royalist guard progresses very slowly." Reports that, regarding the proposed meeting of the Cortes on June 6, Miguel "will defer for a time taking the title of King as immense number of arrests are made." Notes that "the Police have endeavored to arrest those Peers who refused to sign" the address of the nobility in support of Miguel, but "fortunately they have all escaped." Adds in a postscript that the Prince has formally announced that "he would place himself at the head of the army." ALS. DNA, RG59, Dip. Disp., Portugal, vol. 8 (M43, R–T7). Received August 9, 1828.

From FRANCIS T. BROOKE
Richmond, June 2, 1828

I was very happy to receive your letter of the 28h ultimo—but Should have been better pleased if you had informed me that your health was improving—nor do you Say whether I am to have the pleasure of Seeing you at St Julien, there is a rumour here that you will take this in your way to Kentucky—and I am informd that Some preparation is making to receive you at the Oaks[1]—you would I have no doubt receive a warm reception here, at least Lynch & [John H.] Pleasants tell me So—Mr [Edward] Bates informed me when here that you were preparing an answer to the Jackson address[2] of the terretory, nothing is now read with avidity but what comes from your pen, and your determination expressed in your Speech at Baltimore [May 13], to visit and inlighten the people in every quarter when Spared from your public duties, has alarmed [Thomas] Ritchie & Co very much, he is I am told hoping that you will be violently attacked and run down, in retaliation for the attacks on [William T.] Barry in Kentuckey [sic]—the address of our freinds in Congress to which you allude[3] is able and will do Some good, Pleasants has in his possession the correspondence between John Randolph & Mrs [Ann Cary Randolph] Morris which you may have heard of[4]—I heard it read on yesterday and it is the most damning attack upon him [Randolph], that has yet been exhibited but he doubts whether he will publish it though I believe he has Mrs Morris permission—you might give him a jog on that Subject, I Shall leave this in the course of the week and Shall be very glad to know when you will leave Washington and your ultimate decision on your rout[e] if possible I will be in Washington by the 15h our friends here are in good Spirits, [Fleming B.] Miller from Botetourt[5] the Son in Law of your friend [James] Calwell, told me yesterday that he was now convinced that Mr Adams [wou]ld be reelected I think many of the opposition here entertain that opinion.... [P.S.] Mr [Tristam] Burgeses [sic, Burges's] two Speeches[6] will (if circulated) make a favorable impression for the American System every where—I wish I had a few copies more of both of them—

ALS. InU.   1. Probably "Merry Oaks," owned by Hector Davis of Hanover, Va.
2. Clay to Brooke, June 5, 1828.   3. Brooke to Clay, May 28, 1828.   4. This correspondence dealt with an earlier sex scandal involving Randolph's cousin, Ann Cary Randolph (Mrs. Gouverneur) Morris, and Randolph's two brothers. See William C. Bruce, *John Randolph of Roanoke*, 2 vols. (New York, 1922) 2:274-95.   5. Robert Stoner, *A Seed-Bed of the Republic, Early Botetourt* (Radford, Va., 1962), 439.   6. Rep. Tristam Burges of R.I. His speech in the House, specifically on the wool and woolens tariff, was delivered on March 29, 1828; that on the tariff in general was given on April 21. Both were published in pamphlet form.

To ALBERT GALLATIN   Washington, June 2, 1828

Your letters of the 23d and 28th ult have been received. Mr. [William P.] Preble's instructions were forwarded to him some days ago, with instructions to proceed to New Brunswick. I expect to return to this city early in August, and shall remain here unless the then state of my health should require my absence.

The difference in the phraseology between the first and second paragraphs of the third article of the Convention [6:1100-01] had not escaped my observations. To obviate any cavil which might arise out of it, I intend to have the demands for papers, which it authorizes, made both at Washington and London, within the proscribed period.

You will consider yourself authorized to correspond with the Governors of any of the States on the subject of your agency, with the view of procuring authentic copies of any public documents, or other information. As to the Governor of Massachusetts [Levi Lincoln], I have anticipated your wishes, by requesting that he would furnish copies of any documents or information that you may apply for. The Governor of the other States, with whom you may desire to correspond, will, doubtless attend to your wishes, without any special request proceeding directly from this Department.

I sent you a copy of the report of the Secretary of State of Massachusetts, respecting the documents for which application was made to him.[1]

LS. NHi–Gallatin Papers (MR15). 1. On the same day, June 2, Clay acknowledged receipt of Gallatin's letter of May 19, authorized him to travel to Albany or Boston to make "researches connected with your agency," and urged his close cooperation with Preble "in the execution of the joint agency confided to you both." LS. NHi–Gallatin Papers (MR20).

To JOHN McLEAN   Washington, June 2, 1828

I have received your letter of the 31st. ulto.,[1] stating the inconvenience to the General Post Office, resulting from the occupation of a part of the building appropriated to its use by the Patent Office, and offering to rent the house, formerly used by Congress, on Capitol hill, for the accommodation of the Patent Office, and to pay the rent out of the funds of the Post Office.—

I regret that you should be subjected to any inconvenience from the Patent Office, and, if I possessed any legitimate means to obviate it, I would use them with pleasure. But Congress was apprized, prior to its late adjournment, of the condition of both Offices, and it seems it was not thought proper to make any adequate provision for them. The mode, you suggest, of renting the house on Capitol Hill, and paying the rent out of the funds of the Post Office is liable to two objections, the first is, that it would remove the Patent Office an inconvenient distance from the Department of State, and prevent that facility of intercourse, which is necessary to the despatch of the public business; and the other is, that the application of the funds of the General Post Office to the payment of the rent of a building, for the accommodation of another Department is not warranted by law. You Suppose that Congress would sanction such an application of them, but they might not. And, at all events, if the law ought ever to be violated, the case ought to be one of more urgency than any which, I hope, now exists.—

Neither of the above objections would apply, with the same force, to your renting the house on the Hill for some branch of the Post Office establishment. If that should be deemed by you inexpedient, I think it will be best, as the period will not be long, until Congress is again in Session, to do as well as we can, during the intermediate time, and rely upon a satisfactory arrangement being then made.—

Copy. DNA, RG59, Dom. Letters, vol. 22, pp. 212–3 (M40, R20). 1. See McLean to Clay, March 5, 1828.

To BENJAMIN PIERCE   Washington, June 2, 1828

I have the honor to request that Your Excellency will be pleased to cause this department to be furnished with certified copies, duly authenticated, of any grant, or grants, of land, made by the State of New Hampshire to Dartmouth College; and, also, of the act, or acts, of the legislature of New Hampshire relinquishing the claims of that State to territory west of Connecticut river, in favor of the inhabitants of Vermont. These documents are wanted to comply with a demand made by the British Government, in pursuance of the convention [6:1100-01], lately concluded, respecting our Northeastern boundary.[1]

Messrs. [Albert] Gallatin and [William P.] Preble having been appointed agents by the Government of the United States to assist in making preparations for the arbitration provided for by that convention, I have the honor further to request, that if either of them should have occasion to correspond with Your Excellency, on subjects connected with their Agency, you will have the goodness to have proper attention paid to any application they may make.

LS. KyLoF. 1. Similar requests for copies of state-held documents relating to state boundary designations went to Lieutenant Governor (Acting Governor) Nathaniel Pitcher of New York. Clay to Pitcher, June 2, 1828. Copy. DNA, RG59, Dom. Letters, vol. 22, p. 209 (M40, R20). Pitcher complied. Pitcher to Clay, June 12, 1828. ALS. DNA, RG76, Northeast Boundary: Misc. Papers, Env. 4, item 26; and to Levi Lincoln, Governor of Massachusetts. Copy. DNA, RG59, Dom. Letters, vol. 22, p. 211-2 (M40, R20).

From JOSE S. REBELLO, Washington, June 2, 1828. Has learned from a New York newspaper of May 30 that the Customs House in New York has cleared the Buenos Airean warship *Bolivar* for the West Indies. Protests again that this armed vessel was fitted out in the U.S. for a cruise to "make war against . . . Brazil." Seeks assurances for his government that the U.S. government has intervened and that the *Bolivar* is bound instead on a "legal voyage." LS, in Portuguese, with trans. in State Dept. file. DNA, RG59, Notes from Brazilian Legation, vol. 1 (M49, R1).

From JOHN YOUNG, Greenup County, Ky., June 2, 1828. Says he plans to publish in the Maysville *Eagle* "a Question to all Christians thus [:]Is Genl Jackson an Adulterer or not." Notes also that since Luke 16:18 shows that the "Tesimony of mortals dont suffice," Clay must therefore "bear with fortitude the aspersions cast on your well earned reputation" by the "most dangerous monster that has ever appeared in our land." ALS. DLC-HC (DNA, M212, R3).

To JOHN QUINCY ADAMS   Washington, June 3, 1828
The Secretary of State having been directed by the President to report the objects to which the expenditure has been applied, during the years 1825, 1826, 1827, of that portion of the Contingent Fund for Foreign Intercourse, which has been audited at the Treasury, in conformity with the third section of the act of the 1st May, 1810, entitled "An act fixing the compensation of public ministers, and Consuls residing on the coast of Barbary, and for other purposes," so far as those objects can now be disclosed to the public, without prejudice to its interests, has the honor to submit the following statement:

That there was expended and audited, agreeable to the provisions of the above mentioned section in the years

1825 the sum of	$1,700.
1826.	1,666.66
1827.	8,958.01
Making an aggregate of	12,324.67

The whole of this sum was expended in the foreign service of the Government. The sum of $1700, part of it, was paid before the commencement of the present Administration; to wit, $700 on the 4 January, 1825, and $1,000, on the 11 February, 1825. Another part of it, $9124.67 was paid in consequence, and in compensation of services rendered under instructions given by the last Administration. These services related to highly important interests of the United States in the Levant,[1] which were faithfully performed. Their duration was, necessarily, not short; and the only duty which devolved on the present Administration was that of fixing and paying, on the termination of them, the amount of a just compensation. It would not be proper to say more on that subject, at present.

The residue of the above aggregate of $12,324.67, to wit, the sum of $1,500, was paid to the late Daniel P. Cook, Esq. for a confidential service rendered the United States, in relation to the islands of Cuba [6:295–6, 1223].

On the commencement, and during the whole course, of the present administration, no one of the foreign relations of this country has more anxiously engaged the deliberate attention of the Executive, than that of its connexion with, and the possible fortunes of, the islands of Cuba. The great extent of the commerce of the United States with that island; its proximity to our Southern border; the character of its population; the influence which, if it were in the hands of either of certain foreign powers, might be exerted on various interests of the people of the United States and the dangers from without and within, with which it was supposed to be menaced, were well calculated to awaken and keep alive the solicitude of the Executive of the United States. The distracted condition of Spain, and the total reduction of her power on the Continent of America, induced a general expectation that an invasion of the islands would be made, either separately or conjointly, by the forces of some of the New Republics [Mexico, Colombia] which have been organized out of her former American possessions. Information reached the United States of the actual concentration of forces, and the preparation of means, with a view to such an attack. On the other hand, Cuba did not appear to be free from danger on the side of Europe. Large squadrons of two of the greatest maritime powers [Great Britain, France] of that portion of the globe, at different times visited the West Indies, with the purpose, ascribed by rumor to each of them of taking possession and occupying the island. Although contrary assurances from the Governments of both those powers tended to quiet, they did not absolutely remove all, apprehensions on the part of the American Executive [James Monroe]. Whilst the island was thus threatened, on all sides, from without, it was known that a considerable portion of its inhabitants were desirious of breaking the colonial connexion with Spain.

In this critical state of things the American Executive felt itself bound, by the highest and most responsible duties to exert a constant and watchful vigilance. To this cause is to be principally traced several measures of the present Administration. Among others, that presented themselves, was that of deputing a confidential agent [Cook] to Cuba, for the purpose of correctly ascertaining its actual condition. It was desirable that the agent to be selected should be an inhabitant of the valley of the Mississippi, as being the quarter of the Union most interested. Accordingly, on the 7h. day of December, 1825, a letter of appointment and instructions were transmitted to a distinguished citizen [Thomas B. Robertson] of Louisiana, with a request that he would proceed to the islands, and execute the trust offered him [4:882–4]. Although there had been some reason to expect, from indirect information, that he would accept, he declined the appointment. His answer [5:47–8] was received on the 15th day of February, 1826. During the residue of that year, the apprehensions of the Executive, in respect to the fate of Cuba, were somewhat allayed, though they did not entirely subside. It was still deemed an object of sufficient importance to send an agent. And, on the close of the 19th Congress, it being ascertained that the late Mr. Cook would accept the agency, he was accordingly designated. He was recommended by his local position; by his general intelligence; by the integrity of his character; and by his intimate knowledge of the views of the American Government, derived from long participation in its councils. An extract from his instruction, bearing date the 12 March, 1827 [6:295–6], accompanies this report. He was, also, furnished with a letter of introduction to the Captain General of the Islands [Francisco Dionisio Vives], personally and advantageously known to the President, and to the Undersigned, and who, during his administration of the Government of Cuba, has given strong evidences of his desire to maintain friendly relations with the United States. In that letter the general objects of Mr. Cook's agency were communicated. Although the state of his health had been low, during the preceding Session, it was believed to be improving, and to be such as to admit of a satisfactory execution of the trust confided to him. He left the United States in the month of April, delivered the letter to Governor Vives, and made some, if not all, of the inquiries with which he was charged. He returned in the ensuing Summer, bringing with him a confidential letter from the Governor, which he had engaged to deliver with his own hands, and bringing with him, also, the materials for a detailed report of the results of his inquiries. He died on his way from his residence to the seat of Government, to execute that engagement, and to make that report. The letter of the Governor has been since received, and is on file in the Department.

The compensation promised Mr. Cook was the same, in amount, as that which had been offered to the citizen of Louisiana [Robertson], already referred to; the same as that which was received by Mr. [Thomas] Randall [4:377] during the former administration, on an analogous service; the same as that which was received by our agents sent to Spanish America, prior to the formal recognition of the New Republics; and the same that has been allowed, in numerous instances, to our foreign unaccredited diplomatic agents. He had received, prior to his death, $1,500, on account of that compensation, but the final settlement of his account with his representatives remains to be made.

From the preceding statement it results, 1st. That no part of the sum of $12,324.67 has been disbursed in the domestic service of the government. 2dly. That of the $12,324.67, expended according to the third section of the act of the first of May, 1810, the sum of $1,700 was paid in the year 1825, prior to the commencement of the present Administration. 3dly. That the sum of $9,124.67 was paid for services, conceived projected, and ordered, during the last administration. 4thly. That the present Administration is not otherwise responsible for that disbursement, than in having continued and fixed the amount of compensation for services created and begun during the last Administration. And, 5thly. That the only part of the sum of $12,324.67 which has been expended in a service created by the present administration, is the sum of $1,500.

LS. DLC–HC (DNA, M212, R3). Letter marked "Official." 1. These confidential sums were likely related to the attempt of John Rodgers to secure a commercial treaty with the Turks by working through Turkish naval officials. Clay to Rodgers, September 6, 1825. See also, 6:827, 1272.

To JAMES BARBOUR   Washington, June 3, 1828[1]

It is stipulated in the second paragraph of the 3d. Art: of the Convention concluded at London on the 29th. day of September 1827 [6:1100–01] providing for an arbitration of the dispute on our N. Eastern boundary, as follows:

"Each of the Contracting Parties shall be bound, on the application of the other Party, made within six months after the exchange of the ratifications of this Convention, to give authentic copies of such individually specified acts of a public nature, relating to the territory in question intended to be laid as evidence before the Arbiter, as have been issued under the authority, or are in the exclusive possession, of each Party."

The clause does not state whether the application shall be made at London to the British Government, through the American Minister, or at Washington to the British Minister. The first paragraph of the same Article, and the 2nd. Article, have, in this respect, been made definite. They expressly stipulate that the reciprocal communication of the respective statements and replies of the Contracting Parties, and of the evidence which each of them intends to exhibit to the Arbitrator shall be made to the respective Ministers of the two Governments. It is not known why the same precision of language was not employed in relation to the demands to be made for authentic copies of acts of a public nature. To guard against any objection which might be raised on this account, we intend to make the demand both at Washington and London. The object of this despatch is to state certain acts of a public nature, authentic copies of which we desire to possess, and to direct you to make application for them, accordingly, to the British Government.

The demand is to be made within six months after the exchanges of the ratifications of the Convention. That ceremony was performed at London, on the 2d day of October next, when six calendar months will

321

have been completed from the exchange of the ratifications. It had better be made before the 29th of September, so as that it will fall within a period of six months computed in the lunar mode. The Convention does not restrict either Party to a single demand, but, authorizes, as we understood it, as many successive applications for the authentic copies described, as either party may think proper to make to the other, provided they are all made with the time limited.

The copies which it is my present purpose to direct you to demand are the following:

No 1. Grant of Nova Scotia to Sir Wm. Alexander, by James I, dated 10th September, 1621.

2. The Act of confirmation of said grant by Charles I dated 12th. July 1625.

3. Grant of the Province or Countie of Maine, by Charles I, to Sir Ferdinando Gorges (or Georges) dated 3d. April 1609.

4. Charter of the Province of the Massachusett's Bay in New England, by William and Mary, dated October 7th. 1691.

5. Order in Council, or other Act of the crown, by which Nova Scotia, which had been part of the Massachusett's Bay, was, not long after the Treaty of Utrecht, separated from Massachusetts, and erected into a separate Government.

6. Report of the law officers of the crown to the board of trade, on two questions referred to them, being, in substance, whether the charter of Massachusetts had not become vacated, so far as related to the territory between the rivers St. Croix and Kennebeck, and the government thereof and the right to grant lands therein had not reverted to the crown. The report is dated about the year 1730, '31, or '32.

7. The decision of the Board of Trade or Council on the said Report.

8. The Proclamation of His Britannic Majesty [George III], of the 7th. October, 1763, erecting in North America the Government of Quebeck East & West Florida, and for other purposes.

9. Grants by the Crown, or by the Govr. of Nova Scotia, of the Island of Campo Bello in the Bay of Passamaquoddy, or in the Bay of Fundy and of a tract of land of 100,000 acres more or less, to Govr. Bernard and others, or to Francis Bernard and others, lying West and southwest of the river Schuodic, and extending westwardly towards the river Cobscook, erroneously described the river St. Croix. Both these grants are supposed to have been made between 1764 and 1776.

10. Order of survey, from the same authority for surveying the last mentioned tract of land for the said Governor, or Francis Bernard and others.

11. Commission of Richard Phillips, as Governor of Nova Scotia,

			in 1719.
Commission of Edward Cornwallis as	do	do	in 1749.
Commission of Henry Ellis as	do	do	in 1761.
Commission of Montague Wilmot as	do	do	in 1763.
Commission of Francis Legge as	do	do	
in what year, not known.			
Commission of the person who was Governor of Nova Scotia			in 1776.
do. " do.		do.	in 1782.

12. Order in Council, or other act of the Crown, by which the Province of New Brunswick was erected into a separate Government, about the year 1783, '84, '85.

13. Commissions of the several Governors of New Brunswick, from the time it was erected into a distinct province, to the year 1828.

14. Any order in council, or other act of the crown, that may have defined or altered the boundaries of the Province of New Brunswick, from the period of its erection into a separate Government, to the year 1828.

15. Order in Council, or other act of the crown, by which the Province of Quebeck was divided into the two separate provinces, or governments of Upper and Lower Canada

16. Any order in Council, or other act of the crown that may have defined or altered the Southern boundary of Lower Canada, from the period of its erection into a separate province to the present time.

You will apply for authentic copies of the preceding acts being of a public nature, and all of them having more or less relation to the territory in dispute. This instruction is thus early addressed to you to guard against any casualties which might prevent the demand being made within the time prescribed by the Convention. But you need not present a formal application to the British Government until the month of September. It should be made, for the reason already stated, before the 29th. of that month.

No objection to furnishing this Government with authentic copies of any of the preceeding Acts can be anticipated. All of them originated under British authority and most of them are in the exclusive possession of the British Government. They all have a relation more or less intimate to the territory in question. The demand being made within the time limited by the Convention, if, contrary to our expectation, any objection shall be made to furnishing any of them the discussion and consideration of that objection may take place either before, or after the six months limited in that instrument. There may be some mistake in some of the dates of the acts described. Our wish is to obtain them, whatever may be their dates.

Copy. DNA, RG59, Dip. Instr., vol. 12, pp. 109-13 (M77, R7). 1. On May 29, Clay formally notified Barbour of his appointment as Minister to Great Britain, at an annual salary of $9000 and "an outfit" of $9000. Clay to Barbour, May 29, 1828. LS. DLC-HC (DNA, M212, R8). The formal letter of appointment was dated May 23. Adams and Clay to Barbour, May 23, 1828. Copy. DNA, RG59, Ceremonial Communications, 2:85. In mid-June, Barbour reported that he had adjusted his personal affairs and was preparing to depart. Barbour to Clay, June 14, 1828. ALS. DNA, RG59, Dip. Disp., Great Britain, vol. 36 (M30, R32). See also, Clay to Barbour, June 13, 1828. On June 16, 1828, Clay, writing to "the King of the United Kingdom of Great Britain and Ireland [George IV]," introduced Barbour as the new American Minister to London. Copy. DNA, RG59, Ceremonial Communications, 1:86.

From GIDEON JAQUES, Wilmington, June 3, 1828. Has learned that *"Crumb Creek Stone,"* found in Delaware County, Pa., is to be used for the proposed breakwater at the mouth of Delaware Bay. Claims that a better and less costly stone, much more suitable for breakwater construction, can be quarried in the Wilmington area and that it is of a "specific gravity vastly greater." Hopes that the President, upon learning these facts, "will allow our citizens a participation in the contract for this great work." MHi–Adams Papers, Letters Received (MR486). For the Delaware Breakwater project, see Anna T. Lincoln, *Wilmington, Delaware: Three Centuries Under Four Flags, 1609–1937* (Rutland, Vt., 1937), 238–9; Wilson L. Bevan, ed., *History of Delaware Past and Present* (N.Y., 1929), 863; Ralph D. Gray, "The Early History of the Chesapeake and Delaware Canal: Part II: Delay, Debate, and Relocation," *DH* (1958–9), 8:355–97.

From ALBERT GALLATIN, New York, June 4, 1828. Acknowledges receipt of Daniel Brent's letter of May 31 enclosing various ancient documents, colonial charters, and reports pertaining to U.S. preparation for the arbitration of the Northeast boundary question, and solicits still others. Discusses at length the usefulness and authenticity of several of these documents, and says that it "would be highly useful" for him to proceed to Boston and Albany to continue his research. Indeed, he must search for relevant maps in the Harvard University library, find out whether Nova Scotia was detached from Massachusetts at her own request, learn "on what possible grounds the St. John's river had been claimed as its boundary," and discover "what were the understood boundaries of Maine west of Kennebec, &c &c." LS. DNA, RG76, Northeast Boundary: Misc. Papers, Entry 82, frames 69–70. Copy in NHi–Gallatin Papers, vol. 15, pp. 240–2 (MR21).

From JOEL R. POINSETT, Mexico, no. 128, June 4, 1828. Transmits a translation of President Guadalupe Victoria's discourse to the Mexican Congress, relative to his power "to call into service as many battalions of militia as he may think proper" as well as all "the troops of the nation"; but discounts this as a threat of a Mexican invasion of Cuba.

Discusses "the violent excitement and . . . animosity" incited by the translation of the article in the *American Quarterly Review* which caused the rejection of two articles in the Treaty of Limits [Poinsett to Clay, May 21, 1828, January 8, 1828]. Continues: "I did not think it proper to urge the Treaty thus mutilated through the Senate [Obegron to Clay, August 2, 1828]." Regrets the delay but will not "relax my exertions."

Remarks on "the expulsion of a certain class of Spaniards," who "acted as the middlemen between the foreign importer and the retail dealers," charging that "They regard the creoles as rebels and . . . still cherish hopes of seeing the dominion of Spain restored in these countries."

Reports that while "The Treasury remains empty," the Mexican officials "continue to pay and clothe the troops, and so keep things quiet."

Mentions the ratification of the treaties of the Panama Congress [Poinsett to Clay, July 23, 1828]. States in conclusion that the relations between Colombia and Guatemala "are as bad as possible." LS. DNA, RG59, Dip. Disp. Mexico, vol. 4 (M97, R5). Received July 18, 1828. Also as LS, draft. DNA, RG84, Foreign Service Posts, Mexico (R17, frames 503–06).

To JOSE S. REBELLO   Washington, June 4, 1828

The Undersigned, Secretary of State of the United States, has the honor to inform Mr. Rebello, Charge d' affaires from Brazil, in reference to his several notes, particularly that of the 2nd. instant to this Department, concerning the Corvette of War, Bolivar, which was recently detained in the port of New York by the Attorney of the United States [John Duer] at that place, upon the suspicion of being engaged in adding to her warlike equipments, with hostile purposes towards Brazil, in violation of the neutrality which the Government of the United States has always professed, and sincerely wishes to maintain, in the contest between the Government of Brazil and Buenos Ayres, that he has lately received a communication from that officer,[1] a copy of which is herewith transmitted to Mr. Rebello; which states that the Bolivar had been released from seizure by his direction, and the grounds upon which this was done, with the conditions of release; viz, that the Vessel should be stripped of her armament, (number of men) and should sail from the port of New York, with no greater armament than would be sufficient to navigate her, which condition had been fully complied with.

The Undersigned flatters himself that Mr. Rebello will discover in these proceedings on the part of this Government, a new proof of the scrupulous exactness with which it fulfils its neutral obligations, and of the earnest desire which it constantly cherishes to presevere in a course of the strictest impartiality in the unhappy contest prevailing between Brazil and Buenos Ayres. . . .

Copy. DNA, RG59, Notes to Foreign Ministers and Consuls, vol. 4, p. 32 (M38, R4).
1. Duer to Clay, May 31, 1828.

To FRANCISCO TACON, Philadelphia, June 4, 1828. Notifies him that "the Buenos Ayrean privateer, the Juncal, and the brig Reina [*sic, Reyna*] Amelia, have been libelled for supposed violations of law, the former . . . at Baltimore, and the latter . . . in East Florida."

Inquires if he wishes "to present any claim . . . or exhibit any proof" against either of these vessels as "the respective Courts . . . will give such claim or evidence full examination and consideration." Informs him of "the existence of those prosecutions" for presenting claims. Copy. DNA, RG59, Notes to Foreign Ministers and Consuls, vol. 4, p. 33 (M38, R4).

Tacon replied to this note on June 7, saying he had no further case to make on the *Reyna Amelia;* but expresses his distress that the U.S. government has allowed the Buenos Airean privateers *Bolivar* and *Juncal* to sail. LS, in Spanish, with trans. in State Dept. file. DNA, RG59, Notes from Spanish Legation, vol. 9 (M59, R–T12).

From CHARLES R. VAUGHAN, Washington, June 4, 1828. Reviews the exchange of diplomatic correspondence and negotiations related to the case of John Baker of Maine [6:1272-3]. Reports the result of the trial at Fredericton, New Brunswick, on May 8, which found Baker guilty, with a sentence of a "fine . . . of twenty five pounds sterling & . . . imprisonment for two months." Encloses a copy of a letter of the Lieutenant Governor of New Brunswick, Sir Howard Douglas, who regrets "that he cannot remit the punishment of Baker," and moreover wishes not to interfere "with the regular course of the law" unless so ordered by the British government. Encloses report of the trial. LS. DNA, RG59, Notes from British Legation, vol. 15 (M50, R15); also in Manning, *Diplomatic Correspondence . . . Canadian Relations*, 2:714-5, 724.

On January 20, 1829, Clay sent John Q. Adams documents to use in complying with a House Resolution of January 5, 1829 [*Register of Debates*, 20 Cong., 2 Sess., 160-1], directing the President to communicate all the available information concerning the seizure, trial, and punishment of John Baker by New Brunswick authorities, as well as all correspondence between the U.S. and Britain "in relation to the aforesaid arrest." Copy. DNA, RG59, Report Books, vol. 4, pp. 265-6.

To FRANCIS T. BROOKE   Washington, June 5, 1828

I recd. your favor of 2d. inst. My health remains pretty much in statu quo. I do not anticipate any considerable improvement of it until I commence my journey, which I propose doing about the 15th. inst. I shall go through Virginia, but by what route I have not yet positively decided. I think I shall go to the mountains by the shortest.

I have prepared a letter [June 5] to the Central Admn. Comee of K[entucky]. in answer to one received from it, on the subject of Amos Kendall and his correspondence with me. I think some letters from him which I have authorized to be published will fully establish his infamy.

I am not preparing, nor shall I prepare, any answer to the Address[1] of the Jackson Central Comee. of this place. My opinion is that it is unworthy of notice from *me*, But I shall probably publish, by way of Supplement[2], to my former Address [6:1394-6], a Mass of testimony which has since accumulated on my hands, and I may publish it, without comment. I have also addressed a letter [May 24] to K. to a friend [Robert Wickliffe] (which he is authorized to publish) respecting my private affairs, which will relieve my friends from any anxiety on that account.

I should be glad to see published the correspondence to which you allude[3] between Mr. [John] R[andolph]. and Mrs. M[orris].; but I do not think it proper that *I* should urge its publication.

Judge [John] Savage declined the office of Treasurer, & it has been given to Genl. [William] Clark, late Treasurer of Pennsa. who was turned out by the Jackson party last winter, because he is a friend to the Administration. There is some reason to hope that circumstances will hereafter admit of something being done for your friend.

I regret that I have no copies of Mr. [Tristam] Burgess [*sic*, Burges's] two speeches which I have never seen.[4]

I should be extremely happy to see you here, prior to my departure.

Copy. DLC-TJC (DNA, M212, R13).   1. Brooke to Clay, May 20, 1828.   2. Clay, *A Supplement to the Address . . . to the Public*, June 10, 1828.   3. Brooke to Clay, June 2, 1828.   4. Brooke to Clay, May 20, 1828; and June 2, 1828.

From ROBERT M. HARRISON, St. Bartholomew, June 5, 1828. Feels compelled, in spite of "the recent melancholy death of my beloved Son who was drowned in Norfolk sometime in April," to express "my indig-

nation and destestation of those *vile wretches,* the mere *tools* of a *party,* for the *slanderous* and *villainous accusations* against yourself and the President." Continues at length in this vein, citing the loss of liberty in ancient Greece and Rome. Concludes that "at a proper time" means will be found legally and justly to humble "this party *to the dust!*" Hopes "you may defeat all your enemies (which are those of the country also)." ALS. DNA, RG59, Cons. Disp., St. Bartholomew, vol. 1 (M72, R1). Received July 28, 1828.

To JOHN HARVIE   Washington, June 5, 1828

Your letter of the 14th ult. [*sic,* April] as Chairman of the Central Committee of the friends of the Administration in Kentucky, requesting for publication, copies of my correspondence with Messrs. [Francis P.] Blair and [Amos] Kendall, was received shortly before I made a late visit to Philadelphia. My absence from this city, the press of business incident to the close of the session of Congress, and the feeble state of my health have combined to prevent an earlier reply.

I preserved no copies of my letters addressed to either of those gentlemen. Mr Blair has furnished me with copies of several of those directed to him [4:9–11, 46–8], including that upon which, I understand, a reliance is placed to establish the fact of my having made a corrupt agreement, in relation to the late Presidential election. My correspondence with that gentleman was friendly and familiar, and sometimes sportive. It is characterized by a freedom of language which is occasionally admissible in private and friendly intercourse, but which would not be decorous towards the public. Mr Blair has himself refused to exhibit the letter in question, or to testify concerning its contents, upon the principle that he will not voluntarily consent to the violation of private correspondence. That principle must command the respect of all honorable men. So far as regards the charge against me, the publication would benefit instead of injuring me. Such is the opinion of several gentlemen to whom I have shewn the correspondence, and such is my own. But I will not avail myself of this advantage, at the sacrifice of a principle, the preservation of which is a necessary guarantee to social confidence and intercourse. I could not, moreover, publish my own letters to Mr Blair, without some of his, showing the sense in which he understood mine. Although he has given me permission to publish both, he thinks they ought not to be published; and I will not, on the defiance of a profligate editor, be the first to set a mischievous example, which the other party to the correspondence has refused to establish. I must decline, therefore, authorizing the publication of our correspondence. But the Central Committee is at liberty to exhibit to the inspection of any gentleman, of any party, all such portions of it as relate to the late Presidential election, and I will so the same upon any such application being made to me.

My correspondence with Mr Kendall stands upon different grounds. That gentleman has assumed the triple attitude of my accuser, the witness to establish the accusation, and the publisher of it to the world, through the paper [Frankfort *Argus*] which he edits. He has not scrupled to violate private correspondence, and to misrepresent my motives, and the better to enable him to accomplish his purpose, (as I am compelled to believe) he states he has destroyed my letters. If he has really destroyed them, I regret it very much, because I should have preferred their speaking for themselves, instead of their contents being perverted by his enmity and prejudice—Should all or any of them be hereafter found to have been preserved from the flames, he is at full liberty to publish them. Not content with misrepresenting me, I am informed that he has given, in the Argus,[1] an erroneous and faithless version of the testimony delivered before the Senate of Kentucky, in that most extraordinary inquiry which was instituted before that body at its last session.

The obligation to respect the confidence which is implied between man and man, in their private correspondence, must be reciprocal. One party cannot be bound to respect, whilst the other is free to violate it. Still less can such a one-sided obligation exist, when one of the parties has not only violated it, but misrepresented the purpose of the correspondence. Mr Kendall has therefore absolved me from all duty of withholding from the public any portion of the correspondence which has passed between us, if it had ever possessed a character of higher confidence than that which was actually stamped upon it. But I will not avail myself of the privilege which his conduct has thus conferred, further than is necessary to vindicate myself against him and his testimony. Before I proceed to notice the letters from him, which are communicated, it is proper that I should take a rapid survey of the relations which existed between us.

Mr Kendall had been educated at Harvard University, which is among the most respectable, if it be not the most celebrated, of the institutions dedicated to education in the United States. During my absence from my country, on its public service, he was engaged by Mrs. Clay as a private tutor to instruct my children. Upon my return, I understood that he had been attentive to the discharge of the duties of his station, and I ascertained that they had benefitted by his instructions during his residence in my family. Parents know how to estimate such a relation. My personal acquaintance with him was never great, he having left my house prior to my return, and my opportunities of seeing him having been chiefly limited to my occasional visits at Frankfort where he resided. After he became the editor of the Argus, I took, and generally read his paper, which I thought exhibited some talent and much diligence. I have never spoken in any boasting or reproachful spirit of hospitalities or kindnesses, received by him under my roof. If they ever create any obligation it is cancelled whenever they are trumpetted forth by those who dispense them. He has chosen, himself, publicly to avert to this subject, and I leave him in the undisturbed enjoyment of the sophistical distinction between instances of hospitality rendered by a man, and his wife, on which he dwells with so much self-complacency.

The relation which I have described, created a strong interest, on my part, in the personal welfare of Mr Kendall. It was not extinguished or abated by the fact of his taking a part in the local politics of Kentucky, which my judgment did not approve. I have never allowed my private feelings towards individuals to be affected by a mere difference in opinion on political subjects; when the opinion opposed to my own is believed to be honest, and is maintained with proper attention to truth and decency. That interest in the prosperity of Mr Kendall was, moreover, kept alive by frequent expressions from him, of dissatisfaction as an editor of a newspaper, and intimations of his desire to change it for some more eligible public service. I have no recollection of having ever written to him any letter, prior to the late Presidential election, offering to aid him in procuring other public employment. Applications to me for such aid were, however, frequent, whilst I was a member of Congress, as they have been since; and it is quite possible that I may have written to him on that subject. But if I ever did, all inferences from any friendly expressions of mine, that I was subsequently to be appointed to the Department of State, and that I would then provide for him [and such I understand to be the import of the insinuation, contained in his testimony before the Senate of Kentucky,] are as malignant as they are utterly groundless.

After, and not until about a month after, I was appointed to the Department of State, believeing that Mr Kendall would make an useful subordinate clerk in that department, I offered him an employment in that character, with a salary of $1000 per annum; but as the campaign for that year was just opening in Kentucky, on her local politics, I annexed, as an indispensible condition, that, if he determined to accept, he should not quit the field until the campaign was terminated. My motive for this condition cannot be mistaken. The offer led to some correspondence [4:305-6, 719, 746] and conversation between us, in the course of which he expressed a willingness to accept of a place, provided a salary of $1500 was attached to it. As I then had no such place at my disposal, the negotiation terminated. How fortunate the public and I have been in such an issue, let the world now judge!

Among other modes of Mr Kendall's appeal to me for aid to his embarrassed circumstances, was that of his endeavor to prevail on me to effect or make a loan of money to him. I had a sum of Commonwealth's bank paper, belonging to the estate of Colonel [James] Morrison, of which I could make no use in the course of its administration. I resolved not to sacrifice it by a conversion of it into specie, at an enormous discount, foreseeing that it would certainly appreciate in value, if our state should not be afflicted with unwise legislation. Mr Kendall applied to me to borrow a part of that paper. I loaned him, in 1825, for one year, $1500, and took a mortgage for the reimbursement of the loan, with legal interest in the same paper medium. The mortgage was committed to record, thereby demonstrating that I had no wish to throw any mystery or concealment around the transaction. At the end of the year, Mr Kendall expressed himself unable to pay the debt, and I gave him another year, on the condition of his paying the arrear of interest. At the termination of this other year, he was still unable to pay. I informed him that the matter must be closed, but I instructed my agent to extend to him every indulgence, consistent with the security of the debt, about which I entertained some apprehensions. He has paid a part of it, by the sale of some of the mortgaged property; and, at the date of my last advices, a considerable balance remained undischarged.   If I had retained the paper unappropriated in my possession, as I did retain a large sum, the estate would have derived all the benefit of the anticipated appreciation in its value, which has, in fact been realized, without risk of the loss of the capital.   The sole effect produced by the loan, (on the supposition of its ultimate reimbursement,) will be, that the estate will acquire interest upon the sum loaned.   This innocent pecuniary affair has been represented as a disposition on my part to bribe Amos Kendall; and I have been held up, at the same time, as a bankrupt & a griping creditor, seeking to compel my unfortunate debtor to pay in specie, dollar for dollar, that which he had borrowed in paper; and robbing the estate of a deceased friend of the benefit of the operation!

Of the three letters of Amos Kendall, herewith transmitted, the first bears date the 21st of January, 1825 [4:35].   In that letter he states that General Jackson was his second choice, but adds, "If our interest in the west can be promoted by any other arrangement, I shall be content. At any rate, let us have a President.   I would sooner vote for any of the three, than have a viceregent for four years.   Do what you think best; the Argus will not complain, because it has FAITH that you will do nothing to compromit the interests of the western country, or the nation."   What Mr Kendall meant by promoting our interest in the west, by any arrangement other than the election of General Jackson, he does not explain: and never did explain to me.   That at the date of that letter he had not heard from Mr Blair or from any other person, that I had made a corrupt agreement to obtain the appointment of Secretary of State, is manifest, from his explicit avowal of *faith* in me, that I would do nothing to compromit the interests of the western country, or the nation.

The committee will bear in mind that Mr Kendall makes in his testimony before the [Ky.] Senate, and has repeatedly otherwise asserted, that he obtained information from Mr Blair, in January 1825, of the existence of a corrupt bargain, by which I was to be made Secretary of State, in the contingency of Mr Adams election, I have shewn, from his own letter, that he could not possibly have received any such information up to the 21st January, 1825. The next letter from him, herewith transmitted, bears date the 20th February, 1825 [4:81]. In this letter he says, "There is much inquiry," [at Frankfort, where both he and Mr Blair resided and where he pretends he received the alleged information,] "whether you will be offered, or will accept the Secretaryship of State, and much diversity of opinion as to what you ought to do, if it is offered. It seems to me that no man here can tell what you ought to do; because it is impossible for us to know all the circumstances." That which is known is not ordinarily a matter of speculation, although it may lead to speculation.   If it were known, at Frankfort, to Mr Kendall and others, upon the 20th of February, 1825, that I was to be appointed Secretary of State, there could have been no doubts, no uncertainty, no speculative inquiries, about it.   This inference appears to me to be fair and irresistible, from the context of his letter.

But if any one can hesitate, yet, to believe that Mr Kendall never entertained any opinion unfavorable to the purity of my public conduct, and that his charge is a gross fabrication, I invite the attention of such a sceptic to the remaining letter from him, which is now transmitted. Before it is introduced, one word of explanation is necessary. I had heard, in the summer, or September, 1826, that a report had been put in circulation in Scott county, that I had sought to bribe Mr Kendall, and to buy him off by a Clerkship in the Department of State. I addressed him a letter, in consequence of it, in September of that year, communicating the existence of the report, expressing my surprise, and enquiring of him about it. I kept no copy of my letter; and therefore speak from memory. His reply bears date the 11th of October, 1826 [5:776]; more than twenty months after the period when he alleges that he had received, from Mr Blair, the information of my having made a corrupt bargain, in this answer, he states that he had not heard the report; that it had never received the slightest color from any declaration of his, and that he will take prompt measures to put a stop to it. And he adds, "Whatever course I may feel constrained to take, in relation to the Administration generally, I trust I shall not be the means, or the occasion of casting any imputation upon your INTEGRITY or HONOR."

Such is a faithful account of my relations and correspondence with Mr Amos Kendall, so far as the public can feel any interest in knowing them. Had there not been a call upon me, from so respectable a source, it would never have been communicated to the public. This is the only notice in him that I shall ever take. I will not descend to the level of a newspaper controversy, with one who has shewn himself destitute of all principle. It belongs to my temperament to think favorably of my fellow men. But I have not been so often deceived as some of my Kentucky friends imagine, in respect to the dispositions of men towards me. I have long known that several prominent individuals in that State, now my open enemies, cherished, during many years, admidst the most friendly professions of esteem and admiration, a secret hostility against me. Some of these have labored to heighten the effect of their present emnity by the affectation of a former warm friendship. But I acknowledge that I have been deceived in Mr Amos Kendall. The regret which the development of his want of veracity and integrity has occasioned, is mitigated by the conviction that his malignant shafts are harmless and impotent.

Copy. Lexington *Kentucky Reporter,* July 2. 1828. An extract from this letter, dealing with Clay's stewardship of the James Morrison estate, was published in *Kendall's Expositer,* vol. 4, no. 12 (May 28, 1844), 183, in conjunction with issues in the Presidential campaign of that year. 1. Frankfort *Argus of Western America,* July 9, 1828; Kendall to Clay, February 6, 1828.

From MARTIN DURALDE, New Orleans, June 6, 1828
JAMES ERWIN, *ET AL.*
The office of surveyor of this Port having become vacant by the death of Mr William Emerson,[1] a number of candidates have presented themselves and. obtained recommendations, which are without doubt entitled to consideration with the Government; and as there may be some difficulty in deciding upon the comparative merits of the applicants. we have thought it would not be considered intrusive if we were to offer our opinions on this Subject.

We unite in thinking that the appointment of Mr Brainard would be the most acceptable to the friends of the Administration in this city and we are assured, it would be satisfactory to the officers of the Customs over whom Mr. Brainard, in the event of his appointment, would be called upon to act

Mr Brainard has been for six years an inspector of the customs and his fidelity, capacity and general conduct as a gentleman has secured to him the respect of the community—to no portion of which would his appointment be in any way obnoxious.

LS. DNA, RG59, A. and R. (MR1). Letter addressed "Private."   1. The 1824 New Orleans *City Directory* lists Emerson as "Surveyor of the Customs," at 22 Royal.

From JOHN IRWIN, Port au Prince, June 6, 1828. Encloses copy "of a law to be submitted to the Chambre ax Communes," which, if passed and enforced, "must inevitably expel the American trade entirely from the Island." States that American commercial interests on the Island would be advantaged if "a vessel of war would touch here" as often as possible. ALS. DNA, RG59, Cons. Disp., Cap Haitien, vol. 6 (M9, R6). Received June 23, 1828.

A similar letter to Clay from Samuel Israel, dated Cap Haitien, June 7, also complained of possible Haitian trade restrictions on American imports, blaming this on inflation, currency exchange difficulties, and "French influence strongly prevailing with this Government." *Ibid.* Received June 28, 1828.

On June 12, however, Irwin reported that the contemplated law "relative to the payment of duties accruing to this Government on imports an[d] exports . . . has been entirely abandoned." But he also suggested that the U.S. could assist Haiti in stabilizing its economy by adopting "such measures as would effectively prevent the counterfeiting of the currency of this Republic." New York, he charged, was where "this infamous rape is carried on," counterfeit Haitian money being manufactured there almost publicly. *Ibid.* Received July 2, 1828.

From "JUNIUS," June 6, 1828. Refers to Clay's "tirade in the shape of a speech" in Baltimore on May 13, 1828, and links it to his "annual electioneering tour." Predicts that those who respond to such "perversions of truth" are sycophants "who now fawn and flatter around you" but will "soon leave you to your fate." Attacks Clay's references in Baltimore to the dangers of Andrew Jackson's military background, predicts that the Administration will be badly beaten in the coming election, and charges that his trip to Kentucky is designed for the purpose of helping defeat William T. Barry's gubernatorial campaign and to load the state legislature with his friends. Accuses Clay of wanting to supercede Richard M. Johnson as U.S. Senator from Kentucky, and predicts that "all your schemes will be prostrated." Calls attention to President Adams's disgraceful "*Ebony and Topaz*" toast [6:1233] and criticizes the Administration campaign of "last summer" that employed Cabinet members to assault Jackson on the stump. Charges Clay with having organized that operation. Argues that Jackson is not opposed to the American System, as witness his support of the Tariff Act of 1824, and states that Clay's attacks on him in that regard are knowingly irresponsible. Refutes Clay's argument that his speeches for Adams and the American System are primarily designed to "vindicate your character from groundless aspersions and put down calumny." Remarks that Washington, Hamilton, Jefferson, and Madison were all "calumniated"; but that they did not abandon their official duties to "traverse the country making dinner speeches to propitiate the people and uttering denunciations against their opponents?" Recalls that Jefferson outlived the calumnies of his enemies. Notes that if "such should not be your fate, attribute it not to the calumnies of your enemies, but to your own ever reaching ambition and the folly of your friends." Lexington *Kentucky Gazette*, June 6, 1828.

A similar letter, from St. Clair County, Ill., dated June 17, 1828, signed "An American," is in *ibid.,* August 1, 1828, copied from the the Louisville *Public Advertiser*. In it, the writer maintains that Clay's Baltimore speech marked his political death. Indeed, "in it, you exhibit yourself your worst enemy. In it, like a poisonous serpent, you have bitten yourself, even unto a political death." Charges, further, that Clay is a Godless person, that he has "devoted more of your time to the trump card, than to the Holy Bible; but if you do pray, in my opinion, neither God nor man will listen to you." Remarks, also, that "the people of New England ... hate you; yet they may love your act, in electing their favorite President.... Eat the bread of your 'bargain' in peace. The people will do you justice.... Your days are numbered—you die politically on the 4th of March next."

From WILLIAM B. LAWRENCE, London, no. 42, June 6, 1828. Encloses copies of official documents relative to the appointment of the Earl of Aberdeen as Foreign Secretary. Reports meeting him briefly at a "Ministerial levee," where he was assured by Lord Aberdeen that "his personal feelings had always been most friendly" to the United States.

Mentioned to Aberdeen his "unfinished affairs" concerning the choice of a Northeastern boundary arbiter and the "arrest of [John] Baker [6:1272–3]." Recapitulated for Aberdeen his conferences with Lord Dudley on these matters, stressing the American "excitement" and the "greatest sensibility" over the Baker case. Refrained from asking Aberdeen for an immediate private interview, but hoped there would be no further delays.

Submits for the State Department Parliamentary documents, containing "a map of the disputed boundary territory," as well as related "evidence laid before the legislature of Lower Canada." Learns that England is sending, within a few days, a diplomatic delegation to Russia and to Corfu to resume negotiations with her allies in conformity to the Treaty of July 6, 1827 [6:780–2].

Transmits materials, relative to Brazilian–Portuguese affairs, mentioned in his last dispatch. LS. DNA, RG59, Dip. Disp., Great Britain, vol. 35 (M30, R31). Extract in Manning, *Diplomatic Correspondence ... Canadian Relations,* 2:726–7. Received July 26, 1828. The fourth Earl of Aberdeen, George Gordon–Hamilton (1784–1860) devoted his career to politics and diplomacy. He became Foreign Secretary on June 2, 1828. See *DNB*.

From BARON PAUL DE KRUDENER, Washington, June 7, 1828. Notes that while competent Russian authorities have found against the claims of the owners of the U.S. vessels *Commerce* and *Hector,* the Emperor, Nicholas I, has reviewed and overruled those findings in a manner "fully satisfactory to the proprietors," so as "to correspond with the wishes manifested by the President of the United States on this subject." Copy. *Niles' Register* (June 28, 1828), 34:294. An enclosure, from Count Nesselrode to de Krudener, dated March 22, 1828, gives details of the Russian captures of the vessels in the Mediterranean in 1807 and the subsequent claims negotiations related thereto. *Ibid.,* 294-5.

Clay responded to de Krudener, on June 9, 1828, thanking the Emperor for his courtesy and "enlightened deliberations" in the matter. *Ibid.,* 295.

On June 7, Clay informed Eliphalet Loud of Salem, Mass., claimant in the matter of the *Commerce,* that the Russian government had settled his claim in the amount of 50,000 rubles; on the same day, Israel Thorndike of Boston, claimant in the matter of the *Hector,* was told that his claim had been settled in the amount of 207,731 rubles. Copies of both letters in DNA, RG59, Dom. Letters, vol. 22, pp. 219-20 (M40, R20).

To RALPH I. LOCKWOOD, Washington, June 7, 1828. Explains that John Adams Smith, Secretary of the U.S. Legation at Madrid, formerly Secretary of Legation at London, has been assigned to the Legation at Paris [replacing the recently deceased Daniel Sheldon] because of his fluency in both French and Spanish. He cannot, therefore, gratify Lockwood's interest in the Paris post, although it would have "afforded me much pleasure" to have been able to do so. Assures him, however, that "you labor under an entire mistake in supposing that there existed, on the mind of the President, any unfriendly reminiscence which would have constituted a bar to your appointment [3:845-6]." LS. KyU. Letter marked "Private."

Clay informed Smith on June 12, 1828, that he had been appointed, by act of the President, to this post. Copy. DNA, RG59, Ceremonial Communications, 1:84. On June 14, Clay transmitted to Smith his commission. LS, Draft. DLC-HC (DNA, M212, R8). On the same day, Clay wrote James Brown at Paris, in dispatch no. 17, of Smith's appointment and said that Smith was reporting to Paris "with all convenient Despatch." L, draft. *Ibid.* On June 16 Clay informed Alexander H. Everett at Madrid, in dispatch no. 13, of Smith's transfer to Paris and of the appointment of Charles S. Walsh as his successor at Madrid. *Ibid.*

From ROBERT R. STEWART, Trinidad de Cuba, June 7, 1828. Complains of "the system of piracy" in south Cuban waters, reporting specifically that the schooner *Charles,* out of Philadelphia and bound home, had been found "eight leagues at sea, scuttled, boat destroyed, sails and

334

rigging cut up, and the decks stained with blood." ALS. DNA, RG59, Cons. Disp. , Trinidad de Cuba, vol. 1 (M–T699, R1). Received July 6, 1828.

To CHARLES R. VAUGHAN, Washington, June 7, 1828. Calls attention to the decision of the British–American commission of 1822 [4:182], respecting the status of "all the islands" in rivers and lakes demarcated by the designated boundary. Assures him that if any islands assigned to Great Britain are in possession of the United States, this country "is ready to surrender them." Is concerned, in this respect, that the islands "called Drummonds, near the head of Lake Huron . . . [are] yet occupied by British authority." Seeks quick "reciprocal execution" of these transfers, and hopes that Vaughan has received instructions from Great Britain, providing for "the surrender of the islands which belong to the United States." Copy. DNA, RG59, Notes to Foreign Ministers and Consuls, vol. 4, pp. 34–6 (M38, R4); also in Manning, *Diplomatic Correspondence . . . Canadian Relations,* 2:178. Drummond Island is now part of Michigan.

On June 10, Vaughan acknowledged this letter, assuring Clay that having no instructions on this subject, he would transmit his note to the British government. Vaughan to Clay June 10, 1828. LS. DNA, RG59, Notes from British Legation, vol. 15 (M50, R15).

On September 29, 1828, Vaughan informed Clay that he had been instructed by his Government to proceed with the transfer of the islands involved. *Ibid.* On October 20, Vaughan informed Clay that Sir James Kempt, Governor General of Canada, in response to orders from the Colonial Department in London, "has directed the small detachment of troops stationed at Drummonds Island to be immediately withdrawn." Copy. DNA, RG107, Letters Received, Reg. 23, C–208.

On October 22, Clay acknowledged this note, adding that "Drummonds Island was the only one of those adjudged to the United States which subsequently continued in British possession," and pointing out that none of the islands awarded to Great Britain by the Commissioners was still under American authority. Copy. DNA, RG59, Notes to Foreign Ministers and Consuls, vol. 4, pp. 81–3 (M38, R4); also in Manning, *Diplomatic Correspondence . . . Canadian Relations,* 2:186–7.

Finally, on October 24, 1828, Clay wrote to Peter B. Porter, Secretary of War, transmitting copies of Vaughan's notes of September 29 and October 20. He called attention to enclosures in Vaughan's correspondence of these dates pertaining to orders withdrawing British troops from Drummond's Island. LS. DNA, RG107, Letters Received, Reg. 23, C–208.

From DANIEL WEBSTER   Boston, June 8, 1828
You will have seen some proof of the prevailing sentiments, on public subjects, in this quarter. The best possible feeling was indicate[d], at the meeting on the 5th.[1] I do not mean in regard to myself, but on general subjects, & in respect to others. The toast, in which you were named, was recd with the most enthusiastic applause. I do not think I have ever seen

in Boston a meeting comprising so much character, talent, influence & respectability—I hope it may do good.

All that we yet hear from N Hampshire is very well. Mr. [Samuel] Bell, I preceive will be re elected to the Senate, this week.[2] One objection, My Dear Sir, which I have to write to you, is, that your courtesy & kindness lead you always to answer me—& I feel that it is wrong, in the present state of your health, & of your engagements, to impose any new duty, tho' it be a trifling one, upon you. I will really take it as a greater proof of friendship & confidence if, how often or ever I may write, you will forbear all reply, unless when there is something which you wish to say.

ALS. DLC–HC (DNA, M212, R3). Marked "Private."   1. A testimonial dinner for Webster at Faneuil Hall on June 5, given by "a large number of his constituents." Boston *Daily Advertiser*, June 6, 1828.   2. He was.

From THOMAS L. L. BRENT, Lisbon, no. 72, June 9, 1828. Transmits a letter and a statement from Joaquium Antonio de Magalhaes, "charged with the department of foreign affairs by the Provisional Junta," requesting recognition of the junta and the opening of diplomatic relations. Declares he was not authorized to recognize this junta, only the government of Dom Pedro. Asserts, further, "if I did, the policy of the United States would . . . require an entire separation of the interests . . . of Europe and America, and in particular of Brazil and Portugal." Notes that the policy of disregarding Magalhaes's request has been adopted by all the foreign representatives.

Reports that the Cortes did not meet on June 6, as expected, the delay owing perhaps to internal confusion, the advice given by foreign powers, and the protest of the Brazilians. States that the decrees of Miguel are issued with the title, "The Infante Regent." Explains that Miguel "has been gaining in popularity" and courts his troops. Observes that practically "all the troops of the line" have left Lisbon for Coimbra, and that the Prince, in command of the army, will join them shortly.

Reports on the "innumerable arrests . . . made by the government" and says that many Peers "have either left the country or hid themselves."

States that a Regency has been appointed by Miguel to rule during his absence with his troops. LS. DNA, RG59, Dip. Disp., Portugal, vol. 8 (M43, R7). Received August 9, 1828. For the career of Magalhaes, see *GEPB*.

From RICHARD HENRY LEE, Washington, June 9, 1828. Asks for "some employment, under the General Government," with "great embarrassment," but in the knowledge that he is "capable of serving my country, in some respectable situation." Remarks that he is "the only direct and immediate descendant of Richard Henry Lee and the only immediate collateral descendant of Arthur Lee, Francis L. Lee, and William Lee who has applied for, or received any post of 'profit or power' under a Government, the blessings of which, they all hazarded their lives & fortunes, throughout the whole of the revolutionary struggle, to establish." Explains that his need for work stems from "an artful speculation made upon me, on my first entrance into life while yet unacquainted with things, & unsuspicious." ALS. DNA, RG59, A. and R. (MR2). For the several Lees see *DAB*. In spite of his impressive genealogical credentials, Lee did not get a government job.

From GUSTAVUS H. SCOTT, Fairfax County, Va., June 9, 1828. Reports that "We had a meeting of our administration committee on Thursday last & enlarged it by adding thereto every man in the county who will be likely to exert himself in behalf of the administration, & it was unanimously agreed that each & every one should ride about, see the people & use all possible means to secure the votes of this county for Mr Adams—The documents printed by the convention are still sleeping I understand, in Richmond, on account of the expense of transportation—We have sent for our portion, & at our next meeting shall distribute them, probably, with another address better adapted to the understanding of the mass of the people—We shall also have a committee of three or four persons appointed for the express purpose of corresponding with influential & active friends in other counties & to enable us to do this with the greatest effect I must beg you to give *me* the names of some of the most prominent friends of the administration in the different counties—We can get the names of the corresponding committees by reference to the public prints, but it is essential to address ourselves to the most zealous advocates of the administration." ALS. NcD.

To WASHINGTON DAILY   Washington, *ca.* June 9, 1828
NATIONAL INTELLIGENCER
I have witnessed, with very great regret, the unhappy controversy which has arisen between two of my late colleagues [John Quincy Adams and Jonathan Russell] at Ghent. In the course of the several publications of which it has been the occasion, and particularly in the appendix to a pamphlet,[1] which has been recently published by the honorable John Quincy Adams, I think there are some errors, (no doubt unintentional,) both as to matters of fact and matters of opinion, in regard to the transactions at Ghent, relating to the navigation of the Mississippi, and certain liberties claimed by the United States in the fisheries, and to the part which I bore in those transactions. These important interests are now well secured, and, as it respects that of the navigation of the Mississippi, left as it ought to be, on the same firm footing with the navigation of all other rivers of the confederacy, the hope may be confidently cherished, that it never will hereafter be deemed a fit subject of negotiation with any foreign power. An account, therefore, of what occurred in the negotiations at Ghent, on these two subjects, is not perhaps necessary to the present or future security of any of the rights of the nation, and is only interesting as appertaining to its past history. With these impressions, and being extremely unwilling to present myself, at any time, before the public, I had almost resolved to remain silent and thus expose myself to the inference of an acquiescence in the correctness of all the statements made by both my colleagues; but I have, on more reflection, thought, that it may be expected of me, and be considered as a duty on my part, to

contribute all in my power towards a full and faithful understanding of the transactions referred to. Under this conviction, I will, at some time more propitious than the present, to calm and dispassionate consideration, and when there can be no misinterpretation of motives, lay before the public a narrative of those transactions as I understood them. I will not, at this time, be even provoked (it would, at any time be inexpressibly painful to me, to find it necessary) to enter the field of disputation with either of my late colleagues.

As to that part of the official correspondence at Ghent, which had not been communicated to the public by the President of the United States, prior to the last session of Congress, I certainly knew of no public considerations, requiring it to be withheld from general inspection. But I had no knowledge of the intention of the honorable Mr. [John] Floyd, to call for it,[2] nor of the call itself, through the House of Representatives, until I saw it announced in the public print. Nor had I any knowledge of the subsequent call which was made for the letter of the honorable Mr. Russell,[3] or the intention to make it until I derived it from the same channel.

I will thank you to publish this note in the National Intelligencer. . . .

Copy. Washington *United States Telegraph*, June 10, 1828.   1. John Quincy Adams, *The Duplicate Letters and the Fisheries and the Mississippi. Documents Relating to Transactions at the Negotiations of Ghent*. Washington, 1822.   2. Floyd's two resolutions, dated April 18 and May 6, 1822, are in U.S. H. of Reps., *Journal*, 17 Cong., 1 Sess., 468, 576.   3. Letter solicited May 4, 1822, by President James Monroe. See *State Papers* [Misc.], 17 Cong., 1 Sess., no. 131, pp. 3–56.

From THOMAS I. WHARTON   Philadelphia, June 9, 1828

Before the receipt of your letter of the 6th I had ascertained that the appointment of Treasurer [of the U.S.] was given to Mr [William] Clark; And although personally I wished some token of executive good will to have been shown to Col. [Nicholas] Biddle, yet I think the spirit & manliness displayed in giving the office to Mr Clark will be of service to the cause in all parts of the United States.

My present object is to enquire what are the intentions of the Government with respect to the [Delaware Bay] Breakwater.[1] Is there to be a Commission of two or more individuals? If there should be I should like, frankly, to be one of them, or, if it is intended that there shall be a secretary to the Board with an annual salary it would be very convenient to me to have the appointment. I do not like asking an office for myself, but the claims of an increasing family will not allow me to overlook any opportunity of obtaining an increase of a very limited income. And on the score of political services and steadiness I believe you require no evidence. You will not understand me when speaking of a Commissionership as wishing to put myself permanent in competition with Col. B[iddle]. to whose superior claims I yield without a moment's hesitation. His appointment would be highly acceptable to our friends here and eminently serviceable to the community. Indeed I know of no man more intrinsically competent. It is only in the event of more than one being appointed or in case of the appointment of a Secretary by the government that I wish to be considered.

Your good offices in this matter will be very gratefully acknowledged.

ALS. DLC-HC (DNA, M212, R3). Marked "(Private)."   1. Jaques to Clay, June 3, 1828.

To THE PUBLIC   Washington, June 10, 1828
ADVERTISEMENT.

In my Address of December [29] last to the Public, in relation to the charges against me, concerning the last Presidential Election, which originated with General Andrew Jackson and some of his friends, I stated that I had been disappointed in the receipt of some testimony which I had expected; and that, if I should subsequently obtain it, I would present it to the Public. I accordingly received several statements from different gentlemen, some of which were communicated without solicitation. Deeming them highly important, I present them to the Public in this Supplement, without a single comment. I offer only the following explanation:

PART I.

Exhibits the statements of Messrs. William Sample, Isaac Bennett, the Rev. A[ndrew]. Wylie, John Keel, Cuthbert T. Jones, and J[ohn]. U. Waring. Upon perusing them, in connexion with statements on the same subject which I formerly published, the Public will be able to judge of the accuracy of General Jackson's assertion, that "the origin—the beginning of this matter," [the charge of bargain,] "was at my own house and fireside, where surely a freeman may be permitted to speak on public topics, without having ascribed to him improper designs."

PART II.

Consists of the statements of Messrs. George Robertson and Charles S. Todd, of Kentucky, and Daniel Vertner and A[aron]. W[sic, K]. Wooley, of Mississippi, and B[enjamin]. S. Forrest, of Maryland; the four former narrating conversations between other gentlemen and me, long antecedent to the late Presidential Election, in which I freely expressed my opinion respecting Mr. Adams and General Jackson. Mr. Forrest's statement proves that Colonel [Thomas Hart] Benton, on his way to Congress in the Fall of 1824, declared that "it was impossible that Mr. Clay could vote for General Jackson, and expressed much surprise at the suggestion."

I subjoin the statements of Colonel Benton, Mr. [William] Plumer, and Mr. Robertson of Ohio, which have been already published, without having been previously communicated to me; and of D[avid]. White, Esq., the only Representative from Kentucky, voting for Mr. Adams, whose statement was not contained in my former publication: Also, two letters written by me,[1] which had escaped my recollection, and have been published by the gentlemen to whom respectively they were addressed.

Printed Introduction to Clay's, *A Supplement to the Address of Henry Clay to the Public, Which Was Published in December, 1827. Exhibiting Further Evidence in Refutation of the Charges Against Him, Touching the Last Presidential Election, Made by Gen. Andrew Jackson.* Washington, Peter Force, 1828. 22pp.   1. Clay to Brooke, February 4, 1825 [4:55–6]; and Clay to Unknown Recipient, February 4, 1825 [4:54– 5]; both published in *A Supplement to the Address . . . to the Public.*

To **WILLIAM B. LAWRENCE,** London, no. 8, June 11, 1828. Notifies him that James Barbour has been appointed as the new minister to Great Britain and will sail in July for his post. States that the President wishes him to represent the United States until Barbour arrives.

Transmits a copy of a despatch prepared for Barbour [Clay to Barbour, June 3, 1828] relative to obtaining "authentic copies of certain acts and documents" from the British government on the Northeastern boundary issue and authorizes him to apply for them. LS. DLC–HC (DNA, M212, R8); also in DNA, RG59, Dip. Instr., vol. 12, pp. 113–4 (M77, R7).

From **WILLIAM B. ROCHESTER**   Savannah, June 11, 1828
Conformably with the intention indicated in the enclosed envelope communication of the 16th ultimo (brought by the first vessel for the U. States—the *Albion*—the same is which I have made my return passage) I debarked from the Falmouth at Omoa on the 17th ultimo that she might not, on my account be delayed in her cruize, and proceeded thence to English Key in the bay of Honduras.—I did not land at Belize on account of a slight bilious attack super—induced by my recent exposure at Omoa, the intensity of the heat & the necessity, to which I should have been subjected, of going about nine miles in an open boat, not to speak of the probable risque in landing at a place which had the character of being extremely sickly. I took measures however thro the medium of Capt. Vennard of Portsmouth N.H. to obtain all the news which might have reached Belize, of later date than the accounts at Omoa. Besides, I had there an opportunity of seeing another intelligent Gentleman who had spent several months in Guatemala, which city he had left but a few weeks before. From neither of these sources could I procure any information of later date of giving a more favourable aspect to the affairs of the Country—indeed, the latter Gentleman drew a more unpromising picture that had been previously presented—I send herewith an Honduras paper containing scarcely anything and a Guatemala paper containing the exposé on one side, of the causes which produced the failure of the attempt at negotiation, between the two states, adverted to in my letter from Omoa.[1] I left English Key of the 22 ultimo on the sch. *Albion* & arrived here last evening—I am much exhausted, but shall embrace an early oppy after recovering from the fatigue & other effects of my voyage to write more in *extenso* respecting the political condition and prospects of Central America up to the time of my departure, so far forth as I was put in possession of facts and events and enabled to predicate opinions upon them

I find upon searching that I have sent the Hondures [*sic*] newspaper by mistake, with some other papers, to New York—will send it hereafter.

ALS. DNA, RG59, Dip. Disp., Central America, vol. 1 (M219, R2).   1. Reference obscure. Possibly his letter of May 14 from Trujillo.

From **ROBERT M. HARRISON,** St. Bartholomew, June 12, 1828. Summarizes his mission to "the various colonies" in the Caribbean.

Learns while at St. Thomas, that "four Guineamen were fitting out in the Port" and "apparently some of our citizens are interested."

Reports calling at St. Eustatia to find *"two* of *three Prizes* and as many Privateers under the Buenos Ayrean flag . . . nothing more than the worst of Pirates, their commissions being manufactured in Baltimore!" States that "Our citizens trading there have no one to protect them, and are alarmed beyond measure." Observes further that "Our Merchant vessels can scarce[ly] keep a man on board, they being seduced either by the Guineamen or Privateers." Mentions one schooner "belonging to the celebrated John Gooding of Baltimore (who is now on this Island)," and notes that he has recently taken a $30,000 prize. He has also "taken the protection of this Government but how far that can shield him from the *offended laws* of his country which makes the traffic in Slaves a *capital crime* I know not!"

Endorses the request of the resident American citizens engaged in lawful pursuits "to require that a light vessel . . . be sent here, that she might look into and visit the neutral Islands . . . every eight to ten days." Mentions that "the new duty on Rum will be a great inducement to defraud the revenue," a situation which "I have already indicated to the Secretary of the Treasury [Richard Rush]." Recommends the establishment of the post of Consul at St. Eustatia and the introduction of measures to prevent smuggling. Cites particularly the widespread smuggling in the two lower counties, Accomack and Northhampton, in Virginia in which *"Colonels Majors Captains* and *Magistrates"* engage in this business undetected, but different standards are in effect for "any poor man." Cites cases involving "free coloured people and Indians" in which some of them here have "been *towed* out in a *canoe* in the *middle* to the *Chesapeake* and left there!"

Recounts the expenses incurred on this mission, complaining "you cannot live in any of these islands for less that $7" per day. Observes, further, that "In these countries there are only two classes of boarding houses, those visited by respectable people and . . . those where *sailors* and *negroes* resort." Reports that his expenses amount to $1038.

Mentions, in a postscript, that he will provide tables of "a correct return of Imports and exports of the Islands" and will send a local newspaper with accounts of privateering activities. ALS. DNA, RG59, Cons. Disp., St. Bartholomew, vol. 1 (M72, R1). Received July 8, 1828.

On October 18 John Gooding, who by this time had been arrested for his slave trading and privateering activities, wrote Clay requesting that he be allowed to travel to the West Indies to summon several witnesses for his trial in the Maryland Circuit Court. ALS. DNA, RG59, Misc. Letters (M179, R66).

The U.S. District Attorney for Maryland, Nathaniel Williams, wrote Clay on November 1, informing him of Gooding's request that in the pending prosecution "his recognizance may not be forfeited" and that the trial "not be urged before the May term." Believes the President cannot reconcile this request with his sense of duty and concludes that the case "must . . . take the established course of the law." Copy. DNA, RG59, Dom. Letters, vol. 22, p. 325 (M40, R20).

From ISAAC MUNROE   Baltimore, June 12, 1828

I notice in the [Washington *Daily National*] Intelligencer of this day an adv't of the Navy Commissioners, among others, ordered to be published in the [Lexington] Kentucky *Gazette*. That paper vies with [Amos] Kendall's [Frankfort *Argus of Western America*] in its lawless abuse of the Administration & particularly of yourself. I dare say if the commissioners were apprised of its real character they would Substitute the [Lexington *Kentucky*] *Reporter* in future. I have reason to know how painful it is to see by one['s] own Side an opponent patronised instead of a friend. In the Same way the [Richmond] Enquirer is selected instead of the [Richmond *Constitutional*] Whig. These little matters are probably not thought of by those who give the direction, but they are in a measure of some importance.

I think at this moment our prospects are more propitious than at any former period. I deem Mr. Adams' re-election almost as certain, unless we are greatly deceived in New York. There the people are with [us] but our friends ought to be cautioned against the effect of intrigue & party machinery.

The recent appointments[1] have had the most salutary effect upon the feelings of the friends of the Administration, & if things go right, I [hope] after the next election to see a revision of the *political* tariff—acting fully upon the principle laid down by Mr. Jefferson "support & be Supported."

ALS. DNA, RG59, Misc. Letters (M179, R66).   1. Probably a reference to the appointments of Peter B. Porter as Secretary of War and William Clark as Treasurer of the United States.

From PETER B. PORTER   New York June 12, 1828

I arrived in this city an hour ago. I spent yesterday at Albany where I found the Admin Convention (which assembled the preceeding day & closed its labors last evening) in session. It was the most respectable body of men I have ever known assembling in this state in a similiar occasion, and consisted of 104 members—128 being the maximum number that could have been elected. Some counties, decidedly, admn, neglected, for reasons unexplained, to elect delegates, and, in some counties entitled to *several*, it was not deemed necessary for *all* to attend.

They were all in high spirits, & acted with great harmony. The objects of their convening having, by the circular address of last spring,[1] been confined to the admn of the *General* Government, they did not deem themselves authorized to make a nomination for Governor, but have called a new Convention for that express purpose, to meet at Utica, on the 23d of July.[2] They passed, with great unanimity, several appropriate resolutions in relation to the Presidency, & adopted an address to the people which is said to possess uncommon energy, and merit. The whole proceeding, with the address, will appear in pamphlet,[3] in two or three days.

I was much disappointed in not meeting a line from you at Albany, by which I might have, more satisfactorily, regulated my movements. I have some private business to transact in this city which has the most pressing claim to my attention, & which will require about two days. I shall therefore (unless my determination should be changed by advices from you) remain here for that time, & then proceed as rapidly as possible to Washington. In haste. . . .

ALS. DLC–HC (DNA, M212, R3). Letter marked "(Confidential)."   1. Porter to Clay, February 13, 1828.   2. Porter to Clay, March 26, 1828. The call for a convention at Utica on July 23 recommended Smith Thompson [see *DAB*] as the Republican [Administration] candidate for the office of Governor of New York. See New York *Evening Post*, August 8, 1828.   3. *Resolutions and Addresses of the Convention of Delegates from the Counties of New York, Held at Albany June 10, 11, 1828, Nominating John Quincy Adams and Richard Rush for President and Vice President, in Opposition to General Adrew Jackson.* Albany, 1828. 33 pp.

From CHARLES SAVAGE, Guatemala, June 12, 1828. Refers to his March 10 letter. Since then, the Federal army has retired from San Salvador and has been inactive and seems to prefer negotiations "rather to that of arms for peace." Reviews in detail, and in chronological order, the history of the Federation of the Centre of America since 1825, emphasizing the internal political disorder and fighting that has occurred, particularly the events surrounding San Salvador's invasion of Guatemala in March, 1827, Guatemala's immediate counterinvasion, and the destructive war that followed. Discusses attempts to negotiate peace, beginning in January, 1828, which broke down when San Salvador attacked "Federal and Guatemala state troops with 3500 men," only to be "completely routed." Remarks that "At this time the influence of the state Government of Guatemala seems of more importance than that of the Federation, both are bankrupt and destitute of Credit." Notes that "resort is had to loans which are now no less than military actions—very oppressive on the inhabitants and urged against all foreign merchants except those of the U States." Demands for loans have, however, been made on U.S. citizens, by the state of Guatemala, but the policy has apparently not been enforced. Reports that commerce and communication between the states of the Federation have broken down, except "by sea." ALS. DNA, RG59, Cons. Disp., Guatemala, vol. 1 (M-T337, R1).

From WILLIAM TUDOR, Ship *Star*, at Sea, no. 89, June 12, 1828. Recalls a conversation with the late James Cooley, relative to Peruvian affairs, and feels it would be "useful to submit some observations upon it." Refers to the "demand" Cooley was instructed [5:867–8] to make upon Admiral Martin George Guise, the English–born naval hero in the Peruvian War of Independence, who was honored, shortly before Cooley's arrival in May, 1827, with a public dinner on board the *Presidente* by the government. States that Cooley felt awkward about making the demands under those circumstances, especially since Guise had just been placed in command of the Peruvian fleet in an impending struggle with Simon Bolivar. Given these conditions, he advised Cooley to make no demands which the government of Peru "neither could nor would comply with," but instead to "express the strong disgust which his government felt at the outrages committed by Admiral Guise against two American vessels [4:425–6]; & insinuate that in accordance with the friendly feeling of the government of the U.S. toward the republic of Peru, he forbore at that moment to press a requisition he had been instructed to make on this subject, & which in any other circumstances could not have been dispensed with."

Recounts his personal relations with Guise, noting, "I had felt a deep disgust at the outrages he had committed against my countrymen." Reveals, however, that after Guise was brought to Lima as a sick prisoner, he had visited him. Believes that "Guise is a man with stronger passions than judgement," but feels that "In the struggle with Bolivar, he is of importance" because of his loyalty to Peru as a citizen and his marriage "to a lady of the country."

Concludes that he is aware of the hesitant course Cooley adopted, but desires now to submit "all the circumstances of the case." ALS. DNA, RG59, Cons. Dips., Lima, vol. 2 (M154, R2). Letter marked "Confidential." Received August 13, 1828. For Martin Jorge Guise, see *Diccionaria Enciclopedica Del Peru.*

To JAMES BARBOUR   Washington, June 13, 1828

The President having, by, and with the advice and consent of the Senate, appointed you Envoy Extraordinary and Minister Plenipotentiary to the United Kingdom of Great Britain and Ireland, I transmit, herewith, your commission in that character, together with the usual letter of credence, to be delivered on your presentation to the King [George IV]. It is the wish of the President that you should proceed on your mission without unnecessary delay. In the discharge of the duties of the high and honorable trust which is thus confided to you, much reliance is placed on your experience, zeal, ability, and fidelity. You will commence them with the great advantage of a thorough acquaintance with the relations between the two countries, and a knowledge of the views of the President, derived from your long participation in the public councils as a Senator of the United States, and a member of his Administration.

The first and highest duty of a foreign minister is to attend to and observe the instructions which he may receive from time to time from his Government. In cases which may arise, not embraced by them, especially if there be any doubt or difficulty, it is his safest and wisest course to refer to his government for further instructions.

Mr [William B.] Lawrence, Secretary of the Legation, and now acting as Charge d' Affaires, will put into your possession the books, papers, and documents belonging to the mission. These will give you an adequate idea of the existing state of such of our relations with G. Britain, as may require attention from you. Most of the subjects on which Mr [Albert] Gallatin was instructed to negotiate with the British Government, were acted upon by him. Some of them were brought to a satisfactory conclusion, whilst, on others, the British Government declined to treat. Of the latter description are all that class comprised under the first general head of the instructions given to that gentleman, on the 19th of June 1826 [5:440-78], embracing the following.

1. The abolition of privateering.
2. The principle of "Free ships, free goods."
3. Impressment of seamen.
4. The law of Blockade.

5. Contraband.

6. Confiscation of debts, or funds in public stocks.

7. Exemption of persons engaged in trade, in the respective countries from molestation in consequence of the existence of war.

8. Other special provisions, designed to define more precisely the rights and duties of the neutral and belligerent, and, generally, to mitigate the rigors of war.

On all these subjects the government of the U.S. is willing to treat, and to make an arrangement on principles which have frequently been communicated to the British Government. But after all that has passed between the two Governments, the President thinks that the first movement towards such an arrangement, ought to proceed from the Br. Government. In the event of the continuation of the present state of peace, no difficulty is likely to arise, on any of them: but if any war should break out to which G. Britain should be a party, it is possible that the practice of impressment may be attempted to be again applied to us. In that event, you will, in the very first instance of the impressment of any american seaman, remonstrate in strong, but respectful, terms against it, and let the Br: Govt. know, that this Govt. cannot, and will not submit to it.

The necessary arrangements for carrying into effect the Convention of September last [6:1100-01], providing for an arbitration of the dispute in our Northeastern boundary, will require your constant attention. I have addressed a separate letter [June 3] to you, instructing you to make application to the British Government for authentic copies of certain papers, which may be requisite as evidence before the arbitrator. That application ought not to be deferred beyond the 29th. of September next.

I transmit herewith a copy of a Resolution of the House of Representatives,[1] requesting the President to open a negotiation with the Br: Govt., for the recovery of fugitive slaves who make their escape from the United States into Canada. On that subject Mr Gallatin found, in his conferences with the Br: ministers that they were unwilling to treat. You will ascertain if the same indisposition continues to exist. The evil is a growing one, and is well calculated to disturb the good neighbourhood which we are desirous of cultivating with the adjacent British Provinces. It is almost impossible for the two governments, however well disposed, to restrain individual excesses and collisions which will arise out of the pursuit of property, on the one side, and the defence, on the other, of those who have found an asylum. You will find, in the instructions to Mr Gallatin, of the 19th. June 1826, and of the 24th. Feby, and 24th May 1827 [6:229-36, 589], all that was communicated to him on this subject, from the Department. And if you ascertain that the Br: Govt is in a favorable disposition, you are authorized to renew the proposal which he was instructed to make, embracing fugitive slaves, and deserters from the military, naval, and merchant service of the two countries.

During your mission, you may be applied to, from time to time, to interpose on behalf of American Citizens, to obtain satisfaction of claims which they may have on the Br: Govt, or the redress of grievances which they may experience in the course of their dealings and transactions.

345

You will, in all such cases in which the intervention of the Government may be proper, according to the public law, afford such official aid and assistance as may appear to you to be likely to be useful, whether you have special instructions from this Department, or not.

Copy. DNA, RG59, Dip. Instr., vol. 12, pp. 122–5 (M77, R7); also in DLC–HC (DNA, M212, R8). No. 3.   1. U.S. H. of Reps., *Journal*, 20 Cong., 1 Sess., 715. Introduced by Rep. Robert McHatton of Ky.

From JAMES BROWN   Paris, June 13, 1828

I have had no letters from you for some time except that in which the President has been so kind as to give me leave of absence. You have before this time received the news of Mr [Daniel] Sheldons death and consequently will in all probability expect me to prolong my stay. The accounts I have already given you of the improvement in Mrs. Brown's health will leave you at liberty to count upon my remaining here until Spring unless such arrangements have been made to fill my place as would make my return before the close of the Session you have no doubt been beset by numerous applications for the place he has left vacant. As well Mr. Adams as yourself are aware of the importance at this Court, of filling that vacancy, by a man of business, of good manners and temper, and one well acquainted with the language of the Country. If any of your Clerks shall possess these qualifications he would probably make the best Secretary [of Legation], because he would be broken in to steady habits of business and accustomed to labor and confinement. Many young gentlemen of fortune will solicit it, but they are generally impressed with the idea that they have nothing to do except it be going with the Minister to gay parties, and doing the honors of this house. These gentlemen will find themselves greatly disappointed when compelled to remain in the office five hours every day to copy letters and grant Passports—Besides Secretaries are not here as at Washington invited whenever the Minister is asked to dinner or evening parties. In a word the place suits only a man of business and no others ought to have it. I hope the President will exercise his own judgment in this choice without giving too much weight to the recommendations of those who are not as competent judges as himself. It may be of little consequence to me personally but is of much more to the Country than most persons imagine.

The Emperor [Nicholas I] had joined his army, the Turks who had remained in a state of astonishing apathy, had become awakened to the danger, and we shall soon receive intelligence from the East of an important character. It is generally believed that the Emperor will easily overcome any force which the Porte can now interpose between Constantinople and the Russian army. It seems pretty well understood that other nations will remain neutral unless Russia shall push her acquisitions of territory as far as to endanger the Ballance of Europe, in which case some attempt will be made to restore it not by taking from her the conquests she may make but by endeavoring to rake in the spoils of the Barbarous nations.

The Chambers are yet in Session and will not adjourn for some time. It is yet uncertain whether ministry[1] will or will not ultimately gain a majority. In some instances the center has acted with the right, and sometimes with the left, thus inclining at pleasure the majority to the liberals or friends of Villele—[2]

I find General [Samuel] Smith has again endeavored to injure the Administration by his Colonial questions. Much nonsense has been spoken in relation to Guadaloupe & Martinique. The ordinance[3] was passed for the convenience of the Inhabitants of these Islands and not with any view to our advantage or in any hope of favoring their navigation. The present [Martignac] Ministry seems to be better desposed towards us than the last [Villele], and I think will place the intercourse on a fair footing. As to the Claims, they believe that the Chambers would not agree to the appropriation or seem to believe it. The heirs of Beaumarchais some of whom have great influence are becoming advocates for the payment of our Claims as a means of obtaining their own [3:311-3].

Mrs Brown's health is much improved and I now hope will in three or four months be perfectly reestablished.

ALS. DLC-HC (DNA, M212, R3). Printed in *LHQ*, 24:1108-10.   1. Of Jean Martignac, acting President of the Council of Ministers.   2. Jean Baptiste de Villele, President of the Council of Ministers from 1826 to January 3, 1828.   3. See *Sen. Docs.*, 20 Cong., 1 Sess., no. 89, pp. 1-11; and Clay to Adams, January 15, 1828.

To FOREIGN DIPLOMATIC AGENTS   Washington, June 13, 1828
Having found it necessary, for the benefit of my health, to absent myself from the City of Washington a few weeks, I shall, with that object, take my departure in the course of the ensuing week. I hope to return early in August. During my absence, any communications which you may think proper to make to the Department, being addressed to me, and sent to it, will receive due attention from Mr. Daniel Brent, the Chief Clerk.

Copy. DNA, RG59, Notes to Foreign Ministers and Consuls, vol. 4, pp. 40-2 (M38, R4). The names, nationalities, ranks and titles of thirteen diplomats accredited to the U.S. are listed as recipients of this circular letter.

From "JUNIUS," June 13, 1828. Notes that "Ever since you have allied your political destinies with the fortunes of your former enemy, John Q. Adams, and there has been a probability of General Jackson's election to the Presidency, the phantom of Military despotism seems continually and upon all occasions, to haunt your troubled imagination." Cites Clay's letter to Francis T. Brooke [4:45-6] in this regard. Argues, from history, that "Military usurpation" in Republics occurs only when there is widespread corruption "first among the politicians and then with the great mass of the people." Charges that in his Baltimore Speech of May 13, Clay had missed this point and had "outstripped all your former efforts of this kind in the want of candor" and in "the utter falsity and glaring absurdity of your historical deductions." Undertakes, at great length, to instruct Clay in an appreciation of a correct view of history. Begins with the ancient Greeks and Romans and continues through Oliver Cromwell and the French revolutionaries of the Bonaparte era. Concludes this exercise with the charge that Clay has "studied history to little purpose," and that in attempting to overturn "long established maxims," he is "attempting to white wash the Ethiopian." Presents a detailed defense of

General Jackson's genuine republicanism as a "citizen–soldier," pointing out that the General has never endorsed the idea of a "standing army that could prove dangerous to the political stability of our present happy form of government!" Wonders also how an army of 6000, deployed in small detachments of 500 men or fewer from Maine to Georgia, and throughout the "western wilds," could possibly prove dangerous to the liberties of a population of 12,000,000 Americans. States that Jackson asserts his "claim to the Presidency" not by means of "violence and military force," but by the "peaceful suffrages of an enlightened people." Condemns Clay's "morbid imagination" in believing that "the Republic is on the brink of destruction" unless "yourself and Mr. Adams" are retained in power. Suggests a reading list that Clay might profitably consult to improve his knowledge of the basic causes of military usurpations in republics; lists Machiavelli, De Retz, Livy, Salust, Plutarch, Montesquieu, Herodotus, and Thucydides. Copy. Lexington *Kentucky Gazette,* June 13, 1828; reprinted in Washington *United States Telegraph,* June 23, 1828.

SPEECH   Western Virginia, Summer, 1828
I thank you, Sir [Joseph Lovell], and those of my Fellow Citizens, whom you represent on this occasion, most cordially and respectfully, for the eloquent and flattering address with which you have honored my arrival among you. I was not ignorant of the existence of those friendly sentiments, of which you have been the organ, but until I came here I was not aware of their extent nor of the full force of my obligation for the warmth with which they are entertained. They spring from a cause honorable to the hearts and heads of enlightened freemen—an ardent love of Country and an indignant sense of great injustice done to a fellow Citizen.

If a further refutation were still wanting of that calumny to which you have alluded,[1] in such generous terms, it is supplied by the total failure of all the persons, in the House of Representatives who have been concerned in originating, propagating or countenancing it, to bring forward during the late protracted Session [20 Cong., 1 Sess.], any proposition whatever to arraign the alleged political culprit, and to drag him, if guilty, to condign punishment. A majority of that House, it is well known, was composed of members in opposition to the Administration. They possessed the whole power of the House and could direct and control it according to their will. The Speaker [Andrew Stevenson], chosen by their suffrages, would not have done them injustice, in the organization of of [sic] any Committee of Enquiry or Managers of an Impeachment, which might have been ordered, if we are to judge from the arrangement of the other Committees of the House. They could have pushed investigation to the farthest limits. The accused was on the spot. He had openly[2] avowed, in an address to the American public [4:53–4], published in the midst of the Session, and freely circulated among the members, his readiness to submit to any fair trial. The accuser [Andrew Jackson] was not further from Washington than from New Orleans, which he visited in the depth of the winter. Had he been summoned to the Capital to make good his charge, he would have found there "honest George Kremer" willing and ready to support him to his utmost ability,

348

his designated witness, Mr. [James] Buchanan, and all the would-be witnesses, in their respective places. Never was a party impelled by more powerful considerations to accomplish any object than they were to convict the accused, if he were really guilty. They would then have secured the certain triumph of their cause, the elevation of their chief [Jackson], and the vindication of his honor, implicated as it is by the invention and insidious circulation of the calumny. If a single member of the house believed the accusation true, it was the bounden duty of that member, at least to propose an enquiry. With all these advantages for eliciting the truth, and with all these urgent motives for establishing the guilt of the accused, a Session of Congress, of near six months duration, is allowed to pass away without a solitary motion or proposition, touching the accusation! No member, submitted any such motion, because no member really believed to charge to be true. Manufactured for electioneering purposes, it was thought to be safer and more profitable to trust to profligate appeals to credulity, ignorance and prejudice, & to rely upon inflaming and agitating the public, than to meet the accused fairly, face to face, and confront him with witnesses.

I beg pardon for this personal digression. In every part of the Civilized world there is a proper sense of the inestimable value of public character; but if there be any portion of the globe where it is wanting, I am quite sure it is not that State [Virginia] which gave me birth, nor that [Kentucky] which has adopted me with maternal affection.

You appreciate, Sir, much too highly my poor services to my Country. I claim only that they have ever been animated by zeal in its cause, devotion to its liberty, and unsurpassed solicitude for the preservation of its union and institutions.

I believe that system to which you have refered, justly called the American system, which had my best exertions in its establishment, as it now has my anxious wishes for its continuation and improvement, will realize, if not prematurely abolished, every hope of its friends, and ultimately disappoint every fear of its opponents. It is founded on a maxim which the most enlightened nations sanction by their practice if they do not always proclaim through their writers, and which inculcates a patriotic preference of the produce of native to foreign industry. It rests on that principle which, inherent in our nature, has been planted there by the wisdom of our Creator, and felt, if not owned by every one, who retains a consciousness of personal identity, teaches the fair protection of our own interests in any collision with the interests of foreigners. The prosperous state of the manufacture of a necessary of life, in this neighborhood[3] which you have mentioned, illustrates the whole system. I can add my testimony to yours in respect to the very great reduction in the price of it, in the Western States, in consequence of the establishment of these valuable manufactories. If nature, in their origin, interposed, in their behalf, some protection, by the intervening mountains and extended space, which separate you from the ocean, the genius of [Robert] Fulton has conquered both, and brought almost into the bosom of the Allegheny the foreign rival to compete with the native article.

I thank you for the kind interest which is felt in the restoration of my health. Should it continue to improve, during the residue of the period allotted to my relaxation from official duty, as much as it has since I left Washington, I hope to return entirely recovered.

I pray you, Sir, in your own eloquent and interesting manner, to make these my acknowledgments and sentiments acceptable to those whom you represent.[4]

Copy. NBuHi. Printed in Washington *Daily National Intelligencer,* July 25, 1828. Reprinted in Lexington *Kentucky Reporter,* August 6, 1828. Delivered in White Sulphur Springs, Burning Springs (home of William Tompkins), Charleston, and other places in Western Virginia in July and August, 1828. See, below, Clay to Lovell, July 13, 1828. At Burning Springs, for example, the speech was heard by "nearly two hundred of our most respectable citizens."   1. To the alleged "corrupt bargain" between Clay and Adams in Feb. 1825.   2. Word substituted for the word "publicly," which was struck through.   3. Salt works in the Kanawha Valley which, according to Joseph Lovell's remarks when introducing Clay to the audience, had reduced the cost of salt locally, over the past 25 years, from $5.00 per bushel to 25 to 75 cents per bushel.   4. Following his speech, Clay was driven to Charleston, eight miles distant, where he attended a public dinner. The toast he made at that event was to "The valley of the Kenawha [*sic*]—Not more distinguished for the fertility of its soil, than for the enterprize, patriotism, and hospitality of its inhabitants." Lexington *Kentucky Reporter,* August 6, 1828.

To DANIEL WEBSTER   Washington, June 13, 1828

Notwithstanding your kind permission given me in your letter of the 8th instant, to abstain from addressing you, I cannot deny myself the gratification of expressing the satisfaction which we all felt here with the proceedings and speeches of the Boston dinner. I was particularly delighted with two or three circumstances: 1. The harmony which prevailed in respect to the tariff, or, rather, the acquiescence in the measure. 2. Your felicitous defence of your vote.[1] 3. The notice, truly national and patriotic, which you took of the great interest of internal improvements. And 4. The New–England feeling to which you so urgently appealed, and which the whole proceedings were well calculated to excite. Good will come of your work.

I have a letter from General [Peter B.] Porter, who will be here in two or three days. He postpones his decision until he comes here; but I think it will be to accept.

My health continues as it was when you left here. I commence my journey next week, from which I anticipate the best effects. I have been rendered very happy by the company of my only surviving daughter [Anne Brown Clay Erwin], who joined us a few days ago, and who is one of the best of girls. She brought with her her two children [Julia D. and Henry Clay Erwin], whom I had never seen.

Our news from Kentucky continues good.

You will have seen a report on the secret service fund.[2] It was a necessary explanation for the West. I must be held exclusively responsible for its publication, which the President approved at my instance. I hope it will meet your approbation.

My best regards to [Edward] Everett, [Benjamin] Gorham, and Mr. J[ames]. Mason.

Copy. G. T. Curtis, *Life of Daniel Webster,* 1:329.   1. Webster had voted for the Tariff Bill of 1828, the so-called "Tariff of Abominations."   2. Clay to Adams, June 3, 1828.

From JOHN M. FORBES, Buenos Aires, no. 59, June 14, 1828. Reports that the election was temporarily postponed because of irregularities and then was completed without opposition when Bernardino Rivadavia's party withdrew rather than face the possibility of assuming responsibility for a penniless government.

States that Frutuoso Rivera, chief of Banda Oriental [Uruguay], was thought to have allied himself with Emperor Pedro I of Brazil for a second time. Adds that Rivera was cursed throughout Buenos Aires when he conquered the province of Misiones, but then he sent to Buenos Aires trophies of his conquest, including a proclamation inviting the Misiones to join the Republic of Buenos Aires. Predicts they will accept this invitation and says that because of this action the government of Buenos Aires is now hoping for Rivera's success.

Reports that the English Minister to Brazil, Lord John Ponsonby, has suggested a second attempt at peace negotiations at Rio de Janeiro and that the government of Buenos Aires has named Juan Ramon Balcarce and Tomas Guido as ministers, and Pedro Feliciano Cavia as secretary. Also reports that a "tumultuous and premature" revolt occurred in Bolivia, but has been suppressed and that the Bolivian President, General Antonio Jose de Sucre, was seriously wounded in the fighting.

Continues on June 27.

Notes that the ministers nominated to hold peace negotiations with the Emperor of Brazil are expected to sail soon in the British ship, *Red Pole,* and that their chances for success are uncertain.

Points out that members of the National convention have assembled at Santa Fe, not for the purpose of considering a constitution but solely for the purpose of promoting peace and understanding between the provinces. Predicts a constitution will not be considered until "a far distant day." States that the former U.S. acting Consul in Buenos Aires, Dr. Robert Kortright, has submitted his resignation.

Protests that the "scandalous and unblushing abuses" by foreigners to the flag of the United States in the Plate River have "merited a much more energetic resistance than has been given." Gives several examples of this interference with American shipping, and concludes: "The timidity of our consuls in these cases seeks a justification in the absence of direct instructions of the Government, and the reluctance shown to approve the conduct of those who assume this responsibility." Fowards printed message of Governor Manuel Dorrego to the Buenos Aires legislature. LS. DNA, RG59, Dip. Disp., Argentina, vol. 3 (M69, R4). Received September 4, 1828; also in Espil, *Once Anos en Buenos Aires,* 491–3.

From WILLIAM B. LAWRENCE, London, no. 43, June 14, 1828. Reports the results of a conference with Lord Aberdeen. Is convinced the choice of an arbiter will be made at their next meeting on June 16. Alluded in the meeting to Emperor Nicholas I of Russia as his preference, while Aberdeen was apparently thinking of "the King of the Netherlands [William I]." Also exchanged remarks on the Northeastern frontier and learned that Aberdeen must first consult the Colonial Department on what he termed this "extremely difficult" issue.

Mentions that Lord Aberdeen has "more fully avowed," than had Lord Dudley earlier, the maintenance of British "maritime principles" relative to the blockade at Buenos Aires.

Reports on Portuguese matters, noting that the London journals have published a declaration of the Brazilian plenipotentiaries in Europe respecting the "Junta of Oporto" as the legitimate representative of Pedro [IV]. Reports that the Marquis Pedro de Sousa Holstein Palmela is en route home to Brazil where it is rumored he will be named Minister of Foreign Affairs. Believes Palmela's endorsement of the Constitutionists in Oporto must create great confidence in their cause as he "would not have entered into any rash scheme." LS. DNA, RG59, Dip,Disp., Great Britain, vol. 35 (M30, R31). Extract in Manning, *Diplomatic Correspondence . . . Canadian Relations,* 2:728. Received July 20, 1828.

From ROBERT MALLORY, Orange, Va., June 14, 1828. Reports that his poor health has required him to take leave for an indeterminate period from his duties as a clerk in the Department of War, but that he has found a suitable substitute. Notes his close personal relations with the outgoing Secretary of War, James Barbour, and requests that the incoming Secretary, Peter B. Porter, not abolish his job during his absence. "Being solicitous for the safety of my Office, let me pray Yr protection; as my enemies are looking for protection under the hope of a new incumbent to the Presidential Chair; and would buy favour by such prostitution." ALS. DNA, RG59, Accounting Records, Misc. Letters.

From PETER B. PORTER, New York, June 15, 1828. Explains his delay in leaving New York for Washington, hopes to arrive on June 18 and see Clay before his departure from the Capital, and notes "Maj. [Joseph] Delafield will accompany me and is almost as anxious as myself to see you on several points connected with our [Boundary] Commission [1:1006; 4:677-8]." ALS. InU.

From JOHN SERGEANT   Philadelphia, June 16, 1828
I have this moment received your favor of the 13th. inst., and will immediately set about the needful enquiries. The result shall be communicated to you as soon as possible.

It gives me pleasure to learn, from yourself, the state of your affairs. I will acknowledge, however, that solicitude on this subject, occasioned by various accounts,[1] led me to enquire while at Washington from one or two of your most discreet friends, and I was gratified to learn that upon this, as upon many other points, there had been great misrepresentation. Not that I think it any reproach to a public man to be poor. But, as respects your own comfort, it is quite another matter, and I am sincerely glad to find that in this particular you are at your ease.

We are in the midst of an operation here, to consolidate our force. Many little difficulties have embarrassed us. They are only to be overcome, by getting up a strong feeling, and turning it all into one channel, so as to produce a current powerful enough to bear down these petty obstacles. We have begun with a meeting to prepare for celebrating the 4th. July.[2] It went off very well. In a few days, we shall have a general public meeting of the friends of the Administration, to concert measures preparatory to the October elections: and then, we shall have the celebration itself, which will be as comprehensive and imposing as possible.[3] If, after this, we should have good news from Louisiana and Kentucky, Pennsylvania politics will, I hope, assume a new face.

I have not yet seen the Supplemental Address [June 10, 1828].

ALS. InU. 1. Clay to Wickliffe, May 24, 1828; Clay to Biddle, May 28, 1828; Sergeant to Clay, June 23, 1828. 2. See Philadelphia *United States Gazette*, June 28, 1828. 3. *Ibid.*, July 7, 1828.

To WILLIAM H. CRAWFORD Washington, June 17, 1828

I received your letter, under date the 10th ultimo, with its inclosure, both of which I have attentively perused. I regret extremely that an impression should prevail in Georgia, in which you appear to participate, that a spirit unfriendly to her interest animates the General Government. There can be no greater error. The Administration is most anxious faithfully to perform all its duties to Georgia and to the Union, If it has sometimes differed with that State about their accomplishment, the difference has related rather to the means than to the end. I think a candid review of all that has passed between the two Governments would satisfy you that no intentional wrong, or even intemperate language has ever proceeded from the Administration of the General Government towards Georgia. General [Edmund P.] Gaines did permit himself to use co nomine, by almost every president who preceded the present incumbent. I had in my mind the subject of a National University, of which it is not unusual for an Observatory to be an appendage. It cannot, I think, be doubted that the same principle upon which a national University could be established, (especially within the District of Columbia,) would justify the erection of an Observatory. Indeed, this latter institution, considered as a substantive and independent establishment, appears to me to be more clearly within the scope of the duties and powers of the General Government, than an University, because of its direct relation to the commerce and navigation of the United States, to say nothing of the public domain. Mr. Jefferson did more than recommend an Observatory. He actually obtained an appropriation to purchase philosophical instruments, (and they were accordingly purchased,) the acquisition of which was a waste of the public money, without such a Repository as an Observatory would afford. . . . P.S. I shewed your letter, of the 4th of February, to several of our mutual friends, and perhaps to some gentleman who did not stand in that relation to us both. I thought its contents were quite as honorable to you as to me. And it was in that spirit that I exhibited it. I regret that they have been made the subject of newspaper commentary. Should you feel it to be necessary to publish the whole, or any part of our correspondence, you have my full assent to the publication.

LS. KyLoF.

From ALEXANDER H. EVERETT, Madrid, no. 105, June 17, 1828.

Transmits Spanish national budgetary estimates for 1828, noting that the total sum is 448,000,000 Reals, or $22,000,000; but believes that figures from the war and navy departments may not have been included owing to the expected costs of "the war with the colonies." Discusses developments in the Russo–Turkish War as gleaned from newspaper reports, rumors, and his diplomatic contacts. Has been assured by the Russian Minister to Madrid, Pierre d'Oubril, that with regard to neutral commerce in wartime. the policy of the Russian Navy is governed by the 1801 Russian treaty with Britain. Opines that Spain will adopt a more hostile stance toward Miguel and Portugal than will other powers, and that in spite of support of the Portuguese Cortes, which was to have convened on June 9 to proclaim him King, Miguel will fail in his desire to mount the throne because of opposition "by his own army . . . as well as foreign powers." LS. DNA, RG59, Dip. Disp., Spain, vol. 29 (M31, R29). Received August 13, 1828. For the Anglo–Russian Treaty of 1801, see Parry, *Treaty Series,* 56:105–33.

From FRANCISCO DE PAULA SANTANDER, Ocana, Colombia, June 17, 1828. Submits an "important document," dated Ocana, June 11, to the "impartial judgment of the American People, and of the old friend of the cause of Colombia, the Honorable and Illustrious H. Clay." The enclosed document, signed by 51 deputies to the constitutional "Grand Convention" at Ocana, explains the reason why the convention, which convened on April 9, 1828, suspended its deliberations on June 10. In sum, a number of deputies withdrew from the proceedings in early June, giving no reasons, but leaving an inadequate legal number [55] to carry on. The undersigned, however, aver that they "have fulfilled their duties as Representatives of the people of Colombia; and that the misfortunes which may flow from so unlooked for event, can never, with justice, or reason, be imputed to them." Copy, trans. InHi. For accounts of the breakup of the Ocana Convention, see J. B. Trend, *Bolivar and the Independence of Spanish America* (Clinton, Mass., 1951), 197–8; Harold A. Bierck, Jr., ed., *Selected Writings of Bolivar.* 2 vols. (New York, 1951), 2:750.

On June 19, 1828, writing from Philadelphia, Edward Barry, transmitted to Clay a Spanish language version of the June 11 enclosure in Santander's letter of June 17. ALS. DNA, RG59, Notes from Colombian Legation, vol. 1 (M51, R2).

From ALEJANDRO VELEZ, Philadelphia, June 17, 1828. Announces that he will be handling diplomatic matters previously dealt with by Jose Maria Salazar, former Colombian minister to the United States.

Reports that he has obtained a letter "written by Mr. Robert F. Jones, from the dungeons of Carraca, near Cadiz, where he is confined, together with twenty other officers and men of the crew of the Colombian privateer, 'General Armaria,' captured off the coast of Spain." Explains further that Jones and several others of these prisoners are American citizens, "suffering the greatest privations and misery."

With a view toward ending the war between Colombia and Peru [1828–1829] and mitigating further suffering, asks Clay to work through Alexander Everett, American minister to Spain, in obtaining "the exchange of the prisoners in question."

Discusses the legal aspects of the case, dismissing as "obsolete" the Spanish contention based on the 14th article of her 1795 [Pinckney] treaty with the U.S. Cites Everett's earlier success in securing the release from Ceuta prisons of several Americans off the Colombian privateer, *General Soublette*. LS, in Spanish, with trans. in State Dept. file. DNA, RG59, Notes from Colombian Legation, vol. 1 (M51, R2). On February 9, 1829, Clay wrote the Colombian Consul General in New York, Xavier de Medina, reporting that with the interposition of Manuel Salmon, Spanish Foreign Minister to the U.S., "the Prisoners twenty-one in number, have been set at liberty, without exchange, upon engagement on their part not to serve against Spain." Copy. DNA, RG59, Notes to Foreign Ministers and Consuls, vol. 4, pp. 142-3 (M38, R4). The same day Clay wrote William Henry Harrison, U.S. Minister to Colombia, in dispatch no. 4, instructing him to inform the Colombian government that through the good offices of Alexander Everett, Spain has released the prisoners of war captured from the *General Armaria*. Copy. DNA, RG59, Dip. Instr., vol. 12, p. 191 (M77, R7).

From WILLIAM H. D. C. WRIGHT, Rio de Janiero, June 17, 1828. Reports a riot on June 11 of drunken German and Irish mercenary troops, some 2500 to 3500 men, in the employ of the Brazilian government. Describes the tension in Rio de Janiero, frequently involving the killing and wounding of "Negroes (to whom the Irish have a violent hatred), the Negroes in return butchering in the most inhumane manner every Irishman and German who fell in their power." Reports the landing, by request of the Brazilian government, of 600 marines of the English and French vessels of war in port who restored order.

Reports the plunder of the brig, *Fox*, from Gloucester, Massachusetts, which arrived here on June 12. Notes that the ship was "robbed of a thousand dollars of property by a pirate schooner" near the Cape Verde Islands. Mentions, furthermore, that shortly afterwards the same private vessel boarded the brig *Conveyance* from Norfolk but failed to find any suitable goods. ALS. DNA, RG59, Cons. Dip., Rio de Janiero, vol. 3 (M-T172, R4). Received August 2, 1828.

From NICHOLAS BIDDLE Philadelphia, June 18, 1828
As you represent the terrestrial part of the theological interests [Kenyon Seminary] in the joint care of yourself & Bishop [Philander] Chase, I enclose a copy of a letter received this morning from the Bishop—and also my answer which, after reading it—you will have the goodness to seal & forward with any observations, which you may deem necessary.

I read this morning an admirable letter [6:97-100] from you to our late Chargé d'affaires in Brazil [Condy Raguet] published in the [Washington *Daily*] Nat. Intelligencer,[1] and should be glad to have a copy of the whole correspondence, if you have one to spare. We of the working classes cannot aspire to read much of these things—but I wish to send the Book to Commodore [James] Biddle.

ALS. DLC-HC (DNA, M212, R3).   1. On June 17, 1828; also in *ASPFR*, 6:1066-8; see Clay to Biddle, June 21, 1828, and Tudor to Clay, August 20, 1828.

From WILLIAM G. DUNCAN   Louisville, June 18, 1828
& WILLIAM F. BULLOCK

Two colored men, Edward & Samuel who were brought here in irons, from Maryland have induced us to institute suits for their freedom— They say they were Emancipated by their Master Mr. West of Maryland who died in March last leaving a will in the hands of Judge Keys or Keas[1] and that before the will was proved they were run off in irons by their young Master Arthur West—

They say they [*sic*, the] will was to be proven in Marlboro' and that their old Master told them before his death to go [to] Judge Keas—

We consider it due to Humanity to investigate their rights—and on the other hand we do not wish to annoy their master if they are slaves—I must therefore ask of you the favor to Enquire whether there is such a man as Judge Key, or Keas in that part of Maryland Contiguous to Washington and that you will request him or any other person conversant of the facts to give us any information which may be important to these colored men.

With great respect and a desire that your health may soon be entirely regained.... P.S. Your answer in the suit of Nicholas &c vs [James] Morrisons Exor will be prepared as soon as possible[2]

ALS. DNA, RG59, Misc. Letters (M179, R66). For Duncan, see *BDAC*. For Bullock, see H. Levin, ed., *The Lawyers and Lawmakers of Kentucky* (Chicago, 1897), 163.   1. Edmund Key [1771–1857] of Prince George's County, Md., a prominent Maryland Circuit Court jurist and second cousin to Francis Scott Key.   2. On November 4, the Board of Trustees of Transylvania University approved an arrangement Clay had made as executor of the Morrison Estate to refer the case of George Nicholas's heirs to arbitrators for award. KyLxT.

From JAMES RAY, near Newark, Delaware, June 18, 1828. Appeals "on behalf of myself & fellow sufferers, in the shameful plunder of our property by the Spaniards from the brig James Lawrence." Recounts in detail his various appeals to Alexander Everett, U.S. Minister to Spain, to the President, and to others for redress. Asks that these various letters, certificates, and reports "be laid before the President" for submission to the Spanish government as "the proofs of the chicanery of the Spanish officers." ALS. DNA, RG59, Misc. Claims, Spain.

From JAMES B. HARRISON, Lynchburg, Va., June 19, 1828. Seeks a "minor diplomatic station abroad," noting that he and his fellow townsmen are strongly attached to the Administration although Virginia has received no "appointment of this nature" from it. Concludes with the hope of "the complete overthrow of the combination" against the Administration; and to this end quotes the "classical English maxim" that "When Knaves *combine,* honest men should unite." ALS. DNA, RG59, A. and R. (MR2).

From DANIEL McLAUGHLIN   Philadelphia, June 19, 1828
Solely from a desire to contribute my small mite to perpetuating our Institutions (the happiness of our common country I beg leave to mention what has evidentally come to my knowledge of what I consider very

ungrateful & iniquitous conduct of a certain protegee of the Administration I alude sir to Mr Thomas [M.] Rodney our present representative at the port of Havana From a source which I consider entitled to credit I understand that this Gentleman is in the habit of grossly vilifying & misrepresenting the conduct & motives of the present Administration with a view to promote by such means to designs of Gen. Jackson & the Combination that supports him

Mr R being supposed to know whatever the Cabinette has done in regard to Cuba represents that Mr [Daniel P.] Cook of Illinoise [*sic*] was sent thither [6:295–6] for no other purpose than in order to enrich him with the spoils of the public Treasury under pretence of performing secret services for Government   That there was nothing of the kind to perform & that Mr. C. was totally incapable of performing such & did nothing but spend his time there as on a jaunt of pleasure &c & that this favour was confered on him *because* he voted for Mr Adams in the House of Representatives & on that account lost his election to the present Congress &c I know nothing sir of Mr. R. except what I learn from some of his associates but from that I judge that his conduct in his office is not unexesstionable & if it would be easy to discover Misconduct (if any) I think it might deserve notice & lead to more important discoveries My information however is not definite in regard to him I form my suspicions from what I know of his conduct in private life & the revenue that I understand he has said he derives from his appointment being no less a sum than $12000 per Annum & being at loose or profligate habits But my opinion sir of his private & official conduct is founded on what I know of that of his associates & what they report of him Believing that Mr R's place was given him partly from respect to his father [Caesar Augustus Rodney] & partly through charity & that he is become a livid & violent traducer of his benefactors in order to promote the very interested & dishonorable wishes of a few leaders of a faction hostile to the prosperity & dignity of the nation I thought proper to give you this notice of it But if it is not perfectly easy to inspect his official conduct you perceive sir that I have no evidence that would warrant a formal investigation

ALS. DNA, RG59, A. and R. (M531, R7).

To ADAM BEATTY   Washington, June 20, 1828

I received your letter of the 12th instant, and thank you for the very satisfactory information it contains on political affairs. The result of the election in Kentucky, whatever way it may be, will have a powerful, if not deciding influence on the Presidential Election. I think from all the information that has reached me, and judging from the present state of things, we may calculate upon ten out of the eleven votes of Maryland, and upon a majority of at least twenty–four of those of New York. But if the issue of the contest in Kentucky should be adverse, both of those States may be materially affected.[1] To what extent, it is impossible now to say.

I was not aware, until the receipt of your letter, that your son [William Rochester Beatty] had not gone with Judge [William B.] Rochester.

I perceive by a Savannah paper, which arrived this morning, that the Judge has returned to the United States from Omoa. That he was authorized to do, if, upon his arrival there he should find a state of civil war and commotion which should render his presence unnecessary, or hazardous. It is fortunate that your son did not accompany him. I should be very glad to be able to contribute to the accomplishment of your wishes respecting your son. At present there is no vacancy in any office of Secretary Legation. But it is possible that one may occur, before a great while, to the South. In that event, I will take pleasure in presenting his name to the President.

LS. Courtesy of Earl M. Ratzer, Highland Park, Ill.   1. Adams received 6 out of 11 of Maryland's electoral votes, 16 out of New York's 36, and none of Kentucky's 14. Florence Weston, *The Presidential Election of 1828* (Philadelphia, 1974), 181–2. See also 6:360–3.

From "JUNIUS," June 20, 1828. Attributes Clay's decline of political influence to the fact that he is not "an accomplished scholar, profoundly versed by close application to books, with the history of past times." Admits, however, that he has a "thorough knowledge of men," and that he understands well "the springs of human action." Even so, charges that his ambition and "thirst for office" is now clear to all Americans, and that his defense of Adams, which you "elevated by your vote and influence to the Presidency," is not the "voluntary sacrifice of yourself for the good of the country" that you claim it to be. Cites Clay's Baltimore speech of May 13 to the point of Clay's lack of historical understanding. Also comments at length on the corrupt bargain with Adams that has so outraged the American people. Charges that even the "sycophanic partizans" and flatterers who now surround you should not conceal from you the fact that the "purity of your motives are drawn into public question." Points out that "your present [political] situation is one particularly embarrassing," and predicts "your last political throes will be like the convulsive efforts of the mentally maimed Lion." Wonders why it is that "almost every officer in the present administration, from the President and his Secretaries, down to the lowest menial in the park" is "industriously engaged, by means the most corrupt" in attempts to "crush and put down a single private individual [Andrew Jackson]." Especially criticizes the cruelty of their attacks on Mrs. Jackson, and notes that the newspapers "under the immediate patronage of the Executive, have charged General Jackson with murder, cruelty, fraud, and almost every crime in the dark catalogue of human iniquity." Singles out Clay's attacks on Jackson as a "dangerous military chieftain" as beneath the dignity of a man who was once "a beloved favorite of the democracy of the nation." in those days "you were hailed as the patron of liberty, the champion of free principles, and the enlightened advocate of the right of instruction. Now, you are viewed as the friend of autocracy, the advocate of enlarged Executive patronage and power, and the contemner of the right of instruction." Reminds Clay, further, that once he had condemned the members of the Hartford Convention as "enemies to their country, and traitors to their government," whereas now "we see that administration, of which you are a conspicuous member, zealously supported by all the prominent actors and advocates of that dark and wicked conspiracy."

358

Charges, in addition, "once you opposed, with all your influence, the election of a cabinet officer to the presidential chair as a most alarming and dangerous precedent," whereas now, "as if to show the profligate boldness of your inconsistency, you justify your vote for John Q. Adams, on the ground that you had acted in accordance with a 'safe precedent.'" Compares Clay's earlier dislike of Adams with recent of his speeches in which Adams is portrayed as "almost immaculate." Concludes: "How can you calculate that the purity of your motives will not be called in question, when your conduct displays such glaring inconsistency?" Lexington *Kentucky Gazette*, June 20, 1828.

From CHARLES SAVAGE, Guatemala, June 20, 1828. Reports that the contending armies have signed a ten–day armistice and that a treaty has been negotiated between the state of San Salvador and General Manuel de Arce, chief of the Federal army. Encloses a copy of the peace treaty as published in a local newspaper. Has just learned that William B. Rochester arrived at Omoa three days ago enroute to the United States, it being reported that "his return is attributed to personal political motives emmanating from the death of Mr. [DeWitt] Clinton of New York." Adds in a postscript that General Rafael Merino, late Governor of San Salvador, "has been condemned to be shot." ALS. DNA, RG59, Cons. Disp., Guatemala, vol. 1 (M–T337, R1). Received October 11, 1828.

To NICHOLAS BIDDLE   Washington, June 21, 1828
I regretted to learn from your letter to Bishop [Philander] Chase[1] that he had lost his pocket book, which I had not before heard of. I have transmitted to him your letter, to which it did not appear to me necessary to add any thing.

I forwarded by yesterdays mail the published correspondence of Mr [Condy] Raguet, Commodore [James] Biddle &c [5:709, 747; 6:97–100].[2] The Commodore shews himself alike able to command success with the pen and the sword. On one of the topics, which he discussed, he displayed an extent of research, of which I found it useful to avail myself when I had lately occasion to argue the same question.

I invite your perusal of the whole correspondence. I think the friends of Mr. Raguet, and he himself ultimately, must regret that it was ever called for.... P.S. Tell my friend [Nathaniel] Chapman that I am off tomorrow for the West; and that my general health has sensibly improved under the prescriptions of himself and Dr. [Philip S.] Physic[k].

ALS. DLC–Nicholas Biddle Papers (DNA, M212, R20).   1. Biddle to Clay, June 18, 1828.   2. *Ibid.*

From THOMAS L. L. BRENT, Libson, no. 73, June 21, 1828. Submits two translations of documents relative to Miguel's efforts to become King, an act that is anticipated at the forthcoming meeting on June 23 of the Cortes, which is packed with the Prince's supporters. Explains that local attorneys are directed "only to vote in favor of Dom Miguel . . . to the exclusion of [Pedro I] the Emperor of Brazil [Pedro IV of Portugual]," and "to propose that in the default of Dom Miguel . . . the crown should revert to" another line of Portuguese royalty. Reports pressure on Miguel "to take soon a wife" and "to direct his attention to the suppression of masonic societies." Adds that it is not known whether the Prince, upon the decision of the Cortes, "will allow himself to be immediately proclaimed."

Reviews the domestic situation in which "the publick are not allowed to know correctly" the news from the interior, some areas of which are apparently held by hostile armies. Mentions the incident of the "nine students who murdered near Coimbra some professors of that university." Notes that they were hanged yesterday, their speedy executions "owing to party spirit." Reports the actual or impending departure of many foreign ministers—English, Austrian, Russian, Danish and others—resulting from Miguel's efforts to become King. LS. DNA, RG59, Dip. Disp., Portugal, vol. 8 (M43, R7). Received August 27, 1828. Pedro I of Brazil and Pedro IV of Portugual were the same person.

From SIMON HICKEY, Lexington, Ky., June 21, 1828. Explains at considerable length the "real secrets" of a complicated lock Clay had commissioned him to make. Reports that he has mailed the lock to Washington, and that while his asking price of $100 for it is quite low, "My desire has been more to show what Kentucky can do, than to make any money." Notes further that "If Mr. Adams should want an alarm lock I will make him one of the first quality on order." Mentions, in passing, that "the Jackson boys" in Lexington have been "completely discomfited in their attempts" to undermine the integrity of the Adams administration. ALS. DNA, RG59, Misc. Letters (M179, R66).

From WILLIAM B. LAWRENCE, London, no. 44, June 21, 1828. Refers to a debate in Parliament on June 2, relative to "the State of the civil Government of Canada." Concludes from various sources that "the difficulties" in Canada "seem to be of a most complicated character." Mentions the "dissensions between the English inhabitants and the descendants of the French settlers in Lower Canada [Quebec]," and notes a six to one population ratio in favor of the latter. Describes Upper Canada [Ontario], as being predominantly English in origin. Reports on the "discontent" occasioned by religious, political, and economic differences between the two provinces. Observes from both general and private opinions "an increasing belief that Canada will not for many years remain a part of the British Empire." States, however, that England would "hesitate long before acceding to an arrangement repugnant to her pride" regarding any consideration of the sale of Canada to satisfy the public debt. Feels that Britain, given the "choice between incurring the additional expense of sending large forces to Canada or effecting a separation, a new independent state composed of the present British Possessions in North America would be preferred to the annexation of a portion of them to the United States."

Refers to the Russo–Turkish War, and suggests that "delays to discussions under the Treaty of July 6, 1827 [6:780–2]," stem from differences of opinion among the Allies on a "loan or gift to the new Greek state," and on the presence of the Russian fleet in the Mediterranean. Plans to request of Prince Christoph von Lieven, Russian ambassador to London, that he lend his influence in stabilizing the situation.

Announces in a postscript the British selection of the King of the Netherlands, William I, as arbiter for the Northeastern boundary dispute. LS. DNA, RG59, Dip. Disp., Great Britain, vol. 35 (M30, R31). Excerpt in Manning, *Diplomatic Correspondence... Canadian Relations,* 2:731–5. Received August 9, 1828.

From WILLIAM B. LAWRENCE, London, no. 45, June 22, 1828. Transmits "an official correspondence with Lord Aberdeen," announcing the British choice of the King of the Netherlands, William I, as arbiter of the Northeastern boundary question. Reviews and summarizes in detail the prolonged negotiations since March 24, which resulted in the British choice. Explains that Russia or Denmark would not have been satisfactory from their standpoint. States that "the personal character of the King of the Netherlands is well Known ... and we have every reason to conclude that ... a thorough investigation of the case will be made." Believes also that the King is "scrupulous." Reports meeting with Aberdeen on June 19, "in order formally to invite the King ... to undertake the important and friendly office." LS. DNA, RG59, Dip. Disp., Great Britain, vol. 35 (M30, R31); also in Manning, *Diplomatic Correspondence... Canadian Relations,* 2:736–40. Received August 9, 1828.

From B. AYMAR & CO., New York, June 23, 1828. Recommend the appointment of Mr. John James Hall, an English merchant resident in Manzanillo de Cuba, as U.S. commercial agent there. Note that "our vessels are at times subject to vexatious charges and trouble by the lower grade of Spanish officers," and that "Since the close of the B West India trade Manzanillo de Cuba has become a resort for the Jamaica traders & the trade has consequently increased for our vessells." ALS. DNA, RG59, A. and R. (MR2).

From HECTOR DAVIS, Hanover Court House, June 23, 1828. Invites him to visit Henrico and Hanover counties on his way home to Kentucky so that the people there may "have an opportunity of manifesting in some degree their high regard for *one* whose destiny was cast amongst them." ALS. DLC–TJC (DNA, M212, R13). Envelope marked "Private."

From ALEXANDER H. EVERETT, Madrid, no. 107, June 23, 1828. Encloses a translation of a private dispatch by the Council of Castile to the principal courts of Justice in the various provinces warning them "against the mechinations which are supposed to be in train for the reestablishment of a constitutional Government." States that such a rumored plan can be traced to "the Spanish Refugees at London in concert with the Liberal party in France."

Reviews the situation in Portugal and says he has been assured by Manuel Gonzales Salmon, Spanish Prime Minister, that Spain will not interfere in the support of Miguel.

Reports receiving information provided by a private, unnamed source that Count de Ofalia [Narciso de Heredia], Spanish Minister to Great Britain, "advises an attempt to reconquer Mexico, and place one of the Infantes there as Vice Roy," a plan said to be supported by Great Britain financially and militarily. Views this rumor "as a thing impossible that such a proposition should really have been made."

Mentions, in conclusion, that the Consulate of Cadiz drew up "a strong representation" to the King, Ferdinand VII, "in favor of the acknowledgment of the Independence of the American Colonies" but that it never reached Ferdinand.

Adds in postscript on June 25 that he has learned the French are about to evacuate their troops through the port of Cadiz, using "two ships of the Line, four Frigates & about thirty transports." Reports that part of the production of "the silver mines is pledged to France as security" by Spain to pay for the French occupation. LS, with postscript in Everett's hand. DNA, RG59, Dip. Disp., Spain, vol. 29 (M31, R29). Received September 4, 1828; also in Manning, *Diplomatic Correspondence . . . Latin American Nations,* 3:2161–2.

From JOHN SERGEANT   Philadelphia, June 23, 1828
I had the pleasure of writing to you on the 15th. [*sic,* June 16] inst., only to acknowledge your letter of the 13th. Since then, I have made enquiry upon the subject of a loan, and am very sorry to say that there is no probability of being able to obtain one in Philadelphia. Such operations can only be effected with moneyed institutions, or with money lenders. The former, acting upon a system adapted to a limited sphere, and calculated to secure mercantile punctuality, do not adventure abroad, nor without personal security upon the spot, of at least two or three good names. In general, too, they will only lend for short periods—The latter (money lenders) having a commodity which is always in demand, are very precise in their notions of security, and preemptory as well as scrupulous in exacting it—Upon the ordinary footing, therefore, of a business operation (upon which alone you are willing to place it) I am satisfied nothing can be done.

Some months ago, when I was apprehensive that your affairs might be in a state to cause you anxiety, I stated to our friend Col: [William L.] Brent my wish that any such difficulty (if existing) might be removed, and the part I was willing to take in removing it. This is, perhaps, what you allude to, in your late publication. All I need now say upon the subject is, that I am of the same mind still, and will at any time do, cheerfully and with pleasure, what was then proposed. I wish it were in my power to go further, and offer you the whole loan myself. But it is not. I have no doubt of the ample sufficiency of the security. If I might be permitted to offer an assurance, however, I would advise a negociation with Mr. [John Jacob] Astor [2:686]. The additional one per cent for a few years, will not come to much; and as he deals upon the mere footing of business, in his usual line, you will incur no obligation but the pecuniary one. Pardon the freedom of this suggestion.

We are again in motion here, and I hope with effect. The 4th. of

July will find us cordially united, or make us so, and rid us of many petty embarrassments.

I hope some of our friends in Kentucky will give us early information.[1]

ALS. DLC–HC (DNA, M212, R3). 1. The Kentucky state election was held on August 6. Pennsylvania went to the presidential polls on October 31, followed by Kentucky on November 3.

From JOHN HAMILTON   New York, June 24, 1828

I take the liberty of offering to you my services as a charge Des affaires or Minister Plenipotentiary to *any* foreign port—I would perform any duty assigned me correctly, & with aware [*sic*] to the strictest economy, in fact would be willing to serve in the capacity of a travelling gentleman. for *one* half the sum usually in such cases—I can make a Speech of 3 hours in length—and will say anything and everything to advance the interest of my employers—if any office under your control is vacant You will please give it to me—at a small Salary my recommendation is—I am an American—a democrat and an *Adams* man—[P.S.] answer me by next Thursday—at New York City

ALS. DNA, RG59, A. and R. (MR2).

From ABRAHAM B. NONES, Maracaibo, June 24, 1828. Discusses the dissolution of the Grand Convention at Ocana, in which "Twenty two Deputies deserted in a body . . . to the Bolivian party" which disapproved of the "project of the New Constitution." States that President Simon Bolivar is now "off to Bogota."

Is alarmed that this "occurrence . . . will tend to drive the parties to extremities, and increase the confussion already existing." ALS. DNA, RG59, Cons. Disp., Maracaibo, vol. 1 (M–T62, R1). Received July 18, 1828. See Watts to Clay, February 10, 1828.

From PHILIP YOST, JR., Philadelphia, June 24, 1828. Solicits appointment to the post of Commercial Agent at Port au Prince. Reports that the "Political State of the Island [Haiti] is somewhat precarious," and doubts the present regime will last much longer. States: "The most respectable part of [the] community utter loud complaints against the Treaty with France, and I should not be surprised to hear of another cut–throat scene taking place, with Frenchmen alone as all their displeasure is directed against them, notwithstanding they have a most powerful advocate in the French Consul." ALS. DNA, RG59, A. and R. (MR4). The Franco–Haitian Treaty is in Parry, *Treaty Series,* 75:417–23.

From ROBERT M. HARRISON, St. Bartholomew, June 25, 1828. Articulates the problems of the American commercial interests and citizens living on the island. Is concerned that many agents cannot "transact business in the court house . . . without employing a Broker," which they want to avoid. Expresses additional grievances pertaining to the high percentage of governmental taxes in the event of death or "leaving the colony and disposing of their property." Discusses at length the legal intimidations of Americans living there.

Reports "the circumstance of vessels coming out from Baltimore to this place to equip for Privateers[,] Guineamen," proceed to St. Eustatia "to get a dutch flag," return here for "final equipments" and then enter the slave trade "for the [African] *coast* or a piratical cruise!" Exclaims that they obtain slaves, and "make arrangements with purchasers and deliver them at [Dutch] Saba [Leeward Islands]!" Complains that many ships arrive from Baltimore "but as they have not committed at that time any offense *against the U States* I cannot detain their Registers."

Continues on June 30: Reports that "the Ship called *Bolivar* fitted out in August as a Buenos Ayrean cruiser has this moment come ... with American Ensign and Pendant flying!" Describes its armaments and states he had no power or authorization "to compel the captain to deposit anything with me. . . . It is lamentable indeed to see our Seamen on board these Piratical cruises whilst our ships of war experience the greatest difficulties in procuring men." Requests again "the necessity of a light cruiser stationed in these seas."

Concludes on July 2 that the *Bolivar* sailed for St. Eustatia, obviously in search of Brazilian prizes. ALS. DNA, RG59, Cons. Disp., St. Bartholomew, vol. 1 (M72, R1). Received July 22, 1828.

To JOSIAH STODDARD   New Market, Va., June 25, 1828
JOHNSTON
At the moment of my departure from Washington I received two letters (one from [Martin] Duralde and the other from Mr. Duprey)[1] recommending Mr. Gibson,[2] Editor of the [New Orleans] Argus, as Surveyor of the port of N. Orleans I had not time to consult with you and Mr. [Charles J. D.] Bouligny, and directed the letters to be laid before the President. I have no wish on the subject but that a competent person should be appointed—one who is not tainted with Jacksonism, and who may be agreeable to friends. Will you confer with Mr. Bouligny on the matter?

We are now about 120 miles from the City. My horses stand the journey better than I do. The heat is excessive. I shall stop a few days at the White Sulphur Springs in Greenbriar [County, Va.], where a letter, put into the post office, the day you may receive this or the next would overtake me. . . .

ALS. PHi.   1. For Jacques Dupre, see *NCAB*, 10:75.   2. For John Gibson, see Albert A. Fossier, *New Orleans, the Glamour Period, 1800–1840* (New Orleans, 1957), 183.

From WILLIAM B. LAWRENCE, London, no. 46, June 26, 1828. Discusses his meeting with Lord Aberdeen on June 19 in which he mentioned the problem of the "jurisdiction to be exercised over the disputed [Northeast] territory," pointing out that the "settlers on the Madawaska" had established a government, without which the "interposition of either Maine or New Brunswick" would have been necessary to avert "temporary anarchy." Referring to the Convention [6:859–60] "respecting the territory West of the Rocky Mountains," Lord Aberdeen "inquired whether I would enter into a similar arrangement with regard to the country now under consideration." Lawrence replied that he had used the Madawaska reference "merely by way of illustration" to lead into a discussion of his orders from the President to make "a demand for the redress of a specific injury on an American citizen [John Baker, 6: 1272-3]," and an end to Britain's attempt to exercise "exclusive jurisdiction" in a territory the U.S. owns. Continued with a detailed exposition of the principles of law involved in the jurisdiction question, citing supporting historical examples, especially the Treaty of Paris of 1783, to make the points to Aberdeen that "The territory now disputed was never held by Great Britain like a town or a fortress"; nor had the U.S. "held any portion of the territory embraced within the original states as a *'grant'* or *'cession'* from a foreign power." Concludes: "I cannot flatter myself that I have been able to change the views of Lord Aberdeen, but . . . he said that he would give to my observations a full consideration and requested me not to regard what had fallen from him as the final opinion of the British Government." LS. DNA, RG59, Dip. Disp., Great Britain, vol. 31 (M30, R31); also in Manning, *Diplomatic Correspondence . . . Canadian Relations,* 2:741-4. Received September 4, 1828.

From WILLIAM TUDOR, U.S.S. *Macedonia,* Rio de Janeiro, no. 92, June 26, 1828. Reports on the recent uprising in Rio de Janeiro of Irish and German mercenaries who had not received their regular rations and pay promised by the Brazilian government. States that the city "pursued the strange and dangerous course of arming the slaves" and that the British navy protected Emperor Pedro I until quiet was restored and the slaves were disarmed. Notes that the Irish are to be returned to Ireland and German troops sent to the army in the South.

Reports also that a ship arrived two days ago from Bahia with news of a revolutionary conspiracy to murder "all persons in authority" and revolt against the Emperor.

Asserts his regret that Congress failed to pass the appropriation for the U.S. Navy, because the sailors insist on being discharged before their time of service has expired if wages are not paid on schedule. States that sixty or seventy men have been discharged because of this and that many more will have the right in a few days to demand their discharge. Mentions that many of these men will then go into the Brazilian navy where they are promised high wages, "or what is deplorable, engaged on board vessels in the slave trade."

Comments that the Navy sloop, *Boston,* is hourly expected from Montevideo; that there are now in Rio de Janeiro "four Brazilian ships of war in readiness for sea, two English and two French." ALS. DNA, RG59, Dip. Disp., Brazil, vol. 6 (M121, R8). Received August 16, 1828. Letter marked *"Confidential."*

From JAMES BROWN   Paris, June 27, 1828
I have been somewhat alarmed at discovering from the newspapers that you had arrived in Philadelphia for the purpose of consulting Physicians respecting your health. I knew that it had long been delicate, that your

labors had been great and that with all your firmness you could not be altogether indifferent to the shameful attacks which were levelled at you, as well in the publick Journals as on the floor of Congress. Doctor [Samuel] Brown however greatly relieved my mind by assuring me that your complaint was by no means dangerous, and that travelling, abstraction from business and a change of scene, and air, would speedily restore you to health and strength. I beg of you to avail yourself of the recess of Congress, and withdrawing from all business, and selecting for yourself the most agreeable route to endeavor to effect a speedy restoration of your enfeebled Constitution. By no means if you can avoid it return at this time to Kentucky, where party spirit, and lawless violence, are likely to return uncontrouled sway, and sweep away all moderation and good sense. The North where you will find a more calm state of publick opinion, and a higher state of moral and physical culture, will better administer to your cure by more aggreeably occupying your mind and diverting it from political cares. I would were I in your situation, visit the falls of Niagara, and descend the S Lawrence to Montreal, and thence return to New York by Boston. In the course of this journey, you will view at once the most beautiful and diversified scenery in the U States, and the most refined and cultivated society on the other side of the Atlantic excepting perhaps that of Virginia and South Carolina.

I have this moment received a letter from our Consul [Reuben G. Beasley] at Harve who informs me that two Packets ships have arrived and that I shall receive my newspapers and letters to morrow. He announces to me the appointment of Mr James Barbour as Minister at London. You could not have selected an individual within the circles of the Presidents friends, for whom I entertain a greater esteem on account of the generosity and manliness of his character and the excellence of his heart. I am sure that he will please by his kind and candid manners those of our Countrymen who may pass through England. He is a good speciman of the Virginia character which will be something new in England. It is to be regretted that the Salary is so small that if he indulges in his naturally hospitable temper he must greatly impair his fortune. I am told however that Ministers plenipotentiary there do not often[1] give Diplomatic dinners, which are only given by Ambassadors and the Nobility. If this is the case he may live cheaper in London than he could do in Paris where Ministers entertain nearly as much as Ambassodors. I have heard it said, that Mr [William B.] Lawrence would not remain at London after the arrival of a Minister. Perhaps he may apply to be transferred to Paris as the State of society here is more agreeable to him. His character is spoken of in the most favorable manner by all those who have seen him in London. We shall wait with some anxiety to know who will be Secretary of War.[2]

The Russians have passed the Danube on the 7th. and 8th. after meeting with some assistance [sic, resistance]. Their army is full of enthusiasm and in a higher state of discipline. The Turks are preparing to combat every inch of ground and will derive great advantages from the nature of the Country through which the invaders will be obligated to march. The Persians it is said have commenced hostile movements on their side against the Porte and he will have equally to dread the infidelity of the Janizares [*sic*, Janissaries] and the discontents of the Christians. If the Russian shall not be opposed by some European power the Turkish Empire must be of short duration. Its distruction would confer a great benefit on the cause of civilization.

You will perceive that the refusal to discuss our claims has been alledged by Labbay Pompieres[3] amongst the Charges against the late ministry. General Mathieu Dumas[4] who served in our Revolutionary war is connected with Beaumarchais heirs [3:311-3], and as their claim awaits the settlement of ours, he puts an interest in their adjustment. I hardly think our proposal for an arbitration will be accepted but I have some hope that in refusing it ministry will make some proposal for the adjustment of our Claims. If a gross sum smaller than the amount of the Claims as stated by the Claimants could be accepted perhaps it might be offered. Our experience as derived from the last Spanish treaty [2:678, 803-16] proves that claimants exaggerate the amount of their claims. In that instance I think the claims were stated to amount to more than fifteen Millions, and yet when examined, were covered by five—If the claimants had an agent authorized to compromise for them perhaps something might be done—This however is a delicate subject and any Minister who would make a Treaty on that basis would expose his character to suspicion of an unfavorable kind.

Mrs. Brown['s] health which had improved by much, has lately been injured by a severe cold, followed by fever, and difficulty of breathing. She coughs so much that if I did not believe her complaint asthmatic I should fear her lungs were affected. I have been advised that it proceeds from weakness arising from a long regimen and free use of medicine. Her Physicians advise me to take her to the sea shore where she may have the benefit of sea bathing. If her strength will permit I shall accompany her in a few days to Dieppe where I shall leave her and return to Paris. The distance is but a ride of 16 hours. I have passed many anxious days and nights within the last eight months on her account. She is too weak to support a sea voyage. I hope a change of air will relieve her. In addition to the complaint of which I wrote you[5] she suffers from the complaints incident to the critical period of life at which she has arrived. Her spirits are good and she never permits her courage to abandon her. As she is generally beloved by all her acquaintances she has received from all of them daily proof of sympathy and kindness.

The present Ministry[6] having proposed laws conformable to the charter, and in accordance with the publick opinion, have gained much popularity since the opening of the Session. The Count de la Ferronnays Minister of foreign affairs unites great frankness and elevation of character to talents far above mediocrity. Mr de Martignac Minister of the Interior possesses talents as a lawyer and statesman of the highest order. He is a ready and eloquent debater and seems to understand the management of a popular assembly. Mr. Roy[7] Minister of Finance although rather a heavy and uninteresting speaker so far as his manner is concerned yet understands perfectly well the subjects belonging to his Department, and with great wealth, the fruit of his own acquisitions, possesses great weight of character. Mr de Neuville[8] you know perfectly well. He is or he ought to be in *France* a supporter of Legitimacy, but is at the same time an admirer of the charter, a friend to free elections, to equality before the law, and to the liberty of the Press. Mr Vatimesnil[9] Minister of public Instruction has been procureur General du Roi in the Court of Cassation and justly enjoys the reputation of distinguished talents. All the laws proposed have passed the deputies by large majorities composed principally of the liberal party. Amongst these are the law on Elections, on the 80 million loan, and on the Liberty of the Press. The two former have passed in the aristocratic branch of the Legislature. The ordina[nce] of the 17 Inst depriving the Jesuits of taking part in the publick instruction is exceedingly popular and has elevated the King [Charles X] and Ministry in the estimation of the people. The situation of France is much more prosperous now than it has been at any former period. Their navy has advanced with giant strides. They have now nearly 180 vessels of war of all sizes afloat. There has been a rumor for some days that they had obtained as some say Porto Rico others the Balearic Isles from Spain in payment of the debt due to France from that Country. A considerable squadron which sailed from France some days ago was destined as report said to take on board the French troops at Cadiz and with them to take possession of this newly acquired domain. I have not been able to obtain any certain information on this subject. It is not very probable that Spain would give up Porto Rico and the Balearic Isles could be of little utility to France.

Your accounts are regular as to what is passing in Portugal and therefore I shall merely observe that this Government is not disposed to countenance the conduct of Don Miguel however much it may please the Jesuits and friends of Absolute power. It is very possible as the English are very unpopular in the Peninsula that they may ultimately favor the pretensions of this contemtible adventurer.

I find much difficulty in transmitting the Newspapers and documents to Mr [Henry] Middleton at St Petersburg. Few couriers are going to that place and indeed these papers are too voluminous to be sent in that way. It would be well to instruct the Collector at New York [Jonathan Thompson] to send all the Dispatches for Sweden Denmark and St Petersburg by sea to some port in the Baltic.

Mrs. Brown renews to Mrs. Clay expressions of the warmest affection.

ALS. DLC–HC (DNA, M212, R3).   Printed in *LHQ*, 24:1110–4.   1. Phrase "are not expected" is struck through and "do not often" is substituted.   2. Peter B. Porter replaced James Barbour.   3. For Pompieres, a minor opposition politician, see Paul Bastid, *Les Institutions Politiques de la Monarchie Parlemintaire Française* (Paris, 1954), 295. 4. For Mathieu Dumas, see Benjamin E. Smith and William D. Whitney, eds., *Century Dictionary and Cyclopedia*. 12 vols. (N.Y., 1911).   5. Brown to Clay, February 28, 1828. 6. In which Vicomte Jean Baptiste Martignac, Minister of Interior, was the leading figure, since there was no President of Council at this time. The government was thus sometimes referred to as the "Martignac Ministry." For Martignac, see *NBG*.   7. For Comte Antoine Roy, *ibid*.   8. Hyde De Neuville, *ibid.*, was appointed Minister of Navy in 1828.   9. For Antoine François Henri Vatimesnil, *ibid.*

From LUDWIG NIEDERSTETTER, Philadelphia, June 27, 1828. Refers to the treaty he and Clay recently signed [Niederstetter to Clay, May 9, 1828] and recalls that he then asked Clay about fees to be paid to clerks in the State Department for making copies of the document. Recalls that Clay had said there were no funds for this purpose; but he wishes to remind the Secretary of the matter in order to prevent future misunderstanding, and in order to give the correct information in the matter to the Prussian Minister of Foreign Affairs, Count Christian Gunther von Bernstorff. Proposes a mutual allowance be established by Prussia and the United States to be used as a gratuity to the clerks. Discusses procedures for completing this and suggests the United States–Prussian Treaty of 1799 as a precedent. LS. DNA, RG59, Notes from Prussian Legation, vol. 1 (M58, R1). For the U.S.-Prussian Treaty of 1799, see Parry, *Treaty Series*, 55:17–39.

On November 4 Clay wrote Niederstetter apologizing for the delay in replying to his letter of June 27. Responds to the suggestion for a gratuity to be paid to the clerks: "It has been long an established rule with this Government neither to give nor receive presents of any kind on the conclusion of Treaties with foreign Powers." Points out that "This rule results from a provision in our Constitution and the nature of our institutions." States that in none of the treaties signed since he became Secretary of State has a gratuity been exchanged. LS, draft. CSmH. Copy in DNA, RG59, Notes to Foreign Ministers and Consuls, vol. 4, pp. 86–7 (M38, R4).

On about February 6, 1829, Niederstetter wrote Clay again proposing a gratuity to the clerks in the State Departments of the two governments. ALS. DNA, RG59, Notes from Prussian Legation, vol. 1 (M58, R1).

From THOMAS L. L. BRENT, Lisbon, June 28, 1828. Reports that the Cortes met twice, on June 23 and 25, in separate buildings, but that its decisions about Miguel's status remain in doubt.

Mentions that the two armies reportedly "advanced against each other"; and that without a battle, "the troops of the Junta have returned from Coimbra."

Announces that Mr. Frederico Torlade, new Portuguese minister to the United States, has embarked for this country via Liverpool. LS. DNA, RG59, Dip. Disp., Portugal, vol. 8 (M43, R7). Received August 21, 1828.

From FRANCISCO TACON, Philadelphia, June 28, 1828. Reacts vigorously to the news that Commodore David Porter "of the Mexican service" has published a decree commanding the detention and confiscation of Spanish property and contraband of war on neutral vessels.

Declares, in consequence, that Spain will be compelled to adopt toward the United States a policy of reciprocal measures for its "own just defense." LS, in Spanish, with trans. in State Dept. file. DNA, RG59, Notes from Spanish Legation, vol. 9 (M59, R–T12). For Porter's decree, see Manning, *Diplomatic Correspondence . . . Latin American Nations*, 3: 2158–9.

From WILLIAM B. LAWRENCE, London, no. 47, June 29, 1828. Reports that the choice of the King of the Netherlands, William I, as arbiter for the Northeastern boundary issue had already been completed when

Clay's instructions of May 17 were received, but remarks it is "very agreeable to find that, had they been received previous to arriving at a decision, they would not have required any change in the course which was adopted in concluding that important business."

Encloses a schedule of proposed changes in the "acts for granting duties of Customs" which includes an additional duty on unmanufactured, stemmed tobacco and a reduction in duties on cotton wool imports from British colonies. Explains that these two provisions are intended to affect United States staple crops in retaliation to the new [1828] United States tariff. Explains that under the present British tariff law all cotton pays six per cent *ad valorem* except that from Britain's American colonies which are duty free. States that the new law will lay a duty of one shilling per cwt. on cotton wool imports from any British colony while retaining the existing rate for foreign cotton. Notes that this would result in East India cotton paying one shilling and American cotton paying from three shillings sixpence to four shillings.

Encloses London *Gazette,* June 27, 1828, containing a copy of Order in Council, April 28, 1828, opening trade between Spanish and British colonies. Also comments on Britain's supposed attempt at maintaining neutrality between the factions fighting to control Portugal. Contends that the meetings between the Marquis Pedro de Sousa–Holstein Palmela and British Foreign Minister, Lord Aberdeen, were informal and inconclusive.

Reports that Britain, Prussia, and Austria were unable to take concerted action to resist Russia's invasion of Turkey because of Turkey's demonstrated military weakness. Reports that Russian war vessels attached to the Allied squadron are now at Portsmouth, Eng., on their way home, and that Russia will continue to maintain a naval force in the Mediterranean without reference to the Russo–Turkish War.

Mentions the recall of Sir Edward Codrington, the British admiral in the Mediterranean, but says this should not be taken as an indication of a change of policy by Britain nor should it be ascribed to the Battle of Navarino, but rather to subsequent bad management in preventing "almost uninterrupted intercourse between the Egyptian army in the Morea and Alexandria." Adds that Codrington's successor, Sir Pulteney Malcolm, is a devoted partisan of the Duke of Wellington. Concludes with the observation that the coolness between France and England is "believed to have greatly abated." LS. DNA, RG59, Dip. Disp., Great Britain, vol. 35 (M30, R31). Extract in Manning, *Diplomatic Correspondence . . . Candian Relations,* 2:744. Received September 1, 1828.

From ALEXANDER BURTON, Cadiz, June 30, 1828. Reports the evacuation of Cadiz by French troops by "five vessels of war and thirty transports, from Toulon," which embarked "about 4000 men, and 400 horses." Believes that the evacuation of the "whole number of . . . about 11,000" men will be effected by October. ALS. DNA, RG59 Cons. Disp., Cadiz, vol. 4 (M-T186, R4). Received August 30, 1828. Reported on September 25, 1828, that all remaining French forces departed Cadiz the previous day and were replaced by a Spanish garrison of about 2400 men. *Ibid.* Received November 17, 1828.

From **CHARLES W. DABNEY,** Fayal, Azores, June 30, 1828. Submits quarterly list of U.S. ships calling at Fayal and an accounting of funds spent to aid destitute American seamen there. Complains that he does not have enough money to aid these seamen properly and "This Consulate is annually burthened with seamen from whaling vessels" who are unfit for such work to the point that "medical treatment would not avail" them. Reports that he has not received the money to cover the expenses related to the shipwreck of the schooner *Navarino,* out of Bath, Maine, in April. ALS. DNA, RG59, Cons. Disp., Fayal, vol. 1 (M–T203, R1). Received September 8, 1828.

From **CHARLES R. VAUGHAN,** June 30, 1828. Refers to Clay's note of January 7, 1828, regarding the establishment of reciprocity on duties levied in the ports of the Kingdom of Hanover and of the United States. Reminds Clay that the note had stated that the President of the United States was authorized by an act of Congress, dated January 7, 1824 [4:116, 644], to lift discriminatory duties to tonnage and impost in United States ports against the ships or merchandise of any nation which had lifted within its ports duties discriminating against the United States. Says that Clay had further stated that a declaration by the government of Hanover, suspending discriminatory rates and "made through the undersigned, or in some other authentick form, would be deemed a compliance with the intention of the Act of Congress." Encloses a document, signed by the King of Hanover, George IV of Great Britain, granting him the power to make such a declaration. Adds that he "presumes, that the Declaration therein contained, will be deemed such a compliance with the Act of Congress of 1824, as to admit of the establishment of a reciprocity of Duties without delay, by a Proclamation to be issued by the President of the United States." LS. DNA, RG59, Notes from British Legation, vol. 15 (M50, R15).

From **ALEXANDER BURTON,** Cadiz, July 1, 1828. Relates in detail the known facts of the piratical cruise of the Brazilian brig, *Defensor de Pedro,* from November, 1827 to April, 1828. Taken over in January, 1828 by 17 mutineers in her crew, the vessel subsequently plundered numerous merchantmen, among them an unknown American vessel, apparently in the China trade, from which 30 bales of silk goods were taken prior to the burning of the ship and the murder of her entire crew. Thinks the vessel may have been out of Boston bound home from Japan and Canton, China. Asks if "any vessel be missing in the U States." The *Defensor de Pedro* is now being held at Coruna, Spain, her silk and tea cargo having been impounded "until the right owners appear." LS. DNA, RG59, Cons. Disp., Cadiz, vol. 4 (M–T186, R4). Received August 11, 1828.

On July 5, Burton reported further that Spanish legal proceedings against the crew of the vessel have shown, beyond all doubt, the fact of "the destruction of an American ship, and the shocking fate of the unfortunate crew." *Ibid.* Received August 27, 1828.

On July 16 he informed Clay that the U.S. vessel was the *Topaze,* bound from Calcutta to Boston, and that her crew numbered "about 15 persons." *Ibid.* Received September 25, 1828.

From WILLIAM VINCENT HAROLD, Washington, July 2, 1828. Is offended by two letters from Rome, submitted as enclosures. In one of them, written by Joseph Velzi, Master of the Pope's Palace, he is ordered by Pope Leo XII "to leave the city of Philadelphia where I now reside, and to render myself at Cincinnati"; furthermore, he is threatened with unknown consequences if he refuses to obey. Argues at length that although he is a priest, he is, nevertheless, a citizen of the United States with civil rights and liberties. Concludes: "I claim the protection of the President against this novel and unauthorized invasion of my private rights." Begs that the matter be brought to the President's attention. ALS. DNA, RG59, Misc. Letters (M176, R66). On the same date and from the same place, the Reverend John Ryan wrote Clay on the identical subject, noting as well that his own relocation would "postpone my legal ability to become a citizen for one year more." *Ibid.*

On September 22, Fathers Harold and Ryan again wrote Clay, expressing indignation that their protests, intended only for the private viewing of the State Department, the President, James Brown, American Minister to France, and the Papal Nuncio in Paris, had somehow fallen "into circulation," in New York, Philadelphia, and other places. *Ibid.*

James Brown wrote Clay on September 28 [see above, Brown to Clay, August 12, 1828], reporting on his first conference with the Nuncio, Luigi Lambruschini. Notes his surprise at learning that the Nuncio had already obtained copies of Brown's instructions from the State Department on the subject of Harold and Ryan. States that, according to the Nuncio, Pope Leo XII decided on their removal to Cincinnati because dissension in the Catholic Church at Philadelphia necessitated the recall to Rome of the Bishop of Philadelphia, Henry Conwell, and that in order to allow "party Spirit" in the Church to subside the Pope believed it best also to remove the two priests from that city for a short time. Brown explained to the Nuncio "that the President disclaimed any interference [in] the spiritual affairs of the Church, and was willing that the spiritual powers of his Holiness should be fully exercised; but that [in] doing so the President expected he would carefully abstain from interfering in the temporal concerns of the United States or of their citizens—" To this admonition the Nuncio replied "that his Holiness was fully sensible of the limits of his authority in the United States and would in no case transcend them by . . . exercising temporal power over their citizens." Added, however, that "these Ecclesiastics are Missionaries who had made vows of obedience," and any punishment of them for disobedience would "be of a character purely spiritual." ALS. DNA, RG59, Dip. Disp., France, vol. 23 (M34, R26). Letter marked "(private & Confidential)." Probably received November 19, 1828.

On October 10 the Rev. William Matthews, administrator of the Diocese of Philadelphia, wrote Clay, articulating the power of the Pope in such matters and stating that he was "at a loss to know on what grounds the appeal could be made to the President, and at a still greater loss to know on what grounds our Government could consent to intermeddle in the spiritual concerns of our Church." Mentions that he has applied to the State Department to know the nature of the priests' appeal and what measures the U.S. government intends to adopt. ALS. DNA, RG59, Misc. Letters (M179, R66). The following day he again wrote, attempting "to shew, that the direction to these Gentlemen was an exercise of purely spiritual jurisdiction, in no manner connected with the rights of the citizen." Emphasizing that the Pope will not physically force them to move to Cincinnati; but points out that "no one I presume will deny that his Holiness the Pope, has a right to send missionaries to preach the Gospel: but if he has no right to change the residence of his clergymen, how can he send them?" *Ibid.*

James Brown wrote again on October 13 officially detailing his communications with the Nuncio. LS. DNA, RG59, Dip. Disp., France, vol. 23 (M34, R26). Received November 21, 1828.

Clay reported to Brown on November 20 the receipt of Brown's letter of September 28. Apologizes for any embarrassment caused by the Nuncio's having received copies of Brown's instructions. Explains that in his absence from the State Department, Daniel Brent gave a copy to the Rev. William Matthews "under the impression that Mr. Matthews was entitled to it," and that Matthews apparently transmitted it to the Nuncio. Copy. DNA, RG59, Dip. Instr., vol. 12, pp. 166-7 (M77, R7). Letter marked "Private."

Clay on November 21 transmitted to Harold and Ryan a copy of the dispatch he had received from James Brown. Copy. DNA, RG59, Dom. Letters, vol. 22, p. 335 (M40, R20).

Clay notified Brown on November 22 that "your agency in this matter will be considered as satisfactorily closed, except as to the mere transmission to this department of the result . . . from Rome, in answer to the Nuncio's communication to this Government." Copy. DNA, RG59, Dip. Instr., vol. 12, p. 167 (M77, R7).

On November 26 Harold and Ryan acknowledged receipt of Clay's letter of the 21st, together with a copy of Brown's dispatch. They reviewed their objections to Henry Conwell and the statements he had made to the public in newspapers. Also, they reaffirmed their belief that "no vow of ours binds us to recognize in Rome . . . an authority affecting our civil liberty." ALS. DNA, RG59, Misc. Letters (M179, R66). See also, Brown to Clay, December 30, 1828.

From WILLIAM PITT PREBLE, Fredericton, New Brunswick, July 2, 1828. Discusses in detail early land grantees in the area, some of which are registered in the Halifax Registry of Deeds and Conveyances and/or at Fredericton. States that he arrived in New Brunswick on June 28, 1828 and anticipates from provincial officials "the interposition of every obstacle in their power to throw in my way." ALS. NHi–Albert Gallatin Papers (MR15). Received July 17, 1828.

To SAMUEL L. SOUTHARD   White Sulphur Springs, Va., July 2, 1828

Two or three days use of the Water at this place have produced already good effect, especially in relieving me from a complaint which affected me on the journey. I am tempted by it to continue here four or five days longer—[1]

You can expect nothing new from this quarter. I have met one or two Kentuckians who corroborate the information, received at Washington, of the probable success of General [Thomas] Metcalfe. But no stone will be left unturned to defeat him.

I shall be glad to hear from you at Lexington. What has the President finally decided in the affair fo the P. M. General [John McLean]? Wherever I go accounts reach me of his treachery and duplicity—

I understand that Mrs Southards sister and family at Lewisburg [Va.] are well.

ALS. NjP. Endorsed by Southard: "No ans–wrote a few days ago—." 1. On July 9, 1828, while at White Sulphur Springs, a toast was made to Clay: "What is a public man worth who is not ready to sacrifice himself when the good of his country requires it?" Clay replied: "Health to the invalid, and pleasure to the gay, who resort to these salubrious waters." Printed in *Niles' Register* (July 26, 1828), 34:345.

From WILLIAM HENRY HARRISON, North Bend, Ohio, July 3, 1828. Reports that he is ready to depart for Bogota, Colombia, and will leave Ohio for Washington between July 20th and 25th, "unless I shall receive your instructions to go sooner." ALS. DNA, RG59, Dip. Disp., Colombia, vol. 5 (M–T33, R5).

From SAMUEL L. SOUTHARD   Washington, July 3, 1828
Your family is well—I was with them an hour last evening. The news from N. York still continues favorable. Judge [Charles H.] Carroll[1] is here.

Genl. [Peter B.] Porter is getting along extremely well—& the health & spirits of every body are as good as when you left.

I have not been able to write to [Robert P.] Letcher or [Benjamin H.] Buckner but shall (as I yet hope) in a day or two.

Brent[2] has been appointed Clerk by Genl. P[orter]—

I *hear* that Linneus Smith has written to [John H.] Pleasants & that he has replied very harshly—He [Pleasants] has demanded from Mr. [Richard] Rush his letter or a Copy, to publish it, in his paper [Richmond *Constitutional Whig*] with comments. This is very bad—

I hear you forgot my friend [John] Taliaferro before you left us.[3] Do write about him—I feel great anxiety for him.

Thos. P. Moore[4] has demanded an account of the Cadet appointments of this spring. You must defend those made by me. I shall be glad to hear from you—The [Washington *United States*] Telegraph this morning says that you throw Dutch pamphlets out of your Carriage as you travel—to electioneer.[5]

ALS. NjP.   1. *BDAC.*   2. Possibly William Brent who had been a Circuit Court clerk in Washington, D.C. Washington *Daily National Intelligencer,* August 5, 1828.   3. Clay to Brooke, May 18, 1828.   4. *BDAC.*   5. The paper reported in its July 2, 1828 issue that on June 24 Clay had distributed German language pamphlets from the windows of his coach as he passed through Woodstock, Va. The pamphlets allegedly attacked Jackson.

From WILLIAM TUDOR, Rio de Janeiro, no. 93, July 3, 1828. Recounts the details of his introductory audience with Emperor Pedro I on

June 28 and his attendance at a Court Levee on July 2 honoring Maria da Gloria, the 12-year old Queen of Portugal, who will leave Brazil on July 5. Has reviewed Clay's instructions [Clay to Tudor, March 29, 1828] on securing a commercial agreement and hopes to open negotiations on this and various claims issues with the Brazilian Government within a few days. Has learned that the Congress now in session is considering legislation that will establish the principle that in all treaties "every nation shall be placed on the same ground, as to duties, &c." Believes, with Commodore James Biddle, whose guest he is on board ship until he can find a house on shore, that peace between Brazil and Buenos Aires is imminent, for no other reason than "the general one of the folly & mischief of the war for both Parties"; further, it is said that lodgings are being prepared for the peace Commissioners expected from Buenos Aires. Notes that all this has been arranged without British intervention, the British having become "very unpopular here." Copy. MHi–Adams Papers, Letters Received (MR487). Letter marked "Confidential." Written on board U.S.S. *Macedonian*. Received August 19, 1828.

From WILLIAM B. LAWRENCE, London, no. 48, July 5, 1828. Transmits copy of a note by request of Count de Itabayana, Brazilian Minister to Great Britain, relative "to the right of Emperor Dom Pedro [I of Brazil] to the crown of Portugal [as Pedro IV]."

Concerning the new British customs legislation, submits the printed bill of July 1, noting changes in the duties and regulations proposed therein. States: "The additional duty on stemmed tobacco is continued in the [printed] bill." Has learned, however, from recent Parliamentary debates, "that no alteration should be made in respect to this article without ample notice being given." LS. DNA, RG59, Dip. Disp., Great Britain, vol. 35 (M30, R31). Received August 27, 1828.

To JOHN Q. ADAMS   White Sulphur Springs, Va., July 7, 1828
A week's use of the Waters at this place has been productive of sensible benefit to my health. They have relieved me, at least for the present, from a troublesome complaint. I shall resume my journey tomorrow, taking the route by the Kanawha, and trusting to the chance of a passage in a Steam boat at the mouth of Guyandot.[1] Should I succeed in getting one I shall reach Lexington several days earlier than I should have been able to do on the alternative route, by Beans station.[2]

I have avoided the larger villages on the road hither. But I have nevertheless been offered several complimentary testimonies which I have declined accepting.

ALS. MHi–Adams Papers, Letters Received (MR486).   1. Spelled also Guyandotte, a small river that joins the Ohio River near present day Huntington, W. Va.   2. In present day Hamblen County in Eastern Tennessee.

From WILLIAM B. LAWRENCE, London, July 7, 1828. Has learned from American newspapers of the appointment of James Barbour as U.S. minister to Great Britain. Has had no "official information on the subject" and was "unacquainted with the President's views respecting my remaining here." Says he is not interested in being Secretary of Legation again, as he had been under Albert Gallatin. Complains that the "enormous expenses" of London make it impossible to live on a Secretary of Legation's salary, and that even on the salary of Chargé he has been forced to "draw largely upon my private resources." Asks that a new Secretary be appointed, a course that will involve "less personal embarrassment to me." Reports that Jared Sparks is now on the Continent, but that "I gave him every assistance in my power to obtain access to British papers" he may "deem useful to his undertaking [6:899–900, 962]." Refers to "impediments" thrown in his way by British officials. Reports that Mr. Stratford Canning has left London for Corfu, where the Allied Ambassadors will soon assemble, and that Miguel has been elected King by the Portuguese Cortes. ALS. DLC-HC (DNA, M212, R3). Letter marked *"Private."*

On October 14, 1828 in dispatch no. 58, Lawrence informed Clay that with Barbour's concurrence he was leaving London for Paris the following day and that his date of resignation would be effective October 15; also, that given King George IV's poor health there was no reason to stay in London until Barbour had been presented at Court, since that event might lie several months in the future. ALS. DNA, RG59, Dip. Disp., vol. 35 (M30, R31). No date of receipt.

To JAMES MADISON   White Sulphur Springs, Va., July 7, 1828
Mr. J. Caldwell,[1] who will present you this letter, being desirous of the honor of your acquaintance, I take pleasure in introducing him to you as a respectable and intelligent gentleman, and as the son of my particular friend, the worthy proprietor [James Caldwell] of these excellent waters. He is a member of the Convention,[2] about to assemble at Charlottesville, of which I understand you are also a member. I unite my wishes to those of the Citizens of Virginia that your deliberations may result in the advancement of the good cause which they were intended to promote.

ALS. PU.   1. John Bowyer Caldwell (or Calwell) was born in Maryland in 1798. A Lewisburg, Va. [now W. Va.] lawyer and sometime (1837–1839) publisher of the Lewisburg *Western Enquirer*, he was part owner of White Sulphur Springs after his father's death in 1851. He died in 1875.   2. The Convention discussed the problems of and need for internal improvements in Virginia. Washington *Daily National Intelligencer*, July 21, 1828.

From DANIEL WEBSTER   Boston, July 7, 1828
I am in hopes this will find you in Kentucky, in good spirits, & renewed health. If you are as well as we wish you, this way, you need be no better. A strong manifestation of kind feeling towards you, personally, has very generally appeared in all the numerous celebrations of the fourth inst., in this quarter of the Country, which have fallen under my observation. As far as I can judge, the general aspect of things is favourable. A Gentleman of the first character is now with me, from the Genessee [*sic,* Genesee] River, recently, and who saw, on his way hither, Mr. [Francis] Granger, & many other well informed persons, who are all represented as agreeing with him that the best hopes may be entertained respecting that State.

Mr. Lewis Williams[1] writes me a very encouraging letter from

North–Carolina; but you have still better means of judging of that State. After all, I remain of opinion that the battle is to be won or lost where you now are. With Kentucky on our side, we shall get gloriously through the contest. I wish some of our friends there would let us know how the face of things appears. Tell [James] Clarke[2] to write me, but do not take that trouble yourself.

I wish now to say one word on another subject. In the multitude of things which were to be attended to at the breaking up of Congress, a *part of one thing* was omitted. The enclosed[3] is designed to accomplish it, and put it right.[4] I would adopt another *form*, if I could think of a better. When you return to Washington, or chuse to send this there, it may be conveniently used, in the manner indicated on it.

In the mean time, have the goodness to communicate with Mr. C[larke]. and let him understand that the matter is arranged. I would not trouble you with this, if I could well avoid it, and I shall feel more at ease when I know that you have received this Letter.

Have the goodness to acknowledge it in one word.

LS. DLC–HC (DNA, M212, R3). Letter marked "Private & confidential."
1. *BDAC.* 2. Listed in Rossiter Johnson (ed.), *Twentieth Century Biographical Dictionary of Notable Americans* (Boston, 1904). 3. The enclosure reads: "Mr. [Josiah S.] Johnston presents with great pleasure to Mr. Clay two letters from Mr. Daniel Vertner & Mr. A. W. Wooley—Which he is at liberty to use in any way he may think proper. July 7th. 1828." The letters have not been found. For Vertner, who was from Natchez, Miss., see 1:108. For Wooley, from Port Gibson, Miss., see Clay, *A Supplement to the Address . . . to the Public,* June 10, 1828. 4. Clay endorsed this letter on an attached sheet as follows: D. Webster, Sent the check for $500 inclosed to R[ichard] Smith Cash etc Washn. to collect and to pass the amt to my acct." Smith was Cashier of the Washington branch of the Bank of the United States. A second endorsement by Clay, also on the attached sheet reads: "Mr. Johnston, with the letter of Mr. Vertner and Mr. Wooley."

From THOMAS L. L. BRENT, Lisbon, no. 76, July 8, 1828. Reports that as soon as Miguel accepted the throne of Portugal, all members of the diplomatic corps "who had express instructions resolved to cease their diplomatic functions" and made such an announcement through their respective consuls. Notes that only the Papal Nuncio and the Spanish Minister remain without specific instructions from their governments, and he expects that the Spanish decision may be made soon. Says he has decided that it "is my duty to wait for your instructions."

Reports on events in the Portuguese civil war, saying that it now appears after the capture of Oporto that Miguel holds the allegiance of the country and that the war will soon be terminated in his favor. States that on the previous day Miguel's decree of acceptance of the crown was made public and "the three orders of the kingdom" took the oath to support him as king. LS. DNA, RG59, Dip. Disp., Portugal, vol. 8 (M43, R7). Received September 4, 1828.

From ANNE BROWN CLAY ERWIN   Washington, July 9, 1828
I was happy to learn from your letter of the first that your health had somewhat improved since your departure; I hope you will remain long enough at the [White Sulphur] springs to recover entirely from the fatigue of your previous journey.

We have had quite a gay fourth here,[1] or rather I should say the

Gentleman have had, for the ladies as usual on such days of festivity were entirely forgotten. The President acquitted himself in his task of digging to the satisfaction of all his friends; he became so much excited at meeting with a *hickory* stump that he threw off his coat and went regularly to work, which of course quite delighted the laboring class, and many of them who were before unfriendly were heard to say, that they really did not beleive he would [have] done such a thing and that he deserved to be president four years longer for it. About a dozen of our warmest friends had a pleasant little party at a spring near town; in the [Washington *Daily National*] Journal of today you will see some of their toats & a peice of poetry composed by Dr Thomas for the occasion. Our friends are many of them leaving town; Mr & Mrs [Josiah Stoddard] Johns[t]on with General [Simon] Bernard's[2] family started yesterday; General & Mrs [Thomas S.] Jessup[3] go tomorrow, and we are to lose Mr [Charles R.] Vaughan in a few days; the City I suppose will we [*sic*, be] very dull for a month or two; fortunately we are so situated that we are independent of the parties a good deal, having so many neighbors that we can see as often as we wish.

Henry [Clay, Jr.] has been with us about a week; he is much grown since I saw him, but I was disappointed in not finding him as handsome as I expected; he is just from camp however, and at the age when young gentleman are afraid of their dignity being questioned and are therefore obliged to put on a very sage and serious air to remind one of it occasionally; to make up for it, he is quite as amiable and goodhearted as we could wish to see him. He appears to be contented to remain at West Point as long as you may desire him.

Our friends are generally well and all enquiring anxiously about you. Mrs General [John] Mason[4] met with a serious acccident a week ago and has been very ill until yesterday; in getting out of her carriage at the Church door her dress caught in the wheel; she was thrown on the pavement and fractured her hip bone in such a manner that it is supposed she will never be able to walk again and her life even was considered in danger from it for some time.

Our City has been increasing as well as decreasing its population since you left here; Mrs [Joseph] Lovell[5] has a daughter, and the same day Mrs [Charles J. D.] Bouligny[6] presented her husband with a son, thus fulfilling the Scriptures, which orders us to multiply and replenish the earth.

The family are all quite well; Mama joins me in [illeg. word] Grandma [Susannah Hart] and the rest of our relations and friends. Tell Cousin Nannette [Price Smith][7] that I should be extremely happy to hear from her, but it is a pleasure I so rarely enjoy that I never anticipate it. From a letter received this morning from Mr [James] Erwin I expect him on the 25 July; I shall not know until he comes on when we shall go to Philadelphia or how long we shall be able to remain here before we leave for the West....

ALS. Henry Clay Memorial Foundation, Lexington, Ky.; copy in KyU.   1. Ground-breaking ceremonies for the Chesapeake and Ohio Canal were held in Washington on July 4.   2. Thomas Hamersly (ed.), *Complete Regular Army Register* (Washington, 1880), 297.   3. *Ibid.*, 541.   4. *DAB*.   5. *Ibid.*   6. *BDAC*.   7. A niece of Lucretia Clay.

From **JOHN M. FORBES,** Buenos Aires, no. 60, July 9, 1828. "From a highly respectable source," learns about "the sinister views of the British government in the mediation" between Buenos Aires and Brazil. Describes an incident two weeks ago in which a British armed vessel on the coast of Banda Oriental [Uruguay] landed a messenger to the patriots who carried with him an unsigned document, "purporting to be a petition from the Banda Oriental to the Governments of England and France to take that province under their joint protection." Reports that Banda Oriental disclaimed the "project" and that Buenos Aires treated it "with indifference and ridicule." Nonetheless, he has been exposed to "a steady opinion" that the British "constantly covet" an influence over Banda Oriental, in fact, seek "a direct Colonial Government" there. States that the Buenos Airean diplomatic mission of Juan Ramon Balcarce and Tomas Guido is scheduled to leave for Rio de Janiero on a British packet on July 12.

Continuing on July 12, Forbes reports that "the pacificating mission" embarks today for Rio. Believes from conversations with "those gentlemen . . . that, should the present attempt fail, the mediation of the President of the U.S. will be invoked." Also has reason to believe that "such mediation would be extremely efficient and successful." Refers to an incident in which Pedro I, Emperor of Brazil, allegedly expressed, in confidence, "his willingness to accept any respectable American mediation, adding that he wished to have nothing to do with the British in this business." Learns that Pedro's remarks were passed on, "by the treachery of the high officers of this Government [Buenos Aires]" and became known to John Ponsonby and other British officials in the country. Remarks that this incident caused English "jealousy." Has discovered that Ponsonby, former British minister to Buenos Aires, is still in the capital city awaiting passage to his new post as minister to Brazil; and that he now intends to "reach Rio simultaneously" with the Buenos Airean peace negotiators in order to influence the proceedings. LS. DNA, RG59, Dip. Disp., Argentina, vol. 3 (M69, R4). Received September 26, 1828; also in Espil, *Once Anos en Buenos Aires*, 494–6.

From **AMOS KENDALL,** Frankfort, Ky., July 9, 1828. Reviews their 1825 correspondence on the subject of Clay's offer to him of a clerkship in the State Department [Kendall to Clay, May 28, 1828]. Defends himself against the charge that he had improperly made it public, pointing out that Clay had "assented . . . to my disclosing the facts stated." Suggests that Clay's displeasure in having it known that he had offered Kendall a job in 1825 was based on the fact that subsequently "I had drive the giant to the wall" in testimony to the Kentucky Senate. In this testimony [Blair to Clay, January 22, 1828], Kendall reported a conversation between Francis P. Blair and himself in January, 1825, in which Blair had assured him that "MR. CLAY WOULD BE SECRETARY, IF MR. ADAMS WERE MADE PRESIDENT." Points out that Blair had affirmed the correctness of his comment in a letter to Kendall dated July 2, 1828.

Summarizes at length his earlier favorable opinions of President Adams, views that "You [Clay] sought successfully to destroy," and his important assistance to Clay's campaign against Adams in the presidential election of 1824. Calls special attention to Clay's attacks on Adams's position on the New England fisheries vs. Mississippi River navigation question at the Treaty of Ghent negotiations, and reminds Clay that in a series of articles in the Frankfort *Argus* in 1823 [3:409] on this subject, he had "commenced the war upon him [Adams] with all the vigor of which I was *master*." Reminds Clay, further, "You approved of these Letters during the process of their publication. . . . offered me fifty dollars toward defraying the expense" of a pamphlet edition of them, eventually paid $100 to have them printed as a pamphlet in Lexington, and "had an agency in distributing them" after the pamphlet was published [3:543].

Denies that he ever sought a federal government job from Clay, pronounces as "false" Clay's "insinuation" to the contrary, and declares "You first put the thought of public employment into my head."

Maintains that in his personal dealings with himself [Kendall], and in his attacks on Jackson, Clay has shown neither integrity or honor. "*Dishonorably*, you procured at Wheeling a copy of General Jackson's letter to Mr. [Carter] Beverl[e]y and threw it before the public. In violation of integrity, you denied things which I knew to be true, and made charges against General Jackson which you knew to be untrue."

Reviews at length the arguments and evidences demonstrating Clay's bargain with Adams, basing his remarks substantially on the recently revealed Clay–Blair correspondence of January, 1825 [4:9–11, 46–8]. "At last, these famous copies are accessible. I have *seen them*." States that having read that correspondence, "it is impossible for me to conceive how any other construction can be put upon the letter [of January 8] than that the friends of Mr. Adams had promised you the first office in his gift with their future support!; that your friends had determined to vote for Mr. Adams on that account; and that you were using personal exertions to bring the members of Congress into your views." Asks if the real meaning of the letters to Blair be other than that "New England desires to see you in the second office now, and will support you for the first office when Mr. Adams has served out his eight years?" Citing Clay's letter to him of April 16, 1820 [2:822–4], charges that "You think the public good requires that *Henry Clay* shall be President." Claims, on the basis of Clay's letter to him of January 8, 1820 [2:752–3] that he was even then "attempting to organize an opposition to Mr. Monroe's administration, for the purpose of beating" Secretary of State Adams "in the next contest for the Presidency," while "At the same time you and all your friends were denoucing the Secretary succession as dangerous to liberty. . . . Sir, I have now fully exposed your duplicity and a portion of your intrigue." Charges, further, that "every effort of your administration has been directed to secure the re election of Mr. Adams and make you his successor." Concludes with the observation that having "purchased the Secretaryship of State with his vote and influence" in order to "secure to himself the succession," Clay has become a threat to American liberty. Printed in Lexington *Kentucky Gazette*, August 15, 1828; reprinted from Frankfort *Argus of Western America*, July 9, 1828. See, below, Kendall to Clay, July 16, 1828.

From JOHN M. MACPHERSON, Cartagena, July 10, 1828. Discusses the Convention at Ocana, Colombia, which has dissolved, its failure caused by twenty-two delegates who withdrew. Encloses a printed pamphlet which they wrote, describing the reasons for their actions.

Notes that the inhabitants of Bogota have recalled their delegates and have also "proclaimed [Simon] Bolivar Supreme Chief or Dictator," and suggests that this example is expected to be followed throughout the country. Comments: "Whatever may be the future consequences arising from placing absolute power in the hands of Bolivar, the immediate effects will be salutary, in keeping party spirit within bounds, and in placing the Country in a better state of defense against foreign invaders."

Concludes with the reported news that "the Peruvians had invaded the territory of Columbia," over the issue of Azuay, a province which Peru claims was under its jurisdiction "in the time of the Spaniards." ALS. DNA, RG59, Cons. Disp., Cartagena, vol. 1 (M-T192, R1). No date of receipt.

From THOMAS L. L. BRENT, Libson, no. 77, July 11, 1828. Reports that after the British ambassador, Frederick James Lamb, left Portugal a ship arrived bringing dispatches for him and for Captain George R. Sartorius, Commander of the British squadron on the Tagus River. States that Sartorius was ordered to provide transportation to any British subjects who desired to leave Portugal with their property. Notes that this order "produced a considerable sensation" because "it was supposed that this measure implied a probability of war between the two countries." Adds that Sartorius, who received all of the dispatches intended for Lamb, has not explained the British government's motive in issuing the order; consequently, British merchants have been reluctant to accept the offer. Adds that Sartorius has also received orders to respect the blockade of Oporto which is in keeping with a policy of neutrality. Mentions also that Count de La Tour Maubourg remains in Portugal "by . . . an express order from his government, charged with the affairs of the french government: yet without any diplomatick . . . authority." LS. DNA, RG59, Dip. Disp., Portugal, vol. 8 (M43, R7). Received September 4, 1828. For George Sartorius, see *DNB;* for Maubourg, *NBG.*

From CHRISTOPHER HUGHES, The Hague, July 11, 1828. Reports the most recent news of military operations in the Russo-Turkish War, and expresses the opinion that the Turks "will soon come to terms." Warns Clay not to be deceived by heroic Turkish statements of resistance and retaliation and adds that the Anglo-French-Russian Treaty of July 6, 1827 [6:780-2] for "the pacification or independence of Greece" remains in operation. Thinks, however, that "there is a feeling of mistrust & discontent" on the part of the Allies toward Austria's "playing a double, a wavering, a *tricky* sort of game. I *know* this to be the opinion of my Colleagues." Notes, further, that in Portugal Miguel was proclaimed King by the Cortes on June 25, that he accepted the title the next day, and that on the same day a Portuguese mob broke into the hotel where British Minister Sir Frederick Lamb was staying, seized one of his servants and tortured him—"they applied Thumb-screws to Him"—to get information. States that the Duke of Palmela, Portuguese Minister to Britain, and other Portuguese refugees have arrived at Oporto from London where they were received with "acclamation," even though "it is *certain* that the constitutional, the *Pedro* Party, at Oporto, were in great dejection." Believes that the Constitutionalist–Royalist struggle is "tearing the vitals of Portugal." Concludes: "There are stories circulated (& believed) of the immoral habits, & life of Don Miguel & *His Sisters,* not to be committed to paper, at least, *by me;* though *I believe them.*" MHi–Adams Papers, Letters Received (MR486). No date of receipt.

From SAMUEL ISRAEL, Cap Haitien, July 11, 1828. Announces that the President, Jean Pierre Boyer, has stated in a message to his Chambers that "Trade would be equalized with *all* Nations in the year 1830 [and] the discriminating duties on their vessels are to [be] taken off the 1st of January next, so that their vessels pay the [same] as foreign." Believes that Haiti "is disposed to do what is right," but that their involvement with France "hangs heavy upon them."

Concerning U.S. relations with the Haitians, believes that "when all nations are placed upon the same footing" by Haiti "the U States will then no doubt acknowledge their Independence." ALS. DNA, RG59, Cons. Disp., Cap Haitien, vol. 6 (M9, R6). Received July 24, 1828.

From HENRY PERRINE, Campeche, July 11, 1828. Reports the wrecks of several American ships on Mexican islands and river bars in the area. Relates the belief of the American ship masters and traders with whom he comes in contact "that frequent visits of a Naval Vessel of the U.S. would have an influence in preventing the many grievances to which, in person, property, or both, they are universally subject." Mentions that the "animosity" against naturalized Americans of Spanish origin is "so violent" here that their expulsion is often asked. Notes that some vessels, once under the Mexican flag but now under the American, are asserted to be owned by Spaniards resident in this place. Reports that this circumstance creates, among the Mexicans living on this peninsula, *"extreme hostility to our native countrymen."* LS. DNA, RG59, Cons. Disp., Campeche, vol. 1 (M286, R1). No date of receipt.

From JAMES BROWN Paris, July 12, 1828
In consequence of a violent cold attended with fever Mrs Brown has suffered very much during the last three weeks. Her physicians insist that she shall immediately repair to Dieppe where they conceive she may restore her enfeebled constitution by change of air, repose, and sea bathing. My brother [Samuel] and niece [Susan] have just arrived and will go with us the day after tomorrow to the sea side, where I shall leave her in their care and immediately return to Paris to avail myself of the approaching adjournment of the chambers and press on my negocia-

tions. I have not been unemployed in endeavoring to have the way to success by every measure which has suggested itself to my mind as likely to contribute to a favorable result. You will perceive by the Newspapers that some observations have been made on the floor of the Chamber of Deputies in relation to them. It gives me much pleasure to express to you my hope that the complaint of Mrs. B which he has given me so much alarm affords hope for her recovery. She continues to sustain her spirits with admirable firmness.

I am happy to find that you have resolved to absent yourself for some time from Washington and to enjoy some repose rendered so necessary to the recovery of your health. I pray you to avoid as much as you can all subjects of irritation Your life is precious to your friends and family, and as to the attacks so wantonly levelled at your character they will recoil with time on the authors. I think the election will turn upon Kentucky and if the accounts received from that state deserve credit, it will vote in favor of the Administration. At all events the more steady and reflecting portion of the community will support Mr Adams and this will be creditable to him whatever may be the results—

The Russians who from the apathy manifested by the Turks had expected but a feeble resistence are now convinced that the struggle will be difficult and that many obstenate battles must be fought before they can obtain possession of Constantinople. So long as the resistance is great the war will be confined to the two powers and indeed under any state of things I doubt whether it will become general.

Don Miguel has been declared absolute King [of Portugal] under the title of Miguel 1st. The Constitutional troops act with but little vigor and as the nobles the Clergy and Canaille [common people] are opposed to Don Pedro [IV] it is probable the cause of the Constitution will fail of success.

I wait with some impatience to see who will be sent as Secretary of Legation in the room of Mr [Daniel] Sheldon. I can hardly expect a Successor [John Adams Smith] equally qualified for the place. You wil perceive that I have carefully abstained from making any recommendations.

ALS. DLC–HC (DNA, M212, R3). Printed in *LHQ,* 24:1114–5.

From LEVI LINCOLN   Boston, July 12, 1828
I herewith transmit, in compliance with your request, authenticated copies of two Acts of this Government, having relation to the Separation of Maine from Massachussetts proper,[1] and the execution of the former into an Independent State.

I have also much satisfaction in being now enabled to forward a copy of an important Document, in the Report of the King's Attorney and Solicitor General, upon the subject of the title and claim of *"the Province or Territory of the Massachusetts Bay."* The certificate of the Secretary of the Commonwealth [Edward D. Bangs][2], which is subjoined, fully explains the authenticity, and degree of credit, which, under the circumstances, should be attached to this paper.

After a diligent and long continual search, no other Records such as are now, or heretofore have been furnished, are to be found in the Department of this Commonwealth, which can give aid in the management of the controversy, concerning our North Eastern Boundary &c.

ALS. DNA, RG76, Northeast Boundary: Misc. Papers, Env. 4, item 27.   1. For the first Act of Separation of June, 1816, see Banks, *Maine Becomes a State*, 237-44; for the second Act of Separation, see *ibid.*, 270-9.   2. For Bangs, see Norman L. Pidgeon, *The Commonwealth of Massachusetts Manual for the General Court* (Boston, 1971), 374.

To JOSEPH LOVELL   Mr. Maupins, [Cabell Co., Va.],
July 13, 1828

I send you the requested sketch inclosed.[1] It is submitted to you and the gentlemen who expressed a wish to have it, to be dealt with; either by retrenchment or addition, as you may think proper:

I think it best not to publish the letter requesting it, and therefore have not replied to it. That would be giving the affair too much form and importance. I will thank you to give this explanation to the gentlemen [M. Campbell] who concurred, in writing me the letter, as an apology for my forbearance to answer it.

I shall take the chance of sending this letter by some opportunity which I may meet between this place and Guyandotte,[2] or at the latter.

ALS. NBu. Addressed to Lovell or M. Campbell at Charleston, Va. [W. Va.] "Mr. Maupins" or "Mauppin," after Thomas Maupin, was a tavern-inn in Cabell County, Va., about three miles west of present day Milton, W. Va. George Selden Wallace, *Cabell County Annals and Families* (Richmond, Va., 1935), 446-7.   1. A copy of Clay's Speech at White Sulphur Springs, Va., which was subsequently published. See, above, pp. 348-50.   2. Clay to Adams, July 7, 1828.

From LANGDON CHEVES, Lambertsville, N.J., July 14, 1828. Requests permission to resign his place on the St. Petersburg Convention [1:1002, 1011; 3:318] Commission because of a "bilious fever" attack which will prevent his discharging duties which must be performed before September 1. Suggests that the President appoint someone in his place who can start work immediately. ALS. DNA, RG59, Letters of Resignation and Declination.

Daniel Brent replied on July 17 that the President would defer acceptance of the resignation until the other members of the commission could be consulted. Cheves informed Brent on July 21 that he still wanted to resign as soon as possible because of his health. *Ibid.*

From ELIZA S. [Mrs. JOSIAH S.]   Philadelphia, July 14, 1828
JOHNSTON

With infinite pleasure have we heard of the improvement made in your health by the [White] Sulpher [*sic*] Springs—your first letters gave us reason to fear that your were far from being well—but now we are easy on that subject,—& pray you take great care of yourself & return to us quite well—We have been four days in this City which is extremely pleasant—the weather cool—& a gay & agreeable party in the house where I lodge—we sing & talk away the mornings & visit & walk in the Eve[nin]g—there are many persons absent—but enough of our acquantances left to make it agreeable. Long Branch [N.J.] is much visited—& we have had many inducements offered us, to go there—but I have not seen Nahant [Mass.]—& we shall proceed about the 18th. & if I can take my Son, with me, shall go direct to Seratoga [*sic,* Saratoga] for a few days & thence to Boston, to be there about the 12th. of August, & home in Washington, the first week of September—for I shall be tired of this changing scene before that time—& now as Mari[1] sometimes tells me, I have given you, the end of the story, first—you ask? if we travelled alone—not entirely—for Col. Thare [*sic,* Thayer][2] (who happens always, to be in Washington when you are away)—expressed a desire to join us, & remained a day or two for the purpose we took a carriage, & came quietly along to Baltimore where we dined ensemble, & rode & walked about the City until bed time & off at 4 Ock next morning—& truly I felt so unsentimental at that hour that I was *au desespoir* of retaining the impression which I flattered myself I had made—but I rallied after breakfast, & passed a pleasant day on the water & in the Stages & I must do the COl. [Thayer] the justice to say that he is exceedingly well informed—not only relative to his profession, but upon all subjects, that I heard him converse—he has gone to W. Point, to make his arrangements, so he said, to meet us at Boston—my opinion of his very good manners have undergone no change I did not see Capt. [William A.] Gordon[3]—he has been ill & had left the hotel, for more quiet lodgings—& Mari appeared particularly indifferent, & I [am] not particularly anxious—he told me he had left a note for him—but I did not ask what about—so it will be merely accidental if I see him—pray try & get back to the sea-bath, it will be good for you, I am sure & it would be so agreeable to meet you somewhere before September—it is a long, long time—& I did miss you most terribly after your departure—oh, it is sad to be seperated from those whose society give us pleasure—I saw Mrs. [Anne Clay] Erwin as frequently as possible—but not often enough, for really I do like her—I fear she will find Washington a little dull—but Henry [Clay, Jr.] was with them—you would be surprised to see how grave he has grown—he has a countenance which indicates reflection, & the habit of abstraction—which they all acquire I am told, at West Point—COl. Thare speaks very well of him—I am going to send a few pieces of music to Mrs. Erwin, as I did my Books, before my departure, she has a Piano to amuse herself with—

Have I answered all your questions—if I appear to be a great egotist it is your own fault—you never fail to meet some handsome Ladies— wherever you go, I do wish you could see none, but ugly old maids, as the one you met, at the Springs during your absence—I do think you have enough to do—without observing the Ladies so particularly—finish your business & return to your friends at home who estimate you, for yourself alone—I could tell you of a handsome beau who lives with us & who it is said has played the mischief with a fair Lady, already, he is well looking & I will tell you about it when I have the pleasure to see you—& what pleasure it will be to me—let me hear from you again—& tell me all your plans—a letter directed to Northampton [Mass.] will reach us, or be sent by the Post Master to us—. . . . [P.S.] I have been called a dozen times since I commenced writing

ALS. DLC-HC (DNA, M212, R3).   1. Possibly a servant.   2. Col. Sylvanus Thayer was Superintendent of the U.S. Military Academy at West Point.   3. *Biennial Register,* 1827, p. 73; 1829, p. 71.

From JOSIAH S. JOHNSTON   Philadelphia, July 14, 1828

We remained in Washington until the 8th, but no event took place after your departure worth recounting, except perhaps the Canal Ceremonies,[1] which you have read in the papers, Mr. Adams acquitted himself well & the affair was well Conducted—Genl [Peter B.] Porter took very kindly, notwithstanding the hot weather, to the Labors of his office—he will be Capable & efficient—& will be better pleased with it, as he grows more familiar with its duties But I do not think, he enters upon it, with more pleasure than the Governor [James Barbour] left it.

I am delighted with the great revival in this City—A Compleat amalgamation of the two parties has taken place & they are now engaged Cordially & Zealously in the Cause   It has had the effect to animate their spirits & to inspire Confidence—& will diffuse its influence through the State   One of the best Signs here is the liberal Subscription for the expenses—by Which the Cause will be well Sustain[e]d throughout Penna. & Some thing will be done for Ky—

There will be a great Meeting at Valley-forge on the 26th. To which [John] Sergeant & others are invited, This will be a great Occasion—I send you the proceedings at this place—Which speak for themselves—no doubt is entertained of this City—I shall be in N. york on the 16th. & write you again,—You Must Carry Kentucky & We will Do the rest—The State of the Contest is now well understood—Kentucky is necessary to us—Penna. Might save the Country, but neither Penna nor N. york Could be roused to the effort, under the loss of Kentucky—But with Kentucky both may be Carried—I think a great effort ought to be made in this State, even if Ky is lost—She would still have the event under her Controul—but although they are now full of Zeal, her political leaders will dispair of success—but We Must be ready to keep them up to the point, as well from the hopes of success as to preserve our Organization, & it is perhaps a public duty, to hold out firmly to the Last—

The British Cabinet seems unsettled—Huskisson with two others have resigned—but this will not produce any Change of policy—While Wellington is Premier—

Russia pushes steadily on to her object, without regarding the interests of England or France—An Army in Persia another threatening Constantinople, Capo d'Istrias (really no doubt for Russia,) President of Greece—& as yet, they dare not question her—She Seems to Me to have taken her Course & does not intend to be stopped—She has demanded indemnity & will take no refusal, although the payment is impossible, She intends to do herself justice & she will make War How far the Continental powers will permit her to extend his Conquests—does not appear—but the opinion seems to be that they will attempt to set bounds to her—they have as far as We know, taken no stand.

The liberals & the Ultras Seem to move on harmoniously. I have Recd. your Letter[2] from the Springs, you health I hope will be restored—It creates great interest here Your Name has been recd. here on all the Late public Occasions with extraordinary enthusism—

I have engaged your Carriage of [Thomas] Ogle[3] at 700 it will be as good as Mine, & I do not know what improvement $150 more would make—you will Send him the *Colour* of the body & the lining as soon as

386

you please—It will be ready in due time—I met Majr. [John H.] Eaton at
Ogles—I expect to engage a Carriage for the Next President—

ALS. DLC–TJC (DNA, M212, R13).   1. Ground-breaking ceremonies for the Chesa-
peake and Ohio Canal on July 4, 1828.   2. Addressed to the Historical Society of
Pennsylvania.   3. Ogle's carriage business was located at 6 South Sixth Street in
Philadelphia.

From **WILLIAM B. LAWRENCE,** London, no. 49, July 14, 1828. Reports receiving Clay's dispatch no. 8, relative to the appointment of
James Barbour as the new American minister to Great Britain, the notice
of which he has communicated to that government, along with "the acts
and documents" pertaining to the Northeastern boundary controversy.
Discusses the British budget and especially "the new American
tariff," and is glad to report the reduced duty on rice "as found in the
printed schedule." Reports fully on the Parliamentary debates relative to
appropriations of at least three million pounds for public works and
fortifications in Canada. Quotes Sir George Murray, the new Secretary
of the Colonies, who remarked in the debates that "others might despise
America," but he did not, having "not forgotten the achievements of
Americans by sea and land." With reference to the expense of the proposed public works in Canada, notes the reaction of one British newspaper, the *Herald,* which asks, "Could we not sell the Canadas to the
United States? We might save these three millions and perhaps get five
millions more!"
Turns to the subject of Russia and reveals, concerning the choice of
a mediator in the Northeastern boundary controversy, that the Duke of
Wellington is reluctant to consider Emperor Nicholas I, "after he
[Nicholas] became a belligerent." In discussing the Russian invasion of
Turkey, passes on the prevailing opinion in England that "the nature of
the ground and the diseases of the country" will stall the Russian advance into the Ottoman Empire.
Discusses fully the unstable situation in Portugal, and reports "nothing has been done by England to aid" the Constitutionalists in Oporto
against Miguel. Mentions the snubbing of Count de l'Alendia, Miguel's
new minister to England, by almost all of the diplomatic corps in London.
Concludes with news of Charles–Joseph Bresson, former [Second]
Secretary of the French legation at Washington, who is passing through
London en route to Mexico and the states of South America, to effect, it
is understood, "the formal recognition of those countries." LS. DNA,
RG59, Dip. Disp., Great Britain, vol. 35, (M30, R31). Received August
27, 1828; also in Manning, *Diplomatic Correspondence . . . Canadian Relations,* 2:744–5. Bresson was the Commissioner of the King in Colombia in
1828. See *Dictionnaire de Biographie Française.*

From **WILLIAM TUDOR,** Rio de Janeiro, no. 94, July 14, 1828. Reports: "I anticipate some trouble and inevitable abuse respecting some of
the claims presented against this government." States he has learned that
"there are cases in which no American interest is involved but speculations have been made [by] selling vessel and cargo to merchants of

Buenos Ayres, to remain under our flag & in case of accident to be claimed as American property, & our flag is preferred to all others, because our seamen are more enterprizing and skillful, & because our government shows more zeal in defense of its citizens." Gives examples of questionable cases in this regard and says that he will not press them until he has concluded those instances in which the claims are "irreproachable." Expresses his belief that the reference in an American newspaper to "the millions that had been taken from us" is exaggerated, because he "can not make up $250,000" in documented claims. Continues: "Yet there have been instances of wanton violence toward the persons and property of our citizens, which honor, & of course policy, forbids being passed over." Asserts that he "adopted the most courteous & conciliatory tone" with the Brazilian government and that in the case of the *Balloon,* out of Baltimore, he had "a very good opportunity of being punctilious" when Brazil refused to clear the vessel despite the efforts of William Wright, the U.S. consul. States that he wrote a note "which procured the instant clearance of the vessel" and adds that he is going to tell the Brazilian Foreign Minister, the Marquis of Aracaty, that the word of Wright should be sufficient in such cases.

Notes that the treatment of Irish and German mercenaries will "discourage all their countrymen from coming hither and that nothing may be wanting to complete the false policy of this government, they are daily filling the country with materials for future combustion from Africa." Also refers to unrest in Bahia where the chief judge of the police was recently assassinated and "a general insurrection partly political and partly servile was instantly apprehended." ALS. DNA, RG59, Dip. Disp., Brazil, vol. 6 (M121, R8). Received September 5, 1828. Letter marked *"Confidential."*

From THOMAS L. L. BRENT, Lisbon, no. 78, July 15, 1828. Reports that a French frigate was unable to break the blockade of Oporto and that it is now evident the British also accept the blockade as legal. Mentions correspondence between Lord [William Carr] Beresford and Miguel's party which has given the impression to Miguel that the Tory party in Britain is secretly in favor of his success; this in spite of the fact that Beresford had no authority to speak for his government and personally denies favoring Miguel's actions. States that in evacuating Oporto the army of the Junta scattered and that the fortress of Almeida is on the verge of falling; that members of the Junta left Oporto in a British ship which was forced to put in at Corunna where the passengers were arrested by Spanish authorities. Warns of a possible expedition against Madeira which refuses to recognize Miguel's regime. Reports also that the Portuguese government is preparing a manifesto to give to all foreign governments, "setting forth the validity of the rights of Dom Miguel to the throne." LS. DNA, RG59, Dip. Disp., Portugal, vol. 8 (M43, R7). Received September 13, 1828.

From ROBERT M. HARRISON, St. Bartholomew, July 15, 1828. Sends specimens of all woods produced in the forests of British Guiana. Recalls that he had previously suggested ways of reducing or eliminating smuggling into the United States. Gives, as an example of the practice, the case of a ship that had recently cleared for St. Thomas, but was actually bound for Virginia. The Customs House at St. Bartholomew had listed its cargo at two puncheons of rum and two bowls of limes, although the vessel was carrying twenty-two puncheons of rum. Says that the customs officials involved apparently received two dollars for this "shameful collusion," and that he did not discover the true circumstances until it was too late to stop the ship. Such practices, he explains, show the need for enactment of legislation to enable U.S. consuls to demand proper clearance papers from vessels from the United States, and authority to prevent vessels from entering the United States without having to produce at customs either consular clearances or certified manifestoes. Concludes with his opinion of the detrimental effects of British regulations on United States shipping in the West Indies. ALS. DNA, RG59, Cons. Disp., St. Bartholomew, vol. 1 (M72, R1). Received August 14, 1828.

From PETER B. PORTER   Washington, July 15, 1828

Notwithstanding I have been over whelmed with business in the office, ever since you left here, I would have written you sooner, but that from the accounts which Mrs Clay has given me at different times, of your progress. I calculate that you will not reach Lexington sooner than this letter.

For the first two days of my official labours, or rather *reconnaisance,* I found myself located in a field so entirely new & strange, that I could not move a single step without encountering some serious obstacle. I have now become familiarised to a small extent of ground over which I move with tolerable ease; but my horison is yet extremely circumscribed—I hope however to be able, by great assiduity, gradually to extend it.

I call, almost daily on the President who treats me with great kindness. His health & spirits have, I think, both improved since you left us.

Our political prospects are evidently growing better at the North & East. The recent hostile demonstrations in the South, cannot fail fast to produce, & I believe, are already producing the best effects in the Tariff States—particularly Pennsylvania & N. York. In N. York I calculate that all will go well if Judge [Smith] Thompson[1] consents to be the Candidate for governor—otherwise I shall fear the effects of want of unanimity in making the selection. He has not yet made known his determination. Mr. [Samuel L.] Southard & myself have both lately written to him. Mr. Judge [John] Savage still avows himself decidedly in favour of the administration, and a gentleman whom I saw last week from N. York thinks he will concent to be the adm Candidate if solicited.

It seems now to be a common sentiment among the calculating politicians of *both* parties, that the fate of the Presidential election will probably be determined by the result of the approaching state election in Kentucky. If the majority *on either side,* is so great as to inspire confidence in a similar result in the fall election my own opinion is, that it will decide the controversy—for, beside the intrinsic weight of 14 votes in a question so nearly balanced, there are thousands of people in every state who are only seeking to get on the strongest side.

My calculation is, to leave Washington in time to arrive in Kentucky a few days after the election. To go sooner would be imputed to electioneering designs, when, if fact, I could not contract the fiftieth part of a vote.

I sincerely hope you will make your arrangements to return, the latter part of August, by way of Black Rock, which could not but contribute to the restoration of your health. I received a letter a few days ago, from Peter B.[2] who says that our prospects are very fair and expresses great zeal for the Admin, and the most unqualified devotion to your person & fortunes. He says that if you return (as he begs you will) by way of N. York, he will meet you at such place as he shall think "but calculated to produce the greatest[3] results."

Your family are well. Henry [Clay, Jr.] was at my office yesterday, quite thin, but well. He leaves here tomorrow for West point,

I enclose you a silk handkerchief, latemade, as you will perceive at Baltimore. It is, at once, an evidence of the state of our manufacturers, *in actual operation*, and of our internal improvements, in *prospects*.

ALS. DLC-HC (DNA, M212, R3). 1. *DAB*. See above, Porter to Clay, June 12, 1828. 2. Reference obscure. 3. Word "polite," following "greatest," is struck through.

From AMOS KENDALL   Frankfort, Ky., July 16, 1828

The following[1] are the documents omitted last week [Kendall to Clay, July 9] for want of room, to which is annexed the letter of Mr. [William] Tanner. The circumstances detailed by him as occurring in 1822, I had totally forgotten; but I have no doubt of their entire truth.[2] I did not remember that a living man, except Mr. Clay, knew that I was the author of "Wayne," and if Mr. [Francis P.] Blair was apprized of the fact, I know not how he got the information, and if I ever did know, I have forgotten it. The world will now have seen, that had I been disposed to "violate private correspondence," I could have furnished the Washington Jackson Committee with some facts which would materially have aided them in their "Reply"[3] to Mr. Clay's Address [6:1394–6].

Copy. Frankfort *Argus of Western America*, July 16, 1828. 1. Printed are Clay to Kendall, January 8, 1820, April 16, 1820, February 16, 1823, October 18, 1825. See, above, 2:752–3, 822–4; 3:381–3; 4:746–8. 2. Tanner stated that he had served as a young printer–compositor in Kendall's employ in 1822. The letters [3:236–8] signed "Wayne," Kendall informed him at the time they were readied for press, were "written at the request or for Mr. Clay," that "they were first to be published in Ohio," and that "Mr. Clay did not wish it known that they were written by you, and that I need say nothing about it." Recalls that the "Wayne" letters later appeared in the Cincinnati *Gazette*, from which they were reprinted in the *Argus*, and that in the reprinting process "the many corrections which you [Kendall] made in them a little astonished the hands in the office." Tanner concludes that while he had great respect for Clay's "claims to the presidency" in 1822, his "veneration was dissolved" when, in 1825, Clay "voted for the man [Adams] I knew he had lavished such abuse on" in the "Wayne" letters. Tanner to Kendall, July 1, 1828, in *Argus of Western America*, July 16, 1828. 3. Sergeant to Clay, Jan. 2, 1828.

From JOEL R. POINSETT, Mexico, no. 144, July 16, 1828.

Transmits translation of an address by Mexican President Guadalupe Victoria at the opening of the extraordinary session of Congress. Lists and discusses in detail the matters to be considered at the session, viz: regulation of the monopoly of tobacco, the export of gold and silver in ingots, the legality of the Senate of Durango, the regulation of elections in the Federal District and in the territories, pending treaties, the protection of the independence and present form of government in case of attack by armed bodies, and the contribution of $600,000 to the federal government from the states.

Explains that alteration in the election laws furnished the real motive for the extraordinary session and predicts that General Vicente Guerrero will win the next presidential election. Also warns that "if the succeeding administration fails to organize the collection of the public revenues, and to reduce the public expenditure not even its great popularity can save this country from a Revolution, which would probably be attended with a dissolution of the union." Notes that the President has nominated Jose Maria Bocanegra to be minister to the United States. LS. DNA, RG59, Dip. Disp., Mexico, vol. 4 (M97, R5). Received September [19]?, 1828.

From **SAMUEL LARNED,** Santiago, Chile, no. 69, July 17, 1828. Reports submission to the Chilean Minister of Foreign Relations, Carlos Rodriguez, of a proposition calling for a special convention to settle the claims of the United States against Chile in the cases of the *Macedonia* and the *Warrior.* Has not received a reply but hopes the proposition will reopen discussion on the claims.

Asserts that he is no longer anxious to press for the negotiation of a commerical treaty with Chile unless it can be used as a medium in the adjustment of claims. Hopes that the question can be transferred to Washington. Notes that one motive for the treaty negotiations was to prevent Peru from conceding an advantage to the wheat of Chile over that of the United States, and this motive no longer exists because Peru's Congress has prohibited further importation of flour and other articles. Mentions that Chile has not responded by lowering specifically the duties for Peru's sugar, although duties have been lowered generally. Adds that Peru has suggested a mutual defense alliance with Chile, and the desire for this probably accounts for Peru's indirect concession to the staple product of Chile [wheat].

Has protested to Chile the administration of the Estanco [state monopoly on tobacco, spirits, etc.] for which heavy bonds have been required from "the consignee of all vessels having such articles on board" that they would not land these cargoes in Chile. Reports the Chilean government has responded by issuing "a decree prohibiting the Estanco from demanding such bonds." Mentions that the Chilean Congress is discussing a new constitution, "more than one half of which has already been sanctioned by that body."

Has heard reports from Bolivia that the Peruvian army under General Agustin Gamarra has completely routed the Colombian and Bolivian armies under General Antonio Jose de Sucre y de Alcala and that Sucre must evacuate his forces from Bolivia. Notes that this invasion resulted from a revolution in Chuquisaca, capital of Bolivia, against Sucre who was fired upon by his own guards and severely wounded.

States, that the insurrection was suppressed "by the armed force from other quarters," and fifteen or twenty "of the most distinguished persons in the country" were executed. Comments: "The patriotick party, though oppressed by the foreign force having possession of the country . . . called in the assistance of General Gamarra." ALS. DNA, RG59, Dip. Disp., Chile, vol. 3 (M–T2, R3). Received November 22, 1828.

From JOHN SERGEANT   Philadelphia, July 17, 1828

I hope your visit to the West, and relief from official labours will quite restore your health. If every thing should go as we wish, what a glorious time you will have. It will be like the sun bursting out after a long and angry storm. We are doing all we can here, to bring about this result. Our friends are more zealous and energetic than I expected, and seem willing to atone by their present activity for former neglect. We had, as you know, a great many little difficulties to contend with in this City. They are chiefly overcome, and tho' there are some who would be very willing to obstruct us, under various pretexts, I think the current is too strong for them. Our opponents are in a great rage, scolding and abusing us all, outrageously. This is a good symptom—it betrays apprehension. We, on the contrary, are cheerful, good humored and steady, and perfectly harmonious—The public mind of Pennsylvania, generally, is more susceptible than it has been of sound impression. The extravagance of the South is obviously producing good effects. We do not therefore despair, and we are determined at all events to persevere 'till the end. It is of great importance for the future repose of the Country, that Pennsylvania should be brought to the right side, and, if that cannot be effected, that she should not be suffered to go too strongly on the wrong one. Her seeming unanimity in 1824 has been the cause of great mischief. Other States have endeavoured to persuade her, that they are avenging her wrongs, and thus have been enabled to work up her passions against her most obvious policy. Her own citizens, too, and among them, some men from whom one would have expected better things, have thrown themselves into the Jackson current because they thought it would carry them along on its surface. I do not wish to see Pennsylvania placed again in the same offensive attitude towards the Govt.   If the President be reelected (as I think he will be) it ought not to be permitted to factious men to say that it is against the unanimous voice of Pennsa. If we make a strong stand, we shall be able to maintain it, in the event mentioned, and soon become a majority. If we were to surrender, it would be difficult, even in that event, to rally again—There is a still stronger argument, I acknowledge, in favor of exertion, even if there were no hope. Every man who believes that the election of Genl. Jackson will be dangerous to the Country (as I most sincerely do) owes it to that Country, and owes it to himself, not to incur the imputation of having contributed to his elevation, actively or passively.

There is to be a very large meeting in Chester County on the [July] 26th. If the weather should be good, there will be some thousands assembled. I promise myself a gratifying day—As to probabilities in Pennsa., I am afraid to speak, there is so little known. Of those we rely upon, not to be against us, there is a portion that is essentially inert, and very difficult to be excited. Of those professing to be with us, there are a few miserable egotists, who are continually finding fault, charging us with exaggeration, and intimating that after all Jackson's election would not be so bad a thing, by which means they counteract, as far as they can, our efforts to excite the sluggish. Here, (in the City) however, we have succeeded in quickening the whole mass, as well as in thoroughly uniting it, and whatever strength there is, will be fairly produced. Our proceedings will have some influence in New Jersey and Delaware. But the great event will be the election in Kentucky. If we succeed strongly there, it will give a new impulse, which will be felt every where.

I am upon the point of leaving home for a few days, intending to leave my family at Long Branch [N.J.] and return without delay,

ALS. InU.

From C.D.E.J. BANGEMAN HUYGENS, Washington, July 18, 1828. Recounts a robbery committed in his Washington home by three of his servants on July 12. Reports that the thieves fled the District of Columbia, but that two were apprehended in Maryland "with the greater part of the articles stolen," and were ultimately confined in the "gaol" in Baltimore, "where the trial will be held according to the laws of the state."

Reviews the legal technicalities of the case and states that since "the crime was committed within the District," it is desirable to have the trial there to frighten "their abettors or accomplices"; thus "the culprits should be transferred from the Baltimore gaol to one of the District" for this trial. Hopes that the President will "adopt proper measures for that purpose." ALS, in French, with trans. in State Dept. file. DNA, RG59, Notes from Netherlands Legation, vol. 1 (M56, R1).

From JOAQUIM B. PEREIRA, Philadelphia, July 18, 1828. Transmits a decree of May 3, 1828 he has just received from the Department of Foreign Affairs in Lisbon which, be believes, clearly indicates the intention of Miguel's government to usurp the Portuguese Constitution. Gives notice that he is "ceasing henceforth his functions as Diplomatic Agent from the said Government" because he "can not recognize any other authorities" but those acting under the name of Pedro IV and in accordance with the Constitution. ALS. DNA, RG59, Notes from Portuguese Legation, vol. 2 (M57, R2).

From WILLIAM TUDOR, Rio de Janeiro, no. 95, July 18, 1828. Encloses copies of the principal notes which have passed between him and Brazilian Foreign Minister, the Marquis of Aracaty. Reports that the conference of July 17 with him lasted about an hour and "turned principally on the two cases of the Spermo and the Spark as the Ruth had already been ordered by a decree promulgated in June to be given up, with several other damages paid her." Is unable to open the case of the *Spermo* fully because he lacks the necessary information; asks for relevant documents if the State Department has them. Adds that the minister was willing to pay for the *Spark*, but "complained that much passionate exaggeration had taken place in representing transactions here." Asserts that he "complained in turn of the violence & ill treatment exercised toward the officers & crew of the Ruth" and the minister assured him "that the persons who had committed the offense had been punished."

States that the minister agreed to the plan "of making a settlement in each individual case with its agent rather than enter into a formal convention." Comments at length on the indecisiveness of his negotiations with Aracaty, written and oral, in attempts to settle these particular claims. ALS. DNA, RG59, Dip. Disp., Brazil, vol. 6 (M121, R8). Received September 5, 1828.

From WILLIAM TUDOR, Rio de Janeiro, no. 96, July 18, 1828. Reports that the French are also trying to recover claims against Brazil, "backed with the imposing appearance of a considerable squadron & an admiral sent out expressly for that purpose, & not least diplomatic dinners, where the service of plate would have required four or five years of my salary to purchase it." Notes that the obstacle to the recovery of French and U.S. claims can be traced to Brazil's "expenses of the war and a depreciated currency getting daily worse."

Has heard that the French claims had been settled because of the menace of the French squadron, but has found this to be untrue. Has again exchanged notes with the Minister of Foreign Affairs, the Marquis of Aracaty, on American claims. Contends "it is polite to use all the indulgence possible without abandoning any rights, in order to secure a more favorable footing for our commerce which is of great & growing importance with this country." ALS. DNA, RG59, Dip. Disp., Brazil, vol. 6, (M121, R8). Letter marked "Confidential." Received September 5, 1828.

From JOHN HOWARD MARCH, Madeira, July 20, 1828. Reports that on June 22 Governor Jose Lucio Travassos Valdez "proclaimed this island to be independent of the government of D Miguel of Portugal and that it is his intention to endeavour to defend it for D Pedro [IV] against any force that may be sent from Portugal to take possession of it in the name of D Miguel." Transmits copies of Valdez's "Proclamations & Manife[sto]" and adds that he expects no "interruption to the trade of the United States with Madeira." ALS. DNA, RG59, Cons. Disp., Funchal, vol. 1 (M-T205, R1). Received September 2, 1828.

From WILLIAM B. LAWRENCE, London, no. 50, July 22, 1828. Reviews thoroughly the situation in Portugal, noting "the dispersion of the Constitutionalists in Oporto." Regarding British recognition of Portugal, reports a delay as the Duke of Wellington, the British Prime Minister, has stated in a speech the desirability of waiting "to see what line Don Pedro [I, Emperor of Brazil] would take." Concludes on the entire Portuguese question: "The most important result ... will be to deprive this country [England] of the virtual control of a valuable Province."

Reports at length on the arduous return of the Marquis of Palmela,

Portuguese minister to England, which involved seven days' detention of his ship at the Spanish port of Corunna.

Analyzes the ambiguous British mood on "things in the east of Europe." States: "The necessity which obliges England at this time not only to abstain from giving any aid to the Turks, for whose success she is most desirous, but even compels her to cooperate with their enemies" in the Russo-Turkish War. Notes that British public opinion opposes the "large expenditures," involved in any military intervention.

Reports at length on British views of the tariff issue. States that William Huskisson, in the House of Commons on July 18, commented on the American tariff act of 1828 as it affected British manufactured articles and "intimated that this country [England] migh retaliate" either with higher duties on American articles or "by annulling the Commercial Convention [6:826-7]." Mentions the view of Charles Grant that the new American tariff is "an infraction of the late convention." Feels that Huskisson is wrongly representing the recent U.S. tariff law, "as an indication of hostile feelings towards England."

Concludes by noting that Parliament is about to adjourn and that nothing will be done on the tariff issue this session, aside from "the new Customs bill," which shows that "the duty on East India Cotton has been further reduced from a shilling to four pence per cent cwt [hundredweight]." LS. DNA, RG59, Dip. Disp., Great Britain, vol. 35 (M30, M31). Received September 13, 1828.

From HENRY WHEATON, Copenhagen, July 22, 1828. Says that the indisposition of Count Ernst Heinrich Schimmelmann, Danish Minister of Foreign Affairs, has delayed his laying American claims before the Danish government, but Schimmelmann has now proposed that a Foreign Office official "confer with me on the business, informally, and with an understanding that if our conferences did not ultimately result in any thing which might serve as the basis of a formal arrangement, both parties should be at liberty to take such course as each should deem proper." Believes that this is preferable to a formal conference.

Discusses, in a forty-seven page letter, the arguments of both sides on these claims, some dating back to the 1807 war between Denmark and England during which Danish privateers seized U.S. vessels suspected as British. Notes that when the United States sent George W. Erving to protest in 1810-11, he "was obliged to grope his way in the dark, and to support *all* [claims] indiscriminately" because of "the impossibility of distinguishing between his countrymen, their documents, & property, & those which were masked as such. This difficulty was greatly enhanced by the identity of our language, manners, customs, & modes of business with that of the English, & the nations facilities given to the fabrication of ship's papers in London for the purpose of protecting that commerce with the Baltic." States that at his last meeting with Schimmelmann, the Count "mentioned his intention of bringing the whole subject before the King [Frederick VI] & that it would probably be submitted to the deliberations of a Cabinet council." Remarks that the United States accepted Denmark's desire to postpone the question of indemnities, attributing "it to the extraordinary circumstances in which Denmark found herself at that period, rather than to a want of a disposition on the part of the Danish Government to do complete justice." Has told Danish officials that the United States would prefer the establishment of a Joint Commission to hear the claims, but after preceiving "a repugnance to this course" by the Danes, he told them that the United States was willing "to take into consideration any proposition from it of a gross sum to be paid in full satisfaction of all the claims, & to be distributed among the different claimants by Commissioners appointed by the American Government." ALS. DNA, RG59, Dip. Disp., Denmark, vol. 1B (M41, R3). Received September 25, 1828. Letter marked "Private."

From JOEL R. POINSETT, Mexico, no. 146, July 23, 1828. Reports that the Mexican Congress has decided that the Senate of the State of Durango was not constitutionally organized. Predicts that this decision could cause some confusion, "but the Congress could not have come to a different conclusion without violating the principles of the Constitution." Declares that President Guadalupe Victoria has caused "very general dissatisfaction" by his appointment of General Melchor Muzquiz, a leader of the opposition party, as Inspector General of the Army. Predicts: "This country will not be perfectly tranquil until the elections are over, nor then, if the choice should not fall upon General [Vicente] Gurrero." Says that an effort will be made to induce the state legislatures to vote for Victoria for vice president, although this is "contrary to the letter and to the Spirit of the Constitution." Says also that he daily expects Congress to ratify the Panama treaties. Mentions that as soon as his negotiations are over he will "avail myself of the President's permission to leave this country." Notes that he has proposed to the other ministers a meeting at Tacubaya to adjourn the Congress of American Nations and to state their reasons for doing so; but reports they have rejected this suggestion because of resentment against Mexico for its neglect of the Treaties of Panama. Complains that he neither feels he should take the lead in this, nor does he think the project should be abandoned without a public explanation of the reasons therefore. LS. DNA, RG59, Dip. Disp., Mexico, vol. 4 (M97, R5). Received September [?], 1828. While several of the nations at the Panama Congress signed treaties of friendship, as well as several special conventions, none of these was ever ratified by the governments involved. J. Fred Rippy, ed., *History of Colombia* (Chapel Hill, N.C., 1938), 385.

From WILLIAM PITT PREBLE, Portland, Maine, July 23, 1828. Transmits copies of documents obtained in New Brunswick which help to indicate the accepted boundaries of that province, but states "the precise line between New Brunswick and Lower Canada [Quebec] . . . seems never to have been definitely settled and marked on the surface of the earth." Reveals that his goal in selecting the documents is to "seize upon strong prominent facts, susceptable of easy proof" which would provide "the necessary evidence, without resorting to testimony." Reports that although officials in the province extended "every proper courtesy and attention, there was a fixed purpose and understanding among them to note my movements, to be cautious and reserved, and to defeat, if possible, the object the President had in view in sending me into that region." ALS. NHi–Gallatin Papers (MR15).

From CHRISTOPHER HUGHES, Brussels, July 24, 1828. Encloses three papers, "handed to me by General Count [Dimitri] de Wuits . . . [a] resident of this country with news and objects connected with the cause of Greece."

Reports de Wuits's desire "to communicate with my Government, *through me,* having a very important proposition to hold out to the U.S.," that is: the cession of Cyprus to the United States in return for a liberal American government there, free and independent of Turkey. Describes General de Wuits as a man sixty years old, "a Montenegrin by birth, and has been chosen by the inhabitants, his fellow countrymen *Chef Legislateur* of that Principality." Mentions, according to de Wuits, the rumor that "there is a secret understanding between France & Russia to make a partition of Greece between themselves."

Asks for acknowledgement of this dispatch "to keep his word" to de Wuits. Comments: "I have engaged for nothing more." ALS. DNA, RG59, Dip. Disp., Netherlands, vol. 8 (M42, R12). Received September 16, 1828. See, also, Hughes to Clay, July 27, 1828.

Count Demitri de Wuits was a Montenegrin General who had served Napoleon and who lived variously in France, England, and Holland after Bonaparte's defeat and exile. He is mainly described, however, as a "famous adventurer" and confidence man who aspired, first, to the throne of Montenegro and, later, to personal power and position in an independent Cyprus. To the latter end he embraced the Greek independence cause, and in 1824 was in London attempting to arrange a British loan to the Greek revolutionary government, as well as one to Cyprus. Neither the British nor the Greeks trusted him, and his self-serving efforts came to nought. See, Amestasios D. Lignades, *The First Loan of Independence* (Athens, 1970), 118, 137–42, the title and relevant pages of which have been translated from the Greek by Helen Digenis. The editors also acknowledge the assistance of the Cyprus Research Centre, Nicosia, in helping to identify de Wuits.

To JAMES G. BIRNEY Lexington, July 25, 1828
Your favor of the 1st[1] addressed to me at Washington found me here. The effort making in Alabama for the administration, whatever may be its issue, will have exterior effect. I have been highly gratified with the zeal and attachment of my fine friends in that State, among whom I have had the satisfaction to know that I have been permitted to consider you as one of the most distinguished. I am not sure that my feelings have been more affected by the calumnies to which you refer, than those of others would be, under similar circumstances. Desiring to reserve and possess the return of all, it has been certainly painful to me to have been the object of the abuse of any. But I have found a cheering resourse in the sympathy of my friends, and of thousands to whom I do not stand in

that relation. The contest is now drawing to a close, and whatever may be its issue, it will be my duty and inclination heartily to acquiesce in it, and, should it be adverse, I shall hope that my fears may never be realized. There is however much reason to anticipate a propitious result, to which a favorable event of our elections here would powerfully, I think decisively contribute. Of such an event our friends are very confident; but a few days more will give us the fact, one way or the other, which is better than conjecture.

ALS. DLC–HC (DNA, M212, R3).   1. No letter dated the first of any month in 1828 has been found, but see Birney to Clay, January 18, 1828.

From THOMAS L. L. BRENT, Lisbon, no. 79, July 25, 1828. Reports that Miguel's forces are continuing preparation for an expedition against Madeira and possibly against Terceira in the Azores which at first accepted Miguel but later revolted. States that the ship carrying the governor, appointed by Miguel but rejected by Madeira, will probably take part in a blockade of that island. Estimates two thousand troops may be used in this expedition. Adds that he has sent these facts to the commander of the American squadron in the Mediterranean.

Encloses copy of a letter of July 15, 1828 which he has sent to the United States minister in Paris, James Brown, stating his belief that Britain may decide "to acquire the island of Madeira." Asks if this might not also be true for the Azores or Cape Verde Islands.

Notes that most of the Junta's troops which evacuated Oporto have either returned home or accepted amnesty and joined the other side, while the remainder apparently have been admitted into Spain, and that the Junta's troops since their retreat from Coimbra "have behaved in the most disorderly manner and pillaged the country in many places whilst the troops of this government have observed the most strict discipline." Reports that many who opposed Miguel have been arrested and will be tried before a special Tribunal in Oporto without appeal. States that the Spanish Legation may not withdraw from Portugal entirely unless strongly urged to do so by "all the great European Powers."

Mentions an acute shortage of government money which has resulted in a decree asking for voluntary contributions. Explains that this may bring in a considerable sum because "the system of terror is so well practised that there will be among the contributors many who would be willing to decline."

Says that since writing the above, he has learned that the Portuguese refugees in Spain will receive asylum for only one month. LS. DNA, RG59, Dip. Disp., Portugal, vol. 8 (M43, R7). Received September 23, 1828.

From JOHN CHAMBERS   Washington, Ky.,
                                              July 25, 1825 [*sic,* 1828]
The appointment of Maurice Langhorne to the Post office at Maysville[1] is spreading ruin amongst our ranks here and if the continuation of it cannot be averted I greatly fear the administration majority of this county is gone forever. [Adam] Beatty and myself have spent this after-

noon at Maysville in strong exertion to prevent the immediate effects of it there, but there are many who could only be opperated upon by the suggestion that *the evil* might yet be remedied & some not even by that means. John M. Morton was recommended by upwards of fourteen hundred of the voting population of this county beside[s] many individuals of great worth & high standing. It is already urged that the voice of the people has no influence with Mr. [John] Adams and that a few members of congress alike ignorant and regardless of the wishes and interest of the people of this section of the country have procured the appointment of a man of whom perhaps not ten men in the town in which he resides approve. Judge Beatty and myself have written to Mr. Adams, but it is our anxious wish you should join us in trying to avert the calamity with which we are threatened. Beatty will write to you tomorrow [July 26] more fully and I must close my letter or it will be excluded from the mail.... P.S. A Bond has been forwarded to Mr. Langhorne upon the return of which with security he is assured of being commissioned. Mr. [John] McClain [*sic,* McLean] has taken care to let it be understood that the appointment was made by direction of the President. This in a letter to his kinsman Mr. R[obert] Taylor [Jr.] who was an applicant for the office.

ALS. MHi–Adams Papers, Letters Received (MR486). For Chambers, see *BDAC*.   1. See Beatty to Clay, July 26, 1828; Clay to Adams, July 28, 1828; Clay to Beatty, July 28, 1828. Langhorne had been appointed to replace the deceased William Murphy as Postmaster at Maysville, Ky.

To MARK HARDIN Lexington, July 25, 1828

Your favor of the 23d. inst. is received. I am not sure that I shall go to Frankfort. If I do it will be next week and to remain only a single day. Should I go I will notify you.

You did right in dissuading my friends from inviting me to Shelby. I should be happy to see them, but perfect tranquillity is indispensible to the restoration of my health, and to obtain that I must avoid large assemblages, which always excite me too much, especially if I speak in public.

'Though my health is improved, it is far from being as good as I could wish.

I congratulate you on a recent change in your Religious feelings, of which I have heard. I always rejoice when I hear of any friend, undergoing such a change.

ALS. Courtesy of R. S. Sanders, Lexington, Ky.

From RICHARD HIGGINS, *ET AL.*, Lexington, July 25, 1828. Notes that Clay's "former congressional constituents" want him to attend a testimonial dinner in his honor, on a date agreeable to him, because they have "witnessed with pain and indignation the unparallelled persecution, with which you have for the last 3 or 4 years been pursued," and wish to express "their continued and increased confidence in the purity of your heart." Lexington *Kentucky Reporter,* August 6, 1828.

Clay declined this invitation on July 26, 1828, pleading "the yet delicate state of my health." *Ibid.*

A similar dinner invitation, from Willis Field and G. M. Pinckard, Versailles, July 23, 1828, which drew attention to the threat of "military rule" replacing "constituional supremacy" were Jackson to be elected, was similarly declined on July 26. *Ibid.*

From PETER B. PORTER   Washington, July 25, 1828
The N. York Convention met two days ago,[1] and, in about three days more, we shall get the result of its proceedings, of which I will immediately apprise you.

From letters which I received yesterday from N. York & Albany I apprehend that Judge [Smith] Thompson[2] has made up his mind not to be a Candidate, although the writer of a letter from N. York dated on monday, did not yet entirely dispair. [Francis] Granger will probably be the Candidate for Governor, & perhaps, Peter Sharp [*sic*], for Lt. Governor.[3]

Granger is extremely popular in the western parts of the State, in consequence not only of the great zeal he has displayed in favour of internal improvements & the tariff, but from the peculiar *midway* position he occupies between the Masons & [William] Morgan men.[4] Our accounts from every part of N. York continue to be flattering. The recent nomination (which has been accepted) of Mr [Abraham] Van Vachten [*sic*][5] as the Elector for Albany county, is a most favourable circumstance and will secure, beyond question, the three electors of Albany, Rensselaer & Montgomery, all of which have been confidently claimed by the Jackson men.[6] Mr. V. V. is called by the people, what is deemed by them to be a very rare animal "The honest Lawyer" & has stood for 30. year[s] at the head of the profession in that county. Being a dutchman, he has great influence with the electors of these counties who are principally dutch.

All eyes are turned to Kentucky; and I am still of opinion that the result of your approaching Election will decide the presidential contest. Should [Thomas] Metcalf[e] be elected, I shall insist on your returning by N. York—otherwise I would not urge it, as I take it for granted your feelings[7] will not, for a short time at least, be in proper tune to enjoy yourself with political friends. However, happen what may, I shall consider your chance, four years hence, as decidedly better than that of any other man.

Your friends were well two evenings since, & I presume are so still. I was yesterday at a farewell dinner, given by the President to Gov. [James] Barbour, who will leave this for N. York, tomorrow, unless prevented by the State of Mrs B's[8] health, which is very delicate. I calculate to leave here on Monday the 4th of August & shall probably reach Ky about the close of the week. The President intends leaving the same week. Mr. [Samuel L.] Southard will remain somewhat longer, & Mr [Richard] Rush, *throughout*. H[enry]. Eckford[9] of N. York has been here, & dined yesterday at the Presidents. After suffering for two years past, as much persecution as yourself, but in a much more mortifying way, he has reestablished his character and recovered his spirits. He left town this morn[in]g, determined to do what he can for the Admn. and his influence is yet to be felt.

400

I have recently received two letters from [William B.] Rochester, written on his journey through the interior of the country home—which he is performing on horse-back. You have undoubtedly heard from him. I have become somewhat more domesticated in my office. But I find my domestic labours still so arduous that I have scarcely a moment to devote to my friends abroad. . . . [P.S.] Judge [John] Savage still avows himself decidedly for the Admn, and a friend who conversed with him five days ago thinks he would have been [a] candidate for Gov. had it been offered to him. But it was too late

ALS. InU.   1. Porter to Clay, June 12, 1828.   2. *Ibid.*   3. Smith Thompson and Francis Granger [*BDAC*] were the pro-Administration candidates for Governor and Lt. Governor. They were defeated by the pro-Jackson ticket of Martin Van Buren and Enos T. Throop [*BDAC*]. For Peter Sharpe, see *BDAC*.   4. For more on Granger and the Mason vs. Antimason controversy in N.Y., see Ratner, *Antimasonry: The Crusade and the Party*, 64–74.   5. For Abraham Van Vechten, see *NCAB*, 9:162–3.   6. In the Presidential election of 1828, Jackson carried Albany 4195 to 3924 over Adams, Rensselaer 4650 to 4263, and Montgomery 3982 to 3778. Albany *Argus*, November 22, 1832.   7. Word "spirits" struck through and "feelings" substituted.   8. For Mary Thomas Barbour, see *DAB*.   9. For Eckford, see *DAB*.

From ADAM BEATTY   Washington, Ky., July 26, 1828

Inteligence has been received, that Mr. [Maurice] Langhorn [*sic*, Langhorne] is to receive the appointment of Post Master at Maysville,[1] & a bond has been forwarded to be executed by him, preparitory to his receiving the commission. This appointment, if confirmed, will opperate very adversely to the interests of the administration as the popular current runs very strongly in favour of Mr. [John M.] Morton, and against Mr. Langhorn. I have written to the President fully on this subject and also to Josiah S. Johns[t]on, in which I sugested the propriety of suspending the commission of Mr. Langhorn, to give further time for consideration. I have presented a fair and candid view of the circumstances, so as to enable him to act as to his judgment may seem most proper. Many other letters have also been addressed to him on the subject. And I have been specially requested, by a number of the citizens of Maysville & others, to write you on the subject. From the following state of facts you may readily immagine how strong a feeling prevails against the appointment of Mr. Langhorn. . . .

[Comments at length on the circumstances of the death of William Murphy, the former postmaster, the popularity of John M. Morton, Mrs. Murphy's brother, Morton's superior qualifications for the position and the political in-fighting in Maysville between Langhorn and Morton partisans. Continues:]

That the appointment of Mr. Langhorn will opperate adversely to the cause of the administration, in a high degree, is the general opinion; indeed, while at Maysville yesterday, I heard none speak on the subject but were decidedly of this opinion. The Jackson party are already urging it as *proof* that Mr. Adams habitually disregards *the will of the people;* and as *proof* of the correctness of the construction *they* have put upon a clause in one of his first messages to Congress,[2] in which he is alledged to have uttered the sentiment that a representative ought not to be palsied by the will of his constituents   You know the use they [have] already made of this *false* construction of a part of Mr. Adams' first message. And you know also slight circumstances will give *colour* to the charge when so many are interested in sustaining it. The charge of disregarding *the will of the people* is urged with peculiar force, in relation to the appointment of a post master in Maysville, because it is founded upon the fact of Mr. Morton having in his favour the almost unanimous sentiment of the county, whilst Mr. Langhorn has in his favour a very small number; and because this charge is countenanced—under the state of excitement now prevailing—by the friends of the administration, or at least by many of them.

I did what I could, on yesterday, to moderate and allay the excitement which now prevails in Maysville, and hope that no imprudent course will be taken, but I greatly fear that if the appointment of Mr. Langhorn is confirmed, it will opperate very adversely to the administration party. Is it too late yet to remidy this evil? Cannot the President yet correct the mischief by making such an appointment as will give satisfaction? . . .

[Concludes with the observation that "Your judgment will suggest the proper course to be taken. I will only add, that the *Jackson party* are endeavouring as usual to throw the blame of this transaction upon you." Requests that Clay keep the authorship of this letter confidential since Beatty is a candidate for the state legislature].

ALS. MHi–Adams Papers, Letters Received (MR486).   1. See Chambers to Clay, July 25, 1828; Clay to Beatty, July 28, 1828.   2. Richardson, *MPP*, 2:299–317.

From ROBERT M. HARRISON, St. Bartholomew, July 26, 1828. Encloses copy of a petition of Alexander Barclay, agent for certain American vessels, to the Jamaican House of Assembly seeking redress for double charges for tonnage. Contends this document proves the correctness of President John Q. Adams's statement, made to Congress during the last session, "that the orders in Council were not understood by the British Authorities in the Colonies who were to execute them." Believes that if "the cases of those vessels . . . were laid before the British Government the money would be instantly refunded." ALS. DNA, RG59, Cons. Disp., St. Bartholomew, vol. 1 (M72, R1). Received August 14, 1828.

From WILLIAM PLUMER, JR.   Epping, N.H., July 26, 1828
I did not think it necessary to trouble you with my acknowledgments for your letter of the 7th April last, though duply sensible to the friendly terms in which it was expressed. I take the liberty however to request your acceptance of the enclosed Address—in which you will perceive that I have not avoided the great question, which so duply agitates the public mind, in every quarter of the Union. Not that I expect you will find time to read a 4th of July oration, especially the hasty production which at the close of the session of our Legislature I was called upon to prepare—but I have marked one or two passages, in which I have ventured to introduce your Baltimore speech [May 13, 1828]—a speech, which, however abused by the Jackson presses, appears to me to be conceived, & expressed in the true spirit of the revolution.

I do not know whether I sent you, at the time, the newspaper containing my answer to an attempt, which was made here, to prove, by declarations of mine, the corruption imputed to you & Mr Adams in the late presidential election. I am very confident that I never used the language imputed to me, & perfectly certain that nothing I did say could, by any fair construction, be considered unfavourable to your conduct or your motives. While noticing this attack, I thought the best course would be to correct, with a general denial of its truth, certain views of the subject, which appear to me to set many expressions imputed both to your friend & to Mr Adams, in their true & perfectly unexceptionable light.—If you have a spare copy of your late pamphlet [6:1394-6], I should be glad to receive it, as I am not certain that I have seen the whole of it in the public papers.

I hope, & trust, that the election has gone favourably in Louisiana;[1] & that you will follow it up with a still more signal victory in Kentucky. If the summer elections show an increasing strength, on the part of the Administration, in the western country generally the effect of such success on the November elections, in all the doubtful states will be prodigious. The anti tariff proceedings in South Carolina[2] must, it appears to me, have the happiest effects in Pennsylvania & New York, not to speak of Kentucky Ohio, & Indiana—Is there no hope of Illinois?

We think ourselves safe, here in New Hampshire; though there is among us less zeal & activity than there ought to be considering the strength & perservence of the opposition. There is, in fact, no part of New England in the least degree doubtful unless it be this state, & one or two districts in Maine. Still however I think we are safe enough—Measures will be sensibly taken to bring out our whole strength in November. For my own part, I have done little else, for the last year, but labour in this great cause—with little success indeed, but with a zeal proportioned to my sense of its importance—

ALS. DLC-HC (DNA, M212, R3).   1. The state elections in Louisiana were a triumph for the Administration party. The results, according to the New Orleans *Bee* of July 10, 1828, gave the Adams National Republicans the Governorship (Pierre Derbigny), one U.S. Senator (Dominique Bouligny) and two U.S. Representatives (William H. Gurley and Henry H. Gurley). The Jackson party captured one House and one Senate seat.   2. See David Houston, *A Critical Study of Nullification in South Carolina* (Cambridge, Mass., 1896), 71–5.

To TRUSTEES OF TRANSYLVANIA UNIVERSITY, Lexington, July 26, 1828.

As executor of the estate of James Morrison, proposes that instead of Transylvania's taking the full sum [$20,000] of its Morrison legacy the trustees should consider one of two propositions: (1) loan Clay the legacy for an indefinite period at six per cent interest, paid semi-annually in exchange for a real estate mortgage "amply sufficient to secure the punctual payment of the interest" and the ultimate reimbursement of the principal; or (2) for the trustees to receive the full amount of the legacy on January 1, 1829, which would give them time to find a proper investment of the capital. LS. KyLxT.

Transylvania's trustees accepted Clay's first proposition. Minutes of the Board of Trustees, July 28, 1828. *Ibid.*

From CHRISTOPHER HUGHES, Brussels, July 27, 1828. Discusses recent correspondence he has had in fulfilling his duties. States that King William I is "one of the wisest, best and most just men upon earth," but notes that his predecessor in the post, Alexander H. Everett, had treated the King "with pronounced disrespect, in his vapid, vague & vain political works" and had "shocked the society of the country, & of his Colleagues by leading the gloomy, unsocial life of a morose Student." Charges that "Mr. Everett, *when here,* would not pronounce the word Royal Highness, if he could help it!" Claims he has done well in the post considering the "up-hill work left me, by my predecessor."

Discusses at length his social life and local social gossip, then refers to his letter to Clay of July 25 [*sic,* July 24–25] by "*special* Courier," in which he had drawn attention to the possibility of the United States acquiring a "certain Island [Cyprus]" rich in natural resources, on which 30,000 Turks "keep down" 120,000 Greeks who wish to "throw off the moslem yoke, which may be done, with 5 or 6,000 Troops, & at small expense; the Troops are ready." Says he got this information from a "Montenegrew Chief [General Count Dimitri de Wuits]" and that he knows no more about the situation on the island than what he has already transmitted. Suggests that Clay acknowledge receipt of this information in a letter sent in the British diplomatic bag, rather than putting such a letter into the regular mail. "I leave all the rest to the higher powers!" Adds: "If you should give any serious attention to this project of insular cession, I should have no objection to make a trip of reconnaissance," a confidential trip that would take four or five months. States that he worked "very hard" on his July 24–25 letter about this matter; "in 48 [hours], I worked 25 hours; and as I kept no copy, I should not like to have my work lost. You will oblige me by acknowledging it." Complains that Clay does not write him often enough or at sufficient length.

Compliments Clay on his Baltimore speech [May 15, 1828]. Urges him to fight back against the "slanders, lies & malice" that his political enemies have hurled against him, and do so in correct grammar: "I delight in your doctrines; & in every part of your Speech but your 'precipice' an Abyss may, but a 'Precipice' cannot yawn."

Concludes with Court gossip and the information that General Lafayette has summoned him to Paris because "he has something to communicate to me . . . that would take too much writing." ALS. DLC-HC (DNA, M212, R3).

To JOHN QUINCY ADAMS   Lexington, July 28, 1828
You will have received letters from the two gentlemen who wrote the inclosed.[1] Mr. [John] Chambers is the Candidate for Congress, on the side of the Administration, to succeed Genl. [Thomas] Metcalfe. There is no warmer friend nor better man than Mr. [Adam] Beatty. If I had made an appointment,[2] and acted upon my own knowledge, I believe I should have appointed Mr. [Maurice] Langhorne. If I had appointed an other, it would have been a concession to the weight of testimonials in behalf of that other. Without expressing any decisive opinion to Mr. Beatty (that I could not do, unless I possessed information of the grounds of proceeding at the City) I have stated to him that I would

suggest to you the propriety of a reconsideration of the matter. I imagine a good deal of the excitement is the effect of sympathy for the widow and family of the deceased encumbent [William Murphy][3]; and some of it proceeds from disappointed persons. A good deal may wear out with the lapse of time; but it is not to be concealed that the recent appointment is, after making all abatement for the above causes, unsatisfactory to the Maysville and Mason County public. In other parts of the State I believe Mr. Langhorne's appointment will be well received.[4] I have other information, besides that of Mr. Chambers, that the P.M General [John McLean] has endeavored to throw upon you, and to escape himself from, all the consequences of the actual selection.

My health has not improved as much since I left the White Sulphur Springs as it did before. I feel much debility yet. I shall remain here about two weeks longer, and then return leisurely, by what route I have not yet decided.

I think the friends of the Administration will succeed in the election next week unless some adverse events should take place during the present. I apprehend however that the majority will be less than I expected before I left Washington. If Mr. Chambers be right, as to the influence of Mr. Langhorne's appointment in Mason County (hitherto one of the strongest for the administration) it would have a material effect on the issue; but I hope he exaggerated.

ALS. MHi–Adams Papers, Letters Received (MR486).   1. Chambers to Clay, July 25, 1828; Beatty to Clay, July 26, 1828.   2. To the position of Postmaster at Maysville, Ky.   3. Whose widow was sister to John M. Morton, an aspirant for the postmastership. Beatty to Clay, July 26, 1828. Murphy, who died on June 17, 1828, had long served as Postmaster at Maysville. *RKHS*, 39:244.   4. John Green to Clay, September 3, 1828. ALS. DNA, RG59, Misc. Letters (M179, R66). Writing from Stanford, Ky., Green strongly endorsed Langhorne, noting: "The fact of the post office at Maysville being the principal distributing office for Kentucky is a reason why we at a distance feel an interest that it be well filled."

To ADAM BEATTY   Lexington, July 28, 1828

I have recd. your favor of the 26h. I had previously written to Mr. [John] Chambers in answer to a letter from him, on the same subject, and requested him to shew you my letter.[1]

I left Washn. City on the 22d. June and travelled through the Valley to the White Sulphur Springs [Va.], and never heard of the death of Mr. [William] Murphy[2] until I reached Maysville this day fortnight. I have not written one line to any person in favor of or against any applicant.

The full details in your letter make out a strong case for Mr. [John M.] Morton. Of several of them I never before heard. The fact of Captn. [James] Byers[3] and Mr. [Robert] Taylor [Jr.][4] declining in his favor is one of great weight. If Mr. Morton be best qualified, that single circumstance ought to have decided for him. When at Maysville I was told that Mr. Taylor was an applicant. I also understood that many of the most prominent Citizens of the State had recommended Mr. L. [Maurice Langhorne]. Several of these were well known at Washington [Ky.], and I presume much importance was attached to their opinions. If any improper means were employed to procure their recommendations it could not have been known there.

I shall write to the President[5] and suggest the propriety of a reconsideration of the matter. If he is satisfied that the public interest requires the appointment of another, he has the power, as you know, to direct accordingly. As I have not the whole ground before me—particularly as I have not the testimonials on which the appointment was made, you must not understand me as expressing any decisive opinion. I think a full & fair hearing ought to be given. I must add that I think Mr. Langhorne qualified for the office, although Mr. M[orton]. may be better qualified. Of that I have not the means of forming an opinion.

I lament the excitement which has been produced.

ALS. Courtesy of Earl M. Ratzer, Highland Park, Ill.   1. Beatty to Clay, July 26, 1828; Chambers to Clay, July 25, 1828.   2. See, below, Clay to Adams, July 28, 1828. 3. See, G. Glenn Clift, *History of Maysville and Mason Co.* 2 vols. (Lexington, Ky., 1936), 1:161.   4. Chambers to Clay, July 25, 1828.   5. Clay to Adams, July 28, 1828.

From JAMES BROWN   Paris, July 28, 1828

Your letter of the 15 Ulto. informing me that your health had greatly improved, that you only required absence from business and exercise to confirm it, and that you were just setting out on a Journey to Kentucky passing the Virginia Springs, gave me the greater pleasure on account of the alarming reports on that subject which had already reached us. General Lafayette who had just heard that your life was despaired of, called on me and was much gratified at the contradiction of the report contained in your letter. I beg of you to live if by prudence and care you can preserve your life, as well for the gratification of your friends, as to vex, and disappoint, and mortify, some of your inverterate enemies. Not only *live* for these purposes, but be cheerful, and calm, and contented, and happy. Nothing gratifies an enemy so much, as to perceive that his sling is felt, nothing disconcerts him so much as to discover that his malice is impotent.

My brother [Samuel] and my niece [Susan] arrived here just as we were leaving for Dieppe, where Mrs. Brown had been advised to spend a few weeks for the benefit of her health   They very readily agreed to suspend their curiosity, and accompany us—I remained with them until the 20th. and then left them, in order to be in Paris in time to see the Minister of Foreign Affairs [Ferronnays] on the business of our Claims you will see the result of our interview in the despatch[1] which I send by this Ship. We have so often been deceived with hopes of success that I have not ventured to hazard the expression of mine in my official letter but I cannot help thinking that we shall succeed, if the present Ministry, and more especially the Ministers, of F[oreign]. A[ffairs]. and of the Marine, continue in office for some time, and shall receive as the[y] have lately the Confidence of the two Chambers. Our success depends in the event of the continuance of peace, upon the adoption by France of what has been already commenced, a more strict system of ecomony and accountability than has hitherto prevailed   In the event of a Continental war, our weight may do something for us. In the interview which I had with the Count de la Ferronnays, I enlarged upon the liberal measures which had been adopted at the last Session, in relation to the Commerce of France and urged that they ought to be met by at least an honest settlement of debts so long due to our citizens. I was surprized to find

General [Samuel] Smith expressing regret at the turning [out] of the Villele Administration and stating Mr. V. was exceedingly friendly to the United States. If he has been liberal in any one act I have not been made acquainted with it   I labored Eighteen months to obtain restitution of the discriminating duties demanded on two Tobacco and five Cotton Cargoes merely beca[use] they had touched at Cowes in Cork for orders, and because by the act of this Government, forbidding their Consuls to give Certificates of origin to any vessels which should not clear one for a french port they had rendered the obtaining [of] that document impossible—I have renewed the Correspondence with the present [Martignac] Ministry and have better hopes of success. It has been referred to the Minister of Foreign Affairs to the Count de St Creqe [*sic*][2] Minister of Commerce with whom I have asked a conference. He has appointed for it the day after we shall have sent off our despatches, so that you cannot know his decision until the sailing of the next ship. One thing I think will be clear. If I do not gain the cause I shall win the argument.

Mrs. Brown begs me to say that she will when she returns execute your Commissions, and those of our friends Mrs. [Richard] Rush and Mrs. [William] Wirt, at her return to Paris, which will take place early in September, and send them if possible by the Vessel of the 15 of that month. Make yourself perfectly easy about the small sum you say stands to my credit   I have ample means at my disposition until my return. If it was ten aye fifty times as much it would never figure in the scandalous and incredible list of Mortgages published by your Kentucky *friends*   Great God to what a cruel height has malicious immoraltity grown in our Country when such things can be tolerated!—But meet it all firmly and good naturedly—In my youth I was the most irritable of human beings, I am now and have been for several years one of the least excitable—I find my account in this change of temper. Wretches like many of your enemies are unworthy of any sentiment but those of pity and contempt.

Mrs. Brown is fortunate in being absent from Paris at this time because she is too weak to entertain her friends, and too hospitable to abstain from giving them a kind reception. I am told Mrs. Scott & Mrs. Cabell and their mother have arrived at Havre in the last ship. Mrs. Brown and myself have been deeply affected at the loss which we have sustained by the death of Miss Mary Sumter of South Carolina in her 21. year. She was a dear and interesting friend indeed like a daughter to us. At that early age with beauty which would have spoiled any other young lady (for she was universally acknowledged as the greatest beauty in Paris) she spoke and wrote perfectly and with equal ease the Portuguese, French, and English languages, was a fine Musician and to the most excellent heart, united the greatest polish of manners. Her poor father and mother will be broken hearted at hearing of her death—

You ask me will the war in the East become general? It is not very easy to conjecture what will result from the present very extraordinary problem in which Europe is placed. I do not think that either of the great powers, or indeed any power, will make common cause with the Turks, or indeed directly oppose resistance to the march of the Emperor [Nicholas I]. What may however be considered as probable is, that France

England, and perhaps Austria, will endeavor to avail themselves of the moment to take possession, severally, of portions of the Ottoman Empire. It is now reported that France, with the Consent of England is about to send twel[ve] thousand men into the Morea, and I shall not be surprized if she takes possession of some important positions to be held, either as securities that Russia shall not pursue the War for motives of aggrandizement, or as an equivalent for the strength which the Emperor may gain by his victories. England has sunk much in the Opinion of the Continent, on the score of strength, not only by the events which have taken place in the East, and in Portugal but also by the dispending language which has been used in Parliament; and by her Ministry. This, and the popular conduct of the new [Wellington] Ministry, which has united the people and Government, to a degree beyond what has been known since the Restoration, has given confidence to France, and inspired her with the disposition to take a high stand in the European family of nations. It is possible that England, alarmed at the rapid growth of the French Navy, and discovering that the loss of her maritime superiority is threatened, may rouse from her despondency, & make a vigorous attempt to destroy the french fleet. This event is however by no means probable, as in the present distracted state of Ireland, a war with a Catholic power, would, too probably, terminate in the loss of that portion of the British dominions. I rather incline to the opinion that England will endeavor to get up a Congress, and try to arrange all these questions by negociation. Her standing at such a Congress will be very different from what it has been at former meetings of that kind. Lord Granville has been succeeded by Lord Stewart [sic],[3] formerly Sir Charles, who is considered as an able Diplomat. He has just arrived [in Paris] but has not yet been presented at Court.

I am very well acquainted, and much pleased, with [John Adams] Smith, who passed the greater part of a winter in Paris. He would [be] every thing I could wish if he possessed a knowledge of the French language. Too little attention to this circumstance has hither to been given by our Government. In former days, when politicks entered but little into the conversations of the people, and when Representative Governments were not in existence, it was much less important, than it is at this time. Every body here, as with us, converses on the politics, not only of his own Government, but also of every other with which it has relations. Much may be done by judicious conversations, which may have an indirect bearing on questions depending between this Government and that of the Minister, and without writing a single note, many difficulties may, in this way, be removed out of the way of Negociation. The correspondence with the Government is in our language, but that with the Inhabitants who apply for information must necessarily be in French. Many letters are mere matters of form which may as well be written, as copied, by the Secretary of Legation, without an application to the Minister. I shall be happy however when Mr Smith arrives, because he is honorable, amiable, and I believe sincerely attached to me. With application he may in one or two years acquire some Knowledge of the language, perhaps enough to enable him to go on with ease. Mr

[William B.] Lawrence writes me that he will make a visit to this city and then return to the United States.

I am happy that Mrs. Clay has the pleasure of her daughter [Anne Brown Clay Erwin] and grand childrens [Julia D. and Henry Clay Erwin] company during your absence. You speak too modestly of Anne when you say she is a good girl. I always felt convinced from her infancy, that she would be a distinguished woman. To ineffable sweetness of temper, she united great natural grace in her manners, and good sense in all her expressions. When I last saw her about five years ago I thought her very handsome. My brother and niece who met her in Tennessee speak of her in the most exalted terms. I am happ[y] that Henry [Clay, Jr.,], is doing so well—He is at the best institution [U.S. Military Academy] in the United States. I have written to him encouraging him to persevere in his studies, and hope my letter may have some effect.

I am happy to discover that you are still sangu[ine in your] belief that the President will be re elected. If there is time eno[ugh for the] passions and prejudices of the people to subside before the election [there can] be but little doubt as to the result. I am told that [Edward] Liv[ingston] will lose his election in Louisiana.[4]

You do not say how long you intend to be absent from Washington but I presume you will not return before October. Should this letter reach you in Kentucky, be so good as to make my affectionate remembrances to all my relations.

ALS. DLC-HC (DNA, M212, R3).   Printed in *LHQ*, 24:1115-20.   1. Brown to Clay, July 29, 1828.   2. Pierre Laurent, Comte de Saint Cricq. Beach, *Charles X of France*, 253.   3. For Gower Leveson, Lord Granville, and Charles, Lord Stuart, see *DNB*. 4. He did. *BDAC*.

From CHRISTOPHER HUGHES, Brussels, July 28, 1828. Encloses an extract of "the very remarkable speech" of Hyde de Neuville, French Minister of Marine, on the "naval budget," pointing out that "At length, full justice is done to the memory of our old friend [Robert] Fulton, the American Archimedes, in despite of the frauds and lies of the British press." Reports that the "augmentation of the french Marine is enormous," but feels that Neuville is in error in speaking "rather slightingly of other naval powers," particularly the Dutch. "The Navy of the United Netherlands and the talents of the Dutch officers are worthy of more respect." Promises "a report on the Dutch Navy depots–arsenals, income resources soon for our Secretary [Samuel L. Southard]." Mentions the "conceit and vanity" of the French about their Navy since the Battle of Navarino, and reports a conversation with the French minister, Louis-Toussaint, Marquis de la Moussaye, who was "crowing over me the other day about their great superiority to U.S. in numbers." Says he silenced the man with a remark that there was a way that the French Navy "may be decreased one half, in one year." When the minister asked how, Huges replied: "Why—declare war against US." Concludes with detailed reports on Court gossip and his plan to travel to Paris to speak with Lafayette, George Washington's "adopted son." ALS. DLC-HC (DNA, M212, R3).

From **BARON PAUL DE KRUDENER,** Washington, D.C., July 28, 1828. Transmits copy of a circular dispatch, concerning the enforcement of maritime law, which the Czar of Russia, Nicholas I, issued to his naval forces in the Mediterranean following Russia's declaration of war against Turkey [6:1343–4]. States that the United States will find in this document "convincing proof of the deference with which His Imperial Majesty wishes his naval forces to act with respect to neutral navigators" and expresses his belief that American merchantmen and naval forces will reciprocate by observing a policy of neutrality. Assures neutral powers that they have "no legitimate cause of apprehension" about the war, because Russia's intentions are "uniformly moderate." Notes "it is with deep mortification" that he has been deprived until now of the power to inform the United States officially of Russia's declaration of war. LS. DNA, RG59, Notes from Russian Legation, vol. 2 (M39, R2).

On October 14, de Krudener transmitted to Clay copies of the Emperor's declaration of war and related documents. These, he asserted, "are guarantees of the uprightness of his intentions." ALS, in French, with trans. in State Dept. file. DNA, RG59, Notes from Russian Legation, vol. 2 (M39, R2).

From **JAMES BROWN,** Paris, no. 85, July 29, 1828. Refers to his dispatch no. 84 of May 12, in which he reported that Count Pierre de La Ferronnays had assured him that Brown's letter of December 19, 1827 to Baron de Damas [6:1392–3] on American claims would be submitted to the French Council of Ministers and that a decision on the matter could be expected. Notes, however, that the new ministry was then experiencing problems with maintaining a majority in the two chambers; but now its political situation is far more stable. Indeed, "Our claims for Indemnity were mentioned in favorable terms by some members of the Chamber of Deputies and I considered the moment as having arrived when I could press them with some hope of success."

He therefore sought and received an audience with the Foreign Minister on July 24, only to be told again that the American claims, "now of ancient date," should have been presented at the "general settlement" of claims and indemnities worked out in 1818, and to learn that he "could not then offer me a satisfactory answer"; further, that for various reasons further postponements must be expected. Brown protested this, pointing out to Count de La Ferronnays that "the United States had during the long war in which France had been involved preserved their neutrality—that they had no share in the events which led to the settlement which terminated that war." Reminded him also that the Duke of Richelieu, in 1818, had specifically separated American claims against France from those of the European powers, the former "being reserved for discussion at the express suggestion of the Minister of the United States [Albert Gallatin]." In addition, Brown reviewed for Ferronnays the history of the attempts of various American ministers in Paris from 1816 to the present day to present and discuss the claims. "I concluded by mentioning that my efforts to bring the negotiation to a close, had for more than four years been as unremitted, as they had been unsuccessful,

410

and that I could not, under these circumstances, conceive how our claims could be objected to on account of their ancient date." In response, the Foreign Minister "assured me" that he would submit "my letter of the 19th December" to the Council of Ministers as soon as the legislative session was adjourned. ALS. DNA, RG59, Dip. Disp., France, vol. 23 (M34, R26). Received September 24, 1828.

From **WILLIAM CARROLL,** Nashville, July 29, 1828. Recommends Archelaus Hughes of Dresden, Tenn. who "is desirous to accompany the Southern [Cherokee] Indians on their exploring expedition Westward, or to procure the appointment of Indian agent." ALS. DLC–HC (DNA, M212, R3). Several of these "exploring expeditions" were sent out to prepare the Cherokees for voluntary migration westward. The first forcible removals of the Cherokees began in 1832. Duane King, ed., *The Cherokee Indian Nation* (Knoxville, 1979), 135.

From **THOMAS L. L. BRENT,** Lisbon, no. 80, July 30, 1828. Transmits copy of an act of the Cortes "containing an exposition of the Fundamental law concerning succession to the crown of Portugal," an examination of the claims of Pedro and Miguel to the throne, an appeal to foreign powers to accept the decision of the Portuguese nation on this matter, and a declaration that since March 10, 1826 the crown had belonged to Miguel. Adds that Miguel dissolved the Cortes a few days after it passed this act. States that Spain has still not made a decision about withdrawing its diplomatic corps from Portugal and that "from all that I can learn England is the only power at Madrid that had as yet pressed that cabinet to follow the example of Austria and England."

Continues on July 31, saying Count de La Tour Maubourg has received orders from the French government to leave Lisbon immediately; and mentions a meeting yesterday of British merchants to discuss a renewed offer to evacuate them and their property by means of the British squadron on the Tagus River. Adds that none have accepted this invitation although the squadron will probably soon be ordered to leave the Tagus. Reports that the steamboat carrying anti–Miguel refugees from Oporto, which was forced to land at Corunna, Spain, has now sailed from there. LS. DNA, RG59, Dip. Disp., Portugal, vol. 8 (M43, R7). Received July [September?] 22, 1828.

On August 23, 1828 Brent wrote Clay from Lisbon, reporting that on August 21 Spain had recalled her legation. *Ibid.* Received October 27, 1828.

From **ALEXANDER H. EVERETT,** Madrid, no. 111, July 30, 1828. Transmits a translation of a note by Jose G. Lima, Portuguese Minister at Madrid, who remains loyal to King Pedro IV, to Manuel Salmon, Secretary of State in Spain, in which Lima declares suspension of all his relations with Miguel's government. Mentions, as well, Lima's circular to other Portuguese diplomatic agents abroad urging a "pro-test against the usurpation" of Miguel. Explains Salmon's objections to Lima's note. Adds that Don Miguel's minister, Count de Figuera, "has arrived here, but has not yet been formally received."

Announces the "great preparations" being made for the return of King Ferdinand VII to Madrid on August 11, following his tour of the Northern Provinces, and reports that "The interior of the King-dom is perfectly tranquil." LS. DNA, RG59, Dip. Disp., Spain, vol. 29 (M31, R29). Received September 21, 1828.

From ALBERT GALLATIN, New York, July 30, 1828. Sends copies of documents relating to the Northeastern boundary controversy which Judge William P. Preble obtained in New Brunswick, as well as a copy of Preble's list of the documents which should be requested from Britain, and additional specifications for documents already requested. Notes that several documents of the same nature will be requested "in order to show that those acts of jurisdiction were not the result of accident *but* of a constant and uniform understanding with respect to the established boundary of Canada." States that when these documents are obtained "I believe that there is nothing else to be asked from the British Government." Also suggests that the United States Minister to Britain, James Barbour, be instructed to collect all modern British maps of New Brunswick and send them immediately to the State Department. ALS. DNA, RG76, Northeast Boundary (KyU., Special Roll, frames 72–6).

From WILLIAM B. LAWRENCE, London, no. 51, July 30, 1828. Encloses a printed copy of a speech given in the name of King George IV in Parliament on July 28. Quotes a sentence from the speech: "His Majesty relies upon the wisdom of the august Sovereign, the Head of the House of Braganza." Interprets this to mean that Pedro I, Emperor of Brazil, "should amicably arrange matters with Don Miguel, leaving to the latter the Sovereignty of Portugal." On "the affairs to the East [Russo–Turkish War]," mentions France's decision "to send troops to the Morea."

Includes an analysis of the situation in Ireland, stating that "the King is silent" on the issue. He has learned, however, from credible sources, that legislation will be introduced in the next session of Parliament as a "plan of conciliation" to remove "all practical grievances on the part of Catholics," and yet will contain "securities" to satisfy the established [Anglican] Church. Predicts that this bill will pass. LS. DNA, RG59, Dip. Disp., Great Britain, vol. 35 (M30, R31). Received September 10, 1828. In April, 1829, Parliament passed the controversial Catholic Emancipation Bill. See also, Lawrence to Clay, February 28, 1828.

From ABRAHAM B. NONES, Maracaibo, July 30, 1828. Transmits correspondence concerning the case of the American schooner, *William Dawson,* which was boarded, a passenger removed, and was later fired upon by the British schooner *Skip Jack* in territorial waters off Maracaibo, on June 3, 1828. Has protested to Colombian officials and has received their promise "to protect our Flag from any repetition of insult from this vessel." States that the British are trying to deny that the shots were fired.

412

Reports that Simon Bolivar has been named Supreme Power of the State and has returned to Bogota. Predicts that vice president, Francisco de Paula Santander, will be arrested. Notes that Bolivar's partisans expect "great results from his sole legislation," but concludes "I have not the same confidence nor do I see anything to justify the hope of the pacification and regulation of their internal affairs, all which continued in the same grand confusion." ALS. DNA, RG59, Cons. Disp., Maracaibo, vol. 1 (M–T62, R1). Received September 8, 1828.

From JOEL R. POINSETT, Mexico, no. 147, July 30, 1828. Transmits copy of a peace treaty between Guatemala and San Salvador which will deprive "their ambitious neighbors of all pretext to interfere in their affairs." Also encloses copy of a new Mexican law permitting the export of bullion which is "likely to have an important bearing upon our commerce with this Country." LS. DNA, RG59, Dip. Disp., Mexico, vol. 4 (M97, R5). No date of receipt.

From CHARLES DOUGLAS, Tuscumbia, Ala., July 31, 1828. Points out that Rep. William Creighton of Ohio has informed him of Clay's willingness to create a U.S. consulate at Guasacualco [now Coatzacoalcos], Mexico if the commercial importance of the town justifies the act. Seeks appointment as consul there, assuring Clay that it is indeed becoming a place of commercial importance and that the Mexican government has recently declared it a port of entry and has established a "custom House, and other government offices" there. Notes that the Guasacualco River offers "wonderful advantages" to the "Commerce of the United States, Europe and Asia" in the area since it winds through the Isthmus of Tehuantepec and provides "many facilities" to the "contemplated canal for connecting the two oceans." ALS. DNA, RG59, A. and R. (MR2). Letter endorsed by Clay: "Mr. [Daniel] Brent will, with the Presidents assent, make out a Commission for Consul as requested."

From JAMES BROWN, Paris, August, N.D., 1828. Reports at length on the Russo–Turkish war, explaining that the Turks have shown no disposition to capitulate and have inflicted considerable losses on the Russians. Mentions that the first contingent of French troops has left for the Morea where it is believed they "will take position ... with the determination to compel the Turks to evacuate Greece." Notes that the French have taken two American vessels as transports on this expedition and expresses the fear "that furnishing transports for French troops and landing them in Greece ... may put in jeopardy the persons and property of American citizens."

States that heavy rains during harvest have damaged crops in France but not to the extent that France will import grain from the United States. LS. DNA, RG59, Dip. Disp., France, vol. 23 (M34, R26). Letter marked "Private." Received October 8, 1828.

To TRUSTEES OF TRANSYLVANIA UNIVERSITY, August 1, 1828. In a Mortgage Deed to Transylvania University, Clay conveys to the

Trustees certain pieces of property as security for a loan of $20,000 [the sum of the Morrison legacy to Transylvania] borrowed from the estate of James Morrison, "of whose Will the said Clay is the only acting Executor." Chief among these properties is his residence, "Ashland," which contains "by estimation Four hundred acres." Other properties are: 271 acres in Fayette County and "all those lots in the Town of Lexington at the corner of Market and Short Streets extending back to Church Alley." Interest on the loan is set at "6 per cent per annum, payable April 1 and October 1." Debt to be paid off in full within 12 months of demand by Trustees, or upon notice to the Trustees by Clay. DS. Fayette County Deed Book 4, pp. 140-2.

On or about October 1, 1828, Clay paid half [$600] of the first year's interest to the Trustees of Transylvania. KyLxT. Memorandum of Trustees' Minutes, October 7, 1828.

From PABLO OBREGON, Washington, August 2, 1828. Informs Clay that he has received the Treaty of Limits [Poinsett to Clay, January 8, 1828] as ratified by Mexico. Is ready "to exchange the ratifications when convenient to the Secretary of State." LS, in Spanish, with trans. in State Dept. file. DNA, RG59, Notes from Mexican Legation, vol. 1 (M54, R1). The terms of the treaty are found in Parry, *Treaty Series,* 78:33–42.

From RICHARD RUSH   Washington, August 3, 1828
Although I have had little or nothing to say, I should at least have dropped you a line since you went away, if only to tell you that we are all alive here; but you have been whirled about so from post to pillar that I have not known where to aim a letter at you. You have been *bargaining* all over the land, no doubt. No sooner have I heard of your being at one place, but the next mail has fixed you at another, and the third some where else again, but now that you are in Lexington I may hope that you will remain at moorings a while.

First and foremost, I am glad to learn that your health is better. Next, I congratulate you in the issue of the Louisiana election,[1] hoping that you will follow suit in old Kentuck.

My primary object in writing at this late day to you, is to send you the enclosed article signed Julius.[2] One of my objections to publishing it in the winter was, that, in the state in which it then was, it neither satisfied, nor pleased me, and I could not, at that season, find the time to write it over again. But, during the summer, I have; and, for myself, like it better. But it has been out more than a week without republication in the [Washington *Daily National*] Intelligencer, or without that paper or the [Washington *Daily National*] Journal having given it a word of comment or notice in any way, from which I half infer that it has proved a failure, here in Washington at least. Be it so. I must submit. Nobody—all the world over—[is] more apt to deceive himself, than an author about his own piece, and that which he may have supposed something choice, often turns out to be the reverse with his readers, and falls still-born from the press. Mine, thus far, has done so.

The President sets out for the north tomorrow. He expects to be gone a couple of months. I am highly pleased with our new colleague,

General [Peter B.] Porter. If I do not mistake, there is a fine mixture of suavity and energy in him. The former is very apparent and attractive. You would come at the latter, I suspect, as soon as you get below the surface.

Adieu—be sure you bring good tidings from Kentucky, or we will give you no welcome on your return. P.S. August 4 Hearing today that you are expected to leave Lexington on the 10th, and not being sure that this will reach you there, I will just fold it up to wait your arrival

ALS. DLC-HC (DNA, M212, R3).   1. Plumer, Jr. to Clay, July 26, 1828.   2. Enclosure not found; but published in Washington *Daily National Journal*, July 26, 1828. The "Julius" article answered "drunken speeches" by John Randolph in the Senate in 1826, which had included attacks on the character of Secretary of the Treasury Richard Rush and his deceased father, attacks that had resumed in the House in February, 1828. Randolph then published his several remarks in pamphlet form. See, John Randolph, *Speech of the Hon. John Randolph, of Virginia, on the Retrenchment Resolutions. Delivered in the House of Representatives of the United States, February 1, 1828*. Boston, 1828. The "Julius" rebuttal was also published in pamphlet form. See, "Julius," *John Randolph, Abroad and at Home, Being the Only Accurate Delineation Ever Published of That Distinguished Orator*. Philadelphia, 1828. See, also, John H. Powell, *Richard Rush, Republican Diplomat* (Philadelphia, 1942), 216–9; and Allen Nevins, ed., *The Diary of John Quincy Adams* (New York, 1928), 383.

From ROBERT R. HUNTER, Cowes, August 4, 1828. Reports that Joseph C. Delano, master of the American vessel *Columbia*, has arrived at Spithead, bound from London to New York, but has refused to present his ship's papers at the Consulate. Calls this a "defiance" of the "uniform and established surveillance of the Consulate" and requests that measures be taken to "preserve the rights and respect due" his office. ALS. DNA, RG59, Cons. Disp., Southampton, vol. 1 (M-T239, R1). Received September 21, 1828.

On July 30, and again on August 6, 1828, Thomas Aspinwall, U.S. Consul in London, complained to Clay that Capt. Delano had refused to "receive on board his vessel two destitute American seamen" while the *Columbia* was at Portsmouth, and that the behavior of captains like Delano "is placing the exercise of the Consular functions under the control of Ship Masters." Asks if Delano's refusal is "an infringement of the law." LS. DNA, RG59, Cons. Disp., London, vol. 12 (M-T168, R12). Received September 12 and 20, 1828.

Aspinwall wrote again on August 22, explaining to Clay that he was too hasty in his judgment of Delano, that his refusal "was not intentional," and that he possessed an "excellent character" and "a large family to support." *Ibid.* Received September 25, 1828.

Delano informed Clay on September 26 that New York authorities had served him with a writ for allegedly violating U.S. law pertaining to destitute seamen. Encloses a letter from Aspinwall to Clay on August 18 explaining that the error was that of the mate, not Capt. Delano; asks that legal action against him be stopped, since the financial burden on him would be great were he required to postpone a planned sailing to London on October 1. ALS. DNA, RG59, Misc. Letters (M179, R66).

From CHARLES SAVAGE, Guatemala City, August 5, 1828. Sends a copy of his letter of June 20. Reports that San Salvador refused to ratify the treaty of peace with the Federation government, that fighting has resumed, and that the Federation "now appear[s] on the decline" in its "ability to sustain the war," while San Salvador seems to grow militarily stronger. Notes that the "Genl. Government" is still attempting to negotiate a peace with San Salvador. Remarks also that the Governor, Mariano Aycinena, of the State of Guatemala is becoming "extreme[ly] unpopular," and that "the public appear[s] to expect a revolution." Calls attention to a recent proclamation of the "Federal Executive," Manuel Jose Arce, designed to exclude Spaniards and Spanish merchandise from the Federation of the Centre of America, and to end all commercial intercourse with Spain. ALS. DNA, RG59, Cons. Disp., Guatemala, vol. 1 (M–T337, R1). Received October 31, 1828.

Joel R. Poinsett had also reported from Mexico, on August 1, the break down of the Guatemala [Federation]–San Salvador treaty agreement and the renewal of fighting. LS. DNA, RG59, Dip. Disp., Mexico, vol. 4 (M97, R5). Received September 27, 1828. The treaty was never ratified. For Aycinena, see Bancroft, *History of Central America*, 8:150.

From WILLIAM TUDOR, Rio de Janeiro, no. 98, August 5, 1828. Has received this afternoon Clay's despatches numbers 6 and 7 "inclosing me a commission with full powers, to form a treaty [Clay to Tudor, March 29, 31, 1828] of friendship, commerce & navigation with the Empire of Brazil." Discusses in general terms his earnest desire to arrange this treaty to please the President of the United States. Hopes "to remove the disadvantages [Brazil–Buenos Aires war] that our commerce now labours under . . . with this growing country." Although mentioning the "circumstances" surrounding this "arduous enterprise," he is optimistic about entering "at once into the negotiation." LS. DNA, RG59, Dip. Disp., Brazil, vol. 6 (M121, R8). Received September 20, 1828.

From WILLIAM TUDOR, Rio de Janeiro, no. 99, August 5, 1828. Transmits copies of documents and correspondence relating to his negotiation of U.S. claims against Brazil. Comments: "It will no doubt excite your surprise to hear that I have not yet effected the settlement of a single point of the claims." Notes particularly that he has not been able "to procure payment for the Spark & the surrender of the bonds of the Spermo" which "is really a point of honor" for the U.S. Explains that "the two chief obstacles to the settlement of our claims, are the embarrassed state of the finances [of Brazil], & the simultaneous presence of the English & French Ministers, whose claims are so much heavier than ours; & as we watch each other's progress, the moment either gains a point, the others press with increased zeal." Reports that Sir Robert Gordon, British Minister to Brazil, has sailed for England, apparently without accomplishing anything on claims. Adds that a French squadron appeared the day he opened negotiations on U.S. claims, and that it had a "considerable effect" because "these people are very apt to feel a sudden panic." Continues: "The French immediately began to push their negotiations with their usual impetuosity, and expected to carry everything by storm, and it was for a time supposed . . . that they had succeeded." States he has since discovered that Brazil has not settled with the French, and he now believes the French squadron has orders not to use force. Complains: "I never yet met with people so difficult to settle with as these: they have a union of weakness & vanity, that alternately prevent them from persisting or yielding." Hopes that he can use the prospect of a commercial treaty "to urge them into an arrangement of the claims." Believes that U.S. commerce with Brazil would be "greatly increased" by such a treaty, because "the difference of duty is sufficient at present to exclude our cotton goods." ALS. DNA, RG59, Dip. Disp., Brazil, vol. 6 (M121, R8). Letter marked "Confidential." Received September 20, 1828.

From CHRISTOPHER HUGHES

Brussels, August 6, 1828

I have passed several hours this morning reading from news papers. I will not say, how I have been affected by the tenor and spirit of the Election question; nor with what bitterness, and mortification, I have followed of the venemous assaults upon *your* fame, character and happiness. Your letter, giving a view of your private money concerns,[1] and of your substitution of mortgage, for endorsement, almost made me weep, not for you, but for my country. Public life must have charms, when those who are fitted to honour private life, and to enjoy every comfort, happiness and domestic delight, of which their at best, passing existence is capable, sacrifice them *all,* for unprofitable labour & corroding strife. But, I am nor high, nor wise enough to write to you, on this theme!

I have not words, to express to you, my admiration of your Letter of 20th. June [*sic,* January] 1827, to Mr. Condy Raguet [6:97–100]; it is a model of wisdom, gentleness, discretion, peace, and decency, in the course of a public agent; whose transactions, and whose conduct, turn upon, and should be guided by the same principles of moderation & decorum that govern private Individuals; excepting the load of responsibility that rest on the former which should make him, a thousand times, more circumspect, and cautious, *not* to deviate from the road, marked out by those principles of conduct, which, you lay down with such clearness and such good-humour, in your letter of graceful castigation, to that [illeg. word] diplomat; Condy l'enragé If he have any feeling, how severely must he have suffered, under the chastened, things keen rebuke, is conveyed by every line of your (Capital) Letter! I have had, on more than one occasion, conversations with the Superior of Brazil's Representative here; a native of Brazil; but he is a highly educated gentleman & an honourable man; the Chevalier de Sanza Dias! I shall make a point, of showing him your letter of the 20th. January 1827. No doubt, Mr. Raguet was moved by honest & well meant zeal. But his Letter to you [5:709–10, 747, 848], to which, yours is an answer, proves him to be little better than an incurable madman, & his indication, (which I have also seen) where he complains, of not having been employed, *elsewhere,* (on the *British* Principle of promoting insolent and outrageous agents;) developes, what *were* the secret calculations, of the aforesaid *Condy.* Enough of him! [illeg. word] How did he ever happen to be employed?

You will have received various letters and communications from me both from the Hague, & Brussels, written between 4th. July & this date. Some of them, for reasons therein mentioned, were addressed, through

New Yorks Post Office directly, to Mr. Adams! I learned fromMr. [James] Maury at Liverpool, that my memoir of 4th. July & despatch of 8th. did not arrive, but in time for Packet of 25 so that my Letter of "Errata," concerning General [Jan] Verveer's scientific Expedition to the Isthmus of Darrin [*sic*, Darien], may arrive, before the material which it is meant to correct!—²

Mr. [William B.] Rochester's news, as to the state of things in Central America, may cause obstacles to Genl. Verveer; and perhaps, new instructions, from the King [William I] of the Netherlands. I am in hourly expectation of a summons to the Hague; I may go tomorrow, or in two or three days; and if I learn any thing, on the subject, I shall certainly communicate it to you. The British Expeditions to the Pacific,³ and our own⁴ (of which I hope, Mr. Schoolcraft⁵ may have accepted the guidance) offer a striking coincidence, as to *time*, though not as to objects.— with that of General Verveer. I do not remember, if I mentioned to you, that it was known at the Hague about the 6th. or 8th. July, that *two agents*, had been sent by the British Government, to Guatemala, or to *Omoa*, so soon as Genl. Verveer's Expedition was known, in London; & it was surmised, at the *Hague*, that *their* objects, were to throw difficulties in the way, and progress, of the General's Reconnaissance, At all events; this *notion existed* at [the] Hague.

There is no late important intelligence of the movements of the Russian army. But you may *rely* on it, they will conquer, they will advance; and they will conquer. Nothing will stop them, but a Reis Effendi on his knees between the Balkan Mountains & the Emperor Nicholas [I] and the Reis Effendi [Esseid Mehemmed Perter] be sent on this mission of deprecation—

The only important feature, in the King [George IV] of Englands theory of prorogative, is that, where he said that Nicholas hastened round his separate orders from his admiral [Count Lodewijk Heyden] in the Mediterranean; & instructed him to cooperate with the English & French Fleets. Take [the] efficacy to the Triple treaty of 6th. July [6:780-2]. Nicholas in doing this knows what he is doing! England will do *all* she may, to avoid, hot war, but *expenses;* but they main the *same.* Austria is uneasy about Italy; & well may she be! Don Miguel will be left to Himself which is all, that he wants. as to Don Pedro [I, of Brazil; IV, of Portugal], he will soon be forgotten in *Europe.*—and it is believed by *many* driven from America.

I had a letter of *16* pages & a pamphlet from Lord Strangford,⁶ yesterday. Mr. [George] Canning put him on Shelf, after his Petersburg Embassy. Lord Wellington has taken him down, from his niche & offered him to be Governor General of Jamaica & its dependencies, which Strangford refused. He wants new diplomatic employment & will get the Austrian [?] Embassy. He is now a B[ritish]. Peir. He is a dead man; but not *sound.*—I had a letter from Mr. [James] Brown the other day He left Mrs. B. at Dieppe It may be cruel in me but I tell *you* in *candour*, that as to Mrs. Brown prepare Mrs. Clay for the worst. When I return from Hague *I think* I shall go to Paris for a few days, I go incog.

ALS. DLC–HC (DNA, M212, R3).   Letter marked "Private."   1. Clay to Wickliffe, May 24, 1828.   2. Jan Verveer, Netherlands Minister to the Federation of the Centre of

America, was ordered to discuss with that government the prospects of a possible inter-oceanic ship canal via the Lake of Nicaragua as well as the purchase of necessary territory for the project. Webster, *Britain and the Independence of Latin America, 1812-1830*, 344. When Clay learned on October 21 that General Verveer was embarked on his diplomatic and exploring expedition to Central America, he wrote Bangeman Huygens, the Dutch Minister to the U.S., offering passage to Verveer from New York to Curacao in the U.S.S. *Erie*. The sloop was soon to sail to Colombia to deliver William Henry Harrison to his post as U.S. Minister there. Copy. DNA, RG59, Notes to Foreign Ministers and Consuls, vol. 4, p. 80 (M38, R4). On October 29, Bangeman Huygens accepted the offer "with gratitude." ALS, in French. DNA, RG59, Notes from Netherlands Legation, vol. 1 (M56, R1).
3. There were several of these scientific surveys then underway. See Herman R. Friis, ed., *The Pacific Basin: A History of Its Geographical Exploration* (New York, 1967), 249-54.   4. A proposed U.S. Navy exploring expedition to the Pacific and South Seas, under the command of Thomas Ap Catesby Jones, failed to secure the necessary funding from Congress. *ASPFR*, 3:196, 211-2, 308-17, 336-43, 546-56, 684.   5. For Henry Rowe Schoolcraft, see *DAB*.   6. For Percy Clinton Sydney Smythe Strangford, see *DNB*. He received no further appointments after his mission to Brazil in August, 1828 to help mediate the end of the Buenos Aires-Brazil war.

From WILLIAM B. LAWRENCE, London, no. 52, August 6, 1828. Sends copies of Britain's new Corn Law and the new act relating to customs, both of which will affect the United States. States that "it is generally supposed that in ordinary cases, the duties will be prohibitory" but crop damage due to rainy weather may "render this year the provisions of the Corn law of more consequence to foreigners than usual." Notes that in order to prevent grain from the United States being imported to Britain via Canada, a declaration and certificate of origin must accompany any importations from British possessions. Adds that under the general provisions of the Customs Law, goods imported from any British possession in America to any other British colony or to the United Kingdom must be accompanied by a statement as to whether the goods were produced in a British possession or in a foreign country; discovery of a false declaration will result in forfeiture of the goods. Explains that corn and other articles formerly supplied to the British West Indies by the United States will be allowed into the colonies "duty free, if imported direct from a warehouse in the United Kingdom." Discusses at length the new Customs Law, comparing the duties levied on goods from British colonies to the higher duties levied on foreign goods, and concludes that "the new regulations have been made to bear on the consumption of American productions."

States that the papers concerning the United States Tariff of 1828 which William Huskisson requested have not yet been printed, "but the newspapers continue to express themselves on the recent enactments with a good deal of violence and erroneous impressions of the motives of the American legislature seem to be very generally entertained." Comments: "The public are . . . given to understand that our late Tariff was passed in retaliation of the British West Indies restrictions and it may be as well for our future interests that this impression should prevail." LS. DNA, RG59, Dip. Disp., Great Britain, vol. 35 (M30, R31). Received September 20, 1828.

From WILLIAM TUDOR, Rio de Janeiro, no. 100, August 6, 1828. Reports that Juan Ramon Gonzalez Balcarce and Tomas Guido have arrived from Buenos Aires for peace talks and that the news "is rather favorable to their mission." States that Brazil is having a problem with desertions by its German mercenary troops and that the Irish and Germans have played an equal part in recent riots and other disturbances. Adds that the Irish have all been shipped home and seventeen Germans sentenced to be shot. Notes that "the general opinion seems to be that peace will be made." ALS. DNA, RG59, Dip. Disp., Brazil, vol. 6 (M121, R8). Received September 26, 1828.

To JOHN QUINCY ADAMS   Lexington, August 7, 1828
Our Election terminated yesterday, In this, my old Congressional District, composed of three Counties,[1] the majority for [Thomas] Metcalfe is above a thousand. It is greater, by several hundred, than it was last year. In this County [Fayette] it is, this year, upwards of 350, exhibiting a gain of about two hundred. We have heard from several of the adjacent Counties which lead us to believe that Metcalfe is elected, but we cannot, for some time yet, receive returns enough to decide positively. Mr. [John] Chambers,[2] the Admon Candidate, is Certainly elected as Metcalfes Successor. I will write you again before I take my departure next week.

Mr Isham Talbot[3] would accept the place to Peru, declined by Mr. [George] Robertson.[4] If you have thought of no better arrangement, I think it would be advisable to appoint him. He reads with great facility and would soon speak the French Language. Although he does not combine all the qualifications desirable, his standing in society and the important places he has held, would make his appointment acceptable. His hopes about it will be confined to himself.

My health has improved, but not I think in such degree as to justify the resumption of the labors of my office for several weeks.

ALS. MHi–Adams Papers, Letters Received (MR487).   1. Fayette, Jessamine, and Woodford. Metcalfe defeated William T. Barry in Fayette 1422–1069, in Jessamine 614–543, and in Woodford 660–437. See Clay to Whittlesey, August 15, 1828.   2. For John Chambers, see *BDAC*. He defeated Nicholas D. Coleman [see *BDAC*] by 337 votes. Lexington *Kentucky Reporter*, August 13, 1828; *Niles' Register* (August 23, 1828), 34:411. 3. If offered the post, Talbot did not accept it. He continued his law practice in Frankfort. *BDAC*.   4. At this time Secretary of State in Kentucky. *Ibid.*

From WILLIAM TUDOR, Rio de Janeiro, no. 101, August 7, 1828. Reports that "the case of the *Spark* was finally settled today," and hopes that this will lead to the settlement of all U.S. maritime claims against Brazil. Mentions a report of a pirate vessel operating out of the Cape Verde Islands and expresses fear that if this vessel is not stopped, it will encourage other pirate ships to "follow in the same track." ALS. DNA, RG59, Dip. Disp., Brazil, vol. 6 (M121, R8). Received September 26, 1828.

From ROBERT MONROE HARRISON, St. Bartholomew, August 8, 1828. Sends Clay "some mineral specimens from the Mines of Cornwall in England," presented to him "by a *Virtuoso*" in Mineralogy. Asserts that "some of the finest Mineral Specimens in the world" are at the Island of Antigua "consisting principally of *Petrified woods Shells Insects* and *even Vegetables*" which take a fine polish for ornaments. Notes that collections of these specimens would make a great addition to a museum. Suggests: "Should [the] Govt ever make an appropriation for the collection of such things ... much money may be spent at Antigua to useful purposes." ALS. DNA, RG59, Cons. Disp., St. Bartholomew, vol. 1 (M72, R1). Received August 28, 1828.

ACCOUNT WITH MORRISON ESTATE, Lexington, August 8, 1828. Clay's accounting of his stewardship (at 5% commission) of the estate from July 6, 1827 through August 8, 1828. Fayette County Will Book, 1:15-23. On August 16, 1828, he paid Transylvania the sum of $600, the semi-annual interest (at 6%) due on his loan of $20,000 (the entire Morrison legacy) from the Board of the institution. Clay to John Bradford, August 16, 1828. KyLxT.

From JOHN M. MACPHERSON, Cartagena, August 11, 1828. Reports two recent decrees by Simon Bolivar. The first reorganized the nation into five military and civil divisions and seems to be related to military defense in the event of invasion by Spain. The second reestablished the suppressed convents, which was a wise attempt to conciliate the clergy.

Reviews an "unpleasant situation" with local customs officials in which they have demanded payment of $1400 duties on his personal mercantile transactions in 1824-1825. Has unsuccessfully appealed this demand to General Mariano Montilla, Supreme Military and Civil Chief of the Province. Reminds Clay that there is no U.S. minister "near this Republic, whose protection I might claim," and notes that "it is obvious, that I could not extend to others [Americans] that protection denied my own person." LS. DNA, RG59, Cons. Disp., Cartagena, vol. 1 (M-T192, R1).

Adds, on August 12, that he was arrested while "writing my Despatch of yesterday" and was "hurried ... to the common gaol." Reports that he was released after several hours detention upon the intervention of the British Vice Consul, but remains confined to his residence under bail bond. *Ibid.* Both letters received September 6, 1828. Details of MacPherson's altercation with Cartagena customs officials are in his letter to Montilla, August 8, 1828, enclosed.

MacPherson wrote again on September 15, saying that after 30 days imprisonment in his own house, he had "no alternative but to submit and pay the money" which was "unjustly claimed by the Custom house." Adds that if he had not paid, he would have been transferred to the common jail, but "In the absence of a Representative of the United States near this government, to whom I might look to for redress," he wrote to Simon Bolivar "complaining of the treatment I have received."

Encloses a Proclamation and a Decree of Bolivar "pointing out the way the affairs of the Republic are to be conducted until a Congress meets ... January 1830." *Ibid.* Received October 16, 1828.

On December 16 Clay wrote MacPherson's friend, Tench Ringgold, explaining MacPherson's problem with the customs house and the response of the State Department to the matter. Copy. DNA, RG59, Dom. Letters, vol. 22, pp. 347-8 (M40, R20). See also, Clay to MacPherson, November 13, 1828.

From JAMES BROWN   Paris, August 12, 1828

Since the date [July 28] of my last letter I have passed some days with
Mrs Brown at Dieppe where she yet remains with my brother [Samuel]
and Niece [Susan], in the hope that repose, and the sea air, will re
establish her health. Although there is nothing of an immediately
dangerous disaster in her indisposition yet she suffers from so many
causes, that her situation is a source of constant anxiety to me. She has
arrived at a critical period of female life, and in addition to some fears as
to the ultimate result of the tumor [of] which I spoke in former letters,
she has been for some weeks, greatly afflicted by the recurrence of a tic
douleureux, or pain in her face, from which she suffered constantly
before she left the United States. If my correspondence has not, for
some months, been so full and satisfactory as you may have wished, you
will be so good as to impute it to the true cause, the necessity of my
devoting much of my time to one so deservedly dear to me, and whose
situation requires every soothing attention in my power to bestow.

The Russian Army has marched on with rapid strides and have not
hitherto met with any resistance which is calculated to impede its progress, or discourage its hopes. The resistance it is true at Brahilov was
obstinate, but the force was very inadequate to the defence of the place.
The plague is said by the Austrian papers, to rage at Bucharest and in
other places, but these accounts are believed to be greatly exaggerated.
Varna is the next fortress which will be assailed, and although reinforced
will fall before the immense force by which it is invested. The French
army is already embarking at Toulon and will, on board of English and
French transports, shortly be in possession of the Morea. At the latest accounts the army of Ibrahim Pasha much diminished in numbers, was in
want of supplies of every Kind, and as it is believed was proposed to
evacuate Greece—It is said that this fact was urged with this Government
as a motive for suspending the embarkation of the Troops, but was
considered as insufficient to induce France to desist. It is not improbable
that she wishes to place herself in a situation to watch the course of
events, and either dispose Russia to be moderate in her demands by
means of uniting in remonstrances to that effect, with Austria and England, or in the failure of that attempt, to seize upon a portion of the
spoils of the Ottoman Empire. England continues inactive under all this,
and what is yet more provoking, the outrageous conduct of Don Miguel,
who imprisons her subjects, insults her diplomacy, and confiscates the
Estates of her friends. The French papers which attribute this inactivity
and patience to the public debt, the state of Ireland, and a consequent
inability to support a war have been afilled with sarcastic and provoking
articles, which are answered on the other side of the Channel, by attacks
on the Editors, and compliments to the moderate, friendly, and pacific
dispositions, of the French Government, which they represent as acting
in perfect accord with that of Great Britain. *I* rather think that the
influence of the British Government has sunk under the present Military
Premier [Wellington] who derived much of the publick Confidence from
the persuasion, generally entertained, that he would raise the national
character of England on this Continent. It is possible that presuming on
the weakness of Great Britain, she may receive such provocation as may

force her to make war, and with all her embarrassments she is yet capable of making mighty efforts by sea if not by land. The French Marine, although greatly increased in force and discipline, could not yet resist that of Great Britain. Austria finds her situation exceedingly unpleasant situated as she is near the seat of War, anxious for the success of the Turks, and yet afraid to give any direct assistance. Prussia ia believed to be friendly to Russia, and many think that France, by receiving equivalents, might not be disatisfied with the dismemberment of the Ottoman Empire.

The Chamber of Deputies having finished the budget and sent it to the Peers, has left Paris, with the exception of a small portion of it, which still remains. The Peers are engaged in discussing the budget, but are compelled by the absence of the other Chamber to receive it as they find it, and pass it without amendments. The [Martignac] Ministry has done well this Session, and secured the support of a Majority of the nation. The Clergy, that is to say the Jesuits and the Congregation [Knights of the Faith], are organizing themselves, and have lately prescribed as the papers state, a Memorial to the King [Charles X], in which they inveigh in no very measured language, against the ordinance which takes the publick instruction out of the hands of the Jesuits.[1] The Bishops, who belong to those two parties, it is said, refuse to assist in the Execution of the Ordinance, declaring that the publick instruction, and the choice of the instructors, has always appertained to the Church, and that, although they know how to give unto Ceasar [sic] what belongs to Ceasar, they will obey God rather than man. Considering the mild manner in which the Ordinance has been executed, and the large sums devoted to Ecclesiastical instruction (12,000,000 of francs whilst only 50,000 are devoted to primary instruction for all the laity) this discontent on the part of the Clergy would seem to be rather unreasonable. This Ordinance has been represented as an Act of persecution; and threats were uttered that the liberal and liberty loving Jesuits would remove to our Country, where the free exercise of their religion would be tolerated. It would seem as if France was destined to exhibit to the world contrasts the most striking and extraordinary that have ever been witnessed—The transition from a state of incredulity, bordering on Atheism, to religious disputes and wars, in the short space of thirty five years, would be one of the most extraordinary which has been recorded in history—

Whilst touching on this state of things here, permit to mention the receipt of a letter from Mr [Daniel] Brent on the subject of the Complaints of the two Priests in Philadelphia,[2] on account of the papal order, assigning them Cincinnati as their place of residence and menacing them with the consequences of disobedience. On reading the letter of Mr [William V.] Harold, I rather doubt whether his statement of the case is not such, that his admission of the right of submitting to restraints on our liberty voluntarily is not gotten over by the argument to which he has resorted. I am not sure that we, who as a Government take no part in the discipline of any church, can interfere to persecute a Priest from subjecting himself to ecclesiastical censures and ecclesiastical punishment, such as interdiction as a priest, for disobeying the order of his Superior. If the order is contrary to the Canons of the Church, he must resort to authorities purely ecclesiastical to obtain their revocation—If the Pope [Leo XII] attempts to enforce his order by any sanctions not merely spiritual, or if he employs force to remove a citizen from one place to another, then the question would admit of influence on the part of the Civil authority, but if he merely menaces the party with interdiction or excommunication in the event of disobedience, I do not clearly perceive how the laws can be involved to protect him from them. In most European Countries the struggle between the Ecclesiastical and civil Jurisdiction has been long and violent, and has ended pretty generally in concordats assigning to the Pope and Bishops the degree of Jurisdiction, they shall exercise. We engage to protect the liberties persons and principles of all our citizens, whatever religion they may possess. The orders of His Holiness are certainly arbitary and despotic, and are calculated to revolt our republican feelings, but such is the structure of their Hierarchy and so long as by entering on the Priesthood they surrender their reasoning powers and subject their spiritual actions to the Will of a foreign Head they must either abandon their profession or obey the Mandates of their superiors. Such is the first impression which this affair has made in my mind for I have but this day received Mr Brents letter. As I never act of first impressions in delicate matters, I shall acquire all the information I can before I proceed farther and the President may rest assured that I shall carefully abstain from saying or doing any thing which could subject the Government to the imputation of interfering in matters purely spiritual. As a general principal it may be assumed that the best way to neutralize the effects of religious intolleration [in] their principles, is to let them alone as long as they abstain from a violation of the laws. Thanks to what is in often deplored, *divisions in the Church,* we find the number of sects, the best safeguard against Persecution and intollerances.

I hope by the time this letter reaches Washington, you will have returned, and will have the satisfaction of having added to Mr. Adams prospects in the East, the vote of Kentucky. If that State is gone the election is over. If you save it I think Mr Adams has considerable prospects of success. It is unfortunate that the struggle had not commenced at an earlier day in Virginia and Pennsylvania particularly in the last. The tariff will I apprehend destroy all hope of enlisting Virginia under the Administration banners. The result must now soon be known and would to heaven that it would bring with it tranquillity and union. The advantage which the world would derive from the example of our free Republicks is greatly impaired by these dissentions and the menaces of disunion with which they are sometimes accompanied. The prediction so often falsified but so often repeated that our Union was to be short lived, is lately relied on as promising its speedy accomplishment. The tariff made on concessions made to all, if I may judge from what I hear, displeases a majority of the people of the Union. My information however may be incorrect in consequence of the channel through [which] it is derived. Pennsylvania will derive the greatest advantage from it and yet she is apparently opposed to the administration.

The Minister of foreign affairs [Ferronnays] has gone for a few weeks to a watering place in Germany for the purpose of improving his health. He will return about the middle of Septr and I shall again renew my negociations on the subject of the claims. The allegation that they are stale is so void of foundation that I think they must be ashamed again to allude to it. Considering the manner in which France has behaved under the Convention of 1822 [3:53] in relation to the discriminating duty I think General [Samuel] Smith and his friends in Congress have been very generous to her.[3] I have been laboring for two years to have those duties repaid, and have hitherto been baffled under various frivolous pretexts. I hope to have it decided soon and then you will see whether they deserve the treatment they have received in permitting them to land a part of their cargoes in their Islands and be received afterwards in our ports on the footing of equality—Mr St Cricq has engaged to reconsider the decision of Mr [Jean] de Villele and I am in daily expectation of his answer.

I have written to Mr [John Adams] Smith informing him of his translation to Paris and expect soon to hear from him. My occasional short visits to Dieppe rendered indispensable by the State of Mrs. Brown's health make me very anxious that he should arrive.

ALS. DLC-HC (DNA, M212, R3).   Printed in *LHQ*, 24:1120–4.   1. See Beach, *Charles X of France*, 259.   2. Harold to Clay, July 2, 1828.   3. Brown to Clay, July 28, 1828.

From ALBERT GALLATIN, New York, August 12, 1828. States that he can procure the boundary acts of New York "relative to Vermont," but wants to obtain "copies of the Acts of New Hampshire granting land to Dartmouth College." Does not know, however, how these may apply to the Northeastern boundary dispute. Also asks that the U.S. Minister to Britain, James Barbour, request additional documents from the British government. Endorses William Preble's offer to go again to New Brunswick to obtain additional information. ALS. DNA, RG76, Northeast Boundary (KyU., Special Roll, frame 77).

Writing to Clay on August 21, 1828, Gallatin summarizes the history of the boundaries of New Hampshire, Vermont, Massachusetts, and New York. *Ibid.* (frames 79–80). On this same point, William P. Preble believes that it will not be necessary to transcribe the boundary documents he obtained from Maine's archives. Preble to Clay, August 13, 1828. *Ibid.* (frame 78). Additionally, John G. Deane believes that the results of his research in the land office of Massachusetts may help in the John Baker case [6:1272–3]. Deane to Clay, August 25, 1828. *Ibid.* (frames 81–2).

From WILLIAM KILLEY   Cartagena, August 12, 1828
i am Compeled By the felings Witch flows in My Brest To acquaint you With a Carsistance Witch Took place here yeasterday With our Council [John M. MacPherson] he is Now a prisner and the Columbian Government has Taken his Sword from his Hands and if this is alowed To our Council What is a american Subject to Doe   i have property in Columbia

and Who Shell i Call To pretect But My one [*sic,* own] Government i certnly feel that We had ought To have a Minister To pretect us and our propterty[1]

ALS. DNA, RG59, Misc. Letters (M179, R66).   1. William Henry Harrison was appointed U.S. Minister to Colombia in May, 1828, but had not yet arrived there to take up his duties.

From JAMES DAVIDSON, Frankfort, August 13, 1828. Introduces Daniel Mayes of Frankfort, who is seeking appointment to a judgeship in Florida Territory, noting that his appointment "would be gratifying to the friends of good order and correct princip[les] at least in Ky." Congratulates Clay, and the "good people" of Kentucky and the United States on the outcome of the state election on August 6. Thinks that the results in Kentucky and Louisiana bode well for the coming presidential contest. ALS. DNA, RG59, A. and R. (MR5).

Additional letters to Clay in behalf of Mayes stress his legal qualifications and membership on the "Administration Central Committee" in Frankfort, and note that his appointment would help the Adams cause in "this quarter." The recommendation of Mayes by James W. Denny on August 12 added: "The information which we have received in this place [Frankfort] leaves no room to doubt the Election of General [Thomas] Metcalfe as Governor. I most heartily congratulate you upon this event," because it demonstrates "to the world an honorable testimony of the estimation in which you [Clay] are held by the inteligent & patriotic of the State." It also counters "the foul charges which have been propigated in reference to the late Presidential election." *Ibid.* See John Harvie to Clay, August 11; James W. Denny to Clay, August 12; John J. Crittenden to Clay, August 13; John J. Marshall to Clay, August 13; Jacob Swigert to Clay, August 13; William Owsley to Clay, August 21; Benjamin Mills to Clay, August 23; John Boyle to Clay, August 28, 1828. *Ibid.*

From BOYD McNAIRY   Nashville, August 13, 1828
you will have seen in the [Nashville] National Banner of the 12th instant, that I have come out upon [Andrew] Jackson in relation to [Aaron] Burrs conspiracy.

I shall probably pursue the subject still further if the minions of the General reply in the way I anticipate, and I think I shall be able to fasten the charge upon him. My principle object in addressing you at this time is to inform you, that I have learnt that certain letters of Jackson on this subject are in the hands of the executor of one Comfort Tyler,[1] late of the City of New York or of the Town of Geneva. Three letters, if my information is correct, will establish the fact of his connection with Burr in his clandestine enterprise

I have no doubt that if there are such letters in existance, you can procure their publication through some one of your confidential friends, and then, I think, the hero will be thrown from his war horse.

ALS. DLC-HC (DNA, M212, R3).   1. See *NCAB,* 2:449.

426

From JOSE SILVESTRE REBELLO, Washington, August 13, 1828. Acknowledges the receipt of Clay's note of June 4, containing an enclosure of John Duer, Attorney of the United States at New York, which explains Duer's decision to suspend "the trial against the ship General Bolivar," because of insufficient evidence. Notes that he has read in the public newspapers that the *General Bolivar* was, on July 3, at Eustatia "in a state of war, with other vessels all bearing the Buenos Ayres flag." Notes also that Duer gave "legal clearance to the Schooner Maria ... which [carried] to sea the warlike equipments of the said Bolivar," for a renedezvous in the West Indies.

Protests, accordingly, against the "violations of the strict neutrality" the United States is supposely observing in the war between Brazil and Argentina. States that many American citizens or inhabitants are involved in these "damages" against Brazil, and remonstrates against such "seizures." LS, in Portuguese, with trans. in State Dept. file. DNA, RG59, Notes from Brazilian Legation vol. 1 (M49, R1).

To WILLIAM W. WORSLEY   Lexington, August 13, 1828
I shall leave this [place] for Louisville on Saturday. I expect to reach your City on tuesday, and to leave it for Cincinnati on thursday. Will you try and secure me a passage in a Steam boat?

I desire no public entertainment and no parade at Louisville. If I expected any I would not visit it.

ALS. Courtesy of J. Winston Coleman, Jr., Lexington, Ky.

From ALEXANDER H. EVERETT, Madrid, no. 112, August 14, 1828. Acknowledges Clay's dispatch of June 16, giving notice of John Adams Smith's appointment as Secretary of the U.S. Legation in Paris. Praises Smith's work in Madrid and says that he will depart for Paris "tomorrow night." Discusses the status of certain Colombian war prisoners being held in Spain, and recalls that he had earlier represented the Colombian government in their behalf. Notes that an order has been issued to transport them to Havana where, it seems likely, they will be exchanged. Reports the return of King Ferdinand VII to Madrid on July 11 from his tour of Catalonia and the northern provinces. Repeats "what was well known before," that the Spanish government is "well disposed" toward the new regime of Miguel in Portugal. LS. DNA, RG59, Dip. Disp., Portugal, vol. 29 (M31, R29). Received October 8, 1828.

From WILLIAM B. LAWRENCE, London, no. 53, August 14, 1828. States that he has read in manuscript "the report of the committee appointed at the last session of Parliament to inquire into the state of the Civil Government of Canada" and reports that "the committee merely propose some internal reforms of no very great importance" rather than recommending a union of the two Canadas.

Notes Britain's recognition of the blockade of the Port of Funchal, Madeira, by the forces of Miguel. Also discusses in detail Britain's relations with Spain and the attempt of the latter to borrow money from English capitalists.

Contends that the appointment of Lord Percy Strangford as mediator between Brazil and Buenos Aires [Wright to Clay, March 4, 1828] "is regarded by my [Spanish] American colleagues as a gross indignity offered to all the new republics"; this is because in a speech during the last session of Parliament Strangford indulged "in the most violent abuse of all the new States and of the policy which had led to their recognition." LS. DNA, RG59, Dip. Disp., Great Britain, vol. 35 (M30, R31). Received September 21, 1828. Also in Manning, *Diplomatic Correspondence . . . Latin American Nations*, 3:1589–90. On August 30, Thomas L. L. Brent, writing from Lisbon, confirmed Strangford's appointment as British mediator in the dispute between Buenos Aires and Brazil. ALS. DNA, RG59, Dip. Disp., Portugal, vol. 8 (M43, R7). Received November 7, 1828.

From CHRISTOPHER HUGHES, The Hague, August 15, 1828. Discusses at length the birth of a baby to the Princess Fredericke, noting "you may tell Mrs. Clay, that the Baby is to be clad in a Court [christening] dress with a train as long as the Pen[n]sylvanian Avenue, *said* train to be borne by 4 Chamberlains!!!" Reports the steady progress of the Russian army toward Constantinople, the capture of the fortress of Kars in Armenia by General Ivan Feodorvich Paskevich, and the "hourly expectation of news of a decisive battle" that will seal the doom of the Turkish capital.

Mentions a meeting about six weeks ago in Brussels with "Your literary Friend and Protege Mr. Jared Sparks." Assisted Sparks in gaining access to "all the ancient catacombs of dusty archives & folios, within the precincts of the Hague." Reports that Sparks was especially interested in procuring the "very scarce and much sought after" volumes of the *Journal de Leide* from 1774 to 1784, but that an entire set of them, 51 volumes, which Hughes had located in the hands of Mr. Luzac of Leyden, grandson of the editor, were quoted "at an enormous price. Out of the question!" Later he met Luzac socially and "won him over" to the idea of lending Sparks the 10 volumes in which he was most interested. In return for this courtesy Luzac would be presented "with 2 copies of J. Sparks History; one for Mr. L. & one for [the] Royal Library. . . . So you see my d[ea]r. Mr. Clay, I have done every thing, but suffocate, in the service of Jared." ALS. DLC–HC (DNA, M212, R3). Letter marked "Private." For Hughes's assistance to Sparks in the Luzac matter, and Sparks's search for the source in question, see Herbert B. Adams, *The Life and Writings of Jared Sparks.* 2 vols. (Boston and New York, 1893), 2:83, 100, 104–05. Just which of Sparks's many publications is referred to here as his "History" is not clear.

To ELISHA WHITTLESEY   Lexington, August 15, 1828
I have delayed acknowledging the receipt of your favor of the 5h. Ulto. until I could convey some certain intelligence on the subject of our election, respecting which you desired information. I have now the satisfaction to inform you,

That Genl. [Thomas] Metcalfe is elected—[1]

That the Admon Candidate for Lieut. Governor [John Breathitt] is *probably* elected[2]

That the Admon Candidate [John Chambers] is elected as successor to Genl M. in the H. R.[3]

That in [Joel] Yancys and [Thomas] Chiltons districts the Admon has majorities[4]

That the Jackson Speaker [John P. Oldham] has lost his election.[5] On the other hand, we have *probably* lost the majority in the Legislature,[6] owing to the diffusion of the majorities of the Opposition, and the concentration of ours, in the various Counties. In [Richard A.] Buckner's district[7] there is a small majority against us; whilst in [Chittenden] Lyons[8] there is a *small* majority for our opponents. In my old district, our friends have done well, and have increased, by several hundred, upon former elections.[9]

Our friends are confident of success in Novr. and so am I, if the zeal now exhibited remains unabated.

I congratulate you on all the recent events. Indiana has realized our best hopes.[10]

My health is improved, and I leave here tomorrow, by a circuitous route for Washington:

ALS. OC1WHi. 1. Metcalfe defeated William T. Barry, 38,910 tò 38,231. Frankfort *Argus of Western America,* August 27, 1828. 2. Breathitt defeated Joseph R. Underwood, 37,511 to 36,454. *Ibid.* 3. See Clay to Adams, August 7, 1828. 4. In Yancy's district (Simpson and Warren Counties), Metcalfe won 1,136 to 744; in Chilton's district (Muhlenburg and Ohio) he won 793 to 552. *Ibid.* 5. Judge Oldham, of Louisville, retained his Ky. House seat; but on December 1, 1828, when the new legislature convened, he lost his post as Speaker to John Tunstall Quarles [see *BDAC*] of Pulaski County by a vote of 48 to 47. Ky. H. of Reps., *Journal . . .* 1828–1829, p. 5. 6. According to the partisan leanings of the individual winners, as these were detected by the Frankfort *Argus* of August 27, 1828, the pro-Jackson group would control the new Ky. House, 58 to 42, and the new Ky. Senate, 20 to 18. 7. In Buckner's district (Adair, Casey, and Cumberland), Metcalfe won by a 1,290 to 1,225 margin. Frankfort *Argus,* August 27, 1828. 8. Metcalfe carried Lyons's district (Todd, Trigg, and Union), 1,056 to 849. *Ibid.* 9. Metcalfe carried the Fayette–Jessamine–Woodford district, 2,696 to 2,049. *Ibid.* 10. The Indiana election was a signal triumph for the Administration party. The Adams group elected James B. Ray as Governor, Milton Stapp as Lt. Governor, and carried the state legislature. See Lexington *Kentucky Reporter,* August 20, 1828; Indianapolis *Gazette,* December 4, 1828.

From WILLIAM TUDOR, Rio de Janeiro, no. 102, N.D. [Mid–August], 1828. States he has told Brazilian officials that there are "some claims on which I had doubts . . . and that I felt confident that the government of the U.S. would never make a demand, which it would refuse to grant if made upon itself." Does not believe the French have "adhered to this rule, which seems to me to be a sound one in public as well as private transactions." Comments that the French "have insisted in a vehement manner on the payment of all their claims, on the ground that the Brazilian blockade [of Plate River ports] was not efficient." Explains at length the status of that blockade and is certain the United States is willing to acknowledge it a legal blockade. Lists claims he is not going to pursue without further instructions viz: the *Brutus* of New York, the schooner *United States* of Baltimore, and the brig *Caspian* of Boston. Will see if Brazil will pay for the brig *Matilda* of New York, but expresses doubt that it will do so. ALS. DNA, RG59, Dip. Disp., Brazil, vol. 6

(M121, R8). Letter marked "Confidential." Received December 18, 1828.

On August 25 Tudor notified Clay in dispatch no. 103 "that the questions of claims . . . are in a course of adjustment for final settlement, & I have reason to believe that all those in which the demand is just, will be soon concluded." Believes the delay in settling the claims resulted from Brazil's desire to wait until the rate of exchange became more favorable at the conclusion of the war with Buenos Aires. *Ibid.* Received December 18, 1828.

The same day, August 25, Tudor wrote dispatch no. 104, marked *"Confidential,"* enclosing copies of all his correspondence with the Brazilian government since July 21, 1828. Emphasizes again the unfavorable rate of exchange which is also delaying Brazil's settlement of French claims. Admits that the frustrations of the negotiation sometimes disposed him "to resort to . . . force," but that knowing "the magnanimous moderation which governs our policy," he "honestly strove to bring these affairs to an amicable conclusion." Speculates that the use of force would have produced a "political convulsion" that would "probably have produced a servile insurrection, the fear of which is . . . very prevalent in the northern provinces especially." Reports that he has made the overture for negotiating a commercial treaty with Brazil and that the response appears favorable. Notes his plan to ask the President's permission to resign his post after the conclusion of the treaty. *Ibid.* Received December 3, 1828.

From JOHN MULLOWNY, Tangier, no. 56, August 16, 1828. Discusses the well–established custom in Morocco of other foreign countries giving presents "to obtain favors, and thwart others in their concerns of commerce, or other national affairs." Gives assurance that "whatever leaves my hand does not carry with it, an idea of adulation or tribute, it is understood that it is [a] compliment for friendly services . . . any giving me offense, get but little & sometimes . . . nothing." Requests an allowance of $1600 to use for presents, thereby insuring good relations for the United States and protection for her commerce. Notes that Morocco wages a "war in disguise" against the U.S. Believes it is especially important to give the Emperor, Abd–er–Rahman II, a gift on his first visit to Tangier. Comments: "I regret to think I am considered prodigal at home, here I am said to be scanty handed, and marked as penurious." Warns that if the United States relies solely on its treaty rights and ignores the customs of Morocco, American citizens and commerce, as well as her Consul, will be subjected to harrassment. Lists gifts other countries have given to demonstrate that they are larger than what he is requesting. ALS. DNA, RG59, Cons. Disp., Tangier, vol. 4 (M–T61, R4). Received October 24, 1828.

To ROBERT SCOTT, Lexington, August 17, 1828. Reports two suits filed against him in Frankfort as executor of the James Morrison estate. Informs Scott that he has retained John J. Crittenden to represent him in the matter. ALS. DLC–HC (DNA, M212, R3). Written from Frankfort.

From THOMAS L. L. BRENT, Lisbon, no. 82, August 18, 1828. Reports that on August 9, 1828, a Portuguese expedition sailed against Madeira and Terceira with about two thousand troops. Lists the ships which are commanded by Vice Admiral Henry da Fonseia de Souza Prego. Comments: "The activity displayed, and so unusual here, in getting off this expedition, is due to the spirit infused into the navy department by the frequent personal attendance of Don Miguel." Notes that Spain's position with regard to Portugal has not changed.

Reports that the intimacy between Miguel and his mother, Carlota Joaquina, has diminished and speculates that Miguel "since his assumption of the royal dignity . . . may have become jealous of his authority which she has almost exclusively exercised since his arrival." Predicts that "the imperious character . . . of the Queen and her fondness of power" may lead to "a serious coolness" with Miguel.

Notes that by a decree of August 4, 1828, all those against whom "the crime of rebellion shall be proved" will lose their pensions and will have their property confiscated. Mentions that the Portuguese are anxious to see what action the Emperor of Brazil [Pedro I] "may take respecting Portugal." Concludes there is little Pedro could do without first making peace with Buenos Aires and that in any event it is unlikely that he would try to assume the throne of Portugal, as Pedro IV, because "the people of Brazil will be pleased to see an entire separation" of Portugal and Brazil "and would be very unwilling to pay taxes for the execution of . . . such measures." Also predicts it is unlikely that England will "support by force the rights of Don Pedro." LS. DNA, RG59, Dip. Disp., Portugal, vol. 8 (M43, R7). Received October 13, 1828.

From JAMES HALL, Vandalia, Ill., August 18, 1828. Discusses taxes overpaid and due on Clay's Illinois lands.

Reports that General Joseph Duncan has been reelected by over 4,000 votes, or by a margin of 2 to 1 over his opponent [George Forquer]. Warns, however, that this outcome "is not to be considered as any indication of Genl Jackson's strength in Illinois, as many of our warmest administration men support the General, and in some counties the Presidential question was not thought of. The true situation of the case is, that the friends of the Administration were satisfied that they could not elect a candidate on that question, particularly against Genl Duncan, whose course has been inoffensive, and who is personally popular. It was thought better therefore, not . . . to expose their weakness by making the attempt, but rather to aid in electing our present member [Duncan], and to husband our strength, for the ensuing contest. The course has been a concialiatory one; it is possible we may gain by it—and at all events we have lost nothing." ALS. DLC–TJC (DNA, M212, R13). Duncan defeated Forquer in the Illinois U.S. house race by 10,398 votes to 6,166. Theodore Calvin Pease, *The Centennial History of Illinois, The Frontier State* (Springfield, Ill., 1918), 2:128.

From ROBERT R. REID   Augusta, Ga., August 18, 1828
[Asks Clay to forward an enclosed letter to Bremen. Continues:]
    I am tempted by the occasion to acknowledge the reception of your pamphlet[1] sent me long since, upon the subject of the late [1824] Presidential Election, and deem it a duty to say (although the expression of the opinion of one so humble as myself can be of little worth) that I never for a moment entertained the belief that you were governed by other than the best motives in that election. although in this quarter, we are almost unanimously opposed to the reelection of Mr. Adams, yet I trust there is magnanimity and candor enough amongst us, to refuse all credence to the Stories of bargain & corruption which have been so industriously circulated with a view to prejudice the public mind against you. Our opposition to the President arises not from the manner in which he came into office—but from an objection to his opinion upon certain constitutional points, and from the position he occupied in what has been called "The Georgia Controversey."[2] You will pardon me for having said this much. . . .

ALS. DNA, RG59, Misc. Letters (M179, R66).   1. Either that of December 29, 1827 or the supplement thereto of June 10, 1828.   2. "The Georgia Controversy" of 1825-1826, having to do with the removal of the Creek Indians to the west, severely strained relations between Georgia and the Federal government under President Adams. E. Merton Coulter, *A Short History of Georgia* (Chapel Hill, N.C., 1933), 212-5; Wilson Lumpkin, *The Removal of the Cherokee Indians From Georgia, 1827-1841* (New York, 1907), 1:41-2.

From WILLIAM WOODBRIDGE, Detroit, August 19, 1828. Transmits copies of territorial documents relevant to a complaint by Judge Henry Chipman voiced in the body of the letter. Argues at length that he should be the presiding judge of the three justices appointed to the Supreme Court for the Michigan Territory by the President. Complains that the other two judges, Chipman, and Solomon Sibley, will not accept his rightful claim to this position, even though an act of the Legislative Council has sustained him in his view. Assures Clay that he has no "boyish vanity" in the matter and asks him for his assistance. Copy, signed. MiD-B; also in Carter, *Territorial Papers,* 11:1199-201.

From "WAYNE JUNIOR," Louisville, August 20, 1828. Condemns Clay for having attacked John Quincy Adams before and during the 1824 campaign "until your *mad reckless ambition* forced you to coalesce with your ancient enemy." Accuses Clay, further, of vanity, hypocrisy, and authoritarianism. Is convinced that "*divine Providence,* who certainly *more* than *once* has signally *preserved* these *United States,* was also conspicuous in this case, and *forced* you, at the *very* time your *hypocrisy* was *most needful,* to *disclose* your *true character.* Could anything but *proof, damning proof,* have made *me believe* you were so vain, as disclosed in your letters to [Amos] Kendall. You there [3:382-3, 674] *emphatically* say; that 'tis for the interest of the U. States that you should be President. Well may we exclaim vanity! vanity! 'tis all vanity!" Louisville *Public Advertiser,* August 20, 1828.

From WILLIAM TUDOR   Rio de Janeiro, August 20, 1828
The kind opinion which some of my friends write, that you have ex-

432

pressed towards me, leads me to presume on your excusing a private letter, in which I wish to touch on some topic, that I cannot perhaps well introduce into the confidential part even of my public correspondence. If this letter should have too much reference to myself you will for once excuse an egotism that is not wholly disconnected with public affairs.

I have seen with much regret the course pursued by Mr [Condy] Raguet since his return home, I have rarely met with a publication more calculated to injure the author in the opinion of all judicious persons, than his address to the people of the U.S.[1] of which he sent out a great many copies here, to be forwarded to various individuals, his own country men as well as foreigners in public stations. It is quite clear what opinion the latter will entertain of it, & as to the former I have not met with one, who did not regret that he had made such an address.

I do not know that gentleman personally, tho' while at Lima, I exchanged a few letters with him. I respect him as a man of strict integrity, & very pure morality; but who unites with these qualities a disqualification that they cannot always prevent that of possessing more passion than judgement. He discovers in the address before referred to, a fondness for diplomatic life, that vents itself in frank asperity at not being continued in it. There are few persons I should think less qualified for such a career, & so strong was any impression that he wished to retire from it, that more than once before my arrival here, & when the unwarrantable step he took was a subject of conversation, & with great simplicity, expressed the opinion, that he had been induced to take it, from the two-fold motive, that it might be useful to his country, & that having as he thought a fair pretext, he was anxious to make use of it in order to return home & get rid at once of a country & a career, with which he was disgusted. I have seldom been more erroneous in any conjecture.

If Mr. R. had not been entirely blinded by passion, he would have seen what every impartial person has felt, that the President went the utmost length in his power (& farther probably than for Mr R's sake alone he probably would have gone) in shielding him from disapprobation [6:97–100, 295], after taking on his own obstinate will a step of such an extraordinary nature; & where as a subaltern he attempted in a moment of passion by abandoning his post without leave to coerce his government into such a course as he thought most expedient, under the influence of a great deal of personal irritation & private resentment, which as [Edward] Gibbon[2] remarks in speaking of late, very honest men sometimes confound with the legitimate feelings of public policy. Had Mr R. have declined further correspondence with this government, & announced that he should only wait for the orders of his own; it is in the highest degree probable that on receiving orders to ask for his passports, unless an immediate redress of grievances was made by this government, they would not have dared to refuse, & a very prolonged & entangled derangement of our affairs would have been avoided.

Mr R. says that his course was approved of by everyone, which forms the most striking evidence how blind & deaf obstinacy & passion had made him. There was on the contrary not a single individual among his own country men or foreigners whose opinion (on that subject) was worth a straw, who was not opposed to the course he took. The foreign diplomatists, who being [illeg. word] under forms of severe discipline & subordination, were astonished at the rashness of a man in a situation so subaltern, taking a course that almost placed his country against the will of its government in a state of war. Everyone allowed & admired Mr R's upright & fearless character; but there was not a little diplomatic perfidy in applauding what was real indiscretions on his part, so as to keep this government personally indisposed towards him, while they might undercover of his rash, intemperate attacks, negotiate the same subjects in a more conciliatory & successful manner.

I have heard that Mr R spoke without reserve or discretion against the Emperor [Pedro I] in the bitterest manner, & this before officers in his service with the avowed intention, that his opinion should be made known. Allowing all the reputation that such practise may merit on the score of chivalry, I do not know how any man could expect for a moment, under a government where the Sovereign was nearly despotic that he could ever be a successful negotiator for his country. He had the misfortune to have one or two disputes here about houses &c, in which he was unquestionably very ill-treated; & from all I hear about judicial proceedings, I should immediately back out of any dispute at the first moment with the least expence possible. But the outrages Mr R. received were nothing in comparison to those other foreigners have met with to say nothing of some notorious ones of anterior date, Mr [Sir Robert] Gordon[3] was turned out of his house in the rudest manner by the Emperor himself & the list which the English have suffered is truly extraordinary, & nothing could cause them to be overlooked, but the worse than colonial system so far as commerce is concerned, with which they treat this country. I never wish to see my own country men submit to indignities any where, or from any person; but Mr R. may be said to have provoked them & really met with fewer than most other agents.

There was another point in which he erred in judgement he paid too much attention to the [illeg. word] opinions & worse clamours of Masters & supercargoes of vessels; a class not famed for moderation any where, & some of the most noisy of whom were actually engaged in clandestine speculations, covering enemies property. & embarrassing the fair commerce of their country. European officers in every branch of service diplomatic or military, treat all merchants & masters of vessels with an indifference or contempt that our country men would not practise on the one hand or endure on the other. Mr. R. went to the other extreme, he listened with too much reliance to the statements & outcries of these persons, & while in their "resolutions," he was a hero, he in turn thought their representations were to be received with high respect, & be considered as an authority at home. I heard from Como. B [James Biddle] a curious instance of their exaggeration; he was on a visit to Mr. R. at Botafogo, when they both received a letter from a supercargo of a captured vessel, calling for their interference without delay, as he had no doubt he should be murdered that night without it. Com B. immediately returned to his ship hurried off a lieutenant to inquire for the supercargo. He found him late in the evening on board the prison ship & with great difficulty, was allowed to go aboard. He easily found his way to the distressed individuals, who has occasioned others the most painful anxiety, by the cheerful sounds of *Auld lang syne* which they were singing with great glee, cigars &c. being the interludes.

I observe that Mr R. is pertinacious in wishing his correspondence to be published. so far as I may judge, if the government does not save him by its discretion in the selection, the man would not greatly increase his reputation. Mr R. seems to have an ignorance of the world that would have occasioned him severe shocks in most countries. If he would abuse every sovereign who treated his wife ill, he would be obliged to break a lance at most Courts in Christendom, He avowed as a peice of boldness, that republican as he was he could not help shedding tears on the death of the poor Empress [Maria Leopoldina], & that he was not ashamed of it—as if being a republican, prevented feelings of humanity, & that an Empress would not be loved & pitied as a woman if she deserved it, the most cockney demagogue, that had never seen a wider range than a alley would hardly have made such a silly remark as this. I observe also that he seems in one place, confounded with astonishment, & adds a dozen marks of admiration, that the Pope [Leo XII] had acceeded to the desire of Brazil, & named a patron saint [Peter of Alcantara][4] for the empire a peice of antiquated routine like this one of the idle frivolities perhaps of the Catholic religion, was hardly worth so much wonder; and after all ingenious Catholics make a very plausible defence for a custom, which they if superfluous, is at least innocent. But on the score of absurdity, men should not judge one another too hastily. The most eminent & justly revered monk in South America, the head of the Convent of St Francisco in Lima, honored me with his friendship. One day we were conversing in his cell as we sometimes did on religious topics, when he asked, if I understood the doctrines of [Emanuel] Swedenbourg, & whether it were possible for any rational being to believe in such nonsense. I disclaimed all knowledge of the doctrines, but told him there was no end to the waywardness of the human mind, that if I knew there were individuals, very enlightened & excellent in character who did believe in them; & I had in my mind, the gentleman I am now writing upon, who I had formerly heard was an adherent of the mystical.

To add one word more on this subject, I have nearly made up my mind should the President displace me, not to complain in print, whatever grief & indignation I may feel. But with respect to publishing correspondence, I avail myself of this occasion to entreat that mine so far as it is possible, even that which is not marked confidential, may be kept in MS. I cannot flatter myself, that my correspondence would suit many who would make themselves pitiless judges of it; besides the object of this kind of writing, at least I speak for myself, is not that of being published. I know a motion "to call for & print" is the common effort for distinction, by members who can make no other, & that much must be yeilded in this way, which is either superfluous or prejudicial but I am most earnest & sincere in availing myself of this private letter, to request that I may be *exposed* as little as possible.

I recently received a letter from my friend Dr Luna Pizarro,[5] President of the Peruvian Congress, a circumstance that I had also heard from others,—that General [Jose] La Mar [*sic,* Lamar] had written to you expressing a wish that I might be sent back to Peru. Receiving this kind

435

of semi official notice, I thought allowable in writing to the General, to express my thanks for this very flattering proof of his partiality, & at the same time, to say that the obstacles would be probably insurmountable to this I added a suggestion, that in addition to the desire I had to meet again with himself & others for whom I entertained the most affectionate esteem, I should be half tempted to wish for such a destination if I could be instrumental in establishing what I thought would be an enterprize of the highest importance both to my own country & Peru, but to the latter especially, the enterprize of packets to & from the Isthmus, & to be moved in the Pacific by steam.

This is a subject on which I have once or twice written to the Secretary of the Navy [Samuel L. Southard], & to some private individuals. It is perfectly practicable to reduce the present interval of communications between our ports & those of Peru &c—at least two thirds, & to turn the greater part of the trade of the Western coast to Panama, where it was originally established. whenever this is done, a decided preponderance in carrying on all that immense commerce will be decidedly thrown into our hands. Priority of information & proximity of the respective marts, would give us a leading, permanent facility over the merchants of Europe. If a company could be formed in the U.S. with a capital to make it, an insurance, as well as a packet, company they might undertake on a commission the transportation of all the remittances in the precious metals to Europe & doing it in a much shorter period than is at present requisite, the whole of it would fall into their hands. & this business alone in the course of time when those countries are tranquilized, give a commission of a million annually. In good times the exports from the Pacific coast of Mexico, Guatemala, Colombia, Peru & Chile of species & bullion does not fall short of 15 or 16 millions annually, & the time may come when it might be more, Nearly the whole of this may be made to pay us a toll, besides the increased amount we should permanently retain from the increased traffic we should possess, whenever such a communication shall be finally established. It would require a long memoir to point out all the bearing & extent of this business. & such ideas as I possess on the topic, I should gladly communicate to the government, if desired, at some future period. In regard to the foreign commerce of the U.S. you may be assured that there is no branch which is susceptible of such prodigious extensions as this.

I have frequently thought that nothing would take me back to South America if I once get out of it. After curiosity respecting some of its original & sublime natural features is satiated, a mortal ennui follows; physical forces enervated & mental energy extinguished in its lanquid, debilitating atmosphere, which is so, both morally & physically. But if I survive these Brazilian negotiations, and after recovering a little animation by the sight of the friends & the country I love, I should perhaps under a Quixotic impulse of aiding a vast & most useful enterprize, be willing to return to Peru; if a company would be formed for this object, (in which of course I would hold no interest), if the government thought proper to aid in the object, & if the President would be willing to give me such rank as would serve to sustain what little influence I may possess, thro the partiality of some of the present leading men in the government of Peru, & last not least if I should not be expected to remain more than a year on such a duty—Perhaps you will smile at my simplicity in some of these suggestions, but I confess that the importance to my own country as well as to those on the shores of the Pacific, by carrying back the course of trade to the Isthmus of Panama, has made me rather an enthusiastic missionary on the subject—

Tho' I beg you to consider this long letter as strictly confidential, I except the President, if you think it would interest him enough to look it over—

ALS. DLC–HC (DNA, M212, R8). Received December 3, 1828. Letter marked *"Private & confidential."*   1. For Raguet, see *DAB;* for his five letters "To the People," in which he defended his conduct as Minister to Brazil and his resignation from that post, see *The* [Philadelphia] *Banner of the Constitution,* February 12, 17, 20, 24, 26, 27, 1830.   2. *DNB.* 3. *Ibid.*   4. *New Catholic Encyclopedia.*   5. *Ibid.*

From JAMES BARBOUR, Liverpool, August 22, 1828. Announces his safe arrival in England. Reports "great animosity" to the latest [1828] American tariff, and states that "the folly is indulged of speculating on its consequences, in the South, lead by the violence . . . in S. Carolina—" Plans to proceed to London shortly. ALS. DNA, RG59, Dip. Disp., Great Britain, vol. 36 (M30, R32). Received September 27, 1828. Letter marked "Private."

From WILLIAM B. LAWRENCE, London, no. 54, August 22, 1828. Encloses a copy of a letter he has received from British Secretary of State for Foreign Affairs, Lord Aberdeen, concerning "John Baker [6:1272–3] and the exercise of exclusive jurisdiction on the North Eastern frontier," together with his reply. States he had "great doubts" about the propriety of replying, because "the trial of Baker . . . occurred subsequently to the date of my instructions." Decided to respond only because some of the statements in Aberdeen's letter "appeared to require a reply from the same person [Albert Gallatin], who has heretofore conducted the business on behalf of the United States." Notes that he did not have knowledge of the many discussions which have taken place between the United States and Great Britain, but says he "endeavoured to regulate my remarks by the views taken . . . by the American Government, as far as they could be learned from the imperfect sources of information accessible to me."

Mentions also that he has complained to Aberdeen about the fact that the British statement of claims to the territory on the Columbia River contained extracts from dispatches of British officials which had never been communicated to the American Government. ALS. DNA, RG59, Dip. Disp., Great Britain, vol. 35 (M30, R31). Received September 27, 1828; also in Manning, *Diplomatic Correspondence . . . Canadian Relations,* 2:762–3.

From WILLIAM B. LAWRENCE, London, no. 55, August 22, 1828. Reports that the resignation of the Duke of Clarence [William Henry] as Lord High Admiral has "produced but little sensation." Discusses some of the internal political implications of this. Notes, however, that Sir

Robert Peel may also resign as Home Secretary and that this would constitute "a more important secession." Encloses a copy of the Brazilian "Protest respecting Don Miguel's claims to the throne of Portugal." Has also heard that Spain has made an arrangement to pay the claims of British subjects against her. ALS. DNA, RG59, Dip. Disp., Great Britain, vol. 35 (M30, R31). Received September 27, 1828.

From HENRY MIDDLETON, St. Petersburg, August 22, 1828. Encloses copies of correspondence between the "Great Powers" just prior to the outbreak of the Russo-Turkish War. In this connection, draws particular attention to Lord Dudley's [John William Ward, former British Foreign Minister] "long winded, feeble, shuffling despatch" to Karl Nesselrode, the Russian Foreign Minister. Presents an extended historical analysis of Russia's wars, treaties, and national objectives pertaining to securing "water communication" on the Baltic, Black, Caspian, and Mediterranean seas and relates these to the onset of the present war and to specific Russian ambitions in the Black Sea and at the Bosphorus. Sees little prospect that the Turks can turn back Russia's military thrusts. States that "Greece is lost," and notes that Mahmud II, the Sultan of Turkey, "seems to have made up his mind to say nothing about it." Informs Clay that the Sultan is "said to be a besotted predestinarian who believes no harm can happen to him so long as he is in possession of a caftan of consecrated cloth which was brought to him by a holy Imaun [*sic,* Iman] from Mecca—for the rest he passes his time in making reviews & excursions on board a steamboat, when he indulges in copious potations of Champaigne wine. It would be difficult to lose an Empire more gayly than he does, if indeed it is to be lost. If saved it will be so by the same jealousy of the Powers of Europe which has so long protected it." LS. DNA, RG59, Dip. Disp., Russia, vol. 11 (M35, R11). Received November 22, 1828. Also dated August 10, Old Style.

From WILLIAM J. SEAVER, Santa Marta, Colombia, August 22, 1828. Reports the "dreadful falling off of trade" between North America and Santa Marta "has prevented my making the usual Return." Notes that a few small chartered vessels have called, carrying fustic, cotton, and hides as cargoes. Adds: "Some Doubloons and Spanish Dollars have also been shipped but the quantity I cannot say as my means of information are circumscribed." ALS. DNA, RG59, Cons. Disp., Santa Marta, vol. 1 (M-T427, R1). Received October 3, 1828.

From ANTHONY H. DUNLEVY, Lebanon, Ohio, August 23, 1828. Regrets that Clay will not be able to visit with his political friends in the Lebanon area on his way from Kentucky to Washington. Continues: "I congratulate you on the result of the Kentucky elections as well as those of Louisiana and Indiana. The effect of these I think must be considerable in Pennsylvania & other states. But still I felt much apprehension for the final result. New York appears to be so much under the influence of a few designing and artful men that I know not how to calculate upon her, and Virginia is so obstinately bound to her state right scruples and prejudices that I have no hope of her electoral vote. Of Penna and North Carolina there is some encouragement but great cause of fear. In fact the issue is doubtful as it appears to me but we must exert ourselves and never yield while there is the possibility of success." ALS. DLC–HC (DNA, M212, R3). For the Louisiana results, see Plumer to Clay, July 26, 1828. In Indiana the National Republicans elected a governor, lieutenant governor, U.S. Senator, and two of the three U.S. Representatives. Lexington *Kentucky Reporter,* August 20, 1828; Indianapolis *Gazette,* December 4, 1828; Clay to Whittlesey, August 15, 1828.

From JOSIAH S. JOHNSTON
New York, August 24, 1828

We return[e]d two days since from Boston—intend to remain a Week here & as long in Phila. & move slowly back to the Capitol. We are ignorant of your movements & do not know whether you will appear in the North or the South, but we are happy to see your triumphant return—bringing with all the West—My Letters from Loua. say "The Victory is for us. & the Country is Safe—Let Mr. Clay keep a Steady helm, the Storm is over—Let him get health & Serve his Country." "God bless the Country & its friends"—so say we all—The Battle will be fought here—The [N.Y.] Legislature will not touch the Law [3:476-7; 5:988][1]— Although every art & every influence in & out of the State will be essay[e]d to bring them up to the point—The Jackson *Leaders* will press [Martin] Van Buren, & they will be desperate as they are hopeless—He dare not, even if he could influence the Legislature—He will keep up their hopes of Success to the Last, to avoid the necessity of the desperate measure— Thompson[2] is firm—our friends ardent & Confident—Every thing must be done to encourage & Sustain them. It would be well I think now to give the Election to the people by a general ticket The vote of this State would then be decisive

Mr. [Thomas] Ogle will give you your Carriage by the 1 Oct. you must direct about the Colour & Lining—He makes it like mine for $700. If you wish the Lining of finer cloth, it will add only the difference in the price—I can not suggest any improvement   I shall be in Phila. by the first of Sept. & will take your orders—

ALS. InU.   1. See also, Weston, *The Presidential Election of 1828,* p. 173.   2. Probably Smith Thompson, gubernatorial candidate of the Administration party in N.Y. in 1828.

To JOHN SLOAN
Cincinnati, August 25, 1828

Your favor of the 14h. addressed at Lexington found me here. I regret extremely the unpropetious state of things in your district [5:799] which has created a necessity for your retirement from Congress,[1] and I yet hope that the good sense of your Constituents will not allow an event, which the public at large would have just occasion to lament. There is no friend I have in the H. of R. whose absence from it I should more seriously deplore.

[Thomas] Metcalfe i[s] elected, and only elected, but still he is governor, and I do believe that it will be followed by a train of consequences that will ensure success in the more important election in Nov. Some of the elections in the Western States have been unfavorable, but taken altogether, including Louisiana, the result is better for us than for our opponents, and is such as to stimulate patriotism to the highest exertions. We need not despair. Our *chance* (I am sorry to be obliged to use that word) is best.

I leave here tomorrow to return by the Virginia [White Sulphur] Springs with my health so far improved that I hope their use aided by the journey will fully re-establish it.... P.S. I understand from Frankfort that 54, out of 82 Sheriffs who attended to compare the polls, were for Adams; and that they are animated by the greatest zeal.

ALS. MH.   1. Sloane lost the election in the 12th District of Ohio (Wayne County and Wooster) by a "very meager majority." Ben Douglas, *History of Wayne County Ohio* (Indianapolis, 1878), 320.

To SAMUEL L. SOUTHARD   Cincinnati, August 26, 1828
Notwithstanding the result of the K[entucky]. Election has not fulfilled our hopes, [Thomas] Metcalfe is elected, and the State is safe with proper exertions—These our friends are resolved to make, but they will require all the aid that can be given. They are systemazing their efforts, and I anticipate from them the best effects.

I have regretted that the arrangement with Mr. J. A. Jr. with which you were charged was not executed.[1] Can it not now be done?

There is one matter about which there is making a most injurious use. It is a Navy report of your's recommending the employment of native Seamen.[2] It is perverted to mean the exclusion of naturalized Citizens. It would be well if in your clear and perspicuous stile an explanation were made in some prominent print.

I leave here tomorrow via the W. Sulphur Springs for Virginia.

ALS. NjP. Letter marked "(Confidential)."   1. Reference obscure; but possibly concerning John Adams, Jr.   2. *ASPN,* 3:205–09

From JAMES BROWN, Paris, no. 86, August 27, 1828. Reports that the Foreign Minister, Count Pierre de La Ferronnays, has fallen ill, has "repaired to the waters of Baden," and that the duties of his office have been given temporarily to M. De Rayneval, French Ambassador to the Swiss Confederation. Has decided to do nothing more on the U.S. claims question [Brown to Clay, May 12, 1828] until the absent Foreign Minister returns to Paris. ALS. DNA, RG59, Dip. Disp., France, vol. 23 (M34, R26). Received October 8, 1828. For Francois–Maximilien Gerard, Comte De Rayneval, see *NBG.*

From THOMAS T. CRITTENDEN, Frankfort, August 27, 1828. Recommends that John J. Crittenden, his brother, be appointed by the Adams administration to the U.S. Supreme Court; to the seat made vacant by the recent death of Justice Robert Trimble. Notes: "You may suppose, from the extent of his business here, that, in a pecuniary point of view, the office is of no consequence to him—He never can make money from his practice. His liberal and indulgent Spirit forbids the hope. He has a large and most expensive family. It is too but a sad truth, that that same liberal and generous temper has placed him under some

440

embarrassments. I greatly desire to see him released from them. This situation will soon effect it, if given to him." ALS. DNA, RG59, A. and R. (MR1).

Other recommendations were received from Thomas Triplett, August 27, John Harvie, August 27, and Richard H. Chinn, August 28, 1828. *Ibid.* Also, Robert P. Letcher to Clay, September 4, 1828, in DNA, RG59, Misc. Letters (M179, R66). See Kirwan, *John J. Crittenden*, 84.

From JOHN FORBES, Buenos Aires, August 27, 1828. Is awaiting "in the most anxious expectation" the arrival of news about the pending peace negotiations in Rio de Janeiro. Takes the opportunity to nominate Francisco Aguilar as a suitable U.S. commercial agent at Maldonado. LS. DNA, RG59, Dip. Disp., Argentina, vol. 3 (M69, R4). Received December 3, 1828. See, also, Espil, *Once Anos en Buenos Aires*, 497.

From ROBERT P. LETCHER   Lancaster, Ky., August 27, 1828
I am very sorry I did not see you before you left this country, and certainly should have gone to Lex. for that purpose, but for the fact, I learnt from my brother,[1] of your intention to visit the Greenville Springs [at Harrodsburg, Ky.], previous to your departure. I should have liked very much to have had your views of the most efficent means to be employed in the canvass from now until the 2d. Monday in Novr.

Our limited success in the late [August 6, state] election establishes clearly to my mind two propositions 1st. We have the numerical force to beat the opposition in this state. 2d. They have their forces better disciplined, and can bring them to the pools with greater facility than our party can, and will ultimately triumph over us, unless the most vigorous active and powerful exertions are resorted to, to counteract them. The friends of the administration in all this region of [the] country, will do their duty, they are alarmed, but yet entertain a confident belief that activity and concert will lead them to victory. We are endeavoring to follow up our success, with a new zeal and spirit. On the other hand, we have to contend with an untiring eninmy, they are also preparing for active operation, and speak in a tone of the most undoubted confidence. I *think,* (no doubt of the fact) they are preparing more *Amunition.* I always have, and *do now dread* the illegal manner in which they arm themselves. They consider their salvation temporal and eternal at stake and of course stop at nothing.

I regret to hear of the death of Judge [Robert] Trimble.[2] In relation to his successor, allow me to make a single remark. If the President thinks the interest of the public would be best promoted by *taking* or rather by making his selection out of this state to fill the vancancy, I hope, most earnestly hope, he may not act in the case until the meeting of Congress, unless the Public service should require him to do so....

ALS. DNA, RG59, Misc. Letters (M179, R66).   1. Probably Benjamin, who lived in Lancaster at this time.   2. Thomas T. Crittenden to Clay, August 27, 1828.

From JOHN HENRY OWEN, Franklin, Tenn., August 27, 1828. Apologizes for his long silence, but assures Clay of his continuing regard and loyalty. Reports that since seeing Clay in Lexington he has studied law, history, and literature and will soon leave Tennessee and return there. "Indeed, Sir, nothing can exceed my anxiety to leave this state. Although Kentucky is lashed by the billows of contending politics, yet its ocean waves are more grateful to my feelings than this Dead Sea of America." Notes that there has been a severe drought in Tennessee and that the "cotton and indeed [the o]ther crops have failed beyond expectation." ALS. DLC-HC (DNA, M212, R3).

From JOSE SILVESTRE REBELLO, Washington, August 27, 1828. Notifies Clay that Brazil did not receive the newly appointed diplomats of revolutionary Portugal, "as it represented an usurping [Miguel] Government." Argues "it is a matter of duty of all governments to concur" against "those turbulent spirits whose only object is to acquire wealth, and high rank through revolutions, and intrigues"

Requests that the U.S. not receive Frederico Torlade, "who has just arrived at Baltimore announcing himself as a Chargé d'Affairs from Portugal." LS, in Portuguese, with trans. in State Dept. file. DNA, RG59, Notes from Brazilian Legation, vol. 1 (M49, R1).

Torlade wrote Clay from Baltimore on August 26, stating that he was on his way to Washington to present his "Letters of Credence" as Chargé d'Affairs, and that the object of the Miguel government in Portugal is "to strengthen the relations of ancient amity . . . and to promote every means of encouraging commerce." ALS, in Portuguese, with trans. in State Dept. file. DNA, RG59, Notes from Portuguese Legation, vol. 2 (M57, R2).

Joaquim B. Pereira, Portuguese commercial agent in Washington, informed Clay on August 25 that an anti–Miguel provisional junta had been installed at Oporto on May 20, 1828, and that he now represents that government. On August 27, he urged Clay not to recognize Torlade. Both in *ibid*.

Rebello wrote Clay again on September 1, pointing out again that Miguel was an usurper, that "all the Representatives of the Foreign Nations" had left Lisbon, and that the U.S. Minister to Portugal, Thomas L. L. Brent, should also be withdrawn. LS, in Portuguese, with trans. in State Dept. file. DNA, RG59, Notes from Brazilian Legation, vol. 1 (M49, R1). He wrote Clay again on September 22, urging Brent's recall and protesting "against the reception, by the Government of the United States of any Diplomatic Agent appointed by the usurper of the Portuguese Crown." *Ibid*.

From WILLIAM TUDOR, Rio de Janeiro, no. 105, August 27, 1828. Reports that the two commissioners [Diego Souves da Silva de Bivar and Antonio Jose da S. Louveiro] appointed by Brazil to settle United States claims "will commence the business tomorrow." States that Brazil has already settled French claims on the basis that the bills in payment shall "be liquidated when due at the current ex[chan]ge of the day, & I suppose we must assent to a similar arrangement, which is in fact an equitable one."

Mentions that at a meeting with Brazilian Foreign Minister, the Marquis of Aracaty, they discussed a commercial treaty, and the Marquis gave assurances that it would be finished in order to reach the United States in time for ratification by the next session of Congress. Believes the peace between Brazil and Buenos Aires was signed yesterday, but adds in a postscript that Buenos Aires officials deny it. ALS. DNA, RG59, Dip. Disp., Brazil, vol. 6 (M121, R8). Letter marked "Confidential." No date of receipt.

Tudor wrote Clay again on August 29, no. 106, reporting that the peace treaty between Brazil and Buenos Aires was signed on August 28, and that while he had no information on the particulars he had "always understood that the cession of the Banda Oriental [Uruguay] by this government [Brazil] was the sine qua non held out by B'Aryes [sic]." Ibid. Received December 3, 1828. See also, Manning, Diplomatic Correspondence... Latin American Nations, 2:865; and Parry, Treaty Series, 79:1-11.

From WILLIAM H. D. C. WRIGHT, Rio de Janeiro, August 27, 1828. Reminds Clay that during the fourteen month period between the departure of Condy Raguet and the arrival of William Tudor he was the only U.S. representative to the Brazilian government. Points out that because of this "my private concerns were... neglected and expenses were incurred." Asks that he be paid for these additional duties. ALS. DNA, RG59, Cons. Disp., Rio de Janeiro, vol. 3 (M-T172, R4). Received November 24, 1828.

From LAWRENCE DE CRUISE, Paris, August 29, 1828. Reminds Clay of his earlier letter, written shortly after the Battle of Navarino on October 20, 1827, when it had become clear that "the brave but unfortunate Greeks would be free." In this letter he had recommended that the U.S. send a Chargé to Greece to encourage the people there in their continuing struggle for freedom, since he also knew that "nothing was more popular in the United States" than the Greek cause.

Reports that French troops have sailed for the Morea and that "it is pleasing to see, that the french nation has taken to heart the misfortunes of those poor fellow beings, and notwithstanding any thing that the British Govert. may oppose. I think the french will have all the glory." Offers himself for appointment as Chargé to Greece if such a post is now to be established.

Praises Clay's efforts on behalf of South America and hopes "you will now think with me that this is the moment to offer a friendly hand to the poor but brave Greeks." ALS. DNA, RG59, A. and R. (MR1). Received October 8, 1828.

From THOMAS C. FLOURNOY, Columbus, Ohio, August 29, 1828. Has learned of the death of Ohio Federal District Judge Charles Willing Byrd and recommends the appointment of William Creighton, Jr. to fill his place. Creighton "is a man of the finest legal attainments, and undoubtedly the most *popular* man in Ohio. To give him the office, (if he

443

will accept it) would have the best possible effect upon the Presidential Election." ALS. DNA, RG59, A. and R. (MR1).

On September 6 Flournoy again wrote recommending that Adams wait until after the election before appointing anyone to the office, saying "*then*—I should hope that the office may be given to Mr. Creighton, *by all means.*" *Ibid.*

Clay wrote Creighton [see *DAB*] on November 1, offering him the position. Copy. DNA, RG59, Dom. Letters, vol. 22, p. 326 (M40, R20). On November 11 Creighton notified Clay of his receipt of the commission, stating that he had "this day taken the oath of office." ALS. DNA, RG59, Accept. and Orders for Comms. (M-T645, R2). Creighton's appointment, however, was not confirmed by the Senate.

Jackson beat Adams 67,597 to 63,396 in the Presidential election in Ohio, taking all 16 electoral votes there. Svend Petersen, *A Statistical History of the American Presidential Elections* (New York, 1968), 20.

From FRANCISCO TACON, Philadelphia, August 29, 1828. Presents in great detail the facts surrounding the physical and mental harassment of Hilario de Rivas y Salmon, Secretary of the Spanish Legation, at the hands of the family of William Kirk, occupant of an adjoining house. Notes other insults visited upon Salmon by William Kirk and his son, Thomas, even after Kirk had been informed of the privileged status of diplomats.

Appeals to Clay personally "to give more effect to the protection granted by the Law of Nations to Prime Ministers and to secure" this guarantee for Salmon. LS, in Spanish, with trans. in State Dept. file. DNA, RG59, Notes from Spanish Legation, vol. 9 (M59, R12).

On October 13, 1828, Charles J. Ingersoll, United States District Attorney, writing to Clay from Philadelphia, reported that the Grand Jury has presented an indictment against William Kirk in this case. ALS. DNA, RG59, Misc. Letters (M179, R66). Ingersoll wrote again on October 26, stating that the prosecution of Kirk had resulted in an acquittal, "on the ground that the process not having been executed the minister's privilege was not violated." *Ibid.*

On November 19 Tacon again wrote Clay, detailing at length Salmon's grievances and protesting the failure of legal action against Kirk. LS, in Spanish, with trans. in State Dept. file. DNA, RG59, Notes from Spanish Legation, vol. 9 (M59, R12). On the following day Tacon provided Clay with the names of Salmon's household. *Ibid.*

On November 24 William Kirk wrote Clay, requesting him "to lay the enclosed Petition before the President," presenting his legal case against Salmon. LS. DNA, RG59, Misc. Letters (M179, R66). Four days later on November 28, Clay notified Kirk that he had complied with this request, and that the President would adopt such measures to settle this case. Copy. DNA, RG59, Dom. Letters, vol. 22, pp. 336-7 (M40, R20).

Clay responded to Tacon's note of November 19 on December 10, stating that the President desires all members of the Diplomatic Corps to enjoy in the U.S. the full protection and privileges to which they are entitled, but that "it is no less his duty to exercise if necessary all the authority which he possesses to prevent any wrongs from being commit ted upon American Citizens" by members of that corps. Notes that when Kirk was prosecuted, the case ended in acquittal. Encloses copies of a petition sworn to by Kirk and "accompanied by the depositions of three witnesses, which give a very different account of the character of those transactions, from that which you presented at the instance of Mr. Salmon." Points out that these documents allege that Salmon not only beat Kirk's son, but also beat a female domestic "so severely that the blood jellied on her back"; and that on another occasion Salmon entered Kirk's premises and carried off two carpets which he still retains. Attributes these problems to the fact that the Spanish Legation is located in Philadelphia where there is dual federal and state authority rather than in the District of Columbia. Copy. Notes to Foreign Ministers and Consuls, vol. 4, pp. 98–102 (M38, R4).

Tacon replied on December 20, defending Salmon against Kirk's charges, which he alleged were false, and stating that Salmon would shortly be returning to Spain to assume a new office [Everett to Clay, September 17, 1828]. Asserts also that the Spanish Legation will remain in Philadelphia. ALS, in Spanish, with trans. in State Dept. file. DNA, RG59, Notes from Spanish Legation, vol. 9 (M59, R12).

On or about January 8, 1829, Clay wrote William Kirk, enclosing copies of Tacon's reply to the petition and the depositions furnished by Kirk. Concludes: "Should you think proper to furnish any additional testimony, the President will give it attentive consideration." Copy. DNA, RG59, Dom. Letters, vol. 22, pp. 365–6 (M40, R20).

Clay wrote Tacon on February 7, reporting the President's views in "this unpleasant controversy." Referring to Salmon's violence and "passion," asserts that Salmon should "abstain from taking justice in his own hands." Believes he could have obtained "necessary protection" from local authorities. States that the President feels Salmon should respect the laws of the U.S. so long as he remains here, and that he should return Kirk's property. Stresses also "the inconvenience of your residence from the seat of Government is sensibly felt." Copy. DNA, RG59, Notes to Foreign Ministers and Consuls, vol. 4, pp. 139–42 (M38, R4). Tacon acknowledged receipt of Clay's letter on February 16. LS, in Spanish. DNA, RG59, Notes from Spanish Legation, vol. 9 (M59, R12).

From JAMES BROWN   Paris, August 30, 1828

Mrs. Brown returned with me from Dieppe a few days ago, but finding herself too weak to bear the fatigue of receiving company, and justly apprehending that her fondness for it would overcome her resolution if she remained within its reach she went out with my brother [Samuel] and niece [Susan] to spend two or three weeks at Versailles at which place from its proximity to Paris I can see her frequently. She is delighted with the place which affords her so many agreeable means of taking exercise and I wish her to prolong her stay there until the beginning of October. I think she is in a fair way of recovering if she can abstain from company which in her present nervous state, the effect of taking too many and too powerful remedies, is very prejudicial to her—

The affairs of this continent present an aspect so complicated that no statesmen can predict what will arrive or whether we shall have peace or war. The stocks still maintain their stand and such is the conviction every where that no nation, (France perhaps excepted) is ready for war, that perhaps by amicable negociation it may yet be avoided. The unexpected resistance made by the Turks will also have a tendency to induce the Emperor [Nicholas I] to be more moderate in his demands and thus restore tranquility. The French people have always been friendly to the Greek cause and the sailing of the expedition from Toulon ensures its success.

I have not yet received any letter from Mr [Stephen] Pleasonton informing me that my account of last year which I sent by January Packet with the necessary vouchers has been settled. Will you be so good as to urge him to close it as I wish that nothing on my part should give room for the criticisms of Messrs. Chilton & Co. I wish also to pay [Armand] Barnet as soon as [John Adams] Smith may arrive and hope you will say what I ought to allow him.

My brother will leave Paris on the 15 of next month and will bring on what you have ordered for Mrs. [Richard] Rush Mrs. [William] Wirt and Mrs. Clay. I shall direct the articles to you and you can settle with them.

The Louisiana election has gratified me very much and may have some influence on the other elections. I hope Kentucky has done well. It will now depend on New York where Mr. [John Jacob] Astor assures me the Administration gains friends daily. Write me all about these things and more especially tell me how you are because the accounts we have received of your health have given us much uneasiness.

Lieut. Levi [sic][1] of the Navy called on me yesterday and stated that he had obtained a furlough to come to Europe for his health which was now nearly expired, and that he was too unwell to undertake the voyage without exposing his life to great hazard. He says he has been long in actual service. Of this last assertion I know nothing, but I can safely say that his health appeared to be very bad, and you may say so to Mr [Samuel L.] Southard should Mr Levi have asked for a prolongation of his furlough.

Mrs. Brown joins me in love to Mrs Clay. . . .

ALS. DLC–HC (DNA, M212, R3). Printed in *LHQ*, 24:1125–6.   1. For Uriah Phillips Levy, see *CAB*.

From CHARLES J. CATLETT, Washington, August 30, 1828. Encloses a "protest," which has been presented to the Slave Indemnity Award Commission and to the Secretary of the Treasury [Richard Rush]. LS. DNA, RG59, Misc. Letters (M179, R66). In his protest Catlett argued that the members of the Board of Commissioners [Langdon Cheves, James Pleasants, Henry Seawell], operating under the Convention of November 13, 1826 [6:347], were not proceeding along "Solemn & important legal principles." In the first instance, Catlett noted that "Cheves has resigned his seat," without the appointment of another person to fill the vacancy. This event, he claimed, "nullified all the proceedings of the Board." Secondly, he pointed out that Pleasants was "nearly connected with several of the claimants from Virginia" in the admission and rejection of claims, thus rendering "a sufficient objection to the validity of their [the Commissioners] decisions." In a postscript, Catlett declared he had also submitted a copy of this complaint to Rush, objecting to the "payment of any money under any award of the Board." *Ibid.*

On July 14, 1828, Langdon Cheves, writing from Lambertsville, New Jersey, had informed Clay he was resigning his duties as Commissioner because of "a severe fit of bilious fever." ALS. DNA, RG59, Letters of Resignation and Declination.

From ROBERT M. HARRISON, St. Bartholomew, August 30, 1828. Reports that the British brig, *Aurora,* out of Glasgow, was taken by pirates, carried to St. Eustatius, "and as report[s] say, every Soul on Board Murdered, among whom were two Ladies with children!!!" States that the Government of St. Kitts is claiming the vessel and hopes "those wretches at St. Eustalia [*sic*]," long known to aid and equip Guineamen and Piratical cruises, "will be made to feel the effects of *British vengeance.*"

Discusses other examples and incidents of piratical activity. Understands that one vessel "is a Baltimore built Schooner, Commanded and Manned, as those Pirates are in most instances by natives, or adopted citizens of the *U States!*" Details rumored links between American business interests with piracy. Urges strongly, in the interest of protecting American commerce, "the propriety of sending one of our light cruisers into those seas," even though "none of our Merchant vessels have been robbed or plundered" yet. ALS. DNA, RG59, Cons. Disp., St. Bartholomew, vol. 1 (M72, R1). Received October 16, 1828.

From WILLIAM B. LAWRENCE, London, no. 56, August 30, 1828. Reports that James Barbour, the new U.S. minister to Great Britain, arrived in Liverpool on August 21, 1828, and is expected in London in two or three days. Discusses rumors relating to the progress of the Russo–Turkish war but admits that he has "no information on the subject, not to be found in the newspapers."

Notes that new arrangements necessitated by the Duke of Clarence's [William Henry] resignation as Lord High Admiral have not been completed, but it seems to be the opinion of many that "Lord Melville [Robert Saunders Dundas] will resume his place" as First Lord of the Admiralty. Has heard from the East India Company that the merchants of Singapore are anxious to open trade with the United States and "that, if application was made" to the British government, "it would not be declined." Adds that he has not felt himself authorized to take this matter up with the British.

Encloses a copy of a report on the wool trade which will supply information of interest to the United States. LS. DNA, RG59, Dip. Disp., Great Britain, vol. 35 (M30, R31). Received October 3, 1828.

From JAMES PLEASANTS & HENRY SEAWELL, Washington, D.C., August 30, 1828. Report that the Board of Commissioners [6:347] has concluded action, awarding to all claimants "which constitute a just claim upon the Treasury of the United States" the total sum of $1,297,422.18 leaving a balance of $1,204,960. Mentions other disbursements to cover the expenses of the [Slave Indemnity Award] Commision. ALS, by Pleasants except for one paragraph. DNA, RG76, Misc. Claims, Great Britain. They had asked Clay on August 29 for "necessary directions" on how to pay Col. Aaron Ogden the sum of $1,804.45 for serving as Clerk of the Commission, and for the advertisements run by the Commission in the Richmond and Baltimore newspapers. In a second letter on August 29, they also asked Clay what to do with the Commission's "documents and papers" and "public furniture." Both in *ibid.*

From WILLIAM RADCLIFF, Lima, no. 2, August 30, 1828. Reports that Peru has named a new Minister of Foreign Affaires, Jose M. Galdiano, and that he has made through him "the communication intended by the President to have been made through the late Mr. [James] Cooley [Clay to Cooley, April 15, 1828]." Notes that in his role as acting Chargé d'Affaires he has been treated by the Minister "with all the respect due to one representing our Government." States that Peru's President, General Jose de Lamar, is preparing "to resist an invasion expected from Colombia." States also that "a proclamation of [Simon] Bolivar" is responsible for the belief that war between Peru and Colombia is inevitable. Believes some foreign power, friendly to both countries, might be able to mediate and prevent war. Fears a war will jeopardize the independence and republican governments of both countries.

Predicts that the newly elected Peruvian Congress, which will probably meet in November, will be "more liberal and friendly to commerce" than the last Congress which passed an act "prohibiting entirely the importation from the U[nited] States after eight months . . . of all Flour" and other articles, including low–priced cotton fabrics. Comments at length on the various problems he has brought before the Peruvian government. Adds that he has made his son, Alexander H. Radcliff, vice consul in order to give himself more time to deal with "the duties devolved on me through the death of Mr. Cooley." Complains that the distance between Lima and the port of Callao necessitates maintaining two offices and results in extra expense for traveling; asks, therefore, for extra compensation. Inquires about his legal responsibilities in regard to destitute seamen. ALS. DNA, RG59, Cons. Disp., Lima, vol. 2 (M154, R2). Received December 20[?], 1828.

SPEECH   Cincinnati, August 30, 1828
Mr. Chairman [Samuel W. Davies][1]—Although it is not entirely compatible with the precautions which are enjoined by the delicate state of my health, to which you have so obligingly alluded, to present myself in this attitude, I cannot refrain from making a public expression to you, and to my fellow citizens here assembled, of my profound acknowledgments for the hearty welcome, and the cordial, spontaneous, and enthusiastic manifestation of respect and attachment, with which my present visit to your city has been attended. It has been frequently, but not less truly said, that the highest reward for public service, is the approbation of the public   The support of public opinion, is the greatest incentive to the faithful and beneficial discharge of official duty. If, as you have truly

448

suggested, it has been my misfortune for several years to have been abused and assailed without example, I have nevertheless had the satisfaction to have been cheered and sustained in all parts of the Union, by some of the best and most virtuous men in it. And I seize with pleasure, this occasion, to say, that even among my political opponents, many of the moderate and most intelligent, have done me the justice to discredit and discountenance the calumnies of which I have been the object. But no where have I found more constant, ardent, and effective friends, than in this city. I thank them most heartly for all their friendly sentiments and exertions.

Whatever may be the issue of the contest which, at present, unhappily divides and distracts our country, I trust that the beneficial system, to which you have referred, will survive the struggle, and continue to engage the affections, and to cheer and animate the industry of the people of the United States. It has indeed been recently attacked in another quarter of the Union, by some of our fellow–citizens, with a harshness and intemperance, which must every where excite the patriot's regret. It has been denounced as if it were a new system, that sprung into existence but yesterday, or at least with the present Administration, if not during the last session of Congress. But it owes its origin to a much earlier date   The present Administration, though sincerely attached to it, and most anxious for its preservation, has not the merit of having first proposed or first established it. The manufacturing system was quickened into existence by the commercial restrictions which preceded the late War with Great Britain, and by that greatest of them all, the War itself. Our wants, no longer supplied from abroad, must have been supplied at home, or we must have been deprived of the necessaries and comforts of civilization, if we had not relapsed into a state of barbarism. The policy of Jefferson and Madison fostered, if it did not create, the manufactures of our country   The peace brought with it a glut of foreign fabrics, which would have prostrated our establishments, if government had been capable of unjustly witnessing such a spectacle, without interposing its protective power. Protection, therefore, was not merely called for by the substantial independence of our country, but it was a parental duty of government to those citizens who had been tempted by its restrictive policy to embark all their hopes and fortunes in the business of manufacturing   Twelve years ago Congress took up the subject, and after long and mature deliberation, solemnly decided to extend that measure of protection which was alike demanded by sound policy and strict justice. Then the foundations were laid of the American System; and all that has been subsequently done, including the act of the last session of Congress, are but the consequences of the policy then deliberately adopted, having for their object the improvement and perfection at the great work then began. It is not the least remarkable of the circumstances of these strange times, that some who assisted in the commencement, who laid corner–stones of the edifice, are now ready to pull down and demolish it.

It is not the fact of the existence of an opposition to the Tariff, that can occasion any inquietude; nor that of large and respectable assemblies of the people, to express their disapprobation of the policy and their firm resolution to consume only the produce of their own industry. These meetings are in the true spirit of our free institutions, and that resolution is in the true spirit of our American System itself   But what must excite deep regret is that, any persons should allow themselves to speak of open and forcible resistance to the government of their country, and to threaten a dissolution of the Union. What is the state of the case? A great measure of national policy is proposed; it is a subject of discussion for a period of twelve years, in the public prints, in popular assemblies, in political circles, and in the Congress of the United States. That body, after hearing the wishes and wants of all parts of the Union, fairly stated by their respective representatives, decides, by repeated *majorities* to adopt the measure. It is accordingly put into successful operation, improved from time to time, and is rapidly fulfilling all the hopes and expectations of its friends. In this encouraging condition of things, a small number of the citizens composing the minority, (for I will not impute to the great body of the minority, any such violent purposes) threaten the employment of force, and the dissolution of the Union! Can any principle be more subversive of all government, or of a tendency more exceptionable and alarming? It amounts to this, that whenever any portion of the community finds itself in a minority, in reference to any important act of the government, and by high colouring and pictures of imaginary distress, can persuade itself that the measure is oppressive[,] that minority may appeal to arms, and if it can[,] dissolve the Union; such a principle would reverse the established maxim of representative government, according to which, the will of the majority must prevail. If it were possible that the minority could govern and control, the Union may, indeed, as well be dissolved; for it would not be then worth preserving. The conduct of an individual would not be more unwise and suicidal, who, because of some trifling disease afflicting his person, should, in a feverish and fretful moment, resolve to terminate his existence.

Nothing can be more unfair and ridiculous, than to compare any of the acts of Congress of the United States, representing all, and acting for all, to any of the acts of the British Parliament, which led to our revolution. The principle on which the colonies seceded was, that there should be no taxation without representation   They were not represented in the British Parliament, and to have submitted to taxation, would have been to have submitted to slavery, and to have surrendered the most valuable privileges of freemen. If the colonies had been fairly represented in the British Parliament, and equal taxes, alike applicable to all parts of the British Empire, had been imposed by a majority, a case of remote analogy to any act of Congress to which a minority is opposed, might be deduced from the history of the Revolution. But every State of this confederacy is fairly represented, and has the faculty of being fully heard in the Congress of the United States. The representation has been regulated by a joint principle of distribution, the result of a wise spirit of mutual compromise and concession, which I hope never to see disturbed, of which none can justly complain, and least of all those citizens who have resorted to threats of an appeal to arms and disunion.

But there is, I hope and believe, no reason to apprehend the execution of those empty threats. The good sense, the patriotism, and the high character of the people of South Carolina, are sure guarantees for repressing, without aid, any disorders, should any be attempted within her limits. The spirit of [Francis] Marion, and [Francis W.] Pickens, and [Thomas] Sumpter [*sic,* Sumter], of the [Edward, John] Rutledges, the [Charles, Charles C., Thomas] Pinckneys, and of [William] Lowndes, yet survives, and animates the high-minded Carolinians. The [John] Taylors, and the [David R.] Williamses, and their compatriots of the present day, will be able to render a just account of all, if there be any, who shall dare to raise their pa[t]ricidal hands against the peace, the constitution, and the union of the states. Rebuked by public opinion, a sufficient corrective, and condemned by their own sober reflections, the treasonable purpose will be relinquished, if it were ever seriously contemplated by any.

I have no fears of the permanency of our Union, whilst our liberties are preserved. It is a tough and strong cord, as all will find who shall presumptuously attempt to break it. It has been competent to suppress all the domestic insurrections, and to carry us safely through all the foreign wars with which we have been afflicted since it was formed, & it has come out of each with more strength, and greater promise of durability. It is the choicest political blessing which, as a people, we enjoy, and I trust and hope, that Providence will permit us to transmit it unimpaired to posterity, through endless generations.

I thank you, Mr. Chairman, for the flattering opinion which you have expressed of my public services, and especially of those which I have endeavoured to render to the West. Whilst I am sensible that you appreciate them much too highly, it is at the same time true that I have sought, on all occasions that appeared to me proper, to advance the interests of that section, of which I am proud to be a citizen, whenever I have thought it could be done without prejudice to the predominant interests of the whole. I have, nevertheless, in several important instances given my most zealous support to measures (the navy and the late war for example) in which the West could not be regarded as having any distinct or other interest, than that which belongs to the honor, the prosperity, and the character, of the whole Confederacy. During the short period of the present Administration, I hope I may be permitted to say, without the meaning to claim for it exclusive merit, that more has been done and recommended for the West, than ever was done during the whole preceding period of our present Constitution, with the exception only of the acquisition of Louisiana, under the administration of Mr. Jefferson. I have not strength or time to enter into details to establish the general proposition; but those who will take the trouble to examine the appropriations of land and of money, for objects of internal improvement, and education, the measures which have been adopted or recommended, in respect to the public domain, the judiciary, &c., will find that proposition fully sustained.

There are here many who by a too flattering estimate of my capacity, deemed me worthy of the office of Chief Magistrate, and during the last Presidential canvass honored me with their support. To them I take this occasion to say that, if instead of the present abused Chief Magistrate, they had obtained their preference, the measures of the Administration would not have been, in any essential particular, different from those which have been adopted. All the principal acts and measures of the existing Administration have met with my humble and hearty concurrence.

Cultivating a farm in Kentucky, and having other objects of private concern, I have found it necessary, both on that account, and the relaxation from official business, indispensable to the preservation of health, annually to visit this quarter of the Union, during the period of my connexion with the Executive of the United States. In these visits, I have frequently met large portions of my fellow-citizens, upon their friendly and pressing invitations. My object has been called in question, and my motives assailed. It has been said that my purpose was electioneering. If it be intended to charge me with employing improper or dishonorable acts, to secure any election, I deny the charge, and disclaim the purpose. I defy my most malignant enemies to show that I ever, during any period of my life, resorted to such acts to promote my own election, or that of any other person. I have availed myself of these assemblies, and of other opportunities, to defend myself against an accusation, publicly made, and a thousand times repeated. I had a right to do this by the innumerable laws of self-defence. My addresses to the public, heretofore, have been generally strictly defensive. If they have ever given pain to any of my adversaries, they must reproach themselves with its infliction. There is one way, and but one way, in which they may silence me. My traducers have attributed to me great facility in making a bargain. Whether I possess it or not there is one bargain which, for their accommodation, I am willing to enter into with them. If they will prevail upon their Chief [Jackson] to acknowledge that he has been in error, and has done me injustice, and if they will cease to traduce and abuse me, I will no longer present myself before popular assemblies, or in the public prints, in my own defence. That is one bargain which I have no expectation of being able to conclude; for men who are in a long-established line of business, will not voluntarily quit their accustomed trade, and acknowledge themselves bankrupts to honor, decency and truth.

Some have persuaded themselves that they saw in my occasional addresses to the people, incompatibility with the dignity and reserve belonging to the office I hold, I know not according to what standard (it can hardly be any deduced from a popular representative government,) these gentlemen have regulated their opinions. True dignity appears to me, to be independent of office or station. It belongs to every condition; but if there be a difference between private and public life, the more exalted the station, the greater is the obligation of the public functionary, in my humble judgment, to render himself amiable, affable, and accessible. The public officer who displays a natural solicitude to defend himself against a charge deeply affecting his honor and his character, manifests, at the same time, a just respect for the community. It is, I think, an erroneous judgement of the nature of office, and its relations, to suppose that it imposes the duty on the officer, of abstracting himself from society, and a stiff and stately port. Without, I hope, forgetting what was due to myself, my habit, throughout life, has been that of friendly, free, and frank intercourse with my fellow-citizens. I have not thought it necessary to change my personal identity in any of the various offices through which I have passed, or to assume a new character. It may not be easy to draw the line, as to the occasions in which a man should remain silent, or defend himself. In the general, it is better perhaps, that he should leave his public acts, and the measures which he espouses or carries, to their own vindications; but of his integrity he questioned, and dishonorable charges, under high and imposing names, be preferred against him, he cannot remain silent without a culpable insensiblity to all that is valuable in human life.

Sir, I feel that I have trespassed too much both upon you, and myself. If prudence were a virtue of which I could boast, I should have spared both you and me. But I could not deny myself the gratification of expressing my thanks to my Cincinnati friends for the numerous instances which I have experienced of their kind and respectful consideration. I beg you, Sir, and every gentleman here attending, to accept my acknowledgments; and I especially owe them to the gentlemen of the Committee, who did me the honor to meet me at Louisville, and to accompany me to this city. Whatever may be my future destiny, whilst my faculties are preserved, I shall cherish a proud and greateful recollection of these testimonies of respect and attachment.

Copy. Lexington *Kentucky Reporter*, September 3, 1828. Also printed in Colton, *Clay Correspondence*, 5:359–64, under date August 23, with minor changes in punctuation and capitalization.   1. For Davies, see *OHQ*, 70:96–7. His brief speech of welcome to Clay emphasized the unfairness of the "violent attacks made upon your public conduct, by ambitious and disappointed men, who do not themselves believe to be true the charges they have made against you"; and lauded Clay's "efforts to elevate the character and advance the interests of the west." Lexington *Kentucky Reporter*, September 3, 1828.

From LEWIS CHARLES DE LEDERER, Mansion Hotel, Philadelphia, August 31, 1828. Recalls that Clay in a letter of December 20, 1827, suggested that a convention was "the most proper means for removing the obstructions, which . . . prevent the Austrian flag from participating in the trade between the Austrian ports" and the United States. Reports he has now been given "full powers" from his government to conclude "a Convention of Commerce and Navigation on the most liberal principles of perfect reciprocity." Asks Clay to communicate this to the President. ALS. DNA, RG59, Notes from Austrian Legation, vol. 1 (M48, R1). In a memo, dated November, 1828, Clay noted: "This treaty was prepared for signature, and the translation of it was made for examination. It was prepared in conference between the Baron of Lederer and me, and the translation was made by him." Adds that the negotation was then closed when the Baron "stated that he could not conclude and sign it, until he had transmitted it to his Government for their approval." ALS. OHi. The Treaty of Commerce and Navigation with Austria was concluded on August 27, 1829. Ratifications were exchanged on February 10, 1831. See Parry, *Treaty Series*, 80:53–64.

From WILLIAM B. ROCHESTER, Buffalo, N.Y., August 31, 1828. Asks if Clay has received his letters of May 14, May 16, and June 11 reporting on political conditions in Central America. Has heard that "important changes have taken place in that country since my departure from Honduras" and doubts that he can say little about the current situation there that would not be "mere speculation." Encloses a copy of *The Honduras Gazette* [Belize] for May 10, 1828. ALS. DNA, RG59, Dip. Disp., Central America, vol. 1 (M219, R2). Received September 4, 1828.

Clay responded to this letter on October 7, noting: "The President approves your return to the United States from your mission to Guatemala.... In the unhappy and distracted condition of that country, it is not believed that your presence there could have been of any service to the United States." Copy. DNA, RG59, Dip. Instr., vol. 12, p.144 (M77, R7).

From HENRY WHEATON, Copenhagen, no. 4, August 31, 1828. Because Denmark's severe quarantine regulations have hurt American commerce with the Baltic and "I have found it necessary ... to remonstrate against their operations in particular cases." Announces his success in achieving modification of the regulations on American ships coming from Cuba to Denmark. Encloses copies of correspondence concerning the quarantine regulations. ALS. DNA, RG59, Dip. Disp., Denmark, vol. 1B (M41, R3). Received November 7, 1828.

From ALEXANDER H. EVERETT, Madrid, no. 113, September 1, 1828. Reports that "I have occasionally in my interviews with M. Salmon [Manuel Gonzales Salmon] ... reminded him that I was still waiting for an answer" concerning a Convention for Mutual Indemnities [Everett to Clay, February 21, 1828]. Adds that he has not pressed the issue because "any resolution taken under the present disposition of the Govt. would be unfavorable"; also, "I have thought it more expedient to leave the matter temporarily as it is." Mentions that negotiations between Spain and England on the same subject may soon be concluded with Spain agreeing to pay "a fixed sum to be distributed ... among the claimants." Mentions that Count Ofalia, who has been negotiating with the British, "will probably be appointed [Spanish] Ambassador at Paris in the place of the Duke of San Carlos [Jose de Caravajaly Manrique], who lately died very suddenly."

Reports: "Strong rumours have been circulated here ... of a favorable change in the policy of the British Cabinet in regard to Spanish America, and of intimations given by the Duke of Wellington [Arthur Wellesley] ... that he would aid Spain with troops & money in an attempt to establish one of the Infantes on the throne of Mexico." Finds this difficult to credit even though the Duke of Wellington is friendly to Spain. Believes "the present system is too popular" in Great Britain "to be hastily abandoned by any Minister whatever may be his personal feelings." Speculates that Wellington has thrown out hints on this subject "to facilitate the negotiation on the Indemnities."

States that he has told Salmon that a settlement of claims with Britain would be viewed by the U.S. "as a precedent authorizing us to expect an immediate termination of our negotiations on the same subject." To this, Salmon "replied that he did not consider the two cases as exactly parallel." Notes that the House of Representatives will probably take up the matter next session and predicts that "any demonstration of activity at home would enable me to carry through the negotiation without much difficulty." Suggests possible actions by the U.S. Government which might facilitate a speedy conclusion of the matter. ALS. DNA, RG59, Dip. Disp., Spain, vol. 29 (M31, R29). Received November 1, 1828.

From **WILLIAM B. LAWRENCE,** London, no. 57, September 2, 1828. Submits his resignation as Chargé d'Affaires on the arrival of James Barbour as U.S. Minister to Britain and refuses offer, conveyed by Barbour, to resume his position as Secretary of Legation. States that "circumstances, peculiar to my situation and that of my family . . . render it highly desirable that I should retire as soon as possible from the Mission." Expresses gratitude for the offer, but says he has Barbour's permission to leave when Barbour is presented to King George IV or on October 1, 1828, if "that ceremony be longer delayed." ALS. DNA, RG59, Dip. Disp., Great Britain, vol. 35 (M30, R31). No date of receipt.

From **JOHN C. PEARSON,** Urbana, Ohio, September 2, 1828. Requests an enclosed letter be forwarded to William S. Wetmore, administrator of the late James Cooley's estate in Peru. As one of the executors of Cooley's will, Pearson seeks information on his "affairs in Lima."

On political matters, comments: "The cause of the Administration and civil liberty [are?] prospering in this section of the country and I believe throughout the State, the croaking of the opposition to the contrary notwithstanding." ALS. DNA, RG59, Misc. Letters (M179, R66).

From **LEWIS SUMMERS,** Kanawha Court House, Va. [W. Va.]., September 2, 1828. Reports: "I think Mr. Adams' prospects are improving in the Western part of our State, but not to that extent which would authorize a reliance on the voting. From West Pennsylvania I have rece[ive]d very chering & promising comments of the probable results of the fall elections." ALS. DNA, RG59, A. and R. (M531, R8). Summers's intelligence was faulty. Transmontane Virginia cast a landslide 4,811 votes for Jackson to 1,906 for Adams. Lynchburg *Virginian,* November 2, 1828; Stanley B. Parsons, *et al., United States Congressional Districts, 1788–1841,* (Westport, Ct., 1978), 281. The results in Transmontane Pennsylvania also reflected this trend, with Jackson defeating Adams by a 26,252 to 11,022 vote margin. Philadelphia *United States Gazette,* November 19, 1828.

From **ALEXANDER BURTON,** Cadiz, September 4, 1828. Reports that the British government has sent three survivors of the *Morning Star* to Cadiz to identify pirates being held captive on suspicion of having plundered that ship and several others. Relates account of the witnesses' visits to the prison in Cadiz and to Gibraltar where they were able to identify eight of the pirates. Notes that the Spanish government has directed the Tribunal of the Marine to take exclusive jurisdiction of the case. Encloses a letter on the subject from Alexander H. Everett, the American Minister at Madrid. ALS. DNA, RG59, Cons. Disp., Cadiz, vol. 4 (M-T186, R4). Received November 19, 1828.

From JAMES W. DENNY   Frankfort, September 4, 1828
[Forwards recommendations received at Frankfort supporting John J. Crittenden for appointment to the U.S. Supreme Court. States that if Crittenden receives the appointment he (Denny) will become an applicant for the post of U.S. District Attorney. Continues:]

Our Governor [Thomas Metcalfe] entered upon the discharge of the duties of his station the day before yesterday—the former Gov [Joseph Desha] left town yesterday & dined at Georgetown with Mr. [William T.] Barry with a concourse of their friends—drank toasts & Barry made a speech—The appointment of Secretary has been offered to Mr. [George] Robertson[1] he has not however been heard from, he will, no doubt accept—

The Jacksonians have a majority in the house, the Senate is either equally divided, or else they have a majority of one in that body[2]—It is their determination, I have been informed, to turn out every officer favorable to the admn over whom they have any controul, and where the elections may not depend on them, their design is to reduce the Salaries so low as to compel a resignation—

They have even done me the honor to threaten that the contemptible salary which I rece[i]ve shall be reduced to $50.[3]—[Jacob] Swigert is to be placed on the civil list—

The late election has disclosed to us our strength—it may be considered as certain that Barry ran up to the strength of Jackson—The old court Jackson men did support him & I am well assured that he recd. as many admn. votes as did Metcalfe Jackson votes—

We are preparing in good earnest & using all possible diligence & industry for the great battle in Novr   Our arrangements & plans will be calculated to bring the people to the polls, if we succeed in this our triumph is certain—We are aware of the importance of the contest & will not for a moment intermit our exertions—[4]

ALS. DNA, RG59, A. and R. (MR1).   1. *BDAC.*   2. Clay to Whittlesey, August 15, 1828.   3. As Attorney General of Kentucky.   4. In another letter of the same date, Denny enclosed additional recommendations in favor of Crittenden. *Ibid.*

From FRANCIS M. DIMOND, Port au Prince, September 4, 1828. Reports being "cordialy received in my capacity of Commercial Agent." Mentions that the Haitian government is becoming more liberal toward foreigners and that on January 1, 1829, Haitian ships which are now paying one half duties "will pay the same as other Nations (France excepted)." ALS. DNA, RG59, Cons. Disp., Cap Haitian, vol. 6 (M9, R6). Received September 28, 1828.

To JAMES ERWIN   White Sulphur Springs, Va.,
                                           September 4, 1828
I was exceedingly distressed, on my arrival here last evening, by the perusal of your letter of the 19h. Ulto. I had not before heard of the illness of Mrs. Clay and James [Brown Clay], nor of the severe affliction

which you and poor Anne [Brown Clay Erwin] have been visited with. I fear she has borne it ill. The fact of the anxious apprehensions which poor Julia [D. Erwin] excited, from her birth [4:571], and throughout her life, must have heightened her distress. Tell her that she must bear with fortitude and philosophy this dispensation of Providence. Her innocent child is no doubt happy, and has escaped from an existence which, in its best forms, is full of care and vexation.

The state of my health, though improved, is such as to still require some nursing. For that purpose I intend to remain here about ten days, unless advices from the City should hurry me away. I wish much to see you and Anne, prior to your return. How is that to be accomplished? Can you not both remain with us this fall and winter? Such an arrangement would be a source of the greatest happiness to me, and I have no doubt to Mrs. Clay. If that be impracticable, can you not remain at the City until my return? If you determine to leave it by what route will you travel? Should you decide to go this way, I think you will have no difficulty in obtaining a passage in a Steam boat at the mouth of Guyandotte. I went and returned in that way. The river was still boatable, when I landed from the Talisman on friday last, and it was expected to continue so throughout the summer. If you quit the City before my return let me know your route. The best is to this place to keep below. the Blue ridge and come by Lynchburg, or to cross it between Charlottesville and Staunton. The road through the [Shenandoah] valley by Winchester is very rough.

I wish to see you not merely for the gratification of meeting you, but to consult you respecting Mathers' bonds [5:1019-20]. I have some thought of crediting the Estate with them, at their just value, and appropriating them to my own use.

You will have heard of the events in K.[1] My belief is that there is no ground to fear Mr. Adams obtaining the vote of that State in Novr.

ALS. THi.   1. Clay to Whittlesey, August 15, 1828.

From JOHN G. MARTIN   Paris, Ky., September 4, 1828
[With reference to the appointment of a Kentuckian to fill the seat on the U.S. Supreme Court vacated by the death of Justice Robert Trimble, remarks that "It is to be regretted there should be so much division in our state on the subject, as is likely to follow." Suggests that Adams make no nomination for the post "until Congress meet." Continues:]

But little has occured in Kentucky since you left it—In the election of Gen—[Thomas] Metcalfe as Governor, the friends of order & civil rule have gained a great victory—We still however anticipate a severe contest next fall but I feel pretty sanguine that Mr Adams will get the vote of Kentucky—The warm partizans of Gen Jackson here, have in losing [William T.] Barry, lost all that was desirable to them—They have lost the patronage Mr Barry would have had, had he been elected, and of course the great influence they would have had—Under [Joseph] Desha every county had a few *little big men* who must be consulted upon every petition to remit a fine &c [illeg.] write letters to the Gov:—Collectively then that party have very little interest in the election of Gen Jackson—

Nor do I believe the Jackson party will use near the exertion in Novr which they did in & previous to August—But, not choosing to trust too far, the administration party here through the medium of the county committees of vigilence—otherwise intend to have every voter at the polls in Novr—This is far as I can learn is the case every where in Kentucky—

ALS. DNA, RG59, A. and R. (MR3).

To JOHN QUINCY ADAMS
White Sulphur Springs, Va., September 5, 1828

I returned to this place the evening before the last, and I propose stopping here eight or ten days to confirm the re-establishment of my health, prior to my return to the City.

The K. Election did not, in all its particulars, result as I last wrote you.[1] But the main object, the election of [Thomas] Metcalfe, was effected, and that, with its train of necessary consequences, will, in my opinion, ensure success in November. That single fact overturns the clamor and the vituperation of the last three and a half years, founded on his alleged violation of the will of the people of K. in his vote for you [4:79]. On a fair appeal to them a majority of the whole people express, by necessary implication, their approbation of that vote. Coupled with the other fact that my old district has three times (the last by an augmented majority) expressed its satisfaction with my conduct, the bargain story may be considered fully quashed.

Judge [Robert] Trimble of the Supreme Court is dead. I think it will be advisable to postpone the appointment of his Successor. until November. I believe there will be no necessity for one earlier, the first Court commencing, in Kentucky, in that month.

ALS. MHi–Adams Papers, Letters Received (MR487).   1. Clay to Adams, August 7, 1828; see, Clay to Whittlesey, August 15, 1828.

From JAMES BARBOUR, London, no. 1, September 5, 1828. Reports his arrival and first meeting with the Earl of Aberdeen, George Gordon-Hamilton, the British Secretary of State for Foreign Affairs. States that Aberdeen inquired "if the arrangement entered into with Mr. [William B.] Lawrence relative to the North Eastern boundary had been received in the United States, and if . . . it had been accepted." Says that he assured Aberdeen it had not yet been received when he left for Britain. Adds that he asked if the King of the Netherlands, William I, would serve as arbiter, and was told "he would doubtless find great pleasure in acting as Umpire between us."

Notes that he has not yet been presented to King George IV who is out of town, but that Aberdeen has said "he will receive my communications independently of the ceremonial referred to." He therefore plans "to enter fully upon the functions of the mission so soon as my household shall be arranged."

Comments at length on the political situation in Europe, contending that the "tendency of Power here is to the old order of things as far as they will be tolerated." Believes that since the death of Prime Minister

George Canning "liberal principles have ceased to prevail in the Councils of Great Britain." Concludes that the "present Administration is completely Tory, and . . . I deem it the strongest which has existed for years." Predicts that Sir Robert Peel, the Home Secretary, will soon leave the Ministry.

Requests copies of Albert Gallatin's instructions [5:440-78] so that he will have them for reference in future negotiations. Expresses regret that William B. Lawrence is leaving the position as Secretary of the Legation and says it is because of "the inadequacy of his compensation . . . to which is added the repugnance to a retrogression in his position [from Chargé d'Affaires to Secretary of Legation]." States that he is substituting his son, James Barbour, Jr., as Secretary and proposes his permanent appointment to that position. LS. DNA, RG59, Dip. Disp., Great Britain, vol. 36 (M30, R32). Received October 13, 1828. See Manning, *Diplomatic Correspondence . . . Canadian Relations,* 2:763; also Lawrence to Clay, June 6, and June 22, 1828.

From THOMAS L. L. BRENT, Lisbon, no. 85, September 7, 1828. Reports receiving from the State Department a dispatch of July 24 [see below] in which "I learn that the resolution I had adopted of suspending all diplomatick intercourse with the new government that should proceed from the occupation of the throne of Portugal by Don Miguel; and await the instructions of my government—had met the approbation of the President." Regrets this was not accomplished as "opportunely" as the President wished. ALS. DNA, RG59, Dip. Disp., Portugal, vol. 8 (M43, R7). Received October 27, 1828.

On September 9, 1828, no. 86, Thomas Brent reported communicating the dispatch of July 24, which he had received from Daniel Brent at the State Department, to the Viscount of Santarem so that any impression created by the timing of the suspension of diplomatic intercourse would not be regarded as "a disposition to interfere even the most remotely into the internal concerns of Portugal." *Ibid.*

From SAMUEL MIFFLIN, Philadelphia, September 7, 1828. Reports that in Pennsylvania "your friends, are making every effort to overcome preexisting prejudices & altho', their opponents are loud and *apparently* confident, of success, I think, the indications of their disappointment, are very strong—" Believes the appointment of Joseph Hopkinson of New Jersey as District Judge "would have the happiest effect, upon our federal friends, who have been & are still, feared by the ultras, of their party—, with the truth that Mr. A[dams], will continue his system of exclusion, notwithstanding he may owe his reelection, to the federal party." Argues that the time has come for Adams "to shew himself, & give us, a fair opportunity to Judge of his intentions, respecting our party," and hopes that Clay will support the Hopkinson appointment. Assures Clay that the influence of Hopkinson "was the moving cause of the junction of the two parties, in those counties, heretofore known, as federal—Such as Delaware Chester, Lancaster & the City of Phila.—" Is certain that Hopkinson's appointment will have a salutary effect upon "the contest of the day." ALS. DNA, RG59, A. and R. (MR2). Hopkinson [see *BDAC*], a former two-term Congressman, was appointed judge of the United States District Court for the Eastern District of Pennsylvania in October, 1828, and served until 1842.

The party system in Pennsylvania was very confused, with the two major parties—the Federalists and the Democrats—divided into factions, each trying to win control of their respective parties. Support for both Adams and Jackson in 1824 cut across factional and party lines until "the Family" and "the Amalgamation" factions of the Democratic party converged behind Jackson and began to win county elections in traditionally Federalist counties. They succeeded so well that in 1828 Jackson won the usually Federalist Chester County 3,835 to 3,535; Lancaster County 5,186 to 3,719; Philadelphia 12,017 to 6,200; and lost Delaware County 953 to 1,164. Jackson carried Pennsylvania 101,652 to 50,848 for Adams. See Klein, *Pennsylvania Politics 1817–1832*, 188-251; and Weston, *The Presidential Election of 1828*, 73-4.

From JOSE SILVERSTRE REBELLO, Washington, September 8, 1828. Encloses a copy of a paragraph in the Baltimore *Commercial Chronicle* of September 8, "by which it is clearly perceived that the Buenos Ayran Naval Officer [Cesar] Fournier is actually cruising on the coasts of the U. States to aggregate new vessels of war."

Protests "the public infraction of the rights of neutrality which the Government of U.S. professes to maintain" in the war between Brazil and Buenos Aires. Declares that whatever damages are caused by Fournier and his squadron against Brazil "will be indubitably reclaimed" from the U.S. LS, in Portuguese, with trans. in State Dept. file. DNA, RG59, Notes from Brazilian Legation, vol. 1 (M49, R1). On September 15, 1828, from Washington, Rebello sent a similar letter of protest, concerning the *Bolivar,* cruising off the coast of Long Island. *Ibid.*

From EDWARD RUMSEY   Morganfield, Ky., September 9, 1828
I have been informed by letters from Frankfort that Mr. [John J.] Crittenden would be proposed to fill the vacancy occasioned by the death of Judge [Robert] Trimble, and have enclosed a letter signed by the Bar of this district, which, if he should be an Applicant you will please use &c—

The election in this state, altho' it has not terminated so decisively favorable,[1] as I had hoped, has yet satisfied us, that we can, by reasonable activity & exertion, succeed in November; & appearances indicate that every effort will be made in this section of country—Personal considerations out of the question—and with me I admit they are very powerful—I consider the approaching election, on broad national principles, more important than any which has ever occurred in the republic. If the result be such as I hope, it will be a great triumph of reason over passion—of truth & wisdom over error & folly—If the issue be other wise, I shall still hope, & hope with confidence, that before the end of four years, the mists of delusion & prejudice raised by envious calumniators & unprincipled demagogues will have passed away, and that a

460

disabused country in confering her highest honor, will afford some compensation for the merciless persecution & base slanders with which you have been so accrimoniously & perseveringly assailed....

ALS. DNA, RG59, A. and R. (MR1).   1. Clay to Whittlesey, August 15, 1828.

From RICHARD H. CHINN   Lexington, September 10, 1828
[Recommends John J. Crittenden for appointment to the U.S. Supreme Court. Continues:]

It is said [George] Robinson [*sic,* Robertson] will accept the appointment of [Ky.] Secretary of State. It is believed that [Joseph] Desha was much disposed to hold on to the office of Governor (because [Thomas] Metcalfe had not taken the duelling oath), and all he wanted was the countenance of his friends—[William T.] Barry had a dinner given him in Geo Town [Georgetown, Ky.] a week since I was present they dined at a tavern where I stopped & did not chose to leave there. 26 sat down to the first table among whom were 3 or 4 professional black legs with Desha, [Amos] Kendall, [Francis P.] Blair &c. &c. in a word the whole fry of Lex & Frankfort of choice spirits—After dinner they went to the Courthouse rang the bell, and Barry spoke—I did not hear him, but was told he pronounced a highly wrought eulogium upon himself and a violent & virulent phillippic against his enemies—It has been aptly styled his funeral Service—They hold today a metting of delegates at Harrodsburgh [*sic*] to devise ways & means for Novr.—My majority did not hold out at the last election, but I shall struggle the more to produce it in the fall.[1]—There is evidently a favourable feeling prevailing Since the Election. The [Aaron] Burr business is operating upon a few. But more is to be effected by reason of Metcalfes election and a division in their [Jackson's] ranks about Senator.[2] There is a very great number of them who expect to be at the Mercy of the Executive within the Succeeding four years—And they are *politely* inclined towards those whom they expect may exercise any influence in that quarter.

Col. [Richard M.] Johnson is very apprehensive that the admn party will unite upon some Jackson man & oust him from the Senate—So that he will be upon his good behaviour. The Pope's[3] for Jno or Judge [John P.] Oldham's success[4] will also be somewhat reserved—All things considered I cannot for a moment doubt the result in Novr; But it can only be secured by great vigilance.

On behalf of the Centre Committee I wrote to [Thomas] Curry to procure from the Offices an account of all the moneys received from the Govt. by the Johnsons—Jas. & Richd. M.[,] Ward & Johnson[,] Johnson & Taylor, Sebrees & Johnsons—Joel, Edward P. Jno. T.—Wm.—Darwin—Pay—pensions—Congress. Army, Contracts for Supplies—Post office Contracts &c. &c. and I have not heard from him upon the subject.[5]

I think it would be a very important document if it is practicable to procure it.

ALS. DNA, RG59, A. and R. (MR1).   1. Chinn, secretary of the Fayette County committee for the reelection of Adams, had not delivered the anti-Jackson vote at the state elections on August 6 in the expected numbers.   2. The growing division in Kentucky's Jackson ranks resulted, in December, 1828, in the defeat in the Legislature, of incumbent pro-Jackson U.S. Senator Richard M. Johnson and the election to his seat of George M. Bibb. Orval W. Baylor, *John Pope—Kentuckian*, (Cynthiana, Ky., 1943], 318–22; John S. Goff, "The Last Leaf: George Mortimer Bibb," *RKHS* (October, 1961), 59:336–7.   3. Perhaps a pun on "hopes," at the expense of John Pope [1:254].   4. Clay to Whittlesey, August 15, 1828.   5. James, Joel, John T., and William were all brothers of Richard M. Johnson. William Ward, Johnson's brother-in-law, and Benjamin Taylor were partners with James Johnson in supplying the U.S. Army, under government contract, during and after the War of 1812. Edward P. Johnson, son of James, was the nephew of Richard M. Johnson. Uriel Sebree, "a near kinsman" of the Johnsons, who had fought with Richard M. at the Battle of the Thames in October, 1813, was a member of the controversial Yellowstone Expedition. See 2:598–9, 605, 799–800; 3:89, also, James A. Padgett, "The Life and Letters of James Johnson of Kentucky," *RKHS* (October, 1937), 35:301–08; Leland W. Meyer, *The Life and Times of Colonel Richard M. Johnson of Kentucky*, 189–206; William H. Perrin, *History of Scott County* (Georgetown. Ky., 1964), 23.

From SAMUEL LARNED, Santiago de Chile, September 10, 1828. Describes at length a "mutinous military movement" consisting of a regiment of infantry and a squadron of cavalry at San Fernando, Chile, which marched upon the capital on July 17. Despite the valiant armed resistance of Vice President [Acting President] Francisco Pinto with government troops, the revolters entered Santiago the following day. States that the mutinous troops demanded pay, discharges, and the resignation of Pinto, who declared "that he would suffer himself to be cut to pieces before he would descend from the presidential chair." Mentions large public demonstrations in favor of the government and against the rebel occupation. With "public feeling" totally against them, reports that the "revolted chiefs" submitted and received a pardon. This ended the disturbance.

Submits a copy of the new Constitution, sanctioned by the Constituent Congress for promulgation on September 18, which shall divide the Congress into two houses—the Senate and Chamber of Deputies.

Is informed that Grand Marshall Andres Santa-Cruz has just been accredited by Chile as the minister from Peru. Learns as well that General Jose de la Riva-Aguero, former President of Peru, "a person of much notoriety in this quarter," has arrived from France. Speculates that the presence of these two men, both hostile to the present regime in Peru, "together with movements on the side of Colombia," seem to indicate threats to Peru's President Jose Lamar, now "very much indisposed."

Concerning Peruvian-Bolivian relations, notes that a treaty has been ratified by which "General [Antonio Jose de] Sucre and the Colombian troops are forthwith to evacuate Bolivia."

With reference to the reassembly of the dissolved Bolivian Constituent Congress "for the purpose of receiving the resignation of President Sucre," states that the National Assembly will be called "for the revision or rejection of the Constitution forced upon the country by the Colombian bayonets."

Hopes that the treaty negotiations proposed by Chile and transferred by them to Washington, will be successfully concluded there.

Concludes by remarking that he has had several conferences with the Chilean Foreign Minister, Carlos Rodriguez, about American claims, and that "he has been made to understand that the business is not to be allowed to slumber, or be forgotten." ALS. DNA, RG59, Dip, Disp., Chile, vol. 3 (M–T2, R3). Received February 25, 1829. For the Peruvian–Bolivian peace treaty, see Parry, *Treaty Series*, 79:325-8.

From **SAMUEL ISRAEL,** Cap Haitien, September 11, 1828. Encloses copy of a letter from Joseph–Balthasar Inginac, Secretary General of the Republic of Haiti, which shows that their non-acknowledgement of U.S. Commercial Agents "arises more from a Punctilio *not observed* [by] our Government towards the Haytien Government & by them look'd for." Adds that "it is essentially necessary for [the] interest of our Countrymen that we should be acknowledged," because cases "frequently occur that considerable property is jeopardized . . . and unless we are officially known we can" make no claim. ALS. DNA, RG59, Cons. Disp., Cap Haitien, vol. 6 (M9, R6). Received October 5, 1828.

From **JOSE M. MONTOYA,** Washington, September 11, 1828. Informs Clay of "the sudden death of Dr. Pablo Obregon . . . which happened yesterday." States that Obregon's funeral will take place this evening, and hopes that the American government will pay funeral honors to him. LS, in Spanish, with trans. in State Dept. file. DNA, RG59, Notes from Mexican Legation, vol. 1 (M54, R1).

From **WILLIAM TUDOR,** Rio de Janeiro, no. 108, September 11, 1828. Discusses the case of the U.S. Schooner *Haran* which was captured by the Buenos Airean blockading squadron. States that he sees "no plausible reason for demanding restitution" because the ship was not supposed to go to the blockaded shore.

Forwards a translation of the peace convention between Brazil and Buenos Aires.

Reports that Peru "is on the verge of anarchy, & destined like all the republican States of South America to be the prey of factions for a long period." States that the Congress in Peru acted in "the most shameless manner, the last two months of its session" with Dr. Francisco Javier Luna Pizarro's faction losing its majority through "the intrigues of [Ignacio] Alvares, a daring, sordid demagogue, & who there is little doubt is secretly an agent of [Simon] Bolivar's." Discusses an intrigue to separate the three southern departments of Peru and "form an union with the Provinces of . . . Bolivia," and says this might not be fatal to Peru "if the three southern departments of Colombia which naturally belong to Peru & were treacherously forced by Bolivar to aggregate themselves to the former, could be reunited to Peru"; but, if not, Peru "will be a very feeble State." Contends that these movements are noted by Simon Bolivar's partisans "with the hope that the whole will again fall into his power." Repeats ultimatum which Bolivar has issued to Peru which is "unjust and degrading." Contends: "It is impossible to execrate too strongly the unprincipled ambition of Bolivar," who is not "capable of appreciating the immortal renown that was in his power—it has involved his own country & all Spanish South America in the deepest calamities & may even prove its eventual ruin." Adds that Bolivar is anxious to leave

Colombia "where he is detested, except by the military and return to the luxurious climate & sensualities of Lima, & govern that country despotically." Believes Peru need have no fear of fighting Colombia if General Jose de Lamar is able to lead its army, but Lamar's health is poor and it is feared "he cannot long hold out." Complains that "Bolivar has always unfortunately been able by his deep hypocrisy, his ardent vehemence, & his artful representations to gain all the Foreign Agents to his side, which has naturally served to discourage the republican party in Colombia." Hopes General William Henry Harrison, the new minister to Colombia, "may have been ordered to sustain the patriots of Colombia, & animate them in defense of their country." ALS. DNA, RG59, Dip. Disp., Brazil, vol. 6 (M121, R8). Letter marked "*Confidential.*" Received December 3, 1828.

From JAMES BROWN, Paris, September 12, 1828. Itemizes ladies gloves and hats and the costs thereof purchased by his wife for Mrs. Richard Rush and Mrs. Peter B. Porter. Reports that these have recently been packed and shipped via Le Havre. Notes that Mrs. Brown "has been in town expressly to execute these commissions as she is so consciencious in cases of this kind that she would not permit it to be done by any other person." Comments on her continuing "very delicate state of health."

Concludes: "We wait with great impatience to hear from Kentucky elections and even should these turn out as we wish it is still doubtful whether New York will give the number necessary to elect Mr. Adams. Pennsylvania has changed considerably but will I fear vote for Jackson." ALS. DLC–HC (DNA, M212, R3). Printed in *LHQ,* 24:1126–7.

From ROBERT MONROE HARRISON, St. Bartholomew, September 12, 1828. Reports that the local authorities have "assumed the right to themselves of making ordinances ... which greatly conflict with the interests of American citizens and ... in direct opposition to the spirit and meaning of the recent treaty between" Sweden and the U.S. [6:761–2]. Complains that officials of the colony, owned by the King of Sweden, Charles XIV, are paid such "miserable salaries" that they are forced "to make the best of their situation, which they never fail to do in every possible way." Says he especially opposes their fees for granting passports to distressed American seamen who are being sent home. Feels "it is my duty hereafter to resist the charge altogether." Asks that a formal protest be made in Stockholm.

Deplores also the action of the Judge of St. Bartholomew who is usurping the powers and fees of the U.S. Consul by taking "complete control over American vessels Entering into this place in distress, or for sale, as regards documents &c." Reports that the Judge has remarked "that he and the Mayor had been directed by the King to receive me as Consul, but that I was to exercise no rights or duties that would conflict with the interests of any officer in the colony of which they are to be the sole Judges." Discusses recent instances of U.S. citizens' participating in the slave trade and in privateering in the West Indies. ALS. DNA. RG59, Cons. Disp., St. Bartholomew, vol. 1 (M72, R1). No date of receipt.

Writes Clay from St. Bartholomew on September 27, transmitting an account of his "mission or tour through the British West India colonies," and calling particular attention to his correspondence from Antigua. Suggests that if Anglo–American negotiations regarding colonial intercourse are renewed, "it would be advisable . . . to have the powers of our Consuls clearly defined by treaty." *Ibid.* Received October 24, 1828.

Writes again on November 5, reporting the facts of the "prosecution and condemnation of the crew of the Piratical Schooner called 'the Las Damas Argentinas.'" Also calls attention to his dispatches of June 25 and September 25 [*sic,* 27] for which he has not received replies. *Ibid.* Received November 26, 1828.

From JOHN HOWARD MARCH, Madeira, September 12, 1828. Reports that "an expedition from Portugal, consisting of ten men of war with about fifteen hundred troops has taken possession of this Island in the name of D[om] Miguel without meeting with hardly any resistance from D[om] Pedro's [Pedro IV] party." Adds that an American, one Watts, has been imprisoned with a large number of Pedro's adherents. ALS. DNA, RG59, Cons. Disp., Funchal, vol. 1 [M–T205, R–T1). Received October 25, 1828.

On September 26, Charles W. Dabney reported from Fayal, Azores, that "these islands with the exception of Terceira have recognized the Majesty of Don Miguel the first." At Terceira, Azores, "there are about six hundred regular troops who have possession of the Fortress" and will not surrender except by order of Pedro. ALS. DNA, RG59, Cons. Disp., Fayal, vol. 1 (M–T203, R1). Received October 30, 1828.

From JAMES BROWN, Paris, France, September 13, 1828. Reports at length on the Russo–Turkish War, noting that "no decided advantages have been gained on either side." States that the Russian Emperor, Nicholas I, "intended about the first of this month to resume the command of his army at the siege of Varna," and "it is believed that this fortress cannot long hold out against a combined attack by sea and land." Adds that Constantinople is the place where "the Porte intends to repair in the last result, & perish in their ruins, rather than permit the Infidels to profane his Capital." Expresses skepticism at the Emperor's claim that he has no desire to conquer territory. Instead, "it will naturally occur to Nicholas that the best security for the future will be found in retaining the command of the Dardanelles."

States that the Jesuits "are losing ground daily, & many of them are preparing to leave France . . . & it is believed that numbers will fix themselves in the United States." Believes "the ordinances excluding them from public instruction in France will be executed."

Mentions "Mr. [John Adams] Smith arrived here a few days ago" and that "Mr. [William Armand] Barnet who discharged the duties of Secretary of the Legation for four and a half months has agreed that the Department shall decide the amount to be allowed him for his services." ALS, DNA, RG59, Dip. Disp., France, vol. 23 (M34, R26). Received October 25, 1828. Copy in DNA, RG84, Foreign Service Posts, France (MR3, frames 7–8). Letter marked "Private."

From JOHN M. FORBES, Buenos Aires, no. 62, September 13, 1828. Discusses his previous dispatches concerning settlement of the *Ruth* case. Recalls that in dispatch no. 57, dated May 2, 1828, he had reported that the favorable decision of the second court had been appealed by the captors to the High Court of Justice. States that since the "whole affair slept in the hands of Dr. Don Gregorio Tagle," a member of the court who had kept the papers for more than two months, he wrote to the Minister of Government, Jose Roxas, "remonstrating in strong terms against the arbitrary delay, denouncing Dr. Tagle by name, and invoking the authority of the Minister to accelerate the termination" of the case. Adds that six days later he received a dispatch from the State Department ordering him "to make an immediate and most urgent demand of full satisfaction and indemnity in behalf of the owners of the Ruth and her cargo." Reports in detail his various frustrations in dealing unsuccessfully with Buenos Airean authorities.

Continues on September 17: Announces that he is "happy to state that we yesterday received a sentence for the liberation of the [*Ruth*'s] cargo, together with such amount of damages as we shall be enabled to prove."

Mentions that the most important event in Buenos Aires is news of the peace treaty with Brazil. LS. DNA, RG59, Dip. Disp., Argentina, vol. 3 (M69, R4). Received December 3, 1828. See also Espil, *Once Anos en Buenos Aires,* 497–500, and Manning, *Diplomatic Correspondence... Latin American Nations,* 1:663. The State Department dispatch which Forbes received on May 8, 1828, has not been found.

On October 2, in dispatch No. 63, Forbes sent Clay a translation of the Buenos Airean–Brazilian peace treaty [Parry, *Treaty Series,* 79:1–11], and noted that its ratification had been authorized by Brazil. Also reported that the Brazilian blockade had been raised, and that "an active renewal of foreign commerce" was expected. ALS. DNA, RG59, Dip. Disp., Argentina, vol. 3 (M69, R4). Received December 8, 1828.

From FRANCIS T. BROOKE
Near Fredericksburg, Va.,
September 15, 1828

It is Seldom I permit myself to Say anything to you in behalf of any one of my relations, but the affairs of my brother in Law Mr George W Spotswood[1] for whom I entertain the most affectionate feelings, compel him to Seek employment in [one] of the Departmts at Washington for his qualifications I refer you to his letters from Mr [James] Madison & Mr [James] Monroe who are tristees of the University of Virginia have had ample opportunity to know him intimately well I know him to possess great honour and lofty feelings and anything you can do for him will confer a lasting obligation on your friend....

ALS. DNA, RG59, A. and R. (MR3).   1. On September 19 Spotswood wrote to Clay, asking for employment, because "I find it necessary for the advancement of my Six Sons ... to seek a more lucrative situation." *Ibid.* For the erratic and tempestuous George Washington Spotswood, distant cousin of Washington, manager of a hotel near the University of Virginia, see P. A. Bruce, *History of the University of Virginia,* 2:222–4. He received no appointment.

466

From DANIEL MAYES   Frankfort, September 15, 1828

[Recommends John J. Crittenden for appointment to the U.S. Supreme Court and notes efforts to delay the resignations of two U.S. judges in Kentucky in order to "keep off the day of complaint and excitement, and keep in suspence all the expectants of succession to their offices." Continues:]

To some extent the effect of the election of Governor [Thomas Metcalfe] is already felt. Some, indeed not a few little lawyers, who have some influence in their neighbourhoods, and who are as destitute of patriotism as of merit, have long been looking to a commonwealth attorneyship or the bench of the Circuit Court. They believed that by the Success of Mr. [William T.] Barry they could raise themselves to this *ne plus ultra* of their earthly ambition and were most clamorous Jackson men. They have now become entirely inactive and begin in some degree to speak very respectfully of the present admn &C.

On yesterday we had a laborious sitting of the whole day. and matured a system of orgainzation which I fondly hope will bring to the polls the whole of our strength, and of a strength now increasing. Every member of the committee resident in this place is now busily engaged in starting into existance the proposed organization. The *modus operandi* I cannot trespass so far on your time as to explain, but it is efficient & will I doubt not prove effectual.

Mr. [John] Pope is said to be very busy in the Jackson cause. He says (as it is reported) that he will not oppose [Richard M.] Johnson. We think he will if he hopes for success. and he is not difficult to persuade that he can succeed. Most of the admn. men would I think prefer Johnson. If Mr. Adams succeeds we hope for an admn. senator. You may have noticed that a great Jackson Meeting is to take place here today. It is now about 12 oclock and no one has come in. The wire workers are very busy but the people cant be gotten to dance. They advertised that Mr. Barry would make a speech. This has not drawn the expected concourse. Mr. Barry is not here nor is he now expected. The Jackson Managers are most active, but the administration voters seem to be most alert. I fully believe we will beat them by a large majority

Pardon my having so lengthly & [. . .]¹ unnecessarily trespassed on your time. I supposed some of these things might be & doubtless are interesting tho your advices would probably supersede the usefulness of any intelligence from me.

ALS. DNA, RG59, A. and R. (MR1).   1. Manuscript torn. Possibly one word missing.

From JOEL R. POINSETT, Mexico, no. 149, September 15, 1828. Transmits two notes received from Juan de Dios Canedo, Mexican Secretary of Foreign Relations, "on the subject of the instructions for the conduct of their cruisers." [These would allow Mexican privateers to seize goods on the high seas being shipped to belligerents in neutral ships.] Comments: "The Mexican Congress has declared that all the laws and ordinances of Spain, shall be considered valid and in full force, whenever they are not repealed by especial acts and are not repugnant to the constitution." Contends that "it would be unwise to suffer the principles contained in these instructions to be carried into execution against our commerce," and argues that "it will . . . be equally just and politic . . . [for the U.S.] to detain and send in for trial, any Mexican privateer which shall have taken goods belonging to a belligerent, out of an American vessel for trial on the pretext of her having on board goods of a belligerent. . . ." ALS. DNA, RG59, Dip. Disp., Mexico, vol. 4 (M97, R5). Received November 22, 1828.

From FRANCISCO TACON, Philadelphia, September 15, 1828. States his continuing objections to the activities of Capt. Cesar Fournier of Buenos Aires and his sloop of war, the *Bolivar*. The vessel is now "anchored in Long–Pond [Fort Pond Bay, Long Island Sound], completely armed, and is engaged in recruiting seamen in New York itself." Objecting to this case and other alleged violations of U.S. neutrality toward Spain, urges Clay "to obtain from the President the orders and measures necessary to stop their armaments and to punish . . . those who attempt to disturb the peace and harmony . . . between the two Nations." LS, in Spanish, with trans. in State Dept. file. DNA, RG59, Notes from Spanish Legation, vol. 9 (M59, R–T12).

From ALEXANDER H. EVERETT, Madrid, no. 114, September 17, 1828. Reports that "A number of changes have lately been made in the composition of the Spanish diplomatic body" but only two "are immediately interesting to the United States"—the appointment of Francisco de Paula Quadrado as Secretary of the Legation at Philadelphia to replace Hilario Rivas y Salmon and Salmon's appointment as Undersecretary of State. States that the "ostensible motive for the new arrangements . . . is that of economy." Details these changes, among which is the naming of Court Ofalia as minister to France. Notes that Ofalia's appointment, as well as that of Francisco de Zea Bermudez as minister plenipotentiary to London "have given very general satisfaction to intelligent and judicious men." Discusses at length the diplomatic representatives of various European countries in Spain. ALS. DNA, RG59, Dip. Disp., Spain, vol. 29 (M31, R29). Received November 19, 1828.

From DANIEL MAYES, Frankfort, September 17, 1828. Encloses recommendations for the appointment of John J. Crittenden to the U.S. Supreme Court.

Reports, with reference to the coming Presidential election, "that we are very active and full of hope," and that "letters have been written to every prominent friend in almost every section of the state with a view to impart activity." ALS. DNA, RG59, A. and R. (MR1).

From JOEL R. POINSETT, Mexico, no. 151, September 17, 1828. Remarks that he "had hoped before this to have been able to give you an account of the result of the Presidential election, which produced so much excitment here, and which is likely to be attended with fatal consequences." Reports that "So far the result is much in favor of [General Gomez] Pedraza and has disappointed public expectation." Contends that "this result has been produced by the wealth of the [Masonic] Scotch party, and the unwarrantable employment of the armed forces. . . . The people are therefore highly indignant and in some States have appealed to arms, against the decisions of their Legislatures." Mentions that Santa Anna "is in arms in Vera Cruz," and that "Death to the European Spaniards, is a watch word which will rally round the standard of any adventurer four fifths of the population of Mexico." Believes Mexico is "on the eve of a civil war." ALS. DNA, RG59, Dip. Disp., Mexico, vol. 4 (M97, R5). Received November 22, 1828. For the bloody outcome of this election, see Gene M. Brack, *Mexico Views Manifest Destiny, 1821–1846: An Essay on the Origins of the Mexican War* (Albuquerque, 1975), 33-4.

From WILLIAM RADCLIFF, Lima, no. 3, September 17, 1828. Reports receiving a letter from the Minister of Foreign Affairs of Peru, Jose M. Galdiano, "announcing the blockade . . . of all the ports of Colombia on the Pacific." Concludes that war between Peru and Colombia now seems inevitable, and "From the sweeping paper blockade declared by this Government without power to enforce it, may be inferred what neutrals have to expect during the war, if they do not support their rights by force." Adds: "How far our squadron in this ocean, or one of similar force in its relief, will be adequate to that end, and to the general protection of our trade and property afloat in this ocean . . . is at least doubtful, and has to be well considered at home." Mentions that he has notified Peru "that a declaration of blockade without the application of power sufficient to enforce it, cannot be valid or of any effect; and that the true definition of blockade has been settled by our Government in various treaties, particularly in the one with Colombia, which will of course be our role in regard both to Peru and Colombia during their present contest."

Estimates that Peru can field "about eight thousand efficient troops," and notes that President Jose de Lamar of Peru has gathered his forces in the North where they are to be joined shortly by General Agustin Gamarra's forces from Bolivia. Has heard that Simon Bolivar has issued a Proclamation "tantamount to a declaration of war," that he is already at Guayaquil and is preparing to invade Peru. Predicts that Bolivar will triumph and will then unite Colombia, Bolivia, and Peru into either "a grand Empire" or "a confederated Republic." Concludes, however, that if Peru should prevail, she will enlarge her boundaries both in the North and in the Southeast.

Reports having an interview with Lamar and pressing on him the desirability of concluding a commercial treaty with the U.S. States that Lamar conceded that such a measure would be presented to the next session of Congress. ALS. DNA, Cons. Disp., Lima, vol. 2 (M154, R2). Received December 8, 1828. The United States did not sign a treaty of peace, friendship, commerce and navigation with the Peru–Bolivian Confederation until November 30, 1836.

From ALBERT GALLATIN, New York, September 18, 1828. Reports he has just returned from Boston where he selected large numbers of documents to be transcribed and authenticated. Foresees pressure to get the transcribing of all arbitration materials done by January 1, 1829, as required under the Convention [6:1100–01]. States that he has instructed William P. Preble to purchase copies whenever they are available "as any price they may cost will, exclusively of the time saved, be less than that of having manuscript copies made." Asks that Preble be instructed to join him in Washington in November. Requests also that the department ask the Governors of Pennsylvania, Maryland, Virginia, and Carolina for authentic and attested copies of the Proclamation of 1763 and the letter from British authorities transmitting same to the Governor of the Province, Sir Howard Douglas. ALS. DNA, RG76, Northeast Boundary (KyU., Special Roll, frames 87–9).

Preble wrote Clay on November 12 reporting that he had spent a week in Boston gathering maps and documents and would leave tomorrow for Washington. *Ibid.* (frame 96).

From CHRISTOPHER HUGHES, Brussels, September 18, 1828. Praises Clay for vindicating himself so nobly against the "vile slander" of his political enemies and lauds President Adams for his character, private habits, and decency. Reports that in Europe the violence of the presidential election in the U.S. has "not a little stricken confidence in our stability, and in the duration of our internal peace."

Remarks that he has "no very important news to write you," but continues at length to discuss the gossip and social activities of various Royal families in Europe. Hearing of the arrival of James Barbour in London, has written "suggesting to him such persons of the Corps. Dip. at London, as [I] know to be friendly to us, & may be useful to him." Has resisted the "urgent invitation" of Lafayette to visit him for fear it might "give new activity to the malice and flippancy of the opposition" party in Paris. Confides that "I happen to be no small personal favorite" of Count de la Ferronnays, the French Foreign Minister. Asks what the President wants him to do about Lafayette's invitation. Comments at length on the character and backgrounds of a number of political exiles from various nations who have gathered in Brussels for safety. Observes: "I am never disposed to think well of men, who leave their country, in a moment of danger. I know none of these Gentlemen!" ALS. DLC–HC (DNA, M212, R3).

From JOSE SILVESTRE REBELLO, Washington, September 18, 1828. Reports he has received a note from the State Department, dated September 17, in response to his note of September 15, stating that the U.S. government "would transmit to the Attorney General of the United States in New York [John Duer] the instructions to act with the Buenos Ayrean squadron, now at anchor on Long Island Sound."

Concerning the observation of the Laws of Nations with regard to American neutrality in the war between Brazil and Buenos Aires, expects the U.S. to order both its land officers and revenue cutters "to keep a good lookout on the said squadron and to capture the Sloop of War Bolivar, now called the 'Twenty Fifth of May.'" LS, in Portuguese, with trans. in State Dept. file. DNA, RG59, Notes from Brazilian Legation, vol. 1 (M49, R1).

On this same day, William Betts, writing from the U.S. Attorney General's Office in New York City, informed Clay that three Buenos Airean vessels, the *Bolivar* among them, were lying in Fort Pond Bay near Long Island, and that they were allegedly "in our waters augmenting their force in violation of the laws." Notes that at least two American seamen were on board the *Bolivar* under the impression that the vessel was "going on a whaling voyage." LS. DNA, RG59, Misc. Letters (M179, R66). For attorney William Betts, see *CAB*.

From ALEXANDER H. EVERETT, Madrid, no. 115, September 19, 1828. Transmits a communication from Manuel Gonzales Salmon, concerning piracy. Mentions that the goods which the pirates of the *Defensor de Pedro* had deposited at Corunna before wrecking at Cadiz probably came from the *Topaze* and "the necessary measures will be taken by the Consul at Cadiz [Alexander Burton] for securing, as far as may be practicable, the rights of our citizens." Praises Burton for securing the information which brought British witnesses to Spain to identify the pirates who had plundered the *Morning Star*.

Encloses a decree concerning trade between Spain and her American colonies. Reports that a ship carrying Maria da Gloria recently arrived at Gibraltar, probably on its way to Genoa where Maria will wait pending negotiations "on the subject of her marriage & succession to the crown of Portugal." ALS. DNA, RG59, Dip. Disp., Spain, vol. 29 (M31, R29). Received November 19, 1828. See, also, Burton to Clay, July 1 and Sept. 4, 1828; Everett to Clay, Sept. 19, 1828.

From HENRY MIDDLETON, St. Petersburg, no. 81, September 19, 1828. States that he has not heard from William B. Lawrence in London, but says that John J. Appleton, U.S. Chargé in Sweden, has reported that Lawrence and the British have "agreed upon an Arbiter [William I of the Netherlands]" for the Northeastern boundary controversy. Concludes "that objections must have been made by the British Cabinet to *our first choice* [Nicholas I]."

Believes Russia has acted moderately in its war against Turkey, but will not continue to do so. Comments that the war will be pursued "with increased vigor on the opening of a new campaign" and "a blockade of the Dardanelles will be forthwith adopted." ALS. DNA, RG84, Foreign Service Posts, Russia (R23, frames 45–6). Received January 8, 1829.

From "JUNIUS," Lexington, Ky., September 19, 1828. Accuses Clay of leading a host of "venal fools which you have succeeded in making your noisy and devoted partisans by the influence of your patronage" in political attacks on the beloved Jackson. Charges that he has attempted with patronage to subvert the free American press in the interest of maintaining Adams and himself in power. Attacks campaign tactics of Clay and Adams, especially the "loathsome depravity" of the "Coffin Handbills." Recalls Clay's decisive role in the election of Adams by the

House in 1825. Notes that "John Q. Adams was not the choice of the people of the United States," but with Clay's aid had come to power under a "gross violation" of the "spirit" of the Constitution. Refers also to the fact of "your bitter political hostility towards each other previous to the last presidential election," the fact that the Kentucky legislature had instructed Clay to vote for Jackson [3:902], and "the fact of your vote and influence making John Quincy Adams President and his giving you the next highest executive office in the government." Lexington *Kentucky Gazette,* September 19, 1828. For the "Coffin Handbill" broadside, see Marquis James, *The Life of Andrew Jackson.* Complete in One Volume (Indianapolis, 1938), 464–5; see also 5:739.

From F. SYDNOR, *ET AL*. Lynchburg, Va., September 21, 1828. Invite Clay to a public dinner in his honor in Lynchburg, noting that they have no "doubt [of] the final result of the contest which is now going on in the country," and that once it is over all the "friends of good order" will no longer regard him merely "as a conspicuous member of one of two almost balanced parties—but, as a favorite leader of that great Catholic 'party, that loves its country.'" Lynchburg *Virginian,* September 25, 1828. Reprinted in Washington *Daily National Intelligencer,* September 30, 1828.

Clay, who was in Lynchburg, responded on September 22, saying he could not delay his trip back to Washington and would have to refuse the kind invitation. Notes, however, that were Jackson to be elected "my confidence in the great experiment of self-government, which the U. States now almost alone exhibit to the world would be weakened. But if that contingency should unfortunately happen, I would still cherish the hope that the intelligence of the present generation may guard us against its pernicious consequences, and that the wisdom of posterity may protect it against the influence of the perilous example." *Ibid.*

From JAMES BARBOUR, London, no. 2, September 22, 1828. Comments on the anticipated arrival in Britain of the Queen of Portugal, Maria da Gloria, who is to be received "with all the honours usually offered on such occasions to crowned heads." Adds: "The conduct of Great Britain towards Don Miguel has been contradictory and equivocal." Notes that Britain "has lost her hold on Portugal if Miguel be confirmed in his usurpation," but "Should she be mainly instrumental in placing Maria on the throne, British influence will regain its lost ascendancy over the Councils of Portugal."

Reports news on the Russo–Turkish War and transmits maps relating to the Northeastern boundary arbitration. LS. DNA, RG59, Dip. Disp., Great Britain, vol. 36 (M30, R32). Received October 30, 1828. See also Manning, *Diplomatic Correspondence . . . Canadian Relations,* 2:770.

From JOHN J. CRITTENDEN   Frankfort, September 23, 1828 [Discusses legal work he is doing for Clay. Continues:]
The work of preperation, on both sides, for the contest in November, is going on with great earnestness & spirit—In aid of the more

systematic plan recommended by the Administration Central Committee for securing the attendance of its friends & a full expression of the public Will at the November election, they have written letters to influencial men in every county in the State invoking the utmost exertion of their activity & zeal—Stuborn as the contest must be, I trust & beleive that Kentucky will give a good account of herself.

I hope that your health is improving, & that a glorious way will yet be opened for you through that "Sea of troble" with which you have been surrounded.

ALS. NcD.

From THOMAS H. PINDELL, Lexington, September 23, 1828. Remarks on the coming presidential election that "We are, at length, acting with some vigour, and doubt not of success in Novr.—" ALS. DNA, RG59, A. and R. (MR1).

From JOEL R. POINSETT, Mexico, no. 152, September 25, 1828. Reports that both General Gomez Pedraza and General Vicente Guerrero received the vote of ten states in the presidential election. Notes that "this unexpected result has produced great excitement throughout the whole Country and the most serious consequences to their institutions and liberties, appear to be inevitable." States that the "executive will be invested with the powers of dictatorship; and if it proceeds in quelling the rebellion by the exercise of those powers, we must look forward to . . . a military despotism. . . . If on the other hand the opposite party succeed, it can only be by overthrowing the constitution and violating the laws of the Country." Believes that this "is a fatal dilemma," but that it will not lead to much fighting because of inertia resulting from "the natural indolence of the people, and from a disinclination to risk their lives in any quarrel"; also because both the national forces and Santa Anna "are lamentably in want of funds." States that he is "waiting with great impatience for the Senate of Mexico to conclude their discussions on the [Commercial] Treaty, as my intention is to leave this country as soon after as possible." ALS. DNA, RG59, Dip. Disp., Mexico, vol. 4 (M97, R5). Received November 22, 1828.

From WILLIAM B. ROCHESTER Rochester,
September 15, 1828
[Recommends the appointment of Judge Ogden Edwards as Postmaster for New York City, noting that "he was an early friend of Mr. Adams and has always been an unwavering democrat—[DeWitt] Clinton hated him most cordially—nor was there any love lost on the other side—"[1] Continues:]

I take this occasion to felicitate you upon the Election of Genl [Thomas] Metcalfe—as your Friend I would rather see him elected & Mr. Adams fail, than the reverse—let them no longer prate about violence being done to the feeling of Kentucky in the vote of her Representatives—I wish I could say with any kind of assurance that our State will be more than balanced at the next Prestl. Election—My

473

Brother Thos. is confident of 24[2]—I am not so sanguine   We shall do our duty here—but the Anti Masonic excitement is turning every thing topsy turvy—there is no counting upon the result—we shall choose our elector[3] easily—but the knaves are determined to defeat Barnard[4]—I fear they will be but too successful. . . .

[Concludes with a "secret" remedy for dyspepsia which he had at last found after a ten year search: "a teaspoon full of white mustard seed (to be swallowed whole) about an hour before breakfast—the like quantity about an hour after dinner and the like quantity just before going to bed." Recommends this dosage for a three month period]. . . . [P.S.] The Genl. [Peter B. Porter] & his Lady slid through town without my seeing them—

ALS. DNA, RG59, A. and R. (MR2).   1. President Adams appointed James Monroe's son–in–law, Samuel Gouverneur, as Postmaster for New York City. He was a former Adams supporter now turned Jacksonian. Mushkat, *Tammany*, 111.   2. Jackson carried New York with 140,763 popular votes and 20 electoral votes; Adams received 135,413 popular and 16 electoral. Weston, *The Presidential Election of 1828*, 182.   3. James K. Garnsey from New York's 27th District. New York *American*, November 20, 1828. 4. Daniel D. Barnard was defeated for reelection to the 21st Congress. *BDAC*.

From WILLIAM TUDOR, Rio de Janeiro, September 25, 1828. Reports on two informal meetings with the Minister of Foreign Affairs, Marquis of Aracaty, and the Minister of the Marine, Miguel de Souza Melloe Alvin, who have been appointed to negotiate a treaty of Commerce with the U.S. States that they asked him to prepare the plan of a treaty [Clay to Tudor, March 29 and 31, 1828] which he has done, using the U.S. treaty with Central America [4:878] as a model. Has tried to persuade them against making an exception in favor of Portugal on the issue of reciprocity and has also attempted "to awaken them to a resistance to the colonial system of Europe which is extremely injurious to the interest of every state on this Continent." Argues that in renewing existing treaties with European powers, the South American countries "will be obliged in self defense to contend for a relinquishment of the partialities, & restrictions of that system."

Mentions he has just returned from a conference with the negotiators and says his plan for the treaty will probably be accepted with slight modifications, one of which includes an article favoring Portugal. Such a provision has been included in all of Brazil's treaties with other countries. Says he has tried "to urge the [settlement of] claims as a necessary precursor for the success of a Treaty," but as yet the only settlements have been payment for the *Spark* and cancellation of bonds for the *Spermo*. ALS. DNA, RG59, Dip. Disp., Brazil, vol. 6 (M121,R8). Letter marked "Confidential." Received December 3, 1828.

From ALBERT GALLATIN, New York, September 27, 1828. Reports his return from Albany, New York, where he obtained "all that can sustain our equitable claim to the northern boundary from the Connecticut river to the St. Lawrence, as surveyed under the Provincial Governments." Adds that he has had a letter from William P. Preble stating that "he is well assured that there stands, about six leagues from the river St. Lawrence . . . a post with a superscription on it, which was placed formerly, by the British authorities, as being on the boundary of Canada." States: "These facts, if proven, would certainly strengthen our case," but adds that it will be "difficult to obtain authentic evidence of them." ALS. DNA, RG76, Northeast Boundary (KyU., Special Roll, frames 89–90). Copy, in NHi–Gallatin Papers (MR21).

To MURRAY MORRIS, Cuckooville, Va., September 27, 1828. Had hoped to visit with him enroute to Washington, but did not understand the geography of Goochland and Louisa Counties and hence did not pass near enough to Louisa Court House to make a visit possible. Asks if Morris was serious "about purchasing my grey horses"; if so, "let me know immediately by mail" at Washington. ALS. ViU. Dr. James Murray Morris, a graduate of William and Mary College in 1798, was a son of Colonel Richard Morris of Hanover. See Malcolm H. Harris, *A History of Louisa County* (Richmond, 1936), 393; and *VMHB*, 30:242–3.

From WILLIAM TUDOR, Rio de Janeiro, no. 109, September 28, 1828. Reports a three week delay by the commission appointed to settle various claims such as the *Hero, Panther, Ruth, Sarah George,* and *Rio.* States that the agents "who are accustomed to the habits of the country do not consider the delay as extraordinary, nor as mere trifling to defer a settlement," but admits "It excites . . . my anxiety." Believes that there is "slight ground of right" for many of the cases, pointing out that some of the "claimants . . . have been so notoriously doing everything in their power to aid the Buenos Ayreans, that the disposition to cavil at their demands is not unnatural." Repeats as in previous letters that the great obstacle to a settlement is "the extreme embarrassment of their finances" which can be attributed largely to the war with Buenos Aires, and the abuses, especially embezzlement, associated with its management. Also notes that other countries have large claims and that "payment to one party is immediately stated by another as a precedent that cannot be evaded."

Mentions that Emperor Pedro I closed the legislature on September 20 "in a very laconic speech which I enclose & which only contains reproaches for their neglect of his repeated injunctions to attend to the pressing concerns of the Treasury & the Reformation of justice."

Comments at length on the problem of piracy and recommends that the U.S. "lose no time in preparing a force" of vessels to patrol trouble spots and "to prevent piracy from being carried on to a most serious extent."

Reports that a revolution has broken out in Lima and that "prospects for all those countries is gloomy in the extreme." ALS. DNA, RG59, Dip. Disp., Brazil, vol. 6 (M121, R8). Letter marked "Confidential." Received December 3, 1828.

From JOSEPH R. UNDERWOOD Bowling Green, Ky., September 29, 1828
The kind sentiments expressed in yours of the 4th Instant shall be gratefully remembered. I did believe until shortly before the election that

my success was pretty certain.[1] The result did not surprize me, because in July handbills were extensively circulated containing many charges against me, some without the least foundation & others based upon partial & perverted views of my political conduct. I was denounced as any enemy to the occupant, as inimical to the settlement of the Tennessee River [2:770] & as having mainly, by my course in the Legislature, inflicted irreparable injury on the State by compromising the question of disputed boundary between us & Tennessee [2:268-70].[2] These and numerous minor charges were made known too late for refutation. The mendacious spirit of my opponents was not content with the libels which were circulated against me. I was the subject of many "fire side" slanders. Insolvency was imputed to me & mortgages which I had expected in good faith to secure the payment of debts contracted merely as security, were made the pretexts for charging me with fraud. But to you I need not speak of the base means resorted to by knaves for the purpose of deceiving the ignorant & credulous. You have suffered so much more than ever I did from calumny (because your fame too bright & extensive to be viewed by the eye of envy without acute pain has exposed you to a thousand malignant shafts where one has been pointed at me) that you can readily imagine the whole conduct of its propagators & all its consequences. The strength of innocence has already brought you out triumphant & I doubt not, if I live long, that I shall survive the petty slanders that were invented to defeat my election. The office to which I aspired as you remark "is no great affair" & I should never have thought of it but for the unsolicited & even unwelcome nomination of the Administration convention. I regret that my friends & the cause they espoused did not triumph to the extent of their wishes. I am sure that my individual interests will prosper more by my defeat. I shall never permit myself to become miserable because the people will not put it in my power to do them good or evil.

The election of Genl [Thomas] Metcalf[e] is indeed cause for "sincere gratulation" It is proof that the majority of the people of Ky have not yet been blinded by the glare of a warriors sword & epauletts. I shall dispair of the Republic whenever I am convinced that a majority of the people pay more respect to military than civil qualifications in selecting a President. If my public discourses have had a good effect in guarding the people against the fatal error I am more than compensated for the loss of my time & the loss of my election.

Every exertion will be made in this quarter to insure a triumph in November.[3] Our county committees will do their duty. I shall omit nothing on my part to rouse the friends of the Administration to action. I will freely write to you whenever I can make my letters worthy of your perusal

ALS. DLC-HC (DNA, M212, R3).   1. Underwood lost the race for Lt. Governor of Kentucky to John Breathitt. The results were: Breathitt 37,511; Underwood 36,151. Frankfort *Argus of Western America*, August 27, 1828.   2. Underwood was then on the Ky. House Committee for Courts of Justice, to which the bill on the boundary adjustment was given. Ky. H. of Reps., *Journal* . . . 1819-20, p. 139. Concerning the boundary controversy see, further, Samuel Cole Williams, *Beginnings of West Tennessee*, (Johnson City, Tenn., 1930), 105-08.   3. These efforts were successful. Adams carried Warren County (of which Bowling Green is the county seat) by a 674-478 margin over the Jacksonians. Frankfort *Argus of Western America*, November 19, 1828.

To **JOHN S. WELLFORD,** *ET AL.,* Near Fredericksburg, Va., September 29, 1828. Declines with gratitude an invitation from a group of Fredericksburg citizens to attend a public dinner in his honor. Explains that he will be happy to greet Fredericksburg's citizens informally as he passes through the town tomorrow, but that he cannot "deviate from the resolution," made earlier in Lexington, to avoid public political gatherings during his vacation in Kentucky and on his trip back to Washington. Remarks on his Virginia origins and his pride at being "one of her humble sons," and thanks the committee for "the generous indignation which you express on account of the continued and relentless persecution of which I have been so long the object." Washington *Daily National Intelligencer,* October 2, 1828. Reprinted in Lexington *Kentucky Reporter,* October 15, 1828. The invitation, Wellford, *et al.* to Clay, Fredericksburg, September 29, 1828, is in *ibid.*

From **CHRISTOPHER HUGHES,** Brussels, September 30, 1828. Contrary to the doubts expressed in the London *Courier* of September 30, regarding the blockade of the Dardanelles by the Russians, reports "*the fact is positive,*" because he has "this moment received the information from official sources." States: "This measure of the Emperor [Nicholas I] will make a complete change in the face & *footing* of the relations of the Triple Alliance; the Blockade will be enforced by the presence of a powerful Russian Fleet of Ten Ships of the Line." ALS. DNA, RG59, Dip. Disp., Netherlands, vol. 8 (M42, R12). Received November 19, 1828.

From **WILLIAM TUDOR,** Rio de Janeiro, no. 110, September 30, 1828. Reports on his negotiations for a commercial treaty with Brazil. Notes that he has prepared a draft of the treaty based upon the U.S.–Central American treaty [4:878]. Says he has attempted in the negotiations "to awaken them to a resistance to the colonial system of Europe which is extremely injurious to the interests of every state on this Continent, & which receiving its first shock, by the independence of the U.S. has by the subsequent independence of new States, met with additional opponents." States that he has urged the settlement of U.S. claims as a necessary prerequisite to the success of a treaty. Believes his draft will be accepted with only minor changes except the Brazilian insistence that Portugal must be excepted from the terms of reciprocity. Though he has strongly opposed this, concludes that he will probably have to yield on this point, because all of Brazil's treaties with other countries make an exception of Portugal.

Mentions that the only settlement of claims with any nation which Brazil has made definitely is payment for the *Spark* and cancellation of the bonds of the *Spermo.* ALS. DNA, RG59, Dip. Disp., Brazil, vol. 6 (M121, R8). Received December 3, 1828.

From **REBECCA SMITH BLODGET,** [N.P., N.D., Probably Philadelphia, *ca.* October, 1828]. Writes to explain her personal, unexpected visit to Clay in Washington to seek a patronage job for her nephew. Notes that the call was in character, because she is known as "the eccentric" Mrs. [Samuel] Blodget. States that her father, the Reverend William Smith, a "learned Philosopher & Divine, who held the singularly liberal opinion that education & habit made the sole difference between the sexes," encouraged her to read from his library where she learned to love history and "great men." Believes that Aaron Burr, "whose pigmy form commanded so much respect as the Herculean form of Washington . . . yet wd. he make love to every young woman he me[t] married or single—from the first circle down to the kitchen wench," was one of the greatest of all men. Confesses: "I became *intimately* acquainted with him—till he made love to *me*—as he did to every woman he approached—don't suppose I think worse of a great man for loving a beautiful young woman . . . a great man may love as much as he pleases." Has concluded over the years that John Adams, Burr, and her father, provost of the College of Philadelphia during the American Revolution, were among history's few truly great men.

Contends, however, that Clay is now "decidedly the greatest man in the country." States that this is not an attempt at flattery because she did not mention it when she solicited an office from him for her nephew. Asks that he visit her at her house, 95 North 5th St. when next he comes to Philadelphia. Laments that while "I can never have the high gratification of being persona[lly] acquainted with you . . . I hope . . . you will now accept all I have to offer—my respect, esteem, & admiration & that friendship which has seldom been given on demand & never offered but as a tribute to worth & talent. I think there are many traits of Burr in your character . . . you possess the same portion of electric fire." Adds: "You have vanity Mr Clay—for you are a man."

Mentions that all the members of her family are supporters of John Q. Adams except two—her son, John Adams Blodget, and her brother, Judge Charles Smith. Concludes: "Take my letter as it is meant—& believe me with all my faults, my follies & exccentricities *an honest* politician—If I dared I wd send my respects & my love too to Mr Adams—the worthy son of my father's faithful friend." ALS. DLC–HC (DNA, M212, R4). For the controversial William Smith, founder (in 1782) and first president of Washington College, Chestertown, Md., and progenitor of other educational good works, see *DAB*. For Samuel Blodget, see *ibid*. Letter incomplete; first part missing.

To JAMES BRECKINRIDGE   Fincastle, Va., *ca.* October 1, 1828
I intended, on passing by your farm this morning from the Sweet Springs, to have called, but I learnt from your Overseer that you were not at the house and he was not certain whether you were at your Mill or at some other place. I am on my way to the Botetourt Springs to meet there my son in law and daughter [James and Anne Clay Erwin], who are on the road to Tennessee. I shall remain with them tonight, and tomorrow, and return on friday or saturday (most probably friday) immediately after breakfast. I mean then to have the pleasure of visiting you, in company with one or two young friends,[1] my fellow travellers, if you should not have left home. . . .

ALS. Courtesy of Mrs. Abram P. Staples of Roanoke, Virginia. The date of this letter might be October 8, 1828. James Breckinridge was a brother of John Breckinridge of Kentucky.

See further, *BDAC* and *DAB*.   1. Probably Dominique Bouligny and William C. C. Claiborne, Jr.

From BEN DE FOREST & SON, New York, October 1, 1828. Complain of "the oppressions & lawless acts of the Brazilian authorities & Government" against American commerce. Call upon the U.S. government "to obtain redress & ample remuneration, as every Amn. Citizen has a right to expect." Expect additional attacks on American ships "unless decisive measures are adopted by our Govt. to protect it." Discuss in detail the case of the *Exit.* ALS. DNA, RG76, Misc. Claims, Brazil.

Clay replied on October 6, stating that William Tudor, "our Chargé de' Affaires at Rio de Janeiro is instructed to urge the Government of the Brazils to make prompt and full satisfaction for all aggressions upon our lawful commerce." Urges them to send documents concerning the *Exit* and *Telltale* either to the State Department or directly to Tudor. Copy. DNA, RG59, Dom. Letters, vol. 22, p. 297 (M40, R20).

From BETSEY HAWLEY, New York, October 1, 1828. Complains that she is "much the worse" for having applied to the Secretary of State for help in collecting her late brother's [Isaac P. Hawley] estate in Puerto Cabello, Colombia, than she would have been had she earlier sought assistance elsewhere. Believes the reason Franklin Litchfield, U.S. Consul at Puerto Cabello, has not communicated any specific amount for the estate is because he is afraid "lest I should embrace the means which such information would afford me to visit the place where my brother died [in August, 1825]." Asks that Clay notify her if he can give no help except that of writing to the Consul; but suggests that he might help her raise the money for a voyage to Puerto Cabello. Asks him to direct Colombian officials in Washington or New York to give her a list of documents she would need to settle her late brother's estate. ALS. DNA, RG59, Cons. Disp., Puerto Cabello, vol. 1 (M-T229, R1).

The persistent Miss Hawley had written Clay on August 7 and again on September 2, demanding action on her problem. In the latter, she threatened to publish an incriminating letter [not otherwise revealed] from Litchfield unless she received assistance from the Department. ALS. DNA, RG59, Misc. Letters (M179, R66). See also Hawley to Clay, October 27, 1828, *ibid.;* also Hawley to Clay, October 29, 1828, in which she claimed that her brother had a thousand dollars worth of property a few days before he died. ALS. DNA, RG76, Misc. Claims, Colombia.

On October 11, 1828, Franklin Litchfield reported to Clay that Miss Hawley continues to write him concerning her deceased brother's estate, that it is not likely that she can recover any of his property, if indeed he had any, and that she "has been very erroneously informed" about the whole matter. Suggests that "if she is dissatisfied with me, she had better send out an Agent to investigate my conduct in particular, and the affairs in general of her late brother." ALS. DNA, RG59, Cons. Disp., Puerto Cabello, vol. 1 (M-T229, R1). No date of receipt.

Writing again on December 20, Litchfield enclosed "copies of all correspondence, which has passed between . . . the Consulate" and the Colombian government "relative to the deceased Isaac P. Hawley."

479

Hopes this information "will be deemed sufficient proof by Miss Hawley, that her Brother has no property in this Country." *Ibid.* Received January 20, 1829.

On January 6, 1829, Hawley demanded: "I now ask you Sir to restore me the money, and pay me for the time, which I have expended in consequence of relying on your promises as secretary of state." *Ibid.* She announced on January 21 her intention to go personally to Puerto Cabello. Charges: "You perhaps take the liberty to trifle with me on this subject for the same reason that Franklin Litchfield does—because I am a defenceless woman." Warns: "You may think, Sir, that you are too much aloof to fear a woman's resentment—resist if you dare, sir—" *Ibid.*

From WILLIAM R. HIGINBOTHAM, Bermuda, October 1, 1828. Reports the loss on September 19 on the American brig, *Polly* of Baltimore in a storm and the rescue of the crew. Concerning expenses for sending the survivors home, notes that advances "will be at a great loss—as British Govt B[ills] are at but 1½ pr ct premium here and sell at a premium of 12 pr ct in the U.S.—Bills on the U.S. not being wanted in consequence of want of trade are below par." ALS. DNA, Cons. Disp., Bermuda, vol. 1 (M–T262, R1). Received October 27, 1828.

On October 3, 1828, Higinbotham reported he had drawn $302.62 for the relief of the *Polly*'s crew and had seized an opportunity "for sending on the entire crew to Eastport, Maine . . . for the Moderate Sum of $150 for Passage, Provisions &c." *Ibid.* Received October 29, 1828.

From AMOS KENDALL, Frankfort, October 1, 1828. Reviews the background of Clay's letter to Francis P. Blair [4:9–11], and the details of Clay's political "bargain" with Adams in January, 1825, that had put Adams in the White House. Notes that "Many copies of your letter to Mr. Blair have been made out in manuscript and disseminated through this State and probably into others. The people in general cannot be permitted to see it: but it is secretly read by your partizans, who tell the people that they have seen it, and that it is a harmless production." States that he has reason to believe that "the most objectionable passages are entirely omitted." Demands that the letter be published in full.

Vigorously supports Rep. George Kremer's charge at the time that there was indeed a bargain struck between Clay and Adams. Recalls that Clay had initially called Kremer "a base and infamous calumniator, a dastard and a liar [4:48]." Continues: "This was the first step in your defense. It has been followed up ever since by perservering attempts to degrade Mr. Kremer and make the people believe that he had made a false charge. Let us now see who is best entitled to the epithets of 'base and infamous calumniator, a dastard and a liar,' GEORGE KREMER or HENRY CLAY." Defends Kremer's veracity in all particulars, concluding that "Mr. Kremer was neither 'a calumniator' nor 'a liar.'" Charges that "Precedent had made the office of Secretary of State the avenue to the Presidency and the second station in the government, and to attain that, when you failed in your attempts upon the first, was the well known object of your ambition . . . the proof is complete that you were promised the office of Secretary of State and the future support of Mr. Adams and New-England, if you would but transfer to him your support and secure his election."

Concludes: "In your letter to Mr. Blair, you admit, in language that cannot be misunderstood, that Mr. Adams' friend had promised you *any station you might ask. . . .* Thus, sir, every charge made against you by Mr. Kremer is proved to be true by your own letter to Mr. Blair and by the declarations of your friends [David Trimble, Francis Johnson, Thomas Metcalfe]. Yet, for telling what *you knew to be true,* you called him 'a base and infamous calumniator, a dastard and a liar,' and by your promise to challenge him to deadly combat, proved you were ready to *defend corruption and falsehood with your life!* Such is the man who complains of slander and charges me with a want of veracity!" Frankfort *Argus of Western America,* October 1, 1828.

From JAMES M. PORTER   Easton, Pa., October 1, 1828
I enclose you a news paper printed in this place in which is Contained a Statement purporting to be made by an Old Soldier, named Richard Nagle alleging that the president turned him out of His House telling him "to be gone for an impostor and a dirty old rascal, or he would have him horsewhipped." As I have no doubt that this story is essentially untrue, and as the friends or supporters of General Jackson are endeavoring to make a handle of it in this section of the state I am desirous that the President should see it and say whether there is any truth in it.

May I therefore ask the favor of you to exhibit it to the president and ascertain from him whether there is any truth in it or not, in order that I may have it in my power to contradict it.—

ALS. MHi-Adams Papers, Letters Received (MR488). For Porter, see *DAB.*

From DANIEL WEBSTER   Boston, October 1, 1828
I hope this will meet you at Washington, in bettered health, & good spirits. You will have recd. a short letter from me, of date ten days earlier than the present, & also a letter from our friend Mr Welch [*sic,* Robert Walsh]. I am afraid those communications would have done more good, if they could have reached their ultimate destination earlier,[1] but altho yours from the Springs was promptly attended to, some delay, I fear, has, or may have, arisen from communicating with you, instead of writing direct to others. There were objections, however, to the latter course, which we could not well get over. If my letter & Mr Welch were forwarded to you, they would be recd. in tolerable scorn. If they stopped at Washington, it will be less fortunate—

I observe, however, that the election in K[entucky]. does not take place till Novr. 10.

Our friend Mr [Henry Randolph] Storrs has been here & made us a very short visit. His hopes are good. The doubtful Districts, he says, lie in his neighborhood,[2] & great efforts will be made in them, on both sides; & at present the expectation of himself & friends is better than it has been. We were glad to see him, & he was gratified with his visit.—

I believe, My Dear Sir, Mr Adams will be reelected, if K. goes for him. What we hear from Maryland & N York[3] is so encouraging, that no pains ought now to be spared. I think the object is fairly within reach.— You will have seen that there is no fear of losing a vote in N. England. I feel some anxiety for Delaware;[4] but the question will soon be settled there.

Is there any thing further that *I,* or *we* can do?—

ALS. DLC-HC (DNA, M212, R3). Letter marked "Private."   1. Reference obscure; but see Clay to Webster, October 6, 1828.   2. Storrs's neighborhood was the Oneida County District in New York which Adams carried in the 1828 election by 681 votes; Storrs was re-elected.   3. In the 1828 election Adams won 25,527 popular votes and 6 electoral votes in Maryland to Jackson's 24,565 popular votes and 5 electoral votes. For the New York vote, see Rochester to Clay, September 25, 1828.   4. Delaware's legislature gave Adams all 3 of its electoral votes.

From JAMES BARBOUR, London, no. 3, October 2, 1828. Reports having had a meeting on the previous day with Lord Aberdeen, British Foreign Secretary, who apologized for the delay in Barbour's audience with King George IV who is ill. Was assured by Aberdeen that "there was as little regards to etiquette here, as any where else . . . and that he wished me when ever I do so to call on him without ceremony or previous notice." Mentions that Aberdeen stated that Britain would not accede to Russia's blockade of the Dardanelles. Refers to discussions with Aberdeen on the West Indies trade, the tariff, and the problem of slaves taking refuge in Canada. On the latter question, says that he emphasized that "the mischief [of runaway slaves] was by no means confined to the number that escaped; but acted on and much impaired the value of those that remained." Notes that Aberdeen replied that the state of public feeling on the subject in Britain amounted to "a mania" and therefore was a matter of "some delicacy and difficulty." ALS. DNA, RG59, Dip. Disp., Great Britain, vol. 36 (M30, R32). Received November 17, 1828. Also in Manning, *Diplomatic Correspondence . . . Canadian Relations,* 2:771-2.

From JOHN L. BRIDGES, Harrodsburg, Ky., October 4, 1828. Recommends George Robertson for appointment to the U.S. Supreme Court to replace Robert Trimble, deceased. Regrets not having seen Clay when he was last in Kentucky. Presumed he would remain in Lexington "until the meeting of the [Masonic] Grand Lodge." Concludes: "I have not nor never had an unfriendly feeling towards you, and hope I never shall have; parties Still run high in this State, altho. I am for Genl. Jackson, I am temporately so, and am inclined to the opinion that the vote of the State will be given to the administration." ALS. DNA, RG59, A. and R. (MR3).

To THOMAS McGIFFIN   Washington, October 4, 1828
I received your favor of the 29th ult. respecting the charge of my having purchased a negro, a free born Pennsylvanian, and now holding him in illegal bondage. I presume the allusion is to my purchase of Jerry, copies of the papers respecting which are enclosed.

Jerry came to me at Wheeling, with the agent entrusted to sell him,

482

in the Summer of 1824, when I was on my return to Kentucky, and entreated me to buy the remainder of the time of his servitude. I was informed that his mistress was resolved to sell him, for some cause which I do not now distinctly recollect, and he was apprehensive of being sold to some person of whom he entertained a less favorable opinion than of me. I accordingly purchased him, and received the bill of sale, of which a copy is enclosed. The certificate of the two Justices of Washington county (of which a copy is also enclosed) was shewn to, and left with me:

In the Summer of 1825, my son–in–law, Mr. Jas. Erwin, having purchased some of my improved breeds of cattle and horses, wished to have Jerry to conduct them to his farm. I accordingly let him have Jerry with his consent, stipulating in his behalf that Mr. Erwin should pay him $35 when he becomes free, of which a memo. is now before me. I saw Mr. Erwin a few weeks ago, and he informed me that Jerry was well, contented, and happy.

I purchased the boy not merely with his own consent, but upon his earnest solicitation. I purchased him, and he is now held, in conformity of the laws of Pennsylvania as I understood them. I parted from him with his consent. He will be free at the age prescribed by those laws.

In the mean time, he is a more respectable and useful man than the Editor[1] of the paper[2] which you sent me: for he is no calumniator. . . .

Copy. Washington *Daily National Intelligencer*, October 30, 1828. Reprinted in Washington (Pa.) *Reporter*, from which the Lexington *Kentucky Reporter* again reprinted it on November 12, 1828.   1. William Sample, editor of the Washington, Pa. *Reporter*. See George H. Roadman, "Washington (Pa.) Newspaper Battles 1817–1825," *WPHM*, (Fall, 1957), 40:195-7.   2. On October 20, Clay wrote Joseph Gales in reply to Gales's inquiry about the purchase of Jerry. Said Clay: "the calumny refered to . . . has already recd. the *coup de grace* in a letter from Mr. C. to Mr. M'Giffin, published in the Reporter at Washn. Pennsa. The colored man was regularly purchased by Mr. C. accordingly to the Laws of Pennsa., and carried to K. not merely with his consent but upon his earnest entreaty. He had to serve until he is 28, when he will be free." AL. NN.

From WILLIAM P. MATHEWS, Baltimore, October 4, 1828. Solicits an appointment as consul at Chagres, Province of Panama, Colombia. Notes that because he contracted a severe illness in Liberia in February, 1828, while conducting two large groups of emigrants there under the direction of the American Colonization Society, his health is such that he cannot visit in Washington at this time to press his case personally. ALS. DNA, RG59, A. and R. (MR3). For Mathews, a Baltimore shipper, and his earlier interest in securing an exclusive contract from the Colonization Society to transport Negro emigrants to Liberia, see Staudenraus, *The African Colonization Movement, 1816–1865,* 160-1. He did not receive the desired appointment.

From HENRY PERRINE, Campeche, Mexico, October 4, 1828. Transmits the September 27th issue of *El Investigador,* containing an account of two seamen who "were forcibly extracted [on September 19] from [the] American brig Telegraph . . . by order of Charles Rich . . . Commander of the British Sloop of War Harpy." Both were ultimately returned by Mexican officials. States that Rich has made "the repeated declaration . . . not merely of his general right but of his especial *Orders* to take Seamen, Englishmen by birth, wherever he might find them . . . especially should the sailors desire to enter into his Majesty's service." ALS. DNA, RG59, Cons. Disp., Campeche, vol. 1 (M286, R1). No date of receipt. Clay ordered a translation of the article that "relates to the impressment of seamen."

From THOMAS I. WHARTON, Philadelphia, October 4, 1828. Urges the appointment of William Rawle, Sr. as District Judge of the Eastern District of Pennsylvania, and warns against the "danger" of appointing Joseph Hopkinson. Assures Clay that impressions to the effect that Rawle is a supporter of Jackson are incorrect, that he has in the past voted for "friends of the Admn.," and will "At all events . . . vote for Mr. [John] Sergeant." Informs Clay that the Rawle appointment "will conciliate" those "who have been called Federalists while it will be equally agreeable to the Democratic party." Complains that memorials in favor of Rawle that he had sent to the President have not been acknowledged, "nor has he on any other occasion taken the slightest notice of any Communication I have made him." Concludes: "The result of the contest of yesterday has certainly surprised but I hope will not dishearten us. I am still in hopes that we shall be able to carry Mr S[ergeant] into Congress." ALS. DLC–HC (DNA, M212, R3). On October 3 the Adams candidates lost the ward elections in Philadelphia. Sergeant, who was seeking re–election to Congress was defeated in the subsequent Congressional election by Joseph Hemphill.

On October 23, Adams appointed Joseph Hopkinson to the vacant District judgeship. Clay to Hopkinson, October 23, 1828. Copy. DNA, RG59, Dom. Letters, vol. 22, p. 314 (M40, R20).

On October 26, Hopkinson acknowledged receipt of the commission. ALS. DNA, RG59, Accept. and Orders for Comms. (M–T645, R2).

From E. & G. W. BLUNT   New York, October 5, 1828
We have received a few copies of Bouchette's map of Lower Canada[1] which we should be happy to dispose of, the price of which is $30— including his map of Upper & Lower Canada and part of the U.S. The value of this map is no doubt Known to you as containing considerable Topographical information and it has become very scarce in consequence of the British government having suppressed the sale of them, the information contain[ed] in them being favourable to the claim of the U.S. Boundary line

ALS. DNA, RG59, Misc. Letters (M179, R66).   1. Joseph Bouchette, *A Topographical Description of the Province of Lower Canada with Remarks upon Upper Canada, and on the Relative Connexion of Both Provinces with the United States of America.* London, 1815.

From ROBERT MONROE HARRISON, St. Bartholomew, October 5, 1828. Reports having been compelled to pay for passports for distressed American seamen. States: "I am satisfied his Swedish Mejesty [Charles XIV] would not admit of such a charge, if aware of its existence." Mentions that there is a "French Guneaman" in port which has just landed 450 slaves at Guadaloupe and that "This vessel reports that when he left the coast [of Africa], there were seventeen slave vessels off Cape Palmas mounting from 10 to 20 Guns. The Stronger capturing and taking slaves from the Weaker vessel that is to say *Wolf* eating *Wolf*." ALS. DNA, RG59, Cons. Disp., St. Bartholomew, vol. 1 (M72, R1). Received October 30, 1828.

From EDWARD BATES, St. Louis, October 6, 1828. Transmits a certified statement of William Eckert of St. Charles, Missouri, swearing he had heard Thomas Hart Benton, Senator from Missouri, say that he believed Adams and Clay had concluded a corrupt bargain in the Presidential election of 1824. States that Benton and his friends "extensively circulated" this charge in Missouri. Notes that "the Warriors have given me a thorough defeat . . . the Administration stands no chance of getting the three votes of this state; nor need I say that I, indeed all your friends here, were fully as much surprised as mortified." ALS. DLC–HC (DNA, M212, R3). Bates had been defeated by the Jacksonians in his bid for re–election to the House of Representatives. Jackson also won Missouri's 3 electoral votes in the presidential election in 1828, carrying the state by the margin of 8,272 popular votes to 3,400 for Adams.

To RICHARD SMITH, Washington, October 6, 1828. Submits first payment, in the amount of $577.70, on his loan from the Washington Office of the Bank of the United States, with which he had bought a lot in Washington, D.C. ANS. DLC–TJC (DNA, M212, R16).
    Clay's Washington tax bill for 1828 indicates that the property, Square 253, Lot 3, was valued at $1479.00, plus improvements thereon in the amount of $3700. The tax came to $29.00, less $3.10 "for prompt payment." Washington also taxed Clay $11.00 in 1828 on "2 female Slaves and one coacher." W. W. Billing to Clay, December 22, 1828. ADS. *Ibid.*

To DANIEL WEBSTER   Washington, October 6, 1828
I found on my arrival here on the third your favor of the 22d. Ulto. with its contents, which I immediately expedited to the several points where I believed they would be most beneficially employed. They will reach their destination in due season. Be pleased to say to Mr. Welsh [*sic,* Robert Walsh] that I recd his letter. If the fund of which he speaks could be remitted to Mr. J. A.[1] I would advise its transmission, with due precaution, where it might be most properly and usefully applied.
    I recd. also your favor of the first. The decision of the pending contest is now so near at hand that speculation about it will soon be superceded by the fact. I concur with you in thinking that it depends mainly on N. York and Kentucky. I believe we shall prevail in the latter State, although on one or two points the result of the late [state] Elections was not quite as favorable as when I communicated it to you. And there is enough of hope and probability of general success to animate us, to the last, in the highest exertions. Maryland and Delaware will this week let us know what we may count upon from them.[2] I am rejoiced that the land is all dry in N. England. Our friends there may rely upon the most prese-

vering activity in the West, which I think will give Mr. Adams 40 and perhaps 43 votes. . . . P.S. My health has greatly improved

Copy. Courtesy of Messrs. Curtis F. Brown and Hayden Goldberg, Brooklyn, N.Y. Letter marked "(Confidential)." 1. Probably Joseph Anderson, Comptroller of the Treasury. See *DAB*. 2. For the Maryland returns, see Kent to Clay, October 9, 1828. The popular vote in Delaware showed a majority of 428 for Adams; and its Legislature, which chose Presidential electors, voted 19 to 11 for Adams, thus giving him the state's three electoral votes. Baltimore *American and Commercial Daily Advertiser,* October 11, 1828; Philadelphia *United States Gazette,* October 10, 1828; Weston, *Presidential Election of 1828,* 182.

From JOHN M. CLAYTON   Dover, Del., October 8, 1828

As a friend I take the liberty briefly to state to you that the Election in this State yesterday terminated gloriously for the cause of the administration. The County of Sussex gave 450 majority for the administration ticket & Kent gave 294. against this New Castle gave 325 for Jackson, leaving 419 majority for the Administration in this little State. Mr. Johns[1] is reelected by an increased majority. The vote of the Legislature will stand in joint ballot on the Presidential question as follows

For Adams   19
For Jackson <u>11</u>.
majority   8

So our three [Electoral College] votes are secure beyond all question.

As much of the zeal I have felt in this cause has resulted from my feelings in your favour, you will pardon the liberty which though a stranger I have taken in writing to you.

ALS. DLC-HC (DNA, M212, R3). 1. On October 13, Governor Charles Polk of Delaware, and his Secretary of State, John M. Clayton, officially informed Clay that Kensey Johns, Jr. had been elected U.S. Representative to the Twenty-First Congress. ADS. DNA, RG59, Misc. Letters (M179, R66). Johns had been elected to the Twentieth Congress as a Federalist. *BDAC.*

From VINCENT GRAY, Havana, October 8, 1828.

Transmits a copy of the Royal Order admitting flour on the former terms into Havana from Spain in foreign vessels. While believing this order "is favorable to those Americans who have vessels in the Spanish trade to Santander," believes that "it is truly injurious and . . . destructive to the flour trade from the U States." Reports that the intended Cuban military expedition to Mexico "is abandoned for the present." ALS. DNA, RG59, Cons. Disp., Havana, vol. 5 (M-T20, R5). No date of receipt.

On January 1, 1829, Thomas M. Rodney, U.S. Commercial Agent in Havana, reported that 519 American vessels had called at Havana during 1828. *Ibid.* Received February 1, 1829.

From JOSEPH KENT, Rose Mount [Near Bladensburg, Md.], October 9, 1828.

Recommends Mr. Phileman Chew for the State Department clerkship vacated by the death of Richard Forrest. Reports that "Our election for [House of] Delegates is over & as far as the returns have been received, may be considered highly favourable to the Administration & indicative of almost an unanimous vote in this State in favour of

Mr. Adams in November next—In many of the Counties which were decidedly in favour of the Administration the election cou[l]d not be made to turn upon party grounds, which will account for a stragling Jacksonian of great personal popularity being elected in A. A. [Anne Arundel] & P[rince]-Georges Co.s." ALS. DNA, RG59, A. and R. (MR1). Letter delivered by hand, "Politeness of Mr. Chew." The House of Delegates elections on October 7 resulted in the selection of 48 pro–Adams delegates and 31 pro–Jackson. Baltimore *American and Commercial Daily Advertiser,* October 11, 1828. In Anne Arundel County, pro–Adams delegates elected were four; none for Jackson. *Ibid.,* October 8, 1828. In Prince George's County, three pro–Adams and one pro–Jackson delegates were elected. *Ibid.,* October 8, 9, 1828. Adams carried Maryland and six of its eleven electoral votes in the November 10 election by a 25,527 to 24,565 popular vote over Jackson.

From HENRY ECKFORD, New York, October 10, 1828. Reports that the ship, *General Brown* [4:425–6] owned by Peter Harmony and himself was detained [in 1825] by a Chilean squadron off Lima and "afterwards condemned by the authorities of Peru in a most unjustifiable manner." Requests the State Department to press this claim with the Peruvian Government. LS. DNA, RG76, Misc. Claims, Peru.

On October 15, 1828, Eckford suggested to Clay that "A gentleman" who is leaving for Lima be delegated by the State Department to deliver "some official direction in that particular case . . . to the consul [William Radcliff]." *Ibid.*

The following day, October 16, Clay replied to Eckford that the President was seeking a replacement for the late James Cooley as minister to Peru, but promised that if the appointment were delayed, "instructions will be given" to Radcliff concerning the case. Copy. DNA, Dom. Letters, vol. 22, p. 306 (M40, R20).

To JAMES MADISON   Washington, October 10, 1828
I have been informed, through a respected channel, with which I presume you are acquainted, that it would conduce greatly to the comfort of Mrs. [Martha Jefferson] Randolph, the daughter of Mr. [Thomas] Jefferson, if her son in law Mr. [Nicholas P.] Trist[1] were appointed to some Clerkship in one of the Departments here; and that, in that event, she would establish herself in this City. A vacancy having recently occurred in the Department of State,[2] I am enabled to offer him a Clerkship with a salary of $1400. In doing this I should, however, have to overlook those promotions among the existing Clerks, which it is desirable generally to make, on suitable occasions. But my feelings prompt me so strongly to serve the family of Mr. Jefferson that I would, in this instance, deviate from the general rule, if I were assured that Mr. Trist possesses the requisite qualifications. This is an indispensible condition. Unfortunately my knowledge of him does not enable me to decide that point. The object, therefore, of this letter is to ask the favor of you to afford me the advantage of your decision. Your intimate knowledge of the general business of the office, and your presumed acquaintance

with Mr. Trist, will admit of your giving a judgment, with which I should be as well satisfied as with my own, if I knew him well. Should you deem him qualified, I will thank you to forward the enclosed letter, addressed to him.[3]

Mrs Clay unites with me in the tender of respectful Compliments to Mrs. Madison. . . .

ALS. ViU. Letter marked "(Confidential)." No. 1 of this date.   1. See *DAB*.   2. Occasioned by the death of Richard Forrest the previous week.   3. Clay to Trist, October 10, 1828. See also Clay to Trist, October 21, 1828; Trist to Clay, October 18 and 24, 1828.

From JOSE SILVESTRE REBELLO, Washington, October 10, 1828. Reports that "there is at present at Baltimore, a Brig made to carry eighteen Guns, for the service of the Government of Buenos Ayres, and under the Command of one Cottrel." States that when the ship is outfitted, it will sail for one of the West Indies Islands where the Buenos Airean flag will be hoisted and will "cruize against the subjects of H. M. the Emperor of Brazil." Protests that this violates both "the Law of Nations" and U.S. law. Warns that "the acts perpetrated by her will be considered by the [Brazilian] Government . . . as if they had been committed by Citizens of the United States; for the hull, rigging, armaments, and crew" are all American. LS, in Portuguese, with trans. in State Dept. file. DNA, RG59, Notes from Brazilian Legation, vol. 1 (M49, R1).

Clay responded to Rebello's protest on October 11, informing him that he had ordered the U.S. Attorney for the District of Maryland, Nathaniel Williams, to institute an inquiry into the charge. Copy. DNA, RG59, Notes to Foreign Ministers and Consuls, vol. 4, p. 75 (M38, R4). Also on October 11, he wrote to Williams, instructing him to make an investigation. Copy. DNA, RG59, Dom. Letters, vol. 22, pp. 300–01 (M40, R20).

On October 18 Williams replied that "there is no doubt she is peculiarly calculated for a privateer," but stated that "At present, I do not perceive that I can safely or judiciously interfere." ALS. DNA, RG59, Misc. Letters (M179, R66).

On October 21, Clay again wrote Rebello, enclosing a report on the case by Williams, and noting that the vessel will be held in port until "Bonds are given." Considers this "new evidence of the earnest desire" of the U.S. to "preserve unimpaired" its "strict neutrality" in the war between Brazil and Buenos Aires. Copy. DNA, RG59, Notes to Foreign Ministers and Consuls, vol. 4, p. 81 (M38, R4).

On October 22, Rebello acknowledged receipt of Clay's note of October 21. He pointed out that Brazil expects U.S. neutrality in deed as well as word. LS, in Portuguese, with trans. in State Dept. file. DNA, RG59, Notes From Brazilian Legation, vol. 1 (M149, R1).

From CHARLES S. TODD   Stockdale [Shelby County, Ky.], October 10, 1828

I take the liberty of enclosing a letter for General [William Henry] Harrison that it may be sent with the first dispatches forwarded to him—I hope, however, that it may reach him before he leaves our Coast.

I have been waiting sometime to see what our friends in this County

488

[Shelby] would do, in order to advise you of their determinations.—I have urged upon the Committee the policy of a General Meeting as to the proceedings in the South—but the idea has been postponed until the County Court in this month, provided it shall be thought proper to act upon it at all.—Measures have been taken to sectionize the County and ascertain our strength; and I think our friends will come to the polls in as great proportion as our enemies. The real Majority here is between 4 & 500.[1] I will write you on this point before the election.

I send the last publication as to the Chickasaw Treaty.[2] General [Isaac] Shelby has made another attempt by sending Col. [Leslie] Combs to the "Hermitage" but I fear the Hero will stand mute.[3]—perhaps the present attitude of the Controversy may do some good in Virginia, Pennsylvania & New York. Can you conveniently cause an enquiry to be made in the Office as to, this "Secret Journal"?[4]

Mrs. [Letitia] Todd has added another Son to our Stock of blessings and both are doing well. We hope you reached the City safely and in improved health. Our best regards to yourself & Mrs. Clay.

ALS. DLC-HC (DNA, M212, R3). 1. Adams carried Shelby County in the 1828 presidential election by only 1,097 to 946 for Jackson. 2. For the treaty between the Chickasaw Indians and the U.S. government, dated October 19, 1818, see Party, *Treaty Series,* 69:287-91. 3. Jackson and Shelby had served as U.S. commissioners in the negotiation of the Chickasaw Treaty. 4. Two controversies surrounded the Chickasaw Treaty. Col. Robert Butler, secretary to the Commission, kept a "Secret Journal" of the negotiations, including the fact that a $20,000 bribe had been given to the Indian chiefs in exchange for their agreement to the treaty. The journal was kept secret by the Tennessee legislature and the U.S. Senate for fear that its publication might endanger the lives of the chiefs who had personally profited at the expense of their tribes. The second controversy, which became a campaign issue in 1828, resulted from Jackson's involvement in a land speculation company which leased from the chiefs, as part of the treaty, a four square mile area of land containing salt deposits. See also, Todd to Clay, October 30, 1828; Robert S. Cotterill, *The Southern Indians* (Norman, Okla., 1954), 207-08; Williams, *Beginnings of West Tennessee,* 89-93.

To NICHOLAS P. TRIST   Washington, October 10, 1828

Having received assurances of your wish to be appointed a Clerk in one of the Departments here, and confiding in your integrity and capacity, I take pleasure in offering you a vacant Clerkship in the Department of State, with a salary of fourteen hundred dollars attached to it. A strong motive with me, in tendering you this appointment, is that I have reason to believe it may be made to contribute to the personal comfort of Mrs. [Martha Jefferson] Randolph, your mother in law.[1]

Should you determine to accept it, you will repair to this City to enter upon its duties without unnecessary delay; and in that case the Salary will commence on the day of my notification of your acceptance.

ALS. DLC-Nicholas P. Trist Papers (DNA, M212, R22). Letter addressed to Trist at Monticello. No. 2 of this date. 1. Whose husband, Thomas M. Randolph, had died at Monticello on June 20, 1828, leaving her in straitened circumstances. Trist had married Virginia Jefferson Randolph.

To JAMES BROWN   Washington, October 11, 1828

I returned a few days ago from my Western tour with my health some what improved. During my absence and since my return I have received your several letters up to the 30h. Aug. We regret extremely the continuance of Mrs. Brown's ill health, and sincerely hope that her judicious retirement to the delightful gardens of Versailles may restore her health. I found and left all our friends in K. well. Mrs. [Susannah Gray] Hart does not decline faster than is natural to her advanced age. Although I have long time since been without any active means of the Estate of Col. [Thomas, Sr.] Hart, I continue to pay her regularly out of my own the 500$ annuity which he devised to her,[1] and that with what she receives from your generosity makes her and Mrs. [Susannah] Price quite comfortable. Mrs. E[leanor]. Hart occupies the Town house which belongs to her Estate and keeps an excellent boarding house at which I stayed during my sojourn in Lexington. I saw your brother's family at Frankfort & they were well. I met at Lynchburg a fine daughter of Dr. P[reston] Brown who was agreeably passing her time in that quarter among her relations.

I wish I could relieve you and myself from the uncertainty which hangs yet over the P. Election. The elections of this summer and fall have been so far highly favorable to Mr. Adams. Those of Maryland and Delaware have just closed, and their issue realizes almost all the hopes that were entertained of them. The closeness of the vote in K. by which [Thomas] Metcalfe was elected throws some doubt upon the ultimate issue in that State. I believe Mr. Adams will get that vote. If he does, and if he should also receive 20 votes in N. York he will be re–elected. I despair of Pennsa. Virginia and No. Carolina. A few weeks will now decide the contest. Whatever may be the result, the Tariff will be maintained. The violence in the South is pretty much limited to So. Carolina & Georgia. It derives no countenance and will obtain no support in Virginia, which is rapidly becoming a Tariff state. What divisions among the party of Jackson will not immediately arise if Jackson be elected!

In any event, my present inclination is to retire from public life after the 4h. of March. In one, I shall be strongly urged to return to the H. of R. and if I enjoyed the strength and buoyancy of 35 I would return. But there is a great difference between 35 and 52. In that event, I shall have the satisfaction to know that all the great measures of Domestic policy which I have espoused will be firmly established.

You have been authorized to fix the compensation of Mr. [W. Armand] B[arnet]. who acted as Secretary. Whatever you may allow him not excee[d]ing in amount the annual appropriation for a Secretary to your legation will be approved. I think it probable Mr. [John Adams] Smith will be sent to London, to take the place of Mr. [William B.] Lawrence, and some other person sent to Paris. In that case I will endeavor to find one well versed in the French Language.

Your accounts to the close of the last year have been approved and settled.

The King of the Netherlands [William I] has been selected as the Arbitrator of our dispute in the N.E. boundary with Great Britain. I hope it will form as additional motive for the elevation of [Christopher] Hughes's rank.

The Country is generally prosperous. Kentucky is becoming quite so. Virginia and some of the Southern States are exceptions.

Lucretia joins me in affectionate respects to Mrs Brown.

ALS. ViU.   1. See Clay to Brown, August 10, 1828.

From ALEXANDER H. EVERETT, Madrid, no. 117, October 11, 1828. Reports that the Council of States has been reorganized so that it will meet once a week instead of daily and will consider only matters directed to it by King Ferdinand VII. Discusses the internal political scene in Spain which renders the Council a "complete nullity."

States that a "dangerous conspiracy has been suppressed in Catalonia." Discusses the government's position on the independence movement in Latin America, saying that "new forces are constantly despatched to Cuba, no doubt with the ulterior object of attempting an invasion of the [Spanish] main whenever circumstances may appear at all favorable."

Reports he has notified the Minister of State, Manuel Gonzales Salmon, of the President's decision to resume intercourse with the existing Portuguese [Miguel] government which seemed to please the Spanish official. ALS. DNA, RG59, Dip. Disp., Spain, vol. 29 (M31, R29). Received December 5, 1828.

From JAMES BROWN, Paris, October 12, 1828. Recalls mentioning previously that the French Minister of Foreign Affairs, Count de La Ferronnays, had intimated his wish that the U.S. claims be taken up without further delay. Reports that today two gentlemen "who I have every reason to believe possess correct information" called on him and said that the Council had decided to examine the American claims and adjust them if possible and that when Ferronnays returns to Paris "I might expect that he would be ready to open the negotiation." States that France may make some distinction between "adjudicated cases and those arising from spoiliations by destruction at sea and the Antwerp cases," and that the latter two may meet with more favor than the former. Predicts that negotiations will be "slow and will present obstacles" which will not be easy to overcome. Asks for "instructions adapted to the different aspects" of the problems which may arise in the negotiations. Adds that "The disposition of France is more favorable now towards us than it has been at any previous period since my arrival." Predicts that "we may yet obtain something like justice on behalf of the Claimants."

Says that he will probably arrange to sail about May 15, 1829, "at which time a successor might be on his way to France." States that Mrs. Brown has returned from a five–week stay at Versailles with her health improved and will be able to make the voyage home if "she can restrain her fondness for society and remain ... quiet during the winter."

Comments on the progress of the Russo–Turkish War, noting that Nicholas I "has lately notified the English and French Government of his intention to blockade the Dardenelles." Reports that France has "acquiesced" in this and that the British have accepted it with "some reluctance."

Mentions that he waits anxiously for the election returns "of Pennsylvania and New York which will decide the Presidential question." Notes, however, that "Pennsylvania is hardly to be expected to take the side of Mr Adams at this time although it would seem that his cause has gained there very considerably. In New York the battle will be finished." Has heard it rumored that James Monroe and Albert Gallatin are "candidates for the vacant Post Office at New York" because both need the salary to sustain them. "If it be true it is a fact more honorable to them than to the liberality of the Government. . . . I am very sorry for both of those gentlemen." ALS. DNA, RG59, Dip. Disp., France, vol. 23 (M34, R26). Received November, n.d., 1828.

To WILLIAM HENRY   Washington, October 13, 1828
HARRISON

As you have notified the Department that you are ready to proceed on your mission to the Republic of Colombia, I will now communicate the instructions by which you will govern yourself, in conformity with the intimation contained in my note to you of the 29th day of May, last.

The distracted condition of that Republic,—the uncertainty whether a constitutional Government, or a military despotism is existing there, and the disorders which are likely to arise in the contest between the respective parties for supreme power, render the mission one of great delicacy, and impart to it a high degree of importance. Deploring, as the President most deeply does, that unfortunate state of things, it is hardly necessary to say to you, that during your residence there, you will cautiously abstain from identifying yourself with either of the contending parties. Our policy has been long and firmly fixed, to avoid all interference in the internal concerns of any country. The President wishes no deviation from it. It is not, however, inconsistent with it for you to avail yourself of proper occasions to express his sincere regret on account of the dissentions which unhappily prevail in Colombia, and his ardent hope that they may terminate in the establishment of a constitutional Government, so as to secure her liberty, and advance her happiness and prosperity, nor that you should, on proper application, communicate freely and frankly the nature of our institutions, and their practical operation—Your business is mainly with the actual Government of the country where you are to reside, and you should sedulously endeavor, by a frank and courteous deportment, to win its esteem, and conciliate its confidence. Nothing in the general, is more indiscreet than for a foreign minister to attempt to rally round himself, a party for any political purpose, connected either with his own Government, or with that which accredits him.

It is desirable that you should collect, and transmit to this Department, from time to time, any information you can procure in relation to the views of the Colombian Government, of the persons who administer it; of the commercial and other resources of the country; its revenue, army, navy and consumption; and that you should, also suggest such improvements in the commercial relations of the two countries, as may appear to you likely to promote their mutual interest.

You are aware that we have an existing treaty with Colombia, negotiated on the 3d of October 1824 [4:127–8]. Whatever may be the form of the Government of that country, the treaty will be still binding upon both Parties. It should be an object of your constant attention to watch over the fulfilment of the treaty, on the part of Colombia, and promptly to remonstrate against any measure in violation of it. It will also be your duty to afford your official aid and protection, in all cases of injury to the Citizens of the United States, or their property, flowing from acts under the authority of the Colombian Government, in derogation of the public law: and whenever any of our countrymen have just claims upon that Government, in consequence of any of those acts, after satisfying yourself of their justice and propriety, you will use all proper exertions to obtain for them the satisfaction or indemnity to which they are entitled, whether you receive special instructions to that effect from this office, or not. Several cases of claims were under the care of your predecessors in which satisfaction has not yet been obtained. These you will take some suitable and early opportunity to press upon the attention of the Colombian Government. Among these cases are that of the Josephine and her cargo,—the Schooner Ranger and cargo, and the Brig Morris. The papers which relate to these, and all other claims, which have been in the possession of your predecessors, will be found in the Archives of the Legation. That of the Josephine is one respecting which particular solicitude is felt, because the claimants have hitherto failed to obtain full satisfaction of their demand in consequence of a clerical error committed in this Department. The claim was intended to be provided for in an arrangement with the Colombian Government negotiated by the late Mr [Richard C.] Anderson [Jr.], but, owing to that error, the sum allotted to the claimants by that arrangement was only 21.750$, instead of 42.000. Their present demand, therefore, is $20.250 (being $13.500, the amount of the error, and 50 per ct damages thereon) with interest at the rate of 6 per cent. per annum, from the 27th day of January 1819. You will find, in a letter from this Department, of the 18th. June 1825, addressed to Mr [Beaufort T.] Watts, the subject particularly alluded to, and the manner stated in which the error was committed—In a communication from that gentleman, under date the 17th. May, last—he says that, in the interview he had with the Minister of foreign affairs [Pedro Gual], a short time before leaving Bogota, he was informed that the claim would be settled upon the meeting of Congress; and he conveys the assurance that it will be satisfactorily settled. You will find, also, in a letter from this Department of the 16th. September, 1825, addressed to Mr Anderson [4:643–8], that he also had been instructed upon the same subject. The interest felt in regard to this claim arises out of obvious official considerations. But you will extend your exertions to all fair and just claims, on the part of any of our citizens, upon the Colombian Government.

A war is threatened, if it has not been actually commenced, between Colombia and Peru. This government has been requested by that of Peru, to assume the friendly office of mediator. No answer has been yet returned to the application. It is not necessary that you should communicate the fact of the application to the Colombian Government—Whatever may be the nature of the answer, the President feels an anxious wish that the war may be averted, if it has not broken out, or may be honorably terminated, if it has commenced. You will embrace some suitable occasion to communicate this sentiment to the Colombian Government, and to express the gratification which the President will derive from the existence of peace and good understanding between two countries in whose prosperity and happiness the United States must ever feel a lively interest. . . . P.S. Although you will probably find all the papers relating to the claims on account of the Josephine and cargo in the archives of the Legation, it is thought proper to furnish you directly from this Department with the following papers. [Encloses copies of ten documents, dating from June, 1822, to March, 1825, relating to the *Josephine* claims case. Among them are those printed in 4:411–12, 643–8.]

Copy. DNA, RG59, Dip. Instr., vol. 12, pp. 152–5 (M77, R7). No. 2. This letter of instruction is enclosed in Clay to Harrison, Washington, October 13, 1828, no. 1, *ibid.*, pp. 145–52 [not printed herein]. It is document no. 14 in a 15-item package of books, newspapers, personnel lists, various documents, official stationery, letters of introduction, etc. that Clay thought Harrison would need in conducting his ministry in Colombia. Included in the package are standard, detailed explanations of how U.S. ministers are expected to deport themselves abroad, professionally, socially, and sartorially, and how they might best handle the daily mechanics and routines of their jobs.

To ROBERT POTTER   Washington, October 13, 1828

I have duly received your letter of the 30th.[1] ultimo, requesting information, as to the terms on which it might be practicable for the State of North Carolina to contract a loan of half a million of dollars in England, or on the Northern States, and, if in the former, what aid, in the accomlishment of the object, would be afforded by the Executive of the United States. I take pleasure in answering your letter, although it is proper for me to add, that I possess no other knowledge, as to the facility of obtaining the proposed loan, than such as I derive from general observation, and such as is accessible to all.

I do not believe that Money can be borrowed in London, as stated in the "New York Journal of Commerce," at 2 percent, or at any thing like it. Money may be obtained in England, upon English security, satisfactory to the lender, at a much less rate of interest, than it could be procured upon American, or any other distant Security. The same observation is applicable to loans negotiated in the American capitals, Philadelphia and New York, for example. Money, in either of them, can be procured upon security in the city where it is borrowed, upon much more favorable terms, than if the security should be at a distance, even in another state of the Union. This arises out of the caution and timidity of capitalists, the necessity of employing Agents, giving Commissions &c. The best evidence, as to the rate, at which money could be borrowed in England, upon American security is afforded by the price of American Stocks in the London Market, which is always about the same that it is in the New York and Philadelphia Markets, with the difference of exchange for the time being. No Security could be offered by any state in the Union, which would command a higher confidence, among English Capitalists, than that which exists in the funded debt of the United States. The best proof of the terms on which a state could contract a loan in one of our Northern Capitals (say New York) is furnished by the fact, as to the conditions on which similar loans have been obtained. The State of Ohio, to enable it to execute its great Canal, has repeatedly borrowed, within two, or three years past, large sums in New York, at about five per

Cent. It has recently contracted with Mr. [John Jacob] Astor and others for a loan at about that rate.

I am inclined to think that it would be more practicable for the State of North Carolina to obtain a loan, and on better terms, in the United States than in England. Those who have made investments in the debt of the United States, must be anxious, as that debt is paid off, and their Capital liberated, to re-invest it in other stocks, and I should suppose, they would prefer some in the United States to any foreign Stocks. A large amount of the principal of the public debt has been paid during the current year, and unless the operation of extinguishing it should be checked, an equal amount of it will, probably, be paid in the ensuing year. The effect will be to throw a large sum of unemployed Capital into the Market, and I should think that, during the next year, the State of North Carolina might be able to obtain a loan at not a greater rate of interest than five per cent.—

If it be deemed expedient to make the experiment in England of effecting the loan, I should take pleasure in directing our Minister [James Barbour], at the Court of St. James [*sic,* James's], to afford his good offices to any Agent that the State of N. Carolina might employ for the purpose; but the Executive of the United States could neither contract for the loan in their Name, nor guaranty its ultimate reimbursement, without the Authority of an Act of Congress. Whether our Minister could undertake the agency of negotiating the loan, or not, would depend upon himself, it not being a matter of official duty, but of private concern.

Copy. DNA, RG59, Dom. Letters, vol. 22, pp. 302-04 (M40, R20).   1. Writing from Oxford, N.C., on September 30, Potter blamed North Carolina's financial problems on the "iniquitous and illegal proceedings of the local banks in this state." He asked Clay's advice on floating a state loan in London and the availability of "disposable capital in the northern portion of the union." He assured Clay that North Carolinians would "view as their *deliverer* the individual who should effect" such a loan. ALS. DNA, RG59, Misc. Letters (M179, R66).

From ALEJANDRO VELEZ, Philadelphia, October 13, 1828. The Colombian Chargé informs Clay that he will soon be returning home. Expresses his "gratitude for your constant and generous efforts to induce this illustrious and free nation to ackno[w]ledge the independance of my country; and for your endeavours in the cabinet to establish friendly relations with it. Your name is gloriously associated with the noble cause of the emancipation of Spanish-America; and that people will always remember with respect and gratitude your important and valuable services." Notes, further, that "My political opinions, strictly republicain, and by no means favourable to the supremacy of military power, so dangerous to civil liberty, and which in the actual struggle of opinions you so nobly oppose, form a new motive of sympathy, and induce me to offer you the tribute of the highest respect and esteem." ALS. DNA, RG59, Notes from Colombian Legation, vol. 1 (M51, R2).

Clay responded on October 14 that it was "very gratifying to me to know that my efforts to produce the recognition of Colombia, as an Independent State, are Justly appreciated by you." Affirms his continuing interest in the welfare of Colombia and says he will maintain that interest "under all vicissitudes." Copy. DNA, RG59, Notes to Foreign Ministers and Consuls, vol. 4, pp. 76–7 (M38, R4).

From DANIEL WEBSTER   Boston, October 13, 1828

I am obliged to you for yours [October 6], recd two posts back. One part of its objects, you will have seen or heard, had been anticipated, by our friend & neighbor will have before this recd the proper communication.

The favorable results in Maryland & Delaware I am now to put the general object fairly within our reach, with proper exertion, & common good fortune. In my judgment, nothing fair & honorable should be spared. If we hold Kentucky, I have now full faith that we shall get votes enough in New York to ensure Mr A's re election. No doubt every useful mode & communication will occur to our friends, but I take the liberty of suggesting the expediency of letters, written or printed, from friends in Washington to friends in every part of Kentucky, laying before them the true state of things, as it is at present presented, & thus showing them the great probability that the vote of K. will decide the above. Our friends there ought to be made to feel, as the ancient combatants felt, that the issue of the contest may depend on a single arm. I know, at the same time, their zeal & steadiness; & that they will not be likely to omit reasonable exertions. Still, new hope would naturally inspire new vigor. Let me add, in a word, *if any thing remains to be done, to secure the vote of K. do it.*

I have seen David Trimble's publication[1] which, I should think, must do good. The best part of your letter is that which gives assurance of the improvement of your health. May God preserve you—for your own sake & the country['s]

ALS. DLC–HC (DNA, M212, R3). Letter marked "Private." 1. *Address of David Trimble, to the Public, Containing Proof That He Did Not Make Statements Attributed to Him, in Relation to Charges Against the President of the United States, and Mr. Clay.* Frankfort, 1828. Extracts published in the Frankfort *Argus of Western America,* October 13, 1828, and the Lexington *Kentucky Reporter,* October 8, 1828.

From WILLIAM T. WILLIS, Greensburg, Ky., October 13, 1828. Assures Clay that prospects are good for the election of Adams in Kentucky. "County committees are generally organised in the state and very active, and although the heroites [Jacksonians] are attempting something of the same kind of discipline, yet in this part of the state I am sensible they are not effecting any thing, but looseing daily, of my own knowledge. And although our friends may not consider Ky as altogether safe yet I consider it perfectly so & beyond doubt. Should our friends else where do their duty we shall achieve a most glorious trimph—a triumph of reason over corruption and villany." ALS. DNA, RG59, A. and R. (MR1). Willis's optimism was unfounded; Jackson carried Green County in November by a vote of 993 to 524.

To NICHOLAS BIDDLE, Washington, D.C., October 14, 1828. Requests that a line of credit be opened at the Bank of the United States to cover the salaries of William Henry Harrison, U.S. Minister to Colombia, and Edward T. Tayloe, Secretary of Legation there. Harrison's salary is $9000 per annum, Tayloe's is $2000. Copy. DNA, RG59, Dom. Letters, vol. 22, p. 304 (M40, R20). On October 18, 1828, William McIlvaine sent Clay a copy of a letter from Harrison to the Bank "authorizing me to appropriate quarterly three hundred dollars of his salary as . . . Minister . . . to Colombia, towards the payment of his debt to this Bank." LS. DNA, RG59, Accounting Records, Misc. Letters.

From THEODORE W. CLAY   Lexington, October 14, 1828
Yr favors inclosing your bond & a letter to me arrived in due time, for which I thank you. Mr Hill called to me & stated he thought he would pay down the purchase money or most of it, which caused me to write to you; I requested him to wait 'till I heard from you, and I expect in a few days should [Richard?] Hickman not wish to take it, that he will do so. Old Mr [David?] Bryant called to see if you had left any word about his debt, & has left or proposes to leave in a short time money with Mr [James] Harper on Acct of his note. He desired me not to write to you about his business, of a mortgage &c 'till he should see me again, which was made to enable him to encrease his payt I suppose.

Mr [Matthew] Kenneday [*sic,* Kennedy] thinks it necessary to remove the front wall of the back building at the [Kentucky] hotel which was quite dilapedated, & is accordingly having it done.

I saw Petit on my return here, & had rye sowed in the 25 acres preparatory to clover as you desired Mr [Robert] Scott to have done.

I think we are going on with a little more animation at Ashland. We are selling some wood, & I have had a few repairs gates &c essentially necessary.

Mr Scott advanced the quarterly sum of $12.50 cts to the President [Alva Woods] of the college [Transylvania]; who was inaugurated yesterday, and bids fair to please all parties, & succeed.

No doubt you have before this heard of or seen a set of certificates and an affidavit of Jno Downing, as to your being associated with [Aaron] Burr.[1] It is a scandalous business. But from persons I have seen from different parties it will benefit the Ad[ministration] in this state, whatever effect it may produce elsewhere. I am sorry to see that Thomas [Bodley] has so far forgot himself as the Jackson Prints represent he has done. I hope it will be laughed at as it deserves.

The politicians in this quarter seem to be determined to keep up their feelings to the sticking point 'till the election, & will succeed I believe.

I will attend to the contents of your letters, as [*sic,* and] to any other business you may have with the greatest pleasure. . . . PS. Should it be convenient for you to advance me what I desired in my last viz $200. I will scrupulously deposit the sales of wood and the collection of a note of young [Matthias?] Bush's for $200 $50 of which has been paid.

ALS. DLC–TJC (DNA, M212, R13).   1. John Downing, a Lexington mechanic, swore in an affidavit on October 4, 1828, that Burr, on his first visit to Kentucky in 1805, approached him and attempted to enlist him as a spy. Downing charged that Clay had urged him to accept Burr's offer and had said that he himself was engaged with Burr. This affidavit was accompanied by a certificate, signed by a number of Lexington citizens attesting to Downing's good character. These citizens later charged that they had been tricked into signing the certificate. See further, Lexington *Kentucky Reporter*, October 15, 22, 1828; Washington *Daily National Journal*, October 20, 1828.

To NATHANIEL HART   Washington, October 14, 1828
Inclosed is a letter for Mr. [James] Harper, which I hope may answer your purpose.[1]

I trust that K. will not forget herself in the approaching Contest. If she decides against the Chieftain, rely upon it absolutely that he is defeated. Kentucky holds the decision in her hands. And our friends in every County ought to recollect that every Vote will count.

ALS. KyU.   1. Not found; but see T. W. Clay to Clay, October 14, 1828.

To CHRISTOPHER HUGHES, no. 6, October 14, 1828. Instructs
Hughes to apply formally to the King of the Netherlands, William I, asking him to serve as arbiter between the U.S. and Britain on the Northeast Boundary dispute. Directs him to use the form of application devised by Lord Aberdeen, who will apply simultaneously to William on behalf of Britain. LS. DLC-HC (DNA, M212, R8). Also in DNA, RG59, Dip. Instr., vol. 12, p. 155-7 (M77, R7).

On October 16, Clay sent a copy of these instructions to James Barbour in London, directing him to "acquaint the British Government with this instruction given to Mr. Hughes." LS. DLC-HC (DNA, M212, R8). Also in Manning, *Diplomatic Correspondence . . . Canadian Relations*, 2:184-5.

From JOHN M. MACPHERSON, Cartagena, October 14, 1828. Complains that the response to his appeal to Simon Bolivar was unsatisfactory, because it incorrectly assumed that there was not a contest over the equity of the Custom House charges against him [MacPherson to Clay, September 15, 1828].

Reports details of the assassination attempt on Bolivar on September 25. Attributes the plot to Vice President Francisco de Paula Santander. Thinks Santander and General Jose Padilla may be executed as have six other leaders. Has learned that Bolivar hid beneath a bridge in water up to his chin during his escape, "while his enemies were passing over it, crying out Death to the Tyrant—Long live General Santander—" Reports that Bolivia has declared its independence from Colombia. Predicts more disorders in Colombia should Bolivar attempt to restore his power in Bolivia by force of arms. ALS. DNA, RG59, Cons. Disp., Cartagena, vol. 1 (M-T192, R1). Received November 11, 1828. For the assassination attempt on Bolivar, and subsequent disorders, see Salvador de Madariaga, *Bolivar*, 569-75, 584-5.

To JAMES BARBOUR   Washington, October 15, 1828
Mr. [William B.] Lawrence has transmitted to this office[1] a copy of the British Act of Parliament, which passed on the 25th. day of July, 1828, entitled "An Act to amend the laws relating to the Customs"—According to the provisions of that Act, as they are understood here, british vessels

importing cotton into any of the ports of the United Kindom, from anv british colony, without regard to the place of the growth of the article, are subject only to the payment of a duty of 4 d. per cwt., whilst the same article, imported directly from any foreign country, in British or foreign vessels, is liable to the payment of a duty of six per cent. As it respects the navigation of the United States and that of Great Britain the operation of that act, as applied to the article of cotton, the growth of the United States, would be that when it is imported into the ports of the United Kingdom, in American vessels, it would be subject to the higher rate of duty; when imported in british vessels, indirectly, through a British colony, it would be chargeable only, with the lower rate of duty. The British Act, though general in its terms, would be principally, if not exclusively, limited, in its effect on importations into the British ports, to cotton, the growth of the United States; for it is not likely that that article, grown in any other country, would be first introduced into any british colony, and thence imported into the United Kingdom. The cotton of the United States is not wanted in any of the british colonies for colonial consumption, nor is it according to the course of trade to export cotton from the United States to the British Colonies, and thence into Great Britain. The design, therefore, of the British Act of Parliament,—manifestly is, by presenting a motive for the importation of cotton, in the first instance, into the british colonies, from the United States, to give a preference to british shipping, in a competition with American shipping, in the transportation of the article from the United States to Great Britain. This preference could not be given in the direct trade, without a palpable violation of the existing commercial convention between the two countries,[2] and the attempt to give it in the circuitous trade, which is provided for by the Act, is a plain evasion, if not an infraction of that convention. The second article of the Convention provides that "the same duties shall be paid on the importation into the Unites States of any articles, the growth, produce, or manufacture of His Britannic Majesty's territories, in Europe, whether such importation shall be in vessels of the United States, or in British vessels, and the same duties shall be paid on the importation into the ports of any of His Britannic Majesty's territories in Europe, of any article, the growth, produce or manufacture of the United States, whether such importation shall be in British vessels, or in vessels of the United States." The equality of duties stipulate between the vessels of the two countries, in the above article, is without reference to the place of exportation, whether it is direct, or indirect, To entitle the vessels of each country to it, all that is required, is, that the article imported shall be the growth, produce or manufacture of one of them. If that qualification exists, the vessels of the one country have the same right with those of the other, to import the article subject to the same rate of duty. It is not intended to assert that the vessels of the United States have a right to import into British ports, from British colonies, articles the growth, produce or manufacture of the United States, but to contend that, if such circuitous importation be allowed to British vessels, it cannot, under the Convention, be permitted at a lower rate of duty on the article, than when the importation is direct from the United States in American vessels. In other words, that when a british and an american vessel enter, for example, the port of Liverpool, laden with articles the growth, produce or manufacture of the United States, precisely the same duties, and no others, are to be exacted, in both instances, no matter from what place, colony or country the exportation of the article has been made.

The great object of the Convention, as it respects the navigation of the two countries, was to secure a perfect equality in the competition between their respective vessels, and the transportation of the objects of production of the one intended for the consumption of the other. To ensure that equality, various other provisions, besides that recited, are to be found in the Convention, relating to duties and charges in the vessels, themselves, to duties and bounties on exportation, and to drawbacks.

We can hardly suppose that the good faith of Great Britain will allow her thus to violate and evade a solemn national compact. But the subject is too important to our navigation to suffer us quietly to remain in ignorance or uncertainty as to the intention of the British Government. From the British Gazettes which have reached us, it seems to be uncertain whether a British vessel simply touching at a colonial port, without discharging any part of her cargo, will not be permitted to import the article at the lower rate of duty. The difference in the effect upon our navigation will be considerable, whether the british vessel be admitted to entry at the lower rate of duty by simply touching and obtaining new papers, or upon a discharge of her cargo at the colonial port; but the difference will only be in the degree of injury sustained by us. In principle, both modes of proceeding are the same; they are both condemned by the Convention.

The President wishes you officially to enquire whether it be the intention of the British Government to admit the importation of cotton, the growth of the United States from a british colony, in a british vessel, at a lower rate of duty than when the same article is imported, in an american vessel, direct from the United States; and whether the british vessel will be entitled to a exemption from the higher duty by merely touching at the colonial port, or if it will be required that the cotton shall have been imported into a colonial port in a different vessel from that which transports it to Great Britain; or if the British vessel clearing out from the ports of the United States with cotton, will be required to discharge her cargo, or any part of it, at the colonial port? Should the answer be that it is the intention of the British government to give to the act the unfavorable interpretation which has been supposed, you will remonstrate against it, and notify the British Government that such an operation of their law is considered as forbidden by the Convention, that the Government of the United States cannot acquiesce in it; and that if our laws are not already adequate to counteract the effect, we must resort to other remedial measures to secure to our navigation the fair and equal competition which was the object of the commercial Convention.

ALS. DNA, RG59, Dip. Instr., vol. 12, pp. 157-60 (M77, R7). No. 4.   1. See Lawrence to Clay, August 6, 1828.   2. The Commercial Convention of July, 1815 [2:26, 30-7] was renewed in October, 1818 [2:611], and again in August, 1827 [6:826-7].

To RICHARD PINDELL   Washington, October 15, 1828

I observe that some of the Jackson party in Kentucky, for the purpose of withdrawing public attention from the alleged connection between General Jackson and Col. [Aaron] Burr, have gotten up a charge against me, of participation in the schemes of the latter. I have not, myself, thought it necessary to notice this new and groundless accusation, but prompted by the opinions of some of my friends, and actuated also, by the desire to vindicate the memory of an inestimable but departed friend [John Allen] who fell in the service of his country, I communicate the following statement, which you are at liberty to publish:[1]

Public prosecutions were commenced in the Federal Court of Kentucky against Col. Burr in the fall of 1806 [1:256-9, 270, 272]. He applied to me and I engaged as his counsel, in conjunction with the late Col. John Allen, to defend him. The prosecutions were conducted by the late Col. Joseph Hamilton Daviess, a man of genius, but of strong prejudices, who was such an admirer of Col. [Alexander] Hamilton, that after he had attained full age, he (Col. D.) adopted a part of his name as his own. Both Col. Allen and myself believed that there was no ground for the prosecutions, and that Col. Daviess was chiefly moved to institute them by his admiration of Col. Hamilton and his hatred of Col. Burr. Such was our conviction of the innocence of the accused that, when he sent us a considerable fee, we resolved to decline accepting it, and accordingly returned it. We said to each other, Col. Burr has been an eminent member of the profession, has been attorney general of the State of New York, is prosecuted without cause, in a distant State, and we ought not to regard him in the light of an ordinary culprit. The first prosecution entirely failed. A second was shortly afterwards instituted. Between the two, I was appointed a Senator of the U.S. In consequence of that relation to the general government, Col. Burr, who still wished me to appear for him, addressed the note to me [1:256-7] of which a copy is herewith transmitted. I accordingly again appeared for him, with Col. Allen, and when the Grand Jury returned the true bill of indictment not true, a scene was presented in the court room which I had never before witnessed in Kentucky. There were shouts of applause from an audience, not one of whom, I am persuaded, would have hesitated to level a rifle against Col. Burr, if he believed that he aimed to dismember the Union, or sought to violate its peace or overturn its constitution.

It is not true that the professional services of either Col. Allen or myself were volunteered, although they were gratuitous. Neither of us was acquainted with any illegal designs whatever of Col. Burr. A better or braver man, or more ardent and sincere patriot, than Col. Allen never lived. The disastrous field of [River] Raisin, on which he fell, attests his devotion to his country. The affidavit of a Mr. John Downing has been procured and published to prove that I advised him to enlist with Col. Burr, and that I told him I was going with him myself. There is not one word of truth in it, so far as it relates to me. The ridiculous tale will be credited by no one who knows both of us. The certificate of some highly respectable man has been procured as to his character. This affidavit bears date on the 3d, and the certificate on a detached paper on the 4th inst. I have no doubt that it was obtained on false pretenses, and with an entire concealment of its object. I was, at the period of the last prosecution, preparing to attend the Senate of the United States at the seat of Government, many hundreds of miles in an opposite direction from that in which it afterwards appeared Col. Burr was bound. So far from my having sent any message to Mr. Downing, when I was last in Lexington, I did not then even dream that the malignity of party spirit could fabricate such a charge as has been put forth against me. It is not true that I was at the ball given to Col. Burr in Frankfort. I was, at the time, in Lexington. It is not true that he ever partook of the hospitality of my house. It was at that time a matter of regret with me that my professional engagements and those connected with my departure for Washington did not allow me to extend to him the hospitality with which it was always my wish to treat strangers. He never was in my house, according to my recollection, but once, and that was the night before I started to this city, when, being myself a stranger in the place, he delivered me some letters of introduction, which I never presented.

On my arrival in December, 1806, I became satisfied, from the letter in cipher of Col. Burr to Gen. [James] Wilkinson and from other information communicated to me by Mr. [Thomas] Jefferson, that Col. Burr had entertained illegal designs. At the request of Mr. Jefferson I delivered to him the original note from Col. Burr to me, of which a copy is now forwarded, and I presume it is yet among Mr. Jefferson's papers. I was furnished a copy of it [1:257] in the handwriting of Col. [Isaac] Coles, his private secretary, which is with my papers in Kentucky. This, my dear doctor, is a true and faithful account of my connection with Col. Burr.

Printed in H. H. Crittenden, comp., *The Crittenden Memoirs* (New York, 1936), 100–2. 1. Clay's statement was published in the Richmond *Enquirer*, October 17, 1828; see also Clay to Thompson, November 25, 1828.

From WILLIAM RADCLIFF, Lima, no. 5, October 15, 1828. Discusses problems of destitute American seamen and inquires about the legal obligations of ships' masters to transport them home. Notes also that there are frequent "complaints about Captains and Mates illegally punishing their men," underfeeding them, and overworking them. Says that ships' officers deny that consuls have any right to interfere with their crews. Comments: "I am well satisfied there is a domineering & tyrannical spirit prevalent among the officers of our Merchant vessels, which leads to great abuse of authority, and that generally the sailors are more sinned against than sinning." Argues, further, that "there should be better proof required of the desertion of a seaman than a mere entry by the mate in a log book." ALS. DNA, RG59, Cons. Disp., Lima, vol. 2 (M–T154, R2). No date of receipt.

From WILLIAM RADCLIFF, Lima, October 15, 1828. Reports that Peru's Minister of Foreign Affairs, Jose M. Galdiano, has not replied to his letter concerning Peru's blockade of Colombian ports. States that it is not probable that the blockade "will be acted upon or abused to such a degree as was to be expected, its object being chiefly . . . to produce an effect in Colombia by actually blockading Gua[ya]quil only, and nominally the whole coast." Adds that "they have already been foiled" in the attempt to blockade Guayaquil. Believes "that negotiations are on foot between the Governments of Peru and Colombia, and am not without hopes that they may shortly terminate in peace." Mentions that Galdiano has now resigned as Foreign Minister.

Notes that he has opened several packets of mail addressed to the late James Cooley, but adds that he is postponing taking any action until he can receive further instructions. States that he has communicated informally with the Peruvian government concerning Cooley's instructions [5:865-70] to negotiate a treaty of friendship and commerce and that the response he received was cordial. Believes that the war and Peru's "pecuniary embarrassment" will cause its Congress at the next session to revise the tariff which is so detrimental to trade with the U.S. Adds that the government has asked foreign merchants for a loan and has been refused. Predicts that the government will demand a "forced loan" to which all foreign merchants will have to contribute. ALS. DNA, RG59, Cons. Disp., Lima, vol. 2 (M154, R2). No date of receipt. For the Colombian-Peruvian treaty of peace of February 28, 1829, see Parry, *Treaty Series*, 79:325-8.

From JOHN SERGEANT   Philadelphia, October 15, 1828
I regret more than I can tell you the unfortunate issue of yesterday's election,[1] chiefly for the effect it will have elsewhere. It was carried against us by illegal voters and voters brought from other Districts. Local dissensions, too, had some influence, and the tariff was brought to bear against us, that is, to keep some of our friends from the polls.

With my regret, there is mingled a strong wish that our friends every where may be persuaded we have done the best we could. Errors there may have been, but there was no want of zeal,

ALS. InU. Letter marked "Private."   1. The administration candidates, including Sergeant, were soundly defeated in the city, state, and congressional elections on October 14. See the Philadelphia *United States Gazette*, October 15, 1828, for unofficial returns for all offices.

To CHARLES HAMMOND   Washington, October 17, 1828
Prior to the receipt of your favor of the 10h. inst. I had seen [John] Downing's affidavit; and I had written a letter [October 15], for publication, to Dr. [Richard] Pindell of Lexington, a Copy of which I shall cause to be inserted in the papers here.[1] I thought the story almost too ridiculous to notice. Downing is a profligate, street blackguard, as dirty a fellow as you have in Cincinnati, who has abandoned his own family, and keeps a strumpet, in open prostitution. How the gentleman came to give him the *qualified* Certificate which has been published I know not.

I can tell you nothing at present about the Judges. My opinion is that the vacancy in Ohio[2] ought to be filled. But I believe Mr. Adams thinks it most proper to postpone, for obvious considerations, of which the near approach of the Senate is the principal [consideration], the appointments at this time.

The re-election of Mr. Adams is now almost demonstrated to be sure, *if* he gets the votes of K. and 20 in N. York. Of the latter we do not doubt. As to K. you are as good a judge as I am. My friends write very confidently.

ALS. InU.   1. See Washington *Daily National Journal,* October 18, 1828.   2. This vacancy, occasioned by the death of Charles W. Byrd, was a federal judgeship for the District of Ohio. Correy to Clay, October 4, 1828.

From "A REPUBLICAN OF 98," Lexington, Ky., no. 1, October 17, 1828. Recalls the strength of Clay's republicanism during the political crisis [Sedition Act controversy] in Kentucky in 1798 and the acclamation it had then brought him. Contrasts this with Clay's abandonment of republican principles in supporting John Quincy Adams for the presidency in the House election of 1825. "You betrayed them [the people], you abandoned the principles which had given you your influence,— which had raised you to power.... You were found acting with men whom you had long denounced." Charges that Clay paid no attention to the will of the people of Kentucky in his support of Adams, in that their legislature had instructed the state delegation in Congress to vote for Jackson [3:902]. Denounces as "chicanery and sophistry" Clay's contention that he had voted for Adams in obedience to the wishes of the people of his own Congressional district, rather than the wishes of all the people as expressed in the instructions of the legislature. Explains to Clay in this regard the difference between federalism and republicanism: "The federal doctrine is that the representative has the most intelligence, the republican doctrine is that the people are the most honest, and is the safest depository of power." Questions Clay's explanation that given William H. Crawford's poor health and Jackson's unsuitability for the presidency, he had no choice but to vote for Adams. Deems this an expression of the federal doctrine. His duty as a true republican was to disregard "your own personal predilections and opinions" on that question, and be governed instead "by the wishes of the freemen of your state." Promises a second letter on this theme [below, October 24, 1828]. Printed in Lexington *Kentucky Gazette,* October 17, 1828.

To WATERS SMITH, Washington, October 17, 1828. Reports that the President has communicated to the State Department "the Memorial of Peter Mitchell, agent of the Underwriters at Lloyd's, in the case of the ship James Mitchell and cargo, libelled in 1827, on claim of salvage," in East Florida courts. Continues that the memorial asserts Smith sold the ship, but did not pay into the registry of the Superior Court of the Eastern District of Florida, as per its order, the $19,260.05 proceeds of the sale. Furthermore, that he absented himself from the Court's jurisdiction "to elude the operation of an attachment which had been issued against you," leaving Mitchell without remedy to recover those costs. Concludes: "The President expects from you a prompt explanation, in regard to these very serious charges, affecting your official conduct." Copy. DNA, RG59, Dom. Letters, vol. 22, p. 309 (M40, R20). Smith, U.S. Marshall for East Florida, was at this time in Washington.

Following a personal interview with Clay, he addressed to the Secretary of State on October 24, a seventeen-page vindication of himself. He charged that Mitchell Farmer, acting British consul in Florida, headed a small cabal of his "personal enemies" who sought to remove him from his office, and that he was innocent of the charges leveled against him. ALS. DNA, RG59, Misc. Letters (M179, R66).

From THOMAS L. L. BRENT, Lisbon, no. 87, October 18, 1828. With reference to the claim for a cargo of dried beef by the owners of the brig *Osprey* of Boston, reports that the reason Portuguese officials cannot make payment "is very obvious—they have no money." LS. DNA, RG59, Dip. Disp., Portugal, vol. 8 (M43, R7). Received December 19, 1828.

From FRANCIS C. FENWICK, Nantes, October 18, 1828. Reports sentiment in France for the abolition of the state monopoly on tobacco, and an import duty on foreign tobacco instead. Believes the duty will be lower on "inferior quality" tobacco from the Ukraine, Palatinate, and Belgium, and that American tobacco will surely suffer. Notes that the government has already reduced the quantity of superior U.S. tobacco in the mixture currently being produced in the "Royal Manufactories." ALS. DNA, RG59, Cons. Disp., Nantes, vol. 1 (M-T223, R1). Received February 8, 1829.

To RALPH R. GURLEY Washington, October 18, 1828
Mr. Clay presents his respects to Mr. Gurley,[1] and in answer to his note of this day, has to say that he regrets he cannot name any person in Kentucky that he knows would undertake so long a journey for the purpose indicated by Mr. Gurley.[2] If Mr. [John J.] Crittenden, Dr [James] Blythe, or Mr. [Benjamin O.] Peers, could be prevailed upon to attend, either of them would make a highly respectable representative from Kentucky. But Mr. C. does not know that either of them would have it in his power to attend. Supposing neither of those gentlemen to be able to attend, Mr. [John] Chambers, the newly elected member to the House of Representatives would answer very well, if he be a member of any Auxiliary Society, which Mr. Clay is, however, unable to say.

AN. DLC-Records of the American Colonization Society (DNA, M212, R20). 1. For the Rev. Mr. Gurley, see *DAB*. 2. Gurley's purpose was to recruit a qualified Kentucky delegate to attend the 12th annual meeting of the Society which convened in Washington, D.C., on January 17, 1829. R. R. Gurley, ed., *African Repository* (January, 1829), 4:348-9. The *African Repository* was the official journal of the Society. On December 20, 1828, the Kentucky State Colonization Society was launched in Frankfort by John Pope, Benjamin O. Peers, Daniel Mayes, Adam Beatty, James W. Denny, and Samuel Daviess. *Ibid.*, 351. The Rev. Mr. Peers, later President of Transylvania University, was the leading force in this action. Staudenraus, *The African Colonization Movement, 1816-1865*, pp. 137-41.

From ABRAHAM B. NONES, Maracaibo, October 18, 1828. States that yesterday the mail from Bogota brought word of a revolt of the battalion of artillery on September 25, 1828, in which an attempt was made to assassinate Simon Bolivar. Adds that two aides and many guards were killed, but Bolivar escaped, "it is said through a back window." Reports that the infantry "turned out and after a hard contest over powered the assailants." Relates that this morning there is a rumor "that an attempt would be made to get up a revolt here, and implicate all foreigners." Believes that the Colombian officials "meant to avail themselves of the Excitement caused by the news of the Bogota affair" to liquidate the foreigners by implicating them in a revolt which they themselves would foment. Says the authorities will then "plead to the world, that the foreigners were Suspected, and that before they could come to their Succour, the work of death had commenced." Concludes: "Night is coming on, and as a precaution I have traced these hasty lines to the effect—that, Should we Suffer the Govmt & people of the US may not be imposed on by the falsehoods and Statements of those in Command, it is a weak invention to impose on the world but, may be fatal in its consequences." ALS. DNA, RG59, Cons. Disp., Maracaibo, vol. 1 (M–T62, R1). Received November 26, 1828.

Continues on October 21, reporting that the notes which he and other foreign consuls handed to local authorities "seemed to have had the effect most desired, and great precautions were consequently taken to preserve the peace from any revolt." Notes "the most distinguished men of the Country are among those *accused*" in the assassination attempt. Complains that American commerce has recently been annoyed by extra duties and confiscation of allegedly counterfeit money. *Ibid.* Received November 26, 1828.

From NICHOLAS P. TRIST   Monticello, October 18, 1828
Enclosed in one from Mr [James] Madison, I received, by the last mail, your favor of the 10th inst, which I lose no time in acknowledging. If the duties of the office, for the offer of which I have to tender you my thanks, be such as I am competent to, the situation will be very acceptable. To avoid trespassing on your time, engrossed, as it must be, by weightier matters, I shall, by this post, address a request to my kinsman Mr. [Thomas Jefferson] Randolph, to afford me, by return of mail, such an insight into those duties as is requisite to a determination on my part, and this shall be made & communicated, the moment. I hear from him.

As the circumstances on which Mrs [Martha Jefferson] Randolph and I find ourselves at this moment, would render an immediate removal of the family to Washington, very inconvenient, this will be postponed till some time next year—perhaps the fall. There will be nothing, therefore, to detain me, after I shall hear from Mr Randolph, except the situation of Mrs [Virginia Jefferson Randolph] Trist, whose confinement is impending & will, at latest, take place very early next month. My wish is, of course, not to leave her at so critical a moment: but I do not forget that the public service is not to be postponed to private considerations of even this nature, and it will be felt, by me as a favor, if you will drop me a single line, stating whether a delay up to the end of the first week in November would be inconsistent with a due regard for those paramount claims.

Should the duties to which you are pleased to invite me, be such as I shall feel justified in undertaking, I will enter upon their discharge on the determination to justify, as far as in me lies, the confidence with which I am flattered.

506

With a grateful sense of the generous interest which has actuated you on this occasion. . . .

ALS. DNA, RG59, Misc. Letters (M179, R66). Addressed "Private." A draft of this letter is in the possession of Thomas D. Clark, Lexington, Ky. It differs to no important extent from this, the final version.

From FRANCIS T. BROOKE   Richmond, October 19, 1828

I fear that you have either written me, and that your letter has been embezzled at Some of the Post offices, or that your official engagements and private correspondence have been too much for your health, as though you Said on parting I will write you Soon, I have received no letter, however this may be, a letter from you whenever all these things will permit it, giving me an assurance that your health is improving will afford me great pleasure, until the unfavorable news from Penna[1] the Spirits of our freinds here were very high—and though it ought to have had no effect, yet those who entertain that opinion are doing all we can to counteract its influence on others, unless this news reacts on Virginia we Still entertain hopes that the freehold vote will Save her from disgrace—Specific information of great change in many parts of the State encourage our hopes—and if it were possible to get anything that could be relied on from NY we Should feel assured of Success—the elections in Maryland & Delaware have been of much Service in Virginia, and the address of the Central committee here,[2] with the facts which are daily coming out, both as to Genl Jackson and the character of Some of his party are making favorable impressions—you will have Seen what [Thomas] Ritchie Says of your being Counsel for Burr &c is it worth your time to expose the fabrication[3]—I Shall be glad to hear that your health is improving and that Mrs Clay & family injoy good health—

ALS. InU.   1. Sergeant to Clay, October 15, 1828.   2. Brooke to Clay, January 9, 1828; Richmond *Enquirer*, October 21, 1828.   3. Ritchie ran articles on October 10, 14, 16, 17, 1828, in his Richmond *Enquirer*, attempting to implicate Clay in the Burr conspiracy. The most extensive article was that of October 10, taken from the Lexington *Kentucky Gazette* and signed by "Brutus." Clay's most detailed answer to the charge is in Clay to Pindell, October 15, 1828.

From JOHN M. MACPHERSON, Cartagena, Colombia, October 19, 1828. Reports that General Jose Padilla and Colonel Ramon Guerra, Army Chief of Staff, were shot for their participation in the Simon Bolivar assassination plot. Thinks Vice–President Francisco Santander will not be executed because he has too many powerful friends. Notes that a regiment officered by English mercenaries loyal to Bolivar has been sent to the Bogota garrison. Mentions that one of the frigates in harbor has been ordered to sail to the South Sea "to act against Peru." Deplores the "shocking" treatment of foreign seamen and doubts if a complete crew can be found to man the mission to Peru. Hopes no American will be "enticed into this service." ALS. DNA, RG59, Cons. Disp., Cartagena, vol. 1 (M-T192, R1). No date of receipt.

To THOMAS SMITH   Washington, October 19, 1828

I have the satisfaction to inform you that information has this moment reached us from various parts of New Jersey, in letters and newspapers, shewing that at the elections which have just terminated in that State the Administration has obtained a signal and decisive victory. Our friends have succeeded in ten out of the fourteen counties of that State,[1] have obtained a majority in the Legislature of three-fourths, and have, in short, an aggregate popular vote, greater than ever was given there before for the Administration, and such as to put the choice of Electors for Mr. Adams[2] beyond the possibility of doubt.

I hasten to give you this agreeable information, which I shall communicate to various parts of our State, to guard against the circulation of erroneous reports.

Copy. Lexington *Kentucky Reporter*, October 29, 1828. Smith edited the *Reporter*.   1. The Adams Administration actually carried 9 counties compared to 5 by the Jackson forces. The 9 Adams counties with their vote tally were: Bergen, 1393-1231; Burlington, 2315-1055; Cape May, no opposition; Cumberland, 1212-1116; Essex, 2935-1995; Gloucester, 1378-1088; Middlesex, 1688-1228; Salem, 1036-918; and Somerset, 1173-1064. The 5 Jackson counties were Hunterdon, 2257-1839; Morris, 1799-1600; Monmouth, 1848-1685; Sussex, 1602-971; and Warren (ticket unopposed). See *Niles' Register* (November 15, 1828), 35:1.   2. Adams's total popular vote of 23,764, as compared with Jackson's total of 21,951, secured all 8 New Jersey electoral votes for Adams. Weston, *The Presidential Election of 1828*, 182.

From JAMES CLARK, Winchester, Ky., October 20, 1828. [First few lines of letter cannot be read]. "The most of the hands engaged in driving hogs are, Jackson men, they will be absent at the [November] election and to that number we will be the gainer. I cannot say what effect Mr. [Richard A.] Buckners and my address has had. It has been answered by Mr. Benj. Taylor." Notes that Col. John M. McConnell will campaign "in the upper [coun]ties in [Henry] Danls. [Daniel] district." Declares: "My real opinion is that little or nothing can be done at this time by printed addresses. The floating vote, which is now the only disposeable one, can only be secured, by judicious management on the days of the election—We will try to get our proportions of them." Calls attention to John Downing's statement linking Clay to Aaron Burr and apologizes that he was tricked by Downing [several lines of the manuscript cannot be read at this point] into earlier signing a character reference for him. Concludes: "Suspecting no villany in the business, and knowing but little of his character I did not hesitate to give him my name. I need not say to you how much I have been vexed at being thus imposed on—The publication as to yourself is intirely harmless, no person beleives it, and the fraudulent manner, he obtained the signatures to his certificate has increased the infamy of his character." ALS. DLC-HC (DNA, M212, R2). The "Circular Address of James Clarke and Richard A. Buckner, to their Constituents of the 3rd and 8th Congressional Districts of Kentucky," which extolled the record of the Adams administration, defended the Tariff of 1828, and linked Jackson to the Aaron Burr conspiracy, was published in the Lexington *Kentucky Reporter*, "Extra," September 20, 1828, in lieu of issue No. 4 of the *Anti-Jackson Bulletin or Messenger of Truth*. The Benjamin Taylor response has not been found; but for Taylor's other pro-Jackson political activities, expecially his defense of the General in the Tennessee militiamen controversy [5:739], see Lexington *Kentucky Gazette*, October 10, 24, 1828. John M. McConnell was state senator from Greenup County, Ky. The district of Henry Daniel [see *BDAC*] included Lawrence, Lewis, Montgomery, and Pike counties. For the charge that Clay was involved in the Burr conspiracy, see Theodore W. Clay to Clay, October 14, 1828.

From JAMES IREDELL, Raleigh, October 20, 1828. The Governor of North Carolina regrets that Daniel Brent's request for two documents— the Royal Proclamation of October 7, 1763, and a letter from the then British Secretary of State transmitting the Proclamation to the Colony of North Carolina—cannot be honored, since the documents cannot be found in the state's archives. "In the Confusion incident to the change of officers & Government during our revolution," a large number of North Carolina's records and documents "were lost or destroyed & these probably were among that number." LS. DNA, RG76, Northeast Boundary: Misc. Papers, Env. 4, item 28. The famous Royal Proclamation established the so-called "Proclamation Line of 1763" which, in part, defined the western boundaries of several colonies.

To BARON PAUL   Washington, October 20, 1828
DE KRUDENER
I have the honor to acknowledge the receipt of your Note of the 14th. instant, communicating the declaration of the Emperor of Russia [Nicholas I], under the date the 14th. of April last, in which His Imperial Majesty announces the motives which have impelled him to appeal to Arms against the Ottoman Porte, together with a copy of the circular despatch of Count [Karl Robert] Nesselrode, and the accompanying documents. I have submitted to the President of the United States your note, with its several accompaniments, all of which he has perused with great interest. They have brought to him official knowledge of an event, the existence of which had previously reached him through other channels.

Standing as the United States do in an attitude of neutrality, in respect to the existing war, it would not become them to express any opinion on the causes which have led to it, especially as they have received no communication from the other belligerent. But it is not incompatible with that proper and just reserve, to say that the communications which I have had the honor to receive from you present a very strong case, on the side of Russia. The President is fully persuaded that His Imperial Majesty, in resorting to Arms, has been actuated by a clear conviction that he has the support of right and justice, and that the honor and interests of his Empire left him no alternative. Whilst the United States will faithfully perform towards both parties all the duties which appertain to their neutral position, they can never forget that Russia has ever been their firm constant and powerful friend, nor be indifferent to the fortunes which may attend her. The President has seen with much satisfaction the spirit of moderation manifested by the Emperor, according so well with that which ever animated his illustrious Brother [Alexander I]. It must inspire confidence in other powers, and afford a guarranty for a speedy and honorable termination of the war.

It is gratifying to the President that no disturbance of the good understanding which happily subsists between Russia and the United

States is ever likely to occur; but that, on the contrary, there is every reason to believe that their amicable relations, which it will always be his pleasure and desire to strengthen and invigorate, will continue unimpaired. . . .

Copy. DNA, RG59, Notes to Foreign Ministers and Consuls, vol. 4, pp. 78–80 (M38, R4).

From ROBERT P. LETCHER   Lancaster, Ky., October 20, 1828

Yours of the 12h Inst & this inst recd. my horse was in readiness again to visit the interior countries, and daily waited the arrival of the mail. The *cheering* news contained in your short letter arrived at a most fortunate moment. You may rely upon it, the intelligence from Delaware from Maryland, and from the *North* will animate the spirits, and greatly increase the exertions of our friends. Every thing which can be done, to save this state, by honorable means, will be done I believe we shall give a majority in this D[istrict][1] for Mr. Adams, of about 3000—many friends think 3500—and that will be the number if the mountains turn out as well as I have a right to believe they will, but we have lost 250 votes by the Hog Drivers—many of them would not employ the Jackson men.

In [Thomas P.] Moores[2] and [Richard A.] Buckners[3] Districts I am very apprehensive of a little loss compared with the vote for Govr. In [Thomas] Chiltons[4] [Charles A.] Wickliffes[5] and [Joseph] Le Comptes[6] we shall do better.

Upon the whole I am by no me[ans] entirely confident of success, yet I would not exchange chances with the enemy. The truth is, we have the majority, in my opinion, but the other side have the art in many instances, to make one voter count two or three at the Pools. . . .

ALS. DLC–HC (DNA, M212, R3).   1. Letcher's district was comprised of Clay, Estill, Garrard, Harlan, Knox, Rockcastle, and Whitley counties. Adams carried this district 2456 to 1121 for Jackson, less than half the margin Letcher predicted. Thomas Metcalfe had carried the district in the August gubernatorial election by 2918 to 972 for William T. Barry. For returns in all of these counties, see Frankfort *Argus Of Western America,* November 19, 1828.   2. Moore's district was comprised of Jessamine, Lincoln, and Mercer counties. Letcher was correct in predicting a greater loss for Adams than Metcalfe had experienced there. Jackson carried this district by 2354 to 1551 for Adams, while Barry had won it by only 2299 votes to 2020 for Metcalfe.   3. Buckner's district was comprised of Adair, Casey, and Cumberland counties. Jackson carried the district by 1284 to 841 for Adams, while Barry had lost it to Metcalfe by a margin of 82 votes.
4. Chilton's district comprised Muhlenburg and Ohio counties. Letcher was incorrect in predicting that Adams would do better than Metcalfe had done there, because Jackson won the district by 624 to 572, while Metcalfe had carried it by a 793 to 552 margin.
5. Wickliffe's district was comprised of Bullitt, Jefferson, and Nelson counties. Letcher was also incorrect in this prediction, since Jackson carried it by a wider margin than Barry had in August. Jackson won it by 2697 votes to 2085 for Adams, while Barry had carried it by 2580 to 2291 for Metcalfe.   6. Le Compte's district was comprised of Gallatin, Henry, Owen, and Shelby counties. Again Jackson did better here than Barry had. Jackson won 2572 votes in this district to 1893 for Adams, while Barry had defeated Metcalfe by 2506 to 2362.

To HENRY CLAY, JR.   Washington, October 21, 1828

I recd. your favor of the 16h. inst. I have constantly intended to write you, since my return from the West, but I have omitted it from the multitude of my engagements. My health is improved by the trip, but it is not, and I fear never again will be, as stout as I could wish.

I am glad to hear of your success,[1] and particularly of your doing better in drawing than you had expected. All the accounts that reach me are highly creditable to you, and you now constitute one of my greatest sources of happiness.

I think you would do well to refresh your recollection of the dead languages. I never enjoyed the advantage of Knowing them, but I have remarked that those who do find a resource in them throughout life, and some times at a late period of it.

Mr [Alva] Woods, the President of Transylvania has been installed and the Institution has been again opened with good prospects.

Your Mama and family are well.

Thomas [Hart Clay] has been behaving very ill at Philada. & N. York—

ALS. Henry Clay Memorial Foundation, Lexington, Ky.   1. At West Point. Young Clay had entered the Academy on July 1, 1826.

From JOHN McKIM, JR., Baltimore, October 21, 1828. Reports that he and his friends are working "by day and by night" in the good cause that is the Adams campaign; but notes that "when any thing turns up to give our Opponents an advantage like the Peruvian Decree, that Our Administration has not Attended to Our Commercial concerns in the New South American States, does us much Injury." Suggests that "a man of Talents and Respectability, with Commercial Knowledge" be sent immediately to Peru as Chargé to straighten out the problem. Assures Clay that since the Peruvians themselves have no manufacturers and concept of "what we call the American System," the articles they have forbidden to be imported, especially textiles, can only be traced to "British Influence" in the country. ALS. DNA, RG59, A. and R. (MR3). Endorsed by Clay: "To be sent to the President."

On October 23, Clay offered the Chargé post in Peru to Edward Ingersoll, informing him that "no time must be lost in your proceeding on the Mission," and that the public interest required a U.S. representative "at that Republic as soon as may be practicable." AL. DLC-HC (DNA, M212, R12); also in DNA, RG59, Dip. Instr., vol. 12, pp. 161–2 (M77, R7). Letter marked "Confidential." The Peruvian Decree of June 15, 1828, prohibited the importation after 8 months from the U.S. and after 10 months from Europe of all flour and also of those articles that were subject to a duty of 90%, including low–priced cotton fabric produced primarily in the U.S. See, further, Radcliff to Clay, August 30, 1828.

To NICHOLAS P. TRIST   Washington, October 21, 1828
I have received this morning your letter of the 18th. instant, from which I am glad to perceive that you are disposed to accept the appointment in the Department of State, an offer of which I transmitted to you through Mr. [James] Madison. From the favorable accounts I have received from him, and from others, of your capacity, I do not think you need apprehend any want of competency to the discharge of such duties as may be assigned you. I do not know that on this subject, Mr. [Thomas Jefferson] Randolph can afford you any satisfaction. The gentleman [Richard Forrest], whose death created the vacancy that recently occurred, was chiefly employed in making out passports and Instruments of au-

511

thentication. I have not determined to which of the gentlemen that business shall be assigned. If, as I understand, you are well acquainted with the French language, you will be sometimes employed in translating, sometimes in transcribing, and recording diplomatic correspondence &c—

Your presence here at this time, is not so urgent, as to require your leaving your family, under the circumstances of their condition described to you. The public service will not suffer, if you remain at home until the 10th. of November, or even a few days longer, if the state of Mrs. [Virginia Jefferson Randolph] Trist should be such as to require your presence. I shall hope to see you here about that time—

Copy. DNA, RG59, Dom. Letters, vol. 22, pp. 312-3 (M40, R20).

From JAMES BARBOUR, London, no. 4, October 22, 1828. Reports that the Queen of Portugal, Maria da Gloria, is still in Britain and that "her fate is so far uncertain." States that the high officials of Britain and "the whole Diplomatic corps resident at this court" have paid their respects and kissed her hand, but "Not perceiving the propriety of my doing so I have abstained—and being single, it has excited the more attention." Comments at length on the possibility of a Russian blockade of the Dardanelles and Britain's problems with Ireland. LS. DNA, RG59, Great Britain, vol. 36 (M30, R32). Received December 4, 1828.

From JOEL R. POINSETT, Mexico, no. 153, October 22, 1828. Reports that several skirmishes have occurred between Antonio Lopez de Santa Anna and government forces. Notes that the Senate on "the most inconclusive evidence" impeached the Governor of the State of Mexico, Lorenzo Zavala, for abetting Santa Anna, and thus, this man "of talents and of great energy of character, and justly beloved by the people, has been forced to become a rebel to the Government."

Adds that returns from the election of the Chamber of Deputies seem to indicate a victory for the popular [Guerrero] party, and an investigation may be conducted into the presidential election. States that "the manner in which the elections were conducted in some of the States which voted for Manuel Gomez Pedraza, will not bear an impartial" investigation. Has heard Pedraza's party may "prevent the members of the new chamber from assembling, a mode of securing the election of their chief quite characteristic of the principles of that party."

Mentions that the Senate has returned to the Chamber of Deputies the treaty between the U.S. and Mexico [Poinsett to Clay, February 22, 1828], having approved certain sections and disapproved others. Believes the Mexicans "dislike our republican institutions" and "are in reality envious and apprehensive of" the U.S. ALS. DNA. RG59, Dip. Disp., Mexico, vol. 4 (M97, R5). Received December 1, 1828.

From DAVID TRIMBLE   Trimble's Iron Works, Ky.,
                                              October 22, 1828
I came home on yesterday from the hills, and shall leave here for them again on tomorrow. This gave me an opertunity of Seeing yours of the

eleventh Inst. you think I ought to circulate my address through my old district.[1] I have done So, under a belief that I owed it to myself to make known what is there Stated. I have expended about $250, to have it printed & distributed. The money is honestly laid out; because the address tells the truth and gives the people honest information. I did not Suppose it would produce any good effect untill the election is over; but if the publication had been delayed untill after that Event, it would have lost one half of its interest. I Shall no doubt have a torrent of abuse heaped on me from Montgomery [County]. Let it be so. There are people there who can prove any thing.

I suppose it is too late to do any harm by Saying that I have Sometimes doubted whether Mr Adams would get Ohio.[2] Judging from the news papers, letter &c, there is no ground to Doubt, but Judging from what I have seen of the State personally, I am induced to believe that the Administration is not as strong as we are lead to hope. The mail of next Sunday [October 26] will bring us some news of the late Elections there.[3] We have nothing but verbal news as yet, & only from the Country[4] near us. These have done well well [sic] enough, if reports are true; but I still fear the Military fever—

I have less confidence at this time than I had four weeks ago. Assuredly the other side is making great exertions, and I think not without Success. You ought to prepare your mind to hear of our defeat. If Tennessee disgorges 1000 voters upon us, we are gone. We shall have two or three thousand illegal ones of our own. My fears have not had the effect of relaxing my exertions.... P.S. It is not probable that I Shall avail myself, of the Suggestion made in your letter; and Shall therefore say nothing on the Subject.

ALS. DLC-HC (DNA, M212, R3). Letter marked "Confidential." 1. See Webster to Clay, October 13, 1828, for Trimble's "address." His old district consisted of Bath County which Jackson carried in the presidential election 546 to 343; Fleming County which Adams carried 676 to 661; Floyd County which Jackson carried 380 to 92; and Greenup County which Jackson carried 302 to 294. 2. Trimble was correct; for Ohio's vote see Flournoy to Clay, August 29, 1828. 3. Ohio's state election was held on October 14, 1828, with the Adams candidate, Allen Trimble, winning the governorship and the Administration party winning a narrow majority in both houses of the state legislature. The presidential election in Ohio was held on October 31. 4. Trimble's Iron Works was in Greenup County, Ky., directly across the river from Ironton, Lawrence County, Ohio, and Portsmouth, Scioto County, Ohio. Jackson carried Lawrence County by only 1 vote and lost Scioto County to Adams by the vote of 469 to 685. For presidential returns see, Washington *United States Telegraph*, November 21, 1828.

From WILLIAM TUDOR, Rio de Janeiro, no. 111, October 22, 1828.

Reports that he has "been engaged in prosecuting the treaty" and that at the last conference "we . . . finally passed upon all the articles." Hopes that the Brazilian Council will pass it without further alterations and that President Adams will approve it "tho I have been obliged to admit the exception in favor of Portugal."

States that since writing last, he has heard about the capture of seven American vessels. Complains that the Brazilian navy seems "to have made use of the last moments of the war [with Buenos Aires] to perpetrate all the mischief in their power." Adds that he has protested to the Minister of Foreign Affairs, the Marquis of Aracaty, asking that the vessels "be delivered up now that the war was over, & which would save the necessity of paying some heavy additional demands." Says Brazilian officials have "in fact admitted that any orders sent from here would be disregarded."

Reports: "The Commissioners [Diego Souves da Silva de Bivar and Antonio Jose da S. Louveiro] on U.S. claims are now making a progress in the cases before them ... & they agree to settle the amounts on the same conditions with those stipulated for French claims." Notes that "Unfortunately the conduct of many Americans throws doubts on all the claims." For this reason he has told persons with questionable cases that they "must produce clear evidence of the property & the origin of the transactions."

Mentions that Lord [Percy Clinton Sydney Smythe] Strangford, British diplomat, arrived last week to mediate between Emperor Pedro I and Miguel and was yesterday presented to the Emperor. ALS. DNA, RG59, Dip. Disp., Brazil, vol. 6 (M121, R8). Received December 22, 1828. Letter marked *"Confidential."*

From ENOCH LINCOLN, Portland, Maine, October 23, 1828. Reviews the situation of John Baker [6:1272-3], his controversial conviction and his continuing imprisonment in a New Brunswick jail. Details the "unfortunate effect" of his imprisonment on his health, and on the economic welfare of his "numerous and respectable" family. Reminds Clay that Baker "remains a prisoner under the domination of that Government of which the President long since demanded his release with indemnity," and that "he is a solitary American in a foreign gaol." Asks what the U.S. Government is doing about the case. Informs Clay that Maine has advanced $212 for the relief of Baker's distressed family, but that this sum "will be considered as an allowance made on account of the United States, and that to use a mercantile expression it will be honored accordingly." LS. DNA, RG76, Northeast Boundary: Misc. Papers, Env. 4, item 23.

Clay responded on November 6, expressing sympathy for Baker's condition, and stating that the $212 "is considered to be a proper charge against the Federal Government. I am authorized by the President to say that the State of Maine shall be re-imbursed the sum thus advanced." Copy. DNA, RG59, Dom. Letters, vol. 22, pp. 327-8 (M40, R20).

From "A REPUBLICAN OF '98," Lexington, Ky., no. 2, October 24, 1828. Continues his attack [see above, October 17, 1828] on Clay with the observation that Jackson's military background was no good reason for Clay's refusal to abide by the will of the Kentucky legislature in its instructions [3:902] that the state's delegation in Congress vote for him rather than Adams. The real issue was the will of the majority of Kentuckians versus Clay's personal opinions about Jackson's qualification. "This is the doctrine of despotism. It is the doctrine that the people are incapable of self government; that the many must be under the wholesome restraint of the reason and discretion of the few." Quotes Clay's statement that "The military idolitry of the people is the most dangerous to public liberty." Adds: "What sir, the people destroy their own liberty!

Oh! What a falling off is here. Is this the doctrine of the great Republican leader of the west, the advocate of South American Independence, the defender of liberty in every clime? Do I understand you, sir, that it is decisive against the pretensions of a candidate for the Presidency to possess military qualifications only; that the public gratitude must be controuled, and the people must not have the candidate they prefer. We repudiate this odious doctrine sir, from our political code as the doctrine of tyranny and aristocracy." Cites Clay's letter of February 24 [*sic*, 23], 1824 [3:655–6] to Francis T. Brooke to reveal Clay's imperious opinion that it was his obligation to save the nation from the candidacy of the ailing William H. Crawford in the previous election. Cites also Clay's "frantic" speech at Baltimore [May 13, 1828] to show that he has now taken it upon himself to save the republic from a "military chieftain." Charges, therefore, that "Henry Clay believes the *influence* of a successful 'military chieftain' is dangerous; but we are convinced, that he wishes his *countrymen* to believe it; that he is playing the factious demagogue that he is maddened with ambition and despair.... You say you are 'singled out for proscription and destruction.' Not so: sir, you abandoned the principles and rights of the people who have sustained you. You have perverted the purposes of your patronage." Printed in Lexington *Kentucky Gazette,* October 24, 1828.

From NICHOLAS P. TRIST   Monticello, Va., October 24, 1828
Your favor of the 21 inst., just received, removed the only bar to a definitive reply to the kind offer conveyed in that which preceded it; and I hasten to communicate my acceptance of the situation in the Department of State. I hope the partiality of Mr [James] Madison & the other friends to whose favorable representations it seems that I am indebted, may not have led you to form an over estimate of my capacity to be useful; such as I possess, however, shall be as cheerfully as, I am satisfied, it will be agreeably, exerted. With regard to my acquaintance with French—once familiar, it has experienced the effects of disuse; and will, I fear, compare but indifferently with that of Mr [Aaron] Vail, [Jr.] of whose skill, I understand, you have heretofore availed yourself.

As soon as possible, within the very liberal limit for which I have to return my thanks, I shall repair to Washington.[1]

ALS. DNA, RG59, Accept. and Orders for Comms. (M–T645, R2).   1. On November 8, Trist informed Clay that he had fallen ill and would not arrive in Washington until November 13. ALS. DNA, RG59, Misc. Letters (M179, R66).

To DANIEL WEBSTER   Washington, October 24, 1828
Although some of the Congressional results in Ohio[1] are to be regretted, my belief is unshaken that we shall get the State by a large majority. The returns in [Elisha] Whittleseys,[2] Bartletts[3][*sic*, Mordecai Bartley], [Samuel F.] Vintons[4] and McClanes[5] [*sic*, William McLean] districts are not yet fully recd. In them our majorities will be great. [Allen] Trimble will be re–elected by many thousands,[6] and he, you know, was the Admon Candidate for Govr.

My intellegence from K. continues good, very good. I have heard of the safe reception there of what you sent.[7] All has been done, and will continue to be done, that honorable men can or ought to do.

I yet think that Mr. Adams will be re–elected; but it is mortifying, and sickening to the hearts of the real lovers of free Government, that the contest should be so close; and that if Heaven grants us success it will be perhaps by less than a majority of six votes.

I thank you for the hint about Mr. B. who has not yet called.[8]

ALS. DLC-Daniel Webster Papers (DNA, M212, R22). Letter marked "Confidential." 1. For Ohio's vote see Flournoy to Clay, August 29, 1828. 2. Whittlesey's district encompassed the counties of Ashtabula, Geauga, Portage, Trumbull. Adams easily carried this district over Jackson by the vote of 8696 to 2771. 3. Bartley's district was composed of Cuyahoga, Huron, Medina, Richland counties; Adams swept the district 4596 to 2874. 4. Vinton's district was Athens, Gallia, Jackson, Lawrence, and Meigs counties, which Adams carried 2816 to 1887. 5. McLean's district consisted of Allen, Darke, and Mercer which Joseph Crane, the Administration candidate, carried after McLean decided not to seek reelection. Jackson, however, handily carried the district over Adams. 6. Trimble defeated John W. Campbell 53,981 to 51,861. 7. See Clay to Webster, October 6, 1828. 8. Reference obscure.

From FRANCIS T. BROOKE   Richmond, October 25, 1828

I know that your incessant labours render it impossible to attend to your private correspondence, of course I do not look for answers to my letters except when you find it perfectly convenient—your last letter[1] I shewed to [John H.] Pleasants—who expressed a desire to have it, for the purpose I Supposed of noticing the view what it takes of our prospects, I see however that to day he published some extracts[2] from him, this I have no doubt he thought himself at liberty to do, though it was certainly not my intention   I mention this to you, lest you should think I make too free use of our correspondence, no harm I beleive can come of it—and I shall be more cautious in future its effect has been to cheer our frends here though I saw no cause for despondence, as I had taken the Same view, with you of our prospects, was not there a want of tact in Mr Adams coming out with his Statement at this time[3]—[William B.] Giles I learn has contradicted him in the [Richmond] Enquirer of day[4]—he will Stop at nothin—I hope Mr Adams has preserved his letter or letters which he [Giles] denies having written,[5] I shall return home in two or three days for a week so that if you have occasion to write me you can to Fred[ericksbur]g—

ALS. InU. 1. Clay to Brooke, May 28, 1828. 2. In the Richmond *Constitutional Whig*, October 25, 1828. 3. In response to publication of an exchange of letters between William B. Giles and Thomas Jefferson, dated December 15 and December 26, 1825, critical of the President for his past inconsistencies, Adams authorized a public statement explaining why he had shifted from the Federalist to the Republican party in 1808. His decision had to do, he explained, with the resistence of Massachusetts Federalist leaders in 1807–1808 to Jefferson's embargo policy against Great Britain and their talk of possible secession of New England from the Union. He also mentioned in the statement that he had privately communicated these reasons in personal letters to Giles and Jefferson. Washington *Daily National Journal*, October 25, 1828. 4. In a letter published in the Richmond *Enquirer*, October 23, 1828, Governor Giles denied having authorized the publication of the December 26, 1825, letter from Jefferson, which was critical of Adams, while suppressing another letter from Jefferson written one day earlier, on December 25, 1825, "under the extreme pressure of business" which had praised Adams. The latter, he contended, was a badly confused communication written by Jefferson when he was under severe mental strain. 5. Giles denied having corresponded with Adams in 1808 on the subject of the latter's shift to the Republican party. Adams, in turn, insisted that he had. While Adams refused to permit publication of his correspondence with Giles, he did allow the editors of the Washington *Daily National Journal* to read the letters from his copybook. Washington *Daily National Journal*, October 29, 1828.

To JAMES M. MORRIS   Washington, October 25, 1828
Your manager arrived this morning and is preparing to start with the horses. I hope and believe they will prove a most serviceable pair. I bought them in June for five years old each. If they have a fault, I do not know it. I could have sold them here, without difficulty, and probably at a greater price than I gave. The delay in sending for them has had the good effect of enabling them to recover entirely from their late journey.

[Says he will procure information, unspecified, sought by Morris. Continues:]

I hope, if you come to this City, you will be sure to bring Mrs. Morris with you, and both come to my house sans ceremonie. As to your apprehension that Mrs. M. may be infected by political heresies, I protest most solemnly that there shall be no practises upon her. Besides, the question will be decided when you come, and as you will certainly be beaten, you will require all the compassion and kindness which are due to defeat and delusion. You will have a safe reliance on Mrs. M. for consolation, and the humanity of Mrs. C. and myself would prompt us to aid her in preventing you from committing any act of violence or indiscretion. So come to us you must. . . .

ALS. ViU. Addressed to Dr. Morris at Green Springs, Va.

To SIMON BOLIVAR   Washington, October 27, 1828
I have delayed answering the letter which your excellency did me the honor to address me, on the 21st of November last [6:1298-9], and which was delivered by Mr. [Beaufort T.] Watts, to avail myself of the opportunity of conveying an answer afforded by the departure of general [William Henry] Harrison, from the United States, on the mission with which they have charged him, to Colombia. He will deliver this letter, and I beg leave to introduce him to your excellency as a gentleman, who, besides enjoying the confidence of his country, implied in the high trust that has been confided to him, possesses the personal esteem of all who know him, and my particular friendship. Having been one of those who early concurred with me in the expediency of acknowledging the independence of the new republics formed out of Spanish America, he carries with him to Colombia the best and most friendly dispositions.

It is very gratifying to me to be assured, directly, by your excellency, that the course which the government of the United States took on that memorable occasion, and my humble efforts, have excited the gratitude and commanded the approbation of your excellency. I am persuaded that I do not misinterpret the feelings of the people of the United States, as I certainly express my own, in saying, that the interest which was inspired in this country by the arduous struggles of South America, arose principally from the hope that, along with its independence, would be established free institutions, insuring all the blessings of civil liberty. To the accomplishment of that object we still anxiously look. We are aware that great difficulties oppose it; among which, not the least, is that which arises out of the existence of a large military force, raised for the purpose of resisting the power of Spain. Standing armies, organized with the most patriotic intentions, are dangerous instruments. They devour the substance, debauch the morals, and, too often, destroy the liberties of a people. Nothing can be more perilous or unwise, than to retain them after the necessity has ceased which led to their formation, especially if their numbers are disproportionate to the revenues of a state.

But, notwithstanding all these difficulties, we had fondly cherished, and still indulge, the hope, that South America would add new triumphs to the cause of human liberty; and that Providence would bless her, as He had her northern sister, with the genius of some great and virtuous man, to conduct her securely through all her trials. We have even flattered ourselves that we beheld that genius in your excellency; but I should be unworthy of the consideration with which your excellency honors me, and deviate from that frankness which I have ever endeavored to practise, if I did not, on this occasion, state that ambitious designs have been attributed by your enemies to your excellency, which have created in my mind great solicitude. They have cited late events in Colombia as proofs of those designs. But, slow in the withdrawal of confidence which I have once given, I have been most unwilling to credit the unfavorable accounts which have, from time to time, reached me. I cannot allow myself to believe that your excellency will abandon the bright and glorious path which lies plainly before you, for the bloody road, passing over the liberties of the human race, on which the vulgar crowd of tyrants and military despots have often trodden. I will not doubt that your excellency will, in due time, render a satisfactory explanation to Colombia, and to the world, of those parts of your public conduct which have excited any distrust, and that, preferring the true glory of our immortal Washington, to the ignoble fame of the destroyers of liberty, you have formed the patriotic resolution of ultimately placing the freedom of Colombia upon a firm and sure foundation. That your efforts, to that end, may be crowned with complete success, I most fervently pray.

I request that your excellency will accept assurances of my sincere wishes for your happiness and prosperity.

Copy. *Niles' Register* (April 24, 1830), 38:173; reprinted from Washington *Daily National Journal*, April 17, 1830.

From ROBERT MONROE HARRISON, St. Bartholomew, October 27, 1828. Complains that unless a certified manifest from "our Consuls in the Neutral West India Islands" is required by port collectors in the United States, "the *nefarious* and shameful business of *smuggling* will be carried to a greater extent than it ever was before." States that smugglers can obtain at St. Bartholomew "*false clearances,* for the paltry sum of *one* and two dollars." Mentions that many of these vessels carry rum and are "mostly from the Eastern shore Virginia, one of which called the *Walton Gray* a *Schooner* . . . belonging to Cherry Stones [Va.] sailed on the 18th having nearly a full cargo of Rum." Believes the King of Sweden, Charles XIV, would punish local officials if he knew about the false clearances and suggests he be informed. States that the local officials oppose him and "consequently every advantage is taken to annoy me and this they will continue to do with me, or any Consul who may come here ... and does his duty." ALS. DNA, RG59, Cons. Disp., St. Bartholomew, vol. 1 (M72, R1). Received November 26, 1828.

From WILLIAM TUDOR, Rio de Janeiro, no. 112, October 27, 1828. Reports he has been notified by the Marquis of Aracatay that the preliminary peace between Brazil and Buenos Aires has been ratified and that the blockade has been lifted. States that the treaty has been "received here coldly because the vanity of the people is a good deal mortified by the result." Believes, however, that it reflects "wisdom & firmness in the present administration, in putting an end to a calamitous war." ALS. DNA, RG59, Dip. Disp., Brazil, vol. 6 (M121, R8). Received December 22, 1828.

From JAMES BROWN   Paris, October 28, 1828
The Minister ad interim of Foreign Affairs [Francois–Maximillien Gerard] sent me a note last evening informing me that the Count [Pierre] de la Ferronnays had returned from the waters of Baden, and had resumed the Port folio of that Department. I intend this day to pay him my visit of ceremony, and on to morrow address him a note asking an interview for the purpose of ascertaining the views of the French Government respecting our claims for Indemnity. As in my repeated conversations with him he did not seem to insist much on the question growing out of the Louisiana Treaty [3:382–3; Brown to Clay, February 27, 1828] I cherish the hope that he may waive it and proceed to the examination of the Claims.

[Discusses pending changes in the Ministry. Continues:]

I have had the pleasure of seeing Mr [William B.] Lawrence who has lately arrived from London, and who has given me such an estimate of the expences of living in London as induces me to believe that Mr [James] Barbour will not remain there much longer than his his [sic] immediate predecessors. He assures me that he spent at the rate of three thousand pounds per ann whilst he remained in England as charge d'Affaires. If you have to pay an outfit for your Minsiters once a year the salary ought to be increased as a measure of economy. From the best estimate I can make the expences of Paris are nearly as great as those of London particularly on the arrival of a new Minister who is always subject to great impositions which observation and experience alone can enable him to avoid. This however is not a subject on which I have ever Complained because I knew the utter inadequacy of the Salary before I accepted the place and therefore ought witho't a murmur to submit to the sacrifice. I now hope to embark on the 15th. of April or at furthest—on the 15 May for the United States and request the favor of you to take the orders of the President as to the person with whom I am to leave the Legation. I presume it will be Mr [John Adams] Smith who has labored much since his arrival in Europe and has had but a moderate compensation.

[Discusses his wife's health. Continues:]

The long unexpected intelligence of the surrender of Varna arrived this day by Telegraph. It surrendered on the 11 Octr. you will find the account in the Messages des Chambers which are sent you by this opportunity. This event will revive the confidence & hopes of the Russians and induce the Emperor to continue the Campaign through the Winter. Indeed this is become necessary because the Porte having left Constantinople with the sacred Standard cannot return unless after peace or the expulsion of the invaders. The French troops will soon reduce the places held by the Turks in Greece and the recapture of the Morea being complete the French army will return to Toulon

We anxiously wait for the result of the Presidential election. The question rests with New York. In the event of the reelection of Mr Adams who will be my successor?

It is now many months since I have heard from you. I am anxious to have news of your health . . . . P.S. I have several times requested you to be so good as to ask Mr [Stephen] Pleasonton to settle my account for the last year. If there is any difficulty let me know and it shall be explained.

ALS.   DLC-HC (DNA, M212, R3). Letter marked "Private." Printed in *LHQ,* 24:1128–30.

From ROBERT MONROE HARRISON, St. Bartholomew, October 28, 1828. Encloses a local newspaper dated October 21, which reveals "that the Piratical vessel, which took the British Brig *Caraboo,* was owned in Baltimore and that Cabot & Co. of St. Thomas were the agents at that place." Reports that the "execution of *twenty eight* of the Piratical crew at S[t.] Kitts has created a great sensation here." Recommends that "one or two of our *light cruisers*" be sent into those seas. ALS. DNA, RG59, Cons. Disp., St. Bartholomew, vol. 1 (M72, R1). Received November 26, 1828. The "piratical vessel" left Baltimore in September, 1827, as the *Bolivar,* Capt. John D. Quincy; she sailed to St. Thomas where she was fitted out and manned as the Buenos Airean privateer, *Las Damas Argentinas.* After making various captures, she was taken by H. M. S. *Victor.*

From CHRISTOPHER HUGHES, New York, October 28, 1828. Announces his arrival back in the U.S. and that he will soon be in Washington. Has learned of the recent death of Julia D. Erwin, Clay's granddaughter, and has "partaken sincerely in your and Mrs. Clay's sorrow." Mentions that he and his wife had lost a son and a daughter in 1823 and that his "good and pious" mother had recently and suddenly died. Transmits "in the form of a private letter to the President," written on board ship, "a very hasty & imperfect sketch of my general observations during the few last months of my residence" in Brussels. Asks Clay to read it before delivering it to the President. Reports that "I have no very interesting political news to give you!" ALS. DLC-HC (DNA, M212, R3). Letter marked "Private!"

From LAFAYETTE   La Grange, October 28, 1828
The Critical time of presidential Election is Now Come; the Busy time of the Session is Coming on; Yet I know You Ever Have a thought to Spare

for Your Affectionate friend on this Side of the Atlantic. Mr [James] Brown whose Excellent Lady, to our inexpressible Gratification, is Now in Much Better Health keeps You informed of European political News. The Russians Have Met with More dif[f]iculties than Was Expected. it is Said that Mistrusts Relative to the Suppressed Conspiracy[1] Have Some What added to them. Mahmond [*sic*, Mahmud II] is a Spiritual Sultan. Yet at the long Run the power of Russia is Considered to Have the Better Chance, Unless the influence of England and Austria Succeed in patching Up a peace During the Winter. Amidst those Broils and intrigues, france is acting a Noble part quite the Reverse of the Spanish Expedition [3:313], a Contrast Which Has Been observed By ibrahim pasha Himself in His Conversation with the french Generals, Our Session will not open Untill the 20th of January. Some particular points we wish to obtain Have Been Stated in a public dinner at Meaux an Account of which I inclose. there are Some others that will Be Mentionned; But while the present [Martignac] Ministry are less advanced in their own liberalism than we wish them to Be, they find at Court a Heavy draw Back in their endeavour to Move On the popular Road. Some progress However is Made.

Mr [James Fenimore] Cooper is Now on His travels: His Late publication[2] will Give to European Readers More Correct Notions of the U.S. than are found in Most Books on that Matter, and Yet I Hear it is Criticised in America as Being too Complimentary to His own Country men. I don't find it is So, and while foolish Slander is propagated in Almost Every British publication, don't think that feeling, or Rather profession of Humility, to be Seasonable.

I Understand Mr Cooper Has Resigned His Consulship of Lyons. the emolument of the Station do not allow a Special mission from the U.S. I am told applications Have Been Made in favor of My friend Mr [Cornelius] Bradford, a New yorker, Nephew to Mr Philip Hone Late Mayor of that City, and I Hope I don't Break Upon My determination Not to Sollicit preferments, When I tell You that Mr Bradford Whose intimacy With Us Has Given me full Scope to know Him well is one of the Best, most Sensible, and Noble minded Young Gentlemen I ever met in my life. He is Universally Beloved.[3]

Be pleased, My dear Sir, to Remember me very respectfully and afectionately to Mrs Clay and family. . . .

ALS. DLC–HC (DNA, M212, R3).   1. The Decembrist uprising in December, 1825, and January, 1826. See Mikhail Zetlin, *The Decembrists.* New York, 1959.   2. *Notions of the Americans: Picked up by a Travelling Bachelor.* London, 1828.   3. In a letter to Clay, October 27, 1828, James Brown recommended Cornelius Bradford for the consulship at Lyons, noting that it "would afford much gratification to his friend General Lafayette." ALS. DNA, RG59, A. and R. (MR1). On November 24, 1828, Philip Hone also recommended his nephew to Clay for the consulship. *Ibid.* Bradford was appointed to replace Cooper in the post on April 10, 1829. Robert E. Spiller, *Fenimore Cooper, Critic of His Times* (New York, 1931), 102.

From BENJAMIN WATKINS LEIGH
Richmond, October 28, 1828

I have a favor to ask of you, and estimating it by my own feelings, a very great favor—

I have a son,[1] just turned of 14 years of age, for whom I wish to procure a Midshipman's warrant. His heart has been set upon this line of life, ever since he was ten years old; and I have long since resolved to indulge his inclinations. You need not be told that I have been attentive to his education—he reads Sallust, Virgil and Horace without any difficulty—has a little Greek—and a smattering of French and Spanish. He has read plutarch's lives, and all the voyages to be found in Richmond.

I have desired judge [Francis T.] Brooke to make application for the warrant to mr Secretary [Samuel L.] Southard (being unacquainted with him myself) and he has kindly undertaken to interest himself in it. I am very desirous to obtain the warrant immediately, having learned that a ship is fitting out to be sent to the pacific, and that Capt. [Lewis] Warrington is to command her; and he being an old friend of mine, and an excellent officer, as well as a most amiable man, I had rather my son should commence his service upon his quarter deck, than that of any officer in the service. I am sure Capt. Warrington will, for my sake, be attentive to train the little fellow to usefulness and virtue.

What I am afraid of is, that his name may be only put on the list of applicants, and that the appointments may be deferred for years, till it is too late (in prudence) to give him such a destination. I beg you, my dear sir, to take a personal interest in this affair, and (if it be proper that you should do so) to urge the secretary to give him a warrant immediately.... P.S. I have written to mr [William] Wirt also, on this subject, to request his friendly aid in promoting my wishes.

ALS. DLC–HC (DNA, M212, R3).   1. Leigh's son, William, received his commission on November 1, 1828, and was assigned to the frigate *Constellation*. By 1841 he had reached the rank of lieutenant and was serving in the sloop *Fairfield*. See *Biennial Register*, 1829, p. 134; 1835, p. 132; 1841, p. 150.

From JOEL R. POINSETT, Mexico, no. 154, October 28, 1828. States that two letters from Europe have arrived which "alarmed" the Mexican government "very much." One reported that Britain had made a loan to Spain, and it is feared that much of the money will be used "in an attempt to reconquer this Country." The second letter came from Madrid and seems to confirm this fear, stating that "an expedition against Mexico has been resolved upon, by that cabinet." Mentions that Spain decided upon this course of action after some Mexican exiles reported to the king that "the enthusiastic feeling in favor of the Independence of Mexico, had subsided very much, while that in favor of the old country, had augmented." States that the alleged plan for conquest calls for a blockade of Mexico and an expedition of 15,000 Spanish soldiers, supplemented by reserves, who would land at Veracruz and march to the capital "where they would be joined by the loyal in great numbers." Adds in code that he believes such an expedition would have "a fair chance of success" because of the poor state of Mexico's finances and army, but concludes that Spain could not hold "possession of this bounty for any length of time." ALS. DNA, RG59, Dip. Disp., Mexico, vol. 4 (M97, R5). Received December 16, 1828.

From ALEXANDER H. EVERETT, Madrid, no. 118, October 29, 1828. Reports that Spain has concluded with Britain a Convention of Indemnities. Encloses copy of a note he has written to the Minister of State, Manuel Gonzales Salmon, reminding him "of our pretentions of the same kind [Everett to Clay, February 21, 1828]." ALS. DNA, RG59, Dip. Disp., Spain, vol. 29 (M31, R29). Received February 22, 1829. For the Anglo–Spanish treaty, see Parry, *Treaty Series,* 79:181–90.

From DAVID B. OGDEN, New York, October 29, 1828. Informs Clay that his decision not to run for the U.S. House, conveyed in a letter "yesterday," has been reversed. "It has been so strongly represented to me as the only possible means of breaking down the present ruling party [Tammany Hall] in the city, and that with my name it can be done, and without it, the struggle must be abandoned, that I have not felt my self a free agent on the subject—and have been obliged to consent to be a candidate, and to abide the result—" Has been told that he has a "fair chance" of beating Churchill C. Cambreleng. ALS. DLC-HC (DNA, M212, R2). Cambreleng defeated Ogden 14,117 to 12,204. In the presidential contest Jackson received a 6000 vote majority over Adams from a total of 25,000 votes cast in New York City. See, further, Alfred Connable and Edward Silberfarb, *Tigers of Tammany, Nine Men Who Ran New York* (New York, 1967), 94; and *Niles' Register* (November 15, 1828), 35:178.

From JOSEPH DELAFIELD, New York, October 30, 1828. Transmits two maps of North America "which are evidence to support my claim to the Long Lake contended for under the 7th article of the Treaty of Ghent." They are: "The United States of America laid down by the best authorities agreable to the Peace of 1783 published April 3. 1783 by the proprietor John Dublis London," and "America divided into North and South with their several subdivisions and the newest discoveries. London published by Laurie and Whittle May 1800." The first of these was filed with the Boundary Commission [1:1006; 2:162]. Both were appended to General Peter B. Porter's report [6:1238–40]. Considers the first map of "great interest" since it defines as American "a large territory, hithertofore supposed to be British, with the only two routes of communication by which they can pass without the utmost inconvenience and embarrassment." Further, it "is one of the original documents to sustain my claim to the Long Lake of the Kamanistiguia River [Kaministikwia] and has the Boundary line engraved upon it." ALS. DNA, RG76, Northeast Boundary: Misc. Papers, Env. 4, item 31. "Long Lake" consists of a string of lakes in Ontario between the Lake of the Woods and Lake Superior. See Robert Laurie and James Whittle, *The United States of America . . . According to the Preliminary Articles of Peace. . . .* [map] (London, 1794).

From CHARLES S. TODD   Stockdale, [Shelby Co., Ky.],
                                                            October 30, 1828
I had the satisfaction a few weeks ago of informing you[1] that the necessary measures were in progress to bring out the Administration strength

in this [Shelby] County and I am now satisfied from the intelligence collected last evening in a very large meeting of the Corresponding Comee. that we have nearly 2 to 1 in the County; which, on the supposition that there are 2400 voters, will give us a Majority of 800 *all polled*. From the zeal displayed in the Commee. I think that an equal portion of our strength will come to the polls and that we may rely on a Majority of 5 to 600—[2]the news from Ohio which during the last week was so appalling, has become more favorable this week and there is little doubt now that Gov. [Allen] Trimble and a majority of the Legislative is elected. and that Mr. Adams will receive the vote of the State which until the late election we had supposed to be the most decided of all the States south of N. England—

You will have seen that there is an angry Controversy. about the Chickasaw Treaty.[3] and that I have encountered all the Malice of the General and his party. The last Argus[4] contains the statements of his friends and is indeed a feeble defence Considering that he told Col. [Leslie] Combs he was *fortified* &c. His refusal to make the call on James Jackson[5] may do some good—I shall make some further comments in the "Advocate"[6] of tomorrow which shall be forwarded to you—I have no doubt the General has prevailed on his Certificate men to state that Gov. [Isaac] Shelby saw & approved the letters from the General to James Jackson.

Col [Robert] Butler enclosed the deeds[7] to and from J. Jackson to the Secy. of War perhaps you may be able to procure from the War Office a Copy of the letter of Mr. [John C.] Calhoun on the Subject; as I presume some intimation must have been given by the Government of its intention to take the reservations I would like, also, to Know at what time a Duplicate of the Journal[8] was sent to the Govt. if at all—perhaps it has been placed on file lately.

It may be useful, also, to Know what were the proceedings in the Senate on the ratification[9] and whether Geo: Graham[10] yet recollects any thing about it—If our strength can be brought to the polls, Mr Adams will receive the Vote of the State—if not, the result is doubtful

We Congratulate you on your Arrival in the City much improved in health and hope you may be long preserved to your friends and abused Country—What is the Complexion of affairs East of the Mountains?

ALS. DLC-HC (DNA, M212, R3).   1. See Todd to Clay, October 10, 1828.   2. See *ibid.* for results of the election in Shelby County; in Ohio, see Clay to Webster, October 24, 1828.   3. See *ibid.* for discussion of the controversy.   4. Frankfort *Argus of Western America,* October 1, 22, 1828.   5. James Jackson was a business partner with Andrew Jackson in the land company which leased the salt deposits from the Chickasaw chiefs. See Abernethy, *Frontier to Plantation in Tennessee,* 230, 271; and Todd to Clay, October 10, 1828.   6. Shelbyville *Kentucky Advocate.*   7. Deeds to the Chickasaw salt deposits acquired by James and Andrew Jackson. See Charles C. Royce, *Indian Land Cessions in the U.S.* (Washington, 1900), 694.   8. The "Secret Journal" of Col. Robert Butler kept during the Chickasaw Treaty negotiations. See Todd to Clay, October 10, 1828.   9. *Annals of Congress,* 15 Cong., 2 Sess., 205, 227.   10. Acting Secretary of War in 1816.

To ROBERT J. BRECKINRIDGE   Washington, October 31, 1828

I recd. your very friendly letter of the 22d. inst. with many of the views contained in which I entirely concur. Mr. Adams' re-election depends upon the West. The East will do its duty. So far as respects myself, I should care but little if he is defeated, provided I had health and strength. In regard to the Country and our free institutions, I should deplore the election of Jackson as a great calamity.

We hear good tidings at last from Ohio. N.York it is believed will not disappoint our expectations. But it is useless now to speculate. Before you receive this letter the event will be decided. I have no hope South of the Potomac.

I thank you, most sincerely, for your friendly expressions and assurances. I endeavor to calm my mind as much as I can, and to bear up, with philosophy, against the base attacks made upon me.

ALS. DLC–Breckinridge Papers, (DNA, M212, R20).

To HENRY B. BASCOM   Washington, November 2, 1828
Your favor of the 29h. Ulto. is recd. I see you need instead of being able to give consolation, on account of public affairs. Pennsa. is mad and bad enough; but there is yet hope. Whether well or ill founded we now shall soon know. You fear that Providence intends to scourge us. I hope that his mercies hitherto so signally experienced by this people will not now be withheld. Should he bring upon us the impending and dreaded affliction we must submit, and bear it like men....

ALS. Courtesy of Mr. William Stucky, Louisville, Ky.

To ANNA MARIA [Mrs. William] THORNTON, November 2, 1828. Expresses his regret and disappointment at being unable to complete the purchase of the racehorse, Rattler, because he "cannot consent to purchase the horse on the condition" that he not take possession of him until spring. Notes that the mare, Dutchess of Marlborough, which he has purchased from Mrs. Thornton, is on her way to Kentucky now and he had hoped Rattler would join her there. Copy. KyU. On the same day, Clay wrote James Calwell at the White Sulphur Springs of his failure to obtain Rattler. Copy. *VMHB* (October, 1947), 55:306.

Mrs. Thornton on February 16, 1829, gave Clay a receipt for his check of $500 in payment for the Dutchess of Marlborough. She explained that the mare was "gotten by Sir Archy, her Dam by the capital Horse Diomed (imported) her grand–Dam by the imported horse Alderman, her gt. grand–dam by old Clock fast, which was by Jimcrack, the Sire of Old Medley; her gt. gt. grand–dam by old Wild air of Virginia, which was by old Fearnought by Regulus, Kitty Fisher by Cade & both by the Godolphin Arabian"— ADS. Courtesy of Miss Josephine Simpson, Lexington, Ky. Endorsed by Clay on attached sheet: "Mrs. Thornton's bill of Sale for the Dutchess of Marlboro."

The following day, February 17, Thomas Peter wrote Clay, stating that in "the popular opinion" the Dutchess "was a Mare of fine Bottom and great Speed & if she had had an experienced Trainer she would certainly have ranked as a 2d if not a first rate nag." Concludes: "I consider the Dutchess a good Brood mare & one of the very best bred Mares in America." ALS. DLC–HC (DNA, M212, R3).

From JOSEPH LAWRENCE, Washington, Pa., November 3, 1828. Recommends that Judge William Baird be appointed to the position on the U.S. District Court about to be vacated by Judge William Wilkins of Pittsburgh, who has been elected to Congress. Adds: "You are apprised of the defeat of myself and all our administration members in Penna— Still we have strong hopes of the success of our favorite Mr Adams, which is with some of us much more of an object than our own success." ALS. DNA, RG59, A. and R. (MR3). For Lawrence and Wilkins, see *BDAC*. Lawrence was beaten by William McCreery [See *BDAC*] in the 15th District; and Wilkins's victory was in the 16th. Jackson defeated Adams by a 101,652 to 50,848 margin and took all 28 of Pennsylvania's electoral votes. Only one pro–administration congressman, Thomas H. Sill of Erie [See *BDAC*], survived the Democratic sweep. Western Pennsylvania was particularly solid for Jackson. Weston, *Presidential Election of 1828*, 182; Philadelphia *United States Gazette*, October 31, 1828; Parsons, *United States Congressional Districts, 1788–1841*, 269; *Niles' Register* (November 1, 1828), 35:147.

From ROBERT SCOTT, Lexington, November 3, 1828. Discusses cases pending in Clay's legal practice, especially his administration of the James Morrison estate. States that Theodore W. Clay, who will soon take over the operation of the Clay farm, does not anticipate a need for "any advances for contingencies." Adds: "I think however that he will." Reports, on the evening of November 4, that the day's voting in the presidential election shows the Administration to be about 200 votes ahead in Fayette County, "not as much as we ought to be, but will I hope do better to morrow." ALS. DLC–HC (DNA, M212, R3).

From JOHN SLOANE Wooster, Ohio, November 3, 1828
Contrary to my wishes, and expectations when I wrote you at Lexington, my friends so insisted on my being brought out a candidate that I thought it could make our situation no worse though I should be defeated. The defeat[1] has taken place though under circumstances rather calculated to promote my hold on the affections of the sound part of our population   The result was produced by a vilainnous defection of a small squad of my former supporters who owe all their consequence to my countenance such things I need not dilate on to you experience will long since have dictated such occurrences—We have just passed the ordeal of the 31st [October][2] and are enjoying that kind of calm produced by an awful suspense. I wish, most devoutly wish, but dare hardly hope for success   It seems as if some maddening influence is abroad in the land whose cause and modes of operation is too occult to admit of full comprehension—

Sometime since I wrote to the President on the subject of appointing Mr [John] Wright in the place vacated by the death of Judge [William] Byrd. I now take the liberty of naming it to you His recent defeat[3] will make it still more acceptable to him.

You will perceive that I have got into a controversy with the great Leviathan [John Randolph] of the ancient dominion [Virginia][4] I may have acted with temerity in the manner of bringing it on; but I must make up for all such mistakes by the mode of prosecuting it   I shall make one more publication on the subject, but not until I reach Washington. If there has fallen with in your knowledge any thing in the shape of testimony as regards Mr [illeg. initial] cause during the year 25 which you could with propriety communicate it will be to me a favour.

I keep this letter open to give you all I can on the Subject of the election.

Wayne County	Jackson majority		1117 [1120][5]
Columbiana Coy		do	229 [268]
Stark Co			360 [462]
Richland		do	500 [522]
Knox			800 [861]
Holmes		do	600 [629]
			3676 [3862]
Medina	Adams	do	890 [444]
Cuyahoga	do	do	1100 [876]
Geauga	do	do	1850 [1788]
			3840 [3180]

ALS. DLC-HC (DNA, M212, R3). Letter marked "Private."   1. Sloane lost his U.S. House seat to John Thompson. Cincinnati *Daily Gazette,* October 22, 1828. For both men, see *BDAC,* in which Thompson's name is spelled Thomson.   2. Date of the Presidential election in Ohio.   3. John Wright lost his U.S. House seat to John Milton Goodenow. Cincinnati *Daily Gazette,* October 22, 1828. For Wright and Goodenow, see *BDAC.*   4. In mid–January 1828, Randolph and Sloane had clashed in the House over the latter's resolution instructing the Secretary of War to furnish a complete report on Jackson's court martial and execution of six Tennessee militiamen [5:729] in 1815. Randolph's motion to table the resolution was defeated, and it was adopted on January 16, 1828. See, *Register of Debates,* 20 Cong., 1 Sess., 999–1000, 1031–48; *Reports of Committees,* 20 Cong., 1 Sess., no. 140; John Sloane, *View of the Report of the Committee of Military Affairs, in Relation to the Proceedings of a Court Martial, Ordered for the Trial of Certain Tennessee Militiamen.* Washington, [April 26], 1828. 16pp.   5. The bracketed numbers are the official returns later reported in the Washington *United States Telegraph,* November 21, 1828.

From XAVIER DE MEDINA, New York, November 4, 1828. Responds to Clay's note which complained, on behalf of some New York merchants, about the detrimental effects caused by the practice of copying the invoices certified in the Vice Consulate. States that "the Liberator, President of Colombia [Simon Bolivar]," is surprised at the complaint because it is a practice in which England has not met with any objection, nor in Jamaica which has a lively commerce with Colombia. Reports that the Liberator has reluctantly decided to continue the policy in order to "avoid facilitating contraband." LS, in Spanish, trans. by Dr. Kathleen Hill. DNA, RG59, Cons. Corresp.: Notes From Foreign Consuls, vol. 2.

From JOHN M. FORBES, Buenos Aires, no. 64, November 5, 1828. Announces a change in the Buenos Airean ministry, with General Tomas Guido becoming Minister of the Interior and of the Foreign Department. Contends that this action will give "very considerable popularity and strength to the Government," although the "opposition party . . . continues to be active, acrimonious and powerful." Notes that the opposition dislikes the opening of the river trade to Brazil, which was provided in the Treaty of Peace between Buenos Aires and Brazil, as well as the government's large expenditures "at a moment of hopeless poverty in their treasury."

States that he has taken up the subject of the claims for the ship *Ruth* and her cargo with Guido, the new Foreign Minister. Also has requested the government to investigate and take whatever "measures may be deemed proper" concerning the ship, *Sailor's Return* "in which the documents and flag of the U.S. have been abusively employed." Views these abuses with "the bitterest indignation" and would "have remedied the indecision and timidity of the Acting Vice Consul [Robert Kortright] . . . but was kept in check by the promise, in your Despatch No. 4 [6:204] of your decision on the conflicting opinions of Mr. [George W.] Slacum and myself on subjects of official duty. I have still to hope for that decision, and am unwilling to persevere in, or multiply erroneous opinions, if those on which I have before acted should be settled to be of that character."

Continues on November 18: Reports on peace celebrations in which flags of most European countries and all those of the Western Hemisphere, except that of the U.S., were displayed. Announces he protested this slighting of the U.S. to Guido, received an apology, "and forthwith our flag was displayed." Mentions a published letter of Guido, inviting six other Latin American countries to join Buenos Aires in an attempted mediation in the threatened war between Peru and Colombia. Believes that mediation will fail and contends that "it is by no means extravagant to suppose that [Simon] Bolivar's attempts at extensive and absolute power are supported by secret pledges from some of the powers of Europe." Believes that Buenos Aires has decided to invade Paraguay which is "so deadly hostile to them, before . . . Bolivar shall have approached too near."

Continues on November 20: Transmits copy of a note from Guido, requesting him to send documents concerning the proposed mediation between Peru and Colombia to the U.S. Legations in those countries "inviting our agents to lend their friendly efforts to promote the philanthropic views of this Government."

Continues on December 3: Reports on the arrival of "the late National army" on November 27, whose arrival "it had been very generally whispered. . .would be the signal of a violent change of Government." Adds that General Juan Lavalle leads the revolutionary forces and has assumed the title of "temporary Governor" of Buenos Aires after the governor, Manuel Dorrego, fled to the countryside, leaving Guido and Juan Ramon Gonzalez Balcarce in charge. LS. DNA, RG59, Dip. Disp., Argentina, vol. 3 (M69, R4). Received February 21, 1829; also in Espil, *Once Anos en Buenos Aires,* 500–9.

From JOEL R. POINSETT, Mexico, no. 155, November 5, 1828. Encloses translation of a proclamation issued by President Guadalupe Victoria "in consequence of the intelligence which this government had received from Europe, and which I communicated to you in my last [October 28, 1828]." States that the motives of the President for publishing such a paper were questioned, and by some members of the Senate "he was declared to be equally culpable with Santa An[n]a and to have encouraged the revolutionary movement of that chief." Mentions that the Senate is attempting to deprive the Chamber of Deputies of the right to scrutinize the election, as "They are aware that the majority of the votes for their favorite will not bear investigation." Predicts a continuation of the revolution as Santa Anna is being declared by some as "the Deliverer of the people from the tyranny which oppressed them." ALS. DNA, RG59, Dip. Disp., Mexico, vol. 4 (M97, R5). Received December 16, 1828. Also in Manning, *Diplomatic Correspondence . . . Latin American Nations*, 3:1670-1.

From JAMES BARBOUR   London, November 6, 1828

I understand the Prussians feel a little Sore, at the Supposed neglect of our Government, for not reciprocating a diplomatic appointment, corresponding with theirs—If it should be within the view of the Government, to do so, I will take the liberty of Suggesting Mr [William B.] Lawrence, as a proper person for the appointment—He is anxious for some situation abroad; and I think has Zeal and capacity, in a respectable degree—The king [George IV] continues at Windsor—Rumors are continually afloat that he is, seriously, indisposed which are flatly denied by the Court Papers—His death is I believe almost, universally deprecated by the nation—The Duke of Clarence[1] seems to be generally unpopular, and his coming into office esteemed, a national calamity—The scarcity of grain in this Country, and indeed generally on the Continent, threatens the most tenous suffering—nothing but the depreciated value of the grain of the last Harvest, has kept the foreign grain out of the market—You are aware that the reduced average from that circumstance, may keep the import so high as to detract greatly, from the value of foreign grain, and prevent its being disposed of advantageously here—But it must eventually come into market—or the People must starve—Good wheat is equal to 100 sterling (with occasional fluctuations) the quarter and would probably in our market [be] from $2 to 2.25 the bushel—The state of Ireland is truly deplorable—The combustible materials there, are kept quiet by the bayonet, and a Speculation that Wellington means to make concessions—He however maintains it is said great reserve, as to what he means to do—And Judging from the adjournment of Parliament—which it is said will not convene till the last of January, he seems to be in no haste to disclose his views—

The intelligence from the seat of war you will see by the papers, gives Varna to Russia—said here to have been obtained by Treachery—Much Speculation is indulged on the immediate operations of Russia—And great anxiety as to the question whether she will carry on a winter Campaign—The Emperor [Nicholas I] is returning to St. Petersburg, but I know not whether that proves any thing—Dining with Prince [Christoph Andreievich] Lieven the other day, I took occasion to remark to him that his successes did not seem to be highly relished here—to which he replied that his Government would execute its purpose, without regard to the clamors of any one—and added that now [is] the best season for warlike operations in the East—and that having opened the way to Constantinople, the occupation of Schoumla [*sic,* Shumla] by

the Turks would be of no moment; and that if they came down to resist—
the Russians would have them in a Situation they had long wished—the
open Country—It is however I think doubtful whether any further attempts will be made this season, to advance on Constantinople—During
the winter Great Britain and Austria I am persuaded will endeavor to
patch up a peace.

The tariff [of 1828] is as unpopular here as it is in S—Carolina—
From the blustering of [William] Huskisson [in] the last Session I should
not be surprized, if he made it his hobby, to regain influence—A vague
threat at retaliation is indulged by him, and reechoed by some of the
papers—Whether, anything will be attempted, time must decide—I cannot see what policy they can pursue towards us more unfriendly, than
the one they have heretofore followed—The idea of getting their Cotton
from India is idle and any attempt to injure us will fall with a redoubled
weight on themselves—

Long before this reaches you the fate of the Administration will have
been settled—Tho I cannot help fearing the worst my wishes are still
unabated for their success....

ALS. DLC-HC (DNA, M212, R3). Letter marked "Private."   1. Later (1830–1837] King
William IV. *DNB.*

From PHILEMON BEECHER   Lancaster, Ohio,
                                                          November 6, 1828

Adams, Athens—Belmont, Butler—Clermont, Clark—Delaware, Franklin—Fairfield—Green—Guernsey—Hamilton—Hocking—Knox—Lick-
ing—Logan—Montgomery—Muskingm.—Pike—Ross—Warren—Perry
—Pickaway—Clinton.

Majority for Jackson 8330 in the above named Counties[1] which are
all that has been heard from—There are three *heavy* Jackson Counties
to be heard from Clermont Brown and Wayne which will give about 850
majority each—There are several small counties to wit Dark[e] Morgan
Munroe [*sic,* Monroe] and Holmes, which will give Jackson Majorities say
300 each—Jefferson Harrison Richland & Cashockton [*sic,* Coshocton]
that are large Counties and will give small majorities perhaps some thing
larger than for the governor [Allen Trimble] to the same, say, 400 each—
So that Jackson majorities yet to be heard from may be estimated at
5500

The administration majorities to be heard from cannot in my opinion
exceed 11500—There is only one fact that we can hope for to save the
state, that is a very general turn out in the right Counties within the
Connecticut Reserve[2]—If they give three thousand votes more than they
did at the general Election,[3] then we may say that Ohio has paid some
attention to superior talents and intelligence, to tried experiance and
virtue, or otherwise that she has cast these away for comparative im-
bicility and Ignorance, for inexperiance and prominent vices—You will
hear from the North Eastern part of the State as soon as we shall and
perhaps before you will receive this hasty letter—I hope it may be such
as to give you pleasure and our Country profit—

ALS, except for list of Ohio counties in first paragraph, which are in a strange hand. OHi.
For Beecher, See *BDAC.*   1. A breakdown of the Ohio presidential election by counties

is found in the Washington *United States Telegraph,* November 21, 1828. 2. These 12 counties, in northeast and north central Ohio, are identified in W. W. Williams, *History of the Firelands....* (Cleveland, 1879), 9; see also Roseboom, *A History of Ohio,* 94. 3. The state and congressional elections held on October 14, 1828.

To CHRISTOPHER HUGHES   Washington, November 6, 1828
Your several despatches under dates the 13th. June, and 24 & 25 July, and your private letters of the 27 & 28th. July & 5th August have been duly received. That of the 24th July last, transmits three papers, No 1. 2. 3. which you received from Genral Count [Dimitri] de Wuits, and which propose, in substance, acession to the United States of the Island of Cyprus, upon certain conditions. I have submitted them to the inspection of the President, and it is now my purpose to enable you to return the answer which you promised to General Count de Wuits.

The policy of acquiring distant colonial, or other dependencies has not yet been adopted by the United States. Hitherto they have confined themselves and their views to this Continent. A change, in this respect, of their policy, would require the most serious and grave consideration. The president does not think that the time has yet arrived, if it shall ever come, when such a change is to be made. The exertions and the wisdom of Government can be more safely, prudently, and beneficially employed in the population and improvement of the vast territory which the United States possess on this Continent. During the existence of this Government, various propositions have been made, at different times, to cede different Islands situated in several parts of the globe, all of which have been declined.

This view of the proposal of General Count Wuits renders unnecessary an examination into his authority to cede the Island of Cyprus, or the conditions upon which it is proposed.

You will accompany the communication of the substance of this despatch to General Count de Wuits with all proper acknowledgments for his friendly consideration of the United States, which prompted him to offer an island so valuable.

Copy. DNA, RG59, Dip. Instr., vol. 12, pp. 164-5 (M77, R7). Instruction No. 7.

From FRANCIS T. BROOKE, Near Fredericksburg, Va., November 7, 1828. Is departing Richmond for home. Reports: "As far as we have heard from the elections though unusually thin the vote for Mr. Adams has been as favorable as we could expect, and but for the vote on the South of the James River I should anticipate his election by Virginia, his statem[en]t in relation to Mr. Jeffersons letter, though it was too late to do him much injury has done Some, it would have been better to have omitted any notice of the letter & Mr [William B.] Giles for the present [Brooke to Clay, October 25, 1828]." ALS. InU. Jackson overwhelmed Adams in Virginia by a 26,752 to 12,101 margin and captured all of the state's 24 electoral votes.

From ROBERT WICKLIFFE   Frankfort,
October [i.e., November] 7, 1828
Before this reaches you you will learn our defeat   All our efforts have not withstood the Torrent & this State of things *here* no doubt Littles the

question who shall be President favourable to *Jackson*   I deplore this misfortune more than I can or ought to express—but instead of complaints & murmurs shall make the most & best of the future, you & Mr Adams will have the taunts of the vulgar & the unprincipled of the leaders as we have here. But you have the consolation of having contributed mainly to give to the millions over which he has presided a happiness & prosperity never exceed[ed] & which they can never equal under those that succeed you   I could not have our election & on yesterday, arrive]d] here & found Judge [John] Boyle out of Temper & the whole of my chancery business continued &c   this so far deranges our Docket that the Term will do little & you have observed the flying off of [George M.] Bibb in the court of appeals[1] so that our State is becoming peculiarly the subject of contest again, what will be done about our judge I have heretofore cared little & declined interfering but information I have received here induces me to believe that If [John J.] Crittenden is nominated that his nomination will go down the Senate As [Josiah S.] Johns[t]on is understood to be pledged to go for him   Indeed the strong hold we have here upon [two illeg. words] will make it his interest to not offend the Administration party. If so is it not best that he should be nominated immediately on the meeting of the Senate   the Jackson Party have laid out the office for Bibb And are determined to have the Presidents nomination be it whom it may rejected[2] & will in all likelihood succeed   you are too sensible how undeserving Bibb is & how unacceptable he will be to the friends of Mr Adams & yourself not to avert this if possible   I beg you therefore to impress it upon Mr Adams to nominate one that will be strongest with the Senate in reference to their determination to keep in reserve this patronage for the General [Jackson], In the event of Crittenden passing—[Richard] Chinn will make a most excellent officer to succession—[3]If you deem my opinions of any value with the President you can shew him this scrawl   I write without consulting Crittenden & write to avoid the curse of Bibbs appointment

ALS. DLC–HC (DNA, M212, R3).   1. Bibb resigned from the Kentucky Court of Appeals, effective December 23, 1828.   2. This awkward phrase is rendered as written. 3. As U.S. District Attorney.

To FRANCIS T. BROOKE   Washington, November 9, 1828
I recd. your favor of the 7h. as I did the previous one enclosing a letter from Mr. [George] Spotswood. I need not say that it would have afforded me much satisfaction if I could have gratified this gentleman with the appointment to the vacant Clerkship in the Dept. of State. But Mr. [Nicholas P.] Trist came recommended to me by so many powerful considerations, of ample qualification, a knowledge of foreign language &c. the necessity of his appointment to the personal comfort of Mrs. R. [Mrs. Thomas B. Randolph] that I could not decline appointing him. In his behalf, I declined appointing a brother in law of the President[1] who was urged on me.

I can give you no satisfactory news about the Election. The most discouraging aspect of our cause is that it is necessary we should succeed in five or six disputed States[2] to ensure Mr. Adams' Election. It will be wonderful if we do not fail in some one of them. The same mail that carries this letter will take you some information from N. York which will enable you to make an approximation. My solicitude about Kentucky is extreme.

Have you read my [Jonathan] Russell correspondence [3:219-26, 269-72]? I am deceived if the publication of it does not essentially benefit me. I wish, after the smoak of the election is dissipated, that [John H.] Pleasants would republish it.

ALS. KyU. 1. Thomas B. Johnson, brother of Mrs. Adams. 2. The five "disputed" states, all of which Jackson carried over Adams, were: Ohio (67,597 to 63,396), Indiana (22,257 to 17,052), Illinois (9,560 to 4,662), Louisiana (4,603 to 4,076), and Kentucky (39,397 to 31,460). Weston, *The Presidential Election of 1828*, pp. 181-2. See also Clay to Brown, November 12, 1828.

From SAMUEL LARNED, Santiago de Chile, no. 71, November 9, 1828.

Reports receiving State Department dispatch no. 1 [March 22, 1828], together with his commission and other documents. Has been formally recognized by the Chilean government as Chargé des Affaires for the U.S. States that a new constitution has been promulgated in Chile and sworn to on September 18 and "has been received with great satisfaction, and promises to be more permanent than such instruments have hitherto been in most of these new States." Notes: "Some seditious movements have been discovered and defeated here . . . and capital punishment [has] been inflicted on two individuals implicated."

Reports that "General [Andres] Santa Cruz has been chosen President of Bolivia" and that the "Bolivian Code will no doubt be annulled there, and, perhaps, even the name blotted out so far has this celebrated personage [Simon Bolivar] forfeited the good opinion of the people, even in this country of his creation." States that General Antonio Jose de Sucre and the Colombian auxiliaries have departed Bolivia and that Sucre has offered "his personal mediation between the government of Peru and General Bolivar." Adds that Peru has given partial approval to this idea, but that General Jose de Lamar "has sailed from Callao, for the purpose of putting himself at the head of the Army of Peru, which will soon consist of near eight thousand men, a force superior to any that Genl Bolivar can, at present, bring to bear upon that point." ALS. DNA, RG59, Dip. Disp., Chile, vol. 3(M-T2, R3). Received February 14, 1829; also in Manning, *Diplomatic Correspondence . . . Latin American Nations,* 2:1132-3.

From JOHN TAYLOR, Columbia, S.C., November 10, 1828.

Forwards a copy of King George III's Proclamation of 1763 defining the western frontiers of the American colonies. Concludes from the proclamation that the "then province of South Carolina was not a frontier province." Says that he will consult with Stephen Elliott, "who from the Literary pursuits & Antiquarian penchant, I believe is possessed of more knowledge of our early History than any other Gentleman in our State." Will forward whatever information Elliot may have on the Proclamation of 1763. ALS. DNA, RG76, Northeast Boundary: Misc. Papers, Env. 4, item 23. For Stephen Elliott (1771-1830), historian and author, see *CAB*.

In a second letter marked *"Private,"* also dated November 10, Taylor notes that the Proclamation of 1763 found in the archives of South

Carolina may or may not be "perfectly valid & binding—we found other documents of the like kind upon which the Government (provincial) had acted & had received *as perfectly binding*—with no other formalities or Evidences of being the act of the King; than accompanies the Instrument in question viz Emblazoned with the Royal Arms & printed by the Kings Printer, but without the Great Seal or the signature of the King." *Ibid.*

Clay responded on November 16 noting that it would probably not be necessary to have the original document. Copy. DNA, RG59, Dom. Letters, vol. 22, p. 332 (M40, R20).

To DENISON WATTLES, JR., Washington, November 10, 1828. Mentions that had Wattles's "publications appeared earlier, I have no doubt that they would have done good in other quarters, as they have in your own, but I received them too late to be republished so as to produce any effect to the South or West. Henceforward, we shall probably, in any event, hear but little more of that charge. There are seasons when passion and delusion take possession of the public mind. This has been one. When it shall have passed away, and soberness and reason shall again resume their sway, I feel confident [that justice] will be done to the integrity of my motives and the patriotism of my conduct." LS. NN. Addressed to Wattles in Lebanon, Conn. Wattles not identified, his "publications" not found. But the latter probably had to do with the "corrupt bargain" charge against Clay. See, Clay to Wattles, December 6, 1828.

From SAMUEL ISRAEL, Cap Haitian, November 11, 1828. Complains of receiving no reply to his dispatch of September 11. Transmits copy of a "law passed at [the] session of the Chambers, putting the National Flag and its commerce upon the same footing as the Foreign." Inquires if this does not put "the Haytien commerce upon an equal footing with our own [in] America?" Asks "if it does, would it not be advisable to inform [the Haitian] Government of the fact."

Reports that in "these last few days a considerable force has been marched to the Eastern part of the Island, formerly [the] Spanish part, to protect it from an invasion of the Spanish." Believes that if an invasion is made "that territory would fall very easily, as *all* the Spanish inhabitants are disaffected to the Haytien Government." ALS. DNA, RG59, Cons. Disp., Cap Haitien, vol. 6 (M9, R6). Received December 10, 1828.

On January 15, 1829, Israel wrote again, complaining of having received no answer to his dispatches of July 11, September 11, and November 11, 1828. Reports that "the country is in much agitation, and the general commerical interest much distressed," as a result of the Haitian government's calling in its currency and paying merchants "with a Bond of the Government." *Ibid.* Received February 9, 1829.

To JAMES BROWN   Washington, November 12, 1828.
Enough is now known about the P. Election to justify my writing to you that Genl. Jackson is believed to have been chosen. That result must happen even if Mr. Adams obtains the forty votes which were calculated upon from the States of Ohio, Kentucky, Indiana and Louisiana, every

one of which I consider in more or less doubt.[1] The returns from Ohio and Kentucky, as yet partial, render it uncertain whether both of those States have not decided against Mr. A. The most unexampled attendance on the polls in those States has taken place, and the probability is that there will not be a greater difference in either of them than two or three thousand votes. We lost one vote in N. England.[2] Maryland and New York have fallen short of our expectations.[3]

As for myself, I have enjoyed more composure during the last 24 hours than I have for many weeks. I am preparing to return home early in the Spring. What I shall do, must be left to future events. My wish is to remain in retirement, and I shall do so, if I can. Each of the three Counties composing my old Congressional district, has however manifested a friendly feeling by giving a majority for Mr. Adams.[4] I anticipate therefore a strong pressure upon me to return to the H. of R. The point will be whether I can resist it or not.

Dr. [Samuel] Brown has arrived; and we have recd. some of the articles which Mrs. [James] B. was good enough to purchase. The others are on the way. Our health is good; and I sincerely hope that of Mrs. B. has improved. . . .

ALS. KyLxT.   1. See Clay to Brooke, November 9, 1828.   2. Jackson got one (1) electoral vote in Maine, while losing the state to Adams by a 13,927 to 20,733 margin.   3. For Maryland, see Webster to Clay, October 1, 1828; for New York see Rochester to Clay, September 25, 1828.   4. Adams carried Fayette County, 1340 to 1021; Clark County 784 to 537; and Woodford County 647 to 513. Frankfort *Argus of Western America,* November 19, 1828.

From HENRY A. S. DEARBORN, Boston, November 12, 1828. Encloses the statements of Kimball Gallop, commander, and Josiah Gould, supercargo, of the brig, *Monroe,* of Boston. The *Monroe* had recently returned from the coast of Africa where she had had two men taken from her there by the British ship, *Eden.* Feels that it is "my duty" to transmit statements about this incident. LS. DNA, RG59, Misc. Letters (M179, R66).

From ROBERT MONROE HARRISON, St. Bartholomew, November 12, 1828. Reports that there are 66 American seamen present at St. Bartholomew who have been lured off American vessels on to "Piratical cruisers" and then thrown on shore to starve. States they have been implicated in a store break-in and have been ordered off the island. Adds that he has ignored the problem, because "persons of this discription do not properly come within my instructions," and because the authorities asked him to pay for passports for all of them. Asks for instructions, but believes the men should be sent home, "as it would convince them that sailing under their own flag was preferable to all others." ALS. DNA, RG59, Cons. Disp., St. Bartholomew, vol. 2 (M72, R2). Received December 1, 1828.

To JOHN SLOANE   Washington, November 12, 1828
I recd. your favor of the 3d. inst. I need not express to you my deep mortification at the loss of your election. That of no friend could have

given me more pain. But my dear Sir distress on our own accounts is merged in the still greater distress on account of our Country. There is but too much reason, from present appearances, to apprehend the election of Genl. Jackson, than which no greater calamity has fallen to our lot since we were a free people. But however we may deprecate the means which have been used to bring about the event, and deplore its effect and its tendency, acquiescence is the joint duty of patriotism and religion. We must still struggle for our Country, in private life, and hope that Providence may yet watch over and preserve our Liberties.

I have noticed your controversy with Mr. Speaker [Andrew] Stevenson,[1] and I have no doubt that you state what you understood. From a conversation with Col. [William L.] Brent of Louisiana, I am inclined to think that he can furnish strong corroborative evidence.

I hope soon to see you.... P.S. Creighton is appointed Dt. Judge[2]

ALS. MH.   1. On the issue of Jackson's court–martial and execution of six Tennessee Militiamen in 1815 [5:739]. *Reports of Committees*, 20 Cong., 1 Sess., no. 140; Adams, *Memoirs*, 8:107.   2. William Creighton, Jr. was appointed Judge of the United States Circuit Court for the District of Ohio.

To ADAM BEATTY   Washington, November 13, 1828
I received your letter of the 6th instant. From the information which it communicates, and that which I derive from other channels, there is reason to apprehend that the vote of Kentucky has been given to General Jackson. Without that event, there is but too much probability of his election. To this decision of the people of the United States, patriotism and religion both unite in enjoining submission and resignation. For one, I shall endeavor to perform that duty. As a private citizen, and as a lover of liberty, I shall ever deeply deplore it. And the course of my own State, should it be what I have reason to apprehend it has been, will mortify and distress me. I hope, nevertheless, that I shall find myself able to sustain with composure the shock of this event, and every other trial to which I shall be destined.

You kindly promise me the suggestion of your ideas as to my future course. I shall await it with anxiety, and shall receive and deliberate upon it in the friendly spirit by which I know it will be dictated.

Printed in Colton, *Clay Correspondence*, 4:210-1.

From JAMES BROWN, Paris, November 13, 1828. Discusses at length the restrictions and policy decisions affecting U.S. vessels calling at French ports, as these relate to the provisions of the Commercial Convention of 1822 with France [3:53]. Notes he has "sometimes thought that France perceived with some displeasure that the trade between the two Countries was almost exclusively carried on by American Vessels, and that she has felt the wish to cramp our commercial operations as far as she could without dissolving the Convention." States, further, that he is making "little progress in the business of claims"; but adds: "I hope that patience and perservance may yet be successful and therefore in spite of the many petty and vexatious commerical questions which arise I endeaver to keep my temper and pursue a conciliatory course with the Government. By moderation and mildness I hope to pave the way for my successor [William C. Rives] to atchieve what I have not been able to effect, and thus have the consolation of thinking that my mission has not been altogether unprofitable to my country."

Reports the conclusion of Russia's campaign against Turkey; but feels that if England and the Continental powers continue in a neutral stance the war will be renewed "on a great scale at the opening of the next Season. All will depend on the policy of France. Should she feel inclined to permit Russia to try the chances of another campaign, I cannot persuade myself that either Austria or England will oppose the Emperor [Nicholas I] or give direct assistance to the Porte." Says his wife's health had worsened, but hopes she will be able to bear the voyage home in April, 1829. ALS. DLC–HC (DNA, M212, R3). Letter marked "(Private)." Printed in *LHQ,* 24:1130–3.

From CHARLES KING   New York, November 13, 1828
I fear from the result in this State & in Maryland, and from the accounts from Ohio & Kentucky,[1] that the game is all up and that Gen Jackson will have a large majority of the popular votes. If however the two latter States or Even one of them yet be Saved, there is yet perhaps a chance of security, what I cannot but consider still, a great calamity, the success of Gen Jackson—Virginia must do it—Her support of Jackson is known to be an alternative of evils—Let her vote then be given for John Marshall—So as to bring the election into the House,[2] keeping the understanding and the pledge as far as it can now be had, that the friends of Mr. Adams will abandon him there, and give their support to John Marshall. So could the nation be spared the discredit and the dangers of such a President, elected upon such principles, as Genl Jackson—the angry passion of factions would be soothed & hushed, and the dignity and resources of our form of govt be equally vindicated and displayed—I forbear to enlarge upon the Considerations by which this suggestion might be rendered acceptable to Virginia—providing that your own reflection will supply them more forcibly[?] than any thing I could say—but I am so much impressed with the Conviction that Gen Jackson's success, must be of fatal injury to this Country—and so entirely sure, that in the desire I feel to avert it, there is mingled up no selfish or unworthy consideration, that I could not restrain my anxiety to attempt this last Expedient to defeat him and save the nation—Give [illeg. word] & what is to be done at [?] all, must be done quickly—I cannot doubt that Mr Adams himself and Mr. A's friends throughout the nation would gladly adopt this plan, if otherwise feasible—Here I am sure there won't be but one voice—

Excuse the freedom with which I have written—our cause is a common one, & that must be my apology for troubling you. Concerning it—If you think proper to move [?] the business[?], let us hear from you.... P.S. I have only spoken on this subject to one individual Mr. [Stephen] White an elector of [Salem] Massachusetts—who cordially enters into it—By this day, think I shall transmit a Copy of his letter to

Chapman Johnson of Va (with whom I have no acquaintence personally) and ask his concurrence

ALS. DLC–HC (DNA, M212, R3). Letter marked both "(Confidential)" and "Private." Endorsed by Clay on verso: "Answered, disapproving decidedly the project." Manuscript difficult to read. 1. Weston, *Presidential Election of 1828,* 181–2. Adams carried Maryland. 2. See Clay to Brooke, November 18, 1828; Clay to Childs, November 20, 1828.

To JOHN M. MACPHERSON Washington, November 13, 1828
I have the honor to acknowledge the receipt of your letter of the 14th. ulto., accompanied by translations of your representation to the President Liberator [Simon Bolivar], and the answer to it. Your communication of the 15th. September had apprised me of the personal difficulties on your part, which form the subject of that representation, and I regret to find that it has not been successful in removing them. This case has occasioned painful feelings to your own Government; but would not justify its interposition, as your Consular character does not carry with it any diplomatic immunities, and you are consequently liable, like other individuals, to the laws of the country in which you reside. If, indeed, any rigor not warranted by the local law of Colombia, or not usual in other cases, has been exerted towards you, those circumstances would form a proper subject of remonstrance from this Government to that of Colombia. And I have the authority of the President for saying that should such a state of things app[ear t]o have existed, this remonstrance will be made.[1]

LS. CSmH. 1. On January 10, 1829, MacPherson responded to Clay that he did not wish to make his dispute with the customs house a cause for official protest, contending that the slight to his public dignity was of more concern to him than the loss of money. ALS. DNA, RG59, Cons. Disp., Cartagena, Colombia, vol. 1 (M–T192, R1). Received February 11, 1829. See MacPherson to Clay, August 11, 1828. MacPherson to Clay of September 15 has not been found.

From JAMES BARBOUR, London, no. 6, November 14, 1828. Transmits a copy of his reply to Lord Aberdeen's note of October 31, 1828. Comments on the Russo–Turkish War, saying that "Every sympathy is now with the Turks" and noting that England and Austria are making "Great efforts . . . to restore peace." States that the French are rapidly building up their navy "which has become the ascendant passion with the nation." LS. DNA, RG59, Dip. Disp., Great Britain, vol. 36 (M30, R32). Received January 20, 1829. Also in Manning, *Diplomatic Correspondence . . . Canadian Relations,* 2:778.

To HENRY CLAY, JR. Washington, November 14, 1828
I have received your letter of the 9h. instant, and I am truly sorry that you give so unfavorable an account of the prospects of Richard [Shelby].[1] It will distress his parents extremely. I shall send your letter to his father,[2] who must decide what is to be done.

Genl. Jackson, without doubt, will be elected. He will obtain the votes of Kentucky and Ohio, and perhaps of Indiana also. I consider the question as decided.

We shall return to Ashland in the Spring. And now, my dear Son, you are one of my greatest comforts. Indeed there is no object in life about which I have so much solicitude as your success in your studies, which I believe to be so intimately connected with your welfare and future usefulness. I intreat you therefore, by your love for me, and by your own good, to persevere, and do as you have done. My health is now pretty good. That of your mother and the children is also good.

ALS. Henry Clay Memorial Foundation, Lexington, Ky.   1. Cadet Richard Shelby, a weak student, was not graduated with his class (1832) at West Point. USMA, *Register*, 185.   2. Probably James Shelby, son of Gov. Isaac Shelby.

From PETER B. PORTER   Washington, November 14, 1828
I have the honor to enclose a letter from the Chief of the Engineer Corps [Charles Gratiot] to whom your communication of yesterday[1] was referred.

The Officers of the Topographical corps have full employment; but the immediate execution of all the works on which they are engaged is not essential. A plan for the execution of the work required by you with the greatest economy of time, can be best concerted between the officer of your Department [Lt. MacKay] to whom this business is confided, and Lt. Colonel [James] Kearney[2] of the Topographical corps, who has already been instructed on the subject.

Copy. DNA, RG107, Military Books, vol. 12, p. 387.   1. On November 13, Clay wrote Porter asking that the Topographical Corps prepare copies of maps relevant to the Northeast Boundary dispute with Great Britain and noting that such copies would be "submitted to the Arbiter, King William I, as evidence in support of our claim." Copy. DNA, RG59, Dom. Letters, vol. 22, p. 330 (M40, R20). In preparing the Corps for this service to the State Department, Gratiot had written Clay on October 24 announcing that Lt. MacKay had been assigned these cartographical duties. Gratiot to Clay, October 24, 1828. ALS. DNA, RG59, Misc. Letters (M179, R66).

On February 25, 1829, Levin Gale, a Maryland Congressman [See *BDAC*], writing Clay from the House of Representatives, requested the return of a rare copy of *The American Military Pocket Atlas* (London, 1776) which he had left at the State Department during December, 1828, for use in the Northeastern boundary question. ALS. DNA, RG59, Misc. Letters (M179, R67).   2. For Kearney, see Hamersly, *Complete Regular Army Register of the United States. . . .*, 549. Lt. MacKay cannot be positively identified, but is likely the Alexander B. MacKay mentioned in *ibid.*, 595.

From JOEL R. POINSETT   Mexico, November 15, 1828
I transmit herewith a translation of an Extract of the proceedings of this Senate, on the subject of the Treaty[1] between the two Countries. The amendments which had been made in the House of the 16th and 17th articles of the Treaty, were confined altogether to verbal alterations in the Spanish version of them.

I have furnished a member of the House with the necessary arguments to rebut those used by the Senate. It is very vexatious to have to contend with the extreme ignorance and presumption of this body, and it is perfectly impossible to anticipate their objections.

LS. DNA, RG59, Dip. Disp., Mexico, vol. 4 (M97, R5). Dispatch No. 156. Received December 23, 1828.   1. Of Amity, Commerce, and Navigation. See Poinsett to Clay, February 22, 1828.

From FRANCIS T. BROOKE   Richmond,
                                        November 16, 1826 [i.e., 1828]
My pen has been really dumb, Since I heard the news from NY and Maryland and to make it Speak my astonishment is impossible, or I

would have written you Sooner, I am entirely Satisfied with your preference of Mr. [Nicholas P.] Trist, I have no doubt of his Superior qualifications for the office you have given him,[1] indeed I inclosed you the letter from Mr S [George W. Spotswood], that you might judge for yourself of his qualifications believing them myself not Sufficient for any but Some minor office—your whole correspondence with Mr [Jonathan] Russel[l] I have not Seen but I understand from Mr [Philip N.] Nicholas that there is nothing in it that ought to operate against you, and I Shall keep in mind your request to have it republished in the [Richmond *Constitutional*] Whig—I am glad to find that the triumph of the Jackson party here is not over you, with Some few exceptions—I think your course will be a very plain one, you have Sacrificed enough to your country, and as a consequence to Mr Adams, I hope you will calmly continue in the office you hold, until you can no longer Serve your country with credit to yourself and of consequence with usefulness to it, by which you will preserve your influence to be exercised at some more propitious period for its interests—how it is in other States I do not know but I am much mistaken if it is not now greater in Virginia than at any prior time—I hope that Shock has not been so great as to effect in the Smallest degree the course of the Cabinet and that it will move on in the useful and dignified path it has here to fore followed. . . .

ALS. InU.   1. Clay to Brooke, November 9, 1828.

From ROBERT MONROE HARRISON, St. Bartholomew, November 17, 1828. Deplores the fact that U.S. Customs Collectors do not require clearances before goods are landed. Discusses the problem in St. Bartholomew and St. Eustatius with regard to clearances and complains that officials in St. Bartholomew do not show him "the respect which was due to me, as Consul of the U States." ALS. DNA, RG59, Cons. Disp., St. Bartholomew, vol. 2 (M72, R2). Received December 11, 1828.

From RICHARD RUSH, Treasury Department, Washington, November 17, 1828. Encloses a copy of an order of the President, issued in 1818, "by which all public moneys in the hands either of collecting or disbursing officers are to be kept . . . in the Bank of the United States and its branches, or in the State Banks" authorized by the Secretary of the Treasury "in places where there are no branches." States that some new government officers are unacquainted with this regulation which in some instances "has not been complied with." Urges, therefore, full conformity with the law.

In addition, recommends that the officers be instructed "to use . . . in their disbursements of public money the same funds . . . received in payment of the warrants or drafts of this Department." Concludes that the Bank of the United States "will on the application of those officers, discharge the Treasury warrants and drafts in such funds . . . for these disbursements." LS. DNA, RG59, Misc. Letters, (M179, R66).

From JOHN JAMES APPLETON, Stockholm, no. 30, November 18, 1828. States that the Swedish government is increasing appropriations for the army and navy, and for fortifications, and that both the financial situation of the country and the "condition of the People" have improved. ALS. DNA, RG59, Dip. Disp., Sweden, vol. 5 (M45, R6). Received February 1, 1829.

To FRANCIS T. BROOKE   Washington, November 18, 1828
I received your favor of the 16th instant, from which I am very sorry to learn that a late political event has produced on you so serious an effect. It is certainly not very agreeable, and, though feared, was not expected by me. It is undoubtedly calculated to weaken our confidence in the stability of our free institutions. But we ought not to allow this, or any other of the ills of human life, to deprive us of hope and fortitude. For myself, I declare to you, most sincerely, that I have enjoyed a degree of composure, and of health too, since the event was known, greater than any I experienced for many months before. I shall continue at my post, honestly and faithfully discharging my duty, until the 4th of March, when I shall surrender my trust to other hands, which I hope may serve the public with more success—with more patriotic zeal they cannot. In my retirement to Ashland I shall find tranquillity, and whatever my future situation may be, I shall continue to employ my best exertions for the preservation and perpetuation of those great principles of freedom and policy, to the establishment of which my public life has hitherto been sincerely dedicated. I believe the other members of the Administration, including its head, will, in their respective spheres, calmly exercise equal diligence, until the arrival of the same period.

A most wild and reprehensible suggestion has been made, by some anonymous correspondent of the editors of the "Intelligencer", whose letter is published in their paper of this day, to defeat the election of General Jackson by the electroal colleges, or some of them, taking up a new candidate.[1] Nothing could be more exceptionable than any such attempt at this time. It would be a gross violation of the pledge which has been implied, if not expressed, in the choice of all the electors. Calamitous as I regard the election of General Jackson, I should consider the defeat of his election, at this time, by any such means, as a still greater calamity.

I am glad to find that you approve of the appointment of Mr. [Nicholas P.] Trist. It was made without any personal attachment for him, and upon considerations which all good persons must respect.

LS. KyU.   1. Washington *Daily National Intelligencer,* November 18, 1828. See King to Clay, November 13, 1828; Clay to Childs, November 20, 1828. The anonymous correspondent proposed: "Cannot the matter be brought into the House of Representatives by some political legerdemain?" By "inducing five states to vote for Mr. Clay," the House would be compelled to consider three candidates, an act that might serve to overturn the Jackson victory. The editors, Gales and Seaton, branded their correspondent "a sorry Knave." See, also, Weston, *The Presidential Election of 1828,* 179–80.

To JAMES CALDWELL   Washington, November 18, 1828
I received your letter of the 11th instant, and thank you for the information it contains about the progress of my servants.[1] I wish I could communicate to you, in return, agreeable information about the result of the Presidential Election. But I regret to have to inform you than [*sic,* that]

General Jackson is elected by a considerable majority. He obtained the vote of Ohio and Kentucky, and probably Indiana also. And Mr. Adams' vote in the Eastern States was less than anticipated.[2] For myself, I have no reproaches on account of any omission of exertion to avert this calamitous event. I shall remain at my post, calmly and honestly discharging my duty, until the 4th of March, after which I shall return to Kentucky. It is uncertain whether I shall be able to see you in the course of the ensuing year. . . .

LS. *VMHB*, (October, 1947), 55:306. Letter marked "(Confidential)." 1. Clay had sent two of his house slaves back to Kentucky ahead of him, via White Sulphur Springs, Va. 2. Weston, *Presidential Election of 1828*, pp. 181-2.

From DANIEL JENIFER   Port Tobacco, Md., November 18, 1828
The Accounts by yesterdays mail seem to leave no room to doubt the result of the Presidential Election being in favour of Gel. Jackson—. Comment upon this is unnecessary—

Yet I cannot forbear to congratulate you that altho your opponents have succeeded in this contest, they have failed in one of their primary objects; and that the utmost reason of your enemies has not been sufficient for a moment to shake that confidence which your friends have reposed in you—nor has this defeat in any measure rebated that zeal which they have always felt for your success, and which only audits an opportunity hereafter to be excelled. The "developments" which have within the last twelve months been made, have tended to rivet more and more that confidence in you, which facts have compelled to be withdrawn from others—You will I am sure properly appreciate the feelings which have given rise to this communication.

ALS. DLC-HC (DNA, M212, R3).

From C. D. E. J. BANGEMAN HUYGENS, Washington, November 20, 1828. Complains of the "injurious effects of the recent Tariff of the United States upon their commercial relations with the Netherlands," especially "the distilleries of grain and Holland Gin." States that "the Chambers of Commerce of the principal cities in Holland" are alarmed about the situation, believing that the tariff on gin is prohibitive. Warns that when gin, "one of the principal articles of exchange in the commerce of" the U.S. and the Netherlands, is "erased from the list," a reduction "must speedily take place in the direct importation of the produce of the United States" by the Netherlands. Requests "that all cargoes of gin which have been shipped or which had cleared before the new tariff was known in Holland will be considered as having been admitted under the former rate of duties." LS, in French, with trans. in State Dept. file. DNA, RG59, Notes from Netherlands Legation, vol. 1 (M56, R1).

To DAVID LEE CHILD   Washington, November 20, 1828
I have duly received your letter of the 14th inst. Events not known at Boston at its date, but a knowledge of which has been acquired here, demonstrate the loss of Mr. Adams' election, and the success of General Jackson, by a considerable majority. It is known that the latter has re-

ceived the votes of Ohio and Kentucky, probably Indiana, and I should not be much surprised, after all that has occurred, if he gets that of Louisiana also.[1] It is useless to indulge in the expression of mortification and regret on account of this inauspicious event. It has filled me with more than any language could convey. Ardently devoted throughout a life which is now not short, to the freedom of my fellow men, nothing has ever heretofore occurred to create in my mind such awful apprehensions of the permanency of our liberty. I most devoutly pray that they may not be realized.

The duty enjoined by patriotism and philosophy is submission to what has become inevitable. We must bear with fortitude a calamity which we have done all that honest men and sincere patriots could do, to avert. Whilst there is life there is hope, and henceforward we should exert all our energies to preserve those great principles of liberty and of policy to which our best exertions have, hitherto, been zealously dedicated. Such is my own determination, and I am happy to tell you that since the event was known, I have enjoyed a degree of composure, and a bouyancy of spirits, which I have not known for many weeks before. If you had possessed the information which has reached us, you would not, I think, have made the suggestion of the declining of Mr. Adams, and bringing out now a new candidate.[2] Such a measure on his part would expose him to ridicule, if not contempt. Calamitous as I regard the election of General Jackson, any attempt to defeat his election, at this time, would be still more calamitous. It would be the signal of instantaneous civil war. Electoral Colleges which have been constituted with an express understanding to vote for him, would not vote for another, and could not, without dishonour and disgrace. Believing that you would not have made the suggestion if you had known all that we do, I shall exercise my discretion in not forwarding the letter which you have transmitted me for Richmond. I think the bare suggestion of the project calculated to do mischief, and that if it could be supposed to originate with the great body of our friends, it would attach to them lasting prejudice.

I regret extremely that Mr. Adams should have excited such feelings as you describe, by his comments on the letter of Mr. Jefferson.[3] Although I thought them unnecessary and unfortuante, I sincerely hope those feelings will be softened if not eradicated.

I am well aware of the friendly feelings for me which prevail throughout New England. They excite my profound gratitude, and whatever may be my future lot, they will always constitute a source of the most pleasing reflection. It would afflict me if I believed that I should never be able to visit again that interesting quarter of our Union. When I had that happiness, now more than ten years ago, friendly impressions were made on my mind which can never be effaced.

LS. NcD. Letter marked "Confidential." Fon Child, a Boston journalist, see *NCAB*, 2:324.   1. Weston, *Presidential Election of 1828*, 181–2.   2. King to Clay, November 13, 1828; Clay to Brooke, November 18, 1828.   3. Clay to Brooke, October 25, 1828.

From BARON LEWIS CHARLES DE LEDERER, Washington, November 21, 1828. Announces the willingness of the Austrian government to "Suspend and discontinue from the first of January 1829 . . .

all discriminating duties of tonnage or impost" levied in her ports against U.S. commerce, provided the U.S. will reciprocate. ALS. DNA, RG59, Notes from Austrian Legation, vol. 1 (M48, R1). See de Lederer to Clay, August 31, 1828.

The following day, November 22, Clay replied that "the Government of the United States is desirous of applying the principle of equal and unfettered Navigation in their intercourse with all Nations which are disposed to adopt it," either "by Treaty, or by separate and distinct regulation of the two Governments." Notes that under the act passed by Congress on May 24, 1828 [4 *U.S. Stat.*, 308-9], the President must be provided with proof that a foreign nation has already abolished discriminatory duties against the U.S. Concludes that de Lederer's declaration does not announce that the Austrian government has lifted such duties and, therefore does not provide "such evidence as would justify the President" in making a proclamation lifting discriminating duties against Austria. Adds, however, that he is directed by the President "to inform you that whenever the evidence required by the Law is received by him, he will without delay, exercise the power with which he is invested." Copy. DNA, RG59, Notes to Foreign Ministers and Consuls, vol. 4, pp. 89-91 (M38, R4).

To ADAM BEATTY
Washington, November 22, 1828

I received your friendly letter of the 12th inst. and thank you for the kind suggestions about my future course. I shall give them the most deliberate consideration. Unless I should be controlled by circumstances, my present intention is to decide nothing, in regard to myself, until I go to Kentucky next Spring. My first object, in the mean time, will be the state of my health, which I am happy to tell you has been better, since the event of the election was known, than it had been for some time before. I receive, from all quarters, and from individuals of both parties, the strongest assurances of personal confidence and attachment, and the most positive opinions that I will sustain no prejudice by the late event. Some of them even say that they think I will be benefitted by it.

I shall be glad to hear from you, occasionally, from Frankfort, where I hope you will pass an agreeable Winter.

LS. Courtesy of Earl M. Ratzer, Highland Park, Ill.

From HEZEKIAH NILES
Baltimore, November 22, 1828

I have felt myself so completely broken down by unexpected results, that I have not had the heart to correspond with my friends on the business of the election. It is over; and we were to be beaten, perhaps, it may prove most beneficial that a large majority of the electoral votes will be given to gen Jackson.[1] It may keep him, clear of some particular influence, as if however of special obligations, that many of us have dreaded.

It seems to me right, as well as expedient, that our friends should keep themselves aloof from every present party movement. It is very very probable that the opposition to us will divide strong into, at least, great and exceedingly hostile parties. Though defeated as we have been, the *moral power* of the nation is with us, and that will induce when *feeling* has ceased to have effect. I hope therefore, that we shall remain uncommitted—not in the New York meaning of the term, but really so, to rally round those principles which we have felt essential to the prosperity of our country.

I look back with disgust on the means used to overthrow us—not forward with hope, that we shall yet triumph in the success of our measures.

In the midst of the gloomy news last week—"a mere child" was laid to my charge—a very trusty and hearty fellow, and his name is Henry Clay.[2] About five years hence, I hope to have the pleasure of presenting him to you under different circumstances than the present. The mother, child and *myself*—are "as well as can be expected!"

ALS. DLC-HC (DNA, M212, R3).   1. The final electoral vote count was Jackson, 178; Adams, 83.   2. Henry Clay Niles was a child of Niles's second marriage. R. G. Stone, *Hezekiah Niles as an Economist* (Baltimore, 1933), 49.

To JOSEPH NOURSE, Register of the Treasury, Washington, November 22, 1828. Transmits an estimate of $229,800 for the expenses of the State Department for the year of 1829. Includes an itemized list of projected expenditures. Copy. DNA, RG59, Dom. Letters, vol. 22, pp. 338–9 (M40, R20).

On this same date, Clay also sent Nourse an estimate of $57,325 for Department expenses for the first quarter of 1830. *Ibid.*, 341.

From JOSE SILVESTRE REBELLO, Washington, November 22, 1828. States it is his duty to inform the Government of the United States that Pedro IV has abdicated the throne of Portugal in favor of his daughter Maria II, now Queen [5:310]. Expects, accordingly, that the United States will recognize Maria II as Portugal's sovereign. ALS, in Portuguese, with trans. in State Dept. file. DNA, RG59, Notes from Brazilian Legation, vol. 1 (M49, R1).

On November 27, Joaquim B. Pereira repeated the abdication news to Clay, noting further that Maria's title has been "formally recognized" by Brazil and Britain and that recognition "by the other Powers of Europe" is expected soon to follow. Asks for speedy recognition by the U.S. LS, in Portuguese, with trans. in State Dept. file. DNA, RG59, Notes from Portuguese Legation, vol. 2 (M57, R2).

From ASAKEL THOMSON   Ithaca, N.Y., November 22, 1828
From intelligence received from several states of the Union of the results of Electoral Elections there appears not the least probability that the present enlightned and upright chief Magistrate will be re-elected, permit a humble individual therefore who has felt a cordial interest in the present contest whether there is not one measure which may yet be adopted to defeat the election of a despotic military Tyrant—Cannot a third candidate be brought forward in the person of the Hon. Wm. H. Crawford of Georgia who Will secure the votes of all Mr Adams' friends in the electoral Colleges[1] and of many of the nominally Jackson— Electors and thus be chosen by a majority in the Colleges or at least may

not an election by the people be thus prevented and the choice be thus ultimately into the House of Representatives in which the friends of Mr Adams and of Mr Crawford may unite and succeed in electing the latter to the office of President of the United States—To accomplish an object so desirable and so necessary to the safety and welfare of our country as the defeat of those who would elevate Andrew Jackson to the presidency must meet the ardent wishes of every genuine patriot: For this purpose let Expresses and letters be despached without delay to one (or more) influential Electors in each State Friendly to Mr Adams and in each state also whose vote it may be possible to secure to Mr Crawford particularly the states of Virginia North Carolina and Georgia reccommending and urging the choice of that Gentleman by every consideration which can have weight with those to whom it is suggested. Let such letters or Expresses proceed for instance from some distinguished Elector in Maryland proposing this plan and pledging the influence of such Electors in his Own College and stating his undoubting belief that Mr Crawford will receive the votes of all Mr Adams' friends in his College and can and will be elected by the people if a union of the friends of Mr Adams and those Jackson Electors supposed to be friendly to Mr Crawford can be effected for so desirable and important an object.

I hope you will not think me impertinently officious or intrusive in thus writing to you and recommending this measure   I have nothing at stake in this election other than what is common to every citizen of our country   I have been induced to submit this project to you from a sincere regret at the expected defeat of Mr Adams election whose administration aided by able and upright Counsillors I regard as having been Wise and happy and [from] a warm and cordial attachment to my Country Whose safety and happiness will in my opinion be seriously endangered by the elevation of Andrew Jackson to the Presidency

ALS. DLC–TJC (DNA, M212, R10).   1. Clay to Brooke, November 18, 1828; King to Clay, November 13, 1828.

From CHRISTOPHER HUGHES   Brussels, November 24, 1828
I will not attempt to describe to you the gratification I have felt, at the perusal of your private Letter of 6th. October; it might be still more difficult for me to persuade you to believe, that, however desirable and important to me may be the promotion,[1] in perspective, which circumstances seem to promise, (if not to call for) still, the part of your letter, which went most to my heart, and which has given me most pleasure, is to be found, in the terms of approbation of kindness & of affection in which you have had the goodness to express—yourself. . . .

[Assures Clay of his undying friendship and devotion. Continues:]
You say nothing about your health; I learn from others, that you are much better; & a letter of same date, as Yrs., describes you as being in great health & spirits; certain of the Election and talking of a trip through Pen[n]sylvania "N. York & Jersey." in your own letter you say expressly that you consider the result very doubtful; so you see, how much better others know what you think, & what you project, than you do yourself; & I authorize you hereafter, whenever you wish for accusable information, about *yourself* to address yourself to me; it is odd, but it

Seems certain, you see, that Bruxelles & not Washington, is the fountain of accurate Knowledge. And yet it is a proverb that there is nothing "new under the *Sun;*" but the proverb makes no allusion to things under Jack*sun*. . . .

I fear, I shall prove more, than may be discreet, or useful to Mr. Adams in, the progress of my testimony! No body has *ever* doubted, that the eminent person, has a most ungovernable proclivity to aristocratical, and even monarchical institutions & *habits;* every act of his conspicuous career has gone to show this; those, who have lived in his intimacy have seen *hourly* proofs of it, in the lofty, haughty, towering points of his personal carriage; & in that awful distance, at which, he obstinately & disdainfully holds, all who are not endowed with high talents & inducted into high office. The Lord knows that during "the pretty particular considerable" space of time, that it was my unhappy doom, to live under the same roof with him[2] & to be subjected to his high and haughty humours, he led me a life of misery & mortification; never spoke to me with kindness; never allowed me to sit—*plump* & comfortable on the centre of my chair; but kept me, dangling, on the *near edge* of it, with my feet ready to *bounce* up, & show him that sort of standing homage, that domineering natures exact; he never laughed, never committed a joke; or condescended to laugh at mine; in a word, he is the Foe to equality & to the rights of his semblables; & everybody knows it; & so do I. . . .

The choice of the King of the Netherlands [William I] as umpire, in our [Northeast] Frontier interests certainly does give us new "importance," to the mission but, the importance of this mission, should never be considered by us, as "temporary" it may serve as a proper occasion, to give that dignity to the Mission by elevating its rank, that seal political importance of this free & flourishing Government the extent of our commercial relations with this kingdom—the ancient claims of Holland to our respect & the offended pride of the King, of the Orange Dynasty & of the high & influential Society of the Country, has been always clearly pronounced as to the importance, which they attach to this mission. . . .

[Discusses at length the "secondary rank accorded to our Legation" by Netherlanders and urges, in the interest of U.S. commercial relations with Holland, that Congress upgrade the status of his mission. Points out that the selection of King William I as arbitrator of the Anglo–American Northeast boundary further justifies the elevation of his mission to ministerial rank. Complains that as a Chargé, he is patronized and "laughed at" by Dutch government officials and other "powerful men in the country." Complains also that the British minister in Brussels knew of Clay's instruction to him on the arbiter–selection issue before he did and blames this demeaning situation on James Barbour who has thus placed him in a "rather awkward situation." Explains at length the need to upgrade the U.S. mission in the Netherlands. Continues:]

However, all this will be remedied in a few days; or I suppose I shall hear from Mr. Barbour by next mail; and I shall take care; not to allow this affair of Umpirage; to degenerate into one of Umbrage between my worthy Colleague and myself; though I wish, on my own account and on that of the public service, that he had put it in my power, to inform you, by this day's post for Liverpool, that the business was going on; & that one application to His Majesty had been presented; as it would have been, yesterday, had I heard from Mr. Barbour. As it is the wait! . . .

I have not the smallest doubt that the king will promptly and graciously accept the invitation; and even feel a certain satisfaction in having his name associated in historical records & recollections, with that of the last and lamented High Arbiter [Alexander I] who gave judgement in the affairs of the same parties.[3] I believe this; but I cannot as yet, write positively on the point.

Do not quarrel with me if I again recur to the rank of the mission, it ought to be, it must be raised, even if it be at the sacrifice of the actual incumbent; the undersigned! Comity, nay common decency will require it! . . .

ALS. DLC-HC (DNA, M212, R3). Letter marked "Private."   1. To upgrade the U.S. Legation in the Netherlands to the status of a Ministry.   2. At Ghent in late 1814. 3. St. Petersburg Convention of July 12, 1822 [1:1002, 1011; 3:736].

From ROBERT CRITTENDEN, Little Rock, Arkansas Territory, November 25, 1828. Announces the death of George Izard, Governor of Arkansas, and states that as Secretary of the territory he has "taken possession of the executive papers, and assumed his official duties." Asks to be appointed Governor. Feels that if he does not receive the office "I should be degraded in the eyes of my friends, and my own estimation, by being virtually told that I am unworthy [of] the high trust which casualties have alone devolved upon me." ALS. DNA, RG59, A. and R. (MR, Supp.). John Pope received the appointment. See Baylor, *John Pope Kentuckian,* 329–33, for the background of his appointment.

To CHRISTOPHER HUGHES, no. 8, November 25, 1828. Orders him to sell the house and lot owned by the U.S. in The Hague for "the best terms that can be procured." Copy. DNA, RG59, Dip. Instr., vol. 12, pp. 167–8 (M77, R7).

To HEZEKIAH NILES   Washington, November 25, 1828
I received your favor of the 22d the inauspicious time of the Election has shocked me less than I feared it would. My health and my spirits too have been better, since the event was known, than they were many weeks before—And yet all my opinions are unchanged and unchangeable about the dangers of the precedent which we have established   The military principle has triumphed, and triumphed in the person of one devoid of all the graces, elegancies, and magnanimity of the accomplished men of the profession

Our course is a plain one—We must peaceably submit to what we have been unable to avert, firmly resolved to adhere to our principles, and to watch over the Republic, like faithful centinels—We should especially avoid gratuitous propositions of support to the new administration or on the other hand a rash and precipitate opposition—Many of our friends have got under the hostile standard—We should endeavour to recall them to their duty by Kindness—A blind and precipitate attact

548

would produce union where now there is nothing but the elements of discord.

I thank you and Mrs. Niles. for the high compliment you have lately paid me—[1]It is a better evidence of the fidelity of your friendship, than of your discretion, at this time With my best wishes for the mother and son. . . .

Copy. DLC–HC (DNA, M212, R3).   1. Niles to Clay, November 22, 1828.

To GEORGE C. THOMPSON   Washington, November 25, 1828

I received your obliging letter of the 9th inst. The fact adverted to by you of Colonel [Joseph Hamilton] Daveiss' assumption, at an advanced stage of his life, of the name of [Alexander] Hamilton, which is mentioned in my letter to Dr. [Richard] Pindell,[1] was currently reported about twenty years ago. Whether true or not, it was believed by many, and by myself among them. It is not important, but if he is named in his father's will without the addition of Hamilton,[2] I should be glad if you, or some other friend, would have an extract from it published.

I not only recollect the fact stated by you of the compliment paid to *Colonel* [Aaron] *Burr* on the motion of General [Samuel] Hopkins to admit him in the Hall of the [Ky.] House of Representatives; but I recollect, also, as I think you will, that when he was about to appear in Court to the prosecution of Colonel Daveiss, General Hopkins and others waited on him at the tavern,[3] then kept by Mrs. [Thomas] Love, and accompanied him to the Capitol.

You will have heard of the election of General Jackson. It appears that it would have happened if Mr. Adams had received all the western votes which were counted upon for him. Whilst no man can have a deeper sense than I have, of the fatal tendencies of this decision of the people, I feel the full force of the obligation of duty to submit to the will of the majority. There is no inconsistency between such an acquiescence and a firm determination to adhere to our principles, and to do all we can to limit the mischiefs, present and future, of the pernicious example which has been set. I shall remain at my post, in the diligent discharge of my duties, until the 4th of March, after which I shall retire to Ashland, where I hope to find leisure and tranquillity. . . .

LS. NjP.   1. Clay to Pindell, October 15, 1828.   2. Daveiss' mother's maiden name was also Hamilton.   3. "The Love House" or "Love's Inn" in Frankfort, Ky., earlier owned by Major Thomas Love.

From JAMES BROWN, Paris, no. 87, November 26, 1828.

Discusses Lieutenant Denis Hart Mahan of the U.S. Army who has been in France three years and is a student at the Military Academy of Metz. States that Mahan also studied under "Mr de Becquey, Directeur des Ponts et Champees et des Mines." Encloses a copy of a work received from Becquey which Mahan believes "would be useful to the Military Academy at West Point." Requests that the Secretary of War obtain copies of "such reports and facts and information generally in relation to our roads, Canals, and other internal improvements as might . . . be useful or interesting to the French Government." Concludes: "It would be exceedingly gratifying to me to be made the organ of transmitting these to Mr de Becquey." LS. DNA, RG59, Dip. Disp., France, vol. 23 (M34, R26). Received January 18, 1829. For Denis Hart Mahan see *DAB.*

On January 19, 1829, Secretary of War, Peter B. Porter, returned to Clay a copy of the November 26 dispatch from Brown, together with a copy of the correspondence between Brown and Monsieur Becquey. Copy. DNA, RG59, Dom. Letters, vol. 22, p. 374 (M40, R20).

From JAMES BARBOUR, London, no. 7, November 28, 1828. Acknowledges receipt of State Department dispatches, dated October 15 and 16, 1828. Reports that he immediately communicated with the Earl of Aberdeen, conveying the President's approval of the King of the Netherlands, William I, as arbiter, as well as Christopher Hughes's instructions "to cooperate with the British Ambassador near the Court of the Netherlands, in soliciting the King, to accept the office." Says Aberdeen expressed his satisfaction with this action. Reports a discussion with Aberdeen on a law passed by Parliament on July 25, 1828, called "An Act to amend the laws relating to the Customs."

Mentions that he has finally had an audience with the King, George IV, and states that he appeared to be in good health despite rumors to the contrary and the statement of the Duke of Welllington "that the King's waist coat had been diminshed three feet in it's circumference." Comments on the failure of a banking house in Glasgow, Scotland, as an indication of "an alarming state of the trading interest." LS. DNA, RG59, Dip. Disp., Great Britain, vol. 36 (M30, R32). Received January 22, 1829.

From JOHN MARSHALL   Richmond, November 28, 1828
In consequence of my inattention to the post office I did not receive your letter of the 23d. till yesterday afternoon. I need not say how deeply I regret the loss of Judge [Robert] Trimble. He was distinguished for sound sense, uprightness of intention, and legal knowledge. His superior cannot be found. I wish we may find his equal. You are certainly correct in supposing that I feel a deep interest in the character of the person who may succeed him. His superior will of course be designated by Mr. Adams because he will be required to perform the most important duties of his office before a change of administration can take place.

Mr. [John J.] Crittenden is not personally known to me, but I am well acquainted with his general character. It stands very high. Were I myself to designate the successor of Mr. Trimble I do not know the man I could prefer to him. Report, in which those in whom I confide concur, declares him to be sensible honorable and a sound lawyer. I shall be happy to meet him at the supreme court as an associate. The objection I have to a direct communication of this opinion to the President arises from the delicacy of the case. I can not venture, unasked, to recommend an associate justice to the President, especially a gentleman who is not personally known to me. It has the appearance of assuming more than I am willing to assume. I must then, notwithstanding my deep interest in the appointment, and my conviction of the fitness of Mr. Crittenden, a conviction as strong as I could well feel in favour of a gentleman of whom I Judge only from general character, decline writing to the President on the subject. . . .

ALS. DLC–HC (DNA, M212, R3).

From MARQUIS DE ARACATY, Rio de Janeiro, November 29, 1828. Informs Clay that Emperor Peter I has recalled Jose Silvestre Rebello, Brazilian Minister to the United States. In the hope that closer relations between the two nations will develop, announces that Rebello's successor is Jose Araujo Ribeiro, former Secretary of the Brazilian Legation at Naples. LS, in French, with trans. in State Dept. file. DNA, RG59, Notes from Brazilian Legation, vol. 1 (M49, R1).

From NICHOLAS P. TRIST, Washington, November 29, 1828. Understands that Clay may have an incorrect impression of his recent connection with the pro-Jackson Charlottesville *Virginia Advocate.* Submits a lengthy statement designed to correct that impression. Admits that during the Presidential election of 1824 he had held "an exceedingly unfavorable impression of you" because of "your construction of the Constitution"; and that this had included an acceptance of the "corrupt bargain" charge, "a belief that rendered me more hostile to you than ever. This state of feeling continued some time; but it was, long ago, altered." Asserts that he had studied the charge carefully and came to realize that "the evidence of bargain was far from possessing the conclusive character I had, without hesitation, recognized in it"; also, under the guidance of Thomas Jefferson, his father-in-law, he had reconsidered Clay's views in opposition to "the principles of unlimited freedom of commerce" and had concluded that they had been misrepresented in Virginia.

Explains his own financial difficulties and those of Jefferson's family after the former President's death in July, 1826. Notes that he had reluctantly gone to work as an editor of the *Virginia Advocate* mainly because of the salary involved. States that in replacing Thomas W. Gilmer as one of its editors, he did so "with the express understanding that I was to have nothing to do with the Presidential Election" of 1828. Further, he was hired in the knowledge that he was "known to be favorable to the administration." Indeed, he had taken the job even though "To all my tastes & feelings, the proposed occupation was exceedingly repugnant." Reports that when the Richmond *Constitutional Whig* falsely identified him as a Jackson partisan in the 1828 contest, friends had advised him not to answer the charge publicly. Maintains also that he had done nothing in his capacity as an editor to advance Jackson's candidacy during the campaign. Points out that the "paper has been very virulent, ever since I came into it; & its bitterness against *you,* particularly great: but this was neither my work, nor any wise under my control." Asserts this was the doing of the "other editors"; indeed, "I had no right to interfere; & if I had interfered, 'twould have been with the certainty of being overruled." Regrets that the "appearances of my *name,* as one of the Editors of the Advocate" might have led Clay to a misunderstanding of the actual situation. ALS. DLC–HC (DNA, M212, R3). A very rough draft of this letter is in ViU. The Charlottesville *Virginia Advocate* was established in July, 1827, by Thomas W. Gilmer and J. A. H. Davis, professor of law at the University of Virginia. It continued publication until 1861. See the *VMHB* (July, 1894), 2:223; (April, 1901), 8:339.

From FRANCIS T. BROOKE   Richmond, November 30, 1828
I have just seen your friend as he calls himself Doctor [Maury] Morris,   he is they say a very good fellow, but I confess I do not like him half as well as I formerly did—you can conjecture why—I was however much pleased with the favorable account he gave of your health and spirits, and of the health of Mrs Clay   he appears himself to be much delighted with his visit to Washington,—I hope you will continue to preserve your trantquility—I have shown your last letter[1] to some of your friends of both parties and they all expressed great Satisfaction with the temper you preserve and also with your determination to continue to fill the office you hold until the 4h of March and then to go into retirement until the passions of the hour have passed away—and the unfriendly sentiments which have been nurtured by them Shall perish with them—our Legislature will meet tomorrow and I shall be better able after some time to give you an accurate account of the State of public feeling, as yet I have seen no marks of triumph in the inglorious victory they have obtained,   Some of the most intelligent Seem to fear the consequences of it,   our Governor [William B. Giles] is litterally despised and nothing can save him from the disgrace he so well merits, but the idea of some that it will be the cause of triumph to his & their political enemies but he will notwithstanding go out, though it is probable to make room for one as despicable as himself—my sincere respects to Mrs Clay. . . .

ALS. InU.   1. November 18, 1828.

To DANIEL WEBSTER   Washington, November 30, 1828
As I understand that you are not to be here for a month, I wish to say some things which I had intended for a personal interview.

We are beaten. It is useless to dwell on the causes. It is useless to repine at the result. What is our actual position? We are of the majority, in regard to measures; we are of the minority in respect to the person designated as C. Magistrate. Our effort should be to retain the majority we have. We may lose it by imprudence. I think, in regard to the new Administration, we should alike avoid professions of support or declarations of opposition, in advance. We can only yield the former, if our principles are adopted and pursued, and if they should be our honor and our probity afford a sufficient pledge that *we* shall not abandon them. To say before hand that we will support the President elect, if he adheres to our systems, is to say that we will be honest; and that I hope is a superfluous proclamation. On the other hand, if we were now to issue a manifesto of hostility, we should keep united, by a sense of common danger, the discordant confederates who have taken the field against us.

They cannot remain in Corps but from external pressure. The dissentions among them this winter, the formation of the new Cabinet, and the Inaugural Speech will enable us to discover the whole ground of future operations. Above all I think that *we* ought not to prematurely agitate the question of the Succession. The nation wants repose. The agitations of the last six years entitle it to rest. If it is again to be immediately disturbed let others not us assume the responsibility.

We shall here all calmly proceed in our various spheres to discharge our, duties, until the 4h. of March. The message[1] is good. It makes no allusion to the late event. Its strongest features are the support of the Tariff and disapprobation of sentiments of disunion.

I shall retire to Ashland after the 4h. of March, and there consider and decide my future course. I do not mean to look at it until then.

You have all my wishes for success in the prosecution against [Theodore] Lyman.[2] I regretted the publication here which led to the libel; but most certainly I never supposed you to be alluded to in that publication. In the midst of all the heats of former times I believed you, as I have since found you, faithful to the Union, to the Constitution and to Liberty.

Under every vicissitude believe me. . . .

ALS. DLC-Daniel Webster Papers (DNA, M212, R22).   1. Adams's Fourth Annual Message, December 2, 1828. Richardson, *MPP*, 3:973–87.   2. For Theodore Lyman Jr.'s clash with Webster, see *DAB* and Wiltse, *Papers of Daniel Webster, Correspondence*, 2:382–3.

From ABRAHAM B. NONES, Maracaibo, December 1, 1828. Details the case of the American schooner, *Baltic* of Bristol, Rhode Island, Captain J. D. Slocum. Complains that specie brought by the *Baltic* from La Guaira was unjustly confiscated by customs officials in Maracaibo on the ground that it was counterfeit. Regrets that his efforts to aid Slocum were "to no avail." Warns that American merchants should be advised of the risk involved in "the introduction of Specie of any kind" in Maracaibo, because the money alleged to be counterfeit fills the pockets of the customs officials. States that he has sent to William Henry Harrison, American Minister to Colombia, the documents relating to this and previous cases of alleged counterfeit money.

Inquires whether American property on consignment in the stores of a Colombian merchant, captured and used by Spanish forces when they captured Maracaibo in September, 1822, could be considered as claims against the Spanish government. Observes that Spain has acknowledged similar claims for British property. ALS. DNA, RG59, Cons. Disp., Maracaibo, vol. 1 (M–T62, R1). Received January 18, 1829.

From SAMUEL J. DONALDSON, Baltimore, December 2, 1828. Releases Henry and Lucretia Clay from a mortgage loan in the amount of $15,527.88, dated July 2, 1825, held by the creditors of Samuel and Robert Purviance [4:498–9], and secured by "Certain Lots of Ground and Improvements in Lexington in Kentucky." Certifies that the three annual instalments have all been paid. ADS. DLC-TJC (DNA, M212, R16).

From JOHN J. CRITTENDEN　　　　Frankfort, December 3, 1828

Tho' recent occurrences have a good deal depressed my spirits, my principles forbid me to despair. I have yet a strong confidence "that truth is omnipotent & public justice certain," & that you will live to hail the day of retribution & triumph. Your political enemies render involuntary homage to you, by their early & spontaneous apprehensions of your future elevation, & your friends find their consolation by looking upon the same prospect. The combination that has been formed against you, will dissolve—its leaders have too many selfish views of personal agrandisement to harmonise long—Your friends will remain steadfast—bound to you more strongly by adversity—You will of necessity be looked to as the great head & hope of the great mass that constitutes the present administration party—This is the spirit already visible here—And I am sanguine of its final result—

What an excellent philosophy it is which can thus extract good from evil—consolation from defeat!! But enough of it.

You will of course go on with the Administration to the last moment; as tho' Mr. Adams had been reelected, & with all the good temper & discretion possible—But what then? That you should return to your District & represent it again in Congress, seems to be the general wish & expectation of your friends here—It is certainly mine—

Our judges of the court of Appeals, [William] Owsley & [Benjamin] Mills have on this day delivered to the Governor [Thomas Metcalfe] their resignations—It will have the effect of depriving the agitators of one of their anticipated topics—It is probable, I think, that they will both be re-nominated by the Governor—¹There is little doubt but that Owsley's nomination will be confirmed by the Senate—The confirmation of Mills will be strongly opposed, & is very doubtful—Unfortuantely he is very unpopular.

The defeat of [John] Oldham's election as Speaker of our House of Representatives, has been a sore disappointment to the Jacksonians—And has produced some scism among them—The Administration men united in favour of [John T.] Quarles, or rather against Oldham—²

As to the Federal judgeship, to which you say I & others have been recommended—I have only to remark, that should it come to me, neither the *giving*, nor the *receiving* of it, shall be soiled by any solicitations of mine on the subject. The kindness of those friends, who have recommended me, is doubly grateful to my feelings, as it was altogether unsolicited—For tho' I have never been guilty of the affectation of pretending that such an office would be unwelcomed to me, I have certainly never asked a human being to recommend me. Indeed I wrote to Judge [John] Boyle, that I would not permit myself to be thrown into competition with him—but he informed me that he would not have the office—that he preferred that which he now holds—

I have violated all rule in writing so Long a letter to a Secretary of State. . . .

ALS. NcD. A sharply edited version of this letter which omits important phrases and all of paragraph five, is printed in Mrs. Chapman Coleman, ed., *The Life of John J. Crittenden, with Selections from His Correspondence and Speeches*. 2 vols. (Philadelphia, 1871), 1:71–2.
1. Both were. Ky. Sen. *Journal* . . . 1828–1829, pp. 63–4; but both were denied Senate con-

firmation by identical votes of 20 to 18. *Ibid.*, 69–70.   2. For party strengths in the new Ky. legislature, see Clay to Whittlesey, August 15, 1828.

To JOHN M. FORBES, Buenos Aires, no. 8, December 3, 1828. States that the differences between Forbes and George W. Slacum, U.S. Consul in Buenos Aires, "have occasioned the President much regret." Explains: "Disputes and contentions between officers of the Government in a distant foreign country are not merely injurious to the public service, They are prejudicial to the character of our country. The President hopes there will be no recurrence of them between Mr. Slacum & yourself." Emphasizes: "You are the only Diplomatic Agent of the United States accredited there [and] any representations to that Government from our Consuls or private citizens, should be made by you only."

In regard to the case of the wrecked *Merope,* which caused a misunderstanding between the two men, affirms that it was Slacum's duty to try to save as much of the owners' property as possible, but it appears that John H. Duffy, the agent Slacum appointed, "seems to have executed his agency very improperly and fraudulently." Suggests Forbes should have permitted "the undisturbed operation of the laws of the Republic [Buenos Aires] to extract from him [Duffy] the property of others." Criticizes Slacum for making a direct application to the government of Buenos Aires for an exequatur for an agent he appointed to act in his absence and for applying for his own passport in order to return to the U.S. Copy. DNA, RG59, Dip. Instr., vol. 12, pp. 169–70 (M77, R7). Also, LS in DLC–HC (DNA, M212, R8).

On the same date, Clay wrote George W. Slacum, Buenos Aires, an almost identical letter. Copy. DNA, RG59, Cons. Instr., vol. 3, pp. 24–6 (M78, R3).

From THOMAS L. L. BRENT, Lisbon, no. 89, December 4, 1828. Reports on the departure of Maria da Gloria from Rio de Janeiro and her subsequent arrival in Europe. Notes that the original plan had been for her to proceed directly "to Vienna to be placed under the care of her grand Father the Emperor of Austria [Francis I]." Believes, however, that when the news reached Rio de Janeiro of the insurrections in Oporto and Madeira, the court "calculated that on her arrival in Europe she would find Lisbon in possession of the constitutional or Emperor's [Pedro IV] party." Instead, on her arrival at Gibraltar, it was found "that affairs had taken so favorable a turn for Don Miguel" that she proceeded to Britain where the government received her "with all the honours usually paid to crowned heads." Adds that a deputation has been sent from the Portuguese community in Britain to Rio de Janeiro "to lay before the Emperor [Pedro I] the state of affairs in Portugal—to solicit him to allow Donna Maria to be kept in England that she might be near at hand to attend to any call from the Constitutional Party in Portugal— to urge him to support with energy the rights of his daughter, and . . . to insist that all those portuguese who had been zealous in support of the Constitution . . . should be restored to their country and to the possession of their confiscated estates." Mentions that Miguel has suffered a broken leg in a carriage accident.

States that since the arrival of a French frigate at the time of the blockade of Oporto, "french ships of war have often visited this port" for the purpose of protecting "french subjects and property." Adds that they may also be used to "capture or remove from these and the neighbouring seas the south american privateers that have infested them."

Discusses sentences prescribed for those arrested during "the distrubance in July last year." Says that sentences, in addition to other arrests, form "part of the system of terror resorted to" in Portugal in order to keep "in awe the enemies of the government."

Reports that a new decree has been issued to increase substantially "the corps of regular volunteers." Says the primary duties of this corps will be "to support and defend the cause of religion and the throne and to promote the preservation of publick tranquillity." States that "Ever since the return of Dom Miguel from Vienna there has been an unanimous feeling of dissatisfaction at every act of the government on the part of the foreigners generally in this country." Notes that "This has been the case particularly with the British merchants," some of whom have been arrested. States that since the fall of Madiera, Terceira remains the only Portuguese island which does not recognize the authority of Dom Miguel. Believes that although one expedition against Terceira failed, another will be attempted by Miguel's forces.

Mentions that the breach between Miguel and his mother, Carlota Joaquina, has not developed into a complete split as had been expected and that the Queen still exercises some role in the affairs of government, while "a continuance of good will has been manifested" between the two. Attributes this to the "inexperience of the Prince [Miguel] to form a party" of his own "sufficiently powerful to withstand that of the Queen."

Speculates on whether or not Pedro I of Brazil will adhere to his abdication [as Pedro IV of Brazil] in favor of his daughter, Maria, and whether or not Brazilians would support a war against Portugal to preserve Maria's rights. Says that "great reliance" is placed in the mission of Lord Percy Clinton Sydney Smythe Strangford to Rio de Janeiro to produce "an amicable arrangement of the differences" between Pedro and Miguel. LS. DNA, RG59, Dip. Disp., Portugal, vol. 8 (M43, R7). Received February 1, 1829.

From JOHN M. FORBES, Buenos Aires, no. 65, December 5, 1828. Transmits copies of letters he has received concerning the establishment of a provisional government in the province, headed by General Juan Lavalle, together with his reply. Says it appears that Governor Manuel Dorrego is collecting his forces in the country and has written to the three ministers he left in charge—Tomas Guido, Juan Ramon Balcarce, and Vicente Lopez—protesting that the acts of the Junta are null and void. States that Dorrego is apparently counting "on much more extensive support than that of this Province alone." Cannot yet predict the outcome of the impending conflict. ALS. DNA, RG59, Dip. Disp., Argentina, vol. 3 (M69, R4). Received February 27, 1829. Also in Espil, *Once Anos en Buenos Aires*, 509–10.

From WILLIAM TUDOR, Rio De Janeiro, no. 114, December 5, 1828. States that illness has thwarted his plan to investigate conditions in Brazil and make an accurate report to the State Dept. Noting that his information remains "imperfect," he nevertheless, gives a full account of his impressions. Maintains that the slowness in the settlement of claims by Brazil arises from the "embarrassment" of its finances, "the immense demands urged simultaneously by various foreign nations, & to the anomalous operation of their council of state." Summarizes his negotiations with Brazilian officials.

Observes that "The Emperor [Pedro I] is spoken of in very opposite terms by his friends & enemies: the latter hardly permit him to possess a single virtue & the former are too much disposed to conceal his errours." Believes that the Emperor "is extremely attached to his children" and in the early years of his marriage was "reputed to be a good husband, & if this conduct had been continued, many subsequent errours might have been avoided." Notes that in the early years of his reign, he was extremely popular but that the "late war with Buenos Ayres was a beginning of misfortune." Adds that the Emperor's "connection with the Marchioness of Santos, & his consequent indifference and unkind treatment of the Empress [Maria Leopoldina] has been & may continue to be the abundant source of many ... misfortunes." Describes the Marchioness "as a voluptuous, good natured woman, not very refined, & was calculated on that very account to be a successful rival to the late Empress." Believes that another of the Emperor's "greatest failings" is "avarice."

Thinks loyalty to the monarchy in Brazil may be declining rather than increasing, but estimates that the majority of the people in Brazil favor a constitutional monarchy rather than an absolutist or a republican government. Has heard that during the latter part of the war with Buenos Aires, a plan was underway "to effect a revolution, & divide the empire into three or four republics." Contends that Brazil is "less qualified" for a republican government "than the states of Spanish origin, & there is not one of these that is yet sufficiently secure to justify even a moderate confidence in its stability." Believes Brazilians are gradually learning the rights and responsibilities of constitutional representation. Applauds the fact that clergymen have no political influence in Brazil. On the other hand, the "two most prominent evils of this country are the state of its finances & a barbarous system of laws, accompanied by a notoriously corrupt administration of them." Predicts that the country will prosper only "when the crown & the legislature unite their efforts to reform their present system of jurisprudence." Discounts the assertion, often made in the U.S., that Brazil "hates & despises us, on account of our republican institutions," contending instead "that there is no nation which they regard with more respect and good will."

Continues on December 7: Reports that the mission of Lord Percy Strangford who arrived in Brazil a few weeks before is useless because his purpose—to induce the Emperor [Pedro I] to abdicate [as Pedro IV] the throne of Portugal and to send the young Queen [Maria da Gloria] to Europe—had already been accomplished before his arrival. Thinks the Emperor is waiting for news from Portugal before taking further action, hoping that "Miguel will be overthrown & the Queen & the Constitution established." Contends that the Emperor may have to give up the constitution and agree to the marriage of his daughter and her uncle in order to settle the situation. Believes that Pedro might have avoided this situation if he had sent Maria to Portugal earlier, thus giving the Constitutional party a figure to use in attracting "the homage of the people."

Notes that Lord John Ponsonby is "urging the British claims with earnestness," and that both the English and Americans are acting "with a mutual understanding" against Admiral Rodrigo Pinte Guedes, "whose conduct at the conclusion of the war has been particularly outrageous." Says the present Ministry opposes Guedes, but his influence with the Emperor may soon give him a place in the Ministry itself. Adds that despite the very friendly relations between Brazil and Britain, "the English have been worse treated than ourselves."

Comments on piracy and fears that "if every nation does not send a squadron" for patrolling these waters, "this quarter will become the theatre of most extensive & frightful Piracy." Mentions that the "headquarters of piracy are in Cuba & some Spaniards are found on board all these piratical" vessels. ALS. DNA, RG59, Dip. Disp., Brazil, vol. 6 (M121, R8). No date of receipt.

From JAMES BARBOUR, London, no. 8, December 6, 1828. Transmits copies of documents received from James Maury, U.S. Consul at Liverpool, concerning an alleged insult to an American merchant ship, the *John Jay*, by a British warship. States that "I did not coincide with the Consul in his views on the subject." Explains Maury's belief that the British vessel had "done no more," than an American sloop of war would have been expected to do to a British merchantman on the U.S. coast, provided there was "suspicion of smuggling." To Barbour, however, "the case seemed a wanton insult to our flag, and . . . justly liable to rebuke," and he addressed a note to the Earl of Aberdeen to this effect.

States he has heard "that England and her allies have agreed on the emancipation of Greece, and her entire independence of Turkey," although there is still a disagreement on Greece's boundaries. Notes that England wants to limit the continental boundaries of Greece to the Morea, while Russia wants to enlarge them and France seems indecisive. Believes Russia still cherishes "gigantic schemes. . . against the Ottoman Empire."

Mentions that the "affairs of Portugal remain unaltered" and that Miguel is reportedly "recovering from his wounds." Emphasizes that "England does not mean to go to war on account of the young [Portuguese] Queen [Maria]."

Reports that the financial panic "excited in the money market by the fore[clo]sures in Glasgow, that of Fry and Chapman . . . could have been great and extensive, but for the aid so reasonably dispersed by the Bank of England." Believes that confidence is still "not fully established." LS. DNA, RG59, Dip. Disp., Great Britain, vol. 36 (M30, R32). Received January 28, 1829.

To CHARLES R. VAUGHAN, Washington, December 6, 1828. Refers to correspondence with Vaughn on May 8, 1826 [5:344-5] concerning the impressment of two seamen in 1825 from the American brig *Pharos* of Boston by Capt. D. C. Clavering of H. M. S. *Redwing* in Freetown, Sierra Leone. Transmits the deposition of Benjamin Homer, mate of the *Pharos,* which details "a clear case of impressment." States: "The allegation that the two seamen volunteered to enter on board the Red Wing is too thin a veil to cover the wrong which was perpetrated." Says the President anticipates that the British Government will make "reparation."

Mentions, further, "the impressment of four other seamen from American vessels by British Ships of war, also on the coast of Africa," and supports the complaint with enclosed depositions. Cites another instance, on April 28, 1828, at Clarence Bay, Island of Fernando Po, off the West coast of Africa, in which the captain of H. M. S. *Eden* impressed men from the Brig *Monroe* of Boston and the Brig *Juno* of New Bedford. Concludes that this practice "is one to which the American Government cannot submit." Copy. DNA, RG59, Notes to Foreign Ministers and Consuls, vol. 4, pp. 92-7 (M38, R4).

Vaughan responded to this letter on December 8, enclosing additional evidence, and asserting that the *Pharos* "could not be regarded as an act of impressment." Deplores Clay's use of the word "impressment." Promises, however, to ask his government about Clay's other impressment complaints. LS. DNA, RG59, Notes from British Legation, vol. 15 (M50, R15).

To DENISON WATTLES, JR. Washington, December 6, 1828
I have duly recd. your favor of the 24h Ulto with the two [Norwich, Conn.] Couriers accompanying, for which I offer you my sincere thanks.

I am not surprized at the sentiments expressed by you under the signature of Brutus.[1] I regret that there exists too much reason for them. The course of the four Southern States to which you refer has been such as to justify your animadversions. Among the disagreeable incidents of the late Presidential canvass, there is scarcely one which has exerted more painful feelings with me than that of the constant abuse which has been poured out on New England. All good patriots shall unite in condemning sectional reflections, no matter from whence they proceed or against what section they are directed.

Among the circumstances of regret which the present times exhibit, it is a source of some consolation to believe that there is yet a large majority in favor of those great measures of National policy with which the prosperity of the Country is so closely associated. It should [be our] care to [preserve] this majority. If the New administra[tion] [s]hould attempt the subversion of those measures, we must [illeg. wonds]. In the meantime [our best] course is [to avoid] alike [unnece]ssary declarations of hostility, and gratuitous pledges of support to the President elect. If he pursues our policy, our integrity is a guarranty that we shall not abandon it. On the other hand, we ought not to menace him in advance.

The Union; the Constitution; the preseration of the American System; and the subordination of the Military to Civil rule should be our great aims. . . .

ALS. NN.   1. In the Norwich (Conn.) *Courier* of November 19, 1828, Wattles ("Brutus") blamed the election of Jackson on narrow Southern sectionalism, pointing out that since the beginning of the Republic no Southern state electoral vote had ever been cast for a man living north of the Potomac. "And yet Yankees must have no sectional feelings!" he exclaimed. Bemoaning Jackson's election, he characterized the General as nothing more than "a full blooded Irishman, whose only merit consists in his having gained the battle of New Orleans; one too, whose hands are red with the blood of innocence."

To ROBERT MONROE HARRISON, St. Bartholomew, December 7, 1828. Acknowledges receipt of Harrison's letter of November 12 concerning "the case of certain American seamen who had been seduced from American vessels, and who were . . . in a destitute condition." Instructs him to arrange for their passage back to the U.S. "on the most economical terms," making sure not to exceed "the sum limited by law for the transportation of such seamen." States that the complaints made in Harrison's letter of June 28 [*sic*, 25] about the injuries done to Americans at St. Bartholomew will be transmitted to John James Appleton, U.S. Minister at Stockholm, who will be instructed "to make such representations to the Swedish Government as may seem best calculated to remove the causes of complaint."

Notes that a copy of Harrison's letter of October 28, reporting "that the Piratical vessel which captured the British Brig Caraboo, was owned in Baltimore," has been sent to the Navy Department. Requests him "to continue advising this Department from time to time of every case of this sort, which may hereafter unfortuantely arise." Copy. DNA, RG59, Cons. Instr., vol. 3, pp. 26–7 (M78, R3).

From ROBERT MONROE HARRISON, St. Bartholomew, December 8, 1828. In an extensive letter, containing sixteen enclosures, reports on the seizure of the brig *Nymph,* out of Boston, by the Buenos Airean privateer *Federal;* and the landing of the *Nymph's* cargo of dry goods in St. Bartholomew. Says he is not convinced that the captured cargo was Brazilian, as claimed by William Taylor, commander of the *Federal.* Discusses the legal ramifications of the case, particularly his disagreement with Captain Daniel Turner, of the U.S.S. *Erie,* on the point of whether the Navy should seize the *Federal.* Is convinced that the *Federal's* manifests and papers are suspicious, but notes that the vessel left port before a determination of her status could be made. ALS. DNA, RG59, Cons. Disp., St. Bartholomew, vol. 2 (M-T72, R2). Received January 7, 1829.

On December 9, 1828, Harrison reported that the *Erie* had captured the *Federal* off Gustavia, St. Bartholomew. *Ibid.* Received January 8, 1829.

Baron Stackelberg wrote Clay on December 31 notifying him that the *Federal* "had been permitted to enter" port "for the purpose of repairing damages experienced while at sea." Says he is "convinced that this . . . outrage is wholly unauthorized by the Government of the United States," and expects Clay to "lose no time in disavowing a violation of territory as unexcusable as it was unexpected." ALS, in French, with trans. in State Dept. file. DNA, RG59, Notes from Swedish Legation, vol. 3 (M60, R2).

Clay responded on January 2, 1829, that he had "instigated the necessary inquiry to obtain a full and authentic account of all the circumstances of the case." Adds that if the President decides, after obtaining the facts, that a violation of the territorial jurisdiction of the Kingdom of Sweden and Norway has occurred, "he will not fail to cause to be promptly made such reparation as justice and the friendly relations between the United States and Sweden and Norway require." Copy. DNA, RG59, Notes to Foreign Ministers and Consuls, vol. 4, p. 133 (M38, R4). That same day, January 2, he wrote Samuel L. Southard, Secreaty of the Navy, asking for information pertaining to the "alleged capture." LS. DNA, RG59, Dom. Letters, vol. 22, pp. 360-1 (M40, R20).

On January 15, Jose S. Rebello, Brazilian Minister to the U.S., wrote Clay complaining that before her capture, the *Federal,* under the flag of Buenos Aires, had unloaded part of the cargo on board the American vessel, the *Nymph,* under the pretext that the goods were Brazilian. Notes that since the U.S. maintains that the flag covers the property, this excuse could not justify the seizure. Argues that because the ship had sailed from Buenos Aires after news of the peace with Brazil had arrived, her seizures constitute piracy. Asserts that the cargo which the *Federal* took from the *Nymph* "belongs by right [to] the Subjects of H. M. the Emperor [Pedro I]." Declares that as part of the cargo had been landed at St. Bartholomew before the *Erie* seized the *Federal,* the prize and its contents should be sold and the proceeds held by Brazil until the owners provide proof of their claim. ALS, in Portuguese, with trans. in State Dept. file. DNA, RG59, Notes from Brazilian Legation, vol. 1 (M49, R1).

The following day, January 16, Clay wrote Rebello, assuring him that the matter was under investigation and that when the facts have been determined, "the Government of the United States will not fail to perform whatever duties may appertain to it towards all parties concerned." Copy. Notes to Foreign Ministers and Consuls, vol. 4, pp. 136-7 (M38, R4).

On February 19, Secretary of the Navy Samuel L. Southard, transferred to Clay documents concerning the *Erie*'s capture of the *Federal* and the results of his investigation into the matter. States that Capt. Turner had evidence that the *Federal,* "using the flag of Buenos Aires," was clearly a privateer, one which "had committed a violent aggression" upon the American vessel *Nymph*. Adds that although the capture was made "without special instructions, or authority" from the U.S. government, the Navy Department has launched "legal proceedings which will enable Capt. Turner to exhibit the evidence on which he relies for his justification, and secure without unnecessary delay a judicial decision upon the character and conduct of" the *Federal.* Copy. DNA, RG45, Navy Dept., Letterbooks, vol. 1821-1831, pp. 370-1.

From WILLIAM WHITE   Nashville, December 8, 1828

The presidential election having now terminated in such a manner, as to have no room to suspect me of any improper motive in addressing you, and as I have been unable to resist the force of my convictions in reference to various charges which have been made against the president and yourself, during the late contest for political supremacy; I feel myself impelled by a sense of Justice, to tender you with assurances of my highest respect, & undiminished confidence in your political integrity, & personal worth. You will doubtless accord with me in the sentiment, that the recent contest for political ascendency, has been alike derogatory to the character of the American people, and the distinguished individuals, to effect whose removal, from or elevation to office, those angry elements of political strife were set in motion, which have so long distracted, divided and disgraced us a[s] a nation. But as when our distinguished fellow Citizen Genl. Jackson was in my estimation unproperly and unjustly assailed, I hesitated not to lend my feeble aid in his vindication, so have I uniformly tho' surrounded by his Zealous friends & partisans, acquited and defended the president & yourself, against charges of which I believed you guiltless; & that too, when I was fully aware that in doing so, I was incuring strong suspicions of hostility, to our favourite candidate for the presidency.

The truth is Sir, that I never did expect you to vote for Genl Jackson for president, & I have received assurances from many others of his friends, in this state to the same effect, altho' it would have afforded *us* pleasure, to have seen him elevated to that office in the first attempt. *We Knew* that *you* had opposed with your characteristic ability, some of the Genls. Acts. whilst he was in command of the southern division of the Army, and that as a consequence of your animadversions on those acts in Congress [2:636–60], you had incured his high displeasure. *We Knew also* that at a subsequent period, the Genl. had refused to reciprocate the usual civilities which are observed by gentlemen who are acquainted when tendered by you. We were apprised, that a sort of formal reconcilliation had afterwards been effected betwixt him & yourself; as well as some others at Washington, but did not consider it as changing the relation in which you previously stood farther than to restore the usual consistency of politeness.[1] But I will not enlarge farther on this topic for if I had ever entertained a doubt as to the rectitude of your conduct in relation to the last presidential election, your unanswerable defence, & the recorded approbation of your constituents would have left it no ground to rest upon. But notwithstanding many citizens of Tennessee, as well as myself who have ever been friends of Genl. Jackson, are fully satisfied that there was no real ground on which the charge of a corrupt understanding betwixt the president and yourself could be predicated, yet it need not be concealed from you, that there are many honest persons with whom "suspicion light as air, is confirmation strong as proof of holy writ." And now that Genl Jackson is elected president by a large majority over Mr. Adams, it is very material for such persons as well as the more artful and designing, to exalt in the overthrow of the present administration. But "truth is mighty & will prevail" & the time is not very distant I am persuaded, when the delusion by which the people have been deceived, will be dissipated by the light of truth & reason. Although, I have at both of the last presidential elections given my suffrage in Genl Jackson's favour and that too from an honest belief, that he deserves well of his country, and that he will administer our government with a degree of wisdom & propriety, which has been rarely if ever surpassed & yet I am far from believing it possible, that his course will command the approbation, of the heterogeneous mass of political parties, and persons, by whom he has been elevated to office. And although I make no pretensions to the prescience which characterised the prophesy of Old, yet me thinks, I can perceive not what many of Genl Jacksons partisans think they do—that Mr Clay has fallen never to rise again; but on the contrary, if you desire it, I consider your elevation to the presidency as morally certain, when the Genl's. present term expires. Aside from the utter impracticability, of his rewarding one in a thousand of his active partisans, and hungry expectants of office, who will set up claims to his favour; it seems to me, that there will be obstacles in his way, which cannot easily be surmounted or removed, and these will arise out of what is called the American system. As I most sincerely wish the Genl a pleasant and successful voyage whilst he remains at the helm of State, I shall not distress myself with anticipated difficulty, which his may never have to encounter, nor will I detain you with my poor speculations with regard to what I apprehend. But having considered you, as well as the president as objects of much unmerited reproach, and bitter persecutions for the last four years; my object in writing has been, to evince to you both, that there is at least one Citizen of Tennessee, (& I would fain hope many more) who takes pleasure in doing you an act of simple justice.

And whether the enlightened patriot who now fills the highest office in our government or yourself, may spend the ballance of your lives in the walks of private life, or be again called into the service of our country, I feel it my duty to offer you assurances of my best wishes. . . .

ALS. DLC-HC (DNA, M212, R3).   1. Parton, *Life of Andrew Jackson*, 3:46–7.

From JOEL R. POINSETT, Mexico, no. 157, December 10, 1828. Reports that a revolution "broke out a few days ago [December 4] and has terminated in the triumph of the popular party." Notes that the fighting began on the night of November 30, 1828, and that the next morning the revolutionaries "signified to the Government their determination to adhere to the plan of Santa An[n]a, namely the expulsion of the European Spaniards and the removal of [Manuel] Gomez Pedraza from the administration." Mentions that on December 4 the palace fell to the revolutionaries, but that Pedraza had already fled. Says "there has been no blood spilt since the triumph of the popular party" and the "only change made in the Government has been to place General [Vicente] Guerrero at the head of the War Department." Adds that dispatches have been sent to all the states informing them of the changes in administration and ordering "the chiefs of both parties who are engaging in war against each other in different parts of the Country to cease all hostilities." Hopes that "order will be restored throughout these States and that hereafter their affairs will be conducted with more wisdom." Notes that the leading figure in the revolution was Lorenzo [de] Zavala who expressed to him in an interview "great alarm lest foreign powers should interfere." Notes that he assured Zavala "that neither England nor any other power, had a right to interfere in their family quarrels." Believes that the revolution is popular with a majority of the people and predicts that if the government "conduct themselves with tolerable prudence," they will succeed in reestablishing order throughout the Union." ALS. DNA, RG59, Dip. Disp., Mexico, vol. 4 (M97, R5). Received January 4, 1829.

On December 19 George R. Robertson wrote from Tampico reporting essentially the same news and predicting that the States would not accept the new regime. ALS. DNA, RG59, Cons. Disp., Tampico, vol. 1 (M–T241, R1). Received January 1, 1829.

From JOEL R. POINSETT, Mexico, no. 158, December 11, 1828. States that order has now been restored in the capital and in its immediate neighborhood, "but the States are most of them involved in confusion." Reports that in Puebla and Veracruz "people are up in arms against the constituted authorities, and there can be no doubt that the great mass of the people throughout all the States are in favor of [Vicente] Guerrero and his party." Says that the "officers of the army are divided, but the common soldiers are all favorably disposed towards this chief and members daily come over to him." Notes that President Guadalupe Victoria has acquiesced in naming Guerrero head of the War Department although the Senate has not met since the December 4 revolution. Comments: "I take it for granted that this assembly [Chamber of Deputies] will declare Guerrero duly elected President . . . and it is believed that very sufficient proof can be adduced of the use of both bribery and force to effect the election of [Manuel Gomez] Pedraza in some of the States." ALS. DNA, RG59, Dip. Disp., Mexico, vol. 4 (M97, R5). Received January 31, 1829.

To CHARLES R. VAUGHAN, Washington, December 11, 1828. Transmits documents received from Henry Perrine, U.S. Consul at Campeche, Mexico, which show that on September 19, 1828, "two seamen were forcibly seized and taken from the American brig Telegraph, then at anchor in the Bay of Campeachy [*sic*], and within the jurisdiction of the Mexican Government, by order of Charles Rich, Esqr., the commander of the [H.M.S.] Harpy." Adds: "The seamen were, however, notwithstanding the remonstrances and the threats of Captain Rich, restored to the American Vessel to which they belonged." Clay protests this "whole transaction," especially "the repeated declaration which Mr. Perrine represented to have been made by the Commander of the Harpy, 'not merely of his general *right*, but of his especial *orders*, to *take* seamen Englishman by birth, *wherever* he might find them; adding for illustration, even if on board of the Mexican gun boat in port, especially should the sailors desire to enter into His Majesty's service.'" States that were it not for Vaughan's repeated assurances to the contrary, this incident, together with others on the coast of Africa and America would appear to show that "it has been done in pursuance of some system or orders prescribed" by the British government. Demands "an explanation of what has occurred at Campeachy, and . . . the punishment of the Commander of the Harpy." Concludes that he "is charged by the President . . . to express his expectation that the British Government will forthwith put an effective stop to a practice which the Government of the United States can not tolerate." Copy. DNA, RG59, Notes to Foreign Ministers and Consuls, vol. 4, pp. 102–05 (M38, R4).

Vaughan responded to this complaint on December 17. He promised to "endeavour to procure an explanation of this transaction" from his government, but deplored Clay's use of the term "impressment," because "impressment by British officers is not authorized during time of Peace." Asserts that in all cases of this kind referred to his government, "the Officers have been required by the Seamen, representing themselves to be British Subjects, to receive them into His Majesty's Service." LS. DNA, RG59, Notes from British Legation, vol. 15 (M50, R15).

From JAMES BROWN   Paris, December 12, 1828

I have received your letter giving me the result of the Presidential election. You may have perceived from my letters that I was not unprepared for it. It gives me pleasure to find you in such good spirits although it does not surprize me. You are relieved from a heavy load of business, the disgusting abuse of your enemies, and the task too great even for your strength of sustaining a President who although honest, learned, and deeply versed in all Kinds of Knowledge necessary for the due discharge of his official duties, yet has never been, and never will be a favorite with the American people. I am rejoiced that you are once more free and at liberty to resume the floor of the house of Representatives where with urbane manners and your fine talents for debate you cannot fail of success. Your temper must have been soured, your health ruined, and your popularity forever sacrificed had you continued four years longer in the Department of State. The House of Representatives has felt the want of your energy and talents in the Chair, and in the event of your election from your Congressional District will I hope chuse you as Speaker of the next Congress. Do not remain suspended in your choice but decide at once to resume your former position which had you retained it would have held you up more fully to the publick notice than a place in the Departments. But I forget in my zeal for your welfare that you are much more capable of designating your own course than I can be, removed as I am from the means of forming a correct judgment.

[Discusses and justifies the allowances and salaries he paid W.A.G. and Charles Barnet for performing the duties of Secretary of Legation from April 16 to September 5. Continues:]

From every quarter I hear it suggested that my old friend [Edward] Livingston will be my successor.[1] If Mrs. Livingston can obtain her wishes, her brother Doct Davezuc [sic, Auguste D'Avezac] will be named Secretary of Legation, and [John Adams] Smith will regret that he had asked to remain at this Court. If Livingston could raise sufficient means to live, he possesses the qualifications for representing the United States well at Paris. But [Joel R.] Poinsett, and [Robert Y.] Hayne, & [Thomas Hart] Benton, and a hundred others will covet the place and consider themselves slighted if refused it. This will be the case with all the important offices and the President elect will make more enemies that [*sic*, than] friends by the bestowals of them.

The very distinguished attentions which have been shewn me in every circle here, have attached me strongly to many inhabitants of this city of different ranks and standing, and I shall feel much regret in taking my leave of them. The mode of living here and the state of society are such that if Mrs. Brown ever recovers her health and my private circumstances permit I may revisit France in the course of two or three years. The first object however is to endeaver so far to re instate her in health, as that she may be able to support the fatigues of the voyage in April. In *confidence* I may say to you that although Mr Smith is a man of sterling honesty and fulfils in a very satisfactory manner the duties of Secretary of Legation, yet I do not think him capable of conducting any very important affairs and therefore hope a Minister may be ready to supply my place almost immediately after my departure. I am not without hopes that the Government will enter with me on a description of our claims if the present Ministry can once feel themselves sufficiently strong to open a negociation which may possibly end in asking the Chambers, for money. An individual who has access to the best services of information told me that it was intended to appoint Count [Francois-Maximillien Gerard] Rayneval to treat with me on the subject of the Claims. It is evident however that this is not yet decided on or the Count [Pierre-Louis-Auguste Ferron] de la Ferronays would have communicated it to me. I have spared no pains to make friends to our claims and think I have perceived a change in the opinions of men in and out of the Ministry since the last nine months. I talk of these matters without reflecting that three months hence they will be committed to other and I hope more successful negociators.

The Russians have not been successful in their campaign—which has just closed in raising the siege of Selestria [*sic*, Silistria]. The Turks it is said will make a vigorous effort to retake Varna before the opening of the next Campaign. The loss of lives on the part of the Russians has not been less than 80,000 as reports state, but as I think with some exaggeration. The failure of this campaign has diminished much those apprehensions, which have been created by the immense population of the Russian Empire.

I am very anxious to Know how Jacksons Cabinet will be composed, who will get places and who will be disappointed in a word all that passes and is likely to pass. I beg of you to write me freely and to ask my friend [Josiah Stoddard] Johnston to write as often as he can. [Alexander H.] Everett wishes to leave Spain and it is said will be named President of Harvard College. [James] Barbour I am told means to return—[Henry] Middleton will stay as long as he can. [Christopher] Hughes will stay if made a Minister and will stay if left as Chargé d'Affaires. [Henry] Weaton and [John J.] Appleton appear pleased with their situations.[2]

I have never seen so many Americans in Paris at any former period as at the present. Many of them are very genteel and all expect those attentions which we have hitherto shewn to our Countrymen almost without discrimination. This circumstances and the the desire Mrs. B feels to be hospitable to every one retards her convalescence and may possibly delay her embarking for the United States but will not prolong her stay in Paris beyond the 10 of April. If she is then too weak to embark we shall travel in the South of France or Italy.

I had the pleasure of receiving a very well written [letter] from your Henry who seems to promise well. What do you intend to make him Soldier lawyer or Manufacturer? Mrs. Brown hoped to have received a line ocasionally from *Ann* [Erwin] during her stay in Washington. Has she returned to the West?

I have seen the ordinance announcing the opening of the next Session[3] on the 27 Junuary [*sic*]. It will be long and interesting. The Jesuits are making a violent effort to turn out the Ministers and resume their power. Nothing can equal the ambition and perservance of this intriguing order—

Mrs. Brown joins me in Compts. to Mrs Clay. . . . [P.S.] Mr [Francois] Barbe–Marbois has requested me to send on with my despatches three Copies of a work he has lately published.[4] one copy for Mr Adams 1 for [James] Madison & one for [James] Monroe.

ALS. DLC–HC (DNA, M212, R3). Letter marked "(private)." Printed in *LHQ*, 24:1133–7.   1. William C. Rives replaced Brown. For Rives, see *BDAC*.   2. Everett's next position was that of owner and editor of the *North American Review*. Louis McLane replaced Barbour in London, who in turn was elected to the Virginia state legislature in May, 1830. Middleton remained in Russia until 1830. Hughes remained in the Netherlands until January 28, 1830, when he was replaced by William Pitt Preble. He next became U.S. minister to Sweden, replacing John J. Appleton there in August, 1830. He remained in Stockholm until 1841. Wheaton remained in Denmark until 1835. See Richardson Dougall and Mary Patricia Chapman, *United States Chiefs of Mission 1778–1973* (Washington, 1973), 39, 107, 140, 145, 159.   3. Of the Chamber of Deputies.   4. *Histoire de la Louisiane et de la cession de cette colonie par la France aux Etats–Unis de l'Amerique Septentrionale. . . .* Paris, 1829. Translated by William B. Lawrence and published in Philadelphia in 1830. For Francois Barbe–Marbois, see *CAB*.

From WILLIAM TUDOR, Rio de Janeiro, no. 116, December 12, 1828. Transmits treaty signed with Brazil [Clay to Tudor, March 29 and 31, 1828], which has been modeled on the December, 1825, U.S. treaty with Central America [4:878]. Gives a detailed comparison of the two treaties. Believes the treaty has "liberal, fair, reciprocal provisions" which the Brazilian Ministers "have more than once contrasted . . . with the European treaties full of jealousy, restriction, & limited as they say to one object that of the 15 per ct duty." Feels that "the ideas I have mentioned as having thrown out respecting our similarity of interests in some points regarding the restrictive system of some European powers, their navigation laws, colonial system, etc. have taken root, & I have no doubt will fructify in time." Adds in a postscript that the treaty will be signed in the morning. Copy, printed. DNA, RG59, Dip. Disp., Brazil, vol. 6 (M121, R8). Received February 25, 1829.

On February 28, 1829, Jose Rebello, Brazilian Minister to the U.S., reported to Clay that he was "in possession of the ratification of the Treaty of Amity, Navigation and Commerce—signed at Rio de Janeiro on the 12th December" by representatives of the U.S. and Brazil. Extends his regards to Clay, saying that he wants to signify "how painful it is to me to see that the opportunity to express these sentiments may soon terminate." ALS, in Portuguese, with trans. in State Dept. file. DNA, RG59, Notes from Brazilian Legation, vol. 1 (M49, R1).

To JOHN QUINCY ADAMS, Washington, December 13, 1828. Requests, in pursuance of a resolution of December 8 of the House of Representatives [*House Reports*, 20 Cong., 2 Sess., no. 19], information on whether the President "by virtue of a resolution passed on the 10th day of May last . . . has entered into any, and if any, what negotiations with the British Government relative to the surrender of fugitive slaves who may have taken refuge within the Canadian Provinces." States "that presuming it will be satisfactory to the House to be informed of the instructions" which have been given to U.S. Ministers to Great Britain, encloses instructions and replies from Albert Gallatin and James Barbour which he proposes supplying to the House. ALS, partially in Clay's hand. DLC–HC (DNA, M212, R3). Copy in DNA, RG59, Report Books, vol. 4, p. 259.

From WILLIAM TUDOR, Rio de Janeiro, no. 117, December 13, 1828. Reports: "I have made every effort to get the settlement of our claims further advanced." Has learned that the claims will "be liquidated on the same terms as the French that is in four payments, at six months interval." States that if all countries pressed their claims so closely, Brazil "might plead inability to comply with the demands," because the amount would total $6–8 million.

Reports that the cases of the *Ruth, Sarah George, Rio,* and *Kero* have been settled, while those of the *Panther* and the *Pioneer* will be settled soon. Contends that these settlements are fair but even if they do not live up to expectation, "any settlement is desirable in a national point of view."

Asks that his resignation be submitted to the President, saying "Five years constant residence in debilitating climates has almost undermined my strength . . . and the last three months have been passed in constant suffering." Pleads to be allowed to return by spring, and hopes to find a U.S. warship for passage because "piracy will be very rife the coming year . . . & many horrible deeds will be perpetrated." Adds in a postscript that he has heard from the Marquis of Aracaty that "the claims shall be completed by the first of Feby." ALS. DNA, RG59, Dip. Disp., Brazil, vol. 6 (M121, R8). No date of receipt.

From JOHN M. MACPHERSON, Cartagena, Colombia, December 14, 1828. Transmits newspaper account of the court martial of those accused of conspiring to assassinate Simon Bolivar in Bogota on September 25. Notes that all, including General Francisco Santander, were condemned to death but that all sentences have been reduced either to imprisonment or banishment, with Santander receiving the latter. Believes that Santander took no active part in the conspiracy but knew of its existence. Imputes Bolivar's clemency "to political motives," arising from Santander's popularity. Believes that Bolivar's primary support "is in the army and (perhaps) in the priesthood." Lists a number of Bolivar's decrees which have had the "effect of irritating the lower classes, and of changing their former affections for him." Admits his own view of Bolivar is no longer uncritical. Fears that distrust of republican government is growing in Colombia as it has in Europe.

Describes Bolivar's current campaigns against an insurrection in the city of Popayan and against Peru. Warns that Peru has blockaded the port of Guayaquil and expresses doubt that "Great Britain, who has never acknowledged the independence of Peru, would suffer her trade to be interrupted." Expects the "chief injury . . . would fall upon" the United States. Reports hearing that General Santander has "inquired very earnestly for General [William Henry] Harrison—if he had arrived, and when he was expected."

Regrets that his August 10 dispatch "had not been noticed," because he believes the questions he raised involve the national honor. Comments: "If Consuls have privileges and immunities, they ought to be defined. At the present moment I consider myself without any, and I fancy this Government is of the same opinion." Points out he has never received more than $200 per year from his post at Cartagena and suggests that he be transferred "to a more desirable consulate." ALS. DNA, RG59, Cons. Disp., Cartagena, vol. 1 (M-T192, R1). Received January 11, 1829.

From HENRY CLAY, JR.   West Point, N.Y., December 16, 1828
When last in Washington, I mentioned to my mother that it would be in my power to be absent from West Point during the two months of the next encampment; and intimated that it would be highly agreable to me to visit Kentucky. My feelings on this subject still remain the same but I must confess that I am not very eager to go, all things being considered. For If I am to remain in the army it will be of the last importance to me to enter as honourable a corps as possible and as this may in some measure be influenced by my going for it is but reasonable to suppose than my mind will be somewhat estranged from study—you will perceive that I am beginning to lose all other ambition than that of being an honest man. A professorship of Mathematics in some colledge, or lastly a post in the army are all that I now aspire to, my Talents; I am forced to coincide with you in what I have long supposed to be your opinion; are not above mediocrity. This presents to me an insurmountable obstacle to the professorship of Law—for in this profession there is no medium. A Good Lawyer and a great man a poor Lawyer and a contemptible man are synonimous terms—The principal objections to the journey in question are the great expence that it would cause you and that I should lose the office, which I hold in the Corps—[1]The short time that I should have to spend at home would not be an objection since 6 weeks would be long enough to spend at one time with my friends, and this I might do very easily as cadets who live in St Louis still farther from West Point have while on furlough passed 6 weeks at home—The only inducement that can be urged in favour of my leaving West Point is my own enjoyment which would really be great as it will be 3 years since I shall have left home [5:772], and perhaps you and my relations may feel some little

pleasure in having me with you—Having now stated fairly the reason pro and con I leave you to decide on the utility—and I will abide by your decision with pleasure whatever it may be—

I write thus early about my furlough because if you should think proper to advise me to obtain one I shall have many preparations to make and I shall live the more economically on account of it between this and my starting in order to be entirely free from debts when I go—

The examination is coming on. I sit up every night till half after 11 and I assure [you] this time is not spent idly—We shall be examined in about 4 weeks the examination of the class below mine commencing on the 5th proximo—

Give my Love to my mother and the boys—Tell James [Brown Clay] to write to me—

ALS. DLC-HC (DNA, M212, R3). Salutation: "My Dear Father."   1. Cadets in the 1820s rotated the duties of commissioned and non-commissioned officers within the Academy military structure. The length of the various officer tours ranged from a week to a month. The duration of the annual summer encampment (service simulating field conditions) was at the discretion of the Superintendent. It could range from six weeks to three months. Lester A. Webb, *Captain Alden Partridge and the United States Military Academy 1806-1833* (Northport, Ala., 1965), 197-8.

From ALEXANDER H. EVERETT, Madrid, no. 119, December 16, 1828. Encloses translation of an article in the Barcelona *Gazette*, containing an account of a new conspiracy against the government. Reports this plot was "detected and suppressed in the province of Catalonia," and that twelve men, "condemned to death by a court martial," have been executed.

Discusses the negotiations between Spain and France about "the expenses of the French army of occupation [3:313] which by the terms of treaty of occupation were to be defrayed by Spain." States the sum was fixed at eighty million francs, but that the negotiations have broken down and remain suspended.

Informs Clay that Charles Walsh "has recently arrived at this place" as the new Secretary of the Legation.

Adds in a postscript that he has learned through the U.S. consulate at Cadiz of "the release of the crew of the Columbian [*sic*] privateer Genl Armario [*sic*, Armaria], who had been for some time past detained in the prison of the Caracca near Cadiz." Recalls that Clay, in his dispatch of June 21, 1828, had sought this action through an appeal of Everett to the Spanish government. Concludes: "It appears that these prisoners were set at liberty without exchange, upon an engagement not to serve against Spain. They were twenty one in number, mostly citizens of the U.S.," including Robert F. Jones of Baltimore. LS, with postscript as ALI. DNA, RG59, Dip. Disp., Spain, vol. 28 (M31, R29). Received February 8, 1829. Terms of the Franco-Spanish treaty of occupation are in Parry, *Treaty Series*, 63:297-301.

From JOHN HAY, Hollingsworth Store, Frederick County, Va., December 17, 1828. Laments the election to the presidency of the "Military Candidate." This event he attributes to "the instability of popular favour, or, to that malignant spirit of Detraction which feasts upon Slander & Falsehood." Argues that Clay has a duty to the nation to return to the House of Representatives to serve there as a protector of "the fair Fabric of our Liberties." ALS. DLC–HC (DNA, M212, R3). Little is known of Hay save that when Clarke County was carved out of Frederick County in 1836, Hay was appointed to the county court and later served as its clerk.

To HENRY CLAY, JR.   Washington, December 20, 1828

I received your letter of the 16h. instant. With respect to the disposition of yourself during the two months of the approaching encampment, I wish you to exercise your own discretion and to pursue your inclination. You shall be supplied with whatever sum you may want for a journey. I would suggest for your consideration a visit to the falls of Niagara, to Genl. [Peter B.] Porter at Black Rock (to whom I will give you a letter of introduction, if you determine to take that direction) and thence on Lake Erie to the Bay of Sandusky and through the State of Ohio to Kentucky. Or you can come directly to Kentucky by Wheeling or Pittsburg[h] and return by the first mentioned route. We shall leave here some time in March or April and you can inform me of your decision before our departure.

You are greatly mistaken my son in supposing that I entertain a low opinion of your talents. On the co[ntrary], I have thought very favorably of them, and I have [thought?] that, by perseverance in that course of study and regu[larity], which has given me so much happiness, you can make yourself any thing you please. When you shall complete your studies at West point, even admitting that you remain there, as I rather think you had better do, during the usual time you will be arrived just at the proper period to commence the study of the Law, if that shall be thought advisable. On the termination of the four years, you can obtain the customary commission in the Army, and I think I shall be able to procure a furlough for you, during which you may enter on the Study of the law. Should you find it agreeable, and think that you can succeed in making yourself master of the profession, you may continue in it, and resign your Commission in the army. These are suggestions to be thought of hereafter. In the mean time, your great effort should now be to perfect yourself in the Studies which at present occupy you. There are many instances of the elevés of West Point afterwards studying the law, and I believe at ages more advanced than yours' will be

Let me hear from you after the Examination. The family are all well and join me in tendering to you our affectionate regards.

ALS. Henry Clay Memorial Foundation, Lexington, Ky.

To ALLEN TRIMBLE   Washington, December 22, 1828

I owe you many obligations for your very friendly letter of the 10th. inst. which I have duly received. I have perused it with all the interest which belongs to our mutual friendship. It always affords me pleasure to received the suggestions of my friends, as to the course of conduct which I ought to pursue. Your's are entitled to the most deliberate consideration. For the future I have decided nothing, and shall decide nothing prior to my return to Kentucky. Circumstances appear to me to require that I should remain here, in the performance of my official duty, and I have accordingly determined so to remain until the close of the present administration. At Ashland I shall be best able to determine whether it is most proper for me to remain in retirement, either permanent or temporary. In making up my mind it will be necessary for me to examine many considerations, among which, not the least important, will be, the state of my health, which, though now good, may be otherwise at that time. Whatever may be my final decision, my friends may rest assured that they have all my sympathies, and my best wishes for the success of those great principles, fundamental and administrative, to the maintenance of which they and I have devoted our highest exertions.

In regard to the course, under existing circumstances, which they ought to pursue, it seems to me that it would be most proper that they should remain silent until that of the New Administration shall be indicated. Wise men neither throw out rash threats, nor precipate promises. If they are honest as well as wise, their past conduct in life presents the best guarantee for the future. The President elect is the Chief Magistrate of the Nation, duly elected by a majority of the people. Whatever we may think of him, or of the means which have been employed to secure his election, (and on those subjects it is impossible that you and I should differ,) he is charged with a high and solemn trust, on, the execution of which much good or evil may ensue to our country. I hope that no personal dislike of him; no abhorrence of the calumnies which have been used to elevate him; no dread, even, of the perilous tendency of the military principle which has formed the basis of his success, will ever induce us to oppose measures which are calculated to advance the prosperity of the Union. Among these, the two to which you allude, the American System and Internal Improvements, will, I hope, continue to command our support and cooperation in all vicissitudes. Should these be threatened with danger, the line of our duty is clear and distinct.— The perusal of your Message gave me great pleasure on account of the allusions which you properly make to those great interests, and the reprehensible spirit which has been recently manifested in the South.[1] I shall be most agreeably disappointed if General Jackson and a large portion of his party do not aim at the subversion of those measures. They will not less be less cherished by me, should he, contrary to my fears, lend himself to their support.

I heard, with pleasure, of the election of Judge [Jacob] Burnet to the Senate of the United States. If he should exhibit on that new theatre the same talent that he has displayed in his former vocations, Ohio and the Union may be proud of him.

I have no news to offer you from this place. There is nothing but vague speculation in regard to the intentions of the President elect. As to the present Administration, it confines itself to the duty of transacting current business, and of winding up affairs so as to turn the public stewardship, in as good a state as possible, over to their successors....

P.S. This letter is written by a Confidential Amanuensis upon my dictation.

LS. NjP. See postscript to letter. 1. In Governor Trimble's annual message to the Ohio legislature on December 2, he took a strong stand in favor of government support of U.S. industrial development. He noted that the protective features of the Tariff Act of 1828 assisted this goal, that the western states supported this legislation, and that "enactments by our fellow citizens of the southern section of the union" against the tariff were unwise and disruptive. He concluded: "we are unwilling to conciliate their violent and intemperate hostility by an abandonment of the principles and opinions we have uniformly maintained upon this subject." Cincinnati *Daily Gazette,* December 3, 1828.

From **WILLIAM HENRY HARRISON,** "Maracaybo," Colombia, no. 1, December 23, 1828. Reports his arrival in Colombia after "a most boisterous & protracted voyage." Comments at length on the government of Colombia, noting that "The affairs of this country are not only in a most unsettled state, but that the prospect in advance is still more gloomy and ominous of future distress." Refers in particular to the unsuccessful assassination attempt on Simon Bolivar on September 25 [MacPherson to Clay, October 14, 1828], which "far from stifling the disposition to overthrow the existing Government, has produced an open appeal to arms—sooner perhaps than it would otherwise have taken place, the standard of rebellion having been actually raised & the first effort of the Insurgents successful." Describes the subsequent insurrection led by Col. Jose Maria Obando, which broke out on October 15, at Popayan. Speculates about the various troop movements and strategies of both Bolivar and Obando in the civil war, especially the possibility of Obando's seeking cooperation from Peru.

Notes he is leaving on December 26 for Bogota.

Recalling his recent voyage in the Caribbean from St. Bartholomew to Maracaibo, comments: "The participation of the authorities of the neighboring Islands in the shameful robberies committed on the vessels of neutral nations by the privateers . . . is well extablished." Copy. DNA, RG84, Foreign Service Posts, Colombia, (R14, frames 235–9). No date of receipt.

From **JOEL R. POINSETT,** Mexico, no. 159, December 24, 1828. Reports that troops have been removed from the Federal District "in order to give a proof to the States that the Executive is free from all restraint, and commissioners have been sent a second time to Puebla, to treat with the authorities of that State and to . . . prevail upon them to submit to the general Government." Notes that it is expected that the revolutionaries will soon march upon Puebla "in order to attack that place before the army of operations which has been employed against Santa An[n]a can reinforce the garrison." Feels that the effects of the civil war may be "fatal to the Country," because the "resources of the General Government are cut off by the disaffection of Vera Cruz; the internal commerce is destroyed . . . and the whole country presents a scene of anarchy and confusion." Believes the revolutionaries "have no confidence in the cabinet and suspect the President [Guadalupe Victoria] of playing them false." Calls the President "weak and vacillating" and contends that "it would not be difficult for Victoria to put an end to the civil war by a show of determination on one side or the other," but believes this "is not to be expected from a Man of his character." ALS. DNA, RG59, Dip. Disp., Mexico, vol. 4 (M97, R5). Received February 11, 1829.

From ISAAC STONE, Veracruz, December 24, 1828. States that it is nearly impossible to collect accurate information concerning the revolutionary movement in Mexico. Reviews past and present circumstances of the revolt in Veracruz. Details the visit of Vice Governor–General Santa Anna to the legislature of Veracruz on September 1, 1828, the day the legislature met to vote on the presidential question. Notes that Santa Anna used violent language and threatened to dissolve the legislature if they did not vote for General Vicente Guerrero as president. Outlines Santa Anna's troop movements following his escape from arrest by the House of Representatives. Relates events of the December 4 overthrow of Manuel Gomez Pedraza's partisans in the Metropolis. Believes Generals Jose Maria Calderon and Santa Anna have met and "buried the Hatchet." Observes that the states of Veracruz and Puebla have resolved not to recognize the "Supreme Government as now constituted." Recounts the Federal government's attempts to force submission of the state of Puebla. Hopes that there will be no bloodshed in Veracruz but is not optimistic. Expects that the persons and property of foreigners will not be violated, even if fighting breaks out. ALS. DNA, RG59, Cons. Disp., Veracruz, vol. 1 (M183, R1). Received January 24, 1829.

On December 28, Stone reported that the "grand political question" has been settled with the military agreeing to support General Vicente Guerrero. Notes, however, that the decision did not come until the troops "in Garrison here" had laid down their arms and refused to fight, saying: "We have served tyrants long enough and will do it no longer." *Ibid.* No date of receipt.

To JAMES STRONG, December 24, 1828. Submits, upon request of the Select Committee on Retrenchment of the House of Representatives [*House Reports*, 20 Cong., 2 Sess., no. 47], answers to inquiries concerning publication and distribution of the laws of the U.S. States that the number of newspapers in which the laws were published in 1802 cannot be ascertained; that in 1812 they were published in 47 newspapers at a cost of $100 per paper; that in 1822 they were published in 73 newspapers at $92 for each paper; and in 79 papers in 1827 at $95.50 each. Adds that in 1802, 10,000 copies of the laws were published in pamphlet form at the cost of $1,196; in 1812 the same number was published at the cost of $2,150; and the same number in 1827 at the cost of $2,395. Notes also that 1,000 copies of John Bioren and W. John Duane's edition of John B. Colvin's laws, in 4 vols., was published for $15,000, and the continuation by William A. Davis and Peter Force cost $2,200 for 550 copies. Copy. DNA, RG59, Report Books, vol. 4, pp. 260–1. John B. Colvin, comp., *Laws of United States, Mar. 4, 1789–Mar. 4, 1815, Including Constitution of United States, Old Act of Confederation, Treaties, and Many Other Valuable Ordinances and Documents. . . .* 5 vols. (including vol. 5, Index). Published by John Bioren and W. John Duane, Philadelphia, and R. C. Weightman, Washington City, 1815; *ibid.*, Mar. 4, 1815—Mar. 4, 1821 ... vol. 6. Published by William A. Davis, P. Force, Washington City, 1822; *ibid.*, Mar. 4, 1821—Mar. 4, 1827 ... vol. 7. Published by William A. Davis, P. Force, Washington City, 1827.

To ISAAC CURD   Washington, December 25, 1828
I hasten to make my grateful acknowledgements for the friendly senti-ments conveyed in your letter of the 18h instant, just received. The assurance you give of the favorable opinion entertained towards me in Ohio is very gratifying, whatever may be my future fortunes. I shall remain here, in the performance of my official duties until the close of the present administration, when I shall return to Kentucky. I shall then have leisure and light to decide whether I ought ever again to attempt to participate in public affairs. Whatever may be my final decision I shall at least enjoy the satisfaction of witnessing the prosperity of my Country, under the operation of those measures of National policy which have had my honest and best support. These measures will not, I think, be subverted by the new administration, although the hope of such an event was doubtless one of the causes which has led to its formation....

ALS, photocopy. MoU.

To FRANCIS T. BROOKE   Washington, December 26, 1828
Having nothing to offer you from this place, I am anxious to learn from you what is passing at Richmond. Here we are in a political eddy, the currents from which will not break out and show themselves until about the Ides of March. There is nothing but vague speculation in regard to the intentions of the President–elect with which it is not worth while to trouble you. Towards the bottom, indeed, there is some movement in the water already, but it does not shew itself upon the surface. It is said that a good deal of jealousy is felt, and in private circles sometimes manifests itself, among the Partizans of the vice President [John C. Calhoun] and the Gove[r]nor–elect of New York [Martin Van Buren].

I get a great many letters from all quarters conveying strong senti-ments of unabated confidence and ardent attachment. I am frequently, too, favored with the advice of friends, of a directly opposite tenor. One tells me, for example, that I should retire from public life for two or three years; whilst another is equally positive that I should forthwith return to the House of R. I have as yet decided upon no course for myself, and shall decide upon none until my return to Kentucky. In the meantime, I should be glad to be favored with your opinion and that of other friends whom you may think proper to consult—

Mr. [James] Madisons letters[1] are sought after with great avidity. They have produced much effect, and I think are likely to produce much more. This is evidenced by the violence of some of those who are opposed to the tariff. You will be shocked when I tell you that one of them, and one too from Mr Madisons own State [Virginia], I have been told, said that he ought to have died, or that he wished he had died, five years ago.

But to return to Richmond—What will be done with the Convention question?[2] What is the tone of party spirit? Is it a proscription there as in some other places?

I shall be glad to hear from you at your leisure.

Copy. DLC–TJC (DNA, M212, R13). Also printed in Colton, *Clay Correspondence*, 4:215–6.   1. Madison's letters to Joseph Cabell of September 18 and October 30, 1828 were published in the Washington *Daily National Journal* on December 25 and 27, 1828. In the first letter he argued that Congress had the Constitutional power to "encourage domestic products by regulations of commerce." In the second, he discussed situations in which the power to impose a tariff "may be usefully exercized by Congress."   2. A Constitutional Convention recommended by Gov. William B. Giles on December 1, 1828 and approved by the Virginia General Assembly in February, 1829. It convened on October 5, 1829. Its primary purpose was to reapportion seats in the General Assembly, it being widely argued that the western counties of the state were under-represented therein [6:292]. But the problem of slavery in Virginia, its retention or abolition, was also discussed at length. The Convention adjourned on January 15, 1830. Richmond *Enquirer*, December 2, 1828; February 12, 1829. See also, Merrill D. Peterson, *Democracy, Liberty, and Property: The State Constitutional Conventions of the 1820's* (N.Y., 1966), 271–443; Charles H. Ambler, *Sectionalism in Virginia from 1776 to 1861* (New York, 1964), 132–74; *Proceedings and Debates of the Virginia State Convention of 1829-30 . . .* (Richmond, 1830), *passim*.

From JOHN J. CRITTENDEN   Frankfort, December 27, 1828

I have received your letter of the 15th Inst:—In anticipation of my rumoured nomination as judge of the S[upreme]—Court, & the rumoured opposition to it in the Senate, some letters have been, & others probably will be written, by my friends here to some of the opposition Senators Mr [Robert] Wickliffe has I beleive written to [Thomas Hart] Benton & Genl S[amuel]—Smith, & perhaps to some members of the House of Representatives—

I have felt great delicacy in acting at all upon this subject—But tho' for many reasons, I would not solicit such an office, yet when the question may be, whether my nomination shall be rejected, by the Senate, I am warranted upon a principle of self defence in endeavouring to avert such a sentence—In this view of the subject I have written letters to several of my old acquaintances in Congress, claiming the interposition of their liberality & justice in my behalf. I enclose those letters (to [John] McKinley of the Senate & to [Charles A.] Wickliffe & [William S.] Archer,[1] of the House of Repts:) to you to be delivered or not according to circumstances—If the President has nominated me, or intends to do so, they can not be too soon delivered, unless indeed the subject has been acted upon—I submit to you whether the letters had not best be delivered as coming through my friend John Chambers, of the House of Reps:—

I shall in a few days answer your last letter more at large. . . . P—S. Archer will see & converse with my old acquaintance [John] Tyler.

ALS. NcD. Letter marked "(Private)."   1. *BDAC*.

From ALBERT GALLATIN & WILLIAM PITT PREBLE, Washington, December 27, 1828.

Enclose "a list of the written and topographical evidence which we have collected and selected for the purpose of being communicated to the British Government in conformity with the 3d Article of the Convention of the 29th of September 1827 [6:1100-01]." State that they hope "that it will not be necessary to lay the whole of the written evidence before the Arbiter [William I of the Netherlands]. But it having been provided by the Convention, that no fresh evidence should be adduced or even adverted to, which had not been previously communicated, it has been deemed prudent to give the evidence of every fact, however notorious, which it may be necessary to state in the course of the argument and to point out all the authorities intended to be quoted." Add that several documents have been included "to guard against arguments and objections which may not be brought forward or again urged by the other Party." Mention that they have included "maps, surveys and topographical delineations" in case the agreement for collation made with British Minister to the U.S., Charles R. Vaughan, is not carried out. ALS, by Gallatin, signed by Preble. DNA, RG76, Northeast Boundary (KyU., Special Roll, frame 97).

Gallatin wrote Clay again on December 29, listing maps that he had left "in the Archives of the American Legation at London" which he now wants sent to the U.S. for use as "triplicates to be annexed to the first statement of the United States." Also lists maps in the possession of U.S. Consul in London, Thomas Aspinwall, which would be useful, as well as other maps which should be purchased in England and sent to the State Department. *Ibid.*

On January 7, 1829, Clay transmitted Gallatin's request to U.S. Minister to Britain, James Barbour, in dispatch no. 6. Instructed Barbour to give his "immediate attention to the execution of these . . . commissions, in the way, and to the extent suggested by Mr. Gallatin himself." Copy. DNA, RG59, Dip. Instr., vol. 12, p. 180 (M77, R7). Also in Manning, *Diplomatic Correspondence . . . Canadian Relations*, 2:189.

From WILLIAM HENRY HARRISON, "Maracaybo," Colombia, no. 2, December 27, 1828. Encloses "a translation of a Decree of this Government, by which the interdiction of Spanish goods into this country is taken off."

Notes the appearance in a Cartagena paper of a memorial to President Bolivar from local merchants, complaining of the effects of the Colombian commerical treaties with the United States [4:127-8] and Great Britain [4:365]. The memorialists insist the injuries done to Colombia are "much greater than the advantages derived from the recognition of their Independence by those Powers." Believes this complaint may be a ruse by the Bolivar government to discredit the Constitutional Party which had negotiated the accords.

Reports that "proscriptions and banishments" of those who are, or are suspected of being, opposed to the regime continue throughout Colombia, and that prominent men who had supported the Revolution "have been torn from their families without any kind of trial, and without even being informed of the charges against them." LS. DNA, RG59, Dip. Disp., Colombia, vol. 5 (M33, R5). Received February 7, 1829.

From JOEL R. POINSETT, Mexico, no. 160, December 27, 1828. Reports that word was received on December 26 "that the garrison of Puebla had declared in favor of the Federal Government and that the revolution was concluded in that State." Notes that General Vicente Guerrero has set out for Puebla, "and after reestablishing order in that State he will probably march upon Vera Cruz." Contends that there is "now scarcely a doubt as to the result of the contest." Believes the uprising furnishes "practical proof of the advantages of our Federal Institutions," because the whole government might have been overthrown had the revolutionaries not been restrained by the fear of the States. Argues: "I firmly believe . . . that the Federal Institutions alone saved this Country from the curse of a military despotism." Believes, however, that "The violent course pursued by the partizans of Guerrero is to be lamented; but if ever a revolution of this nature can be justifiable, this was so, by the oppression exercised by the oligarchy." ALS. DNA, RG59, Dip. Disp., Mexico, vol. 4 (M97, R5). Received February 11, 1829.

On January 8, 1829, in dispatch no. 162, Poinsett reported that the "Revolution has terminated favorably" with all states giving their allegiance to the national government. Predicts that when the vote is completely counted, "Guerrero will be declared President." LS. *Ibid.* Received February 11, 1829.

From ROBERT MONROE HARRISON, St. Bartholomew, December 29, 1828. Discusses in a lengthy letter the corruption, graft, unfair tariff laws, duties, and use by privateers and guineamen of the island of St. Bartholomew. Regarding the situation of destitute seamen, as requested in Clay's letter of December 7, describes his efforts to obtain passports and fair treatment for them despite "the interference of *crimps* and *landlords*." States that the fees for passports "are regularly divided between the *town Mayor, Judge* & *Notary.*" Notes other venal practices against seamen.

Concerning Swedish vessels sailing to the colony of St. Bartholomew, reports that very few come "from the Mother Country." Declares that the Treaty between Sweden and the United States [6:761–2] is much more advantageous to the Swedes. Asserts: "They . . . can make a *Tariff* at *pleasure to suit* their own *convenience,* which falls entirely on us." Lists prices of foodstuffs and goods on the island.

Adds in a postscript the reaction on St. Bartholomew to Captain Daniel Turner's seizure of the *Federal,* the Buenos Airean privateer. Notes: "Those most violent . . . [against him] are Americans! . . . persons connected with the people who are now, or have been Privateers and principally from Baltimore." Feels the President should protect Turner's reputation. Concludes with a discussion of the ties of St. Bartholomew with the slave trade. States that one owner from Guadeloupe who has outfitted and repaired his Guineamen under French flags at St. Bartholomew "has received on his home island in the short space of *two months* upwards of *1000* Slaves!" ALS. DNA, RG59, Cons. Disp., St. Bartholomew, vol. 2 (M72, R2). Received February 10, 1829.

From COUNT CHARLES DE MENOU, Washington, December 29, 1828. Notifies Clay of "a Royal Ordinance of the 29th September last, opening the ports of Moule (Island of Guadeloupe) and of Grand Bourg

(Island of Marie Galante) to foreign commerce" for the purpose of stimulating American trade with the French West Indies. Points out that "the island of Marie Galante is one of the dependencies of the Island of Guadeloupe," but is not expressly mentioned in the Act of Congress of May 9, 1828 [4 *U.S. Stat.*, 269], and requests appropriate measures "to secure to our commerce the reciprocal advantages." ALS, in French, with trans. in State Dept. file. DNA, RG59, Notes from French Legation, vol. 10 (M53, R9).

On January 5, 1829, Clay replied that he had sent a copy of the ordinance to the Treasury Department "to decide whether the Island of Marie Galante, being one of the Dependencies of that of Guadeloupe will not be considered as comprehended in the Act of Congress of May last." Promises that if it is not included, "the necessary measures will be adopted . . . to extend the provisions of the act to Maria Galante." Copy. DNA, RG59, Notes to Foreign Ministers and Consuls, vol. 4, p. 134 (M38, R4).

On January 22 Clay sent a translation of the ordinance to Samuel L. Southard, acting Secretary of the Treasury. Copy. DNA, RG59, Dom. Letters, vol. 22, p. 384 (M40, R20).

On January 30, 1829, Southard replied to Clay that no special measures were needed to extend the act of May 9 to Maria Galante because "the island is one of the dependencies of Guadeloupe." LS. DNA, RG59, Misc. Letters (M179, R67).

On February 3 Clay transmitted to Menou a copy of the Treasury's authorization for Collectors of Customs "to admit [French] Vessels coming from Grand Bourg . . . upon the same conditions as those coming from the Island of Guadeloupe" under the Act of 1828. Copy. DNA, RG59, Notes to Foreign Ministers and Consuls, vol. 4, pp. 138-9 (M38, R4).

From JAMES BROWN   Paris, December 30, 1828
The Marquis de Marbois has requested me to transmit to you several Copies of his work on the Louisiana Treaty[1] which I have promised him you would hand to his friends to whom he has presented them. By delivering them to the Representatives of the Districts in which those to whom they are addressed reside they will reach their destination.

By the time this letter reaches Washington you will have nearly finished your laborious career and be preparing to quit public life. You will not long be permitted to remain at home. Your district will require your services and your friend [James] Clark will probably be too happy to return to his usual occupation. The immense majority in favor of General Jackson not only proves that he is popular but proves more strongly what I always believed that Mr Adams with all his talents and virtures is not the man of the people. You are not the first statesman who has mistaken the publick feeling and fixed upon the unpopular Candidate. Mr. [Martin] Van Buren in the support he gave to Mr [William H.] Crawford was equally disappointed as to the result but has in the short space of four years enjoyed a triumph in the election of General Jackson. If you enter the decision of the people as the true standard of what is right, and we republicans have no other, and acquiesce goodnaturedly in it, you may soon find yourself in the Speakers chair a situation in my opinion much to be prefered to that you have filled during the last four years. Indeed I think the prospect of being noticed by the people in another way is better when in that situation than when acting as Secretary of State. But you are on the ground and know best how it will suit you to act and therefore I shall dismiss the subject.

We were agreeably surprized two or three days ago by the arrival of poor Henry [Clay] Hart[2] from Toulon. He had obtained from my friend [James] Ramage[3] who in the absence of Commodore [William M.] Crane[4] commands the Delaware leave to spend a month at Paris where he arrived under the care of the Purser of the Ship. Her Hull was in a sound state but her rigging was somewhat damaged by the length of her cruise. This we have more than repaired, and shall lay in a stock sufficient to meet his wants until he returns to America. Poor Boy! His orphan condition and the hard and perilous life he has embraced have intrested our feelings, and we shall do all we can to make him comfortable until he can see his native country. Capt Ramage writes me that he is a fine boy and much beloved by his comrades. I had not heard until his arrival that you had been so good as to provide for him. Our relations have great cause to bless you for your Kindness to all of them The little fellow has had a long journey to see his Aunt [Ann Hart Brown] Toulon being distant six hundred miles from Paris. He will return about the first of February.

I presume but little business will be transacted during the present Session. The new President will have some trouble in forming his Cabinet and in making such selections as will satisfy the people and his adherents who have exerted themselves in the last election. [James] Barbour I hear talks of leaving London. were I in his place I should remain, unless recalled for two years. The outfit will make a great noise if he accepts it and returns so soon. If he is recalled (of which I think he can have no apprehensions) he would escape all animadversion.

I am happy to learn that my account for 1827 has been settled and have expected that Mr [Stephen] Pleasonton would have as usual on former occasions written to me informing me of it. Be so good as to remind him of it. I will send on my account for 1828 by the vessel which will sail from Havre on the 15 and shall feel happy when I close my publick agency forever. You know I never was ambitious and since the decline of Mrs. Brown's health I have anxiously wished to retire from all publick business. The state of society has been such during the last few years that the pleasures of even private life are much diminished. I hope however that I shall be permitted to pursue the noiseless tenor of my way without molestation. I have for years endeavored to live peaceably with all men and have some right to hope that I may enjoy the fruits of my labors in peace.

The French Government or in other words the [Martignac] Ministry feel a strong desire to stand well with the United States and I think are only delaying the discussion of our claims under the fear that they will be obliged to propose a new loan in addition to the eighty millions borrowed at the last Session. It was wise in our Government to suspend the adjustment of the claims of French subjects until France shall agree to discuss the claims of our citizens. The French Claimants have influence, they know that we have a right to do what we have done and they will urge the opening of a negociation which shall embrace all claims. I still hope that before the last of January something may be done to lead to the settlements of all the points about which we have hitherto disagreed. I have done all I could to pave the way to this result and if nothing has yet been done I cannot accuse myself of neglect.

Mrs. Browns health continues to be delicate and gives me much concern. She is now very anxious to return but has great reason to fear that she will not have gained sufficient strength before May to embark for the United States. My Successor [William C. Rives] will probably by that time arrive, as the place will be sought by many candidates all of whom are desirous of visiting this interesting Metropolis. Reports from home and the letters of several of my friends state the [sic, that] Edward Livingston will in all probability be appointed. I am very curious to learn what will be the nominations made to the Senate after the 4th. of March and hope you will write me before you leave Washington.

I fear the two respectable Priests of Philadelphia [William V. Harold; John Ryan] will find themselves involved in serious difficulty with the court of Rome, or to speak more accurately, with his Holiness [Pope Leo XII]. Several priests have lately passed through this place who I have heard were not friendly to those Gentlemen. The Catholics in the U States will experience many difficulties inseparable from their dependence on a foreign See and that they must ultimately either secede from that of Rome, or attempt to obtain a concordat with His Holiness. I am sorry for the situation in which Mr Harold is placed because I find the most respectable Catholics of Philadelphia much attached to him. It is however a delicate subject to be meddled with by a Government like ours founded upon the principle of letting alone all religions.

Mr Adams commentary on Mr Jeffersons letter[5] appears to me at this distance as having been unnecessary and indiscreet. The prosecutions against [Theodore] Lyman will make him a man of importance in the New England States.[6]

ALS. DLC-HC (DNA, M212, R3). Printed in *LHQ*, 24:1137–40.   1. Brown to Clay, December 12, 1828.   2. 6:1089.   3. For Lt. Ramage, who had fought in the War of 1812, was promoted to Commander in March, 1829, and was cashiered from the Navy in September, 1831, see Callahan, *List of Officers of the Navy...*, 451.   4. For Crane, later head of the Navy's Bureau of Ordnance and Hydrography, see *CAB*. 5. Brooke to Clay, October 25, 1828.   6. Clay to Webster, November 30, 1828.

From LEVI LINCOLN, Worcester, Mass., December 30, 1828. Forwards, for special notice of the President, an extract of a letter from George Coffin, a Land Agent of Massachusetts, concerning acts that "are not only gross and most injurious violations of the rights of property of this Commonwealth, but if authorized or countenanced by the British Authorities, are in direct repugnance to the understanding, which has been had between the two Governments, that, pending [settlement of] the controversy concerning the North Eastern Boundary, *Neither party* should Exercise a jurisdiction, or do any act, which might be to the eventual prejudice to the other." Refers to the plundering of timber in the disputed territory and says Massachusetts does not "admit that the title to the soil may be questioned" and will insist that the territory "shall not be depredated upon" while the negotiations continue. Recalls that a short time before, Massachusetts had ceased surveying a road in the disputed area because of the protest of British Minister, Charles R. Vaughan. Demands that the State Department take action to stop the lumbering in the area. ALS. DNA, RG76, Northeast Boundary: Misc. Papers, Env. 4, item 35.

On January 9, 1829, Clay transmitted an extract of Coffin's letter to Vaughan, stating that New Brunswick's issuing of permits for cutting timber in the disputed area is "in opposition to the understanding which has existed between the Government of the United States and Great Britain," and warning that if such actions continue "it cannot be expected that the State of Maine will abstain from the adoption of preventive measures." Asks, by direction of the President, that Britain make an "effectual interposition. . . . Without that, the friendly, if not the peaceful relations between the two countries may be interrupted or endangered." Copy. DNA, RG59, Notes to Foreign Ministers and Consuls, vol. 4, pp. 134–6 (M38, R4); also in Manning, *Diplomatic Correspondence . . . Canadian Relations*, 2:190–1.

On January 12, 1829, Clay responded to Lincoln that immediately upon receiving Lincoln's letter of December 30, he addressed a note to Vaughan, protesting the acts referred to. Anticipates "that our protest on this occasion, will have the desired effects." LS. MWA. Copy in DNA, RG59, Dom. Letters, vol. 22, pp. 369–70 (M40, R20).

Vaughan replied to Clay on January 13, promising to transmit a copy of Clay's note immediately to the Lieutenant Governor of New Brunswick, Sir Howard Douglas, "in order to obtain an explanation of the transaction." ALS. DNA, RG59, Notes from British Legation, vol. 15 (M50, R15); also in Manning, *Diplomatic Correspondence . . . Canadian Relations*, 2:783.

Clay wrote Lincoln on January 14, enclosing a copy of Vaughan's response to his note. LS. MWA.

From JOEL R. POINSETT, Mexico, no. 161, December 30, 1828. Sends "the translation of a letter addressed to me by the former Minister of Central America [Juan de Dios Mayorga] at this Court," complaining of a party in Guatemala which prefers the domination of Mexico over independence. States that he has always been aware of the existence of this group "and of the ambitious designs of Mexico to extend their territories by the acquisition of those provinces." Reports that negotiations have been "carried on between this Government and the chiefs of the servile party in Guatemala" for two months but that he has not "been able to ascertain their exact nature." Comments: "Mexico does not appear to be aware to what she exposes herself by attempting to establish the principle that a part of one federation is at liberty to depart from the original contract and to unite itself to another whenever it may think proper." Disapproves "both . . . the principle and . . . the conduct pursued by this Government with regard to Guatemala." Requests instructions on what action he should take if Mexico interferes in the affairs of Guatemala. Recommends that the U.S. send "an intelligent accredited agent" to Guatemala as soon as possible "to calm the disturbances which distract that Country." ALS. DNA, RG59, Dip. Disp., Mexico, vol. 4 (M97, R5). Received February 11, 1829.

To CHARLES R. VAUGHAN, Washington, December 30, 1828. Transmits the evidence which the U.S. intends to present to the arbiter, King William I, of the Northeastern boundary dispute. Recalls that in a note of October 16, 1828, he informed Vaughan of the President's acceptance of the proposal Vaughan had made in a note of May 15 for the "simple collation and comparison" of the *Atlas* annexed to the Report of the Commissioners under the 5th Article of the Treaty of Ghent. In order "to guard against the possibility of any disappointment in the completion of that agreement," encloses also "copies of some of the maps, surveys & topographical delineations which were filed with the Commissioners." Copy. DNA, RG59, Notes to Foreign Ministers and Consuls, vol. 4, pp. 106–30 (M38, R4); also in Manning, *Diplomatic Correspondence . . . Canadian Relations*, 2:187–9; and in CSmH.

From LESLIE COMBS   Frankfort, December 31, 1828
I recd a few days since your letter of the 18th inst.—From the discordant, selfish materials composing the leading phalanx of the Jackson & *Reform* party, it was to be expected their coherence would not be very remarkable, after the contest was ended, as each would—out of pure patriotism—covet place, power and money—Stand aloof & let them quarrel as much as they please we can laugh at them, and in time, relieve the country from their kind keeping—

Every thing goes on better here, than you would imagine—The Heroites [Jacksonians] cannot trust each other & there are so many *little* great men, among, them, hungry—ravenous—for the fat of the land, that we can generally under their differences, by selecting among them—

If you had a long rough rock to break with a small hammer, you would not Strike it in the centre, for you would thereby exhaust your strength in fruitless efforts, but you would Smack off a corner here & there, until it became manageable—

Our friends are real veterans, and constitute as difficult a minority to be managed by dominant,—tomahawk & Scalping Knife majority as your heart could wish—Our opponents understand this & respect us accordingly—We are happier than they—and succeed often in our wishes & operations.

If Col [Richard M.] Johnson had run agt [George M.] Bibb, we should have thrown the C. J. [Chief Justice] into an appoplexy but his (Col Js.) friends were scared off the track & induced to make pledges, from which they could not recede. Mr [John] Pope was also very coy, and altho he would have been beaten, he now thinks he could have been elected, & is ready to bite off his tongue for refusing [James] Loves nomination.[1] So the matter goes—A report of the election is prepared & will appear in next weeks [Lexington] Ky. Reporter—(*drawn up by several members*) we are anxious to know your views after 4th March, So as to Speak of probabilities &c with some certainty.

How do the Jackson leaders treat you and the prominent men among our friends in congress?

The old court Jackson men are withdrawing from the disorganizers and it is probably in a few days, we shall have a dead majority in the Senate—The Gov. [Thomas Metcalfe] gives two dinners a week and is doing very well. I am for [Benjamin] Mills as C.J. I know not who will be apptd.

ALS. DLC-HC (DNA, M212, R3).   1. Bibb, Chief Justice of the Kentucky Court of Appeals, resigned on December 23, 1828, to take up the U.S. Senate seat to which he had just been elected. The seat, Richard M. Johnson's, had been contested in the state legislature by Bibb, John Breathitt, and John Pope. Both Pope and Breathitt's nominations were withdrawn. Johnson had chosen not to run for re-election. Baylor, *John Pope Kentuckian*, 320–1. For Love, see *BDAC*.

To **FRANCISCO MARIATEGUI,** Washington, December 31, 1828. Acknowledges having received "several months ago, an official Letter under date the 16th of November of last year" in which Mariategui requested the United States to protect the "peace and freedom of Peru" by serving as a mediator between Peru and Simon Bolivar. Explains that the delay in reply resulted from the death of James Cooley, U.S. Chargé d'Affaires in Peru, and a delay in appointing his successor. Reports that Samuel Larned will assume that post and "is charged to communicate the views of the President which I hope will prove entirely satisfactory to . . . your Government." Copy. DNA, RG59, Notes to Foreign Ministers and Consuls, vol. 4, p. 131 (M38, R4); also in Manning, [dated Dec. 30] *Diplomatic Correspondence . . . Latin American Nations,* 1:300. Mariategui was Minister of Foreign Affairs of the Republic of Peru.

From **JOHN ROCHE**   Lexington, Ky.,
                                                    N.D. [Late December, 1828]
I am much obliged by the kind attention you paid my former request. The Hon. Mr. [Edward] Everett so promptly and politely satisfied me on the subject of my inquiry, that I have abandoned the purpose of abridging the Work I named[,] Potter's Grecian Antiquities.[1] Had not the work been already abridged, as well as when working on the same subject existed, I should have undertaken it, and thus continued my connection with Transylvania University. From a variety of causes needless to be named I have resigned my office in the University. I have resolved on removing to Missouri, and turning my attention mainly to agriculture at present.

The reason why I obtrude on your attention a second communication so soon is, that I feel confident you wish well to the University and to Lexington, and that I have determined as well as been advised by my friends to await your arrival, in the hope that you may use your influence with the Board of trustees, who seem disposed to treat me with manifest injustice. Should I resort to compulsory means to extort my right from individuals personally irresponsible, the injury, if any ensued, would fall on the College. It is abhorrent from my feelings to injure in the Slightest degree an innocent community because of the contemptible folly of any little junto, who abuse their petty power to nefarious purposes,

The case, Sir, is this. Having exhausted their means in every project that the late president [Horace Holley] proposed, and having given to him at his departure all that they could scrape together, they fell in debt to me $400; to Dr. [George T.] Chapman[2] 300; and to the Revd. Mr. [Benjamin O.] Peers 400. (I mean nothing disrespectful to the memory of Mr. Holley, for he was my friend, but I do mean that the movements of the great body of trustees was nothing more than Automation antics at his bidding.) I became a subscriber to the College fund to the amount of fifty dollars yearly, for 4 years but with an express understanding that I should be released from my subscription, should I leave Lexington at any time before the expiration of that period. I asked them no interest on the money, I consented to take *Commonwealth* Bank paper—now from 10 to 15 pr. Ct. below par for *Specie.* It would not do. Hear their Resolution; "Resolved that the Chairman be directed to settle with Mr. Roche and pay him the whole balance due him by the University *provided he will pay the full amount of his subscription to the Univy. fund in advance."* Here you see I am called on to pay *contrary to my stipulation* to an institution, I may say, of another State, money, part of which will not and cannot be due in any event, before the year 1832. Is this honourable? is it grateful? I have served the University since *1818* with fidelity, if the trustees themselves have not frequently falsified: and yet in *1828* because I deem it expedient for the good of my family to change my residence, or from some other cause, probably the flatulent caprice of paltry little authority these same trustees wish to exact what will fall due three years and a half hence. This will not do to tell; particularly, when, owing myself and the two other gentlemen already named over a *thousand* dollars; when they are begging money constantly of the Legislature and of private individuals, they with great liberality, intended no doubt to command the admiration of the Union, "advance" to Mr. [Alva] Woods *500* dollars to bring him and his wife and child to Kentucky. Thus before this gentleman has rendered them *any service,* he receives 500 dollars, while I, after a Servitude of more than ten years, cannot get about the same lawfully, as I conceive, my due.

[Continues pleading his case at length, with particular criticism of John W. Hunt[3]—"that fetid mass of swaggering, purse proud folly . . . a creature whose God is money"—and asks that when "you come back, Sir, to Kentucky, I wish this small matter settled." Is convinced that the Trustees "appear inclined at least to *jew* me if not to swindle me."]

Concludes with the observation he has "made known these few things to you, who alone, I believe, can save Lexington and its College. The contents of my letter, Sir, you are not bound to keep secret unless you so chose."

ALS. DLC-HC (DNA, M212, R3).   Roche, a native of Ireland and graduate of Trinity College, Dublin, had migrated to the United States in 1816. After teaching briefly in Maryland, he was appointed Professor of Latin and Greek at Transylvania College in 1818. He resigned from Transylvania in December, 1828, but was reappointed to the faculty in October, 1829. He resigned a second time, in October, 1830, after having been reported intoxicated. From 1830 to his death in October, 1845, he operated a private school in Georgetown, Ky. John Roche File, Archives, KyLxT.   1. John Potter, *The Antiquities of Greece or Archaeologia Graeca*. 2 vols. Oxford, 1697: 1698. Potter had been Archbishop of Canterbury. *DNB*.   2. The Rev. Mr. Chapman, professor of history, geography, chronology and antiquities, had resigned from Transylvania on October 1, 1827.   3. Member of the Board of Trustees of Transylvania University.

To SAMUEL LARNED, no. 1, January 1, 1829. Transmits Larned's commisision as Chargé to Peru and urges him to "proceed, without any loss of time to Lima."

Notes that from Larned's dispatches nos. 68 and 69, it appears he has entered upon a negotiation with Chile for a commercial treaty. Points out that he had no instructions to undertake such a negotiation and that it would have been preferable if he had transmitted the matter to his government and waited for instructions. States, nevertheless, that if a treaty has been signed, the President, if he approves its contents, will send it to the Senate for ratification. Authorizes him, if the negotiation is still pending and there is a prospect for an early conclusion, to stay in Chile until it is completed. Adds that if Peru has repealed its decree prohibiting U.S. produce and manufactures by the time this instruction arrives, "the necessity will not be so great for your immediate departure for Lima," so he is to use his own discretion.

Informs him that the instructions given to the late James Cooley under date of April 15, 1828, are to guide him in negotiating a treaty of commerce with Peru. Notes that the two pressing issues with Peru are claims of American citizens against the Peruvian government and commercial relations which suffer "from unfriendly regulations." States that the Peruvian Decree, passed on June 11 and promulgated on June 13, 1828, will put an end altogether to commerical intercourse between Peru and the U.S. Instructs him to "lose no time in representing in forcible and respectful language its unfriendly and partial tendency" and requesting its revocation. Reports rumors that the decree was adopted at the urging of British agents. Emphasizes that the best deterrent to "partial and unjust regulations of commerce and navigation" is a treaty. Copy. DNA, RG59, Dip. Instr., vol. 12, pp. 172–7 (M77, R7).

To SAMUEL LARNED, no. 2, January 1, 1829. Discusses a communication received from the Minister of Foreign Relations of Peru, Francisco Mariategui, dated November 16, 1828, requesting U.S. mediation to avert an attack by Colombia and Bolivia. Notes that Cooley's death and the delay in appointing a successor "have hitherto postponed the return of such an answer as was due to the important nature of that communication." Reports that General William Henry Harrison has departed for Colombia and is instructed immediately upon his arrival in Bogota "to communicate to the Government of Colombia, the President's anxious wish that the war may be averted if it has not broken out, or may be honorably terminated, if it has commenced." Tells Larned to communicate to the Peruvian government "the solicitude" which the United States "feels for its welfare." On the question of mediation, points out that the U.S. has never undertaken such a mission and deems it proper to await a communication from Harrison as to the desire of Colombia for mediation. Transmits a letter to the Peruvian Minister of Foreign Affairs. Copy. DNA, RG59, Dip. Instr., vol. 12, pp. 172-7 (M77, R7).

On January 10, 1829, Clay wrote instruction no. 3 to Larned, concentrating on the news of the war between Peru and Colombia, and its impact upon the United States. Informs Larned of his duty to protect American neutral rights in "our commercial and other interests," and calls attention to the effects of Peru's "paper" blockade of "the whole coast of the Republic of Colombia on the Pacific." Pointing out that paper blockades are illegal, instructs Larned to protest and to inform Peru that the United States "cannot consent to respect any blockade of either party," and that captors will be held responsible for full indemnities. *Ibid.*

From ROBERT SCOTT, Lexington, January 1, 1829. Presents a lengthy and detailed financial account covering wages paid, repair bills, rental income, plantation supplies purchased, sale of farm products, miscellaneous expenses, etc. from August 18, to December 31, 1828. Among the items are found: $20 paid for 20 gals. of "whisky for use of the Farm [Ashland]"; $37.50 in wages paid to John H. Kerr overseer at Ashland; $1.50 for "a Coffin for a Negro that died at the Farm"; $12.50 quarterly tuition payment to Transylvania Univ. for son Theodore W. Clay; $53 income for lease (at $65 per annum) of "Negro Tom" to J. V. Headinburgh from August 14, 1827, to May 31, 1828; $11.75 spent for shoes and mending for Negroes "Phyllis, A[a]ron & David" in 1827 and 1828; $208 income from sale of 832 bu. of corn meal; $15 paid to "H. Gettings on Acct. of conveying Negro's from Virga. to Ky."; and numerous minor expenditures for "sundry" clothing, blankets, etc. for various slaves. ADS. KyLxT.

To ANTHONY CHARLES CAZENOVE, Washington, January 2, 1829. States that the President cannot agree to the suggestion made in Cazenove's letter of December 31, 1828, for "an exchange of the Ratifications of the additional article to the Convention recently concluded between the U.S. and the Free Hanseatic Republics" until the U.S. Senate approves the treaty. Copy. DNA, RG59, Notes to Foreign Ministers and Consuls, vol. 4, p. 132 (M38, R4).

On January 9, 1829, Cazenove reported to Clay his understanding that the Secretary was quite prepared to exchange ratifications of the additional article as soon as the anticipated U.S. Senate action on the matter was completed. LS[?]. DNA, RG59, Cons. Corresp.: Notes from Foreign Consuls, vol. 2.

On January 12, Cazenove wrote Clay that on January 14 he would wait "on you . . . for the purpose of exchanging the Ratification of the additional article to the Convention." ALS. *Ibid.*

The additional article, signed on June 11, 1828, provided for the extradition of sailors who had deserted "the vessels of their respective countries" and obligated the U.S. and the Hanseatic Republics to provide "all aid and assistance to the said Consuls and Vice-Consuls, for the search, seizure, and arrest of the said deserters." For the text of the

Convention of December 20, 1827, and the additional article see Parry, *Treaty Series,* 77:477-90.

From HENRY CLAY, JR.   West Point, N.Y., January 2, 1829
Your last letter [December 20, 1828] was duly recd and I assure you the contents of it highly delighted me. The doubt which has long preyed upon my mind and which I have hitherto but partially concealed, has been cleared up and I learn that in your estimation my talents are such as entitle me at least to a trial of the law—To know that this is your opinion pleased me beyond measure, and, I confess, incites me to exertion and raises within me a wish to arrive at something higher than a professorship although I consider the employment of professor at least as honourable and much more lucrative than a post in the Army—[1]
    In regard to my going to Kentucky—I feel forcibly the obligation under which I am to you for your kind wish that I should spend my vacation as agreably as possible Yet I am not certain all things being considered, whether it will be proper for me to perform the journey in question or not. The expense which it will cause to you will be great, say $150.00 as together with the usual expenses of the journey must be added that of purchasing citizen's clothes, of which I shall be entirely in want; And I know not whether the transient pleasure which I shall enjoy will compensate for the inconvenience to which you may be put to furnish me such a sum—However if you think it well for me to go I will gladly embrace your suggestion as to the route which I take. Richard [P.] Shelby is still here and I fear is in danger of being found deficient: Poor fellow he has had to labour under great disadvantages—He requested me this evening to write to you and to ask you if there was any chance of his getting a reappointment;[2] were he to obtain it I have no doubt but that in the next class he would hold a high standing—He will write to you however himself and will state his case more correctly perhaps than I could do—[3]
    Is William Claiborne in Washington? or has he gone to New Orleans?
    Give my love and a happy new Year season to mama and to all our friends

ALS. Henry Clay Memorial Foundation, Lexington, Ky.   1. Henry Clay, Jr. to Clay, December 16, 1828.   2. On January 28, 1829, Clay wrote to Peter B. Porter, Secretary of War, recommending Shelby's reappointment to West Point. Notes that if this cannot be done, Porter recommend to Shelby that he resign and return immediately to Kentucky. ALS. NBuHi. See, also, Clay to Henry Clay, Jr., January 14, 1829. Shelby was reappointed and attended the 1829–1830 session but was not graduated with his class (1832).   3. In his earlier letter to Clay, January 4, 1829, Cadet Shelby had remarked on his father's [James] "extreme anxiety for me to remain in my present situation," and asked for a stay of his probable dismissal for inadequate academic performance. He blamed his problem, in part, on an attack of rheumatism which had put him three weeks behind his classmates and on the miscarriage of a letter home in which he had asked for permission to resign before being dismissed. This his father had refused, urging him instead to apply to Clay for reappointment if he failed the mid–term examinations. ALS. InU. Failed, he apparently had.

To AMOS NICHOLS, Portland, Maine, January 2, 1829. Responds to Nichols's letter of December 22, written on order of the Governor, Enoch Lincoln, and Council of the State of Maine, stating that they had been informed that the services of Albert Gallatin and William Preble, American commissioners in the Northeastern boundary question, "will be dispensed with" upon their completion of official papers. Notes that Gallatin and Preble have collected their evidence and that it has been submitted to Charles R. Vaughan, the British Minister, in Washington. Regarding contrary evidence gathered by the British to support their boundary claims, states this information will also be delivered to Gallatin and Preble to help them prepare statements for the Arbiter, William I.

Assures Nichols that the assumption of the Governor and his Council that Gallatin and Preble are being dismissed by the President is erroneous. "No Variation has taken place, nor is any contemplated by him, in the Original design of the Agency." Copy. DNA, RG59, Dom. Letters, vol. 22, pp. 361-2 (M40, R20). Nichols was Secretary of State of Maine.

From FRANCIS T. BROOKE   Near Fredericksburg, Va.,
                                                   January 5, 1829
I have been here unsophisticating and [illeg. word] myself in the Solitude of the country for a fortnight, and Shall remain until the 20th instant So that except what I get from the papers know nothing of what is passing in the bustling world—before I left Richmond I reminded [John H.] Pleasants of his promise to republish your [Jonathan] Russel[l] correspondence [3:219-26, 269-72], and we conversed on the propriety of feeling the public pulse, on the Subject of the next Presidential election, reflecting on the Subject Since, I have thought that it would be best to wait until Some candidate on the other Side was brought out, and the public had time to cool on this Subject I Should like to hear from you, I Should like to know also what use they mean to make of their victory, I think the genl [Jackson] will have Sense enough to See, that they have not elected him, but on the contrary that most of them are indebted to him, for the places they hold in the public mind, if So, he will feel no obligation to gratify them—he must however be indebted to his cabinet Such as it may be for instruction, on the Subjects of our foreign relations and even our domestic concerns, but on party politics he can be at no loss—Should he see this, he may do better than may be for the good of the country ultimately as the example of his Success will confirm the people in the opinion that military renoun is always a pledge for good government and Sooner or later we must travel the down hill road of all republics it would be better that he Should not See it, and that he Should drive the carriage of State like another Phaeton, over Some precipice—in the [Washington *Daily National*] journal you will See that we are in a great crisis, and after the reelection of [William B.] Giles I predict nothing, though I hope as it involves no party question we Shall have a convention,[1] and whether on the white or black population I care not, though I do not perceive how if the latter's entirely abandoned in the new, or a amended constitution, we can long retain it, in the Federal constitution, nor am I now very anxious for the freehold qualification, I once thought, as you know, that it was the best Security for the due weight of the wholesome influence which ought to be felt in every good government, I mean patriotism, evinced by public Service, virtue talents

&c but Since the Presidential election in Virginia I give it up, as old Mr. [Nathaniel] Macon would Say—Some qualification is necessary and I think these influences would be more felt by an extension of the right of Suffrage to other classes, who would more probably be affected by them, than the lower class of freeholders, who are governed by little else than whiskey and demagogues—you will laugh at these Speculations—but if you will, in a letter to me, I shall be repaid amply.

ALS. DLC-HC (DNA, M212, R3).   1. Clay to Brooke, December 26, 1828; also 6:292.

From JAMES BARBOUR, London, no. 11, January 6, 1829. Transmits a letter from Lord Aberdeen together with enclosures concerning the Convention of September 29, 1827 [6:1100–01].

States that the recall of the Marquis of Anglesey, Henry William Paget, the viceroyalty of Ireland is causing a sensation in the United Kingdom, but predicts that it will "pass of in murmurs only." Comments: "Forty thousand bayonets in willing hands, are a rude, but irresistible argument to an unarmed peasantry, however outraged and exasperated." LS. DNA, RG59, Dip. Disp., Great Britain, vol. 36 (M30, R32). Received February 24, 1829; also in Manning, *Diplomatic Correspondence . . . Canadian Relations,* 2:783. For Paget see *DNB.*

To JOHN J. CRITTENDEN   Washington, January 6, 1829
I received your letter of the 27th instant, with its enclosures, which I have sent, through the post Office to their respective addresses. They arrived in time to produce all the good they are capable of effecting. Your nomination[1] was made to the Senate agreeably to the intimation which I gave you in my former letter   It has ever since been suspended there, and its fate is considered uncertain by our firends. It was referred, I understand, to a Committee, which is not a very usual thing with original nominations. The policy of the Jackson party will be to delay, and, ultimately, to postpone it altogether. I believe it is contemplated by some of our friends to move to have the Committee discharged, and the nomination taken up in the Senate. Such a motion will probably be made in a few days. As soon as the result is known, I will inform you. In the mean time you need not be assured that I will do every thing in my power, consistently with propriety to promote its success.

LS. DLC-John J. Crittenden Papers (DNA, M212, R20).   1. To the U.S. Supreme Court.

From JAMES ERWIN   New Orleans, January 6, 1829
I had your letter of the 30th Nov. only a few days since. The Boy Jerry is at my plantation in Tennessee. I shall immediately direct, him to be liberated, unless he prefers to remain where he is. in which case he shall in the presence of Respectable Witnesses and in writing declare such a wish he has been kindly treated while with me & is now contented and happy. his Services have already been adequate to the amt paid by me—& I am perfectly willing to liberate him tomorrow—
    By the Packet of the 15th Inst I shall transmit you the amount, that

will be due on the 15th Feby. had I not recd your letter I Should have paid $1000. on the Bank Stock in the name of John Morrison Clay. do you still wish that done?

I herewith Inclose you a letter addressd. by me to Messrs J. Hinman & Son the principal Money Brokers of this City the object of which was to ascertain the real Cash value of the [George] Mather Bonds [5:1019–20] in this Market. and altho you may Safely rely on the Security being ample, yet, the price named by them is the Best that Could be had were the Bonds thrown into Market. I can at this moment invest $100.000 in the most undoubted paper at the rate of ten per centum per annum. I have a large Amt of my own which I would sell at that Rate equal to any in the City.

The Senatorial election takes place on the 12th Inst   There is no chance I think for [Edward] Livingston. the Contest will be at last between [Henry] Johnson & Mr. [Dominique] Bouligney.[1] until very lately I believed the Chances greatly in favor of the party. But I now think Mr Bouligney's prospects very fair. If the friends of Livingston entirely give him up. on the 1st Ballot. Mr. B. will then likely succeed. So great has been the dread of bad feelings arising between our own friends & Livingston benefitting by it. that at first the great aim was to take the Strongest. & the impression generally was that Gov. J[ohnson] would mos[t] certainly Succeed. this idea added to his Strength. But there is a change taking place   But its impossible yet to Say who will be the man we are trying to keep in [mind?] the great importance of Securing a friend in the Senate that can be relied on

The particular situation of Anne [Brown Clay Erwin][2] at the moment of the arrival of your friends Miss B [illeg. name] & Dr [illeg. name] & the Duke denies us the pleasure of attending to them in the manner that it would have been pleasing to us—Gov [Samuel] Sprigg and his Sons are also here to who I shall render all the civilities my present situation will allow me.

The present Calculation is to join you at Ashland this June next.

As to my Horses would like very much to have an elegant pair of well Broke horses. But the great object was to have them here this winter. If however you can get a good Bargain in a fine pair Say worth 500 I should be pleased to get them in the Summer. but there is no use in troubling you, except you think better & Cheaper can be had with you than at Lexington. exercise your own Judgt. & if a fine pair appear I should be pleased to have them purchased. Anne joins me in her love to Mrs. Clay & the Boys [James Brown Clay and John Morrison Clay].

ALS. DLC-HC (DNA, M212, R3). Endorsed by Clay on verso: "[Certificate as to Mather's debt]."   1. Livingston was elected on the fourth ballot by a majority of one, after leading Bouligney by three votes and Johnson by five votes on the first ballot. *Niles' Register* (February 7, 1829), 35:385.   2. According to the Erwin genealogy given in Thomas S. Erwin's "Clay and Erwin Families," *Filson Club History Quarterly* (Jan., 1929), 3:113–6, Anne Clay Erwin gave birth to Lucretia Hart Erwin on Oct. 22, 1829 and to Andrew Eugene Erwin in October of 1830. A letter, however, from Clay to Clay, Jr., dated Oct. 31, 1830, mentions that Anne has given birth to a "daughter" who has been named for Anne's mother. It seems probable, therefore, that the dates given in the Filson Club article by Thomas Erwin for Lucretia and Andrew Erwin were reversed. On the other hand, although this seems less likely, the 1829 birth-year might have been that of James Erwin, Jr. for whom Thomas Erwin gives neither a date of birth nor death.

To JAMES MAURY MORRIS   Washington, January 8, 1829

Mrs. Clay and I are very much obliged to you and Mrs. Morris for the very acceptable New year's present of a dozen bacon hams, which Mr. Taylor[1] has, at your instance, been good enough to send us from Richmond. I assure you we were not long in making an experiment of one of them, which we found fully sustained the antient and renowned character of Virginia hams. We both agreed that their excellence was to be mainly attributed to the Administration member of your family. And under that conviction Mrs. Clay, who admits that they are superior to the hams which we usually make at Ashland, charges me to request of Mrs. Morris to favor her with directions for preparing them. . . .

ALS. ViU. 1. Possibly Creed Taylor of Cumberland Co., Va.

From ROBERT SCOTT   Lexington, January 8, 1829

I wrote to you on the 5 inst. in answer to your favor relative to Flour &c.—as yet, I have been unable to ascertain the present price of Flour at Cincinnati, but expect to do so in a day or two, and if it can be had within your limit, will attend to your request upon that subject.

Herewith, are your A/C with the estate of Colo. [James] Morrison, and with me, down to the 1st. inst.—After you have looked over the latter, please return it to me, or bring it when you come to Kentucky as it will save going over it again—The expenses of repairing the [Kentucky] Hotel will I apprehend be more than you supposed, as there is yet between 500$ & 600$—to take up—say the bills of the carpenter and Brick layer—I have not yet got a tenant for it—Mrs. [Robert] Boggs speaks of taking it toward spring—It was unlucky that it was not put under repair sooner, as it might in that case have now been under rent, but Mr. [Matthew] Kennedy expected to be able to make a lumping job of the brick work with some one of the brick layers, and under that expectation delayed it—he failed however, and the circumstances made it too late in the season to lease, as those who keep boarding houses have fixed themselves, for the season—

Mr. [John] Beach has not yet paid, but promises fair—

In a few days I will forward to you a statement of our Bagging business—it will not be encouraging—

ALS. KyLxT.

From WILLIAM H. TRACY, Guayama, January 8, 1829. Reports the death of two American citizens—John Adams, a blacksmith, and James L. Hancock, an engineer—who had come to Guayama on November 1, 1828, "for the purpose of putting up a Steam Engine." ALS. DNA, RG59, Cons. Disp., Guayama, Puerto Rico, vol. 1 (M76, R22). Received March 3, 1829.

From HENRY SHAW, N.P. [Probably, Lanesborough, Mass.], January 9, 1829. Offers his views of the "politicks & policy of Mass[achusetts] both in regard to the present and the future." Does not believe that Daniel Webster's opinions on the state's political situation are sound. Argues that the "old Parties are dead" and that the Jacksonians, claiming to be "friends of the people" are everywhere on the march, their highly emotional approach to politics having made the difference in Pennsylvania, New York, and Ohio in the recent Presidential election. Predicts that the Jacksonian surge, if not properly countered, will "change within 3 years the Politicks of this State—It will, next Spring, lose us N Hampshire & probably Maine—It is now making rapid progress in Connecticut and Vermont will soon move—Why is this—" Suggests that the Federalist party is still closely associated in the minds of the people with opposition to Jefferson's embargo policy and support of the Hartford Convention. Does not believe that former Federalist Webster's advice to keep Levi Lincoln as Governor and reelect Nathaniel Silsbee to the U.S. Senate is wise, and points out that while the Federalists can still control Massachusetts for a few years, their days are numbered. Believes that Clay must be "a more Democratick Candidate or you must fail—The feeling of New England is decidedly with you, it can only be turned from you by the too close adherence of old Federalists." Warns that the principles espoused by Clay do not impress "the People" because "they [don't] see danger from Military rule or care much about the Absolut[e] doctrines of Civil Liberty or this or that construction of the [Constitution]!" As for the probable outcome of the coming Massachusetts state elections in the Spring, "Lincoln will be nominated for Gov—Silsbee be elected Senator, & that too before this reaches you— unless an arrangement, which is contemplated, takes place—that is to elect Lincoln for Senator & Silsbee for Govr—this . . . will prevent [Marcus] Morton probably from being put up by Jacksonians—& in this breakup the Federal domination now maintained by Webster through Lincoln—If this does not take place, or if Lincoln is made Gov & Silsbee Senator then I shall advise to the nomination of Morton for Govr & a Clay man for Lieut Gov—If the Jackson Men will agree to this last arrangement, the [illeg.] will look to yourself or Van Buren . . . as the future candidate for Pr[esiden]t. Morton is a Calhoun Man in part. If Lincoln is elected . . . & should hold his power, & Mr. Webster proves true, you are safe as far as Masstt can go—If the other Ticket prevails we must trust to good Management[?] to produce the same result—at least there will be a fair chance of dividing the Democrats—thus far in this State Democrats have toiled, & Federalists have caught the fish." Believes that had Webster been sent to Great Britain as U.S. Minister, instead of James Barbour, "you would not be on your way to Ashland." Feels also that Webster "is wasting, in the public estimation—he never had any hold on the affections of the People, and already a large number begin to doubt both his integrity & ability." Concludes with the prediction that on national political issues "N. York & Kentucky will yet strike hands." ALS. DLC-HC (DNA, M212, R3). In the Spring, 1829, elections in Massachusetts, Levi Lincoln defeated Marcus Morton in the gubernatorial race by a four to one margin; Thomas L. Winthrop, the National Republican candidate for Lt. Governor, defeated Nathan Willis for that office by the same decisive margin; Nathaniel Silsbee was reelected U.S. Senator over token opposition. See, *Niles' Register* (January 24, 1829), 35:345; *ibid.* (April 18, 1829), 36:117; Robert Sobel and John Raimo, eds., *Biographical Directory of the Governors of the United States*

1789–1978 (Westport, Conn., 1978), 2:699; Darling, *Political Changes in Massachusetts, 1824–1848*, 75. The Spring, 1829, elections in Maine, New Hampshire, and Connecticut generally went well for the National Republican and pro–Adams forces. In Vermont, the election of a U.S. Representative in the 5th Congressional District was deadlocked by the appearance of four candidates variously identified with the Jackson, Anti–Jackson, and Anti–Masonic parties. See, *Niles' Register,* (September 13, 1928), 35:45; *ibid.,* (March 21, March 28, May 2, June 20, and July 25, 1829), 36:49, 67, 147, 269, 349; Parsons, *U.S. Congressional Districts, 1788–1841*, 232-3, 246; Washington *Daily National Intelligencer,* April 14, 20, 1829. For the New Hampshire results, see Clay to Plumer, February 23, 1829.

To FRANCIS T. BROOKE   Washington, January 10, 1829

I perceive from your letter of the 5h. inst. at St. Julien that you had not then received one which I addressed to you at Richmond, where I presume it now is awaiting your return.

We are here absolutely without any thing new or interesting. Congress is in no disposition to do business. The present Administration is winding up their public affairs, originating no new measures, and endeavoring to turn their Stewardship over to their successors, in the best state possible. In respect to the purposes of the new administration, or rather the intentions of the President elect, nothing seems to be known here. We have vague speculations only in place of positive information. Washington, therefore, is not at present the source of news. We must look to other quarters for it. And accordingly we have been turning our attention towards Richmond. There appears, in your legislature, to be so many projects, in regard to the basis of the representation in your Convention, that we are at a loss to conjecture whether any thing or what will be done.[1]

As far as I can learn (and on that subject a good deal of information reaches me) there is a good spirit prevailing among our friends every where. They seem to be generally impressed with the belief that our true policy, at present, is to do nothing but look on. That they ought to avoid alike hostility or professions of support towards the new admon. That until it begins to act, there is no means of judging what its course will be. That, in the mean time, holding fast to all our principles, and keeping constantly in view the danger to civil liberty of the predominance of the military spirit, we should preserve stout hearts and be prepared to act, under contingencies, according to the impulses of a genuine patriotism.

In respect to myself the best dispositions every where prevail among our friends, without being exclusively confined to them, unless I am greatly deceived. All, with whom I have conversed concur in the opinion that if my name had been fairly before the public, instead of that of Mr. Adams, the result of the late contest would have been different. On that supposition, my friends from the West assure me that every vote would have been obtained for me, which was anticipated for Mr. Adams. And even in N. England I am assured by several of the representatives and Senators that I would have got a greater aggregate popular vote than

Mr. Adams received. In New York and the Middle States my friends more than his contributed to successful results where they were obtained.

Looking to the future, and judging from things as they now exist, we have every encouragement. Supposing the party of the Admon should think proper to unite on me and present my name as the successor of Genl. Jackson, I should have a greater degree of support than any *one* could obtain of those between whom the party of Jackson would be divided. To that support may be added that large number of persons every where, but especially in the West whose attachment to me could not control their aversion to Mr. Adams.

Whether I ought to be brought out, *and when,* must be left exclusively to my friends. This latter point, supposing the first affirmatively settled, is one of great delicacy. Precipitancy and tardiness should be equally avoided. The public wants tranquillity, after the late agitation. To present formally candidates for the succession, before the P. elect enters on the duties of the office would be premature and offensive to the quiet, that is, the larger portion of the community. It would be otherwise, if the Candidates of the Jackson party were announced.

Where Jacksonism has prevailed and secured majorities in the Legislatures of different States, those majorities are more inimical to me, at this time, than majorities in those legislatures ever will be hereafter. They have been elected under an excitement; and I have remarked always that the representatives of the people, when so elected, are ahead of the people themselves in reference to that particular excitement.

It is less difficult to pronounce that it would be too early now to take any formal measures to announce my name than it is to say when will be the proper time. That will depend upon contingencies; such as the movements of competitors, the course of the new administration, the determination of Jackson as to offering for a second term &c. The time *may* arrive next summer or winter; I should think hardly earlier than the latter.

This prudential course will not prevent Editorial allusions to my name, either by way of defence, or from friendly feelings.

It will be time enough, upon my return to K. after the 4h. of March, to decide whether I shall remain in private or again seek to enter public life. I should be glad to know your views and those of other friends on that point. I presume there will be no difficulty in my returning to the House of R. if I should permit myself to be a Candidate.

The health of Mr. [Samuel L.] Southard has been bad throughout the Session. He is now confined to his house, but I learn is better to day. Without perhaps there being any cause of immediate apprehension, I think his situation is one full of anxiety to his friends and connexions.

Do you not mean to visit us? I need not say that I should see you with great pleasure, and although this City presents less attraction than usual at this Season to the Ladies we should be most happy to see Mrs. Brooke also with you. . . .

ALS. KyU. Partially printed in Colton, *Clay Correspondence*, 4:217–8. Letter marked "(Confidential)." 1. See Brooke to Clay, January 5, 1829; also, see Richmond *Enquirer*, December 2, 1828, and February 12, 1829, on the legislative reapportionment issue.

From LAFAYETTE   Lagrange, France, January 10, 1829

Your Excellent Sister [Ann Hart Brown] and Mr [James] Brown are no doubt writing to You Her Health was better when I last Had the pleasure to See Her. The day is drawing near When I must go to town for the Opening of the Session.[1] What liberal fruits it will produce, I cannot Say. There is a general disposition in behalf of Constitutional institution within the very narrow Circle of a granted Charter.[2] Yes, However illegitimate these two words sound to a Republican Ear, some progress might be made on the Road of freedom, provided there was a majority determined to Say "it shall be So" as to the State of European politics Mr Brown will tell you what His Situation enables Him to ascertain.

Late accounts from America make us Anticipate the result of the presidential Contest. You too will know, I Hope, my affection for You, not to think Yourself Bound to write to me every particulars that may Concern Your actual and future arrangements. I want also to Hear the state of Your Health. I Suppose You Will Soon Have a Session Congress. Should it be advisable for Your Health to make a Short atlantic Voyage, How Happy I Should be to welcome You at lagrange!

I beg You to present my affectionate respects to Mrs Clay; remember me to family and friends. George [Washington Lafayette] is in town, but I may Safely Be His interpreter.

ALS. Phi–Samuel M. Clement, Jr. Collection. Begins, "My dear friend"; and signed "Your affectionate friend."   1. Lafayette had been elected to the Chamber of Deputies in 1827, representing Meaux.   2. The Charter, or National Constitution, was promulgated by Louis XVIII in 1814.

From JOEL R. POINSETT, Mexico, no. 163, January 10, 1829. Reports that Vicente Guerrero has been duly declared President and Ariastasio Bastamente Vice President. States that Gomez Pedraza had received a majority of the votes from the state legislatures, but the voice of public opinion had been so opposed to him "that he had himself even felt the necessity of resigning all claims to that office . . . and in consequence the choice of the House was reduced to the two candidates who had received the greater number of votes after Pedraza." LS. DNA, RG59, Dip. Disp., Mexico, vol. 4 (M97, R5). Received February 11, 1829.

From ABRAHAM B. NONES, Maraciabo, January 12, 1829. Reports that General William Henry Harrison has arrived to take up his duties as Minister to Colombia. Remarks that the political situation is far from tranquil and that Simon Bolivar has left Bogota to go to the scene of action [Popayan]. Notes, however, that he has halted at La Mesa, twelve leagues from Bogota, and awaits re–entry to the city until the regular army arrives there, apparently because he does not trust his militia. ALS. DNA, RG59, Cons. Disp., Maraciabo, vol. 1 (M–T62, R1). Received February 13, 1829.

From JAMES BROWN   Paris, January 13, 1829

[Reports that no progress has been made on the issue of U.S. claims against France. Continues:]

I learn that it is probable that Mr [Edward] Livingston will be my

Successor and that Mr. [Martin] Van Buren will go to London. [Langdon] Cheves will probably be Secretary of Treasury and [Robert Y.] Hayne of the Navy.[1] Let me know immediately how the offices are disposed of. It will be difficult to find places for all the expectants of Office—

Mrs. Brown's health is slowly improving and I still hope we shall embark at latest on the 15 May and see you in Lexington in August.

I send on my accounts to you for the last year. I hope Mr [Stephen] Pleasonton will find no difficulty in settling them—Mr [William Armand G.] Barnets allowance for doing the business of the Legation is the only new charge—

I am happy to hear from all quarters that Mr Adams and you have submitted with cheerfulness to the Change of Administration. Preserve your health cheerfulness and spirits and you will be happy and respected by all whose respect is worth having

ALS. DNA. RG59, Dip. Disp., France, vol. 23 (M34, R26). Received March 13, 1829.
1. See Brown to Clay, December 12, 1828. Samuel D. Ingham [*BDAC*] was appointed Secretary of the Treasury, and John Branch [*NCAB*, 5:295] was Jackson's Secretary of the Navy.

From FRANCIS T. BROOKE

Near Fredericksburg, Va.,
January 14, 1829

My last letter which I make no doubt you have received was by anticipation an answer to the greater part of yours on the propriety of retiring for two or three years from the Service of the public I wish I could give you an opinion that could be much relied on—the public eye is So constantly on you and the malice of your enemies So prompt to prevent your most meritorious acts, that it is not only important that you Should do right but if possible proceed on a line of conduct as little Susceptible of criticism as the nature of your condition will admit of—if I could hazard an opinion it would be that you Should be governed by the will of the people of Kentucky as nearly as it can be ascertained when you get there, but I Should greatly prefer to have the opportunity to converse with you much at large on that topick and other matters in relation to it, I find it impossible now that the court of appeals will be in Session to come to Washington before the 4 of March and I think it would be the best plan for you before you finally Set out to Kentucky to bring Mrs Clay & family here and come yourself to Richmond where I think you would receive the civilities of many of the Jacksonians and of all your own friends, or if you prefer it, though I intend to be at home about the last of Feby for a few days, I would delay it, a little, and meet you here, after the 4 of March when we could feel the pulse of the Jacksonians in this quarter as soon as I know your views on this matter I could sound the folks at Richmond and guess and give you more precise information of the effect of your visit to Virginia, at all counts Mrs Brooke would be delighted to see and entertain Mrs Clay in our plain way, and nothing would be more gratifying to me than to meet you and talk over many matters that cannot be thought of in a letter. I Shall be in Richmd by the 20h and Shall be pleased to hear from you, by the bye I was Surprised and happy to find [William H.] Fitzhugh[1] of Fairfax So warm an admirer and friend of yours—also [Fleming B.] Miller of Botetourt your friend [James] Caldwells [or Calwell] son in law N. B. Mr. [James] Madisons letters[2] can not be too much admired they are an amplification of one I had during the settmt of our convention[3] last winter, in which I was permitted by [Joseph C.] Cabell to shew to [Chapman] Johnson and from which he drew a part of our address on the Subject of the tariff, I am rather pleased that [Thomas] Ritchie has fallen into the error of resisting the force of these letters—it is the effusion of his consummate vanity.

ALS. DLC-HC (DNA, M212, R3).   1. For William Henry Fitzhugh, prominent member of the American Colonization Society, see *CAB*.   2. Two letters to Joseph C. Cabell in the Washington *Daily National Journal*, December 25, 27, 1828, in which he supported the right of Congress to impose a tariff for the protection of manufactures. The letters were also published in pamphlet form. *Two Letters [Addressed to Joseph C. Cabell, esquire] on the Constitutionality of the Power of Congress to Impose a Tariff, for the Encouragement of Manufactures.* Washington, 1829. See, White to Clay, February 15, 1829.   3. Mercer to Clay, August 18, 1827; Brooke to Clay, January 9, 1829.

To HENRY CLAY, JR.   Washington, January 14, 1829

I received your letter of the 2d. instant. I am glad that you are unde-cieved in regard to the opinion which you supposed me to entertain of your capacity. I never thought unfavorably of it. I have always believed that with such application to study as you have made, continued for a sufficient length of time, you could rise to eminence in any of the profes-sions. I never wished you to continue in the Army, unless you should find it the most congenial pursuit. If I could realize my wishes concern-ing you, one of the first of them would be to see you a distinguished member of the Bar. You know that I always thought that, so far from its being too late, it would be the proper time, for you to commence the study of Law, after you had finished your course at West point. And that the recommendation of your taking that course was that you would be then qualified for any of the walks of life. You, at first, were averse to going to West point, fearing, as you did, that you could not afterwards adopt any other line of life than that of the Army. But your repugnance to the Point has been gradually overcome; and in the end you will, I am fully persuaded, rejoice that you have taken my advice, and find too that you are able to study the law exactly at the best period of your life. If I were to say at what age a young gentleman had better commence the study, I should specify twenty, which will be yours' when your course at the Point shall be completed.

In regard to the disposition of yourself at the vacation, I wish you to decide for yourself. There is time enough for that between now and the 10h. March, by which time I expect to leave here with your Mother and family for Ashland. I am obliged to you for thinking of the affair of economy. That is a consideration which I am compelled some times to respect; but you have hitherto occasioned me comparatively so little expence, and I have so much reason to be satisfied with you, that I should be very unwilling to deny you any reasonable indulgence.

W[illiam C. C.] Claiborne remains with us and will go out in our company in the Spring.

I have written to Richard [P. Shelby].[1] I hope he may get a reappointment, but it is far from certain. Could he obtain any recommendation from Col. [Sylvanus] Thayer?[2] It would materially benefit him.

All the family unite with me in affectionate remembrance.

ALS. Henry Clay Memorial Foundation, Lexington, Ky.   1. Not found; but see Henry Clay, Jr. to Clay, January 2, 1829.   2. For Sylvanus Thayer, Superintendent of the Military Academy, 1817-1833, see *DAB*.

From JOSEPH M. STREET, Praire du Chien, Michigan Terr., January 14, 1829. Sympathizes with Clay on the loss of the presidential election, blaming the outcome on the widespread "unpopularity" of Mr. Adams, on the ability of Jackson, "a man of no inconsiderable talents," to exploit that fact, and on a variety of "*original* local causes." Calls attention to Jackson's earlier support of and friendship with Adams and notes: "The moment he believed the time had arrived when he could through his *friend Mr. A*—thurst a thorn in your side—he sacrificed his *friendship* & *his previous political opinions*, to his personal enmity against you.—His course is *detestable*." Lauds Clay's long and devoted service to his country and announces "I have cast politicks aside—and am trying in my poor way to seek preferment in Heaven." ALS. DLC-HC (DNA, M212, R3). Letter marked "(Private)."

From JOHN J. CRITTENDEN   Frankfort, January 16, 1829
By the last night's mail I received your favour of the 6th Inst:, the more agreable to me because my other friends at Washington have strangely neglected to write me—And under circumstances so much calculated to excite my anxieties, have left me to gather information as I casually could—Beside your own, I remember to have received from Washington but two letters during the present session—one from [John] Chambers & the other from [James] Clarke [*sic*, Clark]—

Whatever may be the fate of my nomination in the Senate,[1] I am prepared to bear it with becoming fortitude & resignation—tho' in its rejection there is a tast[e] of dishonor that my nature revolts at. I doubt not but that you will do all you & ought to do in my behalf—I would not expect, or desire, that any account you should transgress in the smallest particular the proprieties of your own Station—Your situation, besides the restraints it imposes, occupies all your time—But there are others there who might have done much for me, if they would have taken the *trouble* of it—I doubt not the friendship of Clarke, Chambers, [Richard] Buckner, or [Robert P.] Letcher, but they have most probably been immersed in other affairs or pleasures—One *active* & *zealous* friend is worth a dozen well-wishers. Please to tell them, that stranger as I am to almost every one in the Senate, I rely on their active friendship—I am there put on my trial, & they must be my defenders.

Some of our Kenty: friends I understand will probably be in Washington early in Feby:, and if the nomination has not been acted on, it would be well, I think, that it could be postponed till then, unless my friends there should be certain of its confirmation.

Our friend [George] Robertson some weeks ago appointed judge of the court of Appeals, was a few days ago nominated as Chief justice in the place of Mr [George M.] Bibb, & Buckner was at the same time nominated to take Robertson's place, if he was confirmed as Ch: justice—Our Senate on today rejected Robertson's nomination by a majority of one—Some Administration man voting against it—As the contemplated vacancy did not occur, the nomination of Buckner goes for nothing—The Govnr [Thomas Metcalfe]: will probably nominate him as Ch: justice, & he will be confirmed, I think, without doubt.[2]

What Robertson will do, I can't tell—I have not seen him since his rejection.

ALS. NcD.   1. To the U.S. Supreme Court. Clay to Crittenden, January 27, 1829.
2. Following Bibb's resignation as Kentucky's Chief Justice to take a U.S. Senate seat [Combs to Clay, December 31, 1828], the post remained unfilled until December, 1829. In the interim, the court consisted of George Robertson and Joseph R. Underwood. Robertson was finally appointed Chief Justice by the Governor at the end of 1829. Lewis Collins, *History of Kentucky* (Lexington, Reprint Edition, 1968), 105.

From MESSRS. BEN DE FOREST & SON, January 17, 1829. Acknowledge receipt of Clay's letter of October 6, 1828, and send a copy of Captain Hinman's protest relating the capture of the *Telltale* by Brazilians. Note that Hinman states that the ship was condemned at Montevideo and an appeal was made to the High Court at Rio de Janeiro. Add that William Tudor "addressed the Govt. on the subject," but when the Brazilians did not respond, Hinman could no longer afford to stay there. Earnestly entreat the U.S. government to seek redress. Also enclose copy of a representation to Captain Beekman V. Hoffman of the U.S. sloop of war, *Boston,* complaining of the "brutal violence committed upon the Steward." ALS. DNA, RG76, Misc. Claims, Brazil.

From WILLIAM FIELDING, Columbus, Ohio, January 17, 1829. Introduces himself as a former Kentuckian, and states "since the delivery of your much admired and truly Eloquent Speech, on the Constitutional authority of the General Government, to foster Domestic manufactures and Internal Improvements [3:683–730]: I have looked on you as the only known friend to whom the Great interest of the West could be safely and justly confided." Continues: "With these impressions and convictions and sincerely desirous, of promoting the cause of our common country; your election to the office of Chief Magistrate of the Union, received my unabating and zealous exertion." Adds that "Your disappointment in that, (much hoped by many) was however to me a source of deep regret, and like many, I still had hopes that your past services might be felt, and your claims to public gratitude be admitted by all." Says he cannot "express the abhorrence and detestation which I felt at the unprincipled slanders and calumniations, which the enemies of our country and the enemies of all good men attempted (and succeeded partially for a time) to throw over your character as a cloud to obscure those talents."

Explaining his support of John Q. Adams in the recent election, states: "Sir my exertions to promote the reelection of the present Chief Magistrate, was on my part more an act of Justice towards yourself and to my country's Glory, than for any particular desire to sustain him Longer in office."

Emphasizes his loyalty to Clay, saying "my dear Sir at a moment like this, when you are unjustly forsaken by many of your friends (such only in name) and when the Proud hopes which your mighty efforts had excited in [our] country's friends have been blasted by a reckless party. At a moment like this, which is a time you Merit and should receive support, I offer you my feeble aid by way of Consolation, sincerely believing that a country Free, Generous and Patriotic, will awake from her Reverie, and yet show to the world that notwithstanding she has been led by false reasonings and fallacious dogmas, to desert her best Friends." ALS. DLC–HC (DNA, M212, R3).

SPEECH TO THE AMERICAN COLONIZATION SOCIETY

Washington, January 17, 1829

Mr. CLAY rose to perform a duty which he had hoped would have devolved on some other member of the Institution. But before he presented the resolution, which he held in his hand, he could not deny himself the gratification of offering to the presiding officer [Bushrod Washington], to the Board of Managers[1] and others here assembled, the congratulations which belong to the occasion. How different is the present triumphant position of the Society from what it was a few years ago! He recollected about twelve years ago, when some fifteen or twenty gentlemen assembled in a room, not eighteen feet square, of a tavern in this place, to consult together about this great scheme. They formed a constitution, and organized the Society. We all remember what scoffs and taunts it subsequently experienced, how the timid were alarmed, how the ignorant misconceived or misrepresented its object, and how both extremes—the partizan of perpetual slavery, and the friend of unqualified, immediate and universal emancipation, united against us. We have triumphed over all these obstacles. Prejudice has yielded, the ignorant have acquired information, and converts are daily made. The Report read this evening shows the flourishing condition of the Colony.

Among the circumstances of the past year, which are worthy of particular felicitation, are the formation of State Societies, in two neighbouring Commonwealths [Virginia and Kentucky].[2] One of these [Virginia] has been organized, in a manner calculated to make a deep impression, in a State which has always exercised, and must ever continue to exert great influence on the affairs of this Confederacy. The other has been formed in a State [Kentucky], her daughter, to which I belong as a citizen. In the constitution of each, some of the most eminent citizens of the respective States concurred. We may anticipate, with much confidence, the best effects from both. The past year had brought forth another most gratifying incident. Our fair countrywomen, always ready to sanction schemes of religion, humanity and benevolence, have manifested a warm approbation of that of the Colonizing Society. They have, in several instances, formed themselves into auxiliary associations, and have otherwise contributed to the promotion of the great object of this Society. Their co–operation was wanted to complete the circle of moral exertion. They are entitled to our grateful thanks. It is to propose the expression of them, in the shape of a resolution, that I have now risen.

Mr. President, we have a cause inherently good. It is supported by some of the best, the most virtuous, and eminent men in our country. The Clergy, of all denominations, almost unanimously support it, and daily offer up their prayers for its success. Our fair countrywomen give us their cheering countenance and encouragement. The God of Heaven, (he believed from his very soul) is with us. Under such auspices, we cannot fail. With zeal, energy, and perseverance we shall subdue all difficulties and ultimately realize every hope.

He offered the following resolution:

Resolved, That the cordial thanks of this Society be presented to our fair countrywomen, who contribute by their countenance, association, and their donations, to the success of the Society.

Printed. American Society for Colonizing the Free People of Color of the United States, *The Twelfth Annual Report....* (Washington, 1829), x–xi.   1. For the names of the members of the Board of Managers, see *Twelfth Annual Report,* xvi. An account of this meeting was carried in the Washington *Daily National Intelligencer,* January 26, 1829.   2. For the formation of these two state societies, see J. Winston Coleman, Jr., "The Kentucky Colonization Society," *RKHS* (January, 1941), 39:1–9; and Beverly B. Munford, *Virginia's Attitude Toward Slavery and Secession* (New York, 1909), 63–5; also, Clay to Gurley, October 18, 1828.

To WILLIAM TUDOR, Rio de Janeiro, no. 10, January 20, 1829. Discusses receiving a protest concerning the seizure of the brig, *Budget,* out of Baltimore, by the Brazilian squadron near Montevideo last August; also, its subsequent condemnation by the Prize Court there. States that the owners of the *Budget* [G. B. Wilson and Co.] deny any intention to violate the blockade of the La Plata River. Adds that, according to their explanation, the *Budget* had discharged part of its cargo at Rio de Janeiro and had sailed to Montevideo when it "struck upon the bank going into the La Plata, in a violent gale, and lost her rudder, that she was actually in sight of Montevideo" when seized. Orders an investigation of this incident and "official interposition" if it is concluded that the owners are entitled to an indemnity. Copy. DNA, RG59, Dip. Instr., vol. 12, p. 182 (M77, R7).

In a letter to Clay of January 16, 1829, Congressman John Barney of Maryland [*BDAC*] had enclosed a letter to himself from G. B. Wilson and Co., giving the facts of the case and protesting the seizure of their vessel. He asked that Clay write Tudor and instruct him to seek redress for the loss of the *Budget.* ALS. DNA, RG76, Misc. Claims, Brazil.

From HENRY CLAY, JR.   West Point, N.Y., January 21, 1829
I have received your letter of the 14th instant. By it all my fears are quieted; and I can now look forward to something honorable. You can hardly conceive of a more wretched state than that in which I was before this letter was received. I have always had an inclination for the law, which arose from an entire conviction that it was the path which led to

distinction. When, therefore, it was first proposed to me to come to West Point, I thought that I saw all my hopes blasted forever, and, though I desired to acquire the education given here, yet I must confess to you that I looked upon my stay at this place with a kind of horror. But now that I see that your intentions have all along been in unison with my wishes, I feel sensibly how much I have erred in the supposition, too hastily formed, that you purposed that I should become a member of the army. Feeling as I now do, I can not but beseech you to forgive me for the uneasiness which my but half-suppressed discontent must have caused you.

Copy. Colton, *Clay Correspondence*, 4:218-9.

From JOHN M. MACPHERSON, Cartagena, Colombia, January 21, 1829. Reports that General Francisco Santander has been moved from his prison confinement in Cartagena to the custody of General Jose Antonio Paez in Puerto Cabello. Notes that Paez and Santander are mutual enemies and concludes that the change will not bring more lenient treatment for Santander. ALS. DNA, RG59, Cons. Disp., Cartagena, Colombia, vol. 1 (M–T192, R1). No date of receipt.

From ROBERT SCOTT, Lexington, January 22, 1829. Acknowledges receipt of a letter from Clay of January 8, 1829. Encloses "an expose of the business of S[cott]. H[enley] & Co. for the last year" which while "not disastrous," is "quite discouraging and pretty much what I have anticipated for some months past." Discusses production costs. ALS. DLC–TJC (DNA, M212, R13).

That things had not gone well for the company [see Scott to Clay, January 11, 1828] is evident from the firm's financial report for the period January 2, 1828 through July 9, 1828. During this period the infusion of new, private capital in the amount of $5,500 brought the company's cash balance up to $13,779.08. Expenditures, however, totaled $12,838.76. These included $2145.92 in "Charges pd for Looms, Wheels etc. and for support of Negroes, their cloathing pd"; and $5281.61 for the purchase of hemp. Cash on hand came to $940.92. Assets, including cash on hand, were $14,664.09. These included "All the machinery, which if we quit the business at the end of the year would not produce more than 200 or 250.$"; also, "5 Negroes which cost 1802"; and "662 p[iece]s Bagging of 53 yds each 35,086 yds @20¢"—7017.20. Even with the infusion of the new capital, the firm was barely breaking even as of mid–1828. AD, in Scott's hand. DLC–TJC (DNA, M212, R16). The document dates *ca.* July 10–15, 1828.

From RICHARD HENRY LEE   Leesburg, Va., January 23, 1829
When I last enjoyed the honor of your company, I took the liberty of asking the favour of you, to prepare for me, a list of all the Treaties, negotiated by yourself, and by our foreign Ministers, during your occupancy of the State Department—You were kind enough to promise me,

the enumeration I desired—I am obliged to you; for the call of my attention to the principle, you mentioned, so favorable to our Navigation Interests; and for the history of it's introduction, into our later Treaties.

Permit me to obtrude again on your attention, so far as to beg, that amid the various and important business constantly engaging your mind, you would not forget the memoranda I want—You will add to the favour, if you will attach a note to the name, etc., of any Treaty, noticing any novel principle contained in it, and elucidating the history & the intention of its introduction, and its actual or probable effect upon our National interests & national relations.

In composing the history, I took the liberty of telling you, I intend to write,[1] if I have the leisure & opportunity of writing, I shall devote no small portion of it, to the first Department under the Executive, and to the labours and character of it's Head. I say this, My Dear Sir, without any purpose of flattery or courtier-like spirit (my republican spirit is above these), but because it's concerns & the character & labours of it's officer, of the period I shall be writing of, belong to the history & glory of my country—When I again have the pleasure of seeing you, I will take the liberty of submitting it to you, whether it would be your wish, that an historian, if thought adequate to his task should take *any* notice of the false & malicious imputations cast upon you & Mr. Adams, of intrigue and corruption—For myself, I am inclined to think, that to notice them, would be beneath the dignity of history, and of your characters.

You were kind enough to say to me, that you would take some occasion to converse with your friend, Gl. [Peter B.] Porter, respecting an appointment in his Dept, which Mr. Adams had requested I might receive. I rely on the explanations *voluntarily* made to me, by G[enera]l Porter, but I hear, that Col. [Nathan] Towson[2] with whom I have no acquaintance opposes my appointment, in favour of some friend—Being absent, and the others always being at hand, I feel, that your good offices might serve me, in keeping my name (a novel one to the Gl to whom, I was an entire Stranger, until your note so pleasantly introduced me) fresh in the mind of the Secretary.

ALS. DLC-HC (DNA, M212, R3).   1. Richard Henry Lee, *Life of Arthur Lee* . . . . Boston, 1829. For Richard Henry Lee (1794–1865) himself, historian, college professor, and later an Episcopal clergyman, see Johnson, ed., *The Twentieth Century Biographical Dictionary of Notable Americans* . . . .   2. *CAB.*

From CHARLES F. MAYER, Baltimore, January 23, 1829. Inquires about the claim of Peter Cave, Jr. against the Spanish government "for his severe sufferings in person and property at Manzanello (Cuba) in 1823." States that Cave made a representation to the State Department in 1824 and was told by John Q. Adams, then Secretary of State, "that Commodore [David] Porter should be instructed to prosecute Captain Cave's claim for redress." Notes that twice he has made inquiries on Cave's behalf and on the last occasion was told that the documents concerning the case were missing from the State Department, leaving him, "to infer that no interposition whatsoever in his behalf had taken place." Asks for a more "diligent search . . . since I cannot persuade myself that Documents . . . can be irretrievably missing in the well–organized offices over which you preside." Encloses "a narrative of the facts of the case" and copies of some of the documents originally given to the State Department. ALS. DNA, RG76, Misc. Claims, Spain.

From WILLIAM H.   Woodlawn, Ga., January 24, 1829
CRAWFORD
[Asks that Clay find a government job in Europe for the Reverend Stephen Olin,[1] son of U.S. Representative Henry Olin of Vermont (see, *BDAC*), so that the Methodist clergyman can afford to take his wife along when he goes there to recover his health. "The (Methodist) Church is very numerous & powerful in this State & indeed in the Southern States. His appointment will therefore be popular in this state at least; & I presume Mr. Adams upon leaving the executive chair would like to do a popular act." Continues:]

The Contest for the Presidency has terminated as was foreseen by almost every intelligent man not actively engaged in the political Arena. Mr. [Washington] Irving wrote to me from Paris in the summer of 1827 That he had recd a letter from the Lieut Governor of Massachusetts [Marcus Morton] an old & firm friend of Mr. Adams that if Mr. Adams friends should be convinced that he could not be reelected, & they were certain that my health was restored I would Receive an overwhelming majority in New England. In reply I said that neither Mr Adams or his friends would be convinced of that fact until the ballots were counted. The result has proven the correctness of my opinion. It is entirely problematic whether it was possible to prevent the election of Genl Jackson. If the administration had treated Georgia with common Justice we should have opposed Jackson but it is possible that we should have been in the minority. By *We* I mean myself & respectable & intelligent friends.

ALS. DLC-HC (DNA, M212, R3).   1. *DAB*.

To JOHN QUINCY ADAMS, Washington, January 26, 1829. Submits copies of a letter from the State Department to the U.S. Minister in Mexico, Joel R. Poinsett, dated January 12, 1828, instructing him "to inquire into the truth of the allegation of the existence of impediments, in Mexico, to the recovery of debts due there to citizens of the United States." Also transmits Poinsett's reply, dated March 15, 1828. Reports that these documents contain the information available for the President to use in his reply to a Senate resolution of January 20, 1829 [U.S. Sen., *Journal*, 20 Cong., 1 Sess., 34], requesting information on this subject. Copy. DNA, RG59, Report Books, vol. 4, pp. 266-7.

To JAMES BARBOUR, London, no. 8, January 26, 1829. Transmits copies of correspondence between the State Department and Charles R. Vaughan, the British Minister, from May 8, 1826 to January 17, 1829, relating to cases of the impressment of American seamen by British naval officers. Details the various cases, including the impressment of two Americans from the *Pharos* of Boston by Captain D. C. Clavering of H.M.S. *Redwing;* of two more sailors from the *Juno* and two from the *Monroe* by Captain William Owen of H.M.S. *Eden,* and of two seamen from the *Telegraph* by Captain Charles Rich of H.M.S. *Harpy*. Notes that the British contention that these men volunteered for the British Navy, or desired to volunteer, is highly questionable and even if true did not justify their forcible removal from an American vessel. Adds that all the sailors had prior contracts to American ships and asserts that in all cases the "American vessels would be exposed to imminent danger, by being deprived of the seamen in question."

Instructs Barbour to "address an official note to the British Government, enquiring whether in all, or any of the instances stated in the correspondence the British officers acted in conformity with orders in the forcible seizure of the seamen." Especially wants to know if Captain Rich has any authority for his declaration that it was "not merely his general *right,* but of his especial *orders,* to take seamen Englishmen by birth, *wherever* he might find them." States: "If these proceedings have had the sanction of the British Government, you will inform it that the American Government cannot tolerate them; that, if persisted in, they will be opposed by the United States; and that the British Government must be answerable for all the consequences . . . which may flow from perseverance in a practice utterly irreconcileable with the sovereign rights of the United States. If these proceedings have taken place without the sanction of the British Government, you will demand the punishment of the several British Naval officers at whose instance they occurred, and the immediate adoption of efficacious measures to guard the navigation of the United States against a recurrence of similar irregularities." Copy. DNA, RG59, Dip. Instr., vol. 12, pp. 182-7 (M77, R7).

To HENRY CLAY, JR.   Washington, January 26, 1829
I received this morning your letter of the 21st instant, and I assure you I am highly gratified with the standing which you obtained at the late examination. You think that in being assigned the third place in mathematics, injustice was done you: but that is a very respectable standing, and one that may fully satisfy a reasonable ambition. I should be sorry that you should cherish any feeling of dissatisfaction upon the notion that you had experienced injustice. There is no mistake which a man commits with more ease than that of judging of the degree of his own merit. There is a disposition in the world to flatter a person by inducing him to believe that he has been ill treated, and then to laugh at him for complaining of the hardship of his case. I do not mean to say that any of your class are persons of that character; but I do most anxiously hope that you will not allow the slightest murmur of complaint to escape from you. Colonel [Sylvanus] Thayer has so often, and to so many persons, spoken in favorable terms of you, that I cannot doubt his disposition to do you justice.—Your standing, in drawing, is very encouraging. All these attainments, my dear Son, will prove valuable and interesting resources to you in future life. They will be of great service to you in that profession to which I am well pleased to find you are disposed to devote yourself. As I think I have heretofore told you, when you shall have completed your course at West Point, you will, in my opinion, have

arrived at the best age in human life, for the commencement of the study of the law.

Richard Shelby arrived here the day before yesterday. He tells us that you have improved a good deal in your health, and that you have grown fatter. I have not yet ascertained whether it will be practicable to get him reäppointed.

I have been confined four or five days to the house by a very severe cold, which has reduced me very much. Your mother is at the same time, unwell with the same complaint. The boys are all very well.

You must bear in mind the propriety of letting me know, before we go to Kentucky in March, how you mean to dispose of yourself in the vacation.

LS. Henry Clay Memorial Foundation, Lexington, Ky.

From LEWIS P. W. BALCH   Frederick, Md., January 27, 1829
[Seeks a recommendation from Clay for an appointment of his son to West Point. Continues:]

Since my return from Washington I have conversed with many of our friends of the first respectability. They are anxious to see you again in Congress. That is of all others, your theatre. By retirement & seclusion, you can never mitigate the unhallowed wrath of your political foes. As well might you attempt to tame the hyena of the desert, in full pursuit of its prey, or soothe the dragon of the deep famishing with hunger. But come before the nation once more, where your abilities will have their proper sphere & not be hid "under a bushel" and you must eventually triumph over a cruel relentless persecution—However I must check myself—the tide of friendship carries [?] me perhaps beyond proper bounds. I hope you will do all you can for our country, consistently with the duties you owe to an amicable family & being better qualified to decide than myself, I leave it in your own hands. We shall look for you anxiously after the Ides of March, which I pray may prove [?] more propitious to our republic than to ancient Rome....

ALS. DLC–HC (DNA, M212, R3). Balch was the son of the noted Maryland Presbyterian minister, Stephen B. Balch. A graduate of Princeton, he studied law with Roger B. Taney and was active in the African colonization movement. Thomas W. Balch, *Balch Genealogica* (1907).

To JOHN J. CRITTENDEN   Washington, January 27, 1829
I received your letter of the 16th instant. I was not aware of the existence of the neglect to write to you, on the part of other friends, of which you complain, or I would have written myself, more frequently. I do not think that you have any ground for apprehending that they have, in other respects, neglected your interests. I believe, on the contrary, that all of them have exerted themselves to get your nomination confirmed.[1] [Robert P.] Letcher has employed the most active exertions for that purpose, direct and indirect. Should your nomination be rejected, the decision will be entirely on party ground; and ought, therefore, to occasion you no mortification. I understand that the Senate is now engaged in considering a general proposition that they will act upon no nomina-

tion during the present Administration, except, perhaps, in some few cases of great emergency. I need not comment on the exceptionable character of such a proposition. It amounts, in effect, to impeding the action of the whole Government. And if the Senate were to resolve that they would not during the rest of the session act upon any business sent from the House of Representatives, such a resolution would not be more indefensible. What will be the fate of the proposition, I cannot undertake to say. There is no doubt that it is principally levelled at the appointment for which you have been nominated. Besides the general party grounds, there are two personal interests at work against you. One is that of Mr. [George M.] Bibb, and the other that of Mr. [Hugh L.] White, of Tennessee. If General Jackson has to make a nomination, I think it probable the Tennessee man will get it.

I wish I could afford you some certain information as to the probable issue of the nomination. I regret to be obliged in candor to tell you, that the more prevailing impression is, that it will be rejected. If the above mentioned proposition should be adopted, it will not be, specifically, acted upon; but if the question shall be directly put on the nomination, I cannot help thinking, (perhaps I ought rather to say hoping,) that it will be approved. [John] Tyler, [John] McKinley,[2] [William] Smith, of So. Car. [Samuel] Smith, of Md. [Richard M.] Johnson, &c. have all, I understand, been repeatedly spoken to. I had a conversation with Tyler and Smith, of So. Car. myself, from which I concluded that they would vote for you, whilst a directly contrary impression has been made upon the minds of others by the same gentlemen. I was told this morning, positively, that Tyler would not vote for you. So uncertain is every thing, you see, here! The best course for you, perhaps is, not to let your feelings be too much enlisted, and to cultivate a calmness of mind to prepare for the worst event.

LS. DLC–John J. Crittenden Papers (DNA, M212, R20). 1. Crittenden was nominated for the Robert Trimble seat on the U.S. Supreme Court on December 17, 1828. On February 12, 1829, the Senate voted to postpone consideration of the nomination. On March 6, 1829, President Jackson nominated John McLean, Postmaster General under Adams, to the seat; the Senate confirmed him the following day by voice vote. 2. *BDAC.*

To HOUSE OF REPRESENTATIVES, January 27, 1829. In compliance with a House Resolution of January 20, 1829 [*State Papers* (Misc.), 20 Cong., 2 Sess.], submits documents, including letters of Andrew Ellicott, commissioner of the U.S. for carrying into effect the Treaty of San Lorenzo el Real [Pinckney's Treaty] of October 27, 1795, a letter to the Secretary of State and enclosures dated Oct. 19, 1799, and January 12, April 5, and July 4, 1800, together with other correspondence "as relates to the ascertainment of the head or source of the St. Mary's river, or the reasons why the same was not ascertained." Regrets that he is unable to comply with the wishes of the House to see portions of Ellicott's Journal or Report and refers then to a Report of the State Department to the President on February 13, 1828, which noted that the Department had requested a copy of that Report from the Spanish government, but had received no response. Transmits also extracts of a letter from Ellicott to the State Department, dated March 23,

1800, together with the copy of a certificate from Ellicott, "concerning the appointment of Patrick Tagart to trace the line between the mouth of the Flint river and the source of the Saint Mary's," since these also come "within the scope of the resolution of the House." Copy. DNA, RG59, Report Books, vol. 4, p. 267.

From JAMES McCULLOCH, Baltimore, January 29, 1829. Warns Clay about Captain John Hammond who is attempting to interest the U.S. government in his behalf in a claim against the Republic of Buenos Aires. States that Hammond is an Englishman, posing as an American, who commanded the Brazilian privateer *Mohawk;* that the vessel had been captured at sea by Buenos Aires and later seized by Spanish authorities in Cuba; and that since Hammond is a "desperate man," it is his duty "to protect the Government from imposition." Asks Clay to keep this information about Hammond confidential. ALS. DNA, RG59, Misc. Letters (M179, R67). McCulloch was Collector of the Port of Baltimore.

To WILLIAM TUDOR, Rio de Janeiro, no. 11, January 29, 1829. Acknowledges receipt of dispatch no. 115, but states that the U.S. commercial treaty with Brazil has not yet arrived. Reports that the President yields to Tudor's desire to retire from office and return home because of ill health. Authorizes him to return home "as soon after the receipt of this despatch as you may think proper." Has been directed by the President "to express to you his entire satisfaction with the diligence, ability and address with which you have executed the duties of your mission." Adds his concurrence in this sentiment.

Instructs him to tell the Brazilian Minister of Foreign Affairs, the Marquis of Aracaty, the reasons for his departure and to assure him that the U.S. will replace him as soon as a suitable successor is found. Tells him to turn over any papers of the Legation which he does not bring home to William H. D. C. Wright, U.S. Consul, "especially . . . any documentary evidence in support of claims of American citizens upon the Brazilian Government." Copy. DNA, RG59, Dip. Instr., vol. 12, pp. 189–90 (M77, R7). Tudor did not return to the United States. He died at Rio de Janeiro on March 9, 1830.

To FRANCIS T. BROOKE   Washington, January 30, 1829
Ten days' confinement, from a severe indisposition produced by cold, has delayed my answer to your favor of the 14th instant. I am now better though I still feel much debility from the attack.

I should be extremely gratified to be able to accept for myself and Mrs. Clay your kind invitation to visit you and Mrs. Brooke at St. Julien. But I regret that it will not be in our power to avail ourselves of it. At the season of the year when we shall return to Kentucky, that is about the 10th of March, we have no alternative but to proceed to Wheeling or Pittsburg[h]. The roads on every other route, will be then almost impassible. From the present time until the period of our departure we shall be constantly occupied with winding up my official business; with packing up, sending off, and disposing of furniture; and with other arrangements for the journey.

I should be very much pleased to visit Richmond. It would afford me much satisfaction to see my friends, and I doubt not that there are many of them that would be happy to meet me: But I must own to you, frankly, that I should not expect to derive any political benefit from such a visit. The contest has been too recent; passions have not yet sufficiently abated; prejudices are yet too high and strong, to make me an acceptable guest at Richmond, where a large majority of the Legislature is of an opposite faith from that which I profess. I should, undoubtedly, find among that majority much of the courtesy which characterizes our native State—I should even, now and then, find a friend; but the great mass would be animated by a spirit positively, if not bitterly hostile. You must have remarked what I have often observed, that when a particular popular current prevails, the representatives of the people elected under its impulse, are in advance of the people themselves in violence. It is on this principle that I am inclined to think that the Jackson majorities in the State Legislatures, this winter, are more adverse to me than they will probably be at any future time.

With respect to any movements in regard to the successor of General Jackson, I believe I have already said to you that I think it would be premature now to commence them. The next six months—the next six weeks—may develope important events, and shed brilliant light upon our path. At all events, I do not wish that our friends should disturb the public in the enjoyment of that tranquillity, of which, after the late violent agitation, it has so much need. As to the danger, which some apprehend, of the separation and dispersion of our friends, I do not participate their fears. The same principles which guided them herto-fore, will continue to unite them together. In every demonstration which has been made during the present winter, (witness the Senatorial elections in Ohio, Delaware, Maine, &c.) they stand firm and unshaken.[1]

Should any thing occur to me, prior to my departure for Kentucky, as being expedient to be done, in relation to the Presidential succession, I will communicate it to you.

I received this morning your letter enclosing one for our Minister in England [James Barbour], which will be forwarded to him with the first dispatches. . . .

LS. KyU. Letter marked "(Confidential.)"   1. The successful campaigns for the U.S. Senate of Jacob Burnet of Ohio, elected as a Federalist, John M. Clayton of Delaware, elected as a National Republican, and Peleg Sprague of Maine, also elected as a National Republican. For these men, see *BDAC*.

To **ELISHA WHITTLESEY,** January 30, 1829. "Agreeably to your request," states "a box containing the publications for the college at Hudson, shall be put in your charge, at any time and place in the city you may appoint." Adds that it affords him pleasure "to promote the convenience of the Institution in question . . . by forwarding directly to it, instead of through the Executive of the State . . . the documents to which they are entitled." Notes, however, that the great labor involved for the Department in corresponding with each separate college normally prevents such action. Copy. DNA, RG59, Dom. Letters, vol. 22, pp. 389–90 (M40,

R20). Western Reserve College, founded at Hudson, Ohio, in 1826, was moved to Cleveland in 1882.

On February 26, Lewis Condict of the House of Representatives acknowledged a February 20 note from Clay "kindly offering to send in separate boxes, such public Documents, as by a Joint Resolution . . . were directed for distribution among Colleges." Requests, further, that the papers for Rutgers and for the College of New Jersey at Princeton be delivered to him "this week, that I may take them with me." ALS. DNA, RG59, Misc. Letters (M179, R67). For Clay's note of February 20, see DNA, RG59, Dom. Letters, vol. 22, p. 406 (M40, R20). For the "Joint Resolution," see 4 *U.S. Stat.*, 321.

From HENRY CLAY, JR.   West Point, N.Y., February 1, 1829

I have this moment received your letter of the 26th. inst [*sic,* ulto.]. May I be permitted to say that it seems to me that you have not taken my assertion, that I was not treated quite right at the late examination in the proper light. To judge correctly of it, you must know my situation in regard to the different members of the class and the Academic Board.   In the first place I see plainly that it will be impossible for me to rise above second in my class: The Gentleman who holds the 1st rank[1] arrived on the Point with a knowledge of most of his course; that time which I spent in thoughtless indulgences, he devoted to those studies which would best second the exertion which he intended to make at this place: Moreover he is at this time preparing himself to become a profr of the sciences which are taught here. With all these advantages, you must perceive, then, that he will have a corresponding success.

Should a standing be made out at this moment I would be 2d without a doubt. This I have from Col. [Sylvanus] Thayer and will be evident to you when you know that the Gentleman immediately below me is 2d in Math. 4th in French and 15th in drawing, whereas I am 3d in Math. 1st in French and 7th in drawing. These things being considered you see that the inconsiderate expression of dissatisfaction which escaped me did not arise from any feeling of jealousy.

I Believe that the Superintendant [Sylvanus Thayer] entertains some friendship for me, for though my imprudent and criminal conduct[2] before I entered the Acady gave him no reason to like me, but on the contrary, full cause to dislike me; Yet my exertions to cancel the ill effects resulting from it, I hope, have in part succeeded: But that the Profr to whom I lately recited was an impartial man I cannot believe, or rather I think that his indolence was such that he was prevented by it from justly discriminating between the merits of his section: However had I thought one moment before I wrote my last letter I should not have uttered one word of complaint, for I am but too well convinced of the truth of your remark, that there is not a mistake which a man commits with more ease than that of judging erroneously of the degree of his own merit, and Hence no one should be more carefully guarded against. The conclusion at which I arrived, and was thoughtless enough to mention to you was that of my own unassisted judgement: It is true that I supposed that it received some confirmation from the opinions of others. I was not the only one that we all thought should have been above the Gentleman who was placed 2d in Math—Hence I could not have been selected as the butt for the jests of my classmates. But setting this aside, my standing among my fellows as a man, for here we all are men, is such as to repel the idea. I know, my dear father, that this was not your meaning, and that you were merely desirous of warning me against a too ready assent to the views of all those who might wish to lead. Yes! I wholly agree with you, no man is so contemptible as he who is ready to follow, and to engage in criminal or even in virtuous pursuits without first consulting his own good sense and prudence. After all, whether I have been justly or unjustly treated, my suspicion will be of advantage to me, for I now conceive that in order to justify it, every exertion should be made on my part to show that at all events I have the capacity to be higher. Every thing is now favourable to a correct decision A transfer of Profrs has been made in the Math. department and I now have one, who I think, is an able one; Besides I assure you my emulation has not been abated. I have written so much about the unfortunate expression of dissatisfaction which in an unguarded moment escaped from me, because I imagine that were I to give way to all the little feelings of jealousy or resentments of supposed injury done me, I should be unworthy of being your son; and [were] you to entertain such an opinion of me as might ha[ve been] conceived from my letter, All that I have been striving [to] do since I have been here would be undone—

I am much distressed about the indisposition of yourself and my mother, but I hope, that you will both soon recover and that a residence in Ky will at length reëstablish your health.

I enjoy perfect health though I am, as I have always been, very weak—I shall ask Col Thayer's opinion about the propriety of my going to Ky in a day or two I am altogether disposed to go myself—

I recd a letter from Theodore [W. Clay] a day ago and another from Anne [Clay Erwin]—They both seem to be in excellent spirits, Anne had taken a house in New Orleans.

Tell Richard [P. Shelby] to write to me often. Remember me to all the family. . . .

ALS. Henry Clay Memorial Foundation, Lexington, Ky.   1. Probably Roswell Park who was graduated at the head of the Class of 1831. He later served in the Corps of Engineers, resigned his commission in 1836, and was a clergyman from 1843 until his death in 1869. USMA, *Register*, 183.   2. Probably the incident described in Henry Clay, Jr. to Clay, May 7, 1827.

From THOMAS HINDE, Newport, Ky., February 3, 1829. Acknowledges receipt of Clay's letter of January 14. Discusses Clay's plans to resume his law practice upon his return to Kentucky from Washington. Explains and apologizes for his decision to make public a brief extract of a letter from Clay, dated December 10, 1828 which read: "It is true, as you [Hinde] remark that the die is 'cast' and Genl Jackson is Elected—whilst all reflecting men ought to deplore that Event—as Indicative, I *fear* of the ultimate fall of the Republic—We are bound to Submit—to the *will of the majority.* I yield to it with patriotic if not Christian resignation—In *private* life, to which I shall *return,* I can at least be permitted to offer up my humble *prayers* for the *good* of my *country.*" Assures Clay "I never heard any other expression, than that of approval as to the expression of yr sentiment in this Extract." Also informs Clay that immediately after the publication of the extract a report spread throughout Ohio "that the Kentuckians were preparing to meet you in greater triumph, than if you had individually succeeded to the presidency—." Cautions, however, "The fact is this—We must look upon things as they are—: Genl Jackson has acquired *Military fame.* The rush to the polls on this occasion, has been from a certain class of people from the best of motives: Gratitude as they conceive toward Genl Jackson for Conspicuous & patriotic Services rendered the nation. In doing this, they lost sight of persons who had stood at the helm and managed the whole *Concern,* and not a military District—yet this course tho' from the best of motives, has set a most dangerous *precedent.*" At the same time, believes that public short-sightedness on the dangers of Militarism has happened before in the nation's history, that even George Washington's cabinet was dominated by "warriors." Congratulates Clay for "bringing *John Quincy Adams* to the Presidency" and argues "if you sustain any degree of *temporary* depression in your political fame you have done an act for which the Republic will Son thank you—and in proportion to the blunders of the approaching administration that of *yours* & Mr. A's will rise in proportion." Is convinced Jackson's "difficulties will be with his own party, and his troubles among his own household. perhaps it is best it is so—His success may have saved the nation from insurrection, rebellion & national division. All the troubles of the *nation* will be in the hands of the new administration, and they will make trouble *enough,* for one *another.*" Expresses regret that he had made public the extract from Clay's letter. "If I have done wrong, *I* must bear it." Reports that he was publicly chastised for thus revealing that he was "corresponding with Conspicious characters," and that the criticism merely proves "you are not dead yet!" ALS. DLC-HC (DNA, M212, R3).

From BENJAMIN PARKE, Salem, Indiana, February 4, 1829. States that he had hoped after the election of 1828 to be able to congratulate Clay "on the success of our friends," but reports instead that the "General [Jackson] passed up the [Ohio] River a short time since on his way to the City [Washington]." Believes "His election may be considered among the wonders of the present time, and possibly affords a precedent that may be the scourge of the times to come." Attributes Jackson's success to "the *espirit de corps* of our military officers, operating upon the gratitude of the public for his military services,—much to the idea artfully disseminated, that the people were defrauded of their choice by the House of Representatives [in 1824]—and a great deal to the unrighteous clamour of a factious opposition." Predicts that public opinion will shift against Jackson. Assures Clay that "as you have been identified, for many years, with all the great leading measures of the Government, your public services cannot be forgot—a re action in public Sentiment must take place—and in less than four years you will be the most popular man in the Union—" ALS. DLC-HC (DNA, M212, R3).

From SYLVESTER S.   Providence, February 6, 1829
SOUTHWORTH

We are making a powerful effort in this State, to introduce a Liberal and
General mode of Suffrage.[1] We propose to be as free as Kentucky. Will
you have the goodness to give me your Views on the subject, and allow
me to place them before the public?—[2]

ALS. DLC–HC (DNA, M212, R3). Letter marked "Private."   1. Rhode Islanders at this
time were considering the reform of the state suffrage law of 1798 which limited the right
to vote to those persons who owned property in the amount of $134. For the protracted
struggle over this issue, see Earl C. Tanner, *Rhode Island, A Brief History* (Providence, 1954),
42; and Peter J. Coleman, *The Transformation of Rhode Island, 1790–1860* (Providence,
1963), 267–8, 285.   2. Southworth was Editor of the Providence *Literary Subaltern*.

From LUKE TIERNAN, Baltimore, February 6, 1829. Encloses the protest of the Captain of the brig *President Adams* out of Baltimore. States
that the vessel was fired upon and captured by Brazilian naval authorities near Montevideo, and was "run ashore and lost." Notes that
documents relating to the case were placed in the hands of William
Tudor at Rio de Janeiro with instructions to seek payment for the loss.
Requests that Tudor be urged to proceed with a claim against the Brazilian government. ALS. DNA, RG76, Misc. Claims, Brazil. The enclosed
protest of Captain Albert P. de Valangin estimates the loss at $57,403.13.

From JOSEPH MORRIS, Mobile, February 7, 1829. Complains, as master and part owner of the schooner, *Widow's Son* of Elizabeth City, North
Carolina, of the treatment he received from Spanish authorities in Cuba
during "a late voyage." Explains that he was "obliged to put in at Saint
Iago [Santiago] Cuba in distress for water" and that upon returning to
his ship with the water, he was "arrested . . . incarcerated in a Dungeon,"
given 50–55 lashes with a whip, and plundered of his money. After
paying port duty at Santiago and "after having been detained for many
days," he was returned to his ship and "put again to sea." After being at
sea some days, he "was overtaken by a storm" and forced to put in at the
port of Trinidad, Cuba, again in distress. Asserts "as if by concert between the officers of the two places he was again subjected to port &
other charges and treated with the grocest indignities." States that his
cargo of salt was damaged and asks for "the aid of the Genl Government
in getting redress for his damages." Encloses a 13–page, notarized
statement together with his claim of $790.17 against the Spanish gov-
ernment. ALS. DNA, RG76, Misc. Claims, Spain.

From JAMES ERWIN, New Orleans, February 8, 1829. Reports that
since his last letter [January 6, 1829] "there has been considerable fluc-
tuation in our market" with flour advancing to $8.25 and then declining
to $7.50. Expects that because a large part is being held in speculation,
"we have every hope to believe there will be a further advance in price."
Notes, however, that it is a "dangerous" game and says he would always
be willing to sell "at a moderate profit."

States that Rene Trudeau has sold his plantation which will necessi-
tate payment of George Mather's bonds [5:1019–20] in order to clear the

title. Inquires how to invest the Mather money if this should happen. Points out that it can be invested at ten percent in "paper secured by a mortgage on [New Orleans] property worth two times the amount," or in local bank stock yielding eight to nine percent. Mentions that Anne [Brown Clay Erwin] and the children [Henry Clay and James Erwin] are doing well and they all "expect to meet you at Ashland in June." ALS. DLC–TJC (DNA, M212, R13).

From LUDWIG NIEDERSTETTER, Georgetown, D.C., February 8, 1829. States that the King of Prussia, Frederick William III, has ratified the treaty signed by the U.S. and Prussia on May 1, 1828, and that the document has arrived in New York. Proposes further negotiation on "certain stipulations left in suspense, relative to the rights of Neutrals and applicable during war, conformably to the last paragraph of the twelfth article of the same treaty." Expresses regret that President Adams feels this must be postponed as it is "too near the end of the session of Congress." Requests an official, written interpretation of the twelfth article of the treaty which Clay had verbally given him at their last conference, so that he might communicate it to his government. ALS, in French, with trans. in State Dept. file. DNA, RG59, Notes from Prussian Legation, vol. 1 (M58, R1).

Clay acknowledged this letter on February 14, 1829, pointing out that the adjournment of Congress in early March might make it impossible to complete negotiations on an adjustment of the wording of a clause in Article 12. Assures Niederstetter, however, that "no obstacle will exist" after March 4, 1829, to continuing the negotiations. Explains further his and Adams's understanding of Article 12 as it stands. Copy. DNA, RG59, Notes to Foreign Ministers and Consuls, vol. 4, pp. 144–6 (M38, R4). Niederstetter's concern over the semantics of Article 12 of the 1828 treaty had to do with the wording of the principle expressed in that article as compared with that found in earlier incarnations of it in the U.S.—Prussian amity and commerical treaties of 1785 and 1799. Specifically, the 1785 version permitted either power, as a neutral, to trade freely with the enemies of the other in time of war. Citing President Adams on the point, Clay explained to Niederstetter that if either signatory had concluded treaties with third parties since 1799 which conflicted with the free ships make free goods principle, "the engagements contracted with such third powers would have full effect, notwithstanding the incompatibility of the revived articles." Clay further explained that Adams considered this a "necessary precaution" for both powers, even though he saw no conflict between the article and "the stipulations of any other Treaty concluded between the United States and a third power." See and compare Parry, *Treaty Series,* 49:341–2; 55:25–6; and 78:288–9.

Niederstetter replied on February 15 that Clay's explanation "will be entirely satisfactory to his Government." ALS, in French, with trans. in State Dept. file. DNA, RG59, Notes from Prussian Legation, vol. 1 (M58, R1). Ratifications of the treaty were not exchanged until March 14, 1829, ten days after the Adams administration had left office.

To HENRY CLAY, JR. Washington, February 9, 1829

I received your favor of the 1st. instant. I am afraid you took too seriously my remark, thrown out by way of caution, in respect to the injustice done you in the position assigned you in the class. It is quite likely that you may have ground for some dissatisfaction; but my intention was to guard you against any manifestation of your feelings. The world does not approve of complaints which emanate from one's self as to the intellectual rank which is assigned him. I knew your general discretion, and my only purpose was to fortify it by the advice of your father and friend.

Why should you despair of the first honor? The young gentleman [Roswell Park], your competitor, has great advantage; but there is nothing which we cannot do when we are firmly resolved.

You asked me in a former letter what I mean to do after the 4h. of March. I shall return to Ashland leaving here between that and the 10h. and I shall reserve f[or] my retirement at home the consideration of the ques[tion] whether I shall again embark in public life.

Richard [P. Shelby] left here two days ago for [the] Point He has the assurance of a re–appointment.

My health has not been as good of late at it was in the early part of the Session.

ALS. Henry Clay Memorial Foundation, Lexington, Ky.

From MATHEW CAREY Philadelphia, February 10, 1829

If in the hurry & turmoil of public life, you can find a moment of leisure, it will highly gratify me if you can furnish me with any materials for the publication referred to in the annexed circular.[1]

It cannot but be satisfactory to you to learn the opinion of a man who never once . . . [ms. torn, word or words missing] his life sacrificed truth to compliment or politeness, and who conscientiously believes, that no individual was ever more calumniously or unjustly assailed than you have been—& that shameful calumny was never more completely & unanswerably put down—& I deeply regret, to so little purpose.

ALS. InU. 1. A printed solicitation for information and comments that Carey intends to use in a series of essays dealing with the proposition: "It is self evident, that as man is an imitative animal, the dissemination of striking instances of the social virtues, charity, generosity, liberality, gratitude, heroism, public spirit, &c. cannot fail to have a salutary tendency, by exciting a spirit of emulation, and approximating the human character to that standard of perfection at which it is frequently exhibited in history." The book he was writing was Mathew Carey, *Miscellaneous Essays*. . . . Philadelphia, 1830.

From THEODORE W. CLAY Lexington, February 10, 1829

I received yrs of 31st Ulto. enquiring of the state of your stock. There are 9 mares in fold I believe, and the other season of the Jack besides your own amounted to $40. The Jack & Jenny & offspring are somewhat improved since they arrived, both in size & plight[?].

I would recommend you to reduce the price of a season with the Jack: $3 to 4 is the highest price I believe any where in the country: and the farmers say that Jack will not justify such a price as $10. $6 for mares and $15 or $20 for Jennies would be as high as would be valuable to you. He went to 16 or 17 including 12 of yours. All the money is as good as cash. I will try and send Aaron [Dupuy] next week. He is yet in Frankfort.

ALS. DLC–TJC (DNA, M212, R13).

From EDWARD EVERETT, House of Representatives, February 12, 1829. Asks on behalf of the House Committee of Foreign Affairs, for "the Official report, or statements relative to the conclusion of the Algerine treaty of . . . 1796." States that there is "a chasm in the history of this Negotiation, concerning the Year 1794," and says that the Committee "desire[s] exceedingly to procure such correspondence of Earl [*sic,* David] Humphrey & or other public functionary, which will show the progress of the Negotiation." Notes that vol. 10 of [Thomas B.] Wait's *State Papers* takes the negotiation up to the end of 1793 and then does not mention it again until two days before the treaty was signed. ALS. DNA, RG59, Misc. Letters (M179, R67). Letter marked "Private." The "Algerine treaty of 1796" is that signed on September 5, 1795 with Algiers. It was ratified in 1796. Parry, *Treaty Series,* 52:461–72. The Wait reference is to his *State Papers and Publick Documents of the United States . . . in Ten volumes . . . 2d edition . . . Including Confidential Documents Now First Published.* Boston, 1817.

From JAMES BROWN, Paris, February 13, 1829. Discusses his health. With reference to the Presidential election of 1828, notes: "I am happy to find that you have borne your disappointment and loss of place with so much true philosophy. If you have lost your office you will regain your health and improve your fortune and therefore I think you may felicitate yourself on the result. I hope as you love a little agitation you will obtain a seat in the House of Representatives, where your weight of talents will be felt and where by resuming your cheerfulness and former popular measures you will again fill a high place in the esteem of the Nation. The outs have acted wisely in resolving not to set up opposition until the new Administration shall have done something which merits opposition. My own opinion is that the new President will disappoint both his friends and his enemies—that he will eject very few persons from office—that he [will] appoint a strong and intelligent cabinet and act in a spirit of wisdom and moderation. I am sure you love your country too much to wish that my expectations may be disappointed."

Discusses British and Austrian diplomatic efforts to prevent another Russian campaign against Turkey and believes "Russia too would seem disposed for peace." Relates details of the flight of Portuguese refugees opposed to Miguel's regime to Terceira in the Azores and their harassment en route by a British warship. Fears "an American Ship which sailed from Havre with one hundred of these unfortunate persons on board may on her arrival at Terceira experience similar treatment." Comments on his wife's improved health and the "brilliant parties" they have recently attended. Concludes with the complaint that "Some few of our country men and country women are not easily pleased and not contented with all you can do for them at your own house insist on being presented at places where you have no right to introduce them. The

617

number of these ambitious and difficult persons is inconceivable and in general I hope to have given satisfaction to the great mass of my fellow citizens. At all events I have done all I could with my limited means, and have I believe kept up an establishment as good at least as has been kept by any former Minister of my country." ALS. DLC–HC (DNA, M212, R3). Printed in *LHQ*, 41:1140–2.

From BARBARA O'SULLIVAN, Philadelphia, February 13, 1829. Declares her friendship and admiration for Clay and reminds him that "many months back I gave you my opinion respecting the Election." Notes that she was correct in predicting the outcome. Because "of my *unusual* dress, I mixed much among the mass, and had positive grounds to build my opinion on."

States that "In the former Election you most assuredly sacrificed your interest to your love of your country's good," and argues that his "former enmity to Mr Adams" on the subject of U.S. policy toward Great Britain on the eve of War of 1812 had hurt his cause in 1824. Believes, however, that his future presidential prospects remain bright. Adds that Clay is not the only person to be treated unjustly, pointing out that the Senate, out of "party spirit," is squabbling over the appointment of Judge Joseph Hopkinson, a man of great talent, patriotism, and virtue. Asserts that the charge that Hopkinson is a monarchist is a "falsehood."

Discusses Mrs. Shedden's School on Pennsylvania Avenue and suggests that "if your Lady has an opportunity to Influencing the prosperity of Mrs. Shedden's school" she do so. Also requests Clay to do all he can to promote Hopkinson's nomination. ALS. DLC–HC (DNA, M212, R3). The widow Shedden ran a seminary for young ladies on the south side of Pennsylvania Avenue between 10th and 11th Streets.

From JONATHAN ROBERTS, Reedsville, Pa., February 14, 1829. Is convinced that "There must be an ebb ere long," because "There is nothing sound in Jacksonism." Believes the Jacksonians "will take their own course," and predicts "they will be decreased in their strength & they will hasten a crisis." ALS. DLC–HC (DNA, M212, R3).

From FRANCIS T. BROOKE   Richmond, February 15, 1829
I received your letter Sometime ago, and should have impugned to you my regrets that it, disappointed my hopes of again Seeing you before you went to Kentucky—but I have nothing to offer against your reasons assigned on it, but my feelings which though Stronger than your reasons, could not be weighed against them, Since then nothing has occurred here worth communicating except what you have Seen in the papers—until the report of the committee on the Georgia & S Caroa. resolutions[1] which also you have by this time in the papers, it has excited among the friends of the Tariff more activity and my friend Jo[seph C.]. Cabell & myself have been getting up, an answer to it,[2] and a defence of Mr [James] Madisons letter, it consists of a publication of Mr Madisons Letters in Pamphlet form[3] with an appendix containing extracts from Gen Washingtons messages Mr Madisons Speeches, Mr Jeffersons re-

ports & Messages, & letter to Austin,[4] and especially from his report on the Fisheries, which comprehends the foundation on which you have been erecting the edifice for what you have been applauded by Some and abused by others—as soon as it comes from the press I will send you a copy of it, it will place Mr Jefferson along side of Mr Madison clearly in Support of your policy and not Govr [William B.] Giles & [Thomas] Ritchie, as regards the report of the committee here, you will rightly say that it was unnecessary—for certainly there is nothing in its, matter or manner worthy of a reply in times gone by—but farewell to them we are in a new and wonderful age, when the Pigmy takes the giant by the beard, and is not afraid, when vice laughs virtue out of countenance, and Giles & Ritchie take the field against James Madison &c &c. . . . [P.S.] Mr J Cabell presents his cordial regard & high respect to you—

ALS. DLC-HC (DNA, M212, R3).   1. A Select Committee of the Virginia General Assembly, had just reported that each state had the right to interpret the Constitution of the U.S. for itself. It condemned the Tariff Act of 1828 as "not authorized by the plain construction . . . of the Constitution" and called for its repeal. Richmond *Enquirer*, February 14, 1829. For the "South Carolina Exposition and Protest," and a similar reaction to the Tariff of 1828 from the Georgia legislature, see Houston, *A Critical Study of Nullification in South Carolina*, 79; Coulter, *A Short History of Georgia*, 230; "Memorial Addressed by the General Assembly of the State of Georgia . . . on the Subject of the Late Tariff," in Washington *Daily National Journal*, December 30, 1828. See, also, Clay to Brooke, February 21, 1829.   2. Joseph C. Cabell, *Speech on the Anti-tariff Resolutions Passed at the Session of the Legislature of Virginia 1828–9*. Richmond, 1831.   3. Brooke to Clay, January 14, 1829.   4. For Benjamin Austin, see *DAB*. Jefferson's letter to Austin, January 9, 1816, in which he renounced earlier views against the need for a protective tariff to support domestic manufactures, is in Ford, ed., *The Works of Thomas Jefferson*, 11:500–05.

From JOHN J. CRITTENDEN   Frankfort, February 15, 1829

I have long delayed writing to you, because I wished to avoid that temptation to be egotistical, with which I felt myself beset while the fate of my nomination to the Senate was in suspense—I feel now pretty clear of that encumbrance, for I consider the proceedings of the Senate, of which my friends have informed me, as equivalent to a rejection—Be it so—I feel that I can smile, tho' there may be some ire mixed with it, at the political *game* that is now playing—

I am grieved to hear that you are sick—You must be well before the 4th of March—that you may all bear your parts with unconquered spirits.

I will not say of Mr. Adams & his cabinet, that in their administration, "nothing became them, like the leaving of it," but I have been greatly gratified by all that I have seen & heard of the dignity & good temper which has characterised the closing & trying scenes of the Administration—There is wisdom, & a Roman spirit, in such a course,—But stop, sir—I have said too much, I fear—for it is contrary to all the rules of those who would thrive by politics, to praise fallen ministers or their administration—

It is a constant enquiry among your friends here, "What will Mr Clay do after the 4th of March?" "What is best for him to do?" All these questions suppose that you are again to be a public man, and the only question is *when* you are to appear as such, & *how*— But no matter *when* or *how,* you first reappear, the predictions of many are confident that you are to be the next President—That is to be the finale, whatever the beginning—As to the questionable point, there is some diversity of opinion. There is a pretty general concurrence[1] that you should remain quiet for a time, to observe the course of things, & to give a cooling time to the passions that the late controversy has excited. Some who concur in this, think it would not be inconsistent with it, for you to permit yourself to be returned to our Legislature from your county [Fayette]—They say it would afford you an opportunity of that sort of familiar intercourse with the people of every quarter of the State which is alone necessary to your regaining all that you have lost in the late contests—Others say you can have all those advantages by attending our courts during the session of the Legislature—without the danger of those collisions that might happen if you were a member—collisions which might produce irritation, & in which the completest triumphs could bring you no honor—They therefore think that your first effort should be to return to Congress from your district about two years hence—I concur in this latter opinion—But after all that can be thought or said in the abstract—much must depend on future circumstances—You will have no difficulty in returning to Congress whenever you please—Of that there is no doubt—

Your presence among us will be most salutary—From our political contentions of the last four or five years, there has sprung up a spirit of proscription, which I think is utterly condemnable, & which I am sure is adverse to the general tenor of your sentiments—This spirit of proscription is no where more strongly felt than on the part of the old court men (who are generally your friends) towards the new court men who have been taught to look on you as their *enemy*—It was publicly announced by many of our State Senators during the last session, that no new court man ought to be trusted as a judge of our Court of Appeals—And constituted as our State government now is, the condition of the new court men is one of hopeless proscription,—They feel it very sensibly—And while it could not offend your friends, I am sure that nothing would more conciliate the new court party, than to know that you did not concur in any proscriptive sentiment towards them—If such is the fact, as I am certain it is from the liberality of your principles as well as from what I have heard you say, you would have opportunities enough of making your sentiments known and of contributing thereby to bring back to us a better & more generous state of public feelings—

Strong signs of disunion among the Jackson party in our Legislature, were evident before the close of the last session—[Tunstall] Quarles & his friends are much alienated—John T. Johnson was gratified, as it was most natural for him to be, at the Governor's [Thomas Metcalfe] nomination of him as judge of the court of Appeals, and as much dissatisfied at the conduct of his Jackson friends in rejecting him—And I do think there is a disposition rising up among us to lay aside all our present political distinctions & heart-burnings, & to re-unite again under the old standard of Kentucky republicanism—That old party of which you were so long the standard bearer—and would again be—Many of our old republicans, who in our late subdivisions have fallen into the Jackson party, are tired of some of their company—tired of Mr. [John] Rowan,

[John] Pope &c—Added to all this, there is a belief prevailing among many of our calculating politicians, that as Jacksonism has nothing further to atchieve, it must decline, and that in two years, there will be a Clay Party decidedly predominant in the State. This anticipation has its influence—Ben: Hardin who believes in it, declares openly for you as next President—From what I have heard, I think it probable that Tom Moore will have at his next election[2] *a formidable competition from the Jackson ranks,* who will take the field expressly as your friend, & upon that ground vindicate his opposition to Moore—And will beat him, as I firmly beleive—I know nothing of it myself, but I am told that [Benjamin] Pleasants, of Harrodsburg, will be the competitor above alluded to, & will be elected. He is a son in law of Genl [John] Adair—Judge [John L.] Bridges who is another son-in-law, & all the family, I beleive, tho Jackson men, are your declared political friends—How the old General is I know not.

Thinking it might be agreable, and perhaps not useless to you, I have endeavoured to give you a sketch of our parties & politics—And have been led into a most tedious & immeasurable letter—To shew my contrition, I will only add another line to say, I am. . . .

ALS. NcD. Letter marked "(Private)." 1. Phrase "in the opinion," following the word "concurrence," is struck through. 2. Thomas Patrick Moore, a vigorous pro-Jackson U.S. Congressman, did not run soon again. Instead, on March 13, 1829, President Jackson appointed him U.S. Minister to Colombia, where he remained until 1833. *BDAC.*

From THOMAS W. WHITE   Richmond, February 15, 1829

It is needless for me to say how gratified I was to hear from you last evening.—My attachment for you is stronger than ever, and my great regret is that I fear it will be out of my power to see you personally before your departure from Washington.

When you shall have read Edge Hill,[1] I shall be pleased to hear your frank opinion of it   I must tell you that it is from the pen of your estimable friend J. E. Heath tho' I make the disclosure to you in strict confidence. His object, and a very proper one it is, is to keep the authorship a mystery.—As I have this Morning, sent 90 copies to Pishey Thompson, you may have it in your power to promote its sale among your friends and acquaintances for me, which I hope you will do.

I enclose you the pamphlet alluded to. The old cock has engaged me to print another—subject, of course, the unconstitutionality of the Tariff—and against Madison.[2]

I am also printing a pamphlet from Madison's late letters[3]—to which will be appended much valuable matter selected from Jefferson, &c.—This is our cause—it is the cause of any American—and only I am greatly deceived it will have a most salutary and desirable effect.—The people are already opening their eyes, and the day is not far distant, when the American System will be hailed with acclaimation as of joy from one end of the Continent to the other.

I do not print this for profit—Jos. C. Cabell,[4] is at the bottom of it.—I furnish paper, composition & pass out and deliver them by the 500 and 1000 copies for 3 cts per copy.—It will make as much as 24 large

octavo pages. They ought to be distributed throughout the whole Southern County.

ALS. DLC–HC (DNA, M212, R3).   1. *Edge–Hill, or The Family of the Fitzroyals*, a two-
volume romance of Virginia plantation life published anonymously by James Ewell Heath
in 1828. For Heath, see *DAB*.   2. Enclosure not found; pamphlet reference obscure.
But see comment on "Giles & Ritchie . . . against James Madison" in Brooke to Clay of this
date; and Brooke to Clay, March 3, 1829.   3. *Letters on the Constitutionality and Policy of
Duties, for the Protection and Encouragement of Domestic Manufactures*. By James Madison, late
President of the United States. Richmond, printed by T. W. White, 1829.   4. Brooke to
Clay, January 14, 1829.

From JAMES CALWELL
White Sulphur Springs, Va.,
February 16, 1829

As the time is drawing near when you will be preparing for leaving
Washington I have no doubt you are allready tired out with seeing the
worshipers of Military renown indeed it has been most wonderfull, its
calamitious effects I fear will be memorable, the friend[s] of the Genl.
and those that are looking forward to succeed him—will keep a watchful
Eye upon you perhaps you may think that it is time enough for your
friend[s] to begin to look out but be assured Sir [that] that alone was one
of the great causes of the defeat of Mr. Adams the friend[s] of the admrn
was too slow & long taking their stand they let the combination be
formed & the mind of the people made up is verry hard afterward to
change, you know how important it is to be in the bustle where offices is
given out—from the highest to the lowest it is something like directors of
Money after helping them selves of any left divide with customers—your
friends of course wait with anxiety for some movement the sooner you
return to the capitol the better that is the opinion of your humble friend,
I hope you know him well enough to believe they are honest if they
should not be correct—we have at length got to the time that Mr. Jefferson spoke of in his inaugural address[1] the moments of error & we should
be trying as soon as possible to retrace our steps I shall be glad to hear
from you before you leave Washington if the roads remain as good as
they now are I think this would be as good a rout as any & much the
nearest what would give me more pleasure than to afford you a half way
return place.

ALS. DLC–HC (DNA, M212, R3).   1. Richardson, *MPP*, 1:324.

To U.S. CIRCUIT COURT
FOR THE DISTRICT OF COLUMBIA
Washington,
February 18, 1829

I have received this morning a copy of the petition, filed in the Circuit
Court by my slaves, and I transmit, herewith, an answer to it,[1] which, for
obvious reasons, I wish put upon the file of the Court. I suppose I would
have a right to do that independent of any call upon me in the petition
itself: But the petition expressly requires an answer from me.

ALS. MdHi.   1. See following document.

To U.S. CIRCUIT COURT   Washington,
FOR THE DISTRICT OF COLUMBIA   February 18, 1829

The Answer of Henry Clay to the Petition exhibited to the Circuit Court of the District of Columbia, for the County of Washington, by Charlotte, alias Lotty, Charles, and Mary Ann, persons of the African race, now in the possession of this respondent, and held by him as slaves.

This respondent does not admit, but expressly denies, that the petitioners, or either of them, have any right, or just claim whatever, to their freedom: That the petitioner, Charlotte, is the mother of the other two petitioners: That about twenty-three years ago, this respondent then residing in the town of Lexington, State of Kentucky, was informed that a negro man belonging to him, named Aaron, had married the petitioner, Charlotte: That she was at that time in the possession of a certain James Condon, who held and claimed her as his slave: That this respondent being desirous that Aaron and Charlotte should live together, proposed to Mr. Condon to purchase her of him, and actuated by that object, finally did purchase her, at the high price of four hundred and fifty dollars. That thereupon Mr. Condon executed a bill of sale for the woman [1:236–7], to this respondent, which he will be ready to produce to this court, whenever required, and a copy of which is now annexed to this answer: That subsequent to this purchase, the other two petitioners were born, and raised in this respondent's family: That this respondent never had the remotest suspicion that Charlotte had any title whatever to her freedom, nor does he yet believe she has any: That the sincerity of this conviction is evinced by the conduct of this respondent in regard to her: That he understands she was born on the eastern shore of Maryland; That about twelve or thirteen years ago, he brought her and her husband, as servants in this respondent's family, to this district, where she remained upwards of a year: That during his abode in the city of Washington, at that time, she paid a visit to her relations on the Eastern Shore of Maryland of several weeks duration; and again, during the Summer before this last, she visited them a period of equal, if not greater, length: That these facts are adverted to, as tending, conclusively, to shew that this respondent could not have had the least idea of her having any just pretensions to her freedom.

And this respondent further says, that he has resided between three and four years last past, in the city of Washington, and never heard of any intention to institute this proceeding until about ten or twelve days ago: That he has reason to believe that it has been instigated by motives distinct from the desire of liberating the petitioners, for the purpose of injuring and embarrassing this respondent, who expects to depart from this district, for his residence in Kentucky, in the course of three or four weeks: But from whatever motives it may have been commenced, this respondent acknowledges his subjection to the laws of the District and his obligation to obey them;[1] and he shall readily submit to such order, or orders, as this honorable Court, may, under all the circumstances of the case, deem to be just and proper.

Copy, signed. NcD.   1. On March 9, 1829, Clay assured the Court that while he would soon be taking the three slave petitioners with him back to Kentucky, he would liberate them there if the decision went against him. Clay to U.S. District Court for the District of Colombia, Washington, March 9, 1829. Copy, signed. NcD.

To JOHN QUINCY ADAMS   Washington, February 20, 1829

Mr. Clay's respects to Mr. Adams, and in answer to the enquiry which he made of Mrs. Clay, he has the pleasure to inform him that the Case of Silver[1] which was sent to Mr. A. yesterday was purchased by Mrs [James] Brown for his sister and cost

	2071 francs
Duties on the case—	258:12
total cost—	2329:12

exclusive of insurance, freight &c.

Mr. Clay is willing to take the above for the Case.[2]

ALS. MHi–Adams Papers.   1. The lot consisted of two dozen each of dinner spoons, dinner forks, dessert spoons, dessert forks, dessert knives, and tea spoons.   2. Clay was also in the process of packing and sending other household goods home to Kentucky, as well as selling other items. On February 23, 1829, he wrote Peter Force, editor of the Washington *Daily National Journal*, requesting the insertion of "the advertisement of my furniture," for publication in the newspaper from February 24 to 27. ALS. DLC–HC (DNA, M212, R6). P. Mauro & Sons Auctioneers on February 27 listed sales for Clay amounting to $2886.37. D. DLC–HC (DNA, M212, R3). The sale of his extensive wine closet realized another $405.00. Account of sale, March 12, 1829. D. DLC–HC (DNA, M212, R3). For a list of the items shipped from Washington to Lexington, *ca.* March 4, 1829, see D. DLC–TJC (DNA, M212, R9).

From MATHEW CAREY, Philadelphia, February 20, 1829. States that he has received Clay's letter of February 17 and has "examined the evidence for & against the accusation brought against you." Asserts: "You are right . . . never was one more completely disproved. The wonder has been how, under all the circumstances of the case, it has been possible to produce such a mass of evidence." Concludes: "The issue of the election proves to my mind that we are neither better, nor wiser, than republics that have preceded us—& I fear we shall, at no distant day, share the same fate." ALS. DLC–HC (DNA, M212, R3). The "accusation" was probably that of the Clay–Adams "bargain" in February, 1825.

To FRANCIS T. BROOKE   Washington, February 21, 1829

I received the last letter[1] which you did me the favor to write me, and I have since received the publication relating to the tariff, to which it refers. From the course which that business is taking in your legislature, I apprehend that a majority will oppose itself to the opinions of Mr. Madison.

After a great deal of speculation in relation to the new Cabinet, an arrangement of it is now spoken of, with great confidence. If that be executed, it will consist of Mr. [Martin] Van Buren, for the State Department,—[Samuel D.] Ingham, for the Treasury; [John H.] Eaton, for the War; —[John] Branch, for the Navy; —[John M.] Berrien, for Attorney General, [John] McLean to continue Postmaster General, or to be put upon the Bench of the Supreme Court; and, in the latter case, Colonel [Richard M.] Johnson, of Kentucky, to be appointed Postmaster General.[2] Van Buren, has, from the first, run upon all the tickets for the

State Department; and I conclude, therefore, that he will be appointed. I was at first incredulous as to the other persons spoken of as Secretaries; but I have been compelled at last to believe that they are, at least at this time, designed for those respective places.

I should be glad to hear from you after the decision of the Tariff Resolutions in your House of Delegates.[3] Let me know if there is any diminution in the number of those who heretofore opposed the power. From your silence in your last letter, I infer, as I had anticipated, that the tone of the Jackson portion of your Legislature, with two or three exceptions, is decidedly hostile to me.

LS. KyU.   1. Brooke to Clay, February 15, 1829.   2. Clay's information was correct, save that John McLean was almost immediately appointed to the U.S. Supreme Court and William T. Barry of Ky. was appointed (March 9, 1829) Postmaster General in his stead.   3. On February 21, 1829, the Virginia House of Delegates voted overwhelmingly for resolutions condemning the Tariff Act of 1828 and asserting its unconstitutionality. The Senate followed suit on February 24. Richmond *Enquirer*, February 26, 1829.

From NATHANIEL CHAPMAN

Philadelphia,
February 22, 1829

I have been disabled by a rheumatic affliction of my hand from sooner answering your letters. I have even immediately directed a box of pills, with one of the ingredients in mass, which I was apprehensive might not elsewhere be present of such good quality to be transmitted to you by mail, which, I hope, were duly received. Annexed, you will also find a prescription for the preparation of the pills.

Your letter was shown to Dr. [Philip S.] Physick who unites with me in sincere regret, that your health is not more improved, though released as you will soon be from the cares & vexations of office, we confidently believe in its entire reestablishment. Need I renew to you the assurances, which on the part of Dr. Physick I am specially instructed to give, of the happiness we should derive from seeing you, and once more applying our attention to your care. Why can you not escape from the approaching turmoil at Washington and appropriate a few days for us? There are some reasons, independently of the consideration of health, to induce you to visit this city, where, as a public man, you will be cordially entertained. You have among us many more warm & devoted friends than perhaps you are aware of, eager in the present posture of affairs to manifest their confidence & attachment.

I return the check which you had the goodness to enclose to me. On consultation with Dr. Physick, we at once determined to do so. There were circumstances in your case, which take it out of the professional mill. You will recollect that you came hither at my invitation, and then D. Physick was called in by me as my friend. As he truly says, moreover we thought your ill health owing exclusively to official labours, and bitter indefatigable persecutions, and that such was a proper occasion, on public grounds to lend you our services. These are our views on the matter, and by a just appreciation of them, we wish to escape from the appearance of indelicacy towards you. I have written this with an aching head & [illeg. word] much indisposed in bed, though with a heart full of warm &

affectionate feelings for you. I am requested by D. Physick, who called to see me a few minutes ago, to express to you his gratification at your kind remembrance of him, and to assure you of his sincere personal attachment.

ALS. DLC-HC (DNA, M212, R3).

From FRANCIS T. BROOKE   Richmond, February 23, 1829
I hasten to answer your letter of to-day.[1] The intelligence it gives of the proposed Cabinet had reached here on yesterday and filled the Jackson party with consternation. Some affect not to believe it, and some few to palliate it; you will see the vote [in Virginia] on the tariff, the minority has increased from forty-nine to 75 and would have been higher but for the absence of some members[2]—You have not drawn the intended inference from my letter there can be little doubt that a large portion of the Jackson party are favorable to you at least, this is my information from every quarter, I think the people must say with Hamlet, "Look at this picture and look at that," and for this only has been the mighty Strife, I confess I am myself disappointed, I thought genl Jackson if he could not get, splendid talents and information he at least would have brought around him great moral worth, as those who have least of it, are not insensible to its value, feeling must have superseded this instinct, I think that now his future course will not be doubtful, he must put himself into the hands of the Secretary of State [Van Buren], who will be de facto, President, &c.

ALS. DLC-HC (DNA, M212, R3). Copy with different punctuation and capitalization, in Colton, *Clay Correspondence,* 4:222-3.   1. Clay to Brooke, February 21, 1829.   2. *Ibid.;* and Brooke to Clay, February 15, 1829.

To WILLIAM PLUMER, JR.   Washington, February 23, 1829
Your favor of the 26 July last was received by me in Kentucky, amidst popular movements which left me no leisure, and which I believe prevented my acknowledgment of it. I received at the same time and perused, with much satisfaction, the address which accompanied it. I had also received the news paper containing your answer to an attempt to prove by your declarations the corruption imputed to Mr. Adams and me. For all these instances of kind attention I pray your acceptance of my sincere thanks.

Since the date of your letter events have gone very adversely to our hopes and to the cause of human freedom. Speculation upon their sources is useless, except in so far as it may enlighten the future. I have been unable to view the election of Genl. Jackson, under any aspect whatever, without awful apprehensions. Still, we have yet our liberty. And it should be our aim, by the exertion of all our energies, to preserve it, and to destroy the pernicious influence of the example which a majority of our Countrymen have passionately and thoughtlessly established. For myself I desire life no longer than I possess liberty.

We are beginning already here to witness some of the consequences of this fatal election, in the motley host of greedy expectants by whom the Genl is environed; in the vulgar, audacious and proscribing tone of the official paper [Washington *United States Telegraph*] of the new administration; and in the composition of the new Cabinet which may be considered as almost officially announced—V. Buren, [Samuel D.] Ingham, [John] Eaton, and [John] Branch the four Secretaries, in the order in which the departments are usually ranked.[1] I do not think that the present state of things can last long. Our friends, as far as I can learn, are firm in their resolutions and stedfast in their principles. If they remain so, a change must be effected. Much depends on New England. And we are accordingly looking with deep interest to the approaching Election in your State, which is considered as the most doubtful of that section.[2]

I shall return to my farm in Kentucky shortly after the 4h. of March. I reserve for tranquil consideration there the question whether I shall offer for a seat in the H. of R.

I pray you to communicate my best regards to your venerable father and to be assured that they are constantly entertained for yourself....

ALS. MB. Printed in *PMHB*, (1882), 6:356-7.   1. State, Treasury, War, Navy.
2. The election of a governor, Benjamin Pierce, and six members of the U.S. Congress "friendly to the present administration" was reported in *Niles' Register*, (March 21, 28, 1829), 36:1, 67. It was thus a Jacksonian sweep in New Hampshire. See, also, Shaw to Clay, January 9, 1829.

From LEWIS P. W. BALCH, Frederick, Md., February 24, 1829. Reports receiving Clay's letter of February 21 and thanks him for his efforts on behalf of his son. Assures him that the dinners to be given in his honor at Hagerstown and Frederick "will greatly assist your cause & tend to consolidate and unite our friends." Warns him to be prepared to make an address at both towns, but cautions him to avoid as much as possible any reference to Jackson. Notes that the ruling party at present "is flushed with victory" and have as yet done nothing Clay can criticize, so "it is vain to augment their wrath." Contends that the Jackson coalition will soon split up, because it is made up "of such discordant materials." Hopes that Clay will return to Congress in "due season," since "*That* is your theatre, & there your friends will be best enabled to rally on you at a proper period—However, this is 'entire news' [*entre nous*]." ALS. DLC-HC (DNA, M212, R3). Clay accepted several invitations to speak on his way home to Kentucky in March, 1829. The Frederick speech was on March 18; that in Hagerstown was delivered two days later. See, further, Clay to Adams, March 3, 1829.

To JAMES CALWELL   Washington, February 24, 1829
I received this morning your obliging favor of the 16th instant. You are right in supposing that I am anxious to quit Washington and be on my return home. There is nothing here, at present, to gratify patriotism. The President–elect, feeble in body and mind, and irresolute, is surrounded by a host of ravenous expectants of office, & a corps of newspaper editors, gathered from the four quarters of the world. His intended cabinet is almost officially announced. It is to consist, as is believed, of [Martin] Van Buren for the State,—[Samuel D.] Ingham for the Treasury—[John] Eaton for the War—and [John] Branch for the Navy Department. Upon such a Cabinet, comment is unnecessary.

I would return by the White Sulphur Springs but for the greater length of the land travel, and the bad state of the roads. These circumstances will determine me to go by Wheeling. With regard to my return to Congress, to which you allude, that is a question the decision of which I reserve for Ashland, where I can tranquilly weigh all the considerations on both sides of it.

My friends convey to me, from various quarters, assurances of their continued attachment and support. They are confident of yet realizing hopes which they have all along cherished in regard to me. But the most judicious of them that have spoken to me, think it would be premature to make any movement, towards the accomplishment of their wishes, until the New Administration is formed, and its course of policy more distinctly indicated. They are sensible, with you, of the inexpediency of delay. Events may happen within a short time to accelerate or retard the commencement of operations. On all these matters I consider myself as incompetent to decide, and as being bound to remain perfectly passive. . . .

LS. ViHi. Letter marked "(Confidential)." Also printed in *VMHB* (October, 1947), 55:306–07.

To EDWARD EVERETT[?]　　　　　Washington, February 24, 1829

I recd. your friendly note about the proposed Call for the Panama instructions [5:313–44], and I am anxiously waiting to hear of its being made. The principal part of the Copying is already executed. I begin to have fears that the resolution[1] may not be offered, without doubting, in the smallest degree, your kind intentions. If there be a doubt about an opportunity occurring in the House, could you not prevail upon Mr. [Josiah S.] Johnston, Mr. [Daniel] Webster or some other friend in the Senate to offer it?

If the publication be desirable, as I think it is, now is the time or never.

Why don't you apply the previous question to those interminable morning discussions of resolutions?

ALS. MHi. Letter marked "(Confidential)." Presumably to Everett, with whose papers this letter is filed.　　1. The resolution was introduced in the Senate by Daniel Webster on February 27, 1829. It asked that the President "communicate to the Senate, *confidentially and in its Executive character,* copies of the instructions given to the Ministers of the United States" to the Panama Congress. *Register of Debates,* 20 Cong., 2 Sess., 38–49, 64–70.

From NATHANIEL F. WILLIAMS　　　　　Baltimore,
February 24, 1829

This is the first political letter I have written Since the mortifying result of the late election, not that, I am dispared to Surrender the ship forever to a Mutining crew, but, I thought, & still think, the true policy is, to be calm & united for a short time at least, for it is impossible for Such a heterogenous mass to hang together if left to themselves. Altho' every Wish of my heart leads me to retire altogether from the political world, and in a pecuniary point of benefit to do so, but I have no hesitation in Saying, if I should be alive four years hence, & you should be the Candidate of the friend of Civil & religious Liberty, I shall feel myself called upon to Contribute my mite towards restoring the people, which call will not be disregarded by me. On your return to Kentucky, I am pleased to learn, it is possible we may have the pleasure to see you in this city, a pleasure that will be very gratifying to your numerous friends here.

ALS. DLC-HC (DNA, M212, R3).

From CHARLES STERETIZ RIDGELY, Font Hill, Waterloo, Anne Arundel County, Md., February 25, 1829. Analyzes South Carolina political leaders who have opposed the Adams administration, noting that "they are unprincipled Demagogues, devoid of honour or honesty and governed only by selfish motives; and are for *Men* & not measures—in short [John C.] Calhoun for himself. [George] McDuffie for Calhoun & himself & so on through the whole catalogue." Assures Clay that he, on the other hand, has "always been for measures and not men." Says he voted for Jackson in 1824, "but as he was not my first choice I was not active & felt almost perfectly indifferent when the matter was transferred to the House of Representatives, but after the [George] Kremer [4:48, 52-4]—Panama [5:277-9] & [Carter] Beverl[e]y [6:448-9] conspiracies—I again took side with my Country, or rather with her best friends & truest Patriots." Has since supported the Adams administration because "I considered Genl. Jackson as totally unqualified for office" and because "he placed himself in the attitude of a slanderer—" Notes that since Clay's "triumphant defense [6:1394-6]" against the charge of corrupt bargain was published, "I claimed the honour of ranking myself amongst your most zealous friends—" Concludes with the observation that for "the honour & good of my country, I yet hope to see you where you ought to be, at the head of a free & patriotic people." ALS. DLC-HC (DNA, M212, R3).

On December 27, 1828, James L. Hawkins of Baltimore had written Clay, recommending Charles S. Ridgely's son, Randolph, for appointment to West Point. Stated that General Ridgely "will probably be the next Representative in Congress" from the Anne Arundel County, Maryland, district. ALS. DNA, RG59, Application Papers of Cadets. Ridgely did not become a congressman. For the Ridgelys, father and son, see *MHM*, 12:236; 22:378.

To EDWARD EVERETT   Washington, February 27, 1829
In reply to your note of today, I have to state that Mr. [Charles R.] Vaughan has not addressed to me any official note on the subject of the road referred to; but he conversed with me about it, and concluded that, pending the resolution before Congress,[1] and in the uncertainty as to its passage, and as to the direction which might be finally given to the road, it would be premature for him to interpose. He would, beyond doubt, strongly interpose if any attempt should be made to open a Road through the disputed territory.

ALS. MHi. Letter marked "(Private)."   1. The Senate Resolution of January 2, 1829, inquired into "the expediency of continuing the Military Road from Mars Hill to the mouth of the Madawascou, in the State of Maine." U.S. Sen. *Journal,* 20 Cong., 2 Sess., 61. See, also, *ibid.* (January 8, 1829), 69; (January 20, 1829), 84. No legislation affecting the road was passed in this session.

To JOHN HOLMES   Washington, February 27, 1829
I have received your note under date the 25th instant requesting me to inform you "whether our ministers at Ghent would not have been satisfied to have obtained what the Commissioners under the fourth article did in fact obtain—the status ante bellum, and any particulars in regard to the Islands in the Bays of Fundy and Passamaquoddy which you recollect."[1]

I take pleasure in referring you to the Ghent correspondence published in the ninth volume of State papers.[2] From an examination of that you will perceive that the American[s] offered to the British Commissioners to treat on the basis of the status ante bellum. In their letter to their British associates under date the 24th of August 1814, they state "the undersigned to have been accordingly instructed to agree to its termination (the war) both parties restoring whatever territory they may have taken." In their letter of the 18th of October 1814 adverting to the previous note of August they repeat that they have been authorized to agree to a mutual restoration of territory—again, in their note of the 24th of October they explicitly "decline treating on the basis of uti possidetis or upon any other principle involving a cession of any part of the territory of the United States, as they have uniformly stated that *they can treat only on the principle of a mutual restoration of whatever territory may have been taken by either party.*"

These letters sufficiently establish the willingness of the American Commissioners to treat on the basis to which you allude—the small deviation from it to which the American Commissioner subsequently consented, so far as related to the mere possession of the American islands in the Bay of Passamaquoddy of which the British forces had taken possession during the war, would not have been yielded to by the American Commissioners but for the stipulations contained in the 4th article. According to these, provision was made for the settlement of the question of right, and the island of Grand Menan which had always been in the British possession and never in ours was included in the arrangement. *We thought that our risk of losing the Islands taken from us during the war by the decision of the tribunals to be constituted in virtue of that article was compensated by the chance of a decision in our favour in respect to Grand Menan. . . .*

MHi–Adams Papers, Letters Received (MR491). Unidentified newspaper clipping.
1. John Holmes [see *DAB* and *BDAC*] served as U.S. Commissioner and Thomas Barclay as the British Commissioner in the subsequent negotiations required by Article IV of the Treaty of Ghent to divide the islands in Passamaquoddy Bay and the Bay of Fundy between the two nations. This letter, solicited from Clay, was used to rebut political charges in Maine that he had given the British more territory than they were entitled to receive. At this time, Holmes was U.S. Senator from Maine.   2. *State Papers and Public Documents of the United States . . .* (Boston, 1817), 9:319–432.

From CHARLES STUART WAUGH, Culpeper County, Va., February 28, 1829. Inquires about Clay's future political plans, assuring him that he has many devoted supporters in Virginia who are "sincere in the belief that you will be at no distant day, our high Magistrate." Hails him as "the putative father of the American sistem," about which his Virginia friends will want to know more. Entreats him "to return to the council of the Nation, as we consider you the Apostle of Liberty," and asks if one of his Virginia supporters "can be of service to you, by taking a seat in the Virginia Legislature." ALS. DLC–HC (DNA, M212, R3).

From JAMES CONDON   Nashville, March 1, 1829

Your letter dated Washington 11th Feby 1829 address[e]d. to me[1] was receiv[e]d. by the hands of Mr Jno P Erwin of Yesterday; and I hasten to answer its contents.[2] you say that Charlotte or Lotty a female Slave whom I sold to you sets up a claim to her freedom & is about to assert it in a Court of Justice, that you understand her claim to be that her Mother & Grand-Mother were free. that I was only entitled to her service untill she was 18 years old; and that I had carried her from the Eastern Shore of Mary-land, and sold her illegally.

The degree of moral turpitude that would necessarily attach to the foregoing charge if sustained by any responsible accuser, would certainly be exceedingly painful to the feelings of an old Man, who has pass[e]d. a life of more than 60 years without ever having been call[e]d upon to answer before a Court of Justice. or any other earthly Tribunal for any Crime what-ever,—I infer however from the language of the letter referr[e]d to, that your information is exclusively drawn from the Slave in question hir-self. And shall now proceed to give you the information sought for. I will just add that I am happy to say my recollection of the facts of which I shall speak are as clear in my mind as if they had transpired but yesterday.

1st. you ask "was Lotty's mother free"? I answer she *was* free at the time I purchased Lotty.—2ndly "was she born free, or did She become so before or after Lottys birth? ["] Answer the Mother was *born* a *Slave* and remained such for several years after the birth of Lotty.—3dly "who did you buy Lotty of, and whose property was she when born"? Answer I purchased her of Daniel Parker then residing in Cambridge Dor-chester County Mary land said Parker resided about 3 miles from Cambridge.—*She was born his Slave*—I have a distinct recollection that the name of the husband of Lottys mother, was either, James or Ezekiel Stanley and that said Stanley purchased Lottys Mother from said Daniel Parker a short time before I purchased Lotty. You no doubt are aware that by the Laws of Mary-land (at that time) when the husband pur-chased a Slave for a wife, that she thereby became free

I became the purchaser of Lotty in the year 1795 or 96 of the aforesaid Parker, to whom I paid $100 dollars, which at that time *in that County* was Considered by every body as a very high price.—some time in the month of May or June 1805 when I came to Lexington wishing to comply with what I understood to be the law of the land, I had Lotty registered as my Slave, this was done by Thomas Wallace Esqr. in Con-formity with the laws of Kentucky.—I presume you will find the Record thereof by application to the proper office

Lotty was about 18 years old, when I moved with my family from Mary land, and such was the strict & rigid regulations of the Abolition Society at that time, that if there had been any illegal or fraudulent Conduct in relation to this woman, it would have been next to impossible to have eluded detection by that Institution.—

I must Confess that I was truely astonished at the Contents of your letter, and cannot account for the origin of this business in any other way, than that of some evil disposed person opperating upon the mind of Lotty improperly.—There is however another Circumstance that upon reflection has occur[re]d to my mind & perhaps it may have had some influence upon her mind. I did once promise Lotty freedom (when I do not now remember) but this promise was predicated upon the Condition of long & faithful services, this she voluntarily relinguished by marying Your Servant Boy Aron [*sic*]³ and by her own pressing solicitations I sold her to you. You perhaps do not recollect the particulars, but I have no doubt Mrs Clay will be able to remember, that it was with much reluctance I sold her, & in fact never would have sold her had it not been for the cause already mentioned. after she married your servant, she repeatedly express[e]d. her fears that I would move away & part her from her husband You Came to me and asked my price. I replied $400 you paid it without hesitation

I still cannot for a moment entertain the belief that any serious attempt will be made to bring you or my self into a difficulty about this matter.—If however it should turn out otherwise; I shall feel my self bound to do every thing in my power, to have the subject fully and Clearly understood.—It is now 33 Years since I purchased this Woman, many of my old neighbors & acquaintances, who were at that time knowing to all the circumstances of the purchase are now no doubt Numbered with the dead, & if evidence of that kind should become necessary it may be very difficult to adduce, I will however now refer to such persons as are probably living, and if they are no doubt their testimony would at once put this question to rest, as to where they are if still in existance. I cannot Speak with any degree of Certainty Constantly engaged for many Years as I have been providing for a Numerous family. I have not attempted to keep up a Correspondence with my old friends in Mary land. John Mobry was a Young Man who Commenced his Appreprentiship with me a short time after I purchased Lotty   I left him Carrying on the Tayloring business in the same house that I previously owned in Cambridge. Some Years ago I was informed that he had maried & perhaps is still living in that Country.—William Flint (occupation sadler) lived next door to me in that place and was well acquainted with my domestic Circumstances   Daniel Parker the former Master refer[re]d. to above, died before I left that Country   He had two sons then young Men, named Daniel & Ezekiel. where they are I know not. but was informed many years ago that Daniel had moved some where into the Country on the lower Mississippi—I think it probable that there is a record in Dorchester County Court of the purchase of Lottys Mother from Parker, by her husband before named.—You will pardon this tedious detail. I have been influenced by a sincere desire to serve you, and, to do an act of justice to my self,—I am informed that William Bond Martin is the present Governor of Mary land. If I must take the liberty of refer[r]ing you to him for information as to my Character & Standing when residing in that State,—he knew me well. I might refer you to many others there but is very uncertain whether they are yet in the land of the living, as to my character in Lexington I trust that a reference to your self would be sufficient—I have been living in this County 21 Years, & I believe I could with safety refer you to every Citizen of good standing in it

In Conclusion I have only to add that every statement I have made in this letter as fact I would at any moment be ready to depose upon oath, before any Tribunal on this Earth, or before my God If I were now in Mary land I have no doubt but the necessary evidence Could soon be had in this Case, but there I am unable to go.—Altho now an old and infirm Man, If I could be of any service, I would yet, endeavor to ride up to Lexington & see you personally—Sensible that I am rapidly approaching the borders of the Grave it would be a source of much affliction to me If I could for a moment believe that I am destined to descend into that mansion with the slightest imputation resting upon me in relation to this matter.—I shall anxiously look for further information from you.

ALS. DLC-TJC (DNA, M212, R3).   1. A native of Cambridge, Md., Condon had moved to Lexington, Ky. in 1805, and then to Nashville in 1809 where he subsequently served as police chief, high constable, and (in 1820) mayor of the town. Henry McRaven, *Nashville, "Athens of the South"* (Chapel Hill, N.C., 1949), 275.   2. See, Clay to Unknown Recipient, February 18, 1829; Clay to U.S. Circuit Court for the District of Colombia, February 18, 1829.   3. Aaron Dupuy [1:73].

To JOHN QUINCY ADAMS
Washington, March 3, 1829

I do hereby resign the office of Secretary of State of the United States, to which with the concurrence of the Senate, you did me the honor to appoint me; and I respectfully request that this my act of resignation may be accepted, and preserved on file, in the Department of State—I have the honor to be. . . .[1]

Copy. DNA, RG59, Dom. Letters, vol. 22, p. 410 (M40, R20).   Endorsed by John Q. Adams on March 3: "The resignation of Mr. Clay is accepted."   1. Clay had been invited to stop in many different places on his way home to Kentucky and to participate in events planned in his honor. On February 12, 1829, Alexander Wilson, *et al.* of Washington, Pennsylvania, requested his attendance at a dinner they planned for him when he passed through their town. ALS. DLC-HC (DNA, M212, R3). On February 18, John McPherson, *et al.* of Frederick, Maryland, wrote offering Clay "a public entertainment at this place on any day to be appointed by Yourself" so that they could "Express to you their undiminished confidence in Your wisdom as a statesman, and the unsullied purity of your public course." ALS. DLC-TJC (DNA, M212, R10). William Price, *et al.* of Hagerstown, Maryland, wrote on February 19 stating that Clay's friends in Hagerstown and Frederick would like to honor him with a testimonial dinner. ALS. DLC-HC (DNA, M212, R3). Peter Little inquired of Clay on February 24 if he planned to go through Baltimore on his way home, and, if so, whether or not he would agree to a public dinner there in his honor. *Ibid.* Samuel Barnes and M. Bradley Tyler notified Clay on March 2 that they would provide "the necessary arrangements for an escort to receive and attend you to Frederick Town" and ask "to be informed of the day you expect to reach Frederick Town, and, if practicable, the hour." *Ibid.* That same day, March 2, William Price again wrote from Hagerstown to inform Clay that the "entertainments" at Frederick and Hagerstown would be separate and that friends would escort him to Frederick and "thence to Hagers Town." Price also outlined the toasts to be offered, one of which would express support for Clay and his policies of tariff protection and internal improvements. He remarked, further, that the Hagerstown committee had also considered a toast mentioning "the heartless persecution of which you have been the subject for the last four years," but finally decided to omit "every thing calculated to frighten off any who may feel disposed to atone for the injustice they have done you." *Ibid.*

Clay left Washington on March 14, 1829, arriving in Lexington on April 6. For his journey home see, Epes Sargent, *The Life and Public Services of Henry Clay, Down to 1848.* Edited and Completed [1852] by Horace Greeley (New York, 1860), 130-1. An undated list of personal effects and furniture he shipped back to Kentucky is in DLC-TJC (DNA, M212, R19). See, also, Balch to Clay, February 24, 1829.

From FRANCIS T. BROOKE   Richmond, March 3, 1829

I am to day leaving Richm[on]d. for a few days and it would have afforded me great happiness to have met you & Mrs. Clay at St. Julien, but
as I can not flatter myself that, that event is possible I must content
myself to Say to you by letter Some few of the things on which I Should
have had a more free communication—Things at Washington to us here
Seem to open better prospects than we expected   There are very few
of the former friends of the genl [Andrew Jackson] who do not admit
that they are deeply mortified, the new cabinet is a bitter pill, and to my
astonishment men who I thought prepared to swallow anything coming
from the gen to Attract, incapacity—this and the antitariff resolutions
has and will go on to weaken their cants, indeed I hear from Some of the
meetings at court houses, that with few exceptions, there is an universal
disgust manufactured that could not have been anticipated, [William B.]
Giles and [Thomas] Ritchies attacks[1] on Mr. [James] Madison has had a
powerful effect, the pamphlet a copy of which I Sent you is grately
Sought after, a new edition is in press with Some additional letters from
Mr Jefferson to the manufacturing companies in the north, which will
add much to the effect, between you & me, there have been furnish[ed]
by Mr [William C.] Rives, but the matter which most deeply interests me
and the country is the course that it will be proper for you to take
advantagously to meet the coming change in public opinion, I think it a
plan[?] only when you return to Kentucky—if the State through its public men of both parties indicates a wish, to have your Support of the
american System which it can hardly fail to do, you must come up once
into Congress by that time I think the day of repentance will have arrived and our institutions and our long cherished principles, though lost
for *a while* in the glare of military fame may be insured, and an example
will be furnished of lasting benefit to the present & future generations,
Giles I was told this morning is in a paroxysm of rage at what is doing at
Washington, and also complains bitterly that he will again be obliged to
publish his own pamphlet[2] (as in the case in which he published also your
Speeches[3] in which he rendered you some Service,) whilst Mr Madisons
letters &c are published at the expense of the purchasers if you have
leisure let me hear from you and do not omit, the picture of things at
Washington. . . .

ALS. DLC–HC (DNA, M212, R3).   1. Brooke to Clay, February 15, 1829; White to Clay,
February 15, 1829.   2. Probably William B. Giles, comp., *Political Miscellanies*.
Richmond, 1829. The earlier pamphlet was his *Plain Matters of Fact, Undenied and Unde-
niable . . . From the Richmond Enquirer of 1828*. N.p., n.d. [Richmond, 1828].   3. William B.
Giles, *Mr. Clay's Speech Upon the Tariff: or the "American System," So Called; or the Anglican
System, in fact. . . .* Richmond, 1827. This pamphlet was a critical answer to Clay's stance on
the protective tariff and its relationship to the American System.

634

CALENDAR OF UNPUBLISHED LETTERS

Letters deemed to have little or no historical importance to an understanding of Henry Clay and his career are listed below. Copies of them are on file in the offices of *The Papers of Henry Clay* at the University of Kentucky, Lexington, and may be consulted by interested persons. The locus of the original manuscript of each letter has been included below, as has an indication of the general subject matter of each. Subject classification code numbers have been employed as follows:

1   Requests for general and government assistance, information, documents, reports, correspondence, and books.
2   Transmission of routine information, and documents, including that between and within the Executive and Legislative branches.
3   Applications, recommendations, appointments, and resignations, pertaining to government employment.
4   Acknowledgment of receipt of mail, information, reports, documents, and correspondence.
5   Correspondence and transmission of information relating to private citizens' claims on the U.S. and foreign governments.
6   Correspondence relating to routine consular functions, viz: quarterly reports, and reports concerning distressed seamen, marine disasters, financial disbursements, and consular personnel.
7   Correspondence relating to routine diplomatic functions, financial disbursements, courtesies, ceremonial proclamations, announcements and invitations.
8   Correspondence concerning military appointments, commissions, promotions, dismissals, postings, courts-martial, and admission to West Point.
9   Routine government financial correspondence and documents, viz: bills, receipts, checks, bank drafts, vouchers, and payments.
10   Routine correspondence relating to:
     a. Forwarding of mail
     b. Interviews and audiences
     c. Introductions
     d. Social invitations, acceptances and regrets, condolences.
     e. Letters of appreciation, gratitude, and thanks.
11   Correspondence relating to routine professional services rendered politicians, constituents, colleagues, friends.
12   Routine correspondence relating to:
     a. Publication of U.S. laws and documents
     b. Patents and copyrights
     c. Pardons

      d. Census matters

      e. Subject matter not clear.

13 Routine correspondence and documents relating to Clay's law practice.

14 Routine correspondence and documents relating to Clay's land, business, and real estate holdings.

15 Routine Clay bills, receipts, checks, bank drafts, promissory notes, tax notices, payments.

16 Miscellaneous

JANUARY 1828

nd To William R. Morton, DNA, 15.

nd To Charles R. Vaughan, All Souls College, Oxford, England, 16.

1 To B.U.S., Wash. Branch, DLC-TJC, 15. From Dr. Henry Huntt, DLC-TJC, 15. From Theodore Ladico, DNA, 6. From W. Newson, *et al.*, DNA, 3. From Robert Scott, KyLxT, 14. From Robert Scott, KyLxT, 14. From Beaufort T. Watts, DNA, 7. From William G. Wetherall, DNA, 6.

2 From Ninian Edwards, DNA, 2. From Christopher Neale, DNA, 3. From Ambrose H. Sevier, DNA, 3. To Samuel L. Southard, DNA, 1.

3 From John Barney, DNA, 3. From E. F. Brown, DNA, 3. From William B. Giles, DNA, 4, 10a. From Isaac Leffler, *et al.*, DNA, 3. From William Paulding, DNA, 3.

4 To Thomas Appleton, DNA, 6. To Nicholas Biddle, *et al.*, DNA, 3. To B.U.S., Wash. Branch, DLC-TJC, 15. From John Davenport, DNA, 1. From William Fowle, *et al.*, DNA, 3. From Robert W. Fox, DNA, 6. From Benjamin Grist, DNA, 7. From Edmund J. Lee, DNA, 3. From Thomas Swann, DNA, 9. From Norman Williams, DNA, 2. From Levi Woodbury, DNA, 3.

5 From R. G. Beasley, DNA, 6. From Thomas L. L. Brent, DNA, 7. From Langdon Cheves, *et al.*, DNA, 15. To James Barbour, NBuHi, 8, 10c. From Willink & Van Staphorst, DNA, 9.

6 From J. Pemberton Hutchinson, DNA, 6. From Enoch Lincoln, DNA, 3.

7 To B.U.S., Wash. Branch, DNA, 15. To B.U.S., Wash. Branch, DNA, 15. From Ezekiel F. Chambers, DNA, 3. From R. H. Douglass, DNA, 6. From William F. Thornton, DNA, 3. From John C. Wright & John Sloane, DNA, 3.

8 From A. Blondel, DNA, 3, 10a. From W. R. Higinbotham, DNA, 6, 9. From Wilson Lumpkin, DNA, 5. To Robert Tillotson, DNA, 1, 4.

9 To B.U.S., Wash. Branch, DNA, 15. From Alexander H. Everett, DNA, 9. To John Hallock, Jr., DNA, 2. From Bernard S. Judah, DNA, 3. To William Tudor, DLC-HC, 7, 10c. To Charles R. Vaughan, DNA, 7.

10 From James Andrews, DNA, 6. From Francis M. Dimond, DNA, 3. From Jonathan Elwell, DNA, 5. From Daniel Hay, DNA, 3. From Nathan Levy, DNA, 6. From William Paulding, DNA, 3. From Lewis Shoemaker, DNA, 6. From Jonathan Thompson, DNA, 1, 15. From Lewis Williams, DNA, 3. From James Witherall, *et al.*, DNA, 3. From John C. Wright, DNA, 3, 6.

11 From George Washington Biscoe, DNA, 5. To A. Blondel, DNA, 4, 10a. From John Davenport, DNA, 3. From Ariana F. Johnston, DNA, 3. To William B. Lawrence, DNA, 5. From Isaac Leffler, DNA, 3. From William Wilson, DNA, 3.

12 From Rufus Southworth, DNA, 3. From William Tudor, DNA, 9.

13 From James Lynch, DNA, 3.

14 From George B. Adams, DNA, 3, 4, 6. To John McNairy, DNA, 3. To Robert Purdy, DNA, 3. From Robert Tillotson, DNA, 3. From David Walker, DNA, 6.

15 From John James Appleton, DNA, 9. To Frank W. Armstrong, DNA, 3. To Alexander Caldwell, DNA, 3. From William T. Cogswell, DNA, 12b. To William Crawford, DNA, 3. To Lucius Q. C. Elmer, DNA, 3. From Henry Johnson, DNA, 3. From Ramez [?], DNA, 10a. To Benjamin Reeder, DNA, 3. From Isaac Stone, DNA, 6. From Bushrod Washington, DNA, 3, 10c.

16 From Dennis Davis, DNA, 5. From Samuel C. Hyslop, DNA, 3. From Samuel Mickum, DLC-TJC, 14. From John Mitchell, DNA, 1. From William Spicer, DNA, 3. From John W. Thompson, DNA, 1.

17 From Martin Duralde, Jr., DNA, 3. From Alexis Joseph Elder, DNA, 10a. From Josiah
   S. Johnston, DNA, 1, 9.
18 From Charles D. Dutellet, DNA, 8.
19 From James Brown, DNA, 6, 9. From Gabriel Moore, DNA, 3. To Thomas Newton,
   KyU, 3.
20 From Charles Savage, DNA, 6. From A. S. Thruston, DNA, 3.
21 From James Andrews, DNA, 3. From Churchill C. Cambreling, DNA, 3. From C. D.
   Coxe, DNA, 6. From John Douglas, DNA, 3, 12a. From Richard H. Wilde, DNA, 10a.
22 From Samuel B. Barrell, DNA, 2. From Elias K. Kane, DNA, 3. From Edmund J. Lee,
   DNA, 3. To Gabriel Moore, DNA, 3, 6.
23 From Thomas H. Benton, DNA, 1. To Edward Everett, DNA, 4, 5. From Thomas B.
   Reed, DNA, 3. To Charles R. Vaughan, DNA, 4, 10e. From A. E. Wing, DNA, 3.
24 From Joseph Anderson, DNA, 2. From Rufus McIntire, DNA, 5. From Benjamin
   Russell, DNA, 4.
25 From Lucius Q. C. Elmer, DNA, 3. To Richard Rush, DNA, 1, 2.
26 From Samuel K. Collier, DNA, 16. From John W. Parker, DNA, 6. From William
   Woodbridge, DNA, 2.
27 From Heman Allen, DNA, 1, 7. From John Mitchell, DNA, 16.
28 From William L. Brent, DNA, 3. From Josiah S. Johnston, DNA, 3. From Josiah S.
   Johnston, DNA, 3. From Robert Wickliffe & W. T. Barry, Fayette Co. Circuit Court,
   File 823, 13.
29 To Richard Hawes, Jr., DLC-TJC, 15. To Enoch Lincoln, DNA, 2. From Stephen
   Pleasonton, DNA, 2, 7. From James Riddle, DNA, 8.
30 From Joseph Duncan, DNA, 3. To John Mitchell, DNA, 2, 4.
31 From John Barney, DNA, 5. To Gen. Alexander Macomb, DNA, 8. From MacDonald
   & Ridgely, DNA, 15. From James Noble, DNA, 12a. From Thomas M. Rodney, DNA,
   6. From Willink & Van Staphorst, DNA, 9.

FEBRUARY 1828
[ca] From Richard Ward, DNA, 3.
 1 From J. Pemberton Hutchinson, DNA, 6. From Alexander Macomb, DNA, 8. From
   James Maury, DNA, 6, 10a. From Elisha Phelps, DNA, 1, 11. From Asher Robbins,
   DNA, 5, 6. From Benjamin Ruggles, DNA, 5. To Beaufort T. Watts, ScU, 7. From
   Elisha Whittlesey, DNA, 5.
 2 From M. Alexander, DNA, 3. From William Brown, DNA, 10a.
 3 From Samuel C. Reid, DNA, 8.
 4 To John Duer, DNA, 3. From Edward Everett, DNA, 5. From Daniel & John M. Faust,
   DNA, 12a. From Robert Purdy, DNA, 3. To Elisha Whittlesey, DNA, 5. From A. E.
   Wing, DNA, 3.
 5 From Pryor Lea, DNA, 9, 12a. To Daniel Strobel, DNA, 5. From Bushrod Washington, DNA, 3.
 6 To Reuben G. Beasley, DNA, 6. To George Corbin Washington, DNA, 10d.
 7 From Thomas Aspinwall, DNA, 6. From William Haile, DNA, 12a. From Bernard S.
   Judah, DNA, 1, 3. From Joseph Richardson, DNA, 5. From William Woodbridge,
   DNA, 2.
[ca] 8 From Noyes Barber, DNA, 1.
 8 To William Brown, DNA, 4, 10a. From George W. Kouns, DLC-TJC, 15. From Samuel McRoberts, DNA, 3. From James Maury, DNA, 6. From Josiah Snelling, DNA, 3.
   From Stephen Whitney, DNA, 5.
 9 From William McLean, DNA, 1. From Josiah Snelling, DNA, 3.
10 From Leonard Corning, DNA, 6. From James H. Forsyth, DNA, 3. From Edward
   Livingston, DNA, 3. From Joseph Ridgway, DNA, 6.
11 To Nathaniel B. Blunt, DLC-HC, 3. From John Duer, DNA, 3. From Joseph Pulis,
   DNA, 2. From Joseph Pulis, DNA, 3. From Robert Purdy, DNA, 3.
12 From Samuel Butman, DNA, 12a. From James G. Dana, DNA, 12a. From Jonathan
   Jennings, DNA, 12a. From Thomas Metcalfe, DNA, 16. From Joseph C. Morgan,
   DNA, 5.
14 From J. M. Baker, DNA, 6. From Francisco Xavier de Cato [?], DNA, 6. From David
   Crockett, MHi, 10a.
15 From George Forquer, DNA, 3. From Elias K. Kane, DNA, 3. From William W.
   Worsley, DNA, 12a.

16 From Nathaniel B. Blunt, DNA, 3. To Joaquin Campino, DNA, 7. To Stephen Pleasonton, DNA, 9. To Jeremy Robinson, DLC-Jeremy Robinson Papers, 10d. From
[Joseph?] William & May Torrey, MiD–B, 3. To Beaufort T. Watts, DNA, 7. From
William Woodbridge, MiD-B, 3.
17 From Solomon Sibley, MiD-B, 3.
18 To Nathaniel B. Blunt, DNA, 16. To B.U.S., Wash. Branch, DLC-TJC, 15. To B.U.S.,
Wash. Branch. DLC-TJC, 15. From Samuel Heap, DNA, 6. To Joseph Kershaw, DNA,
5. To Robert P. Letcher, DLC-TJC, 15. From Asher Robbins, DNA, 6. From William
Woodbridge, MiD-B, 3.
19 To B.U.S., Wash. Branch, DLC-TJC, 15. From Samuel Butman, DNA, 12a. From
Francisco Xavier de Cato, DNA, 6. From Matthew St. Clair Clarke, DNA, 2.
20 From Thomas Backus, DNA, 6. From Elijah C. Berry, DNA, 3. From Nathaniel B.
Blunt, DNA, 16. From B. & J. Bohlen, DNA, 5. From Edward Everett, DNA, 1. From
George McDuffie, DNA, 1, 5. From John C. Wright, DNA, 1.
21 From Heman Allen, DNA, 7. From Theodorus Bailey, DNA, 16. From John Bell,
DNA, 3. From James L. Hodges, DNA, 6. From Felix Huston, DNA, 3. To George
McDuffie, DNA, 5. From Stephen Van Rensselaer, DNA, 3.
22 From A. Blondel, DNA, 5. From Edward Coles, DNA, 3. To John A. McKinney, DNA,
3. From Daniel Webster, DNA, 3.
23 From Arthur L. McIntire, DNA, 3.
25 From Charles P. Butler, DNA, 3. From Matthew St. Clair Clarke, DNA, 1. To F. R.
Hassler, MH, 12b. To Richard Rush, DNA, 1.
26 To William S. Archer, DNA, 5. From Edward Everett, DNA, 2. From William Haile,
DNA, 12a.
27 To House of Representatives, DNA, 2. From Stephen Pleasonton, DNA, 9. From
Deborah S. Warnier, DNA, 5.
28 To John Q. Adams, DNA, 2. To B.U.S., Wash. Branch, DLC-TJC, 15.
29 From John Cuthbert, DNA, 6. To Samuel Larned, DNA, 3. From Richard Rush,
DNA, 2. From Philemon Thomas, DNA, 3.

MARCH 1828
1 To James Barbour, DNA, 8. To Henry M. Brackenridge, DNA, 3. From Nathaniel
Childers, DNA, 1. From I. F. Flemmish, DNA, 6. From J. E. Davis & L. Marshall, DLC-
TJC, 14. To George Izard, DNA, 3. To Henry Wilson, DNA, 3.
2 From B.U.S., New York, NN, 15.
3 From William Frain, DLC-TJC, 15. From J. Hamilton, Jr., DNA, 1, 2. From Thomas
L. McKenney, DNA, 3. To Stephen Pleasonton, DNA, 1.
4 From John Anthon, DNA, 5. From George W. Slacum, DNA, 2. From William Woodbridge, DNA, 3.
5 From Dutee J. Pearce, DNA, 3. From J. F. Sutherland, DNA, 3. From Francisco
Tacon, DNA, 4, 10a.
6 To Charles R. Vaughan, CSmH, 2, 10a.
7 To Pearson Cogswell, DNA, 3. To Edwin S. Duncan, DNA, 3. To Isaac Ilsley, DNA,
10a. From Benjamin Reeder, DNA, 3. To John S. Sherburne, DNA, 3. To Jonathan
Thompson, DNA, 10a.
8 From Robert Monroe Harrison, DNA, 6. From David Kizer, DNA, 1, 3. From W. G.
Lyford, DNA, 5.
10 From Edward J. Coale, DNA, 10a. From Kendrick Gray, DNA, 9. To Nathaniel
Pitcher, DNA, 1. From Condy Raguet, DNA, 7. From Samuel L. Southard, DNA, 2.
From Hooper Warren, DNA, 12a.
11 From Edward Everett, DNA, 1. To Carlos Rodriguez, DNA, 7. From Thomas Young
Spicer, DNA, 3.
12 From John Cuthbert, DNA, 6. To Col. J. Thomas, DNA, 5.
13 To John Q. Adams, DNA, 2. From F. & A. Brunel, DNA, 6. To Gales & Seaton, DLC-
TJC, 15. From John Owings, DNA, 3. From William Wheelright, DNA, 6. From H. A.
Worth, DNA, 9.
14 From Joaquin Campino, DNA, 7. To Charles R. Vaughan, DNA, 7. From William
Wheelright, DNA, 6. From John W. Wyman, *et al.*, DNA, 10c.
15 To House of Representatives, *ASPFR*, 6:218, 2. From Elisha Phelps, DNA, 4, 10a.
From Nathaniel Potter, DNA, 3.

17 From Michael Beyley, DNA, 3. To Henry Conner, DNA, 3. To Nathaniel Pope, DNA, 3. From George Sullivan, DNA, 16.
18 From John Blair, DNA, 1, 9. From Heinrich Janson, DNA, 3. From John A. McKinney, DNA, 3.
19 To Joaquin Campino, DNA, 4, 7. From Matthew St. Clair Clarke, DNA, 5. To Beverly Daniel, DNA, 3. To William P. Duval, DNA, 3. From House of Representatives, DNA, 1, 5. To Henry Potter, DNA, 3. From Peleg Sprague, DNA, 12a.
20 From Thomas Aspinwall, DNA, 6. From Michael Beyley, DNA, 3. From Joseph Delafield, DNA, 9. To Alexander Macomb, DNA, 8. From Alexander Macomb, DNA, 8.
21 From William Blackledge, DNA, 3. To B.U.S., Wash. Branch, DLC-TJC, 15. To House of Representatives, DNA, 2. From Felix Huston, DNA, 3. From Robert Jacques, DNA, 3.
22 From Theodore S. Fay, DNA, 3. From Nathan Sanford, DNA, 3.
23 From Peter Isler, DNA, 9, 10a. From William Taylor, DNA, 6.
24 From Joseph Nourse, DNA, 9. To Pablo Obregon, DNA, 7. To Arthur Ware, DNA, 3. From Henry Wilson, DNA, 3.
25 To John Blair, DNA, 2, 9. From W. S. Bodley, Fayette Co. Circuit Court, Box 823, 14. To Benjamin Greene, DNA, 3. From William B. Rochester, DNA, 4, 10a. From Nathaniel Silsbee, DNA, 2, 10a. To Charles R. Vaughan, DNA, 1. From Robert Wickliffe, DNA, 13.
26 To B.U.S., Wash. Branch, DLC-TJC, 15. From Thomas Walker Gilmer, DNA, 1. From Thomas H. Perkins, DNA, 6. From Ambrose H. Sevier, DNA, 1. From E. Simms, Jr., DNA, 3.
27 From Edward Everett, DNA, 2, 5.
28 To James Barbour, DNA, 8. From Ludwig Niederstetter, DNA, 7. From Isaac Roberdeau, DNA, 3.
29 To James Cooley, DNA, 7. From S. A. Elliot, DNA, 3. From John P. Gilroy, DNA, 3. From John Hepburn, DNA, 1. From Samuel L. Knapp, DNA, 3. From Thomas L. McKenney, DNA, 3. From J. Robinson, DNA, 3. From John D. Simms, DNA, 3. From George Taylor, DNA, 3. From William H. Tracy, DNA, 3, 6. To Whom It May Concern, DNA, 7.
30 From Philemon Chew, DNA, 3. From Joseph Kent, DNA, 3. From George Taylor, DNA, 3.
31 From Matthew St. Clair Clarke, DNA, 2. From Gabriel Duvall, DNA, 3. From George Bethune English, DNA, 16. To Elisha Phelps, DNA, 5. From Viscount Santarem, DNA, 7. From Ann S. Simpson, DNA, 3. From J. Simpson, DNA, 3. From Ichabod L. Skinner, DNA, 3. To Baron Stackelberg, DNA, 7. From Luke Tiernan, DNA, 3. From John S. Williams, DNA, 3. From John C. Wright, DNA, 3.

APRIL 1828
[ca] April From George Taylor, DNA, 3.
1 From Henry W. Dwight, DNA, 3. From Joseph Edison, DNA, 4. From George Howard, DNA, 3. From Peter Little, DNA, 3. From Edward Livingston, DNA, 3, 6. From Aaron Ogden, DNA, 3. From Benjamin Ruggles, *et al.*, DNA, 3. From Robert Scott, KyLxT, 15. From William H. Tracy, DNA, 3, 6. From Willink & Van Staphorst, DNA, 9.
2 From Stevenson Archer, DNA, 3. From Joshua Bond, DNA, 6. To B.U.S., Wash. Branch, DNA, 15. From John Irwin, DNA, 6. From John Jackson, DNA, 3. From James W. McCullock, DNA, 3. From Henry Moore, DNA, 3. From John Mullowny, DNA, 6. From Calvin Willey, *et al.*, DNA, 3.
3 To House of Representatives, DNA, 2, 12a. From Thomas Kell, DNA, 3. From William Tudor, DNA, 7. From Nathaniel F. Williams, DNA, 3.
4 From James L. Edwards, DNA, 2. From Alexander H. Everett, DNA, 7. From James Ray, DNA, 5.
5 From John S. Ellery, DNA, 5. From Nathan Levy, DNA, 6. To Joseph Nourse, DNA, 9. To St. John's Church, DLC-TJC, 15. From John H. Sargent, DNA, 5. From Charles A. Wickliffe, DNA, 12e.
6 From Heman Allen, DNA, 5. From David Barton, DNA, 3. From Thomas Davidson, DNA, 3, 6.
7 From William H. Hendricks, *et al.*, DNA, 3. From Jesse B. Thomas, DNA, 3.

8 From Langdon Cheves, *et al.*, DNA, 9. From William Cranch, DNA, 3. From Gideon Davis, DNA, 3. From Edward Everett, DNA, 1. From Robert Monroe Harrison, DNA, 6. From Ralph Ingersoll, DNA, 3. From George Izard, DNA, 3. From Nehemiah Rice Knight, DNA, 3. From Francis W. Taylor, DNA, 3. To Whom It May Concern, DNA, 7.

9 From C. E. Haynes, *et al.*, DNA, 3. From William McLean, DNA, 3. From N. Waterman, Jr., DNA, 9.

10 From John Gill, DNA, 1.

11 From John Peter, DNA, 3.

12 From Lewis M. M. Raison de la Gente, DNA, 10a. From Antoine Leger, DNA, 6.

14 From Richard Bibb, Jr., DNA, 9. To B.U.S., Wash. Branch, DLC-TJC, 15. To Joseph Marti y Nin, DNA, 3. From Sampson C. Russell, DNA, 3, 6. To Samuel L. Southard, CtHi, 3. From George C. Washington, DNA, 3.

15 From Solomon Etting, DNA, 3. From Henry Pratt, DNA, 5.

16 From Abraham Gibson, DNA, 6. From Kendrick, Gray & Co., DNA, 9. From Charles F. Mercer, DNA, 3. From Joseph Richardson, DNA, 5. From Robert Scott, DNA, 15.

17 From H. D. Chapin, DNA, 3.

18 From Henry Conner, DNA, 3, 4. From Charles Edmonston, DNA, 4, 5. From House of Representatives, DNA, 5. From Joel R. Poinsett, DNA, 7. From Robert Scott, DLC-TJC, 14. From Ephraim Shaler, DNA, 3. To Whom It May Concern, DNA, 7. From John S. Williams, DNA, 3.

19 To James Barbour, DNA, 8. From Stephen Kingston, DNA, 1. From Hezekiah Niles, DNA, 9, 12a. From Benjamin Ruggles, DNA, 3, 12a.

21 To John Q. Adams, DNA, 2. From Susan Decatur, DLC-TJC, 15. From William P. DuVal, DNA, 3. To James H. Peck, DNA, 3. To John Simonds, Jr., DNA, 3.

22 From John Binns, DNA, 3, 10c. From George Graham, DNA, 14. From Abner Hill, DNA, 10a. From Elisha Phelps, DNA, 3. From James Renwick, DNA, 10c. From Gulian C. Verplanck, DNA, 10a.

23 From William S. Archer, DNA, 3. From Jeromus Johnson, DNA, 3. From David Kizer, DNA, 3. From Joel R. Poinsett, DNA, 7.

24 From Beaufort T. Watts, DNA, 7.

25 From Jonathan Jennings, DNA, 12a. With Robert Scott & Ozborne Henley, DLC-TJC, 14. From Wilkins Tannehill, DNA, 3.

26 From Thomas Backus, DNA, 6. From Charles J. Ingersoll, DNA, 2. From Robert Taylor, DNA, 1.

27 From Thomas L. L. Brent, DNA, 7.

28 To William Bristol, DNA, 3. From Leonard Canning, DNA, 6. To Daniel M. Christie, DNA, 3. To James Mitchell, DNA, 3. From J. Pemberton Hutchinson, DNA, 4, 6.

29 From Edward Everett, DNA, 1. From Ralph Ingersoll, DNA, 1. To Matthew Hall McAllister, DNA, 3. From John Mountz, DNA, 2, 3.

30 From James R. Mullany, DNA, 9.

MAY 1828

1 From Reuben G. Beasley, DNA, 4, 6. To B.U.S., Wash. Branch, DLC-TJC, 15. To William Thornton, DLC-TJC, 15. From Nehemiah Knight, DNA, 1, 6. From John Howard March, DNA, 6. From Pablo Obregon, DNA, 4, 7. From Stanhope Prevost, DNA, 6.

2 From John J. Appleton, DNA, 7. From William A. Davis, DNA, 16. To Francis M. Dimond, DNA, 6. From Joseph Duncan, DNA, 3. From George W. Slacum, DNA, 6.

3 From James C. Dunn, DLC-TJC, 15. From Gabriel Duvall, DNA, 3. From J. L. Skinner, DNA, 12b.

5 To John Chambers, IHi, 3.

6 From Alexander H. Everett, DNA, 3, 6.

7 To Baring Brothers & Co., DNA, 9. From John William Fay, DNA, 3. From William B. Lawrence, DNA, 7. From George McDuffie, *et al.*, DNA, 3.

8 From John Floyd, DNA, 3. From Daniel Strobel, DNA, 3.

9 From Thomas H. Carson, DNA, 1. From Francis M. Dimond, DNA, 3, 6. From David Erskine, DNA, 6. To Albert Gallatin & William P. Preble, DNA, 3. From C. E. Haynes, DNA, 3.

10 From John M. Forbes, DNA, 2, 7. From Samuel L. Southard, DNA, 1, 9.

11 Due bills from Robert Scott, DLC-TJC, 15.
12 From Heman Allen, DNA, 4. To J. A. Brooks, DLC-TJC, 15. From James Brown, DNA, 3. From Beverly Daniel, DNA, 3. To Robert Oliver, DNA, 5, 10a. From Samuel F. Vinton, DNA, 1.
13 From Thomas Pennant Barton, DNA, 3. From A. Blondel, DNA, 10a.
14 From Peter L. Parsons, DNA, 5. From John Simonds, Jr., DNA, 3.
15 From John Q. Adams, DNA, 7. From John H. Bryan, DNA, 3. From E. W. DuVal, DNA, 3. From Kensey Johns, Jr., DNA, 3. From James W. Rowland, DNA, 3.
16 To Joshua Grady, DNA, 12c. To House of Representatives, DNA, 2. To House of Representatives & the Senate, DNA, 2. From Bernard S. Judah, DNA, 3. From Aaron R. Levering, DNA, 3. From Mathew H. McAllister, DNA, 3. From G. W. Owen, DNA, 3. From James Richardson, DNA, 5. From John Sergeant, DNA, 1. From John Taylor, DNA, 9. From Richard Henry Wilde, DNA, 1.
19 From Daniel D. Barnard, DNA, 3. To B.U.S., Wash. Branch, DLC-TJC, 15. To B.U.S., Wash. Branch, DLC-TJC, 15. From William Coolidge, Jr., DNA, 3. From C.D.E.J. Bangeman Huygens, DNA, 6. From William Massicot, DNA, 5. From Joseph L. Smith, DNA, 3. To Samuel L. Southard, DNA, 1. To Unknown Recipient, PHi, 15. To Wash., Alex., Balto. Steam Packet Co., DLC-TJC, 15.
20 To John Q. Adams, DNA, 2. To Daniel Brent, DLC-TJC, 15. From Peter Hagner, DNA, 5. From Bernard Henry, DNA, 6. From J. Mason, DNA, 3. From Joel R. Poinsett, DNA, 7. From John M. Sanderson, DNA, 1. From Nathaniel Silsbee, DNA, 3. From Samuel L. Southard, DNA, 2. From William Wirt, DNA, 3.
21 From Thomas Aspinwall, DNA, 6. To B.U.S., Wash. Branch, DLC-TJC, 15. From Nathaniel Chapman, DNA, 8. From Charles Hay, DNA, 3. From Asher Robbins, DNA, 3. From Austin E. Wing, DNA, 3.
22 From William Cranch, DNA, 3. From James Mitchell, DNA, 3.
23 From Stanislas Vergara, DNA, 7.
24 From Thomas L. L. Brent, DNA, 7. From Philip Yost, Jr., DNA, 3.
26 From August Neale, DNA, 3. To Joel R. Poinsett, DNA, 4. To Joel R. Poinsett, DNA, 2, 5. From Ambrose H. Sevier, DNA, 3. From James L. Stabler, DNA, 3. From Samuel L. Southard, DNA, 1. To Edward J. Taylor, DNA, 3, 7.
27 From Robert Carr Lang, DNA, 3. From John Rowlett, DNA, 12b.
28 From Andrew Armstrong, DNA, 6. From John McKee, DNA, 3. From Joaquim B. Pereira, DNA, 7. From Beaufort T. Watts, DNA, 7.
29 To Baring Brothers & Co., DNA, 9. From Peter L. Parsons, DNA, 5.
30 From H. L. Barnum, DNA, 3. From Lafayette, DLC-Lafayette Papers, 10c. From Thomas W. White, DLC-HC, 16.
31 From Department of War, DNA, 7. From Paul Froberville, DNA, 6. From Samuel L. Southard, DNA, 7.

JUNE 1828
1 From John Mullowny, DNA, 6. From James S. Thompson, DNA, 3.
2 To B.U.S., Wash. Branch, DLC-TJC, 15. From Lewis Maxwell, DNA, 3. To Peter L. Parsons, DNA, 5. From William L. Reaney, DNA, 3. To James S. Thompson, DNA, 3. From G. Washington, DNA, 3. From Joseph M. White, DNA, 1.
3 From Thomas Finley, DNA, 3. From Bern Henry, DNA, 6. From Joseph Karrick, DNA, 5. From Theodorick Lee, DNA, 3. From Thomas Moore, DNA, 1. From John Stricker, Jr., DNA, 3. From Luke Tiernan, DNA, 3.
4 To James Woodson Bates, DNA, 3. To Henry M. Brackenridge, DNA, 3. To Henry M. Brackenridge, DNA, 3. To Adam Gordon, DNA, 3. From Robert M. Harrison, DNA, 6. From James L. Hawkins, DNA, 3. To Henry Johnson, DNA, 2. From Walter A. Jones, DNA, 5. From Baron Paul de Krudener, DNA, 7. To William McRae, DNA, 3. To Thomas Randall, DNA, 3. To Joseph L. Smith, DNA, 3. To James Webb, DNA, 3. To James Webb, DNA, 3. From William White, DNA, 1. To Henry Wilson, DNA, 3.
5 From James H. McCulloch, DNA, 10a. From Jacques Villere, DNA, 8.
6 From Joseph Kent, DNA, 3. From Stanhope Prevost, DNA, 2, 6. From Stanhope Prevost, DNA, 6. From Samuel L. Southard, DNA, 2. From James Young, DNA, 5.
7 From Rollin C. Mallary, DNA, 3. To Marshals of the U.S. for States & Territories, DNA, 1. From Peleg Sprague, DNA, 3.
8 From Daniel Webster, DNA, 3.

9 To B.U.S., Wash. Branch, DLC-HC, 15. From Charles Ellet, Jr., DNA, 1. From Frederick Frey, DNA, 6. From Joseph Hill, DNA, 9. From David B. Ogden, DLC-HC, 3. From William T. Simons, DNA, 3.

10 From John Barney, DNA, 3. From Samuel Brents, DNA, 3. From Benjamin Greene, DNA, 3. From Beaufort T. Watts, DNA, 3.

11 From George S. Bourne, DNA, 3. From Matthew St. Clair Clarke, DNA, 3. From Benjamin P. Smith, DNA, 3.

12 From Thomas Aspinwall, DNA, 6. To William G. Merrill, DNA, 3, 6. To Charles S. Walsh, DLC-HC, 3.

13 To B.U.S., Wash. Branch, DLC-TJC, 15. From William Clark, DNA, 3. From Christopher Hughes, DNA, 7.

14 To Gerard C. Brandon, ViU, 12a. From John H. Bryan, DNA, 3. To B.U.S., Wash. Branch, DLC-TJC, 15. To James Collier, DNA, 12a. From Frederick Gebhard, DNA, 3. From Robert M. Harrison, DNA, 9. From J. W. Townsend, DNA, 12a.

16 To George B. Adams, DNA, 3, 6. To Albert Davy, DNA, 3, 6. From Thomas W. Fox, DNA, 6. To Henrich Janson, DNA, 3, 6. To John Pulis, DNA, 3, 6. To William Radcliff, DNA, 3, 6. To Samuel L. Southard, NjP, 10c. From Baron Stackelberg, DNA, 7.

17 From Samuel Brent, DNA, 5. To B.U.S., Wash. Branch, DLC-TJC, 15. From Samuel D. Heap, DNA, 6. From William Steele, DNA, 3.

18 From Jonathan Elliot, DNA, 3. From Alexander H. Everett, DNA, 5, 10a. From Kensey Johns, Jr., DNA, 3. From David McKeehan, DNA, 3. From Richard Peters, DNA, 12a. From Francisco Tacon, DNA, 4. From Michael Tiernan, DNA, 6.

19 From Joaquin Campino, DNA, 4. From George Graham, DNA, 2. From Robert M. Harrison, DNA, 6. To Robert Jaques, DNA, 3. From Alejandro Velez, DNA, 4.

20 From George S. Bourne, DNA, 3. To B.U.S., Wash. Branch, DLC-TJC, 15. To B.U.S., Wash. Branch, DLC-TJC, 15. To B.U.S., Wash. Branch, DLC-TJC, 15. From William L. Reaney, DNA, 3. From William Wirt, DNA, 3.

21 To B.U.S., Wash. Branch, DLC-TJC, 15. From Daniel M. Christie, DNA, 3. From Joseph O. Gales, Jr., DNA, 3.

22 From Thomas L. L. Brent, DNA, 2, 7. From Kensey Johns, Jr., DNA, 3. From J. H. Wingate, DNA, 5.

23 From William Tudor, DNA, 7. From R. H. Weyman, DNA, 1.

25 From Eliphalet Loud, DNA, 5. From Thomas Tyson, DNA, 5.

26 From William Tudor, DNA, 7.

30 From George B. Adams, DNA, 6. From George Moore, DNA, 6.

JULY 1828
[?] From Robert Scott, KyLxT, 14, 15.

1 From Charles Barnet, DNA, 6. From Reuben G. Beasley, DNA, 6. From Thomas L. L. Brent, DNA, 7. From James L. Kennedy, DNA, 6. From William McRea, DNA, 3. From G. Theodore Sadio, DNA, 6. From Isaac Stone, DNA, 6. From Willink & Van Staphorst, DNA, 9.

2 From Beverley Chew, DNA, 6. From Joseph Lovell, et al., Lexington Ky. Reporter, 10d. From James Webb, DNA, 3.

3 From M. R. DaSilva, DNA, 6. From Alexander H. Everett, DNA, 7.

4 From Henry M. Brackenridge, DNA, 3.

5 From Thomas Cox, DNA, 1. From John Cuthbert, DNA, 6. From Thomas Randall, DNA, 3. From Count Ernst H. Schimmelmann, DNA, 7. From John Vawter, DNA, 4. From William H. D. C. Wright, DNA, 6.

6 From Gabriel Richard, DNA, 3.

7 To Joseph Lovell, et al., NBu, 10d.

8 From Alexander H. Everett, DNA, 7. To Peter B. Porter, NBuHi, 12e. From Samuel Upham, DNA, 9.

9 From Thomas Dove, DLC-TJC, 15. From Joseph Peck, DNA, 3. To St. John's Church, DLC-TJC, 15. From Griffin Stith, DNA, 3.

10 From Joseph Blunt, DNA, 12a. From William H. Tracy, DNA, 6.

11 From Adam Gordon, DNA, 3. From George R. Robertson, DNA, 6. From Henry Wilson, DNA, 3.

12 From Henry Johnson, DNA, 16.

13 To Joseph Lovell, NBu, 12e.

14 From Joel R. Poinsett, DNA, 2. From Joel R. Poinsett, DNA, 7. From Joel R. Poinsett, DNA, 6, 7. From Joel R. Poinsett, DNA, 7.
15 From John Cuthbert, DNA, 6. From James Maury, DNA, 6. From Joel R. Poinsett, DNA, 7. From Joel R. Poinsett, DNA, 7. From Joel R. Poinsett, DNA, 7. From Joel R. Poinsett, DNA, 2, 7. From Joel R. Poinsett, DNA, 7. From Joel R. Poinsett, DNA, 7. From Joel R. Poinsett, DNA, 7. To Whom It May Concern, DNA, 7.
16 From Thomas Aspinwall, DNA, 6. From Joel R. Poinsett, DNA, 7. From Thomas M. Rodney, DNA, 6. From Samuel L. Southard, DNA, 16.
17 From Francisco Tacon, DNA, 7. From William Taylor, DNA, 6.
18 From J. W. Baker, DNA, 6.
19 From James W. Bates, DNA, 3. From John W. Parker, DNA, 6.
20 From Thomas Backus, DNA, 6. From J. J. Debesse, DNA, 6.
21 From Thomas Stringfield, DNA, 15.
22 From Samuel L. Southard, DNA, 3, 4.
24 From Samuel Jayne, DNA, 12a.
25 From Frederick J. Wickelhausen, DNA, 6.
26 From James H. McCulloch, DNA, 16. From Christian F. Goehring, DNA, 6. From Mat. D. Patton, DNA, 3, 12a.
28 From William Gordon, DNA, 3, 6.
29 From Albert Davy, DNA, 3, 6.
30 From Thomas Aspinwall, DNA, 6. To John Brown, CtY, 10d. From James Maury, DNA, 6.
31 From Charles W. Dabney, DNA, 6.

AUGUST 1828
1 From A. & H. Wilson, DNA, 12a.
2 To Nathan Hale, KyU, 12b. From James Maury, DNA, 6.
3 From Thomas L. L. Brent, DNA, 5, 7.
4 From Samuel Redd, DLC-TJC, 15. From William Tudor, DNA, 7.
6 From Thomas Aspinwall, DNA, 6. From William Brown, DNA, 3. From John H. Kerr, DLC-TJC, 15.
7 From James Maury, DNA, 6. From Beaufort T. Watts, DNA, 5, 6.
8 To Thomas Corwin, KyLoF, 14.
9 From James E. Davis, DNA, 3. From Benjamin Mills, DNA, 3. To William North, Fayette Co. Deed Book 4, 14. From Robert Trimble, DNA, 3.
11 From Will S. Dallam, DLC-TJC, 13. From James E. Davis, DNA, 3.
12 From James K. Cook, DNA, 12a. From Thomas Culbreth, DNA, 2. From David Walker, DNA, 6.
14 From Pablo Obregon, DNA, 7. To Samuel L. Southard, DNA, 3.
15 From Robert Jacques, DNA, 3, 6. From Robert Scott, KyLxT, 15. From Robert Scott, KyLxT, 15. From Robert Scott, KyLxT, 15
16 From James Maury, DNA, 6.
18 From George G. Barrell, DNA, 6. From John Adams Smith, DNA, 7.
19 From Thomas L. L. Brent, DNA, 5, 7.
20 From Robert Blackwell, DNA, 12a. From W. Burritt & E. B. Clayton, DNA, 1. From Willink & Van Staphorst, DNA, 9.
21 From R. H. Gist, DNA, 8.
22 From James K. Cook, DNA, 9, 12a.
23 From T. I. Wharton, DNA, 3.
28 From Bern Henry, DNA, 6. From Bushrod Washington, DNA, 3. From Ebenezer [?] Wentworth, DNA, 2.
30 From John Cuthbert, DNA, 6. From William Radcliff, DNA, 6. From H. F. Von Lengerke, DNA, 7.

SEPTEMBER 1828
[ca] 1 From George H. Dunn, et al., DNA, 12a.
1 From Robert Taylor, DNA, 15.
2 From J. Harper, DNA, 3.
3 From William Key Bond, DNA, 3. From William Radcliff, DNA, 6.
4 From John F. Anderson, DNA, 3. From Samuel Bell, DNA, 3. From Samuel Brents,

DNA, 9. From Joseph Emerson, DNA, 5, 6. From William Gordon, DNA, 6. From David Trimble, DNA, 3.

5 From James Dill & Noah Noble, DNA, 3, 12a. From John Rainals, DNA, 6. From Baron Stackelberg, DNA, 7. From William H. Tracy, DNA, 6.

6 From Thomas C. Howard, DNA, 3. From James H. McCulloch, DNA, 6.

8 From John Barney, DNA, 3. From Gabriel Duvall, DNA, 3.

9 From C. Blythe, DNA, 2.

10 From J. Burnet, DNA, 3. From William Hardin, DNA, 5. From John C. Jones, Jr., DNA, 6. From John M. McConnell, DNA, 3.

11 From John Breathitt, DNA, 3. From Thomas McAllister, DNA, 8.

12 From Peter Pedersen, DNA, 7.

13 From Francis M. Dimond, DNA, 6. From Frederick Frey, DNA, 7. From Seth Sweetser, DNA, 12e.

14 To B.U.S., Wash. Branch, DLC-TJC, 15. From John C. Wright, DNA, 3.

15 From Joseph F. Benham, DNA, 3. From G. W. Boerstler, DNA, 16. To Hilliard, Gray, Little, & Wilkins, Gregg M. Sinclair, 12b. From Thomas C. Owings, DNA, 3. From Joel R. Poinsett, DNA, 7.

16 From Francis Dunlevy, DNA, 3. From C. Snell, DNA, 1. From Thomas P. Spierin, DNA, 1.

17 From William Gibbs Hunt, DNA, 9, 12a. From Daniel Mayes, DNA, 3. From William P. Preble, DNA, 2. From William Shaler, DNA, 6. From Xavier de Medina, DNA, 7.

19 From Charles J. Nourse, DNA, 2.

22 From Gregg & Culley, DNA, 12a. From William Hendricks, DNA, 3. From John R. Thornton, DNA, 3.

23 To B.U.S., Wash. Branch, DLC-TJC, 15. From Joaquin Campino, DNA, 7. From James G. Dana & Albert G. Hodges, DNA, 12a. From Henry Farrow, DNA, 3. From Thomas H. Pindell, DNA, 3.

26 From John Reed, DNA, 12c. From John P. Sheldon, DNA, 12a.

27 From Francis Brooke, DNA, 3. From A. W. Paulding, DNA, 3. From John Sergeant, DNA, 1, 3.

28 From James H. Causten, DNA, 5.

30 From Jesse L. Holman, DNA, 12a. From Samuel Larned, DNA, 7.

OCTOBER 1828

1 To Simon Bolivar, DNA, 7. From William Prince, DNA, 16. To Whom It May Concern, DNA, 7.

2 From Edward Church, DNA, 3. From Charles W. Dabney, DNA, 6. From John I. DeGraff, DNA, 3. From Alexander F. Grant, DNA, 12a.

3 To B.U.S., Wash. Branch, DLC-TJC, 15. To B.U.S., Wash. Branch, DLC-TJC, 15. To B.U.S., Wash. Branch, DLC-TJC, 15. From R. H. Douglas, DNA, 3.

4 From Dabney Carr, DNA, 3. From Theodore W. Clay, DLC-TJC, 15. From Thomas Clay, DLC-TJC, 15. From William Corry, DNA, 3. From John F. May, DNA, 5. To Edward Tiffin, MiD-B, 3.

6 From Nathaniel Beasley, DNA, 3. To Isaac Bell, DNA, 5. To B.U.S., Wash. Branch, DLC-TJC, 15. To B.U.S., Wash. Branch, DLC-TJC, 15. From Thomas L. McKenney, DNA, 3. To John F. May, DNA, 5.

7 From Samuel W. Davies, DNA, 3. From J. C. Wright, DNA, 12a.

8 From John M. Baker, DNA, 9. From David Fullerton, DNA, 3. From William Hebb, DNA, 3. From William Lee, DNA, 3. From William G. Merrill, DNA, 3, 6. From William Ruffin, DNA, 3. From Alexander Scott, DNA, 3. From John A. Smith, DNA, 3.

9 To B.U.S., Wash. Branch, DLC-TJC, 15. From B. L. McCarty, DNA, 3. From James McCloskey, DNA, 3. From David McKeehan, DNA, 3. From A. K. & D. S. Smith, DNA, 6. From George Taylor, DNA, 3.

10 From Alexander H. Everett, DNA, 7. From Waters Smith, DNA, 2. From Willink & Van Staphorst, DNA, 9.

11 From Thomas Aspinwall, DNA, 6. From J. F. Clement, DNA, 12a.

12 To B.U.S., Wash. Branch, DLC-TJC, 15. From George Jones, DNA, 6. From Baron Lewis de Lederer, DNA, 7.

13 From Henry Middleton, DNA, 5, 7. To St. John's Church, DLC-TJC, 15. From John Todd, DNA, 3. From Hooper Warren, DNA, 12a.

644

14 From Thomas Law, DNA, 3. To Baron Lewis de Lederer, DNA, 7.
15 From Gideon Beck, DNA, 12a. From John Binns, DNA, 12a. From Richard Rush, DNA, 1. From Arthur Shaaff, DNA, 2. From Samuel Sitgreaves, DNA, 5. To Charles R. Vaughan, All Souls College, Oxford Univ., 10b.
16 From Henry Baldwin, DNA, 1. From Charles E. Clark, DNA, 3. From James Jones, DNA, 3. From R. Temple, DNA, 12a.
17 From John B. Butler, DNA, 12a. From James B. Causten, DNA, 5. From J. B. Clapp, DNA, 12a. From Charles L. Harrison, DNA, 8. From John M. Talbot, *et al.*, DNA, 8. From Charles Thruston, DNA, 8.
18 From Samuel Wheeler, DNA, 5.
20 From Will Fox, *et al.*, DNA, 3. From William P. Preble, DNA, 2. From John I. Stull, DNA, 3. From James I. Thornton, DNA, 2. From Arthur Ware, DNA, 2.
21 From Charles Babcock, DNA, 12a. From Tristam Burges, DNA, 3. From Peter Hagner, DNA, 5. From Baron Lewis de Lederer, DNA, 7. From C. Smith, DNA, 3.
22 From Andrew Armstrong, DNA, 3, 6. To B.U.S., Wash. Branch, DLC-TJC, 15. From James G. Dana, DNA, 12a. From Jose M. Montoya, DNA, 7. From John Pegram, DNA, 8.
23 To Henry Baldwin, DNA, 2. From Samuel C. Crafts, DNA, 3. From John Cuthbert, DNA, 6. From Charles D. McLean, DNA, 12a. To Jose M. Montoya, DNA, 7. From H. Ariel Norris, DNA, 8. From Andrew Smith, DNA, 3.
24 From Robert Crittenden, DLC-TJC, 15. From William Gordon, DNA, 6. From Aaron Ogden, DNA, 9. From Peter Pedersen, DNA, 7. From George Ristoa, *et al.*, DNA, 1. From John P. Sheldon, DNA, 12a. To Whom It May Concern, DNA, 7.
25 From Joaquin Campino, DNA, 7. From Joseph Edson, DNA, 4. From Albert Gallatin, DNA, 7. From William Pearce, Jr., DNA, 3.
27 From Francis Brooke, InU, 12e. To N. C. Buck, DNA, 7. To B.U.S., Wash. Branch, DLC-TJC, 15. To B.U.S., Wash. Branch, DLC-TJC, 15. To Tristam Burges, DNA, 3. From A. & C. Cunningham, DNA, 6. From N. Edouard Fowl, DNA, 7. From Jones & Simons, DNA, 12a. From Jacob B. Moore, Jr., DNA, 12a. To Peter Pedersen, DNA, 7. From Henry Wilson, DNA, 3.
28 To Joseph W. Ingraham, DNA, 2. From L. Lederer, DNA, 7. From James Noble, DNA, 3. From Samuel Pleasonton, DNA, 5. From George C. Sibley, DNA, 3.
29 From Chipman & Seymour, DNA, 12a. From Robert Johnston, DNA, 2. From Thomas Smith, DLC-TJC, 15.
30 From Samuel D. Harris, DNA, 4. To Baron Lewis de Lederer, DNA, 7. From John W. Post, DNA, 3. From Francis Wyeth, DNA, 12a.
31 From William Bradley, DNA, 3. From William Doherty, DNA, 2. To Samuel L. Southard, DNA, 10d. From Thomas Stapp, DNA, 12a.

NOVEMBER 1828
3 To C. D. E. J. Bangeman Huygens, DNA, 7. From Charles J. Ingersoll, DNA, 10a. From Calvin Spaulding, *et al.*, DNA, 12a. To Wa–ri–ga & Chick–hong–sic, WHi, 12c.
4 From Joseph M. Hernandez, DNA, 3. From Joseph M. Hernandez, DNA 3. To Baron Paul de Krudener, DNA, 7. From Andrew Smith, DNA, 3.
5 From Thomas Douglas, DNA, 3. From John Rodman, DNA, 3. From John Sergeant, DNA, 2.
6 From James Barbour, DNA, 7. To J. B. Harrison, DLC-Burton Harrison Papers, 3. From John H. Norton, DNA, 3. From Joaquim Pereira, DNA, 7. From David Rogers & Son, DNA, 3. From Benjamin Russell, DNA, 12a.
7 From Francis Brooke, DNA, 3. From Baron Paul de Krudener, DNA, 7. To Baron Paul de Krudener, DNA, 7. From L. Marchand, DNA, 1.
8 From John Duer, DNA, 2. From Samuel Jayne, DNA, 12a. From Peter Pedersen, DNA, 7. From Sampson C. Russell, DNA, 2.
9 From Benjamin W. Leigh, DLC-HC, 3.
10 From Jacob B. Moore, Jr., DNA, 12a.
11 From George F. Clarke, DNA, 3. From N. Edouard Fowl, DNA, 7. From Peter Hagner, DNA, 2, 5.
12 From Peter B. Porter, DNA, 1. From Thomas P. Saul, DNA, 3. From John Rodman, DNA, 3. From John S. Simpson, *et al.*, DNA, 12a.
13 To B.U.S., Wash. Branch, DLC-TJC, 15. To B.U.S., Wash. Branch, DLC-TJC, 15. From Thomas P. Green, *et al.*, DNA, 12a. From A. & Henry Wilson, DNA, 12a.

14 From Thomas L. L. Brent, DNA, 5. From Henry Bruce, DNA, 3.
15 From Carlos Rodrigues, DNA, 4, 7. From John Test, DNA, 3. From John Test, DNA, 12a.
16 From William Moncure, DNA, 3.
18 From James Dill, DNA, 3. From J. B. Ferand, DNA, 3.
19 From Charles W. Ernest, DNA, 3.
[ca] 19 To Peter B. Porter, DNA, 10c.
19 From James Wilson, DNA, 12a.
20 From Joseph F. Benham, DNA, 3. From Pedro Gual, DLC-TJC, 10c. From Francisco D. Vives, CSmH, 10c. From William S. J. Washington, DNA, 3.
21 From Joshua Bond, DNA, 6. From Alexander Campbell, DNA, 3. From Francis J. Fatio, DNA, 3.
22 From Daniel Palmer, DNA, 3.
24 From Seth Cushman, DNA, 3. From J. B. Harrison, DLC-HC, 2. From Margaret C. Meade, DNA, 5.
25 From S. Burch, DNA, 3. From L. Marchand, DNA, 1. From Andrew Scott, DNA, 3.
26 From Samuel Brents, DNA, 1. From Nathaniel Law, DNA, 12a. From Daniel Webster, DNA, 3.
27 From Robert Barnard, DNA, 3. From John Green, DNA, 3. From John Irwin, DNA, 6.
28 From James Noble, DNA, 12a. From William Tudor, DNA, 7.
29 From James Lanman, DNA, 3. From [?] Owen, DNA, 12a. From Thomas Searle, DNA, 7.
30 From Edward P. Roberts, DNA, 9.

DECEMBER 1828
1 From Henry Channing, DNA, 12a. From William Elliot, *et al.*, DNA, 9. From Jacob B. Gurley, DNA, 3. From Thomas Skidmore, DNA, 1. From George W. Slacum, DNA, 2. From Samuel L. Southard, DNA, 2. From John B. West, DNA, 9.
2 From Stephen P. Hosmer, DNA, 3. From John Irwin, DNA, 6. From Robert Porter & Son, DNA, 12a.
3 From Joseph Gales, Jr., DNA, 3. From William B. Rochester, DNA, 3. To William Tudor, DNA, 4, 7. From Joseph F. Wingate, DLC-HC, 16.
4 From Richard Collins, DNA, 3. From William Hendricks, DNA, 12a. From Theodore Hunt, DNA, 3. To Thomas Searle, DNA, 7. From Ambrose H. Sevier, DNA, 3. From Joseph Wingate, DNA, 5.
5 From John R. Hurd, DNA, 5, 7. From Levi Woodbury, DNA, 1.
6 From Charles Barnet, DNA, 6. From J. W. Edwards, *et al.*, DNA, 3. From Henry Johns, Jr., DNA, 12a. From James Noble, DNA, 12a. From John Russ, DNA, 3. From Joseph M. White, DNA, 3. To Levi Woodbury, DNA, 2.
7 To John James Appleton, DNA, 7. From Joseph F. Caldwell, DNA, 12a. From James Partridge, DNA, 5.
8 To John Q. Adams, DNA, 2. To John M. Forbes, DNA, 5, 7. From Susannah Foster, DNA, 10a. From William Hendricks, DNA, 12a. From B. L. Lear, DNA, 3. To Xavier de Medina, DNA, 4. From Timothy Pitkin, DNA, 5. From William B. Swett, DNA, 5. From Gulian C. Verplanck, DNA, 1. From John C. Wright, DNA, 12a.
9 From Franklin Ferguson, DNA, 12a.
10 From John Dunlap, *et al.*, DNA, 3. From Asa May, DNA, 3. From John Nichols, DNA, 3. From Joseph Vance, DNA, 1. From John S. Wills, DNA, 3. From Ebenezer Young, DNA, 3.
11 From Thomas P. Eskridge, DNA, 3. From Nathanial Law, DNA, 12a. From William Tudor, DNA, 7.
12 To B.U.S., Wash. Branch, DLC-TJC, 15. From John Fitch, DNA, 3. From Ebenezer Stoddard, DNA, 3. From James Strong, DNA, 1, 12a.
13 From Ephraim Batemen, DNA, 12a. From Demetrius A. Gallitzin, DLC-HC, 1. From Hezekiah Huntington, DNA, 2, 3. To Joseph Vance, DNA, 2.
14 From J. B. Clapp, DNA, 12a. From William R. Higinbotham, DNA, 6.
15 From Alexander Allyn, DNA, 3. From David Doggett, DNA, 3. From Edward Everett, DNA, 1, 5. From William B. Giles, DNA, 2. From Nathan Smith, DNA, 3. From John Stricker, DNA, 3. From Norman Williams, DNA, 2.

16 From John Barney, DNA, 3. From F. G. Fish, DNA, 3. From Joseph Gales, DNA, 2. From John Hyde, DNA, 3. To Timothy Pitkin, DNA, 5. From James Powell, DNA, 16.
17 From Mason Campbell, DNA, 12a. To Edward Everett, DNA, 5. From Roger Huntington, DNA, 3. From Henry Meigs, DNA, 8. To Joel R. Poinsett, PHi, 6. To Samuel L. Southard, NjP, 3. From Anthony Woodward, DNA, 5, 6.
18 From Isaac C. Barnet, DNA, 6. From G. W. Boestler, DNA, 16. From Josiah Isham, DNA, 3. From Lyman Law, DNA, 3. From Elias Perkins, DNA, 3. From Thomas L. Perkins, DNA, 3. From Charles H. Pond, DNA, 3. To John Adams Smith, DNA, 3, 7.
19 From Noyes Barber, DNA, 12a. From Jose S. Rebello, DNA, 7. From Samuel L. Southard, DNA, 9. From Henry Wolcott, DNA, 3.
20 To B.U.S., Wash. Branch, DLC-TJC, 15.
[ca] 20 To Jesse Burgess Thomas, IHi, 10d.
20 From Christopher Hughes, DLC-HC, 10c. From William Ladd, DNA, 3. From John S. Peters, DNA, 3. To Jose S. Rebello, DNA, 4, 7.
21 From Adams & Hudson, DNA, 12a. From Noyes Barber, DNA, 3. From Stephen Henderson, Jr., DNA, 12a. From George C. Washington, DNA, 3.
22 From James Barbour, DNA, 7. To B.U.S., Wash. Branch, DLC-TJC, 15. From Noyes Barber, DNA, 12a. From Edward D. Ellis, DNA, 12a. From R. I. Ingersoll, DNA, 3. From Charles King, DLC-HC, 3, 6. From Joshua Mezick, DNA, 5. From William B. Rochester, DNA, 7. From Squire Turner, *et al.*, DNA, 3.
23 From Noyes Barber, DNA, 3. From Anthony C. Cazenove, DNA, 1. From Jonathan Jennings, DNA, 3. From Bob McHatton, DNA, 1. To Richard Rush, DNA, 9. From Joseph M. White, DNA, 16.
24 To Bob McHatton, DNA, 1, 4. From E. Phelps, DNA, 3. To Charles S. Walsh, DNA, 3, 7.
25 From John S. Peters, DNA, 3.
26 To Baring Brothers & Co., DNA, 6, 9. From Theodorick Bland, DLC-TJC, 13. From Daniel & John M. Faust, DNA, 12a. From Charles P. Huntington, *et al.*, DNA, 12a. From John Kennedy, DNA, 8. From David M. Randolph, DNA, 10a. From Littleton W. Tazewell, DNA, 1, 7.
27 From Noyes Barber, DNA, 3. From Charles Gratiot, DNA, 2. To Littleton W. Tazewell, DLC-HC, 2, 7. From Joseph F. Wingate, DNA, 3, 6.
28 From James Barbour, DNA, 5. From Isaac Stone, DNA, 6.
29 From Francis Cooke, DNA, 3. From James G. Dana, DNA, 12a. To Samuel Larned, DNA, 3, 7. To Francisco Mariategui, DNA, 7. From Nathaniel Silsbee, DNA, 3. To Samuel L. Southard, NjP, 12e. From Benjamim F. West, DNA, 1. To Whom It May Concern, DNA, 7.
30 From Lewis Williams, DNA, 5.
31 From Alexander Burton, DNA, 6. From Anthony C. Cazenove, DNA, 7. From Thomas Davidson, DNA, 6. From Charles B. Goddard, DNA, 3. From Robert Scott, DLC-TJC, 15.

JANUARY 1829
[ca] 1829 To William S. Dallam, DLC-TJC, 15.
[ca] 1829 From Drake & Co., DLC–TJC, 15.
[ca] 1829 To Edward Everett [?], MHi, 10d.
 1 From Reuben G. Beasley, DNA, 6. From Edward Everett, DNA, 1, 5. From G. Theodore Ladico, DNA, 6. From George McDuffie, DNA, 9. From George R. Rogers, DNA, 6. From Robert Scott, KyLxT, 15. From Ambrose H. Sevier, DNA, 3. To Whom It May Concern, DNA, 7.
 2 From Noyes Barber, DNA, 3. From John Blair, DNA, 1, 9. From Samuel J. Donaldson, DLC-HC, 13. From P. A. Karthaus, DNA, 5. From B. Shackelford, DNA, 3.
 3 From Beverley Chew, DNA, 2. To James Finley, DNA, 5. To Ralph R. Gurley, DLC-HC, 1. To John R. Shaw, DLC-TJC, 15. From Baron Stackelberg, DNA, 4. From George R. Tompkins, DLC-TJC, 14, 15.
 5 To John Q. Adams, DNA, 2, 5. From Peter Care, Jr., DNA, 5. To Edward Everett, DNA, 2, 5. From Enoch Lincoln, DNA, 9. To Peter B. Porter, NBuHi, 8, 10c. From Oliver H. Prince, DNA, 3. From John C. Wright, DNA, 3.
 6 From Daniel D. Barnard, DNA, 5. From Nehemiah Foster, DNA, 5. From Charles King, DLC-HC, 3, 5. From William Trimble, DNA, 3.

7 To Daniel D. Barnard, DNA, 5. To John Blair, DNA, 2, 9. From Xavier de Medina, DNA, 7. To Peter B. Porter, NBuHi, 3. From Nathan Sanford, DNA, 2.
8 To Nicholas Biddle, DNA, 3. To Charles A. Davis, DNA, 3. To Eleuthere DuPont, DNA, 3. To William B. Giles, DNA, 4, 10a. To Benjamin Hatcher, DNA, 3. From Dutee J. Pearce, DNA, 1. To Nathan Sanford, DNA, 10a. To John B. Trevor, DNA, 3.
9 From Edward Everett, DNA, 1, 5. From Edward Everett, DNA, 1. From Ralph R. Gurley, DNA, 3. To Duncan McArthur, DLC-HC, 10d. From Peter B. Porter, DNA, 1. From Oliver H. Prince, DNA, 5.
10 To John Q. Adams, DNA, 2. From Lewis Shoemaker, DNA, 6. To Whom It May Concern, PHi, 2.
11 To Peter B. Porter, DNA, 2. From Joseph Richardson, DNA, 5.
13 From Andrew Armstrong, DNA, 3. From William Creighton, Jr., DNA, 3. From C. D. McClean, DNA, 12a. From Thomas C. Worthington, DNA, 8.
14 From J. Buchanan, DNA, 3. From Edward Everett, DNA, 1, 5. From William Gordon, DNA, 6. From Stephen Kingston, DNA, 10a. To Levi Lincoln, MWA, 2.
15 To Edward Everett, DNA, 2, 5. From Bernard S. Judah, DNA, 1, 3. From Richard H. Wilde, DNA, 3.
16 From John Barney, DNA, 5. From William J. Brown, et al., DNA, 3. From Charles Dabney, DNA, 6. From Charles Dabney, DNA, 6. From Chauncey Goodrich, DNA, 2. To Oliver H. Prince, DNA, 5.
17 To John Barney, DNA, 5. From Joseph Emerson, DNA, 5. To Edward Everett, MHi, 2, 3. To Edward Everett, MHi, 2. From Harvey Gregg, DNA, 3. From John S. Wills, DNA, 3.
20 To Antonio Alvarez, DNA, 3. From Matthew St, Clair Clarke, DNA, 1. From Edward Coles, DLC-HC, 2. From Stephen Kingston, DNA, 5. From Lewis Maxwell, DNA, 3. To Jonathan Sizer, CtY, 12b. From John W. Smith, DNA, 3. To Increase Wilson, CtY, 12b.
21 To Count Charles de Menou, DNA, 7.
[ca] 22 To President & Mrs. John Q. Adams, MHi-Adams Papers, 10d.
22 From P. R. Beverly, DNA, 10a. From John Downing, DNA, 1. From Jose M. Montoya, DNA, 7.
23 To Jose M. Montoya, DNA, 7. From Joel R. Poinsett, DNA, 9, 10a. From Charles R. Vaughan, DNA, 1.
24 To Charles Douglas, DNA, 2. From Samuel L. Southard, DNA, 10c. To Charles R. Vaughan, DNA, 2.
25 From Joshua Lewis, DNA, 3.
26 From Noyes Barber, DNA, 5. To James Barbour, DNA, 7. To Samuel R. Betts, DNA, 3. To Alexander Brackenridge, DNA, 3. To Anthony Burrington, DNA, 3. To Alfred Conkling, DNA, 3. From Susan Decatur, DLC-TJC, 14. To William A. Griswold, DNA, 3. To John W. Livingston, DNA, 3. To Thomas Morris, DNA, 3. To John H. Norton, DNA, 3. To John Pitman, DNA, 3. To Peter Randolph, DNA, 3. To Samuel C. Roane, DNA, 3. To George Washington Scott, DNA, 3. To Ether Shipley, DNA, 3. To William Trimble, DNA, 3. To Nathaniel Williams, DNA, 3.
28 From Joseph Anderson, DNA, 2. From Ezekiel F. Chambers, DNA, 5. To Benjamin Johnson, DNA, 3. To Samuel Larned, DNA, 10c.
30 From J. M. Huntington, DNA, 2.
31 From Edward Everett, DNA, 1. From Tucker & Thompson, DLC-TJC, 15. From Joseph F. Wingate, DNA, 12a.

FEBRUARY 1829
1 From Anthony Burrington, DNA, 3.
2 To Congress, DNA, 2, 9. To Edward Everett, DNA, 2. From Eliphalet Loud, et al., DNA, 5. To Peter B. Porter, DNA, 8. From R. Makepeace Ransom, DNA, 1. From Joseph F. Wingate, DNA, 12a.
3 To John Gadsden, DNA, 3. To John W. Smith, DNA, 3.
4 To Cornelius Bradford, DNA, 3, 6. To John Davis, DNA, 3. To Charles Douglas, DNA, 3, 6. From Samuel D. Harris, DNA, 3. To Samuel D. Harris, DNA, 3. To Henrich Janson, DNA, 3, 6. To John Pulis, DNA, 3, 6. To Ernest Schwendler, DNA, 3, 6.
5 From Ebenezer Sharpe, DNA, 8. To Jonathan Thompson, DNA, 1. From Nathaniel Williams, DNA, 3.

6 From Theodore W. Clay, DNA, 5.
7 To Thomas Swann, DNA, 1. To Joseph M. White, DNA, 4.
9 From Alexander Brackenridge, DNA, 3. To Orlando Brown, CtY, 3. From Nehemiah Foster, DNA, 5. From Dixon H. Lewis, DNA, 3. To Xavier de Medina, DNA, 7. From Ether Shipley, DNA, 3.
10 To George IV, DNA, 10d. From William A. Griswold, DNA, 3. From Thomas Morris, DNA, 3. From Jonathan Thompson, DNA, 2. From T. W. Woodbury, DNA, 9.
11 From Antonio Alvarez, DNA, 3. From John Gadsden, DNA, 3. To John Marshall, DNA, 2.
12 To James Barbour, DNA, 10d. From Elisha Phelps, DNA, 12b. From Peleg Sprague, DNA, 10a.
[13?] To John Q. Adams, MHi, 10d.
14 From William Cranch, DNA, 3. From George R. Gilmer, DNA, 1. To George R. Gilmer, DNA, 2.
16 From Eliphalet Loud, DNA, 5. To Richard Rush, DNA, 1. To George Watterson, DNA, 2.
17 From Joseph Anderson, DNA, 9. From D. S. Bernard, DNA, 3. From Matthew St. Clair Clarke, DNA, 2.
18 To John Q. Adams, DNA, 2. From John Davis, DNA, 1, 3. From H. D. Dwight, DNA, 5. From Samuel A. Foot, DNA, 3. To George McDuffie, DNA, 7. From Jacob C. Treadwell, DNA, 5.
19 To Henry Middleton, DNA, 10d. To Nicholas I, DNA, 10d.
20 From E. E. Peterson, DNA, 7. To E. E. Peterson, DNA, 7. To Nathan Smith, DNA, 3. From Gulian C. Verplanck, DNA, 1. From John Watts, DNA, 8.
21 From Richard H. Wilde, DNA, 1, 3.
23 From John W. Livingston, DNA, 3.
24 To House of Representatives, House Reports, 20 Cong., 2 Sess., p. 141, 2.
25 To Ezekiel F. Chambers, DNA, 6.
26 To John Q. Adams, DNA, 2. From William Carter, DNA, 1.
27 To John Q. Adams, DNA, 2. To Peter B. Porter, NBuHi, 12d.
28 To Owners of ship *Mentor*, RPB, 16. From Thomas H. White, DNA, 10a. [misdated Feb. 29]

MARCH 1829
3 To Daniel Brent, 12 *VMHB* (1911), p. 207, 10e.

NAME & SUBJECT INDEX: VOLUME 7

For abbreviations used in index, see page 691.

652

Chile (continued):
221, 462; Senate, 462; internal instability, disorder, revolution, civil war in, 38, 108, 462, 533; mentioned, 9, 96, 134, 204, 238, 260, 280, 436
—U.S. relations with: nature & extent of US trade with, 222, 391; US claims against, 38, 181, 391, 462; negotiations of commercial treaty with, 221–22, 269, 391, 462, 586; blockade, contraband, privateering & other US neutral rights problems, 487; US diplomat helps draw up constit. of, 221; tariff, duty, fee discrim. against US shipping & trade, 222; C. chides Larned for acting sans instructions, 586
Chillicothe, Ohio, 35, 103
Chilton, Thomas: role in retrenchment issue in 1828 campaign, 70–71, 224; mentioned, 117, 196, 446, 510
Chilton, Thomas J., 117, 429
China, 244
China: US trade with Peru via, 9; US trade with Canton, 371; US consular relations with Canton, 261; English language newspaper in Canton, 261
Chinn, Richard H.: analysis of Ky. politics (1828), 461–62; analysis of Pres. election (1828), 461–62; mentioned for US Dist. Atty. for Ky., 532; from, 441, 461; mentioned, 29, 39
Chipman, Henry, 432
Chipman, Ward, 115
Chippewa Indians, 296
Chowan Co., N.C., 182
Christy, William, 62
Chuquisaca, Bolivia, 391
Cincinnati, Ohio, 17, 26, 372–73, 423, 427, 453, 503, 592
Cincinnati *Gazette*, 390
Claiborne, William C. C., 54, 588, 598
Claiborne, William C. C. Jr., 479
Claremont, N. H., 34
Clarence, William Henry, Duke of, 437, 447, 529
Clark Co., Ky., 128, 535
Clark Co., Ohio, 530
Clark, James: from, 508; mentioned, 579
Clark, Joseph Hill: from, 149, 162

Clark, William, 120, 326, 338, 342
Clarke Co., Va., 571
Clarke, James, 277, 599
Clavering, D. C., 559, 605
Clay Co., Ky., 510
Clay, Henry
—personal items: boasts of personal impact on US domestic policy, 490; C. gambling, 333; C. on US capitalists, 494–95; C. alleged Godlessness, 333; C. ego & pomposity, 478, 541; death of close kinsmen, 456–57, 520; too old to serve again in US H. of Reps., 490; Ashland as security for loans, 413–14; plans after leaving State Dept., 490; ladies' man, 385, 478; rental costs in Wash., D.C., 268; lives on salary as Sec. State, 266; political attacks on, 27, 383; rentals & repairs on Lex. properties, 28, 29, 136, 207, 497, 592; on public speaking, 399; toasts, 273, 335, 350, 374; on travel routes to & from D.C., 375, 457, 609; sense of political humor, 517; C. support of national university & observatory, 353; patron of arts & literature, 221; identification with Span. Am. independence movements, 280–81; eating habits, 243; clothes, 263; carriages, 386–87; land speculation, 154; buying, selling, and breeding horses, 475, 483, 517, 525, 616–17; courtesy & kindness to Rom. Catholic church, 303; on being a Mason, 186–87; on his economic status, 298–99, 303–04, 309, 313, 315, 352, 362, 413–14, 417; personal economics, 188, 285, 298–99, 303–4, 352, 362, 497, 553; compassion & good manners, 192–93; vacations at the Springs, 305, 364, 440, 478; C. reaction to Sedition Act of 1798, 504; kindness to & support of relatives, 580; on weakness of constit. concerning Pres. elections, 2; opposition to free trade, 11, 12; sells silver service to JQA, 624; criticism of admin. of State Dept., 404, 604–5; suit of Geo. Nicholas's heirs against Morrison Estate (*see* Morrison Es-

tate); real estate in Wash., D.C., 485; Ashland operations & livestock, 187, 497, 587, 592, 616–17; hams produced at Ashland, 592; character of, 478; sued by slaves, 356, 622–24, 631–33; on keeping slave families intact, 623; slaves of in D.C., 485, 623–24; books & articles read, 155, 358; as House Speaker, 565; work for Kenyon Seminary, 138–39, 355, 359; support of GB travelers in US, 314–15; health of, 243, 262–64, 270–73, 278, 284–85, 290, 297, 300, 309, 313–15, 326, 336, 349–50, 359, 365–66, 375, 383–84, 399, 405–6, 420, 440, 446, 457, 486, 507, 510, 546, 572, 609, 616, 619, 625; attacks on his personal financial integrity, 298–99, 315, 329–30, 407, 417; friends offer to bail C. out of debt, 298–99; enters bagging business, 29, 30, 119, 592, 603; social life in Wash., 266 (*see also* Washington, D.C.); land holdings in Ill., 34; business matters in Lex., 231, 497, 587, 603; rumored as Min. to GB, 39, 188; references to God & religion, 100–101, 399; work for Episcopal Church, 113–14; supports Mrs. Hart & H. C. Hart, 490, 580; on dishonesty & misbehavior in public office, 71; on violence in politics, 610; on the inevitability & cyclical nature of war, 81; children named after, 194; on principle over popularity, 100; on his Va. origins, 349, 361, 477; on his patriotism, 100, 541; on his early education, 358, 511; boasts of no. of treaties signed as Sec. State, 278. *See also* "Corrupt Bargain" controversy; Election (Presidential) of 1828: Clay role in
—involvement in political patronage appointments & concerns: William Clark, 120, 326, 338–39, 364; Charles Douglas, 413; John Duer, 59, 71, 93; Ogden Edwards, 32, 59, 61, 71; Robert Y. Fairlie, 83, 84; John Gibson, 364; Archelaus Hughes, 411; Nathaniel W. McGiffin,

122–23; Hezekiah Niles, 210–11; John Savage, 207–8, 280, 326; Mathew Stewart, 67; Isham Talbot, 420; Peter G. Washington, 296

Clay, Henry Jr.: C. personal relations with, 80, 81, 510–11, 538–39, 598–99; at West Point, 385, 409, 510–11, 538–39, 569–70, 588, 598–99, 606–7, 611–12; C. career–counseling of, 80, 81, 511, 571, 588, 606–7; C. financial assistance to, 81; C. urges to study hard at USMA, 539, 571, 616; C. advice to, 606–7; death of (1847), 81; future career hopes of, 569, 588, 602–3; attempts to help fellow cadet, 538, 588, 598–99, 607, 616; health of, 607, 612; academic success at USMA, 611–12; scrapes at USMA, 611; dislike of West Point, 603, 611–12; considers resigning from USMA, 80, 81; considers career in law, 588; complains of academic discrim. at USMA, 611–12, 616; from, 569, 588, 602, 611; to, 80, 510, 538, 571, 598, 606, 616; mentioned, 378, 390, 567

Clay, James Brown, 456, 570, 591

Clay, John Morrison, 591

Clay, Lucretia Hart (Mrs. Henry): health, 188; social life in Wash., 188; impact of 1828 campaign on, 129, 130; living arrangements (Decatur House) in Wash., 159–60; mentioned; 73, 83, 104, 120, 126–27, 168, 194, 196, 236, 279, 285, 290, 297, 301, 328, 378, 389, 409, 428, 446, 456–57, 488–90, 507, 511, 517, 520–21, 539, 552–53, 567, 569, 570, 591–92, 597, 607, 609, 618, 624, 634

Clay, Theodore Wythe: C. financial assistance to, 28, 118–20, 497; accompanies C. to Wash., 217; bad character & habits of, 28, 217; accused of impropriety as messenger to Mex., 119, 143; on his political independence, 118–19; involvement in politics, 118–19; love of Lex., 119; on marriage, 119; involvement in C.

business affairs, 118–20, 497; manages Ashland in father's absence, 497, 526, 616–17; from, 38, 118, 497, 616; mentioned; 29, 81, 187, 587, 612

Clay, Thomas Hart: C. criticism of, 81, 511; in trouble in Phila., 511; mentioned; 290

Clayton, Augustin Smith, 268–69

Clayton, John M.: role in 1828 Pres. election, 486; from, 486; mentioned; 610

Clermont, Ohio, 236

Clermont Co., Ohio, 95, 530

Cleveland, 611

Clinton Co., Ohio, 530

Clinton, DeWitt: C. on death of, 101, 103; political effects of death of, 93, 110, 136, 164, 188, 243; mentioned; 22, 73, 76, 113, 359, 473

Coatzocoalcos, Mexico, 413

Cobnook Bay, 294

Cobscook River, 322

Codrington, Edward, 262, 370

Coffin, George, 581

Coimbra, Portugal, 336, 360, 369, 398

Coimbra, Portugal, College of, 198, 360

Colchagua, Chile, 38, 108

Cole, Henry S. (not identified), 165

Coleman, Edward, 253

Coleman, Nicholas D., 420

Coles, Isaac, 502

College at Hudson. *See* Western Reserve College

College of New Jersey. *See* Princeton University

College of Philadelphia, 478

Collier, James: from, 161; to, 183

Colombia (including Ecuador & Bolivia): Bolivar as dictator of, 381, 413, 498, 577; corruption in; 241–42; support for Bolivar in, 146, 251–52, 381, 413, 568–69; opposition to Bolivar in, 3, 88, 157, 240, 413, 463–64, 568–69; Negro slave disaffection in, 79; military posture of, 251–52; Min. to GB slighted in, 96; forced loans on foreigners in, 79; treaty with GB, 79, 577; economic problems in, 79, 80, 146, 157, 252; national constit. conv. in (Ocana), 88, 89, 146, 226,

240–41, 244, 251, 354, 363, 381; threat of Spanish invasion, 146; war with Spain, 88, 354–55, 421, 427, 570; war with Bolivia, 462, 498; Bolivar–Santander struggle in, 226, 413, 498, 507, 568–69, 603; role of clergy in, 421; freedom of press in, 244; war with Peru (*see* Peru); Senate in, 88; constit. of, 240; condition of army in, 146, 492; navy of, 226, 492; trade with Spain, 577; prisoners of war in Spain, 427, 570; GB mercenaries fight for, 507; assassination attempt on Bolivar (*see* Bolivar, Simon); internal instability, disorder, revolution, civil war in, 9, 69, 70, 79, 80, 88, 89, 108, 146, 157, 185, 226, 240–42, 244, 251–52, 363, 413, 421, 492–94, 498, 505–7, 568–69, 573, 577, 596, 603

—U.S. relations with: US citizens serve in privateers of, 354–55, 570; US policy toward & in, 492–94; US claims against, 24, 25, 88, 312–13, 493–94, 553; US interference in internal affairs of, 69, 70; US non–interference in internal affairs of, 492; 1824 General Conv. of Peace, Amity, Navigation & Commerce with, 32, 79, 200, 202, 227, 229, 469, 492, 577; US recognition of, 495; violation of US treaty rights, 79; isthmus of Panama railway project, 88; C. criticizes Bolivar's hostility to democracy, 518; protection of US citizens in, 251; tariff arrangements with, 82, 83; extend consular courtesies to in Barbary ports, 214; advancing the cause of US democracy in, 492; US neutrality in Colombian–Spanish war, 222, 427, 527, 553; Wm. H. Harrison appointed Min. to, 308; US mediation in maritime incident with Spain, 354–55, 427, 570; dangers to US citizens in, 506; arrest of US Consul (MacPherson) at Cartagena, 421, 425, 498, 538; US dip. assistance to in Spain, 427, 570; blockade, contraband, privateering & other US neutral rights

627, 629; AJ as demagogue, 460–61; AJ as land speculator, 250; AJ execution of Tenn. militiamen, 152, 155, 245, 285, 471–72, 508, 527, 536 (see also 5: 739); appt. of Rufus King to GB, 306; Rachel Jackson issue, 318, 358; Treaty of Ghent issue, 75–76, 141, 339, 380, 532, 540; Indian policy & problems, 103–4, 432, 489, 524, 605; trade with Span. Am., 511; nationalism, 460, 472, 559; national univ. & observatory, 268–69, 353; slavery issue, 482; AJ involvement in Burr Conspiracy, 27, 175, 190–91, 211–12, 216, 225, 426, 461, 501–2, 508, 549; C. involvement with Burr, 461, 497–98, 501–3, 507–9, 549; Anti–Mason movement as issue, 129, 186, 400–401, 474; JQA inconsistency, 516, 531; JQA unpopularity, 600; C. debts as issue, 303–4, 309, 313, 315, 352–53, 362, 417; Am. System, 5, 63–64, 98–99, 102, 185, 210, 243, 299, 316, 332–33, 349, 390, 449, 600, 613; tariff, 22, 64, 93, 95, 97, 99, 102, 104, 136, 164, 186, 191, 207, 210, 212, 225, 263–64, 285, 342, 350, 389, 403, 424, 449–50, 490, 508; retrenchment (economy in govt.) issue, 70, 92, 117, 130, 169–70, 193, 196, 254, 283; various foreign policy issues, 33, 75, 141, 159, 339; "Corrupt Bargain" between JQA & C. in 1824 election, 5–6, 17, 25, 54, 62–63, 81, 86, 95–96, 99–100, 104–7, 110–11, 118, 121, 135, 139–42, 144–46, 151, 154, 156, 174–75, 179–82, 188, 191–93, 194–96, 204, 216–17, 225, 227, 248, 254–5, 266, 285–86, 306–7, 326–27, 330, 333, 348–50, 358, 390, 399, 426, 432, 449, 458, 460–61, 471–72, 480–81, 485, 496, 504, 508, 515, 525, 534, 562–63, 600–601, 604, 613, 616, 624, 626, 629. See also "Corrupt Bargain" controversy; Election (Presidential) of 1824: "Corrupt Bargain" dimension of

—campaign activity in states & sections; prognoses & outcomes: Ala., 45, 397–98; Del., 393, 482, 486, 490, 496, 510; Ga., 77, 432, 605; Ill., 45, 299, 403, 431, 533; Ind., 45, 403, 429, 438, 533–34, 538, 542–43, 613; Ky., 37–39, 43–45, 54, 62–63, 76, 104, 113, 117–18, 121, 128–29, 144, 162, 168, 182–83, 185, 188, 192–93, 225, 227, 248, 278, 290, 305, 310, 314, 316, 326, 350, 357, 360, 363, 376, 383, 386, 389, 393, 398, 400–401, 403, 405, 424, 426, 438–39, 441, 446, 456–58, 460–61, 464, 467–68, 472–73, 476, 481–82, 485, 489–90, 496–98, 503–4, 508, 510, 513, 524, 531–33, 535–38, 542–43; La., 26, 82–83, 311, 403, 414, 438, 440, 446, 533–35; Maine, 403, 535; Md., 4, 182, 235, 252, 262, 273, 357–58, 482, 485–87, 490, 496, 510–11, 535, 537, 539; Mass., 264, 281, 335, 350; Mo., 171, 485; N.H., 217, 336, 403; N.J., 393, 508; N.Y., 22, 32, 36–37, 71–73, 83, 92–94, 101–2, 110, 136, 155, 164, 168, 182–83, 186, 188, 191, 207, 210–11, 216, 225, 247, 266, 284–85, 290, 300, 311, 342, 357, 374, 376, 386, 389, 400, 403, 438–39, 446, 464, 473, 482, 485, 489–91, 496, 503–4, 523, 525, 537, 540, 593; N.C., 36, 64, 94, 129, 182, 225, 278, 377, 439, 490; Ohio, 25, 43, 45, 403, 443–44, 455, 513, 515–16, 524–27, 530,533–35, 537–38, 542–43, 575, 593; Pa., 4–6, 18, 22, 36, 53, 64, 67, 70, 94, 96, 98–99, 117, 122, 129, 155, 158, 168, 210, 253, 262, 266, 278, 352–53, 362–63, 374, 386, 389, 392, 403, 424, 438, 455, 459–60, 464, 481, 484, 489–91, 503, 507, 526, 593; S.C., 403; Tenn., 18, 185; Vt., 35; Va., 23–24, 33–34, 36–38, 45, 53, 64, 70–71, 86, 94, 99, 110, 117–18, 124, 129, 135, 158, 168, 174, 182, 224, 247, 250–51, 266, 278, 285, 337, 356, 424, 438–39, 455, 472, 489–90, 507, 516, 531, 537, 540,

590; East, 389, 525, 542; New England, 217, 281, 350, 376, 389, 403, 481–82, 535, 543, 559, 605; North, 389, 510; South, 389, 393, 525, 559; West, 439–40, 451, 455, 485–86, 525, 600; sectional dimensions of outcome, 525, 594–95 (for outcomes, see espec. 397, 443–44, 460, 473, 485, 508, 526, 531–33, 535, 539; also, 6: 362–63); hostile reactions to & explanations of AJ victory, 532, 537, 544–46, 558–60, 599, 612–13, 622; support for AJ victory, 562–63; analyses of AJ victory, 593, 613, 622; political implications of AJ victory, 490, 543, 548–49, 552–53, 612–13, 624, 626–27; scheme to nullify AJ victory in Electoral College, 537, 541, 543, 545–46; C. accept. of AJ victory, 472, 559; C. belief he could have won, 594; sympathy notes to C. after AJ victory, 542, 562, 565, 570–71, 599–601, 613, 618, 622; C. analysis of AJ victory, 525, 534–36, 540–42, 544, 548–49, 552–53, 559, 594–95, 610, 612; advice to C. after AJ victory; 540, 552, 554, 565, 571, 575, 579, 597, 607, 617, 619–20, 628, 630, 634; C. future Pres. prospects in light of AJ victory, 542–44, 554, 563, 589, 593, 595, 610, 618–20, 628–30; C. plans for future, 490, 525, 535–36, 542, 544, 549, 552–53, 565, 572, 575, 595, 612, 616, 627–28, 634; C. resigns as SecState, 633; trip home, 627

Elizabeth City, N.C., 614
Ellicott, Andrew, 72, 80, 91, 253, 608–9
Elliott, Stephen, 533
Ellis, Henry, 322
Emerson, William, 331–32
Emily, 61
English Channel, 101, 422
English Key, Honduras, 340
Erie, 419, 560–61
Erie, Pa., 526
Erving, George W., 395
Erwin, Andrew Eugene, 18, 591
Erwin, Anne Brown Clay (Mrs. James): character of, 456–57; children of, 456–57, 520, 591; visits C. in Wash., 350; comment on Wash. social scene, 378; plays piano, 385; from, 377; mentioned, 290, 478, 567, 612, 615
Erwin, Henry Clay, 350, 409, 615
Erwin, James: recommends political appt. to C., 331–32; buys cattle from C., 483; C. sells slave to, 483; death of daughter (Julia D.), 457, 520; financial dealings with C., 591, 614, 615; manumits slave, 590; from, 331, 590, 614; to, 290, 456; mentioned, 29, 378, 478, 631
Erwin, James Jr., 591, 615
Erwin, Julia D.: death of, 457, 520; mentioned, 350, 409
Erwin, Lucretia Hart, 591
Escambia Co. Court (Fla.), 88
Escoseses party (Mexico), 153
Espinosa de los Monteros, Juan Jose, 21
Essex Co., N.J., 508
Esteva, Jose Ignacio, 21, 84, 114, 153
Estill Co., Ky., 510
Ethiopia, 193
Eubank, James T., 109
Europe, 6, 8, 9, 11, 36, 46, 84, 88, 90, 101, 125, 127–28, 131, 133, 149, 150, 152, 156, 169, 170, 172, 187, 190, 197, 214–16, 220, 227, 238, 266, 278–79, 286–87, 289, 291, 302, 310, 320, 336, 346, 352, 367, 395, 398, 407–8, 410, 413, 418, 424, 436, 438, 446, 458, 468, 470, 474, 477, 499, 511, 519, 521–22, 528, 545, 555, 557, 567, 569, 596, 605
Everett, Alexander Hill: character & personality of, 404; from, 16, 60, 111,

137, 187, 213, 249, 253, 302, 353, 361, 411, 427, 468, 471; to, 72; mentioned, 9, 10, 24, 52, 73, 85, 91, 214, 276, 334, 354–56, 362, 454–55, 566–67. *See also* Spain: U.S. relations with
Everett, Edward: from, 79, 617; to, 220, 270, 276, 279, 282, 628, 629; mentioned, 350, 584
Exit, 479

Fairfax, Va., 597
Fairfield, 522
Fairfield Co., Ohio, 530
Fair Trader, 17
Fairlie, James: to, 83
Fairlie, Robert Y., 83–84
Falmouth, 168, 174, 251, 274, 275, 277, 340
Faneuil Hall (Boston), 336
Farmer, Mitchell, 505
Fayal, Azores, 371, 465
Fayette Co., Ky., 128, 207, 298, 414, 420, 429, 461, 526, 535, 620
Fayette Co. (Ky.) Corresponding Committee, 192
Featherstonhaugh, George W.: to, 101
Federal, 560–61, 578
Federation of Centre of America. *See* Centre of America, Federation of
Feestown, Ohio, 95
Fendall, Philip R.: from, 77; mentioned, 170
Fenwick, Francis C.: from, 505
Ferdinand VII of Spain, 16, 80, 88, 137, 214, 362, 412, 427, 491, 522
Ferguson, James, 177
Fernando Po Islands, 559
Ferronays, Pierre de la, 91, 121–22, 126, 224, 248, 271, 282, 311, 367, 406, 410, 424, 440, 470, 491, 519, 566
Field, Willis: from, 400
Fielding, William: from, 600
Fingal, 242
Fitzhugh, William H., 597–98
Flaget, Bishop Benedict Joseph, 303
Fleeming, Charles E., 112
Fleming Co., Ky., 128, 513
Fleming, Mr. _____ (not identified), 268
Flint River, 609
Flint, William, 632
Flor de Mayo, 8, 147, 157, 161
Florida: boundary dispute with Ga., 68, 73, 78; fed. marshal dishonesty in, 504; Superior Court of,

504; mentioned, 6, 55, 72, 222, 253, 325, 426, 505
Flournoy, Thomas C. (not identified): from, 443–44
Floyd Co., Ky., 513
Floyd, John, 338
Foot, Samuel A.: from, 9
Forbes, John M.: from, 40, 260, 350, 379, 411, 466, 527, 556; to, 6, 555; mentioned, 138, 160–61, 189, 197
Force, Peter: to, 624; mentioned, 204, 574–75
Forquer, George (not identified), 431
Forrest, Benjamin S., 339
Forrest, Richard, 143, 486, 488, 511
Forsyth, John: urges C. to accept SecState in JQA admin., 99; mentioned, 100
Forsyth, Samuel D., 240
Foster, Thomas, 31
Fournier, Cesar (not identified), 297, 460, 468
Fox, 355
Fox Indians, 296
Fox, Thomas W.: from, 92
France: Dept. of Finance, 367; Academy of Medicine, 130; army, 422, 520, 570; Chamber of Deputies, 158–60, 172, 267, 383, 406, 410, 423, 566, 567; Chamber of Peers, 406, 410, 423; constit. of, 596; Council of Ministers, 271, 346–47, 491; C. on outcome of 1827 elections in, 3; popularity of Greek cause in, 248–49; policy toward Span. Am. independence movements, 7; withdrawal from Spain, 137, 362, 370; 1828 elections in, 91, 157–58, 249; political instability in, 91, 158, 310, 346–47, 410, 596; financial instability in, 271, 580–81; military intervention in Spain, 9, 92, 362, 521, 570; political & military involvement in Russo–Turkish–Greek crisis, 92, 126, 159, 195, 223, 247–49, 286, 309, 310, 407–8, 412, 422, 443, 446, 465, 520, 558; treaty with GB & Russia (7/6/27), 126, 162 (*see also* Russia: Treaty of London July 6, 1827); rumored policy in Mex. as ally of Spain, 267; policy in & war with Algiers, 195, 221, 263, relations with & policy toward Miguel govt. in Portugal, 411; relations with

Haiti, Chambre ax Communes, 332, 382, 534
Halifax, Nova Scotia, 67, 373
Hall, Basil: from, 314
Hall, James: from, 34, 431
Hall, John James, 361
Hall, Nathan H., 39–40
Hallett, William P., 13–14
Hamblen Co., Tenn., 375
Hamburg, 150
Hamburg, Senate of, 114
Hamilton, Alexander, 333, 501, 549
Hamilton Co., Ohio, 25, 530
Hamilton, James A., 261
Hamilton, James Jr.: from, 92, 183; to, 130, 188, 253; mentioned, 169, 245, 285
Hamilton, John: from, 363
Hamilton, Ohio, 17
Hammond, Charles: supports JQA in 1828 election, 17, 314; to, 314, 503; mentioned, 116
Hammond, John, 170–71, 609
Hammond, Thomas: from, 4
Hampden–Sydney College, 28
Hampton Roads, Va., 168
Hancock, James L., 592
Hanover: trade reciprocity with US, 15, 371
Hanover, Va., 316
Hanover, Co., Va., 361, 475
Hanseatic Republics: trade treaty with Br., 137; commercial treaty with US (1828), 114, 137, 150, 201, 228, 278, 587; additional article to commercial treaty with US, 587–88
Haram, 463
Hardin, Augustine B., 230–31
Hardin, Benjamin: role in Ky. Sen. inquiry into "Corrupt Bargain", 141–42; mentioned, 74–75, 192, 621
Hardin, Benjamin F., 230–31
Hardin, Benjamin W., 230–31
Hardin, Mark: from, 399
Hardin, Swan, 230–31
Hardin, William, 230–31
Harlan Co., Ky., 510
Harmony, Peter, 487
Harold, William Vincent: from, 372; to, 373; mentioned, 423, 581
Harper, James, 303, 497–98
Harpy, 483, 564–65, 606
Harriet, 31, 274
Harrisburg, Pa., 5–6, 98
Harrison Co., Ohio, 530

Harrison, James B.: from, 356
Harrison, Robert Monroe: complains of lack of respect for himself as US Consul, 464, 540; fact–finding mission on impact of GB trade restrictions on US in BWI, 465; from, 138, 146, 221, 302, 326, 363, 388, 402, 420, 447, 464–65, 484, 518, 520, 535, 540, 560, 578; to, 560
Harrison, William Henry: appointed Min. to Colombia, 308, 374, 496–97; C. instructions to, 492–94; problems faced in Colombia, 464; indebtedness to BUS, 496–97; support of Span. Am. independence, 517; view of internal Colombian situation, 573, 577; from, 374, 573, 577; to, 25, 308, 492, 494; mentioned, 24, 109, 355, 419, 426, 488, 553, 569, 586, 596
Harrodsburg (Ky.) Central Watchtower, 76
Harrodsburg, Ky., 441, 461, 621
Hart, Eleanor, 490
Hart, Henry Clay: career in USN, 168, 580; C. subsidizes, 580
Hart, Nathaniel: to, 498; mentioned, 15
Hart, Susannah Gray, 126–27, 378, 490
Hart, Thomas Sr.: estate of, 490
Hartford, Ct., 9
Hartford Convention, 358, 593
Havana, Cuba, 9, 10, 85, 93–94, 153, 274, 357, 427, 486
Harvard University, 11, 324, 328, 566
Harvie, John: from, 227, 441; to, 327, 426; mentioned, 191–92
Hawes, Richard Jr.: from, 62
Hawkins, James L.: from, 629
Hawley, Betsey: from, 479–80
Hawley, Isaac, 479–80
Haxton, Washington M.: from, 10
Hay, John: from, 570; mentioned, 571
Hayne, Robert Y., 566, 597
Hazard, 70
Headinburgh, J. V., 587
Heath, James Ewell, 621–22

Hector, 209, 334
Hellas, 90
Hemp: price of, 29; C. enterprise in Lexington, 29, 30; shipments of from Italy to GB, 166
Hemphill, Joseph, 484
Hempstead, Charles S.: from, 10
Hempstead, Cornelia: from, 10
Hempstead, Thomas, 10, 253
Henderson, Joseph, 5, 98
Henley, Ozborne, 29–30
Henley, Scott, 119
Henrico Co., Va., 361
Henry Co., Ky., 104–5, 510
Henry, Patrick, 119
"Hermitage," 489
Hermon, 255
Hero, 174, 475
Heron, 260
Herries, John Charles, 96
Hertslet, Lewis, 36
Heyden, Count Lodewijk, 418
Hickey, Simon: from, 360
Hickman, Richard, 497
Higgins, Richard: from, 399
Higinbotham, William R.: from, 480
Hill, Isaac, 120
Hill, _____ (not identified), 497
Hinde, Thomas: from, 612
Hinman, Capt., _____ (not identified), 189, 600
Hinman, J. & Sons, 591
Hocking Co., Ohio, 530
Hodgson, William B.: from, 221; mentioned, 263
Hoffman, Beekman V., 160, 600
Holding, John W., 88
Holland, 41, 397
Holland, Edward, 12, 55–56, 86, 107–8, 112
Holley, Horace, 585
Holley, Mary Austin (Mrs. Horace), 119, 290
Holmes Co., Ohio, 527, 530
Holmes, John: to, 630; mentioned, 284
Homer, 165
Homer, Benjamin, 559
Honduras: army, 359; mentioned, 84, 340, 454
Honduras Gazette, 454
Hone, Philip, 521
Hopkins, Samuel, 549
Hopkinson, Joseph: from, 484; to, 484; mentioned, 459–60, 618
Hopkinsville, Ky., 193
Horton, Wilmont, 130
Houlton, Joseph, 162

314–15, 326–30, 332, 339, 346, 349–50, 353, 357–58, 360–61, 363, 366, 374, 376–77, 379, 383, 386, 389–90, 393, 400, 403, 405–7, 409, 414–15, 424, 426, 438, 440, 442, 446, 452, 456–58, 461, 464, 467, 472–73, 476–78, 480–83, 485, 490, 496–98, 501–5, 514–15, 524–25, 533–38, 542–44, 549, 553, 569, 571–72, 575, 585, 587–88, 592–93, 595, 597, 601, 607, 610, 612–14, 618, 623–27, 629, 631, 633–34
—State elections: JQA party nominating convention & controversies in, 43–44, 47–49, 50–51, 62, 144, 227; C. role in, 332; Am. System issue in, 39; patronage activities relating to, 404–6, 456; New–Old Court issue in, 48–49, 456; Metcalfe prospects in, 225, 305, 374; duelling as issue in, 461; importance of state elections to national pres. canvass, 185, 377, 386, 389–90, 393, 398, 400, 403, 404–6, 414–15, 424, 426, 428–29, 438–39, 456–58, 460–61, 464, 467, 476, 481, 485, 498; performance of JQA party in, 404–5; C. role in Metcalfe election, 426; outcome of, 47–51, 405, 424, 426, 428–29, 438–41, 446, 456–58, 460–61, 467, 473, 476, 485, 490; Maysville postmastership controversy in, 398–99, 401–2, 404–6; Lt. Gov. race, 476; House Speakership, 63; US Sen. election in, 461–62, 467, 583–84, 600; attacks on Barry in Gov. election, 316; 1828 state elections in, 278, 332, 400, 428–29, 446, 461–62, 476, 554–55; Admin. Central Committee, 144, 326–27, 330, 426, 461, 473; AJ party nominating conv., 467; AJ Central Committee, 144–46; judicial elections in, 554; C. declines testimonial dinners during 1828 contests, 399–400; Old Court Jacksonians support Barry for Gov., 456; Speaker of Ky. House election, 554; split among Jacksonians, 583–84
Kentucky, Circuit Court of, 117

Kentucky, Constitution of, 49
Kentucky, Court of Appeals of, 532, 554, 584, 599, 620
Kentucky, State Colonization Society, 505
Kentucky State Legislative Committee of the College, 39
Kenyon College (Theological Seminary of the Protestant Episcopal Church in the Diocese of Ohio), 113, 139, 355
Kero, 568
Kerr, John H., 27–28, 187, 587
Kerr, Nathaniel, 27
Key, Edmund, 356
Key, Francis Scott, 356
Key West, Fla., 12, 55, 60, 93, 112–13, 191, 222, 255
Killey, William (not identified): from, 425
King, Charles: suggests scheme to deprive AJ of his election (1828), 537–38; from, 537
King, Edward, 25
King, John, 224, 265
King, O. V. (not identified): from, 135
King, Rufus: political opposition to appt. as Min. to GB, 306; JQA admin. favors to family of, 265; mentioned, 189–90
Kingston, Mass., 67
Kircheval, Robert: from, 35
Kirk, William: from, 444; to, 445; mentioned, 444–45
Kirkland, John T.: from, 11, 218
Knight, Jonathan, 94
Knights of the Faith (France), 423
Knox Co., Ky., 510
Knox Co., Ohio, 527, 530
Kortright, Robert, 70, 351, 528
Kremer, George, 5, 38, 62, 348, 480–81, 629
Krudener, Paul, Baron de: from, 120, 183–84, 334, 410; to, 184, 209, 334, 509; mentioned, 206, 233

Laborde, Angel, 79, 146, 288
Laennec, Rene T. H., 197
Lafayette, George Washington, 3, 596
Lafayette, Marie Joseph Paul Yves Roch Gilbert du Motier, Marquis de: comment on "Corrupt Bargain" charge, 1–2; on Russo–Turkish War, 524; C. favors to, 11; on Fr.

domestic politics, 521, 596; health, 188; recommends US consular appt. at Lyons, 521; family matters, 311; proposed meeting with Christopher Hughes, 470; on James Fenimore Cooper, 521; service in Chamber of Deputies, 596; on US Pres. election (1828), 596; C. advice to on participation in Fr. politics, 3; on Fr. invasion of Spain, 521; from, 520, 596; to, 1; mentioned, 103, 404, 406, 409
La Guira, Colombia, 241–42, 251, 553
Lake Charles, Mo., 62
Lake Erie, 78, 571
Lake Huron, 335
Lake of the Woods, 523
Lake Superior, 523
Lamar y Cortazar, Jose de: C. lauds election of as Peru pres., 2–3; mentioned, 226, 435–36, 448, 462, 464, 469, 533
Lamb, Frederick James, 197, 381–82
Lambertsville, N.J., 447
Lambruschini, Luigi, 372–73, 377
La Mesa, Colombia, 596
Lancaster, Ky., 309
Lancaster, Pa., 158, 160
Lancaster Co., Pa., 158, 160, 253, 459–60
Langhorne, Maurice, 398–99, 401–2, 404–6
Lansingburgh, N.Y., 232
Lantista, 297
La Paz, Bolivia, 157
La Plata, Argentina, 258
Larkin, Elijah: from, 95
Larned, Samuel: from, 38, 108, 221, 269, 391, 462, 533; to, 181, 586–87; mentioned, 584
La Rochelle, N.Y., 90
Las Damas Argentinas, 465, 520
Latin America. *See* Spanish America
Laurens, Henry, 180
Laurie & Whittle (publishers), 523
LaValle, Juan, 528, 556
Lavergne, H., 275
Lawrence Co., Ky., 509
Lawrence Co., Ohio, 516
Lawrence, Joseph: from, 526; mentioned, 64, 97–98
Lawrence, William B.: complains of low pay, 225–26, 376; high cost of living in London as US Chargé, 366, 376, 459, 519; resig-

671

Marseilles, France, 159, 195–96, 224, 237
Marshall, John: supports C. "Address" on "Corrupt Bargain", 12, 216–17; supports JQA in 1828 campaign, 217, 235; misquoted in Baltimore *Marylander* on planned participation in 1828 election, 216–17; mentioned as alternative candidate in Electoral College plot to deny AJ the election, 537; on Crittenden appt. to Supreme Court, 550; C. asks for Crittenden patronage recommendation, 550; from, 12, 254, 550; mentioned, 91, 225
Marshall, John J.: to, 426
Marshall, Louis, 29
Marshall, Thomas, 142
Mars Hill, Me., 293–94, 629
Marteli, _____ (not identified), 108
Marti y Nin, Joseph: from, 127
Martignac, Jean Baptiste, 347, 367–68, 407, 423, 521, 580
Martin, Alexander, 25
Martin, John G.: from, 457
Martin, William Bond, 632
Martinique, 37, 111, 120, 138, 147–48, 347
Mary (daughter of James II) of England, 322
Mary, 27
Mary Ann, 241–42
Maryland: Gov. election in, 53–54; failure to benefit from JQA patronage, 120; state elections in (1828), 486–87, 490, 496, 507, 510; Pres. campaign in Wash. Co., 4; mentioned, 182, 207, 252, 282, 339, 356–58, 393, 470, 482, 285–88, 535, 537, 539, 546, 585, 602, 607–8, 623, 631–33
Maryland Circuit Court, 341, 357
Maryland Militia, 5th Company, 211
Mason Co., Ky., 405
Mason, James (not identified), 350
Mason, _____ (Mrs. John), 378
Massachusetts: states rights stance on NE boundary issue, 46, 291; state elections in (1829), 593; property stakes in NE boundary controversy, 581–82; interest in NE boundary settlement, 184 (*see also* Great

Britain: U.S. relations with); mentioned, 87, 102, 123, 163, 209, 264, 305, 317–18, 324, 383–84, 425, 516, 592, 605
Massachusetts Bay, 322
Matagorda, Tx., 237
Mather, George, 457, 591, 614–15
Mather, Thomas, 299–300
Mathews, William P. (not identified): from, 483
Matilda, 429
Matthews, William: from, 372–73
Maupin, Thomas, 384
Mauro, P. and Sons, 624
Maury, James, 418, 558
Maury, Richard Brooke, 248
Mayaguez, Puerto Rico, 53
Mayer, Charles F.: from, 604
Mayes, Daniel: from, 467–468; mentioned, 426, 505
Mayorga, Juan de Dios, 582
Maysville, Ky., 398–99, 401–2, 404–5
Maysville (Ky.) *Eagle*, 318
Maysville, Ohio, 236
Meaux, France, 521, 596
Mecca, 438
Medina, Co., Ohio, 516, 527
Medina, Xavier de, 171, 355, 527
Mediterranean, 115, 166, 210, 214, 334, 361, 370, 398, 410, 418, 438
Meigs Co., Ohio, 516
Melville, Robert Saunders Dundas, Lord, 447
Menard, Pierre, 296
Mendonca, Luis de Paula Furtado do Rio de, 137
Menou, Charles Jules, Count de: from, 578; to, 111, 579
Mentelle, Augustus W., 127
Mentelle, Charlotte, 127
Mercer Co., Ky., 128, 510
Mercer Co., Ohio, 516
Mercer, Hugh, 33
Mercersburg, Pa., 194
Merino, Rafael, 359
Meriwether, James, 268–69
Metcalfe, Thomas: in Ky. Gov. election, 39, 47, 51, 118, 278, 305, 374, 420 (*see also* Kentucky: state elections); elected Ky. Gov., 404, 420, 426, 429, 438–41, 446, 456–58, 473; vote for JQA in 1825 House election, 458; refuses to take dueling oath, 461; role in "Corrupt Bargain" issue, 481; mentioned, 44, 47–48, 51, 104, 124, 192, 225, 305, 400, 404, 467, 476, 490, 554, 584, 600, 620

Methodist Church, 63, 128, 605
Metternich, Prince Klemens Wenzel Nepomuk Lothar von, 289
Metz, France, Military Academy of, 549
Mexican War, 81
Mexico (including Calif. & Texas): internal instability, disorder, revolution, civil war in, 239, 391, 396, 468–69, 473, 512, 539, 563–64, 573–74, 578; commercial treaty with GB, 85; relations with GB, 238; economic difficulties in, 288, 324, 391, 522; hostile Indians in, 287; US military incursions into, 288; continuing war with Spain, 233, 288, 362, 369, 467–68, 522; rumored invasion of Cuba by, 324; shake up in govt. of, 53–54; rumored invasion by Spain from Cuba, 288, 362, 486; commercial treaty with Fr., 239; isthmian (Tehuantepec) canal project, 413; export of specie from, 237, 288, 413; role of Santa Anna in; 512, 529, 563, 574; hostility toward Spain in, 469; ratification of Panama Congress treaties, 396; character of people of, 473; expulsion of European Spaniards, 324, 469, 563; sentiment in for return of Span. colonial govt., 324, 454, 522; role of army in, 469, 522, 564; role of navy in, 153; Pres. election in (1828), 468, 473, 512, 528, 563–64, 578, 596; federalism in, 478; Masonic political power in, 469; designs on Guatemala, 582–83; maritime policy legis., 467–68; army interference in domestic politics, 469; mentioned, 76, 85, 94, 96, 99, 115, 120, 138, 143, 199, 222, 241, 267, 271, 286–87, 320, 362, 382, 390, 416, 436, 454, 469, 483, 486, 522, 582–83, 605
—U.S. relations with: 1831 Treaty of Amity, Commerce & Navigation with, 21–22, 32, 84, 87, 114, 153, 164, 231, 238, 288, 473, 512, 539; 1828 Treaty of Limits with, 21–22, 33, 84, 173, 198, 238, 244,

675

Patent Office, 210–11; on Am. System, 210; on Tariff of 1828, 210; on election & support of JQA, 210–11; reaction to AJ victory (1828), 544–45; names son after C., 545, 549; wife of, 548; on circulation of *Register*, 210; from, 210, 235, 273, 544; to, 548

Niles' Register, 23, 124, 210

Nimble, 12, 55, 60, 112, 314

Nones, Abraham B.: from, 79, 146, 363, 412, 505, 553, 596

Norfolk, Va., 168, 326, 355

North America, 130, 149, 245, 280, 314, 322, 360, 438, 523

North American Review, 155, 187, 288, 567

North Carolina: JQA Electoral–State Conv. in, 181–82; campaign of 1828 in, 181–82; state seeks to borrow money in GB or in North, 494–95; banking crisis in, 494–95; state archives of, 509; mentioned, 36, 64, 94, 129, 225, 278, 377, 439, 470, 490, 546

Northumberland Co., New Brunswick, 294

Northeast boundary, 46, 60, 87, 89, 102, 108, 114, 116, 131, 135–36, 150, 152, 155, 185, 198–99, 204, 213, 215, 220, 227, 233, 235, 250, 262, 273, 275, 278–79, 283, 289, 291, 305, 308, 312, 318, 321, 324, 333, 340, 345, 351, 361, 364, 369, 384, 387, 412, 425, 458, 471–72, 474, 490, 498, 539, 547, 581, 583, 589

Northeast Boundary Commission, 352, 523

Northeastern frontier, 437, 547

Northern frontier, 99, 163

Northampton, Mass., 385

Northampton Co., Va., 341

North Point, Md., 211

Northwest Territory, 262, 274

Norway, 213, 561

Norwich (Conn.) *Courier*, 559–60

Nourse, Joseph: to, 545

Nourse, Michael, 285

Nova Scotia, 123, 130, 187, 293–94, 322, 324

Nymph, 560–61

Oakley, Thomas J., 32, 71

Obando, Jose Maria, 573

Obregon, Pablo: from, 173, 251, 414; to, 251, 255; mentioned, 31, 33, 463

Ocana, Colombia, 88, 157, 226, 240, 251, 354

Ocana, Colombia, convention of, 79–89, 146, 226, 240, 244, 251, 354, 363, 381

Ofalia, Narciso de Heredia, Count of, 137, 213, 362, 454, 468

O'Fallon, John, 62

Offley, David: from, 97, 236; mentioned, 57–58

Ogden, Aaron, 448

Ogden, David B: from, 18, 297, 523

Ogden, vs. Saunders, 15

Ogle, Thomas, 386–87, 439

Ohio: split in AJ forces in, 25; JQA patronage activities in, 536; borrows private capital to build canal, 494–95; nominating convention in, 43; state elections in (1828), 513, 515–16, 524, 526–27, 530–31, 535–36; reaction to (1828) tariff in, 572–73; county vote for Pres. in (1828), 527, 530–31; mentioned, 17, 20–21, 45, 65, 236, 308, 339, 374, 390, 403, 413, 440, 443–44, 503–4, 525, 533–35, 537–38, 542–43, 571, 575, 593, 613

Ohio Co., Ky., 429, 510

Ohio Co., Va., 86

Ohio, Diocese of, 113–14, 139

Ohio River, 153, 212, 375, 613

Oldham, John P., 429, 461, 554

Olin, Henry, 605

Olin, Stephen, 605

Omoa, Honduras, 15, 84, 168, 173–74, 340, 358–59, 418

Oneida Co., N.Y., 482

Only Son, 67

Ontario (Upper Canada), 323, 360, 427, 484

Ontario (Upper Canada), Parliament of, 79

Oporto, Portugal, 289, 304, 313, 352, 377, 381–82, 387–88, 394, 398, 411, 442, 555–56

Osage Indians, 311

Osprey, 79, 505

O'Sullivan, Barbara (not identified): from, 618

Ottawa Indians, 296

Ottoman Empire. *See* Turkey

Oubril, Pierre de, 16, 214, 354

Owen, John Henry: from, 441

Owen, William, 605

Owsley, William: to, 426; mentioned, 554

Oxford, N.C., 495

Pacific Coast, 1, 154

Pacific Ocean, 418–19, 436–37, 469, 522, 587

Padilla, Jose, 157, 185, 226, 240, 498, 507

Paez, Jose Antonio, 240, 252, 603

Pakenham, Richard, 25

Palacios, Leandro, 148

Palatinate, 505

Palmela, Pedro de Sousa Holstein, Duke of, 239, 307, 352, 370, 382, 394

Palmer, Aaron H., 15

Palmerston, Henry John Temple, Viscount of, 311–12

Palmyra, Ky., 128

Panama: importance of US communications, 82; mentioned, 24, 33, 238, 436, 692

Panama Congress: domestic politics of US participation in, 159, 628–29; ratification of treaties of, 324, 396; mentioned, 120, 132

Panama, Isthmus of, 88, 436–37

Pannill, Samuel, 27–28

Panther, 475, 568

Papal States: Leo XII appoints Patron Saint for Br., 435; foreign policies of, 377; pretensions of, 423, 444

—U.S. relations with: Wm. V. Harold–John Ryan case, 372, 423–24, 581

Paraguay: threatened by Buenos Aires, 528

Paris, 23, 124, 128–29, 148, 160, 187, 223, 237, 239, 246, 266–68, 279, 302, 310–11, 367, 376, 382, 398, 404, 406–10, 418, 423, 427, 440, 445–46, 454, 470, 490–91, 519, 566–67, 580–81, 605

Park, Roswell, 612, 616

Parke, Benjamin: from, 613

Parke Co., Ind., 17

Parker, Daniel, 631–32

Parker, Daniel Jr., 632

Parker, Ezekiel, 632

Parrish, Jasper (not identified), 89

Paris *Constitutionnel*, 160, 162

Pascal, _____ (not identified), 241–42

Pasha, Ibrahim, 290, 422, 521

Paskevich, Ivan F., 17, 199, 428

677

Pitcher, Nathaniel, 318
Pitt Co., N.C., 182
Pittsburgh, 18, 253, 526, 571, 609
Pittsylvania, Va., 27
Pizarro, Francisco Javier Luna, 435, 463
Pleasants, Benjamin, 621
Pleasants, James: from, 276, 447; mentioned, 446, 448
Pleasants, John H.: from, 250; mentioned, 38, 154, 174, 183, 188–90, 316, 374, 516, 589
Pleasonton, Stephen, 82, 142, 159, 268, 446, 520, 580, 597
Plumer, William, 103, 217, 339
Plumer, William Jr.: works for JQA ticket in 1828, 402–3; supports C. on "Corrupt Bargain" charge, 626; from, 18, 402; to, 58, 103, 216, 626; mentioned, 59, 217
Plymouth, England, 92
Plymouth, Mass., 174
Pogue, William, 266
Poinsett, Joel R.: attempt to buy northern Mex. territory, 21; on European anti–US propaganda in Mex., 84; knowledge of Mex. agriculture, 76–77, 99; opinion of Mexicans, 288, 473, 512, 539; opinion of Santa Anna, 512; role in Panama (Tacubaya) Cong. treaties, 396; on Central Am. internal problems, 416; involvement in Mex. internal affairs, 539; from, 18, 25, 52, 84, 87, 114, 152–53, 163, 231, 237–38, 244, 288, 324, 390, 396, 413, 416, 467–68, 473, 512, 522, 528, 539, 563–64, 573, 577–78, 582, 596; to, 31, 231; mentioned, 33, 55, 143, 153, 173, 231, 566, 605. *See also* Mexico: U.S. relations with
Poland, 223
Political parties & factions (US)
—Adams, 18, 38, 43, 45, 314, 403, 420, 429, 441, 458, 503, 532, 554, 595
—Anti–Jackson, 18, 594
—Anti–Masonic: C. relation to, 186–87; in N.Y. (1828), 400–401, 474; C. opinion of, 186–87
—Anti–Relief (Old Court): in Ky. Gov. election (1828), 48, 62; in Pres. election (1828), 48, 62;

mentioned, 51, 306, 456, 584
—Jackson Clintonians, 22
—Jacksonian, 4, 6, 18, 22, 25–26, 44–45, 49, 58, 75, 92, 95–96, 98, 104, 110, 112, 118, 122, 129, 140, 145, 156, 164, 179, 182, 186, 188, 191, 193, 211–12, 216, 224–25, 312, 326, 360, 364, 400–403, 429, 439, 441, 456, 458, 467, 474, 476, 485, 487, 490, 496–97, 501, 508, 524, 532, 540, 551, 554, 583–84, 590, 592–95, 597, 618, 620–21, 625–26
—National Republican, 242–43, 439, 594, 610
—Relief (New Court): in Ky. Gov. election (1828), 49, 63; in Pres. election (1828), 63; mentioned, 51, 62, 303, 306, 620
—Republican, 35, 93, 139, 164, 191, 212, 272–73, 343, 516
Polk, Charles (not identified), 486
Polk, James K.: from, 231; to, 230
Pollard, Joseph (not identified): from, 42; mentioned, 43
Polly, 480
Pompieres, Labbay, 367–68
Ponce, Puerto Rico, 53
Ponsonby, John, 351, 379, 558
Popayan, Colombia, 569, 573, 596
Pope, John: in Ky. Sen. inquiry into "Corrupt Bargain", 141; supports AJ in 1828, 467; appointed Gov. of Ark. Territory, 548; withdraws as US Sen. candidate, 583–84; mentioned, 63, 75, 461–62, 505, 621
Portage Co., Ohio, 516
Port au Prince, Haiti, 26, 363
Port Gibson, Miss., 377
Porter, David: licenses Mex. privateers to prey on US Puerto Rican (Span.) shipping, 52–53; proclaims open war at sea on Span. shipping, 55; mentioned, 369, 604
Porter, Isaac H., 231
Porter, James M.: from, 481
Porter, John: from, 111; mentioned, 112
Porter, Joseph B., 231
Porter, Peter Buel: service on US/GB Boundary Commission, 176–79, 186, 300; delegate to N.Y. state JQA

conv., 300, 303, 342, 343; family, 300; wife of (Letitia Preston Breckinridge Grayson), 300, 301, 464, 474; appointed SecWar, 386, 389, 401, 414–15; performance as SecWar, 374; work for JQA ticket in 1828, 389; on Pres. election (1828), 389–90, 400; C. asks patronage favors of, 588; visits Ky., 390; from, 22, 32, 92, 164, 176, 190, 216, 300, 342, 352, 389, 539; to, 36, 71, 136, 175, 186, 211, 225, 300, 302, 335, 550; mentioned, 79, 83, 110, 113, 118, 121, 368, 415, 474, 523, 571, 604
Porter, Robert: from, 111; mentioned, 112
Portland *Eastern Argus*, 135
Portsmouth, England, 370, 415
Portsmouth, N.H., 340
Portsmouth, Ohio, 513
Portugal: European attitudes toward, 289, 304, 360, 377, 411; role in Buenos Aires–Br. war, 8, 151; rumored war with GB, 381, 558; GB withdrawal from, 68, 69, 115, 137, 161, 181, 195, 197, 206, 213, 223, 232, 235, 239, 259, 286, 381, 411; tensions within the nobility of, 23, 72; policy toward Spain, 411, 427; special commercial concessions to Br., 205–6; military forces of, 556; constit. of 1826, 195; Constit. vs. Royalist struggle in, 36, 72, 85, 115, 137, 161, 176, 198, 232, 259, 286, 289, 313, 315, 352, 359–60, 369, 382–83, 387, 393–94, 398, 555–56, 558; economic conditions in, 23, 72, 232, 289, 398, 505; royal family scandals in, 382; Miguel rise to absolute power, 115, 137, 161, 176, 181, 195, 198, 222–23, 232, 239, 249–50, 259, 264, 271–72, 289, 304, 307, 310, 313, 315, 336, 354, 359–60, 368–69, 376–77, 381, 382–83, 393–94, 398, 411, 418, 431, 555–56; Br. Emperor Peter I abdicates crown (as Peter IV) for, 165, 304, 375, 545; relations with Spain, 286; internal instability, disorder, revolution, civil war, 197–98, 289, 304, 313,

Portugal (continued): 315, 336, 352, 359, 360, 369, 377, 382–83, 387–88, 394, 398, 411, 422, 431, 555–56; decline of GB influence in, 382, 394, 422, 555–56; Miguel hostility toward GB, 422; role of Maria da Gloria in, 249–50, 471, 512, 545, 556–58; Masonic societies in, 360; student activism in, 198, 360; justification of Miguel govt. legitimacy, 388, 411; Miguel–Carlota tension in, 431, 555–56; GB influence & policy in, 387, 394, 431, 472, 512, 545, 555–56, 558; Fr. policy in, 556; role of Carlota Joaquina in, 431, 526; Span. policy in (*see* Spain: relations with & policy toward Miguel govt. in Portugal); Azores opposition to Miguel govt., 398, 431; invasion of Azores by, 398, 431, 465; Madeiran opposition to Miguel govt.–independence movement, 388, 394, 398, 465, 555; invasion of Madeira by, 465; pirates out of Cape Verde, 420; mentioned, 8, 200, 267, 333, 361, 370, 395, 408, 412, 419, 438, 474, 477, 513, 617

—U.S. relations with: attempts to get commercial treaty with, 26–27, 151; US claims against, 45, 79, 505; maritime policy toward US, 61, 151; US violations of maritime policy of, 151; protest privateers fitted out in US, 151; US non–involvement in internal affairs of, 264–65, 459; US commercial interest in Madeira & the Azores, 289; US trade with the Azores, 371; Provisional Junta seeks US recognition, 336; treatment of US citizens in Madeira, 465; US attitudes toward recognition of Miguel govt., 259–60, 264, 271–72, 442, 491, 545

Portugal, Constitution of, 23, 72, 85, 115, 137, 161, 176, 250, 383, 393, 555, 558

Portugal, Cortes of, 23, 115, 161, 259, 271, 304, 313, 315, 336, 354, 359–60, 369, 376, 382, 411

Portugal, Dept. of Foreign Affairs of, 393

Portugal, Dept. of War of, 161

Portugal, House of Deputies of, 161, 176

Portugal, House of Peers of, 161

Port Vincent, La., 59

Potomac River, 525

Potowatomi Indians, 296

Potter, Robert: from, 495; to, 494

Poughkeepsie, N.Y., 18

Pratt, Henry: from, 160; to, 161

Preble, William Pitt: from, 308, 373, 396, 470, 576; to, 283, 291, 308; mentioned, 135–36, 152, 284, 289, 291, 296, 316–18, 412, 425, 470, 474, 567, 589

Presbyterian, 63, 128, 193–94, 607

President Adams, 614

Presidente, 1, 343

Prevost, Stanhope (not identified): from, 136, 165, 244, 279; mentioned, 9, 288

Price, George, 252

Price, Susanna Hart, 126–27, 490

Price, William: from, 633

Prince George's Co., Md., 356, 487

Princeton, N.J., 192

Princeton Theological Seminary, 194

Princeton University, 607, 611

Proclamation Line of 1763, 509

Protestant Episcopal Church, 113, 139

Providence *Literary Subaltern*, 614

Providence, R.I., 11

Province of Coahuila & Texas, Mexico, 231, 238

Prussia: King of (Frederick William III) as possible arbiter of NE boundary, 200, 279; reaction to Russo–Turkish War, 370, 423; mentioned, 310, 370

—U.S. relations with: US treaty with, 244, 264, 278–79, 368–69, 615; Prussia proposes free trade arrangement, 264; US Treaty of 1785 with, 244, 615; US Treaty of 1799 with, 369, 615; US slights on protocol issue, 529

Pruth River, 159, 195, 223, 309

Puebla, Mexico, 564, 573–74, 577–78

Puerto Cabello, Colombia, 252, 479–80, 603

Puerto Rico: increase of US trade with, 53; US technicians work in, 592; Fr. interest in acquiring, 368; mentioned, 10, 53, 368

Pulaski Co., Ky., 128, 429

Pulis, Joseph Jr.: from, 90; mentioned, 290

Purviance, Robert, 553

Purviance, Samuel, 553

Quadrado, Francisco de Paula, 468

Quarles, John Tunstall, 429, 554, 620

Quebec (Province of Lower Canada), 44, 114, 216, 292–93, 323, 333, 360, 396, 427, 484

Quebec Act, 293

Quillota, Chile, 108

Quincy, John D., 520

Radcliff, Alexander H., 448

Radcliff, William: from, 288, 448, 469, 502; mentioned, 88, 136, 165, 279, 487

Raguet, Condy: resigns as US Min. to Br., 172, 217, 295, 355, 359, 433; defends decision to resign, 434; character & personality of, 417, 433; mentioned, 173, 189, 200, 259, 435, 437, 443

Rahahman, Abdul (Moroccan slave), 31

Raleigh, N.C., 182

Ramage, James, 580–81

Ramsey, George, 295

Randall, Richard, 31

Randall, Thomas, 320

Randolph Co., N.C., 182

Randolph, Edmund, 128

Randolph, John: attacks C. on "Corrupt Bargain", 110–111, 113, 151; C. dislike of, 154, 182; physical problems of, 154, 182; on Jackson's execution of Tenn. militiamen (1815), 526–27; scandals in family of, 316, 326; conflict with Richard Rush, 414–15; mentioned, 135, 152, 155, 174, 281

Randolph, Martha Jefferson (Mrs. Thomas M.), 487, 489, 506, 532

Randolph, Thomas Jefferson, 506, 511

Randolph, Thomas M., 489

Ranger, 493

Rawle, William, 484

Wing, Charles Fox (not identified), 194
Winnebago Indians, 16, 296
Winthrop, Thomas L., 593
Wirt, William: from, 237; to, 237; mentioned, 198, 522
Wirt, _____ (Mrs. William), 407, 446
Woodbridge, William: from, 56, 432
Woodbury, Levi: from, 120; to, 147
Woodford Co., Ky., 128, 420, 429, 535
Woods, Alva: to, 153, 301; mentioned, 11, 207, 218, 302, 497, 511, 585
Woods, John, 17

Woodstock, Va., 374
Wooley, Aaron K., 339, 377
Wooster Co., Ohio, 440
Workman, Samuel, 5
Worsley, William W.: to, 427
Worth, William Jenkins, 80–81
Wright, John, 526–27
Wright, Silas, 22–23
Wright, William H. D. C.: from, 14, 74, 148, 165, 180, 234, 252, 355, 443; mentioned, 174, 208, 295, 388, 609
Wuits, Dimitri de, 397, 404, 531
Wylie, Andrew, 63, 96–97, 339

Xavier, Candido Jose, 26
Xenia, Ohio, 236

Yancy, Joel, 117, 183, 429
York Co., New Brunswick, 294
Yorkinos party (Mexico), 153
Yost, Philip Jr.: from, 26, 363
Young, John: from, 16, 128, 318

Zanesville, Ohio, 94
Zavala, Lorenzo, 512, 563–64
Zulme, 222

690

SUBJECT INDEX: VOLUMES 1–6

Abbreviations used in the index follow.

AJ	Andrew Jackson	GB	Great Britain	Ru.	Russia
Am.	America	Gr.	Greece	Sp.	Spain
Amen.	Amendment	JQA	John Quincy Adams	TU	Transylvania Univ.
Appt.	Appoint(ed)	Lex.	Lexington, Ky.	Tur.	Turkey (Ottoman
BA	Buenos Aires	Mfgr.	Manufacture		Empire)
BEI	British East Indies	Mex.	Mexico	US	United States of
BWI	British West Indies	MFN	Most favored nation		America
Br.	Brazil	N.O.	New Orleans	USMA	U.S. Military
BUS	Bank of the United	Nom.	Nominate		Academy
	States	P.O.	Post Office Dept.	USN	U.S. Navy
C.	Clay (Henry)	Port.	Portugal	VP	Vice President
DWI	Danish West Indies	Pres.	President	Wash.	Washington, D.C.
Fr.	France	PR	Puerto Rico		

Adams (John Q.) administration (*cont*.):
726, 748–9, 788, 853, 885, 971, 994 (*see
ibid*.). General opposition to: **5:** 565; **6:**
369–70. Clinton opposition to & views of:
4: 129–30, 286–7, 318, 364, 547, 551,
858, 900; **5:** 113, 126, 143, 348, 428, 492,
675; **6:** 130, 245–6 (*see also* Clinton,
DeWitt; Election of 1828). AJ opposition
to & views of: **4:** 84–5, 114–5, 122, 333,
336, 364, 465, 618; **5:** 30, 221, 396, 428,
968; **6:** 369–70 (*see also* Jackson, Andrew;
Election of 1828). Van Buren opposition
to & views of: **4:** 318; **5:** 113, 126, 143–4,
175, 186, 207, 346–8, 410, 676–7,
945–6, 995, 1032; **6:** 141, 245–6, 544.
Eclectic nature of opposition to: **4:** 889,
891, 895–6, 900, 905; **5:** 126, 143–4,
174, 186, 289, 354, 428, 431, 650, 799; **6:**
125, 258. Vigor of opposition to: **5:**
209–12, 259, 381–2, 383; **6:** 991, 994.
Opposition majority in Sen.: **5:** 117–8,
122, 126, 158. Admin. majority in Sen.:
5: 273, 388, 994, 1023; **6:** 169. Admin.
majority in House: **5:** 118, 122, 126, 158,
273, 388; **6:** 361. Choice of newspaper
printers & editors to publish the laws: **5:**
991, 994; **6:** 209–12, 259, 381–2, 383 (*see
also* above politics & patronage relationship during). Attitude toward Federalist
party: **5:** 526. Corruption in: **6:** 331–2,
384, 502. Choice of VP candidate for
1828: **6:** 472–3 (*see also* Election of 1828).
Disloyalty to of John McLean (*see*
McLean, John). Maneuvering for expected new fed. judgeships: **5:** 64–5, 75,
118–9, 254. Porter court martial (*see* U.S.
Navy; Porter, David). Role of VP Calhoun in: **4:** 336; **5:** 7, 113, 126, 158, 191,
233, 307, 350, 428, 664, 788, 853–4; **6:**
125, 258–9 (*see also* Calhoun, John C.).
Cabinet appointments: **4:** 68, 73, 75–6,
88, 90, 92; **5:** 286. C. analysis of 1826
mid–term Cong. elections: **5:** 568, 584–5,
710–11, 742, 755–6, 756–7, 761–2, 804,
810, 888–9, 950, 972, 979, 987, 1000–01,
1023. C. detachment from Ky. politics
during: **5:** 159
—"Corrupt Bargain" controversy during:
C. defense of his role in (*see espec.* **4:**
143–66; **5:** 655–8): **4:** 178, 193–4,
196–8, 210–3, 221, 226–8, 230, 234,
268, 286, 301–2, 317, 335, 387, 392–3,
404, 408, 415–6, 418, 434, 439, 445, 462,
498, 520–22, 530; **5:** 565–6, 655–8, 746,
756, 788, 791; **6:** 18–9, 25, 566–7,
644–5, 763–6, 775, 957–8. C. conspiracy
thesis on: **4:** 211, 318, 382, 408, 413, 418,
447, 522. Support of C. position on issue:
4: 97, 122, 178, 189–90, 205–6, 211–3, 221,
225–28, 230, 234, 236, 257, 264–5,
268–9, 285–6, 301, 316–8, 333, 335,
364, 381–2, 387, 389, 391–3, 400, 401,
405–6, 408, 412–3, 427, 429–33, 437,
440, 442, 489, 553, 561, 567, 572, 576,
698, 722; **5:** 23, 144, 155, 280, 402,
439–40, 561, 563–4, 642, 650, 745, 748,
775, 885, 970, 1009, 1154; **6:** 10, 25, 144,
173 (*see also* Election of 1824: House

election phase; Election of 1828: issues,
charges, & counter—charges in campaign). Attacks on C. position on issue: **4:**
84–5, 191–2, 198–200, 207–8, 221,
282–3, 308, 318, 333, 335, 389, 392–3,
403, 408, 412–3, 429–30, 436, 439, 447,
462, 521, 531, 567; **5:** 279–80, 724, 756;
6: 703, 706 (*see ibid.*, & Eaton, John H.).
C. assertion of purity: **4:** 163, 165, 269,
521; **6:** 1177. C. burned in effigy: **4:** 145,
165, 312, 447. Old Court–New Court
reactions to: **4:** 134–5. C. Cong. district
supports his choice of JQA: **6:** 775–6,
1276. Reaction to controversy in Lex.,
Ky.: **4:** 305; **6:** 776. Newspaper speculation on & role in: **4:** 68, 145, 429; **6:**
778–9. Toasts denying C. role in: **4:** 393,
408, 421, 431, 442, 498, 515, 528; **6:** 777
—policies & legislation: Foreign policy (*see*
various nation entries). Failures in foreign policy feared: **6:** 1082–3, 1139, 1144
(*see also* Brown, James). Ga. (Creek Indian) policy: **4:** 426, 501–2, 585–6, 615,
618, 632, 638, 674, 676–9, 794, 823, 846,
868, 891; **5:** 55, 186–7; **6:** 185–6, 242.
Internal improvements: **4:** 543–4, 807,
872; **5:** 410, 417, 421, 618, 738, 768; **6:**
188–90, 321–2 (*see also* American System:
internal improvements). Constit. amen. to
reform Electoral College: **4:** 781, 783–4;
5: 187, 278–80, 531–2, 650–1. Public
land policy: **4:** 569, 807. Militia reform:
6: 53–4, 119. Bankruptcy law: **5:** 651,
1041; **6:** 192. Tariff attitudes: **5:** 423,
738; **6:** 692, 1303–4. Extinguish public
debt: **6:** 674. King appt. (*see* King,
Rufus). Gallatin appointment (*see* Gallatin, Albert). Offer ministry to Clinton
(*see* Clinton, DeWitt). General policies: **4:**
114–5. *See also* Congress of the United
States: nineteenth congress; twentieth
congress
—Annual Messages: 1825: **4:** 569, 807, 823,
851, 859, 872, 889–90, 905, 920, 931; **5:**
28, 73, 105, 152, 184, 242–3; **6:** 208,
469. Fr. spoilation claims: **4:** 823, 831,
896, 937, 959; **5:** 28–31, 123, 419–20 (*see
also* France: U.S. relations with). Panama
Cong. participation: **4:** 889–90, 892; **5:**
186–7, 253, 273, 281, 421, 428, 531,
658–9, 969, 980–1; **6:** 141 (*see also* U.S.
diplomacy: Panama Congress). National
university: **4:** 872; **5:** 9, 195. National
library: **5:** 195. National observatory: **4:**
872; **5:** 7. National exploring expeditions:
4: 872. Canal construction: **4:** 544, 920.
Trade reciprocity: **4:** 931; **5:** 1. Internal
improvements: **4:** 872. Military post in
Oregon: **6:** 723. Support for 1825 Message: **4:** 895, 920, 924, 948; **5:** 7, 28.
Criticism of 1825 Message: **4:** 895, 906,
948; **5:** 7, 724, 738; **6:** 208, 469. Omissions in 1825 Message: **4:** 920. 1826 Message: **5:** 984, 987, 997. Trade controversy
with GB: **5:** 984, 988, 1027. Militia reform: **6:** 53–4. Neutrality in Br.–BA war:
6: 170. Commercial treaty with Sweden:
6: 183. Recognition of Span. Am. inde-

pendence: **6:** 183–4. Reduction of national debt: **6:** 674, 676. Internal improvements: **6:** 676. Support for 1826 Message: **6:** 185–6. Reception of 1826 Message in Europe: **6:** 128, 183, 674. 1827 Message: **6:** 1157. C. recommends subjects to be treated: **6:** 1256. JQA ducks tariff issue in: **6:** 1303–4, 1350–1, 1384–5

Adams, John: Mission to Fr.: **6:** 242. C. on admin. of: **1:** 36, 94, 720; **2:** 649; **6:** 644. C. on Alien & Sedition Acts (Va.–Ky. Resolves): **1:** 94, 350, 596, 760; **2:** 450, 469–71, 474; **3:** 163–4, 170, 478, 581, 738. War policies against Fr.: **1:** 672–3, 760; **2:** 649. Bankruptcy legis.: **5:** 651–2. C. personal dislike of: **2:** 614. Role of JQA in admin. of: **4:** 934; **6:** 25–6. On Am.–Canadian (Northern) boundary: **4:** 677. Death of: **5:** 545, 577, 622, 640–1, 735, 743. C. on death of: **5:** 554, 567, 762

Adams, John Quincy: Supports Jefferson on 1807 U.S. Embargo: **6:** 818. Shift from Federalist to Dem. party (1808): **6:** 818, 897–8. US Min. to Ru.: **1:** 799, 861, 880; **6:** 413. US Min. to Hague: **3:** 60. Payment for services at Ghent: **3:** 54–5. Doubts favorable outcome of Ghent peace talks: **1:** 940. Conflict with C. over disposal of Ghent conference documents: **1:** 1012; **2:** 1, 2. Appt. Min. to GB: **2:** 12, 13, 23, 25, 43, 54. As Harvard professor: **2:** 80, 761; **3:** 185. US Min. to Prussia: **3:** 60. C. conflict with at Ghent on Miss. River navigation vs. fisheries issue: **2:** 372–3, 427; **3:** 204; **6:** 816–7 (*see also* Election of 1824: issues). C. social intercourse with: **2:** 433; **3:** 22, 181, 899. C. criticizes cautious Sp. policy of: **2:** 499–500, 513. Supporters of hostile to C.: **2:** 672. C. patronage favors to: **2:** 322–3. Conflict with C. over Anglo–Am. Commercial Treaty (1815): **2:** 54. C. patronage requests of: **2:** 400, 764–5; **3:** 103–4. Criticized for sectional biases at Ghent: **2:** 75–8; **3:** 204, 210, 237–40, 254, 256, 270, 283, 292–4, 315, 323–4, 341, 350, 358, 368, 378, 409, 543; **4:** 158–61; **5:** 656; **6:** 816–7 (*see also* Election of 1824: issues). Resignation (1808) from US Sen.: **6:** 818. Political career boosted by Ghent role: **2:** 77–8. C. opposes appt. as SecState: **2:** 258. Russell opposes appt. as SecState: **2:** 428. C. favors rendered to: **2:** 322–3. Sounds C. out on mission to Span. Am.: **3:** 198, 202. Russell condemns role of in Span. Treaty: **2:** 755–58, 782, 784. C. criticism of in negotiating Span. Treaty: **2:** 769, 770–1, 797, 815, 823, 857. Criticism of foreign policy of: **3:** 184. Blocks C. attempt to get payment for Ghent service: **3:** 55, 70. Anglophobia of: **3:** 107, 200. On proper social protocol in Wash.: **3:** 201. C. on character of: **3:** 107; **6:** 816. Various comments on character of: **3:** 196, 808; **5:** 650, 675, 707. Pres. candidacies of (*see* Elections of 1824; & 1828). Opposition to

internal improvements (1807): **3:** 569. Opinion of Wm. H. Harrison: **6:** 473–4. Writes article on Anglo–Am. trade controversy: **5:** 1048. Pres. JQA as his own Sec State: **5:** 1058. Opinion of John Mclean: **6:** 373. Philosophy of patronage: **4:** 321, 568, 615, 858, 799, 820; **6:** 1204. Admin. of (*see* Adams (John Q.) administration)

Alabama: Fertility of fields & forests of: **1:** 593. Territorial status conferred on (1817): **2:** 318. C. recommends Gov. for Ala. Territory: **2:** 318. Prospects for lawyers in: **2:** 418. Proposal to plant Fr. emigrant colony in: **2:** 318–9, 328, 331. University in: **4:** 798–9. Wealth of: **2:** 418. Need for more Fed. courts in: **5:** 18. Views of JQA admin. in: **4:** 688. Poor cotton crop in: **4:** 688. Fraudulent sale of Span.–owned slaves in: **4:** 701; **5:** 146–7, 151, 154, 179–80, 192–3, 218. Pro–AJ sentiment in: **4:** 798–9; **6:** 1367. Attitude toward Panama Cong. in: **5:** 223. U.S. Sen. campaign in (1826): **5:** 702–3, 1023. Adams admin. patronage problems, opportunities, decisions in: **6:** 1367

American Colonization Society. *See* Slavery & slaves

American System
—general (*see espec.* **2:** 512–39, 826–47, 858, 860): Military preparedness dimension of: **2:** 70, 119–21, 157, 793, 844; **3:** 724; **4:** 29; **6:** 700. Speed recovery from War of 1812: **2:** 157–8. Economic nationalism element of: **2:** 157–8, 468, 827–8, 835–6; **3:** 720–2. Foreign policy dimensions of: **5:** 857–8, 867–8. Isolation from European wars: **2:** 828, 836. Handmaiden to US continental expansion: **3:** 584. Aimed mainly at GB: **2:** 174–5; **6:** 745. Factor in recovery from 1819 depression: **4:** 29. Sectional needs for: **3:** 479–80. Key to US prosperity: **3:** 701; **4:** 29. Relationship to industrial revolution: **3:** 695–6, 710. Constit. of: **2:** 469–70, 630; **6:** 701, 706 (*see also below* internal improvements). *Federalist Papers* support: **2:** 476. Relation of national revenue system to: **2:** 410, 831. BUS as dimension of: **2:** 202–3 (*see also* Bank of the United States: second B.U.S.). Favorable balance of trade element in: **2:** 831–2; **3:** 479. Creation of new markets: **6:** 700. Contribution to balanced factory–agricultural economy: **2:** 831–2; **3:** 479, 694–5, 711. No danger to rural–agricultural life in US: **2:** 833–4; **3:** 718. Make–work feature of: **4:** 268. Book, article, newspaper accounts of: **4:** 882; **5:** 37. Impact of 1830 census on: **6:** 654. Interests opposed to: **3:** 727 (*see also* Election of 1824: issues; American System; Election of 1828: issues, charges, & countercharges in campaign). As a political issue: **3:** 727; **5:** 417; **6:** 1372 (*see also ibid.*). C. praised & damned for conceiving & advancing: **2:** 572–3; **4:** 437, 527; **5:** 417, 642–3; **6:** 712–3, 745 (*see also ibid.*).

American System (*continued*):
Toasts associating C. with: **3:** 778, 780; **4:** 421, 498, 523, 531–2; **5:** 661; **6:** 705–6, 712–3, 734, 777–8, 783, 796
—domestic manufactures: Growth of: **2:** 840; **4:** 529. GB threat to: **2:** 174–5, 828; **3:** 642–3, 647, 649. Role in foreign policy: **1:** 396–7, **2:** 486. Key to US isolationism & economic self–sufficiency: **1:** 460–2; **2:** 157, 183, 835–6; **3:** 81, 699. Contribution to international peace: **2:** 836. Relationship to tariff: **2:** 174–5, 182–3, 410, 831; **3:** 711–2 (*see also* below protective tariff). Require stable domestic prices & markets: **3:** 649. Relationship to population growth: **2:** 826–7. Advantage to army & navy: **1:** 462; **3:** 677. Military needs assist development of: **2:** 840; **3:** 696, 700, 741–2; **6:** 1212. Increase US taxation base: **2:** 832; **3:** 698–9. Will help stabilize fluctuating agriculture crops & prices: **2:** 836. Advantages of machine production: **2:** 829–30; **3:**710. Provide employment opportunities: **3:** 709–10. Employ idle women & children: **2:** 830. Factory labor no worse than farming: **2:** 830–1. Will replace foreign trade as basis of US economy: **2:** 835–6. Will not lead to undesirable urban–mfgr. society: **1:** 459–60, 828–9; **3:** 711, 718. C. sees balanced farm (rural) & factory (urban) society & economy in US: **1:** 459–60, 828–9; **2:** 831–6; **3:** 479, 694–5, 711, 718. Use of slave labor in Southern factories: **3:** 701–2, 728. Relationship to immoral capitalism: **3:** 718. Will bind sections together: **2:** 836. National advantages of outweigh sectional disadvantages: **3:** 725–6. Importance to West: **2:** 869 (*see also* below internal improvements). C. urges buy American: **2:** 896. Improvement in technology & quality in US mfgrs.: **6:** 653 (*see also* U.S. Patent Office)
—internal improvements: Will assist agricultural development: **1:** 463. War of 1812 problems show need for: **2:** 462, 476–7, 478. Interstate commerce dimensions of: **2:** 309, 487; **3:** 619. Will unify & strengthen nation: **2:** 309–11, 449–50, 458–9, 468–9, 481, 484; **3:** 588, 592; **4:** 24–6, 31–2, 529; **6:** 1045. C. constit. arguments for: **1:** 285; **2:** 446–55, 457–60, 462–4, 468–9, 474–80, 482, 488, 630; **3:** 568–9, 573–88, 619–26, 779, 881. Constit. arguments against: **2:** 311, 468, 475, 483–4, 869; **3:** 568–9, 573–4, 719. Constit. amen. to authorize: **2:** 464, 483; **5:** 7, 9 (*see also* U.S. Constitution). Relation of constit. war powers to: **2:** 476–7. C. personal experience with river & turnpike travel: **2:** 573, 697–8, 800–1; **5:** 618. Relative costs of: **3:** 574; **4:** 28–9. Use of soldier labor to build: **2:** 485–6, 491, 626–9. Fed. expenditures on helping economy of states & sections: **3:** 589–91; **4:** 22. Fed. vs. private financing of: **2:** 311, 451, 486–7; **4:** 22, 25, 31; **5:** 46, 688; **6:** 188–9. BUS involvement in: **5:** 271–2, 302 (*see also* Bank of the U.S.:

second B.U.S.). Lottery support: **5:** 974. Ky. stake in: **1:** 215–6; **2:** 572; **4:** 22; **6:** 1149–50. Benefit of to West: **2:** 459, 461; **3:** 589–92, 779; **4:** 21, 24–5, 31, 528–9 (*see also* Election of 1824: issues; Election of 1828: issues, charges, & counter-charges in campaign). New England on: **3:** 737–8. Sectionalism & development of rivers, canals, & turnpikes: **2:** 120, 187–8; **3:** 22, 29–30, 529, 779; **4:** 31. Military dimensions of canal & turnpike construct.: **2:** 157, 449–50, 462, 464, 475–8, 484, 626; **3:** 588, 593, 619, 624; **4:** 29; **5:** 328. National vs. state obligation in supporting: **5:** 245. Impact of steamboat on: **2:** 459. Impact of on land values: **4:** 561. Pa. Society for Promotion of: **4:** 102. Improvement of Ohio River navigation: **2:** 310, 793; **3:** 673, 749–50, 779, 810; **4:** 29. Improvement of Miss. River navigation: **2:** 793; **3:** 673, 749–50, 779; **4:** 715–6; **5:** 245. Need for Cumberland (National) Road: **2:** 188, 310, 479–80, 486–7, 563; **3:** 23, 56, 575, 592; **4:** 19–33. Condition of Cumberland Road: **1:** 548; **2:** 188; **3:** 14; **6:** 253–4, 261. Extension of Cumberland Road west of Wheeling: **4:** 21, 268, 304–5, 529, 561, 807; **5:** 45–6, 417. Detroit–Chicago Road: **4:** 99, 268. Hudson River–Buffalo Road: **5:** 663; **6:** 140. James River– Kanawha Road: **5:** 661–2. Lake Michigan–Ohio River Road: **5:** 892–3. Little Rock–Cantonment Gibson Road: **4:** 226. Me.–La. Coastal Road proposal: **2:** 310–11. Maysville—Lex. Road: **2:** 562; **6:** 1174 (*see also* Lexington, Ky.). Shawnee-town–Kaskaskia Road: **2:** 214–5. St. Louis–Santa Fe Road: **4:** 176, 213, 226, 240, 283, 448, 549 (*see also* Mexico: U.S. relations with). Wash.–Lake Ontario Road: **5:** 1037–8. Wash.–N.O. Road: **4:** 21–2, 32, 328–30, 807, 901; **5:** 881; **6:** 1372. Zanesville–N.O. Road: **5:** 881–2; **6:** 1150. Controversy & competition over road routes: **4:** 304, 314, 328–30, 901. Claims related to construct. of: **5:** 46–7. Champlain–St. Lawrence Canal: **5:** 459, 477. Chesapeake & Del. Canal: **1:** 284, 845; **2:** 309, 478, 486–7; **3:** 575, 593; **4:** 29, 31–2. Chesapeake & Ohio Canal project: **3:** 575, 593; **4:** 29–30, 314; **5:** 688, 974, 983; **6:** 188, 322. Del.–Raritan (N.J.) Rivers Canal: **1:** 845; **3:** 575, 593. Dismal Swamp (Va.–N.C.) Canal: **5:** 974. Erie Canal (*see* New York State). Hiwassee (Tenn.) canal proposal: **6:** 490. Ill.–Mich. Canal: **4:** 543–4; **6:** 502. Morris (N.J.) Canal: **3:** 575, 593. Muscle Shoals (Ala.) Canal: **4:** 29, 32–3. N.O.–Pontchartrain Canal: **5:** 635–6. Ohio & Erie Canal: **4:** 112, 529, 531, 547, 836; **5:** 188, 322. Ohio Rapids (Falls of the Ohio River; Louisville–Portland) Canal: **1:** 162, 267–8, 274, 284–7; **3:** 569; **4:** 29, 33, 523; **5:** 590, 965. Oswego (Syracuse–Oswego) Canal: **5:** 459, 477. Pittsburgh–Philadelphia Canal proposal: **6:** 292. Wabash & Erie Canal: **4:** 543–4; **5:**

82. Potomac Toll Bridge: **1:** 273. Importance of railroads to sectional unity: **6:** 1045. Baltimore & Ohio Railroad: **6:** 339. *See also* Election of 1824: issues; Election of 1828: issues, charges & counter–charges in campaign

—protective tariff (*see espec.* **3:** 682–730): Assists the growth of domestic mfgrs.: **1:** 461–2, 470; **2:** 157, 174–5, 179, 182–4, 826–41; **3:** 81, 479, 636, 687–8, 692–3, 701, 703, 709–10, 741; **4:** 28. Will reduce public debt: **3:** 707–9; **4:** 27–8. GB competition necessitates: **2:** 174; **3:** 642–3, 647, 649–50, 659–60, 670–1, 689, 695–6, 703, 713. Aid to domestic agriculture: **3:** 636, 678, 692. Major support of US Treas.: **1:** 625–6. National defense dimensions of: **3:** 724, 741–2. Key to national wealth, power, glory: **3:** 636, 680, 684, 699, 707–9, 727–8, 770; **4:** 789. And the prosecution of war: **2:** 134, 157. US economic foreign policy dimensions of: **2:** 839–40; **3:** 686, 694. Impact on US Merchant Marine: **3:** 705. Sectional differences on: **1:** 462; **3:** 629, 636–7, 639–40, 648, 650, 681, 701–2, 723–6, 738–9, 779; **5:** 655 (*see also* Election of 1824: issues; Election of 1828: issues, charges & counter–charges in campaign; Congress of the United States, various sessions). Will help reduce unemployment: **3:** 692–4, 709–10. Retard international monopolies: **3:** 683, 688–9, 712. Reduce land taxes: **2:** 134, 138–9. Key to economic nationalism & isolationism: **3:** 684, 686, 692. Constit. arguments: **2:** 842; **3:** 719. Arguments against: **3:** 740–2. C. on free trade: **2:** 828; **3:** 714–5. C. cites Smith & Malthus on: **2:** 841, 846. And balance of trade: **3:** 706, 728, 742. Level of trade: **3:** 705–6. Help create stable domestic market: **3:** 649, 693–4, 712. C. support of: **1:** 523; **2:** 134; **3:** 479–80, 683–4, 692, 694, 699, 727. Dutch competition necessitates: **5:** 825. Impact on US trade with BWI: **3:** 635, 637, 714 (*see also* Great Britain: GB restrictions (1822–1825) on US trade with GB American Colonies; GB interdiction (1826) of US trade with GB American Colonies). Specific tariff schedules, viz: books: **2:** 825; coal: **2:** 185; copper: **3:** 733–4; various cottons: **2:** 178–9; **3:** 639, 642–4, 647–51, 659–60, 666–7, 683, 703, 713, 725, 745; **4:** 789; flax: **3:** 667; gunpowder: **3:** 639; hemp: **1:** 524, 596; **2:** 180; **3:** 639, 643, 659–60, 667, 676, 745 (*see also* Clay, Henry: hemp culture); ironware: **3:** 639, 648, 651, 745; lead: **2:** 183; molasses: **2:** 825, 843; **3:** 677–81, 707, 726, 828; sailduck: **3:** 676–7; salt: **2:** 825; saltpetre: **3:** 639; silk: **3:** 667 (*see also* France: US relations with); spirits: **2:** 185–6, 303, 832, 843; **3:** 635–7, 675, 678; sugar: **2:** 303; **3:** 650–1, 678, 680–1, 828, 855; textiles: **2:** 840; **3:** 639; wheat: **3:** 663–5; wool: **2:** 180; **3:** 639, 667, 682, 756. Schedules of 1824 Tariff Act: **3:** 756; **4:** 363–4

Anderson, Richard C., Jr.: Family: **2:** 620; **4:** 378; **5:** 870, 890; **6:** 76–7. Health: **5:** 379. Service in Am. Rev.: **5:** 870–1. On pay & mileage for US House members: **2:** 423–4. Min. to Colombia: **3:** 335, 414; **4:** 167, 213, 235, 378, 680; **5:** 62, 169 (*see also* Colombia: US relations with). Praise for as diplomat: **4:** 637. Min. to Panama Cong.: **4:** 646, 851, 905; **5:** 170–1, 419 (*see also* US Diplomacy: Panama Congress). C. instructions to on Panama Cong.: **5:** 313–44, 375–6. On internal conditions in Colombia: **5:** 378–9. Death in Colombia: **5:** 572, 578, 595, 667, 679, 761, 870, 890, 925. Article on Colombia constit.: **5:** 750. Money owed by State Dept.: 5: 890–1

Argentina. *See* Buenos Aires

Arkansas Territory: C. recommends friends as Gov. of: **2:** 676–7. Borrows money from BUS to pay for initial govt. operations: **3:** 234–5. Boundaries of: **3:** 763–4. National road in: **3:** 624, 627; **4:** 226. Indian land titles in: **3:** 752, 763. Dueling law in: **6:** 56. Duels in: **6:** 56, 68–9. Land claim problems in: **3:** 753, 763–4. Incursions into Mex. mounted from: **6:** 995, 1005, 1155–6

Astor, John Jacob: C. borrows & repays money from: **2:** 686, 863, 884–5; **3:** 83–4, 250–1, 402–3, 454, 533, 795, 797, 803–4, 813, 857, 874, 887, 895; **4:** 38; **6:** 242. Extends repayment time of C. loan: **3:** 83. Sees European war as aid to Am. business: **2:** 863. "Ashland" secures C. loan from: **3:** 813. On Depression of 1819: **2:** 863. Supports C. in 1824 campaign: **3:** 402–3. Shipping business of: **6:** 488. Son–in–law Rumpff (*see* Rumpff, Vincent); Rumpff as Hanse Min. to US: **6:** 273, 275, 726–7, 823, 940 (*see also* Hanseatic Cities: US relations with). C. friendship with: **6:** 726–7. C. favors to: **6:** 940, 1056. On campaign & election of 1828: **6:** 1028. Fur trading operations in Oregon: **4:** 354; **6:** 1127

Austria: Disinterest in Anglo–Am. War (1814): **1:** 921, 923. Policy & actions in Gr. revolution against Tur.: **4:** 204, 277, 703, 735; **5:** 368, 401–2, 406, 432, 552, 781, 784; **6:** 1138. On ending Sp. wars in Span. Am.: **4:** 630–31; **5:** 83, 125. Policy & actions in Italy: **4:** 205, 434. On Br. independence: **4:** 241. On recognition of Span. Am. independence: **4:** 535, 774. Royal family problems: **5:** 51, 189. Commercial treaty with Br. (*see* Brazil). Relations with Netherlands (*see* Netherlands). Policy & actions in Port. (*see* Portugal). Relations with Sp.: **6:** 226. Policy & actions in antecedents of Ru.–Tur. War: **6:** 1264, 1332, 1399

—U.S. relations with: USN courtesy extended Emperor of: **2:** 853, 859. Trade reciprocity offered: **4:** 903, 931. Arrests of US citizens: **4:** 407, 486–7, 519. Tariff, duty, fee discrim. against US shipping & trade: **4:** 903. US discrim. against Autrian shipping: **4:** 903

Baltimore, Md.: GB repulse at (1814): **1:** 995–6; **2:** 69. Mrs. Aaron Vail's School in: **2:** 323–5. Support for Am. Colonization Society in: **6:** 86, 96. Corruption in BUS branch at: **2:** 623–4, 698. Impact of 1819 depression on: **2:** 698; **3:** 739–40. Privateering vessels for Span. Am. built in: **4:** 537, 675; **6:** 590. JQA political strength in: **6:** 355, 467. Piracy & privateering operations out of: **4:** 123, 537; **5:** 125; **6:** 440, 860. 1826 elections in: **5:** 255–7, 761. University of Md. Medical College in: **2:** 567; **6:** 953–54. Agriculture society & journal in: **6:** 1007–8. Library Society in: **6:** 215. Bible Society in: **6:** 215. Temperance Society in: **6:** 215. Cultural life of: **6:** 1293. Criticism of JQA patronage policy in: **6:** 355. JQA political conv. at (7/23/27) (*see* Maryland). Silk industry proposed for: **6:** 1007–8. Merchants in protest US restrictions on GB trade: **5:** 631; **6:** 131, 425, 577. AJ political strength in: **5:** 756; **6:** 1100. JQA visits: **6:** 1152

Banda Oriental. *See* Uruguay

Bank of the United States

—first B.U.S.: Initial C. support: **1:** 537. C. arguments in opposition to recharter: **1:** 527–39; **2:** 200, 216–7. Ky. support of: **1:** 523. Confidence in notes of: **1:** 288. Constit. basis for: **1:** 530–3, 537–8, 543. Power of states to tax branches: **1:** 532–3. Too much wealth & power centered in: **1:** 538, 543. Unnecessary functions: **1:** 534–5. Dominated by foreigners: **1:** 538–9; **2:** 217. Currency value variations: **1:** 649–50. Cong. splits on recharter: **1:** 522, 524. Cong. debates on recharter: **1:** 903; **2:** 6, 7, 11, 169–70, 217. Relation to onset of War of 1812: **2:** 217. *See also* U.S. Supreme Court; Congress of the United States: eleventh congress

—second B.U.S.: C. opposes all banks on principle: **2:** 673. C. arguments supporting: **2:** 169–70, 173, 177, 199–205, 216–9, 623–4, 673, 721, 731. C. explains shift of position on: **2:** 200–05, 210, 216–19; **3:** 620. "Bonus" feature of Charter: **2:** 309, 311. Specie payments issues related to: **2:** 195, 346, 722, 728–9. Paper money: **2:** 729; **4:** 40. Stock purchasing requirements: **2:** 287–8, 792–3. Functions of: **2:** 323, 621. Relation with US Public Land Office: **2:** 722–3. Constit. questions relating to: **2:** 201–5, 435, 446–65 (456), 473–4, 478–9, 623, 673–4, 721; **3:** 596 (*see also* US Supreme Court: *McCulloch* vs. *Maryland*). Need for branching: **2:** 369. State taxing of branches: **2:** 435, 442, 456, 721; **3:** 61, 114–5 (*see also ibid.*). Right to sue in Federal courts: **3:** 549, 560, 646–7, 655. As handmaiden to Am. System: **2:** 202–3, 271–2. Party & sectional political considerations related to: **2:** 277, 281, 283. **5:** 967. C. considers, rejects directorship in: **2:** 262, 276, 282–3, 323, 433–4. C. buys, sells stock in: **2:** 262, 276, 283,

721. C. indebtedness to: **2:** 876–7; **3:** 342, 402, 432–3, 548–9, 886; **4:** 498–500, 513; **5:** 282–3; **6:** 1–2. Favors sought by, rendered to C.: **2:** 722; **4:** 454–5; **5:** 26–7. C. brother connection with: **3:** 248, 264, 272–3. Branch in Lex.: **2:** 235, 257–8, 281, 307, 346, 635, 687–8; **4:** 824–5. C. equates prosperity of BUS with prosperity of US: **2:** 410. Relationship to state & local banks: **2:** 204–5, 435, 621, 665–6, 722. Operational & integrity problems of Western branches: **2:** 687–8, 722, 730, 773–4; **3:** 12–13. Impact of 1819 panic & depression on: **2:** 698. Corruption & mismanagement in: **2:** 201, 623–5, 673–4, 698, 903–4. C. suggests procedural reforms in: **2:** 722, 728–31. Cong. investigates procedures & policies of: **2:** 623–5. Acquires extensive real estate collateral from debtors: **3:** 139–41, 231–4, 245, 874–5. C. legal work for: **2:** 720, 723, 731, 794–5, 873–5, 888, 900–2, 907–10; **3:** 7, 11–13, 20–1, 24–6, 60–3, 88–9, 99, 102–3, 107–8, 111–3, 128–9, 139–41, 143–44, 155–6, 228–34, 245, 347–8, 353, 355, 359–60, 386, 426–7, 429–31, 498, 539–40, 596, 750–1, 759, 804–5, 811–12, 874–7; **3:** 881; **4:** 41–2, 49–50, 62, 72–3. C. resigns BUS job: **4:** 93, 103, 454. C. pay for BUS work: **3:** 25–6, 47–8, 50–1, 57–8, 129, 238, 345, 408, 417; **4:** 93. C. cases won for BUS: **3:** 286, 429, 804. C. cases lost for BUS: **3:** 805. Pro–creditor bias in BUS suits: **3:** 429–30; **5:** 68–9. C. assistance to debtors: **3:** 795–6; **4:** 45. C. criticized for BUS connection & work: **3:** 102–3, 245–6, 259; **5:** 222. Denies pro–BUS prejudices: **3:** 260. C. helps BUS handle GB payments under 1826 slave–indemnity conv.: **5:** 1013–4, 1022, 1044–5; **6:** 23. Role in refunding public debt: **6:** 543

Barbary States: Character of people: **6:** 1033. Prey on Span. shipping: **5:** 857. Procure naval stores from Scandinavia: **6:** 736. Peace treaty with Sp.: **6:** 101. Demand consular presents: **6:** 542. Naval forces of: **6:** 170, 736. Dislike of GB consul in Tangier: **6:** 583, 1033. Price of slaves in: **6:** 351. Internal disorder in various states: **6:** 583, 666. GB naval attack on Algiers: **6:** 605. Safety of resident Christians in: **6:** 1297. Follow US lead on recognizing Span. Am. states: **6:** 1033. Fr. naval operations against Algiers: **6:** 605, 663, 678, 723, 726, 731, 741, 781, 831, 959, 980, 990–1, 1033, 1113, 1170. Colombian privateers welcome in: **6:** 722. Greek cruisers attack: **6:** 736

—U.S. relations with: US assistance to Span. political exiles in Tangiers: **4:** 117, 224, 338–9. Treaty with Algiers (1816): **2:** 80; **6:** 511, 1316–8. Friendly gestures towards Americans: **4:** 209, 277–8, 377; **6:** 559. Navy of no threat to USN: **4:** 621. US courtesies to: **4:** 315. Gifts to leaders of: **4:** 377, 754; **5:** 133, 260, 266, 399; **6:** 169–70, 238, 511, 583, 666, 736,

1222–3, 1297. Cost of gifts: **4**: 816; **5**: 933; **6**: 1307. Consul Shaler writes history of Algiers: **4**: 395. Good relations with: **4**: 415; **5**: 260; **6**: 735, 959, 1033. Misbehavior of US consul in Tripoli: **6**: 939, 1223. USN operations against (1804): **1**: 767; **6**: 1318. Wish to buy US warships: **4**: 628. Commercial treaty with Morocco: **4**: 752. Privateering operations of Morocco: **5**: 564. Schooling for consular service in: **4**: 956; **5**: 37, 260, 266, 411, 971; **6**: 101, 511, 559–60 (*see also* Hodgson, William B. in Name Index). US interests in Tripoli: **4**: 724. Clash of US diplomats serving in: **5**: 133. Christian cemetery in Algiers: **5**: 196, 498. Disease & famine in Morocco: **5**: 223. Anglo–Fr. trade advantages in: **5**: 366. Seek treaty with Span. Am. republics: **4**: 851; **5**: 564. Americans in: **6**: 583. Commercial treaty with Tunis: **6**: 238. Return of US slave "Prince" (Abduhl Rahahman) to native Morocco: **6**: 158, 351–2, 933–4. Nature & extent of US trade with: **4**: 511; **5**: 223, 399–400; **6**: 238, 583, 1033. US war against (1815): **2**: 79–80, 142, 149, 160, 553, 561. USN ceremonial gun salutes to: 6: 1319. *See also* Shaler, William

Barbour, James: US Senator (Va.): **4**: 215; **5**: 1031. Member of "Richmond Junto": **3**: 341. Supports Crawford in 1824: **3**: 341. Involvement in Rufus King controversy: **4**: 843, 852–3, 855–6. Speculation in Ky. land: **4**: 552. Educational subsidies to Indians: **4**: 786. Appt. SecWar: **4**: 90. Patronage relations with C.: **4**: 111, 215, 238, 268, 491; **5**: 276; **6**: 926–7, 999. Supports JQA in House election (1825) of Pres.: **6**: 900. Involvement in Ga. (Creek Indian) vs. US crisis: **4**: 501–2, 677, 891. Plan for integration of Indians into US: **4**: 891. Criticizes AJ press; **6**: 696, 698. On Feb. 1825 "Corrupt Bargain" issue: **6**: 900. Supports JQA in 1828 election: **6**: 924. Mentioned as possible VP candidate on JQA ticket in 1828: **6**: 1291

Barry, William T.: Vote on 2nd BUS: **2**: 205. Legal & financial dealings with C.: **2**: 235–6. C. suggests as director of Lex. Branch, BUS: **2**: 281. Studies public educational needs in Ky.: **3**: 351. Supports C. in 1824 election: **3**: 823. Advises C. on Pres. vote (2/9/25) in H. of Reps.: **4**: 11–2. Supports C. SecState decision: **4**: 77. Chief Justice of Ky. Court of Appeals (New Court): **4**: 59, 67, 673–4. Role in Old Court vs. New Court conflict: **4**: 713 (*see also* Kentucky: New Court (Relief) party; Old Court (Anti–Relief) party). Attacks on C.: **5**: 991. Works for AJ in 1828 campaign: **6**: 841

Batavia. *See* East Indies

Bavaria: U.S. relations with: **4**: 661

Bayard, James A.: Supports establishment of 2nd BUS: **1**: 467. Appt. to Ghent Peace Commission: **1**: 799, 853, 862, 863, 866–7, 877, 879. Fears defeat of Fr. as dangerous to US in War of 1812: **1**: 882.

Doubts favorable outcome of Ghent peace talks: **1**: 935. Criticism of US war leadership challenged: **1**: 996, 997. Appt. Min. to Ru. **2**:17. On military importance of Chesapeake & Del. Canal: **2**: 477–8. Seeks payment for service at Ghent & London (1814–5): **5**: 350–1. Death: **2**: 26, 129, 172

Beatty, Adam: Family: **6**: 1130. C. advises against running for US Sen.: **2**: 586–8. Experiments with Merino wool: **1**: 473; **4**: 638. Offers to buy C. Merino flock: **4**: 638, 679, 753. Political career of: **1**: 473, 480. Urges C. to run for Gov. of Ky.: **2**: 766. Urges Am. System benefits for Ky.: **6**: 1150. Supports & advises C. on 1824 campaign: **3**: 446–7. Legal work for C.: **4**: 491, 637, 679; **5**: 141, 608. On Old Court–New Court fight: **4**: 638. On JQA Ga. (Creek) policy: **4**: 638. Recommended for Fed. Dist. judgeship in Ky.: **5**: 140–1, 146, 210. Analysis of coming 1824 campaign & Pres. election: **3**: 192–5. Urges Fed. road from Maysville to Lex.: **6**: 1150

Bell, John: Elected (1827) to US House: **4**: 847–8; **6**: 515, 799–800

Benton, Thomas Hart: Kinship to Clay: **1**: 447; **6**: 362. Legal business with C.: **1**: 446–7, 490–1, 494, 734, 819–820; **2**: 96. Urges C. to become Speaker of House of Reps.: **1**: 447. On the possibility of war (1810): **1**: 447. Altercation with AJ (1813): **1**: 820; **6**: 811–2. On his law practice: **1**: 491. Seeks commission to fight in War of 1812: **1**: 734. Military career in War of 1812: **1**: 805, 806. On GB aims in War of 1812: **1**: 805. On Federalist loyalty & disloyalty in War of 1812: **1**: 805–6. Condemns Mo. congressman for voting for JQA in 1825 House election of Pres.: **6**: 1226–7. Visits C. at "Ashland": **2**: 892. Connection with C. half–brother (N. W. Watkins): **2**: 892. Assists C. in 1824 campaign: **3**: 202, 204, 460. Recommends patronage appts.: **4**: 285; **5**: 251. Sees C. as hope of JQA admin. on western land policy: **4**: 325. Reelection (1826) of to US Sen.: **5**: 755, 853, 888, 991; **6**: 46. Shifts of pro–AJ stance: **5**: 815; **6**: 604. Decline of popularity in Mo.: **5**: 852–3. Financial problems with Bank of Mo.: **5**: 955–6. Characterization of: **5**: 991. C. break with: **5**: 1001; **6**: 362, 604, 725. Opposes Panama Cong. (Tacubaya): **6**: 127. Verifies C. statement on "Corrupt Bargain" issue: **6**: 1342. Attacks C. admin.: **6**: 544. Works for AJ in 1828 campaign: **6**: 811. On how C. would vote in US House election of Pres.: **6**: 1226–7

Binns, John: Philadelphia alderman: **5**: 352–3. Tells C. truth about Pres. politics: **6**: 492. Analyzes Pa. politics for C.: **4**: 84–5; **5**: 352–3; **6**: 492. Work for reelection of JQA; **4**: 333; **5**: 352–3; **6**: 110, 119, 304, 355, 479. JQA admin. patronage for: **4**: 864, 880; **5**: 265, 352–3; **6**: 175, 304, 320, 433, 814. Seeks patronage

Binns, John (*continued*):
for Philadelphia: **5:** 191, 196. Distrust of Post Master General McLean: **5:** 265. Recommends patronage appt. to C.: **4:** 377, 384–5. Sues Bache for assault: **6:** 813–4, 1301
Birney, James G.: Boyhood recollections of C.: **5:** 120. Patronage recommendations to C.: **5:** 118–20, 702. Supports JQA admin.: **5:** 702–3
Blair, Francis Preston: Personal life of: **4:** 65, 860; **5:** 6. C. courtesies to: **3:** 10; **4:** 65. Connection with Bank of Commonwealth: **3:** 10–11. In Old Court–New Court struggle: **3:** 10; **4:** 65, 67, 603–5, 859–62; **5:** 4–6; **6:** 1404. Clerk of Ky. Court of Appeals: **4:** 65, 67, 605, 860–1; **5:** 4. In AJ admin.: **3:** 11. C. chides on political analysis: **4:** 64. C. confides in on decision to support JQA for Pres. in House (2/9/25): **4:** 9–10; **5:** 989. Controversial letters of C. to on decision to support JQA: **4:** 9–11, 46–8; **5:** 989; **6:** 1121, 1136, 1206, 1260–1, 1265–6, 1363, 1403–4. On Old Court party victory (1825) in Ky.: **4:** 603–5. Works to release Ky. House delegation from Ky. General Assembly instructions to vote for AJ: **4:** 41, 66; **6:** 1071, 1106. Supports JQA in US House election of Pres. (2/9/25): **4:** 41. Supports C. performance as Sec-State: **4:** 399. On compromising Old Court–New Court issues: **4:** 604–5, 859–60; **5:** 4–5. Considers removal to Fla.: **4:** 860; **5:** 6. Identifies with New Court faction in Ky.: **5:** 4. Urges C. to effect compromise in Court fight in Ky.: **5:** 5. Breaks with Crittenden: **6:** 1261. Breaks with C.: **6:** 222, 1106–7, 1163–4, 1261. Leads Frankfort Junto: **6:** 413–4. View of & relationship to "Corrupt Bargain" controversy: **4:** 9–11, 46–8; **5:** 989; **6:** 1071, 1106–7, 1121, 1260, 1264, 1266, 1286, 1362–3, 1363, 1403–5. On the two–party system in US: **6:** 1107. Personal vs. political opinions of C.: **6:** 1106–7, 1404. C. regrets break with: **6:** 1163–4. Criticizes C. for deserting Dem. for alliance with old Federalists: **6:** 1261. Lectures C. on separating political preferences & personal friendships: **6:** 1404
Biddle, Nicholas: C. advises on BUS tactics against Ohio & Ky. relief laws: **3:** 347–8. Appointed Pres. of BUS: **3:** 355. Turns down C. securities for debt to BUS: **3:** 548–9. Interest in Mex. markets: **4:** 100, 118, 126. Lauds C. service to BUS: **4:** 103. C. passes European dip. & financial information to: **6:** 174–5, 180. Brother Thomas killed in duel: **6:** 220. Writes pamphlet on Thomas Jefferson: **6:** 533–4, 567. Handles funds for Kenyon Seminary (College): **6:** 707–8. *See also* Bank of the United States
Bibb, George M.: Role in "Corrupt Bargain" (1825) controversy: **4:** 41. Opposition to TU: **4:** 266. As US Sen.: **1:** 68. Involvement in Burr treason case: **1:** 299,
338. In Ky. State legis.: **1:** 338, 343. As 1812 warhawk: **1:** 473, 697. In US House: **1:** 473. As Chief Justice of Ky. Court of Appeals: **1:** 701. Personal relations with C.:**1:** 871; **2:** 82, 770. Legal business with C.: **2:** 591, 871, 902, 914–5; **3:** 6, 628. On the Fla. (Adams–Onis) Treaty: **2:** 732. Ky. Commissioner in Occupying Claimant Law dispute with Va.: **3:** 151, 158–61, 171, 176–7, 207–9, 357. Nom. & appt. of as Chief Justice of Old Court: **6:** 16–7, 22, 24, 28, 37, 40
Bolivar, Simon: Military activities of in Span. Am. revolutions: **2:** 557, 584–5; **6:** 688. Lauds US leadership in Span. Am. independence movements: **6:** 124, 126. C. advises on proper military tactics: **2:** 557–8. Key to public order in Span. Am.: **5:** 226, 368, 422, 646, 747, 957, 996; **6:** 255, 306. Recruits European "foreign legion" to fight for Patriot cause: **2:** 585. On education of females: **5:** 184, 191. On emancipating slaves: **2:** 860; **6:** 161. Lauds GB for recognition of Colombia: **4:** 907. Saluted as the "Washington of South Am." & Champion of Liberty: **4:** 1, 313; **5:** 184, 1017; **6:** 221, 872, 1308. Praises C.: **6:** 1298–1300. Dislike of in US: **6:**27. C. criticizes: **5:** 422; **6:** 312, 872–3. Fear of in Span. Am.: **4:** 284, 649; **6:** 404, 484. Brings Upper Peru (Bolivia) under his control: **4:** 321, 493, 944. Victory over Span. & Royalists in Peru: **4:** 104, 138, 174, 240–41, 249. Proclaimed Dictator: **5:** 813, 931. To lead expedition against Cuba: **5:** 194; **6:** 548. Urges Panama Cong. (*see* U.S. Diplomacy: Panama Congress). Popularity of in Colombia: **4:** 811. Popularity of in Peru: **5:** 517, 1033. Adulation of: **5:** 373, 526. Attitude in BA–Br. war: **4:** 833. Hatred of Br.: **4:** 585. Ambitions in Bolivia (*see* Bolivia). Influence & ambitions of in Peru (*see* Peru). Ambitions in Chile: **5:** 517, 526–7, 649. As tyrant: **5:** 373; **6:** 161, 351, 1257. Breakdown of unification plans: **6:** 562, 873. Imperial & dictatorial ambitions of: **5:** 373, 391, 426, 527, 572, 594, 647, 670, 793, 931, 999, 1029, 1049; **6:** 27, 78, 101–2, 161, 196, 218, 255, 312–3, 324, 404, 484, 586, 868, 872–3, 1054, 1346. Ambitions in BA: **5:** 527. Napoleon as model: **5:** 527, 647. European opinions of: **5:** 801, 837, 1049. Lafayette lauds: **5:** 837. Disbands army & navy of Colombia: **5:** 1002. Pleas for unity by: **5:**982. Compared with AJ: **5:** 1029; **6:** 221. Personal charm of: **6:** 34. Character of **6:** 306. B. T. Watts favorable opinion of (*see* Watts, Beaufort T.). Resigns as Pres. of Colombia: **6:** 306, 317, 325, 351, 380, 560, 684, 694–5, 868. Resumes Presidency: **6:** 1087, 1123, 1222, 1269, 1308. Attack on Guayaquil: **6:** 404. As economist: **6:** 325. Ambitions in Ecuador (*see* Ecuador). Love life of: **6:** 345–6. Conflict with Santander: **5:** 225; **6:** 161. 305, 374, 684, 1123. Manipula-

tion of Rom. Catholic Church: **6:** 382–3. Brings order in Venezuela: **6:** 255, 684. Key to order in Colombia (*see* Colombia). C. acquires bust of: **6:** 829, 1307–8. *See also* Colombia; Peru; U.S. Diplomacy: Panama Congress; Watts, Beaufort T.

Bolivia (Upper Peru): Triumph of Bolivar forces over Span. & Royalists: **4:** 321, 443. Tension with Peru (*see* Peru). Independence movement in: **4:** 416, 488, 650. Border tensions with Br. (*see* Brazil). Independence proclaimed: **4:** 650, 694–5, 863. Span. Am. reactions to independence of: **4:** 694. Bolivar influence in: **4:** 737, 944; **5:** 129, 527, 594, 670; **6:** 346, 873. Bolivar writes constit. for: **5:** 594, 670, 747, 931; **6:** 78, 81, 873. Internal instability, disorder, revolution, civil war in: **5:** 715; **6:** 82, 368, 484, 522, 683. Tension with BA (*see* Buenos Aires). Bolivar constit. as model for all Span. Am.: **5:** 931. Colombian troops in: **6:** 33, 250. Uprising against Bolivar constit: **6:** 161, 250, 484. Colombian expulsion from: **6:** 250, 346. New constit. (1827) for: **6:** 688. Sucre govt. in: **6:** 81–82, 522. Outlet to the sea: **5:** 129. Alliance with Peru: **6:** 688

Boston: Charles River bridge issue: **6:** 530–2, 584. General Court elections to legis. (1827) in: **6:** 565–7, 584, 603. Decline of Federalist strength in: **6:** 565–7. Lottery issue in: **6:** 584, 586. Morality in politics in: **6:** 586. Clergy in: **6:** 586

Branch, John: Attacks C. for "Corrupt Bargain": **6:** 1004–5, 1160. On C. confirmation by Sen. on SecState nom.: **6:** 1003–4, 1203

Brazil: War of independence from Port.: **4:** 104–5, 409, 643. Port. recognition of independence (1825): **4:** 104–5, 122, 222, 231, 244, 385–6, 406, 642, 714, 820, 828, 833, 854, 875, 952; **5:** 41–2, 104–6, 150, 183, 395, 556, 562. Court & family life of Emperor Peter I: **4:** 409–10, 936; **5:** 236, 506, 716, 849, 959, 975, 978, 1022; **6:** 276, 801, 1145. Internal instability, disorder, revolution, civil war in: **4:** 104, 231, 371, 409–10, 562, 597, 714; **5:** 104; **6:** 630, 1337. US citizens involved in rebellions in: **4:** 104–5, 231, 371, 562; **5:** 986. Liberty & democracy in: **2:** 445; **4:** 409–10; **5:**19. Monarchy launched: **4:** 786. Economic problems of: **4:** 104; **5:** 518, 668, 670; **6:** 171, 533. Sp. military operations against in Uruguay: **4:** 320, 386, 394. Navy: **4:** 104, 231, 768; **5:** 747; **6:** 318, 616. Army: **4:** 231, 394; **5:** 395; **6:** 616. Military defeat in Uruguay (*see* Uruguay). Border tension with Bolivia: **4:** 488, 585, 597, 649–50. Tariff & navigation laws: **5:** 236, 506, 816. Role of Cong.: **5:** 507. Role of church in: **2:** 445. Slave trade in: **4:** 104, 231, 253–4, 371, 844; **5:** 63, 1022. Character of people & institutions: **5:** 506, 747, 848–9. Capital punishment in: **4:** 231. German emigration to: **6:** 268, 802–3. Hires German mercenaries: **4:** 394, 409. Relations with

Port.: **4:** 104, 252, 371; **5:** 19, 41–2, 106, 176, 183, 539, 959; **6:** 276, 411, 633. GB recognition of: **5:** 27. GB claims against: **6:** 989, 1060. GB treaties with: **4:** 104–5, 252, 254, 562, 643, 714, 768, 821, 844; **5:** 41, 63, 183, 235, 959, 1022. GB influence in: **4:** 104, 371, 597, 714, 777, 833, 844; **5:** 104–5, 412, 816, 841; **6:** 1184. GB mediation of Br.–BA war: **5:** 438, 506, 548, 556, 588, 668, 670, 710, 716, 828, 959; **6:** 271, 441, 578, 589–90, 732, 801, 880, 938, 1214, 1264, 1337 (*see also* Ponsonby, Lord John Brabazon in Name Index, *espec.* **5:** 438). GB policy in Br.–BA war: **5:** 395, 438, 506–7, 538, 556; **6:** 616, 1214. Treaty with Austria: **5:** 506, 556. Treaty with Fr.: **4:** 936; **5:** 41–2, 506, 548, 556. Treaty with Hanse States: **6:** 82, 267–8. Treaty with Port.: **5:** 539. Treaty with Prussia: **6:** 1399–1400. Fr. recognition of: **5:** 42, 504. Fr. influence in: **5:** 816; **6:** 1184. Fr. claims against: **6:** 592–3, 989, 1060. War with BA: **4:** 231, 284, 320–1, 370, 386, 394, 409, 488, 514, 537, 597, 643, 653, 737, 768, 792, 821, 833, 845, 865, 936, 943; **5:** 41, 51, 62–3, 105, 183, 215–6, 223, 235–6, 438, 506, 548, 556, 716, 719–20, 849, 959; **6:** 171, 270–1, 533, 578, 616, 841–2, 881, 938 (*see also* Uruguay). Colombian mediation of Br.–BA war: **5:** 538, 846. Interference with European maritime neutral rights: **6:** 98. Peace negotiations with BA: **5:** 441, 537, 592, 616, 716, 732, 750, 861, 880, 1178, 1336

—US relations with: Report of US fact–finding mission to: **2:** 443–6. US recognition of: **4:** 244, 252, 255, 853. Exchange diplomats: **2:** 428, 554, 624. C. instruction to Raguet: **4:** 251–5; **5:** 816 (*see also* Raguet, Condy). Nature & extent of US trade with: **4:** 251–2, 410, 853; **5:** 62, 224, 412, 549, 647; **6:** 1180, 1262. Amazon exploration: **6:** 685–6. Trade reciprocity considered: **4:** 253; **5:** 105; **6:** 37. Protection of US lives & commerce: **5:** 104, 184, 295, 371, 507, 518, 959 (*see also* U.S. Navy). Harassment of US shipping: **4:** 104–5, 737, 792–3; **5:** 395, 637, 809, 848; **6:** 295, 317–8, 532–3, 592, 603–4. Tariff, duty, fee discrim. against US shipping & trade: **5:** 816; **6:** 36, 1184, 1400–1. US act of piracy: **6:** 881, 950, 989, 1060. Impressment of US seamen: **4:** 362, 395, 959–60; **5:** 518, 709–10, 848; **6:** 56, 100, 335–6, 375–6, 533. Encourage desertion of US seamen: **6:** 532. Arrest US citizens: **6:** 989, 1182. US commercial treaty with: **4:** 245, 252–3, 821, 844–5; **5:** 228, 709, 816; **6:** 36, 1179, 1184, 1399. Seek alliance with US: **4:** 222–3, 244, 252, 261. Abolition of slave trade: **4:** 253–4. Purchase, build, outfit warships in US: **5:** 364, 849; **6:** 295, 317, 972, 1181–2. US citizens serve in Br. armed services: **4:** 105, 768; **5:** 364, 424, 750; **6:** 318, 593. US neutrality in Br.–Port. war: **4:** 244. US mediation in Br.–BA war: **5:** 135, 290–1, 538, 846.

Buenos Aires (*continued*):
Reincorporation of Uruguay: **4:** 763 (*see* Uruguay)
—U.S. relations with: C. support of independence & US recognition: **4:** 233, 552, 554, 556, 560–1, 652. US fact–finding mission visits prior to US recognition: **2:** 443–6, 509, 593, 618, 855. C. arguments for US recognition: **2:** 512–62, 590, 667–8, 855; **6:** 495–6. C. portrait presented to BA: **4:** 495–6. US maritime neutral rights in BA–Sp. war: **2:** 156, 159, 501, 505. Nature & extent of US trade with: **2:** 555; **4:** 248–9, 652, 675. Commercial treaty with: **4:** 179, 197, 247–9. US citizens in harassed: **2:** 618–9. Harassment of US shipping: **6:** 1387. Blockade, contraband, privateering & other US neutral rights problems in BA vs. Br. war (*see* Brazil: US relations with). Forbes requests policy guidance on BA–Br. war: **5:** 670. C. instructions to Forbes: **4:** 246–51. Clash between US diplomats (Forbes & Slocum) serving in: **5:** 66–7, 139–40; **6:** 21, 134–5, 162, 202, 204, 306, 517, 543. BA requests interpretation of Monroe Doctrine: **6:** 938–9 (*see* U.S. Diplomacy: Monroe Doctrine). Purchase, build, outfit warships from & in US: **6:** 1181–2, 1262. US citizens serve in privateers of in war with Br.: **6:** 1262–3. Tariff, duty, fee discrim. against US shipping & trade: **4:** 197, 768, 833. US claims against: **4:** 192, 250; **5:** 214, 266–7, 364, 381, 425, 588, 859–60, 924, 981; **6:** 881, 1002, 1191–2, 1336–7, 1401 (*see espec.* the *Ruth* claim: **6:** 1191–2, 1214, 1336; & the *Merope* claim: **6:** 162, 202, 307, 440, 488, 543 (*see also* claims associated with following vessels: *Grace Ann, Hannah, Hope, Mohawk, Patrick Henry, Pizarro* in Name Index). US missionary activity in: **5:** 806
Burr, Aaron: Engages C. as atty. in Mex. conquest charge: **1:** 253, 256–7, 262. Cheats on fee owed C.: **1:** 288. Unpopularity in Ky.: **1:** 254, 337, 341, 364. Land speculation in La.: **1:** 260, 274. Assures C. of his innocence: **1:** 256–7, 333. Charges against: **1:** 270, 272–3, 281, 289, 332–3, 337–41, 362, 535. C. defense of Burr: **1:** 257–9, 274–5, 332–3, 340, 361–2, 366. C. shifts position on Burr: **1:** 272–5, 280, 311, 332–3, 339, 362–3. Declared innocent: **1:** 341–2. Burrism as Ky. political issue: **1:** 329–34, 337, 351–2. Criticism of C. for association with Burr legal defense: **1:** 273, 280, 336–41, 364–5, 375. Burr connection with Blennerhassett: **1:** 274–5. C. connection with Blennerhassett: **1:** 298–301. C. refuses to represent govt. in prosecution of: **1:** 311. Financial problems of: **1:** 341. Duel with Hamilton: **3:** 366. Connection with AJ: **6:** 409–10, 489–90. Fed. trial of: **6:** 409–10

Calhoun, John C.: Conflicts with Randolph on war (1812) issue: **1:** 669. Abortive duel with Grosvenor: **1:** 844. Supports repeal of embargo non–importation policy (1814): **1:** 909. Supports charter of 2nd BUS: **2:** 170. Conflict with C. on wartime property claims–compensation: **2:** 273–4. Supports Internal Improvements: **2:** 309–11. Monroe appts. Sec War: **2:** 391. Votes against Neutrality Act of 1817: **2:** 497. Appts. C. son to USMA: **3:** 82–3. Indian policy as Sec War: **2:** 599; **3:** 185, 187. Pres. & VP candidacy (*see* Election of 1824: John C. Calhoun candidacy). Policies & accomplishments as SecWar: **3:** 187. Attacks on as SecWar: **4:** 635, 678; **6:** 116, 258–9. C. opinions of: **3:** 891; **5:** 158, 1001. Hostility to C.: **5:** 307. Lee post office appt.: **4:** 651–2. Elected VP: **4:** 63, 75. Role in JQA admin. (*see* Adams (John Q.) administration). C.–Randolph duel blamed on: **5:** 233. Rumored duel with C.: **5:** 277. Alleged bargain with AJ in 1824 election: **5:** 280. Cong. investigation of: **6:** 258–9. Political strength in Pa.: **6:** 284. As VP nominee in 1828: **6:** 473, 824–5, 1141 (*see* Election of 1828: general). As presiding officer of US Sen.: **5:** 307–8; **6:** 825
Cambreleng, Churchill C.: Role in 1828 campaign: **3:** 334–5. C. patronage favors to: **5:** 983; **6:** 28. On the tariff: **3:** 676. Involvement in US–GB colonial trade problem: **5:** 76, 905, 941–2, 1010–11; **6:** 131, 423
Cameron, Simon: On election of 1828 in Pa.: **5:** 983; **6:** 821–2. C. patronage favors to: **5:** 86, 647; **4:** 568. On AJ movement in Pa.: **5:** 87. On Panama Mission: **5:** 87. On Pa. politics: **4:** 563. Explains 1824 AJ victory in Pa.: **6:** 822
Canada. *See* Great Britain empire: Canada
Canary Islands. *See* Spain empire: Canary Islands
Canning, George: Boasts that he insured success of Span. Am. independence movements: **5:** 1050–1; **6:** 106, 714–5, 979. C. opinion of: **4:** 323–4, 349. Anti–Americanism of: **6:** 714–5, 979, 1068. Attitude toward Monroe Doctrine: **5:** 317, 341. Negotiations with US as GB Foreign Secretary: **4:** 94, 212, 220, 270, 341–2, 348–9, 619, 733, 858, 944; **5:** 64, 102, 683. View on GB & European recognition of new Span. Am. republics: **4:** 142, 212, 231, 241, 571–2, 574, 595, 691, 733, 739, 777, 858, 907; **5:** 816; **6:** 979. On abolition of African slave trade: **4:** 255, 341–2. On Gr. independence: **4:** 277; **5:**432. Support of liberal principles in GB & Europe: **4:** 324, 595; **6:** 979. Exemplifies character of GB nation: **5:** 1000. On Catholic emancipation: **6:** 225. Personal favor to Rush: **4:** 444, 577, 808. Health of: **4:** 538, 550; **5:** 441; **6:** 167, 224, 226, 305, 344, 468, 806, 854–5. Supports Span. retention of Cuba & PR: **4:** 572, 590–1, 739 (*see also* Spain empire: Cuba; Puerto Rico). On GB & European efforts to end Sp. wars in Span. Am.: **4:** 653, 896, 946; **5:** 27, 132. On proposed

Anglo–Fr.–US guaranty of Cuba & PR to Sp. (*see* Spain empire: Cuba; Puerto Rico). On Anglo–Am. trade restriction legislation & policy: **5:** 84, 630–2, 653, 685–8, 696–7, 705–6, 831–2, 864; **6:** 131–2, 169, 579–80, 715 (*see also* Great Britain: maritime & trade issues). Approves commercial & Oregon conventions with US: **6:** 867. Attitude toward GB nobility: **6:** 136, 138. Political & foreign policy implications of his becoming Prime Min.: **6:** 224–5, 372, 447–8, 476, 481, 495, 536–7, 670, 790. Campaign speeches: **6:** 569–70, 715–6. Ministers of Canning Cabinet: **6:** 784–5. Hypocrisy of: **6:** 715–6. Performance as Prime Min.: **6:** 784, 867, 959, 1041–2. Death of & dip.–political implications thereof: **6:** 167, 854–5, 867, 895, 902, 979, 1041–2, 1068, 1086, 1306, 1319. Supports constit. in Port.: **5:** 998, 1027; **6:** 438. GB intervention in Port. attributed to character of: **6:** 1145. *See also* Great Britain

Carey, Mathew: C. quotes in House speech on tariff: **3:** 716–7. Recommends patronage appts. to C.: **4:** 596; **5:** 804. C. supports views of: **3:** 745. Problems with newspapers: **5:** 971. Supports C. in 1824 campaign: **3:** 816, 829, 836. Attacks GB trade policy: **4:** 416–7; **6:** 563, 568. Supports protective tariff: **4:** 688–9; **5:** 971–2. Rom. Catholic work: **6:** 588–9. On Harold suspension case: **6:** 588–9, 1061, 1379 (*see also* Papal States: U.S. relations with). Asks anti–pirate convoys for US supply ships to Greece: **6:** 256–7, 270, 277–8. Advises C. on newspaper patronage in Pa.: **6:** 1379

Carroll, William: Ambivalence on AJ candidacy (1828): **4:** 716–7, 846–7; **5:** 955–6. C. seeks support of in 1824 campaign: **3:** 243. Asks patronage favors of C.: **3:** 385–6; **4:** 434; **5:** 939. Opposes JQA: **4:** 717. On Tenn. state politics: **3:** 157, 243, 265, 492; **4:** 434, 716–7, 846–7; **6:** 515. On AJ election as US Sen.: **3:** 492. C. recommends as Gov. of Fla.: **3:** 53–4. Caught between AJ & C. in 1824 campaign: **3:** 292, 301, 361, 537. Influence in Tenn. state politics: **4:** 900. Duel with Benton's brother: **1:** 820. Flees Phila. to avoid arrest: **6:** 514–5

Cass, Lewis: Supports C. in "Corrupt Bargain" controversy: **4:** 257

Centre of America, Federation of the: Proposes Isthmian canal via Nicaragua: **4:** 263–4; **5:** 520, 948, 961. Independence of: **4:** 278. Mex. aggression against (*see* Mexico). GB acquisition of Belize: **5:** 589. Consider attack on Cuba & PR: **5:** 229. Friendship treaty with Dutch: **5:** 520. Army of: **5:** 589. Govt. & constit. of: **4:** 124. Tariff policy & schedules of: **5:** 589, 643, 948; **6:** 254, 548. Political parties in: **5:** 948; **6:** 26. Isthmian "Canal Bubble": **6:** 159, 255. Am. contract to build canal: **6:** 159–60, 255. Emancipation of slaves in: **5:** 589. Sentiment in to rejoin Span. Empire: **6:** 254. Foreign officers lead uprisings in: **6:** 822. Indian aborigines in: **6:** 281. Internal instability, disorder, revolution, civil war in: **5:** 589, 931, 948; **6:** 26, 150–1, 159, 254–5, 262, 341, 374, 416, 453, 458, 538, 548, 564, 643, 822, 1003 —U.S. relations with: US consul drafts national bank charter of: **5:** 643. Nature & extent of US trade with: **5:** 961, 1042; **6:** 250. Laud C. for support of independence for Span. Am.: **4:** 103. C. instructions to Miller: **4:** 278–82; to Williams: **5:** 93–4. San Salvador seeks US annexation: **4:** 278–9, 282, 812; **5:** 249. Strategic & commercial importance to US: **4:** 280, 813. US interest in Isthmian communication: **6:** 360. Role in Panama Cong. (*see also* U.S. Diplomacy: Panama Congress). Commercial treaty (Guatemala Treaty) with: **4:** 281–2, 627, 841, 878–9, 887–8; **5:** 93–4, 228, 271, 311, 324, 360, 467, 588–9, 654, 761, 839–40, 948; **6:** 280, 895. Commercial treaty (1825) as model treaty: **4:** 887–8; **5:** 324–6, 328, 467, 722, 761, 839–40, 845, 852, 912, 995, 1042; **6:** 49–52, 183, 273, 612, 823, 1397. Weakness of Commercial treaty with: **5:** 589. Communications problems with: **5:** 228. C. supports in boundary dispute with Mex.: **5:** 339. Exclusion of US products from: **5:** 589, 643. Arrests of US citizens (John Marshall—the Gualan outrage): **5:** 654, 948, 971; **6:** 159–60, 254. Little US trade with: **5:** 961, 1042; **6:** 250, 377. US seeks knowledge of: **6:** 280–1. Am. property is threatened: **6:** 341. US interest in Isthmian canal project: **4:** 263–4, 279–80; **5:** 336, 961; **6:** 159–60, 255, 865

Charleston, S. C.: Outrage by GB navy at in 1807: **1:** 622, 627. Impact of non–importation & embargo on: **1:** 741. JQA political success in (1826): **5:** 804. Opposition to JQA admin. in: **5:** 891

Cheves, Langdon: Family: **3:** 317. As a warhawk in 1812: **1:** 614, 616, 621, 627, 658. As Pres. of 2nd BUS: **1:** 616; **2:** 679. Resigns BUS presidency: **3:** 188, 264, 291–2, 317, 386. Assists C. in BUS legal work: **3:** 386. Supports C. in argument with Randolph: **1:** 700–1. On non–importation & embargo policies: **1:** 739–41. Pres. aspirations: **3:** 188. Neutral in 1824 campaign: **3:** 292, 317. Advises C. on hemp & flax production techniques: **2:** 889–90. On C. pay as lawyer for BUS in Ohio & Ky.: **3:** 47–8, 57–8. On the meaning & future of Mo. Compromise: **3:** 58. US Commissioner for Art. I, Ghent Treaty (slave indemnities): **3:** 318

Chile: History of: **4:** 640. C. on backwardness of: **5:** 750. Independence movement in: **2:** 502, 505, 528, 540, 561, 854–5; **4:** 614, 792. US citizens fight in war of independence of: **5:** 83–4, 425. Internal instability, disorder, revolution, civil war in: **2:** 550, 561; **4:** 125, 632, 733, 791; **5:** 58, 83, 129, 517, 750, 822; **6:** 205–6, 295, 559, 1188. Knowledge of US in: **4:**792; **5:** 177. High wheat production

Chile (*continued*):
potential: **3:** 690. Govt. commodity monopolies: **4:** 324; **5:** 300. GB influence in:
4: 324, 791; **5:** 58. Centralized vs. fed.
political structure debated: **4:** 324, 394,
463, 632, 792; **5:** 648, 894, 1026; **6:** 683,
879. Economic problems of: **4:** 325, 733;
5: 183, 822; **6:** 984. GB recognition of: **4:**
325, 648. Influence of clergy in: **4:** 614;
5: 425. Two–faced attitude toward US:
4: 614, 648. Influence of aristocracy in:
4: 632; **5:** 538, 649. Fr. educational offer
to: **5:** 138; **6:** 1057, 1251. Fr. recognition
of: **4:** 648; **5:** 931. Fr. interest & influence in: **6:** 205, 1057, 1281. Continuing
war (Chiloe Expeditions) with Sp. and
Chilean Royalists: **4:** 875; **5:** 58, 83, 138,
238, 262. Commercial regulations of: **6:**
1061. Interest in Panama Cong. (*see* U.S.
diplomacy: Panama Congress). O'Higgins
ambitions in: **2:** 505; **5:** 425, 517, 526–7,
594, 648, 670, 715. Military weakness of:
5: 517, 822. Movement for constit. in: **5:**
538, 894, 931; **6:** 205, 476, 683. Election
of Pres. in: **5:** 567. Opposition to Bolivar
in: **5:** 649; **6:** 295. Treaties with Buenos
Aires: **5:** 1026; **6:** 205–6, 1052. Treaty
with Peru (*see also* Peru). Support for in
Sp.: **6:** 205–6. Character of people: **6:**
683. Activities of Congress: **6:** 800, 1362.
Internal reform movements in: **6:** 800.
Anti–foreign sentiment in: **6:** 1052. Suggests Span. Am. preferential tariff system: **6:** 1054
—U.S. relations with: Tariff, duty, fee discrim. against US shipping & trade: **4:**
648; **6:** 984. US diplomat helps write
constit. of: **5:** 538, 648, 894. Seeks US
recognition: **2:** 560–1. US claims against:
4: 125–6, 463–4, 632, 733, 875; **5:** 129,
425, 572, 578, 583, 863, 1020–1; **6:** 683,
983–4 (*see also Macedonian* & *Warrior*
cases in Name Index). US should chas-
tise: **4:** 614; **5:** 58, 856. Blockade, contraband, privateering & other US neutral
rights problems in Chile vs. Sp. war: **4:**
125–6, 791–2; **5:** 58, 62. Recip. trade
relations with: **4:** 324. Nature & extent of
US trade with: **4:** 325; **5:** 300, 346; **6:**
250. US seeks commercial treaty with: **4:**
614, 632, 733; **5:** 58, 129, 931; **6:** 1052,
1221. Impressment of US seamen: **4:**
792. Grade of US mission to reduced: **6:**
68. US should offer educational assistance to: **6:** 1281. *See also* Allen,
Heman in Name Index
China: GB trade with: **3:** 714; **5:** 192. Insurrection in Cochin China: **6:** 306. GB
seizes US ship at Singapore: **4:** 653. US
consular relations with at Canton: **4:** 881,
926, 960; **6:** 1052. Nature & extent of US
trade with: **3:** 714; **5:** 192, 954; **6:** 488
Cincinnati: C. lauds as leading western city:
3: 279. C. work for BUS branch office in
(*see* Ohio). Transportation system in &
near: **5:** 871. Political resentment of C.
in: **3:** 331. AJ political strength in: **5:**
723–4. C. on future of: **3:** 504–5. Museum in: **5:** 230–1. Jacksonians in on

attending Harrisburg Conv. to Promote
Domestic Mfgr.: **6:** 797 (*see also* Pennsylvania). P.O. patronage politics in: **6:**
1204. Drunken AJ rally in: **6:** 1210–11
Clay, Henry
—amusements & diversions: Addiction to
"segars": **1:** 308, 437–41, 999; **4:** 707.
Drinking: **1:** 157–8, 188–9, 221, 360,
418, 437–43, 554, 590, 708; **2:** 122, 221,
244, 719; **3:** 79, 172, 637; **4:** 507, 512,
707; **5:** 666; **6:** 696, 1191. Gambling: **1:**
158, 406, 437–44, 708, 751; **2:** 210, 248,
814; **3:** 241; **5:** 974. Vacations at various
Springs: **1:** 149, 193, 252; **2:** 885; **3:** 252,
257, 274, 277, 459, 821–2; **5:** 433, 644,
1047; **6:** 668–9. Physical exercise: **5:** 707.
Patron of arts, artists, writers: **2:** 230; **3:**
103–4, 496; **5:** 77, 145, 230–1, 236, 296,
397–8, 571, 678, 852; **6:** 154. Book dedicated to: **6:** 1102–3, 1220. Interest in
natural history: **3:** 104. Books & magazines read: **1:** 308, 708; **2:** 707, 789, 841,
856; **3:** 143, 358–9, 681–3, 696, 700,
712, 715–6, 720, 722, 728–30; **4:** 9, 34,
41; **5:** 387, 750,1011; **6:** 15, 580. Newspapers read: **3:** 450–1, 496, 868, 907; **4:**
494–5; **5:** 106; **6:** 378. Hospitality rendered at "Ashland": **3:** 177, 781; **4:** 570;
5: 88 (*see also* Washington, D.C.). Extent
& cost of correspondence: **2:** 378; **3:**
450–1, 496, 780, 868. Family carriages:
3: 183, 263, 281–2, 503, 509, 850; **4:**
2–4; **5:** 494, 499; **6:** 567–8. Portraits of:
2: 163–4, 166–7, 683; **3:** 241–2, 413; **4:**
374, 495–6; **5:** 77; **6:** 432–3, 524. Sense
of humor: **2:** 109; **3:** 637; **4:** 34. On
grammar & semantics: **3:** 581, 613, 621.
On public speaking **1:** 274; **2:** 700, 781;
3: 313, 497, 550, 682–3, 894. Harvard
honorary degree: **4:** 674, 703. Babies
named after: **6:** 1247. Taste in clothes: **6:**
1034. Horseracing (*see* below horses).
Toasts given by Clay: **1:** 406, 697, 855; **2:**
61, 62, 71, 82, 344, 355, 573, 588, 697; **3:**
171, 219, 405; **4:** 1, 384, 386–7, 393,
409, 415, 431, 498, 502, 515, 523, 531–2;
5: 548, 661, 703, 706, 713. Toasts given
to Clay: **1:** 696–7; **2:** 61, 62, 68, 70, 71,
343–4, 353, 573, 588, 692, 697, 869; **3:**
68, 79, 209, 218, 279, 403, 498, 778, 780,
797; **4:** 383, 386, 393, 408, 414, 421, 431,
442, 498, 515, 520, 528; **5:** 547, 559, 654,
661; **6:** 700, 763, 778, 783, 796
—character, personality, social attitudes:
Humble origins: **4:** 922. On his youth: **3:**
161, 621, 663; **4:** 922. Women: **1:** 126–7,
458; **4:** 431; **6:** 1241, 1359–60. Marriage:
1: 631. Sex: **1:** 458; **4:** 34. Matchmaker:
5: 987. Children: **1:** 129–30. Anecdotal
stories & sayings: **1:** 528–9, 532, 758; **2:**
60, 70–1, 259, 629, 744, 747; **3:** 432; **4:**
783. As duelist: **1:** 397–401; **5:** 208–9,
211–2 (*see also* Duels & dueling). Man of
destiny: **3:** 89–90. Subject of biographers
& historians: **2:** 605–6; **3:** 452–3. Frugality: **2:** 363. Temper: **2:** 231; **4:** 621; **5:**
392. Memory: **6:** 884. On death & funer-
als: **3:** 105, 493; **4:** 585, 589. On getting
old: **6:** 1194. Forebodings of death: **4:**

522, 598. Modest military career: **1:** 122, 124; **4:** 46. On the purity of his motives: **2:** 581; **3:** 359, 364–5, 464, 506–7, 641, 777, 825, 857, 870–1; **5:** 655 (*see also* Adams (John Q.) administration: "Corrupt Bargain" controversy during; Election of 1828: issues, charges, & counter-charges in campaign; corrupt bargain issue & related campaign literature). Opinions of self: **4:** 447; **5:** 655. Abandons his principles: **2:** 209–10, 469–70. Arrogance: **3:** 613–4. Genius: **5:** 107, 776–7. Decisiveness: **5:** 212. His political contradictions: **3:** 615–6, 620; **5:** 279. His name a household word: **4:** 287, 370. Moral looseness: **5:** 279. Corrupt politician: **6:** 153. Liar: **1:** 338–9, 360
—economic & financial affairs: Economic theory & ideas: **1:** 308. Economic prospects & status: **1:** 180, 220; **4:** 38, 206, 619; **5:** 282–3. Assets as of Dec. 1822: **3:** 345–6. Impact of 1819 panic & depression on: **2:** 589, 662, 685–7, 795, 868, 876–7, 886–7, 892, 899; **3:** 54–5, 59–60, 72, 548–9, 886; **4:** 38; **5:** 983–4. Indebtedness to BUS (*see* Bank of the United States). Sells "Ashland" household furnishings: **4:** 435, 458–61, 489. Pays off debts: **2:** 589; **3:** 886; **5:** 282–3, 389; **6:** 362. Salary as Congressman & Sec State: **2:** 171; **4:** 814; **6:** 362. Investments & speculations in: La. sugar: **2:** 693–5, 719–20, 824; Olympian Springs resort: **1:** 782, 793; **5:** 550; brick–making machine: **1:** 555–6; cotton bagging: **3:** 735; Ky. bank stocks: **2:** 575–6, 866, 894, 902; cotton textile machinery: **1:** 38; hemp mfgr.: **1:** 345–6; merchandizing: **1:** 489, 822; **2:** 159–60, 162–3, 184, 249–50, 373–4. Residential & commercial properties bought, sold, leased, rented in Lex.: Mill St. houses: **1:** 50–1, 55–6, 58, 92–3, 175, 204–5; **2:** 716–7; **3:** 152–3; **6:** 1366; Mill St. office building: **1:** 114, 142, 201–2; Upper St. houses: **1:** 169–70, 194, 251, 377; Short St. store & house: **1:** 795; **2:** 106–7, 169, 184; **3:** 880; **4:** 449, 455–6; Market St. houses: **1:** 348, 355–6, 383, 561; **2:** 236, 241; **4:** 507–9; brick house at Short & Market: **4:** 259–60, 642, 703–4; **5:** 601–2, 847; house on Boonsborough Rd.: **2:** 103; "Ashland" (*see* Name Index). Construction Costs: **1:** 92–3, 132–3, 173–5, 191, 203–5, 794–5. Insurance costs: **1:** 730, 950–1; **2:** 100
—land purchases, grants, exchanges, speculations: **1:** 1, 31–2, 49, 73–4, 79–80, 89–90, 119–20, 135–6, 138–9, 141–2, 144, 148–9, 169–70, 192, 195, 200–01, 209, 241–3, 247–9, 261–2, 264, 297, 300, 306–7, 310, 321, 348–9, 355, 373, 377–8, 394, 405–7, 484, 486–8, 492, 495–7, 556, 559–61, 573–4, 577–8, 580–5, 589, 592, 597–8, 628, 634, 725–6, 731–2, 781, 783, 785–6, 793, 795–6, 814–5, 825, 829; **2:** 90–1, 103, 127, 197–8, 211–3, 238, 242, 251, 337, 349–50, 364, 407–8, 465–7, 578, 592, 717; **3:** 74–5, 104–6, 130–1, 134, 141,

151–2, 291, 296–8, 342, 346, 489, 627–8, 806–7, 880; **4:** 502–3, 505–6, 513, 788; **6:** 1273. C. on land speculation: **1:** 95, 413. *See also* Illinois, Indiana, Missouri
—land sales, divestments, speculations: **1:** 44–5, 135, 153–4, 169, 190, 192–3, 247, 257, 303, 305–6, 314, 348–9, 361, 371–4, 377, 379, 383, 407, 410, 448, 476, 488, 556, 558–9, 561, 578, 583, 593, 668, 738, 776, 781–2, 796–8, 803–5, 820–1, 829; **2:** 90, 92, 97–8; **3:** 92, 108, 138, 153, 244, 272, 806–7; **4:** 464; **5:** 584, 586; **6:** 1273. C. land holdings: **1:** 217–8, 276, 402, 526, 628; **3:** 346
—income from rental & leased properties: **1:** 46, 96–7, 103–4, 355–6, 369, 478, 481, 485–6, 489, 499, 553–5, 590–1, 716, 786–9, 822, 826, 828, 831–3, 878–9, 936–7, 997; **2:** 18, 86–7, 103, 234, 250–1, 340, 342–3, 353, 355–7, 362–3, 367, 394, 398–9, 507–8, 577, 600–1, 684, 690, 714–5, 717, 719, 723–4, 787, 798–9, 866, 882; **2:** 890–1, 893–4, 902; **3:** 97, 136–7, 153–4, 175–6, 182, 235–6, 349, 452, 520, 665, 681–2, 752–3, 777–8, 880, 885; **4:** 51, 259, 449, 642, 703–4, 732, 758–9; **5:** 601–2, 847; **6:** 63, 310–11, 1366 (*see espec.* **2:** 367). *See also* Kentucky Hotel in Name Index
—Clay family: Housekeeper for (*see* Hall, Sarah in Name Index). C. as guardian of his nieces: **1:** 850–1. Expenses of: **2:** 399, 898. Slave owners in: **1:** 277, 370, 395; **3:** 500. Dangers of childbirth: **3:** 432; **4:** 34. C. admin. estates of kin: **6:** 871, 1104–5. General observations on life & death within: **1:** 274, 289, 482, 698; **2:** 306, 356–7, 726–7; **3:** 430–1, 459; **4:** 585–6. *See also* Name Index, Vols. 1–6, for following: Martha Watkins Blackburn (half–sister); William B. Blackburn (husband of C. half–sister); Eliza Clay (daughter); George Clay (brother); Henrietta Clay (daughter); Henry Clay, Jr. (son); James Brown Clay (son); John Clay (brother); John Clay (father); John Morrison Clay (son); Julie Duralde (Mrs. John) Clay (sister–in–law & sister to C. son–in–law) Laura Clay (daughter); Lucretia Hart Clay (daughter); Lucretia Hart Clay (wife); Porter Clay (brother); Theodore Wythe Clay (son); Thomas Hart Clay (son); Henry Clay Duralde (grandson); Martin Duralde, Jr. (son–in–law); Martin Duralde III (grandson); Susan Hart Clay (Mrs. Martin Jr.) Duralde (daughter); Andrew Erwin (father–in–law of C. daughter); Anne Brown Clay (Mrs. James) Erwin (daughter); Henry Clay Erwin (grandson); James Erwin (son–in–law); John P. Erwin (brother of son–in–law); Julia D. Erwin (granddaughter); Henry Clay Hart (nephew of wife); John S. Hart (nephew of wife); Susannah Gray (Mrs. Thomas H. Sr.) Hart (mother–in–law); Thomas P. Hart (nephew of wife); Elizabeth Watkins Wooldridge (Mrs. John) Moss

Clay, Henry (*continued*):
(sister of C. stepfather); Elizabeth Clay
(Mrs. Henry W.) Watkins (mother); Henry W. Watkins (stepfather); John Watkins
(half–brother); Nathaniel W. Watkins
(half–brother)
—farm & farming at "Ashland": Purchase
of Hereford cattle in GB: **2:** 252–3,
314–5, 329–30, 334–7, 345, 380–1, 703;
3: 277–8, 305–8. Flowers, trees, shrubs;
2: 333, 720; **3:** 98. Cattle types & selec-
tive breeding: **2:** 381. Scientific agriculture: **4:** 34; **6:** 1311. Pests infest: **2:** 346.
Merino sheep: **1:** 473, 479, 524, 586; **3:**
384, 442, 464; **4:** 435, 638, 679, 753, 785;
5: 615, 941; **6:** 1058, 1151. Cashmere
goats: **6:** 536. Livestock sales: **2:** 602–3,
689, 887, 899; **3:** 527; **4:** 435, 458–9,
489, 638, 679, 753, 844; **5:** 941. Stud
fees: **2:** 703, 864, 899. Hog production &
prices: **5:** 941; **6:** 63–4. Livestock equipment & inventories: **4:** 7–8. Jackasses: **6:**
992, 1151, 1296. Harvests: **3:** 735. Overseers & their wages: **4:** 7; **5:** 623; **6:** 1150
(*see also* Kerr, John H.). "Ashland" income & expenditures: **5:** 590–1; **6:**
785–6. Interest in new farm machinery:
2: 896; **3:** 735. Purchase of "Ashland": **1:**
474–5, 596–7. Descriptions of: **1:** 475,
597. Land of rented & leased: **2:** 718–9;
5: 155–6, 283. Hemp culture at (*see* below). Slaves & slavery (*see* Slavery &
slaves)
—hemp culture: C. as expert on: **3:** 798; **6:**
8. Quality of C. crop: **6:** 993. C. as producer of: **1:** 524, 708–10; **3:** 33, 658; **6:**
112, 1150. Comparison of US & Ru.: **3:**
906; **6:** 1055, 1057. US competition with
Ru. hemp: **2:** 379, 890, 896; **3:** 659, 903;
4: 60–1; **6:** 8, 1057. Imports from Ru.: **1:**
462. Duties on Ru. hemp: **1:** 524. C.
urges protective tariff on Ru.: **1:** 459; **2:**
180; **6:** 1057. C. as supplier to USN: **1:**
549, 817, 836–7, 840, 844–5; **3:** 775–6,
830, 844, 853, 903–6; **4:** 267, 269, 271.
C. sales of: **1:** 548–9, 562–3, 565–6, 571,
695, 708, 711, 776, 817, 834, 843; **2:** 95;
3: 117, 541, 775; **4:** 267, 269, 271, 435;
6: 63. Prices fetched: **1:** 462, 549, 563,
776, 831, 837; **2:** 95, 379; **3:** 117; **4:**
60–1, 271; **6:** 63. Hemp industry in Ky.:
1: 315–6, 344–5, 458, 463, 524, 625,
811, 817; **2:** 379, 889–90, 896–7; **3:** 219,
648, 659; **4:** 60. Production problems &
techniques in Lex. area: **2:** 889–90, 896;
3: 219, 658–9, 735, 775, 830, 903; **4:** 34,
61; **6:** 8. Use for slave clothing: **6:** 8
—horses: As medium of exchange in Ky.:
1: 57, 114, 139, 144, 152, 170, 200, 206,
227, 240, 243, 293, 377–8, 383, 435, 481,
731, 788, 790, 795, 825–6; **3:** 247. Horse
racing in Lex.: **1:** 97, 272–3. C. dealings
in: **1:** 113, 117–8, 234, 293, 323–4,
377–8, 481, 731, 790, 832; **2:** 86, 163,
246, 603; **3:** 668. Number owned by C.:
1: 171, 218, 276, 402, 526. Price fluctuations: **1:** 85, 98, 482, 790, 795, 826, 832;
2: 86, 163, 603; **4:** 457–8. C. interest in
breeding & racing: **1:** 272–3, 282, 322–4,

412, 706, 708, 710, 712, 731, 794; **4:** 461;
5: 605. Stud fees: **2:** 348
—salt: C. production & sale of: **1:** 153–4,
176, 184, 197, 247–8, 481, 579–80, 634;
2: 465–7. As medium of exchange in
Ky.: **1:** 170, 191, 380, 420, 489–90. C.
opposes tariff reduction on: **2:** 825, 833
—health & medical history: Importance of
C. health to nation: **5:** 725, 746; **6:** 167.
Gunshot wound: **1:** 400, 402. Fatigue &
exhaustion: **2:** 512; **4:** 302. Impact of
political acrimony on: **5:** 746; **6:** 604,
724–5, 1007, 1257, 1356. Rumors of
death: **3:** 301, 318, 372. Health while in
Wash.: **1:** 655; **2:** 462; **4:** 337, 590,
617–8, 906, 943, 953; **5:** 114, 117, 122,
165, 187, 389, 393–4, 396, 400, 413, 420,
422, 433–4, 481, 491, 494, 504, 523, 568,
570, 578–9, 610–11, 679, 725; **6:** 155,
167, 604, 1052, 1063. Various illnesses:
3: 183, 301, 308, 318, 335–6, 372, 471,
481, 485, 495, 500, 506, 548, 737, 750,
780–1, 842, 895; **4:** 38, 88; **5:** 117, 122.
Physicians consulted: **1:** 16; **2:** 89; **3:**
500–1, 813–4, 861, 883–4. Cures recommended to C.: **4:** 701. C. on medical
profession: **6:** 319–20
—law practice: C. training: **1:** 2–3, 25. Formula for becoming a successful lawyer: **1:**
281; **2:** 393. As teacher of law: **1:** 427; **2:**
341, 347; **4:** 757–8, 795; **6:** 3. Easy entry
to Ky. bar: **2:** 393. Questions of legal
ethics: **1:** 311, 779. On use of GB legal
precedents in Ky. courts: **1:** 318. Conflict
between practice & politics: **1:** 261,
752–3; **2:** 393, 591, 900; **3:** 750. Debt
drives out of Cong. & back into practice:
2: 795, 869; **3:** 54, 68, 279. Legal–professional opportunity in Ky.: **1:** 180, 811;
2: 393. Political reputation attracts clients: **3:** 9. C. shaky grasp of international
law: **4:** 832. Practice before Supreme
Court (*see* U.S. Supreme Court). Clients
& cases handled: Vol. **1,** *passim* (*see also*
Scott, Robert). Clay as litigant: **1:** 95–6,
98, 154, 206, 211, 219, 302, 325, 349,
357–8, 414, 419, 431, 448, 495–6,
550–1, 577–8, 581, 711, 776, 794–5,
833–4, 849, 865, 994; **2:** 18, 82, 98, 127,
288, 325–6, 348–9, 383, 416, 465–7,
695; **3:** 127, 796–7, 882; **4:** 507–9; **5:**
427, 507–9, 545; **6:** 216, 272–3, 390–2,
882. Fees quoted & income from practice: **1:** 3, 9, 10, 15, 19, 24, 37, 41, 46–7,
52, 56–8, 60, 62–5, 67, 76, 83, 86,
88–90, 102, 105–10, 113, 131, 146–7,
151, 154–5, 181–5, 189–91, 227, 233,
236–8, 241, 262 (*see also* Burr, Aaron),
279, 291, 296, 305, 310, 317–8, 387,
409–10, 417, 430, 434, 448, 489–90, 558,
568–9, 616–17, 705, 710–11, 732,
735–6, 812; **2:** 233–4, 870–1; **3:** 84, 126,
128, 135, 397, 417, 428–9, 449, 465, 490.
C. complains of high fees: **6:** 216. Slaves
& slavery in Clay law practice: **1:** 9, 19,
41, 59, 178, 230, 235, 291, 402, 405, 417,
433, 485, 552, 585. 632. 726. 819–20: **2:**
236–7, 579, 711; **3:** 98, 100, 118, 174,
310, 438–42, 455, 488–9, 508, 563, 893;

4: 499, 512, 549–50; 6: 935, 1017
—observations on politics, society, & American institutions: Am. character: 1: 605, 626; 6: 730. Nature of constit.: 1: 13; 2: 521. Nature of US Constit.: 2: 413, 470–1; 3: 738. Military powers of Pres.: 2: 184. Freedom of the press: 1: 350. Mankind: 1: 508; 2: 827. The higher law: 1: 511. Nature of justice: 1: 352. Liberty & space: 2: 521–2. Nature of society: 2: 278–9, 837. Monarchy & aristocracy: 1: 508; 2: 377, 521; 3: 608. On the Union as Republic: 2: 771, 775; 3: 728, 779, 792; 4: 24; 5: 804. US as confederacy: 2: 471. Majority not always right: 4: 676. State legis. instructions to their Cong. delegates: 1: 529–30; 2: 199–200, 216–17, 284, 732; 4: 155–6, 166; 6: 775 (*see also* Election of 1824: House election phase). Secession: 1: 167; 2: 474; 3: 58–9; 4: 24. On States Rights: 1: 615, 740; 2: 468–9, 472–3; 3: 168; 4: 20. Patriotism: 2: 444; 6: 703. Treason: 1: 332–3, 759–60. Disadvantage of public office: 1: 328–9; 3: 68–9. Guilt by association: 1: 757. Citizenship & naturalization: 1: 766; 2: 609–11. Extension of suffrage: 4: 521. Capacity for self-govt.: 5: 804; 6: 703. Two–party system: 5: 889. US as world model: 4: 530–1. After the election: 4: 162, 747. C. on his political "principles": 6: 700–3. View of newspapers & their duties: 1: 343, 674, 801; 4: 227. *See also* Bank of the United States; U.S. Supreme Court
—religion: Assists Presbyterian church: 1: 212–3. Roman Catholic church & human freedom: 2: 522. Separation of church & state: 2: 522. Freedom of religion: 5: 337–8. Literal purity of Bible: 1: 537. Disgust with denominational bickering: 2: 595–6; 3: 738. Disinterest in theological doctrine: 2: 613. Stereotypes Jews: 2: 839; 3: 626. On immortality: 3: 901. Roman Catholic church & European prosperity: 3: 718. Respect for Am. Indian religions: 2: 638–9. Pacifist nature of Jesus: 2: 638. On the Quakers: 2: 751. God aids US in battle: 1: 773. God & the tariff: 3: 684. God & Texas annexation: 2: 814. Member of St. John's Episcopal Church. Wash., D.C. (*see* Name Index)
Clay, Henry Jr. (son): Birth: 1: 557. Character: 5: 772. Health: 2: 394. Considers career in law: 6: 385. On a career in the army: 6: 365–66, 385, 718. Attends preparatory dept. at TU: 3: 121, 272; 5: 603–4. Interest in European travel, education: 6: 365, 385. C. career advice to: 6: 385. Views on the military life: 6: 718. Family hopes rest upon: 6: 385. Engages in violent altercation at USMA: 6: 524–6. Suspended from USMA: 6: 525. Officially enters USMA: 5: 772; 6: 718. Friends at USMA: 6: 689–90. C. pride in: 6: 1379–80. C. financial support of: 5: 604; 6: 1380
Clay, John (brother): Character: 1: 180. C. recommends for patronage jobs in N.O.:

1: 125, 152, 159, 215–6, 228, 546, 557, 575; 3: 248, 264. Patronage appts.: 1: 139. Business ventures: 1: 144–5, 159–60, 172, 199; 3: 248, 339; 6: 875. Commercial relations with C.: 1: 140, 144, 172, 175, 549; 2: 898–9; 3: 72. C. posts bond for: 1: 18. Membership in Masonic Order: 1: 140–1. Legal (debtor) problems in Lex.: 1: 198–200, 217; 3: 338–9. Recommends patronage appts. to C.: 4: 391. Slaveowner: 1: 277, 370. Buys cattle from C.: 2: 899. Buys BUS stock on condition of job at N.O. branch: 3: 272–3, 338. C. legal work for: 3: 338–9; 6: 875. Financial difficulties: 3: 338–9; 6: 875–6. C. asks for loan: 3: 339. Disinterest in Ky. politics: 6: 876. Realty transactions in association with C.: 6: 1149–50
Clay, Lucretia Hart (wife): Medical problems: 1: 187, 504; 2: 394; 5: 494. In childbirth: 1: 557; 2: 379, 399. C. on impregnating: 4: 34. Accompanies C. to Wash.: 1: 482, 522, 652, 737, 870 (*see also* Washington, D.C.). Dislike of Wash. society: 1: 870; 3: 538; 4: 38. Takes Lex. townhouse while C. in Wash.: 3: 33–4. Frugality of: 4: 38. Interest in Paris fashions: 4: 336. Withdraws from "society": 4: 336; 5: 494. Indiana ladies salute: 4: 527. Travel between Wash. & Lex.: 5: 494
Clay, Porter (brother): Biographical: 1: 96, 175. Land transactions of: 1: 175, 373. Legal & other business with & for C.: 1: 573, 776–7, 886, 994; 2: 228, 371, 567, 911–2; 3: 457; 4: 713–4; 6: 223, 1149. On Old Court–New Court conflict: 4:713; 6: 28, 1150. Analysis of Ky. politics for C.: 6: 28–9, 982, 1149. Supports C. Negro colonization stance: 6: 222. Laments extent of corruption in US: 6: 222, 1149–50. Realty transactions in association with C.: 6: 1149–50. On Jacksonian corruption: 6: 1149–50
Clay, Theodore Wythe (son): Sent to Lewis Bancel school in N.Y.: 2: 231–2, 253–4. Musical interests: 2: 242. Money from father: 2: 243, *passim*. Father visits at Cambridge, Mass.: 2: 593, 596, 614. Enrolls at Harvard: 2: 598. Costs of attending Harvard: 2: 619–20, 725. Room & board costs in Lex.: 2: 893–94. Travel: 3: 842. Illnesses: 3: 842. Attends Carnahan school (Wash., D.C.): 4: 727 On death of sisters: 4: 817. On Old Court vs. New Court fight in Ky.: 4: 817. Graduate of TU: 6: 48. Derogatory political information solicited from: 5: 431. Courtesies to in Mex.: 6: 541. Bearer of dispatches to Mex. City: 6: 307, 313, 365, 512, 538, 540, 542, 613. C. has little hope for: 6: 385
Clay, Thomas Hart (son): Sent to Lewis Bancel school in N.Y.: 2: 232, 253–4. Money from father: 2: 243, 682. Suffers accident: 2: 261–2. Room & board costs: 2: 724, 893–4. C. admonishes on performance at TU: 2: 781. C. buys textbooks for: 2: 913–15. Appt. to USMA: 3: 82–3.

Clay, Thomas Hart (*continued*):
Runs up bills at USMA: **3:** 209. Fails USMA entrance exam: **3:** 83. Reads law under Judge John Boyle: **4:** 13, 705. Poor reading habits: **4:** 705. Characterizations of: **4:** 705. Attends Carnahan school: **4:** 727. Considers law practice in Miss.: **5:** 969–70; **6:** 139. Assists C. in business transaction: **6:** 242–3. Dissipation of: **6:** 291, 385

Clinton, De Witt: Family: **4:** 497. Recommends mathematician to C. for job in Western Colleges: **2:** 369–70. Patronage recommendations to C.: **5:** 145. Bucktail opposition to in N.Y.: **3:** 147, 150, 185, 357. General opposition to in N.Y.: **4:** 129–31. Possible Pres. candidate in 1824 (*see* Election of 1824: DeWitt Clinton candidacy). Supports AJ in 1824 campaign: **3:** 769, 771, 776; **5:** 348, 664 (*see also* Election of 1824). C. condemns anti–war of 1812 stance: **3:** 364, 366. Albany Regency attacks: **3:** 776. Erie Canal builder: **4:** 529, 531, 919–20; **6:** 885. In N.Y. 1824 Gov. election: **3:** 846–9, 852; **4:** 129; **5:** 347. Declines job as Min. to GB: **4:** 112, 129–30, 193, 286, 858; **5:** 174, 348, 410, 492; **6:** 1129. Attitudes towards JQA admin. (*see* Adams (John Q.) administration). Opinion of Rufus King: **4:** 547. C. opinion of: **4:** 551, 858. Compared with C. as politician: **4:** 551. Possible Pres. candidate in 1828 (*see* Election of 1828). C. asks favor of: **4:** 723. Attempts to build new political following: **5:** 113, 143–4, 175, 186, 346–8, 675–6, 764; **6:** 502, 692 (*see also* New York State). Re-elected N.Y. Gov. (1826): **5:** 207, 347, 349, 650, 665, 676–7, 759, 763, 872, 876, 885, 936–7; **6:** 130, 140–1, 245. Daughter solicits patronage favor of C.: **5:** 497. Interest in Macadam roads in N.Y.: **4:** 663. Decline of influence in N.Y.: **5:** 872. Opposition to US financed internal improvements: **6:** 123–4. Involvement in Isthmian canal: **6:** 160. Role in 1828 campaign (*see also* Election of 1828). Opposition to JQA–C. admin.: **6:** 528. Urged as replacement for JQA or AJ as Pres. candidate (1828): **6:** 1307. Possible compromise candidate in 1828 (*see* Election of 1828). Possible VP candidate on AJ ticket in 1828: **6:** 123, 1046–7, 1062. Supports AJ candidacy in 1828 campaign: **5:** 664; **6:** 457, 754–5, 761, 837, 1046, 1059, 1197, 1200, 1232, 1234, 1265, 1270. Drinking problem of: **6:** 837. Death of: **5:** 759

Columbia: Formed by merger (1819) of New Granada & Venezuela: **2:** 855, 860; **6:** 560. Independence movements from Sp. in New Granada & Venezuela: **2:** 494–5, 502, 504–7, 511–2, 531, 541, 551–2, 557, 584–5, 702, 855, 860; **3:** 143, 172; **5:** 198, 391; **6:** 347, 380, 391, 560. Racial & social structure of: **2:** 531, 585. **6:** 380. Negro troops in army: **4:** 711; **5:** 334, 380; **6:** 27. Emancipation of

slaves in: **2:** 551, 858, 860. C. explains US govt. structure to: **4:** 127. Esteem for C. in **3:** 261, 414. C. esteem for: **5:** 960. C. personal connections in: **3:** 172, 261–2. Progress in: **5:** 378–9, 750. Economic problems in: **5:** 13, 309–10, 378, 587, 813, 878, 927, 1002; **6:** 255, 317, 325–6, 351, 1048, 1087, 1268. Constit. of: **5:** 750; **6:** 196, 724, 860. Amend constit. to provide fed. system: **6:** 724, 860, 1378. Constit. conv. at Ocana: **3:** 172; **6:** 34, 860–1, 1378, 1406. Incapable of running a republic: **5:** 747; **6:** 724. Sentiment for monarchy: **6:** 196. Misrule & corruption: **3:** 414; **6:** 255. Religion in: **5:** 42, 694. Anti–slave trade stance: **4:** 127, 136; **5:** 519. Tariff legis. & policy: **6:** 1378. Elections in: **4:** 811, 863. Bolivar seen as key to order in: **5:** 368, 520, 559, 695, 747, 813, 878, 957, 960–1, 1002, 1005, 1010, 1039–40; **6:** 255, 306, 684, 724, 1196, 1269 (*see also* Bolivar, Simon). Fear of Bolivar in: **6:** 218. Internal instability, disorder, revolution, civil war in: **5:** 225, 368, 422, 500, 520, 527, 536, 559, 573, 587, 747, 927, 982, 1005; **6:** 161, 255, 305, 374, 377, 380, 404, 484, 538, 562, 586, 684, 694, 724, 1048, 1057, 1196 (*see also* Bolivar, Simon; Paez, Jose Antonio; Santander, Francisco de Paula). Venezuelan separation (Paez revolt) movement: **5:** 368, 391, 519, 527, 536, 552, 559, 587, 606, 623, 649, 653, 686, 691, 695, 735, 747, 750, 793, 813, 827, 849, 878, 953–4, 957, 960–1, 981, 996, 1005, 1010, 1039–40; **6:** 33–4, 150, 196, 255, 262, 306, 317, 375, 380, 391, 538, 684, 1048 (*see espec.* **5:** 391). Possible dissolution of the nation: **6:** 374, 724, 1269. Causes of political chaos: **6:** 255, 538–9. Sp. naval operations against: **5:** 479, 520, 606, 653, 740, 809, 1025; **6:** 127, 657, 1262, 1336. Naval & privateer operations against Sp.: **4:** 374, 406, 493, 575, 643; **5:** 22, 500, 653; **6:** 195, 411, 722, 735, 911, 1349. Seek end to war with Sp.: **5:** 877, 957. Fear of Sp. invasion: **5:** 378. Fr. advises to end war with Sp.: **5:** 424. Interest in & threat to conquer Cuba & PR (*see* Spain empire: Cuba; Puerto Rico). Navy: **5:** 309, 334, 378, 479, 813; **6:** 351, 380. Army: **4:** 711; **5:** 334; **6:** 326, 380, 861. Seek to buy warships abroad (*see* Sweden). Arrest Dutch nationals: **6:** 326. Interest in Panama Isthmian canal & railroad: **4:** 810–1; **5:** 224. Mediator in Br.–BA war: **5:** 538, 846. Treaty with BA: **5:** 291. Policy in Peru (*see* Bolivar, Simon; Peru). Bolivar resigns as Pres. of Colombia (*see* Bolivar, Simon). Policy in Ecuador (*see* Ecuador). Border tensions with Br.: **4:** 585; **6:** 1269. Relations with Vatican: **6:** 382. Treaties with Mex.: **4:** 724–5. Interest in Panama Cong. (*see* U.S. diplomacy: Panama Congress). Fr. recognition of: **5:** 24, 816. GB recognition of: **4:** 94, 364–5, 500, 907. GB influence in: **5:** 13, 42; **6:** 326, 465,

538, 1378. Commercial treaty with GB: **4:** 364–5, 378, 500, 612, 620, 643, 654, 680–1, 777, 828; **5:** 42, 79–80, 198, 242, 518, 752, 1006–7. *See also* Bolivar, Simon
—U.S. relations with: US citizens fight in war of independence of: **6:** 1012. Seek US recognition of independence: **2:** 668–9. C. support of independence of: **2:** 494–5, 504. US influence in: **5:** 42, 414, 424, 429–30, 496. US recognition of: **2:** 552, 556; **3:** 182, 186, 398; **4:** 299; **6:** 27, 126. Blockade, contraband, privateering & other US neutral rights problems in Sp. vs. Colombia war: **4:** 122–4, 284, 293, 299, 699; **5:** 13, 400, 479, 500; **6:** 39, 70, 120, 190, 316, 324, 330, 353, 359–60, 384, 411, 414, 483, 656–60, 722, 744, 911, 1135–6, 1349 (*see espec.* the *Zulme* case & related claims, viz: **5:** 500; **6:** 39, 70, 120, 190, 316–7, 324, 330, 411, 483, 589, 657, 710, 744, 825–6, 852, 1327–8, 1349, 1374). Warships for built in US: **5:** 813. US firms provision troops of: **6:** 317. US citizens serve in armed forces & merchant marine of: **4:** 123, 284, 558, 654; **5:** 151, 479, 500, 520, 559, 851; **6:** 351, 411, 414, 480, 495, 560, 635, 722, 911. Seek US peace–truce mediation in war with Sp.: **4:** 326, 647, 691; **5:** 180–2, 229–30, 238, 262, 319, 335, 373–4, 424, 429–30. US assists in prisoner exchange with Sp.: **6:** 1353–4. Nature & extent of US trade with: **6:** 635, 1406. Colombian concept of "del Sistema Americano": **4:** 958. Extension of commercial privileges to US: **4:** 365; **5:** 42, 79–80. US–Colombia commercial treaty: **4:** 118, 120, 127, 168, 248, 558, 643–5, 680–1, 699, 804, 851, 887; **5:** 42, 62, 324–5, 329, 560, 878; **6:** 288, 384, 1135. Treaty as model: **5:** 722. Weak features of commercial treaty: **6:** 288. Restrictions on US trade: **4:** 284. Harassment of US trade & business: **6:** 317, 563, 647. Privateers attack US shipping: **6:** 353. USN needed in waters of: **5:** 559–60, 587, 623, 958. Tariff, duty, fee discrim. against US shipping & trade: **4:** 612, 644; **5:** 79, 694, 878; **6:** 563. US claims against: **4:** 105, 122–4, 142–3, 245–6, 284, 411–2, 416, 421, 454–5, 591–2, 606, 612, 615, 621, 637, 646–7, 654, 749–50, 752, 863, 880; **5:** 13, 25, 50, 83, 108, 115, 139, 198, 226, 230, 271, 500–1, 669, 741, 768, 806–7, 813, 939; **6:** 15, 153, 270, 317, 353, 359–60, 384, 589, 647, 684, 832–3, 921, 1024, 1036–7, 1135–6, 1300, 1378. Murder of US consul: **5:** 558, 578, 1040. Arrest US citizens: **5:** 15; **6:** 317, 326, 560, 684. Military despotism in: **6:** 27 (*see also* Bolivar, Simon). Protecting US life & property in: **5:** 735, 827; **6:** 317. US interest in isthmian trade & communication development: **6:** 360. US arbitrator of US–GB dispute on NE boundary: **5:** 447; **6:** 828. US urges suspension of planned attack by on Cuba & PR: **4:** 174–5, 930, 950; **5:** 19, 138, 237,

335, 386, 397, 424, 429, 437, 709, 1025 (*see* Spain empire: Cuba; Puerto Rico). Failed convention between to suppress slave trade: **4:** 127–8, 136, 217, 246, 341. US diplomat interferes in internal affairs of (*see* Watts, Beaufort T.). *See also* Anderson, Richard C.; Bolivar, Simon; Watts, Beaufort T.

Congress of the United States
—ninth congress (Spec. Sess: 3/4/05; 1 Sess: 12/2/05–4/21/06; 2 Sess: 12/1/06–3/3/07): C. elected to: **1:** 254–5. C. well received: **1:** 274. C. as orator: **1:** 274. Dull session: **1:** 280. Expansion of Fed. court system: **1:** 264, 268–9, 274. Ohio Rapids (Falls of the River) Canal: **1:** 267–8, 274, 284–7. Chesapeake & Del. Canal: **1:** 284–6. Potomac Toll Bridge: **1:** 273. Foreign trade: **1:** 280. Amending constit. **1:** 283
—eleventh congress (Spec. Sess: 3/4/09–3/7/09; 1 Sess: 5/22/09–6/28/09; 2 Sess: 11/27/09–5/1/10; 3 Sess: 12/3/10–3/3/11): C. on Non–Intercourse Act: **1:** 448–52. Public lands: **1:** 458–9. Domestic mfgrs: **1:** 459–63. Protective tariff: **1:** 523. Trade with Indians: **1:** 466. Amend. BUS bill: **1:** 467. Recharter BUS: **1:** 522–4, 527–40, 542–4. La. statehood: **1:** 467–70, 522. Miss. statehood: **1:** 522. Pickering censure: **1:** 517–8. Occupation of West Fla.: **1:** 505–16, 522. Occupation of East Fla.: **1:** 520–2, 544 (*see* Spain empire: Florida, East; Florida, West). Military preparedness: **1:** 523. Maritime relations with GB & Fr.: **1:** 523–4, 526. C. shifts from Sen. to House in 12th Cong.: **1:** 471–3, 491, 498
—twelfth congress (1 Sess: 11/4/11–7/6/12; 2 Sess: 11/2/12–3/3/13): C. elected Speaker: **1:** 594, 598. Criticized as Speaker: **6:** 1371, 1373. Hailed as Speaker: **1:** 778–9. 12th Cong. most memorable in US history: **1:** 779. Decorum in: **1:** 628. C. interprets House rules: **1:** 660–3, 668–73, 753. C. clash with Randolph (*see* Randolph, John). Military preparedness & capability: **1:** 602–10, 613–6, 618–27, 654, 748, 751–2, 754–74. C. wants war with GB: **1:** 636, 660–3, 665. Embargo on GB imports: **1:** 637, 641–3, 738–47; **6:** 1373. Protect US seamen: **1:** 665. Prize vessels: **1:** 775–6. Yazoo land claims: **1:** 778. Tariff issues: **1:** 596. Public land legis.: **1:** 653–4. *See also* Great Britain: War of 1812
—thirteenth congress (1 Sess: 5/24/13–8/2/13; 2 Sess: 12/6/13–4/18/14; 3 Sess: 9/19/14–3/3/15): C. as Speaker: **1:** 798–9. Interprets House rules: **1:** 800–1. Resigns as Speaker to join peace commission: **1:** 853–4; **2:** 205. Wartime taxes: **1:** 812. Embargo & Non–Importation legis.: **1:** 814, 844, 909, 915. Assistance to vessels of nations at war with GB: **1:** 838. C. on length of war: **1:** 844. Foreign trade legis.: **2:** 31, 37. BUS issue: **1:** 903, 916. Honoring USN heroes: **1:** 845–6. Yazoo land claims: **1:** 903, 909, 916. Assist US

Congress of the United States (*continued*):
merchant mariners: **2:** 32, 37. Fed. assistance to canal construction: **1:** 845
—fourteenth congress (1 Sess:
12/4/15–4/30/16; 2 Sess: 12/2/16–3/3/17):
C. reelected to while in Ghent: **1:** 990; **2:**
72. Elected Speaker: **2:** 105, 320. Salary
as: **2:** 171. C. interprets House rules: **2:**
132–3. Debate on chartering 2nd BUS:
2: 6, 7, 11, 169–70, 173, 177–8, 181,
216–9, 257–8 (*see also* Bank of the United States). Compensation (pay raise) Bill
for members: **2:** 171–2, 187, 197,
208–10, 219, 258–9, 284–8, 311, 376–7,
615, 795. Need to end commercial warfare with GB: **2:** 31, 37, 55–6. Tariff Bill
& Act of 1816: **2:** 173–5, 178–80, 182–6,
826, 846; **5:** 134, 1016–7; **6:** 1028–9. GB
reaction to 1816 tariff: **5:** 1016. Adjust
tariffs to conform to 1815 commercial
treaty with GB: **2:** 809–10, 816. Debate &
action on taxation measures: **2:** 178,
180–1, 194, 219–20, 316–7, 832. C. on
need for strong military: **2:** 135, 141,
150–2, 156–7. Financing US military establishment: **2:** 134, 150, 282, 881; **5:**
388–9. Need for additional US military
academies: **2:** 119–22. Cumberland
Road: **2:** 187–9, 310. Internal improvements: **2:** 308–11. C. defense of War of
1812 & Treaty of Ghent: **2:** 140–9; **3:**
257. C. explains features of 1815 commercial convention with GB: **2:** 123–4,
293–4, 295–305. Reaction to exclusion of
US shipping from GB colonial trade: **2:**
293–4, 296–305; **5:** 910. Exclusion of GB
seamen from US merchant marine: **2:** 32,
36–7. War of 1812 claims & compensation: **2:** 110, 164, 167, 194, 214, 268–75,
278–80. Proposals to finance Fed. Govt.
& retire public debt: **2:** 134–40, 149–50,
158, 259. C. on independence movement
in Span. Am.: **2:** 135, 155–6. US neutrality in Sp. Wars in Span. Am. (Neutrality Act of 1817): **2:** 289–92, 493–4,
496–7, 499, 503; **6:** 1005. Accomplishments of 14th Cong.: **2:** 259, 277, 321
—fifteenth congress (1 Sess: 12/1/17–
4/20/18; 2 Sess: 11/16/18– 3/3/19): C. duties & performance as Speaker: **2:** 400,
679–80. Criteria in appt. committees: **2:**
423. Slow progress on legis.: **2:** 439. C.
on US recognition of new nations in
Span. Am.: **2:** 513–62, 667–9. US policy
in Span. Am.: **2:** 508–12. C. on retaliation to GB exclusion of US from colonial
(BWI) trade: **2:** 564–5, 846. Cong. investigation of BUS: **2:** 623–5. Contempt of
Cong. charges: **2:** 424, 428–30. Fugitive
slave problems: **2:** 432–3. War of 1812
claims & compensation: **2:** 411–17,
563–4. Am. Revolution Pension Bill: **2:**
681; **3:** 480–1; **4:** 853; **6:** 400. Pay of
members: **2:** 423–4, 581. Bankruptcy
Bill: **2:** 440–1. Debate on internal improvements ("Bonus Bill"): **2:** 446–65,
467–91, 627. Debate on AJ invasion of
Fla. (Seminole War): **2:** 612–3, 624,
631–2, 636–62, 667; **6:** 914, 1114–5 (*see*

also Jackson, Andrew; Election of 1824:
issues; Election of 1828: issues, charges,
& counter–charges in campaign). Neutrality Bill (Neutrality Act of 1818) debate: **2:** 402–5, 492–507; **6:** 1062, 1108,
1113, 1216–7. Cumberland Road: **2:** 563,
667. Mo. Statehood Bill: **2:** 669–70. Tax
reductions: **2:** 409–10
—sixteenth congress (1 Sess: 12/6/19–
5/15/20; 2 Sess: 11/13/20–3/3/21): C. as
Speaker: **2:** 726, 802, 820. Resigns seat &
speakership: **2:** 680, 752, 769, 794–5,
821–2, 859, 862, 867–8, 870, 895; **3:** 54,
279. C. on House rules: **2:** 784; **3:** 35.
Speakership election in 2nd session: **3:**
57. C. arrives late for 2nd sess.: **2:** 895;
3: 14. Counting 1820 electoral vote: **3:**
36–41. Tariff Act of 1820: **2:** 824–47; **3:**
313. Admission of Me. & Mo. to statehood: **2:** 740–8, 752, 766, 768–9, 771,
774–7, 781, 785–6, 788, 898 (*see also*
Missouri Compromise). Debate on "Second" Mo. Compromise Bill: **2:** 911; **3:**
14–5, 18–22, 35–6, 46–7, 49–50. Concern with panic & depression of 1819: **2:**
739, 819, 845; **3:** 20, 53. Financial problems of Fed. Govt.: **2:** 751, 754, 766, 780,
787–9, 791–2, 819, 845, 850–1, 861; **3:**
46. Army approp. bill: **2:** 789–93, 847,
861; **3:** 15, 52. Navy appropriation bill:
2: 736–40, 788–9. General approp. bill:
2: 847. Relief for public land buyers: **3:**
47, 50, 52; **6:** 858. Public land price: **3:**
247–8, 569. Salary reductions of members: **3:** 46. Cumberland Road: **3:** 23, 56.
Navigation Act (1820): **3:** 729; **4:** 219–20,
421–5. Bankruptcy Bill: **2:** 845, 847; **3:**
53, 81. East India trade: **2:** 839, 846.
Adams–Onis Treaty: **2:** 803–16, 818, 823
(*see also* Spain empire: Florida, East). Tariff concessions to Fr.: **3:** 52–3. Slave
trade deemed piracy: **4:** 220. Recognition
of independence of new Span. Am.
states: **2:** 817, 853–60; **3:** 22–4, 29–31,
42, 44, 80
—seventeenth congress (1 Sess: 12/3/21–
5/8/22; 2 Sess: 12/2/22–3/3/23): Fight
over speakership: **3:** 147, 150, 201. C.
leadership missed: **3:** 150. Many new
members: **3:** 148. C. visits D.C. during: **3:**
154–6, 208, 210, 294. Slavery issue in
Fla. territorial govt. question: **3:** 147, 150.
Recognition of new nations in Span. Am.:
3: 184, 186. Cumberland Road: **3:**
189–90, 581; **6:** 253–4. USN approp. &
anti–piracy policy: **3:** 337–8. Trade Act
(1823): **3:** 729; **4:** 421–5; **5:** 687–8; **6:**
429. Pres. election (1824) politics in: **3:**
148, 185, 195, 205–6, 336 (*see also* Election of 1824)
—eighteenth congress (1 Sess: 12/1/23–
5/27/24; 2 Sess: 12/6/24–3/3/25): C. elected to: **3:** 274, 276, 278, 284, 292. C.
elected Speaker: **3:** 494–5, 524, 528–9,
534–5, 541, 545–7, 601, 640. Duties of
Speaker: **3:** 529, 758. C. clash with Bartlett: **3:** 606, 612–4, 616–8, 655. Increased size of House: **3:** 528–9.
Stenographers: **3:** 758. C. assigns com-

mittees: **3:** 530–1, 546–7, 662–4. Pres. politics in: **3:** 535, 543, 545, 553–4, 560–1, 613–4, 629–30, 654, 736–7, 743, 869; **4:** 62–3. Internal improvements: **3:** 568–71, 573–93, 619–27, 632–3, 655, 673, 744, 749–50, 779, 810; **4:** 19–33, 39, 268, 544, 872. Tariff Bill & Act (1824): **3:** 560–1, 629, 635–9, 642–4, 647–51, 657–60, 663–7, 670–1, 675–731, 733–4, 738, 740, 744, 756, 770, 779; **4:** 363–4, 688, 706, 955; **5:** 741, 944; **6:** 109, 144–5, 692, 706, 1016–7, 1029, 1304–5. Corruption in govt.: **3:** 571. Settlers & fortifications in Oregon: **6:** 388, 723. Naval approp.: **4:** 31, 33, 39, 86. Monroe Doctrine: **3:** 541–2, 597, 606–7, 764–5. Sentiment on Gr. independence: **3:** 597–9, 603–12, 614. Return of fugitive slaves from Canada: **5:** 234–5. Cherokee removal from Ga.: **6:** 676. Tributes to Lafayette: **3:** 893–4, 899–900; **4:** 1–2, 39. Trade recip. legis. (1/7/24): **4:** 116; **6:** 538, 614, 1394. Codification of penal law: **6:** 869, 914. Judiciary Bill: **3:** 550–1; **6:** 791–2, 799. National economic depression: **3:** 635. Aid to public land buyers: **6:** 858. Supreme Court structure & procedures: **3:** 746, 753–6. Distressed merchant seamen: **6:** 393–4. War of 1812 claims: **4:** 18. Postal rates & commissions: **5:** 742. C. farewell address as Speaker: **4:** 86–7. *See also* Election of 1824: House election phase
—nineteenth congress (Spec. Sen. Sess: 3/4/25–3/9/25; 1 Sess: 12/5/25–5/22/26; 2 Sess: 12/4/26–3/3/27): Sen. approves C. as SecState: **4:** 90, 162, 164, 166, 179, 189, 521; **6:** 773–4, 779, 1003–4. JQA admin. majority in: **5:** 118, 122, 126, 158, 273, 388, 994, 1023; **6:** 169, 361. Anti–admin. majority in: **5:** 117–8, 122, 126, 158; **6:** 361–2, 545. Stormy session: **6:** 439, 453, 544. Panama (Tacubaya) Cong. Mission debate in Sen.: **4:** 851, 870; **5:** 20, 81, 105–6, 117–8, 122–3, 126–7, 158, 164, 171–2, 174, 187, 209, 220–1, 223, 277–8, 289, 309, 375, 379, 404; **6:** 126–7, 141, 449. Panama Mission debate in House: **5:** 81–2, 164, 167–8, 171–2, 174, 186, 273, 289, 310, 395, 404, 1017; **6:** 500. Increase in anti–admin. forces: **6:** 544. Choice of printers to Cong.: **5:** 373, 453–4. Constit. amendment to reform Pres. electoral process: **5:** 278–80. Judiciary Bill: **5:** 7, 9, 45, 64–5, 75–6, 91, 118, 159, 199, 221, 254, 360, 528–9, 955; **6:** 102–3. Woolen Bill: **6:** 200, 283, 291, 300–1, 340–1, 370, 373, 435, 452, 497, 499, 515, 634. Trade legis. in response to exclusion of US shipping from GB "Colonial Trade" (BWI): **6:** 239–40, 330–1, 354, 383, 424–6, 432, 452, 520, 582, 941, 1037 (*see also* Great Britain: maritime & trade issues). Tariff adjustments: **6:** 313, 437, 497, 499, 501. Internal improvements: **4:** 543–4. *Biennial Register* authorized: **6:** 417. Fr. spoliation claims: **6:** 596–7. Oregon issue with GB: **5:** 865; **6:**

388, 723. "Corrupt Bargain" of 1825: **6:** 211–2, 743 (*see also* Election of 1824: issues). Aid to buyers of public lands: **6:** 857–8, 1212. Improve communication with Span. Am.: **6:** 816. Corruption in US courts: **6:** 331–2. Various public & private claims concerns: **6:** 590, 627, 651, 1026. Criticisms of JQA: **6:** 738
—twentieth congress (1 Sess: 12/3/27–5/26/28; 2 Sess: 12/1/28–3/3/29): Division of parties in: **6:** 472. Tension & tumult in: **6:** 472, 544. Election of Speaker: **6:** 640–1, 1011, 1085, 1098, 1142, 1147, 1156, 1200, 1229, 1252, 1331, 1342–3, 1372. Selection of printer to Sen.: **6:** 373, 1372. Implications of AJ majorities in both Houses: **6:** 1363, 1377, 1384. Splits within AJ party: **6:** 1363. Tariff Act of 1828: **6:** 877, 1304, 1363, 1385. Fr. reaction to wine schedule: **5:** 288. GB reaction to iron schedules: **5:** 1016–7. Tariff as issue in 1828 Pres. election (*see* Election of 1828: issues, charges, & counter–charges in campaign). Reciprocity Act (1824) amended: **6:** 1393–4. Patronage contracts: **6:** 634. Aid to public land buyers: **6:** 858. AJ Pres. campaign in: **6:** 1326–7. Susan Decatur claim: **6:** 1039. Claims on Fr.: **6:** 667, 835. US occupation of Oregon: **6:** 723. Colonial (BWI) trade issue with GB: **6:** 667 (*see above* nineteenth congress). US neutrality problems (blockades) in Br.–BA War: **6:** 1098, 1145 (*see also* Brazil: U.S. relations with)
Connecticut: Opposes movement of mail on Sundays: **2:** 469, 490. School for Deaf & Dumb in: **2:** 568. JQA admin. slights on patronage: **5:** 97. *See also* Election of 1824; 1828
Constitution of U.S. *See* U.S. Constitution
Cook, Daniel Pope: Spy mission to Cuba: **6:** 295–6 (*see also* Spain Empire: Cuba). Payment for State Dept. work: **6:** 1388–9. On "Corrupt Bargain" issue: **4:** 147–8; **5:** 761. Defeat in 1826 Ill. Cong. election: **4:** 541, 544; **5:** 481, 568, 585, 700–2, 710, 723, 757, 761, 792. Attacks SecTreas Wm. H. Crawford: **3:** 187. Seen as US Sen. candidate: **5:** 701. Votes for JQA in House: **5:** 761 (*see also* Election of 1824: House election phase). Handles taxes for C. on land in Ill.: **5:** 481, 884, 895. Attitude on JQA: **5:** 524. Report to C. on mission to Cuba: **6:** 1223. Illness & death: **5:** 700, 702; **6:** 296, 1223, 1300
Corwin, Thomas: Recommends patronage appts. to C.: **4:** 259, 539–40, 936. Evaluation of John McLean sent C.: **6:** 940–1. On Pres. election (1828): **6:** 941–2. Supports C. on "Corrupt Bargain" charge: **6:** 941–2
Cotton: As medium of exchange: **1:** 420, 583. Tariffs on US cotton abroad: **1:** 925; **2:** 31–2, 57; **4:** 100–1, 106, 177, 375; **5:** 818. Import tariff on: **2:** 178–9 (*see also* American System: protective tariff). Rise & fall of US price: **4:** 601. Declining European market for: **2:** 827, 835. Fu-

Cotton (*continued*):

ture of profitability clouded: **3:** 691–2. Connection between Southern producer and GB manufacturer: **3:** 702–3

Crawford, William H.: Basic biography: **1:** 867, 878. Duel with John Clark: **3:** 150. C. criticizes pro–BUS stance of: **1:** 529–30, 539. Service on Ghent Peace Commission: **1:** 867. Impact of North Am. military events on Ghent negotiation: **1:** 910. C. advises on Ky. land titles: **1:** 898–9. Sees impressment issue as key to Anglo–Am. peace: **1:** 907–8. C. patronage requests of: **2:** 727–8. On the nature & character of Fr.: **1:** 927. Doubts favorable outcome of Ghent peace conference: **1:** 904–5, 908, 910–11, 932–5, 941–5, 948, 975, 977, 980, On US military incompetence during War of 1812: **1:** 910, 945. Recommends C. for Min. to Fr.: **1:** 972, 990, 993. Loses Republican caucus Pres. endorsement to Monroe: **2:** 176. Gift of seeds to C.: **2:** 346. Pres. candidacy of (*see* Election of 1824: William H. Crawford candidacy). JQA approach to for support in House election: **6:** 182–3. On the tariff: **3:** 666–7. Collapse of health during 1824 campaign (*see* Election of 1824: William H. Crawford candidacy). Health after campaign of 1824: **4:** 214, 308. Mentioned for Panama Cong. mission: **4:** 8. Support courted by AJ Dems. in 1828 election: **5:** 500. *See also* Van Buren, Martin

Crittenden, John Jordan: Family: **3:** 488; **5:** 625; **6:** 1287. Marriages: **5:** 949, 952, 994. Death of wives: **3:** 841. C. assistance to brothers of: **3:** 234–5, 287; **5:** 625–6, 732, 821, 999; **6:** 166. Brother Henry runs for Cong.: **5:** 951–2; **6:** 258, 499–500. Legal business with C.: **3:** 884; **4:** 550–1,750; **5:** 158; **6:** 54, 819. Seeks patronage favors: **4:** 236–7, 288–9. Elected US Sen.: **2:** 419. Seeks BUS branch for Russellville, Ky.: **2:** 419. Owed favors by BUS: **4:** 92. Consistent friendship with & support of C.: **5:** 70. Supports C. in 1824: **3:** 823; **5:** 951–2, 994; **6:** 1207. Leans to AJ in 1825 House election: **6:** 992, 1207, 1260. C. confides in on decision to support JQA for Pres. in House election: **4:** 10. Supports C. decision to vote for JQA in House election: **4:** 68; **5:** 5. Work to release Ky. House delegation from Ky. legis. instructions to vote for AJ in House election: **4:** 41. Recommended for patronage appt. in JQA admin.: **4:** 92. C. recommends for BUS job: **4:** 189. Elected to Ky. House: **4:** 585–6, 673. Resigns as Pres. of Bank of Commonwealth: **4:** 606. On Old Court–New Court struggle in Ky.: **4:** 673–4, 942; **5:** 4, 6, 278–9, 950–1. On Ga. *vs.* US on Creek Indians: **4:** 674. Defeated in 1826 Ky. House election: **4:** 942–3; **5:** 592–3. Supports JQA admin.: **4:** 948. Recommends patronage appts. to C.: **5:** 212, 625; **6:** 54, 57, 1010, 1263, 1282. Candidacy for US Supreme Court appt.: **5:** 70, 193. On C.–Randolph duel: **5:** 277. On Panama Cong.: **5:** 277–8. On 1828 Pres. election in Ky.: **5:** 950–1; **6:** 1207. Attacks Duff Green: **5:** 951–2, 991. Attacks Amos Kendall: **5:** 950. Appt. US Dist. Atty. for Ky.: **6:** 17, 24–5, 29, 38, 65, 73, 117–8, 341, 385. Personal economic problems: **6:** 29, 38. Mentioned for Ky. Gov.: **6:** 38. Seeks end to court fight in Ky.: **6:** 53. On US militia reform: 6:53. On John Tyler: **6:** 258. Victim of dirty tricks in 1828 Pres. campaign: **6:** 1265–6. Runs in US House election (1827) in Ky.: **6:** 927. Gets USMA appt. for son (George B.): **6:** 1286–7. Advises C. to cease participation in "Corrupt Bargain" controversy: **6:** 1265, 1363. View of & relationship to "Corrupt Bargain" issue: **4:** 948–9; **5:** 5; **6:** 992–3, 1009, 1206–7, 1260–1, 1264–6, 1329, 1362–3, 1403–5. Advises C. on Ky. & national political developments (1827): **6:** 1265–6

Crockett, David: Political opposition to AJ: **6:** 892, 1098. Elected to US House in Tenn. (1827): **6:** 892, 1098, 1315. Character of: **6:** 1098. Uncouthness of: **6:** 1098. C. urged to cultivate politically: **6:** 1098

Crowinshield, Benjamin W.: Undertakes political fact–finding trip for C.: **6:** 303–4. Reports on politics of Pa.: **6:** 303–4

Cuba. *See* Spain Empire: Cuba

Decatur, Susan Wheeler (Mrs. Stephen): Death of husband in duel (1820): **2:** 803, 815; **3:** 107; **6:** 1302, 1316–7. C. rents home of (*see* Washington, D.C.). Asks & receives C. help in reentering society: **6:** 1302, 1314, 1316. Monroe snubs socially: **6:** 1302

Delaware: JQA support in: **6:** 179, 374, 496, 1011, 1062. AJ support in: **6:** 370, 374, 1062. AJ fusion ticket (1827) in: **6:** 1050–1. Am. System issue in: **6:** 373–4. Two–party structure: **6:** 1050–1, 1062. Federalist party in: **6:** 445, 494, 556, 1011, 1050. US Cong. election in (Oct. 1827): **6:** 556, 1011, 1050–1, 1062, 1085, 1099, 1112, 1148, 1156, 1161, 1171, 1192, 1194, 1207. Federalist support for AJ in: **6:** 370, 373, 494, 1011. Federalist support for JQA in: **6:** 1011. General Assembly election (Oct. 1827) in: **6:** 1011, 1034, 1062, 1148, 1156, 1161, 1171, 1192, 1194, 1207

Denmark: Attacks on US commerce prior to 1812: **2:** 142. GB colonial trade policy benefits (1826–27): **6:** 626. Refuses submission to GB regulations on colonial trade: **6:** 1298. Benefit to from GB–US trade controversies: **5:** 1041–2; **6:** 131. Trade with GB: **5:** 38. Commercial treaty with GB: **5:** 244, 857–8. Harvests in: **5:** 579; **6:** 143, 975. Commercial treaty with Sweden: **5:** 856, 970, 977, 1014; **6:** 51, 142, 184. Give naval stores to Barbary States: **6:** 736. Depression & poverty in: **5:** 38, 350, 386; **6:** 390, 1298, 1376.

Recognition of Span. Am. states: **6:** 1298. Turks permit ships of to pass through Straits: **6:** 1320, 1375–6
—U.S. relations with: US commercial treaty with: **4:** 109, 141, 212, 576, 670, 686, 776, 796–7, 808, 834; **5:** 19, 22, 45, 215, 244, 251, 270, 273–5, 345, 357–8, 360, 363–4, 372, 380, 388, 567, 578, 624, 637, 741, 761, 794–6, 848, 857, 924, 997; **6:** 142, 172, 183, 392, 404, 617, 624, 626, 895. As model treaty: **5:** 467, 761, 795, 839; **6:** 50, 53, 183, 823. US claims against: **4:** 128, 138–40, 566, 580, 809, 820, 886; **5:** 270, 386, 624; **6:** 71–2, 143, 172, 323, 390, 534, 590–1, 617–26, 652, 848, 861, 898, 1256, 1297–8, 1376 (*see espec. Ariel, Fair Trader, Minerva, Smyth* in Name Index). US interest in acquiring St. Johns in DWI: **4:** 566. US consular relations with St. Thomas (Virgin Islands): **4:** 223–4, 808; **5:** 203, 219. Nature & extent of US trade with: **5:** 567; **6:** 617, 975. Tariff, duty, fee discrim. against US shipping & trade: **5:** 22, 45, 270–1, 741. Adjustment of Art. 7 in 1826 commercial treaty with: **5:** 843–4, 857, 893, 916, 927; **6:** 142, 172. Henry Wheaton appt. US chargé in: **5:** 933; **6:** 319, 323, 337, 389–90, 442, 450, 534, 636, 652, 654–5, 1256. C. instructions to Wheaton: **6:** 616–27, 652. US claims & indemnity conv. with: **4:** 886; **6:** 534, 590–1, 848. Mode of settling claims issue: **6:** 624–5. History of US spoliation claims problems with: **6:** 616–24
Desha, Joseph: Enthusiasm for attack on N.O. (1803): **1:** 122. Opposition to US direct (land) tax: **2:** 135. Class analysis of Ky. political–economic issues: **4:** 817–8, 825. On pay raises for Congressmen: **2:** 197. Elected (1824) Gov. of Ky.: **3:** 803. Supports New Court faction: **4:** 817–8. Compromise position on Court fight: **4:** 859. Murder trial of son Isaac: **4:** 64–7, 77–8, 817–8, 825. Isaac Desha suicide attempt: **5:** 537, 554. Criticizes BUS branches in Ky.: **4:** 915–6. Criticizes C. for BUS connection: **4:** 916. Blocks Old Court vs. New Court compromise: **4:** 948. Jacksonians in Ky. support: **4:** 949. Criticizes TU faculty salaries: **5:** 125. On constit. amendment to exclude H. of Reps. from Pres. elections: **5:** 25
Duels & dueling: C. attitude toward: **1:** 844; **4:** 75. C. courage as duelist: **1:** 401. Strother vs. Luckett: **1:** 168. C. duel with J. Randolph (*see* Randolph, John). C. duel with Marshall: **1:** 397–9, 400–2. C. considers with Kremer: **4:** 48, 75, 146; **6:** 1276. Abortive Eppes vs. John Randolph: **1:** 545–6. Nathaniel G. S. Hart vs. Samuel E. Watson: **1:** 613. Jesse Benton vs. Wm. Carroll: **1:** 820. Breckinridge vs. Wickliffe threatened: **3:** 488; C. attempts to stop: **3:** 488. Biddle–Pettis duel: **5:** 215; **6:** 220. Mc Duffie–Cumming duels: **5:** 234. Scott–Selden duel: **6:** 56, 1163. Hamilton–Burr duel: **3:** 366. Metcalfe–Mc Duffie: **6:** 435–6. Rumored

C.–AJ duel: **6:** 850, 863. Impressions of in Europe: **5:** 354, 356. Laws prohibiting: **6:** 56. Choice of weapons tradition: **6:** 435–6. Rumored AJ–Southard duel: **6:** 926. Threatened T. M. Randolph–C.: **6:** 977, 988. Decatur–Barron duel: **2:** 803, 815; **3:** 107; **6:** 1316–7. Maddox vs. Wells (Sand Bar Fight): **6:** 1122–3
DuPont, E. I.: On the tariff (1824): **3:** 638–9, 640. Supports C. in 1824: **3:** 845
DuPont, Victor: Opposes (1816) lowering tariff on cloth & cotton: **3:** 173–5
Duralde, Martin, Jr.: Sisters of: **4:** 659–60. Shock of wife Susan's death: **4:** 659, 665; **5:** 282. Work for C. in 1824 campaign: **3:** 823, 828, 854, 862. On outcome of 1824 election: **4:** 15. Business & legal work for & with C.: **4:** 14–5; **5:** 880–1, 1019–20; **6:** 100–1, 576, 960–1. Suggests political appt. to C.: **4:** 397. Character & reputation of: **6:** 1249

Eaton, John H.: Opposes Morrison claim bill in H. of Reps.: **3:** 195. Role in "Corrupt Bargain" controversy: **4:** 146, 265. Clash with C. on own role in "Corrupt Bargain" controversy: **4:** 191–2, 196–7, 198–200, 201–2, 207–8, 221, 227, 265, 282, 318, 333. Biographer of AJ: **4:** 146, 165. Jacksonian leader: **4:** 847; **6:** 10. On direct election of Pres.: **4:** 846. US Sen. campaign (1826): **4:** 717–8, 847–8, 901; **6:** 10. JQA newspaper seeks to blast: **5:** 431. Defends Rachel Jackson: **5:** 1023; **6:** 5–6. Helps finance AJ newspaper: **5:** 181–2, 573. Seeks patronage favors from C.: **6:** 34, 158. Attempts to harmonize Buchanan & AJ explanations of their relationships in 1825 "Corrupt Bargain" controversy: **6:** 949, 1009, 1049, 1098–9, 1118–9, 1125–6, 1146–7, 1199
Ecuador: Bolivar ambitions in: **6:** 346, 1054. Opposition to Bolivar in: **6:** 346. Peru assists independence movement of: **6:** 694, 728. Bolivar declared Dictator: **5:** 813. Movement in for independence from Colombia: **6:** 345–6, 465, 484, 522, 562, 586, 683, 694, 728, 741, 1048, 1054. Flores named Pres. of: **6:** 1048
Education: Ky. land grants in support of: **1:** 582. C. opposes establishment of N.Y. school for deaf & dumb: **2:** 750–1. Of deaf & dumb in Fr.: **5:** 191–2, 251, 295, 369, 546–7, 580–1. C. supports for free Negroes: **2:** 683, 685. Schools for deaf & dumb in US: **5:** 251–2, 295, 367, 369, 546–7, 580, 632–4. C. on Columbian College (GWU) & States Rights: **3:** 21. C. support for Lex. Female Academy: **3:** 265–6. C. assistance in establishment of Kenyon College (Seminary) in Ohio: **3:** 470–1, 789, 865, 872; **4:** 44, 385, 388; **5:** 114–5, 717–8, 842; **6:** 257, 358–9, 390–1, 707–8, 829, 923, 944, 993. US land grant sought for Kenyon: **5:** 115. US land grants for in West: **3:** 625; **5:** 634. Harvard honorary degree to C.: **4:** 674, 703. US land grants to schools for deaf & dumb: **5:** 367. Kenyon Seminary:

Education (*continued*):
Indian (Mohawk) students at: **4:** 786; **5:** 156; **6:** 390–1. US P.O. sought for Kenyon College: **5:** 717. US subsidies for education of Indians: **4:** 786; **6:** 390–1. US subsidies for education of females: **5:** 184–5. Benefactors of Kenyon College: **6:** 842, 851. Univ. of Va. (*see* Virginia, University of). Litchfield (Conn.) Law School: **5:** 480–1. Ky. Asylum for Deaf & Dumb: **5:** 632–4. C. on Yale: **5:** 997. Trinity College, Hartford, Conn.: **6:** 829–30, 851. General Theological Seminary of Episcopal Church: **6:** 829–30, 851. *See also* Chase, Philander; Transylvania University; U.S. Military Academy

Edwards, Ninian: Chief Justice of Ky. Supreme Court: **1:** 408. C. legal work for: **1:** 33–7, 47–9, 52–3, 58, 68–9, 629. C. recommends for Gov. of Ill. Territory: **1:** 408–9. Salary claim on Fed. Govt.: **2:** 165–6; **4:** 540–4, 912–4. Service in War of 1812: **1:** 774. Represents C. interests in Ill.: **3:** 104. Attacks Crawford as Sec-Treas: **3:** 744–5, 799–800, 808, 818; **4:** 540, 542, 544, 911–2, 914; **5:** 699, 702. Supports C. in 1824: **3:** 744–5. Resigns US Sen. seat: **3:** 745. Appt. & resigns as US Min. to Mex.: **3:** 745; **4:** 542. Elected Gov. of Ill. (1826): **4:** 541, 544; **6:** 46. Politics of canal building in Ill.: **4:** 543–4. Supports JQA admin.: **4:** 543. C. opinions of: **4:** 912. Opinions of C.: **5:** 699–700. Criticizes Jacksonian political tactics in Ill.: **5:** 700–2. Criticizes JQA patronage errors in Ill.: **5:** 701. Popularity of in Ill.: **6:** 46. On Pres. election of 1828: **5:** 701. Accused of lying: **4:** 542, 544

Egypt. *See* Turkey
Election of 1800: C. supports Jefferson: **1:** 36. N.Y. state clinches Jefferson election: **1:** 36. Future of Republic in jeopardy if Jefferson elected: **1:** 536. C. lauds Jefferson admin: **1:** 759
Election of 1804: Opposition to Jefferson in Ky.: **1:** 196
Election of 1808: Monroe seen as likely victor: **1:** 230. C. supports Madison candidacy: **1:** 320–1
Election of 1812: C. sees large majority for Madison as vote also for war with GB: **1:** 771
Election of 1816: Possible JQA candidacy seen: **2:** 77–8. C. supports Monroe–Tompkins ticket: **2:** 176–7, 181, 216. C. on issues in campaign: **2:** 216–22
Election of 1820: C sees need for new policies in White House: **2:** 819. Republican Cong. caucus nomination fails: **2:** 820, 823. C. mentioned as possible VP nominee: **2:** 820, 823. C. view of Pres. nom. by Cong. caucus: **2:** 823–4. Electoral vote of Mo. contested: **3:** 37–41
Election of 1824
—general: Vagaries of various state electoral laws: **3:** 213, 337, 445, 462, 476, 552, 769–70, 783–4, 858, 866. Contro-

versy over Cong. caucus nominations: **3:** 201, 206, 244, 317, 321, 365, 420–1, 434–6, 445–6, 467, 472, 479, 486–7, 494, 517, 524, 535, 537, 543–5, 551–4, 560–2, 572, 602–3, 614–5, 628–9, 630–2, 634, 640–1, 645, 654, 655–6, 662, 667–8, 788. Political sentiment of & nominations by various state legis.: **3:** 226, 265, 268, 282, 285, 308, 330–1, 337, 340–1, 350–1, 413, 419–20, 446, 461, 471, 476, 486–7, 517, 523, 614, 662, 666, 673, 732, 734, 758, 782–3, 787, 800–1, 807–9, 820–3, 825, 831, 838, 847–8, 859–61, 864, 866, 869. State & sectional alliances, problems, prospects in selecting nominees: **3:** 148–9, 191, 194, 196–8, 200, 241, 265, 267, 274, 290, 317, 334, 362–3, 468–9, 545, 808, 839. State legis. choosing Pres. electors: **6:** 749. Demands for Pres. electoral reforms: **3:** 476–7, 501 (*see also* New York State). Social & economic class considerations in: **3:** 201, 241, 469, 523, 836; **4:** 17. Campaign techniques: **3:** 213–4. Favorite son syndrome: **3:** 826. Traditional Federalist vs. Republican stances in: **3:** 486, 634. Arithmetical predictions of outcome: **3:** 375. Role of newspapers, pamphlets, books in campaign: **3:** 198, 206, 214, 237–8, 290–1, 294–5, 309–10, 314, 316, 356–7, 366–7, 372, 374, 376, 421–2, 435–6, 436, 447–8, 460, 463, 467–8, 471, 473, 486–7, 500–2, 506–7, 543, 745–7, 758, 641, 744–5, 758, 787, 790, 793, 808–9, 816–7, 820–1, 823, 827–8, 831–2, 840–1, 843–6, 851–2, 855–6, 861–3, 871; **4:** 121–2, 133, 146, 165, 378–9, 402–3, 590, 769, 848, 854–5; **5:** 885; **6:** 1077. Politics, possibilities & problems if election goes into US House: **3:** 237, 317, 365–6, 535, 547, 554, 561, 603, 629–30, 641, 645, 654, 662, 666–7, 673–4, 676, 731, 743–4, 781, 787, 814, 818–9, 822–4, 827–8, 833–5, 845, 851–2, 860, 862–3, 867, 871. Possible C. candidacy in House: **4:** 317 (*see* below House election phase)
—C. candidacy: Early support for: **3:** 148–9, 156–7, 183–6, 192, 194, 196–8, 200–4, 210–3, 243–4, 249, 258–9, 321–2, 324–5, 333, 337, 361, 392, 398, 419–20, 423, 425; **5:** 285, 765–6, 952; **6:** 475. Works to line up support: **3:** 183, 190–2, 211, 251, 264, 321, 427, 518. As Western sectional candidate: **3:** 191, 194, 205, 226, 241, 246, 252, 267–8, 274–6, 284–5, 292, 300–1, 315–6, 321–2, 325, 359, 362–3, 387–8, 401, 428, 523, 630, 645, 654, 673–4, 676, 743, 758, 776, 816, 822, 825, 834, 841, 851–2; **6:** 1014. C. view of Cong. caucus nomination of Pres. candidates: **3:** 434–5, 517. C. would accept Cong. caucus nomination or House election: **3:** 365–6, 603, 614–5, 628–9. C. political opportunism: **3:** 737. C. campaign tactics: **3:** 205–6, 226–7, 241, 243, 291, 301, 321, 333, 341, 382–3, 467, 491, 746, 785, 809, 843, 852, 859, 870; **5:** 885.

Resumes US House seat as campaign device: **3:** 193, 205, 227, 244–6, 249, 259, 264, 274, 276, 284, 292, 321. Value of House speakership to: **3:** 535, 537, 541, 545–7. C. analyses of his prospects & problems: **3:** 192, 292–3, 300–1, 350–1, 359, 362–6, 382–3, 387–8, 392, 398, 432–5, 472, 477–81, 494–5, 501, 506–7, 517–8, 534–5, 537, 543–5, 553–4, 561, 603, 628–30, 631–2, 634, 640–1, 645–6, 654–6, 661–2, 666–9, 673–4, 676, 731, 734, 743–4, 758, 776, 781–3, 798–9, 821–3, 825, 831–5, 838–9, 842–3, 854–5, 870–2. Analyses of & reports to C. on his prospects: **3:** 147–50, 156–7, 184–6, 192–3, 196–8, 199–206, 210–4, 237, 241, 243–4, 251–2, 284–5, 290–1, 294–5, 308–9, 313–7, 321–2, 333–7, 340–1, 356–7, 361–2, 366–7, 371–6, 412, 419–22, 427–8, 435–7, 445–7, 460–3, 466–9, 475–7, 485–7, 490–1, 510–2, 523–4, 551–2, 614–5, 731–3, 768–72, 787–90, 793–4, 800–1, 804, 807–9, 814–21, 824, 827–9, 831, 836–7, 840–1, 843–9, 851–3, 857–61, 866–7, 869. Only viable slave state candidate: **3:** 656. On his own political purity: **3:** 359, 364–5, 464, 506–7, 641, 777, 825, 857, 870–1. Rumored withdrawal of C. from race: **3:** 676, 823, 845, 851, 869, 872, 887–9. Denies connection with Russell Letter: **3:** 237–40, 252–3, 256, 283, 350, 358, 367, 547. Problems with Relief (New Court) Party in Ky. (*see* Kentucky: New Court (Relief) party). Campaign trips & appearances: **3:** 422, 435, 487, 495, 506, 855. Campaign speeches: **3:** 675–730, 778–80. C. campaign circular: **3:** 823, 827, 842, 845, 854, 856, 861; **5:** 765–6, 951–2, 991, 994. Problems & errors in C. campaign: **3:** 817, 820, 822, 827–8, 832, 837, 845, 856; **4:** 17. C. patronage maneuvers: **3:** 804, 819–20, 823–4. Tactics of C. opposition: **3:** 817–8; **4:** 16. C. faction view of AJ during: **3:** 274, 282, 284–5, 428. C. view of JQA & his prospects: **3:** 322–4, 350–1, 358, 367–9, 501. C. view of Clinton during: **3:** 364–5. C. urged for Cabinet post in next admin.: **3:** 511. As SecState in a Clinton admin.: **3:** 196. Possible Clay–Sanford ticket: **3:** 822. Reactions to C. defeat: **4:** 4–5, 16–8. C. explains his defeat: **3:** 887–9, 891–2, 895–6, 898–900, 904–5; **4:** 38
—J. Q. Adams candidacy: Organization & Prospects: **3:** 149, 156, 185, 196–7, 200–2, 210, 212, 237, 243, 267, 284, 292–4, 315–7, 334, 336, 341, 357, 363, 373–5, 382–4, 388, 421–2, 427, 432–4, 436, 445–6, 460, 463, 467, 472, 476, 486, 491, 501, 505, 510, 517, 523, 543, 547, 552, 630, 641, 645, 655–6, 666, 732, 781–2, 789–91, 799, 807–8, 814–6, 818, 822, 824, 826, 831, 836, 838, 841, 845–6, 851–2, 858, 860, 862, 871; **4:** 17, 641 (*see also* below House election phase)
—John C. Calhoun candidacy: **3:** 157, 182–3, 185, 195–7, 200, 202–6, 210,

211–2, 227, 259, 273, 284, 290–2, 294, 314–6, 321–2, 325, 335–6, 363, 373, 375, 383,436–7, 445, 467, 476, 486, 506, 510–11, 523, 645–6, 653–6, **5:** 7–8, 789
—DeWitt Clinton candidacy: **3:** 156, 185–6, 196–7, 200, 211, 331, 341, 419, 512, 523, 535, 545–7, 554, 561, 601, 614, 673, 744, 769–71, 776–7, 783, 808, 831, 846–7
—William H. Crawford candidacy: **3:** 149, 156, 185, 187, 196–8, 200–3, 205–6, 210–12, 249, 264, 267, 284, 290–4, 309, 314–6, 321, 334, 336–7, 356, 362–3, 366, 374–5, 382, 384, 388, 401, 412, 420–2, 427, 432–4, 445–6, 460–1, 463, 467, 472, 476, 479, 486–7, 494, 505–6, 510–1, 517, 523, 535, 537, 546–7, 560–2, 615, 629–30, 634, 640–1, 645, 655–6, 662, 666–9, 673–4, 676, 731–3, 744, 769–70, 781–2, 784, 788–90, 793–4, 807–8, 815–6, 818–20, 824, 831, 833, 838, 840–1, 845–8, 851–2, 854, 858, 860, 862–4, 867, 869, 871, 879, 901; **4:** 285–6, 426, 542, 544, 911–2; **6:** 32, 130, 641. *See also* below House election phase
—Andrew Jackson candidacy: **3:** 156–7, 197, 243–4, 265, 268, 274–5, 282, 292, 294, 300, 315, 361, 375, 419–20, 427, 436–7, 460, 463, 466–7, 476, 490–2, 501, 505, 511, 517, 537, 545–6, 601, 630, 641, 645–6, 654–5, 658, 662, 666, 669, 674, 730, 732, 743, 758, 769, 771, 781–2, 799, 801, 814–6, 824, 828, 837–9, 845, 854, 860, 888; **4:** 16, 781; **5:** 285; **6:** 177. Jackson–Calhoun ticket: **3:** 846. *See also* below House election phase
—Rufus King candidacy: **3:** 148–9, 203, 357
—William Lowndes candidacy: **3:** 194, 200–1, 237, 249, 292, 315, 335, 413, 415
—VP candidates & ticket pairings: C. as possible VP candidate: **3:** 148–9, 196–8, 334, 356, 364–5, 371, 669, 806, 815–6, 818–9, 826–7, 829, 833–4, 836–7, 851–3, 862, 867, 869–70, 891. Calhoun VP candidacy: **3:** 653, 669, 814,819, 833, 846, 853. Albert Gallatin candidacy: **3:** 562, 640–1, 662, 666, 669, 806, 815, 818, 829, 833, 837, 867, 890. Others mentioned: JQA: **3:** 630; William Findlay: **3:** 669; AJ: **3:** 546, 601; Lafayette: **3:** 827; Nathaniel Macon: **3:** 733, 890; Daniel Montgomery: **3:** 669; Peter B. Porter: **3:** 641, 667, 731; Nathan Sanford: **3:** 733, 744, 776, 799, 822, 833, 835, 841, 853, 858, 864; Smith Thompson: **3:** 641, 733; John Tod: **3:** 669; Joseph C. Yates: **3:** 511; Samuel Young: **3:** 641. Ticket pairings: JQA–C.: **3:** 334; Clinton–C.: **3:** 196–8, 356, 364–5, 371; Crawford–C.: **3:** 815, 818–9, 836, 862, 867, 869–70; **4:** 285–6; King–C.: **3:** 148–9
—issues: American System: **3:** 185, 194, 237–8, 309, 325, 423, 461–2, 479–80, 634, 675–730, 732, 737, 743, 778–80, 789, 801, 828; **6:** 1131. Tariff: **3:** 469, 666–7, 675–730, 744–6, 758, 778–80, 782, 789–90, 793, 815, 827–8, 855, 858,

Election of 1824 (*continued*):
861, 867. Reform of system of choosing Pres. electors: **3:** 475–7, 494; **6:** 181 (*see also* New York State). Span. Am. independence: **3:** 197, 325. States Rights: **3:** 469, 478. Slavery: **3:** 200, 467–8, 655–6. Mo. Compromise: **3:** 212, 294, 423. Depression of US economy: **3:** 211. JQA–Kerr controversy: **3:** 845–6. JQA anti–West performance at Ghent (Russell letter): **3:** 204, 210, 237–40, 254, 256, 270, 283, 292–4, 315, 323–4, 341, 350, 358, 368, 378, 409, 543; **4:** 158–61; **5:** 656; **6:** 816–7, 1071. JQA surrender of Texas in Adams–Onis treaty: **3:** 238. JQA treatment of Edwards: **3:** 799–800, 808, 818. C. pro–West performance at Ghent: **3:** 202, 409. C. close connection with BUS: **3:** 245–6, 259–60, 276. AJ invasion of Fla.: **3:** 284–5, 423, 469; **6:** 1071. AJ military background: **3:** 282, 658; **6:** 702, 1071. AJ character & personality: **3:** 730. Crawford health: **3:** 744, 767, 769, 781–2, 789–91, 793–4, 806, 808, 818, 834, 836–7, 851, 854, 867, 871
—campaign activity in states & sections: prognoses & outcomes: Ala.: **3:** 361, 427–8, 490–1, 835. Conn.: **4:** 315. Del.: **3:** 212, 674, 815, 818, 845. Fla. Territory: **4:** 316. Ga.: **3:** 818. Ill.: **3:** 744, 871, 889; **6:** 748. Ind.: **3:** 517–8, 551–2, 603, 744, 854, 889, 904; **4:** 756–7, 795. Ky.: **3:** 183, 196, 203, 226, 237, 293, 301, 315, 333–4, 337, 494, 501, 505, 545, 783, 799, 822–3, 842, 854; **4:** 155, 166; **5:** 852; **6:** 748. La.: **3:** 200–1, 249, 362, 387, 392, 744, 799, 821–2, 828, 839, 854–5, 891–2, 895–6, 900, 904–5; **4:** 15, 144, 194, 301, 313; **6:** 822, 885, 1275–6, 1346. Me.: **4:** 121–2. Md.: **3:** 210, 213–4, 337, 630, 654, 674, 744, 782, 788, 814–5, 818, 825, 835, 838, 855; **4:** 166; **5:** 756; **6:** 20. Mass.: **3:** 774, 806, 814, 816–7, 826, 857–9, 869–70. Miss.: **3:** 266–7, 505, 630, 835. Mo.: **3:** 413, 494, 501, 505, 744, 843, 871–2, 889; **4:** 378–9; **6:** 748. N.J.: **3:** 334, 655, 674, 676, 758, 782, 787–8, 799, 814–5, 825, 831, 838, 845–6, 852, 869; **5:** 755. N.Y.: **3:** 185–6, 191–6, 200, 203, 211–2, 251–2, 264, 268, 274, 290–1, 300–1, 314–5, 334, 336, 356–7, 359, 362–3, 365–6, 371–2, 373–5, 379, 388, 392, 398, 401, 412, 415–6, 419–22, 433–7, 461–3, 472, 475–7, 485–7, 494, 501, 505, 510–11, 517, 523–4, 545, 547–8, 561, 572, 614–5, 631–2, 634–5, 641, 645, 654, 656, 662, 666–7, 673–4, 676, 731–4, 744, 758, 768–71, 781–3, 787–8, 798, 800–1, 807–9, 814–6, 820–2, 824–5, 831, 834, 838, 840–1, 846–9, 852, 856, 859–64, 866, 869, 888–91, 904; **4:** 17, 34, 39, 128–30; **5:** 718–9, 885, 1032; **6:** 130, 177, 545, 1015. N.C.: **3:** 788, 790, 824, 852, 869, 889; **4:** 166; **6:** 743. Ohio: **3:** 191, 196, 205, 226, 237–8, 246, 258–9, 274, 282, 285, 290, 292, 294–5, 300–1, 308–9, 330–1, 333–4, 340–1,

350–1, 361, 365, 472, 506, 517, 545, 561, 601, 603, 654, 673, 743, 798–9, 854, 871, 884–5, 887, 890; **4:** 97, 154–5, 317, 530, 532; **5:** 7, 284–7, 417, 723–4. Pa.: **3:** 193, 196, 201–2, 205–6, 213, 241, 264, 268, 273, 290, 292, 294, 313–7, 321–2, 324–5, 331, 336, 359, 361, 363, 419–20, 436, 466–8, 506, 517, 603, 645–6, 654–5, 666–9, 732, 743, 758, 785, 815, 828, 835–6, 844, 856; **5:** 353; **6:** 208, 478, 702–3, 822. R.I.: **3:** 661, 804, 817, 824–5, 832, 838. S.C.: **3:** 335, 337, 433, 814, 818, 824, 835, 839, 845. Tenn.: **3:** 156–7, 243, 265, 268, 274–5, 292, 294, 300, 315, 361, 427, 460, 492, 505, 511, 535, 537, 545, 572, 601, 834; **6:** 32. Vt.: **3:** 186. Va.: **3:** 185, 194, 197, 200, 237, 240, 314–5, 319, 334, 341, 358, 384, 387–8, 433, 468–9, 477–81, 505, 561–2, 634, 641, 645, 653–6, 662, 666–7, 669, 673–4, 676, 731, 758, 781–2, 789–91, 793–4, 808, 822, 825, 834, 838, 854, 867, 871, 879, 884, 888, 890. East: **3:** 241, 336. Middle States: **3:** 852. New England: **3:** 212–3, 315–6, 336, 341, 645, 656, 816–8, 824, 826, 832, 851–2; **6:** 641. North: **3:** 241–2, 334. South: **3:** 336, 434, 462, 468–9, 662, 666, 784. West: **3:** 243, 267–8, 275, 284, 300–1, 308–9, 325, 334, 362–3, 387–8, 401, 434, 468–9, 505, 523, 645, 673–4, 676, 743, 758, 776, 781, 783, 788, 799, 808, 816, 824–5, 834, 841, 871, 887, 895; **5:** 284–5, 532; **6:** 1014. For electoral vote returns, *see espec.* **3:** 885, 887–91, 895–6, 904; **4:** 166
—House election phase (Dec. 6, 1824—Feb. 9, 1825): C. holds balance of power in House choice of Pres.: **3:** 806, 862, 867, 871, 892, 895, 901; **4:** 9, 11, 38, 55, 59, 144–5. C. tactics: **3:** 871; **4:** 46. Political difficulties facing C. in House election: **3:** 901, 904; **4:** 45–6, 59, 68, 152, 1133–4. C. future Pres. prospects: **3:** 80, 194, 313, 722, 757. Value of a Cabinet seat to C.: **3:** 859; **4:** 39, 56, 68–9, 73. C. rejects idea of a post in next admin.: **3:** 901; **4:** 11, 56. Candidates court C. vote & influence: **3:** 899, 901; **4:** 11, 38, 47. Advice to C. on whom to support: **4:** 17–8. Ky. legis. instructs Ky. Cong. delegation to vote for AJ: **3:** 901–2; **4:** 10–12, 19, 35, 41, 66, 91–92, 134, 155–6, 489–90; **6:** 775–6, 1071, 1106–7, 1172–3, 1276, 1381 (*see espec.* **3:** 902). C. rejects interference from Ky. on his choice: **3:** 904; **4:** 155; **6:** 1131, 1276. Crawford candidacy in House: **3:** 871; **4:** 17, 55, 67–8, 151–2, 317; **6:** 1127. Crawford health as factor: **3:** 808, 891; **4:** 9, 34, 38, 45, 55–6, 151–2, 317; **5:** 655–6; **6:** 764, 874, 892, 1127, 1133, 1154, 1275. Proposed Crawford deal with JQA: **6:** 182–3. Crawford faction approaches to C.: **4:** 9, 11; **6:** 144, 1403. Alleged Jacksonite approach to C. with deal on SecState post: **6:** 144, 448–9, 557–8, 572–3, 648, 682, 718–9, 728–30, 738, 742–3, 754–5, 778, 797–8, 892,

Election of 1844 (*continued*):
of 1824: House election phase; & Election of 1828: Corrupt Bargain issue & related compaign literature). Revival of Beverley Carter "Fayetteville Attack" charges against C.: **6**: 573 (*see also* Election of 1828: Corrupt Bargain issue & related campaign literature)

Election of 1856: Ky. native declines Am. Party nomination: **6**: 82

Erwin, James: Family: **3**: 496, 868. Children: **6**: 1099. Relations with wife, Anne: **3**: 502; **4**: 15. Father, Andrew, fails election: **3**: 496; **4**: 601, 716. C. legal work for: **4**: 81. In mercantile business & land speculation: **3**: 496. Buys slave from C.: **3**: 773. C. discusses politics with: **3**: 781–2, 895. Performs business & legal tasks for C.: **3**: 895; **5**: 1019–20; **6**: 60, 69–70, 471, 575–6, 642, 798, 849, 1098, 1345. Advises C. on patronage & politics: **4**: 798–9. C. explains SecState offer from JQA to: **4**: 82. In newspaper business: **4**: 901. C. criticizes personal habits of: **5**: 282. On David Crockett: **6**: 1098. Evaluates Tenn. politics for C.: **6**: 798–9, 1098–9

Erwin, John P.: Advises C. on Tenn. & national politics: **4**: 900–2; **6**: 11–12, 892–3, 1292. In newspaper business: **4**: 901. Urges C. for Pres. in 1832: **4**: 901. Quarrel with Sam Houston: **5**: 699; **6**: 11. Works for BUS branch in Nashville: **6**: 12. Controversial Post Master of Nashville: **5**: 699; **6**: 11, 30. Informs C. on patronage problems & opportunities in Tenn.: **6**: 893, 1291–2. Answers attack on C. in 1828 Pres. campaign: **6**: 1049

Everett, Alexander H.: Appt. US Min. to Sp.: **4**: 119, 292. C. instructions to: **4**: 292–300, 322, 440. Wants brother as his Sec. of Legation: **4**: 267, 275, 289. Does not want John Adams Smith as Sec. of Legation: **4**: 275, 289. Performance as Chargé in Netherlands: **5**: 1043; **6**: 106. Supports C. in "Corrupt Bargain" controversy: **4**: 440. Founds Boston newspaper: **4**: 440–1. Low opinion of Sp.: **4**: 440. Unpopularity of in Brussels: **5**: 1043. Book by criticizes Europeans: **5**: 1043–4; **6**: 106. On Bolivar threat to US: **6**: 27. Writes controversial history of W. Hemisphere: **6**: 569–70, 580

Everett, Edward: Family: **5**: 423. C. on public speaking skills of: **2**: 781. Career in H. of Reps.: **2**: 598; **5**: 804; **6**: 579–80. Connection with TU: **2**: 597. On US trade problems in BWI: **5**: 805; **6**: 579. Founds Boston newspaper: **4**: 440. Defends C. on "Corrupt Bargain" issue: **5**: 155. Patronage requests of C.: **5**: 829; **6**: 108. On Fr. spoliation claims: **5**: 805, 829. Writes political pamphlet for National Republicans (1827): **6**: 401, 445, 536, 579. Attacks GB interdiction of US trade in BWI: **6**: 579–80. Reviews C. published speeches: **6**: 859, 962

Fayette County (Ky.): Economic distress in: **1**: 85, 98–9. C. legis. (1804) affecting: **1**: 158, 159, 165; (1805): **1**: 213; (1806): **1**: 253; (1807): **1**: 313, 315; (1809): **1**: 397. C. taxes paid to (*see* Lexington, Ky.). C. acres owned in: **1**: 217–8, 402; **2**: 306–7. War of 1812 tax levy upon: **1**: 803. AJ movement in: **6**: 223. 1827 elections in for Ky. House: **6**: 952 (*see also* Lexington, Ky.)

Featherstonhaugh, George William: Supports C. in 1824 election: **4**: 34. C. advises on Pres. election by House (1825): **4**: 34

Federalist party: C. early hostility toward: **1**: 94–5, 123–4, 129, 481, 756–7. C. castigates Anglophilia & Francophobia of: **1**: 481, 539, 757–60. Class nature of struggle with Dem.–Republicans: **1**: 335–6. On US occupation of W. Florida: **1**: 508, 514, 516. On War of 1812 issues: **1**: 609–10, 641, 677, 727–8, 759, 805–6; **2**: 6, 138. Alleged plot to dismember the Union: **1**: 760–2, 805–6. C. on collapse as national force: **5**: 798–9. *See also* Election of 1824; 1828; New York State; Pennsylvania

Fendall, Philip R.: Work for State Dept. on spoliation claims: **6**: 270. Attacks Calhoun in support of JQA admin.: **5**: 191. Friendship with C.: **3**: 360. Patronage jobs in Wash.: **5**: 191, 667

Fisher, Redwood: Supports Am. System: **6**: 633–4

Flaget, Bishop Benedict Joseph: Collects art treasures for Diocese: **4**: 669; **6**: 462–3. Work as Bishop of Bardstown: **4**: 669; **6**: 462–3. C. helps with import duty problem: **6**: 462–4

Florida, East. *See* Spain empire: Florida, East

Florida Territory: Temporary US govt. organized in: **2**: 678; **3**: 147. C. patronage recommendations for offices in: **2**: 677, 679; **3**: 16, 42, 53–54, 764; **4**: 52, 200. Misconduct of Fed. officials in: **4**: 591, 599, 748, 894–5, 940; **5**: 179–80, 218–9, 225, 271, 533; **6**: 155, 906–7, 1026, 1362, 1383, 1401. Records of Span. land grants in: **4**: 677, 811. Descriptions of: **5**: 128. Boundary controversy with Ga.: **5**: 1027; **6**: 986–8. West Fla. land claims: **6**: 1026 (*see also* Spain, empire: Florida, West)

Florida, West. *See* Spain empire: Florida, West

Floyd, John: Rushes Am. settlement of Oregon: **6**: 388. Supports recognition of independence of Span. Am. states: **3**: 24. Break with C.: **6**: 725. On Mo. vote in Electoral College (1821): **3**: 37, 39–40. Unsuccessful run for Gov. of Va.: **6**: 185–6, 200. Involvement in Russell vs. JQA controversy on Ghent: **3**: 204, 323. In US Cong.: **6**: 200. Mentioned as Gov. candidate: **4**: 857. Sees "Combination" of tariff & anti–tariff support for AJ in 1827–8: **6**: 185, 740–1. Personal relations

with C.: **6:** 725. Member of strict–con-structionist "Richmond Junto": **3:** 341. Supporter of W. H. Crawford: **3:** 341
France: US would support (1794) in war with GB: **5:** 127. Defeat of (1814): **1:** 866–7, 872–5, 877–8, 882, 885, 896–7, 903, 916; **2:** 143. Reactions in to defeat by Allies: **1:** 911–2, 923–4, 938, 945, 949, 967, 996; **2:** 12–3. Restoration of the Bourbon monarchy: **1:** 822–3, 882, 885, 896, 897, 906, 922; **2:** 113–4, 143, 381–2; **6:** 1325. C. on Bonaparte: **2:** 11–13, 377–8, 477, 648; **3:** 720–2. The Hundred Days & Bonaparte exile to St. Helena: **1:** 866–7, 872–5, 877–8, 882, 885, 896–7, 903, 916; **2:** 11–15, 59, 377, 648, 805–6; **3:** 683, 720; **5:** 54. Post–war foreign policy attitudes: **2:** 533. Harvests: **2:** 378; **6:** 1139. Church (Jesuit) vs. state relations, tensions, attitudes: **1:** 949; **4:** 898; **5:** 72, 189, 356–7, 502–3, 619, 639, 800, 964, 998, 1049; **6:** 111, 113, 226, 490–1, 546–7, 670, 1195, 1359. Indus-trial development: **5:** 885–6; **6:** 1001, 1005–6, 1093–4. Interest in Span. Am. trade: **4:** 656; **5:** 99, 125, 710. Education in: **5:** 191. Freedom of press in: **5:** 72, 998, 1049; **6:** 59, 113, 226, 438, 490, 667, 725, 781, 1094–5, 1255, 1359. Domestic politics in (1825–29): **4:** 205, 302–3, 535, 656–7, 775, 820, 897–8, 938; **5:** 29, 71–2, 97–8, 164, 205, 356–7, 430, 502–3, 619, 639, 964, 1027, 1049; **6:** 59, 193–4, 343, 490–1, 546, 725, 781, 1094–5, 1195, 1255, 1319, 1329, 1332, 1337–9, 1399–1400. Economic conditions in: **5:** 72, 98, 800, 998, 1027; **6:** 193, 1139. Connection with Egypt: **4:** 849–50; **5:** 638–9, 641. Internal disorders in: **5:** 639; **6:** 1329. Revolution of 1830: **6:** 439, 490. Am. Indians exhibited in: **6:** 980–2, 1258–9, 1399. Military intervention (1823) in Sp. (*see* Spain). Recognition of Span. Am. republics: **4:** 402, 594, 675, 849; **5:** 24, 29, 708–10; **6:** 447. On set-ting up Bourbon kings in Span. Am.: **4:** 675; **5:** 132, 216, 339–40. Urges Sp. to recognize Span. Am. independence: **4:** 575, 593–5, 640, 656, 774–5; **5:** 167, 189–90, 414, 429; **6:** 447. Plan for politi-cal reorganization of Sp. Am.: **5:** 957. Mediate truce in Sp.–Colombia war: **5:** 373–4. Commercial treaty with GB: **5:** 29, 31, 97, 101. Benefits from An-glo–Am. trade controversy: **5:** 1046. Re-lations with Br., Haiti, Mex., Port. (*see* separate entries). Sentiment in for Gr. cause (*see* Greece). Suppression of slave trade: **6:** 113, 193–4, 406. Growth of navy: **5:** 71–2, 165–6, 840; **6:** 1139. Fleet operations in West Indies: **4:** 685, 762, 935; **5:** 22, 202, 291, 349. Connection with Holy Alliance on Span. Am. inde-pendence issue: **4:** 574; **6:** 693. Interest & policy in Cuba (*see* Spain empire: Cuba). On privateering: **6:** 1027. Rumor of war with GB.: **6:** 175. *See also* Brown, James

—U.S. relations with: Offers US mercenary troops to help fight GB in North Am.: **1:** 986–8, 990–1, 1002. US seeks loan from: **1:** 1001. Initial US reaction to Fr. Revolu-tion (1789): **2:** 289, 500; **3:** 606. US viewed as agent of world revolution: **4:** 898. Menace of Bonaparte: **1:** 275, 607, 757–8. US caught in middle of An-glo–Fr. wars: **1:** 449–51, 607, 670, 673–4; **2:** 289–90; **3:** 721–2. On going to war with: **1:** 499, 481, 657, 670. On maintaining peace with: **1:** 526, 641, 645, 659–60, 670, 674–5, 677, 690, 692. Men-ace to US in Gulf: **1:** 453–4. Treaties of 1778 with: **5:** 383–4; **6:** 527. Maritime neutral rights issues with: **1:** 228–9, 388, 396–7, 481–2, 523, 527, 563, 574, 657, 659–60, 668, 763–4, 774; **2:** 142, 297, 501, 505; **3:** 721–2; **5:** 31. US non-im-portation policy: **1:** 396–7, 574; **2:** 297. Undeclared naval war with: **1:** 622, 672, 760, 767, 774; **2:** 649; **6:** 1318. Conven-tion of 1800: **4:** 599, 917–8; **5:** 382–3. Berlin & Milan Decrees: **1:** 280, 288, 388, 526–7, 557, 574–5, 761. US stake in Fr. victory in Ru.: **1:** 742. Rambouillet De-cree: **1:** 523. Fr. role in Anglo–Am. peace negotiation: **1:** 905–7. Fr. post–war attitudes toward US: **1:** 905–7, 926, 949. Fr. urges US peace with Sp. (1820): **2:** 798. Fr. good offices in Adams–Onis negotiation: **2:** 783–4. US tariff, duty, fee discrim. against Fr. ship-ping & trade: **2:** 839, 846; **3:** 52–3, 287–8, 934–5; **5:** 624, 934–5; **6:** 301, 306, 327, 333, 342, 563–4, 591–2, 722, 1028–9, 1082, 1140, 1357. Fr. tariff, duty, fee discrim. against US shipping & trade: **1:** 523; **2:** 839, 846; **5:** 101, 624, 640, 678, 690, 815, 923, 934–5. **6:** 333, 725–6, 894–5, 977–8, 1029, 1083, 1093, 1140, 1377–8. US tariffs on Fr. wine & silk: **2:** 185–6; **5:** 287–8, 934–5; **6:** 1028–9, 1082, 1140, 1194. Mutual trade concessions: **3:** 52; **5:** 101; **6:** 301. Beau-marchais claims against US: **3:** 312–3, 498, 750; **4:** 850; **5:** 244, 250, 436, 491, 505, 963. Other Fr. claims against US: **4:** 330–1, 764–5, 808; **5:** 249–50, 739–40; **6:** 305, 374, 464, 761. Other US claims against Fr.: **4:** 124–5, 311; **5:** 268; **6:** 534. Nature & extent of US trade with: **5:** 678, 815; **6:** 652–3, 726. Trade reci-procity issue with: **4:** 247; **5:** 29, 71; **6:** 301. US maritime spoliation claims against Fr.: **1:** 527, 641, 643, 659, 878, 905; **2:** 846; **3:** 154–5, 313; **4:** 287–8, 334, 374, 466, 599, 656, 686, 691, 694, 745, 775, 809, 823, 831, 896–7, 937, 959; **5:** 2, 28, 49, 62, 74, 132, 216, 239–40, 268, 273, 275–6, 311, 381–4, 419–20, 653, 681–2, 727, 752, 777, 805, 829, 858, 887, 917, 935–6, 942, 962–3; **6:** 3, 108–9, 143, 343, 596–603, 666, 825, 835, 1013, 1256, 1332, 1357, 1369, 1376, 1398. Rumors of war over US claims: **6:** 343, 1193. Possible arbitration of spolia-tion claims: **6:** 1013–4, 1193. Suggested

721

France (continued):
US special mission on claims issue: **4:**
831–2; **5:** 123, 239–40, 388. Problems &
tension over US–Fr. Convention of
Nagivation & Commerce of June 24,
1822: **3:** 52–3, 313, 382–3; **4:** 247, 336,
467, 477, 693–4, 720, 799–800, 832, 925,
939; **5:** 3, 11, 19, 29, 38, 78, 80, 216,
431, 624, 640, 678, 690, 815, 923; **6:**
120–1, 301, 319, 327, 333, 563–4,
591–2, 599–600, 608, 722, 726, 894–5,
978, 1028–9, 1082–3, 1094, 1140, 1144,
1193–4, 1397. US merchants demand
claims settlement: **4:** 831; **5:** 123, 243. Fr.
tactics in stalling, avoiding, confusing US
claims issues: **4:** 656, 686, 693, 862, 897;
5: 71, 240, 962–4; **6:** 599, 1027–8, 1193,
1357, 1398. US considers maritime re-
prisals for Fr. stalling: **4:** 823; **5:** 123.
Desertion of seamen problems: **4:** 924–5,
939; **5:** 3, 11, 33, 39–41, 418–9, 431. Fr.
harassment of US shipping: **5:** 443,
470–1, 476; **6:** 735. US stake & interest
in Haitian claims payments to Fr. (*see*
Haiti). Claims & commercial treaty of
1831: **1:** 643; **5:** 132, 1015. Proposed
salvage convention: **6:** 249. Currency exchange rates: **5:** 30. Cooperate in returning intercepted slaves to Africa: **6:** 406.
Negotiations on persuading Sp. to end
her wars in Span. Am.: **4:** 373, 535–7,
574–5, 593, 630, 653, 684, 739–41, 762,
766–7; **5:** 24, 169, 189–90, 216, 319,
504, 710. US cautions on ambitions in
Cuba (*see* Spain empire: Cuba). Opposition to US recognition policy in Span.
Am.: **3:** 398; **4:** 694. Protocol problems:
5: 137–8. Fr. view of US–GB friendship:
4: 694. C. too busy to study US–Fr.
relations: **5:** 388
—claims problems under Louisiana Purchase Treaty (1803): Mutual claims &
related negotiations stemming from Art.
8 of treaty: **4:** 136, 204, 302–3, 467, 656,
686, 775, 897; **5:** 29–30, 48–9, 71, 135,
239–40, 963; **6:** 599, 612, 666, 835, 895,
1013, 1256, 1357. US on arbitration of
Art. 8–related claims: **6:** 600–3, 612,
895, 978–9, 1013, 1027, 1193, 1392.
Controversy over commercial clause (Art.
8) in treaty: **3:** 313, 382–3; **4:** 169; **6:**
599. Claims (debts) absorbed by US un-
der treaty: **4:** 917–8, 925; **5:** 164, 166; **6:**
113–4. *See also* Brown, James
Frankfort, Ky.: Fever epidemic in: **3:** 493.
Attempts to remove state capitol from: **1:**
124, 314; **3:** 880–1; **4:** 45, 415. Capitol
building in burns down: **3:** 878–9, 880;
4: 59. Rebuilding of capitol building: **3:**
878–9, 881; **6:** 53. Descriptions of: **3:** 879
Fulton, Robert: Steam engine introduced
into Europe: **6:** 1001–2. Monopoly charter on Hudson River: **3:** 627. C. lauds: **2:**
459, 831; **3:** 711

Gales, Joseph & Seaton, William W.: C.
legal work for G.: **3:** 289. Masonic connection of S.: **3:** 178. Support Crawford
in 1824: **3:** 645–6, 744–5, 808, 818; **6:**

453–4. Opposition to C. in 1824: **3:**
827–8. As public printers: **3:** 645; **6:** 316,
453. On the tariff: **3:** 770. Support JQA
in 1828: **6:** 453–4. Link Van Buren to
spirit of 1798 Sedition Act: **6:** 454
Gallatin, Albert: Opposition to naval expenditures in 1798: **1:** 622. Treas. Dept. has
no power to control slave trade: **1:** 632.
Appt. to Ghent Peace Commission: **1:**
799, 862, 866–7, 876–7, 879, 881, 883,
889, 892. On runaway slave problem: **5:**
610. Defeat of Fr. threatens US in War
of 1812: **1:** 883–4. As Min. to Fr.: **2:** 17;
5: 511; **6:** 546. Role at GB criticized: **2:**
74–5, 77. Hostility to Monroe: **2:** 77.
Expenses as delegate to Ghent: **2:** 100–1.
Astor business offer to: **2:** 109–10. On
Anglo–Am. Commission Convention
(1815): **2:** 124–7. As VP nominee (*see*
Election of 1824: Vice Presidential candidates & ticket pairings). Supports C. in
1824 campaign: **3:** 818. On worthlessness
of Pacific NW: **5:** 480. Declines mission
to Panama Cong.: **4:** 801, 813–4, 826,
905. Appt. Min. to GB: **5:** 273, 293–4,
296, 302–3, 360–1, 363, 379, 388, 419,
428, 440–1, 583, 610; **6:** 237. C. instructions to as Min. to GB: **5:** 365, 367,
424–5, 437, 440–78, 484–91, 504–6,
508, 596–601, 610, 679, 761, 774, 804,
810, 832, 843–5, 895–916; **6:** 229–36.
Reactions to appt. to GB: **5:** 407, 417,
571. Comments on & questions to C.
instructions: **5:** 495, 508–16, 843, 926; **6:**
412. Requests more power & flexibility in
negotiating with GB: **5:** 510–11, 521,
561, 596, 843; **6:** 412. Understanding of
Anglo–Am. colonial trade issue: **5:** 515,
833–5. Requests recall from London: **5:**
1058; **6:** 236–7, 412, 467, 556, 1086,
1108. C. criticizes: **5:** 567, 600–1, 610, **6:**
467, 908, 975. C. rebukes: **6:** 467. Too
poor to serve well as US Min. in GB: **5:**
571. Urges US compromise on BWI
trade issue with GB: **5:** 833–5. Urges US
compromise on NW (Oregon) boundary:
5: 843. C. instructions to on Colonial
trade issue with GB: **5:** 895–916; **6:**
418–32, 908. Concludes Convention with
GB on slave property (*see* Great Britain:
St. Petersburg Convention). On difficulty
of Oregon negotiations with GB: **5:** 958,
1058. On GB–US–Fr. agreement to support Sp. retention of Cuba: **5:** 1057 (*see*
Spain empire: Cuba). On possibility of
general European war: **6:** 235. On the
nature of arbitrators: **6:** 365. On GB
interdiction of US trade in BWI (*see*
Great Britain: maritime & trade issues).
On theoretical nature of GB govt.: **6:**
495. Requested recall from London not
convenient: **6:** 446–7, 556. Coachman of
arrested in London: **6:** 582–3, 615. C.
criticizes for handling of Colonial trade
issue with GB: **6:** 908, 975. Suggests
postponing Colonial trade talks with GB:
6: 577, 646, 826–7. Signs Commercial &
NW boundary conventions: **6:** 854–5.
Departs London for home: **6:** 1108,

1137. Assists C. in NE Boundary dispute: **6:** 1335, 1352, 1354, 1374 (*see also* Great Britain)

Genoa: Role of church in: **5:** 161. Economic situation of: **5:** 162

Georgia: Yazoo land claims issues: **1:** 228–9, 778, 903, 909, 916; **4:** 270–1; **5:** 179, 501; **6:** 14–5, 475. C. on relief for victims of Savannah fire: **2:** 818. Crawford–Clark factional political struggle in: **3:** 149–50. State colonial history project: **4:** 117, 194–5, 239, 270; **5:** 1046. Boundary controversy with Fla.: **5:** 1027; **6:** 986–8. Ga. vs US on Creek land cession & removal (*see* Adams (John Q.) administration: policies & legislation). Gaines–Troup clash: **4:** 676–7, 678–9, 794, 846; **5:** 55. Gov. election in (1825): **4:** 676–7, 794. Secession of rumors abroad: **4:** 768, 845. Sale of slaves illegally brought into: **5:** 1040. Cherokee removal: **6:** 674, 676. Clash with Fed. Govt. on state sovereignty claim: **6:** 186–7

Giles, William Branch: 1812 Warhawk: **3:** 737. Resigns from US Sen.: **3:** 737. Candidate for US Sen. (1825): **4:** 827, 857, 867; **5:** 737. Attacks C. candidacy in 1824: **3:** 737. On BUS: **1:** 528–9. Leads anti-JQA faction in Va.: **4:** 857; **6:** 144, 185–6. C. opinion of: **4:** 867. Clash with C. on issue of personal honor: **5:** 116–7. Attacks C. on States Rights issues: **3:** 737. Resolutions in Va. Legis. for States Rights & against tariff & internal improvements (1827): **6:** 144–5, 164–5, 185, 187, 200, 283, 401, 445, 566, 682, 701, 1035–6, 1175, 1331. Elected Gov. of Va. (1827): **6:** 185–6, 200. On JQA admin.: **5:** 737. Publishes book attacking C. tariff views: **6:** 1331. Speech to Va. General Assembly: **6:** 1138.

Gilmer, Thomas Walker: Edits Jacksonian *Va. Advocate* (Charlottesville) in campaign of 1928: **6:** 974. Political career: **6:** 974

Granger, Francis: In 1826 N.Y. elections: **5:** 347

Great Britain: Industrialism in: **1:** 460. Economic depression, recession, unemployment, class unrest in: **1:** 538, 540, 657; **2:** 105, 252–3, 332–3, 346; **3:** 693; **4:** 933–4; **5:** 84, 98, 126, 189, 232, 288, 355–6, 435, 562, 624, 626, 749–50, 814, 840, 927, 958, 1002, 1016; **6:** 226, 353, 438–9, 670, 958, 980. Descriptions of: **1:** 913. Cabinet changes, crises & implications of: **1:** 526, 630, 677–8; **5:** 230, 288; **6:** 224–5, 265, 376, 447–8, 450, 476–7, 495–6, 521, 536–7, 545, 556, 577, 670, 709, 714–5, 867, 902, 943, 958–9, 983, 1010–11, 1041–2, 1068, 1306, 1319, 1323, 1375, 1390–1, 1400. Canning ministry (*see* Canning, George); Goderich ministry (*see* Ripon, Frederick John Robinson in Name Index). Weaknesses of Parliament: **2:** 171, 376–7. Leader of liberal principles in Europe: **4:** 320, 323–4 (*see* Canning, George). Political influence on Continent: **4:** 205 (*see also* Portugal).

Harvests: **2:** 378, 397; **5:** 624. Cotton prices & imports: **4:** 267, 562. Tariff protection vs. free trade (Corn Laws) issue in: **2:** 828, 838–9, 846; **3:** 689, 698; **5:** 86, 423, 1051; **6:** 224, 226, 437, 680. Flour prices in: **2:** 379, 397. Corn & flour from Canada: **6:** 437, 680. Catholic emancipation issue (*see espec.* **6:** 265–6): **6:** 224–6, 439, 537, 556, 979. Revision of criminal code: **6:** 351, 520, 758–9. Navigation laws: **6:** 1024 (*see also* below maritime & trade issues). Aid to slaves in BWI: **6:** 94. Abolition societies in: **5:** 1016; **6:** 913–4. Irish problems: **5:** 189; **6:** 101, 439, 476. Alien act (1826): **5:** 562. Theory of govt.: **6:** 495. Boxing in: **6:** 1391–2

—foreign policy: Role & size of Royal Navy (command of the sea): **1:** 620–2, 758, 891, 945–6; **2:** 79–80, 653–4; **5:** 165; **6:** 14, 101, 194–5. Role of East India Co. in: **2:** 47; **3:** 714. Trade privileges extended foreign govts.: **6:** 943–4. Popularity of mercantilist–colonial trade policies in: **2:** 300 (*see also* below maritime & trade issues). General European hatred of GB: **2:** 533. Trade with China (*see* China). Stake in Adams–Onis Treaty (*see* Spain empire: Florida, East). Interest in acquisition of Cuba: **1:** 624; **2:** 783; **3:** 383, 388; **4:** 242 (*see also* Spain empire: Cuba). Economic impact of war upon: **1:** 740–1, 945–6. Foreign industrial competition: **5:** 355–6. Post-war (1815) economic recovery: **2:** 398; **3:** 697–700. Post-war economy: **3:** 696–9. Adjusting to peace after 1815: **2:** 172–3, 252–3, 332, 346. No interest in acquiring Span. Fla.: **2:** 173. Tension with Sp. at Pensacola: **2:** 6. Contest ownership of Key Sal with Sp.: **5:** 973, 994. Suppression of slave trade: **1:** 949, 1005–6; **2:** 431; **4:** 104–5, 219, 236, 254–5, 416, 524–5; **5:** 242–3, 653, 740, 959; **6:** 495, 755. Establishes slave colony in Sierra Leone (1792): **2:** 263–4. Slave trade treaties with Br.: **5:** 959, 1022; Fr.: **6:** 193–4; Sp.: **5:** 243; Sweden: **4:** 416, 524–5 (*see also* Slavery & slaves: slave trade). Suppression of piracy: **4:** 299. Policy toward Ru. in Pacific NW: **4:** 212–3, 416. Policy toward Sp.: **4:** 322, 907; **5:** 1010. Colonial policy in W. Hemisphere: **4:** 180. Neutrality in Span. Am. wars of independence: **2:** 536. Assistance to Span. Am. revolutions: **2:** 156, 499, 504, 534–6, 541, 584–5; **3:** 184, 187. Recognition of independence of Span. Am. republics & European reactions thereto: **2:** 499, 533–5; **3:** 184; **4:** 94, 126, 133, 142, 180, 204, 212, 231, 242, 245, 277, 303, 324, 535, 619–20, 821, 828, 849, 858, 907; **5:** 1005, 1050–1; **6:** 714–5 (*see also* Canning, George). Canning boasts paternity of Span. Am. independence movements: **5:** 1050–1; **6:** 106, 714–5. GB commercial interests in Span. Am.: **2:** 535; **4:** 249, 324, 751, 777; **5:** 125, 1005. Urge Sp. to recognize independence of Span. Am.

Great Britain (*continued*):
nations: **4:** 774; **5:** 132, 167, 216, 414, 429, 877. Urge Sp. to end wars against former Span. Am. colonies: **4:** 571–2, 656; **5:** 27, 877 (*see also* Spain: U.S. relations with). On Sp. retention of Cuba (*see* Spain empire: Cuba). Threat of war with Sp. over events in Port.: **5:** 998, 1002, 1005, 1021, 1035, 1044, 1048, 1052; **6:** 26, 58, 101, 111, 113, 124, 151, 165–6, 180, 195, 265, 296, 302, 324, 353, 663. Military intervention in Port. (*see* Portugal). Relations with Holy Alliance: **4:** 204. Neutral rights problems in Br.–BA war: **5:** 506–7, 556 (*see also* Brazil; Buenos Aires). Interest in isthmian canal: **4:** 810–11. Rumors of war with Fr.: **6:** 174–5. Commercial treaty with Fr.: **5:** 29, 31, 97, 101, 242. Tension with Fr. in Iberian Peninsula: **6:** 1145 (*see also* Portugal; Spain). Reaction to Battle of Navarino: **6:** 1323–4, 1390 (*see also* Greece). Domestic politics of US exclusion from GB colonial (BWI) trade: **2:** 565 (*see* below maritime & trade issues). Peacemaker in Sp.–Colombia war: **5:** 27 (*see also* Colombia). War with Burma: **5:** 135. For GB relations with Br., BA (Argentina), Chile, Colombia, Denmark, Gr., Hanseatic States, Mex., Port., Ru., Sp., Sweden, and Tur., *see* separate entries.
—misc. Anglo–American concerns: US cultural, political, economic identification with: **1:** 757; **5:** 156. Establishes businesses in US: **4:** 267, 369. GB citizens dominate BUS: **1:** 538–9. Establishes white settlements in US West: **3:** 459–60. C. lauds parliamentary procedures of: **1:** 662–3, 670–1, 673. C. Anglophobia: **1:** 890, 950. Kentuckians called "savages" by: **1:** 715. GB sends Bibles to US: **4:** 940. GB merchant seamen desert in US ports: **5:** 828–9
—War of the Am. Revolution: Causes of: **1:** 765–6; **2:** 517; **4:** 355–6. Compared with Span. Am. revolutions: **2:** 517, 520, 529, 548–51, 557, 859. US military glory in: **2:** 149, 354. Factions & intrigues in: **2:** 529. Andrew–Arnold treason episode: **2:** 376, 378. Invasion of Canada: **1:** 450. Dip. recognition of US: **2:** 526. Assistance from Fr. during: **2:** 404, 526, 558, 855–6; **3:** 405; **5:** 436. Dutch aid during: **2:** 526. Clark campaign in Ill. country: **2:** 354–5. Battle of Blue Licks (Ky.): **4:** 505. Battle of Cowpens: **6:** 923. US slaves carried off by GB during: **2:** 263. Loyalists in: **6:** 964. GB debt stemming from: **2:** 836. Proposal for establishing a monarchy in US after: **4:** 843, 852–3, 855–6, 889 (*see also* King, Rufus). Articles of Confederation: **3:** 576, 584, 622. Military bounty lands for vets: **6:** 923. Lafayette on veterans claims: **4:** 850. Beaumarchais claims against US (*see* France: U.S. relations with). Claims, pension laws, applications, litigation growing out of war: **2:** 316–7, 376, 378, 577, 594, 603–4, 680–1, 739, 772, 795–6, 844, 876; **3:**

118, 133–4, 480–1, 563–4, 566; **4:** 505, 588, 621, 850, 914; **5:** 770, 793; **6:** 71–2, 166, 400 (*see espec.* **2:** 681). GB claims on US stemming from: **5:** 489–90; **6:** 1142–3. Dip. correspondence of (*see* Sparks, Jared). Secret journals of Continental Cong. during (*see* Wait, Thomas B. in Name Index). Tension among US diplomats during: **6:** 297
—Treaty of Paris (1783): US concessions in: **2:** 82. Navigation of Miss. River (Art. 8) issue: **2:** 82, 144–5; **3:** 254, 256, 381–2; **4:** 160; **5:** 455–7, 477. GB trade with Indians resident in US: **2:** 82. US fishing rights (Art. 3) issue: **2:** 144–5; **4:** 160; **5:** 86. NE & northern boundary issues (Art. 2): **2:** 147–8; **5:** 596–7; **6:** 265, 329–30, 1100. GB recovery of pre–war debts in US (Art. 4): **5:** 489–90; **6:** 1142–3. Land claims problems stemming from: **2:** 490
—Jay's Treaty (1794): C. opposition to: **1:** 94. BUS support for: **1:** 539. US Cong. debate on: **2:** 682. Arbitration provisions in: **6:** 601. Trade with Canada (Art. 3): **2:** 55; **5:** 461, 478. Trade with BWI (Art. 12): **5:** 900, 915. Trade with BEI (Art. 13): **2:** 35, 37, 118–9, 123. Claims & compensation procedures (Arts. 6 & 7; *see espec.* **6:** 627): **5:** 257; **6:** 624–5, 627, 1183. Neutrality in wartime provisions (Arts. 17, 18, & 19): **2:** 493–4. GB trade with Indians resident in US (Art. 3): **2:** 145. GB recovery of pre–Am. Revolution debts in US (Arts. 6 & 7): **5:** 489–90; **6:** 1142–3. Recovery of private debts in wartime (Art. 10): **5:** 473. Provisions for extradition (Art. 27): **5:** 471, 516. St. Croix River as boundary (Art. 5): **6:** 142, 610. Restrictions on US participation in GB colonial trade (Art. 12): **2:** 299; **5:** 897. Land claims problems stemming from: **2:** 490. US constit. issues involved in: **2:** 809
—Abortive Monroe–Pinkney Treaty (1806–7): **1:** 271–2, 288; **2:** 26, 29, 31, 35, 55; **5:** 78. Trade with BEI: **2:** 123. Trade with BWI: **2:** 126. Exclusion of US from GB colonial trade: **2:** 299
—War of 1812: GB motives in provoking: **1:** 608–9, 805, 884. GB acts leading to: **1:** 633, 653, 674–5, 696–7, 715, 756, 760, 763, 765, 771. Role of US Cong. in bringing on: **1:** 672, 696, 763. C. on possibility of war: **1:** 328, 574, 598, 605–6, 611, 613, 633, 636, 653, 657, 659–60. C. calls for war: **1:** 499–50, 609–10, 641–2, 645–8, 653; **2:** 141–2. Viewed as just, righteous, defensive, & victorious for US: **1:** 642, 751, 760, 763, 765–6; **2:** 141–3, 146–9, 220–1, 807, 867; **4:** 30. Goals & objectives of: **2:** 63, 220. Impressment issue: **1:** 288, 449, 539, 606–7, 642–3, 665, 765–9; **2:** 145–7. US neutral rights issues: **1:** 232, 275, 278, 288, 388–9, 449–51, 463, 472, 481, 514–5, 524, 526, 539, 563, 574, 600, 607–8, 622, 642, 761, 764–5; **2:** 142, 145–7, 297, 905–6; **5:** 442–6, 848. GB–Am. Indian connection: **1:** 450, 599,

609, 621, 642, 664–5, 674, 769; **2:** 145. US conquest of Canada as war goal: **1:** 450, 516, 603–4, 615, 625, 769–70, 773, 841–2, 945, 978, 983–4; **2:** 220. US declaration of: **1:** 674–7, 742–3, 763, 765, 858, 967; **2:** 142, 807. On including Fr. in declaration: **1:** 449, 481, 641, 655, 657, 659–60, 674, 690, 692, 763–4. Economic origins of: **1:** 606, 619, 625–6. US preparations for: **1:** 388, 403, 598–600, 603–9, 611, 618–27, 637–8, 653; **2:** 6. Economic impact of on US: **1:** 741–2. Financing war: **1:** 600, 620, 630, 633, 653, 657, 755, 802–3, 806–9, 812, 871, 938–9, 1001; **2:** 6–7, 9, 70. Raising troops: **1:** 697–8, 749, 751–2, 773, 780, 877. Battle of Tippecanoe (11/7/11): **1:** 599, 609, 621, 642, 644–5. Strategic dimensions of: **1:** 605, 621, 623–5; **2:** 221, 270–1. C. on strategy & tactics of: **1:** 713, 729, 749, 770, 783, 846. New England opposition to: **1:** 692–4, 727–8, 740, 759–60, 768–9, 771, 773, 805–6, 884, 892, 909, 916, 920, 941; **2:** 220, 243. C. on Hartford Convention during: **2:** 6, 220, 222. West supports: **1:** 216, 625, 642, 696–8, 703, 751, 769; **2:** 6, 220, 222; **3:** 590–1; **4:** 30. Ky. supports: **1:** 318, 455, 696–9, 703, 712, 715, 720. Indian support: **1:** 980–1. Federalist party opposition: **6:** 20, 1267. C. toasts relating to: **1:** 696–7, 855; **2:** 61, 62, 82, 344. GB sentiment pro & anti–war: **1:** 741, 771, 882, 884, 899, 996. GB financial problems in pursuing: **1:** 740–1. US stake in Fr. victory in Ru.: **1:** 742. Fr. offer of troops: **1:** 986–8, 990–1, 1002. US wartime relations with Fr.: **1:** 754, 757, 838; **4:** 464. C. critical of Madison during: **1:** 750, 782. US logistical problems & failures: **1:** 717, 720, 722, 747, 749, 783–4, 801, 816. Poor condition, training, supply of US troops: **1:** 723, 729, 740. Problems with short–term US militia: **1:** 748–9, 751. Pay & bounties for troops: **1:** 751–2, 777, 783. Ky. troops not paid: **1:** 809, 815–6. US successes on land: **1:** 770–1, 802, 841, 992–3; **2:** 69. US defeats on land: **1:** 988–90. Ky. troop participation in: **1:** 712, 715, 717–24, 726, 729, 734, 780, 784, 799, 801, 819, 841; **2:** 642; **3:** 164. US invasions of Canada: **1:** 516, 603–4, 625, 646, 696, 712–13, 715, 717–23, 726, 728–9, 734, 740, 750–1, 769–70, 773, 839–42, 859, 877, 888, 897, 903, 909–10, 945, 964, 978, 980–1, 983–4; **2:** 6–7, 462 (*see also* Hull, William in Name Index; Wilkinson, James). Battle of River Raisin: **1:** 715, 813–4, 817, 821; **2:** 131, 178, 417, 432, 622–3, 675; **3:** 164; **4:** 237–8; **5:** 990; **6:** 777. Battle of the Thames: **1:** 721, 841–2, 847; **3:** 164. Battle of Horseshoe Bend: **1:** 938. GB repulse at Baltimore: **1:** 996; **2:** 69. Battle of New Orleans: **1:** 995, 997, 999; **2:** 11–12, 69, 148, 221, 693; **3:** 164, 566; **6:** 777. Ky. militia cowardice at N.O. battle: **2:** 11–12; **6:** 777. Battle of Mobile: **2:** 19. Battle of Lundys Lane: **1:** 981, 990, 993–4; **2:** 69.

"Dudley's Defeat": **2:** 167, 234. GB sack of Wash.: **1:** 982, 988–9, 993–4, 996–7; **2:** 275, 440, 462, 594; **3:** 68; **4:** 587. Indian dimensions of war & US operations against: **1:** 713–5, 719, 723, 728–30, 740, 749, 769, 770–1, 774, 782–3, 799, 800, 807–9, 816, 842, 846–8, 938; **2:** 131, 642. Recovery of Indian captives after: **2:** 131–2, 139–40, 160–1. Naval policy & planning: **1:** 748, 751, 775, 777, 938–9; **2:** 6. GB navy in: **1:** 621, 647. GB control of Lake Erie: **1:** 722, 750, 783. Battle of Lake Erie: **1:** 842, 846–8, 877, 910, 945, 992; **2:** 430, 659. Battle of Lake Champlain: **1:** 945–6, 992–4, 996; **2:** 69. Naval actions: **1:** 683–5, 727–8, 751, 767, 770–1, 774, 842, 846–8, 900, 949, 974–5, 981, 992; **2:** 6, 148, 158, 436–7 (*see espec. Chesapeake vs. Shannon:* **1:** 802; **2:** 158). Naval construction problems: **2:** 478. US privateering activities: **4:** 124–5, 464; **5:** 78–9; **6:** 495. US military incompetence during: **1:** 945. C. on USN needs in war: **1:** 621. GB too civilized to bombard US coastal towns: **1:** 647. Disrupts Ky. trade: **2:** 206. War taxes on Ky.: **1:** 803. Unpopularity of in US: **1:** 782–3. Prize law policy during: **1:** 775–6. C. on GB atrocities during: **1:** 800. Prisoner exchanges: **1:** 813–4, 867–8, 1001; **2:** 19–21, 24, 30. Treatment of US prisoners at Dartmoor: **2:** 19, 20–2, 24, 30, 37–8, 53. Dartmoor "massacre" inquiry: **2:** 190–3. Sentiment for, proposals for, conditions of & efforts to obtain peace: **1:** 728, 741, 755, 761–2, 765, 768–9, 771–3, 779, 841–2, 844, 852–3, 857, 860–2, 881, 903, 908–10, 917, 920, 935–6, 938. US slaves carried off by GB: **4:** 109 (*see also* below St. Petersburg Convention). Support & criticism of C. role in: **4:** 437; **5:** 655. C. proud of warhawk role in bringing on: **2:** 141–2, 220. C. pride in helping end: **2:** 692–3. C. personal sacrifices during: **2:** 221. C. sees in retrospect as glorious, wise, & useful: **2:** 70, 82, 141–3, 146–9, 220–1; **3:** 711. C. on post–war policy of US: **2:** 70. War stimulates US mfgrs.: **2:** 826, 840–1; **6:** 1068. Economic & banking crisis after: **1:** 806–7; **2:** 202–3. Anglo–Am. commercial competition after: **2:** 174–5. GB "dump" surplus mfgrs. on US market: **2:** 840; **3:** 643–4; **6:** 1068. Pension & bounty laws growing out of: **1:** 817, 843; **2:** 110, 178, 214, 411, 432, 579; **4:** 18. Exchange of veteran land grants for cash: **2:** 411–7. Land bounties to vets: **6:** 1155. N.Y. civilian property claims ("Niagara Frontier") growing out of: **2:** 270–2, 275, 563–4; **4:** 18. C. assistance to constituents & others with war–connected claims: **1:** 863; **2:** 177, 330, 337, 342, 344, 347–8, 366–7, 375, 380, 385, 399, 414, 416–7, 428–30, 432, 437–8, 491–2, 567–8, 571, 583, 586, 674–5, 677, 681, 732, 780; **3:** 5–6, 69, 170–1, 534, 541–2; **4:** 14–5, 476, 635, 650; **6:** 80–1, 116. *See also* Hagner, Peter & Lee, Richard Bland

Great Britain (*continued*):
in Name Index: and *see* below maritime
and trade issues
—maritime & trade issues: Peace of Amiens
felt in Ky.: **1:** 99. Role of F. J. Jackson in:
1: 456–7, 515, 517, 756; **3:** 30. US investments in GB: **1:** 654. US non–importation, non–intercourse, & embargo: **1:**
227–8, 396–7, 451, 524, 653–4, 657,
670, 738–47, 756, 778, 814, 840, 842,
844, 877, 920; **2:** 297 (*see also* above War
of 1812). US trade restriction legis. repealed: **1:** 903, 909, 915, 920, 924.
Erskine Agreement: **1:** 743, 746, 756; **2:**
756; **6:** 715. *Chesapeake vs. Leopard* incident: **1:** 481, 514, 539, 622, 642–3, 756,
773; **2:** 154; **3:** 107; **5:** 78. Embargo Act
(1807): **1:** 388–9, 515, 642, 739, 756; **2:**
297; **3:** 737. Macons Bills: **1:** 488, 451–2,
457. Embargo Act (1812): **1:** 637, 641–3,
688; **2:** 297. Impressment (after 1815): **2:**
16–7; **5:** 176–7, 179, 344–5, 358, 390,
399, 419, 435–6, 444–6, 476. 482,
492–3, 516, 1021; **6:** 55–6, 234–5, 345,
359, 522, 705, 826, 830–1, 903–6,
908–10, 932–3, 942–3, 952–3, 963, 973,
1086–7 (*see also* above War of 1812; below Treaty of Ghent; *Redwing* & *Pharos* in
Name Index). Broken vs. continuous voyages: **1:** 608, 610; **5:** 902. Tariff as US
dep. weapon: **2:** 304–5. Trade rivalry in
Span. Am.: **4:** 249; **5:** 226. GB tariff
schedules affecting US: **6:** 679–80. GB
undersells US mfgr. goods: **5:** 626 (*see
also* American System: protective tariff*).
Mutual surrender of deserted seamen: **6:**
195 (*see also* Merchant Marine, US). Problems with piracy & privateering: **5:** 443,
471. US trade with BWI: **4:** 422–3; **5:**
834, 899, 910. Trade policy differences:
4: 319–20, 332, 338; **5:** 464–5, 779–80,
895–916. Trade reciprocity: **4:** 680–1,
941; **5:** 121, 143, 466–7, 469–70, 900,
909–12; **6:** 231–4, 520, 582. US claims:
4: 301, 527–8, 809; **5:** 50, 67, 85, 172,
177, 848, 946, 1037; **6:** 80–1, 251, 376,
393, 642, 654–6, 782–3. GB harassment
of US shipping: **4:** 101, 484–5, 575, 586,
611, 653, 723, 726; **5:** 281, 518, 575,
922–3, 946; **6:** 344–5, 359. US harassment of GB shipping: **4:** 485; **5:** 695–6,
817, 821, 830, 878, 882, 948, 1012; **6:**
233. GB tariff, duty, fee discrim. against
US shipping & trade: **4:** 570, 933; **5:** 115,
905, 921, 1016, 1341. US tariff, duty, fee
discrim. against GB shipping & trade: **4:**
89, 933–4; **5:** 1016; **6:** 609, 695, 704,
722–3, 907, 975–6, 1037, 1086, 1088–9,
1096, 1251
—US Restrictions (1817–1824) on GB
Trade from GB to BWI via US (*see espec.*
the relevant restrictive legislation, viz: Act
of 9/30/17: **5:** 910; Act of 4/18/18: **2:**
564–6; Act of 5/15/20: **2:** 846; **3:** 729; **4:**
421–5; Act of 1/21/23: **4:** 475; Act of
3/1/23: **3:** 729; **4:** 421–5; **5:** 687–8; **6:**
943; Act of 1/7/24: **5:** 475): **2:** 564–6,
839, 846; **3:** 714, 729; **4:** 319, 421–5,
472–3, 478–9; **5:** 121, 131, 464–5,

466–7, 469–70, 475, 631–2, 687–8, 706,
744, 777, 790, 831, 902–3, 909–10, 913;
6: 131, 239–40, 316, 322–3, 330, 423,
535, 1335. US opposition to Am. restrictive policy: **5:** 121, 143, 631; **6:** 131,
425, 577. Proposed US retreat from restrictions: **5:** 75–6, 631–2, 779. US Cong.
involvement in restrictive policy: **5:**
631–2, 731, 779, 791; **6:** 131–2, 237,
330–1, 424–7, 429, 520, 577
—GB Restrictions (1822–1825) on US
Trade with GB American Colonies: (*see
espec.* the relevant restrictive legislation,
viz: Act of 7/24/22: **3:** 729; **5:** 835; Acts
of 7/17/23 & 7/18/23: **3:** 729; **4:** 942; Act
of 3/5/24: **4:** 942; Acts of 6/27/25 &
7/5/25: **4:** 180, 941–2): **3:** 729; **4:** 180,
319, 328, 332, 338, 342, 417, 469–75,
478–85, 533, 588, 601–2, 607–8, 626,
632–3, 695–8, 702, 789, 810, 933,
941–2, 944; **5:** 84, 86, 115–6, 142–3,
178, 395, 418, 437, 441–3, 462–8,
475–6, 482, 515, 584, 600, 626, 630–2,
687–8, 804, 806, 808, 810–2, 831–5,
864–5, 879–80, 883, 899, 902–10, 913,
921, 985, 1016, 1045; **6:** 131–2, 169, 232,
237, 239, 330–1, 353–4, 376–7, 420,
424, 427, 429, 437, 535, 551–2, 680, 943.
Related warehousing regulations: **4:** 180;
5: 437; **6:** 1362, 1375. Reaction of GB
shipping interests to restrictions: **6:** 520,
551–2, 943. Commodities affected by restrictions: **4:** 626, 632–3; **5:** 465, 834.
Linked to St. Lawrence navigation issue:
5: 468–9, 835
—GB Interdiction (1826) of US Trade with
GB Am. Colonies (*see espec.* the relevant
interdictive legislation, viz: Acts of 7/5/26
& 7/27/26: **5:** 632; Act of 9/11/26: **5:**
913): **5:** 629–32, 653, 685–8, 697, 702,
706, 716–7, 731, 733–4, 751, 761, 770,
772–5, 779–80, 790–1, 801, 804–5, 810,
833, 844, 855, 895–6, 903–9, 913–4,
926, 940, 958, 967, 1008, 1028, 1041–2,
1046; **6:** 131–2, 239–40, 421–2, 477,
495, 520, 545, 577, 655, 680, 715, 723,
826–7, 943, 1375. US efforts to circum-
vent by indirect trade with BWI: **5:** 812;
6: 331, 518, 536, 626, 647, 739, 802,
867–8, 912–3, 1104, 1191, 1378. GB justification of: **6:** 131–2. GB will not discuss changing: **5:** 1042; **6:** 131, 520, 545,
577, 1178. GB motives: **6:** 823. GB right
to interdict: **5:** 896, 899; **6:** 418–9, 680,
1037. GB domestic politics relating to: **5 :**
1016; **6:** 1037. Exemption of Canada: **5:**
686. Possible GB compromise on: **5:**
1016; **6:** 1037. GB shipping interests support: **6:** 520, 943. Popularity of in GB: **6:**
577: 943. Problem of supplying BWI: **5:**
697, 706; **6:** 151, 536, 595–6, 867, 1037,
1104. GB enforcement of: **6:** 655–6. Economic impact on BWI people: **5:** 1046; **6:**
151, 302, 687, 912–3, 1104, 1377–8. Reaction to in BWI: **6:** 943. US trade with
BWI: **5:** 899, 910, 1046. Minor relaxa-
tions of: **6:** 1219–20. GB conditions on
lifting: **6:** 535, 551–2, 1037, 1086, 1107.
Grain market losses to US: **5:** 706,

Great Britain (*continued*):
sioners toward achieving peace: **1:** 884,
932–5, 943–4, 963–4, 971–2; **2:** 66, 69,
354. US pessimism on favorable outcome
of negotiations: **1:** 904–5, 908, 910–11,
921, 932–5, 940–5, 948, 975, 977, 980,
996. Terms and counter–terms presented
(Aug. 1814): **1:** 953–6, 959–60, 968, 973,
974–5, 991. *Uti Possidetis* proposal
(11/4/13): **1:** 954, 991–2, 995, 998–9,
1001; **2:** 66–8. Relation of negotiations to
Vienna Cong.: **1:** 980, 989, 995. GB stalling tactics: **1:** 963, 965, 989, 995. C. on
US tactics: **1:** 939, 942–3. C. given wrong
cypher code: **1:** 896. Formal protocol
used: **1:** 952. Unacceptable GB demands:
1: 971–2. US demands *status quo ante:* **1:**
973, 983–4, 991, 1001, 1003, 1006; **3:**
219, 255. C. on US must "conquer
peace": **1:** 996. C. threatens to quit talks
& go home: **1:** 972–4, 977. Fatiguing
negotiations: **2:** 17. Peace strategically
necessary to US: **2:** 143, 221, 354. US
valor forces GB to accept peace: **2:** 354.
Harmony within US Commission: **1:** 966,
996. Conflict within US Commission: **2:**
74–7, 372–3; **5:** 656 (*see also* Election of
1824; issues). C. conflict with JQA on
Fisheries & Miss. River issues: **2:** 372–3,
427; **3:** 204, 210, 219–26, 239, 253–7,
269–71, 283, 322–3, 409; **5:** 656 (*see also*
Russell, Jonathan; Election of 1824: issues). Final version of treaty: **1:** 1006,
1008. Disappointment with final treaty:
1: 1007. Pleasure with final treaty: **2:** 5,
141, 221. US Commissioners praised: **2:**
6–8, 62–3, 65–8, 195, 354; **4:** 437. Sen.
ratification: **2:** 11–2, 14. Struggle among
US Commissioners for main credit for
negotiating treaty: **2:** 74–5, 77–8. C. wel-
comed home & praised: **2:** 61–2, 67–71,
92–3, 195; **6:** 745. C. proud of role at
Ghent: **2:** 221, 693–4. C. subsequent defense of treaty: **2:** 141–6, 221, 354; **3:**
257. C. reelected to US House while at
Ghent: **1:** 990, 1008
—Commercial Treaty of 1815: **1:** 853–4,
955, 959, 1009–10; **2:** 14, 26, 30–7, 57–9
(*see espec.* **2:** 26, 30–7). C. social life in
London during negotiations: **2:** 16–7, 25,
43; **3:** 172; **5:** 717. C. fatigued & home-
sick during talks: **2:** 17, 19, 26, 78. No
instruction to US negotiators: **2:** 18, 25,
29. Such a treaty of little importance: **2:**
12. GB concerned with weightier matters:
2: 18. Relationship to possible renewal of
European war: **2:** 22, 25–6. Preliminary
talks: **2:** 20, 73. US constit. issues involved in: **2:** 809–10
—issues discussed: Impressment: **2:** 25–6,
28–9, 32–6, 55. MFN principle (Art. 2):
2: 26, 28, 29, 31–2, 34–5, 41–2, 45–8,
51, 55–8, 73; **3:** 670–1; **4:** 644, 680–2; **5:**
329, 844–5; **6:** 231–4, 582, 973–4, 1086,
1088. Blockades: **2:** 26, 29, 33, 35. US
trade with BWI: **2:** 26, 31, 34–5, 46, 55,
58, 124–7, 565; **5:** 464–5, 697, 773,
844–5, 900–1; **6:** 437. US trade with
BEI: **2:** 26, 28–9, 31–2, 34–5, 41–2,

44–51, 56–8, 73, 118–9, 123–4; **5:**
900–1; **6:** 233, 437. US trade with Canada: **2:** 26, 29, 31, 35–6, 46–7, 49, 55, 58,
73–4; **5:** 464–5, 773, 901. GB trade with
US Indians: **2:** 36, 45, 48, 74. US trade
with colonies of GB enemies during war:
2: 33, 35. Trade on Great Lakes, Lake
Champlain, & St. Lawrence River: **2:** 42,
47–9, 55; **5:** 443, 461. Continuing controversy on exclusion or restriction of US
trade from various GB colonies: **2:**
293–4, 296–305, 523–4, 564–6, 839; **3:**
714, 729; **4:** 180 (*see also* above maritime
& trade issues). C. remedies for US exclusion from GB colonial trade: **2:** 300–5,
564–5; **3:** 714, 729. Time limitations on
treaty provisions: **2:** 51–2, 56–7, 59, 73.
C. conflict with JQA over treaty wording:
2: 54. St. Helena clause: **2:** 759. Continuous vs. broken voyage: **6:** 319. MFN vs.
recip. principles in negotiations: **6:** 582.
Final version of treaty: **2:** 57–9. Model
characteristics of: **4:** 296. C. explains
treaty to US House: **2:** 123–4, 293–4,
295–305. Rolled iron vs. bar iron tariff
controversy under: **5:** 1016–7; **6:** 609,
704, 907, 975–6. C. later (1821) seeks
payment for personal services related to:
3: 54–5, 59–60, 70, 182, 188–9, 257–8,
263–4, 268–9; **4:** 913. So. Carolina defies
Art. 1 of: **5:** 1016–7. Commercial Treaty
of 1815 renewed as Art. 4 of Convention
of 1818 (*see* below Convention of 1818).
See also above War of 1812; Treaty of
Ghent
—Convention of 1818: Renewal of Commercial Treaty of 1815 as Art. 4 of: **2:**
565–6, 611; **3:** 60; **5:** 475, 773, 844, 934,
977, 1016; **6:** 231–2, 609, 704, 716, 806,
826–8, 854–5. Renewed again as Commercial Convention of 1827 (*see* below
Commercial Convention of Aug. 6,
1827). Northwest boundary–joint occupa-
tion of Oregon (Art. 3): **2:** 611; **3:** 60; **4:**
180–1, 485; **5:** 288, 449–50, 475, 480,
511–2, 843, 926, 977; **6:** 230–3, 477,
608–9, 704, 716, 750, 804, 826–7,
854–5, 975. Colombia River claims: **4:**
179, 485; **5:** 933. Free navigation of Colombia River: **5:** 450, 934. Impressment:
2: 609, 611; **5:** 444. Fishing provisions: **2:**
611; **3:** 60; **4:** 484–5, **5:** 67–8, 86, 443,
470–1. Impact of US tariffs on trade
with BWI: **3:** 635, 637, 714. US trade
with BWI: **5:** 773, 844–5. Restitution for
slaves seized in War of 1812: **2:** 611. GB
protests US duty discrim. under: **4:** 89.
US claims stemming from: **5:** 67–8, 85.
Northern boundary discussions: **2:** 611;
3: 60; **4:** 180–1, 485; **5:** 443, 449–50,
934 (*see also* below Northern boundary
controversy; Northwest boundary–
Oregon controversy & convention of
1827 to Regulate)
—free navigation of St. Lawrence River: C.
instructions to Gallatin on: **5:** 451–64,
477–8, 598–9, 888–9. Gallatin view of: **5:**
512–5, 835, 926; **6:** 1060, 1103–4. C.
view of: **5:** 567, 599, 888. JQA view of: **5:**

596, 598. US citizens interest in: **4:** 412–3, 425–6, 437, 485. US position on: **4:** 609–10; **6:** 1103. US Cong. involvement in: **5:** 1017. GB position on: **3:** 382. GB refusal to discuss: **6:** 1087, 1103. Relation to positioning of Northern boundary: **5:** 850–1, 860, 864, 921, 930; **6:** 1060. Concessions & compromises considered: **5:** 463–4, 468–9, 599, 835, 864; **6:** 1103–4
—abortive Convention for Suppression of Slave Trade (1824): GB policy & arguments for: **4:** 219, 236. US arguments against: **4:** 218–20, 246. Related US domestic problems: **4:** 217. Slave trade as piracy: **4:** 219–20. Right of search at sea complications: **4:** 246. C. lectures GB on Senate treaty–making function: **4:** 217–8. Failure of negotiations: **4:** 136, 341
—St. Petersburg Convention: Origin of: **3:** 736; **4:** 342–3; **5:** 148, 484; **6:** 35, 122 (*see also* above Treaty of Ghent). Work of Joint Commission under: **4:** 94, 109, 201, 239, 245, 291–2, 344–8, 448, 838; **5:** 3, 67, 147–9, 273, 358, 486, 873, 980; **6:** 108, 128, 315, 369, 576, 642. Value of slaves adjudicated by: **4:** 292, 351–3. Value of slave property seized by GB: **4:** 292, 351–3; **5:** 255; **6:** 122–3. GB arguments, delay, & obstructionism: **4:** 109, 201, 291, 343–50, 733, 777, 781–2, 858; **5:** 67, 86, 102, 148–9, 246–8, 257, 345, 371–2, 415, 432, 485–8, 629, 683, 782, 792, 903. Arbitration procedures under Art. 5: **4:** 109, 343; **5:** 148, 225–6, 247–8, 263, 304, 484, 486–8, 629, 683, 696, 781–4, 792; **6:** 123, 347. Arbitration by Czar Alexander: **4:** 733, 777; **5:** 86, 102, 246, 255, 304, 488, 781–4; **6:** 122–3, 389, 405. C. criticism of GB handling of issue: **5:** 781–7. C. suggests terminating work of Joint Commission: **4:** 351, 354, 619. Work of Joint Commission suspended: **4:** 733; **5:** 442, 690; **6:** 360. *See also* Jackson, George & Cheves, Langdon in Name Index; *see espec.* **3:** 736; **5:** 923; **6:** 347, 360, 405
—Slave Indemnity Convention of Nov. 13, 1826: Negotiations moved to Wash.: **5:** 102, 142, 203, 304, 441, 484, 683. Principal points of contention: **5:** 262–3, 304–5, 486, 696, 780–2, 786–7. US legal positions on points of contention: **5:** 304–5, 371–2, 485–6. GB legal positions on points of contention: **5:** 696; **6:** 122–3. Negotiation of a compromise settlement amount of money: **5:** 49, 63–4, 84, 102, 235, 246–8, 251, 254–6, 485, 487, 490, 630, 683, 686, 690–1, 811–2, 863, 916; **6:** 405. Settlement by conv. & subsequent GB payments: **5:** 916–7, 923, 926, 933, 935, 1013–4, 1039, 1044–5; **6:** 35–6, 71, 107, 122, 133–4, 166–7, 243, 330, 347, 388–9, 815, 836, 1202, 1256, 1374. US Cong. involvement in: **5:** 147–8; **6:** 107–8. BUS handles GB payments under convention: **5:** 1013–4, 1022, 1044–5; **6:** 23. US Commissioners handle claims for slave property lost: **6 :**

123, 243, 347, 360, 452–3. *See also* Cheves, Langdon; Pleasants, James; & Seawell, Henry in Name Index; *see espec.* **6:** 122–3
—Northeastern boundary controversy & Convention of 1827 to Arbitrate: Encroachments & depredations by GB subjects in disputed area: **4:** 181–2, 197, 390, 484–5, 800, 881, 910; **6:** 994, 1036–7, 1047–8, 1067–8, 1190, 1224, 1251, 1272–4, 1283, 1348. Encroachments & depredations by US citizens in disputed area: **4:** 828–9, 851, 875; **6:** 73, 79, 134, 1047, 1053, 1055, 1190. John Baker incident (*see espec.* **6:** 1272–4): **6:** 1272–4, 1283, 1288, 1299–1300, 1338, 1348, 1379. GB claims & attitudes: **4:** 875; **5:** 996; **6:** 142, 265–6, 364, 828, 1100, 1190, 1299–1300, 1322. Commission to fix boundary fails: **1:** 1006; **4:** 182; **5:** 447, 476. GB bad faith & delay: **6:** 142, 650. US attitudes toward: **5:** 596; **6:** 134, 1067–8 (*see also* below role & involvement of Maine in Northeastern boundary controversy & role & involvement of Mass. in Northeastern boundary controversy). Cartographical (John Mitchell Map & Map "A") bases for conflicting claims: **5:** 146, 1021; **6:** 265–6, 334, 364–5, 450, 609; **6:** 1100–1, 1105–6, 1335. Maps, reports, documents, historical data pertaining to: **5:** 495, 511, 597–8, 778, 1021; **6:** 265–6, 329, 334, 522–3, 1205–6, 1335, 1374. Rumors in Europe of war over: **6:** 343. Mutual pleas for peace, patience, forebearance: **5:** 43; **6:** 1284, 1300, 1322. Linked to St. Lawrence navigation issue: **5:** 463–4; **6:** 1060. C. instructions to Barrell fact–finding mission to disputed area: **6:** 1282–4, 1287–8, 1338, 1403. States Rights issues in: **5:** 843; **6:** 329 (*see also* below role & involvement of Maine in Northeastern boundary controversy). US errors made during negotiation: **5:** 509
—role & involvement of Maine in Northeastern boundary controversy: **4:** 852, 875, 910, 951; **6:** 329, 459, 522–3, 609–10, 994, 1053, 1055, 1224, 1251. Claims relating to controversy: **4:** 951; **6:** 994–5. John Baker incident: **6:** 1272–4 (*see also* above Northeastern boundary controversy & Convention of 1827 to Arbitrate). C. problems, relations, & negotiations with Me. & Gov. Enoch Lincoln on boundary issue: **4:** 910–1; **5:** 11, 43, 597, 843; **6:** 134, 329, 363–4, 459, 522–3, 609, 655–6, 1053, 1055, 1064, 1102, 1205–6, 1272, 1284, 1321–3. Legis. of on issue: **5:** 80–1, 460; **6:** 1348. States Rights stance on: **6:** 459–60, 609, 1272, 1348. Threat to use military force: **6:** 1348. River rights affected: **6:** 994–5. Fear of settlement by arbitration: **6:** 460, 609, 995, 1272, 1321. C. solicits facts from state on boundary: **6:** 1251, 1273. C. on Me. claims: **6:** 656. C. criticism of Gov. Lincoln: **6:** 1064, 1323. C. urges logic of arbitration on: **6:** 1321–2. State

729

trade with GB American Colonies; Harrison, Robert Monroe
—Antigua: Tariff, duty, fee discrim. against US shipping & trade: **4:** 812, 834, 886; **5:** 141, 201, 625; **6:** 341, 389. Harassment of US shipping at: **4:** 101; **5:** 104, 374, 777, 821. Obstruction of foreign business enterprise in: **6:** 341, 389. US seamen at encouraged to desert: **5:** 104, 141; **6:** 341. Extent of US trade with: **5:** 1046; **6:** 341. Indirect US trade with: **6:** 518, 802. Impact of Anglo–Am. trade controversy on: **5:** 1046; **6:** 912. Fr. ships admitted to direct trade with: **5:** 625. GB naval build–up at: **6:** 13–4. Planters in on verge of rebellion: **6:** 302
—Bahamas: US vessels excluded from: **5:** 632. GB relaxes interdict on US vessels trading with: **6:** 1219–20
—Barbados: Nature & extent of US trade with: **5:** 559. Tariff, duty, fee discrim. against US shipping & trade: **5:** 559, 740. Impact of Anglo–Am. trade controversy on: **6:** 912, 1377–8. US vessels excluded: **6:** 151. US vessels admitted: **6:** 301. Slavery in: **6:** 913–4
—Dominica: Impact of Anglo–Am. trade controversy: **6:** 912
—Jamaica: Need for US consul at: **5:** 3; **6:** 956. GB naval build–up at: **6:** 194–5. Indirect US trade with: **6:** 739
—St. Lucia: Impact of Anglo–Am. trade controversy on: **6:** 912
—Trinidad: Slavery in: **6:** 913–4
—Bermuda: Nature & extent of US trade with: **5:** 493, 500, 507. US vessels excluded from: **5:** 632. US merchant seamen stranded in: **6:** 1354–5. Legal problems with US ships in: **6:** 22. GB naval build–up in: **6:** 14, 194–5
—British Guiana: Replaces US suppliers of BWI: **6:** 1135. Nature & extent of US trade with: **6:** 1191. Formation of colony: **6:** 1191. Timber industry: **6:** 1288. Unpopularity of GB merchants in: **6:** 1191
—Canada: US invasions of (*see* Great Britain: War of the Am. Revolution; War of 1812). Spies on US: **1:** 635–7, 642. No military threat to US. **1:** 646. Volunteers from in US army: **2:** 164, 167. Army deserters: **4:** 118. Land prices in: **3:** 665. GB compensation for war damage: **2:** 271. Competition with US wheat: **3:** 664–5. US fugitive slave problem with: **5:** 234–6, 472–3, 600, 610, 1016: **6:** 235–6, 589, 750, 1073. GB development & settlement of: **4:** 180, 212. Canal development in: **6:** 680. Fortification of US border: **4:** 180. GB naval build–up in: **6:** 194–5. Tariff relations with US: **5:** 985; **6:** 584. Indirect US trade with GB colonies via: **5:** 437; **6:** 680, 1104. Indian control problems on US–Canadian border: **6:** 1340, 1369, 1374
—East Indies (British): Potential US trade with: **4:** 225 (*see also* Great Britain: Commercial Treaty of 1815). War with Burma: **5:** 135

—Honduras (British Mosquito Coast): US vessels excluded: **5:** 632, 1018; **6:** 318. Timber operations in: **5:** 589. Slavery in: **5:** 589. As part of Guatemala: **6:** 318
—Newfoundland: US vessels excluded from: **5:** 632
Greece: C. supports independence & US recognition of: **3:** 597–9, 603–14, 608–9; **4:** 437; **5:** 388–9, 494; **6:** 872. Popular US sentiment for independence: **3:** 598–9, 604; **4:** 71–2, 437, 526–7, 958; **5:** 401; **6:** 256–7, 670–1. US opposition to independence: **3:** 606, 612. US organizations aid: **4:** 958; **6:** 256–7. US sympathy for: **3:** 615–6; **4:** 671. USN evaluation of: **4:** 612. Seek GB protection of independence: **4:** 655, 730, 735. Undemocratic nature of revolutionary movement in: **3:** 612; **5:** 938; **6:** 1092. National constit. govt. established in (1822): **3:** 612. Internal disorders: **4:** 730, 905; **5:** 681. Am. arms to Gr. revolutionaries: **4:** 195, 388–9; **6:** 14, 201. Attacks on US ships: **4:** 454; **6:** 14. War for independence against Tur.: **3:** 87, 311–2; **4:** 126, 204, 407–8, 527, 556, 575, 595, 612, 624–5, 640, 655–6, 702, 729, 735, 737, 773–4, 899, 905–6; **5:** 10, 36, 53, 98, 137, 204–5, 241, 281, 283–4, 289, 356, 391–2, 401, 404, 408, 479–80, 494, 552, 618–9, 681, 816, 923; **6:** 345, 491, 667, 677–8, 725, 727, 731, 781, 784, 823–4, 872, 895, 1092, 1134–5, 1138, 1255, 1257, 1329–30. Ru. political & military policy relating to: **3:** 87, 312–3, 611; **4:** 204, 277, 361, 702, 934, 938–9; **5:** 10, 36, 98, 137, 204, 241, 281, 356, 392, 401, 404, 408, 432, 494, 552; **6:** 491, 501, 564, 574, 716, 725, 780, 807, 821, 823–4, 895, 980, 1033, 1092, 1138–9, 1195, 1255, 1280 (*see also* Russia). Fr. political & military policy in: **4:** 655, 702, 729–30, 735, 849; **5:** 137, 204–5, 401–2, 404, 432, 564, 670, 781; **6:** 823–4, 895, 1092, 1195, 1255. GB political & military policy in: **3:** 311–3; **4:** 204, 277, 640, 702, 730, 735, 774, 907, 939; **5:** 98, 137, 204, 241, 281, 368, 393, 401, 404, 408, 422–3, 432, 618–9, 681, 816, 938; **6:** 201, 491, 501, 564, 577, 678, 716, 784, 823–4, 855, 1195, 1361. Protocol of St. Petersburg relating to: **5:** 432; **6:** 781, 784. European reactions to Gr.–Tur. War: **4:** 134, 204, 612, 735; **5:** 137; **6:** 667, 1092. European peace mediation efforts in Gr.–Tur. War: **4:** 241, 277, 303, 655; **5:** 204, 241, 816, 923. Somerville mission to Gr.: **4:** 624–5. Somerville death enroute to Gr. (*see* Somerville, William C.). Rumored US assistance to: **4:** 774, 776, 849. Purchase warships in US: **5:** 388–9, 401, 422–3, 595, 671. US citizens fight for Gr. independence: **5:** 10, 549, 938; **6:** 14, 501–2, 542. Buys ships in GB: **5:** 682. Navy of: **5:** 53, 681–2; **6:** 14. Privateers of attack GB & US shipping: **6:** 1306, 1319, 1324. European protocol to sustain Gr. independence: **5:** 137, 204, 230, 241, 408,

Greece (*continued*):
432. Holy Alliance principles applied to: **6**: 677. Fr. sentiment for Gr. independence war: **4**: 729; **5**: 137, 204, 241, 281, 401–2, 404–5, 681. European sympathy for: **5**: 435, 552. Monarchy seen for an independent Gr.: **6**: 667–8, 678. GB sentiment for Gr. independence war: **5**: 11, 681; **6**: 1145. USN in waters of: **6**: 14. Anglo–Am. trade rivalry in: **6**: 201. Pirates attack US supply ships bound to: **6**: 256–7, 270, 277–8. European disinterest in problems of: **6**: 670–1. Austrian policy toward: **6**: 677, 1092. Prussian policy toward: **6**: 677. Anglo–Fr.–Ru. Treaty of London to end Gr.–Tur. War & establishment of Gr. self-rule: **6**: 564, 667, 677, 716, 725, 727, 731, 780–1, 784, 824, 855, 872, 895, 1041, 1043–4, 1092, 1096–7, 1132, 1134–5, 1138–9, 1145, 1177, 1195, 1241, 1264, 1324, 1329–30, 1335, 1343, 1361. President of: **6**: 780–2. Fall of Athens: **6**: 727, 731, 784, 872. Ru.–Tur. Treaty of Ackerman (*see* Russia). US detachment from affairs of urged: **6**: 1145. Battle of Navarino—influence & reactions to: **6**: 1241, 1255, 1257, 1264, 1280–1, 1297, 1319, 1323–5, 1329, 1332, 1334, 1361, 1389–90, 1392. Fr. attack Gr. for armistice violations: **6**: 1398, 1400. Ru.–Tur. War (*see* Russia). Manumitted US slaves might fight for: **3**: 615 (*see also* Brown, James)
Green, Duff: Attacks C. on "Corrupt Bargain": **4**: 567, 576; **6**: 841. Attacks C. role in preparing "The Ky. Address" (1824) in his own behalf: **5**: 765–6, 951–2, 991. Characterizations of: **5**: 991. Charges JQA–Crawford attempted bargain in 1824 election: **6**: 182–3. Newspaper of supports AJ: **6**: 220, 841, 956. Ownership of *U.S. Telegraph*: **6**: 572–3. In 1828 election: **6**: 220, 841. Elected printer to US Sen. (1827): **6**: 373, 1372. Solicits Cong. printing business: **6**: 453. Defends AJ in "Corrupt Bargain" controversy: **6**: 841. Controversial mail route contracts with US: **6**: 1126, 1153, 1155
Grundy, Felix: Characterizations of: **6**: 70. Differs with C. on banking function of Ky. Insurance Co.: **1**: 166–8, 171–2, 180, 212, 214–5; **5**: 293–6; **6**: 293. Legal business with C.: **1**: 781, 799; **3**: 895; **4**: 417; **5**: 60–3, 66, 155, 1345; **6**: 60–3, 66. Opposition to Burr scheme (1806): **1**: 338. Service in US House: **1**: 491. As 1812 warhawk: **1**: 641, 643. Defeated in 1827 US House election in Tenn.: **4**: 847–8; **5**: 65; **6**: 515, 799, 892. Financial business with C.: **6**: 60–3, 66, 69–70, 155. As commissioner in later Ky. vs. Va. separation compact problems: **3**: 249–50. Solicits patronage favors from C.: **4**: 540; **5**: 65. Supports AJ in 1824 Pres. campaign: **3**: 361, 494. Shifts to AJ party: **6**: 515. Opposes Pres. nom. by Cong. caucus: **3**: 494–5. Opposition to private banks in Tenn.: **4**: 900, 902. On Old Court–New Court struggle in Ky.: **5**: 64

Guatemala. *See* Centre of America, Federation of the

Haiti (Santo Domingo): Whites in flee to US during slave rebellion: **4**: 760–1. C. on slave rebellion against Fr. in: **1**: 516; **2**: 494; **4**: 361, 760. C. on nation not vital to US security: **1**: 516. Attempt to supply naval aid to Christolphe: **1**: 642–3. Sp. attempt to reconquer: **2**: 494, 504. Internal disturbances in: **2**: 494, 504; **4**: 575; **6**: 278. US–Fr. commercial competition in: **6**: 224. US involvement in civil war in: **2**: 494, 501, 504. Concessions to GB shipping: **4**: 234, 441, 539. Concessions to Fr. shipping: **4**: 733; **5**: 281. Educational progress: **4**: 441. Fr. naval squadron visits: **4**: 506, 524, 539, 935. Fr. recognizes independence of: **4**: 524–5, 535, 539, 547–8, 575, 594, 640, 723, 775, 779, 935; **5**: 29, 83; **6**: 200, 224. Commercial treaty with Fr.: **4**: 524, 539, 723, 905; **5**: 36, 281, 355, 357. Character of natives of: **5**: 60. US slaves resettled in: **4**: 557. Fr. influence in: **4**: 723, 905; **5**: 281, 337, 343, 412; **6**: 74, 200–1. Legis. activities in: **5**: 36; **6**: 410. US merchants in: **6**: 693. Smallpox epidemic in: **5**: 179. As Fr. pseudo–colony: **5**: 281, 337, 343, 355, 412, 434–5, 494, 837. Fr. military pressure on: **6**: 200–1. Economic problems of: **5**: 430; **6**: 410. GB interest in: **6**: 74. Commercial treaty with GB: **6**: 159. Tariff policy of: **5**: 412; **6**: 74, 410. Free Negro (US) emigrants to: **6**: 92, 96. Hostility toward US: **6**: 410
—U.S. relations with: Proposed commercial treaty with: **4**: 506, 548; **5**: 60–1; **6**: 488. Nature & extent of US trade with: **4**: 441, 539, 548; **5**: 60; **6**: 74, 278, 410. US dominates merchant marine of: **6**: 74. Commercial recip. with: **4**: 548. On US recognition of: **4**: 723; **5**: 222, 281, 337, 434–5, 837. Lack of consular relations with: **5**: 101, 412; **6**: 74. Racial issue in: **5**: 60–1, 222, 332, 337; **6**: 410. Stake of US citizens in Fr. claims against: **4**: 539, 613, 640, 760–2, 921; **5**: 20, 97–8, 101, 163–4, 172, 241, 281, 355, 357, 366, 399, 430, 432, 528, 592, 607, 636, 647, 652, 686, 688, 796, 798, 818, 837; **6**: 193, 296, 565, 678. Unpopularity of US in: **5**: 412; **6**: 74. JQA opinion of Haiti: **5**: 28, 355, 434, 837. Consul Armstrong opposes US policy toward: **5**: 434–5. Armstrong requests recall: **6**: 250. US claims against: **4**: 235, 441, 548, 760–1, 809; **5**: 60, 163, 232–3; **6**: 693, 990. US Negro seamen desert ships in: **4**: 441. Tariff, duty, fee discrim. against US shipping: **4**: 723, 733. Harassment of US shipping: **5**: 101. Repeal export duties on US shippers: **6**: 248
Hammond, Charles: Family: **5**: 221, 223. Supports & advises C. in 1824 campaign: **3**: 244–6, 471, 505, 654–5, 758, 870–2. Hatred of AJ: **3**: 730. Legal business with C.: **3**: 13, 20–1, 114–5, 245, 259, 355, 549, 560. Opposition to BUS: **3**: 13, 20–1, 51, 112, 245, 259. Linked with

BUS: **5:** 69; **6:** 1200. Debt to BUS: **5:** 887. Failure of election to Cong.: **3:** 259, 309–10. Becomes Cincinnati newspaper editor: **3:** 310, 504. Temper of: **4:** 316. Interest in establishing Kenyon College: **3:** 471, 865. Supports C. in "Corrupt Bargain" controversy: **4:** 211, 285–6, 316, 387, 781. C. sanitizes political letter (**3:** 870) of: **4:** 285–6, 316, 387, 676. C. urges to attack AJ: **4:** 781, 783, 794. On Jacksonism in Ohio: **5:** 830. On AJ "Swartwout letter": **4:** 211, 286, 781. Newspaper of supports JQA admin.: **2:** 220–1; **4:** 472, 929. Newspaper read in White House: **6:** 632. C. opinion of: **6:** 929. C. assists with financial difficulties: **5:** 830, 887–8, 954–5; **6:** 929, 1084, 1156. On US trade difficulties with GB: **5:** 955, 1028. Advises C. on patronage: **5:** 955–6. On Rachel Jackson: **5:** 1023–4; **6:** 697–8. On 1826 Cong. elections: **5:** 1028–9. Compares Bolivar with AJ: **5:** 1029. On nature of anti–JQA coalition: **6:** 369–70. Analysis of coming 1828 Pres. election: **6:** 369–73, 1161. On C. as VP nominee in 1828: **6:** 371, 472. Attacks AJ expenditures while Gov. of Fla. Territory: **6:** 631–2. Writes & works for JQA reelection (1827–8): **6:** 631–2, 719, 1232–3, 1270. Analyzes Ohio politics for C.: **6:** 1199. Urges second US House investigation of "Corrupt Bargain" charge: **6:** 1160, 1200

Hammond, Jabez D.: Analyzes & advises C. on N.Y. politics: **3:** 415, 800–1; **5:** 175–6; **6:** 129–30, 386, 433–4, 451, 1246–7. Seeks public office: **6:** 338, 386, 434. C. discusses possible patronage appt. with: **6:** 386. Friend of Clinton: **6:** 550–1. Sees JQA victory in 1828: **6:** 551. Urges C. to campaign for JQA in N.Y.: **6:** 973–4

Hanover, Kingdom of: Commercial treaty with Prussia: **6:** 693. With Mex.: **6:** 880. US trade recip. with: **5:** 27; **6:** 1382. 1398

Hanseatic City States (Bremen, Hamburg, Lubeck): Trade with GB & Canada: **4:** 446, 562; **6:** 653. Commercial treaty with GB: **5:** 85, 94, 242. Commercial treaty with Mex.: **6:** 880. Trade mission with Br.: **6:** 82, 267–8. Commercial treaty with Br.: **6:** 82, 267–8. Depression in: **5:** 362, 554. Character of people: **6:** 517. German immigration to US: **6:** 802–3 —U.S. relations with: Recip. principle extended to: **4:** 116, 644, 931; **5:** 329, 504, 911. Commercial treaty with: **4:** 247; **6:** 273, 276, 392, 517–8, 521, 548, 605, 823, 1097, 1135, 1318–9, 1370–1. Shortage of US seamen in: **5:** 554. Extradition of US criminals from: **5:** 720, 1010; **6:** 36. Hamburg interpretation of recip.: **5:** 209. Tariff, duty, fee discrim. against US shipping & trade: **5:** 269, 504. Rumpff appt. Hanse Min. to US: **6:** 392, 517, 521, 548, 605, 981, 1370. Gallatin criticism of: **6:** 517. US tariff, duty, fee discrim. against: **6:** 521. Nature & extent of US trade with: **5:** 133–4, 362; **6:** 653, 802. US

consular relations with: **6:** 1097. *See also* Astor, John Jacob; Rumpff, Vincent

Hardin, Benjamin: Opposed US direct (land) tax to support military: **2:** 134. Brother serves as US Dist. Atty. for Ill.: **6:** 268

Hardin, Martin D.: Personal relations with C.: **2:** 344–5. Legal business with C.: **1:** 629, 799, 800, 801–2; **2:** 96, 161, 193, 238–9, 440; **3:** 238–9, 431, 438. Sec-State for Ky.: **1:** 721; **2:** 382. Deals with Indian problem during 1812 War: **1:** 807–8, 816. Political patronage, pension business with C.: **1:** 817, 841, 843–4, 863; **2:** 177. C. asks political advice of: **2:** 71–2. Connection with Bank of Ky.: **2:** 161. Opposes new bank in Louisville: **2:** 161–2. Urges C. to run for Gov. of Ky.: **2:** 439, 674, 753. Role in C. candidacy in 1824: **3:** 238–9

Harrison, Robert Monroe: Family & financial problems of: **4:** 446–7; **6:** 565, 757. Works to assist US seamen: **6:** 757. Poor opinion of Gov. of St. Bartholomew: **4:** 237; **6:** 1019. Analysis of GB trade policy in BWI: **4:** 702; **5:** 625, 697. Death of son Charles: **5:** 669. Seeks transfer from Antigua: **5:** 12, 141, 197, 669, 697, 716; **6:** 496. Anglophobia of: **5:** 625. On impressment & slave trade in West Indies: **6:** 202. Appt. US Consul at St. Bartholomew: **6:** 496, 565, 578, 665, 804–5, 834, 1019 (*see also* Sweden: U.S. relations with). Conducts intelligence mission through BWI for C.: **6:** 552–4, 785, 802, 912–3. Information sent C. on impact of GB & US trade–restriction legislation in BWI: **6:** 595–6, 802, 867–8, 912–4, 1191, 1288, 1377–8. Persona non grata at St. Bartholomew: **6:** 762. On the character of Swedes: **6:** 578

Harrison, William Henry: Family: **1:** 811; **4:** 495; **5:** 222–3. C. recommends for high command in War of 1812: **1:** 698–9, 713–4, 720, 724. Popularity in the West: **1:** 698–9, 713, 720. Plans for prosecuting War of 1812: **1:** 713–4. Commissioned Major General in Ky. Volunteers (1812): **1:** 719–21, 723, 724. Army of lacking in artillery & training (1812): **1:** 723. Opinion of Ky. volunteer militia troops (1812): **1:** 724. Summons C. to his headquarters to discuss operations & politics: **1:** 724–5. C. critical of generalship of: **1:** 799. Opposes brevet officers pay bill (1817): **2:** 312. On militia legis. after 1812 War: **2:** 477, 490. Ladies' man: **5:** 413. C. elector in 1824 Pres. election: **3:** 872. Considered for appt. as Min. to Mex.: **4:** 107; **6:** 473. Debt to Morrison Estate: **3:** 889–90. BUS rescues from bankruptcy: **5:** 396, 413. As Whig Pres. candidate in 1836: **4:** 494. JQA low opinion of: **6:** 473–4. Supports JQA admin.: **5:** 723, 918. Sponsors customs legis.: **6:** 192. Covets VP nomination in 1828: **6:** 473–4. Recollection of alleged C. "Corrupt Bargain" with JQA: **6:** 1003–5. On Sen. vote (3/7/25) on confir-

733

Harrison, William Henry (*continued*):
mation of C. as SecState: **6:** 1160,
1202–3
Hawaii (Sandwich Islands): Nature & extent
of US trade with: **4:** 749; **5:** 345; **6:** 736.
US whaling operations out of: **4:** 749; **6:**
736. Lawlessness of: **4:** 809; **6:** 736. GB
interest in: **4:** 749. US consular relations
with: **4:** 749–50, 760, 793. Destitute US
seamen in: **4:** 793. USN protects US commerce at: **5:** 345; **6:** 737. Fr. colonizing
effort in: **6:** 487. Consul requests USN
show flag: **6:** 736. US commercial treaty
with: **6:** 737
Hayne, Robert Y.: Elected (1822) US Sen.
in S.C.: **3:** 335. Opposes US participation
in Panama Cong.: **5:** 220, 222. On US
recognition of Haiti: **5:** 220, 222. JQA
newspaper seeks to blast: **2:** 431. On Fed.
bankruptcy legis.: **5:** 651
Hemp. *See* Clay, Henry: hemp culture
Hill, Isaac: Opposition to JQA admin.: **4:**
854–5; **5:** 152, 692. Contract to publish
laws during JQA admin.: **6:** 1361. Support of Crawford: **5:** 152–3. Control of
N.H. politics: **6:** 566, 603. Elected to
N.H. State Sen. (1827): **6:** 566–7
Holland. *See* Netherlands
Holley, Horace: Family: **2:** 594, 596; **3:**
904–5; **4:** 58; **5:** 124–5; **6:** 1244–5,
1267–8. Appt. Pres. of TU (*see* Transylvania University). Unitarian views of: **2:**
583; **6:** 461, 945. C. personal courtesies
to: **2:** 595. Political services to C.: **3:** 854;
4: 264–5. C. advice to on how best to run
TU: **2:** 613–4. Faculty criticism of: **4:**
266. Attack in Ky. legis. on: **2:** 780–1.
Dismissed from TU (*see* Transylvania
University). Supports C. in "Corrupt Bargain" controversy: **4:** 264–5. Criticized by
New Court–Reliefers: **4:** 265–6. Stays out
of local politics: **4:** 265–6. C. criticism of:
6: 385. Nephew & son aspire to USMA:
3: 904–5; **4:** 7; **6:** 1244. Brother Myron
in Anti–Mason & Liberty parties: **3:** 905.
Widow (Mary Austin Holley) seeks
USMA appt. for son: **6:** 1244–5, 1249,
1267. Death: **6:** 909, 1244–5, 1259,
1267–8. *See also* Transylvania University
Houston, Sam: Gov. candidate (1826) in
Tenn.: **5:** 699. Duel with White: **5:** 699.
Conflict with James Erwin: **5:** 699. Feels
it pointless to recommend patronage
appts. to C.: **6:** 103. Suggests (1824) C. as
AJ SecState: **6:** 573
Hughes, Christopher, Jr.: Family: **4:** 107,
451, 770, 784, 872, 874; **5:** 233; **6:** 105,
277. Wife (Laura Sophia Smith Hughes):
2: 260; **4:** 872; **6:** 275, 277. Aspires to
election to Cong.: **2:** 232. Attached to
Ghent Peace Commission as Sec.: **1:**
866–7, 1009; **4:** 451. C. recommends for
dip. appt.: **1:** 1009. Appt. as Sec. of
Legation in Stockholm: **2:** 231–2, 259,
315; **4:** 451. Economics of being Sec. of
Legation: **2:** 231–2. Importance of C.
role at Ghent: **2:** 74. Mission to Span.
Am.: **2:** 231. C. advice to as young diplomat: **2:** 259, 390, 817. Conflict with Rus-

sell in Ghent Legation: **2:** 426. Appt.
Chargé in Netherlands: **4:** 85–6, 138,
450; **5:** 280. C. instructions to in Netherlands: **5:** 280. C. supports career of: **1:**
1009; **4:** 324, 331, 731; **5:** 273. JQA
opinion of: **4:** 324, 331. Obsequiousness
to C.: **4:** 450, 771; **5:** 231, 1044. Impatience: **4:** 324. On his own long–
windedness: **4:** 451. Dip. successes of: **4:**
957; **5:** 1043. Writes unnecessary letters:
5: 620, 626; **6:** 670. Self–esteem: **4:**
517–8, 537, 956–7; **5:** 1043; **6:** 106,
135–6, 275, 675. C. fobs off: **4:** 784, 923.
On Swedish sale of warships to Mex.: **4:**
873. Shops for Mrs. C. in Baltimore: **4:**
873, 923, 949. C. refuses to support running for Gov. of Md.: **4:** 923. On Randolph defeat for Sen.: **6:** 277.
Congratulates C. on duel with Randolph:
5: 231–2. On political instability in Germany: **5:** 232. Reports on social & court
gossip & govt. events in Netherlands: **5:**
551, 555–6, 627; **6:** 106, 137, 672–5,
1043, 1110–1. Criticism of Alexander H.
Everett: **5:** 1043; **6:** 106. On threat of
war in Iberian Peninsula: **5:** 1044; **6:** 276,
1041. Predicts general European war: **5:**
1044; **6:** 105, 136. Sees no general European war after Navarino: **6:** 1323–5. On
Gr. independence & related wars: **6:**
670–1, 1041. Collects manuscript letters
of famous people: **6:** 1293–4. Anglophobia of: **6:** 671. On coming 1828 Pres.
election: **6:** 673–4. Canning toasts: **6:**
715–6. On Canning: **6:** 1041–2. On Port.
internal politics: **6:** 1041. On GB internal
politics: **6:** 1041–2, 1390–1. Class arrogance of: **6:** 276. Expense of living in
Brussels: **6:** 105, 274–5. Criticizes wife's
uncle (former SecState Robert Smith): **6:**
135–6, 138. Pursues US claims against
Denmark: **6:** 623–4. Lends money to in-
digent Americans in Europe: **6:** 274. Social life abroad: **6:** 274–5. On Fr. internal
politics: **6:** 670, 1325. Seeks promotion
from Chargé to Min.: **4:** 324; **6:** 275,
449. Has portrait painted: **6 :** 675

Illinois: Land–tax laws of: **3:** 104, 134. C.
land ownership in: **3:** 104, 134, 291, 346;
4: 491; **5:** 884; **6:** 1352. C. on quality of
land in: **3:** 105. Slavery controversy in: **4:**
534. Land taxes paid in: **3:** 104; **5:** 481,
884, 895; **6:** 1352. Cong. elections in
(1826): **4:** 541, 544; **5:** 481, 568, 584–5,
700, 710–11, 723, 755, 757, 761, 792; **6:**
46. AJ movement in: **5:** 700–1; **6:** 46–7,
808. Legis. endorses AJ candidacy: **6:** 47.
Anti–JQA sentiment in: **6:** 46–7, 808. Ill.
& Mich. Canal in: **6:** 506, 543–4, 807,
810. Indian lands in acquired by US: **6:**
1154–5. Change Pres. electoral laws: **6:**
46–7. Lead mines in: **6:** 1154. Politics of
Am. System in: **6:** 807, 809. JQA support, organization, prospects in: **6:** 46–7,
807–8, 1154. JQA patronage concerns in:
6: 269, 808–9, 1388. Gov. election (1826)
in: **4:** 541, 544. Selection of Pres. electors
in: **6:** 809–10. Jacksonians in support

"Virginia doctrines": **6:** 809. *See also* Election of 1828

Indiana: Lead mines in: **1:** 283. Swiss wine–growers colony in: **2:** 331, 333. Admission to Union: **2:** 332. Impact of Depression of 1819 on: **4:** 561–2. C. political popularity in: **4:** 561. Opposition to Pres. nominations by Cong. caucus: **3:** 551–3. Favors National Road extension to Miss. River: **3:** 570–1. Land of & taxes on C. land (Vigo Co.) in: **2:** 407–8; **3:** 134, 346, 456, 489, 877; **4:** 553, 560–1. Ladies of eulogize C. political accomplishments: **4:** 526–7. JQA admin. patronage concerns in: **4:** 488, 708, 710–11, 720–2. Cong. elections in (1826): **4:** 561–2; **5:** 711, 723, 757, 761, 792, 918–9, 1028. JQA popularity in: **5:** 561, 585. Slavery issue in: **4:** 866. Lake Erie–Wabash Canal project: **4:** 543–4; **5:** 82, 892–5. Depression in: **6:** 1211. Land acquisition treaties with Indians: **5:** 82. C. urged to campaign for JQA in: **6:** 516. Legis. of urges US aid to public land purchases: **6:** 857–8. JQA reelection organization & prospects in: **6:** 1061

Indians: C. resolution (1804) for relief of Chickasaws: **1:** 160–1. C. resolution (1807) for payment to whites for depredations by: **1:** 276, 278. C. racist views toward: **4:** 891–2. C. on as brutal savages: **1:** 334, 609, 846, 848; **2:** 160; **3:** 163. C. on why they fight white men: **1:** 729. C. on connections with GB: **1:** 450, 599, 642, 646, 674, 729 (*see also* Great Britain: Treaty of Ghent). C. would subject to extra–territoriality: **1:** 466. Ky. Volunteers march to fight in Indiana: **1:** 664–5 (*see also* Great Britain: War of 1812). Depredations of in Ky. during War of 1812: **1:** 807–8, 816. Recovery of captives of after War of 1812: **2:** 131–2, 139–40, 160–1. White hatred of: **2:** 138. White treatment of: **2:** 638–42. Attacks on Lewis & Clark Expedition: **2:** 229. Henderson Co. land purchase from in Ky.: **2:** 436–7. Self–govt. of as the natural govt. of man: **2:** 521. Portrait gallery of in D.C.: **6:** 676. As factor in Am.–Mex. relations (*see* Mexico: U.S. relations with). Not independent or sovereign nations: **2:** 657. Applicability of US law to: **5:** 770. Disorderly behavior of in Ark.: **3:** 631. Creek removal from Ga. (*see* Georgia). Indian students at Kenyon Seminary (*see* Education). Sale of lands blocking internal improvements: **5:** 82, 892–3. Allied with Texans in Fredonian Rebellion: **6:** 114. Senecas sell N.Y. state lands to white man: **6:** 487–8, 489, 558–9. Cherokee removal from Ga. (*see* Georgia). Patronage & corruption in US Dept. of Indian Affairs: **6:** 1153–4. Civil war in St. Regis tribe: **6:** 1340, 1369, 1374. Osage troop exhibited in Europe: **6:** 980–2, 1258–9, 1399–1400

—U.S. relations with: White prisoners of: **4:** 137. War with Seminoles (*see* Jackson, Andrew). Creek land cession: **4:** 426,

501–2. Indian Springs Treaty (Creeks): **4:** 501–2. C. on Indian Springs Treaty (Creeks): **4:** 585–6. US conflict with Ga. on (*see* Georgia). Black Hawk war (1832): **6:** 1155. Negotiations with for Indian lands: **5:** 82. Threatened war & treaty with Winnebagos: **6:** 1087–9, 1154–5, 1295. Claims growing out of wars & treaties with: **6:** 637–9. US–Cherokee treaties (1816; 1819): **6:** 490, 505. US–Creek Treaty (1814): **2:** 638–40, 660–1. Constit. of treaties with: **2:** 545. Vagueness of US treaties with: **6:** 1295

Inventions: C. law cases related to new: **1:** 145, 297. Nail-making machinery: **1:** 145, 297. General C. interest in: **2:** 896. Stronger gun–powder: **1:** 281–2. Hemp machinery: **3:** 219, 735, 775, 830 (*see also* Clay, Henry: hemp culture). Brick machine: **1:** 555–6, 562, 566. Steam–driven water pump: **2:** 397. Lighthouse lanterns: **2:** 459, 465. Steamboat: **2:** 459, 831; **3:** 711. Oliver Evans steam engine: **2:** 570–1. Spinning jenny: **2:** 829, 831. Cotton gin: **2:** 831. *See also* U.S. Patent Office

Ingersoll, Charles Jared: On canal development: **1:** 845. As JQA admin. candidate in Pa.: **5:** 704. Appt. US Atty. for E. Pa.: **5:** 208; **6:** 356–7. Professional incompetence (Tea Cases): **6:** 356–8. Political ingrate: **6:** 356

Ingersoll, Edward: Family: **6:** 889. Character: **6:** 1364–5. Supports C. in 1824 election: **3:** 829, 836; **4:** 333. Supports C. in "Corrupt Bargain" controversy: **4:** 333. Advises C. on Jacksonian activities in Pa.: **4:** 333; **6:** 282–3. Anti–AJ political activities in Pa.: **5:** 703–4. Works for JQA in 1828 campaign: **5:** 703, 886, 947. On JQA patronage appts. in Pa.: **6:** 282. Solicits information on St. Lawrence navigation issue: **5:** 412–3. Analyzes Pa. politics for C.: **4:** 333–4; **5:** 407–8, 703–4, 885–7. Seeks Chargé appt. in Denmark: **6:** 281–2, 1365. Analysis of "Corrupt Bargain" issue: **6:** 885–8

Isacks, Jacob C.: Involvement in Berkely attack on C. "Corrupt Bargain": **6:** 1161–2, 1219 (*see also* Election of 1828: Corrupt Bargain issue & related campaign literature)

Jackson (Andrew) Administration: Claims Convention (1831) with Fr.: **5:** 1015. Claims Convention (1833) with Br.: **5:** 1022. Claims Convention (1834) with Sp.: **6:** 194. Proscription of JQA appointees: **6:** 168, 195

Jackson, Andrew: C. first impression of: **6:** 1114. C. represents in land claim suit: **1:** 250. On Alien & Sedition Acts (1798): **6:** 580. Entertained at C. home: **6:** 1115. Interest in training & breeding race horses: **1:** 250, 712. Shoot–out with the Benton brothers (1813): **1:** 820; **6:** 811–2. Duels & brawls: **1:** 820; **5:** 416–7; **6:** 811–2. Execution of six Tenn. militiamen (1814): **5:** 739 (*see also* Election of

Legal problems of: **3**: 3–4, 120–1. Proposal in US House to raise troops for War of 1812: **1**: 748–50. Favors additional military academies: **2**: 123. C. assists brother of to obtain govt. contract: **2**: 598–9, 605, 799–800; **3**: 89. Establishes school for Indians (Choctaw Academy): **2**: 605. Financial problems of: **3**: 89, 99–100, 102, 124–5, 418, 485, 559, 811–3; **4**: 573. Urged to run for Ky. Gov.: **2**: 671. Suit against by Ky. BUS branch: **2**: 773–4; **3**: 89, 99, 121–2, 430–1, 812–3. C. supports BUS in Johnson matter: **3**: 99, 103. C. awkward position in BUS–Johnson matter: **3**: 102–3. C. works out compromise in BUS–Johnson matter: **3**: 121–3, 141, 144, 418, 485, 557–60, 597, 811–2. Assists C. in claims matter: **3**: 182, 189, 195, 257–8. Supports C. in 1824 campaign: **3**: 182–3. Patronage recommendations to C.: **6**: 40, 207, 1389. Supports Jacksonians in 19th Cong.: **6**: 395. Supports US House legis. of personal interest to C.: **3**: 195. Support of JQA admin.: **5**: 158–9. On Fed. bankruptcy legis.: **5**: 651. Wins US House seat (1827): **6**: 971. Supports Jacksonians in Ky.: **6**: 724, 727, 877, 917, 1142. Supports AJ in 1828 campaign: **6**: 1129

Johnston, Josiah S.: Family: **5**: 805–6; **6**: 387, 408. Supports & advises C. in 1824 campaign: **3**: 787–8, 807–9, 814–6, 817–21, 824–5, 829, 836–7, 840–1, 843–5, 851–3, 854, 856, 859, 861–2, 869–70. Slave owner: **3**: 439. Campaign for Sen. (1824) in La.: **3**: 823, 854. Friend of C.: **3**: 776. Philosophical attitude toward political victory or defeat: **3**: 837. Leans toward AJ (1826): **5**: 267. Financial problems of: **6**: 568. On GB trade restrictions: **6**: 239–40, 387. Reading habits of: **6**: 569–70. Not interested in being Gov. of La.: **6**: 570, 576. Speculation in US slave indemnity claims: **6**: 576. Recollection of US House vote for Pres. (2/9/25): **6**: 1275–6. Supports JQA & advises C. on 1828 election: **6**: 568–9, 796–7, 1035. Financial support of JQA reelection campaign: **6**: 1243

Kendall, Amos: Family: **4**: 78, 943; **5**: 535. C. hires to tutor his children: **2**: 53–4, 116, 392–3; **4**: 747. C. family kindness to: **2**: 54, 116; **3**: 237; **4**: 77–8; **5**: 989. C. assistance to newspaper of: **2**: 632–4, 674–5. Urges C. to run for Ky. Gov.: **2**: 768. Interest in "Lancaster system" of education: **2**: 822–3. Supports C. in 1824 campaign: **3**: 236–8, 240, 409, 543, 674; **4**: 134–5. On Pres. contest in US House (1824–5): **4**: 35. Connection with Ky. Relief Party: **3**: 237; **4**: 35. Supports relief legis.: **3**: 675; **4**: 78–9. Financial indebtedness to C.: **5**: 534–5; **6**: 993. Cowan assault on: **3**: 674–5. Works to release Ky. House delegation from Ky. legis. instructions to vote for AJ (2/9/25): **4**: 41. Supports C. SecState decision: **4**: 77, 81,

134–5. Sees AJ–Clinton alliance in 1828 election: **4**: 81. In Old Court vs. New Court fight: **4**: 134–5, 719, 942. Personal financial problems: **4**: 135–6, 306; **5**: 534–5. Advises C. to withdraw from Ky. state politics: **4**: 134–5. Opinion of AJ: **4**: 719. C. disagrees with Ky. state politics of: **4**: 747–8. Considers job in State Dept.: **4**: 305–6, 718, 746–7, 943; **5**: 776, 950. Break with C.: **4**: 719. C. charged with attempt to bribe: **5**: 989. As slave owner: **5**: 534; **6**: 993. Political enemies bring suits against: **5**: 534. Characterizations of: **5**: 989, 991. Supports AJ in 1828: **5**: 989–90. Editorial policy of newspaper of: **5**: 994. Leads "Frankfort Junto": **6**: 413. On 1827 Woolen Bill: **6**: 373. Campaign ethics of: **6**: 1121. *Argus* loses public printing contract: **5**: 991, 994; **6**: 381–2. Supports (1827) "Corrupt Bargain" charge against C.: **6**: 1071–2, 1121, 1131–2, 1136, 1206–7, 1260

Kent, Joseph: Patronage suggestions: **4**: 137–8, 709; **5**: 608, 1015; **6**: 124, 191–2, 493. Elected Gov. of Md. (1826): **4**: 923; **5**: 55. On JQA admin. support in Md.: **6**: 123. Political power of in Md.: **6**: 124. Supports C. on "Corrupt Bargain" charge: **6**: 742–3

Kentucky:
—general: Becomes state: **3**: 162, 169, 215. Class dimensions of Constit. of 1792: **1**: 8, 11, 14. C. on Constit. of 1792: **1**: 3–8, 10–14. Indian policy: **2**: 436–7, 566, 605. Prison legis. **1**: 431–2; **3**: 881. Educational system: **4**: 818. Teaching opportunities: **6**: 237. Master–slave relationship in: **3**: 438–40, 563. Ky. Colonization Society: **6**: 31 (*see also* Slavery & slaves)
—agricultural & economic development: Economic distress: **1**: 85, 98–9, 150; **2**: 699 (in 1819); **3**: 328, 330, 440, 465. Economic boom in: **1**: 458, 489; **2**: 383 (in 1817). Panic & Depression of 1819 in: **2**: 699–701; **3**: 12, 76, 107, 123, 328, 330, 440, 465, 734–5. Relief of debtors in: **1**: 124–5 (*see also* below New Court (Relief) party). Payment of debts owed state: **1**: 211–2, 215, 391. State burns worthless paper money: **3**: 330. Importance of N.O. to: **1**: 99, 140, 453, 455, 623–4, 828; **2**: 111, 206 (*see also* New Orleans). Importance of Miss. River trade to: **1**: 623–4. Shortages of specie in: **1**: 702–3; **3**: 328, 330. Relation of US tariff policies to: **2**: 303; **3**: 703, 728 (*see also* American System: protective tariff). Wealth of Ky. is in its land: **3**: 318. State land legis.: **1**: 252, 391, 396, 399, 582, 803, 898, 900. Land sales & prices in: **1**: 150, 525; **2**: 383. Complex & overlapping land titles in Ky.: **1**: 898–9. C. work as Ky. Commissioner to Va. (Va.–Ky. Conv.) under Occupying Claimant Law (1797): **3**: 151, 153–6, 158–70, 175–7, 207–9, 215–8, 249–50, 288, 301–5, 326–7, 340, 343–4, 350, 352, 357–60, 377–8, 384–5, 389–90, 398, 512–5,

737

lutions in Italy: **3:** 87. On revolutionary leadership of Fr. in Europe: **3:** 87. On Span. Revolution (1820): **3:** 311–2, 498. Portrait of presented US House: **4:** 12–3, 193, 362. Biographies of: **4:** 210, 700. Wants USN squadron in Eastern Mediterranean: **3:** 311–2; **5:** 137, 401. Lauds Bolivar: **5:** 837. Doubts Bolivar: **6:** 1133. On Beaumarchais claims against US: **3:** 312–3, 498; **4:** 850. Mentioned as VP of US in 1824: **3:** 827. Tour (1824–5) of US: **3:** 816, 853, 855–6, 867–8; **4:** 12–3, 56–7, 226, 618, 624–5, 627, 632, 700, 848, 865, 905; **5:** 284. Visits Ky.: **4:** 12, 19, 56–7, 82, 226, 489. Reception, tributes & gifts in Wash.: **3:** 893–4, 899–900; **4:** 19, 39, 227, 850; **5:** 837; **6:** 43. Linked to AJ candidacy in 1824–5: **4:** 39. Visits Lex. (*see* Lexington, Ky.). Urged not to enter Fr. domestic politics: **4:** 735–6, 905; **5:** 72, 429, 1049; **6:** 438, 1258. Elected to Chamber of Deputies (June 1827): **6:** 438–9, 725, 1132, 1258. On US policy in Haiti: **5:** 837. On Holy Alliance: **5:** 51. On Austria: **5:** 51, 401. On growth of civil liberty in Fr.: **5:** 72. On republican institutions: **5:** 198. On penal reform: **5:** 401–2. On agricultural reform: **5:** 402. On future of liberty & equality in Europe: **5:** 836–7. Supports C. on "Corrupt Bargain" charge: **6:** 870, 873–4, 1091, 1133–4, 1194, 1258, 1357, 1363, 1385, 1399. On European counter–revolutionary movements: **5:** 1050. Dunned by Americans in Fr.: **5:** 1050–1; **6:** 43. Urges silk industry in US: **6:** 1008. In Revolution of 1830: **6:** 439. C. presents published speeches to: **6:** 613, 981. On Fr. domestic politics: **6:** 1132, 1134. On European intervention in Gr.–Tur. war: **6:** 1132–3. Son (George Washington Lafayette) elected to Fr. Chamber of Deputies: **6:** 1258–9. Secures copies of his war letters to George Washington: **6:** 1293

Latrobe, Benjamin Henry: Consulted on TU building: **1:** 652, 655, 676, 678–83. Work for USN Dept.: **1:** 655–6. Proud of his college buildings: **1:** 656, 678–9. Builds steam engine for N.O. water works: **1:** 658. Designs wings of "Ashland": **1:** 791, 818, 823, 851. Steamboat building venture: **1:** 818, 848–9. Designs & consults on Lex. buildings for C.: **1:** 818, 820, 823, 851–2. Legal business with C.: **1:** 835. Offers to design new statehouse for Ky.: **1:** 848–9. Family problems of: **1:** 835–6. Designs Decatur House in Wash.: **5:** 207 (*see also* Washington, D.C.)

Law, Thomas: Family: **6:** 322–3. Seeks patronage favors from C.: **6:** 272. Sees God's immutable principles in every science: **6:** 1045. Scheme for financing US internal improvements: **6:** 188–90, 321–2. Urges Chesapeake & Ohio Canal: **6:** 188, 322. On fluctuations in national economy: **6:** 1044–5

Lawrence, William Beach: Mentioned as sec. to Panama Cong. delegation: **4:** 889–91, 904. Connection with Rufus King family: **4:** 889–90. Appt. US Sec. of Legation in GB: **4:** 890; **5:** 379, 480, 494–5, 527, 638, 728, 731. Appt. US Chargé in GB: **6:** 1108, 1137, 1309. Urges US non–involvement in Gr.: **6:** 1145. Studies legal bases of GB commercial system: **6:** 1255. *See also* Great Britain

Leigh, Benjamin Watkins: C. legal business with: **2:** 726–7, 733, 735–6, 749, 754, 767, 796, 821, 849; **3:** 320, 378, 499–50, 550, 801–2, 897, 900. As Va. Commissioner on Va.–Ky. land problems (Occupying Claimant Law): **3:** 177, 209, 217, 219, 249, 318. C. instructs on best way to travel from Va. to Ky.: **3:** 177. Political philosophy of: **3:** 318–9. Position in 1824 campaign: **3:** 867. Activity in 1828 campaign: **3:** 591, 1307. Defends JQA: **6:** 186. Urges Clinton replace JQA and/or AJ as Pres. candidate (1828): **6:** 1307

Letcher, Robert Perkins: Family: **4:** 433. Resigns as judge for Arkansas Territory: **2:** 764–5. Role in "Corrupt Bargain" controversy: **4:** 41; **6:** 967, 1014. Retains US House seat (1827): **6:** 960, 966. Criticizes US Supreme Court on *Green vs. Biddle*: **3:** 746, 753–6; **4:** 43. Supports JQA over AJ in House vote (2/9/25) for Pres.: **4:** 79. Supports Panama Mission: **5:** 81–2. On Buchanan role in AJ charge of "Corrupt Bargain" against C. (*see* Buchanan, James). On JQA prospects in 1828 election: **6:** 1034. C. financial dealings with: **6:** 1355

Lexington, Ky.: Cultural life in: **1:** 121, 281, 435, 563–4, 840; **2:** 230; **6:** 734. Dancing school: **3:** 753. Beck Academy: **1:** 322. Lex. (Lafayette) Female Academy: **3:** 265–6. English & Classical Academy: **3:** 885. Free school for Negroes: **2:** 683, 685. Sayre Female Academy: **4:** 713. Stickney School for Girls: **5:** 546. C. work for library in: **1:** 563–5, 708–9; **2:** 338. Theater in: **6:** 734. Newspapers in: **4:** 265–6, 305; **5:** 750–1; **6:** 734, 1173–4. Gossip in: **1:** 126. Lunatic Asylum: **4:** 552. Attempts to move State capital to: **1:** 124, 314; **4:** 415 (*see also* Frankfort, Ky.). C. legal work for: **1:** 201–3. C. legis. affecting: **1:** 161, 212–3. Street improvements: **1:** 406, 419–20. Lottery–supported town improvements: **1:** 406. Canal construction: **1:** 445. Interest in Maysville–Lex. road: **2:** 569; **5:** 881–2; **6:** 1150, 1174. Courthouse building: **1:** 652–3. Superior land near: **1:** 898. Land prices: **2:** 383. Health problems in: **1:** 53, 850; **3:** 260; **6:** 1360. C. popularity in: **2:** 406; **6:** 734. Horse–racing in: **1:** 97, 272–3. Climate & weather: **6:** 112. Crime & jail in: **1:** 473–4; **2:** 227, 338, 589; **3:** 777–8; **4:** 265–305. C. town & county taxes paid: **1:** 63, 171, 217–8, 276, 402–3, 526, 573, 628, 735; **2:** 225–6, 306–7, 361, 585–6, 665, 774; **3:** 203,

Lexington, Ky. (*continued*):
877; **4:** 511, **5:** 566, 569. Industries & enterprises in: **1:** 345, 480, 484; **2:** 67, 159–60, 163, 371–2, 875–6. Textile & cotton bagging industries in: **1:** 264, 298, 473, 479–80; **2:** 876, 878–80, 887, 890; **3:** 236, 442, 644, 648, 659–60; **5:** 216–7, 847. **6:** 1210–11. C. Tammany Mill in: **2:** 806–7, 886–7, 893, 899; **3:** 72, 75, 235–6. **4:** 503, 667–8, 732, 758–9, 764. Tammany Mill labor costs: **2:** 893. Paper–making: **2:** 570–1; **6:** 1211. Gunpowder mfgr.: **3:** 521. Distillery business: **3:** 509. Rope–making in: **1:** 484; **3:** 443, 648; **4:** 758–9; **5:** 216–7 (*see also* Clay, Henry: hemp culture). Sail cloth mfgr.: **2:** 875–6, 877–81. Sail cloth sold to USN: **2:** 876–81. Publishing business: **1:** 254, 327, 747; **3:** 74, 360; **4:** 80. Insurance business: **6:** 112. Consumer prices in: **2:** 388, 394. C. property owned in (1807–12): **1:** 217–8, 276, 402, 526, 628; (1826): **5:** 178. C. ownership of Kentucky Hotel (*see* Kentucky Hotel in Name Index). Slave trading in: **2:** 215, 237, 707, 893; **3:** 488–9. Slave labor in Lex. industries: **3:** 443–4, 642, 649. Free Negroes in: **1:** 79, 300, 418, 445. **2:** 123, 363. Support for Am. Colonization Society in: **6:** 840–1 (*see also* Slavery & slaves). Response to War of 1812 in: **1:** 698, 713, 718–9, 782–3, 821, 997; **2:** 254, 256 (*see also* Great Britain: War of 1812). C. visualizes as leading western banking center: **2:** 903. BUS branch in: **2:** 235, 257–8, 262, 276–7, 281, 287, 307, 346, 635, 687–8, 699, 876–7, 903–4. Politics in BUS–Lex. Branch: **2:** 277, 281, 699–700. Threat to close BUS–Lex. Branch: **4:** 824–5. Banking industry in Lex.: **2:** 729. Banks in resume specie payments: **2:** 346. C. as share holder in Farmers & Mechanics: **2:** 575–6. Financial support in for TU: **1:** 77–8; **6:** 883 (*see also* Transylvania University). Pro–AJ & Relief Party sentiment in: **4:** 265, 305–6. Reaction in to "Corrupt Bargain" charge against C.: **4:** 305; **6:** 776 (*see also* Adams (John Q.) administration: "Corrupt Bargain" controversy during"). Attitudes in toward Am. System: **6:** 734. Pres. election (1828) politics in: **6:** 839–41, 1120–3, 1360. Major C. campaign (1828) speeches in (6/29/27; 7/12/27; 7/21/27): **6:** 728–31, 733, 763–9, 840–1, 948, 1203 (*see also* Election of 1828: "Corrupt Bargain" issue & related campaign literature). Disorderly elections in Lex.: **6:** 876. Postmaster patronage politics in: **1:** 839, 842; **3:** 33–4; **6:** 915–7, 1121–2, 1204. Prominent natives of: **4:** 206–7. Distinguished visitors to: Lafayette: **3:** 855–6, 868; **4:** 56–7, 82, 226; Monroe: **2:** 700–1; Poletica: **2:** 885; **3:** 74; Winfield Scott: **4:** 502

Liberia: Origin of name: **6:** 95. Am. Colonization Society founds colony in: **6:** 85, 95. US assist: **6:** 95. As a sovereign nation: **6:** 85. Population (1827): **6:** 85. War with neighboring tribes: **6:** 95. C. sees as an "Am. Colony": **6:** 88. Negro emigrants to will carry Christianity, civilization, liberty: **6:** 92–3. US commercial potential in: **6:** 222. *See also* Slavery & slaves: Am. Colonization Society

Livingston, Edward: Family: **3:** 422; **4:** 334, 555; **5:** 88. Life & success in N.O.: **1:** 172–3. Batture claim of: **1:** 456. Elected (1822) to Cong.: **3:** 249. Legal work for John Clay: **3:** 338–9. On the tariff: **3:** 658–60; **5:** 971–2. Supports AJ in 1824: **3:** 828; **4:** 555. Defeated (1825) for US Sen.: **4:** 15. Recommends patronage appt. to C.: **4:** 600; **6:** 207. Leans to support of JQA admin.: **5:** 71. Reelected to Cong. (1826): **5:** 635, 815

Louisiana Purchase Treaty (1804): C. on inclusion of West Fla. in: **1:** 508, 510–2. C. on inclusion of Texas in: **2:** 771. Transfer from Sp. to Fr. to US: **1:** 983. Sale of Fed. land acquired in: **6:** 636, 963. Slavery in Mo. Compromise debate: **2:** 742. Slavery in: **6:** 90. Cheap price paid by US: **6:** 1014

Louisiana: Advantages of internal improvements to: **2:** 310; **5:** 635. Pushes Miss. River improvements: **5:** 245. Lafayette's landholdings & claims in (*see* Lafayette, Marquis de). Slavery issue in politics of: **5:** 635. Sugar crop in: **2:** 899. Cotton crop in: **2:** 899. Judgeship, patronage, politics in: **5:** 267. US Cong. elections (1826) in: **5:** 568, 584–5, 635, 711, 815; **6:** 177. Legis. problems in: **3:** 352–3. Climate: **5:** 982. Prospects for lawyers in: **5:** 982. Boom & bust in cotton prices in: **6:** 568–9. Gov. election (1828) in: **6:** 568–70, 576. State Conv. (11/5/27) to elect JQA Pres. electors: **6:** 796–7, 1159. JQA political organization & prospects in: **6:** 796–7, 1159, 1332. Crawford political faction in: **6:** 797. AJ political organization & prospects in: **6:** 545, 724, 797

Louisiana (Orleans) Territory (1804–1812): US military pressure on Sp. to relinquish La. after purchase from Fr.: **1:** 122–3. C. opinion on Am. settlement of La.: **1:** 122, 124–5. Am. emigration to: **1:** 228, 453, 467–8. Political organization of: **1:** 141, 160, 289, 375, 454. C. interest in La. lands & land titles: **1:** 122, 216–7, 222–6, 468. Proposed Span. reconquest (1814): **6:** 1169. Confusion of land titles (Span., Fr., Indian) in: **1:** 222–6; **2:** 331, 853. Land policies of legis. of: **1:** 224–5. Descriptions & impressions of: **1:** 226. Govt. of: **1:** 289, 375–6, 453–4, 470. Weak judicial system in: **1:** 454. Incorporation of West Fla. into: **1:** 455, 456, 640; **3:** 353. Boundary problems of: **1:** 455. C. supports statehood for: **1:** 469–70, 522, 524, 639. La. Constit. Conv. (1811): **1:** 596, 635, 639–40. Earthquakes in: **1:** 651–2, 659, 663. Slave prices in: **3:** 439. *See also* Burr, Aaron; New Orleans

Louisville, Ky.: C. supports state bank for & in: **2:** 162. C. purchase of real estate in: **1:** 261–2, 306–7. C. supports branch of

742

BUS in: **2**: 369, 599, 710. C. on growth & commercial prospects of: **2**: 369; **4**: 523. Stake in internal improvements by US: **2**: 487, **4**: 523. Louisville (Falls of the Ohio) Canal: **4**: 29, 33, 523; **5**: 590, 965. Shipbuilding (steamboats) industry in: **2**: 800–1. Distillery industry in: **3**: 1–3. Marine hospital for river seamen: **4**: 779. Newspapers in: **5**: 861–2. Lack of JQA support in: **5**: 861. Relief & Anti–Relief parties ally behind AJ in: **5**: 861. AJ sentiment in: **5**: 861, 990

Lowndes, William: Possible Pres. candidate (*see* Election of 1824: William Lowndes candidacy). 1812 warhawk: **1**: 621. On Mo. Compromise: **3**: 20. Opposes recognition of Span. Am. nations: **3**: 24, 548. On the tariff: **2**: 138, 173, 175, 183, 839, 846. On constit. of internal improvements: **2**: 446. Monroe admin. supporter in US House: **2**: 851–2. Death: **3**: 201, 470

McArthur, Duncan: Service in War of 1812: **2**: 6–7. Legal business with C.: **3**: 7–9, 16; **5**: 972; **6**: 310–1, 454–6, 557, 999–1000. Supports C. in 1824 campaign: **3**: 205, 258, 309. Explains vote for JQA in 1825 House Pres. election: **4**: 163; **6**: 557–8

McDuffie, George: On motives of officers & men in service: **3**: 565–7. On tariff on whiskey: **3**: 635–6, 638. Sectionalism of tariffs: **3**: 648. Opposes C. on tariff: **3**: 703, 728. Duels of: **5**: 233–4, 354. Support of AJ: **5**: 234. Opposition to Panama Cong.: **5**: 278. Possible duel with D. Trimble: **5**: 278, 309, 354, 360. Attack on JQA admin. use of patronage: **5**: 658, 661–2, 725. Personal political attacks on C.: **5**: 232; **6**: 931–2. Supports "Corrupt Bargain" charge against C.: **4**: 85; **5**: 279–80, 656; **6**: 840–1, 886, 888, 931, 1160–1

McGiffin, Thomas: Advises C. on Pa. politics: **6**: 209–12. Recommends patronage appt. to C.: **4**: 877. Low bidder on govt. contracts: **4**: 714. Assists C. fight on "Corrupt Bargain" charge: **6**: 1205, 1396

McLane, Louis: On C.–Randolph duel: **5**: 231. Recommends patronage appt. to C.: **4**: 377. Urges C. acceptance of SecState post: **4**:74. Supports Crawford in 1824: **4**: 74. On Panama Mission issue: **6**: 498, 500. Stance in 1828 election: **6**: 381, 445, 507, 531. Shift to AJ camp: **6**: 370, 374, 381, 445, 531. Elected to US Sen. (1827): **6**: 361–2, 555. On Federalist party in Del.: **6**: 445

McLean, John: Family: **4**: 892–3. Obligation to Calhoun: **6**: 1155. Supports Calhoun in 1824 campaign: **3**: 259, 436; **5**: 7–8. Close connection with Calhoun: **3**: 259; **6**: 210, 373, 971. Appt. Postmaster General: **3**: 436–37. Patronage concerns of: **4**: 892–3. Opposition to in Ohio: **5**: 7–8. Sentiment for his removal as Postmaster General: **5**: 175, 265; **6**: 372–3. Mentioned for US Supreme

Court: **5**: 221–3. Loyalty to JQA admin. questioned: **5**: 221, 253, 265; **6**: 210–1, 372–3, 473, 940–1, 1153, 1155, 1161, 1204. Views on Panama Cong. Mission: **6**: 941. Views on Anglo–Am. trade: **6**: 941. Opposition to JQA admin.: **6**: 941. Professes loyalty to JQA admin.: **6**: 1161. Deceives JQA: **6**: 1204. As possible VP candidate (1828): **6**: 970. Views on tariff: **6**: 941

McNairy, Boyd: Asks C. for patronage favors: **5**: 922. Supports JQA admin.: **5**: 922. Political advice to C.: **5**: 922

Madison, James: On Alien & Sedition laws: **2**: 469–70; **3**: 738. C. supports for Pres. in 1808: **1**: 320–1. C. supports admin. of: **1**: 557; **2**: 480. View of US Constit.: **3**: 738. White House parties of: **1**: 458. On internal improvements: **2**: 479–81; **4**: 32. C. supports West Fla. policy of (1810): **1**: 513–4, 522. East Fla. policy of: **1**: 519–544. Cabinet shake–up (1811) of: **1**: 557, 563. On USN needs (1811): **1**: 618. C. urges to war against GB: **1**: 637. C. fears political impact of military defeats on admin. of: **1**: 713, 770. C. influence on war policies of admin. of: **1**: 723, 727. Criticism of for disasters in War of 1812: **1**: 725, 750, 770, 782. Clerks in admin. critical of during War of 1812: **1**: 119–20. Reorganizes Cabinet better to prosecute war: **1**: 750–1, 777. Cabinet shake–up (1814): **1**: 866, 877, 888, 895, 897. Admin. of accused of pro–Fr. orientation: **1**: 754, 757. C. criticizes war leadership of: **1**: 750, 782. C. eulogizes personal qualities of: **1**: 763; **2**: 480. Supports 2nd BUS: **3**: 620, 626. Offers C. Sec War post in Cabinet: **2**: 226, 233; **4**: 56; **5**: 657. Offers C. Min. to Ru. post: **2**: 88–9; **4**: 56; **5**: 657. On neutrality in Sp. wars in Span. Am.: **2**: 292. Pro–Span. Am. attitudes of: **2**: 497. Vetoes Bonus (internal improvements) Bill (1817): **2**: 311, 468, 480–2. On the tariff: **3**: 740–3; **6**: 1175–6, 1386. C. personal relations with: **3**: 888. Correspondence with Lafayette: **5**: 875–6. Writes pamphlet on maritime neutral rights (1806–8): **6**: 349–50, 394, 418. Assistance to Univ. of Va. Library: **6**: 349–50, 394. Efforts to involve in 1828 Pres. campaign: **6**: 1077, 1157, 1175–6, 1356, 1386. Opposes extreme Va. states rights stances on protective tariff: **6**: 1175–6. *See also* Spain empire: Florida, East; & Florida, West; Great Britain: War of 1812

Maine: JQA admin. support in: **5**: 726. AJ movement in: **5**: 726–7, 748. Cong. delegates support JQA in House election (2/9/25): **5**: 726–7. Tariffs levied on products by New Brunswick: **6**: 584. US Cong. elections (1827) in: **6**: 820–1, 1085. Arguments for admission to statehood: **2**: 740. Statehood linked to Mo. admission: **2**: 740–3, 744–6; **3**: 15. Constit. of admission: **2**: 745. Land taxes rise after statehood: **3**: 78. JQA admin. patronage policy in: **5**: 721, 726–7. *See also*

743

Maine (*continued*):
Great Britain: role & involvement of Maine in Northeastern boundary controversy

Mangum, Willie Persor: Supports Crawford in 1824: **4:** 74. Urges C. acceptance of SecState post: **4:** 74

Marcy, William L.: Characterized: **5:** 764. Supports Van Buren: **5:** 348, 764

Markley, Philip Swenk: Defends JQA–C. on "Corrupt Bargain": **4:** 84. Analyzes Pa. politics for C.: **4:** 423–30; **6:** 283–4, 493–4, 571. Urges AJ (Jan. 1825) to appt. C. as SecState if elected by US House: **6:** 1162. Episcopal church work: **6:** 493. Work for JQA reelection: **6:** 283–4, 304, 493–4, 571. Appointed to Philadelphia Custom House patronage position: **6:** 282, 355, 955, 1105, 1394. C. defends appt. of to Philadelphia Custom House: **6:** 1394. Character of: **6:** 841. Explains Buchanan role in events (1824–5) leading to "Corrupt Bargain" charge against C.: **6:** 840–1, 850, 954–5, 1023, 1030, 1034, 1105, 1112, 1152, 1162, 1212–3, 1218–9, 1225, 1231–2, 1237, 1247 (*see espec.* **6:** 1218–9; *also* Election of 1828: Corrupt Bargain issue & related campaign literature)

Marshall, Humphrey: Family: **1:** 246; **3:** 133, 138. Ethics of: **1:** 238–9. Financial dealings with C.: **2:** 399. Leads Ky. Federalists: **1:** 245. Legal business with C.: **1:** 587; **2:** 705, 911–2. Associated with C. in land transactions: **1:** 247, 310. Conflicts with C.: **1:** 260, 320. C. attacks: **1:** 329, 351. C. duel with: **1:** 397–9, 400–2. Defeated in Ky. General Assembly election (1810): **1:** 480. Volunteers to fight Indians: **1:** 664. Cheers Old Court faction victory in Ky. election: **4:** 611. *See also* Marshall, John J.

Marshall, John: Supports C. against "Corrupt Bargain" charge: **4:** 211–2, 221. Jarvis portrait of: **5:** 77. Trial of Burr: **1:** 351. Involvement in Pres. campaign (1828): **6:** 1225

Marshall, John J.: Family: **3:** 133, 138. Gets USMA appt. for son: **6:** 1286–7, 1363. Law opponent of C. as BUS debtor: **3:** 233, 287, 331–2, 348, 386, 389, 417, 430. Recommends patronage appts. to C.: **6:** 16–7, 72. Pres. of Ky. Commonwealth Bank: **4:** 406, 888, 942

Maryland: Leading role in turnpike construction westward: **2:** 188, 310. Harvest (1817) in: **2:** 397. Cumberland Road (*see* American System: internal improvements). Pursuit of runaway slaves: **5:** 100–1. C. patronage favors to: **5:** 134–5. Hagerstown postmastership: **6:** 164–5. US Sen. elections (1826): **5:** 419. State legis. elections (1826): **5:** 742–3, 748. US House elections: **5:** 742–3, 748, 755–7, 761, 788–9, 804, 854, 950; **6:** 177. AJ movement in: **5:** 788, 854; **6:** 24, 473–4, 1161. Soft–crabs of: **6:** 493. JQA political support & organization in: **5:** 788; **6:** 451, 467, 507, 526, 536, 603, 853, 866.

JQA party conv. at Baltimore: **6:** 526, 556, 866–7. AJ party conv. at Baltimore: **6:** 866–7. State legis. elections (1827): **6:** 1021–2, 1034, 1099–1100, 1147–8, 1156, 1161, 1171, 1192, 1194, 1207, 1333. *See also* Baltimore; Election of 1824: campaign activity in states & sections; & prognoses & outcomes; Election of 1828: campaign activity in states & sections; & prognoses & outcomes

Massachusetts: C. sees treasonable & secessionist elements in: **1:** 693–4. Has had too many Presidents & VPs: **2:** 78. US House elections in: **1:** 757, 773. Sectional arrogance of: **2:** 78. Free Blacks in want to return to Africa: **2:** 265–6. Recovery of militia expenditures in War of 1812: **2:** 433, 471, 617–8. Stance on Alien & Sedition laws: **2:** 471. Opposition to War of 1812: **2:** 471–2. US Sen. politics in (1826): **5:** 420–1, 434, 650. Cong. election (1822) in: **3:** 372–3. Gov. election (1823) in: **3:** 373, 409. Cong. election (1826) in: **5:** 791–2, 872, 889. US Sen. election in (1827): **5:** 420–1, 889; **6:** 401, 446, 507, 530–1, 555, 566, 585, 603, 639–40, 653–4, 708–10, 947. Special election for Webster House seat (1827): **6:** 820. Opposition to JQA admin. in: **5:** 650, 791. Support for JQA admin. in: **5:** 650, 791; **6:** 506–7. AJ movement in: **5:** 791, 872. School for blind in: **6:** 502. Adamsites in hate C.: **6:** 1279. Gov. election (1827) in: **6:** 401, 555. Free bridge (Warren) vs. chartered bridge (Charles River) issue in: **6:** 530–2, 556. State legis. election in (1827): **6:** 565–77. Opposition to Republican–Federalist alliance in: **6:** 816–7, 947–8. Split in National Republican–Federalist coalition: **6:** 565–7, 820. *See also* Election of 1824: campaign activity in states & sections; & prognoses & outcomes; Election of 1828: campaign activity in states & sections; & prognoses & outcomes; Great Britain: role & involvement of Mass. in Northeastern boundary controversy

Masons and Masonry: C. connection with: **1:** 140–1; **4:** 110, 455. C. assistance to: **6:** 4. C. as Grand Master (Ky.) & Master (Lex.): **2:** 916; **3:** 74, 844. Expulsions from: **6:** 4. C. participation in ceremonies of: **3:** 74; **5:** 95–6. C. role in establishing General Grand Lodge for US: **3:** 177–81. Assist Am. Colonization Society: **6:** 95. C. pride in history of: **3:** 178–80. As contributor to international peace: **3:** 179. Masonic lottery in Ky.: **4:** 455. Maxims & philosophy of: **3:** 179–80. Oaths of: **4:** 115. In Mex. politics: **5:** 14, 125; **6:** 752–3, 832 (*see also* Mexico). *See also* Clay, Henry: religion

Mercer, Hugh: Legal business with C.: **3:** 393–6, 399–400, 406–8. Son (Hugh Weedon Mercer) in "Eggnog Riot" at USMA: **6:** 326, 348. Supports & works for JQA in 1828 election: **6:** 924. Predicts a future C. presidency: **6:** 925. Dines in C. home in Wash.: **6:** 1159.

Merchant Marine, U.S.: No competition to from Span. Am. republics: **2:** 524. C. on arming, convoying merchantmen: **1:** 451. US hospitals for seamen of: **4:** 779. Seamen in fearful of GB aggressive maritime policies: **1:** 609. Nationality quotas in: **2:** 32, 37; **4:** 726. Depression in industry after War of 1812: **2:** 296, 298, 834. Influence of protective tariff policy on: **3:** 705; **4:** 955. C. on importance of: **5:** 39. C. on historical bases of world seapower: **2:** 524. General condition of US merchant seamen: **5:** 518; **6:** 494. C. on decline of as major US industry: **2:** 834–5. Laws relating to seamen in: **4:** 271, 371–2, 854, 903; **5:** 33, 40–1, 145, 224, 374, 518, 606, 691; **6:** 393–4, 805, 1024, 1249, 1263, 1345, 1354. Passenger limit law: **6:** 89, 96, 708, 921–2. Captains exploit seamen of: **4:** 548, 749. Desertion of seamen from: **4:** 277–8, 441, 464, 760, 885; **5:** 40, 57, 91, 104, 157, 518, 606, 768, 967; **6:** 14, 74, 393, 441–2, 532, 592, 1263. Desertion into GB navy: **6:** 494. Negro seamen in: **4:** 441. Recruitment of foreign seamen into: **4:** 885. Inadequate consular funds to assist seamen: **6:** 956–7, 1249–50 (see also US State Dept.: consuls & consular activities). Desertion of foreign seamen in US ports: **2:** 607–11. Ability to carry Negroes back to Africa: **6:** 90. Desertion of foreign seamen into: **5:** 39. Foreign recruitment of seamen of: **6:** 195, 1354. Wage competition with foreign seamen: **5:** 39. Reform of US laws pertaining to merchant seamen: **5:** 518–9, 606. Crimes of seamen of on shore & at sea: **5:** 694, 715, 808, 817, 947, 970; **6:** 1263. Distressed seamen (see US State Dept.: consuls & consular activities). Captains abuse, abandon, & illegally discharge seamen abroad: **4:** 370, 626, 903; **5:** 22, 33, 145, 224; **6:** 377, 393, 441, 680–1, 806, 898–9, 939, 1263. Distressed seamen recruited into GB merchant marine: **6:** 1354–5

Metcalfe, Thomas: Supports JQA in US House election of Pres.: **4:** 79, 163. Patronage recommendations to C.: **6:** 103, 381. Reports to C. on Ky. political events: **6:** 381. US House campaign & election (1827): **6:** 381–2, 435–6, 926–9, 966. As duelist: **6:** 435–6. Political philosophy: **6:** 435–6. Nom. for Gov. in Louisville: **6:** 1121–2, 1380

Mexico: Independence movement in: **2:** 505, 511–2, 547. C. popularity in for support of independence & US recognition: **2:** 505–6; **3:** 206–7, 235, 242, 327, 474–5. US sentiment for independence from Sp.: **2:** 405; **4:** 167–8, 804. US citizens serve in wars & armed services of: **2:** 405, 664; **3:** 69, 241–2; **4:** 126; **5:** 291, 535; **6:** 250–1, 629, 1113, 1320. Grain production: **2:** 524, 546; **3:** 690. Controversy over constit. & form of govt. in: **3:** 242, 474–5, 567; **4:** 175; **6:** 823. Future of: **4:** 167; **6:** 149. Character of the people: **4:** 583–4, 733; **5:** 649; **6:** 125, 148, 540. Mining industry in: **4:** 554, 581–3. Continuing war with Sp. & Mex. Royalists: **4:** 176–8, 326, 661, 835, 837, 840, 844, 876, 879, 885, 921; **5:** 16, 24, 63, 89, 91, 215, 262, 291, 335, 544; **6:** 127, 169, 288, 325, 465, 677, 681, 694, 903, 1114, 1120, 1198, 1336 (see also Porter, David; Spain empire: Cuba). Strategic security of: **6:** 149. Tension with native–born Spaniards in: **4:** 444; **5:** 544; **6:** 126, 148, 548, 1002–3, 1120, 1250. Expulsion of European Spaniards: **6:** 1224, 1250, 1320, 1347, 1376. Attempt to restore Span. rule—Arenas (or Orenas) Conspiracy: **6:** 124, 126, 146, 151, 169, 217, 325, 352, 486, 548, 688, 752–3. Sp. recognition of Mex. independence: **5:** 350; **6:** 148–9 (see also Great Britain; France; Russia; Spain). Seeks leadership of Span. Am.: **4:** 734. Army: **4:** 876; **5:** 812. Navy: **4:** 555; **5:** 57, 268, 291, 334, 491, 535; **6:** 149–50, 694, 1113, 1320 (see also Porter, David; Sweden). Role of Santa Anna in: **4:** 326–7, 584. Church & State relations in: **5:** 88–9, 544; **6:** 124–5, 146, 148, 417, 787, 1251. Promotes Pan–Span. Am. preferential tariff system: **4:** 640–1, 699–700, 734, 802–5, 887, 921; **5:** 325. Tariff policy & schedules: **4:** 100–1, 118, 375, 545, 583, 844, 874; **6:** 374–5, 486, 735, 1120, 1376. C. quoted on Am. System in: **4:** 583. Merchant marine of: **5:** 409, 722, 1053. Foreign loans: **5:** 16, 649; **6:** 1250. Economic difficulties in: **4:** 641; **5:** 16, 649, 812; **6:** 149, 443, 540, 688, 693, 1120, 1250, 1344, 1347. Internal instability, disorder, revolution, civil war in: **4:** 326, 415, 567, 733; **5:** 10, 349–50, 409, 812, 931, 999; **6:** 101, 124–5, 146–7, 150, 161, 352, 443, 458, 486, 548, 693, 705, 752–3, 798, 823, 832, 865, 889–90, 1002–3, 1101, 1120, 1186, 1224, 1250, 1347 (see also below Texas). Indian control problems: **6:** 443, 483, 735, 1115–6. Survey of border with US: **5:** 544, **6:** 1120. Colonization Act of 1824: **6:** 1341–2. Abolition of slavery in: **6:** 218. Masonic movement in: **6:** 752–3. York Mason (Yorkinos) party in: **5:** 649, 812; **6:** 147, 150, 486, 753, 832, 890, 1284–5, 1347. Scotch Mason (Escoceses) party: **5:** 649; **6:** 483, 486, 752, 832, 880, 890, 1250. Struggle between Masonic factions: **6:** 752, 832, 890, 984 (see also Poinsett, Joel R., espec. **6:** 752). Mex. govt. legislates against Masons: **6:** 832. Los Piadosos party in: **5:** 649. Arizpe party: **5:** 812–3. Pedraza party: **6:** 486–7. Sentiment for monarchy in: **6:** 146, 880. Military rule in: **6:** 146–9. Opposition to Bolivar in: **5:** 670; **6:** 375. Disputed state elections in: **6:** 101. Guerrero bid for Pres.: **6:** 146–7, 150, 1224, 1250, 1347

—foreign policy: GB recognition of: **4:** 94, 500; **5:** 224. GB influence in: **4:** 100, 415, 567, 573, 592, 683, 699, 733, 863; **5:** 16, 121; **6:** 262, 1128. Commercial treaty (1826) with GB: **4:** 235–6, 326–7, 339,

Mexico (*continued*):
393, 620, 681–2, 699, 777, 803, 844, 851, 888, 971; **5:** 10, 80, 125, 179, 544, 1005; **6:** 218, 288, 317, 335, 417, 458, 540, 1221, 1355, 1376 (*see espec.* **5:** 1005).
Buys, outfits warships in GB: **4:** 661, 667; **5:** 535. Tension with GB: **6:** 711. GB opposition to Fr. designs on: **4:** 674. GB suspicion of US ambitions in Mex.: **5:** 224. Seek GB aid in ending their war with Sp.: **5:** 877. Fr. political & economic interest & influence in: **4:** 675, 944; **5:** 24, 115, 268, 816; **6:** 447, 491, 693, 705, 889–90. Commercial treaty with Fr.: **6:** 447, 693, 705, 880. Treaties with Colombia: **4:** 724–5. Recognition by Ru.: **5:** 1005. Commercial treaties with Hanover, Hanse States, Prussia: **6:** 693, 880. Commercial treaty with Netherlands: **6:** 1376. Dip. relations with Vatican: **6:** 705, 787, 1250. Annexing San Salvador: **4:** 278, 282. Aggressive policy toward Guatemala: **4:** 278, 443, 565, 584–5, 734; **5:** 339, 409, 589, 643. Security of Yucatan: **5:** 80. Participation in Panama Cong.: **6:** 318, 540–1 (*see also* U.S. diplomacy: Panama Cong.)
—California: US immigration to: **6:** 1155. US consular problems in: **6:** 201
—Texas: C. on US annexation of: **2:** 769, 771, 804. La. Purchase conveyed to US: **2:** 771, 797, 800, 810–11, 813–4. Adams–Onis Treaty improperly surrenders to Sp.: **2:** 800 (*see also* Spain empire: Florida, East). US should risk war with Sp. to acquire: **2:** 771. More valuable to US than Fla.: **2:** 811–2. God wills to be part of US: **2:** 814. US will carry democracy & civilization to: **2:** 814. US emigrants carry slaves into: **6:** 594. US emigrants settle in: **3:** 226; **4:** 556; **5:** 61, 482. Mex. land grants in: **5:** 179; **6:** 9, 308. Mex. attempts to control US emigration into: **6:** 1341–2. US purchase of considered: **4:** 871; **6:** 308–9, 540. US trade with: **6:** 1341. Indian rebellion in: **6:** 218. Am. independence movement in: **3:** 342–3; **4:** 755; **6:** 9. Fredonian Rebellion (1826) in: **6:** 9, 114, 192–3, 209, 217–8, 262, 271, 305, 308–9, 325, 352, 483. Mex. military operations to subdue Texans: **6:** 262, 271, 325, 486, 688, 693. Constit. (1827) of: **6:** 483. Texas war of independence (1836): **4:** 573; **6:** 995. *See also* below US relations with
—U.S. relations with: C. instructions to Poinsett: **4:** 106, 166–78, 182–8; **6:** 285–90. Nature & extent of US trade with: **2:** 547; **4:** 100–1; **5:** 16–7, 519; **6:** 39, 250. US trade with Santa Fe & N.M.: **4:** 240; **6:** 269. US commercial treaty with (7/10/26): **4:** 168–70, 247, 545, 549, 578, 640–1, 644, 680–1, 690, 699–700, 802–5, 851, 887–8; **5:** 116, 124, 409, 438, 543–4, 679, 722, 761, 812, 1038, 1053; **6:** 77, 102, 286, 317, 361, 417, 540, 1349 (*see espec.* **5:** 543–4). Mex. non–ratification of 1826 commercial treaty with US: **5:** 544; **6:** 285–9, 335, 417,

540, 542, 812, 880, 950, 1018. Tariff, duty, fee discrim. against US shipping & trade: **4:** 100–1, 106, 118, 177, 375, 545, 682, 724–5, 874, 908, 918, 931–2, 950; **5:** 9–10, 182–3, 291, 412, 491, 544–5, 812, 882, 946, 972, 980, 993, 998–9, 1016, 1039, 1053; **6:** 39, 121, 267, 518, 687–8, 889. Tariff concessions to US: **6:** 651. Harassment of US shipping: **4:** 393; **5:** 182–3, 266, 291, 495–6, 544, 812, 874, 1027; **6:** 687, 889, 1248 (*see* case of *Fair American* in Name Index). US smuggling into: **4:** 777; **5:** 649. US claims against: **4:** 126, 177, 236, 322–3, 325, 560, 636, 690–1, 837, 844; **5:** 23, 36, 60, 80, 90, 182–3, 194, 200–1, 361, 438, 483, 714, 874, 882, 946, 961, 972–3, 975, 1011, 1027; **6:** 3, 8–9, 20–1, 250–1, 443, 662–3 (*see espec.* cases of the *Liberty* & *Superior*, in Name Index). Mex. claims against US: **5:** 154, 715; **6:** 8, 9, 21, 406. US claims agreement (1842) with: **5:** 874. Claims issues under Treaty of Guadelupe Hidalgo (1848): **4:** 323; **6:** 1248. Blockade, contraband, privateering & other US neutral rights problems in Mex. vs. Sp. war: **4:** 176, 178, 262, 764; **5:** 10, 154, 291, 491, 495, 535, 690, 715; **6:** 134, 287–9, 405–6, 575, 1061–2, 1113, 1158, 1248. On ending Mex. war with Sp.: **4:** 683–4, 921; **5:** 169. Mex. purchase, outfit, staffing war vessels in US: **3:** 207; **5:** 491, 535; **6:** 1113, 1145, 1186–8, 1196, 1202, 1215–8; 1313 (*see espec.* case of *Kensington* in Name Index). US urges suspension of plans & preparations for proposed attack on Cuba & PR: **4:** 174–5; **5:** 9, 19, 80, 153, 169, 237, 261, 335, 386, 404, 415, 424, 429–30, 437, 496, 709, 1025 (*see also* Spain empire: Cuba; Puerto Rico). US seamen in navy of: **5:** 291; **6:** 442, 681, 1113, 1151. Impressment of US seamen: **5:** 291. US resists Pan–Span. Am. preferential tariff system proposed by Mex.: **4:** 640–1, 699–700, 734, 802–5, 887–8, 921; **5:** 325–6; **6:** 1221. Application of Monroe Doctrine in Mex. (*see* U.S. diplomacy: Monroe Doctrine). Treaty of Limits (boundary) with: **4:** 171–3, 176, 448, 545, 549, 578, 666–7, 681–3, 851, 871; **5:** 10, 179, 394, 1038; **6:** 269–70, 308–9, 417, 1250, 1349. US desire to shift border farther toward SW: **4:** 173, 556, 567, 666; **6:** 308–9. Mex. fear of US expansion in SW: **4:** 549, 556, 682; **5:** 10; **6:** 262. Acquisition of Tex.: **4:** 556, 871; **6:** 262, 308–9. US (JQA) considers purchase of Tex.: **6:** 308–10, 540, 950. Santa Fe–St. Louis road: **4:** 176, 213, 226, 283, 448, 549, 578, 682, 851; **5:** 36, 44, 496. US gun traffic in: **5:** 483. Mex. seeks US neutrality in Fredonian uprising: **6:** 271 (*see also* above Texas). US denies involvement in Fredonian Rebellion in Tex.: **6:** 209, 214, 271, 309–10, 950 (*see also ibid*). Indian depredation & control problems: **4:** 173–4, 213; **5:** 415, 418, 483, 671, 714; **6:** 9, 20, 71, 271, 443. US recovery of fugitive slaves: **4:** 174; **5:** 679, 1038; **6:**

235. US incursions into, border violations, filibustering: **6:** 170, 364–5, 368–9, 376, 442, 482, 486, 804, 995, 1005, 1155–6. Extraterritoriality issue (*Eagle* case): **5:** 495–6; **6:** 405–6. Extradition of criminals: **5:** 679. Collection of debts from US citizens in: **5:** 1038. US disregard of Mex. law & national sensitivity: **5:** 495–6, 715. Mex. friendship for US: **4:** 415; **6:** 102. Mex. hostility to US: **4:** 573; **5:** 291, 491, 567; **6:** 202. Poinsett meddles in internal affairs of: **4:** 733; **5:** 10, 14, 125, 752–3, 798, 880, 897, 950, 984 (*see also* Poinsett, Joel R.). C. questions Poinsett reports & assurances: **5:** 201–2, 496. US peace treaty (1848) with: **6:** 663

Michigan Territory: Elections to Legis. Council of: **5:** 15, 162; **6:** 261. JQA admin. problems in: **5:** 204. Delegate to US Cong. election (1825) in: **6:** 496–7. Judicial politics & patronage in: **6:** 1164–8, 1197–8

Mifflin, Samuel: Family: **6:** 79. Interest in internal improvements: **6:** 79. Supports JQA in 1828. **6:** 478–9. Legal business with C.: **6:** 391, 477. Analyses of Pa. & national politics for C.: **6:** 340, 397–9

Mississippi: Creation of Territory of: **1:** 522, 524. Enters Unions as state: **2:** 318. C. supports application for statehood: **1:** 634–6. West Fla. issue in admission to statehood: **1:** 635–6. C. on division of West Fla. between Miss. & La.: **1:** 636. Conflicting land claims related to old Span. grants: **2:** 176. Proposal to plant Fr. emigrant colony in Miss. Territory: **2:** 318–9. Decline of state paper money values: **3:** 199. AJ movement in: **5:** 585, 969. Cong. election (1822) in: **3:** 266–7, 285. Support in for Panama Cong.: **5:** 362. US Cong. election (1825) in: **5:** 584–5, 711. US Sen. elections (1826) in: **5:** 756–7, 918, 969. Methodist involvement in politics of: **5:** 918–9. Support for JQA in: **5:** 969. *See also* Election of 1824: campaign activity in states & sections; & prognoses & outcomes; Election of 1828: Campaign activity in states & sections; & prognoses & outcomes

Missouri: Opening of US Land Office in: **2:** 261. C. ownership of land & speculation in: **2:** 578, 598; **3:** 346, 627–28. Statehood linked with Me. admission: **2:** 740–3, 744–6; **3:** 15 (*see also* Missouri Compromise). Constit. of admission: **2:** 746. Slavery permitted in: **2:** 748. Legality of casting electoral vote of in 1820 election: **3:** 37–41. Legis. nom. C. for Pres.: **3:** 413. Cong. elections in (1826): **5:** 568, 584–5, 710–11, 723, 755–7, 761, 853, 919–991. Land claim problems in: **3:** 753. Vote in House in 1824 Pres. election: **4:** 567–8. Interest in internal improvements: **4:** 576. C. political popularity in: **4:** 576; **6:** 1124. US Sen. election (1826): **5:** 755, 853, 888, 991: **6:** 46. Legis. of supports JQA admin.: **6:** 72. Politics of Am. System in: **6:** 811. JQA

admin. patronage problems, opportunities, decisions in: **6:** 1125–6, 1318. Infant iron industry in: **6:** 1212, 1301, 1318. Arms mfgr. in: **6:** 1212, 1301, 1318. *See also* Election of 1824: campaign activity in states & sections; & prognoses & outcomes; Election of 1828: campaign activity in states & sections; & prognoses & outcomes

Missouri Compromise: C. opposition to Tallmadge Amen. to statehood bill: **2:** 669–70, 740–2. C. support of slavery on Tallmadge Amen. debate: **2:** 670. Linking admission of Mo. to that of Me.: **2:** 740–5. Slavery legal in La. Purchase sector of: **2:** 742. Ky.–Vt. analogy in Me.–Mo. dual admission proposal: **2:** 741–4, 747. Slavery restriction efforts: **2:** 781–2, 784; **5:** 121. Right to holding slaves in Mo. linked to right to self–rule: **2:** 745, 777; **3:** 702. US House seats apportionment issue in: **2:** 743, 745–7. Sectional aggression involved in: **2:** 752, 766, 777. Threats of civil war & disunion: **2:** 766–7, 775, 780–1; **4:** 437. Threat of emergence of sectional parties: **2:** 774–5. Constit. of slavery in Mo.: **2:** 771; **3:** 82, 168, 702. Compromise formula suggested: **2:** 775–6, 781. Compromise finally adopted: **2:** 788. C. hails Compromise as finally adopted: **2:** 788–9, 797. Distinction between immorality of slavery & its legality under the US Constit.: **6:** 701–2. States Rights dimension of: **3:** 168. Tallmadge Amen. limitations on state sovereignty: **2:** 740. Compromise permits slavery in Mo.: **2:** 748. Roberts Amen.: **2:** 775. Thomas Amen.: **2:** 775–76. Taylor Amen.: **2:** 776, 784. C. opposes Taylor: **2:** 786. Storrs Amen.: **2:** 786. C. supports Storrs: **2:** 786. "Second" Mo. Compromise: **2:** 911; **3:** 15, 18–22, 26–9, 32–3, 42, 46–7. C. supports Free Negro exclusion from Mo.: **3:** 19. C. role in compromising Free Negro exclusion issue: **3:** 22, 26–7, 32–3, 46–7, 49–50. C. pessimism in getting a 2nd compromise: **3:** 42. C. on the meaning & importance of the 2nd compromise: **3:** 49–50, 57–9, 81–2, 168. Praise for C. role in: **3:** 70–1, 79, 90; **4:** 437; **5:** 5, 25, 655; **6:** 745. Criticism of C. role in: **3:** 294–5; **5:** 655. C. pleased with role in: **3:** 81. C. pro–South tilt during: **3:** 294–5. Issue in 1824 election (*see* Election of 1824: issues). Reaction to in Pa.: **6:** 702–3

Monroe, James: Min. to GB: **3:** 60. C. legal business with: **1:** 497–8. Eagerness for War of 1812: **1:** 645–8. Visits Lex., Ky.: **2:** 700–1. As land speculator: **1:** 497–8. Policy toward East Fla.: **2:** 418. Stunned by Hulls surrender of Detroit: **1:** 722–3, 726–7. Convinced Canada can be conquered: **1:** 727. Seeks military service in the field: **1:** 723, 727. Instructions to Ghent peace Commissioners: **1:** 857–62, 865. Claims on US for salary & expenses: **3:** 59–60, 189–90; **5:** 61, 105, 108–9. Criticisms of as Pres.: **2:** 439–40. S.C.

Monroe, James (*continued*):
opposition to: **5:** 891. Opposition to Bonus–concept (BUS) funding of internal improvements: **2:** 447. Credited with victory at Battle of N.O.: **6:** 925. Tour to heal national sectional–political divisions: **2:** 372–3, 452–3, 484, 701; **4:** 902. Concept of a national non–partisan party: **3:** 770. C. doubts existence of an era of good feelings: **2:** 452. Wants constit. amen. to permit internal improvements: **2:** 464, 483; **3:** 190, 573, 576–8, 582–3. C. criticizes position on internal improvements: **2:** 482–5, 489, 630. On US neutrality in Sp. wars in Span. Am.: **2:** 497, 504, 733, 753, 769, 804, 854, 856, 860. Procrastination of Span. Am. policy of: **2:** 513, 752–3, 804, 807, 854, 857, 870; **3:** 80. Opposes recognition of Buenos Aires: **2:** 590. C. rumored to be forming opposition party to: **2:** 588–9. C. on his political independence from: **2:** 489, 630, 732. C. political attack on: **2:** 630, 636, 769; **3:** 198. Growth of anti–Monroe feeling: **2:** 774–5, 819; **3:** 197, 199, 241–2. Embarrassed by AJ invasion of Fla.: **2:** 590. Orders to AJ respecting Fla. incursion: **2:** 652, 655. Role in Fla. incursion issue: **2:** 652, 655–7. Politics of C. anti–Monroe stance: **2:** 671–72. On Gr. independence: **3:** 604–5, 611. On Adams–Onis Treaty: **2:** 733, 804. Stance in 1824 Pres. campaign: **3:** 471. C. on lack of admin. leadership: **2:** 819. Product of Cong. caucus nom.: **2:** 823–4. Reelection of (1820): **3:** 36. Endorses recognition of Span. Am. republics: **3:** 186. Refuses to consider C. for Span. Am. mission: **3:** 197–8. Tardiness in appointing US Mins. to Span. Am.: **3:** 242. Kindnesses to James Morrison: **3:** 410, 424. Offers C. post as Min. to Ru.: **2:** 88–9; **4:** 56. On Anglo–Am.–Ru. relations: **2:** 88–9. Urged by C. to reward converted Federalists with patronage: **2:** 138. Recommends pay raises for US Mins. & Consuls: **2:** 190. Cabinet appts.: **2:** 258, 277, 288, 316, 391, 398, 427; **3:** 471–2. C. not offered SecState: **2:** 488, 491. Inauguration locus controversy: **2:** 320, 491. C. involvement in patronage issues & appts. in admin. of: **2:** 322–5, 333–4, 351, 400, 418–9, 727–8, 733, 764–5; **3:** 16, 53–4, 84. Sends fact–finding mission to Span. Am.: **2:** 387, 443–6, 497 (*see also* Brazil: U.S. relations with; Buenos Aires: U.S. relations with). Relations with Am. Colonization Society: **2:** 385. Interest in Span. Am. independence: **2:** 733; **3:** 44. Offers C. SecWar Cabinet post: **2:** 391, 488; **4:** 56; **5:** 657; **6:** 782. Offers C. post as Min. to GB: **2:** 391, 488; **4:** 56; **5:** 657. Ambivalent on suppression of piracy: **4:** 273–4. Possible US Min. to Panama Cong.: **5:** 761. Federalist support for admin. of: **6:** 550. Snubs Mrs. Decatur socially: **6:** 1302. Sounded out on VP nom. (1828): **6:** 1386. Attempts to involve in 1828 Pres.

campaign: **6:** 926, 1356, 1386. Role in 1824 Pres. election: **3:** 471–2.

Morrison, James (Morrison Estate): Slave owner: **5:** 705. Political advice to C.: **2:** 671–2. On Jefferson admin.: **1:** 230. Service in War of 1812: **3:** 46. 1812 War claim: **3:** 195. On Pres. election (1808): **1:** 230. As Navy Agent at Lex.: **3:** 656; **5:** 199, 208. Legal business with C.: **2:** 165, 315, 670–1; **3:** 9–10, 17–8, 33–4, 43, 45–6, 170–1, 195, 409. C. land speculation in partnership with: **2:** 578; **3:** 116–7. Connection with BUS: **2:** 277, 825; **3:** 122, 558, 569–70, 631, 652. Death: **3:** 409–11, 424–4, 426, 739. Emacipates slave: **4:** 499. Connection with Jefferson: **3:** 280. Provisions of last will & testament & legacies bestowed: **3:** 425, 426, 441, 496, 538, 556, 602, 631, 668, 735, 739–40, 788, 882–3; **4:** 449, 507, 565; **5:** 812–3, 941. C. legal work as executor of Morrison estate: **3:** 426, 441, 443–4, 455, 458, 466, 473, 484, 488–9, 496, 499, 507–8, 515–6, 518, 531, 593–4, 602, 656, 669–70, 734–5, 739–40, 756–9, 774–5, 786, 864, 878, 882, 893; **4:** 35, 50–1, 97–8, 109, 111, 394, 417, 436, 492, 496–7, 499, 506–7, 549–50, 564–5, 724, 806, 892; **5:** 158, 173, 182, 185, 208, 399, 533, 543, 560–1, 575, 580–2, 609, 611–2, 683–4, 704–5, 734–5, 758, 880–1, 941, 1019–20, 1034–5; **6:** 54, 63–4, 100, 112, 118, 471, 474, 643–4, 750–1, 788–9, 812–3, 818–9, 843–5, 901, 935–6, 945–6, 960, 991, 997–8, 1016–8, 1039, 1081–2, 1104–5 (*see also* Scott, Robert; Transylvania University). C. use of land of: **3:** 541–2. C. commissions, fees, & income from estate of: **3:** 774–5; **4:** 436; **5:** 399, 533–4, 611–2. New Court & related estate legal problems: **5:** 158

Naples, Kingdon of: Influence of Span. Revolution of 1820 on: **2:** 863. Revolution in (1820): **2:** 863; **6:** 677. Holy Alliance intervention in: **3:** 80–1. Character of King & nation: **5:** 103. Govt. monopoly on tobacco: **4:** 497. GB influence in: **4:** 626. Turks permit ships to pass through straits: **6:** 1320. Claims against Fr.: **5:** 963 —U.S. Relations with: Nature & extent of US trade with: **4:** 369, 497; **5:** 1020; **6:** 47, 1369. General US policy toward: **4:** 367–9. US claims against: **2:** 505; **4:** 243, 367–9, 409, 497, 536; **5:** 103, 141–2, 355, 421–2, 594, 666, 864; **6:** 143. Tariff policy with: **6:** 12–3. Attacks on US commerce prior 1812: **2:** 142; **4:** 626. Reciprocity extended to: **5:** 13. Tariff, duty, fee discrim. against US shipping & trade: **4:** 626; **5:** 153; **6:** 13, 694, 1369. Skill of Neopolitan diplomats: **5:** 103. US tariff, duty, fee discrim. against Sicilian shipping: **5:** 1020

Nashville, Tenn.: Bar involvement in politics: **6:** 10. BUS branch in: **6:** 12. *See also* Erwin, James; Erwin, John P.

Negroes (Free): In Lex., Ky.: **1:** 79, 300, 418, 445; **2:** 123, 363. In N.O.: **1:** 277. C. represents: **1:** 80. Awkward social status of: **2:** 263, 266, 384, 422. C. support free school for in Lex.: **2:** 683, 685. Enumeration in 1820 census: **2:** 750. Issue in Mo. Compromise controversy: **3:** 18–20. *See also* Slavery & slaves: American Colonization Society

Netherlands, Kingdom of: Established in 1814: **5:** 553. Neutrality policy in Span. Am. wars for independence: **3:** 595–6; **5:** 520. GB protection of: **5:** 627. Importance of foreign trade to: **5:** 621. Interest in isthmian canal in Nicaragua: **5:** 520. Relations with Austria: **5:** 551, 553, 620, 627. Claims against Fr.: **5:** 963. Power of Netherlands Trading Co. in: **5:** 621. Pro–US stance during War of 1812: **1:** 882, 888. GB occupation of: **1:** 938, 967, 996. Relations with GB: **1:** 946, 947. Independence of: **2:** 525–6. Acquisition of Belgium: **1:** 946. Dutch question at Vienna Cong.: **1:** 967. Church–State relations in: **6:** 1109–10. Popularity of William I: **5:** 801. Disease in: **5:** 803. Trade policies of: **5:** 1009; **6:** 1330. Concordat with Vatican: **6:** 1109, 1113–14. Numerous GB nationals resident in: **6:** 274. Science education in: **6:** 275–6. King's interest in things Am.: **6:** 674. King speculates in foreign–owned businesses in: **6:** 1042. Commercial treaty with Mex. (*see* Mexico). Tariff discrim. against Prussia: **6:** 1330. Prosperity of Belgian & Dutch sectors of Kingdom compared: **6:** 1393
—U.S. relations with: Neutral rights problems: **3:** 595–6, 600, 618–0, 775. Treaty of Commerce (1782) with: **4:** 612–3; **5:** 184, 187, 308, 916, 995. Hughes appt. US Chargé in (*see* Hughes, Christopher). C. instructions to Hughes: **4:** 138–9. Tariff policy of: **5:** 916, 995; **6:** 449–50. Recip. principle extended (1824): **4:** 116, 644, 894, 939; **5:** 329, 541–2, 622, 690, 803, 818, 824, 826, 911, 916, 995–6; **6:** 104–5, 1330, 1397. Arrest of US citizens: **4:** 517, 829; **5:** 44, 50. Commercial treaty with: **4:** 247; **5:** 280, 995. Nature & extent of US trade with: **5:** 542, 621–2, 689, 823–5, 1397; **6:** 450, 671, 1176, 1330. Maritime complaints against US: **4:** 615–6, 629, 951; **6:** 389, 399–400. US claims against: **4:** 119, 691, 831, 950–1; **5:** 280, 435, 574–5, 829, 935; **6:** 143, 1044. Tariff, duty, fee discrim. against US shipping & trade: **4:** 893–4, 939; **5:** 280, 541–2, 550, 620–2, 689–90, 822–6, 916, 995; **6:** 78, 104, 273, 449–50, 671–2, 1176, 1330, 1397. Problems with deserting seamen: **4:** 951; **5:** 40, 61–2, 280, 689, 825. Protectionism factor in US trade with: **5:** 825. State Dept.–owned Am. Hotel at Hague: **4:** 641, 884; **5:** 151, 790, 801, 996; **6:** 105, 254, 273, 448–9. US tariff, duty, fee discrim. against Dutch shipping & trade: **5:** 542, 621–2, 689, 803, 818, 823, 825, 916; **6:** 1176

Netherlands empire
—East Indies: Native rebellion in: **4:** 653; **5:** 135. Role of Netherlands Trading Co. in: **5:** 135–6. No trade monopolies in: **5:** 135. Potential US trade with: **4:** 225, 653. US trade agreements with native rulers in: **4:** 653; **5:** 135. USN punitive expedition to Sumatra: **4:** 899. Piracy in: **6:** 306. US trade with Java: **4:** 653; **6:** 306. Rebellion in Java: **4:** 653; **5:** 135. European intervention in: **6:** 306
—West.Indies: US trade with Curaçao: **5:** 1009
New Granada. *See* Colombia
New Hampshire: Pro–JQA & C. organization & sentiment in: **5:** 152–3, 692–3; **6:** 446–7, 467, 566, 603, 709–10. Isaac Hill influence in: **5:** 152–3, 692; **6:** 566, 603, 820. AJ press in: **6:** 1301. AJ movement & strategy in: **5:** 692; **6:** 447, 820. Federalist party in: **6:** 447, 566, 709. Gov. election in (1827): **5:** 692–3; **6:** 530, 532. US House election in (1827): **5:** 894. Legis. nom. JQA for Pres. (1827): **6:** 446–7. National Republican tactics in 1828 election: **6:** 566. Incompetence of JQA leadership in: **6:** 709. Gov. election in (1828): **6:** 820. Botched JQA party patronage opportunities in: **6:** 1301
New Jersey: US House elections in (1826): **5:** 708, 710–1, 742, 755–7, 804, 810, 872, 888–9, 950; **6:** 177. JQA patronage problems in: **5:** 711, 714–5, 841; **6:** 1331. US Sen. election (1826): **5:** 841–2. AJ movement in: **6:** 24, 1083. C. urged to campaign in: **6:** 1083–4. JQA admin. organization & support in: **6:** 1083–4, 1331. State legis. elections (1827) in: **6:** 1171, 1192, 1194. AJ newspaper support in: **6:** 1331. *See also* Election of 1824: campaign activity in states & sections; & prognoses & outcomes; Election of 1828: campaign activity in states & sections; & prognoses & outcomes
New Orleans: C. interest in land in: **1:** 122. Negative impact on Ky. economy of Sp. suspension of US right of deposit at: **1:** 99, 624. Importance of European war to economy of: **1:** 172–3, 453. Fourth of July (1804) celebration at: **1:** 140. Growth of Am. population in: **1:** 172, 453. Unhealthiness of: **1:** 144, 180, 220; **2:** 899; **4:** 571; **6:** 1099. James Brown description of: **1:** 164–5 (*see also* Brown, James). John Clay description of: **1:** 172–3. C. visits to: **2:** 688–9, 691–2, 700–1, 800–1. Defense of against Burr schemes: **1:** 270. Burr scheme hurts economy of: **1:** 277. Wilkinson rule in: **1:** 375, 377, 454. Implications of Fr. reoccupation of: **1:** 453. Military defensibility of: **1:** 453, 624, 636. Growing Fr. immigration to & influence in: **1:** 453–5. Importance of Span. Am. independence to security of: **2:** 525. Importance of commerce of to New England: **1:** 455. C. on need for USN defense of (1812): **1:** 623–4. C. on post–1812 war defenses of: **2:** 194. C. on future of: **2:** 693, 698. Impact of

New Orleans (*continued*):
non–importation & embargo on: **1:** 741.
AJ imposes martial law on: **5:** 738–9. Ky.
trade with: **1:** 828; **2:** 111, 206, 407,
693–4, 899. C. sells steam engine in: **2:**
887, 899; **3:** 72; **5:** 282; **6:** 798, 849–50.
Fall of wheat–flour prices at: **2:** 379.
Marine hospital at: **4:** 779. Impact of
1819 Depression on: **2:** 691; **3:** 117, 339.
Military pay claims relating to 1815 defense of: **3:** 44–5. C. interest in buying
sugar plantation near: **3:** 116–7. AJ political (1824) strength in: **3:** 821, 823. Speculation & business failures in: **4:** 819–20;
5: 71, 123, 165, 239, 282, 388. C. patronage problems in: **4:** 954. High legal fees
in: **6:** 100. AJ campaign visit to (1828): **6:**
569–70. Dislike of AJ in: **6:** 569–70.
US–N.O. conflict on ownership of allu-
vian riverfront land: **6:** 636, 963. Paves
streets & quays: **6:** 636
New York City: C. visualizes bombardment
of by GB navy (1812): **1:** 622. Museums
in: **5:** 231. Opposition to Van Buren in:
3: 475–6. Foreign business opportunities
in: **4:** 267. 1824 political divisions in: **3:**
486, 523, 787, 860. C. political strength
in (1824): **3:** 869–70. Tammany Hall in
1824 election: **3:** 869–70. JQA newspapers in: **4:** 112. Political hostility to AJ
in: **6:** 503. AJ strength in: **6:** 1234. Medical education in: **6:** 953–4. GB business
in: **4:** 267–369. Privateers & warships for
Span. Am. built, outfitted in: **4:** 675, 918;
5: 813. Federalist partisans in: **6:** 964.
Vote in 1826 gov. election: **6:** 140. Clinton partisans in: **6:** 961, 964. AJ philosophy of patronage in: **6:** 1254. Tammany
Hall divisions in 1828 campaign & election: **6:** 503–5, 607, 1090, 1131. C. confidential source in: **6:** 1196–7. Crawford–
JQA alliance in: **6:** 606–7. Jacksonian
victory in 1827 local elections: **6:** 1185.
JQA admin. patronage problems in: **6:**
961, 963–4, 1254. Two–party system in:
6: 503, 1189, 1197. Disaffected AJ support for JQA: **6:** 961. Party structure in:
6: 503. Postmaster patronage in: **4:** 198,
287; **5:** 297; **6:** 961, 963–5, 1022. Elections for state legis. (1827): **6:** 1234. Un-
decided on AJ vs. JQA in 1828 campaign: **6:** 1022. JQA political support,
organization, prospects in (1827): **4:** 112,
606–7, 961, 1090, 1130–1, 1189, 1204.
Rally of pro–JQA Tammany men (1827):
6: 1131. Struggle for control of Tammany in 1827: **6:** 503, 505, 1131, 1181.
See also Clinton, DeWitt; New York State;
Van Buren, Martin
New York State: Compensation for War of
1812 losses: **2:** 271. Penal policy (Auburn
Plan): **5:** 402. Erie Canal: **2:** 310–1, 357,
459; **3:** 194; **4:** 20–1, 32; **5:** 459; **6:** 32,
674, 676. Canal systems & politics: **3:**
356–7; **4:** 919–20; **5:** 180, 328. Elections
for state legis. (in 1822): **6:** 529; (in
1824): **5:** 718–9; (in 1825): **4:** 112, 129,
131, 227, 859; (in 1826): **5:** 746, 876; **6:**
140–1, 177; (in 1827): **6:** 1046–7, 1185,

1189, 1197, 1234, 1237–8, 1240–1, 1243,
1252, 1270, 1290, 1303–4, 1329, 1333,
1351, 1357, 1363–4, 1372–3, 1377, 1399
(*see espec.* **6:** 1046–7); (in 1830): **4:** 877.
Legis. vote (1824) for Pres. electors: **3:**
819, 822, 888–9; **5:** 718–9, 885, 1032.
Legis. session (1826): **5:** 113–4, 143–4,
346. Confused party structure in 1827
state legis.: **6:** 1046. Pro–JQA legis.
(1827): **6:** 433, 451, 457, 467, 502, 1046,
1252. State legis. fails (1828) to endorse
Pres. candidate: **6:** 1373. Jacksonians in
legis. caucus (1/31/28) to nom. AJ for
Pres.: **6:** 1373. Controversy over system
of choosing Pres. electors: **3:** 475–7, 501,
510, 512, 523, 547, 554, 570, 614, 669,
673, 732, 768–9, 781, 801, 820–2, 866; **4:**
920; **5:** 719, 885, 988; **6:** 545, 760, 1185,
1234, 1238, 1252, 1290, 1357, 1364, 1399
(*see espec.* **3:** 475–7, **4:** 988, **6:** 1185).
Caucus system of nom. Pres. candidates
in: **5:** 676, 718–9, 1032; **6:** 545. 1822
state constit.: **3:** 185–7, 373–4; **5:** 175.
Elections for Gov. (in 1824): **3:** 846–9,
852; **4:** 129; **5:** 347; (in 1826): **5:** 207,
346–9, 650–1, 663, 676–7, 759, 762–4,
771–2, 876, 878, 885, 889, 936–7, 943;
6: 130, 140, 245, 968 (*see espec.* **5:** 936–7;
also Clinton, DeWitt; Rochester, William
B.). Elections to US House (in 1820): **3:**
147, 150; (in 1822): **3:** 290, 420, 445, (in
1826): **5:** 746–8, 872. N.Y. Cong. delegation key to US House election of Pres.
(2/9/25): **6:** 1156. Election to US Sen. (in
1827): **4:** 131; **5:** 492, 676–7, 945, 1032;
6: 129–30, 141, 245, 394, 435, 1021.
Working Men's Party in: **4:** 877. Federalist party faction in: **6:** 445, 1252–3.
"Bucktail" Dem. party faction: **3:** 147,
150, 185, 357, 373; **5:** 676, 746, 759; **6:**
130, 433, 451, 930, 1046, 1252, 1270 (*see
espec.* **3:** 150). Bucktail–AJ alliance: **5:**
746; **6:** 1252. Clinton faction in: **6:** 433,
446, 451, 528, 1270 (*see also* Clinton,
DeWitt). Van Buren–Clinton coalition
(1827): **5:** 143–4, 174, 186, 207, 346–7,
650, 1032; **6:** 245–6, 397, 405, 433, 446,
457, 502, 504, 692, 760–1, 824, 930–1,
1090, 1185, 1189, 1197, 1200, 1240,
1252, 1265, 1270, 1303, 1332, 1363 (*see
also* Van Buren, Martin). Van Buren shift
to AJ (1827): **6:** 457, 606, 1252. Clinton
lean toward JQA in 1828 campaign (*see*
Clinton, DeWitt). Clinton–AJ alliance
(1827–8): **6:** 457, 837, 1046, 1059, 1197,
1234, 1270. Sentiment for Crawford in:
5: 676; **6:** 606. Baffling politics of N.Y.:
5: 492, 872, 876; **6:** 176–7, 397, 405,
457, 1197, 1204, 1213, 1252, 1329. Lack
of party discipline: **5:** 175, 763, 1032.
Party discipline: **6:** 1270, 1303. C. explains political party system in: **6:** 1270.
Confusing party nomenclature: **6:** 1197.
Anti–Mason movement in: **6:** 1234–5,
1339. States Rights political current in: **6:**
1046, 1252 (*see also* Van Buren, Martin).
Patronage factor in politics of: **6:** 606.
Tariff issue in: **6:** 1350–1. Navigation of
St. Lawrence River: **5:** 514 (*see also* Great

Britain: free navigation of St. Lawrence River). Domestic mfgr.: **4:** 363; **6:** 1290. Wool bill: **6:** 435. Hudson River–Buffalo turnpike: **5:** 663; **6:** 140. Anti–slavery movement in: **5:** 674–5, 679, 695. Am. System: **6:** 760, 1046. C. seeks 1824 electoral vote of: **5:** 885 (*see also* Election of 1824: C. candidacy; campaign activity in states & sections: prognoses & outcomes). Clintonian faction in 1824 Pres. election (*see* Election of 1824: DeWitt Clinton candidacy). Political impact in N.Y. of JQA election to Pres. by US House: **4:** 318, 363 (*see also* Election of 1824: House election phase). N.Y. seen as key to outcome of 1828 Pres. election: **6:** 516, 1021, 1047, 1185. C. urged to campaign in: **6:** 458, 489, 836–7, 968, 973–4. JQA admin. patronage problems in: **6:** 21, 337–9, 386, 433, 446, 451, 764, 772, 807, 877, 943, 961, 963–5; **6:** 837. JQA political support, organization & reelection prospects in N.Y.: **5:** 988, 1032; **6:** 6–7, 129–30, 140–1, 176, 246, 315, 387, 395, 433, 446, 489, 503–4, 527–8, 549–50, 554, 640–1, 692, 754–5, 760–1, 836–7, 1022, 1046, 1090, 1141, 1189–90, 1197, 1204, 1234–5, 1237, 1241, 1244, 1253, 1303–4, 1377, 1384–5 (*see also* Election of 1828: J.Q. Adams candidacy; campaign activity in states & sections; prognoses & outcomes). Mismanagement of JQA political cause & campaign in N.Y. (1827): **6:** 1235, 1238, 1253, 1270, 1303. AJ party support, organization, tactics & prospects in N.Y.: **5:** 746–7; **6:** 6, 24, 141, 177, 433–4, 692, 824, 1185, 1237–8, 1240, 1270, 1282, 1303, 1332, 1357, 1363–4 (*see also* Election of 1828: Andrew Jackson candidacy & campaign). *See also* Clinton, DeWitt; Election of 1824; Election of 1828; New York City; Van Buren, Martin

Nicholas, George: C. handling of estate of (*see* Nicholas, George in Name Index)

Niles, Hezekiah: C. kindness & assistance to: **3:** 246, 390. Newspaper of cautious on C. Pres. bid: **3:** 467. Support & promotion of Am. System: **6:** 373–4, 1231–2. On violations of US neutrality laws by Americans: **6:** 411

Noah, Mordecai M.: Removal as editor, N.Y. *National Advocate*: **3:** 831–2; **4:** 112; **5:** 207; **6:** 505. Editor of N.Y. *Enquirer:* **6:** 141. Supports Clinton for Gov. (1826): **5:** 207, 764, 876; **6:** 140. Abandons Clinton for Gov.: **5:** 885, 937. US Consul in Tunis (1815): **4:** 307. State Dept. subscribes to paper of: **4:** 614. Leans to Clinton in 1824 election: **3:** 831. On AJ resignation from US Sen.: **4:** 794. Slanders Rufus King: **4:** 843, 852–3, 855–6. Supports Crawford in 1824 election: **3:** 290, 356, 366, 374, 831. Considers support of C. in 1824: **3:** 300. Seeks patronage as N.Y. state printer: **3:** 366, 371, 379. Supports JQA in 1828: **6:** 505

North Carolina: GB sends Bibles to: **4:** 940 On colonization of free blacks: **6:** 96.

Project to write history of colony & state: **6:** 466, 962. US Cong. elections (1827) in: **6:** 944–5, 1011, 1085. JQA reelection prospects in: **6:** 1377. *See also* Election of 1824: campaign activity in states & sections; & prognoses & outcomes; Election of 1828: campaign activity in states & sections; & prognoses & outcomes

Norway. *See* Sweden & Norway

Oakley, Thomas Jackson: Political shifts of: **6:** 468, 640, 1252. Importance to JQA reelection campaign in N.Y.: **6:** 555–6, 567, 603. Importance to JQA admin. in US House: **6:** 579, 585, 640. Vote for Speaker of US House: **6:** 1011. Political views of: **6:** 640, 654. Shifts to AJ: **6:** 1252

Ohio: State taxes BUS branches in: **2:** 721, 723, 794; **3:** 41, 60–3, 114–5. State debtor relief laws & BUS: **3:** 760–3. C. represents BUS in suits against: **2:** 794–5, 873–5, 888, 900–2, 907–10; **3:** 20–1, 41, 60–3, 75, 99, 111–3, 115–6, 128–9, 155–6, 228–34, 286–7, 348, 353–5, 359–60, 368, 389, 430, 539–40, 549, 596, 675, 751, 781, 783–4, 804–5 (*see also* U.S. Supreme Court). Criticism of C. work for BUS in: **3:** 102–3, Impact of 1819 Depression in: **3:** 76. Pro–BUS public opinion in: **3:** 113. Sentiment for creditors grows in: **3:** 155. Move to reopen BUS branch in Cincinnati: **3:** 157–8. Harvest (1822) in: **3:** 245. Cong. redistricting in: **3:** 245–6. US House elections (1822) in: **3:** 245, 294, 301, 309. US House elections (1824) in: **3:** 871–2. Establishment of public education for: **3:** 351–2. Reaction to JQA election in: **4:** 87–8. C. popularity in: **4:** 836, 942. Ohio–Erie Canal project: **4:** 112, 529, 531, 547, 836; **5:** 271–2, 302, 717, 800. Support for national roads in: **5:** 881–2. Seeks BUS loan to develop canal: **5:** 271–2, 302. C. support "band of brothers" in: **5:** 359. Criticism of JQA patronage appts. in: **5:** 416–7. US House elections (1826) in: **5:** 568, 585, 711, 723–5, 742, 755–6, 792, 799–800, 804, 810, 830, 872, 888–9, 919, 955, 972, 1028; **6:** 177. Va. lands in: **5:** 979, 1002–3. Gov. election (1826) in: **5:** 1029. Tax reform in: **5:** 1029–30. Hemp machinery in: **6:** 8. C. urged to campaign for JQA in: **6:** 516, 758. Cong. delegation of supports JQA in House election: **5:** 280. JQA political strength in: **6:** 682. Railroad development in: **6:** 691. C. speech in Steubenville: **6:** 690–1, 694, 712–3. JQA party support, organization, prospects in election of 1828: **6:** 1242, 1244, 1247, 1269. JQA admin. patronage problems in: **6:** 971–2, 1161. Special US Cong. election (1827) in: **6:** 1147–8, 1160–1, 1199, 1213. State legis. elections (1827) in: **7:** 1199–1200, 1242, 1244. Conv. to choose JQA Pres. electors: **6:** 1199–1200. Conv. to select AJ Pres. electors: **6:** 1210–1. C. nom. for Pres. by legis. of (1822–3): **3:** 341, 351; **6:** 941. AJ

Ohio (*continued*):
party support, organization, election prospects in: **5:** 723–5, 799, 830, 919; **6:** 370, 682, 971–2, 1160–1, 1210–1, 1269. Support for Am. System in: **6:** 1376–7. *See also* Cincinnati; Elections of 1824: campaign activity in states & sections; & prognoses & outcomes; Election of 1828: campaign activity in states & sections; & prognoses & outcomes
Oldenburgh, Dukedom of: US extends tariff recip. principle to: **4:** 116, 247, 644; **5:** 329, 911

Papal States: Concordats with new Span. Am. states: **6:** 382–3, 1246. Role of Rom. Catholic church in Span. Am.: **6:** 382–3. Dip. & spiritual relations with new Span. Am. states: **6:** 382, 705, 710, 781, 787, 1246. Relations with Sp.: **6:** 710–1, 786–7, 910, 1246. Attention to affairs of church in US: **6:** 787. Concordat with Netherlands (*see* Netherlands)
—U.S. relations with: US trade recip. with: **6:** 316–7, 538, 614, 1096. US dip. relations with: **6:** 574, 588. Suspension of the Rev. Wm. Vincent Harold in Philadelphia: **6:** 588–9, 1061, 1379 (*see espec.* **6:** 589). Nature & extent of US trade with: **6:** 1096
Paris, Ky.: C. political speeches in: **6:** 753, 796
Patronage: C. family involvement in: **1:** 125, 139, 152, 159, 215–6, 228, 546, 557, 575; **3:** 82–4, 248, 264, 842; **4:** 391, 397, 448, 798–9, 821; **5:** 140, 699; **6:** 11. C. philosophy of: **5:** 658, 851; **6:** 110, 444, 491–2. Advice to C. on patronage philosophy: **6:** 31–2, 119–20. C. warned & criticized for patronage decision errors: **4:** 954; **5:** 100, 174; **6:** 21. Cong. inquiry into publication of laws contracts: **5:** 37–8, 136. Restrictions on patronage dispensation: **5:** 213. Complaints of mal–distribution of appts.: **5:** 97, 174; **6:** 154. Cong. concern with under JQA admin.: **5:** 136, 146, 242; **6:** 212 (*see also* Election of 1828: J. Q. Adams candidacy & campaign). JQA disinterest in: **4:** 864. JQA philosophy of: **4:** 864; **6:** 120, 320, 1253–4. Corruption in public service: **6:** 220. AJ philosophy of: **6:** 1254. C. political expectations from an appt.: **6:** 110. C. uses as political weapon: **6:** 212. C. proscriptions from office: **6:** 163. C. criticized for dismissals: **6:** 153. Publication of laws as device of: **6:** 291–2, 320, 454, Kentuckians beseech C. for jobs: **6:** 293–4. Size of Wash. Civil Service: **6:** 337. C. on flexibility of territorial patronage appts.: **6:** 1389
Peace: Attainable only by an efficient war: **1:** 773. Negotiation of related to military realities: **1:** 842. Must be conquered: **1:** 996. C. on need for: **5:** 321. US population growth assures peace & power: **2:** 513. Capitalist–mfgrs. favor: **2:** 836. *See also* War

Pennsylvania: Canal development in: **5:** 100–1; **6:** 79, 292, 368, 634, 669. Poor roads: **2:** 681–2. Penal policy & reform: **5:** 401–2. Popularity & political importance of Am. System in: **4:** 102; **6:** 181–2, 208, 211, 291–2, 320–1, 367–8, 373–4, 397, 401, 408, 445, 515, 587, 614, 633–4, 654, 679, 687, 698, 701, 706, 822, 1376–7. Canal conv. (8/4/25): **6:** 291–2. State conv. to promote domestic mfgrs. (6/27/27): **6:** 320, 698. National conv. to promote domestic mfgrs. (7/30–8/3/27): **6:** 320, 760, 797, 948, 1231–2, 1372–3 (*see espec.* **6:** 320). Philadelphia City–County conv. to promote domestic mfgrs. (5/14/27): **6:** 320, 633–4 (*see also* Philadelphia). Pa. Cong. delegation opposes JQA in US House election (2/9/25) of Pres.: **3:** 645; **5:** 353; **6:** 702–3. Reaction to JQA election to Pres.: **4:** 84–5, 318. Politics of "Corrupt Bargain" in: **4:** 333, 429–30; **5:** 87 (*see also* Election of 1824: House election phase). Popularity of C. in: **4:** 381–3, 430; **5:** 87. Pres. nom. conv. (3/4/24) in: **3:** 645–6, 668–9 (*see also* Election of 1824: campaign activity in states & sections; prognoses & outcomes). Election to US House (in 1826): **5:** 729–31, 744–5, 755–6, 766–7, 796–8, 819–20, 1028; **6:** 177. Election to US Sen. (1826): **5:** 1001, 1028. Elections to state legis. (in 1826): **5:** 87, 353–4, 710; (in 1827): **6:** 1148–9, 1156, 1171, 1174–5, 1192, 1194, 1242. Geo. Kremer campaigns for Gov. & US House: **4:** 84, 333, 429; **5:** 87, 797 (*see also* Election of 1824: House election phase). "Democratic" party split (1826) in: **5:** 730, 744–5, 766–7, 819. Confused party labels in 1827 in: **6:** 1149. Federalist party strength in (1827): **5:** 408, 730, 745, 767, 798–9, 819; **6:** 284, 304, 494, 571, 698, 1079. Federalist–Quid faction alliance: **6:** 284. Federalist–National Republican alliance: **6:** 571–2, 1079. Quaker vote: **6:** 304. German–speaking vote: **6:** 283, 304, 401, 479, 492, 494, 566, 571, 579, 886, 1035, 1063, 1072, 1174, 1385–6. Gov. Shulze support of JQA admin: **5:** 988; **6:** 125, 175–6, 284, 304–5, 366, 571, 714. Shulze mentioned for VP (*see* Shulze, John A.). Calhoun sentiment in: **5:** 204–6, 669; **6:** 284. Anti–Masonic movement: **6:** 304. Pa. seen as key to outcome of 1828 Pres. election: **6:** 367 (*see also* Election of 1828: campaign activity in states & sections: prognoses & outcomes). Newspapers in on "Corrupt Bargain": **4:** 84–5, 429–30 (*see also* Election of 1828: House election phase). Newspaper roles in politics of: **6:** 210–11, 304, 571, 813–4, 846–7, 853, 1030–1, 1063, 1072, 1175, 1213, 1379 (*see also* Election of 1828: general). National Republican conv. (1/4/28) to choose JQA Pres. electors: **6:** 571, 1050–1, 1213, 1338, 1342, 1402. JQA political support, organization & reelection prospects in: **5:** 352–4, 396, 407–8, 796–7, 988; **6:** 110, 119–20, 125,

Peru (*continued*):
84, 666, 867–8, 942; **6:** 903. Ask US mediation in war threat from Colombia: **6:** 1271, 1297, 1346, 1352
Philadelphia: Economic distress in 1804: **1:** 158. C. purchase furnishings for "Ashland" in: **2:** 169. Artist Joseph H. Bush in: **2:** 230, 294–5, 359–60. C. political rally in 1824: **3:** 829. Anti–JQA sentiment in: **6:** 110, 119. Arms & munitions for Span. Am. shipped from: **4:** 675. Merchants want claims settlements abroad: **4:** 831. Support for isthmian communication in: **6:** 360. Midterm elections in 1826: **5:** 729–31, 755, 766–7, 797–8. Courtesies to C.: **5:** 947, 949. JQA patronage concerns & problems in: **5:** 100–1, 265, 270, 353–4; **6:** 110, 120, 175–6, 282, 320, 355–6, 383, 444–5, 633–4, 813–4, 846–7, 886, 1301. AJ political strength & activity in: **5:** 407–8, 413, 704, 744, 766, 954–5; **6:** 125, 846–7. AJ press in: **6:** 1112. Support for Gr. independence in: **6:** 256–7; Rev. Harold suspension case: **6:** 588–9 (*see also* Papal States: U.S. relations with). US House election in 1826: **5:** 729–31. Politics & social class in: **6:** 1030. Anti–AJ Dem. support JQA in: **6:** 1030–1, 1050, 1118, 1385. Federalists for AJ in: **6:** 1059. Federalists for JQA in: **6:** 1030–2, 1035, 1059. Federalist party & factions in: **6:** 445, 1023, 1049, 1059. Binns letter on proposed C.–AJ bargain (1825): **6:** 448–9. Binns reputation a problem for JQA in: **6:** 886. Bache assault on Binns: **6:** 813–4, 1301. Sergeant defeats Hemphill in special US Cong. election: **5:** 731; **6:** 555, 579, 1023, 1030–2, 1035, 1049–50, 1059, 1063, 1072, 1085, 1099, 1105, 1112, 1118, 1148, 1152, 1156, 1171, 1174, 1194, 1200, 1332. City–County conv. to domestic mfgrs.: **6:** 320, 633–4. Controversial C. political visit to: **6:** 909, 919–20, 924, 954–5, 1030, 1063, 1148. JQA political visits to: **6:** 847, 897, 915, 953, 1148–9. JQA admin. political support, organization, activity in 1827: **6:** 120, 355–6, 444, 955, 1023, 1030–2, 1402. JQA newspaper needed in: **6:** 853, 1031. Tensions within JQA party in: **6:** 846–7, 864. City elections in 1827: **6:** 1023, 1034, 1049–50, 1171, 1174. Philadelphia county elections in 1827: **6:** 1023, 1174, 1191 (*see also* Pennsylvania)
Pierce, Benjamin: Elected Gov. (1827) of N.H. as Jacksonian: **5:** 692–3. Loses Gov. election (1828): **6:** 820
Pittsburgh: In election of 1824: **6:** 478. Paper money circulation in: **2:** 169. Growth of: **6:** 208, 367. Prosperity of: **6:** 696. As trans–shipment point to Ky.: **2:** 169, 394. C. visits: **2:** 681–2; **6:** 694–5, 699. C. invited to speak in: **6:** 208, 367, 603, 694–5. Pro–JQA political sentiment in: **6:** 478, 719. C. campaigns in: **6:** 603, 694–6, 699, 708, 713, 719, 798, 807. Paper mill industry in: **6:** 695. Textile

industry: **6:** 703. Support for Am. System in: **6:** 208, 698–9, 701. C. campaign speech in: **6:** 700–3, 708, 713, 1210–1
Pleasants, James: US Sen. prospect (1825) in Va.: **4:** 857, 867, 906. As Gov. of Va.: **3:** 620, 626. Mentioned as VP nominee in 1828: **6:** 1386. C. toast to: **4:** 386–7. Supports BUS: **3:** 620, 626
Pleasants, John Hampden: Founds Richmond (Va.) *Constitutional Whig:* **3:** 791. Supports JQA in 1824: **3:** 790. Opposes Crawford–C. ticket in 1824: **3:** 867. C. personal & patronage favors to: **4:** 250, 254, 261–2, 515, 904. Mission to BA: **4:** 515–6, 613, 652, 654, 753–4, 826–7; **6:** 199. Wants vindication for disastrous mission to BA: **4:** 777, 827. C. criticism of: **4:** 826–7. On Va. politics: **4:** 827; **5:** 1030–1; **6:** 199–200. Mentioned as VP on JQA ticket (1828): **6:** 1386. Supports JQA admin. in 1828 election: **6:** 519, 637, 1187. Congratulates C. on duel with Randolph: **5:** 227–8. Dislike of Randolph: **5:** 984, 1030. Critical of Tyler: **5:** 1030. Suggests C. as VP nominee in 1828: **6:** 519. Attacks AJ immorality: **6:** 637. C. on need to finance faltering newspaper of: **6:** 1187, 1201, 1243. JQA party financial support of Richmond *Constitutional Whig:* **6:** 1187, 1201, 1233–4, 1243. And blackmail scandal: **6:** 1373
Poindexter, George: On public attacks on C.: **5:** 968. Supports C. on "Corrupt Bargain": **5:** 970. On party discipline: **5:** 968. On Panama Cong. Mission: **5:** 969. Kindness to Thomas Hart Clay: **5:** 969–70
Poinsett, Joel Roberts: Horseback tour of the west: **2:** 237–8. Writes book on Mex. (1824): **3:** 562. Appt. Min. to Mex.: **4:** 101, 106, 166, 182–4. On Gr. independence (1824): **3:** 599, 603. C. on effectiveness of: **6:** 361, 871. C. acknowledges as expert on Span. Am.: **3:** 690. C. instructions to as Min. to Mex.: **4:** 166–78, 182–8; **6:** 285–90. Agricultural & botanical interests of: **4:** 563. On European designs on Mex.: **4:** 675, 733. On US annexation of Cuba: **5:** 224 (*see also* Spain empire: Cuba). Would send US agents into Peru & Guatemala: **5:** 14. On ambitions of Bolivar: **6:** 101–2 (*see also* Bolivar, Simon). Forms pro–US Masonic political party in Mex.: **4:** 733; **5:** 10, 14, 125; **6:** 1284–5. Cong. investigates security assurances of to Mex.: **5:** 201–2. C. questions accuracy of reports of from Mex.: **5:** 496. As US Min. to Panama Cong.: **5:** 761, 1050; **6:** 127, 248. Lafayette lauds: **5:** 1050. No outfit for as Min. to Panama Cong.: **6:** 248. Secret sources within Mex. govt.: **6:** 540. Requests permission to return to US: **6:** 711, 1140, 1285, 1399. C. would remove as Min. to Mex.: **6:** 915, 950–1. JQA opposes his recall from Mex.: **6:** 984–5, 1101–2, 1284–5. C. opposes his recall from Mex.: **6:** 1064, 1284–5. Mex. sentiment for recall of: **6:** 838–9, 864, 871, 880, 897, 906, 914–5, 950–2, 984, 1064,

1101, 1284–5. Mex. dislike of: **6:** 1130.
Charged as ineffectual diplomat: **6:** 890.
Accused of meddling in Mex. internal
affairs (*see* Mexico: U.S. relations with).
Analysis of political factions in Mex.: **6:**
752–3

Poland. *See* Russia

Polk, James K.: Elected to US House (1825
& 1827): **4:** 716; **6:** 799–800. Solicits
patronage favor from C.: **4:** 880; **5:** 1040.
Helps finance AJ newspaper: **6:** 573

Pope, John: Family: **5:** 5–6. Service in US
House: **1:** 459, 511; **2:** 895. Service in
Ky. House: **1:** 254. C. defeats in Cong.
election (1816): **1:** 254; **2:** 181–2, 216,
231; **4:** 411. Woodson defeats (1820): **2:**
886. Involvement in Burr conspiracy politics in Ky.: **1:** 352–3. Service in US Sen.:
1: 653. As Ky. Sec State: **2:** 382–3. Censured by Ky. legis.: **2:** 440. C. passes over
for Ky. US Dist. Atty.: **5:** 951. Works for
AJ in 1828 campaign: **6:** 841. Leans to
AJ (& New Court): **4:** 713; **6:** 24–5, 28.
Political clashes with C.: **5:** 5. Patronage
favors to C.: **1:** 546. Opposes War of
1812: **1:** 254. On pre–War of 1812 foreign policy: **1:** 653. Supports TU: **1:** 78;
2: 591. Lex. civic duties: **1:** 126–7. C.
opposes for Lex. postmastership: **1:** 839.
Legal business with C.: **2:** 349, 870. Defends AJ invasion of East Fla.: **2:** 671–2.
Work of BUS: **3:** 122, 558. Support of
domestic mfgrs.: **1:** 459. Ridicules C.: **6:**
28

Porter, David: Commands USN pirate suppression campaign in Gulf–Caribbean: **3:**
337–8. Sp. protests activities of at Foxardo, PR: **4:** 224–5, 320. Span. reaction to
trial of: **4:** 738. USN Court of Inquiry to
investigate actions at Foxardo: **4:** 298–9,
311, 320, 327, 331, 501, 520, 610–1, 632,
676, 738; **6:** 217, 324. Support for JQA
handling of Porter issue mixed: **4:** 823.
Accepts command of Mex. Navy: **4:** 555;
5: 491, 531. Sympathy for: **4:** 610–1; **5:**
18. C. compares with AJ: **4:** 618. Reaction to suspension from USN: **4:** 676. To
lead Mex.–Colombia naval attack on
Cuba: **5:** 194. Mex. naval operations
against Sp. under command of: **5:** 535,
1033; **6:** 39, 134, 149–51, 325, 575,
628–9, 658–9, 821, 1108, 1198, 1263,
1320, 1344. Violates US neutrality: **6:**
134, 575, 594–5, 628–8, 659–60, 821–2,
856, 969–70, 1114, 1198–9. Sp. protests
US toleration of unneutral acts of: **6:**
628–9, 658–9, 856, 1108. Sp. naval operations against: **6:** 677, 681, 694. Recruits
seamen in N.O.: **6:** 694. Commissions
Mex. privateers: **6:** 1320. Threatens joint
Mex.–Colombian naval attack on Sp.
coast: **6:** 1344. Threatens violations of US
maritime neutral rights: **6:** 1344. *See also*
Mexico: U.S. relations with; Spain empire: Cuba; & Puerto Rico

Porter, Peter Buell: Family: **2:** 162; **3:** 134,
422, 431–2, 860; **6:** 208–9, 399, 931–2.
C. supports as Commissioner under

Treaty of Ghent: **2:** 162. Randolph attacks: **2:** 162. C. legal business with: **3:**
133–4. Works for Black Rock outlet of
Erie Canal: **3:** 356–7; **5:** 112–3. Work
for Black Rock harbor improvement: **4:**
491–2; **6:** 504–5, 549. Service on St.
Lawrence–Lake of Woods Boundary
Commission: **3:** 251, 524, 553, 860; **4:**
677, 830–1, 859; **5:** 113–4, 144, 712,
769; **6:** 342, 404, 469–70, 931, 1208–10,
1303. Leans towards a N.Y. favorite son
candidate in 1824: **3:** 251. Elected to
Cong. (1822): **3:** 290. Supports & advises
C. in 1824 campaign: **3:** 291, 356, 367,
371–2, 378–9, 421–2, 485–7, 523–4,
614–5, 731–3, 859–61. Analysis of C.
defeat in 1824: **4:** 16–7. Political enemies
in N.Y.: **3:** 733. C. supports Cabinet post
for: **4:** 286. C. patronage favors for: **3:**
904–5; **4:** 321–2, 918–9; **6:** 208–9.
Wife's patronage requests of C.: **6:**
208–9, 399. Patronage recommendations
to C.: **4:** 746. Analyses of N.Y. state
politics: **5:** 113–4, 143–4, 1032; **6:**
245–6, 405, 502–4, 549, 760–1, 930–1.
Importance to JQA admin. in N.Y. Sen.
election (1827): **6:** 130. Candidate for
N.Y. State Assembly (1827): **6:** 1229,
1235, 1240, 1303–4. Labors for JQA in
1828 campaign: **6:** 433, 489. Analyses of
Pres. campaign & election (1828): **6:** 930

Portugal: Reactions in to Br. independence
movement: **4:** 833, 854. Recognition of &
relations with Br. (*see* Brazil). Flight of
Court to Br.: **6:** 711. Connection with Br.
under single crown: **5:** 176, 189, 310,
358, 539, 556; **6:** 983. Port. separation
from Br.: **5:** 358, 502. Port.–Br. dynastic
relations & adjustments: **4:** 104–5; **5:**
106, 310, 395, 502, 545, 586, 1035; **6:**
911, 937, 983, 1040, 1136, 1335 (*see espec.*
5: 310). Death of King John VI: **5:** 146,
160–1, 176, 310, 518, 735. Democracy in:
5: 19; **6:** 1092, 1136. Constit. of 1822: **5:**
358. Constit. of Apr. 29, 1826: **5:** 310,
502, 533, 545–6; 554, 559, 562, 571, 578,
586, 618–9, 626, 638–9, 647, 680, 777,
828, 859, 923; **6:** 105, 324, 344, 663–4,
824, 895, 1146 (*see espec.* **5:** 310). Elections in: **5:** 828. European reactions to
1826 constit.: **5:** 586, 619, 626, 639,
667–8, 680, 777, 923, 940, 964; **6:** 1146.
Miguel stances on 1826 constit.: **5:** 923,
1027, 1035; **6:** 663, 824, 937, 1043, 1139,
1255, 1361. Regency of Maria da Gloria:
5: 146, 151, 153, 176, 310, 358, 502, 539,
545, 554, 562, 586; **6:** 481, 512, 663, 911,
937, 1136. European reaction to Maria
da Gloria regency: **5:** 502, 518. Ambitions of Queen Carlota Joaqunia in: **5:**
160, 167, 176, 358, 518; **6:** 1139, 1335.
Marriage (11/29/26) of Miguel & Maria
da Gloria: **5:** 310, 502, 1035. Personal
behavior of Maria da Gloria: **6:** 1136.
Austrian influence on Miguel & policy of
in Port.: **5:** 518, 859; **6:** 314, 663, 895,
911, 937, 980, 1041. Economic conditions
in: **6:** 1361–2. Army: **5:** 588, 647. Fr.
policy in: **5:** 792, 940, 992–3, 1021, 1027,

981. On Span. Am. republics: **5:** 981.
Erratic behavior of: **5:** 627–8, 645–6. C.
duel & opinions theron: **5:** 208–9,
211–2, 227–8, 231–4, 253–4, 259, 270,
277, 306–7, 309, 354, 359–60, 392, 403,
416, 499, 585; **6:** 588
Randolph, Thomas Mann: Character &
habits of: **6:** 974, 988, 1010, 1025. Break
with his father–in–law Jefferson: **6:**
1025. Inserts Jefferson opinions into
1828 campaign: **6:** 924–5, 974–5, 1010,
1048–9. Altercation with C.: **6:** 986–8,
1025. Threatens C. with duel: **6:** 977,
988. Serves on Ga.–Fla. Boundary Commission: **5:** 1027; **6:** 986–8. Son apologizes to C. for behavior of: **6:** 1025, 1038
Rhode Island: Free Blacks in want to return to Africa: **2:** 265–6. Politics & JQA
admin. patronage in: **4:** 869–70. US Sen.
& House elections in (1825): **4:** 870. US
Sen. elections in (1826): **5:** 728–9 (*see also*
Election of 1824: campaign activity in
states & sections; & prognoses & outcomes; Election of 1828: campaign activity in states & sections; & prognoses &
outcomes)
Richmond, Va.: Interest in hemp production: **6:** 8. C. on theater fire in (1811): **1:**
601–2, 638
Ritchie, Thomas: Member of "Richmond
Junto" (1822): **3:** 341. Supports Crawford
in 1824 campaign: **3:** 237, 315, 341, 867;
4: 55, 214. On "Corrupt Bargain" controversy: **4:** 213–4. Joins AJ party: **4:**
213–4. Leads anti–JQA forces in Va.: **5:**
1023; **6:** 550. Supports Randolph in 1827
US Sen. race: **5:** 1031. Predicts AJ victory
in N.Y. in 1828 Pres. election: **6:** 1059,
1065, Poor health of: **4:** 310, 712
Robertson, Thomas B.: Offered & declines
spy mission to Cuba (*see* Spain empire:
Cuba). On ethics of spying: **5:** 47–8. Report on internal conditions in Cuba: **4:**
271–4. Supports independence movements in Span. Am.: **3:** 249; **5:** 48. On
the tariff: **2:** 185. Encourages C. candidacy (1824): **3:** 49, 744. Predicts AJ
victory in La. (1824): **3:** 828. Protests
judicial appt. in La.: **5:** 267. Suggests
patronage appt. to C.: **4:** 445. Fed. judgeship: **5:** 88, 267
Rochester, Nathaniel: Explains complex
N.Y. State politics to C.: **6:** 140–1
Rochester, William B.: Family: **6:** 548, 969.
Father founds city of Rochester: **3:** 771.
Elected in 1822 Cong. election in N.Y.: **3:**
445, 447. Appt. N.Y. State district judge:
3: 375, 377, 447. Resigns US House seat
to accept judgeship: **3:** 462–3, 476, 511.
Supports & advises on C. candidacy in
1824: **3:** 192–3, 445, 510–2, 546–8,
768–72; **5:** 885. Sees Crawford electoral
victory in N.Y. (1824): **3:** 864. Appt. secretary to US delegation to Panama
Cong.: **4:** 871; **5:** 304, 373, 389, 393, 398,
663, 878, 885, 932, 936, 938–9. Delays
departure to Panama Cong.: **5:** 878, 932.
Salary of as secretary: **5:** 393, 932, 939.
Considers withdrawing from Panama

Mission: **5:** 398, 400, 403, 406, 415, 878,
936. Returns home from Panama Cong.:
6: 613, 643. Appt. US Chargé to Central
Am.: **6:** 280–1, 548. C. instructions to as
Chargé to Central Am.: **6:** 280–1, 548.
On job of US Min. to Colombia: **5:** 936;
6: 1129. Returns slowly to Guatemala: **6:**
903, 940, 967–8, 973, 1047, 1061, 1099,
1127, 1388. Opinion of Central Am.: **6:**
1129. On Mex.: **6:** 146–50. Opinion of
Poinsett: **6:** 1130. Unsuccessful candidate
for Gov. of N.Y. (1826): **5:** 347, 349, 677,
759, 762–4, 769, 771–2, 876–7, 878,
885, 936–7; **6:** 140, 245, 968. Analyses of
N.Y. State politics for C.: **6:** 836–7,
1046–7. Urges C. to run for VP on JQA
ticket: **6:** 1141, 1228. On Pres. election of
1828: **6:** 836–7, 1228–30. Resists nom. as
candidate for Gov. of N.Y. (1828): **6:**
1230. Patronage recommendations to C.:
5: 694, 939, 945; **6:** 968. Political attacks
on: **5:** 937. Visits Lex., Ky.: **6:** 778, 836,
838
Rochester, N.Y.: Railroad development: **6:**
529
Rodney, Caesar Augustus: Asks C. to prosecute Burr for US Govt. (1807): **1:**
310–1. C. urges patronage job for John
Clay: **1:** 546, 557, 575. Advises C. not to
run for US Sen. (1810): **1:** 472. C. discusses foreign policy issues with: **1:** 481,
522, 557, 574. Wants to buy Ky. carriage
horses: **1:** 482. Loses household furniture
& books in shipwreck: **1:** 522–3. Resigns
as US Atty. Gen.: **1:** 557, 574–5. C.
offers to assist politically: **1:** 574. Opposes
BUS: **2:** 258; as Director of BUS: **2:** 258.
Assist in locating branch of BUS in Lex.:
2: 258. Suggests C. as SecState: **2:** 258.
Death of son: **2:** 386–7. C. high regard
for personally: **2:** 593. Candidate for US
House speakership: **3:** 147. US Min. to
BA: **3:** 335, 406. Appt. to Span. Am.
fact–finding commission: **2:** 387
Rowan, John: Pledges money to TU: **1:**
77–8. Criticizes TU trustees: **1:** 198–9.
Opposes TU: **4:** 266. C. sells land to: **1:**
192. Elected to US Cong. (1806): **1:** 246.
Opposition to separatist Span. Association: **1:** 246. Role in Ky.–Tenn. boundary adjustment: **2:** 770. Role in Ky.–Va.
dispute on pre–1790 land titles: **3:** 326,
350, 377–8, 392, 512–5, 543–4. Association with C. in *Green vs. Biddle*: **3:** 342,
392, 512–5, 543–4, 791. Supports C. in
1824 campaign: **3:** 822–3. In Relief vs.
Anti–Relief clash: **4:** 265–6, 611, 676; **5:**
531. Opposes JQA admin.: **5:** 158–9,
360, 528–9, 532. Opposes Panama
Cong.: **5:** 278. Opposes R. Trimble appt.
to US Supreme Court: **5:** 360–1. Attacks
US Supreme Court: **5:** 532. On Fed.
bankruptcy legis.: **5:** 651. Attacks on C.:
5: 991. C. opinion of: **5:** 360
Rumpff, Vincent: Appt. Hanse cities Min.
to US (*see* Hanseatic City States: U.S.
relations with). Delivers box to Mrs. C.
from Europe: **6:** 823, 1056, 1058, 1067,
1258 (*see also* Astor, John J.)

757

Rush, Richard: Serves in GB as US Min.: **2:** 372, 387, 391. Returns home: **4:** 307; **5:** 903. Conv. of 1818: **3:** 60. C. asks patronage favors of: **2:** 333. Courtesies to C.: **3:** 320. Atty. Gen. in Madison Cabinet: **1:** 877. Russell high regard for as diplomat: **2:** 427. Condemnation of Geo. Canning: **6:** 714–5. JQA appt. SecTreas: **4:** 92, 101, 257–8. Feels inadequate as SecTreas: **6:** 915. Overworked as SecTreas: **6:** 1367–8. Negotiates with GB on Colonial trade: **5:** 902. Work for Am. Colonization Society: **6:** 86, 96. Conflict with House Ways & Means Committee (1827): **6:** 169. Report on protective tariff: **6:** 1304, 1384. Seeks to replace Poinsett as US Min. in Mex.: **6:** 915, 950, 952. Mentioned as VP candidate in 1828: **6:** 926, 970–1. Clays entertain: **6:** 1367
Russell, Jonathan: Problem of pay for service on Ghent Peace Commission: **1:** 869–70. Doubts favorable outcome of Ghent peace conference: **1:** 921. Criticizes Gallatin & JQA roles at Ghent: **2:** 74–7. Pro–West role at Ghent: **2:** 373, 427; **3:** 204. Supports importance of C. role at Ghent: **2:** 74–5. Files libel suits on Ghent charges against him: **3:** 271–2, 283. Notes flaws in Conv. of 1815 with GB: **2:** 73–4. Analysis of return of Bonaparte to power: **2:** 14–5. Bored & fatigued with Sweden mission: **2:** 78–9, 390, 426. Recalled as US Min. in Sweden: **2:** 755. On inferior quality of US Mins. abroad: **2:** 427. Conflict with Hughes within Legation: **2:** 426. On the proper negotiation of treaties: **2:** 761–2, 778–9. Instructs C. on Adams–Onis Treaty matters: **2:** 851. Criticism of dip. procedures of JQA in Adams–Onis Treaty: **2:** 755–63, 770–1, 782, 784, 802, 851, 852. Lauds C. stance on Adams–Onis Treaty: **2:** 852. Dislike of JQA: **2:** 427–8, 758, 761, 782, 784, 851; **3:** 204, 224, 269. "Duplicate letter" controversy with JQA: **3:** 204, 219–26, 237, 238–9, 252–7, 269–72, 283, 292–3, 315, 322–4, 341, 350, 547; **4:** 159 (see espec. **3:** 204). Attacks JQA & C. for "Corrupt Bargain": **6:** 1280. Service in US House: **3:** 154, 186. Assists C. in 1824 campaign: **3:** 202, 204. C. favors & courtesies to: **3:** 907. Sends scientific instruments to US: **2:** 10. Anglophobia of: **2:** 13. Second marriage of: **2:** 372–3, 427, 784; **3:** 271. See also Great Britain: Treaty of Ghent; Spain empire: Florida, East; Election of 1824: issues
Russia: Competition with US hemp: **1:** 462; **2:** 379. C. on impact of Fr. victory over on GB export trade: **1:** 742. Maritime neutral rights interests: **1:** 920. Wartime (1812) devastation of: **2:** 271. Power position after Napoleonic wars: **2:** 532–3. Plots against Alexander I: **5:** 188–9, 241. Death of Alexander I & succession problems: **4:** 923–4, 933–4, 937–8, 944, 950; **5:** 10–11, 24, 28–9, 32, 36, 72–3, 103, 164, 169, 237, 260–1, 269, 318. Elevation

of Nicholas I to throne: **5:** 24, 49, 51–2, 241–2, 579, 691. Class structure of: **5:** 96. Decembrist uprising in: **4:** 924; **5:** 2, 14, 28–9, 32, 51–2, 72, 96, 137, 188, 223, 578, 626, 685; **6:** 759. Problems facing Nicholas I: **5:** 96, 230. Economic problems: **5:** 52. Constit. reforms: **5:** 51, 96. Famine: **6:** 716. Public opinion: **5:** 812. Role of army in: **5:** 29, 52, 72, 98, 188, 356. Naval ambitions in Mediterranean Sea: **2:** 533. Policy in Gr. (see Greece). Commercial treaty with Sweden (see Sweden & Norway). Acquisition of Finland: **2:** 805, 815. Relations with Sp.: **2:** 533 (see also Spain). Policy in Iberian Peninsula: **5:** 800; **6:** 226, 278, 314, 1097. Policy in Span. Am.: **5:** 318, 691, 1005. On Br.–BA war: **5:** 215. On recognizing independence of New Span. Am. nations: **4:** 535, 572, 574, 774; **5:** 1005, 1298. Role in persuading Sp. to end warfare against former Span. Am. colonies: **4:** 929–30; **5:** 19, 125–6, 131–2, 386, 579, 691, 697, 877, 966 (see also below U.S. relations with). War with Persia: **5:** 691–2, 708–9, 792, 801, 812, 816, 966; **6:** 501, 716, 1097, 1343–4; 1361 (see espec. **5:** 691–2). Treaty of Turkmanchai (Feb. 1828) with Persia: **5:** 692; **6:** 1334, 1343. Russian annexations from Persia: **6:** 1334. Interest in absorption of Tur.: **2:** 533; **4:** 203. Sentiment in for war on Tur.: **5:** 29, 52–3, 72, 98, 137, 230, 241, 356. Treaty of Ackerman (10/7/26) with Tur.: **5:** 937, 1036–7. Origin & onset of Russo–Turkish war: **5:** 28–9, 52, 98, 137, 204, 230, 241, 356, 368, 385–6, 392–3, 432, 543, 552, 618, 708, 792, 800, 812, 816, 937; **6:** 345, 1096–7, 1255, 1257, 1280, 1332, 1334, 1343–4, 1357–9, 1398–9 (see espec. **6:** 1343–4). Austrian policy in Russo–Turkish war: **6:** 1399. Fr. policy, aspirations & activities in Russo–Turkish War: **5:** 356, 792, 800; **6:** 1332, 1339. GB policy, aspirations & activities in Russo–Turkish War: **5:** 356, 393, 792, 800; **6:** 1332, 1399. Military operations: **6:** 1356–7. Ru. war aims: **6:** 1332, 1334. Policy in Pacific Northwest: **4:** 141. See also Greece
—Poland: Condition of peasantry: **1:** 460. Discussed at Cong. of Vienna: **1:** 967. Ru. acquisition of & policy in: **2:** 805, 815; **4:** 277, 456. Independence sentiment in: **6:** 759.
—U.S. relations with: Ru. offer to mediate, help end War of 1812: **1:** 799, 844, 853, 857, 860–2, 904, 907, 918–9, 921, 923, 927–8. US seeks dip. recognition from (1781): **4:** 242. Role of Lafayette in Am.–Ru. relations: **1:** 926–8. Ru. importance to US as balance to power of GB: **2:** 88–9. C. offered US mission to: **2:** 88–9. Kosloff affair crisis (1815–6) with: **2:** 255, 260, 511. Lewis–Harris conflict in Ru.: **2:** 265. Behavior of Ru. diplomats in Wash.: **5:** 205–7. No threat to US leadership role in Span. Am.: **2:** 533. Urge peace during (1820) US–Sp. tension over

Fla.: **2:** 798, 804–5. C. on hypocrisy of foreign policy of: **2:** 804–5. C. instructions to Middleton: **4:** 355–62, 630. US claims against: **4:** 108, 141, 207, 240, 261, 269–70, 275–6, 284, 288, 292, 320, 917, 926, 934, 936, 951–2; **5:** 97, 112, 162, 263–4, 386, 478–9, 579, 980; **6:** 132–3, 172–3, 187, 191, 277, 501, 999, 1281. Tariff relations with: **4:** 216, 223, 226. Recip. principle extended to Ru.: **4:** 116, 216, 247, 644; **5:** 911. Access of US shipping to Black Sea: **5:** 691. Tension with in Pacific NW: **4:** 141, 179, 269–70. Treaty of demarcation with (4/17/24): **4:** 213; **5:** 449. Nicholas I as arbitrator of NE boundary: **5:** 447. Dip. immunity of Ru. Min. in Wash.: **6:** 958, 963. Publication of a history of US–Ru. dip.: **6:** 241–2. Friendly dispositions toward US: **6:** 1140. US cooperation with Ru. in helping end Sp. wars against former Span. Am. colonies: **4:** 355, 357, 361, 556, 574, 627, 630–1, 647, 653, 683–4, 691, 702, 739–42, 745, 751, 766, 828, 879, 896, 903, 921, 929–31, 944, 946–7, 950, 957–8; **5:** 19, 36–7, 78, 83, 163, 169, 181, 229, 236–7, 261–2, 318–9, 331, 335, 386, 397, 399, 414, 424, 504, 579, 691, 697, 966, 1024–6; **6:** 35, 183–4
Rutgers, Henry: Key to JQA political hopes in N.Y.C. in 1828: **6:** 606. C. works to recruit to JQA reelection campaign: **6:** 644–5

Salt: Price decline(s): **1:** 497. Price of: **1:** 580; **2:** 833. *See also* American System: tariff
Sandwich Islands. *See* Hawaii
Sandford, Nathan: VP prospect on C. ticket in 1824: **3:** 733, 744, 776, 799, 822, 833, 835, 841, 853, 858, 864. In 1826 N.Y. Gov. elections: **5:** 347. On N.Y. legis. choice of Pres. elections: **3:** 866. C. opinion of: **3:** 776; **5:** 126. Chairman, Sen. Foreign Relations Committee: **5:** 1037. Lack of political decisiveness, courage, & energy: **6:** 434, 1253. Mentioned as VP nominee on JQA ticket (1828): **6:** 1142
Sardinia, Kingdom of: Treaty with Tur.: **4:** 277, 434. Nature & extent of US trade with: **5:** 161, 624; **6:** 142, 782. Fr. trade advantage in: **6:** 142. Consular relations with US: **2:** 862–3; **5:** 1006; **6:** 271, 325. US extends tariff recip. to: **4:** 116, 247, 644; **5:** 329, 911. Extends MFN status to US: **6:** 142. Holy Alliance crushes revolution in Piedmont: **2:** 863; **3:** 81, 87
Scott, Robert: Service as agent for James Morrison: **2:** 315, 578. Recieves legacy from Morrison Estate: **3:** 499, 508, 556, 835, 869, 882–3; **5:** 543; **6:** 812–3. Brother & sister of receive Morrison legacies: **6:** 812–3. Speculates in Mo. land: **3:** 578–9. Business, legal & plantation agent for C. while in Wash.: **3:** 349, 410, 527–8, 531–2, 541, 555, 563–4, 593–4, 627–8, 633, 665, 667–8, 734–5, 752, 788, 889; **4:** 7–8, 50–1, 723–4; **5:** 543, 683–4, 704–5, 758, 940–1, 1034–5,

1058; **6:** 63–4, 111–2, 818–9, 935–7, 945–7, 1016–8, 1039, 1081–2, 1104–5, 1151. Supports C. political career: **3:** 541. Comments on Ky. state politics: **3:** 555–6; **4:** 8, 724; **6:** 946. Slaveowner: **3:** 508, 869. Drinking habits: **5:** 1035. *See also* Morrison, James (Morrison Estate)
Scott, Winfield: Service in War of 1812: **1:** 993, 994; **2:** 158. C. praises War of 1812 role of: **2:** 148. Meeting with Lafayette: **2:** 114. Author of drill manual: **2:** 913–4. Commands Western Dept., US: **4:** 502. C. toasts on visit to Lex.: **4:** 502. Hopes C. will run for VP in 1828: **6:** 1141
Sergeant, John: Family: **6:** 1105. Character of: **3:** 210. C. opinions of: **3:** 355; **4:** 373. Opposition to Mo. Compromise: **2:** 776–7, 786; **3:** 21. On protective tariff: **2:** 843. Work for BUS: **3:** 144, 353, 355, 596–7, 647. On Patent Office matters: **4:** 367, 373. Supports Mex. claims by Philadelphia business men: **4:** 724–5; **5:** 961. Patronage recommendations to C: **4:** 777–8; **5:** 667, 939, 957, 1033–4. Appt. delegate to Panama Cong.: **4:** 832–3, 851, 905; **5:** 303–4. Support staff requests for mission to Panama: **5:** 77–8, 939. Declines mission to Panama Cong.: **5:** 346, 361. Accepts mission to Panama Cong.: **5:** 367. On growth of JQA admin. political strength: **5:** 396. C. instructions to on Panama Cong.: **5:** 708, 925. Ties US House election in Pa. (1826): **5:** 729–31, 745, 755, 766–7, 798, 819–20, 897. On Bolivar: **6:** 78. On Mex.: **6:** 125, 169, 491. On GB interdiction of US trade in BWI colonies: **6:** 169. Disgust with Tacubaya delays, plans departure: **6:** 542–3, 613, 711. Urges C. to campaign in Pa.: **6:** 864. On outcome of US House elections in Ky. (1827): **6:** 1032. Briefs C. on Philadelphia & Pa. politics: **5:** 729–31; **6:** 897, 1023, 1049–51, 1213, 1402. On sectional factor in VP choice for 1828: **6:** 1063. Mentioned as possible speaker of US House: **6:** 1142, 1200, 1229. Role in & views of 1828 Pres. campaign: **6:** 125, 864, 1213, 1402
Shaler, William: Health problems: **4:** 242, 415; **5:** 107, 971; **6:** 101, 559–60, 831, 898, 991, 1170. Visits Hawaii (1804): **1:** 918. Courier to Ghent Peace Commission: **1:** 865–6, 875–80, 897, 904, 925, 1000, 1002; **2:** 129. Sees importance of C. role at Ghent: **2:** 74. Suggests buying carriage for C. in Paris: **1:** 912. Analysis of European power politics (1814): **1:** 922. Undertakes history of Algiers: **4:** 395. On Gr. war of independence against Turks: **4:** 415. Journals of as historical source material: **4:** 944. On Fr. naval operations against Algiers: **6:** 831, 1170. Proposed secret agent to scene of Vienna Cong.: **1:** 989–90. On advantages of US–Sp. commercial treaty: **6:** 831–2
Shaw, Henry: Patronage requests of C.: **5:** 608, 675, 942. On Mass. state politics: **5:** 650–1, 943–4; **6:** 947, 1278–9, On N.Y. State politics: **5:** 650–1, 675–7, 943–4.

1034. Leased out: **1:** 2, 73, 92–3, 326; **2:** 86, 128, 724; **3:** 520, 555, 563; **6:** 223. Leased in: **1:** 353, 435, 709; **2:** 339, 363, 683, 706, 754. In C. law practice (*see* Clay, Henry: slaves & slavery in Clay law practice)
—sale & lease prices of slaves: Sale prices: Year 1800: **1:** 41, 54; 1806: **1:** 236–7; 1807: **1:** 289, 303–4; 1808: **1:** 370, 384; 1809: **1:** 395–6, 404; 1811: **1:** 560; 1812: **1:** 708, 716, 725; 1813: **1:** 824–5; 1814: **1:** 949; 1816: **2:** 247; 1817: **2:** 417; 1820: **2:** 893; 1821: **3:** 73, 127; 1822: **3:** 310, 342; 1823: **3:** 439, 442, 4: 721; 1824: **3:** 773, 872; 1826: **5:** 218; 1827: **5:** 64, 576, 935, 993. Lease costs: Year 1815: **2:** 86; 1816: **2:** 128; 1819: **2:** 706; 1820: **2:** 754; 1823: **3:** 520, 555, 563; 1827; **4:** 223; **6:** 1164.
—slave trade: Origins of African: **2:** 266. C. sees as brutal practice: **2:** 421; **4:** 254; **6:** 90, 94. Opposition to & arguments against: **2:** 420–1; **4:** 253–4. US positions, laws & policies on: **4:** 127, 136, 220, 246, 253–4. US attempts to enforce anti–slave trade laws: **5:** 369–71, 1056–7; **6:** 3, 4–5, 439–40, 483. US Supreme Court & slave trade: **5:** 1057; **6:** 4–5, 77, 168, 196–7, 269. US citizens involved illegally in: **4:** 273, 275; **5:** 369, 1057; **6:** 384, 394, 400. US rejects slave trade suppression treaty with GB (*see* Great Britain). Returning intercepted slaves to Africa: **6:** 406, 646, 751–2. European attempts to suppress (*see* Brazil; Buenos Aires; Colombia; France; Great Britain; Great Britain empire: Canada). Deemed piracy: **4:** 220. Va. ends: **6:** 90
Sloane, John: Supports C. in BUS legal issue in Ohio: **3:** 129–30. Campaigns for C. (1822–3) in Ohio: **3:** 294, 308, 340–1. Analyzes & advises C. on upcoming 1824 Pres. election: **3:** 294–5, 341. Analyzes Ohio & national politics for C.: **3:** 294–5, 340–1; 4: 799–800. Election to US House: **3:** 871–2; **5:** 799. Supports C. on "Corrupt Bargain" issue: **4:** 226–7, 282–3; **6:** 572–3. Supports canal projects in Ohio: **5:** 800. Patronage recommendations to C.: **5:** 1015. Connection with Carter Beverley "Fayetteville Attack" on C.: **6:** 572–3
Smith, Samuel: Transactions in Ky. land: **1:** 194–5, 230, 475; **2:** 108, 118, 579, 698. C. legal work for: **1:** 194–5, 230. On Non–Intercourse Act: **1:** 448. C. purchases "Ashland" from (1807): **1:** 474–5, 596–7; **2:** 96, 686. On non–transfer of East Fla.: **1:** 520. Markets C. Ashland produce in Baltimore: **2:** 95–6, 118. On BUS: **2:** 170. On Tariff Act of 1816: **2:** 179–80, 183–6. On Tariff Act of 1820: **2:** 824–5. On National (Cumberland) Road: **2:** 187–8. On independence of Span. Am. republics: **2:** 291, 500, 503–4, 542, 546–7, 556, 558–9. Candidate for US House Speaker: **2:** 401. On US access to Dardanelles: **2:** 552. Business failure in 1819: **2:** 698; **4:** 451. On US trade to East Indies: **2:** 118–9. On military ap

prop.: **2:** 790. Calls Cong. caucus to nom. Pres. & VP: **2:** 820. Aids career of son–in–law Hughes: **4:** 85–6, 119, 120, 324, 331. Estimates possible Electoral vote in 1824 Pres. election: **3:** 373, 375. Asks C. for patronage favors: **4:** 85–6, 95, 120–1, 376–7, 426–8; **5:** 1007; **6:** 184. On US trade in Span. Am.: **4:** 118, 120; **5:** 818, 830. Will give JQA admin. a fair trial: **4:** 119. C. asks opinion on Anglo–Am. trade issues: **4:** 332, 337–8. Advises C. on Anglo–Am. trade issues: **4:** 469–75. Reelected to US Sen. (1826): **5:** 419. C. warned against: **6:** 124. On GB restriction on US shipping: **6:** 240, 354, 357, 426. Miscalls Md. state elections (1827): **6:** 1333
Somerville, William C.: Family: **5:** 157, 173, 210. Mission to Gr. (*see* Greece). Chargé in Stockholm: **4:** 255–6. As slave owner: **5:** 210. Illness & death in Paris enroute to Gr.: **4:** 334, 772–3, 849, 862–3, 898–9, 938, 956; **5:** 24, 31, 51–3, 74, 137, 173. Will & estate of: **5:** 210, 483
Southard, Samuel L.: Family: **5:** 710–11. Pro–Calhoun in 1824 campaign: **3:** 436. C. patronage favors for: **5:** 1019. Appt. SecNavy: **3:** 436–7; **4:** 67. C. patronage correspondence with: **5:** 935, 1019. Obliges C. patronage request: **3:** 538–44. C. asks favors of: **6:** 79. Partisan criticism of: **4:** 906. Praise for as SecNavy: **5:** 797–8. C. personal & social relations with: **4:** 911; **5:** 173; **6:** 1159. C. inquires of about N.J. politics: **5:** 710. On 1828 Pres. campaign & election **6:** 754, 864–5, 944
South Carolina: Impact of non–importation & embargo on: **1:** 741–2. Opposition to Monroe admin. in: **5:** 891. Hostility to BUS in: **2:** 731. Support for JQA in: **5:** 577, 673; **6:** 179, 202. US Sen. elections in (1822): **3:** 335, 337. AJ movement in: **5:** 576–7, 673, 892. Opposition to JQA admin. in: **5:** 891. JQA patronage errors in: **5:** 576–7, 673. US Sen. election in (1826): **5:** 673, 892, 1001. State legis. elections in (1826): **5:** 804. US House election in (1826): **5:** 891–2. Law against free Negroes coming to ports of: **5:** 1016–7; **6:** 70–1, 233. Calhoun following in: **5:** 891–2. Origin of Nullification issue: **5:** 1016–7. Defies Article I of Anglo–Am. Conv. (1815): **5:** 1017. *See also* Election of 1824: campaign activity in states & sections; & prognoses & outcomes; Election of 1828: campaign activity in states & sections; & prognoses & outcomes
Southworth, Sylvester S.: Supports C. for Pres.: **5:** 258–9; **6:** 350. Edits Providence *Literary Cadet:* **5:** 258; **6:** 350. Deplores C. duel with Randolph: **5:** 259. Plans to skewer leaders of opposition to JQA admin.: **5:** 431
Spain: Character of people: **5:** 619. Contempt for Ferdinand VII: **2:** 507, 807; 4: 594. Character of Ferdinand VII: **6:** 999, 1358. History of colonialism in Span. Am.: **2:** 515–6. Revolutions in Span. Am.

761

Spain (*continued*):
against: **1:** 624; **2:** 494–5, 504, 531. Too weak to suppress revolutions in Spain. Am.: **2:** 531, 701–2, 704, 858–9; **4:** 296–8; **6:** 465. War atrocities in Span. Am.: **2:** 517–9, 854. Holy Alliance will not support in Span. Am.: **2:** 532; **5:** 319. Difficulty of holding Cuba: **2:** 783 (*see also* below Spain empire: Cuba). Interest in regaining La.: **1:** 911. No threat to US (1814): **1:** 996. C. dislike of: **2:** 492, 515–6, 814; **4:** 742. C. on future of: **4:** 741–2, 896. Internal instability, disorder, revolution, civil war in: **1:** 911, 922, 924, 927, 996; **4:** 594–5, 616, 640, 656, 751–2, 767–8, 772, 778–9, 841, 849, 896; **5:** 252, 394–5, 578, 636, 992; **6:** 112, 465, 911, 998–9, 1056, 1092, 1119–20, 1139, 1168–9, 1195, 1245–6, 1319, 1358. Unprepared for democracy: **6:** 1092. Revolution of 1820: **2:** 789, 802, 807, 858, 863; **3:** 30–1, 313, 404; **6:** 677. Fr. conquest (1808) of: **2:** 527; **4:** 356. Fr. military intervention in (1823), occupation, influence, withdrawal from: **2:** 789; **3:** 312–3, 383, 399, 403–5, 606–7; **4:** 117, 290, 493, 556, 570, 594, 640, 763, 778; **5:** 189, 710, 857, 1051; **6:** 26–7, 59, 112, 128, 447, 491, 646, 678, 735, 878, 895, 937, 979, 1041, 1043, 1097, 1119, 1145, 1178, 1245–6, 1255, 1319, 1330 (*see espec.* **3:** 313). Policies of Ferdinand VII: **4:** 209, 290, 402; **5:** 252, 595; **6:** 1092. Collapse of constit. govt. in: **3:** 313, 498, 606–7; **4:** 290, 639; **5:** 144, 595, 647, 923 (*see espec.* **4:** 290). Incompetence of govt. of: **5:** 579, 800; **6:** 382. Economic problems of: **2:** 513, 530–1, 542–3, 704; **4:** 402, 525, 616, 689, 903; **5:** 24, 44, 91, 517–8, 559, 578; **6:** 664, 1195. Grain shortages: **4:** 117, 209. Sale of import monopolies: **5:** 857. Imports & exports: **6:** 80. Tariff policy & schedules: **5:** 194–5, 517. Trade restrictions: **4:** 596. Trade in Span. Am.: **5:** 414, 668. Slave trade: **5:** 242–3. Clerical opposition to Ferdinand VII: **6:** 1358. Role of Rom. Catholic Church & Apostolical party in: **5:** 252; **6:** 194, 911, 1139, 1246, 1358. Relations with Vatican (*see* Papal States). Army: **6:** 194, 663, 1195. Navy: **4:** 447–8, 463; **5:** 809; **6:** 994. Recognition of Br.: **4:** 875; **5:** 710. Hope & prospects of recovering lost Span. Am. colonies: **4:** 209, 751; **5:** 131, 164, 167, 216, 414, 545, 552, 559, 720; **6:** 465 (*see also* Chile; Colombia; Mexico; Peru). Continuing military efforts to crush revolutions in Span. Am.: **4:** 104, 174, 240–1, 249, 357; **5:** 167, 465; **6:** 664, 1133 (*see also ibid.*). European & Holy Alliance role in shaping Sp. policy in Span. Am.: **2:** 856–7; **4:** 241, 575, 741, 751, 896, 930; **5:** 83, 102, 131–2, 189, 215–6, 317–8, 386, 414; **6:** 1217–8 (*see also* Austria; France; Russia). Debate recognition of independence of former Span. Am. colonies: **5:** 101–2, 125, 131–2, 154, 157, 162–3, 189, 215, 414, 429, 691; **6:** 382, 1360, 1406. Ad-

vantages to of peace with Span. Am.: **4:** 326, 358–60, 366–7, 372; **5:** 83, 189, 229, 414. Consider selling recognition to new Span. Am. states: **4:** 640; **5:** 83, 102, 414. Internal political implications of recognition of Span. Am. states: **4:** 774, 778, 896; **5:** 101–2, 163, 189, 414–5, 429; **6:** 465, 664. On Br.–BA war: **5:** 215–6. Open Cuba & PR to foreign consuls: **6:** 646 (*see also* below Spain empire: Cuba; Puerto Rico). Swiss troops in Fr. service withdraw from: **6:** 26–7, 59, 112, 128. Threat of war with Port. (*see* Portugal). Threat of war with GB over Port. (*see* Great Britain)
—U.S. relations with: Burr role in: **1:** 253, 256–7, 259, 263 (*see also* Burr, Aaron). "Spanish Conspiracy" separatist movement in Ky.: **1:** 244–7, 269–71, 329, 331, 336–8, 343, 648–9. C. on independence of Cuba: **1:** 624 (*see also* below Spain empire: Cuba). Strategic threat to US in Gulf: **1:** 514. Sp. control of Miss. River (1802): **1:** 515–6. Hostility toward US: **1:** 945; **2:** 155, 502. Pinckney Treaty (1795) with: **2:** 636, 660; **4:** 173–4, 296; **5:** 1349–50; **6:** 384, 403, 628, 658. War–like acts against US: **2:** 142, 502, 513–4. C. wants no war with over Span. Am. issues: **2:** 512–3. Sp. too weak to fight US: **2:** 513, 530–1, 542, 782–3. Sp. seeks recovery of West Fla.: **2:** 155. US seeks East Fla. from (*see* below Spain empire: Florida, East). Issue of SW boundary: **2:** 634–5 (*see also* Spain empire: Adams–Onís Treaty). JQA policy toward as SecState: **2:** 499–500, 504, 513 (*see also ibid.*). Maritime neutral rights problems: **2:** 492–3, 502, 560; **5:** 809. US recognition of independence of New Span. Am. states issue: **2:** 553, 753, 797, 802–3, 815, 854, 860; **4:** 442. US urges Sp. to end military operations in Span. Am. & recognize independence of former colonies: **4:** 296–8, 322, 326, 336, 366–7, 372, 571–2, 574, 595, 629, 639–40, 647, 653, 684, 689, 739–44, 751, 841, 875–6, 896, 903; **5:** 1, 43–4, 78, 80, 83, 91, 101–2, 131–2, 169, 189–90, 216, 249, 261–2, 349, 414, 424, 429, 437, 504, 533, 545, 552, 691. Problems of US citizens involved in Span. Am. revolutions & wars: **2:** 664, 672–3; **4:** 699 (*see also* Buenos Aires: U.S. relations with; Colombia: U.S. relations with; Mexico: U.S. relations with). Capture of US citizens in Span. Am. service: **6:** 411, 414, 464, 860. Blockade, contraband, privateering & other neutral rights problems in Sp. wars with former colonies: **4:** 406; **6:** 656–60, 1158, 1349 (*see also* Colombia: U.S. relations with; Mexico: U.S. relations with; Porter, David; Vessels *Kensington* & *Zulme* in Name Index). Protests US unneutrality in wars in Span. Am.: **4:** 675, 864–5; **6:** 628–9, 656–60, 677, 1108, 1113, 1145, 1186–8, 1196, 1198–9, 1202, 1215–8, 1255, 1313 (*see also* Porter, David). Protests building & outfitting of Sp. Am.

warships & privateers in US ports: **4:** 675, 734, 738, 745, 864–5, 916–7; **6:** 628, 657, 660, 1113, 1145, 1186–8, 1196, 1202, 1215–8, 1313. US attempts to control building of Span. Am. war vessels in US ports: **4:** 675, 734, 738, 866, 916–8. Protests US arms shipments to Span. Am.: **4:** 675. US suggests truce–armistice formula to halt Sp. wars in Span. Am.: **5:** 229–30, 238, 261, 318–9, 504, 877. US policy on Cuba & PR (*see* below Spain empire: Cuba; Puerto Rico). C. instructions to Everett: **4:** 292–300, 322, 440. Nature & extent of US trade with Sp. & colonies: **4:** 563; **6:** 403, 831–2 (*see also* below Spain empire). Tariff reciprocity: **6:** 2. Commercial treaty with Sp. sought: **4:** 296, 629, 841; **5:** 91, 195, 415, 424, 877; **6:** 194, 246, 645, 831–2, 851–2. Tariff, duty, fee discrim. against US shipping: **4:** 93, 192, 224, 261, 290, 295–6, 299–300, 382, 401, 443, 493, 563, 570, 616, 629, 642, 660, 875–6, 921; **5:** 12–3, 22, 25, 91, 560, 694, 857; **6:** 2, 246, 265, 331, 826. US tariff, duty, fee discrim. against Sp. shipping: **6:** 246, 826. Harassment of US shipping: **4:** 113, 327, 789; **6:** 324, 646, 744, 821, 848, 877–8, 1119, 1169, 1246. Concessions to US shipping: **5:** 652–3, 670; **6:** 202, 214. Restrictions on US imports: **4:** 242, 493, 573; **5:** 22, 91, 195. US claims against: **4:** 239–40, 290, 293–4, 299, 307, 327, 376, 625–6, 629, 780, 809, 812, 841–2, 875, 904; **5:** 209, 252, 349, 385, 415, 533, 636, 668, 683, 690, 800, 843, 877, 973, 981, 985, 992, 1010; **6:** 3, 27, 128–9, 157, 190, 194, 249, 324, 382, 411, 482, 604, 821, 851–2, 903, 1251–2, 1349–50 (*see espec. Antelope, Zulme* in Name Index). Seek indemnities (claims) conv. with Sp.: **5:** 992, 1010; **6:** 194, 382, 411, 464, 645, 710, 851–2. Sp. claims against US: **4:** 295, 738, 812; **5:** 160, 298, 311, 690, 769–70, 827, 862, 1015, 1046–7; **6:** 313, 480, 1026, 1349, 1373. US citizens arrested: **4:** 558, 699, 829; **6:** 1202, 1288–9, 1298; US assistance to Sp. political exiles: **4:** 117, 224, 338–9. Piracy suppression in West Indies: **4:** 224–5, 293, 296, 300, 307 (*see also* U.S. Navy). Foxardo (Fajardo) incident (*see* Porter, David). US loan to Philadelphia legation of Sp.: **4:** 237, 257, 260, 525, 634–5, 443, 545, 629, 689, 778; **5:** 16, 91, 528, 533, 956–7. Sp. interest in building warships in US: –5: 252, 595. Slavery & slave trade issues: **5:** 160

Spain empire
—Canary Islands: Condition of natives: **5:** 1059. GB plot to seize: **6:** 665, 920, 1353, 1360. US citizens imprisoned at: **4:** 442–3. Protecting US interests at: **5:** 1059. Harassment of US shipping at: **4:** 768; **5:** 1059. US trade with: **5:** 1059
—Cuba: Natural wealth & resources: **4:** 272, 883. Backwardness of: **4:** 273; **5:** 32. Depression: **4:** 272, 840; **5:** 242. Socio–political structure: **4:** 272–4. Class

attitudes toward independence: **4:** 272–3. Internal disorders: **4:** 882. Independence of: **4:** 175, 181, 272–3, 442, 711–2, 743, 883; **5:** 89, 237, 331–2. Slavery & slave trading in: **4:** 181, 273; **5:** 242, 653, 690, 740; **6:** 91. US citizens involved in slave trade: **4:** 273. Clergy in: **4:** 273. Piracy in: **4:** 273–4, 293, 298, 326, 361, 374, 402, 762; **6:** 1163. Nature & extent of US trade with: **5:** 528, 740; **6:** 206, 303, 403, 725, 739, 1169. US wants Consul at Havana: **4:** 689, 841, 875, 903; **5:** 415, 606; **6:** 206, 403, 646, 710, 744. Harassment of US shipping in: **4:** 726, 824, 939; **6:** 332. US citizens imprisoned, insulted in: **4:** 143, 181, 314–5, 596, 726, 776, 824, 925, 939; **5:** 50, 740; **6:** 332, 595, 681, 821, 860, 1151, 1289, 1296–8. USN shows flag in: **4:** 575, 925; **5:** 14 (*see also* U.S. Navy). Military defensibility: **6:** 519. As logistical base for Sp. attack on Span. Am. Attitudes toward US in: **4:** 272–3. Desires connection with US: **4:** 711–2. C. on importance of to US South: **5:** 659. Base for Negro attack on US South: **6:** 27. Fr. interest & policy in: **4:** 360, 524, 537, 572, 574–5, 578–9, 584, 640, 685, 744–5, 763, 766–7, 777, 935–6; **5:** 22, 67, 202, 237–8; **6:** 166. US cautions Fr. on ambitions in: **4:** 763, 767, 935–6; **5:** 21, 237–8; **6:** 166. GB interest in & dip. tactics regarding: **4:** 360, 742–3. GB plot to seize: **6:** 664–5, 801, 920–1, 1057, 1353, 1360. Rumored GB–US war over: **6:** 801. GB regards as US colony: **6:** 1335. US cautions GB on ambitions in: **4:** 175; **5:** 237. GB spies in: **4:** 274. Attitudes toward GB in: **4:** 272. Sp. desire to retain: **4:** 532, 570, 685, 742; **5:** 1, 242. Pro–Sp. sentiment in: **4:** 883. People of seek peace & Sp. recognition of new Span. Am. states: **4:** 272, 367, 372–3, 712, 885, 946; **5:** 63. General US interest in: **4:** 359–61. Strategic importance of to US: **4:** 174–5, 298, 360; **5:** 659. US annexation of: **4:** 175, 361, 579, 691, 711, 884, 947; **5:** 224; **6:** 1353. US opposes transfer of to third power: **4:** 174–5, 297–8, 360–1, 442–3, 525, 584, 630, 946; **5:** 84–5, 242–3, 331, 493, 1005, 1021, 1025; **6:** 193, 303, 519, 1353. Abortive Robertson spy mission to & report on: **4:** 271–4;, 310, 712, 731, 882–4; **5:** 47–8; **6:** 295 (*see espec.* C. instructions: **4:** 882–4; & Robertson, Thomas B.). Cook spy mission to: **6:** 295–6, 302–3, 315, 519, 1223, 1300 (*see also* Cook, Daniel P.). Opposition to C. policy of non–transfer of: **5:** 493. US urges Sp. retention of Cuba & PR: **4:** 298, 360–1, 442–3, 630, 691, 739–44, 762–3, 767, 946; **5:** 21–2, 80, 102, 237, 243, 331, 1025, 1169. US neutral attitude toward: **4:** 883–4, 947. GB supports Sp. retention of Cuba & PR: **4:** 572, 590, 739; **5:** 27, 36, 67, 1005; **6:** 166 (*see also* Canning, George). Joint GB–US support of Sp. retention of Cuba & PR: **4:** 572, 574, 640, 653, 739, 742–4, 767, 935–6; **5:**

Spain empire (*continued*):
1057. US declines unilateral self–denying pledge of future hands off Cuba: **4:** 640, 742–4; **5:** 1057. Proposed joint GB–Fr.–US guaranty of Cuba & PR to Sp.: **4:** 572, 590, 640, 653, 742, 766–7; **5:** 36, 238, 1057 (*see* Canning, George). Status of in event of GB–Sp. war: **5:** 998, 1005, 1021, 1057; **6:** 165–6, 193, 296, 303, 664, 1169. Proposed joint GB–US–Span. Am. guaranty of independence of: **5:** 1005. Colombia & Mex. threaten military invasion & liberation of: **4:** 181, 272, 298, 313, 327, 359, 443, 493, 563, 567, 578–9, 584–5, 641, 711–2, 724, 734, 777, 811, 840, 864, 876, 882–3, 930, 946–7, 950, 957–8; **5:** 1, 9, 16, 19, 27, 65–6, 73, 80, 89, 91, 102, 133, 138, 153–4, 157, 164, 179, 181, 194, 215, 229, 237, 261, 281, 291, 309, 332–5, 349, 378, 386, 397, 414, 496, 535, 649, 709, 1025; **6:** 193, 548, 851, 1344. Proposed Sp. military buildup in Cuba to thwart aggressive Colombia & Mex. designs: **4:** 493, 720, 925, 957; **5:** 22, 44, 63, 80, 88, 215, 229–30, 242, 291, 333; **6:** 994, 1120
—Florida, East: US interest in purchasing: **2:** 545, 560, 657. C. urges (1811) US occupation: **1:** 516, 520–2, 544. Strategic importance of to US: **1:** 624. Non–transfer of to third power: **1:** 520. Madison policy toward: **1:** 519, 522, 771, 774. Rumor of Sp. transfer of to GB: **2:** 155, 159, 173. Monroe policy toward: **2:** 418, 514. Sp. too weak to hold militarily: **2:** 531–2. GB dimension in US decision to seize: **2:** 534–6, 806, 816. Sp. responsible for US invasion of: **2:** 580, 636–7. US responsibility for invasion: **2:** 590, 641. AJ invasion (Seminole War) of & military operations in: **2:** 477, 490, 612–3, 636–62; **3:** 284–5, 469; **4:** 426, 701; **5:** 416; **6:** 367–8, 591 (*see espec.* **2:** 612–3). C. criticizes AJ invasion of Fla.: **2:** 636–62 (*see also* Jackson, Andrew; Election of 1824: issues; Election of 1828: issues, charges & counter–charges in campaign). Ky. troops with AJ invading force: **4:** 426. Constit. issues in AJ invasion: **2:** 580; **6:** 367, 777. Sp. slave property captured: **4:** 701; **5:** 218
—Adams–Onis Treaty Negotiations: Purchase of East Fla.: **2:** 673, 677–8, 682, 782; **3:** 748. JQA errors in negotiating: **2:** 755–6, 762–3, 757–8, 760–1, 769, 783, 815, 823, 857. No US sentiment for war with Sp. during negotiations: **2:** 754, 766, 788, 797. Threat of war with Sp. during: **2:** 783, 802, 815. C. opinion of treaty: **2:** 704, 732, 808, 813, 818–9, 823. Slowness in Sp. ratification: **2:** 678, 731–3, 766, 769, 778–9, 783, 814, 855, 860; **6:** 191. Sp. strategic purpose in delay of ratification: **2:** 704. Sp. ratification linked to US non–recognition of Sp. Am. independence: **2:** 704, 797, 802–3, 814–5, 854, 860. US disregards Sp. ratification delay & occupies Fla.: **2:** 732–3, 752–3, 758–9, 762, 766, 769, 783, 788, 792–3, 796, 802,

804, 807, 812, 819–20. Onis handling of Sp. negotiations: **2:** 496, 756–7, 771–2, 782, 823. GB strategic interest in ratification: **2:** 783. C. resents European involvement in US–Sp. relations: **2:** 806–7, 857. Value of Fla. to US: **2:** 812, 852. Constit. issues involved in: **2:** 800, 808–10. Ratification (Feb. 1821): **3:** 45. Financing purchase payment to Sp.: **3:** 747–8. Claims issues under treaty: **2:** 677–8, 755–6, 760; **3:** 66–7, 370–1, 380–1, 748–9, 897–8, 902; **4:** 380, 677, 701; **5:** 12, 154, 181, 218; **6:** 324, 482, 835. Problem of fresh Sp. land grants in Fla.: **2:** 755–64, 779, 784, 813. Trade concenssions: **4:** 169–70. Northwest coast (Oregon) agreement: **5:** 448, 450; **6:** 388. Southwest boundary agreement: **2:** 810; **4:** 171–2, 545; **5:** 394; **6:** 417 (*see also* Mexico: U.S. relations with). US surrender of Tex. agreement: **2:** 769, 771, 782–3, 788, 800, 810–4, 823, 852; **3:** 763; **6:** 330
—Florida, West: C. arguments for US occupation of: **1:** 507–17, 634–6, 640; **2:** 807, 813 (*see also* Congress of the United States: eleventh congress). US annexation (1810): **6:** 1026. Incorporation into La.: **1:** 455–6, 640. Boundary problems: **1:** 455. Encourage US immigration into: **1:** 455. US would purchase: **2:** 545, 560. Sp. seeks recovery of after War of 1812: **2:** 135–7, 155. Separatist–independence movement in: **1:** 601; **6:** 595. Sp. land grants in: **2:** 812–3, 816. Claims on US by Sp. inhabitants & land grantees: **5:** 298, 311, 827, 1015, 1046–7; **6:** 313, 480, 542, 1026, 1372 (*see also* Losada, Juan Miguel de in Name Index)
—Philippines: US consul in Manila: **6:** 1040, 1215
—Puerto Rico: US annexation of: **4:** 361. Independence of: **4:** 442. Fr. interest in: **4:** 685, 767 (*see also* above Cuba). GB designs on: **6:** 151. Piracy in: **4:** 293, 296, 300, 326, 361, 374, 402, 762. Foxardo (Fajardo) incident (Nov. 1824): **4:** 224–5, 298–9, 311, 320, 327, 331, 520, 533–4, 738, 812; **6:** 324, 337, 375 (*see also* Porter, David; U.S. Navy). Sp. seeks to retain: **4:** 532, 685 (*see also* above Cuba). Colombia–Mex. threats against (*see* above Cuba). US supports Sp. retention of (*see* above Cuba). US opposes transfer of: **4:** 361 (*see also* above Cuba). General US interest in: **4:** 359–61. US wants Consuls in: **6:** 646. US claims against Sp. originate in: **4:** 140, 307
—Santo Domingo: Sp. recognize independence of: **4:** 689. US consular relations with: **4:** 93
Spanish America: C. supports independence of & US recognition of new republics in: **1:** 624, 758; **2:** 135–6, 155–6, 289–92, 343–4, 402–5, 492–507, 511, 515, 525, 538, 541–62, 572, 581, 667–8, 817, 854–9, 867–8, 870; **3:** 22–4, 29–31, 44, 80–1, 143, 186, 404; **4:** 103, 167–8, 247; **5:** 278, 307; **6:** 714, 1102–3, 1222,

1298–9, 1393. C. lauded for stance on Span. Am. independence & recognition: **2:** 343–4, 385–7, 572–3; **3:** 184, 405, 414, 481, 778; **4:** 1, 103, 526, 778; **5:** 661; **6:** 745, 783. C. criticized for stance on independence & recognition: **2:** 593. C. equates Span. Am. revolutions with Am. Revolution: **2:** 517, 520, 529, 548–51, 557, 859; **4:** 356–7. Future of Span. Am. republics: **5:** 189, 1049. C. on US commercial stake in independence of Span. Am.: **2:** 519–20, 522–4, 535, 540, 546–8, 558–60, 856–7; **5:** 659; **6:** 82. C. on US political leadership of Span. Am. independence: **2:** 520, 530, 856–7; **3:** 80; **4:** 249; **6:** 714, 751. On liberty & democracy flowering in Span. Am.: **2:** 291, 520, 551, 557, 858; **4:** 655; **5:** 649; **6:** 312–3, 751, 1092, 1257. Origin of independence movements in: **4:** 356. Leadership & class basis of revolution movements in: **2:** 291, 443–6, 520, 522, 551, 557, 584, 858. Character & genius of Span. Americans: **2:** 520–1, 858; **5:** 214–5. US institutions as models for Span. Am.: **4:** 249, 522, 530–1. Emancipation of slaves in Span. Am.: **2:** 858. US influence on revolutions in: **2:** 445, 520. C. on legal, moral, political bases for US recognition: **2:** 525–7, 530, 543–4, 552–3, 556, 565, 797, 854–9; US enthusiasm for recognition policy: **2:** 590; **4:** 442. Ky. favors independence–recognition policy: **5:** 278. European reactions to US recognition: **4:** 212. Holy Alliance as threat to US policy in Span. Am.: **2:** 532–4, 538. **3:** 80–1, 325; **4:** 168, 177, 714. C. on Christianity in: **2:** 522. Condition of natives in: **2:** 548. Importance of independent Span. Am. to security of N.O.: **2:** 525. Wars in stimulate US economy: **3:** 690–1, 705. Burden of armaments in: **6:** 102. C. on selling US vessels to both sides: **2:** 498. US aid to Span. Am. republics: **2:** 155–6, 498–9, 525. US citizens fight in liberation wars of: **2:** 499; **3:** 390–1. Unneutral behavior of US citizens in independence wars in: **2:** 495, 550, 664; **3:** 380, 484, 595–6. US domestic politics of independence–recognition issue: **2:** 543–4, 558, 590. GB–US tension in Span. Am.: **2:** 534–6, 538, 542, 797–8; **4:** 249; **5:** 226. Precious metals exports of vital to US & GB: **2:** 548. Nature & extent of US trade with (*see* entry for specific Span. Am. nation: U.S. relations with). US cotton exports to: **3:** 705, **4:** 100, 177, 249, 375; **5:** 519, 818. Liberal US commercial treaties with (*see* entry for specific Span. Am. nation: U.S. relations with). C. on US non–involvement in internal affairs of Span. Am. states: **2:** 530; **4:** 249. C. urges US neutrality in wars of: **2:** 156, 159, 289–92, 402–5, 441–2, 496–505, 525, 536; **4:** 356, 684, 804; **5:** 316; **6:** 656–60 (*see also* entry for specific Span. Am. nation: U.S. relations with). Preferential tariff system for Span. Am. considered: **6:** 1054 (*see also* Mexico). Monroe sends

fact–finding commission to: **2:** 387, 443–6, 497, 508–11, 556–7, 584–5, 590–1, 592–4, 618–9, 855. C. on inevitable triumph of Span. Am. cause: **2:** 704; **4:** 174. *See also* U.S. Diplomacy: Monroe Doctrine; Panama Congress; Various Span.–Am. States: U.S. relations with

Sparks, Jared: Publication of Shaler consular journal: **4:** 944–5. C. suggests bibliography to: **5:** 387, 406. C. assists research of: **5:** 750. On Hamilton–Jefferson differences: **3:** 415; **6:** 527. C. entertains: **6:** 110. On C. speeches: **6:** 415, 962. Edits out embarrassing data on Am. Revolution: **6:** 297. Edits US dip. correspondence of Am. Revolution under State Dept. contract: **6:** 154, 297–9, 414, 526–7, 717, 859, 899–900. Compensation for editing: **6:** 299, 414. Publishes George Washington correspondence: **6:** 414–5, 526–7. Refuses to assist Timothy Pitkin research on US history: **6:** 717, 859, 899–900. Research in Europe: **6:** 962

St. Louis, Mo.: C. declines invitation to speak in: **6:** 757–8, 810–11, 856–7. Popularity of JQA admin. in: **6:** 810, 1124. C. popularity in: **6:** 1124

Street, Joseph M.: Family: **1:** 246; **6:** 45–6. Attacks "Span. Conspiracy" in Ky.: **1:** 244–6, 329–33, 347–8, 349–50, 648–9; **6:** 45. Federalist sympathies: **1:** 246, 329–30. C. defends in law suit: **1:** 246. Splits with co–publisher John Wood: **1:** 244–6, 259–60. Links C. to Burr conspiracy: **1:** 329, 334 (*see also* Burr, Aaron). C. attacks: **1:** 329–30. Verbal & legal attacks on: **1:** 295–6, 330, 357–8, 649–50. Flees Ky. for Ill. Territory (1812): **1:** 649. Works for US Land Office: **2:** 215. Apologizes to C. for 1806–7 attacks: **6:** 45, 185. C. recommends for public office: **6:** 45. Financial problems: **6:** 45. C. helps secure fed. job: **5:** 46–7. C. forgives for earlier attacks: **6:** 185. Reports to C. on Ill. politics: **5:** 46

Swartwout, Samuel: Involvement with Aaron Burr: **1:** 272–5, 280–1. Supports AJ in 1824: **3:** 888. AJ blasts C. in "Corrupt Bargain" letter to: **4:** 46, 122, 161–4, 211, 286, 403, 781. Authors anti–C. pamphlet: **6:** 396–7, 434

Sweden & Norway: Kingdom of: C. would abolish US Legation in Stockholm: **2:** 232. Annexation of Norway from Denmark (1814): **1:** 885–6, 890, 892, 919, 926; **2:** 240. Attack on Norway: **1:** 862. Pro–US stance of: **1:** 887–8, 902, 919. Interest in US version of maritime neutral rights: **1:** 901, 920, 925–6. C. social life in (1814): **1:** 894, 902. Economic conditions in: **2:** 240–1; **5:** 941. US prize–condemnation problems in Norway: **1:** 900, 926, 940. Usefulness to US dip. declines: **1:** 919, 925–6. Revision of constit.: **6:** 358. King's attitude toward US: **4:** 452. Suppression of slave trade: **4:** 524–5. Seek sale of warships to Mex. & Colombia: **4:** 257, 518–20, 525, 548, 575, 616, 702, 753, 802, 873; **5:** 309, 970,

765

Texas. *See* Mexico: Texas

Thruston, Buckner: C. aids US Sen. race (1804): **1:** 196

Todd, Thomas: Horse breeder: **1:** 282, 322–4. Linked to Span. Assoc. conspiracy: **1:** 246–7, 295–6, 300. Pro–Fr. stance (1793): **1:** 353. C. legal work for & with: **1:** 76, 295–6, 361, 788. Role in War of 1812: **1:** 721. Elected Chief Justice of Ky.: **1:** 271–2. Appt. to US Supreme Court: **1:** 27. Service on Ky. Court of Appeals: **1:** 221–2. Appt. US District Judge: **5:** 31–2. Founder of anti–George Washington admin. Lex. Dem. society: **1:** 353. Support of TU: **1:** 77–8. Political support of C.: **2:** 588. Abstains in *Green vs. Biddle:* **3:** 393. On legal restrictions on BUS: **3:** 751. Death: **5:** 70, 114, 159. *See also* U.S. Supreme Court

Transylvania University: Origins of: **1:** 182. Relation with Bank of Ky. & Bank of Commonwealth: **1:** 431; **3:** 324. C. opinion of: **1:** 71; **2:** 595, 613–4, 735. C. role in finding Pres. of: **1:** 71–2, 77–8, 840–1; **2:** 64–5; **5:** 124–5, 185; **6:** 180–1, 257, 460–1, 518, 661–2, 882–3, 896–7, 900–1, 908–9, 942, 944, 965, 1090, 1146. Economic problems of: **1:** 77–8, 436; **3:** 324, 328–30; **6:** 180–1, 882–3. Faculty members of: **1:** 32, 97, 127, 146, 147, 148, 305; **2:** 594–6, 613–4, 724–5, 868; **3:** 43, 137–8, 447–8; **4:** 609; **6:** 953–4, 1008. Medical school at: **2:** 508, 724–5; **3:** 136–7, 448, 452; **4:** 58, 79–81, 407, 805–6; **5:** 124–5, 185; **6:** 953–4. Academic reorganization of (1818): **2:** 582. Student enrollments: **1:** 78; **4:** 58; **5:** 124–5; **6:** 181. Legal problems of: **1:** 146, 182–4, 564, 734. C. assistance to faculty members of: **2:** 868–9. Tuition costs at: **2:** 582; **3:** 121, 155, 272, 406, 492, 562, 730; **5:** 603–4. Construction of buildings at: **1:** 652, 655–6, 676, 678–83; **3:** 137; **5:** 185, 537. C. interest in general educational reform: **1:** 942. C. work as trustee of: **2:** 198–9, 508, 591; **3:** 324, 330, 351, 843; **4:** 79–80; **6:** 180. Grammar school division of: **3:** 330. Lex. town support of: **1:** 77–8; **6:** 883. State support of & admin. involvement in: **2:** 198–9, 582–3, 735, 780, 782; **3:** 324, 329, 351; **4:** 818; **6:** 883. Board of lauds C. Ghent treaty success: **2:** 67–8. Establishment of dining facilities at: **2:** 582. Law instruction at: **4:** 266. Horace Holley as Pres. of & dismissal of: **2:** 583, 594, 597–8; **4:** 265–6, 461; **5:** 124–5, 185; **6:** 180, 461, 945, 954, 1245. Student opposition to Holley: **2:** 613; **3:** 33, 43. Robert H. Bishop as Acting Pres. of: **2:** 596. James Blythe as Acting Pres. of: **2:** 596. Thomas Johnson Matthews as Acting Pres. of: **3:** 849. C. on church connections of: **2:** 613. Denominational problems & infighting at: **2:** 583, 595, 613; **3:** 738; **5:** 181, 945. Military professorship at: **6:** 882–4, 1016. Faculty salaries: **2:** 594, 597; **3:** 329, 330, 738, 849; **4:** 818. Faculty infighting: **2:** 595–6. Faculty recruitment: **2:** 597–8,

614; **3:** 738, 791, 829–30; **4:** 79–80, 668. Faculty resignations: **4:** 266, 336; **6:** 953–4. Reputation outside Ky.: **2:** 690, 735; **5:** 185. Tenure concept: **3:** 849. Faculty vs. Board on governance of: **3:** 44. Gifts to: **3:** 98, 329 (*see also* below Morrison bequest to). C. rents lecture rooms to faculty of: **2:** 724; **3:** 136–7, 452; **5:** 603–4. Impact of 1819 Depression on: **3:** 328. Staff–student political support for C.: **3:** 447–8. C. houses students of: **3:** 780. Morrison bequest to: **3:** 496, 738, 849; **4:** 724; **5:** 185, 611 (*see espec.* **3:** 496). Morrison Professorship: **3:** 849; **5:** 683. Jacksonians–Reliefers attack curriculum: **4:** 265–6. Relief Party opposition to: **4:** 818; **6:** 883. Thomas McAuley elected Pres.: **6:** 986–7, 1090, 1146. Alva Woods elected Pres. of: **6:** 461–2, 485, 508–11, 516–7, 882, 896–7, 900–1, 908–9, 942, 945, 965, 1016 (*see espec.* **6:** 461–2)

Trimble, David: Land business with C.: **1:** 578–80, 634, 732, 738, 797; **2:** 379, 393–4, 465–7. On military approp.: **2:** 630, 632. On a national loan: **2:** 850. Supports US dip. missions to Span. Am.: **3:** 24. On the tariff: **3:** 707, 728. Service in Cong.: **2:** 569, 627. Elections to Cong.: **3:** 246–7; **5:** 568. Work for C. in 1824 election: **3:** 843–4. Work for JQA in 1828 election: **6:** 1073. Supports JQA for Pres. within Ky. delegation: **4:** 79; **5:** 568. Hostility to in Ky. for JQA vote in US House: **4:** 134. On legis. to handle deserting seamen: **5:** 41. Charges AJ–Caloun bargain in 1824 election: **5:** 280. Possible duel with McDuffie: **5:** 278, 307, 354, 360. Later involvement in C.–JQA "Corrupt Bargain" charge: **6:** 891–2, 1070–1. Loses US House seat (1826): **6:** 568, 959, 966, 970–1

Trimble, John: Seeks US Dist. Atty. in Ky.: **6:** 29, 39–40. Service in Ky. House: **6:** 40

Trimble, Robert: Family: **1:** 222; **4:** 66. Legal work for & with C.: **1:** 261, 374. Interest in & work for TU: **2:** 591. Rejects TU faculty appt.: **4:** 668. On legal restrictions on BUS: **3:** 751. Appt. as US Dist. Judge: **2:** 307–8; **5:** 31–2. Appt. to US Supreme Court (1826): **1:** 222; **5:** 69, 114, 146, 149–50, 193, 210, 221, 254, 279, 360–1, 405. Ky. political dimensions of Supreme Court appt.: **5:** 279. Jacksonians castigate judicial appt.: **6:** 841. Nephew turned down for USMA appt.: **6:** 999

Tucker, Henry St. George: Family: **6:** 815. Candidate for US Sen. in Va. (1825): **4:** 857, 867

Turkey: C. hatred of: **3:** 608, 610. Turco–Egyptian war with Gr. (*see* Greece). European mediation efforts in Gr.–Tur. War (*see* Greece). Treaty with Sardinia: **4:** 277. Treaty with Fr.: **4:** 623. Revolt of Janissaries in: **5:** 482, 543, 552, 571, 618, 638, 680–1. Treaty of Ackerman with Ru. (*see* Russia). Ru.–Tur. War (*see* Russia). Modernization of army: **5:** 638–9. Heavy military losses in Gr.: **5:** 681. De-

preservation: **1:** 514. Territorial expansion: **1:** 516; **2:** 458, 523, 814; **3:** 584. US moral leadership of world: **2:** 530; **5:** 28, 137, 202, 283. US harbors no spirit of conquest: **1:** 982. Secret dip.: **1:** 517–9; **5:** 810. On spies & spying: **2:** 509–11; **4:** 907; **5:** 47–8; **6:** 127 (see Cook, Daniel P.; Robertson, Thomas B.; McRae, Alexander G. in Name Index). On carrying democracy abroad: **2:** 517, 814; **5:** 340; **6:** 312–13. Isolationism & non–involvement abroad: **1:** 758; **2:** 530, 806; **5:** 319; **6:** 1139–40, 1257. Devious ways of diplomats: **2:** 805. Flattery in: **4:** 740. MFN vs. recip. in commercial relations & relations abroad: **4:** 168–9, 245, 248, 477–8, 797, 803; **5:** 866; **6:** 12–3, 582 (see also various nations: U.S. relations with). State interference in execution of: **4:** 764–5, 808; **5:** 249, 431, 1016–7. Shipwreck & salvage issues in: **4:** 292, 330–1, 764–5, 808, 866; **5:** 292, 249–50, 474. Legis. vs. executive roles in: **2:** 536–8, 544–5, 553–6; **4:** 217–8; **5:** 105–6. De facto recognition: **3:** 606–7. Fr. as language of dip.: **5:** 185. See also U.S. State Dept.

—Monroe Doctrine: Promulgated (12/2/23): **3:** 541–2. Principles of: **3:** 597, 764–5; **4:** 170–1, 355, 579; **5:** 201–2. GB reaction to: **5:** 317, 341, 1014–5. Holy Alliance relation to: **3:** 607, 609–10, 765; **5:** 202. C. on impact of: **5:** 317. Relationship to US sentiment for Gr. independence: **3:** 606, 612. Stimulus to US trade in Span. Am.: **3:** 690. US spy reports on impact of in Europe: **4:** 907. As applied generally to Span Am.: **4:** 699–700, 804; **5:** 201–2, 310, 404–5 (see also below Panama Congress). Applied to Br.: **4:** 244, 252–3, 261; **6:** 938–9. Applied to Br.–BA war: **6:** 938–9. Applied to Cuba: **4:** 579. Applied to Mex.: **4:** 170–1, 699–700, 804–5; **5:** 201–2, 310. C. fuzzes implications of: **5:** 202. Cong. consideration of (see Congress of the United States: eighteenth congress)

—Panama Cong.: Origins of: **4:** 242, 397, 443, 559, 645. Scope of: **4:** 397, 443, 565, 567, 585, 725. Agenda: **4:** 788. Attendance at: **5:** 573, 939. US interest in: **4:** 243, 493, 645–6, 684, 827–8, 851, 859, 868, 926–7; **5:** 168, 264. US leadership at: **5:** 183, 202. US moral leadership at: **5:** 137, 283. Limited issues US permitted to discuss: **4:** 645–6, 684–5, 788, 859, 868–9, 927; **5:** 168, 314–5. US delegates to: **4:** 646, 801, 813–4, 826, 832–3, 851, 871, 892, 905; **5:** 8, 77, 183, 303–4, 346, 377–8, 924–5. C. instructions to US mission (Anderson, R. C., Sergeant, J.) to: **5:** 313–44; **6:** 127. Delay in departure of US mission: **5:** 122, 283, 346, 351, 361, 363, 375–8, 389–90, 404, 496, 663. Anderson death en route to: **5:** 572–3, 578, 595; **6:** 267. Cong. debate on sending a US mission to (see Congress of the United States: nineteenth congress). Domestic politics of sending US mission to: **5:** 407,

410, 428, 889, 980–1. Sectional reactions to US participation in: **5:** 220, 253, 273, 660. Ky. support of US participation: **5:** 278, 530. Cost of US mission: **5:** 192, 194–5, 256–7, 303. Unhealthy site of: **5:** 257, 363, 375, 378. Prospects of success or failure: **5:** 183. C. on importance of: **5:** 313. Support for US participation: **5:** 86–7, 99–100, 278. C. urged to represent US at: **4:** 892. Ground rules for decision-making at: **5:** 314–5. Delay in convening: **5:** 378, 390. GB role & interest in: **4:** 777; **5:** 44, 74, 181, 214, 244, 373, 981 (see espec. **6:** 74). Fr. role & interest in: **5:** 24, 74, 244. Sp. role & interest in: **5:** 44. Port. interest in: **5:** 94. Ru. interest in: **5:** 164. Bolivar role & interest in: **4:** 585; **5:** 42, 378, 670–1, 931, 981; **6:** 78, 312. Bolivar criticized at: **5:** 671; **6:** 312. Br. interest in: **5:** 89, 104, 159–60, 244, 295, 556; **6:** 36. Central Am. (Guatemala) interest in: **4:** 585, 788, 827–8, 928; **5:** 169; **6:** 77–8. Chile interest in: **5:** 169, 183, 214, 931, 947–8. Colombia role & interest in: **4:** 443, 559, 585, 684, 725, 788, 892, 927, 958; **5:** 44, 157, 168–9, 212. Mex. interest in: **4:** 645–6, 684, 725, 790, 805, 868, 927; **5:** 168–9, 291. Peru interest in: **4:** 397; **5:** 183, 214, 947, 1026; **6:** 512. Span. Am. delegates to: **4:** 892–3. Inter–Span. Am. tensions at: **5:** 44, 671. Lafayette view of: **4:** 848–9, 905; **5:** 51, 137, 202, 283, 1050. Isthmian canal possibilities discussed: **4:** 877; **5:** 74, 335–6, 343. Liberation of Cuba & PR discussed: **4:** 958; **5:** 66, 133, 157, 181, 220–2, 331–5, 343, 409, 437, 496, 649, 709; **6:** 1344. Continue wars of independence against Sp.: **4:** 788, 927; **5:** 168, 316–7, 320–1, 671, 925. Recognition of Haiti: **4:** 788, 905; **5:** 222, 281, 332, 337, 343, 355. Discuss abolition of African slave trade: **4:** 788; **5:** 220, 222, 253, 342–3, 671. Sp. recognition of Span. Am. independence: **5:** 169, 318–9, 321, 340, 342. End Br.–BA War: **5:** 340–1. Address Mex.–Guatemala border tensions: **5:** 589. Non–colonization by Europe: **4:** 778; **5:** 330–1, 404–5. Monroe Doctrine: **5:** 310, 313, 317, 330–1, 341. International maritime commercial & neutral rights: **4:** 788; **5:** 168, 314, 320–9, 341. Monarchy in Span. Am.: **5:** 339–40, 344. US claims issues: **5:** 193. Freedom of religion: **5:** 337–8, 671. US constit. form as export to Span. Am.: **5:** 340. Defensive alliance against European aggression considered & signed: **4:** 877; **5:** 319–20, 670–1, 709, 939–40; **6:** 540, 1054 (see espec. **5:** 939–40). Treaty attempt to restrain Bolivar: **6:** 101–2, 1054. Treaties drawn up at not ratified: **6:** 77, 125–6, 168, 201, 238, 305, 312, 318, 334–5, 368, 453, 512, 538, 540, 613, 646–7, 699, 741, 872, 1053–4, 1109, 1243, 1345–6. Secret Mex.–Colombia treaty for joint naval attack on coast of Sp.: **5:** 709; **6:** 1344. Accomplishments: **5:** 670. Portraits of delegates to: **5:** 77, 698

—Tacubaya (Mexico) phase of Panama Cong.: Transfer of site to: **5:** 315–6, 535, 595, 670, 679, 707–8, 713, 722, 751, 761, 925, 940; **6:** 36, 540–1. US mission to (Poinsett, J., Rochester, W. B., Sergeant, J.): **4:** 840; **5:** 724, 761, 821–2, 874, 878, 925, 930–1, 935; **6:** 248, 284, 458, 542. C. instruction to US mission: **6:** 248, 311–3. Limitations on US mission: **6:** 311–2. Delays in convening: **6:** 82, 126, 146, 168, 201, 267, 305, 318, 368, 491, 512, 540–2, 563, 647, 822–3, 872, 1108–9. Casual pace of: **6:** 335, 368, 375, 453. Historical hopes for: **6:** 512. US would expand free institutions in: **6:** 312–3. Chaos in Central Am. during: **6:** 453. Irrelevance of US presence at: **6:** 201–2. GB presence: **6:** 77, 82. Colombia presence: **6:** 82, 201, 453. Mex. presence: **6:** 82, 201, 318, 334. Peru disinterest in: **6:** 453, 688, 741, 1053–4, 1242–3, 1345–6. Chile role in: **6:** 205. Bolivar influence on: **6:** 201, 312. Dutch disinterest in: **6:** 77. Delegates to: **6:** 82, 146, 311, 313. Commerce & navigation discussions urged: **5:** 866–7. Sp.–Span. Am. armistice discussions urged: **5:** 877. Defensive alliance signed at Panama not ratified (*see* above Panama Cong.). Failure at Tacubaya: **6:** 238, 453, 613, 688

U.S. Land Office: Patronage in: **4:** 102, 315, 363, 545; **6:** 279. Laws dealing with public lands: **1:** 653–4 (1812); **3:** 247; **4:** 568–9 (1820); **6:** 857–8 (1821, 1824, 1826, 1827). Politics of price & distribution: **4:** 568–9. C. support of right of preemption: **1:** 458–9. C. support of modest public land prices: **2:** 836. C. support of land grants to encourage US immigration to La.: **1:** 467–8. Use of land bounties to raise troops: **1:** 653–4. Land prices & values: **1:** 653; **2:** 407, 884; **3:** 248, 839; **4:** 568–9. Yazoo land–claim issue: **1:** 778, 903, 916 (*see also* Georgia). Exchange of War of 1812 veteran land bounties for cash: **2:** 411–17. C. supports more efficiency in office operations of in Ky.: **1:** 166. Relationship of annual sales of & increase of Miss. River navigation: **1:** 625. Land speculation by US Govt.: **2:** 412–13. C. criticism of crooked land speculators: **2:** 415. Corruption in US Land Office: **5:** 200. Grant of public lands to educational institutions: **2:** 756–1; **3:** 625. C. on relief of debtor-purchasers of public lands: **3:** 47, 50, 52. Purchases drain Western wealth to East: **3:** 591, 626. Location of local offices: **5:** 439. Confirmation of western land titles: **4:** 325. Graduated prices for western public lands: **4:** 568. Salaries of employees of: **6:** 811–2. Trespass on public land: **6:** 268

U.S. Library of Congress: Books acquired: **5:** 988. Librarian Watterson writes books: **6:** 212–3. Services provided states: **6:** 1158–9, 1173, 1202, 1222, 1346, 1350. Jefferson gives books to: **6:** 1173. Books donated to "National Library": **6:** 1236

U.S. Marine Corps: C. opinion of: **1:** 653. Ease of commissioning in: **1:** 653. Patronage importunities: **1:** 653–4; **4:** 259, 769; **6:** 5, 157. West Point graduates desired as officers: **4:** 769. In Am. Revolution: **6:** 71–2. In War of 1812: **6:** 72

U.S. Military (general): Need for additional military academies: **2:** 119–22. Maritime vulnerability of US: **1:** 604. Cong. opposition to financing: **2:** 134. Constit. & the military: **2:** 471–2, 627. Constit. & overseas deployment of: **1:** 614–5. C. on US defensive tactics: **2:** 477–8. C. financial–legal business with War Dept.: **1:** 298. Pension obligations threaten US economy: **2:** 739; **3:** 566–7. Needed to repel future attack: **2:** 152–3, 156–7. C. on principle of pensions: **3:** 565–6. Expenditures on & relationship to Am. System: **2:** 157, 626–7, 793. War of 1812 a lesson in unpreparedness: **2:** 157. C. on dangers of worship of military heroes: **3:** 565–6 (*see also* Jackson, Andrew; Election of 1824: issues; Election of 1828: issues, charges & counter–charges in campaign). C. on need for economy of operation of: **2:** 312. C. offered SecWar post by Monroe: **2:** 391. Calhoun policies as Sec War: **3:** 187. C. on huge military potential of US in event of invasion (1824): **3:** 607, 610. Not a solution to unemployment: **3:** 693. Establishment of armories: **4:** 115. Arms procurement: **6:** 1301. Politics of arms procurement: **6:** 1318

U.S. Military Academy (West Point): Faculty at: **1:** 657; **2:** 163; **5:** 245 (D. H. Mahan). Appt. process: **5:** 1047. C. support of: **2:** 120, 794. C. criticism of: **2:** 120–1. Student sectional distribution at: **2:** 120–1; **5:** 1047. C. opposes Cong. setting admission standards at: **2:** 614–5. Competition to enter: **3:** 736. Interest of Span. Am. in admission to: **5:** 942; **6:** 1281. "Eggnog Riot" (12/25/26) at: **6:** 264, 326, 348, 366. Politics of Board of Visitors appointees: **6:** 356–7. Academic performance of Ky. cadets: **4:** 491. H. Clay, Jr., attends (*see* Clay, Henry Jr.). Chaplains at: **6:** 661–2. Patronage importunities regarding: **4:** 110–1, 207, 236–8, 282, 288–9, 316, 607, 765, 787, 832, 855, 858, 876, 886, 888, 918–9; **5:** 127–8, 134–5, 225, 300–1, 497, 608, 883–4, 922, 995, 1000, 1018–9, 1047, 1054; **6:** 57, 81, 168, 178–9, 184–5, 208–9, 247, 396, 399, 513, 630, 668, 707, 779–80, 814–5, 976–7, 999, 1244, 1305–6, 1363, 1396

U.S. Militia (state): As issue in US domestic politics: **1:** 228. And States Rights: **1:** 615. As supplement to Regular Army: **1:** 604–5, 614–5. Appt. of officers in: **1:** 615. Constit. & overseas deployment of: **1:** 614. Constit. & calling out of: **2:** 471–2. Increase of on eve of 1812 War: **1:** 637. State maintenance of: **1:** 403. Superiority of Ky. militia will conquer Canada: **1:** 450. Need for effective after 1812 War: **2:** 153, 477. Pay for militia

captured during 1812 War: **2:** 167. Pensions for medically disabled from 1812 War: **2:** 177–8. Poor discipline of: **6:** 14. Reform of: **6:** 53–4, 119. Domestic politics of militia reform: **6:** 53
U.S. Navy: Outmatched by GB navy: **1:** 620–2. Constit. of providing: **3:** 584. C. on history of seapower: **5:** 322, 328, 334. C. proud of his support of: **1:** 618–27; **4:** 30. Future challenge to GB naval supremacy: **1:** 608–9. C. on command of the sea: **5:** 334. Seapower arguments for & against: **1:** 619, 621, 625. Role in transporting US diplomats: **2:** 387; **6:** 129. As issue in domestic politics: **1:** 375; **2:** 150. Life & commerce protection function ("Showing the Flag") sought & performed: **1:** 625–6; **2:** 298, 839; **4:** 225, 386, 488, 514, 563, 586, 612, 623, 653, 737, 792, 936; **5:** 135, 184, 295, 310, 345, 368, 391, 395, 507, 518, 559–60, 587–8, 623, 938, 959, 1005; **6:** 14, 74, 201, 306, 393, 465, 604, 736–7, 821, 1281. Upholds US rights in Br.–BA War: **6:** 1262 (see also Brazil: U.S. relations with; Buenos Aires: U.S. relations with). Protecting US maritime neutral rights: **4:** 648, 660, 929; **5:** 66, 395, 959, 1011 (see ibid.; Great Britain: maritime & trade issues). Dip. functions of officers of: **2:** 853–4; **3:** 483; **4:** 137, 612, 623, 687, 736–7, 792, 909, 929, 944; **5:** 58, 84, 139, 311, 558, 822, 829, 942; **6:** 74, 1178–9. Ceremonial activities of: **6:** 835. Arguments to increase on eve of War of 1812: **1:** 618–27. Submarine warfare proposal to: **6:** 21. Classes of warships: **1:** 228, 375, 748, 621; **2:** 157, 194. Books purchased by: **5:** 977. Intelligence gathering by: **6:** 127. Arguments to reduce size of peacetime: **2:** 150. Arguments to augment size of peacetime: **2:** 150, 156. Operations against privateers in Br.–BA War: **6:** 881 (see also Brazil: U.S. relations with; Buenos Aires: U.S. relations with). USN & recruitment by impressment: **2:** 608. Reputation after War of 1812: **2:** 150. Steam frigates & batteries of: **2:** 157, 194. Role in defending N.O.: **2:** 194. Role in defending Chesapeake Bay: **2:** 194. Role in defending coasts & inland waters: **2:** 157. Pres. prerogative in deploying: **2:** 194. GB navy seamen desert into: **6:** 195, 378. Bureaucratic mismanagement of budget of: **2:** 738–9. Arms & supplies procurement at home & abroad: **2:** 765, 767, 875–6, 877–81; **3:** 84; **5:** 959, 975, 1013; **6:** 74, 99–100, 1055, 1301. C. sales of hemp to: **1:** 549, 817, 836–7, 840, 844–5; **3:** 775, 786, 830, 844, 853, 903–6; **4:** 267, 269, 271. USN supports Ky. hemp production: **6:** 1055. C. would weaken presence in Mediterranen: **2:** 788. Unneutral involvement in Peru independence war: **3:** 482–3; **4:** 501. Anti–piracy operations in Mediteranean **6:** 256–7, 270, 277–8, 1281. Interest in Western suppliers: **2:** 877, 881. Interest of the West in: **2:** 876; **4:** 30. C.

opposes relief of family of Oliver Hazard Perry: **3:** 15, 564–8. Foxardo Incident: **4:** 224–5 (see also Porter, David). James Barron court–martial problems: **3:** 107. Charles Stewart court–martial problems: **3:** 483; **4:** 622, 632, 687. Operations against West Indian pirates: **3:** 337–8; **4:** 29, 33, 39, 119, 224–5, 273–4, 296, 300, 330, 373, 533–4, 762. Economic benefit of shipbuilding to ports involved: **3:** 589–90. David Porter court–martial (see Porter, David). Navy yard at Pensacola: **4:** 86. Monitors GB shipping in Mediterranean: **5:** 695–6. Desertion of seamen from: **6:** 845, 1151, 1158. Officers of insulted abroad: **4:** 327. Protecting US fishing fleet: **5:** 390. Fee earned on specie & money transported on ships of: **3:** 483; **4:** 380, 687. Punitive expeditions of: **4:** 899 (see also Porter, David; Spain empire: Puerto Rico). Death of Oliver H. Perry: **5:** 735–6. Supply depots abroad: **4:** 586, 629; **5:** 300, 959. Health of crews: **6:** 129. Nephews of Mrs. Clay serve in (see Hart, Henry Clay; Hart, John S. in Name Index). Patronage related to: **1:** 638, 641, 649, 666–7, 677, 813; **2:** 107, 110, 601, 620, 733, 889; **3:** 16, 56, 327–8, 842; **4:** 282, 315–6, 332, 397–8, 400, 402–3, 408, 414, 490, 572, 661, 730, 746, 780, 854, 894; **5:** 12, 17–8, 37, 60, 85, 197, 397, 584, 720; **6:** 16, 661, 1069, 1089–90. Enforce US neutrality against Porter in Key West: **6:** 660. Turn down steam battery maintenance invention: **6:** 1310, 1388. Chaplains in: **6:** 661–2. Growth during JQA admin.: **6:** 674, 676. European opinions of: **6:** 1110–2. Operations against Barbary States: **2:** 815; **4:** 621; **6:** 1317–9. Decatur–Barron duel (1820): **2:** 803, 815; **3:** 107; **6:** 1302, 1316–7. Susan Decatur claim: **6:** 1039. Duty levied on naval stores warehoused on foreign shores: **6:** 1401. See also Biddle, James; Elliott, Jesse Duncan in Name Index; Great Britain: War of 1812
U.S. Patent Office: C. law cases on new inventions: **1:** 145, 297. Criticism of procedures of: **4:** 92–3, 239, 367, 579, 628, 650. Application for patents: **5:** 923. Criticism of officials of: **4:** 181, 195, 210, 275, 373; **6:** 218–9, 251, 263, 272, 450–1, 989. C. philosophy of patent awards: **4:** 692–3. Applications for copyrights: **4:** 232; **6:** 890. Specific patents submitted & considered: **4:** 370, 628, 650, 715; **6:** 339, 459. Legal problems relating to procedures of: **4:** 258–9, 262, 636, 692–3; **6:** 543–4. Patent conflicts: **4:** 577, 622, 633, 692–3, 745; **6:** 218–9, 251, 263, 271–2. Failure to record patents: **5:** 1018; **6:** 41. Legal assistance sought from: **5:** 498 **6:** 543–4. Patents issued: **4:** 609, 628; **5:** 754, 776–7, 811, 923; **6:** 42–3, 506, 969, 990, 1310, 1388. Great discoveries claimed: **4:** 876, 880–1, 931; **5:** 405, **6:** 339. C. on genius of US inventors: **5:** 811. Rapid increase in business of: **5:** 35, 1018. Ap-

U.S. Patent Office (*continued*):
peals to Pres. for relief from decisions of: **5:** 924. Need for more clerks: **5:** 35, 961, 1018; **6:** 23, 40–2, 256, 262. Finances of: **5:** 961; **6:** 42–3. US Cong. interest in: **5:** 35, 1018; **6:** 41–3. Publications ordered by: **6:** 417. Proposed new Home Office should absorb: **6:** 42 (*see also* U.S. State Dept.). Pay scale in: **4:** 814; **6:** 42–3. C. studies Anglo–Fr. patent practice: **6:** 47, 305. Appeals to Cong. for patent rights over head of Patent Office: **6:** 342. Journal about published: **6:** 855–6, 1301–2. Business journal copyrighted: **6:** 891. Weights & measures: **6:** 962. Thomas P. Jones as Supt. of: **6:** 1008. Patronage importunities: **5:** 1004, 1018; **6:** 23, 117, 154, 252, 256, 266–7, 272, 966

U.S. Post Office Dept.: Corruption in: **6:** 593, 1153, 1161. Postal rates: **3:** 713; **5:** 741–2. Patronage issues in: **6:** 1153, 1161. Number of applicants for jobs in: **6:** 293. Disrupted by storm (1817): **2:** 372–3. Transportation of mail on Sunday: **2:** 469, 490. Regular service to Isthmus of Panama: **5:** 226, 402–3, 427, 583: **6:** 816. Cong. legis. concerning: **3:** 746–7. Poor service of on dip. mail: **4:** 874, 902, 907–8, 934; **5:** 583. Job applicants: **1:** 598–9, 839; **4:** 198, 287, 651, 821–2, 838–40; **5:** 299, 481; **6:** 164–5, 209–12

U.S. State Dept.
—organization, functions, duties: Organization & personnel: **4:** 109–10, 112–3; **5:** 33–5, 752–3; **6:** 39, 171–2, 756, 849. Admin. obligations: **5:** 33–5, 72–3, 109–12. Printing, bookbinding & publications: **4:** 587, 815; **6:** 383–4, 416–8. Books, journals & documents ordered: **4:** 815; **5:** 195, 425, 500, 536, 608, 623, 919, 977, 981, 985; **6:** 59–60, 191, 351, 392, 562, 592, 758–9, 1024, 1068, 1086–7, 1137 (*see espec.* **5:** 195). Newspaper subscriptions: **4:** 119–20, 258, 334, 378–80, 592, 614, 815; **5:** 411, 418, 431; **6:** 383, 496. Financial agencies used abroad: **4:** 375; **5:** 749, 967; **6:** 105, 323, 852. Budgets & expenditures: **4:** 814–6; **5:** 932–3; **6:** 65, 68, 171–2, 590, 1306–7. Contingency funds: **2:** 510–11; **4:** 816. Spies (*see* Cook, Daniel P.; Harrison, Robert M.; McRae, Alexander G.; Robertson, Thomas B.). Use of cyphers: **1:** 986–8; **6:** 401. Assistance to botanical study: **6:** 279. Printing & distribution of US laws: **4:** 815; **5:** 932; **6:** 465–6, 1306. Passports: **6:** 532, 805. Recording & preserving the business of Cong.: **5:** 34–5. Home Dept. (Dept. of Interior) proposed to lessen work load of: **5:** 72–3, 111–2; **6:** 19, 42, 896. Few patronage jobs in: **4:** 379–80; **6:** 185, 452. Need for more clerks: **5:** 33–5, 290, 757–8; **6:** 39, 184, 191, 213, 220, 361. Salaries of employees: **2:** 190–1, 510–11, 817; **3:** 55; **4:** 204, 328, 337, 368, 545, 814–6; **5:** 14, 536, 932–3; **6:** 75, 152–3, 756, 985, 1019, 1033, 1300, 1306–9. Perks of US diplomats abroad:

5: 816; **6:** 97. Cong. economy moves against: **6:** 65, 67–8. Census taking: **5:** 214, 493; **6:** 654. Responsibility for patents (*see* U.S. Patent Office). No gift–taking by US diplomats: **2:** 853; **4:** 187; **6:** 780, 1020. Quality & behavior of US diplomats abroad: **2:** 427; **6:** 98–9. Dip. immunity of foreign diplomats: **5:** 209; **6:** 958, 963. Protection of foreign diplomats residing in US: **4:** 660–1, 686, 727–8, 745, 778–81, 788–9, 894; **5:** 203, 208, 300. Transmission of dip. dispatches: **4:** 546; **5:** 245; **6:** 194, 1340, 1343. Ceremonial functions: **4:** 99, 112, 117; **5:** 3. Citizen claims against: **5:** 493; **6:** 102, 109. Extradition of criminals: **1:** 760, 774; **4:** 142, 790, 811, 818, 925, 955; **5:** 133, 250, 292, 471–2, 515–6, 679, 715, 720, 808–9, 817–8, 925, 955, 1010; **6:** 36, 314, 405–6, 1309–10, 1320–1, 1337, 1344, 1348–9, 1351, 1400 (*see also* Neilson, Michael; Snelson, Nathaniel). Missing persons problems: **5:** 292, 312; **6:** 1349, 1355, 1360. Aid to US citizens with estate, investment, insurance & claims problems abroad: **4:** 579–80, 591–2, 596, 599, 606, 612, 614–5, 617, 620–1, 631, 635, 637, 641, 650, 842, 854, 945, 950; **5:** 16, 22–3, 25, 484; **6:** 78, 404, 480–1, 635–6, 834–5, 958, 1092, 1128, 1137–8, 1247, 1369–70, 1381, 1393 (*see also* Hawley, Betsy in Name Index). *See also* U.S. diplomacy

—Consuls & consular activities: Tensions with shipmasters: **4:** 231, 370, 527, 534, 548, 752, 904, 909; **5:** 22, 374, 432, 479, 482, 535–6, 606; **6:** 14, 680–1. Handling crimes involving US citizens: **4:** 230–1, 311, 407, 410, 566; **5:** 558, 592, 595, 720 1010. Protection of US life, property & rights abroad: **4:** 566, 660–1, 733, 894; **5:** 129–30, 694, 1059. Problems of distressed US merchant seamen abroad: **4:** 271, 311, 339, 370–2, 749, 793, 833, 894, 903; **5:** 22, 84, 145, 213–4, 411, 439, 479, 507, 547, 559, 570, 606, 608, 667, 851; **6:** 47, 376–7, 1024, 1163, 1249–50, 1263, 1345, 1554. Cost of relief of distressed seamen: **4:** 816; **5:** 933; **6:** 956–7, 1307, 1354–5. Control of smuggling: **5:** 247–8, 435, 545. Tension with native (local) businessmen: **4:** 835; **6:** 1055. Control of privateering: **5:** 435, 535–6; **6:** 441. Confer citizenship on US babies born abroad: **6:** 1068. Fly US flag at consulates: **6:** 1119, 1127, 1186. Problems with accounts with State Dept.: **4:** 628, 631, 634, 691; **5:** 79, 84, 107, 203–4, 213–4, 411, 438–9, 498, 507, 547, 591, 873; **6:** 511, 717, 756, 985, 1002, 1010, 1051, 1244, 1271–2. Requests for policy guidance from State Dept.: **4:** 632, 749, 793, 829; **5:** 300, 391, 424, 558. Complain of poor support & guidance from State Dept.: **4:** 339, 371–2, 511, 886. Dishonesty & incompetence of: **4:** 229, 276, 364, 534, 554, 566, 581, 647, 666, 811, 909; **5:** 49, 415, 438, 591, 623, 698; **6:** 214, 1378–9. Criticism of job performance: **6:** 800, 898–9, 939, 1378–9, 1393. Seen as soft jobs: **5:** 1015; **6:** 75–6. Improper personal behavior of: **6:** 898–9, 939, 1055, 1355. Murders & duels: **5:** 558, 578, 939, 1040. Conflict between US diplomats residing abroad: **5:** 66–7, 139–40; **6:** 21, 134–5, 939. Low status of: **6:** 341. Foreign govts. restrict functions & authority of: **4:** 287–8, 296, 464, 566, 833; **5:** 12, 104, 141, 345, 411, 435; **6:** 74, 159, 206, 635, 718, 988. Low pay of: **4:** 545, 791; **5:** 13, 361–2, 370, 399, 1004; **6:** 383, 448, 1222. Need to reform function, pay & status of: **2:** 190; **5:** 361, 370, 435, 438, 482, 518, 606, 608, 743, 993, 1006–7, 1308–9. *See also* Merchant Marine, U.S.

—Clay performance as Secretary of State: Complains of heavy work load: **4:** 221, 269, 289, 302, 318, 335–6, 342, 522, 567, 618, 621, 699, 896, 955; **5:** 72, 110–11, 272, 360, 388, 440, 565, 746, 757, 791; **6:** 361, 378, 896. Asserts harmony with JQA on principles & policies: **4:** 221, 227, 269, 286. On press & foreign policy: **5:** 955. On tactics & technique of negotiations: **4:** 336. His sacrifice in taking job: **4:** 318. Lives on salary: **4:** 814; **6:** 362. SecState as stepping stone to Pres.: **6:** 371, 373. Anglophobia of: **5:** 1000. Executes policy made by JQA: **4:** 366–7, 372, 645, 684, 686, 799, 859, 928; **5:** 210, 246, 567, 596, 722, 728, 743, 769, 778, 1048; **6:** 132, 308, 316, 327, 615, 627–8, 975. Affirms his policy–making role: **4:** 896; **5:** 761, 839–40. Boasts of treaties concluded: **5:** 360, 839–40. Slowness in carrying on official correspondence: **4:** 466–7, 618, 621, 687; **5:** 58, 62, 75, 104, 273, 289–90, 300, 361–2, 368, 400, 466, 494, 618, 709, 761, 835–6, 840, 1001; **6:** 111, 132, 167, 238, 647, 666. Casual admin. of Dept.: **5:** 200–2, 212–3, 1017; **6:** 22, 412, 460. Instructions deemed inadequate: **6:** 744. Relations with Cong.: **5:** 958, 1001; **6:** 151–3. Seeks advice on GB–US trade controversy: **4:** 337–8, 421, 468, 477, 601, 607, 676, 695, 810. Blamed for BWI trade problem: **6:** 373. Move to impeach as SecState: **6:** 1270–1. Lauded for performance as: **4:** 398–9, 401; **5:** 25, 452. C. on own performance as: **4:** 953. C. impatience as: **4:** 621. Lectures Mex. on treaty ratification: **6:** 285–6. Gallatin criticisms of (*see* Gallatin, Albert). *See also* U.S. diplomacy

U.S. Supreme Court: C. favors increasing number of justices of: **1:** 269, 274. On slave trade issues: **5:** 1057. On slave–property issues: **4:** 701. Neutral rights & neutrality cases: **2:** 495, 500–1, 504–5. Relief of judges of from Circuit Court duty: **2:** 673–4; **3:** 551. Webster would reform: **3:** 754–5. Salaries of judges of: **2:** 674. C. practice before: **2:** 721; **3:** 129, 143, 206, 208, 284, 301, 342–3, 347, 348, 359, 360, 386, 388–9, 397, 401, 540, 601–2, 646, 655, 791; **4:** 13, 229, 713–4; **6:** 610, 1081–2, 1200–1. On state

bankruptcy laws: **2:** 748–9; **4:** 13–14. On state taxation of BUS branches (*McCulloch vs. Md.*): **2:** 435, 623, 625, 673–4, 723; **3:** 61, 355. *BUS vs. Osborne* (1824): **2:** 721, 723; **3:** 14, 51, 112, 114–5, 355, 549, 560, 646–7, 655, 675, 751, 782; **4:** 62 (*see espec.* **2:** 723). *Cohens vs. Va.* (1821): **3:** 61, 63, 478–9. *Green vs. Biddle* (1821): **3:** 90–1, 151, 162–3, 207–8, 228, 302, 343–4, 390, 392–3, 478–9, 514, 550–1, 556, 746, 802; **4:** 43; **5:** 1029–30. *Fleckner vs. BUS* (1823): **3:** 540. *Ogden vs. Saunders* (1824, 1827): **4:** 13, **6:** 610, 1081–2. On Ky. debtor relief laws: **3:** 260–1, 348–9, 556, 596, 675, 746, 760, 805; **4:** 5; **6:** 1081–2. On jurisdiction in BUS cases: **3:** 245, 549, 646–7, 655, 751. C. would reorganize structure & procedures of: **3:** 550, 753–4. *Gibbon vs. Ogden* (1824): **3:** 622, 624, 739, 754–5. Charles River Bridge Case (1827–8): **6:** 530–2, 556. C. on dangers in interpretive powers of: **3:** 755. C. criticizes age of justices: **3:** 393. Inadequate service rendered by: **4:** 42–3. Ignorance of local law in West & South: **4:** 43. Wheaton's *Reports of Decisions* of: **6:** 389–90 (*see also* Wheaton, Henry). Appt. of justices to: **5:** 69–70, 149–50, 221. Attempts to limit power of: **5:** 528–9. Slave trade (*see* Slavery & slaves: slave trade). And patronage: **5:** 81, 114, 133, 149–50, 193, 221, 284, 287, 584. States Rights: **1:** 166–7, 283; **2:** 472–3, 490; **3:** 168, 245, 469, 478–9, 500–1, 556, 754–5; **5:** 532

U.S. Treasury Dept.: Attempts to stabilize US currency: **2:** 248. Distribution of surplus in: **2:** 280. Extinguishing the national debt: **2:** 332. C. influence on policies of: **5:** 955. Patronage importunities: **4:** 430–1; **6:** 380–1

U.S. War Dept.: Insufficient clerical support in: **2:** 626, 628. Patronage importunities: **5:** 174. Books purchased by: **5:** 977. *See also* U.S. Army; U.S. Military Academy; Great Britain: War of 1812

Upshur, Abel P.: Role in Va. politics: **5:** 1031

Uruguay (Banda Oriental): *Casus belli* in Br.–BA war: **2:** 445–6, 702; **4:** 177, 320–1, 514, 562, 821, 936; **5:** 438, 506, 556, 588, 716, 828, 1022; **6:** 98, 441, 616, 1178, 1264. Revolution in: **4:** 386, 409, 506, 562, 737. Bolivar influence in: **4:** 737. Reincorporated by BA: **4:** 768, 936. Br. defeat in: **4:** 821, 845, 936; **5:** 51, 63. Independence of: **5:** 438, 506, 588, 828, 1022; **6:** 1178, 1264. GB interests & ambitions in: **5:** 438, 506, 556, 588, 716, 1214. GB support & guarantee of independence of: **5:** 828; **6:** 1178. *See also* Buenos Aires

Van Buren, Martin: Role & maneuvering in 1824 election: **3:** 186, 211, 290–1, 314–5, 356, 373–4, 401, 432, 475, 820; **4:** 17. Supports Crawford in 1824 campaign: **3:** 412, 420, 421, 436, 445, 461, 486, 511, 523, 535, 537, 547, 820, 831, 846–8, 863,

Van Buren, Martin (*continued*):
869; **5:** 718; **6:** 550. Characterizations of:
3: 186, 211, 373, 420, 461, 476, 768; **6:**
544. Attempts personal bargains with
1824 Pres. candidates: **3:** 863. C. distrust
of: **3:** 432; **5:** 945–6. C. personal relations with: **3:** 535, 554, 733. Popularity
among N.Y. Dem.: **3:** 445. Emphasis on
party discipline: **3:** 523. Political opposition to in N.Y.C.: **3:** 475, 494. On
Crawford's health in 1824 campaign: **4:**
308. Attitude toward JQA admin.: **4:**
318; **5:** 126, 207; **6:** 141, 245. Political
connection with Calhoun: **5:** 113, 126.
Political connection with Clinton: **5:**
143–4, 175, 186, 207, 346–8, 650,
675–7, 764, 1032; **6:** 123, 182, 245–6,
397, 405, 433, 502, 692 (*see also* Clinton,
DeWitt; New York State). Opposition to
JQA admin. (*see* Adams (John Q.) administration). Reelection to US Sen. (1827):
5: 492, 676–7, 945, 1032; **6:** 129–30,
141, 245, 394, 435, 1021. On US bankruptcy legis.: **5:** 651. Pro–South tilt
(1826): **5:** 676–7; **6:** 123, 397, 435, 545,
549–50, 692, 1046, 1252, 1279 (*see espec.*
6: 549–50). Control of N.Y. Legis.: **5:**
1032; **6:** 1252. Opposition to Panama
Cong. mission: **6:** 141. Role in 1828 campaign (*see* Election of 1828: general).
Opposition to Wool Bill (1827): **6:** 435.
Financial investments of: **6:** 435. Would
revise laws respecting public printing: **6:**
454. Pro–AJ tilt of N.Y. supporters of: **6:**
457, 489, 1046, 1252. Campaigns for AJ
in South in 1828: **6:** 550. Weakness of
N.Y. political base: **6:** 606. Strengthens
AJ ticket (1828) in N.Y.: **6:** 666. Reaction
to AJ to Beverley Letter (*see* Election of
1828: issues, charges & counter–charges
in campaign). Role in N.Y. state elections
(Nov. 1827): **6:** 1240, 1252. Contract with
Jared Sparks: **6:** 154
Van Ness, Cornelius P.: On Northern
(45°N.) boundary question: **6:** 142, 265.
Attacks JQA admin.: **6:** 408–9, 432.
Loses US Sen. election in Vt. (1827): **5:**
650–1; **6:** 408–9, 432, 530. Switch to AJ
camp: **6:** 408, 432
Van Rensselaer, Stephen: Family of: **3:**
214; **5:** 334, 426. Thought to lean toward
C. in 1824 election: **3:** 476, 511. Largest
agriculturist in US: **3:** 662. Patronage
favor for C.: **3:** 904; **4:** 7. Seeks patronage favors from C.: **6:** 247, 297–8, 315–6,
334, 1012. Nom. for US Sen. (1827): **6:**
129–30, 141. Supports reelection of JQA:
6: 129–30, 315, 433–4, 527, 641
Vance, Joseph: Reports Ohio support for
C. in 1824 Pres. campaign: **3:** 258–9.
Supports Niagara civilian claims for 1812
war losses: **4:** 18. Seeks patronage favors
from C.: **4:** 99; **5:** 140. C. patronage
favors for: **4:** 268. Supports C. on "Corrupt Bargain" issue: **4:** 268; **5:** 280. Supports Harrison as US Min. to Colombia:
6: 473. Reveals popular political concerns
to C.: **4:** 807. Financial arrangements
with C.: **6:** 649. JQA admin. must pay

more attention to West & SW: **4:** 807.
Confrontation with McDuffie on Pres.
election reform: **5:** 278–80, 354. Reelected (1826) to US Cong.: **5:** 723, 725.
On campaign & election of 1828: **6:**
640–1
Vatican. *See* Papal States
Venezuela. *See* Colombia
Vermont: US Sen. election in (1827): **5:**
650–1; **6:** 408–9, 432, 530. AJ movement
in: **6:** 408–9, 432. JQA admin. patronage
operations in: **6:** 409. Distribution of US
laws to: **6:** 442. Canadian fugitives harbor
in: **4:** 118. C. political support in: **6:**
947–8. Direct popular election of Pres.
electors in: **6:** 1238
Vienna, Congress of: C. speculation on
problems & decisions of: **1:** 866, 891,
899. On limiting maritime power & pretensions of GB: **1:** 891, 899, 926, 941,
948. Maritime neutral rights questions at:
1: 902, 906, 918, 925. Slavery & slave
trade questions at: **1:** 927, 949. Legitimacy issue: **1:** 927; **2:** 135. Preliminary
peace treaty with Fr.: **1:** 926–7, 938, 949.
Results of in terms of US military & dip.
goals: **1:** 945. Relation of to Ghent negotiations: **1:** 980, 989, 995. Fr. colonial
issues at: **1:** 949, 967. Fr. maneuvers at:
1: 996–7. Nationality questions raised at:
1: 967. Plan to sent US spy to gather
information about: **1:** 989–90. Return of
Bonaparte to power during: **1:** 945–6,
967; **2:** 13–15
Virginia: C. love of as birthplace: **2:** 472.
Land fever (1795) in: **1:** 238. Harvest
(1817) in: **2:** 397. Land laws in: **3:** 90–1.
Jefferson popularity declines in (1806): **1:**
230. Decline of the aristocracy in: **3:** 718.
C. denies ambition of to monopolize US
presidency: **1:** 763. Debate on Cong. salaries in 1788 Va. constit. ratifying conv.:
2: 285. Resolutions of 1798: **2:** 170; **6:**
1225. C. on danger of States Rights doctrines of: **2:** 472–3, 490. C. lauds States
Rights principles of: **6:** 1312–3. Attack
on Fed. judiciary: **2:** 490; **3:** 469. Hostility to internal improvements in: **6:** 144–5.
Attitudes toward Mo. Compromise in: **2:**
780. Interest in hemp production: **6:** 8.
Individuals in emancipate slaves: **3:** 91.
Hostility to tariff in: **6:** 144–5, 200 (*see
also* Giles, William B.). C. on the chivalry
& integrity of Va.: **3:** 169. Attitudes toward US Supreme Court in: **3:** 169,
478–9. US Sen. election (1825): **4:** 827,
857, 867, 906. C. criticism of: **3:** 478–9.
US Sen. election (1827): **5:** 737, 739, 815,
984, 1001. State–level approach to internal improvements: **3:** 620. Parochial
self–interests of: **3:** 665. Development of
Wheeling: **4:** 95–6. Criticism of BUS in:
5: 967. Bank of Va. solicits business with
State Dept.: **5:** 967. C. political speech at
Lewisburg (8/30/26): **5:** 654–63, 746, 788,
791; **6:** 18–19, 25, 566–7, 775, 957–8.
On colonization of Free Blacks: **6:** 96.
Reaction to C. speech (1/26/27) on colonization: **6:** 144. On constit. basis of State

Rights: **6:** 144–5, 164–5, 187. Turnpike development in: **5:** 661–3. Development of Charleston: **5:** 59. Kanawha Colonization Society: **5:** 59. General Assembly & Gov. elections in (1827): **6:** 185–6, 445, 451. Political factions in (1827) in: **6:** 185. AJ newspapers in: **6:** 199, 227. US House election (1827) in: **6:** 445, 451, 467–8, 473, 507. Constit. conv. movement in: **6:** 291–2, 863, 1065. Hostility to Pres. nom. by caucus in state legis.: **6:** 545. Western Va. political attitudes: **6:** 200, 291–2. Hostility to Am. System in: **6:** 144, 320, 401, 435. AJ political fraud in: **6:** 468–9. Van Buren political tilt toward: **6:** 435. JQA patronage rewards to: **6:** 468–9. Legis. on States Rights vs. Am. System: **6:** 144–5 (*see also* Giles, William B.). JQA party support of Richmond *Constitutional Whig* (*see* Pleasants, John H.). Party & political fragmentation in (1827): **6:** 185. East vs. West sectional divisions: **6:** 291–2, 1065. Political impact of Beverley "Fayetteville Attack" in: **6:** 861–3, 865, 944 (*see also* Election of 1828: issues, charges & counter–charges in campaign). JQA admin. political support, reelection prospects, & organization (1827–8) in: **5:** 644; **6:** 185, 291, 467, 519, 862–3, 865, 944, 1157, 1187, 1204, 1213, 1225, 1237, 1241–2, 1265, 1270, 1326, 1338, 1342, 1364, 1377. AJ party political support & organization (1827–8) in: **5:** 984; **6:** 185, 200, 227, 389, 519, 925–6, 1065, 1194, 1292, 1399. Anti–AJ sentiment in (1827): **5:** 738–9; **6:** 185, 291, 902. Anti–JQA admin. sentiment in (1827): **4:** 857; **5:** 7, 738, 1023; **6:** 185–6. Richmond conv. nom. JQA & Rush & choosing Pres. electors (1828): **6:** 924–6, 1058, 1065–6, 1077, 1157–8, 1194, 1225, 1265, 1291, 1307, 1312, 1338, 1356, 1386. Politics of Pleasants blackmail scandal: **6:** 1323 (*see also* Pleasants, John H.). Population vs. geography in Va. political structure: **6:** 1065, 1077. German vote in Valley of: **6:** 1385. Richmond Junto ("Virginia School" States Rights): **3:** 341; **6:** 186, 1141. Importance of to outcome of election of 1828: **6:** 1312–3. AJ swamps JQA at polls in (1828): **6:** 863

Virginia, University of: Jefferson work for: **5:** 365–6. C. interest in: **5:** 365–6, 370, 652. Fr. assistance to: **5:** 365–6. Cuts into TU enrollment: **6:** 181

Walsh, Robert Jr.: Recommended for USMA Board of Visitors: **6:** 357–8, 445. Advises JQA on Pa. patronage: **6:** 358, 445. Character: **6:** 847, 953. Federalist political roots of: **6:** 847. Personal friendship with JQA: **6:** 847. JQA writes article for: **6:** 1047–8. Newspaper of leans toward AJ (1827–8): **6:** 847

War: Commercial origins of: **1:** 619; **2:** 835–6. Need for military ardor in US: **1:** 450, 619–20. Economic arguments for: **1:** 606, 625–6. National happiness &: **1:** 619–20. Evils of: **2:** 514. No terror in: **1:** 641. C. hatred of: **2:** 512. Patriotism part of human character: **1:** 642. Popularity of in Ky.: **1:** 216. Acceptable reasons for launching: **1:** 765. Quaker views of: **5:** 521–3. Definition of: **1:** 770. C. on conquering peace: **1:** 996. Civilized dimensions of: **1:** 770. As a means to achieve peace: **1:** 855; **2:** 157. Prefers an armed citizenry **2:** 136. Causes public debt: **2:** 140–1, 149. Supports US independence against foreign monarchial aggression: **2:** 141. C. on necessary preparedness for: **2:** 141–2, 149, 157, 477. C. on limits to preparedness: **2:** 477. C. on war & martial glory: **2:** 149. Stages of legis. leading to: **2:** 321. Inevitability of continuing wars with GB: **2:** 152. In time of peace prepare for war: **2:** 157, 462. C. offered & refuses SecWar Cabinet post: **2:** 226, 233. Inevitable to all new settlements: **2:** 264. Difficulty of legis. during: **2:** 321. AJ attacks C. for dodging military service: **4:** 163. C. on treatment of war instigators: **2:** 647–8. C. on need for national unity during: **2:** 803. C. on as a last resort: **6:** 98. C. on "My country right or wrong" in: **2:** 803, 815. C. on tactics in Indian wars: **6:** 1088. C. on historical intervals of: **2:** 833. Threat of in Europe helps US business & commerce: **2:** 863; **3:** 86; **5:** 16. Impact of European on US economy: **1:** 172–3; **3:** 686–7, 700

Warfield, Henry R.: Family: **5:** 54, 56; **6:** 18, 20. Education: **6:** 19. On C. role at Ghent: **3:** 210. Praises C. as House Speaker: **2:** 861. On vote for Speaker (1821): **3:** 147–8. On C. Pres. prospects (1824): **3:** 148–9, 210–13, 336. Supports C. for Pres. (1824): **3:** 148–9, 210–13, 815. Housing arrangements in D.C.: **3:** 150, 210, 336. Defeated for reelection to Cong. (1824): **5:** 54, 57. Financial difficulties: **5:** 53–6, 523; **6:** 17, 19. Problem with liquor: **5:** 54. On the Jacksonians in Md.: **5:** 55, 523. Law practice: **5:** 54–6. Asks C. for fed. job: **5:** 56, 307, 525; **6:** 19–20, 187. On C. duel with Randolph: **5:** 306–7. On Calhoun: **5:** 307. On C. sponsorship of Span. Am. independence: **5:** 307. Votes for JQA in US Pres. election (2/9/25): **5:** 523, 526; **6:** 18, 20

Washington, D. C.: C. support of physical development of: **2:** 193. Indian Portrait Gallery in: **6:** 676. Specie payments of banks in: **2:** 820–1. C. on future of: **3:** 68. Rebuilding Capitol: **4:** 790, 885; **5:** 793. Public office building shortage in: **2:** 734–5. "Six Buildings" complex in: **6:** 128. C. opinion of: **2:** 734. Architects of the Capitol: **5:** 293, 793–4. Penitentiary built in: **5:** 401–2. Remodeling of House chamber: **5:** 793–4, 851, 857; **6:** 178. C. housing arrangements, rental costs in: **2:** 418; **3:** 69; **4:** 309, 336, 580, 590, 601, 616, 702, 728–9, 756, 823; **5:** 24, 72, 162, 253, 282, 844, 853; **6:** 386–7, 471, 537, 612, 642, 649, 653, 1038–9, 1262 (*see espec.* **6:** 728–9; & Decatur, Susan

Washington, D.C. (*continued*):
W.). C. purchases property in: **5:** 1026; **6:** 992, 1387. C. taxes on property in: **6:** 1387. C. buys furniture in: **6:** 537. C. social life in: **1:** 458, 482, 870; **2:** 221, 418, 433, 672, 848; **3:** 549; **4:** 570, 657, 910–11; **5:** 1, 79, 81, 97, 173, 253, 816, 979, 1001; **6:** 35, 110, 157, 1159, 1302, 1314, 1316, 1367–8. Lex. friends visit C. in: **5:** 1001. C. family members in: **1:** 522, 652, 737, 751, 870; **2:** 259, 356, 418; **4:** 210, 287, 336, 489, 512, 571; **5:** 253; **6:** 643, 849–50, 871, 991. C. plan to build house in: **4:** 336, 366. C. use of slaves in: **5:** 188, 1026; **6:** 261, 1387. Disorderly behavior at White House functions: **6:** 172, 207. C. membership in St. Johns Episcopal Church: **4:** 494, 881; **5:** 736, 1059; **6:** 733, 881, 1100, 1176 (*see also* Clay, Henry: religion)
Watkins, Tobias: Family: **4:** 102. Would purchase & edit Wash. *Daily National Journal* (1827): **6:** 1081. C. patronage favors to: **4:** 102. Comment on fed. funding scheme for C. & O. Canal: **6:** 188–90. Assists C. with pamphlet denying "Corrupt Bargain" charge: **6:** 572, 681–2, 1396
Watts, Beaufort T.: Requests pay raise: **5:** 536, 932; **6:** 1300. Opinion of Bolivar: **5:** 793; **6:** 255, 306, 1196, 1269. Appt. Chargé to Colombia: **6:** 270. Requests permission to return to US: **6:** 270, 921. Interference in Colombian internal affairs: **6:** 684–5, 723–4, 738, 868, 889, 956, 1069, 1123, 1243, 1269, 1368–9. C. considers firing: **6:** 738. Bolivar praises: **6:** 1299
Webster, Daniel: Family: **6:** 710, 1085. Opposition to War of 1812: **4:** 203; **6:** 816, 818. Supports charter of 2nd BUS: **2:** 170. On Am. System: **4:** 790. On tariff: **2:** 183; **3:** 664, 706, 728, 745–6. On internal improvements: **3:** 737, 739. On Gr. independence: **3:** 598–9, 603–5. On reform of US Supreme Court: **3:** 754–5. C. respect for: **3:** 604. Opposes C. before US Supreme Court: **4:** 13. Rumored as JQA SecState choice: **4:** 203. On "Corrupt Bargain" issue: **6:** 819–20, 948–9. Supports C. "Corrupt Bargain" defense (3/26/25): **4:** 230, 232–3, 698. Lauds C. character: **4:** 233. Seeks post as Min. to GB: **4:** 230. Urges merger of Federalist & National Republican parties: **4:** 232. Connection with Boston newspaper: **4:** 440–1. On Anglo-Am. trading policy conflicts: **4:** 695–8. Patronage recommendations to C.: **4:** 835, 882, 904; **5:** 822; **6:** 121, 215, 355. C. lauds for remaining in US House: **5:** 434. Role in US House election of JQA (2/9/25): **5:** 526. US Sen. ambitions of: **5:** 434, 650. On bankruptcy law: **5:** 651. On C. anti–AJ destiny: **5:** 791. On C. using amanuensis: **5:** 791. Reelected to US House (1826): **5:** 872. Elected to US Sen. (1827): **5:** 420–1, 889; **6:** 401, 446, 507, 530–1, 555, 566, 585,

603, 639–40, 653–4, 708–10, 947. Supports JQA in 1824 Pres. election: **6:** 1201. C. supports for US Sen.: **5:** 889; **6:** 555, 579, 603, 653–4. JQA supports for US Sen.: **6:** 555. Analysis of upcoming (1828) Pres. election: **6:** 354–6, 445–6, 530, 640–1, 820, 948–9, 1085. On Charles River bridges: **6:** 530–2. On National Republican tactics in N.H.: **6:** 566. Campaigns for JQA reelection: **6:** 556–7, 1085. Involved in political pamphleterring in 1828 election: **6:** 445, 566. Solicits Federalist support for JQA in House election (2/9/25) by promising patronage: **6:** 1199–1201. Fund raiser for JQA campaign in 1827–8: **6:** 1201, 1233–4, 1243. On outcome of N.Y. state elections (Nov. 1827):**6:** 1234–5
Weed, Thurlow: Purchases Rochester newspaper: **4:** 464. Seeks printers contract: **4:** 597
Wharton, Thomas I.: Assists C. publish speeches: **6:** 1. Supports C. in 1824 election: **3:** 466–7, 829, 836. On BUS: **6:** 1. Patronage recommendations to C.: **4:** 832; **5:** 128, 195; **6:** 16. C. explains JQA House vote to: **4:** 59. On US claims on Fr. & Netherlands: **4:** 831–2. Analyzes of Pres. politics for C.: **3:** 467–8; **6:** 846–7. Asks favor of C.: **6:** 846. Works for JQA reelection (1828) in Pa.: **6:** 846–7
Wheaton, Henry: As US Supreme Court reporter: **2:** 915; **4:** 102; **6:** 163, 610, 655. As US Chargé in Denmark (*see* Denmark: U.S. relations with). Politics of appt. as Chargé: **6:** 282, 446. Considered for judgeship: **5:** 877. Urges patronage appt. on C.: **4:** 891. As N.Y. State legislator: **3:** 820–1. Supports C. campaign in N.Y. (1824): **3:** 840–1. As lawyer: **6:** 610
Whisky: US excise tax on: **2:** 178, 180–1 (*see also* American System: tariff). Markets for Western whisky: **2:** 178, 185; **3:** 680. Foreign wine healthier drink than Ky. whisky: **2:** 185–6. Prices of: **3:** 79, 680. Prohibition debate: **2:** 186; **3:** 635, 637, 678
White, David, Jr.: Supports JQA in US House election of Pres. (2/9/25): **4:** 10–11, 41, 79, 91, 134; **6:** 1207, 1260. Supports AJ in 1828: **6:** 1207. Denies C. made a "Corrupt Bargain" with JQA: **6:** 1207, 1260. Runs for Pres. of Bank of Commonwealth: **4:** 605–6, 895, 942–3. C. friends fail to support for Bank of Commonwealth job: **4:** 942–3
White, Hugh L.: Declines appt. as Commissioner to settle Ky.–Va. land dispute: **3:** 326, 350, 514. Claims commissioner under Adams–Onis Treaty: **3:** 326. Character of: **4:** 846, 901. Elected to US Sen.: **4:** 846, 900–1. Reelected US Sen.: **6:** 1098. Mentioned for fed. judgeship: **5:** 65. Opposes US participation in Panama Cong.: **5:** 220–2. Leading Jacksonian in Tenn.: **6:** 10. Supports Tenn. applicant for C. patronage: **6:** 76, 78, 115, 122, 955–6. Seeks patronage favor from C.: **6:** 158

Wickliffe, Charles A.: Defends need in Ky. for protective tariff: **3:** 728. Votes for AJ over JQA in US House election (2/9/25): **4:** 79, 490; **6:** 1014–5, 1380–1. On Ky. fugitive slaves to Canada: **5:** 234–5. Runs for US Cong. (1827): **5:** 861–2, 990; **6:** 73, 500. Supports AJ in 1828: **5:** 990–1; **6:** 24. Switch to AJ: **6:** 395

Wickliffe, Robert: Lex. estate ("Ellerslie"): **5:** 685. Legal business with C.: **1:** 612–3, 617, 629, 649, 664, 737. Litigation against C.: **1:** 349. C. litigation against: **4:** 507–9, 817; **5:** 581–2. Sends political news to C.: **1:** 664. On New Court vs. Old Court issue in Ky.: **5:** 685. Opinion of 1817 election for Ky. General Assembly: **2:** 382–3. Criticism of as lawyer: **4:** 36. Attacks Desha on son's murder indictment: **4:** 64–7, 77–8. Sees Trimble appt. to US Supreme Court as key to Old Court victory in Ky.: **5:** 149–50. Patronage recommendations to C.: **5:** 684–5, 687; **6:** 41

Wilkinson, James: Criticism of: **1:** 289, 375–6. Military despotism of in N.O.: **1:** 376, 454. Supported by Jefferson in N.O. rule: **1:** 454. Cong. investigates for possible treason & incompetence (1810): **1:** 470. Disastrous campaign in Canada in War of 1812: **1:** 839–40, 841–2, 877, 888, 897, 903, 909, 981. Court–martial of: **2:** 6, 7. Claims against Mex.: **4:** 835. Western land ownership: **6:** 997–8. Suit against James Morrison estate: **6:** 997–8

Wirt, William: Appointed Atty. General in Monroe admin.: **2:** 398. Role in fed. trial of Aaron Burr: **2:** 398; **6:** 409

Women: C. attitudes toward: **1:** 126–7, 458; **6:** 1241, 1359–60. Problems with securing jobs: **5:** 281–2. No rights to make contracts: **1:** 532. *Mrs. Colvin's Weekly Messenger:* **5:** 282. C. gallantry to Mrs. Decatur (*see* Decatur, Susan W.)

Woods, Alva: Chosen Pres. of TU (*see* Transylvania University)

Wright, John C.: Legal business with C.: **2:** 874; **3:** 7, 14, 51, 647. Elected to US Cong. (1822): **3:** 245, 259, 294, 309, 871; **5:** 755–6, 799–800. Analyzes Ohio state & national political concerns for C.: **3:** 308–9. On Gr. independence: **3:** 614. Work for C. nom. & candidacy in 1824 Pres. election: **3:** 308. Patronage recommendations to C.: **4:** 235; **6:** 415–6, 813. Patronage go–between in Ohio: **6:** 395. Role in Huntington "scandal": **6:** 332, 384. Defects to AJ cause in Ohio: **6:** 632–3

Wurttemberg, Kingdom of: Ask C. for documents dealing with Wurttemberg emigrants to US: **6:** 294–5

Wythe, George: Protector of & mentor to young C.: **1:** 22; **3:** 161. C. eulogies to: **2:** 270; **3:** 161. On sharp Am. division of opinion on Declaration of Independence: **2:** 551. In Va. Constit. Conv.: **3:** 161, 170

Yazoo Lands. *See* Georgia